Between Sahara and Sea

BY HIS WILL, MR. THOMAS SPENCER JEROME endowed the lectureship that bears his name. It is jointly administered by the University of Michigan and the American Academy in Rome, and the lectures for which it provides are delivered at both institutions. They deal with phases of the history or culture of the Romans or peoples connected with the Roman Empire.

F. E. Adcock, *Roman Political Ideas and Practice*
Larissa Bonfante, *Images and Translations: The Etruscans Abroad*
G. W. Bowersock, *Hellenism in Late Antiquity*
Joseph Coleman Carter, *Discovering the Greek Countryside at Metaponto*
Jacqueline de Romilly, *The Rise and Fall of States According to Greek Authors*
Anthony Grafton, *Commerce with the Classics: Ancient Books and Renaissance Readers*
David J. Mattingly, *Between Sahara and Sea: Africa in the Roman Empire*
Fergus Millar, *The Crowd in Rome in the Late Republic*
Claude Nicolet, *Space, Geography, and Politics in the Early Roman Empire*
Jaroslav Pelikan, *What Has Athens to Do with Jerusalem? Timaeus and Genesis in Counterpoint*
John A. Pinto, *Speaking Ruins: Piranesi, Architects, and Antiquity in Eighteenth-Century Rome*
Lily Ross Taylor, *Roman Voting Assemblies: From the Hannibalic War to the Dictatorship of Caesar*
Mario Torelli, *Typology and Structure of Roman Historical Reliefs*
Paul Zanker, *The Power of Images in the Age of Augustus*

JEROME LECTURES TWENTY-SIXTH SERIES

Between Sahara and Sea

AFRICA IN THE ROMAN EMPIRE

David J. Mattingly

University of Michigan Press
Ann Arbor

Published in the United States of America by the
University of Michigan Press
Manufactured in the United States of America
Printed on acid-free paper
First published August 2023

A CIP catalog record for this book is available from the British Library.

Library of Congress Cataloging-in-Publication data has been applied for.

ISBN 978-0-472-13345-1 (hardcover : alk. paper)

For all the peoples of North Africa,
past and present

CONTENTS

LIST OF FIGURES

LIST OF TABLES

PREFACE AND ACKNOWLEDGEMENTS

The current work, which has its genesis in my 2013 Thomas Spencer Jerome Lectures, is to some extent a companion piece to two earlier books. In *An Imperial Possession: Britain in the Roman Empire*, I sought to challenge orthodox academic and public perceptions of the history and archaeology of a Roman province.[1] The methods employed there were further elaborated in *Imperialism, Power, and Identity: Experiencing the Roman Empire*, reflecting on various aspects of identity presentation and the operation of Roman colonialism.[2] All three books mark the culmination of my academic and practical explorations of Iron Age and Roman archaeology across more than 40 years. This has been a long journey through changing intellectual and physical landscapes. While many specialists on "Roman Africa" have taken as their focus of study the region's ancient cities (replete with extraordinarily preserved monuments and artworks) or the unusually rich epigraphic sources, my career has progressively carried me out into the countryside and then beyond the desert fringes.

In this book I seek to offer a fresh perspective on the interactions between the Roman Empire and the indigenous peoples of North Africa. This is not a conventional history of "Roman Africa" therefore, though I shall contextualise my study within a clear chronological framework (see Appendix 1), and there are some major historical implications arising from the themes explored. A first point of divergence in my perspective is that I shall focus on "Africa in the Roman Empire," which I construe as something quite distinct from "Roman Africa." Readers are advised that this book offers a personal view, though in acknowledging this subjective element, I would also question the assumed objectivity of more conventional studies. As we shall see, the scholarly discourses and agendas of any age are complex and inimical to absolute objectivity.

To understand this objectivity problem, we need to examine the construction of the modern colonial perspective of North Africa (the Maghrib and Sahara). The Maghrib is generally understood to comprise the somewhat mountainous

1. Mattingly 2006a.
2. Mattingly 2011a.

Mediterranean lands (Tell) of north-west Africa; that is, the parts of northern Morocco, Algeria, and Tunisia.[3] To the south and east along the Libyan coast, Saharan landscapes are more prevalent and predominant, with isolated areas of cultivated landscape, whether in oases or close to the Mediterranean. As we shall see, the often-assumed duality of Maghrib/Tell and Sahara/desert elides a greater complexity.

A good starting point on the colonial perspective—and the inspiration of my title—is Eugëne Fromentin. His book *Between Sea and Sahara: An Orientalist Journey* is a classic of the Western romanticising view of North Africa, played out under the shadow of the modern European imperial adventures.[4] It was a work of fiction, but masqueraded as a colonial travelogue. Orientalising stereotypes abound, albeit the narrator's view is somewhat sympathetic to the landscapes and people of North Africa. The narrator is closely associated with Fromentin the artist, representing one end of the spectrum of European engagement—with painterly descriptions (evocations) of landscapes and human tableaux. The narrator's fictional friend, Vandell, represents paternalistic "colonial science" (the other end of the spectrum). However, despite his love for the country and thirst for knowledge of it, Vandell has selfish motivations and seemingly more attachment to the land than the people:

> You see, this land is mine: it has adopted me and to it I owe unique freedom and an unparalleled life. I'll pay back this bounty, if I can, with a modest piece of work composed during my leisure time.[5]

Between these two extremes, Africa was fetishised in art and imagination and exploited through the power of colonial knowledge.

Especially for the French in Algeria and Tunisia, and the Italians in Libya, the Roman period marked a prior episode of colonial rule to which the modern imperial adventures were seen as hereditary successors. The modern colonial discourse thus became deeply entangled with the ancient one, leading to strong feelings of disassociation and alienation with the Roman heritage for the region's non-European majority population. The long-term legacy of this is still with us, with postcolonial thinking having made less headway than might be expected in reshaping the traditional agendas of study. This problem is further exacerbated by increasingly urgent and angry debates within Classical studies about perceptions

3. Some authors use the term "Maghrib" in a narrower sense to refer just to its eastern part (Algeria and Tunisia), or in a more elastic way to include the coastal regions of Libya as well. When I write of the Maghrib in this book, I am generally referring to the totality of Mediterranean north-west Africa; that is, including the Moroccan Maghrib al-Aksa.

4. Fromentin 2004, from the French original published in 1859 as *Une année dans le Sahel*. This book followed the success of his 1857 book *Une été dans le Sahara*.

5. Vandell, as "quoted" in Fromentin 2004, 77.

of racism, sexism, and elitism, whose ultimate origins can be traced back to the formative impact of the modern colonial era on the emergence of the discipline.[6] White supremacist groups and right-wing anti-woke commentators have been prominent in defending "traditional Classics," which should give academics serious pause for thought about the company they keep.[7] The direction of travel in academic studies more broadly over the last century has been from colonial to anti-colonial, to postcolonial, and now decolonial approaches. The issues arising from this are further discussed in Chapters 1 and 2, but the point about the agenda of study is relevant to my explanation here of the decolonising approach adopted in this book. Now, more than ever before, there is a general move to challenge engrained colonialist assumptions and make the study of the Roman Empire more inclusive.[8]

Most previous work on "Roman Africa" (or "l'Afrique romaine" or "l'Africa romana") has tended to present a view of Africa seen from an outside, essentially Roman, perspective. The approach highlights above all the influence of the Mediterranean Sea and the external people, technologies, and contacts that came across it to transform the landscapes and communities of North Africa. Indigenous agency has been minimised, and the influence of the desert on the society and civilisation that emerged has been seen as purely environmental rather than cultural. In the 21st century, 60 years beyond the end of the last European empires in North Africa, I think it is vital that the study of Africa in the Roman era recalibrates its agendas and specifically takes the necessary steps to decolonise the scholarly discourse. To move forward, it is necessary to challenge the status quo and, while I hope I have appropriately shown my admiration for the enormous scholarly achievements of the past, I have tried to demonstrate, sometimes with direct quotation, how outmoded assumptions and unconscious biases still impact scholarly work. My inversion of Fromentin's title is a deliberate attempt to change the emphasis—not to the exclusion of more traditional understanding of the impact of several groups of colonisers of ancient North Africa (Greeks, Phoenicians, Romans), but rather to give due consideration also to the contributions of the autochthonous peoples and the influence of the deep and broad desert hinterland. In offering a critique of the current state of the subject, I hope to demonstrate that the meticulously assembled data at our disposal can be animated in new ways by revising the underpinning agenda of study.

6. Leading to highly publicised clashes, as at the 2019 US Society for Classical Studies conference session on the future of Classics, Poser 2021. See also Appiah 2016 for a broader assault on the idea of Western civilisation; Padilla Peralta 2020; 2021 on the racist underpinnings of Classical studies.
7. Poser 2021, 1.
8. As evident, for instance, in conference sessions on "Decolonising Classical Archaeology: a view from North Africa" at the 2023 AIA, and a 2022 French conference on "Antiquité classique et postcolonialismes: tensions, inspirations, évolutions."

Two further aspects of my approach need to be highlighted. The first is an emphasis on profound regionalism, in part tied to the hugely varied landscapes of North Africa, but also a product of the diversity of the human population across time and space. There is a tendency in most historical writing towards oversimplification of such differences, to smooth the narrative. Yet the historical aggregation that results can produce misleading stereotypes of "average" people and their behaviours. Ryszard Kapuściński captures well what I am trying to articulate here:

> This is therefore not a book about Africa, but rather about some people from there ... Only with the greatest simplification, for the sake of convenience can we say "Africa." In reality, except as a geographical appellation, Africa does not exist.[9]

Of course, it is hard to avoid such convenient umbrella terms in a grand narrative such as my book will attempt to develop—North Africa, Romans, Libyans—but we need to recognise that these entities combine a multiplicity of subunits.

The final dimension, linked to the previous ones mentioned, concerns the way different groups presented their identities. This was certainly in part linked to regionality, but it also had a relationship to social memory, cultural groupings, and hierarchy. In the very broadest terms, I shall combine an exploration of the pre-Roman differences with a review of the specificities of military, urban, and rural communities during the Roman era. At the same time, while a good deal of attention will be devoted to demonstrating the diversity of behaviours and regional peculiarities, I do not make any claim to comprehensiveness (that would require a far bigger book and this one is big enough as it is). Rather I hope to demonstrate the potential of a different approach to the study of Africa and the Roman Empire, utilising varied methods that others may care to emulate and expand on in the future if the ideas and insights prove useful.

My involvement in North Africa began in 1979, with the UNESCO Libyan Valleys Survey investigating the Libyan pre-desert region of Tripolitania. In the course of the following 40-plus years, I have had the good fortune to travel extensively through all parts of North Africa from the Nile to the Atlantic and have directed field projects in Libya, Tunisia, and Morocco. At different times I have worked on a wide range of issues, including the Roman military deployment, olive oil production, urbanisation, field survey and rural settlement, the economy, burial traditions, indigenous peoples, Saharan trade. This book is inevitably a product of that specific, and to some degree atypical, career trajectory.

Another significant stimulus to me in working on the book has been an awareness of the lack of a good English language synthesis on Rome's southern

9. Kapuściński 2002, vii, foreword.

provinces. It is twenty-five years since I co-wrote with Bruce Hitchner a lengthy survey article on "Roman Africa," and the gaps in the bibliography have widened dramatically in recent years.[10] The *Companion to Ancient North Africa* edited by Bruce Hitchner has now partially addressed this need, but with its multiple authors it does not attempt to provide a unified vision.[11] While my book is not a conventional "provincial history" by any means, I hope it will serve as an entry point for more detailed explorations of a wide range of topics that can only be dealt with briefly here. I also include reference to comparative work from other provinces and to more theoretical works that I have found helpful in moving forward my own understanding of the Roman Empire.

I am particularly grateful to the committee responsible for planning the Thomas Spencer Jerome Lectures in honouring me with the invitation to deliver the 2013 series in Rome (21 February–1 March 2013) and Ann Arbor, Michigan (8–17 April 2013). My advertised theme was "Africa under Rome: Relationships, Identities, and Cultural Trajectories." It was a great opportunity (and a challenge) to start shaping my accumulated experience of ancient North Africa into a coherent synthesis. In Rome I must acknowledge the superb hospitality of the American Academy, under its then Director, Christopher Celenza, and with the organising oversight of Professor Kim Bowes, at the time the Andrew W. Mellon Professor there. In Michigan, the Department of Classical Studies, under its chair Professor Ruth Scodel, provided an equally warm welcome and hugely stimulating discussion with staff and students, including many former colleagues and friends. Professor David Potter has played a particularly significant role both in the arrangements for my lecture visit and subsequently as my contact with the Jerome Lecture committee. A highlight for me in both locations was an animated seminar discussion session with doctoral students and early-career researchers on "Romanisation and Discrepant Identity." My first lecture in the Jerome series, which has been developed as Chapters 3 to 5 here, was also first rehearsed in November 2012 as the 2nd Annual Percy Ure Lecture at the University of Reading. I am grateful to many individuals who attended the various lectures for stimulating discussion of the ideas presented.

I must also acknowledge Ellen Baule's editorial guidance at University of Michigan Press and her considerable patience while I have been working on the book. In final stages, I have benefited from the efficient work of the production manager Erin Ivy at Newgen and my indexer Pam Scholefield. The book has been far longer in gestation than I would have liked due to other major commitments. Since it was commissioned following my delivery of the lectures, I have served a five-year term as Head of School and completed publication of four volumes for the Trans-SAHARA Project—funded by a European Research Council grant that

10. Mattingly and Hitchner 1995.
11. Hitchner 2022a.

employed numerous postdoctoral researchers. With limited research time (and in the interests of the careers of the postdocs) the Trans-SAHARA publications have had to be my priority for a number of years. I must also gratefully acknowledge the support of the University of Leicester in granting me a semester of leave in 2012 ahead of the Jerome Lectures and a full year of study leave to complete this book after I finished my period as Head of School. Special mentions are due to Henrietta O'Connor (Head of College), Huw Barton (my successor as Head of School) and many other colleagues in the School. That my 2019–20 study leave also coincided with the COVID-19 pandemic was both a blessing and a curse, in that the circumstances of lockdown in my attic study freed me of many physical distractions to focus on finishing the first draft of this book, while of course also being a rather stressful and mentally distracting period.

There are more than the usual numbers of people to thank when a book like this essentially spans one's entire academic career. I must start with the late Barri Jones, who through his teaching first inspired my interest in North Africa and its frontiers and then gave me my first exposure to its magnificent archaeology on the ground. Barri was co-director of the UNESCO Libyan Valleys Survey with Graeme Barker, and Graeme was responsible for broadening my horizons thematically and methodologically, inspiring the sort of interdisciplinary projects I have subsequently run. Other scholars who took an interest in me at an early stage of my academic development and whose work was highly influential include Olwen Brogan, Joyce Reynolds, Phillipe Leveau, Pol Trousset, Charles Daniels, John Humphrey, Jean-Pierre Brun, Gabriel Camps, Jehan Desanges, Brent Shaw, and Lisa Fentress. I have also benefitted enormously from more than 35 years of close friendship and animated discussion about all manner of topics related to North Africa with R. Bruce Hitchner. During the final stages of revising my book manuscript, we co-taught an experimental transatlantic seminar class on "Decolonising the Classics: Ancient North Africa," involving students from Leicester and Tufts University in the sort of debates explored below (and with Brent Shaw and Matt McCarty also participating).

Special mention is also needed for a few close colleagues with whom I embarked on my exploration of postcolonial theory starting in the 1990s: Richard Hingley and Jane Webster, Chris Gosden, Michael Given, Andrew Gardner, Simon James, Martin Millett, and Peter Wells. Among many other friends and close colleagues (including some now departed) who have generously shared their ideas and publications with me, I must mention Aomar Akkeraz, Sue Alcock, Maria Antonietta Rizzo, Samir Aounallah, Stefan Ardeleanu, Sadok Ben Baaziz, Nejib Ben Lazreg, Paul Bennet, Sami Ben Tahar, Nacera Benseddik, Bob Bewley, Anthony Birley, Veronique Blanc-Bijon, Youssef Bokbot, David Bomgardner, Michel Bonifay, Anna Boozer, David Breeze, Claude Briand-Ponsart, Cyprian Broodbank, Veronique Brouquier-Reddé, Silvia Bullo, Jesper Carlsen, Salem Chaker, Michel Christol, Michelle Colletani-Trannoy, Jonathan Conant, Orietta Cordovana, Luk de Ligt, Mariette de Vos,

Savino di Lernia, Antonino di Vita, Ginette di Vita Evrard, Monique Dondin-Payre, Ali Drine, Xavier Dupuis, Noel Duval, Stephen Dyson, Abdulhamid Ennabli, Maurice Euzennat, Sergio Fontana, Yves Gauthier, Elena Giusti, Stéphanie Guédon, Christine Hamdoune, Colin Haselgrove, Tamar Hodos, Henry Hurst, Antonio Ibba, Mohamed Jerary, Nabil Kallala, Dennis Kehoe, Philip Kenrick, Robert Kerr, Katherine Lafrenz Samuels, Jean-Pierre Laporte, Andre Laronde, Jean-Marie Lassère, Yann Le Bohec, Jean-Loic Le Quellec, Mario Liverani, John Lloyd, Monique Longerstay, G. Lucarini, Matthew McCarty, Kevin MacDonald, Michael Mackensen, Attilio Mastino, Andy Merrills, Vincent Michel, Richard Miles, Peter Mitchell, Yves Modéran, Jennifer Moore, Lucia Mori, Pierre Morizot, Abdulatif Mrabet, Massimilio Munzi, Louisa Musso, Emilio Papi, Dan-el Padilla Peralta, Ted Peña, David Potter, Tim Potter, Jonathan Prag, Jo Quinn, Frederik Rakob, Rene Rebuffat, Michel Reddé, Stefan Ritter, Alan Rushworth, Joan Sanmartí, Gareth Sears, Graham Shipley, Hedi Slim, Susan Stevens, Niccolo Terrenato, Pol Trousset, Peter Van Dommelen, Cinzia Vismara, Philip von Rummel, Susan Walker, Colin Wells, Dick Whittaker, John Whitehouse, and Andrew Wilson.

My PhD students with North African interests include Muna Abdulhamid, Leonardo Bigi, Ahmad Buzaian, Emily Drummond, Ahmad Emrage, Mireya González Rodríguez, Muftah Haddad, Mohammed Hesein, Matt Hobson, Anna Leone, Niccolo Mugnai, Julia Nikolaus, Mohammed Omar, Ruth Pelling, Irene Schrüfer-Kolb, David Stone, and Andrea Zocchi. My debt to them all will be manifest in the references of this book, but many have also supported me in tracking down references and discussing ideas. Other research collaborators in my projects of particular relevance to the subject matter of this book include Touatia Amraoui, Tertia Barnett, Fran Cole, Aurélie Cuénod, John Dore, Nick Drake, Chloe Duckworth, Cori Fenwick, Rob Foley, Maria Gatto, Marta Lahr, Victoria Leitch, Charles Le Quesne, Stefania Merlo, Fares Moussa, Ronika Power, Nick Ray, Louise Rayne, Toby Savage, Katia Schörle, Nichole Sheldrick, Lea Stirling, Martin Sterry, and Kevin White. Many ideas in this book have developed out of conversations between us or from seeds they have planted in my mind by questioning the basis of prevailing knowledge and assumptions.

I need to thank Martin Sterry and Mike Hawkes for producing many of the illustrations in the following chapters. Martin, in particular, deeply engaged himself in interpreting and often improving on my rough ideas in his beautiful maps. I also want to acknowledge the generosity of many other scholars in allowing me to reproduce their figures here.

In the final stages, I was particularly grateful to a range of colleagues who agreed to take on the role of informal readers, feeding back many helpful comments and pointing out embarrassing errors and typos. Bruce Hitchner and Andy Merrills read and commented on first drafts of sections of the book, and David Stone and Lisa Fentress read an entire draft. Their rapid and insightful comments have enabled me to strengthen and clarify the argument in many places. For certain issues they encouraged me to carry my deconstructionist analysis further and I have tried to acknowledge this in the footnotes. The particularly thorough and encouraging comments from the two UMP reviewers of the initial submission have enabled me to restructure some parts of the argument, to improve the flow and cut down repetition. This is undoubtedly a better book than it would otherwise have been, but I must retain sole responsibility for any remaining slips and in a few instances for having stuck doggedly with my original ideas regarding the structure.

Beyond the limits of my own library, at various times I have benefitted from access to materials in the Centre Camille Jullian (Aix-en-Provence), University of Manchester, University of Leicester, University of Birmingham, Bodleian and Sackler Libraries (Oxford), Faculty of Classics library (Cambridge), the Joint Library Institute of Classical Studies (London), Society for Libyan Studies and SOAS library (London), University of Michigan library, Whitehouse library (Sydney), DAI Rome, American Academy in Rome, British School at Rome, Ludwig Maximilian University Munich, the Ausonius library at University of Bordeaux Montaigne, and the Paris IV University. In the circumstances of repeated COVID-19 lockdowns I became acutely grateful for the advances in digital access afforded by Africa Antiqua, Ancient World Online, *Antiquités africaines* (OpenEditions), Academia, *Encyclopédie berbère*, JSTOR, Persée, the Perseus Digital Library Project, ResearchGate, and much more now findable online through the wonders of Google search…

Finally, as ever, I owe more than I can repay to my family for all the time taken from them by the demands of researching and writing this book.

David J. Mattingly
June 2022

NOTE ON THE TRANSLITERATION OF NAMES AND SPELLING OF TOPONYMS

In line with my decolonising agenda for the book overall, I have adopted some approaches in relation to the presentation of names (ancient and modern) that require explanation. Where ancient place names are known, these are generally used in preference to modern toponyms and are given in italics. Names of ancient peoples are also italicised along with ancient terms, but not names of ancient gods and goddesses or individual personal names. In a few cases I have used an unfamiliar form of name for narrative effect—thus *Qart Hadasht* for Punic Carthage, but *Karthago* for Roman Carthage, as they were two completely separate cities built at different times at the same location. Similarly, I think that Tiqfarin better conveys the African identity of the man known in Roman sources as the rebel Tacfarinas.

Where modern toponyms are given, I have tried to avoid using the forms made canonical by the modern colonial powers following their own transliteration conventions. Instead my approach has been to try to use current transliteration practices from the *Encyclopaedia Islam* or Standard Arabic, which are more accepted in many Arabic speaking countries today (thus I use Jabal (for mountain) instead of Djebel in French, Gebel in Italian). While afficionados of the *Guides Bleu* or *Michelin* maps may be horrified, this is a *deliberate* attempt to move away from the modern colonial geographies and to employ postcolonial place name forms that are more familiar to users of tools like Google Earth or Wikipedia (though practice is by no means standardised there also). This leads to some possibly unfamiliar forms of names (al-Qurrayyat al-Garbia/Gheriat al-Garbia and Bu Nijim/Bu Njem), but, as these examples show, the original colonial name is not too hard to recognise in the revised spelling, and I generally give both spellings on first occurrence. The diversity of past and present place name transliteration systems from Morocco to Libya (with the added complexity of both Arabic and Amazigh toponyms) means that total consistency is impossible, but I make no apology for having tried.

Part 1: Introduction

Chapter 1

FROM THE DESERT TO THE SOWN

An African Journey

Introduction

North Africa formed the remarkably successful southern territory of the Roman Empire. It was a surprising and paradoxical land, in that its richness—based on agricultural productivity and its high urban density—belied its sometimes difficult mountainous terrain and its deep desert backdrop. Although seemingly far from a central concern at Rome (the literary sources on Africa are fairly meagre in some respects), by the 2nd century CE Africa had become a critical driver of the Empire. In economic terms, this is reflected in its major contributions to Rome's grain supply, but also in the evident boom in olive oil production, along with large exports of wine and fish products. The political and social impacts centred on hundreds of men who entered imperial service as equestrians and senators, including several who became emperors or would-be emperors. When Christianity became the official religion of the Empire in the 4th century, Africa was one of its main seedbeds and produced a series of key figures in the early Church. Its late antique history was dynamic and profoundly different to the rest of the western Empire. The cultural vivacity of the African provinces, as revealed in its brilliant mosaic art and its extraordinary Classical cities, is readily appreciated by visitors today. There are thus many reasons why the study of Africa in the Roman Empire commands our attention. There is an exciting and instructive story to tell that is entangled with Rome's own story. That is certainly an important part of my endeavour in this book.

However, there is a second narrative that I seek to explore, which bears on my reading of the first. This concerns the historiographical tradition and the agendas of study. I am going to offer some radical rereadings of the evidence, but, in doing so, I shall have to explain the problems with traditional approaches. This analysis has wider relevance to the study of the Roman Empire overall, as my account attempts to decolonise the discipline of questionable and outmoded assumptions. I hope that readers will welcome some unfamiliar angles and insights that at times will challenge their prior assumptions about Rome.

A key theme of this book concerns colonial and postcolonial historical discourses, and it is important to note several distinct approaches to and phases of debate. The scholarly consensus view of Africa in the Roman Empire has tended to be closely aligned with the view from Rome.[1] The victor's version of history has prevailed in most ages, of course, and the Romans made doubly sure of this by their destruction of much of the library of *Qart Hadasht* (Carthage).[2] Although a number of the Libyan peoples had a written alphabet, there is no evidence that they ever used it to document their own version of history.[3] The modern colonial regimes in North Africa (Spanish and French in Morocco; French in Algeria and Tunisia; Italian, British, and French in Libya) gave further impetus to the Romano-centric vision, with a particular emphasis on the notion of a cultural transformation (Romanisation), seen as both palliative and compensation for subjugation.[4] The modern European view of ancient North Africa was thus firmly built on a *colonialist* discourse. In reaction to this model, in the first decades of postcolonial independence, some Maghribian historians constructed an *anti-colonial* reading of history, presenting a version of the past that was more attuned to the nationalist agenda of irreconcilable opposition to imperialism, including Marcel Bénabou's notable account of resistance to Romanisation that heralded a more subtle attempt at *postcolonial* interpretation.[5] The problem is that these historiographical tendencies are products of the modern colonialist discourse and thus opposite faces of the same counterfeit coin. Both agendas have led scholars to perceive the evidence through the filter of ideological preconceptions and neither really does justice to the cultural complexity present.

In the early 21st century, studies of "Roman Africa" might seem rejuvenated, with a glut of new overviews appearing. Many of these works reflect a middle ground between earlier conflicting views of Romanisation and resistance, but Romanisation in a slightly modified form has remained the central paradigm. It should be noted that while Classical archaeologists from Maghribian countries are often broadly supportive of the orthodox agendas (as a result of their training within this tradition), for most inhabitants of North Africa the Roman past remains something alien, perhaps useful in terms of tourism revenues, but not truly an integral part

1. Trousset 1986a, 60 for a map that literally turns Africa on its head, while at the same time emphasising the colonial bulwark centred on major coastal centres such as *Karthago*, *Lepcis* and *Caesarea*, with a vast and an increasingly arid hinterland beyond a 500 km circle drawn on *Karthago* and 250 km circles drawn on *Lepcis* and *Caesarea*.
2. In this book I shall normally refer to Punic Carthage as *Qart Hadasht* and Roman Carthage as *Karthago*, since they were in effect completely different cities, following the complete destruction of the former by Rome in 146 BCE.
3. Aghali-Zakara 2006; Galand 1989; Ghaki 1995; Chaker 2013b.
4. Mattingly 1996a, reprinted as 2011, 43–72; Munzi 2001.
5. Bénabou 1976; for further discussion, see Chapter 2.

of their own cultural heritage.[6] In this book, I attempt to move postcolonial debate to a new stage, by explicitly addressing the need to *decolonise* the discipline, in line with broader scholarly developments in Classical studies that seek to address charges of racism, elitism, sexism, and white supremacist thinking.[7] Similar debates are taking place in other areas of archaeology, history, and the humanities.[8]

What's in a Name: Roman Africa or Africa in the Roman Empire?

The choice of words matters in that terminology often encodes cultural assumptions, especially when we apply essentially modern terms and concepts to the past. A feature of this book is that I have consciously set out to try and define my terms carefully and, for reasons I shall explain, to avoid the use of some common vocabulary that is often applied to the Roman past.[9]

In its broadest sense, the term "Roman Africa" conveys a huge space and a very long chronology. Modern textbooks have generally attempted to cover Africa north of the Sahara between the Atlantic coast of Morocco and the Syrtic gulf of Libya and to provide an account from 146 BCE to 439 CE (Vandal conquest) or 533 (Byzantine conquest). Describing such a vast temporal and geographical range is bound to be impressionistic in places. I reiterate that my intention here is not to present a blow-by-blow political and cultural history, but rather a revised framework for the study and improved understanding of Africa in the Roman Empire.[10]

Stéphane Gsell's eight-volume *Histoire ancienne de l'Afrique du Nord* remains one of the most stunning academic achievements, not least for the depth in which

6. Fenwick 2008; Lafrenz Samuels 2010; 2012; 2015. Note also similar comments on need to enhance "local" involvement in agendas of study in Stone 2022.
7. See notably Eccleston and Padilla Peralta 2022; Padilla Peralta 2020; 2021.
8. On the academic frameworks that "rationalise and maintain unfair social structures," see Tuck and Yang 2012. On decolonising archaeology more generally, see for example, Schmidt 2017.
9. For a variety of reasons (explained at different points below) I have tried to exclude a range of terms from this book; for example: Roman Africa, Romanisation, tribe, native, protohistoric, frontier, slave. It has been an interesting exercise, going further than I have done before in this regard, but absolutely necessary to my project of trying to decolonise the story. It has also been chastening at times, as I have repeatedly encountered my own unconscious biases, with these terms recurrently popping up in my drafts. I hope in the end that my alternative terminology and concepts will find favour with readers, and that what they have replaced will not be missed.
10. The bibliography is vast and disparate. Literature searches are helped by the existence of annual compilations such as *Archéologie de l'Afrique Antique 19XX. Bibliographie des ouvrages parus en 19XX et compléments des années antérieures* (now defunct but covering 1964–1985); *Bibliographie Analytique de l'Afrique Antique* (1963f., but now running some years behind and appearing less regularly). See also, inter alia, Benseddik and Bel Faïda 2015; Ennabli 1985; Laubenheimer-Leenhardt 1971; Le Bohec 1979; 1990; Mattingly and Hitchner 1995; Rebuffat et al. 1980. For Iron Age and prehistoric eras, see also Ferhat and Taveron 2001. Although it is not possible to go into every topic in full detail, the footnotes and bibliography are designed to allow readers to follow up on the state of the field in its many sub-areas.

it attempted to study the pre-Roman era and to explore the initial stages of Rome's colonial entanglements there.[11] The approach was well ahead of its time in that it focused on the rise of the Carthaginian empire and Punic civilisation in Africa (vols. I–IV) and on the appearance of indigenous kingdoms by the latter centuries BCE (V–VIII). Yet, because of Gsell's death, it cut off just when the story of Africa under Roman rule was starting to really get going, with Caesar's victory over the combined forces of his Roman opponents and Juba I at Thapsus in 46 BCE.[12] It must also be recognised that Gsell's perspective on the antecedents of Rome's domination of the region was very much conditioned by the writings of the Greco-Roman sources, due to the non-survival of written accounts of the Carthaginians, *Numidae* and *Mauri*, and was also a product of Gsell's colonial present.[13] His "ancient history" was constructed from the Roman victor's perspective and in the context of particular colonialist discourses, and should thus come with a health warning attached. As I explore further in Chapters 2 to 5, the sources are not neutral documents, but products of a colonial mentality, and in our acceptance or interpretation of this evidence we are liable to add further layers of assumptions. It is also worth emphasising that the longevity of the modern colonial perspectives is in part related to the shape given to the discipline by the sheer volume of data on "Roman Africa" that was compiled under the auspices of modern empires.

Perhaps intimidated by or simply satisfied with Gsell's monumental work, later generations of Roman historians and Classical archaeologists have not devoted much attention to the antecedent peoples,[14] and have generally been content to extol the glory of "l'Afrique romaine" or "l'Africa romana."[15] The emergence of postcolonial perspectives, especially in Algeria after its bitter war of independence, challenged this cosy consensus, notably with the work of Marcel Bénabou.[16] The initial responses to the postcolonial critique of "l'Afrique romaine" were a stern rebuke of those challenging the orthodox position, and to some extent studies of "Roman Africa" have continued in much the same way as before.[17]

11. Gsell 1913; 1918a/b; 1920; 1927a/b; 1928a/b.
12. Gsell 1928b. The final stages of the Mauretanian kingdom to 39 CE are followed in the last section, but the major part of the book ends with the annexation of the Numidian kingdom.
13. See Leveau 2020a for an insightful discussion of Gsell's "colonialist" blindspots.
14. For example, Le Bohec 2005a, 13–15, 21–27, covers the pre-Roman era in just ten pages, of which six relate to *Qart Hadasht* and the Punic Wars.
15. Until recent years, the main contenders as general histories of "Roman Africa" were Albertini 1950; Julien 1978; Picard 1959 (with updated 1990 edition); Romanelli 1959. For shorter general surveys of "Roman Africa" in "handbooks," see Law 1978; Lepelley 1998b; Mahjoubi and Salama 1981; Quinn 2009; Whittaker 1996.
16. Bénabou 1976; note also the less nuanced but influential attack of Laroui 1970. See also Decret and Fantar 1981; Février 1989; 1990 for early attempts to bridge the historiographical divide.
17. The evolution of the subject over recent decades can be judged by scrutinising the contents of the major conferences on "Roman Africa": *L'Africa romana*; the CTHS series (CTHS Perpignan 1984; CTHS Grenoble 1985; CTHS Montpellier 1986; CTHS Strasbourg 1990; 1991; CTHS Avignon 1992; CTHS Pau 1995a; 1995b; CTHS Nice 1999), continued as SEMPAM (SEMPAM Tabarka 2003; SEMPAM Tripoli 2008; SEMPAM Caen 2014); L'Afrique dans l'Occident romain 1990.

The addition of "L'Afrique romaine de l'Atlantique à la Tripolitaine (69–439)" as a subject for the French university *concours* in 2005 had the effect of greatly increasing the teaching of the subject and stimulated a wide range of new "textbooks."[18] In terms of sheer heft, Lassère's posthumous masterwork *Africa, quasi Roma* has set the benchmark for these broad surveys.[19] There have also been a number of more popular illustrated books on all or part of "Roman Africa."[20] A number of the most influential scholars of the last century have also been honoured with "collected papers" volumes, which to some extent present overviews of important bodies of work.[21]

With the plethora of recent overview accounts, do we need another? A first justification is that reflections in English on "Roman Africa" have been rarer.[22] I also aim to do something other than to retell a now familiar story. I hope to provide a different perspective on Africa in the Roman Empire, by approaching the evidence from novel directions.

Another argument for the timeliness of this book is that the pace of research has picked up notably in the last 20 years, with Maghribian archaeologists and historians more and more to the fore. Important new syntheses of data have appeared, and some highly significant new discoveries have been made. However, I would argue that their full impact is constrained by the underlying weaknesses of the interpretative frameworks commonly deployed. While most of the recent French titles cited above still highlight their key theme as Romanisation,[23] I have explicitly rejected that paradigm in my recent work and sought to replace it with the concept of "discrepant identity" in exploring the evidence of cultural interactions and changes (further explained in Chapter 2).[24] All the same, I believe that my vision is complementary to the more orthodox approaches and, of course, this study is dependent for much of its detail on the work of innumerable others, working in different scholarly traditions.

---

18. See for example, Bertrandy and Colletoni-Trannoy 2005; Briand-Ponsart and Hugoniot 2006; Cabouret 2005; Corbier and Griesheimer 2005; Géroudet and Ménard 2005; Ibba and Traina 2006; Lafond 2005; Le Bohec 2005a; Prévot et al. 2006. Note Sanghera 2021, 225 for the observation that "the 2005 law compelled places of education to teach the 'positive' aspects of French imperialism."
19. Lassère 2015.
20. Baratte 2012; Delpont 2003; Di Vita et al. 1999; Lancel 2003; Laronde and Golvin 2001; Sintes 2010; Sintes and Rebahi 2003; Slim 2004.
21. Christol 2005; Desanges 1999a; Février 1996; Gsell 1981; Lepelley 2001; Leschi 1957; Di Vita 2015a; 2015b; 2017; Pflaum 1978; Romanelli 1981; Shaw 1995a; 1995b.
22. The Blackwell Companion volume is now the key starting point, Hitchner 2022a. Apart from that, there are comparatively few books in English devoted to "Roman Africa," all now rather out of date: Broughton 1929; Raven 1993; Warmington 1954 are probably the best, though very much influenced by the French colonial tradition. Barton 1972 is a thoughtful but brief historical and socially focused summary. MacKendrick 1980 is an uncritical and descriptive collage and Manton 1988 is slight and unscholarly. A substantial article by Mattingly and Hitchner 1995 provides an entry point into the vast bibliography up to that date.
23. See for example, Briand-Ponsart and Hugoniot 2006, 12–13; Cabouret 2005, 6–8; Prévot et al. 2006, 15–20.
24. See Chapter 2 for a detailed discussion of theoretical approaches.

This book's subtitle highlights a crucial difference in perspective, rather than a clumsy synonym for "Roman Africa." I shall argue that "Africa in the Roman Empire" has different meanings and connotations to "Roman Africa," the latter being a shorthand term for a rather top-down perspective on the history and archaeology. The distinctions will become clearer as we progress.[25]

The Geographical and Climatic Context

The Geographical Framing of This Book

The geographical and chronological framing of this study need explanation and justification. North Africa spans the entire southern shore of the Mediterranean (Fig. 1.1). In many ways it would be appropriate to consider it as a whole, from the Atlantic coast in Morocco to the Nile (or indeed the Red Sea) in Egypt and extending partly into the northern Sahara as well as along the Mediterranean margins (an area of over 2 million km^2).[26] To give an idea of comparative scale, the area is covered by 13 sheets of the Barrington Atlas, mostly at 1:1,000,000 scale, compared, for example, to 12 sheets covering Britain, Gaul, and Iberia combined.[27] Interconnections across this zone were as important in some respects as the Mediterranean connectivity to the north. Three-quarters of this vast area was desert or semi-desert, and direct Roman territorial control at its maximum is likely to have covered about 600,000 km^2. Allowing for hegemonic control over Saharan peoples, the effective Roman Empire in North Africa could have approached 900,000 km^2 at its greatest extent (though the Sahara as a whole occupies c.9 million km^2).[28] Moreover, the Roman acquisition of territory in North Africa occurred piecemeal across five centuries from 146 BCE, when the initial territory of *Africa Vetus* may have been as small as 20,000 km^2, and even with the addition of the Tripolitanian *emporia* and *Africa Nova* by 46 BCE the total African provinces was at that stage no more than c.80,000 km^2 (Fig. 1.1b). What is striking about these numbers is the relatively small size of the provincial territory when viewed against the immensity of the Maghribian and Saharan backdrop. This echoes a feature of the Roman sources on

25. Hugoniot 2000 and Ibba 2012 from their titles are outliers among French and Italian books in apparently addressing "Rome in Africa," but are actually less distinctive in approach than they sound.
26. The calculations that follow were made using the polygon-measuring tool in Google Earth Pro and must be treated as rough estimations, but accord quite well with figures cited by Shaw 2003, 95–96 (after Courtois 1955, 66–67), with the more habitable portion of the Maghrib and pre-desert estimated at 900,000 km^2 and the limit of Roman territorial control 450,000 km^2 (but excluding *Cyrenaica*).
27. Talbert 2000.
28. Laureano 1991, 23.

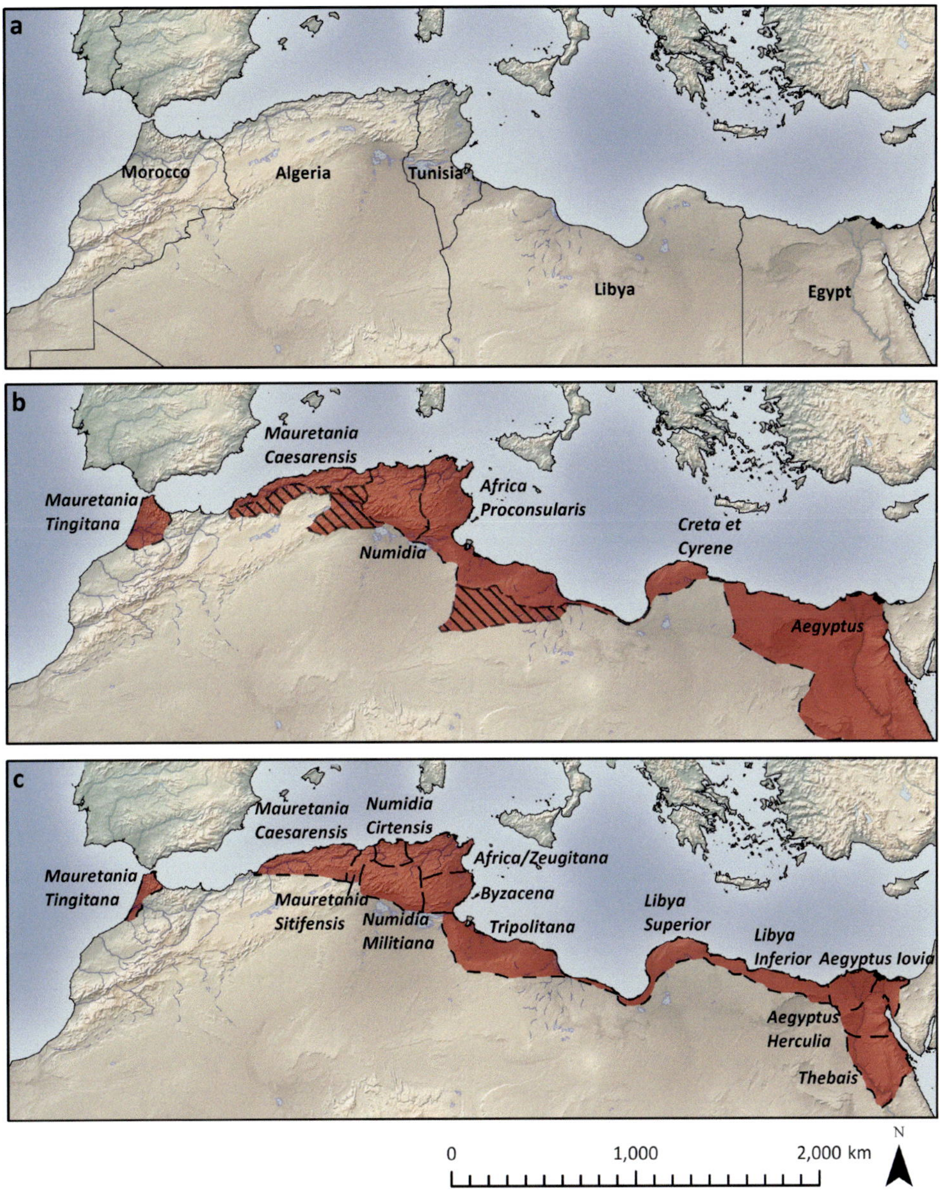

Figure 1.1. North Africa in the Roman Empire. a) Topographic map showing modern countries of Maghrib and Sahara; b) Provinces in the mid-2nd century CE (cross-hatched shading indicates areas of later Severan expansion); c) Provinces in the 4th century (Martin Sterry, after author's roughs).

Africa in that they prioritised the challenging geography and "barbarian" ethnography of the fringes over careful record of society in the heartland provincial territory.[29] In this way, a concerted effort was made to accentuate the difference and the difficulty of North Africa in comparison to other core "Mediterranean" territories of the Roman world. The tropes employed had more in common with those used in relation to the northern heavily garrisoned provinces, for example.

The administrative structures imposed by Rome were complex and ultimately based on the jurisdiction areas of their governors, which changed considerably over time. Thinking about them as tightly bounded and fixed geographical entities is thus not entirely helpful. The African provinces in late Roman times were split between the eastern and western dioceses: the provinces of *Mauretania*, *Numidia* and *Africa* belonged to the Latin Western Empire, whereas *Cyrenaica* (later *Libya Superior* and *Inferior*) and *Aegyptus* were part of the Greek-speaking Eastern Empire (Fig. 1.1c). Moreover, Egypt was always a place apart because of its unique annual river floods and deep Pharaonic backstory and Nilotic culture. There were also significant differences in pre-Roman colonial encounters—Persians and Greeks in Egypt, Greeks in eastern Libya, Phoenicians in western Libya, Tunisia, Algeria, and Morocco. While there were linguistic commonalities (or similarities) for the Libyan peoples in greater North Africa, trying to encompass in any detail the range of cultural variety that is encountered between Atlantic and Nile would be challenging for writer and reader. It has thus made sense to follow the model of many of the recent French textbooks and to make my primary geographical focus the provinces between the Atlantic and the Greater Syrtes (in sequence: *Mauretania Tingitana, Mauretania Caesariensis* (also later *Mauretania Sitifensis*), *Africa,* including the later subdivisions of *Numidia* and *Tripolitana*), but with occasional forays to east and south.

In recent years I have led a large overview of what I define as the trans-Saharan region, generating significant new insights by starting with the Sahara and looking out to north (to the Mediterranean and its civilisations), east (to the Nile valley civilisations), south (to the early farmers and states of sub-Saharan Africa) and west (to the Atlantic world).[30] The presence of a massive hyper-arid desert is undeniably a key part of North Africa's history, though as recently as 2004 it has been wrongly construed as an empty and absolute barrier in the Roman period:

> Thus, the two regions—north and south of the Sahara—though parts of the same continent, remained inaccessible and unknown to each other (terrae ignotae) ... Things changed only with the Arab Middle Ages.[31]

---

29. See in particular Woolf 2014, 8–13 on "Pliny's African safari"; cf. also Shaw 1981d; Whittaker 2009.
30. Duckworth et al. 2020a; Gatto et al. 2019a; Mattingly et al. 2017a; Sterry and Mattingly 2020a.
31. Ennabli 2004, 24: "Ainsi, les deux régions—nord et sud du Sahara—tout en apartenant au même continent, sont restées inaccessible et inconnues l'une à l'autre, des *terrae ignotae* ... Les choses change avec le Moyen Age arabe." Cf. Desanges 2003; Gearon 2011.

As we shall see, such views can be contradicted by reference to the archaeological evidence, and this has implications for the story I want to tell. Africa *in* the Roman Empire can only be properly understood to some extent by exploring its 1st millennium BCE antecedents and the political, social, and economic impacts of all its component micro-regions and its vast desert hinterland, thus making this book also an evaluation of Africa *and* the Roman Empire.

Some Environmental, Climatic, and Conceptual Frameworks

The long-term environmental and climatic conditions of this vast zone need to be understood.[32] For a long time, the perception of the Mediterranean's southern shore in prehistory has been that this area lagged far behind the northern and eastern shores during later prehistory.[33] In a study focused on the Mediterranean parts of Africa, Broodbank and Lucarini have summarised new evidence for the period 10000–1000 BCE.[34] This is relevant to my story, because, as we shall see, later prehistory shaped the North African Iron Age in ways that had long-term impacts into the Roman era.

There has been a resurgence of interest in thinking about the Mediterranean as a distinctive climatic, environmental, and cultural zone, albeit one made up of many micro-regions.[35] The micro-regional approach is well suited to North Africa. While it was part of the Mediterranean climatic and environmental zone, it also stands apart in certain respects. Within the Mediterranean it is the region most subject to arid conditions and droughts, due to the influence and proximity of the Sahara.[36] Climatic change is often raised as a possible explanation for the apparently greater productivity of the North African landscapes in antiquity. However, the most recent scientific data suggests that that climate, after the ending of the last Saharan pluvial phase (c.3000 BCE), has been broadly similar to that of modern times, with high aridity, though perhaps with a slightly higher and more predictably distributed rainfall in the period 2nd century BCE

32. Leveau 2022 for an excellent short summary in English. See also his detailed studies 2009a; 2013; 2018; 2021.
33. See most recently the great synthesis of Broodbank 2013, but note his caution (for instance, 36–40 "North Africa, the great lacuna") about whether in Africa we are looking at evidence of absence or absence of evidence.
34. Broodbank and Lucarini 2019.
35. Following the lead of Braudel (1972; 1973), see now Abdulafia 2011; Broodbank 2013; Harris 2005; Hauschild et al. 2007; Horden and Purcell 2000; Morris 2003; Shaw 2001. Wickham 2005 partially extends an economic grand narrative to the early medieval Mediterranean.
36. For older views (but with a focus on relevance for Classical antiquity), see Shaw 1981b. For the impact of drylands in general, see Barker and Gilbertson 2000.

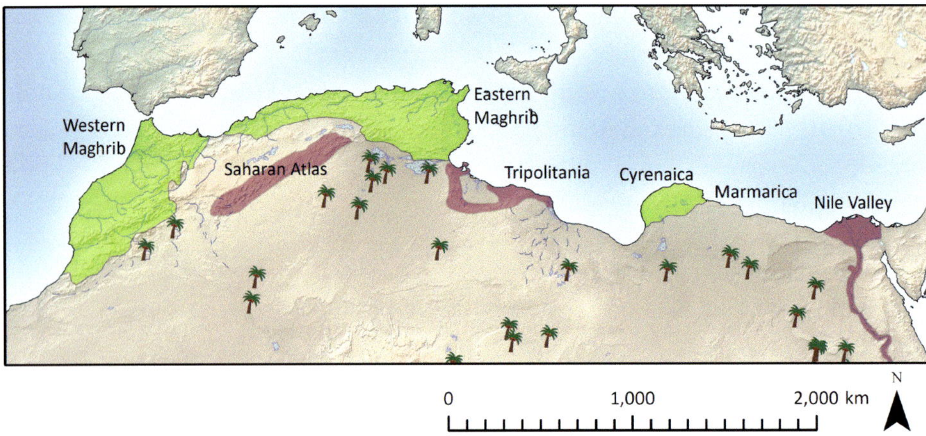

Figure 1.2. North African "islands" and "the sea beyond the sea." The green blocks denote Shaw's North African "islands"; blue blocks are suggested additions of high population density; and palm trees indicate the location of the major Saharan oasis clusters, which may have functioned as minor "islands" (Martin Sterry, after author's rough—developing from Shaw 2003, 98).

to 3rd century CE.[37] As we shall see, rainfall varies markedly across the Maghrib. Despite the likelihood that there have been some minor climatic oscillations over the last few thousand years that may have provided amelioration of generally arid conditions, the starting point for debate now is that the climate in Roman times was, much as today, in general more of a constraint rather than an opportunity.

The Sahara in some respects represents a second "sea" to the south of the Mediterranean, within which the major high relief areas of the Maghrib and *Cyrenaica* stand out like islands (Fig. 1.2).[38] Moreover, the pattern of winds and currents and the natural topography of Africa's Mediterranean coastline makes it less suited for maritime activity than parts of the northern Mediterranean.[39] The landmass of North Africa thus differs from Mediterranean Europe and the coastal zone of Asia Minor/Levant in that those were more readily connected

37. For some recent data/case studies on climatic changes in the Sahara and Maghrib, see inter alia Barker et al. 1996a, 49–80, 291–362; Brooks et al. 2005; Cremaschi 2003; Cremaschi and Zerboni 2009; 2011; Kuper and Kröpellin 2006; Le Quellec 2006; Leveau 2009b (for the argument of marginally higher rainfall); 2013; 2018; Mattingly 2003a, 37–74, 327–46; Mattingly and Sterry 2020a, 8–12. See also Harper 2017 for a rather deterministic view of a Roman climatic optimum and a downturn in late antiquity, but with a good deal of relevant bibliography.

38. Lichtenberger 2016; Shaw 2003; 2006.

39. Broodbank 2013, 72–79. The drawbacks were noted in ancient times, see Pliny, *NH* 5.1: "no other part of the world offers fewer harbours"; Sallust, *Jugurtha* 17.4: "The sea is dangerous and there are few harbours"; Polybius, *Histories* 1.39. Nonetheless, there is ample evidence for maritime activity along the North African coast, see Shipley 2011, on Pseudo-Skylax.

spaces by land and sea. Although it was part of a greater Mediterranean world, Africa has been subject to different ecological rhythms and environmental conditions, contributing to some disjunctures with cultural and economic developments observed elsewhere.

Climatic changes were a recurrent feature of the early prehistory of North Africa.[40] Much as they determined a series of glacial and interglacial periods in Europe, in Africa these events created huge swings between hyper-arid and pluvial conditions. Because of shifts in the northern limits of monsoonal rain, the Sahara went through cycles of having running rivers and large lakes to phases when it was a hostile desert that was inimical to human and animal life.[41] Hominin/human colonisation and development in northern Africa was thus subject to interruptions and discontinuities. Parts of the Sahara that show considerable activity in earlier times appear to have been virtually emptied of people between about 70000 and 20000 BCE. The last pluvial phase began at the start of the Holocene and though the lakes of this period were less spectacular than the great inland seas that had characterised parts of the Pleistocene, the relative availability of water and grazing encouraged the rapid reintroduction of a wide range of fauna, with human hunter-gatherer groups following on their heels. Three main phases can be identified in the early Holocene prehistoric story.[42] The first (9600–6200 BCE) was essentially a period of specialised hunting and foraging strategies. Around 6200 BCE there was a climatic fluctuation, which contributed to a radical and fairly generalised take up between 6200–4000 of a range of domesticated animals (primarily sheep, goats, and cattle). To some extent, both of these strategies seem to have been driven, or at any rate tightly bound up with, people operating in highly connected Saharan spaces.[43]

Agriculture was not as early in date nor as widely practised initially on the Mediterranean's southern shore as it was on the east or northern shores.[44] However, nor was it entirely absent in the period 6000–1000 BCE, though unfortunately much of this crucial period is poorly documented archaeologically in North Africa.[45] A further incident of dramatic climatic change started around 4000 BCE, with a move back to hyper-arid conditions in the Sahara. The full effects of this were not felt until around 3000 BCE, but by that date many of the lakes of the Sahara were dried up, with major implications for the herding communities

40. For discussions of the impact of climate and environmental changes, see Broodbank and Lucarini 2019, 202–06 for an up-to-date synthesis with further references.
41. Drake et al. 2010; 2018.
42. Broodbank and Lucarini 2019, 202–06, 210–38.
43. Di Lernia 2013.
44. Barker 2006; Broodbank 2013.
45. The crucial nature of the *lacuna* is flagged up in Broodbank 2013; Broodbank and Lucarini 2019.

that frequented them.[46] This marked the onset of the hyper-arid conditions in the Sahara that have persisted to the present day—in other words, the start of the environment that pertains to the story of Africa and Rome. The switch to an alternative subsistence strategy involving agriculture in the environmental niches where this was possible can be observed in Egypt and the depressions of the Western Desert from the 4th millennium BCE onwards. However, to some extent this remained an isolated phenomenon and the spread of agriculture across the rest of North Africa appears to have been slow and fragmented geographically.[47] Part of the problem may be absence of evidence as much as evidence of absence, as there is quite simply a dearth of data for human activity in many parts of North Africa between the 4th and early 1st millennia BCE. One area where we have early evidence of agricultural experimentation was at the extreme western end of the Maghrib in Morocco, almost certainly due to contacts across the straits of Gibraltar. There are finds of botanical remains from a number of cultivated crops from multiple Moroccan caves dating as early as the 6th–5th millennium BCE, but this does not seem to have immediately marked a wider dissemination of cultivation eastwards into other parts of the Maghrib.[48] The eastern Maghrib is another area where we might reasonably expect some early experimentation, given the feasibility of marine contacts across the Sicilian straits, but the first agricultural evidence from there dates to the very start of the 1st millennium BCE. However, the explanation may lie in the lack of investigation of open sites of the period 4000–1000 BCE in the Maghrib—this is certainly a situation where a single excavation could change our model. On the other hand, in *Cyrenaica*, the minutely detailed excavation of the Haua Fteah cave sequence has revealed nothing similar to the Moroccan Neolithic sequences with domesticated plants, and the first evidence of agriculture there does not seem to have been before the Greco-Roman era.[49] An important conclusion here is that North Africa was not a uniform socio-economic space in the Holocene in line with its fragmented geographical nature.

One of the great mysteries in North African history is the apparent absence of a significant Bronze Age (at least to west of the Nilotic civilisations). Archaeologically, we seem to encounter instead a continuation of the Neolithic societies with their lithic technologies until the emergence of iron-using societies in the 1st millennium BCE.[50] However, some actual finds of bronze swords and numerous rock carvings of recognisably bronze weapons from Morocco are certainly suggestive of local

46. Cremaschi and Zerboni 2009; 2011.
47. Broodbank and Lucarini 2019, 227–35 for an up-to-date region-by-region survey.
48. See inter alia, Ballouche and Marinval 2003; Linstädter and Kehl 2012; Martínez Sánchez et al. 2018; Morales Mateos et al. 2013; Peña Chocarro et al. 2011; Zapata et al. 2013.
49. Barker 2019; Barker et al. 2012; Hunt et al. 2011.
50. Broodbank 2013, 265–68; Camps 1992b for the scant evidence for the 3rd–2nd millennia BCE; Greene 1997, 155 is categorical about the absence of a Maghribian Bronze Age.

engagement with metallurgy at earlier dates.[51] The problem is lack of identified and excavated settlements of this period, and given what will be discussed about early 1st millennium developments below, the question must remain open.

However, on the basis of the currently available evidence, we do not seem to have a generalised pattern of the spread of agriculture from a single point of origin (whether in the extreme east or west of the continent) outwards across North Africa. Agriculture seems to have been separately transferred to the region from the Levant into Egypt, from Iberia into Morocco and perhaps from Italy, Sardinia, or Sicily into northern Tunisia, with considerable time lags before its ultimate extensive uptake. On the other hand, there is now evidence to suggest that agriculture was more widespread in the Maghrib by around 1000 BCE, with possible multiple foci linked to points of contact with external lands. As we shall see later, there is also evidence of a progressive spread of oasis agriculture along Saharan routes in the 2nd–1st millennium BCE, but this most likely represents a separate tradition of farming to the Mediterranean coastal zone and the Maghrib.

The initially dislocated and retarded development of agriculture in Mediterranean Africa in part reflects the diversity and the fragmented nature of the topography and the general aridity of climate.[52] Shaw's idea of conceptualising North Africa as a series of islands, rather than a single connected continental landmass has much to recommend it.[53] The Arab name for the region, *Jazirat al-Maghrib* ("Island of the West") hints at something similar.[54] As Shaw points out, this is essentially a result of plate tectonics, with the collision of the African plate with the European plate, throwing up the great mountain ranges of the Maghrib, running broadly parallel to the Mediterranean coast, and which Shaw divides into two "island" blocks (one broadly equivalent to Morocco, the other to Northern Algeria and Tunisia). The severe nature of the tectonic action has created a barrier into and out of the Mediterranean coastland of the Maghrib. East of Cap Bon in Tunisia, the African plate has pushed much farther north beneath Italy, Greece, and sundry islands, leading to the much lower-lying landscapes of the Tunisian Sahel and the Libyan *Syrtica* and *Marmarica*. The notable exception to this is the uplifted area of *Cyrenaica*, forming an isolated eastern "island" of classic Mediterranean landscape that looked north towards Crete and the Aegean.[55] One could argue for further small "islands" to be added to the group discussed

51. Bokbot 2020.
52. Lassère 2015, 22–26 for instance, uses terms like *tormentée, diversifié, fragmentation, opposition brutale* to describe the mountains, and *irregularité, instabilité, capriceuses jusqu'à la catastrophe, un cancer toujours renaissant, séverès* to characterise the climate.
53. Shaw 2003; 2006.
54. Shaw 2003, 98.
55. Shaw 2003, 96–99. Greek colonisation of *Cyrenaica* is discussed in Chapter 3. In Roman times, *Cyrenaica* was part of a twinned province with Crete.

by Shaw—the Jabal area of Tripolitania, for instance, while not outstanding for its relief and rainfall in Maghribian terms, is unusual for western Libya on both counts.[56] Not every "island" needs be large to be of significance. If we recognise that Saharan communications have historically been governed by similar "rules" to those of maritime routes, the interconnectedness of all these African "islands" relied on the development of knowledge and experience of both Sahara and sea.[57] Shaw recognised the importance of connectivity, but his overall conclusion about his "islands" is that they were essentially cut adrift from the rest of the Mediterranean and the region was primarily occupied by "transhumant nomadic pastoralists" until the mid-1st millennium BCE, which seems to be an attempt to cloak an old colonialist trope with some environmental determinism.[58] While the island metaphor seems useful, his ideas about context and connectivity are thus more questionable.

A further key distinction between North Africa and other parts of the Mediterranean relates to its harbours and maritime connections. In general, the southern coast is much less abundantly supplied with natural harbours. The coast is much straighter than the northern shore, and with onshore prevailing winds the lack of sheltered anchorages is a serious limitation.[59] Currents are another factor in that they run west to east, imposing further difficulties on sailors to move in counter direction to prevailing winds from the north-west (Fig. 1.3).[60] Broodbank's configurational analysis of the modern Mediterranean coastline, essentially a measure of its relative indentedness, highlights this difference perfectly, with the Aegean standing out as an exceptional area of coastal topography offering multiple possibilities of sheltered harbours and with numerous intervisible island masses within the seascape.[61] In North Africa, there are a number of magnificent natural harbours, such as Algiers, Oran, and Tripoli, but in reality these places are few and far between. The maritime exploitation of the African shore has generally required significant investment in artificial harbour works, perhaps best exemplified by *Karthago* and *Lepcis Magna*.[62] Down the Atlantic coast of North Africa there were a number of important river ports, in part facilitated by the presence of several navigable inlets (*Lixus, Thamusida, Sala*).

---

56. Despois 1935; Mattingly 1995, 5–11.
57. Shaw 2003, 96: "As far as the movement of animals, persons, goods, and ideas was concerned, the Sahara was an environment much like the Mediterranean: one had to navigate across it in convoys along favoured routes that functioned much like sea lanes."
58. Shaw 2003, 101–02. The analysis of this flaw in Shaw's island model by Stone forthcoming is particularly cogent. See also Horden 2012.
59. Kiesling, B. and Isaksen 2014 for the text of the *Stadiasmus Maris Magni*; Shipley 2011, 80–87, 185–210 for the African section of Pseudo-Skylax.
60. Fulford 1989.
61. Broodbank 2013, 72–79, with Fig. 2.9.
62. Stone 2014b; 2016a.

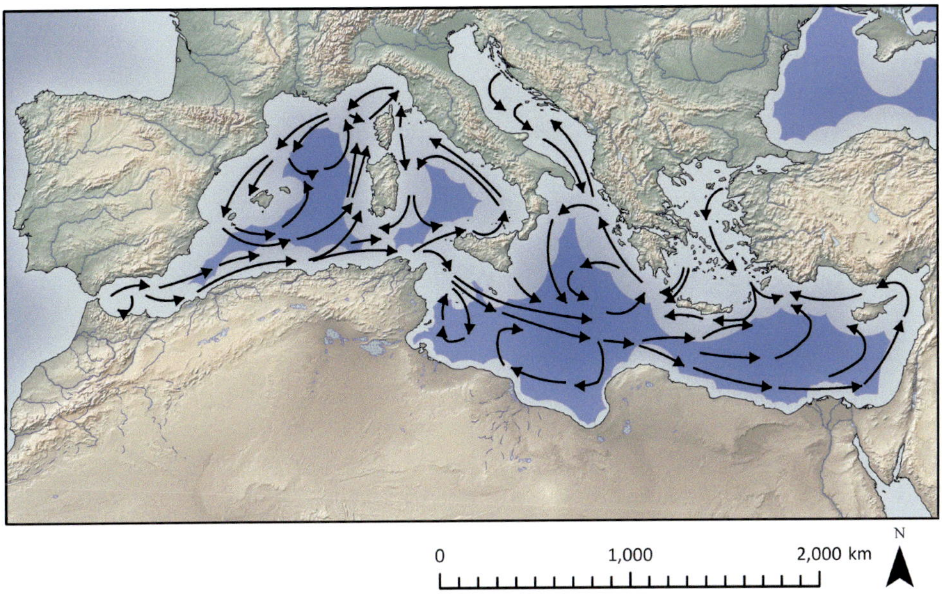

Figure 1.3. Navigational aspects of the ancient Mediterranean sea. Arrows indicate predominant currents and dark blue shading areas of sea out of sight of land (Martin Sterry, after Broodbank 2013, 8–9).

Coastal navigation in antiquity was heavily dependent on visible landmarks and though for much of the Maghrib the high inland relief fulfilled these criteria, this was much less the case moving east. The eastern Tunisian coast, the Libyan coasts of Tripolitania and Syrtica extending into the Marmarica and Egypt are generally very flat with limited relief visible, meaning that ancient mariners would have more often been out of sight of land than on the northern side of the Mediterranean (Fig. 1.3).[63] An added hazard is that in some of the areas where coastal navigation was thus obliged to stick close to the land, the sea was shallow with dangerous shoals (notably in the Lesser and Greater Syrtic gulfs).

A further factor that may have worked against the early development of extensive maritime networks is the fact that there are comparatively fewer offshore islands visible from the coast. For longer-range maritime ventures towards the northern shore, having landmarks in view across the water was a strong motivation for exploration. In the far west, the Iberian landmass can be plainly seen from the Moroccan coast, and from the Nile Delta mariners could follow the eastern shoreline north. Between the two, the next most favourable area for early maritime connections was the sea between Tunisia and Sicily. In the Last Glacial Maximum this had been a much narrower gap, but even as sea level rose again in the early

63. Broodbank, 2013, 8–9; Horden and Purcell 2000, 126–27.

Holocene this was a rare location where the space was broken up by a number of islands (Malta, Pantelleria, Lampedusa, Kerkenna, and so on).

In combination, the shortage of good natural harbours, the prevailing winds and currents, the interrupted visibility of the coastline from the sea, and the small number of close islands did not favour early development of navigational skills and extensive maritime contacts. On the other hand, the sea provided important economic resources. The annual tuna migration through the straits of Gibraltar followed a course close to the African shore and there were important fish spawning grounds in the shallow seas of the Tunisian Sahel and Lesser Gulf of Syrtes.[64] The prehistoric exploitation of shellfish was to lead to the large-scale purple dye production from the murex trunculus mollusc.[65] As we shall see, although maritime activity was less precocious than in the Aegean, by the 1st millennium BCE parts of Africa were increasingly connected by sea with other parts of the Mediterranean, and this should be understood as multidirectional.[66] For instance, the language and culture of the population on the Canary Islands clearly demonstrates links with peoples on the African mainland.

A Topographical Survey: From West to East

The c.4,500 km that separate the Atlantic from the River Nile take in a huge range of landforms and different climate zones (Figs. 1.4 and 1.9).[67] The Maghrib is normally defined as the fairly mountainous region encompassing Morocco, northern Algeria, and Tunisia. All of these regions contain significant mountainous relief, often channelling and hindering overland communications. In general, in the west the mountains are much higher, they are variably aligned, and have higher rainfall supporting a more varied ecology.[68] North Africa is often characterised in terms of binary oppositions between its mountains, whether with the desert or with plains.[69]

It is also conventional to distinguish between two broadly continuous or sequential parallel lines of mountain front in the Maghrib, the more southerly one situated 150–200 km behind the first, which lies directly behind the Mediterranean coast itself (Figs. 1.4–1.7). Between the two there are high uplifted plains, especially in

64. Broodbank 2013, 334, 574–75.
65. Broodbank 2013, 377–78
66. Cf. Broodbank 2013, 572–73 for a more cautious evaluation of the maritime capacity of Africans at this time.
67. For general overviews of the geography and topography the following are still essential starting points, Capot-Rey 1953; Despois 1949; Despois and Raynal 1967; Sherwin-White 1944.
68. Despois 1949, 31–70.
69. Courtois 1955; Mattingly 1987a; Rebuffat et al. 1986; Shaw 1987; Trousset 1987a.

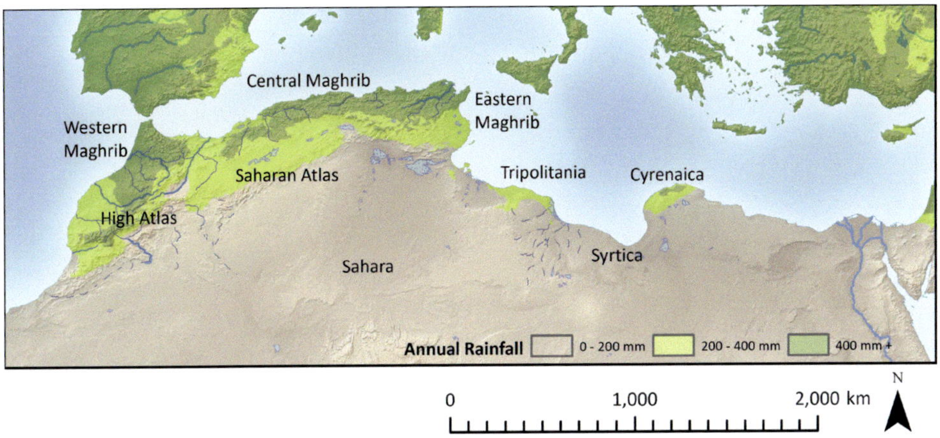

Figure 1.4. Physical geography of North Africa. Relief topography, rivers, chotts/sabkhas, and rainfall isohyet data (200 mm indicates approximate northern limit of desert) (Martin Sterry, after author's rough).

Algeria. The second, more inland sequence of ranges comprises the High Atlas, Anti Atlas, Middle Atlas (curving northwards towards the east so as to almost connect with the coastal ranges), Saharan Atlas (Monts des Ksour, Jabal Amour, Monts des Ouled Nail, Zab), the Hodna, Aurès, Nemenchas, and the Tunisian Dorsal (diverging north-north-east to meet the coast and form the Cap Bon peninsula). The nature of the tectonic uplift means that the main valley systems tend to run approximately east to west or west to east (as with Wadi Chelif and Wadi Medjerda), with relatively few major south-to-north breaks between the ranges through which rivers reach the Mediterranean.[70] Because the coastal zone is so steeply backed by hills and mountains between Tunisia and the Straits of Gibraltar, some of the most important east-to-west routes thus run some way inland from the coast.

The mountains of the Maghrib are best considered in three topographic blocks: a western part focused on northern Morocco; a central zone encompassing much of north-western and north central Algeria; and an eastern part, comprising north-eastern Algeria and most of Tunisia (Figs. 1.4–1.7). In Roman times, the three divisions of the Maghrib from west to east equated with the Roman provinces (and their borderlands) of *Mauretania Tingitana*, *Mauretania Caesariensis*, and *Africa/Numidia* (Fig. 1.1b). As these provinces underlie much of what is to follow, the next section will try and relate the topography to these three main units, with a brief consideration of the lands of *Tripolitana*, *Syrtica*, *Cyrenaica*, *Marmarica*, and the wider Sahara to follow.

70. Despois 1949, 31–72; Despois and Raynal 1967, 9–18.

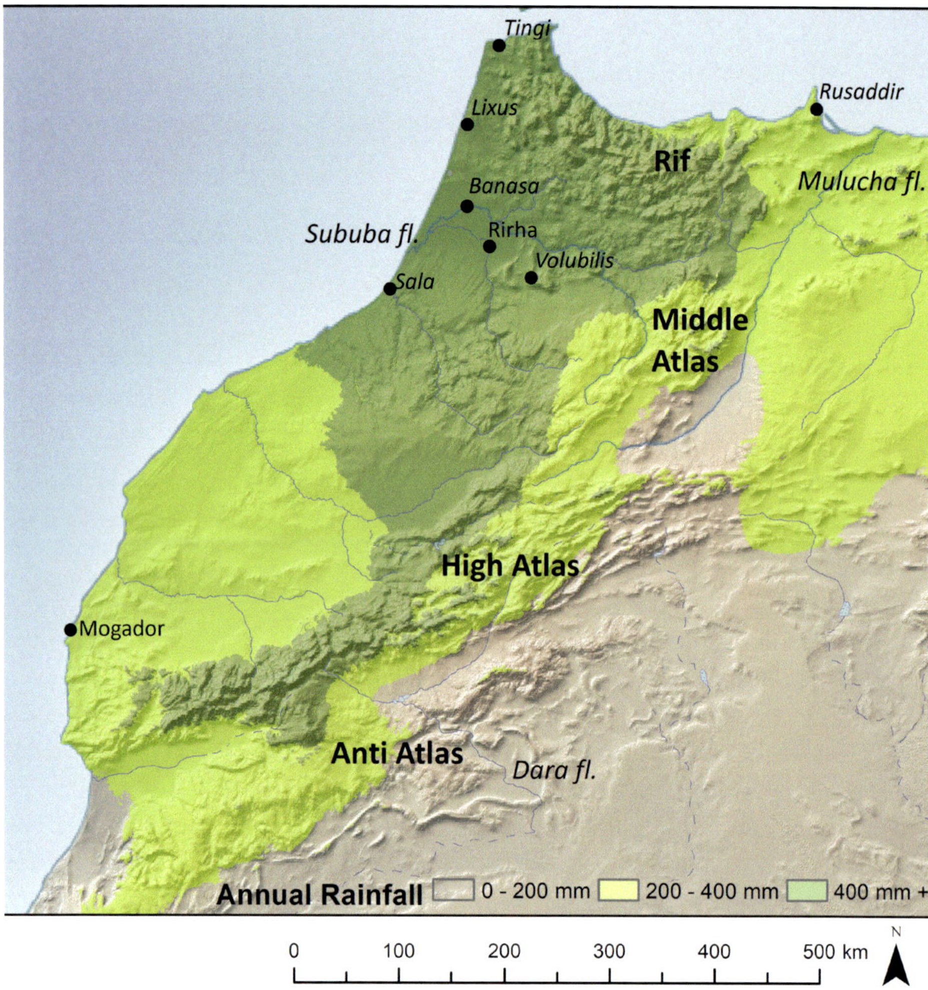

Figure 1.5. The western Maghrib, showing principal mountain ranges, rivers (with ancient names), and some major Roman sites (Martin Sterry, after author's rough).

The Moroccan "island" of the western Maghrib is defined by mountain ranges to the east and south (Fig. 1.5). These ranges separate the rolling plainlands of what was to become *Mauretania Tingitana* from the Sahara, the classic example of one of the most famous historiographical dualities: the *Bilad as-Siba* (literally "land of anarchy") and the *Bilad al-Makhzan* ("land of order").[71] The major historical paradox of Moroccan history is that the people from the "land of anarchy" have periodically overthrown

71. Gellner and Micaud 1972; Pennell 2000, 28–29, though noting that the sharp distinction between orderly Arab cities and plains and disorderly Berber mountains and deserts is in itself a product of French colonial discourse; cf. also Leveau 1986; Rouighi 2019.

and then replaced the dynasties of the "land of order." The High Atlas ranges (with the peaks of Jabal Toubkal and Ighil Mgoun more than 4,000 m) and the main passes across at over 2,000 m) are frequently snow-covered in winter and form an imposing barrier, running south-west to north-east for a distance of c.600 km.[72] The Middle Atlas on the north side of the eastern end of the High Atlas has high peaks of over 3,000 m, while the Anti Atlas, on the south-west side of the High Atlas, still has summits of over 2,000 m.[73] All the major routes across the Atlas thus have to cross a double mountain range. The Moroccan coastal mountains can also be disruptive of easy east–west movement, as in the chaotically broken terrain of the Rif (with peaks of over 2,000 m), which lies between the Middle Atlas and the Mediterranean coast. The main west-to-east corridor sandwiched between the Middle Atlas and the Rif is known as the Taza gap.[74] This upland overland route connects Fez and Oujda, but in antiquity linked *Volubilis* in *Mauretania Tingitana* with the western end of the Roman garrison deployment in *Mauretania Caesariensis*.[75] The heartlands of *Tingitana* comprised a roughly triangular area of c.17,000 km^2 of plains and low hills in north-west Morocco. This is an area with high rainfall (over 600 mm/annum) and generally fertile soils suited to dry cultivation.[76] However, along the Atlantic coast, the presence of ridges of fossilised dunes (al-Bahara), sandy soils, and some marshy areas made the littoral less conducive for settlement, which has thus tended to follow the main river valleys. There has been substantial alluviation in these river valleys since antiquity, leading to the build-up of flood levees and vast marshy areas in the Sebou (*Sububa*) valley basin (the *merjas* of the Rharb).[77] Bordering the Rharb to the south, the Marmora forest is also believed to have covered a substantial area in antiquity.

To the south-west of Rabat (beyond the southern limit of Roman territory) the coastal plains widen, and rainfall remains above 400 mm for some distance in that direction. Looking to the east, although there are also some feasible west-to-east routes through the Rif, the difficulty of all these overland connections meant there was an effective gap of c.200 km between the core territory of the two Mauretanian provinces, though some coastal settlements existed (as at *Rusaddir*).[78] There is also a communication axis that runs south-west to north-east between the Moroccan mountain ranges and those of neighbouring Algeria along the valley of the Wadi Mouloya (ancient *Mulucha*). The mountain bloc to the west creates a partial rain

72. Despois and Raynal 1967, 340–43.
73. Despois and Raynal 1967, 354–56 (Anti Atlas), 372–74 (Middle Atlas).
74. Despois and Raynal 1967, 359–62; On the difficulty of communications in the Rif, see Coletti 2018; Coletti and Guspini 2017.
75. The use of this route in antiquity has been disputed at times, see Euzennat 1977a, 429–34; Rebuffat 1971a. However, the location of the inland city of *Volubilis* is likely to reflect the early development of the land communication between eastern and western *Mauretania*.
76. Carcopino 1944; Despois and Raynal 1967, 299–301; Euzennat 2000.
77. Martorella 2020.
78. Euzennat 2000, 456.

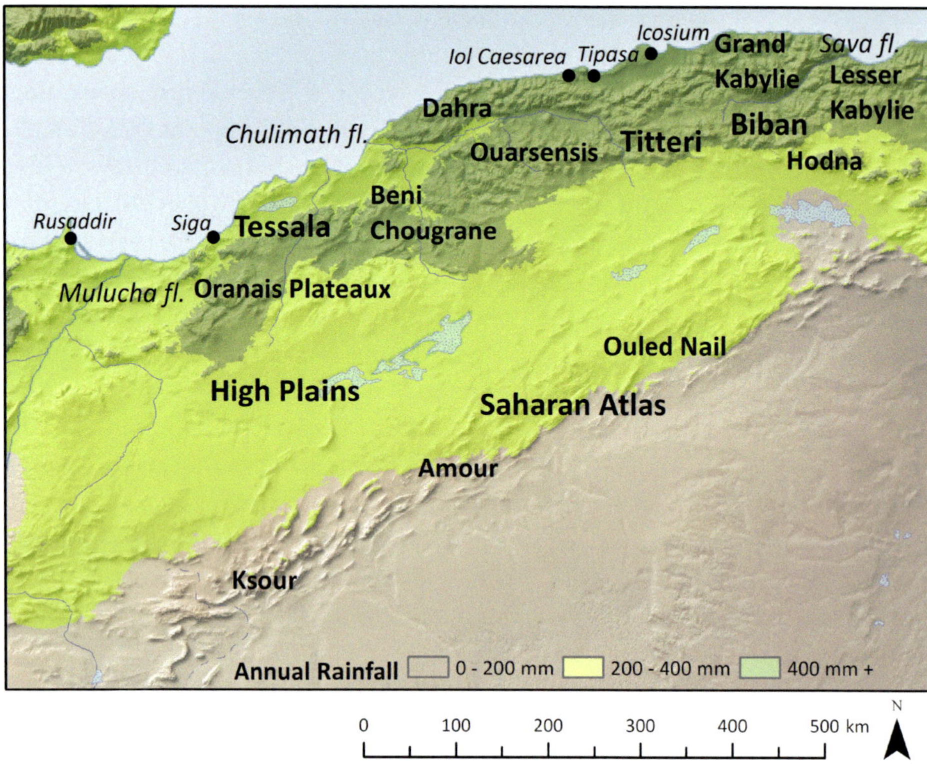

Figure 1.6. The central Maghrib and some major Roman sites (Martin Sterry, after author's rough).

shadow in the Mouloya valley (200–300 mm isohyet), so the agricultural potential of this lower lying strip is somewhat diminished. The historical significance of the river as a boundary is unsurprising.[79]

Across the river and proceeding further east into the area of *Mauretania Caesariensis*, there is a sequence of east–west aligned mountain ranges, extending 100 km south from the coast (Fig. 1.6).[80] Moving east from the *Mulucha,* the major coastal mountain ranges are sequentially Tessala, Dahra, Ouarsenis, Titteri, Grand Kabylie, Biban, Lesser Kabylie. The coastal plain is generally of limited extent, but between the ranges of the Dahra and Ouarsenis, the east-to-west Chelif (ancient *Chulimath*) valley is a significant and broad zone of agricultural land. East of Algiers, the direct coastal route is again impeded by the imposing bulk of the Grand and Lesser Kabylie (peaks in excess of 2,000 m) and the incised valleys of the Wadi Soummam (*Sava*) and Rhumel/Khabir (*Ampsaga*).[81]

79. Desanges 1980b, 154–57.
80. Potter 2000a; 2000b
81. Despois and Raynal 1967, 88–91, 95–97, 106–14; Lawless 1972.

Returning to the west and moving further inland across the high Oranais plateau, there is a parallel line of mountains, effectively the continuation of the Anti Atlas range. This forms the Saharan Atlas (comprising the Monts des Ksour, the Jabal Amour, the Monts des Ouled Nail, and the Zab).[82] Between the Saharan Atlas (which cumulatively runs for c.800 km south-west to north-east) and the coastal Tell, there is a 140–160 km broad zone of high plainlands generally above 1,000 m altitude, with numerous saline lakes (chotts) due to the limited outflow towards the sea caused by the wall of the northern Tell. The high plains lie in a partial rain shadow and are somewhat steppe-like in character.[83]

The Lesser Kabylie, Babor, and Kroumirie mountains fill the land between the Wadi Soummam (*Sava*) and Wadi Rhumel (*Ampsaga*), while a set of broadly north-west to south-east trending ranges (Biban, Hodna, and Belezma) connect the coastal Tell with the Aurès. From the *Ampsaga* eastwards extended the province of *Africa* (Fig. 1.7).[84] The ranges of the northern Tell continue behind the coastline into Tunisia, but with diminishing elevation (the peaks of the Tunisian Tell generally fall below 1,000 m).[85] However, running north-eastwards out of the Tell runs the most significant river of the Maghrib, the Wadi Medjerda (*Bagrada*)—its principal valley and those of secondary tributaries (Mellegue and Siliana) were the heartlands of North Africa's fabled grain production.[86] South of the Medjerda valley there is a fertile region of rolling hills and high plains, broadly centred on the area between *Sicca Veneria* (El Kef), *Ammaedara* (Haidra), and *Mactaris* (Maktar). South of Constantine (*Cirta*) in eastern Algeria, there is another region of high plains, delimited to the south by the ranges of the Aurès (peaks over 2,000 m) and Nemencha (peaks approaching 1,500 m).[87] The Aurès high plain at an elevation of over 1,000 m can receive winter snow, but is better watered, again leading to seasonal lakes, and more suitable for cultivation than the High Plains further west.

North-east of the Nemencha, the southerly mountain chain continues as the Tunisian Dorsal, gradually converging on the coast, where the Cap Bon peninsula forms a final spur of hilly terrain beyond the Bay of Tunis. This again had good potential for farming, but was more suited to vines and olives than cereals.[88]

South of the Dorsal lies the High Steppe region of the Kasserine to Gafsa area, with decreased rainfall making the land somewhat less suited to agriculture.[89] *Capsa*

82. Despois and Raynal 1967, 133–37.
83. Despois and Raynal 1967, 114–32.
84. Fentress 2000a; 2000b; Hitchner 2000a; 2000b.
85. Peyras 1991 for a detailed archaeological study of part of the eastern Tell that relates well to the topography.
86. Despois and Raynal 1967, 237–40
87. Despois and Raynal 1967, 191–93, 195–97; Fentress 2000a; 2000b; Morizot 1997.
88. Despois and Raynal 1967, 219–20; Hitchner 2000a.
89. Despois and Raynal 1967, 243–49; Hitchner 2000b.

Figure 1.7. The eastern Maghrib and some major Roman sites (Martin Sterry, after author's rough).

(Gafsa) sits in a gap through further sharply defined west-to-east running ranges, and south of these the countryside fairly quickly moves through pre-desert to desert conditions. The area between the high steppe and the east coast of Tunisia is known as the Lower Steppe with much of the area receiving below 300 mm rainfall.[90]

Tunisia's eastern coast between the base of Cap Bon at Nabeul and the Gulf of Gabes is notably low-lying, but its plainlands are less well watered than the Dorsal and Tell to the north and west. The area between Sousse (*Hadrumetum*) and *Thaenae* (Sfax) corresponds with ancient *Byzacium* and comprises the best land

90. Despois 1955, 9–96.

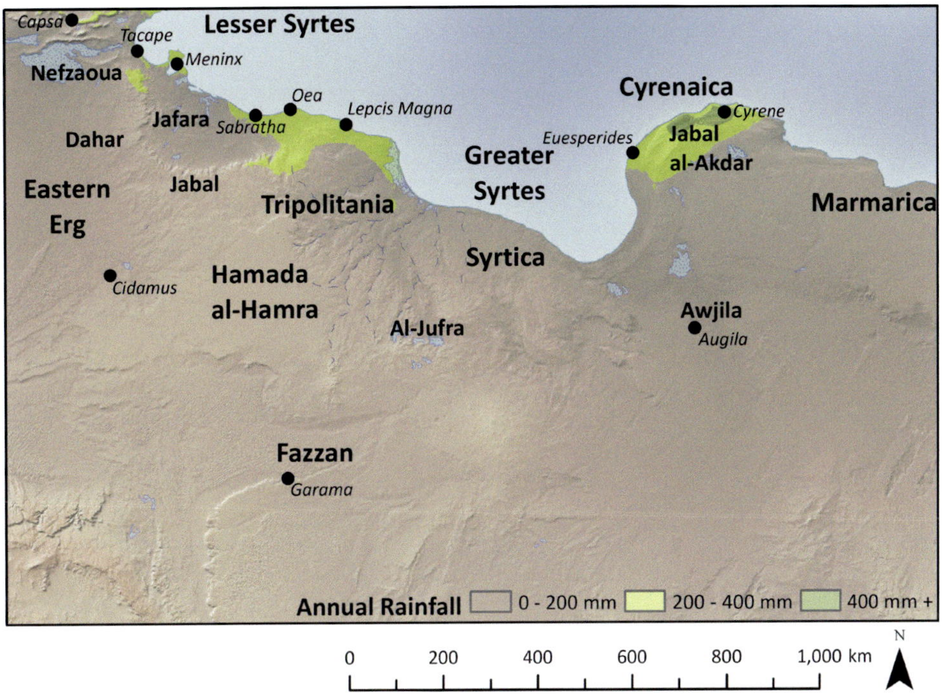

Figure 1.8. Tripolitania, *Syrtica*, *Cyrenaica*, and *Marmarica*, and some major Roman sites (Martin Sterry, after author's rough).

in the region (soils are better here and rainfall rises above 300 mm).[91] South and south-west of Sfax the coastlands are increasingly arid. The landscape is broken up by a number of large seasonal lakes (sabkhas) fed by seasonal run-off in wadis that do not reach the sea. While in modern times the coastal region is most notable for its extensive olive groves, it was evidently also exploited for cereal cultivation in antiquity.[92] The sea is shallow off the eastern Tunisian coast and attractive as a spawning ground for fish, and the exploitation of marine resources has been an important part of its economy through time.[93]

East of Gabes at the foot of the Lesser Syrtic Gulf, the Mediterranean coast lies considerably further south than the zones just discussed (Fig. 1.8), and more generally the coastal zone borders on semi-arid or desert lands directly, with some slight amelioration in a few restricted zones of higher relief (the Tripolitanian Jabal Nafusa/Tarhuna and the Cyrenaican Jabal al-Akdar). This part of North Africa is mostly excluded from standard definitions of the Maghrib, and I shall refer to the

91. Despois 1955, 19–21, 56–74.
92. Despois 1955, 209–24, 235–51; Despois and Raynal 1967, 224–30; Mattingly et al. 2011, 214–19.
93. Slim et al. 2004; Mattingly et al. 2011, 205–14.

Figure 1.9. Topography of the Sahara: massifs and sand seas (Martin Sterry, from Mattingly et al. 2017a, 9).

coastal area and hilly hinterland immediately east of the Maghrib as Tripolitania.[94] To the east again, around the southern side of the Greater Syrtes, is the desert landscape of *Syrtica*.[95] On the east side of the deep embayment of the Greater Syrtes, there is another northward projecting area of land with higher relief and a more typically Mediterranean climate, *Cyrenaica*.[96] The Jabal al-Akdar (Green Mountain) in particular has good soils and receives comparatively elevated rainfall. The zone between *Cyrenaica* and Egypt is once again relatively low-lying and arid steppe lands and is known as *Marmarica*.[97]

Just as the landscapes of the Mediterranean regions of North Africa are very variable, so the vast desert hinterland of the Sahara must also be considered region by region (Fig. 1.9). Only c.20% of the Sahara comprises the sand seas (Ergs, Dahan, or Edeyen) of popular imagination, though the major sand seas are formidable barriers. From west to east the largest are Erg Iguidi, Erg Chech, the Grand Erg Occidental, the Grand Erg Oriental, Dahan Ubari, Dahan Murzuq, the Tenere, and the Great Sand Sea. There are also some significant Saharan mountain enclaves: again from west to east the most important are Adrar des Iforas, Ahaggar, Aïr, Tassili n'Ajjer, Tadrart Akakus, Tibesti, Ennedi, and Jabal Uweynat.

94. Despois 1935; Mattingly 1995, 1–13; 2000a.
95. Mattingly 2000c; cf. Mastino 2020; Quinn 2011; Wilson 2013.
96. Horden and Purcell 2000, 65–74; Johnson 1973; Mattingly 2000d.
97. Mattingly 2000e; Purcaro Pagano 1976 on the *Stadiasmus Maris Magni* for this section of coast.

The mountains have an undeniable savage beauty in their overbaked and wind-eroded state, and, importantly, they function as human and animal *refugia*, due to some limited rainfall that collects in seasonal pools (gueltas) and provides sporadic grazing in water-eroded wadis (a reminder that at times the Sahara has been far wetter). However, the great majority of the Sahara comprises rocky plateau lands (*hamada*, such as al-Hamada al-Hamra in Libya), vast alluvial or gravel plains (*serir* or *reg*), and dusty depressions—many of which are closed basins with springs, relict lakes, or a shallow water table that can be easily reached. Some depressions have seasonal lakes or traces of long-evaporated lakes in them.[98]

In the absence of any regular or significant level of rainfall, the key to movement and survival is the availability of groundwater, mostly accessed through wells or springs. Exceptionally, in times of rare rainfall, desert landscapes can be transformed into a semblance of a savannah environment. Even without human intervention, the Saharan environment is not completely inimitable to life. The cooler winter months are the easiest time for travel and pastoral exploitation, but the possibility of seasonal rainfall in the mountain ranges is important not only for the generation of pasture in the valleys and outflows, but also for the creation and topping-up of the water holes that can contain water all year round. These various types of natural *refugia* within the Sahara have been an important focus of human activity since the last major climatic change 5,000 years ago. Many of them have been developed as oases in the course of time, and this will be an important focus later in this account.[99]

The rainfall isohyet data works with the topographical features to define the limits of the possible (Fig. 1.10). The highest annual rainfall is, as one might expect, associated with the High Atlas range in Morocco, with peaks at over 4,000 m and frequent snow cover in winter. The rainfall and snowmelt of the Middle Atlas feeds a number of perennial and navigable rivers, notably the Loukkos, Sebou, and Bou Regreg (in the fertile valleys of which were situated the Roman sites of *Volubilis*, *Lixus*, *Banasa*, *Thamusida*, *Sala*). The Sebou river (*Sububa*) was navigable at least as far inland as *Banasa* in Roman times, and with its major tributaries formed the most extensive basin in Morocco.[100] There are also some important wadis on the south side of the Atlas that flow south into the northern Sahara, notably the (perennial) Wadi Draa (*Darat*) and the seasonally significant Wadis Rheris, Ziz, and Gir.[101]

There are few perennial rivers in Algeria and Tunisia, but the *Sava* (Soummam), *Chulimath* (Chelif), and the *Bagrada* (Medjerda) are important exceptions (Figs. 1.5–1.7) and again their valleys have been a focus for settlement

98. For desert landforms, see for instance Capot-Rey 1953, 102–60; Gautier 1970, 34–52; Laureano 1991, 22–45; Mattingly 2017, 6–12.
99. Purdue et al. 2018b.
100. Pliny, *NH* 5.5: *amnis Sububus magnificus et navigabilis*. On the Sebou valley in antiquity, see Akerraz et al. 1995.
101. Sterry et al. 2020a, 252–63.

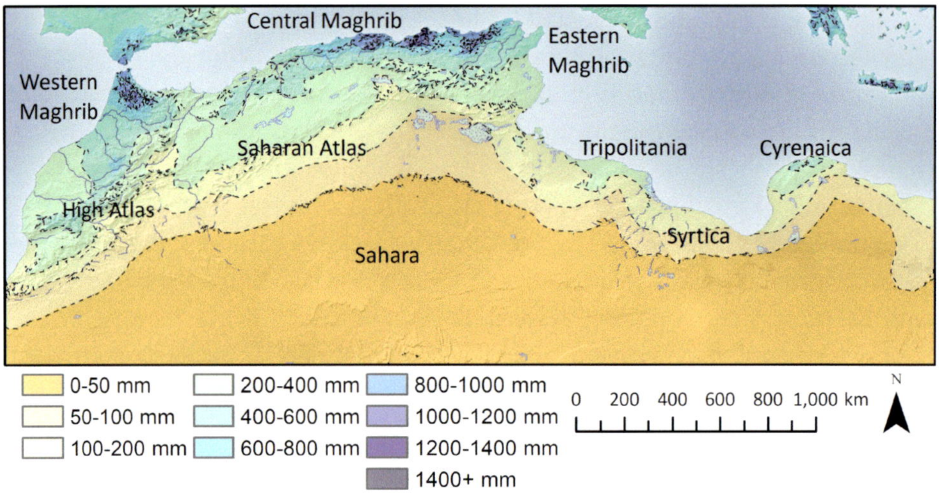

Figure 1.10. Rainfall isohyet data for North Africa and the northern Sahara (Martin Sterry; data from worldclim.org).

over time. More common across North Africa are seasonal rivers (wadis), which are reduced to at most a trickle of water in the hottest months of the year, but can carry spectacular flash floods after autumn or winter rains. Travelling in Algeria and Libya for the first time in 1979, two formative experiences involved dangerously close encounters with flash floods. The power and unpredictability of such floods are not easily forgotten, but another flash flood in Libya in 1998 still nearly caught me unawares (Fig. 1.11). Flooding can affect land adjacent to river and wadi systems.

Some of the rivers and seasonal wadis empty into the sea, but others into flattish areas of seasonal lakes (variously described as chotts or sabkhas—Fig. 1.4 for largest examples). The largest of the chotts in southern Tunisia and Algeria are below sea level.[102] Although they often exist as shallow lakes or mudflats in the winter months, in the summer they are salt flats, hostile environments for travel or pastoral exploitation.[103] The chotts thus channel communications or at any rate seasonally limit them. Their low elevation, however, means that groundwater is often close to the surface in their environs. To south-east and north-west of the largest example (Chott Jarid), extensive spring-fed oases have developed, known as the Nefzaoua and the Jarid.

In general terms, areas receiving more than 400 mm rainfall per year are considered suitable for dry farming, but this needs to be moderated by two important

102. Peyras and Trousset 1988.

103. On the seasonal crossing of the Chott Jarid, Trousset 1982a. On chotts and sabkhas, see Capot-Rey 1953, 137–41; Despois and Raynal 1967, 29–30, 424–25

a b

Figure 1.11. Wadi agriculture. a) Flash flood in the Wadi Beni Ulid, Libya in March 1998. The river bed is cultivated and irrigated by such periodic flood events, with wadi walls directing and helping control the floodwaters. b) Abandoned wadi wall systems in another pre-desert wadi (Photos: author).

provisos in the case of North Africa.[104] First, the annual average figures mask the fact that rainfall is very unevenly distributed within the year, and year on year does not follow a consistent and reliable pattern.[105] If anticipated autumn rains do not arrive in fact till January or February, this has implications for the growing season to follow. Extended droughts are not uncommon, as demonstrated by the propitious rainfall that marked the visit of Hadrian to Africa in 128 CE (HA, *Hadrian* 22.14: "it rained upon his arrival after five years of drought which earned him the affection of the Africans"). A related issue is that a large proportion of the annual rainfall can arrive all together in a single downpour and accompanying flash flood. Such floods are difficult to control and can erode soil, endanger homes and livestock, and the rapid passage of the water deprives the subsoil of the opportunity to absorb a larger reservoir of moisture. The second proviso is that the isohyet is an average across years and in fact reflects a pattern of drastically unequal annual totals, with years of abundant rainfall interspersed by others of serious dearth. Farming in North Africa has thus depended on careful water management to a much greater extent than farming in the European Mediterranean.[106]

Parts of the Tripolitanian coastal plain (Jafara) as well as *Syrtica* and *Marmarica* are poorly watered areas, receiving little rainfall and with relatively few springs and oases. The highest rainfalls in Tripolitania (>300 mm per year) and *Cyrenaica* (>400 mm per year) are quite restricted to the immediate area of *Lepcis Magna* and

104. Capot-Rey 1953, 36–68; Despois and Raynal 1967, 18–32; Hobson 2020, 308–09 for a strong correlation between the 400 mm isohyet and the areas of strongest settlement development in the North African provinces of Rome.

105. Illustrated in relation to Tripolitania in Mattingly 1995, 8–11.

106. Barker et al. 1996a, 191–225; Ibba and Mastino 2011a; Shaw 1984.

Cyrene—the two major ancient cities of these regions. Much of the rest of these areas lies below the 150 mm threshold that marks pre-desert and desert conditions. The only perennial stream in Libya is the *Cinyps* (Wadi Caam) near *Lepcis Magna*. In a European context it would not merit the appellation "river." The coasts of *Syrtica* and *Marmarica*, extending close to the Nile Delta, had much in common with the Tripolitanian coastal lands in terms of the paucity of watercourses.

The River Nile is an exceptional geographical phenomenon within North Africa and the Mediterranean. Its high-volume flow, its annual floods, and its complete south-to-north passage across the Sahara make it a river unlike any other.[107] For much of its length it is in effect an extended river-fed oasis, with some notable offshoots where topography and canalisations allowed, as in the Fayum basin. The Nile Delta represents another very different environment again, with its intensively irrigated cultivation.[108] Because of its utter difference to other parts of North Africa, it makes sense to treat the Nile Valley as outside the scope of this book, while noting that some ancient geographers believed its source lay in the far west.[109]

Our view of North Africa's climate and geography is not wholly objective in that it in part enshrines emphases and assumptions of both the ancient sources and modern colonial science.[110] It is easy to overstate the constraints and difficulties of terrain and climate—as my own account above may do in places. However, we need to carefully re-evaluate what we know and what we assume. Despite its deserts and mountains, North Africa contains significant areas of land suited to agriculture and arboriculture. Where rainfall is sufficiently high and reliable, this has allowed extensive agricultural development, helped also by a long growing season, though high summer temperatures and hot desert winds can pose problems. The main Mediterranean cultivars do well in North Africa, bread wheat and barley are the principal cereal crops, accompanied in many regions by olive trees. Vines thrive better in some locations than others, as do a range of other fruit trees (figs, pomegranates, peaches, apricots, almonds, and so on). On the other hand, the date palm is queen of the desert landscapes, which have also been made fruitful by human ingenuity.

Figure 1.12 shows the prime areas of cultivation of a range of crops: cereals, olives, vines, and date palms.[111] In general, cereals seem to have had greatest importance on larger plainlands and where rainfall was highest or more reliable. While wheat cultivation has traditionally been rare outside the highlighted areas, barley and hardier cereals have a somewhat wider distribution. As a fairly drought-tolerant species that can grow on hilly terrain also, olives thrive in a wide range

107. Merrills 2017a for Roman geographical understanding and reception.
108. Mattingly et al. 2020c, 115–21.
109. Merrills 2017a on the supposed source in the Moroccan Wadi Draa (ancient *Darat*)
110. Davies 2007; Vatin 1984. See also the excellent studies by Leveau 2018; 2021.
111. Data compiled from multiple sources, including Camps-Fabrer 1953; Despois and Raynal 1967, 199–209, 258–64, 394–405; Le Glay 1966b, 193.

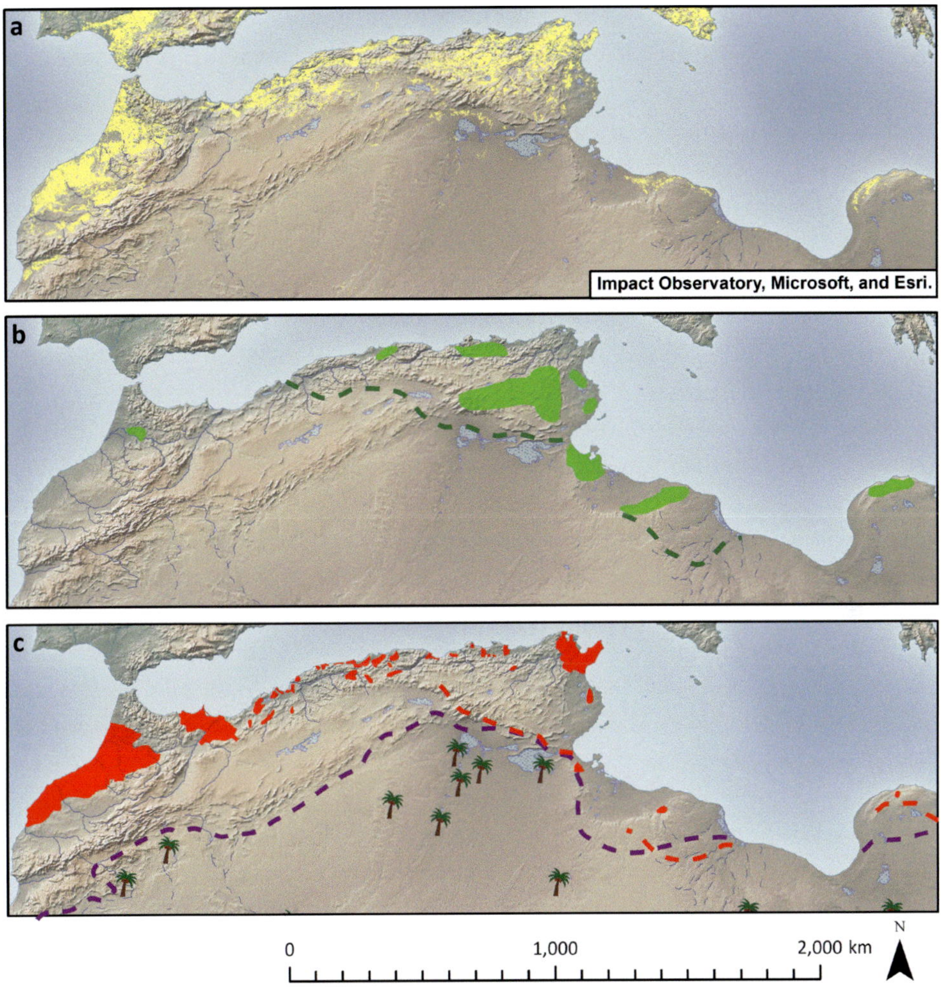

Figure 1.12. Main areas suited to cultivation. a) Cereals. b) Olives (green line = ancient southern limits). c) Vines (red line = ancient southern limit) and dates (purple line = northern limit of main productive oases) (Martin Sterry, after author's roughs, drawing on Despois 1949, 370 and other modern sources).

of topographical conditions in North Africa, from pre-desert wadi cultivation to high-altitude plantations in the Aurès (well above the modern limits).[112] In principle, viticulture can follow fairly closely the pattern for olives, but intensive and more specialised cultivation relies on niche locations where soils and rainfall are optimal. There is evidence that viticulture in North Africa was in general much more extensive than its modern limits. The date palm is predominantly a crop of

112. Mattingly 1988b; 1996b.

the Sahara and its oases, though in places the bulk cultivation of comestible dates overlaps with the limits of floodwater and irrigated cultivation of the vine and olive (Fig. 1.12c).

Soil quality is another key determinant of subsistence and economic strategies, and the most productive regions of North Africa generally combine higher rainfall with good quality soils. In some cases it was the contrast with the surrounding area that may have favoured the more intensive development of a particular ecological niche. This is what makes some areas stand out: the plains of *Tingitana*, the Chelif and Medjerda valleys, the Constantine area, the Aurès plateau, the Tunisian Tell and Dorsal, Cap Bon, the Tunisian Sahel, the Tripolitanian Jabal, the Jabal al-Akhtar.

The animal resources of North Africa were varied and played important roles in the story.[113] As noted already, domesticated cattle, sheep, and goats were well established throughout North Africa from around 6000 BCE. Pigs, chickens, donkeys, mules, horses, and camels were later introductions, but were all present during the 1st millennium BCE.[114] While some of these animals are well suited to the transhumant pastoral lifestyles that have been often assumed for the bulk of the pre-Roman indigenous population, we need to interrogate the evidence more closely. Cattle, horses, pigs, and chickens, for instance, are best reared by people with ready access to water and relatively fixed bases. It is certainly true that parts of the North African landscapes were suited to pastoral forms of exploitation, but we might expect at certain times and places to see evidence of more sedentary communities and mixed farming communities as well. Horses and camels have played a particularly important role in facilitating the interconnectedness of the vast trans-Saharan spaces of North Africa.[115]

Wild animals in North Africa were both an economic opportunity for hunters and a hazard for farming communities. This country (if we consider its Saharan parts as well) supported elephants, lions, a range of other big cats, ostriches, giraffes, antelopes, gazelles, and Barbary apes. The capacity of North Africa to supply some of Rome's needs in wild and exotic beasts was celebrated in the ancient sources as well as in vivid mosaic art (Fig. 12.3).[116] At another level, the concept of a "wild beast zone" was often deployed in the ancient sources to portray a negative vision of the landscape encountered by Rome—essentially focusing on it as a waterless desert, made even less hospitable by its ferocious beasts and insidious snakes and scorpions (e.g. Pliny, *NH* 5.22; Strabo 2.5.35).[117]

---

113. See now Blanc Bijon et al. 2021 for a range of relevant studies.

114. Fothergill et al. 2020; Mattingly and Hitchner 1995, 196–97; Mattingly et al. 2021.

115. Bernus 2006; Daumas 1968; Devisse 1995; Mattingly et al. 2021; Shaw 1979a.

116. Vismara 2021; Laporte 2021; Lochin 2021 for a series of recent studies.

117. Borca 2004; Corbier and Griesheimer 2005, 81–85; Desanges 1980b, 205–208; Gsell 1913, 100–37.

Chronological Framing

Another of the challenges with writing about "Roman Africa" is to know where to draw the chronological limits. There is no simple answer to this, though the sample of recent French textbooks suggests 69–439 CE (five titles), 146 BCE–439 CE (two titles) or 256 BCE–711 CE (one title). Arguments in support of all of these can be advanced, no doubt (though many of the chronological termini relate to events external to Africa and thus emphasise the extent to which the books look at Africa from Rome's perspective). From the First Punic War (264–241 BCE) onwards, it can be argued, that Rome's destiny was tied to some degree to that of its great rival, *Qart Hadasht* (Punic Carthage). The battle of Zama in 202 BCE on African soil confirmed Hannibal's defeat in the Second Punic War. Rome's eventual victory in the Third Punic War in 146 BCE and the destruction of *Qart Hadasht* led to annexation of territory and continuing responsibilities and entanglements in Africa. At the other extreme, the Vandal invasion of North Africa in 429 CE and their eventual capture of *Karthago* a decade later marks a political end to Roman rule. On the other hand, many aspects of life continued as before under the rule of the Vandal kings, up to the Eastern Roman Empire's reconquest of 533 CE, and Byzantine Africa can in some ways be seen as a prolongation of the earlier imperial project. The Arab invasions from the 640s CE onwards led to another long transitional phase, culminating in the fall of *Karthago* in 698 CE (and 711 CE marked the surrender of the final Byzantine outpost far to the west at *Septem*/Ceuta in Morocco). There was undoubtedly considerable continuity across many of these event horizons—there was, for instance, certainly an important Christian afterlife in some areas. Overall, there is a case for studying "Roman Africa" across approximately one thousand years from the 3rd century BCE to the start of the 8th century CE.[118] Appendix 1 (at end of the book) presents some of the essential chronological framing as an expedient alternative to a long narrative description.

One of the problems of chronology is that there are always precursors and repercussions to take into consideration, especially in a study that is more culturally than politically focused. In the preceding section I have already ventured back to the start of the Holocene and attempted to draw out some of the main environmental factors that made the human development of North Africa somewhat different from other regions of the Mediterranean.

The main chronological focus of this book is on the early imperial period, broadly the later 1st century BCE to the 3rd century CE. However, at times the discussion must range much more broadly. In Part 2, for instance, I look back in detail at the archaeology of the 1st millennium BCE in North Africa, which is absolutely

118. Though note that the chronological implications of my study of "Roman Africa" extend to the 21st century.

crucial to understanding the cultural and economic evolution of the region under Roman rule. Archaeological evidence to supplement historical sources is much more limited for the Roman Republican phases in comparison to the Principate.[119] I shall also draw on information from the late Roman and subsequent phases, where it illuminates aspects of life in the earlier period. In focusing on discrepant Roman imperial experience I have taken the decision to largely ignore the story of Christianity in Africa. Christianity and post-Roman political change created new manifestations of identity that are beyond this study.[120] Similarly, the Islamic era lies well outside my scope, yet still provides a wide range of relevant material to compare and contrast with the Roman era.[121]

The Human Backdrop to Africa in the Roman Empire

Who were the inhabitants of North Africa at the time of Roman annexation? And how should we characterise them? How far back in time did ethnic identities extend?[122] As a starting point I want to differentiate three very broad groupings, though further subdivisions will become apparent as we proceed.[123] I must acknowledge at the start that these broad divisions are essentially externally observed ones, and that the communities that the Romans defined by these terms did not necessarily see themselves as having a primary attachment to such large entities, but rather traced their cultural identity to a multiplicity of smaller urban and rural population groups.[124] Nonetheless, the larger blocks of peoples recognised by Rome as sharing linguistic and cultural traits are relevant to an analysis that seeks to explore different identities at play.

First, we need to recognise that the Phoenician/Punic settlements were from quite an early date in effect populated by ***Libyphoenices***, through intermarriage of Phoenicians with local Africans—indeed, ethnically some of these communities may have been more Libyan than Phoenician. A second important point is that differences between the Libyan groups may have resulted in a lack of an overall sense

119. Hobson 2019a; 2022; Stone 2013b.
120. See, inter alia, Leone 2022; Mandouze 1982; Shaw 2011. Conant 2012a; Rebillard 2012; Whelan 2018 all show that questions of identity have relevance to the later periods.
121. Fenwick 2020; Levtzion and Hopkins 1981.
122. This question is not easy to resolve on current evidence, but I strongly believe that the earlier 1st-millennium BCE developments were highly pertinent to what emerged in the last centuries BCE. In this sense I may talk about proto- or early Numidian society long before we have the evidence of a Numidian state to solidify our sense of a Numidian ethnic group.
123. The bibliographic starting point for any evaluation of the peoples of North Africa in antiquity is the remarkable work of Jehan Desanges, starting with his 1962 catalogue of references in Classical sources. See also Desanges 1978a; 1980b; 1999a; 1999b. The work of Bates 1970; Brett and Fentress 1996; Camps 1960; 1980; 1987a; 1987b; Hamdoune 2018; Modéran 2003 are also essential reading.
124. Cf. Fentress 2006; Shaw 2014.

of a common Libyphoenician identity.[125] As the pre-eminent centre, *Qart Hadasht* was somewhat distinctive in cultural terms compared to the Libyphoenician *emporia*, and we need to be cautious about assuming evidence from there can be applied equally to other Libyphoenician centres.[126] Some scholars have started to question the cultural significance of the term Punic, as conventionally understood, because of this African cultural context.[127] It is certainly clear that Punic language, institutions, and culture became widely disseminated within Africa beyond the original coastal *emporia*. Nonetheless, there is a sense, I think, that those coastal settlements retained a cultural character long after the Roman provincialisation of Africa that was distinctive from Roman colonies or inland towns.[128]

The second group comprises peoples who are often referred to today as Berbers, to use an externally applied collective term of the medieval period, or as Amazigh (plural, Imazighen) to employ a self-determined (modern) term.[129] The term Amazigh clearly relates to an ancient ethnic, *Mazices*, but this was just one of many known from antiquity.[130] Berber heritage remains politically contentious in many countries of the Maghrib, and Ramzi Rouighi has recently argued that the idea of collective Berber identity was largely a construct of the Arab conquest of the region, which was subsequently adopted as a key element of French colonial discourse.[131] While the linguistic and cultural connections between the local populations of North Africa pre- and post-Arab conquest are undeniable, we need to be careful not to assume they constituted a monolithic cultural entity. A key argument of this book is that there were significant and long-running differences between a number of distinct Amazigh groups in North Africa, and that these profoundly shaped regional societies in the Roman era. One solution would be to use in preference to Amazigh or Berber the ancient term ***Libyes***, meaning in essence the indigenous inhabitants of Africa north of the Sahara. These people were predominantly "Mediterranean" Africans, rather than Black Africans—who were designated as *Aethiopes* in the ancient sources (though in reality, as we shall see, such a binary division of populations is not supportable by the evidence).[132]

125. Mattingly 1995, 25–29. The *Libyphoenices* are a prime focus of Chapter 3, though consideration there will also be given to other Mediterranean "settler" groups, Greeks in Cyrenaica, and Romans more generally.
126. Ben Younès 2007; Ennabli 2020; Fantar 1993a/b; Fumadó Ortega 2022; Lancel 1995; Quinn and Vella 2014.
127. Quinn 2018, with in depth discussion below in Chapter 3.
128. Modéran 2011, 15; cf. St Augustine *Letters* 138.4.19 reprimanding Maxim of *Madauros* for making derogatory comments about people with Punic names.
129. Brett and Fentress 1996, 1–49; Modéran 2010; Sanmartí 2022.
130. Modéran 2010; Rebuffat 2011a, 74–76.
131. Rouighi 2019, for instance, makes clear that we need to be aware of the potential back-projection of a colonialist discourse on the Berbers derived from the 19th-century reception of Ibn Kaldun's *Kitab al-ʿibar*.
132. This is discussed in more detail in Chapter 5.

There was no universal Amazigh language base, but rather the development of lots of regional dialects and strong perceptions of local differences. The reality on the ground was that the *Libyes* were represented by a vast number of smaller groupings of people, with their own specific names and identities. Pliny (*NH* 5.29), for example, wrote of 516 distinct *populi* between the *Ampsaga* river and the Greater Syrtes, of which he specified 53 as urban populations and commented that, of the remaining 463, many were more appropriately thought of as *nationes* than *civitates*. He only named 10 of these groups by name, so that leaves around 450 peoples living under Roman authority in the 1st century CE within *Africa* whose names he did not copy from his sources.[133] There were also, of course, many other peoples who at this time lived outside Roman control. In his great catalogue of North African peoples, Jehan Desanges listed 24 peoples geographically associated with *Mauretania Tingitana*, 60 with *Mauretania Caesariensis*, and 107 from *Africa Proconsularis* (including *Numidia* and Tripolitania).[134] That is a grand total of 191 ethnonyms, well short of the 463 for *Africa* alone, and the discrepancy must be wider still as his *Catalogue* included many names that are either earlier or later than Pliny.

While many of these peoples perhaps represented relatively small-scale communities (often designated "tribes" in colonial and more recent scholarship), some were evidently much larger and complex societies. In fact, the more northerly peoples were coalescing into states by the late 3rd century BCE, based around two main self-identifying groups, the *Numidae* in western Tunisia and eastern Algeria, and the *Mauri* further to the west.[135]

The peoples living to the south of the Carthaginian, Numidian, and Mauretanian heartlands were known by myriad names, but had the capacity for periodic confederated action. The Roman sources tended to refer to them in broad terms as *Gaetuli* and I shall argue that this was a meaningful cultural distinction. Beyond them lay other Libyan peoples of the deep Sahara, including the *Garamantes*.[136]

Aethiopes were Black Africans in the Classical sources, and though sometimes presented as remote in space from the core territory of the Roman provinces in Africa, they were clearly a recognised element of the population on the fringes and in the northern Sahara.[137] The neat separation of *Aethiopes*, *Gaetuli*, and *Garamantes* may be suspected as a *topos* of our sources and, as I shall argue in more detail in Chapter 5, from an early date Saharan communities

133. Desanges 1980b, 276–349 for detailed commentary on Pliny's list.
134. Desanges 1962; Ibba and Traina 2006, 81 for a neat tabulation of the names in relation to provinces.
135. These groups are the focus of Chapter 4.
136. The *Gaetuli* and the *Garamantes* will be examined in detail in Chapter 5.
137. Desanges 1976; 1999a, 215–27, 229–38 on the issue of whether the *Aethiopes* attested in the sources in the northern Sahara were Black or melanomene.

comprised mixed populations of varied levels of skin pigmentation. Through migration, forced or voluntary, Black Africans were also present within the provincial territories.

Modern scholarship follows the judgement of our ancient sources in according the *Libyphoenices* a reasonably high degree of civilisation, based on their having embraced urbanisation, agriculture, legally constituted communal regulation, anthropomorphic gods, epigraphic practices, and so on.[138] A more sceptical view has been taken of the level of civilisation of the *Libyes* more generally, and they have tended to be characterised as "tribal" societies, even when there is evidence, as with the Numidian and Moorish kingdoms, of a rise in urbanism, agriculture, magistracies, epigraphic practices, and so on.[139] The use of the term "tribe" stereotypes these societies with a range of negative connotations in modern colonial discourse.[140] Neo-evolutionary paradigms (band, tribe, chiefdom, state) are now widely discredited in the anthropological literature.[141] My practice here is thus to avoid use of the term "tribe," because it leads us to prejudge their social makeup in a way that continues a colonialist discourse. In many instances, as we shall see, there is archaeological evidence to call into question the prejudices of ancient and modern writers about these peoples. From the 3rd century BCE, Rome had regularly encountered Libyans on the battlefields, whether as troops fighting for the Carthaginians or as allies recruited by Rome. The prowess of Numidian and Moorish light cavalry was well known and well respected.[142]

Aethiopes in the Sahara were generally assumed by Roman and modern writers to be essentially primitive, though the evidence advanced in support looks like literary tropes for the most part. The extent to which the population of the North African provinces included Black or mixed-race individuals is uncertain, but their presence is not to be doubted, and this may be demonstrated more fully as aDNA research advances. I think there are interesting stories to tell about the mixing of human communities that went on in Africa, blurring the hard lines of categories like Roman, Punic, Libyan, Black African. Later migrants included groups of Roman colonists and other settlers from outside Africa who were settled there, particularly under Caesar and Augustus. Once again, we need to be aware that through

---

138. Picard 1990, 35 equates Phoenician, Greek, and Roman cities as a sort of holy trinity, contributing to the ancient city.

139. See Chapter 4.

140. Berque 1953; Broughton 1929, 91; Fentress 1982a. Here I must note with regret my own use of the term "tribe" in my early work (e.g. 1995, 17–49, "The Tribal Background"). The dangers of employing such terms loosely can plainly be seen in my initial underestimation of the social structure of the *Garamantes*.

141. See notably Moore 2011 for a deconstruction of the modern colonialist concept of Iron Age tribes in Britain. Also Yoffee 2005, 4–21 for broader anthropological debates.

142. Aït Amara 2013.

normal societal interactions and intermarriages the distinctiveness and separation of all these categories of people may have gradually lessened.[143]

A further issue with traditional approaches to the autochthonous peoples of North Africa concerns the terminology used to refer to the pre-Roman period. The "Carthaginian era" or "Punic era" gives overall priority to *Qart Hadasht* and the Libyphoenicians at the risk of ignoring or obscuring the interior peoples. "Protohistory" is at one level an accurate term for a time when, in common with many other areas of the Mediterranean, societies were in transition to becoming recorded in written sources. However, the term has a good deal of colonial baggage in the North African context, not least the way it has been used to enforce binary oppositions between a supposedly more primitive African society and more advanced Phoenician, Greek, and Roman settler societies.

> What we call Punic civilisation—religious and funerary practices, lifestyles, craftsmanship—was born from the encounter on African soil of a Libyco-Berber substrate still immersed in *protohistory* and a Semitic culture already tested through *history*. It is, in some ways, the product of a successful transplantation.[144]

Although I have referred to the Protohistoric period in many of my past publications, essentially indicating the 1st millennium BCE in the Maghrib (and extending into the 1st millennium CE for extra-provincial lands of the Sahara), for dialectical consistency with my aims in this book I now propose a more neutral label of North African Iron Age (normally abbreviated hereafter as NAIA).[145] This is a deliberately broad chronological and geographical term, referring to the Iron Age in all parts of North Africa, but by no means implying cultural uniformity across this vast zone and its long Iron Age chronology. However, my starting position is that the NAIA is not to be assumed to have lagged far behind other areas of the Mediterranean Iron Age in terms of development in the early 1st millennium BCE, unless this can be explicitly demonstrated. As we shall see, the NAIA was a dynamic period of socio-economic development and change. Where finer grained chronology is possible, I think that this can most appropriately be defined in terms of more localised cultural units (thus at various points below I describe early, mid, and late Numidian or early, proto-urban, classic, and late Garamantian phases).

143. Lassère 1977 remains the classic demonstration of this. See also Lassère 1982a; 2005b.

144. Lancel 1992, 52: "Ce que nous appelons la civilisation punique—des pratiques religieuses et funéraires, des modes de vie, un artisanat—est né de la rencontre en terre africaine d'un substrat libyco-berbère encore immergé dans la protohistoire et d'une culture sémitique déjà éprouvée par l'histoire. C'est, en quelque sorte, le produit d'une greffe réussie." (my italics). I am grateful to David Stone for urging this extra step on me and pointing me to this quote.

145. In British archaeology it is conventional to refer to the Late Pre-Roman Iron Age (LPRIA) for the immediate pre-Roman conquest period, but for North Africa it makes more sense to use an acronym that covers the long formative period of the 1st millennium BCE and early 1st millennium CE.

Issues with the Primary Evidence

"Marvellous Stories": The Literary Sources

The Greco-Roman literary sources on Africa are relatively meagre considering the size of the territory, and in many respects their use is complicated by numerous *topoi*.[146] Much of the material focuses on moments of warfare and revolt, and even then very incompletely. Strabo's great geographical work devoted only a few chapters to the region, and Pliny's account in his *Natural History*, so fundamental to modern scholarship, is also extremely laconic. Most sources deal only briefly with the heartland provincial territories and people, and present Africa instead as primarily a desert land populated by pastoral nomads.

To illustrate further how the Roman view of Africa and Africans was constructed and to demonstrate the key *topoi* of such accounts, I am going to focus on just a few instances, with further examples in the following chapters. Strabo (17.3.3) sums up our difficulty in reading these accounts, for though aware that factual accounts of the country had become intertwined with fabrications, he asked his readers' pardon for "introducing marvellous stories, if perchance I digress into material of that sort, since I am unwilling wholly to pass them over in silence and in a way to cripple my history." Sometimes these invented aspects are clear, as in the case of "flying scorpions" (Strabo 17.3.11), but the problem is that the line between fact and fiction is by no means always so apparent.[147] My sense is that many modern commentators have tended to place too much trust in the textual evidence, rather than recognising in the stereotypical accounts, the operation of an ancient colonial discourse about the "other."[148]

Some particular themes I want to look at are binary oppositions between "tribes" and states, urbanisation (and its absence), agriculture and nomadism, the sown and the desert, tamed land and land plagued by wild beasts/vicious serpents, and water abundance and water scarcity. It is not uncommon to find all these elements combined together in a single schematic caricature. Strabo (17.3.1) stated:

> The greater part of the interior [of Africa] and the Ocean coast is desert, and it is dotted with small and scattered settlements and mostly nomadic, and in addition to its deserts it being a nursery of wild beasts drives out people even from land that could be inhabited.

---

146. Giusti forthcoming a, forthcoming b for decolonising analysis of ancient sources.
147. Giusti forthcoming b for an excellent analysis.
148. For critical commentary on the framing of the "other" in the ancient sources, Camps 2007, 95–101; Dauge 1981; Hartog 2009; Mattingly 2011a, 34–37; Woolf 2014.

Here we see the key ingredients of a Roman view of Africa as a sparsely populated desert land, home to wild beasts and nomadic people, though with some potential for agriculture if occupied by the right sort of people. While in a continuation of that same passage, Strabo qualified his account by confirming that the part of Africa previously occupied by the Carthaginians was "settled and prosperous," he noted that even some coastal sectors were "destitute of water" and this water poverty is a repeated theme in Roman sources.[149]

The notion of the wild beast zone is another very prevalent one in the sources, often allied to burning hot deserts and veritable plagues of deadly snakes and scorpions.[150] The subliminal message in all this is that Africa before Rome was lightly occupied by people who struggled to overcome the challenges of the land. There was limited urbanisation or permanent agriculture and arboriculture outside a few restricted zones until Roman pacification and colonisation opened up the country and turned it to more profitable use—so the standard narrative goes. No wonder this sort of agenda was embraced enthusiastically by the modern colonising powers, seeking ancient authority for their own assumptions about land development and the perceived limited capabilities of African subjects.[151]

The Epigraphic Imbalance

North Africa is incredibly rich in epigraphic evidence, with over 60,000 Latin inscriptions on stone.[152] The material is exceptionally well published in a series of major corpora and regionally focused studies.[153] The numbers are greater still if the Greek and Latin texts from *Cyrenaica* are added,[154] as well as Punic/Neo-Punic[155] and Libyan texts.[156] By way of comparison, Britain has yielded fewer than 4,000

149. On water poverty, see Shaw 1984; 1991a.
150. Leigh 2000.
151. Corbier and Griesheimer 2005, 17–19 for examples.
152. Bertrandy and Coltelloni-Trannoy 2005, 24 for the number.
153. The main general collections are *CIL* 8 (and supplements); *ILAf*; *ILS*; *AE*. Regionally focused corpora are: *IAM*$_{lat}$ *and IAM*$_{lat}$*2* (Morocco); *ILAlg 1 and 2* (Algeria); *ILT* (Tunisia); *IRT* (west Libya): online version *IRT2021* includes supplementary material since original publication). See also Mastino 1984; 1986; 1987; Rebuffat 1992a. For focused studies on pagan texts and onomastics, Ben Abdallah 1986; Ben Abdallah and Sebaï 1983; Ibba 2001 (*Uchi Maius*); Khanoussi and Maurin 1997; 2000; 2002 (*Thugga*). There are additional Christian-focused corpora, for example, Duval 1975 (*Ammaedara*); Ennabli 1975; 1982; 1991 (*Karthago*); Prévot 1984 (*Mactaris*).
154. *IRCyr2020* (Greek texts from Roman Cyrenaica).
155. *IPT* (Punic west Libya); *IAM*$_{pun}$ (Morocco); Fantar 1992; Jongeling 1994; 2008; Jongeling and Kerr 2005; Kerr 2007; Marcy 1936; Rebuffat 2007; Wilson 2012b.
156. Ait Kaci 2007; Aghali-Zakara 2006; Chabot 1940 (*RIL*); Camps 1993a; 1996; Chaker 2013a; Galand 1966 (*IAM*$_{lib}$); 1989; 2005; Marcy 1936; Rebuffat 1975a; 2007; 2013 (*RIL* supp).

Latin texts on stone. In addition to the stone inscriptions from Africa there have been some important discoveries of wooden tablets, pottery ostraca, and lead curse tablets (*defixiones*).[157] By any standards this is an amazing and invaluable resource, but we need to be aware of some biases and imbalances with the data that have the potential to distort interpretation. The superabundance of inscriptions has led to a distinctive scholarly apparatus for the study of "Roman Africa," in which the epigraphic evidence has been unusually prominent in the construction of the narrative of these Roman provinces, with literary sources and archaeology being used primarily to provide confirmatory testimony. In contrast to the epigraphic riches, there is a relative dearth of literary and historical texts pertaining to Africa from the early Roman era; this also makes the narrative over-reliant on a few historical windows (such as Sallust's account of the Jugurthan war and the allusions in Tacitus to African campaigns and revolts).

The strong emphasis on the Latin epigraphic habit also has the potential to deflect attention from other language use in society at large and the fact that some sectors of society may not have chosen to employ inscriptions on stone to convey information about their identity or status. Although it has been often observed that even as late as Saint Augustine in the 5th century there were Punic and Libyan speakers active in the countryside, researchers have often been surprised when hard epigraphic evidence of this emerges.[158] It is interesting, nonetheless, to explore the differences in epigraphic practice and literacy between different communities. Because of reduced levels of fieldwork in recent decades (and particularly since 2011) the rate of new discoveries has also slowed, and a good deal of scholarly effort is directed at revisiting previously published texts.[159] Scientific excavation across a range of sites also remains somewhat divorced from the epigraphic studies, which often occurred at different times or are separately interpreted. To give just one example, despite the wealth of funerary texts, very few inscriptions can be directly related to excavated human remains to provide a combined picture of the deceased person's life as commemorated on stone and their biological identity.

157. Bronze tablets: Sherwin-White 1973 (*Banasa*); *CIL* 16 and supplements; *RMD 1–4* (military diplomas). Wooden tablets: Courtois et al. 1952; Rothenhöfer and Blänsdorf 2016. Ostraca: Marichal 1992 (Bu Nijim); Peña 1998 (*Karthago* harbour); Varhelyi and Bagnall 2009 (*Meninx*); Ziegler and Mackensen 2014 (al-Qurrayyat al-Garbia). Curse tablets: Jordan 1996 (*Karthago*).

158. For discussions on mixed language usage and bilingualism, see inter alia Adams 1994; 2003; Cooley 2012, 250–68; Courtois 1950; Lengrand 2005; Mullen 2013; Wilson 2012b. See also Chapters 9 and 11.

159. *L'Africa romana* 1–20 (1980–2015) contains numerous epigraphic contributions. See also Aounallah and Mastino 2020 (=*L'Africa romana* 21); Perea Yébenes and Pastor Muñoz 2020 for two recent epigraphically focused volumes..

Biases and Lacunae in the Archaeological Record

The archaeological record for ancient North Africa is far from perfect, and there is a pressing need to decolonise its agendas.[160] The archaeological record across North Africa is as fragmented and heterogeneous as its topography, in part reflecting historical differences in heritage management.[161] Early colonial travellers were struck by the density and preservation of Roman remains in the landscape.[162] The registration and mapping of the region's archaeological sites began early in Algeria and Tunisia, through the work of the "brigades topographiques"[163] and early pioneer work in relation to Roman "frontiers" and land survey schemes.[164] Ancient Libya was mapped by a team led by Richard Goodchild in the post-war years.[165] There were also somewhat disjointed initiatives in Morocco.[166] However, none of the colonial-era mapping projects was fully completed. Modern mapping programmes are now underway in Tunisia and Morocco, though coverage is still far from complete, while in Algeria and Libya there has been no systematic collation of records in recent times.[167] New tools of remote detection are available, such as high-resolution satellite imagery, but modern development is also accelerating rapidly, and the existence and preservation condition of many sites is now under grave threat.[168]

Much of the early interest in mapping the Roman period remains focused on establishing the ancient name for the sites whose ruins were such a prominent feature of the 19th-century landscape. The high preservation of inscriptions helped here, and though many ancient roads in North Africa were unpaved, their stone milestones were an invaluable guide to routes and to the location of places named on the milestones or in the Roman itineraries.[169] An updated version of Salama's 1952 map of the road network and the various sheets of the Barrington Atlas have continued the tradition of mapping towns, roads and road stations, and their ancient toponyms to a much greater extent than they are able to reflect the nature

160. For relevant comparanda and reflections on decolonising archaeology for other periods and places, see inter alia Atalay 2006; 2007; Nicholas 2006; Schmidt 2017.
161. See Stone 2022 for a useful overview of the development of archaeological research.
162. For example, Guérin 1862.
163. See Cagnat and Merlin 1914/1932 for the *Atlas Archéologique de la Tunisie*; Gsell 1901a; 1901b; 1911 for the *Atlas Archéologique de l'Algérie*).
164. Baradez 1949a; Caillemer and Chevallier 1959; Chevallier 1958.
165. Goodchild 1952; 1954b; 1954c.
166. Luquet 1966; Ponsich 1970a; Souville 1973.
167. *Atlas Prehistorique de la Tunisie (APT)*; Ben Baaziz 2005; Carte (Tunisie); Carte (Maroc).
168. Sterry and Mattingly 2020a for use of remote sensing in the Sahara. Hobson 2019b; Rayne et al. 2017a; 2017b for the work of the Endangered Archaeology of the Middle East and North Africa Project.
169. Salama 1951 remains the classic work. See also Mrabet 2016; Salama 1987.

of rural settlement.[170] We are much less well informed about minor tracks and desert trails, or about the pack animals and wheeled vehicles deployed on the roads.[171]

There is a huge imbalance in the archaeological evidence at our disposal, in large part due to the priorities established in the modern colonial period. These were predominantly focused on the urban centres (see Chapter 8) and especially the monumental public buildings and elite houses that promised to be a rich source of inscriptions and artworks, whether fixed (like mosaics and wall paintings) or portable (like sculpture).[172] This bias is also reflected in the national museums of the Maghrib, where displays tend to be dominated by the great artworks (sculpture and mosaics) and less attention on everyday items of material culture.[173] The fact that many ancient cities were not overlain by medieval and modern settlements facilitated the identification of their key public buildings from surface traces. We thus have a large corpus of excavated forum/basilica complexes, public temples, baths, markets, and theatres. Amphitheatres and circuses were less common amenities, but again we have some key excavated examples from the African provinces. For later antiquity, churches have been a prime focus of interest, with hundreds of examples. In a few cases, the scale of urban excavation has been much more extensive, and entire quarters have been exposed, including housing of different social levels, shops, and workshops alongside the cherry-picked monuments already mentioned—classic examples are *Volubilis* in Morocco and *Thamugadi* in Algeria. It must be emphasised that the large-scale clearance operations were generally excavations of poor technical quality, involving large numbers of unskilled labourers under limited supervision. Relatively little publication from the colonial era provides any detail of stratigraphic contexts or associated finds, apart from the occasional statue or inscription. These were primarily treasure-hunting exercises, and though they provide us with some impressive-looking overall plans of towns and their key monuments, they rarely allow much scope for tracing phases of development or looking at the material culture and behaviours associated with the architecture recorded. Solid walls and solid floors were generally well recorded; timber structures, earthen floors, and occupation deposits or mud walls (mudbrick or rammed earth) much less so.[174]

---

170. For the update on Salama, see Desanges et al. 2010; for the Barrington sheets, see Euzennat 2000; Fentress 2000a; 2000b; Hitchner 2000a; 2000b; Mattingly 2000a; 2000b; 2000c; 2000d; 2000e; Potter 2000a; 2000b. See further discussion in Chapter 10.
171. Förster and Reimer 2013; Guédon 2010; 2012b; Rebuffat 1970c; 1970d; 2003.
172. Mattingly and Hitchner 1995, 179–87. North African examples feature in standard overviews of Roman architecture, but often with scant attention to the local context; see, for example, Yegül and Favro 2018.
173. See Catalogue Alaoui 1897–1922; Yacoub 1996 (Bardo). See also descriptions of the museums in Algeria and Libya in Blas de Roblès et al. 2019, 38–49, 71–74, 77–87, 129–37, 154–60, 214–21, 246–51; Kenrick 2009, 21–34, 135–40; 2013, 239–50.
174. Sears 2011; Wilson 2020.

Military sites of all types are also less well known (see Chapter 6). In part this is a simple and understandable consequence of the postcolonial era of North African countries, where investigation of sites associated with Roman imperialism has been deprioritised by the Maghribian nation states, anxious to find their own identity.[175] But even at the height of French and Italian colonial rule in the early 20th century, Roman military studies had played second fiddle to urban-focused ones. The long-lived legionary base at *Lambaesis*, with its associated *canabae* and town (which also served as a provincial capital from the early 3rd century CE) is an important exception, though even there, the decision to build a prison across a large portion of the fortress caused a massive loss of evidence.[176] During the modern colonial era many interventions were carried out by serving military personnel, but again these tended to target features thought likely to produce epigraphic evidence, such as headquarters' buildings or gates.[177] Relatively few auxiliary forts have been extensively excavated and, as with towns, the rare examples of substantial clearance, such as *Rapidum* in *Mauretania Caesariensis* or *Castellum Dimmidi* in Algeria, were of poor quality.[178] Two important exceptions to this general rule are Bu Nijim (Bu Njem) in Libya and *Thamusida* in Morocco, though there remain important gaps in the publication record of the former.[179] More surprising still has been the failure to systematically follow up the discovery of linear earthworks and walls built by Rome in Morocco, Algeria, Tunisia, and Libya—the lack of excavations leaves open to question their construction date and periods of operation.[180] If we look beyond the epigraphic records, compared to the scholarly effort expended in other provinces, our knowledge and understanding of the military community in the African provinces are constrained.

The situation is even starker in relation to rural communities (see Chapter 10). In many other provinces, the luxurious elite rural dwellings (often referred to as villas) have attracted particular attention. It is striking that we know more about the physical appearance of the African examples of this type of site from mosaic representations, found in urban settings, than from actual excavations of rural buildings.[181] Since the late 1970s the rapid growth of rural surveys has expanded knowledge of the ancient landscapes and settlement patterns.[182] Some types of rural activity are now much more fully understood, notably olive oil production, where the extent,

175. Mattingly and Hitchner 1995, 174–76.
176. Effros 2018, 125–67. Effros does note (2018, 187) the ingenious attempt at safeguarding many inscriptions at *Lambaesis* by embedding them facing out in the walls of the penitentiary, but many others originally recorded at the site were lost, along with a substantial area of the legionary base.
177. Dondin-Payre 1991; Effros 2018, 139–50.
178. Laporte 1989; Picard 1944.
179. Akerraz and Papi 2008; Euzennat 1989, 70–98 (*Thamusida*); Rebuffat 1989 (Bu Nijim).
180. Baradez 1949a; 1967; Mattingly 1995, 106–15; Mattingly et al. 2013a; Trousset 1984b; 1997b.
181. Duval 1986; Rind 2009; Wilson, R. 2018.
182. Mattingly 1997c; Mattingly and Hitchner 1995, 189–96; Stone 2004.

technology, and scale of olive cultivation and oil pressing have all been a focus of research.[183] The excellent preservation conditions in some parts of North Africa mean that plans of many rural structures can be recorded from surface remains, a distinct advantage over the plough-zone signals of partly destroyed sites on the northern side of the Mediterranean. Yet the relative lack of excavation of rural sites remains a critical limitation of our understanding of them and their occupants. This is true even of olive oil production, where a handful of sites have been properly excavated out of the thousands recorded in survey. Although there have been a number of major infrastructure projects in North Africa in recent decades, with the construction of major roads, rail links, and the Great Man-Made River in Libya, there has not been systematic survey and excavation of the representative selection of archaeological features encountered. In Europe, these sorts of project have provided a fascinating glimpse of the overall range of rural settlement, countering the older bias in favour of just the largest or most prestigious sites and monuments.[184]

Material culture studies related to the Roman provinces in Africa have had a strong focus on the extraordinary wealth of mosaic art, this being one of the pre-eminent regions for the production of figural polychrome mosaics.[185] They are among the great treasures of Classical antiquity anywhere. Equally, many sites have produced significant finds of ancient sculpture, and if perhaps not in the same abundance or quality as the provinces of the Greek world or mainland Italy, this is an extraordinary dossier. A number of sites stand out as exceptional—*Iol Caesarea* (Cherchel, Algeria) was the showcase town of the Roman-educated Mauretanian king Juba II and liberally adorned with extraordinary sculptural works.[186] *Lepcis Magna* (Libya) is another city that combines grandiose sculptural acquisitions with the good fortune of many pieces escaping late antique lime kilns.[187]

I return in Chapter 13 to the question of what is missing in the archaeological record. The most important *lacuna*, I shall argue, is the lack of detail on the African background to the Roman era achievements and highpoints. I explore this in more detail below, but fundamentally this relates to the lack of a developed archaeology of the pre-Roman Iron Age across much of North Africa. That leaves the Roman evidence strangely decontextualised from its African setting.

While we cannot ignore the biases and weaknesses of the archaeological evidence, the quality and quantity of these data now available also need to be recognised. Despite the fact that much was gathered to fulfil specific colonialist agendas supporting a vision of "Roman Africa," it is still feasible to tell a different sort of story about Africa in the Roman Empire.

---

183. For up-to-date reviews, see Brun 2004, 185–259; Hobson 2015a, 63–102.
184. Allen et al. 2017; Smith et al. 2016; 2018.
185. See for example, Blanchard-Lemée et al. 1996; Dunbabin 1978.
186. Landwehr 1993; 2000; 2006; 2008.
187. Di Vita et al. 1999; Kenrick 2009, 21–32.

The Structure of This Book

The book is divided into six broad sections, including the introductory discussions. This introductory chapter is complemented by Chapter 2, where I shall give a fuller explanation of my objections to and rejection of the Romanisation paradigm. I shall instead continue to explore the possibilities of an alternative approach, which I have called discrepant identity.

Part 2 of the book seeks to establish a secure context for the Roman experiences by looking at three broad groups of peoples who were influential in shaping the cultural character of Africa in the 1st millennium BCE. The first group comprises a number of incomers from elsewhere in the Mediterranean: Greeks, Phoenicians (and Libyphoenicians), and Romans. Chapter 3 explores what these terms meant in historical and archaeological terms, with a particular focus on deconstructing colonial discourses relating to outsider groups. In Chapter 4, I examine the two most important indigenous cultural groupings beyond the territory of the Libyphoenician settlements—specifically the *Numidae* and the *Mauri*. These comprised numerous population groups of the northern Maghrib. By the later centuries BCE, these had undergone state formation and were able to challenge (at times) the might of *Qart Hadasht* or Rome. By contrast, the people of the southern Maghrib and northern Sahara are much more shadowy. I focus in Chapter 5 on two broad groups, the *Gaetuli* and the *Garamantes*, and challenge the conventional picture of their social organisation and technological capabilities. This has major implications for the rest of the book, in which I look in turn at three major groupings: the military, urban, and rural communities of the Roman provinces.

In Part 3, I focus on the military community, first looking at how the garrison deployment was physically constituted and how the army functioned. In describing the deployment I have tried to avoid use of the term "frontier." Although it is clear that the Roman Empire did have a sense of its territorial limits, I think "frontier," with its modern connotations of demarcated lines, focuses our attention excessively on the idea of a garrison defending imperial territory from external peoples, whereas I want to explore the impacts of that garrison within broad "security zones" that extended considerable distances to either side of any notional boundaries. In Chapter 7, I turn to the shaping of military identities and how these were specific to the army and its close civilian associates.

Part 4, on the urban communities, is again divided into two distinct sections, with Chapter 8 looking at the different types of towns and varied urban trajectories encountered in Africa. Far from being the product of a unified urban ideology, I argue that the towns fall into a range of diverse types, in part reflecting differing traditions and understandings of what was urban. In Chapter 9, I look at the cultural and behavioural correlates of these different types of towns and reflect on some of the key differences between the urban and the military and rural communities.

In Part 5, attention passes on to the rural communities. Through a detailed overview in Chapter 10 of a range of diverse landscapes and forms of rural settlement, I shall first illustrate the fundamental heterogeneity of rural communities. Chapter 11 expands on this by considering how the different behaviours and cultural manifestations demonstrate profound roots in the pre-Roman past.

In Part 6, Chapter 12 is an attempt to look at the different sorts of economic relationships that operated across, and complicated the relationships between, the three broad communities described in the previous sections. Finally, Chapter 13 draws together the arguments about the diversity of cultural identities in North Africa and explores how the picture of Africa in the Roman Empire has opened up a new world to view.

Chapter 2

DISCREPANT IDENTITY AND OTHER THEORETICAL APPROACHES

History is not an exact science with a single objective truth to be reconstructed. Precisely because of the incompleteness of the record, it is open to subjectivity in filling in gaps and underlying subconscious assumptions in the shaping of the narrative. Each generation of scholars will reinterpret the historical record, in part reflecting changes in the modern world. Nor is archaeology immune from such biases—especially when in earlier times its agendas have been strongly shaped by prevailing socio-political concerns, as in colonial North Africa in the 19th and early 20th centuries.[1] It is ever more important for historians and archaeologists to reflect on the unconscious bias that lies behind the evidence and the way it has been presented, to acknowledge their own influences, and to recognise and deconstruct the hidden discourses of the presentation of history. Having grown up through the end of European empires and engaged with changing narratives about imperialism, I am more sceptical than my (ancient historian) father or grandfather would have been of the universal benefits the Roman Empire is sometimes claimed to have brought to its subject peoples. In the 21st century, I think it is incumbent on scholars to adopt more critical approaches to Roman imperialism and to attempt to frame debate about Rome's provinces in new ways. This chapter sets out some problems with the historiographical tradition of study of "Roman Africa" and proposes some different approaches to address them.

Theoretical Challenges: Romanisation

The standard paradigm through which to present the development of Roman provincial societies has been Romanisation. The understanding of this term varies (which is one of its problems), but generally it is taken to be a process by which

1. For two pioneering attempts at this sort of historiographical reflection, Février 1989, 21–90; Shaw 1980. See also Hitchner 2022b.While a descriptive critique of the historiography has now become more common in the French tradition, active steps to decolonise the subject are less clear; see, for example, Corbier and Griesheimer 2005, 7–33; Géroudet and Ménard 2005, 7–64.

cultural differences within provincial societies were smoothed and a common sense of Roman identity emerged, backed up by reorientation of religious and other social behaviours. However, the appropriateness of this concept has been increasingly challenged, especially in Anglophone scholarship, and I am one of the advocates of an alternative approach. I shall first outline some of the problems with the way Romanisation is used within current scholarship on North Africa and then explain in more detail the nature of my opposition to the Romanisation paradigm in general.[2]

Romanisation underpins much of the traditional agenda of studies of the Roman Empire and in particular its western provinces and has proved remarkably resilient to change, despite its widely recognised problems.[3] A classic statement of Romanisation was given by the term's inventor, Francis Haverfield, capturing both its universality and also its vagueness:

> What, then, was the general civilisation of the western Empire, the conditions of which were so similar in all its districts? The general answer is easily given. The whole area in varying degrees became Romanised. In speech, literature, in fashions, in art and architecture—in short in the whole fabric of life—it adopted Roman ways. Put that broadly, the statement is almost too familiar to convey any definite impression.[4]

There is no ancient exact equivalent term for Romanisation, and the invention of the concept is tied to the modern imperial age and ultimately much influenced by the idea of a "civilising mission" of colonial powers.[5] As such, Romanisation has to be understood as part of modern colonial discourse and thus ought to be intellectually/scientifically suspect today.[6] Attempts to update the concept, by moving the emphasis away from Roman intentionality to focus instead on the agency of local elites have not really helped, because the multiplicity of different highly nuanced meanings that now exist for Romanisation fundamentally undermine its utility as a paradigm.[7] The modern colonial heritage of Romanisation theory and its multiple meanings are two major obstacles to continuing attempts to reboot the concept: "Romanisation 2.0," as Versluys terms it, does not address these fundamental objections.[8] Further deficiencies of Romanisation are its emphasis on the "Roman" aspect of what were often extremely complex and multidirectional cultural exchanges. There is a tendency for analysis to default to consideration of the

---

2. See in particular, Mattingly 2002; 2004b; 2006a, 14–19; 2010b; 2011a, 38–41, 203–07; 2014a, 19–20.
3. Inglebert 2005; Keay and Terrenato 2001; Lepelley 1998a.
4. Haverfield and MacDonald 1924, 173.
5. Haverfield 1912; Hingley 2007; James 2001a.
6. Gardner 2013; Mattingly 2002; 2011a, 38–39; Van Oyen 2015; Webster 2001.
7. Belvedere and Bergemann 2021; Keay and Terrenato 2001; Millett 1990; 2021; Metzler et al. 1995; Woolf 1992a; 1994; 1995; 1997; 1998.
8. Versluys 2014.

unilateral spread of what is deemed "Roman" culture in the provinces (with inbuilt binary assumptions about "civilised" and "less civilised"), rather than a consideration of how culture changed in multiple directions within and beyond the space occupied by the Roman Empire and how it was never the same everywhere. The emphasis also tends to be on elite elements of culture (monumental and prestige architecture, art, epigraphy), which automatically excludes a substantial part of society. The focus on the elite and on the degree of sameness across provinces undoubtedly does highlight an important, but unsurprising, truism of the Roman Empire—there were elements of cosmopolitan culture within the Empire.[9]

However, there are other models that can be used to explore this dimension, notably globalisation theory.[10] A further critique of Romanisation is that the way the concept is used often underestimates the manner in which Roman culture was transformed by its imperial encounters, with the singular exception of contacts with the Greek world.[11] Such analyses have tended to privilege some cultural voices over others—intertwining Romanisation with Hellenisation—to the exclusion of proper consideration of more varied influences and material impacts.[12] This is perhaps best witnessed in the religious sphere, where Rome's pagan pantheon of the gods was vastly expanded and iconographically transformed between the late centuries BCE and the early centuries CE.[13] In later chapters I show how the religious transformations in Africa are particularly poorly served by the notion of religious Romanisation.

Yet, modern commentary on the cultural transformations remains somewhat blind to the directionality of change within the Empire. To select just one example, from an essay accompanying an exhibition on *Roma Caput Mundi* that coincided with my Jerome lectures in Rome, the paradigm of Romanisation remained to the fore:

> since [the Romans] were convinced that their culture was superior, they thought it natural that foreigners should make it their own. Individuals chose to become Romanised because they were attracted to Roman culture, because it raised their social status, because it allowed them access to local and public offices.[14]

The implication is that it was the culture of the dominant power that was ultimately alluring and seductive for provincials, determining a circulation of Roman

9. Hingley 2010 supports my emphasis on the need to investigate the heterogeneity of cultural response to empires like Rome.
10. Belvedere and Bergemann 2021; Hingley 2005; Geraghty 2007; Hitchner 2008; Hodos et al. 2016; Pitts 2008; Pitts and Versluys 2015; Witcher 2000. Applying globalisation theory to the Roman Empire, of course, brings with it additional baggage.
11. Best exemplified in Wallace-Hadrill 2008.
12. Mattingly 2010b, 285–87.
13. Rives 2007.
14. Giardina and Pesando 2012a, 33–34; note also the short (and quite traditional) essay on Romanisation in the volume by Wallace-Hadrill 2012.

culture outwards from the metropolitan heart of empire. However, what was really striking about the *Caput Mundi* exhibition and its catalogue was the extent of the cultural flows in the reverse direction. The exhibition presented finds from Italy representing the integrationist success of the Roman Empire, with long sections on the impact of a range of different cultural markers.[15] The migration (forced or voluntary) of people from all over the Empire saw the import of many new cultural practices, languages, and religions, and these are all too visible in the archaeological record, much as later imperial capitals, such as Paris and London, are marked in the 21st century by the cultural specificities of former colonies.

The Romanisation concept has led to a highly simplistic characterisation of the population of the African provinces:

> One can distinguish three groups in the population: the Romanised people (by origin or adoption), the unmanageable Africans and those who were partially Romanised, forming the largest and most important group.[16]

After more than a hundred years of Romanisation, the agendas of Roman studies need refreshing, with a greater focus on the cultural impact throughout society, not just at its top, investigation of cultural continuities with pre-existing traditions, and exploration of cultural diversity and different identities rather than similarities.[17]

The Entanglement of Romanisation and Modern Colonialist Discourse

For me, the primary problem with Romanisation is that the concept is entangled with modern colonialist discourse and agendas of study, and should thus be "handled with care" in a postcolonial age.[18] It is also somewhat unidirectional in directing our gaze towards aspects of material culture and behaviour that

15. Giardina and Pesando 2012b, 17–20, 49–64, Eastern religions; 39–42, foreigners in the army and senate; 43–48, Greeks and Greek culture; 65–68, enslaved people.
16. Groslambert 2011, 15: "On distingue des lors trois groups dans la population: les romanisés (d'origine ou d'adoption), les africains réfractaires et les romanisés partiels, groupe le plus nombreux, dont le role fut determinant." Baratte 2012 tells a similarly schematic story, 22–70 an urban civilisation, 71–97 a Romanised society, 98–114 a diverse rural society. Briand-Ponsart and Hugoniot 2006, 426–76, recognise the cultural diversity but then conflate it into a collective "Romano-African identity," which is not meaningful either.
17. Mattingly 2011a, 39.
18. A difficulty here is that most defences of the traditional Francophone position on "l'Afrique romaine" do not recognise the problems posed by the maintenance of the Romanisation discourse as the key paradigm of analysis; see, inter alia, Bertrandy and Coltelloni-Trannoy 2005, 8–9; Briand-Ponsart and Hugoniot 2006, 12–13; Cabouret 2005, 6–12; Géroudet and Ménard 2005, 39–40; Lassère 2015, 246–55; Prévot et al. 2006, 15–20. For more explicit critiques of Romanisation and its application in Africa, see Le Roux 2004; 2006; Quinn 2003. Cf. Hingley 2021 for reflections on the progress of postcolonial debate in the context of Britain in the Roman Empire.

are construed as being more "Roman" and by implication more relevant to our understanding of "Roman Africa." Here I return to my alternative formulation of "Africa in the Roman Empire," which is explicitly intended to provide a more wide-ranging overview across society, including peoples whose material culture and lifestyles were less conventionally "Roman," but who nonetheless should feature in the story if we are to fully appreciate the impacts of imperial incorporation and government.

There is no doubt that Romanisation is a concept with a lot of modern imperial baggage, and it is first necessary to understand how this affects the study of the Roman past. Its influence is clear in the fact that studies that extol the benefits of Roman civilisation tend to far outnumber those that reflect on the exigencies of Roman domination.[19] In a 1996 article I attempted a first exploration and deconstruction of some aspects of the colonialist discourse on "l'Afrique romaine" and "l'Africa romana."[20] The French and Italian archaeological ventures in North Africa in the 19th and 20th centuries were deeply entangled with the modern colonial projects. I showed how the colonial discourse operated to present modern colonial regimes and settlers as direct inheritors and successors of Rome (with the concomitant necessity of disinheriting "native" Africans from this history) and how emulation of Rome was a powerful motor of the modern colonial regimes. The visual framing of romantic ruins evoked a land of once great promise that had undergone a cataclysmic end. Through colonial excavation and reconstruction, the skeletal remains of lost buildings were given new meaning and importance.[21]

Interestingly, French archaeologists applied the concept of Romanisation in different ways in Africa compared to France, producing a markedly different narrative about the incorporation of indigenous peoples into the Roman Empire in the former compared to the latter. This required a crude characterisation of the limitations of some North African societies when it came to their appreciation or participation in the perceived advantages of civilised Roman life. Some aspects of the colonialist model are more patently absurd than others, in particular the claims of French and Italian colonial regimes to be the direct inheritors of a great, but long interrupted, imperial project in Africa:

> The natives call us *roumis*; they regard us as the descendants and heirs of those who have ruled for so long and whose memory they vaguely acknowledge. Accept the inheritance, Messiers, we will find our profit there. We come to continue a great work

19. Bénabou 1976; Kotula 1976; Leveau 1978a; 2020a.
20. Mattingly 1996a, reprinted in Mattingly 2011a, 43–72, with some minor changes. For other work in the same spirit, see Balice 2010; Dondin-Payre 1988; 1991; 2002; 2005a; Effros 2018; Effros and Lai 2018; Frémeaux 1984; McCarty 2018; Munzi 2001; 2004; 2012; Stone 2022.
21. Yelles 2020.

of civilisation interrupted for centuries. We have retaken possession of an ancient domain and these old monuments, in front of which the Arab does not pass without a feeling of respect and fear, are precisely our title deeds.[22]

Another key construct of the colonialist vision of "l'Afrique romaine" was the idea of a "permanence berbère"—implying an inherent backwardness and lack of capacity in indigenous societies on the margins of "Romanised" territory.[23] One manifestation of this was to create binary oppositions between nomads and sedentary peoples, between hostile montagnards and settled populations in the plains.[24] Despite a much greater awareness of the problems and subjective dimensions of such binaries in academic discourse, these models still remain influential themes in some modern work.[25] A further tendency in colonial-era scholarship was to exaggerate the numbers and impact of Roman colonists to the ancient imperial project, with the consequence that colonists were seen as behind the great achievements and monuments of "Roman Africa" that were being revealed by "colonial science" at centres like *Lepcis Magna* or *Karthago*.[26] In areas where there was not much evidence for overseas settlers, the Roman army was seen as a good stand-in, and where there was a lack of certain evidence for regular troops, then unofficial "soldier-farmers" could be invented.[27] Emulation of Rome was a major preoccupation of the modern colonial regimes, leading to constant comparing of achievement, and further increasing the alignment of the study of the Roman past with the external power.[28] Indigenous resistance was generally conceptualised in terms of wilful or perverse opposition to Romanisation from the irredeemable "permanence berbère."[29]

22. Corbier and Griesheimer 2005, 18 (citing G. Bossier addressing the 1891 Congrès des societés savantes for North African researchers): "Les indigènes nous appellent des roumis; ils nous regardent comme des descendants et les héritiers de ceux qui ont si longtemps gouverné et dont ils gardent confusément le souvenir. Acceptons l'héritage, Messiers, nous y trouverons notre profit. Nous venons continuer une grande oeuvre de civilisation interrompue pendant des siècles. Nous reprenons possession d'un ancien domaine et ces vieux monuments devant lesquels l'Arabe ne passe pas sans in sentiment de respect et de frayeur, sont précisément nos titres de propriété." See Mattingly 2011a, 45–47 for further examples of the European colonisers as inheritors of Rome.
23. Mattingly 2011a, 49; cf. Corbier and Griesheimer 2005, 18–19. While the colonial categorisations of modern Maghribian peoples have been more thoroughly deconstructed (see, for example, Lorcin 1995; Rouighi 2019), the equivalent stereotyping of ancient peoples applying similar criteria has been less investigated.
24. See, inter alia, Courtois 1955; Rachet 1970. Brett and Fentress 1996, 6–7; Fentress 1983 for critique.
25. Géroudet and Ménard 2005, 36–50; Le Bohec 2005a, 14–15; Prévot et al. 2006, 49–55.
26. Mattingly 2011a, 50–51.
27. Mattingly 2011a, 55–56. Cf. Dondin-Payre 1991; Effros 2018. For "soldier-farmers" see Goodchild 1949; 1950a; 1950c
28. Mattingly 2011a, 54–57. Note, however, Dondin-Payre 2020 for the observation that in comparing imperial armies, the "native" auxiliaries in the modern colonial armies were largely excluded from the comparative perspective, and the main focus was on "legionaries," ancient and modern.
29. Fentress 1983; 2006; Leveau 2005; Mattingly 2011a, 57–59; Sheldon 1982.

Modern scholars from former colonising countries are now starting to recognise the distortions engendered by such deliberate and self-serving falsification of the past in the service of modern colonial projects.[30] Yet there remains a general unwillingness fully to deconstruct the discourses underpinning 19th- and 20th-century studies of "Roman Africa" or of the need to decolonise the agendas of 21st-century study.[31] As we shall see in subsequent chapters, there are many points at which analysis is still hamstrung by outmoded assumptions derived from the colonialist discourse that shaped the early agenda of study.

The net result of these varied elements of the modern colonial discourse was an effective disinheritance from their Roman past for the vast majority of the Maghreb's non-European population.[32] "Native" peoples were consistently denied agency in Rome's African past, whether within the provinces or beyond the desert borders—and here we need to recognise the colonialist power of the term "native" itself.[33] The long-term legacy of that remains with us today and continues to inform the postcolonial debate. The importance of the European settler communities, in Algeria and Libya in particular, in polarising attitudes to the Roman past must also be recognised. When the first post- or anti-colonial reinterpretations of Maghribian history started to appear in the 1970s,[34] their emphasis on resistance to Rome and a sort of proto-nationalist ambivalence to Roman civilisation elicited a hostile, at times vitriolic, response from the academic "establishment," typically accusing the Maghribian scholars of constructing an anachronistic "nationalistic" discourse ("l'histoire inversée"). To emphasise resistance as the primary response to colonialism above all others presents a narrow base for understanding the complex social interactions of such imperial settings, but by the same token nor should we exclude consideration of resistance in its various active and passive forms.[35] In objecting to the anachronistic potential of a nationalistic view of resistance to Rome, French scholars have often failed to recognise that the same subjective issues might underlie their established orthodox positions as well.[36]

---

30. Corbier and Griesheimer 2005, 19: "Ces thèses sont aujourd'hui réfutées avec une meilleure connaissance de la géographie de l'influence romaine." The authors believe that more data is what is needed rather than new frames of analysis. See also Christol 2015.
31. Cf. Giusti forthcoming a; Perkins and James 2000 for attempts to teach "Roman Africa" from a more postcolonial perspective.
32. Mattingly 2011a, 47–49, 58.
33. Wheeler 1954 for a colonialist reading of the *Garamantes*. I have tried to remove colonialist vocabulary from my writing in this book—terms such as "native" and "tribe" have been more neutrally expressed as "local" and "people."
34. See in particular, Bénabou 1976; 1977; Kaddache 1971; Laroui 1970.
35. Such varied strategies of peoples living under colonial rule are well theorised; see Mattingly 2014a; Scott 1990; Stark and Chance 2012; Webster 2001.
36. Euzennat 1986, 576; Thébert 1978. Reflections on the debate in modern textbooks may recognise the polarised postcolonial positions, yet, while critical of anachronisms of postcolonial writers, do not always break free from the underlying colonialist discourse, see Briand-Ponsart and Hugoniot 2006, 7–13; Corbier and Griesheimer 2005, 16–19;

The eminent French scholar Jean-Marie Lassère attributed controversies affecting the ancient history of "Roman Africa" to the legacy of the Algerian war of independence rather than the long-term impact of colonialist historiographical distortions.[37] My point is that there are undoubtedly problems with the inverse history that has emerged, in that it too is a product of and a response to the modern colonial discourse that shaped the 19th-century agendas. But the only way to address those adequately is in fact to deconstruct the larger underlying issues of the modern discourse. Part of the way in which the colonial discourse is to be deconstructed is through a franker acknowledgement of the negative impacts of empires, including that of ancient Rome—whether through war, enslavement, provincial exploitation, or petty acts born out of the power inequalities present in everyday situations.[38]

However, decolonising the discipline is not yet very far advanced. Despite the recognition that different perspectives on "Roman Africa" could exist,[39] many traditionalists continue to assert the superiority of their own approaches and intellectual probity, while calling into question the objectivity of those who challenge the orthodoxy. In particular, the work of Bénabou has been effectively written off in some quarters, without his important ideas about Roman imperialism being addressed.[40] There is an unwillingness to engage with theoretical work on imperialism and colonialism (and consideration of how this may affect our reading of the Roman past) and a contradictory insistence that negative comparisons with modern colonialism are anachronistic, while allowing the colonialist thinking that still underpins much Classical scholarship to go unchallenged.[41] As a result, the longevity of elements of the colonialist discourse is still evident in much scholarship on "Roman Africa." Even in the most scholarly and important works of recent years, one finds awkward self-justifications of the traditional approach and perspective

37. Lassère 2015, 10 with n. 24: "Il y a eu des historiens estimables qui ont en quelque sorte continué la guerre d'Algérie sur le terrain de l'Afrique romaine," with specific allusion to Bénabou and Kaddache.
38. On the predatory nature of the Roman Empire, see Fernández-Götz et al. 2020; on the impacts of military force: Mattingly 2011a, 22–37, 94–96, 118–21; on financial exploitation: Mattingly 2011a, 125–45; on slavery: Webster 2005; 2008. In this book I have used the term "enslaved person" rather than "slave" to emphasise the individual impact of the institution of slavery and that someone in this position was more than a possession.
39. As exemplified by the three-cornered debate between Bénabou 1978a; Leveau 1978a; Thébert 1978. For some further interesting reflections on Bénabou and the debate he provoked, see Fenwick 2008; Lamirande 1976; Lawless 1978; Sebaï 2005; Whittaker 1978b.
40. In addition to works cited above, see Bénabou 1978b; 1980; 1981; 1982. Bertrandy and Coltelloni-Trannoy 2005, 8 for an example of the overly dismissive rejection of his decolonised ideological perspective.
41. Lepelley 2004, 27: "It was therefore clear that any retrojection of the contemporary colonial situation into Roman North Africa was a false problem and meaningless." I am grateful for Andy Merrills for pointing out this reference.

combined with an insinuation that, while the personal experiences of scholars offering alternative views are fraught with danger of anachronism and error, their own critical judgement is objective.

> So please forgive me, I hope I have rejected in these pages, as I have done non-aggressively for 60 years, the "politically correct" in favour of a free examination without presuppositions, and to have avoided, as much as I could, an emotional approach while inserting personal reflections on the long developments: if I have throughout my life had a dialogue with Africa, I have also discussed it with myself.[42]

> My book is a continuation of this tradition of work, a synthesis of reflections carried out for many years on ancient sources relating to the world of tribes in the western part of North Africa and nourished by fruitful discussions with Y. Modéran on the social and cultural mechanisms underlying the construction of multiple identities, on which we have focused particular attention, both enriched by the personal lived experiences and distanced by the spirit of critical analysis proper to our training as historians.[43]

The reference to "political correctness" is here meant to undermine the academic credibility of postcolonial approaches, while the repeated claims of academic "objectivity" by traditional Roman scholars are to my mind hard to reconcile with the still present residue of the highly subjective (and sometimes racist) thinking of the 19th-century framing of the subject. There is a need to scrutinise the basic assumptions of the conventional models of "Roman Africa" and to be open to attempts to decolonise the subject.

42. Lassère 2015, 758: "On voudra donc bien me pardoner, je l'espère d'avoir, comme je l'ai fait sans aggressivité pendant une soixantaine d'années, refusé dans ces pages le 'politiquement correct' au profit du libre examen sans présupposés, d'avoir évité, autant qu'il m'était possible, une démarche émotive tout en insérant dans les longs développments des réflexions personnelles: si j'ai pendant toute ma vie dialogué avec l'Afrique, j'ai aussi discuté avec moi même." This concluding passage of his great book is accompanied by a footnote: "Fidèle à la terre natale, aux hommes qui l'ont habitée et qui l'habitent encore, avec discrétion, mais aussi conviction, sans mélanger les genres, sans confondre les périodes."

43. Hamdoune 2018, 13: "C'est dans la continuité de ces travaux que s'inscrit cet ouvrage, synthèse des réflexions menées depuis plusiers années sur les sources antiques relatives au monde des tribus dans la partie occidentale de l'Afrique du nord et nourries par des fructeuses discussions avec Y. Modéran sur les méchanisms sociaux et culturels sous-tendant la construction des identités multiples, sur lesquels nous portions un regard particulier, à la fois enrichi par les expériences personnels que nous avions vécus et distancié par l'esprit d'analyse critique proper à notre formation d'historiens," with accompanying footnote seemingly questioning the historical validity of the perspective of a Maghribian historian: "Voir Bénabou 2004 [2014], pour l'influence de sa situation personnelle dans son approche et sa compréhension de l'Afrique romaine." To me, Bénabou's autobiographical note about growing up in Meknes in a multicultural (Muslim, Christian, and Jewish) and multilingual society under colonial rule seems highly pertinent to his perspectives as an ancient historian.

In the rest of this chapter, I shall examine some broader developments in postcolonial studies and archaeological theory that are enabling the development of alternative analytical frameworks to Romanisation.[44] To be clear, my proposition is not that we abandon study of what is currently covered by the term "Romanisation," but rather that we expand and recontextualise this discussion as part of a broader-based study of society, material culture, and behaviours, informed by identity theory.

Postcolonial Theory and Colonial Discourse

The Roman Empire cannot be understood in isolation, but rather it needs to be reviewed as one example among other systems of imperialism and within comparative frameworks of study.[45] Archaeological studies of colonialism and the impacts of colonisation have broadened the scope of research.[46] Empires represent a key development in the structural embedding (and scale) of inequality in societies, and this gives significance to our efforts to understand their operation in both political and cultural terms.[47] My approach to the Roman Empire thus involves a critical engagement with both rulers and ruled, and with both positive and negative impacts of empire.[48] Some traditional Roman scholars have confused my critical stance with anti-Roman sentiment and questioned the validity of my views on the grounds that "Mattingly does not like the Romans."[49] While I find this characterisation of my position absurd, if we turn this argument around, surely as historians we should be even more concerned about the potential bias inherent in work by scholars whose analysis is constrained by an over-strong "liking" for the Romans. After all, the facts of Rome's negative impacts on its subject peoples are not really in doubt from our ancient source material: wars, sackings, enslavements, extortion, abuses of power. The historian's job, it seems to me, is not to make moral judgements about whether the Empire was a good or a bad thing, but rather to delineate how it achieved what it did, for the benefit of which people and at the expense of

44. On the growth of theoretical approaches in Roman archaeology, see, inter alia, Dyson 1993; Gardner 2013; Terrenato 2005; and the annual proceedings of the UK-centred Theoretical Roman Archaeology Conference.

45. Mattingly 2011a, 3–26; see, inter alia, Alcock et al. 2001; Burbank and Cooper 2010, 23–59; Doyle 1986; Parsons 2010; Terrenato 2019, 1–30, 249–72.

46. Dietler 2010; Given 2004; Gosden 2004; Hodos 2006; Hurst and Owen 2005; Lyons and Papadopoulos 2002; Stein 2005; van Dommelen 1998; van Dommelen and Terrenato 2007.

47. Altaweel and Squitieri 2018; Flannery and Marcus 2012.

48. Woolf 2014, suggests that a common failure of postcolonial approaches to the Roman Empire has been the replacement of the emphasis on the civilising process with a focus on domination and exploitation. I would argue that decolonising history involves striking a balance in making a critical analysis of both the positive and negative aspects of ancient imperialism.

49. Selkirk 2006, 31: "[T]he author follows the modern fashion of not liking the Romans. He does not like them at all and loses no opportunity to disparage them throughout the book."

Table 2.1. Comparison of different drivers and locales of imperialism and cultural impacts in the Roman Empire (building on models of imperialism discussed in Mattingly 2011a, 16).

Imperialism model	**Key locale**	**Behaviours related to imperialism**	**Cultural driver**	**Behaviours related to cultural exchanges**
Metrocentric	Metropolitan core	Imperial actions	Metropolitan fashion	Diffusion of Roman elements
Pericentric	Peripheral or frontier zones	Provincial reactions	Provincial/ Regional tradition	Assimilation and spread of regional cultures
Systemic	Dispersed/ widespread	Transgressive abuses	Globalisation effect	Systemic effects of cultural change in a globalised world

which others. Much of the worst impact was not deliberate policy, of course, but rather what I have termed "systemic consequences" of imperial systems, with parallels in empires of every age.[50] Put simply, colonialism's huge power imbalances and opportunities work against the best behaviour of its servants, and this is periodically disruptive of governance and justice.[51] These sorts of interacting factors are represented in Table 2.1, reflecting on metropolitan and peripheral locales and the impact of systemic effects.

The table presents the three elements of the power dynamic: intentional acts of the imperial state; the consequential acts or responses of the provincial community; and the systemic effects that often complicate the business of empire.[52] For an example of such transgressive acts, a fragment of a rescript of Severus Alexander from *Vazaivi* (Henchir Zoui) addressed complaints by provincials against officials and military personnel abusing their power and demanding "illicit exactions" (*CIL* 8.17639). This illustrates how the ideal operation of power can easily be thrown off track by individual transgressive actions provoking acts of resistance.

In the same way, I argue that the scale and diversity of the Empire complicated its cultural impacts. It is debatable that there was ever a coherent cultural mission of the Roman Empire, though the cosmopolitan ruling elite and the military

50. Some eminent Roman historians (for example, Ando 2016; Woolf 2012, 23–26) seek to deny the possibility of drawing comparisons between the Roman and modern empires on the grounds of structural dissimilarities, but I think such comparisons are perfectly possible and appropriate if we consider the overall strategies for control and exploitation of conquered peoples and territories employed by empires and the systemic impacts from the huge power imbalances that empires create.

51. Mattingly 2011a, 33–37, on transgressive behaviours within imperial systems; 2014a, 25–26, for a schematic modelling of the interplay between imperial actions, local reactions and systemic factors in Roman imperial government.

52. Mattingly 2014a, 25–28.

community were two groups that built ideas of identity more explicitly on perceived "Roman" norms, albeit often with a narrowly defined group focus, rather than a desire to transform society at large.[53] My model suggests that the cultural patterns that emerged in Roman provinces reflected not just intentional transmissions of key elite culture, but strong resilience of local traditions and a systemic mixing due to the very interconnectedness and globalising effect of empire. In what follows I shall not explore globalisation theory in detail, as I am most interested in the interplay between Roman cosmopolitan practices and the cultural preferences of Africans in terms of identity formation.

As noted above, a complaint about the postcolonial debate on ancient North Africa is that it has had quite a narrow focus, primarily on the theme of resistance. There is potential in the now well-developed field of postcolonial studies for a much broader range of themes and approaches.[54] One of the key tenets of postcolonial writing across the last 50 years has been the need to let the subaltern speak—to allow access to the platform for people denied a voice in the conventional, top-down, and patronising history of colonised territories that was set as a template by colonial era historians.[55]

> Perhaps in the future there will be some African history to teach ... at present there is none: there is only the history of Europeans in Africa. The rest is darkness ... and darkness is not the subject of history ... [History] is not ... the unrewarding gyrations of barbarous tribes in picturesque but irrelevant corners of the globe.[56]

On the other hand, for remote antiquity it is no easy task to give voice to the subaltern, and there are attendant risks in placing responsibility on past actors and ignoring our own scope for action:

> Peoples without History, are usually those who have been deprived of it by force. Pretending to restore it is a condescension that trivialises the original theft.[57]

As an archaeologist, I am less pessimistic about the possibility of achieving a different perspective, but I am also more concerned by the alternative of simply persisting

53. Terrenato 2019, is particularly good on the cynical manipulations of the ruling elite to preserve the status and power in the rise of the Empire.
54. I have found the works of Said 1978; 1992 a particularly useful entry point. For a range of other classic studies, see Ashcroft et al. 1995; 1998; Schwarz and Ray 2000. For some early explorations of postcolonial thinking in Roman archaeology, see Gardner 2013; Hingley 2005; Mattingly 1997a; 2011a; Scott and Webster 2003; Webster and Cooper 1996.
55. Haeussler and Webster 2020; Webster 2001; Wells 1999.
56. This classic denial of history to Africans and cultural disparagement of subjected peoples is from a 1963 radio broadcast by Hugh Trevor Roper, quoted in Sanghera 2021, 177.
57. Woolf 2014, 3.

with traditional top-down narratives. While our literary sources and epigraphic data are inevitably slanted in favour of people who by social status or education were situated more towards the "Roman" end of a broad social spectrum, there are a number of ways in which I have tried to counter these imbalances in the evidence. The first is to make greater use of a wider range of archaeological evidence than is often considered—looking beyond the monumental architecture and high-end art—to reflect on local and discrepant ways in which material culture was used and prioritised. The second has been to develop a step-by-step critique of the written sources, focused on the identification and disentanglement of colonial discourse that underlies the way in which material has been presented and understood.

I have already mentioned this idea of discourse, but now I need to specify that there are in fact three separate colonial discourses to take account of. The first relates to how the Romans considered and justified their own imperial power. This was no doubt less sophisticated than modern analyses of imperialism and colonialism, but nonetheless there are common elements. The Romans frequently cited divine sanction of their Empire and of their civilising mission. The imperatives of ruling far-flung provinces, no matter that territorial acquisition was in some instances eschewed in the Late Republic, were typically expressed in terms of advancement for provincials and the Pax Romana. The economics of imperial exploitation are almost never mentioned, and Roman interventions are generally presented as defensive reactions to external enemies or fanatical rebels. The symptoms of such a discourse are evident in the distortions of the texts that portray Africa's landscapes as desertic, empty, undeveloped, and its peoples as barbaric or unsettled (recurrently encountered in Chapters 3 to 5). The Africa "discovered" by our sources was in effect presented as a virgin landscape in need of sensible and intelligent outsiders to allow it to be developed for the benefit of benighted Africans. The echoes with modern colonial discourses on Africa should be very apparent.[58]

My second discourse concerns the modern colonial justifications of contemporary imperial projects. This was especially important in the late 19th and early 20th centuries in that it created a body of dogma about the appropriateness of imperialism and the rights and duties of colonising powers.[59] There was much direct drawing of parallels and lessons from ancient to modern colonialism and vice versa.

In North Africa the close collaboration between the modern colonial regimes and archaeologists, epigraphers, and historians studying the rich evidence of the Roman past inevitably developed this further into a third specific discourse, in which the interpretation of the ancient sources and of past history was underpinned by a host of shared "understandings" and value judgements about the moral rectitude of the imperial project. This was the intellectual climate in which Haverfield

58. Mattingly 2011a, 19; cf. Pakenham 1992.
59. See for instance, Baring 1910; Bradley 2010; Hingley 2000; Vasunia 2013.

produced the concept of Romanisation—the perfect tool for eliding history to best fit a preconceived sense of the lessons of imperial history and the benefits of colonial rule.[60] The surprising part of the story is that the Romanisation concept has so long outlasted the colonial age that spawned it. This is not to say that the evidence collected across the modern colonial age (and beyond, with scholarship continuing to follow similar agendas) is of no value. However, the twin challenge is to broaden the range of data under consideration and, through the deconstruction of the underlying discourses that shaped the collection and prioritisation of evidence, to allow a different reading to emerge.

To illustrate the way that the conventional narrative of "Roman Africa" has been constructed around specific sets of assumptions as part of a colonialist discourse, I shall present two aspects briefly here.

The Conventional Narrative (i): The Rise of Urbanism and Sedentary Agriculture as Key Elements of a Roman Success Story

Bearing in mind the difficulties and constraints of the topography and climate of the Maghrib, a key part of the modern colonial discourse relates to the extraordinary nature of its transformation into a richly productive land in Classical antiquity:

> Given these conditions, it must be noted that the wealth of Africa ... has only one explanation: the work of men. They alone have made possible what deserves to be called the "African miracle."[61]

A central element of the "colonial" story of "Roman Africa" is thus that a desert land thinly populated by uncivilised nomads experienced a veritable boom in agriculture and urbanisation under Roman rule. While such accounts had to recognise that there was some evidence of agriculture and towns in pre-Roman Africa, these were mainly considered to have been a coastal phenomenon (the Libyphoenician *emporia* and their territories), stimulating a few farming and urban experiments in emulation by Numidian and Mauretanian kings in the last centuries BCE.[62] Urbanisation has thus been seen as essentially an imported concept that was part of a package of Punic, Hellenistic, and Roman culture. The conventional wisdom is that these successive waves of Mediterranean civilisation were passively embraced

60. For the colonialist context in which Haverfield wrote, see Freeman 2007, 1–42.
61. Le Bohec 2005a, 13: "Dans ces conditions, il faut bien constater que la richesse de l'Afrique ... n'a qu'une explication: le travail des hommes. Eux seuls ont rendu possible ce qui mérite d'être appelé le *miracle africain*."
62. For typical expressions of this viewpoint see, inter alia, Le Bohec 2005a, 22–23. For a more nuanced view, Briand-Ponsart and Hugoniot 2006, 24–25.

and adopted by Libyans in the Roman period, with an important element in Rome's success being the transformation of nomads into sedentary farmers.[63] I shall examine this in some detail across the next three chapters.

A strong sense of emulation of Rome is apparent in many 19th- and early 20th-century accounts of North Africa, aimed at demonstrating the interconnection between the Roman and modern colonial discourses. French and Italian archaeologists and historians enthusiastically took on the idea that it was "outsiders" who were primarily responsible for the miraculous transformation of African deserts into productive and civilised lands, eventually supported by Africans who became "Romanised." According to this view, "Roman Africa" was a land of 400–600 towns and these settlements were hotspots of profound Romanisation—generally understood in Africa to be represented by the wide adoption of Latinity, the epigraphic habit and an investment in cultural markers of *Romanitas*, such as mosaics, statuary, the urban amenities of comfortable Roman towns, and so on.[64] Leaving aside issues relating to the Romanisation label, there is another question that begs to be asked. If Africa was so un-urbanised in the pre-Roman period, how is it that the province achieved such a density of towns in comparison to other areas of non-existent or low pre-Roman urbanisation, such as Britain or Northern Gaul?[65] Similar questions are also pertinent in relation to the agricultural boom witnessed in Africa under Rome.[66] Again credit is predominantly given to Roman initiative, building on Punic foundations, with little consideration of Libyan contributions. As noted already, the conventional narrative stresses instead the prevalence of pastoralism across large swathes of the Maghrib in the pre-Roman period and credits Rome with a massive and successful programme of sedentarisation:

> The African miracle is explained by several causes and in particular by historical reasons, foremost among which was the legacy of Magon. By this expression, we mean that the Carthaginians, people of the sea as we know, had also become a people of the earth. They developed a brilliant agriculture, recorded in the treatise of the famous agronomist. However, the Romans were not outdone. One of their essential contributions was to delimit the lands of semi-nomads and thus cause the decline of that kind of life.[67]

63. Picard 1990, 66–68 links the Roman extension of agriculture to a progressive sedentarisation of pastoral groups.
64. See Chapter 8.
65. On urban density in Gaul and Britain see Bekker Neilsen 1988; Mattingly 2006a, 255–91.
66. Mattingly 1988c. Now Hobson 2015a.
67. Le Bohec 2005a, 137: "Le miracle africain s'explique par plusiers causes et en particulier par des raisons historiques, au premier rang desquelles se plaça l'héritage de Magon. Par cette expression, nous voulons dire que les Carthaginois, people de la mer comme on sait, sont devenus aussi un people de la terre. Ils ont développé une agriculture brillante, consignée dans le traité du célèbre agronome. Cependant, les romains n'ont pas été en reste. Un de leurs apports essentials a été de delimiter les terres des semi-nomades et de provoquer le déclin de ce genre de vie."

One of the dangers here is that the close correlation of urbanisation and agricultural intensification with successful Romanisation is that both propositions rest on assumptions of prior underdevelopment. While these propositions have proved remarkably resilient in late 20th- and early 21st-century studies of "Roman Africa," I argue that there is now sufficient data to support a radically different appraisal of the situation of the NAIA and that this has profound implications for our understanding of the following period. If urbanisation and agriculture were already widespread in the NAIA, the explanatory power of two key instruments of Romanisation theory has to be rejected, with fatal consequences for the overall concept.[68] The urban and agricultural development and achievements of the Roman era in Africa were indeed remarkable, but my discussion in Chapters 8 and 10 will start in a different place to the conventional one.

The Conventional Narrative (ii): The Evolution of a Roman "Frontier" in Africa and the Nomad Paradigm

Ideas about nomads have always been central to debate concerning the Roman "frontiers" (*limites*) in Africa.[69] In the French colonial period, there was an obsession with the idea of a pervasive "nomad menace" that demanded tactics of exclusion and repulsion on the part of the Roman army.[70] According to this view, linear barriers were erected in places to define and protect the limits of the sedentary agricultural project of the Roman province against nomad raids and depredations.[71] Such views also elided with a broad perception that beyond the "semi-civilised" Numidian and Mauretanian kingdoms, most of the territory eventually occupied by Rome comprised the unstructured range lands of "nomadic tribes" who needed to be tamed to ensure the security of the agricultural zone and the Libyphoenician towns and Roman colonies. In the last decades an alternative view has gained currency that stresses the fixed (or transhumant) nature of the pastoral migrations made by the "nomadic" peoples in North Africa (Fig. 2.1a).[72] The geographical incompleteness of the linear "frontier" works and their unsuitability to completely exclude pastoral migrations suggests instead that their function was more one of control rather than defence, building on traditional symbiotic relations between

68. Leveau 2005, 85–87 noted the circularity of the Romanisation and agriculture argument.
69. For overviews of the nomadism debate, see Devallet 2003; Ibba and Mastino 2011b; Leveau 1988; Rebuffat 1990a; Shaw 1981c; 1983a; Trousset 2012b. Cf. also discussion on more recent periods in Aurenche 1984; Johnson 1969; Scheele 2017.
70. See, for example, Frézouls 1957; 1980.
71. Capot-Rey 1942; Daumas 1968; 1971; Leschi 1942; Rachet 1970. See now, Still-Simon 2006.
72. Mattingly 1995, 37–38; Trousset 1980a; 1980c; 1982b; Whittaker 1978a.

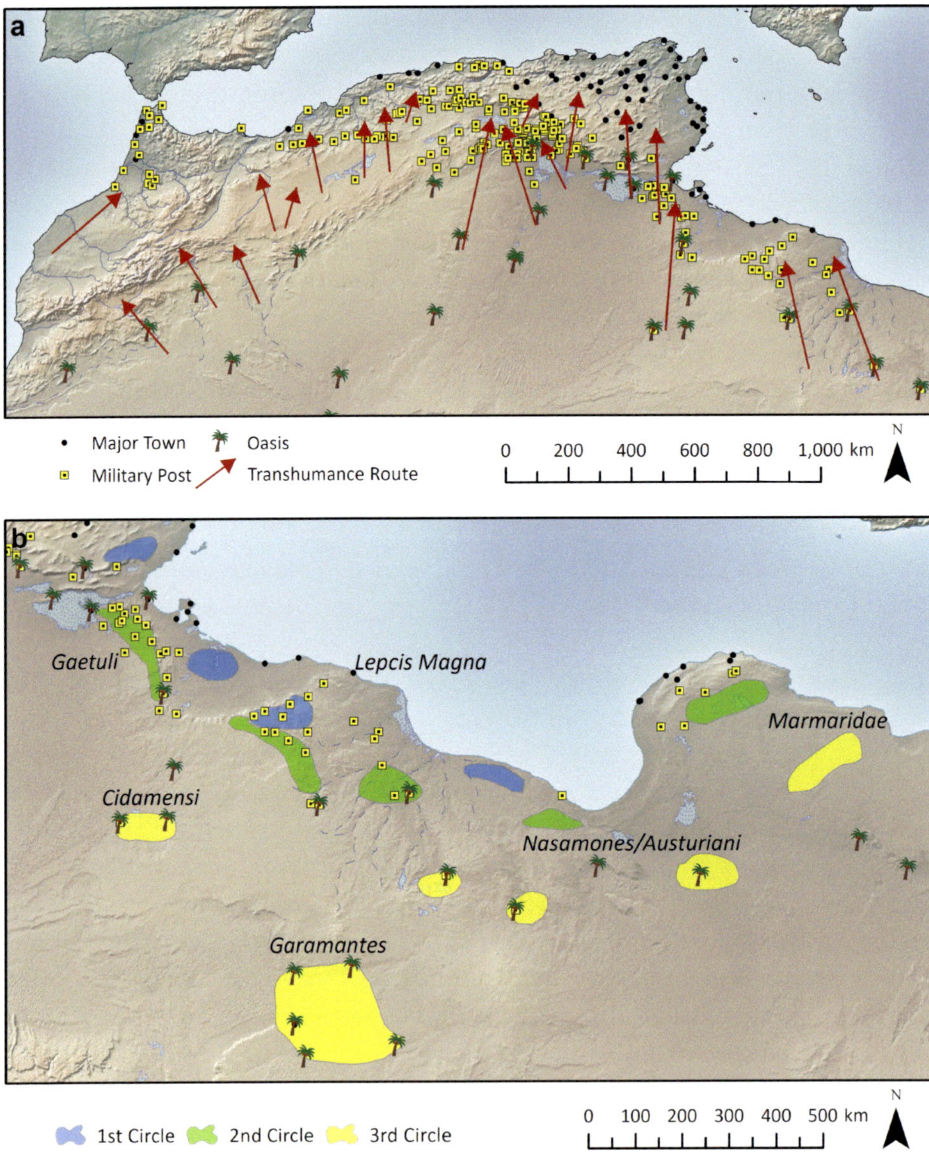

Figure 2.1. Models of nomadism in relation to Africa in the Roman period. a) Transhumance routes (arrowed) between desert and sown (Martin Sterry after Leveau 2018, 78; Whittaker 1978a). b) Revision of Modéran's three circles of nomadism model (Martin Sterry, from author's rough after Modéran 2003, 268).

pastoralists and settled farming communities. While still stressing the close interrelationship of garrison deployment and pastoral movements, C.R. Whittaker's model saw the "frontier" as a permeable membrane rather than a point of repulsion. Transhumance movements are of undeniable importance in Maghribian history, though more recent studies also suggest that in terms of length, seasonality, and specific character these have actually been very varied across North Africa.[73]

The most recent iteration of the nomadic pastoralist model by Yves Modéran talks of Rome dealing with three circles of nomadism in "Roman Africa," involving different scenarios and solutions.[74] In Figure 2.1b I have reversed his order of presentation of the three circles, as more logical chronologically and spatially. The first circle involved groups whose activities were entirely focused within provincial territory, with progressive transformation into sedentary farmers achieved by first demarcating and constraining water and grazing rights, then concentrating groups in reservation-type zones and promoting sedentarisation through enhancing the position and status of the elite. The second circle involved groups, including montagnard communities, whose transhumance carried them across the "frontier," necessitating the need for control and customs exaction at key transit points between desert and sown. The third circle involved the peoples of the desert outside the province, who needed to be intimidated and persuaded to keep their distance by the presence of sufficient forces in outpost forts. Rome also needed to demonstrate a continued ability and willingness to launch long-range campaigns when necessary. Trade relations were developed and maintained with some of these peoples.

The three circles of nomadism model is certainly more nuanced than the nomad menace model with its ideas about how Rome managed relations with pastoral groups. However, the model is seriously flawed in a number of ways, not least in its reliance on the notions of a well-defined Roman "frontier," the "tribal" nature of society, and the assumed overwhelmingly pastoral lifestyle. The problems with this caricature of Libyan nomadic pastoralists is explored in more depth in Chapters 4 to 5, with significant implications for the interpretation of Rome's military strategy discussed in Chapter 6.

Alternatives to Romanisation: Hybridity, Ethnicity, and Identity

My favoured alternative to Romanisation is to use well-established frameworks of postcolonial and identity theory to look afresh at the cultural changes within the Roman Empire.[75] I examine Africa in the Roman world in terms of its multiple and changing identities, drawing on ideas of social memory and articulated social relations.[76] This was a world where there were profound regional differences, informed by their varied historical trajectories. Communities and individuals

73. Leveau 2018, 76–78, with Fig. 9, p. 78 discussing work of A. Bourbouze.
74. Modéran 2003; Trousset 2012b. See also Merrills 2018.
75. Said 1978; 1992; Sen 2006.
76. My approach is best explained in Mattingly 2011a, 203–45; 2014a.

engaged in practices of code-switching, from local to cosmopolitan identity (and vice versa). Cultural change was multidirectional rather than following a single inexorable movement in one direction (colonial emulation). There have already been a number of explorations of the theme of identity in relation to North Africa, though generally lacking a strong theoretical underpinning.[77] While we need to recognise the potential difficulties implicit in the varied ways of defining social/group identity, identity has been a key concept in archaeological research.[78] There has been considerable interest in the potential of investigating identity representation through archaeological evidence in general, with a particular focus on how this relates to cultural hybridity.[79] Identities can perhaps be thought of as flexible, like the choice of clothing, or strategies of bilingualism.[80] By changing costume or language, people can signal a switch in their identity display. Code-switching has been recognised as an important aspect of plural identity presentation.[81] The idea is also being applied to artefacts and other aspects of identity construction.[82]

The idea of ethnicity was probably far less developed than in later eras, and ethnic boundaries in consequence more fluid.[83] In any event we also need to be aware that ethnic identities are ambiguous and complicated in imperial contexts by colonial misunderstandings, inventions, and misrepresentations.[84] In such circumstances ethnicity was also something that was often externally observed and applied—thus, groups like the Phoenicians, Celts, Germans, and Britons were primarily constructs of the Greeks and Romans.[85] Such differences between emic and etic ascriptions of identity in our literary source material are still not always recognised in scholarly discussions.[86] Regional populations were more likely to self-identify in relation to smaller-scale pre-existing states and peoples at the level of the city or the "ethnic unit," though these units might share a language and aspects of material culture in common with other groups.

77. The work that is closest to my own in focusing on the often hybrid nature of identity is by Shaw 2014; 2021. Cf. Briand-Ponsart 2005a; Briand-Ponsart and Crogiez 2002; Briand-Ponsart and Modéran 2011.
78. Brubaker and Cooper 2000.
79. Díaz-Andreu et al. 2005; Gardner 2002; Hales and Hodos 2010; Insoll 2007a; 2007b; Meskell 2006; Shennan 1994. For some specific applications in Roman history and archaeology, see Bauduin et al. 2008; Berry and Laurence 1998; Gardner 2002 (following Giddens 1984); 2004; Hope 2001; Huskinson 2000; Pitts 2007; Revell 2009; 2016.
80. Clothing, Rothe 2009; bilingualism, Adams 2003; Millar 1968.
81. Mullen 2013; Wilson 2012b.
82. Perring and Pitts 2013; Revell 2013; 2016; Van Dommelen and Knapp 2010; van Oyen and Pitts 2017; Winther-Jacobsen 2013.
83. For a range of views and approaches to ethnicity, see Brubaker 2004; Derks and Roymans 2009; Emberling 1997; Geary 1988; Hall 1997; Isaac 2004 (for the related issues of racism); Jones 1997; Roymans 2004. Shaw 2014; 2021, for important discussions of North African ethnicity.
84. Richard and MacDonald 2015, for a series of papers relating to African pasts.
85. See, inter alia, James 1999a (Celts); Quinn 2018; Van Dommelen 2002 (Phoenicians). For Africa, see also Shaw 2014, 527–30.
86. Hall 1997.

In many parts of the Mediterranean the prevalence of city states informed later cultural preferences for stressing the city of birth as an identity marker.[87] Local loyalties and affiliations continued long into the Roman Empire, especially in the Eastern provinces, with its ancient urban cultures and distinctive traditions.[88] The evolution of "Greek" identity under Roman rule has been a particular focus of discussion.[89] Overall, the Roman Empire has yielded little evidence of an enthusiasm for individuals to self-identify in terms of provincial units like *Britannia, Mauretania*, or *Africa*, and so on.[90] Religion always had the potential to create a sense of groupness, but in reality this was more relevant to the monotheistic communities of Jews, Christians, and, later, Muslims than the accommodating accretions of paganism, but even then identities were often multiple and situationally defined.[91] Roman citizenship was an important discriminator of status that cut across geographical, language, ethnic, social, and cultural groupings.[92] Because of the massive expansion of the Empire and its citizenship by the 1st century CE, it is debatable to what extent Roman citizens really constituted an identity group as such, as opposed to a diverse set of people with specific legal rights and privileges—they were more akin to a privileged subgroup, like platinum credit card holders, than a community.

Some groups in society stand out for their constructed identities. The Roman army is the best example from the ancient world of an "imagined community"—though widely scattered through the provinces and composed of a polyglot and culturally diverse manpower, the garrisons exhibited a distinctive set of behaviours and cultural preferences that had the effect of setting them apart from ordinary people.[93] Some groups of civilians who were closely associated with the army became culturally enmeshed in the military community (especially those living adjacent in garrison settlements), but the wider rural community exhibited fewer signs of engagement.[94] In the army and beyond, linguistic and literate skills served to set some people apart from others in society—creating cultural groupings that were highly dependent on the imperial power networks. Apart from soldiers, some minority groups—such as enslaved people—proved adept at constructing identity in the narrow spaces allowed them, sometimes taken to further extremes in their self-reinvention as freedmen and freedwomen.[95] Gender and age are important

87. Hall 2002.
88. Ball 2000; Hoffman 2011.
89. Wallace-Hadrill 2008; Whitmarsh 2010; Woolf 1994.
90. Modéran 2011. See also Shaw 2014.
91. Rives 2007; McCarty 2022; though cf. Webster 1997a; 1997b; 1999 for a postcolonial critique of how conventional approaches to religion in the provinces may misrepresent its social resonances. On Christian and Jewish identity, see Conant 2012a; Rebillard 2012; Stern 2008.
92. Dench 2005.
93. Anderson 1991; cf. Goldsworthy and Haynes 1999; James 1999b.
94. James 2001b.
95. Webster 2005.

division lines in many societies; these were overtly deployed in projecting higher-order identity in Roman society.[96]

How can we best operationalise the investigation of identity in imperial societies? One approach is to explore evidence for different identity groups in provinces under Roman rule.[97] This involves recognising differing levels of social conformity in Roman society and in delineating some broad communities (the military—this group including imperial servants and officials—along with urban communities and rural populations are obvious starting categories). The investigation needs to take account of both inter- and intracommunal differences.[98] Such approaches highlight internal variability in the use of material culture and dynamic change across time (with many actors evidently having a plurality of identities).

My research has led me to consider two crucial aspects of identity. First, I draw attention to how the different ways of being "Roman" reflected the place of an individual within the imperial power structures.[99] The second important observation is that identity was often used in a relational manner, to mark boundaries and differences between people, rather than similarity.[100] Romanisation theory has obscured this, but an important advantage of identity theory is the way it allows us to appreciate that differentiation and the creation of distance from other groups in society was often more important than emulation for some groups.[101]

Discrepant Experiences and Discrepant Identities in the Roman Provinces

In these introductory chapters, I have discussed some of the difficulties with traditional approaches to studying "Roman Africa." I believe strongly that there is both scope and need to advance new agendas, well though the old agendas may be thought to have served. In the 21st century we have the intellectual tools for deconstructing key elements of the colonial discourse that underlies the consensus history of "Roman Africa," established in the 19th- and 20th-century modern colonial heyday.[102] We also have little excuse not to undertake this decolonisation of the

---

96. Herring and Lomas 2009; Harlow and Laurence 2002.
97. The importance of recognising plural and diverse identities is alluded to in Briand-Ponsart 2005a, 7–11.
98. For an insightful case study of cultural diversity at Dura-Europos, Hoffman 2011.
99. Mattingly 2011a; cf. also Gardner 2013; 2017.
100. Barth 1969.
101. One of the most interesting aspects of the *Apologia* of Apuleius is that the conflict between the Numidian/Gaetulian author and his Tripolitanian in-laws reveals the distance between different North Africans in the Roman era and how this could be exploited and accentuated.
102. For an earlier attempt to reflect on the appropriateness of the academic agenda, see Mattingly and Hitchner 1995.

narrative. Although my engagement with this agenda dates back 25 years now,[103] while I was in the middle of the writing of this book, a series of events raised the heat of debate among American Classicists about decolonising the curriculum.[104] There is not just a moral imperative to act, but also a real danger to the future vitality and standing of our subject if we continue to ignore problematic aspects of the modern historical discourse on ancient imperialism.

A key element of my work on Roman imperialism has been to highlight different experiences and impacts of conquest and incorporation for subject peoples. This is consistent with what the Roman sources themselves say. Strabo (*Geography* 17.3.12) in talking of Africa stated:

> for the divisions of the country have been made in various ways, inasmuch as its occupants have been several in number and the Romans have dealt with them in different ways at different times, treating some as friends and others as enemies, the result being that different parts were taken away from, or presented to, different peoples, but not in the same way.[105]

In other words, the Roman Empire did not have standard "terms of membership" and much depended on the circumstances and timing of incorporation. This could work at the level of specific people or at an individual level, in terms of the balance of merits/demerits—with wildly varying outcomes: enslavement, advancement and enrichment, harsh tax imposition, generous tax status, favourable settlement of land rights, loss of direct control or ownership of land, and so on. The terms of engagement offered by Rome, highly varied over time and dependent on the character of powerful actors, shaped the medium- to long-term trajectory of communities under Roman rule, with the potential for positive or negative change in the event of service rendered to the state or participation in acts of rebellion.

A second stage in this line of argument is to recognise how this diversity of experience of a relationship with Rome may have contributed to the cultural

103. Explicit decolonising of the Classics remains relatively underdeveloped; see Bradley 2010; Goff 2003; Munzi 2001; 2004; Vasunia 2013. However, Perkins and James 2000, 5, specify among the aims of their Open University module on "Roman Africa": "consider the validity of making value judgements about cultural traits; develop a critical framework for the understanding of cultural history (whose point of view? African or Roman? Colonised or colonial?; and practise a critical approach to cultural history written from a colonial viewpoint." That pretty much sums up my objectives in this book.

104. See, for instance, Poser 2021. The controversy about racism and sexism include the 2019 SCS conference (whose programme highlighted wider concerns for the future of Classics), the Mountaintop Coalition, and the Black Lives Matter movements that led to criticism in 2020 of the attitude of the Bryn Mawr Classical Studies department by its own students. On the broader social movements of direct action that are challenging the status quo on colonial attitudes, see, for instance, Sanghera 2021; Getachew 2020.

105. English translation from H.L. Jones Loeb edition.

hybridity already remarked on. I have thus suggested that we can replace the term Romanisation with a more subtle interpretative framework, based on the concept of "discrepant identity."[106]

In a number of publications I have articulated an approach to discrepant identity—also to be understood as "hybrid," "plural," or "different identities." My idea of discrepant identity needs a few words of introduction for anyone unfamiliar with it or perturbed by the concept of "discrepancy." The underlying principle here is that people experienced the Roman Empire in many very different ways, rather than in a standard relation.[107] I like the fact that the term "discrepant" hints at both range and sometimes sharply contrasting approaches to identity projection.[108] I believe "discrepancy" is an appropriate term for this range of difference as it emphasises that the possible responses can go beyond variations of consensual adaptation of behaviour and material culture. I have shown how there were many different ways for people to express both association and disassociation with the Roman Empire. In particular, I illustrated how broad groups in Roman provincial society, like the army or town dwellers, actively sought to differentiate themselves from other groups rather than pursuing supposedly uniform cultural norms, which are so often the focus of Romanisation analysis. Yet, as we shall see, there was also considerable variation within these broad communities, reflecting differences in past cultural history and a range of different ways of formulating identity. My arguments in this book build on the basic working principles of the discrepant identity model.

The complexities of multiple identities require us to reflect on how higher-order group identities might have been shaped in the Roman Empire.[109] A series of higher-order identity markers can be suggested that may have operated individually or in combinations to define identity groups: ethnicity, pre-existing states and kingdoms, Roman citizenship, language (multilingualism/bilingualism: Latin, Greek, many others), association with particular cities, *civitates*, *nationes*, provinces, religion/religious preferences, communities (real and imagined), and gender and age groups. The crucial point is that for most people in antiquity, there was no singular identity affiliation that outweighed all others. This is something that makes the Roman Empire very different from the modern world, which has been much more prone to nationalistic or overarching religious affiliations (though these are also far from universal). The interplay between local and global influences is particularly pertinent in the case of imperial and colonial societies.[110]

106. Mattingly 2004b; 2006a; 2011a.
107. Mattingly 2011a, 203–45.
108. For the evolution of the idea, see especially Mattingly 1997b; 2004b; 2006a; 2010b; 2011a; 2014a.
109. Mattingly 2014a.
110. Hodos 2010; Mattingly 2010b.

Part 2: Early Cultural Encounters in North Africa

1000 BCE – 40 CE (and Beyond)

Chapter 3

INCOMERS: PHOENICIANS, GREEKS, AND ROMANS

Introduction

As explained in the introduction, the conventional history of "Roman Africa" has prioritised the roles of outsiders in transforming the southern seaboard of the Mediterranean into a cultural and economic powerhouse of the Roman Empire. In this chapter I present a reconsideration of the evidence underlying such colonising perceptions, before exploring in detail in the two following chapters alternative narratives relating to the role of indigenous peoples in key developments of the 1st millennium BCE. While chronologically those African stories began earlier than the colonial ventures discussed in this chapter, thematically it makes more sense to me to present the problems with the orthodox model of exogenous agency first.

Migration undoubtedly did have a part to play in the story, and there is clear evidence to attest the presence of outsiders in North Africa during the 1st millennium BCE (Fig. 3.1). Though literary sources suggest still earlier origins, the archaeological story begins with Phoenician seafarers around 900 BCE, who are associated (with varying degrees of certainty) with coastal settlements or *emporia* that eventually stretched westwards from Tripolitania to the Atlantic. The most influential of these settlements was Carthage, which by the 6th–5th centuries BCE had established its hegemony over many others and was starting to build an empire. Indeed, the story of the western Phoenicians is indivisible from that of the "new city"—*Qart Hadasht* in Phoenician, *Karkhedon* in Greek and *Karthago* in Latin.[1] Meanwhile from the mid-7th century BCE, Greek colonists settled in eastern Libya (*Cyrenaica*). The city of *Cyrene* was at times a dominant partner among the five cities (*Pentapolis*) that resulted from this colonisation (though over time there were

1. Lancel 1992, 34. When talking about the modern location I use Carthage and for the Roman city *Karthago*; otherwise in this book I privilege *Qart Hadasht* as the name its first citizens used for the pre-Roman city. It is an irony that we do not know the indigenous North African name for Carthage. Miles 2010 is a recent and fairly comprehensive attempt to tell the story of Carthage and its eventual demise at the hands of Rome, employing both the ancient sources and archaeological evidence. See also Ennabli 2020; Fantar 1993a; 1993b; Lancel 1995. Fumadó Ortega 2022 for a good short summary of recent research.

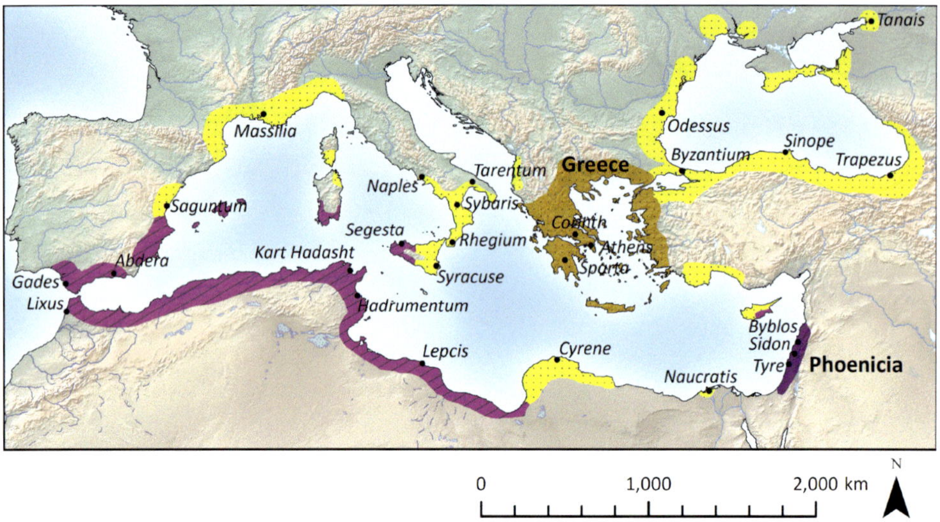

Figure 3.1. The traditional view of Mediterranean colonisation in the 1st millennium BCE: purple: "Phoenician"; yellow: "Greek" (Martin Sterry from author's rough).

in fact more than five main centres). While the geographical location of the Greek settlements in North Africa makes them somewhat marginal to my story, their historiographical significance in helping shape modern agendas and colonialist assumptions is important. Finally, there is unequivocal evidence of the settlement of several waves of Roman colonists subsequent to Rome's acquisition of North African territory. We shall return to their role in the subsequent history later in the book, but a few introductory comments are offered here in relation to my general consideration of colonisation by outsiders as a theme.

This chapter will set out a contextualised account of the nature and landmarks of the early "colonial" ventures. While arguably only a small minority of the population in the 1st millennium BCE were of wholly external ancestry, the potential impacts of these privileged actors are hard to dispute. This external influence is unsurprisingly reflected in multiple ways in the history, languages, religions, institutions, architecture, economic contacts, and material culture of these regions. But the emphasis placed on such factors may impede a more measured assessment of the contributions made by autochthonous groups or individuals. Even where we have clear evidence of the adoption of external aspects of Hellenistic or Mediterranean culture, the question needs to be asked whether the responsibility for introducing it lay entirely with outsiders (and their direct descendants). We know, for instance, that some Africans had themselves travelled outside the region and been exposed to the wider cultures of the Mediterranean world and potentially brought new ideas back to Africa. The obvious examples are the Numidian kings Syphax and Massinissa, who served in Carthaginian armies in Spain (see the next chapter). Many Libyphoenicians were active in Carthaginian imperial service, of course, including some renegades like Marcus Valerius Muttines, who profited from his multiple betrayals by gaining Roman citizenship (Livy 26.40; 27.5).[2]

Colonialism

There has been considerable debate in recent years about the nature and cultural impacts of early colonial ventures, especially the Phoenician and Greek settlements.[3] There is a traditional view that Greek colonies were from the start much more about establishing a home away from home (*apoikia*), whereas Phoenician enterprise focused on maritime trading centres (*emporia*).[4] Greek colonies, in particular, have long been viewed as conscious attempts to create daughter settlements, with close links to established cities, where a Greek identity was strongly maintained and celebrated.[5] Similar ideas have been advanced to explain why Phoenician cities in the Levant sent out surplus population to establish trading settlements in the western Mediterranean.[6] Both of these colonial models incorporate a lot of retrospective tradition and "after the fact" justification to make sense of what may actually have been much more varied and less coherent ventures, especially in the initial stages. A classic case study concerns *Pithekoussai* and *Cumae* in southern Italy. The island of *Pithekoussai* (Ischia) was clearly a focus of mercantile activity in the early 1st millennium BCE, especially from the 8th century, before eventually being supplanted by the mainland settlement of *Cumae*.[7] The historical sources evoke a foundation legend linking back to Euboean Greece and there are certainly some striking attestations of a Euboean presence on *Pithekoussai*, including the celebrated "cup of Nestor" with its Greek inscription. But the evidence from *Pithekoussai* also indicates a much more mixed community, with material culture connecting strongly with Etruria, the Phoenician Levant, and Egypt as well as to the Aegean. The motivation of the island settlement also seems primarily connected to trading and manufacturing activity, rather than to the establishment of a conventional Greek city (*polis*) with associated agricultural lands (*chora*). The location on

2. I am grateful to David Stone for reminding me of this example.
3. For works that engage with the idea of more complex interactions with indigenous populations in the early colonial encounters, see, inter alia, Broodbank 2013; Dietler 2010; Dietler and López-Ruiz 2009; Gailledrat et al. 2018; Gosden 2004; Horden and Purcell 2000; Hurst and Owen 2005; Stein 2005; Tréziny 2010.
4. Broodbank 2013, 524.
5. For more traditional accounts of Greek colonisation, Boardman 1999; Carratelli 1996; Tsetskladze 2006a; 2006b.
6. For more traditional accounts of Phoenician colonisation of the western Mediterranean, see Aubet 2001; Bonnet 2004; Moscati 1988.
7. See Ridgway 1992 for a classic account.

a mountainous volcanic island highlights the importance here of maritime connections and protection from mainland forces. Although *Pithekoussai* is still commonly referred to as the first Greek colony, its early phase looks much more like a cosmopolitan trading settlement in which different cultural groups coexisted. The political organisation, Greek culture, and development of a formal agricultural territory of *Cumae* clearly reflect a somewhat later stage of development.

Views on Greek and Phoenician colonisation have thus been changing in recent years, though, as with the Romanisation debate, there is something of a split between those who continue to insist on the traditional models (despite their modern colonialist baggage) and those who are attempting to explore the greater complexity of the archaeological record. Interestingly, the great modern accounts of the ancient Mediterranean have relatively little to say about colonies and *emporia*, but much more about connectivity, interaction, and trade.[8] As Cyprian Broodbank's magisterial *Making of the Middle Sea* demonstrates, the complexity of developments in this period necessitates a cross-cultural approach, looking at a multitude of different actors in each area and each phase.[9]

Another controversial issue concerns the extent to which the early "colonies" are identifiable simply by imported trade goods and by the implication that imports equate with incomers, as opposed to already present local peoples. Again, older views about the cultural integrity of these communities and their adherence to external norms have perhaps been overstated, and in any case reflect their more evolved character rather than their initial moments. In reaction to this approach, Tamar Hodos, for instance, has argued persuasively for a much higher involvement of local peoples in the early Greek colonies on Sicily and elsewhere.[10] In a similar way, indigenous engagements with externally sourced goods are also now more explicitly recognised in Michael Dietler's work at *Lattara* in southern Gaul.[11] Such possibilities have been less explored in relation to the 1st millennium BCE North African settlements marked by imported goods, but as we shall see, there are some telling hints in the historical and archaeological record.[12] When we talk of Greeks in Cyrenaica and Punic cultures of West Libya and the Maghrib, this needs to be understood as a hybrid mix of incomers and local peoples and culture. The old tendency to associate any and all external material culture as indicative of incomers must be resisted.

A particular problem of reconciling the historical sources with the archaeological evidence for these "colonial" settlements is that there is often a disjuncture

8. Broodbank 2013, 524–50, 550–56; Horden and Purcell 2000, 395–400.
9. Broodbank 2013, especially 445–610 for the "long" 1st millennium BCE.
10. Hodos 2006.
11. Dietler 2010.
12. The essays on Greek colonies and indigenous peoples in Tréziny 2010 span from Spain to the Black Sea, but omit any study on the African colonies. To some extent, discussion of the Greek cities of Cyrenaica is thus left behind mainstream debate.

between the historically claimed origin (in general, recorded by sources dating to several centuries after the event) and the earliest archaeologically documented activity. This raises several separate issues. There was certainly a (competitive) antedating of urban origin myths that were frequently presented in a manner designed to establish lineage with a mother city. Such *post facto* historical creations may not have corresponded with historical reality (or were designed to provide a simplified narrative) and unsurprisingly there is often a lack of exact correlation with the archaeological evidence for the earliest phases at sites. There is a related issue of cultural convergence in Mediterranean societies in the later 1st millennium BCE. Broadly this is what is often understood by the term "Hellenisation"—though in many ways this is as problematic a concept as Romanisation and, like the latter, encourages us to look at North Africa narrowly in relation to external stimuli.[13]

A further problem is that Greek and Phoenician colonisations, though recognised as being somewhat distinct from one another, are often perceived as being relatively uniform and coherent "programmes" within their individual cultural domain. On the contrary, it can be argued that the subsequent rationalisation in antiquity of the histories and cultural trajectories of these sites (amplified in modern scholarship) has created a false impression that there was a standard template for Greek or Phoenician colonialism. This of course, disregards the fact that the overseas settlements traced their links with a multiplicity of mother cities in the Aegean and Levantine worlds (though many of the Phoenician *emporia* in the west do not seem to have developed a special foundation myth linked to a mother city at all).

This is not to deny, of course, the reality of human migration in the Mediterranean in the first half of the 1st millennium BCE, which clearly had significant historical consequences. But rather than being the product of a deliberate export of a fully fledged cultural identity, we need to recognise that the diaspora of Greek- and Phoenician-speaking communities helped create in the long term a more marked sense of Greek or Phoenician identity, not only in the "colonies" but also in the homelands. While it is still conventional in many historical accounts to partition the 1st-millennium BCE Mediterranean into separate zones of "Greek" and "Phoenician" colonisation (as graphically represented in Fig. 3.1), such an assumption of uniform cultural blocks is misleading. For a start, it ignores the fact that the basic patterns of winds and currents and ancient maritime technologies meant that in conducting trade and making long-range voyages in the Mediterranean, there were not separate shipping lanes under Greek and Phoenician colonial control.[14] Most east-to-west movements were obliged by prevailing winds to follow routes along the northern waters, and

13. Prag and Quinn 2013; Bonnet 2014.
14. Broodbank 2013, 73–79, 445–49, 482–95.

many west-to-east routes exploited the favourable winds and currents nearer the southern shore. Both Greek and Phoenician ships (and Etruscan, Roman, Iberian, Egyptian, African, and whoever else was active in longer-range shipping) followed essentially the same sets of routes, albeit potentially with different preferences for stopping points along the way.[15] It is no wonder that the material culture of Mediterranean seaports in the 1st millennium was culturally highly diverse, often with as much Greek pottery as "Phoenician" material at Punic centres in the west. Indeed, in the earliest levels at *Utica*, Greek ceramics predominated among the imports.[16] This highlights that material cultural markers cannot necessarily be assumed to provide ethnic identifiers, with considerable complexity and overlap emerging through trade and imitation of goods produced in areas that were brought into contact during this formative period.[17]

With the above provisos in mind, I now give some description and explanation of Phoenician and Greek involvement in the south and west Mediterranean. Here I focus on "outsider" explanations of these sites, before turning in the following chapter to the evidence that suggests more endogamous involvement in the early maritime settlements.

Phoenicians

French colonial sources had no doubts on the importance of the Phoenicians:

> The true discoverers of North Africa were the Semites, the Phoenicians. It is with them that Africa enters into history.[18]

The Phoenician homelands lay on the Levantine coast, focused primarily in modern Lebanon. The main cities of *Tyre*, *Sidon*, *Berytus*, *Byblos*, and *Tripolis* generally had a somewhat constrained hinterland due to the Lebanese mountains and to some extent always looked to the sea. The fact that some of the most important centres, such as *Tyre*, were located on offshore islands emphasises their connection with the sea and relation with maritime trade. These Levantine cities were generally independent of one another, though on rare occasions *Tyre* seems to have aspired for ascendancy among them.[19]

15. The maps of Phoenician trade routes in Lancel 1992, 29; Miles 2010, 63.
16. Ben Jerbania and Redissi 2014.
17. Broodbank 2013, 491–95.
18. Albertini et al. 1955, 36: "Les véritables découvreurs de Afrique du nord furent des Sémites, les Phéniciens. C'est avec eux qu'elle entre dans l'histoire."
19. On the Phoenicians in general, see Bonnet 2004; López-Ruiz and Doak 2019; Krings 1995; Moscati 1988.

There is a strong ancient tradition supporting the idea of widespread Phoenician colonisation of the western Mediterranean. Diodorus Siculus (5.20) summarises this neatly for us:

> The Phoenicians, who since distant times have navigated the seas in pursuit of commerce, have founded many colonies on the Libyan coasts and a certain number of others in the western regions of Europe.[20]

One of the paradoxes of the Phoenician diaspora, but also potentially a contributing factor to it, was the periodic domination of the Levantine coast by the early empires of Mesopotamia, such as the Assyrians. For extended periods during the 1st millennium the Phoenician cities were essentially subjugated and tribute-paying to the Assyrians, the Persians, and later Alexander, his Hellenistic successors, and the Romans. Their towns were centres of trade and skilled craftwork, often more in the sea than attached to the land.[21] Phoenicians spoke a Semitic language and were early adopters of an alphabet. It is this linguistic conformity that essentially underlies the ancient and modern identification of "the Phoenicians" as a distinct group. Since the pioneering work of Sabatino Moscati, there has been a general acceptance that Phoenician identity went further than this, also being a distinctive and shared cultural package of materials, gods, and behaviours.[22] The orthodox view of the Phoenicians still emphasises cultural homogeneity over heterogeneity and sees some coherence and overall purpose in the pattern of settlement and economic activity.[23]

However, as Jo Quinn and Nicholas Vella have recently argued, the idea of a Phoenician identity was largely an imposed one, based on Greek sources,[24] and while there are signs that the idea of "being Phoenician" was to a degree explicitly used within their society, this cannot be detected until long after the initial diasporic migrations, which seem to have been much more individual initiatives or related to a specific city, rather than being a more coordinated programme of Phoenician colonisation. For instance, the adoption of the imagery of the date palm as a symbol of Phoenician identity references a Greek play on words, where *phoenix* could stand either for a Phoenician or a date palm. The adoption of the palm tree as an iconographic device was a late 5th-century BCE development at

20. See also Pseudo-Skylax 111.9 for a similar reference to numerous "Carthaginian" colonies between the Syrtis and the Atlantic.
21. As reflected in their apparent preference for establishing settlements on offshore islands or peninsular locations projecting into the sea; Broodbank 2013, 482–88.
22. Moscati 1963; 1988; 1993; but cf. Quinn 2018, 22–24.
23. Aubet 2001 (though successive editions of Aubet's great work have toned down the colonialist assumptions); see also Maraoui Telmini et al. 2014, 114–15. Cf. also Sommer 2010.
24. Quinn 2018; Vella 2014.

Qart Hadasht, reclaiming a Greek cultural identifier of "Phoenicians" as an element of Carthaginian self-identification—most notably on its coinage.[25]

It is also clear from recent scholarship that the idea of the Phoenicians and Phoenician identity has been further distorted in modern political discourses.[26] Similar ambiguities and cultural baggage attach to the ancient term *poenus* (Punic), which was variously employed to describe speakers of a language, to identify someone as broadly Phoenician (east or west), to refer in general to west Phoenicians, to Carthaginians or to a hybrid North African/Phoenician identity.[27]

The key building blocks of Punic identity are generally held to be shared language, social and political institutions, and religious practices and specific deities, but how are we to securely identify it?[28] Do we accept ancient literary testimony alone or, if we prioritise archaeological evidence, what were the primary material markers of a Punic identity?[29] While the term is often restricted in its wider use to the 6th century BCE and later, at *Qart Hadasht* a case has been made for describing the earliest activity in the 8th–6th centuries as Early Punic I, II, and so on.[30] In any case, there is a good deal of ambiguity, bearing in mind that "Punic" was not an ethnic term and, as we shall see, that some indigenous African communities also adopted the Punic language and aspects of material culture and practices.[31] In reluctantly continuing to use the shorthand terms, "Phoenician" and "Punic," I want to emphasise that these cover a range of cultural encounters. Within North Africa, people described in this way were always to some extent mixed communities of outsiders and Africans, as reflected in antiquity by their common identification as *Libyphoenices* (for example: Strabo, *Geography* 17.3.19; Pliny, *NH* 5.24). A final important consideration is to recognise that the reception of the Phoenicians in modern times has been part of a wider discourse, involving both colonial and nationalist perspectives.[32]

25. Alexandropolous 2000; Frey-Kupper 2014; Jenkins and Lewis 1963; Quinn 2018, 86–90. Cf. also Cherif 2006 for wider usage of the iconography. One of the reasons the imagery may have had such salience in the Carthaginian world relates to the state of development of North African oases, on which see Chapter 5.
26. Quinn 2018; Van Dommelen 2014.
27. Prag 2014; Gómez Bellard 2014, 69–70.
28. Quinn 2018; but cf. Filippo Bondi 2014 who, while noting great regional differences, nonetheless makes a case for "recognising the very strong elements that unite the Punic culture of different Mediterranean regions" (quote from p. 68 in an extended passage that sounds very like the standard Romanisation defence).
29. Van Dommelen and Gómez Bellard 2008.
30. Maraoui Telmini et al. 2014, 117.
31. On the cultural ambiguity of Punic settlement in Sardinia, see Van Dommelen 2002.
32. Quinn 2018; Van Dommelen 2014. In Tunisia, for instance, Punic studies (exemplified by, inter alia, Fantar 1993a; 1993b) took on a strongly nationalistic aspect as a reaction to the French colonial emphasis on the Roman period. In Morocco, despite a generally lukewarm attitude among Classicists towards the Phoenicians, they provided a useful colonial antecedent to the Roman interlude, seemingly kick-starting developments that would be taken further under Rome, Carcopino 1944; Gsell 1913; 1918a/b; 1920.

There are some strange elements in the pattern of Phoenician expansion in the Mediterranean, not the least that the majority of their "colonies" or *emporia* lay so far from the homelands. Indeed some of the earliest archaeological evidence has emerged at the western extremity—on the Atlantic coast of Spain at Huelva, where Phoenician pottery and other imports occur in deposits dated to the 10th–9th centuries BCE.[33] The Phoenician activity at Huelva and nearby Cadiz, an offshore island settlement, was close to a major zone of mineral resources and early metallurgy. It is clear that local populations with advanced technical knowledge were also involved at these sites, so their characterisation as Phoenician colonies is potentially misleading. Interestingly, some of the other instances where we can detect the early presence of "Levantine" interests in the early 1st millennium BCE were also associated with mineral resources and metallurgical centres: Cyprus, *Pithekoussai*, Sardinia. Access to metals thus seems to have been one of the factors behind the long voyages made by Levantine ships in this period. At least in the early period, the main routes took a relatively northerly course that ran west past Cyprus, Crete, Sicily, Sardinia, the Baleares, and the Straits of Gibraltar.[34] Although there are legendary origin dates for sites like *Utica* on the North African coast around 1100 BCE, the earliest archaeological evidence from North Africa, as we shall see, dates to the late 10th and 9th century, but activity at so early a date is limited to a very small number of sites.

Themes to be looked at as potentially defining Punic identity include funerary practices, religious rites (in particular those related to Melqart and Baal Hammon/Tinnit), language, and civic institutions (as demonstrated through epigraphic records). To start with funerary practices and traditions, in broad terms Phoenician societies in the Levant appear to have used both cremation and inhumation, but most of the first Phoenician settlements in the west were cremating, whereas at *Qart Hadasht* burials were inhumations from the start.[35] After the mid-6th century, other Punic settlements seem to have by and large adopted the Carthaginian practice of supine inhumation and this is potentially an indication that the power or cultural hegemony of *Qart Hadasht* over the other "western Phoenicians" had intensified at this time. From the late 4th and early 3rd centuries, cremation in distinctive types of cinerary urns was again widely adopted, though without fully replacing inhumation everywhere. A wide range of grave goods (notably pottery, lamps, perfume flasks, jewellery, and other metal artefacts like mirrors and razors) were routinely included with burials, but again with a lot of regional, social,

33. Broodbank 2013, 483–84.

34. Broodbank 2013, 446–47.

35. Bénichou-Safar 1982; Ferjaoui and Redissi 2019; Gómez Bellard 2014; Morel 2010. But cf. Ben Younès and Krandel-Ben Younès 2014 for a detailed review of the North African evidence which raises issues with how we isolate Punic from Libyan.

and temporal variation.[36] While there is a clear expectation that a Phoenician or Carthaginian material culture existed, it must be recognised that this varied from place to place and over time, that some canonical emblems (such as the "symbol of Tanit/Tinnit") did not appear until the 5th century BCE, and that at all times the "Punic" aspects were mixed up with artefacts originating in other parts of the Mediterranean—Iberia, southern Gaul, Italy, Sardinia, Sicily, the Aegean world, the Levant, Egypt.[37] In other words, there was a great deal of cultural heterogeneity across the Punic world, which we will undervalue if we focus principally on the more homogenous aspects.

The Semitic origins of the main cults in Punic North Africa have been much discussed, but whatever the links with ancient "Phoenician" practices, it is clear that "Punic" religious practices also diverged significantly.[38] Melqart (later equated with Herakles/Hercules) was seemingly a diasporic cult with Mediterranean reach.[39] However, *Qart Hadasht* was the dominant influence in development in the central Mediterranean of a "circle of the Tophet" (to use Quinn's phrase), involving the worship of Baal Hammon in Tunisia (initially at *Qart Hadasht* and Sousse), Malta, western Sicily, and southern Sardinia.[40] The development of the tophet was a characteristic of this central Mediterranean region. These were originally open-air ritual and sacrificial enclosures associated with Baal and later also with the allied cult of Tinnit (Tanit). The interior of the tophet enclosures were filled up with multiple layers of ritual stelae and urns containing cremated remains of children.[41] Over time the tophets were augmented by other religious structures.[42] Tinnit (to use the fuller expansion in Greek texts of Punic "*TNT*") seems to have been linked to the earlier Phoenician cult of Astarte.[43] Even if the names Baal and Tinnit are encountered at an early date in the Levant, the specific development of the cult and ritual in the central Mediterranean was very distinctive. These chthonic divinities became arguably the most significant at *Qart Hadasht*, especially with their associations with child sacrifice.

The Carthaginian practice of sacrificing children to the gods is a strong and consistent feature of the ancient sources dealing with *Qart Hadasht*.[44] Before we accept this unquestioningly, we should recognise that the Greco-Roman sources had specific agendas in portraying the otherness and brutality of the Carthaginians.[45]

36. Bisi 1990; Gómez Bellard 2014, 72–73.
37. Quinn 2018, 107.
38. Bonnet and Xella 1995; Ferjaoui and Redissi 2019; Lipiński 1995.
39. Bonnet 1988; Quinn 2018, 113–31.
40. D'Andrea 2014; Fantar 1990b; Quinn 2018, 91–112; Xella 1991; 2013.
41. On the stelae, see Amadasi Guzzo 2002; 2008; Bisi 1967.
42. On tophets, see now Bénichou-Safar 1995; 2004; D'Andrea 2014; Xella 2013.
43. Quinn 2018, 97–98. Cf. Bonnet 1996.
44. D'Andrea 2014, 328–30; Xella 2009, 63–88 for detailed discussion of the source evidence.
45. Mosca 2013; Quinn 2018, 92–98; Xella et al. 2013, 1202–03.

However, there is evidence from the tophets in the form of engraved and inscribed stelae and the cremated remains of children, which might support an interpretation as sacrificial acts. The issue has been much debated by modern scholars and broadly there are two schools of thought. The first argues that the ancient source evidence deliberately misrepresented an aspect of Carthaginian society, whereby children were subject to different funereal rites to adults and their cremated remains placed in the tophets serving essentially as infant burial loci. If there were sacrifices, these were generally animal substitutes, and the vast majority of the huge numbers of children are to be interpreted as a normal pattern of neonate and early childhood mortality.[46] The alternative view is that the explicit sacrificial language of the stelae (referring to things given to the gods in fulfilment of vows) are in full concordance with the testimony of the ancient sources.[47] That animals were sometimes used to substitute for a human child is illustrated by references on stelae to *mlk 'mr* ("sacrificial offering of a sheep") alongside references to *mlk b'l* or *mlk 'dm* ("sacrificial offering of a human"), since such expressions cannot be read as "offering by a sheep" and "offering by a person."[48]

The two schools of thought (child sacrifice vs child burial) remain irreconcilable, and attempts to use detailed analysis of the cremated remains of infants can take opposing views of the same evidence, with Schwartz et al. arguing that these are consistent with a normal pattern of infant mortality, and Smith et al. that there is an abnormal peak of infants dying in the first month or so of life.[49] On balance, the evidence is in favour of accepting that child sacrifice was an important element of the cult of Baal and Tinnit, with children often pledged in advance and sacrificed in fulfilment of a vow that the gods had already honoured. A related and equally important question is the extent to which such practices changed over time or were eradicated under Roman rule. Again, there is a tendency to want to believe that such a practice had no place in a Roman province, despite hints in the Christian writers that it was indeed a continuing feature of pagan practice (for example, Tertullian, *Apologia* 9.2–4).[50] As we shall see in Chapter 11, the question of child sacrifice has important resonances in the later story of Africa in the Roman Empire.

The Phoenician language was clearly a key element of defining a Punic identity—even if that identity was externally applied by Greeks to their Mediterranean trading rivals and partners. Punic was widely disseminated in the western Mediterranean by the late 1st millennium BCE, but did speaking Punic make you Phoenician? The adoption and use of the language certainly extended beyond the settler communities

46. Bénichou-Safar 2004; Moscati 1987; Ribichini 1987.
47. Brown 1991; D'Andrea 2014; Stager 1980; Xella 2009; Xella et al. 2013.
48. Xella et al. 2013, 1202–04.
49. Smith et al. 2011; Schwartz et al. 2010; 2012; Xella et al. 2013, 1200–02.
50. McCarty 2017; 2019.

in North Africa (see Chapter 4). Given that *Qart Hadasht* had emerged as a regional superpower by the 3rd century BCE, these sorts of cultural impacts are not unexpected, but they relate to a very different phenomenon to the idea of Phoenician colonisation where we started.

The eventual distribution of "Phoenician" colonial settlements is skewed towards the central and western Mediterranean, notably the North African coastline from western Libya to Morocco, western Sicily, Sardinia, and south-western Spain (Figs. 3.1–3.2). There are some explicit references in the sources to deliberate Phoenician foundations on the African coasts, including some very early claimed dates: c.1100 BCE, *Utica* (Pliny, *NH* 16.216) and *Lixus* (along with Cadiz in southern Iberia); 814 BCE, *Qart Hadasht* (Cicero, *De republica* 2.23.42).[51] The early phases of urban evolution in Africa have been inadequately explored, whether in terms of matching up the traditional literary foundation dates for sites like *Utica* and *Qart Hadasht*, or in assessing the scale and sophistication of early sites, their economic bases and connectedness, or the lifeways of their inhabitants (diet and material culture). However, in general, Punic specialists have found it difficult to demonstrate archaeologically dates as early as the literary traditions imply for foundations. Although the expectation is that more of the Libyphoenician sites should date to the first half of the 1st millennium BCE, at present the evidence suggests that the main expansion of their numbers came after 500 BCE. Part of the problem is that many early towns went on to be successful Roman towns, replete with monumental architecture and in situ mosaic floors, which have discouraged deeper sondages. At any rate, it is apparent from the mid to late 1st-millennium origins of many Phoenician/Punic settlements that they must relate to multiple episodes and potentially to a range of different scenarios—from predetermined colonial towns to settlements that evolved and grew out of trading contacts. To some extent the architectural traces of these early cities and the material culture reflect a broad engagement with Mediterranean societies, not simply "Phoenicians."[52]

A persistent scholarly idea that there were regularly spaced Phoenician stations all along the African coast from the Atlantic to the Syrtes has long since been discredited due to the lack of evidence at many postulated sites.[53] However, there are still a number of locations that merit closer scrutiny. "Phoenician" sites along the North African coast can be divided into several distinct groups: sites in northern Tunisia (*Qart Hadasht*, *Utica* and Cap Bon); sites of the Lesser Syrtes (*Hadrumetum* to *Lepcis Magna*); sites of the Algerian coastline; and sites in Morocco.[54]

51. Lancel 1992, 30–38.
52. Ward-Perkins 1971.
53. Lancel 1992, 111–12; Mederos Martín 2019.
54. Gsell 1918a, 93–181 is now outdated but has useful summaries of ancient source evidence. See Laronde and Golvin 2001, 16–35 for some good reconstruction drawings of *Qart Hadasht* and Kerkouane.

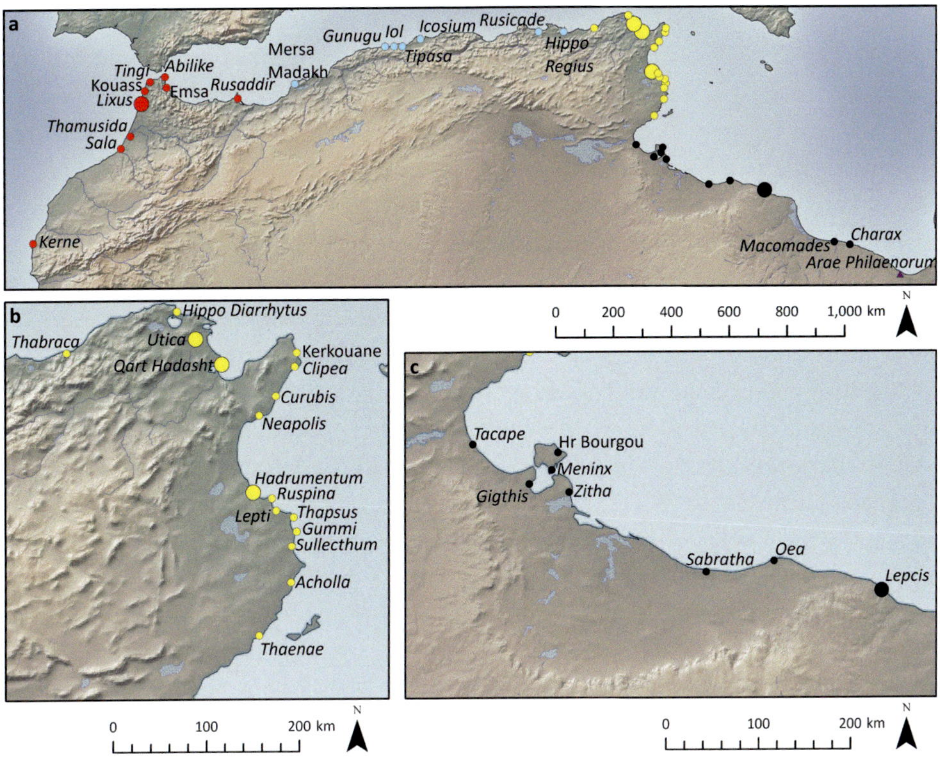

Figure 3.2. "Libyphoenician" settlements in North Africa. a) Overall map showing named locations from Morocco to Algeria and in Greater Syrtes. b) Detail of north and east Tunisian sites. c) Detail of Tripolitanian sites (Martin Sterry from author's rough).

Northern Tunisia: Utica, Qart Hadasht and Their Immediate Hinterland

The emergence over time of a dominant "Phoenician" city among the *emporia* in the west at *Qart Hadasht* is an important theme.[55] In a North African context, the story of *Qart Hadasht* dominates the 1st millennium BCE, though nearby *Utica* appears to have been an earlier foundation.[56] At present the earliest archaeological evidence from *Utica* relates to some late 10th-century burials and other features (compared with the literary date of the late 12th century BCE), and for many years there has been a disparity between the earliest buildings at *Qart Hadasht*—dated

55. For older views, see Chifman 1963; Sznycer 1976; Warmington 1969.

56. Four of Gsell's eight volumes covering the period are devoted to *Qart Hadasht*: 1913 (Phoenician colonisation); 1918a (the Carthaginian state); 1918b (military history); 1920 (Carthaginian civilisation). For more up-to-date accounts, see Aubet 2001; Docter et al. 2015; Ennabli 2020 (especially important as summary account of all key sites); Fantar 1993a; 1993b; Fumadó Ortega 2022; Lancel 1995; Miles 2010.

to the late 8th century BCE (compared with the literary foundation date of the 9th century BCE).[57] Carthage has been subjected to intense archaeological investigation including a number of deep excavations that have reached the underlying subsoil (Fig. 3.3).[58] Of particular importance are the excavations at three nearby locations: Niemeyer's pioneering sondages beneath the crossroads of the Decumanus Maximus and Cardo X, followed up by the more extensive trenching at Bir Massouda and Rue Ibn Chabâat ("Quartier Didon").[59] These sites, located on the east side of the acropolis hill (Byrsa) towards the sea, have produced the earliest stratigraphic sequences, though the ceramic assemblages and the associated houses appear to go no earlier than the later 8th century BCE.[60] However, radiocarbon dates on animal bones related to make-up levels on which the mid to late 8th-century Punic houses were built now confirm that there was activity at the site by the second half of the 9th century, most likely relating to nearby structures (perhaps on the Byrsa hill, that have been completely erased by subsequent activity there, or an original low-lying settlement core slightly north of the excavated sequences).[61]

Within the early Punic period (760–480 BCE),[62] several subphases of buildings have been recognised at *Qart Hadasht*. These were complex, multiroomed, rectilinear structures, with stone-footed walls or mud-brick construction. Roofs were mostly flat and most buildings single-storey.[63] Despite the relatively low number of excavations that have penetrated to the lowest levels, the extent of the urban area is starting to become better defined. It can be assumed that the Byrsa was used as an acropolis from early times, with settlement also extending on its east side to the seashore. Early Punic cemetery areas, encountered in multiple areas, define to some extent the maximum southern and northern limits of the built-up area and the Bir Massouda side has yielded traces of what appears to have been a 7th-century BCE casemate wall defending the south side of the settlement.[64] Outside the wall

57. Chelbi 1996; Lézine 1971; López Castro et al. 2016 (*Utica*); Flügel and Dolenz 2018, 28 (*Qart Hadasht*).
58. For a good summary of early discoveries, see Lancel 1992, 49–93.
59. Docter et al. 2003; 2006; Flügel and Dolenz 2018; Maraoui Telmini et al. 2014; Niemeyer et al. 1996; 2007.
60. Niemeyer 1990; Rakob 1990.
61. Docter et al. 2005; 2008 for the radiocarbon dating results from the Bir Massouda site; Flügel and Dolenz 2018, 28 for discussion of new dates from the rue Ibn Chabâat site; Maraoui Telmini et al. 2014, for overall discussion of dating issues.
62. Maraoui Telmini et al. 2014, 117 for a dating table of all subphases of Early, Mid and Late Punic periods. NB that the earliest dating here follows the ceramics rather than the latest radiocarbon dates, with a noted disjuncture between the two.
63. On the early buildings, see the forthcoming volume *Karthago V*; also Docter et al. 2003; 2006; Flügel and Dolenz 2018, 28–34; Maraoui Telmini et al. 2014, 118–22.
64. Maraoui Telmini et al. 2014, 121–22. For the existence of 8th-century burials within the Bir Massouda site, see Chelbi et al. 2006b.

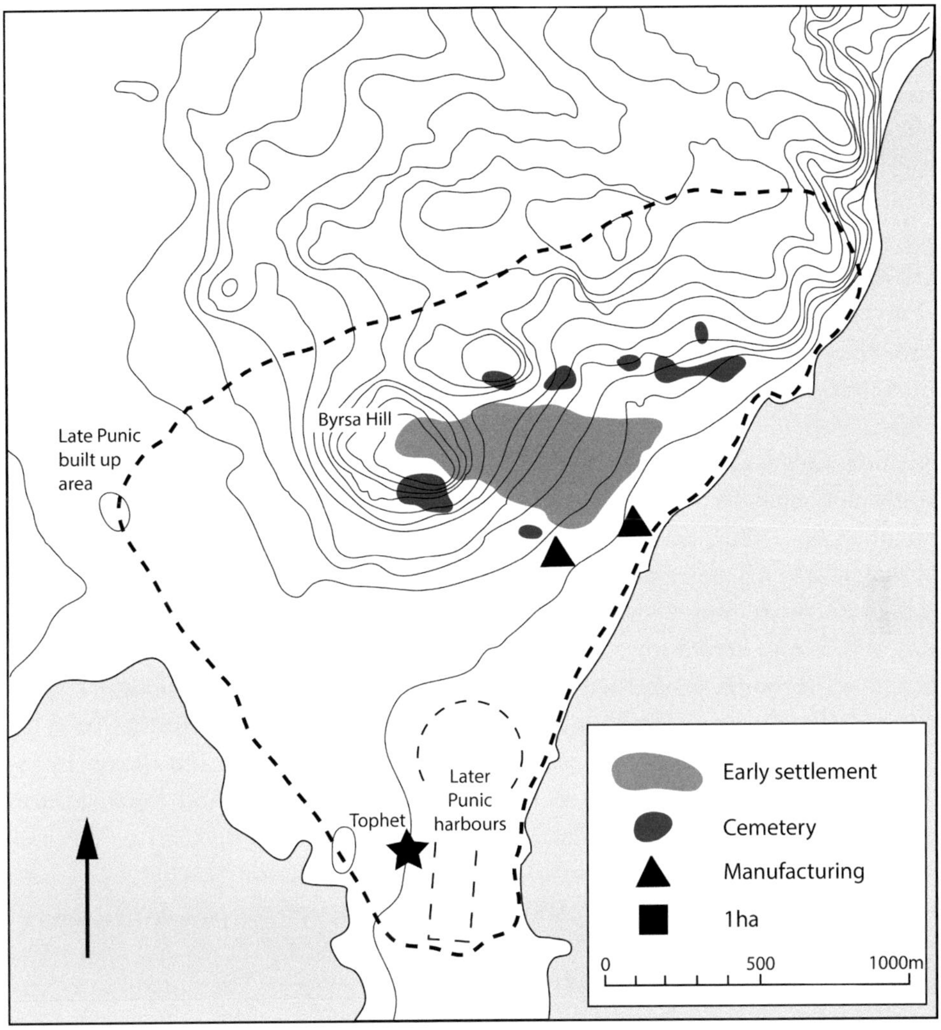

Figure 3.3. *Qart Hadasht* in the 1st millennium BCE (Mike Hawkes, from author's rough after Telmini et al. 2014, 119).

towards the south and also towards the sea there appear to have been zones of metalworking and other manufacturing activity—principally purple dye production. Further to the south outside the urban core was the large tophet, site of child cremation and possible sacrifice, covering an area of 0.3 ha, with an estimated 10,000 markers and 20,000 cremation urns spanning the 8th–2nd centuries BCE.[65] The identification of a southern limit of the early city has necessitated some

65. Bénichou-Safar 2004; D'Andrea 2014, 33–67); Lancel 1992, 40–44; 247–76; Quinn 2018, 94 for the size); Stager 1980; 1992.

downward revision of the overall size of early *Qart Hadasht*, but at c.25 ha, and a proposed population of 5,000–8,000, this was still quite a sizable settlement among known Phoenician centres in the western Mediterranean. The size of early *Utica* can be approximately estimated from its known cemeteries at 12–14 ha, but *Lixus* appears to have been no more than 10 ha, and the core of early Cadiz only 5–6 ha.[66] *Qart Hadasht* thus seems to have been unusually large from an early stage and its special status among the cities of the west is also reflected by the fact that it appears to have had specific foundation myths from early times.[67]

By the Mid Punic period (480–300 BCE) there were signs of urban growth and a restructuring of the townscape, with residential quarters now extending over the early industrial areas and new industrial activity appearing on the southern slopes of the Byrsa hill. The new residential units appear to have been more orthogonally planned and were built over fairly homogenous orange-yellow levelling layers, both implying a strong centralised control.[68] In longer-established quarters, it is not unusual to find later phases of construction reusing the stubs of walls of earlier phases as foundations and thus preserving building alignments. Domestic housing of this phase, best represented at the Bir Massouda and Magon excavations, was increasingly standardised and regular in plan, with houses typically comprising suites of rooms around a central open court containing an oval/cigar-shaped cistern.[69] The interior decoration of houses was also increasingly elaborate from the Mid Punic period, with painted wall plaster, solid mortar floors, and already by the late 5th century the first experiments with mosaics.[70] In this period, the first traces of public buildings have been identified, so interpreted from distinctive aspects of their plan and the use of ashlar masonry from the al-Haouaria quarries.[71] Two conjoined structures at the Quartier Didon site had broad rubble and clay foundations below ashlar walls (the more complete structure measured 14.74 × 10.12 m, with a symmetrical internal layout focused on two oval cisterns). The function of these buildings is uncertain; the initial identification of the first to be found as a temple is no longer thought probable.[72] There is also evidence for the construction of impressive city walls enclosing a wider area by the late 5th century.[73]

The Late Punic period (300–146 BCE) marked the apogee of *Qart Hadasht*, with new residential quarters laid out on a systematic grid (as on the south slopes of the Byrsa hill),[74] the great harbour complex taking its final shape (with its inner

66. Maraoui Telmini et al. 2014, 118, 143–45 for comparisons with other earlier sites.
67. Maraoui Telmini et al. 2014, 145–46.
68. Flügel and Dolenz 2018, 29–36; Lancel 1995, 136–37, 154–55; Maraoui Telmini et al. 2014, 122–26.
69. Chelbi et al. 2006a; Docter et al. 2003; 2006; Rakob 1991.
70. Rakob 1991; Maraoui Telmini et al. 2014, 129–30.
71. Flügel and Dolenz 2018, 33–36, Edifices I and II.
72. Maraoui Telmini et al. 2014, 123.
73. Rakob 1991.
74. Lancel 1983; 1992, 172–92; Lancel and Morel 1992.

Figure 3.4. Late Punic buildings on the flank of the Byrsa hill, burned during the Roman sack in 146 BCE (photo: author).

circular naval base),[75] and its enhanced land and sea defences that were to frustrate the final Roman siege efforts for three years.[76] The densely inhabited part of the city did not extend to the full area enclosed by the walls, but was still an impressively large and populous site. The burnt-out buildings of this city on the south slopes of the Byrsa hill bear witness to the final outcome and the catastrophic circumstances of its eventual fall (Fig. 3.4).

There is no doubt that *Qart Hadasht* stands out among other presumed Phoenician or Punic colonies in North Africa. The archaeological evidence confirms the primacy accorded to the city in the literary sources, especially from the late 6th century. The picture of *Qart Hadasht* on the eve of the Third Punic War provided by Strabo (*Geography* 17.3.15) in many ways presents a mirror image of Rome's own discourse about its African empire:

> Carthage was founded by Dido, who brought a host of people from Tyre. The colonisation proved so fortunate an enterprise ... they also gained possession of all that part of Libya which men can live in without living a nomadic life ... they had 300 cities in Libya and 700,000 people in their city.

75. Hurst 1985; 1992; Lancel 1992, 192–211; Panero 2008; Stager 1992, 75–78.
76. Fantar 1998, 2–3 (reconstruction drawing of the city and its defences); Lancel 1992, 434–46.

The 300 cities in Africa mentioned here far exceeds the numbers of potential coastal *emporia* subject to Carthaginian hegemony, and I shall return to the significance of this comment in later chapters. For other sites on the north Tunisian coast, including Cap Bon, several ancient sources are relevant (Pliny, *NH* 5.22–24; Pseudo-Skylax 110–111.4; Strabo, *Geography* 17.3.13–16; Sallust, *Jugurtha* 19.1). Following the Tunisian coast from north-west to south-east, Phoenician or Punic origins have been proposed at numerous sites, sometimes based on the identification of "Punic"-type tombs and cemeteries (Fig. 3.2).[77]

Thabraca (Tabarka) has yielded no especially early evidence, though the name is Libyan and is also attested in Punic texts. There were Roman-style magistrates in 37–36 BCE.[78] *Hippo Diarrhytus* (Bizerte) is mentioned as *Hippou Akra* in Pseudo-Skylax (11.5) at the end of the 4th century, but there is no corroborating archaeological evidence. As already discussed, despite the legendary 12th-century BCE foundation date, *Utica* has produced nothing archaeologically that predates the later 10th century.[79]

There is a cluster of sites around the Cap Bon peninsula (*Hermaia*) to east of Carthage with plausible Punic origins, mostly known from Punic tombs.[80] *Clipea* (Kelibia) has yielded traces of Punic fortifications.[81] *Curubis* (Korba) had *sufetes* as magistrates, but has no other evidence to suggest a date for its origin.[82] *Neapolis* (Nabeul) appears to have originated by the 5th century BCE and appears in Pseudo-Skylax (110).[83]

The best-preserved and most extensively excavated Punic town in North Africa apart from Carthage is Kerkouane (ancient name unknown). Lacking a harbour, this small coastal settlement, c.12 km north of Kelibia, is possibly atypical of "Phoenician" settlements. It was evidently founded in the 6th century BCE, with its main phase of structural development in the 4th–3rd centuries BCE, but with a sudden abandonment shortly before 250 BCE.[84] The extensive excavations have revealed an oval walled settlement (c.5 ha)[85] with a densely built up interior packed with relatively standardised housing units and with a possible temple, but relatively few other candidates for public buildings and little monumental architecture (Fig. 3.5).[86] Although central parts of the settlement were laid out relatively

77. Fantar 2002; cf. also Fantar 1995. For tophets, see D'Andrea 2014, 146–50 (northern Tell); 120–38 (Cap Bon); 68–119 (Sousse and Sahel); 256–60 (Lesser Syrtes); 261–64 (Libya).
78. Desanges 1980b, 203–04.
79. Chelbi 1996 (8th-century burials); Desanges 1980b, 214–16; Lancel 1992, 30–31; Lézine 1971. See now López Castro et al. 2016, for the earliest dated material.
80. Fantar 2002.
81. Desanges 1980b, 222–24; Desanges et al. 2010, 137–38.
82. Desanges 1980b, 225; Desanges et al. 2010, 140–41.
83. Desanges 1980b, 225–26 (stating that mentioned by Thucydides, *PW* 7.50); Desanges et al. 2010, 186.
84. Most likely as a result of the campaign of the Roman general Regulus in 256–255 BCE, Lancel 1992, 289.
85. Fantar 2012 for the defences.
86. Fantar 1984; 1985; 1986.

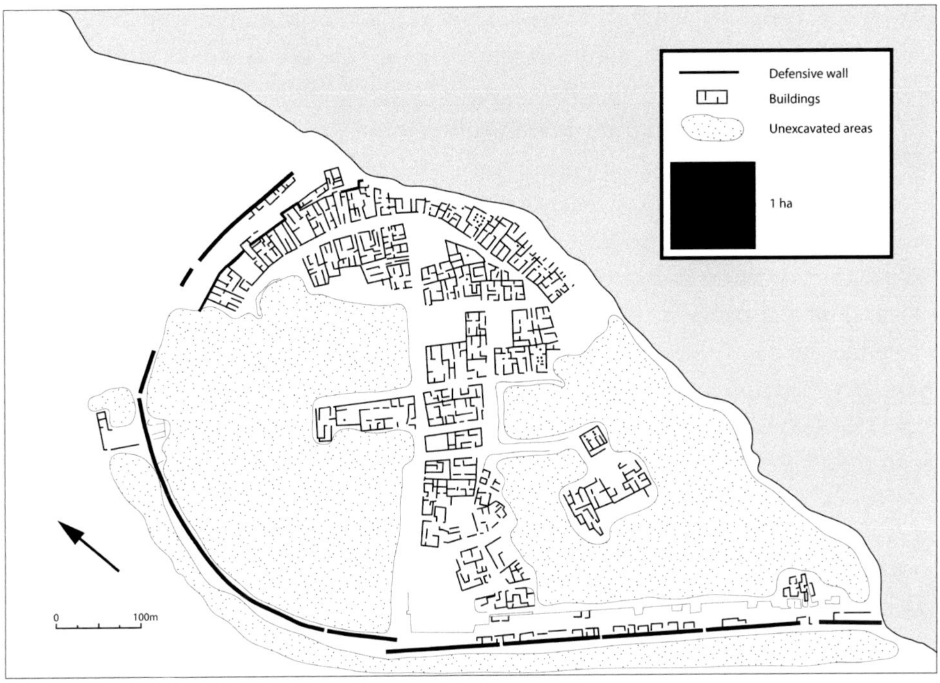

Figure 3.5. Plan of Punic small town at Kerkouane, Cap Bon (Mike Hawkes after Fantar 1984).

regularly to a rough grid, the curving outer wall influences the orientation of the peripheral buildings and contributes an overall impression of radiating outer blocks. The stone-built houses, with mortar floors including some early mosaic and tesserae decorations (including one "Tinnit symbol") and domestic bath installations, are directly comparable to material at *Qart Hadasht*. Kerkouane was little more than a large village, though the domestic architecture and material culture suggest quite a well-to-do community. The site is also associated with a large cemetery of Punic style rock-cut tombs.[87]

South-Eastern Tunisia and North-Western Libya

The sea is very shallow along this sector of the coast and there was a notable engagement with the development of port facilities and exploitation of marine resources in the region.[88] The Punic centres of the Tunisian Sahel and the north-west Libyan coast are specifically associated in the literary sources with the people described as *Libyphoenices* (Pliny, *NH* 5.24–25; Pseudo-Skylax 109.4–110.8; Strabo, *Geography*

87. Gallet de Santerre and Slim 1983; Lancel 1992, 308, 312.
88. Slim et al. 2004.

17.3.16–18).[89] That might imply some perceived differentiation between these settlements and those of northern Tunisia just reviewed. The review below takes a north-west to south-east order.

The Phoenician foundation of *Hadrumetum* or *Adrumetum* (Sousse) is explicitly mentioned in Sallust (*Jugurtha* 19.1) and Solinus (27.9), and it appears in Pseudo-Skylax in the late 4th century. Though the Punic town is deeply buried beneath the Roman, medieval, and modern city, evidence from a Punic necropolis and tophet attests to activity here from the 6th century BCE.[90] The early date of the tophet and Punic tombs of *Hadrumetum* stand out in the region as being more like those of *Qart Hadasht* and having less in common with other sites of *Byzacium*.[91] *Ruspina* (Hr Tennir, near Monastir) was on a hill about 5 km distant from the sea. Recent survey there has found pottery of 5th-century BCE date.[92] *Leptiminus* (Lamta) is described as a possible Phoenician foundation, due to the relative lack of ancient source references to it, though there is archaeological evidence from extensive cemeteries of Punic-style rock-cut tombs and some finds of Punic pottery (but not pre-5th century).[93] The lack of evidence for a tophet or for Punic inscriptions stands in contrast to the scale and extent of the Punic cemeteries.[94] Certain aspects of the material culture in the Punic tombs at *Leptiminus* highlight Libyan aspects of the tradition.[95] Similar burials have been recorded at *Thapsus*[96] and a number of other sites along this stretch of coast (for example, Mahdia, Salakta) and also inland (Smirat, al-Hkayma), but the large rock-cut tombs seem to date to the second half of the 1st millennium BCE, so do not inform us regarding earlier origins.[97] *Thapsus* was mentioned in Pseudo-Skylax in the late 4th century BCE, but there is no archaeological evidence to push the date back further.[98] Mahdia (*Gummu*?) has one of the largest "Punic" cemeteries with 311 tombs, so looks to have been an important site, though the urban remains are deeply buried beneath the medieval centre.[99] *Acholla* (Ras Boutria) was allegedly a colony of Phoenicians from Malta (Stephanus Byzantinus, Meineke edition, p. 152), but there is little archaeological data to ascertain when it was established.[100]

89. Desanges 1980b, 226–38; Mattingly 1995, 25–29; Shipley 2011, 191–94).
90. Desanges 1980b, 232–33; Desanges et al. 2010, 156–57; Lancel 1992, 108 (tophet).
91. Ben Younès 1995, 74; D'Andrea 2014, 68–119; McCarty 2011 (tophets).
92. Desanges 1980b, 233; Desanges et al. 2010, 200.
93. Ben Younès and Sghaïer 2018 for the most comprehensive study on the tombs and associated ceramics, 103–10 for summary of dating evidence.
94. Desanges 1980b, 231–32; Desanges et al. 2010, 164–65; Mattingly and Stone 2011, 272–74.
95. Ben Younès 2016.
96. Younes 1999.
97. Ben Younès 1981; 1995; 1996; Lancel 1992, 314–23.
98. Desanges 1980b, 233–34; Desanges et al. 2010, 237–38; Younes 1999.
99. Ben Younès 1995, 76; cf. Ben Younes 1985 (tombs of 4th-2nd century BCE).
100. Desanges 1980b, 234 (not mentioned by Pliny); Desanges et al. 2010, 92–93 (the reference to *Maltais* would certainly suggest a secondary phase of Phoenician colonisation).

The port of *Thaenae* was first mentioned in the mid-3rd century BCE (Ptolemy 1.15.3), but again we lack confirmatory archaeological evidence on the site's ultimate origins.[101] No less than 707 Punic-style tombs have been recorded at just seven of 27 "Punic" sites from the coast and the hinterland of *Byzacium*: Mahdia (311), *Thapsus* (120), *Leptiminus* (113), el-Alia (67), el-Hkayma (49), *Gurza* (26), and Smirat (21). Some of the other 20 sites have just a single tomb.[102] The overall distribution reflects a dense development of the wider landscape away from the coast in the later 1st millennium BCE, though it remains uncertain how far their origins predate the Roman period. With the exception of *Hadrumetum*, there is a striking lack of archaeological evidence for early Punic origins in this region.

The coastal centres of Tripolitania include several where a case can be made for the Phoenician origin and where there is some evidence to attest the character of these centres. However, these sites again seem somewhat different to the northern group of Libyphoenician sites described thus far.[103] *Tacape* (Gabes) is relatively poorly known as an urban centre, but Punic stelae have been recovered within the oasis, indicating the presence of a tophet.[104] As a result of recent survey and excavation, we know that the town of *Meninx* on the island of Jerba was a Libyphoenician centre, with simple stelae to Tinnit discovered in a suburban sanctuary.[105] However, the town does not appear to have been founded before the 4th century BCE.[106] Two other sites on Jerba, Henchir Bourgou and Ghizène, have earlier ceramic material (8th, and 6th or 5th century BCE respectively), but may be more appropriately thought of as Libyan centres of even earlier date—suggested by handmade impressed "basket-ware" pottery (see next chapter).[107] Geophysical survey at Bourgou has revealed a more or less circular walled site of c.4–5 ha, with a radiating internal layout of streets and buildings somewhat reminiscent of Kerkouane.[108] From the dating of Kerkouane, that settlement phase at Bourgou is most likely to date to the 6th century BCE or later and further excavation is needed to determine the nature of the earliest occupation.

On the mainland facing Jerba, the site of *Gigthis* has sometimes been posited as a Libyphoenician centre, on the basis of some Punic-era tombs.[109] Another mainland

101. Desanges 1980b, 235–36; Desanges et al. 2010, 232–33.
102. Ben Younès 1995, 73–74.
103. Gharbi 2020.
104. Desanges 1980b, 237; Desanges et al. 2010, 224; Ferchiou 1990c, 66–70; Krimi 2005 ("Punic" tombs and anepigraphic stelae from santuary).
105. Drine 2002 (anepigraphic stelae); Fentress 2009a; Fentress et al. 2009 for wider survey of Jerba.
106. Desanges et al. 2010, 177; Ritter and Ben Tahar 2020 (for dating).
107. Ben Tahar 2018.
108. Ben Tahar et al. 2022, for an extended overview.
109. Ben Tahar 2004 ("Punic" tombs); Desanges et al. 2010, 150–51.

site, *Zitha* has also yielded Punic stelae from an open-air sanctuary to Tinnit.[110] Once again, these sites seem to be comparatively late foundations, with significant Libyan aspects.

The three main centres of north-west Libya were known collectively as the *emporia*.[111] *Sabratha/Abrotonon* (Sabratah), *Oea* (Tripoli) and *Lepcis Magna* (Lebda) all have well-established Libyphoenician character.[112] The foundation of *Sabratha* cannot be pushed back before the late 5th century BCE, and the structures the Greek and Punic pottery relates to were relatively ephemeral ones.[113] Later Hellenistic features of the town, including two obelisk mausolea and a tophet, are evidence of impressive growth and prosperity. The city's coins identify the town in Punic as "*SBRTN*".[114] Although relatively inaccessible beneath modern Tripoli, the Punic cemeteries of *Oea* have also yielded pottery starting from the 5th century.[115] *Lepcis Magna* is a rare example among the second rank of Phoenician colonies in asserting a clear connection with a mother city, Tyre. That might suggest an early date for its establishment; however, the earliest archaeological evidence (urban buildings beneath the Old Forum and a burial ground beneath the theatre) is later 7th-century and the bulk of early finds are 6th–5th century BCE. The site is identified with the city called *Neapolis* in Pseudo-Skylax (109).[116] Punic inscriptions ("*LPQY*") show that the Latin spelling of *Lepcis* reflected the local pronunciation better than *Leptis*, which represented an Italianisation of the name.[117]

East of *Lepcis*, the Punic world met the Greek world—first at a contested and abortive late 6th-century Greek colony at the *Cinyps* river (Wadi Caam), where according to Herodotus (5.43) the attempt by the Spartan Doreius to establish a colony was eventually rebuffed by a combination of *Macae* (local Libyans) and "Carthaginians" (surely the people of nearby *Lepcis*?). There are other minor sites in the Syrtic gulf for which a Punic origin has been posited, but without much

110. Drine 1991.
111. Di Vita 1982; Rebuffat 1990c.
112. Di Vita et al. 1999, 6–181; Sintes 2010, 86–99.
113. Desanges 1980b, 237–38, 260–61; Desanges et al. 2010, 200–02; di Vita 1969; di Vita et al. 1999, 33 (tophet) 146–51; Mattingly 1995, 125–26.
114. Di Vita 1969; 1971; 2015a, 303–54 (Punic mausolea); Kenrick 1986, 10–12, 141–50, 312–14 (late Hellenistic urbanism); Dore and Keay 1989 and Fulford and Tomber 1994 for the pottery evidence.
115. Desanges 1980b, 256–27; Desanges et al. 2010, 189; di Vita 1969; di Vita et al. 1999, 33 (tophet at Gheran); Mattingly 1995, 122.
116. Carter 1965; Desanges 1980b, 259–64; Desanges et al. 2010, 162–64; de Miro 2002; de Miro and Fiorentini 1977; de Miro and Polito 2005; di Vita 1969, 197; di Vita et al. 1999, 50; Lancel 1992, 108; Masturzo 2013; Mattingly 1995, 117; Zocchi 2018a, 11–13.
117. *IRT*, p. 74–76. While the local inscriptions speak uniformly of *Lepcis* and *Lepcitani*, the Classical authors often refer to *Leptis* and *Leptitani*, which we may consider an overt colonialist discourse (both ancient and modern). Nonetheless, many modern scholars still persist in imposing the "colonial" version of the name.

concrete evidence.[118] The final location is the Altars of the *Philaenus/Philaeni* deep in the Greater Syrtic gulf. The location was mentioned in singular form by Pseudo-Skylax in the late 4th century, but by the 1st century BCE had become the subject of a developed myth involving a pair of Carthaginian brothers who allowed themselves to be buried alive by a rival Greek deputation in order to fix their mutual boundary in a way more favourable to Carthaginian interests. As recorded by Sallust (*Jugurtha* 79), the story has elements that suggest he was drawing on a written Punic tradition.[119] The legend mentions a long-running conflict between Cyreneans and Carthaginians by land and sea ("after many armies and fleets had been put to flight"). Although the mythical story explains the remote desert location of the altars in terms of the point where the rival embassies from the two cities met and the Carthaginian brothers were buried and memorialised, a more plausible explanation is that a decisive sea battle took place off the Syrtic coast and the location of the monuments effectively marked the recognition of Phoenician domination of the Syrtic Gulf.[120] In any event, the Punic/Greek divide did not prevent subsequent trade and there is now more positive evidence of commercial exchange across the Syrtic Gulf that was once apparent.[121]

The investigation of Libyphoenician urbanism has thus far not fully matched expectations, though some caveats need to be considered.[122] Many of the sites mentioned above have not been investigated archaeologically in a systematic way, and it is possible that other sites not listed here might prove in future to have had origins in the 1st millennium BCE. The characterisation of cemeteries and tombs as of "Punic" type is in part a rather subjective one. Although the typologies of the rock-cut tombs bear some resemblance to Punic *hypogea* at *Qart Hadasht* and *Hadrumetum*, in reality there were significant divergences between the funerary complex at sites of undoubted Phoenician origin, like *Utica*, *Qart Hadasht*, *Hadrumetum*, *Lepcis Magna*, and other centres of the later 1st millennium BCE. The typical "Punic" tomb comprised a vertical shaft, sometimes with access facilitated by rock-cut steps, giving access to a subterranean chamber (Fig. 3.6).[123] However, there was a good deal of local variation in the provision of rock-cut or built features in the tomb chambers (beds, benches, podia, niches, and so on).[124] But there are aspects of the funerary rite and grave goods that are quite distinctive, including the fact that many burials

118. Di Vita et al. 1999, 18 (*Macomades* and *Charax*).
119. Quinn 2014 for a discussion of the interesting possibility that Sallust drew on Punic sources preserved in the libraries of the Numidian kings after the fall of Carthage (*Jugurtha* 17.7).
120. Quinn 2014, 175 makes a similar argument, noting the statement of Polybius (3.39.2) that the Carthaginians were masters of the Mediterranean coast of Africa from the Altar of Philaenus to the Pillars of Herakles.
121. Fulford 1989; Quinn 2011; Wilson 2013.
122. Ben Younès 2013.
123. Ben Younès 1995, 74–82.
124. Ben Younès and Krandel-Ben Younès 2014, 150–53.

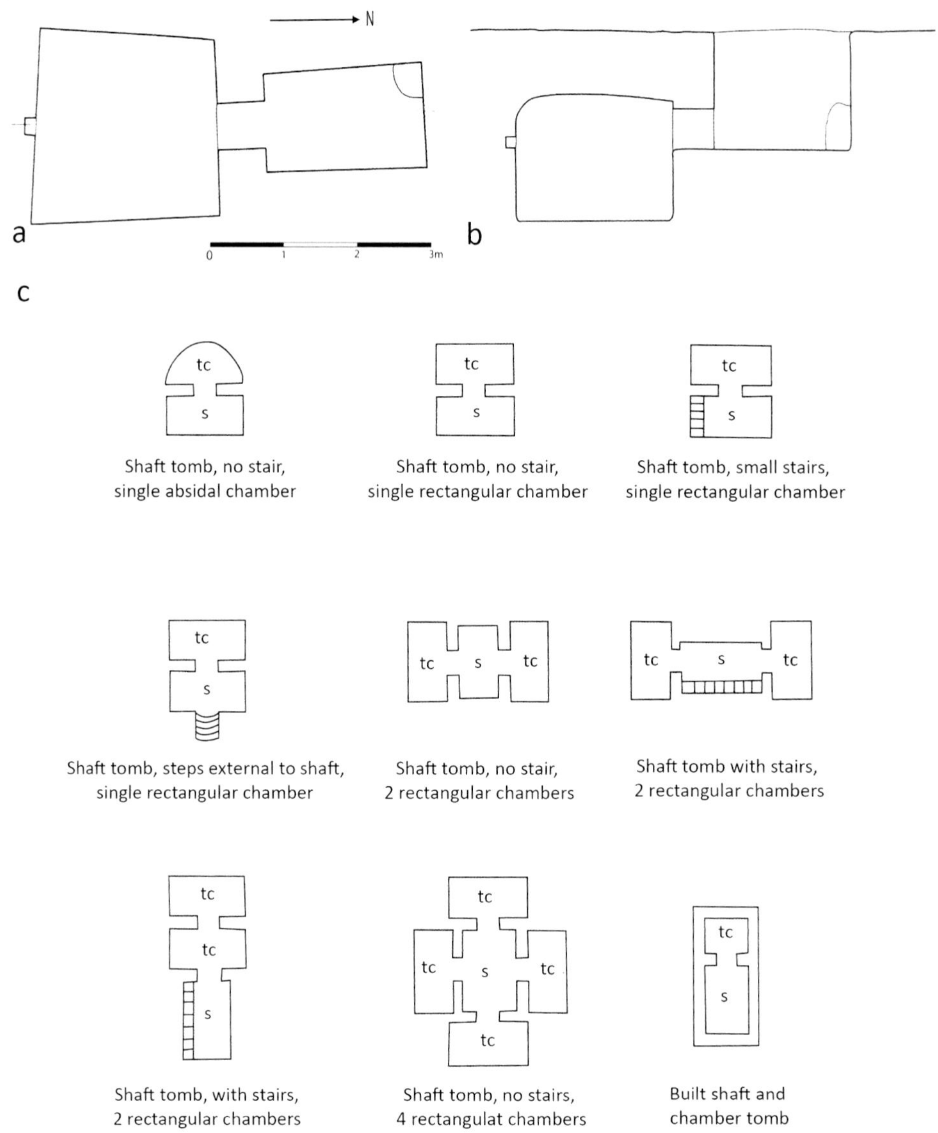

Figure 3.6. Typical examples of Punic tombs from *Leptiminus* (author's montage after Ben Younès and Sghaïer 2018). a) Plan of typical rock-cut shaft tomb. b) Cross section of same tomb. c) Schematic plans of other Punic tombs.

were laid on their side rather than their back, there was extensive use of red ochre in burials, and a high rate of inclusion of handmade pottery.[125] In this case, Punic identity must be recognised as encompassing a much broader range of people and

125. Ben Younès 1995; 1996; Ben Younès and Krandel-Ben Younès 2014; Ben Younès and Sghaïer 2018.

behaviours than the traditional conception of Phoenician settlers and their alien culture. As we shall see in the next chapter, similar Punic identity traits also appear in the context of Numidian inland communities in the latter centuries BCE. It is not always clear where the dividing lines between Punic and Libyan actually lay—at any rate the Liby- element in Libyphoenician appears to have been substantial and more consequential than has sometimes been recognised.[126]

Moreover, given that it is hard to push the earliest origins back before the later 7th or 6th centuries, and quite a number of sites do not seem to have been active until the 5th or 4th centuries, the Libyphoenician "colonisation" appears to have been later than that of northern Tunisia and to have gained its greatest momentum when *Qart Hadasht* was already in the ascendancy and extending its political dominance, especially in the central Mediterranean.[127] The Tripolitanian *emporia* were certainly paying a tax (*vectigal*) to *Qart Hadasht* in the later 3rd century and this was subsequently claimed by the Numidian king, Massinissa, when he wrested control of the region away from *Qart Hadasht* in the early 2nd century BCE (Livy 34.32.3–5; 34.62.1–18). The evidence for the spatial extent of the earliest phases of the Libyphoenician *emporia* also suggests that these were generally quite small in size, between 5 and 10 ha.[128]

Northern Algeria

Parts of the Mediterranean coast of Algeria offer limited possibilities for harbours or safe anchorages, so the natural harbours have special importance and generally long histories (in turn making their earliest phases less visible). In this section, I follow an east-to-west route away from Carthage.[129] *Rus-* place names are believed to be derived from the Punic word for a cape, and there are a good number on this stretch of coast, though by no means all have yielded any archaeological evidence of early activity.[130] Once again, the most significant evidence from many sites relates to so-called Punic tombs, though again the distinction between true "Phoenician" communities and Libyan groups who had adopted similar aspects of funerary architecture is not always easy to determine. The presence of imported pottery is not in itself evidence of incomers, though it has often been assumed to be so.[131]

126. Ben Younès 2007; Ben Younès and Krandel-Ben Younès 2014.
127. As argued long ago by Whittaker 1974; 1978c.
128. Consideration of published plans and GoogleEarth imagery suggests the following rough estimates: Kerkouane 5 ha; *Leptiminus* 3–6 ha; Henchir Bourgou 12–14 ha; *Meninx* 5 ha; *Sabratha* 5 ha; *Lepcis Magna* 5–7 ha.
129. The area is covered by Mederos Martín 2019.
130. Desanges 1980b, 169–72, 194; Lancel 1992, 112 (*Rusguniae, Rusucurum, Rusazus, Rusicade*).
131. Krandel-Ben Younès 1988, 2–3 draws together material from Rachgoun (earliest material 7th century), Les Andalouses (3rd), Gouraya (5th), *Tipasa* (6th), Jilel (4th), Collo (3rd), Beja (3rd), *Bulla Regia* (4th).

There was an early tradition for a harbour called *Hippo* between *Qart Hadasht* and the Pillars of Herakles (Sallust, *Jugurtha* 19.1), but which of the two sites called *Hippo* (*Dhiarrytus* or *Regius*) is uncertain. *Hippo Regius* (Annaba) is missing in Pseudo-Skylax but is mentioned in connection with the campaigns of Agathokles at the end of the 4th century BCE. There is no archaeological evidence earlier than the 2nd century BCE.[132] The next major port to the west is *Rusicade* (Ras Skikda), sometimes identified as *Thapsa* in Pseudo-Skylax (111), but the order of citation and identification of sites listed in this section of that work is uncertain.[133] *Icosium* (Alger) certainly had pre-Roman origins (*Ikosim*), though the finds from there only go back to the 3rd century BCE and the site is not obviously mentioned in Pseudo-Skylax.[134] To the west, *Tipasa* is another site evidently absent from Pseudo-Skylax, but where there is clear evidence of occupation from the 6th century BCE, marked by two widely spaced cemeteries.[135] *Iol* (Cherchel) has also yielded 5th-century pottery from pre-Roman burials adjacent to the modest harbour.[136] Another small port around 15 km west of *Iol* is *Gunugu* (Gouraya) where 5th-century pottery has been excavated from a necropolis.[137] Finally, in the far west of the Algerian coastline, there is a cluster of sites with early imported material, Les Andalouses, Mersa Madakh, and the island of Rachgoun, where finds as early as the 6th century have come from.[138]

Although it is possible that some of these sites represent Punic or Phoenician settlements, in other cases it is equally plausible that indigenous African communities were in the lead, as we shall see in the next chapter when we consider the early history of the *Numidae*. At any rate, the natures of the tombs and funerary rites, while somewhat different from the inland *Numidae* groups, are also differentiated from those of the sites with greatest claim to be Phoenician colonies, like *Qart Hadasht* and *Utica*.[139]

Morocco

There is similar debate today about the scale and extent of Phoenician colonisation along the Mediterranean and Atlantic coasts of Morocco.[140] The ancient sources must bear some responsibility for the modern conviction that there were

132. Desanges 1980b, 201; Desanges et al. 2010, 157–58; Lancel 1992, 14; Shipley 2011, 197.
133. Desanges 1980b, 194; Desanges et al. 2010, 198–99; Shipley 2011, 197.
134. Desanges 1980b, 166–69; Le Glay 1968b, 10–16.
135. Desanges 1980b, 165–66; Blas de Robles et al. 2019, 52–74; Lancel 1965; 1968; 1992, 112–16;
136. Desanges 1980b, 162–64; Blas de Robles et al. 2019, 29–31; Lancel 1992, 116; Leveau 1984, 9–11.
137. Desanges 1980b, 161–62; Lancel 1992, 116.
138. Lancel 1992, 116; cf. also Vuillemot 1965.
139. Krandel-Ben Younès 1988, 16–19.
140. Mederos Martín 2019; Marzoli 2018; Papi 2014.

numerous Phoenician *emporia* in Morocco. The *Periplus of Hanno* (1–6) mentions the foundation of six "Carthaginian" colonies on the Atlantic coast, with a total population of 30,000 migrants.[141] Even in antiquity the authority of such claims of Phoenician *emporia* was questioned on the grounds that no trace of them could be found (Pliny *NH* 5.8; Strabo, *Geography* 17.3.3). Writing in the later 4th century BCE, Pseudo-Skylax (111.5–112.12) describes only two cities on the Mediterranean coast of Morocco, *Akros* (later *Russadir*?) and *Abilike* (at or near Ceuta), before mentioning several Punic *emporia* founded on the Atlantic coast beyond the Pillars of Herakles (a "city in a river," *Pontion*, *Lixus*, *Thymiateria*), with trading activity also being carried out further south at *Kerne* Island (plausibly Mogador, though still much debated).[142] There is some doubt about whether Mogador was an island or a promontory in the 1st millennium BCE, but there is strong evidence there for purple dye production and trading activity, linked to Mediterranean circuits from the mid-7th century, along with handmade wares of local tradition.[143] Strabo's discussion of the coast west of the Pillars (*Geography* 17.3.2) mentions a town with an African name, *Tinx* (later *Tingi*) and refers to other Phoenician settlements south of *Lixus* (which he has confused with *Tinx*, so the geographical location of these additional sites is a bit ambiguous).

A secondary debate has also developed concerning the interconnections between sites in Morocco and those in southern Iberia, with the main argument being that the two sides of the Straits of Gibraltar were much more intimately linked economically and culturally than sometimes appreciated ("the circle of the Straits").[144] This is in some ways an improvement on earlier views that tended to look far to the east towards *Qart Hadasht* or the Levant for an understanding of the activities of Phoenician colonies, but it is not without its critics.[145] Settlements on both sites of the Straits were undoubtedly more closely connected and interacting in this period, but there is still a tendency to see the drivers of the exchange systems and interactions as coming from outside Africa, or at any rate to privilege the role of the Phoenician *emporia* around the Straits.

Archaeologists and ancient historians have enthusiastically followed up these promptings by trying to locate and identify Phoenician/Punic settlements in relation to imported pottery and other finds of the first half of the 1st millennium BCE.[146] Archaeologically, there is some limited evidence of late 8th-century

141. Lancel 1992, 119–26.
142. Shipley 2011, 199–210; Pappa 2009.
143. Bokbot 2020, 482–84; Jodin 1987; Marzoli 2018; Marzoli and El Khayari 2010; 2018.
144. See especially Coltelloni-Trannoy et al. 2016.
145. Papi 2014, 204–05; 2016. See also Bridoux 2014 for a useful survey of trade contacts between sites in Morocco and the Carthaginian world further east.
146. Cintas 1954; Luquet 1956; 1975; Ponsich 1988a. But see now Arharbi 2003; el-Azifi 1995; el Khayari 2007; Papi 2014 for more sceptical views on the "Phoenician" status of many sites.

occupation at Ceuta and 8th-century pottery from the region of *Tingi*.[147] There is apparently 8th–7th-century activity at *Lixus*, suggesting, in line with the literary tradition, that these were three key sites; though despite large-scale excavations at *Lixus*, the evidence of the early "Phoenician colony" is still rather scanty.[148] Ksar as-Sghir, between Ceuta and *Tingi*, has been suggested as the unnamed city in a river from Pseudo-Skylax, and other "Phoenician" *emporia* have been identified along the Mediterranean coast and the Rif hinterland at Sidi Abdesalem del Behar, Wadi Emsa, and Sidi Driss.[149] Close to the mouth of the *Mulucha* river, the settlement of *Rusaddir* (Mellila) has some finds that go back as early as the 6th century. Several important sites down the Atlantic coast were located a few miles upstream on navigable rivers (*Lixus*, *Thamusida*, and *Sala*/Rabat). All these sites are best known for their Roman remains, but have yielded finds of earlier date and are often referred to as "Punic" foundations.[150]

The site of Kouass lies directly on the Atlantic coast to the west of *Zilil*, between *Tingi* and *Lixus*, and is currently the most extensively investigated of the supposed Phoenician *emporia* in Morocco. Focused on a prominent circular hill, standing 40 m above sea level but of only c.2 ha extent, the site was first investigated by Ponsich in the 1960s, yielding evidence for fish salting and pottery production between the 5th century BCE and the 3rd century CE.[151] The recent excavations have revealed well-preserved stratigraphy for the pre-Roman occupation on the central hillock, as well as a range of structures and activities spread over a wider area.[152] The date of occupation on the mound site, which may have been fortified, has been revised (end 6th to end 1st century BCE). One of the structures excavated appears to be some sort of shrine or religious structure. Other rectangular buildings show some regularity of layout from early phases, with construction employing a mixture of ashlar blocks, river cobbles, and mud-brick. Among finds recovered from the debris of a fire was jewellery of typical Phoenician/Punic type.[153] The finds from both phases of excavation attest to intense commercial activity at the site and wide contacts in the Mediterranean world, but especially focused on the Circle of the Straits. However, interestingly, the latest dating schema for the site characterises the pre-Roman as archaic, early, middle, and late Mauretanian, revealing an important

147. Ponsich 1967; 1969; 1970a—though note that these sites are from tombs and rural settlements around Tangiers, which has erased trace of the assumed *emporion* site. Papi 2014; 2019, in any case questions the "Punic" ascription of the burials due to differences from Phoenician practice elsewhere.
148. Aranegui Gascó 2001; 2005; Aranegui Gascó and Hassini 2010; Papi 2014, 210–12.
149. Desanges 1978b, 108.
150. See for instance, Lugan 2000, 22.
151. Ponsich 1970b; cf. Bridoux and Kbiri Alaoui 2013; Bridoux et al. 2011.
152. See annual reports by Bridoux et al. in the *Melanges de l'Ecole Francais de Rome* since 2008.
153. Bridoux et al. 2011, fig. 5.

shift in interpretation.[154] The site is of particular importance for its ceramic assemblage, which demonstrates contacts not only with *Qart Hadasht* and especially Punic Spain, but more widely with the Greek world, Italy, Sardinia, and Sicily.[155]

Concluding Comments on Phoenician Colonisation

Several main conclusions arise from the preceding survey. First, it is no longer appropriate to think in terms of a systematic and programmatic colonisation of the North African seaboard by Phoenicians and/or Carthaginians. That is not to deny the importance of settlements of the 1st millennium within which the language, culture, and ethnicity of some inhabitants made them outsiders. These were undoubtedly gateway sites that created multiple connections between North Africa and the wider Mediterranean world.[156] A number of these sites were evidently established (to follow the archaeological evidence) early in the 1st millennium (*Utica, Qart Hadasht*), with others reasonably dated to the 8th–7th centuries (*Lixus*, Mogador, *Hadrumetum, Lepcis Magna*). However, it is striking that the vast majority of supposed Phoenician *emporia* were evidently not established until the 5th century BCE or later. The question of Carthaginian influence and organisation being behind this late wave of foundations remains open, as does the extent of Carthaginian control over them. The written language of these settlements was Punic, but these sites also had Libyan speakers, and the populations later display a mixture of Punic and Libyan names. The ancient sources explicitly recognise the mixed nature of their populations by describing them as *Libyphoenices*—the term seems to have been particularly applied to the coastal populations of *Byzacium* and Tripolitania.[157] Punic municipal institutions were evidently well developed and disseminated across multiple sites, though the detailed evidence from most of the Punic towns is slight.[158]

While the majority of the Libyphoenician centres were coastal settlements, there is increasing evidence from the second half of the 1st millennium BCE that these were actively associated with agricultural development in their hinterlands as well as with the traditional mercantile and manufacturing concerns of *emporia*.[159] By the time of the Punic Wars with Rome, Carthaginian agriculture was well established and codified in the treatise of Mago (Pliny, *NH* 18.22), one of the few Carthaginian works to have been translated by Rome from the library of

---

154. Bridoux et al. 2014.
155. Bridoux 2014.
156. Ferjaoui 1993a.
157. Diodorus Siculus 20.55.4; Livy 221.22; Strabo 17.3.19; Pliny NH, 5.24; Ptolemy 4.3.6.
158. Belkahia and di Vita-Evrard 1995; Fantar 1988.
159. Ferjaoui 2010a for a range of studies reflecting on the African dimensions of Punic culture and its adoption.

Qart Hadasht.[160] The main areas of agricultural development were evidently in the large hinterland territory of *Qart Hadasht* itself (extending into Cap Bon and far up the Medjerda valley), in *Byzacium* and around the Tripolitanian *emporia*.[161]

The idea of a unified Libyphoenician ethnic identity is a misleading construct when applied to the entirety of the 1st millennium BCE North African coastal settlements from Morocco to western Libya. These communities were very varied in terms of the material culture, despite some commonalities, such as evidence of the Punic language and early imports from other parts of the Mediterranean. Under Carthaginian domination, the term might have had some measure of political meaning and the Roman writers clearly saw the term as a useful way of distinguishing coastal communities from inland ones. I shall return in the next chapters to the involvement of indigenous African groups in sedentary agriculture and nucleated settlements prior to and alongside the establishment of "Phoenician" *emporia*. In later chapters I shall also demonstrate how the different Libyphoenician sites can be split into several distinct groups, relating to the underlying African Iron Age pattern. For the moment, it is simply necessary to highlight that the underlying process of "colonisation" has much in common with the complex settler/local people interactions that are now well documented in the European zone of the ancient west Mediterranean.[162] Finally, it must be admitted that by the late 1st millennium BCE many of the key markers of Phoenician identity—Punic inscriptions, tophets, sacrifices to Baal Hammon and Tinnit, assimilation of a wide range of Mediterranean material culture, and architectural motifs were not restricted to the sites discussed in this section as *emporia*. These aspects had a very long afterlife in Africa in the Roman Empire.[163] As we shall see, disentangling Punic from Numidian or Mauretanian is far from straightforward.

Greeks

As Greek colonists were essentially restricted in Africa to eastern Libya and Egypt, and these regions will be more peripheral to my later chapters, this section will be much shorter than the previous one. The early florescence of civilisation in the Aegean has been much remarked upon, though often explained largely in relation to itself with the full weight of historical hindsight. One of the more interesting aspects of Broodbank's evaluation of this, in its Mediterranean and deep-time context, is that the region was particularly suited for the growth of maritime activity.

160. Fantar 1997; Gsell 1920, 1–52;
161. Manfredi 2003, 407–84.
162. Dietler 2010; Hodos 2006.
163. Fantar 1990a; 1992; Millar 1968; Mattingly 1987b.

The length and indentations of coastline, the vast number of intervisible islands, the hilly and mountainous inland communications all favoured the evolution here of seaborne communications and navigational skills.[164] The relative lack of extensive plainlands for cereal cultivation also created conditions where growing populations had either to look to import staple food or to export surplus population. As with the Phoenicians, it is misleading to present this as a uniform process. Greek colonisation, in its initial phases at least, is a term that covers a range of quite diverse activity from individual mercantile ventures, to collective actions by small groups of citizens, to (perhaps) *polis*-level initiatives.[165] There are indications that Greek traders were going to some of the same locations as Phoenician ships—trading sites or *emporia,* including the metal-rich areas of the Tyrrhenian Sea, the Iberian peninsula, and Cyprus—but in the course of time a pattern emerged for the creation of cities on the Greek model (*apoikia*, literally "home from home"), with attached agricultural territories. This is more characteristic of the "Greek" settlement in the Black Sea region, in southern Italy (Magna Graecia), Sicily, southern France, and north-east Spain and Cyrenaica.[166] One of the most striking differences between studies of Greek colonies in North Africa and those elsewhere concerns the limited extent to which the countryside beyond the monumental towns has been explored.[167]

In North Africa, Greek colonisation began in the later 7th century, traditionally attributed to a group of Theraen adventurers looking for land and establishing a first settlement on an offshore islet of *Platea* in the Gulf of Bomba in 631 BCE (Herodotus, *Histories* 4.151–159).[168] After an unpromising start there (and subsequently on the adjacent mainland), the group were eventually led inland by local Libyans to the ecologically better-supported Jabal al-Akdhar (Green Mountain), where *Cyrene* was founded at some point in the 620s BCE beside an abundant natural spring. Herodotus asserts that *Cyrene* was initially ruled by a line of eight kings down to c.440 BCE, these being alternately named Battos (after the founder of the dynasty) and Arkesilaos. Further Greek cities appear to have been founded by separate settler groups already by the late 7th century (*Taucheira*).[169] Another inland city at *Barca* was also most probably a 7th-century foundation, as a result of internal schism within the royal line of *Cyrene*, though the historical sources seem to date the events to the 6th century. However, a port for *Barca* seems to have

164. Broodbank 2013, 75–76.
165. Boardman 1999 for the traditional view. See also references in the introductory section above on coloniation.
166. On Cyrenaica, see the detailed discussion in Horden and Purcell 2000, 65–74.
167. See Carter 2006, for a study of the *chora* of *Metapontum*, achieving a level of detail that has hitherto not been attempted in Cyrenaica.
168. For the history, see Chamoux 1953; di Vita et al. 1999; Kenrick 2013; Laronde and Golvin 2001.
169. Boardman and Hayes 1966.

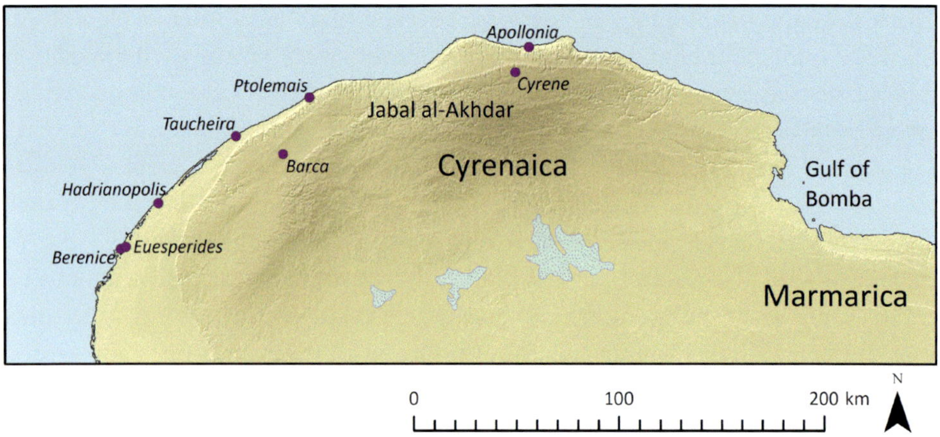

Figure 3.7. Greek and Roman cities in Cyrenaica (Martin Sterry, after author's rough).

existed by the late 7th century (this is the site later known as *Ptolemais*). *Euesperides* appears to have been the last founded in the 6th century BCE, though it was evidently abandoned c.250 BCE in favour of a new urban centre about 3 km to the south-west, adjacent to the modern harbour of Benghazi. The move to the new site (*Berenice*) is believed to have been necessitated either by the siltation of the original harbour of *Euesperides* on a coastal lagoon or a sack of *Euesperides* in civil war.[170] *Cyrene*'s port, which must have existed from the foundation of the inland city, eventually also emerged as an independent city, *Apollonia*, certainly by the 2nd century BCE.[171] In the Roman period there was a further urban foundation on the coast between *Berenice* and *Taucheira* at *Hadrianopolis*, in honour of the reigning emperor's measures to restabilise the region after the Jewish Revolt (Fig. 3.7).

Land ownership/access was evidently a cause of periodic tension and fighting between the "Greeks" and local Libyan peoples, as is common in such colonisation situations. It is a repeated feature of the Herodotean account (*Histories* 4.160–161), but so too were incidents of civil strife and outright war between rival Greek cities (*Histories* 4.161–165). The negative impact on relations between Greeks and the local Libyans is explicitly attributed by Herodotus to the arrival of fresh waves of colonists to reinforce the original settlers under Battos II (*Histories* 4.160). In the reign of Arkesilaos II, after a period of civil discord, at *Cyrene* the citizen body was divided into three parts relating to the Theraens, to settlers from Crete and the Peloponnese, and to other islands (*Histories* 4.162). Attempts by Greek settlers to establish themselves further west in North Africa were several times rebuffed—most notably in the late 6th century BCE when a group of Spartans led by Doreius

170. Wilson 2020, 405.
171. Wilson 2020, 397

established a settlement by the *Cinyps* river (Wadi Caam), close to Libyphoenician *Lepcis Magna* (*Histories* 5.43). After two years they were ejected by a combination of local Libyans and "Carthaginians." At various points, the Cyrenaican cities came under Persian overlordship (*Histories* 4.201–204) and later Hellenistic/Ptolemaic suzerainty from Egypt.[172]

Although several of the main Cyrenaican cities were established in coastal locations to develop harbour facilities—as at *Taucheira* (Tocra), *Apollonia* (Susa), *Ptolemais* (Tolmeita), and *Euesperides*/*Berenice* (Benghazi)—it is striking that *Cyrene* and *Barca*, the two most powerful cities historically lay c.15 km inland up a steep escarpment, occupying the best-watered and highest-quality agricultural land in the area. *Euesperides* by contrast appears to have been in a much more marginal agricultural zone, though potentially in a position to capitalise on Saharan trading possibilities. Most of the major cities of Cyrenaica have been the subject of considerable investigation, already initiated prior to the Italian colonial era,[173] but massively increased between 1911 and 1943, with continuing engagement of Italian missions and others since.[174] The archaeological work has focused primarily on the monumental buildings of these cities and on their architectural and sculptural treasures.[175]

There were in addition a large number of smaller towns and many village settlements, whose ultimate origins are for the most part uncertain.[176] However, Greek-period temples and tombs in association with some of these indicate that the Roman settlement landscape built on that of the Greek era.

What were the primary markers of the Greek colonies in North Africa? The obvious starting point is their similarity to the Greek *poleis* of the Aegean world,[177] though of course even there the idea of the city covered a multiplicity of variant or divergent forms.[178] For the Cyrenaican cities of the Greek era, archaeology has not generally explored much beyond the major temples, theatres, public squares (*agora*), and rock-cut tombs, and the sites are (with the important exception of *Euesperides*, see below) overlain by the impressive remains of their Roman-era successor cities. This reinforces a view of the Greek city as a place of monumental architecture, regular layout, and extensive use of ashlar masonry in construction.[179]

172. Laronde 1987.
173. Rekowska 2016 for an overview of the history of research from the first antiquarians to the start of the Italian colonial era.
174. See, inter alia, Barker et al. 1985; Bonacasa and Ensoli 2000; Catani and Marengo 1998; Fabricotti and Menozzi 2006; Gasperini and Marengo 2007; Laronde 1987; Luni 2006; 2010; 2014; Stucchi 1975; 1976; Stucchi and Luni 1987.
175. For short summaries of the major sites, see di Vita et al. 1999, 183–238; Kenrick 2013; Laronde and Golvin 2001, 74; Sintes 2010, 12–85.
176. Mattingly 2000d (Cyrene); Ward-Perkins and Goodchild 2003.
177. Wilson 2020, 401–06.
178. Osborne 1998; Osborne and Cunliffe 2005.
179. On the archaeology and architecture of the Cyrenaican cities, see, inter alia, Luni 2006; 2014; Sintes 2010; Stucchi 1975.

Some urban building forms at *Cyrene* were unmistakably inspired by monuments of the Greek homeland zone—as, for instance, the huge Doric temples of Zeus and Apollo, and the Greek theatre.[180] The original settlement at *Cyrene* probably focused on an *acropolis* (little investigated archaeologically) on the northern edge of a steep escarpment. The city core seems to have soon spread down from the acropolis hill to the adjacent plateau area, where an *agora* was laid out and a huge Doric temple of Zeus erected on a gentler northern hilltop in the early 5th century.[181] To the north of the acropolis a spring issued at a lower elevation and this became developed as the Sanctuary of Apollo. Another external sanctuary of Demeter (on the south side of the Wadi Bel Gadir that provided a natural defence on that side of the city) has also been explored on a substantial scale.[182] The rock-cut tombs of the Greek city are especially impressive.[183]

Cyrene's port at *Apollonia* grew to be an impressive city in its own right, though occupying a constrained site around a double harbour basin. The results of a long-term French mission at the site are not yet published in detail, but comparatively little of the early city has been recorded, with the exception of some Classical burials outside the west gate.[184] Some evidence has been found of an early sanctuary area in the centre of the town, but little else is known of the extent or monumentality of the early phases.[185]

As already noted, *Barca* was reputed to be the second city of the *Pentapolis* but has not been accessible for archaeological investigation, being deeply buried beneath and no doubt quarried in the construction of the early Islamic capital of *Barce* and Ottoman al-Marj.[186] The early modern town was destroyed by an earthquake in 1963, and excavations by John Dore in the 1990s, while confirming the likely association of the site with the Greco-Roman city, did not penetrate sufficiently deeply to access the early stratigraphy. Much more impressive remains survive at its harbour site on the coast to the north, *Ptolemais*. However, the visible remains are primarily of the Hellenistic era and later, when the city was vastly expanded.[187] Recent work at *Ptolemais* has included methodological innovation, including extensive geophysical survey and aerial photography to explore more fully the urban context of the monuments.[188] The city's enlargement in the 3rd century BCE was on a grand scale, with elongated rectangular insulae, but little is known of its prior layout.

180. See Bonacasa and Ensoli 2000 and works referred to in n.174 for *Cyrene*.
181. Di Vita et al. 1999, 196–227.
182. Though the structure long presented by White 1984/2012 as the sanctuary now appears to have been just one small element within a vast sanctuary, Luni 2010.
183. Thorn 2005.
184. Di Vita et al. 1999, 228–32; Humphrey 1976a.
185. Di Vita et al. 1999, 228 (to Callicrateia)
186. Dore 1994.
187. Kraeling 1962.
188. Jaworski et al. 2015; Zelazowski 2012.

To the west of *Ptolemais* is another coastal city at *Taucheira*, though lacking a good harbour and on a very exposed shoreline in the winter months.[189] Traces of an early internal sanctuary, the Hellenistic walls, and rock-cut tombs in the faces of the city's quarries attest to its pre-Roman phases, but most of the visible archaeology relates to the Roman, Byzantine, and early Islamic city.[190]

The seemingly unpromising modern state of the site of *Euesperides* in the suburbs of Benghazi allows us to nuance our view of the early Greek city in Libya somewhat. The site is notable for the rarity of monumental buildings of archaic or Classical date, and the excavations have revealed a small walled settlement of relatively simple type, with unpaved streets and buildings mainly of mud-brick on pebble foundations and beaten earth.[191] The town appears to have been extended to the south in the 4th century BCE, with a more carefully gridded (though not entirely regular) plan (Fig. 3.8). This gives us our most detailed picture of a Greek city in the Classical era. The plan of *Cyrene* at this time can be reconstructed, with its far greater size, three large external sanctuary areas, and much greater evidence of monumental architecture revealing the gulf in status between the sites. Where the other Cyrenaican cities sat between these extremes during the Classical period is harder to say.

As already noted, study of the rural landscape and settlement beyond the Greek cities of Cyrenaica is very underdeveloped. There are some exceptionally well-preserved field systems on the upper plateau to the south, east, and west of *Cyrene* that seem to relate to the original Greek land division.[192] The construction at an early date of an orthogonal system of long linear walls is paralleled, for instance, in Greek colonies in southern Italy.[193] Pioneering research on oil and wine production in Cyrenaica has focused primarily on the Roman era, but it is clear from the epigraphic sources that agriculture was well established during the Greek period.[194] While the deep prehistoric sequence in the Haua Fteah cave near *Apollonia* does not reveal any evidence for pre-Classical agriculture in the vicinity, it cannot be absolutely excluded that there was some pre-existing agriculture before the arrival of the Greeks.[195] However, on the balance of available evidence, it does seem more likely that the Greek colonies were responsible for the establishment of extensive sedentary agriculture in this region.

---

189. Bennett et al. 2004 for a discussion of ongoing coastal erosion of the site.
190. Boardman and Hayes 1966.
191. See, inter alia, Buzaian and Lloyd 1996; Lloyd et al. 1995; 1998; Wilson 2005; 2006b; 2020, 402–06.
192. Jones 1989a. The material was mapped in detail by a team led by Martin Webb in the 1960s, but, apart from the sample image in Jones's article, remains unpublished at present (materials are now in the archive of the Society for Libyan Studies/BILNAS, Leicester).
193. Cf. Carter 2006 91–127 for the great land division scheme at *Metapontum*, probably initiated in the 6th century BCE.
194. Abdelhamed 2018; Buzaian 2022 for two Libyan theses on the rural economy and landscape.
195. Barker 2019; Barker et al. 2012.

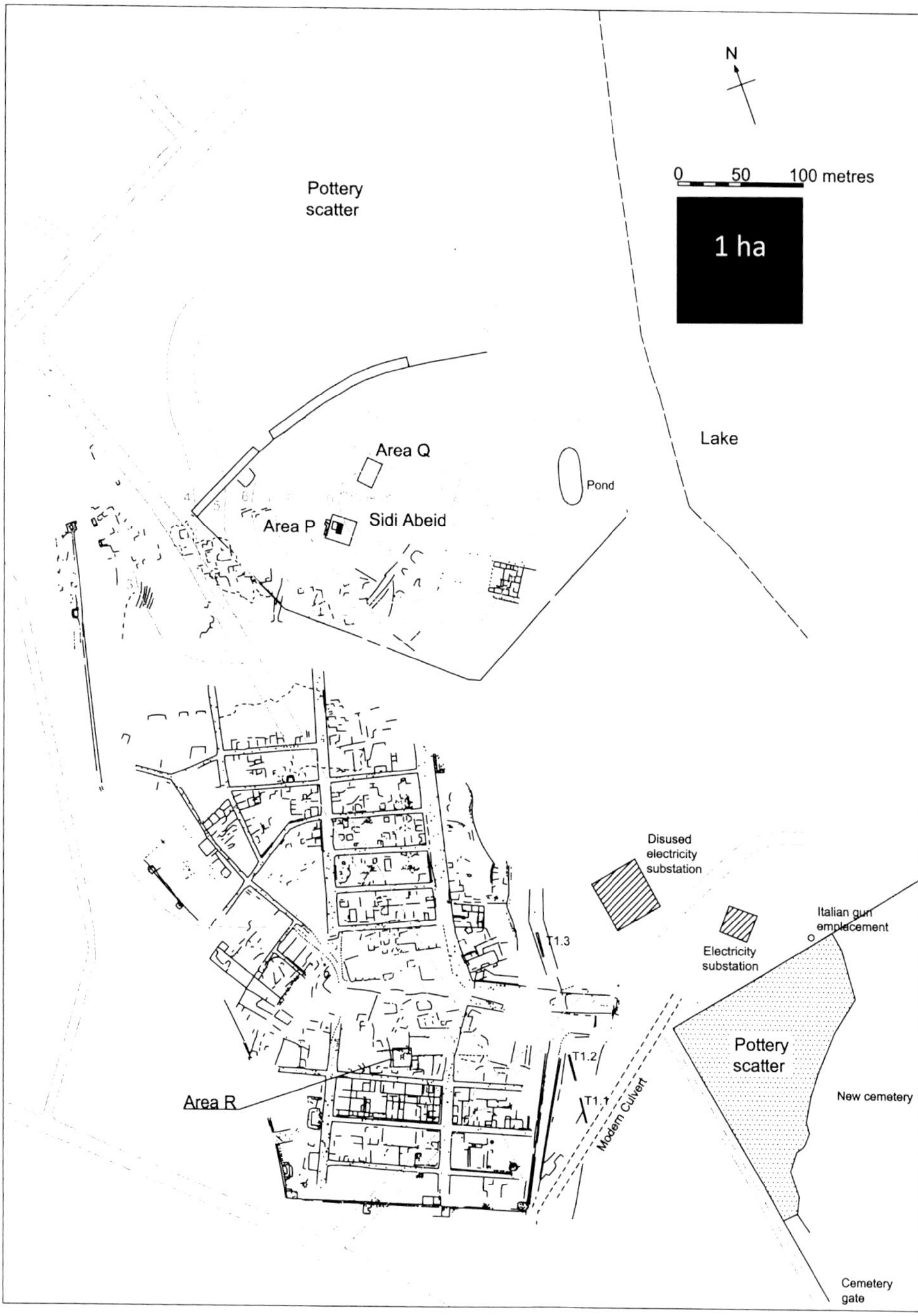

Figure 3.8. Plan of *Euesperides* (Benghazi) in the Greek period. The older part of the site lies on the hill to the north, with Hellenistic expansion following in the southern orthogonally planned area (from Wilson 2020, 402).

Other indications of the "Greek" identity of the cities and major settlements of Cyrenaica were the predominant use of the Greek language in inscriptions, the importation and production of statuary and architectural elements following Greek models, the introduction of Greek Olympian gods and the construction of sanctuaries that followed the ritual layout and practices of those from the Aegean world, the construction of theatres and *gymnasia* and related institutions, such as the Ephebic training of young men, and participation in the great festivals of the Greek world—with Cyrenaicans on numerous occasions winning the top prize for chariot racing.[196]

But it is also apparent that the populations at the Greek cities soon incorporated many individuals of mixed ethnicity. The bronze head of a young Libyan man from *Cyrene* now in the British Museum is one example of this, seemingly representing someone of status within the town.[197] There are rural sanctuaries with Greek inscriptions but Libyan divinities. The cemeteries of *Cyrene* were ornamented by statues of a unique goddess of death that have no exact parallels in the Greek world and seemingly touch on local rites and beliefs. Libyan and Jewish names occur as well as Greek and Roman. Even among the Greek onomastics, there are some distinctive regional patterns. For instance, there are numerous horse-linked names in Cyrenaica, reflecting a particular affinity with horse-rearing, perhaps.[198]

Finally, what of the presence of Greeks elsewhere in North Africa? There were evidently Greek traders active in the Punic Mediterranean and in some cases forming small communities in residence. This continued also into Roman times.[199]

Roman Settlers

The presence of substantial numbers of Roman era settlers in some areas of North Africa is well attested in the historical sources and epigraphic data.[200] Because of the specific conditions of its territorial conquest, Rome acquired blocks of lands—notably from the violent destruction of *Qart Hadasht* and enslavement of its surviving population in 146 BCE, to the overthrow of the Numidian king Juba I in the aftermath of the concluding battle of the civil war in Africa in 46 BCE. When Roman sources mentioned the establishment of colonies they tended to focus on the specific allocations to colonists and the numbers of allotments,

196. Sintes 2010, 12–85.
197. https://www.britishmuseum.org/collection/object/G_1861-1127-13
198. Abdelhamed 2018.
199. As is evident in presence of Greek speakers at *Cirta*, *Karthago*, *Lepcis*, and many other towns (Lassère 1977).
200. Demougin and Scheid 2012.

rather than providing the full social picture of such settlements. There is thus a tendency to assume that colonies were new towns with an associated territory, set up for the benefit of Roman settlers, often discharged legionaries or land-hungry Italian peasants.

As we shall see later in this book, the availability of *ager publicus* or other lands in the gift of emperors and commanders made Africa a favoured venue for the establishment of Roman colonies. These took various forms, from the early (and troubled) attempts at colonial deductions under C. Gracchus and C. Marius in the late 2nd century BCE, to the settlement by Caesar and, later, Octavian of thousands of discharged legionaries at the end of the civil wars in the 40s–20s BCE, to the somewhat informal assignment by Caesar of territory around *Cirta* to an Italian adventurer Sittius and his Campanian and Spanish followers, to additional establishment of veteran colonies in the 1st and early 2nd centuries CE (notably at *Thamugadi*).[201] However, quite a number of early Roman colonial deductions in Africa involved groups of Roman citizens being sent to join pre-existing communities, rather than to found sites *de novo*. We know little about the original inhabitants (*Libyphoenicians*, *Numidae*, *Mauri*) and how their lives were impacted, but the important point to bear in mind is that they were also present in these colonial landscapes.

The wealth of surviving epigraphy from North Africa has allowed detailed onomastic study of the long-term impacts of such settlements, and it is clear that if we think of North Africa as a great patchwork quilt, then certain segments of the design comprised concentrations of incomers (and their descendants).[202] However, other elements of the patchwork were much less impacted by colonial settlement and again this is strongly reflected in onomastic studies.

Beyond the tens of thousands of colonists who were settled on conquered land or in new or rebranded cities, there were other groups of outsiders, most notably merchants, migrant craftsmen, and other "carpetbaggers" of empire—serving, servicing, or exploiting the imperial project. For example, at the outbreak of the Jugurthan War, the massacre of a group of Italian *negotiatores* at *Cirta* was an important *casus belli* (Sallust, *BJ* 21.2, 26.3). There were also some unusual clusters of people originating from a specific area of the Roman Empire, suggestive of some settlements of close-linked groups, like Etruscans, in the hinterland of Carthage.[203] As with all other groups of Mediterranean migrants in Africa, there was a tendency over time for the distinctions to diminish through intermarriage, especially in the more cosmopolitan cities.[204]

201. These issues will be discussed in Chapter 8 and 9.
202. Lassère 1977.
203. Heurgon 1969; Lassère 1977, 132; cf. also Leglay 1962 on Gauls.
204. Lassère 1977.

Cultures of Colonialism

If we look at the changes in material culture of the 1st millennium BCE and early 1st millennium CE in North Africa, we have to acknowledge the importance of the Mediterranean contacts. The Phoenician and Greek "colonies" were undoubtedly hubs for the import and replication of distinctive and (at the time) novel forms of material culture, whether things like Greek decorative pottery or Phoenician amphorae.[205] Some new pyrotechnologies reflect contacts with the east Mediterranean, most notably glassworking, with distinctive artefacts such as eye beads and miniature heads.[206] Three-dimensional sculpture in stone and terracotta, including small-scale figurines, generally followed Mediterranean models.[207] The alphabets and epigraphic behaviours of the colonial settlements emphasise contact and continuity with external communities in important respects. As already noted, the architectural models for key monuments of the coastal urban communities were often based on Phoenician, Greek, and, later, Roman exemplars. Carthaginian coinage, when it appeared in the late 5th century BCE, followed in the steps of the spectacular Sicilian Greek coinages.[208] Nonetheless, the precise iconography adopted for the coins was distinctively "Carthaginian" and the various combinations of "Tinnit," horse, and palm tree were as iconic as the Athena and owl combination from Athens.[209]

This highlights an important aspect of the way material culture evolved on the southern shore of the Mediterranean in the 1st millennium BCE. The flow of innovations was not simply from "mother city" to "colony," or even from "Greek world" or "Phoenician world" to Greek colony and Phoenician *emporion*. Rather, they reflected the interconnectedness of the Mediterranean world as the millennium progressed and the profound artistic and stylistic cross-cultural borrowings that went on. A remarkable gilded bronze Campanian-style cuirass from a tomb at Ksour-Essaf in the Tunisian Sahel was found in a wooden coffin, associated with a metal-bound wooden casket and a small wooden vessel (echoing a black glaze ceramic cup, but containing ochre)—perhaps suggestive of a Libyan mercenary.[210] Such mixed assemblages reveal the complexities of identity as expressed through material culture. In the early stages of the establishment of trading settlements in the central and western Mediterranean, eastern influences were pronounced (what is commonly known as an Orientalising phase), while by the later centuries BCE

205. Cf. inter alia Ben Tahar 2014; 2018; el-Rashedy 2002; Quinn 2011; Ramón Torres 1995; Wilson 2013.
206. Fantar 1972.
207. For example, Paribeni 1959; Traversari 1960; Yacoub 1996.
208. Hoyos 2010, 120–21; Jenkins and Lewis 1963, 11–12.
209. Alexandopoulos 2000; Frey-Kupper 2014.
210. Ben Younès 1997.

the Mediterranean was an interconnected "Hellenistic" world,[211] unconstrained by ethnicity or geography.[212]

Political changes also had their impact, as in periods when the Cyrenaican cities were subject to Egyptian, Persian, or Ptolemaic rule from Egypt, with potential impacts for cultural engagement with the Nile Valley civilisations. In a somewhat different way, when *Qart Hadasht* started to exert its own imperial ambitions on cities in Sicily, Sardinia, and southern Iberia, the nature of the "Phoenician" *koine* was also affected. The rise of Carthaginian imperialism has long been recognised as a key political moment for the central Mediterranean, but it was also culturally significant as the period when Phoenician identity became better defined at *Qart Hadasht* and other centres under its hegemony.[213] In other words, what we recognise in the archaeological record as "Phoenician" or "Punic" culture was to a large extent contingent on the emergence of a major state on the North African coast, with significant territorial and mercantile interests in the central and western Mediterranean, but less direct contact with the notional east Mediterranean homeland.

Any and all of these aspects mean that the cultural contours were a good deal more complex than the neat division of the Mediterranean into separate spheres of Greek and Phoenician influence might lead us to expect. Both the traditional emphasis on cultural movement from outside Africa and the characterisation of the social context of cultural change as resting on external civilisation and internal passive receptors are demonstrably false paradigms.[214] Greek pots did not necessarily equate with consumers who identified as "Greeks" and even though some inhabitants of the "colonial" cities were undoubtedly the descendants of outsiders, many others were evidently of more local or mixed heritage. Punic culture is best thought of as Libyphoenician culture, as the ancient sources suggest, and, indeed, aspects of Greek culture in Cyrenaica also need to be recognised as reflecting cultural hybridity. Such cultural mixing is even more identifiable in the story of Africa in the Roman Empire, as we shall see.

A Globalised Roman Empire?

That last point reminds us of an important aspect of the Roman Empire in Africa. Already by the time the provincial territory and government was reaching a more fixed state under Augustus, the region was extremely mixed ethnically and

211. Broodbank 2013 for a good survey of these phases. See also various papers in Prag and Quinn 2013; Quinn and Vella 2014.
212. Purcell 2013.
213. Quinn 2018, 65–90.
214. Euzennat 1965 as an example of the potential for outsider culture to be emphasised at the expense of the emic.

culturally; it was polyglot and diverse, with intense regional and communal characteristics. From Hellenistic times the region—not simply its coastal "Phoenician" and "Greek" cities—had been firmly attached to a pan-Mediterranean cultural world. This trend was to be dramatically reinforced under Roman rule. Yet, too often in the past, the emphasis in accounts has focused on the abilities and know-how of outsiders in the making of "Roman Africa."[215] In the final analysis, the presence of tens of thousands or low hundreds of thousands of people of migrant descent among a population of millions still leaves a large majority of people to be accounted for in the history of the region under Rome. It is to the indigenous or autochthonous elements that I now turn.[216]

215. Le Bohec 2005a, 34: "Cette masse d'immigrants permit à l'Afrique de connaître une grande prospérité, charactérisée par une économie nettement monétaire."
216. Mattingly 2016 and Chapters 4–5.

Chapter 4

NUMIDAE AND *MAURI* OF THE TELL

Rehabilitating the North African Iron Age and Indigenous Agency

One of the biggest challenges to advancing new agendas in the Classical archaeology of North Africa relates to the underdevelopment of its Iron Age archaeology as a discipline.[1] Roman and Iron Age archaeologists do not always read from the same page in other areas of the Empire, but there is no doubt that the existence of these disciplines side by side provides a wealth of data for both groups to reflect on in testing their models.[2] As explained in Chapter 1, in this book I refer to the period that is sometimes known as protohistory as the North African Iron Age (NAIA). Our level of ignorance about the physical reality of the vast majority of the African peoples mentioned by authors like Strabo, Pliny, or Ptolemy ought to be profoundly worrying for specialists of "Roman Africa." All too often it limits us to vague discussion about where to place the large capital letters denoting supposed "tribal" units on archaeologically blank maps. Modern scholarship has expended vast efforts in trying to locate the African peoples mentioned by the sources, with an emphasis on confirming the veracity of the texts, but has done very little to research the archaeological evidence pertaining to these societies. A typical example of this tendency concerns a number of peoples associated with the province of *Mauretania Tingitana*, specifically the *Baquates*, *Bavares*, and *Macenites*.[3] The *Baquates* alone or in combination with the other two groups are recorded as participants in regular *colloquia* with the Roman provincial governors confirming peace agreements from the 2nd to 3rd

1. The pioneering work of Camps in the 1960s–70s remains fundamental, but that fact alone reveals the attenuated growth of the discipline in subsequent decades. See, in particular, Camps 1960; 1961; 1973a; 1980; 1981; 1987a. For an early attempt to write a Libyco-Berber history of the early Maghrib (but desperately lacking in hard evidence), see Désiré-Vuillemin 1964. A major new study in German by Ardeleanu (2021) appeared too late for me to fully reference it in my discussion, though it shares many ideas in common with what I present below and will be an essential point of reference. See also the perceptive survey by Sanmartí 2022.
2. For a snapshot of the state of Iron Age studies in Britain, for comparison, see Haselgrove and Moore 2007; Haselgrove and Pope 2007.
3. Cf. Christol 1988; Desanges 1962; Euzennat 1984; 1995a; Hamdoune 1993; 2014; 2018; Rebuffat 2001; 2011a; Sigman 1977.

centuries CE.[4] There has been endless speculation as to the location of these peoples in respect of the provincial territory—just to the east or just to the south are the most favoured options (though more radical solutions are possible).[5] While a considerable amount of scholarly ink has been spilt on this question, there is still not a shred of archaeological evidence that can be firmly associated with these peoples, or (alternatively) that can be used to develop an *archaeology* of the people who occupied the zones ascribed to them. If these people were important enough to have had regular treaties with Rome and for some of their leaders to be accorded Roman citizenship, it is improbable that they should be archaeologically invisible, and the fault lies with archaeological fieldwork priorities. In the absence of hard archaeological data, we are left with the literary tropes about "tribal barbarians."

The most vibrant field in NAIA archaeology, perhaps unsurprisingly, concerns the Punic sphere—partially reviewed in the previous chapter. Yet here the intellectual divisions (and rivalries) between Romanists and Punic specialists have been particularly unhelpful, and Punic experts have tended to eschew study of the non-Punic NAIA, or only to study those aspects where direct Punic influence is evident.[6]

In the next two chapters I shall address what we know of two distinct broad groups of autochthonous peoples in North Africa (Fig. 4.1). In this chapter, the focus will be on the Libyan (Berber/Amazigh) peoples who came to be known by the late 1st millennium BCE as the *Numidae* and *Mauri*, with their leaders recognised by Rome as kings and the kingdoms exhibiting the characteristics of early states.[7] In Chapter 5, I then turn to the peoples of the more marginal pre-desert and desert lands. However, some of this introductory section is of relevance to both groups and indeed also to African dimensions of their Libyphoenician neighbours.

As noted already, it has long been conventional to characterise these ancient Libyan peoples as "tribes," but it is important to reflect on what we understand by that term and how appropriate it is at any given moment.[8] The sociological assumptions that underlie a term like "tribe" need to be carefully considered, because it is a relic of two interlinked modern scholarly discourses. The first of

4. Shaw 1987; Hamdoune 2014, 430–31; 2018, 90; Mattingly 1992; for the inscriptions of the "altars of peace" see IAM_{lat} 348–50, 356–61, 376, 384, 402. See also Fig. 6.16 below.
5. The possibility that the *Baquates* included people based some distance from *Volubilis*, even on the south side of the Atlas range in oasis communities, seems never to have been seriously considered. Work in the Wadi Draa shows it to have been an area with numerous NAIA funerary monuments and settlements (see for example, Bokbot 2003; 2019; Mattingly et al. 2017b). On the other hand, applying the same intensive survey methods to other areas bordering the Roman province might equally reveal a "busy" NAIA landscape.
6. Ben Younès and Krandel-Ben Younès 2014; Fantar 2006.
7. On the Berbers, see, inter alia, Ardeleanu 2021; Brett and Fentress 1996; Camps 1980; 1987a; Chaker 2013a; Hachid 2000; Onrubia-Pintado 2013; Skounti 2012.
8. Berque 1953; cf. Moore 2011.

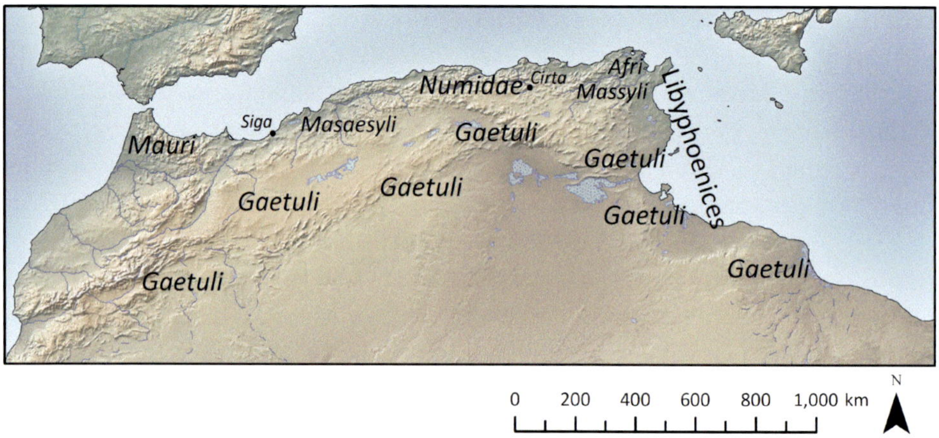

Figure 4.1. The principal indigenous population groups of the 1st millennium BCE (Martin Sterry, after author's rough).

these is a tendency to categorise ancient peoples in a hierarchical or evolutionary schema, through whose levels societies are assumed to have gradually risen from small disorganised bands to sophisticated state-level societies. Typically in such schemes, the "tribe" is somewhere near the bottom of the scale, and this sort of neo-evolutionary categorisation will almost invariably lead us back to the colonial-era stereotypes of inferior "native" peoples.[9] The second discourse relates to the practice of modern imperial regimes in places like Africa, the Middle East, or the Indian subcontinent to impose the category on "native" peoples (both contemporary and historic) and thus to relegate them deliberately to a remote stage of social evolution. For these reasons, I have become increasingly uneasy about using the word "tribe" in my own writing and prefer the more neutral "people." The fact that some of these societies could at a certain point be recognised by Rome as states (typically in the form of client kingdoms) raises important questions about exactly when (and how) this development of greater social complexity occurred.[10] Since the Roman sources, as already noted, are not entirely to be trusted in the way in which they characterised and described the ancient African peoples, this is likely to be very difficult to ascertain from the literary accounts alone and emphasises why we need more archaeological evidence. In any case, when our ancient sources employed terms like *gens*, *ethnos*, *natio*, *populus*, or *tribus*, there is inconsistency in the way these terms are understood and translated by modern scholars, often depending on whether we are dealing with an autochthonous group or a settler community of "Phoenicians" or Greeks.

9. Yoffee 2005, 17–21.
10. Buck 1984; Camps 1960; Smadja 1983.

It is clear that the ancient sources were at times both ambiguous and stereotyping in the way they depicted the ancient peoples of North Africa.[11] In many ways they are surprisingly uninformative about the lifestyles, customs, and beliefs of these peoples.[12] Epigraphic attestations are potentially more revealing in that the terminology and titles describing such autonomous groups and their leaders may be construed as reflecting actual usage. Rome was by no means consistent or systematic in her approach to such relationships and labels, and just like modern imperial powers, Rome was also predisposed to downplay the civilised status and organisational capabilities of indigenous societies. For this reason, where we have references to kings and kingdoms, especially when accorded client status by Rome, we should recognise that such societies had passed some sort of threshold test of social complexity.[13]

The most important of the ancient sources for our understanding of the state of African society are Herodotus, Polybius, Sallust, Diodorus Siculus, Livy, Strabo, Pomponius Mela, Pliny the Elder, Tacitus, and Ptolemy. There are many additional allusions in other writers, including the epic poems of Virgil and Silius Italicus, but these have to be recognised as yet a further step away from factual accounts. With its extensive engagement with indigenous peoples, the late antique epic poem of Corippus is both immensely valuable and problematic.[14] A recurrent trope of these sources is the categorical identification of the Libyan peoples as primarily nomadic, even though the same sources cite contradictory evidence at times. Herodotus, for instance, described the Libyan peoples of the broad zone from Cyrenaica to the *Lacus Tritonis* (Chott Jarid in southern Tunisia) as nomadic, but noted that the Libyan peoples from *Lacus Tritonis* to the west were not nomadic (*Histories* 4.186–87); and while seeming to place the *Garamantes* of the Sahara in the nomadic grouping, he also wrote of them cultivating land (*Histories* 4.183). Another of the striking aspects of the different sources is how little correspondence there is between them when it comes to the names of ancient peoples they locate in any given topographic zone.[15] One could easily conclude that the last centuries BCE and early centuries CE were marked by massive instability of ethnic groups and other forms of social organisation. It is highly probable that the arrival of Rome on the scene did spark significant changes in the autochthonous societies its armies

11. See the argument as first developed in relation to the *Garamantes*, Mattingly 2003a, 76–79; 2011a, 34–35. Cf. also Whittaker 2009; Woolf 2014 for overviews of some of the structural distortions of Roman ethnography.
12. Desanges 1962; 1980b; Gsell 1927a/b for the classic syntheses.
13. Braund 1984 on client kingdoms in general; Mattingly 2006a, 47–84; 2011a, 75–93 on the British client kingdoms disrupted by the Roman conquest—also regularly referred to as "tribes" in the modern literature.
14. I am grateful to my Leicester colleague Andrew Merrills for several enlightening conversations on Corippus in advance of a forthcoming monograph length treatment. See also Merrills 2019.
15. See, for instance, the maps in Bates 1970; Desanges 1962.

encountered, notably higher levels of confederation or grouping under the leadership of charismatic or imposing individuals. However, factors of social organisation may have been significant.

As already noted in Chapter 1, there is a great disparity between the overall number of named peoples of *Africa Proconsularis*, perhaps over 460 (Pliny, *NH* 5.29–30), and the actual number of names preserved in our sources and in epigraphy for that region (about 109).[16] However, if we examine the underlying structures of traditional Amazigh societies, they offer an important clue towards understanding the multiplicity of different names for people seemingly occupying the same landscape spaces.[17] The typical segmented and hierarchical structures of Amazigh "tribal" societies may well map against the ancient patterns of population groups named in the ancient sources. Many of these societies comprised of a multitude of lineage groups that existed within a broad framework of latent alliances and social obligations that could lead to higher levels of confederation at times of need. An individual being questioned on what social unit they belonged to could answer in several different ways, depending on whether he or she referenced their immediate family unit, clan group, extended lineage group, or a larger entity whether under the authority of a powerful individual or a looser regional confederation of peoples. An explanation of the frequent inconsistencies between different sources describing the peoples of the same area could be that they were referencing different levels of this hierarchy, rather than a situation in which "tribal" groups were regularly replaced by new groups. Roman administrative convenience was also a potential factor in the eventual solidification of some of these ethnic names within the provincial structures.

Another problem with much of the historiography on the ancient peoples of the Maghrib and Sahara has been the assumption that these names were to a large extent equivalents of each other, producing a reified image of "tribes" that misses the significant differences between groups—some of which were very localised bands and others proto-states. A fundamental concern of both ancient and modern listings of peoples has been where they were located in relation to the Roman territory. In the analysis that follows across the next two chapters, I shall attempt to extend analysis beyond such limited questions of ethnic geography and also deconstruct the stereotypical assumptions about "tribes," especially concerning their assumed tendency towards nomadism.[18]

These are still persistent issues, even in the most recent syntheses. Christine Hamdoune's detailed analysis of the sources and epigraphic data relating to the

16. Desanges 1980b, 276–349.
17. Mattingly 1995, 19–21.
18. Colin 2000 is a good example of an analysis that relies almost entirely on the ancient sources and keeps defaulting to a discussion centred on nomadism, despite an awareness of there being some indications of sedentarisation.

indigenous peoples of the western Maghrib (*Mauretania*) followed up Yves Modéran's work that had focused more on the late antique *Mauri* of the eastern Maghrib and Libya.[19] We should note here that the geographical employment of the term *Mauri* in late Roman and late antique times was much broader than is evident in the earlier sources where it mainly denoted people of the western Maghrib. Hamdoune and Modéran provided a careful historiographical review of past study and recognised the problems inherent in some of the traditional models, for instance relating to the assumed nomadic character of these people and the idea of a "permanence berbère."[20] However, while both scholars recognised the potential range of meanings of the Latin terms deployed in relation to the Berbers, they chose to generally translate these by the catch-all French word "tribu" and to some extent focused on creating catalogues of "Berber tribes."[21] To do so, they founded their work on a fundamental distinction between the Romano-African provincial population, who they depicted as having embraced *Romanitas* (including urban living), and groups of *Mauri* or Berbers who lived on the fringes of the provinces and who periodically caused political and military difficulties for the state.[22] While "tribu" is a convenient shorthand no doubt, the problem is that it invites the reader to impose the assumption "barbarian tribe," rather than allowing other possible meanings to be considered. One of the most interesting aspects of the history of these groups is that they do show clear signs of evolving in terms of scale and complexity, with some of their leaders being recognised by Roman and Byzantine authorities as "kings."[23] That implies the emergence of polities—not just with the Numidian and Mauretanian kingdoms that we shall review in this chapter, but also with some of the late Roman and late antique peoples both within and beyond the Roman garrisoned regions. This is a really crucial aspect—not least because it shows up the fallacy of the old colonial-era beliefs in the lack of indigenous capacity for achieving sociopolitical complexity.

Another problem with differentiating between two broad groups—Romans/Romano-Africans and Berbers—is that it emphasises two worlds in opposition and denies the possibility of intermediate positions and behaviours, or for people to have crossed from one group to another. The hinterland zones of *Mauretania Tingitana* and *Caesarienses* appear to have been great population reservoirs, spawning peoples like the *Baquates*, *Bavares*, *Macenites*, *Quinquegentanei*—who are generally held to

19. Hamdoune 2018; Modéran 2003. See also summaries in Merrills 2022; Shaw 2014, 536–37.
20. Hamdoune 2018, 9–17; Modéran 2003, 1–23.
21. Hamdoune 2018, 15. Note also that her overall title evokes the "tribal worlds" in relation to the Mauretanian provinces; Modéran 2003, 18: "La priorité était tout d'abord de constituer un corpus le plus complet possible des textes évoquant les tribus berbères du Maghreb oriental."
22. Hamdoune 2018, 64: "pour désigner les communautés qui n'ont pas adopté le modèle socio-politique de la cité ... on emploie par défaut le mot tribu, traduction du latin *gens*'; Modéran 2003, 12.
23. Hamdoune 2018, 68; Modéran 2003, 15. Cf. the astute analysis of Sanmartí 2022, 41–47.

have been a recurrent source of trouble for the Roman provinces.[24] There is a danger that "tribal resistance" becomes a trope of the "permanence berbère" here.[25] The antecedents of these groups were at some points linked in to the Moorish and Numidian kingdoms, and their leaders certainly shared in some of the cultural reference points of the settled provincial territory. As an example, there are clear indications that some of the most famous 4th-century Moorish leaders (the sons of Nubel—Firmus, Gildo, Sammac) were at the same time high-ranking imperial servants—that is, both Romans and Berbers under the traditional definitions. The fortified residence at Kasr al-Kaoua (Ammi-Moussa) is a wonderful example of this investment in the architectural trappings of Roman power by an individual from a similarly high-ranking Moorish family.[26] The idea of a dichotomy between "civilised Romans" and "barbarous Libyans" is something that is strongly present in Greco-Roman sources on North Africa (with echoes also in Arabic narratives).[27] That does not make it an accurate representation of society; rather, it was more plausibly a convenient simplification of a broad spectrum of attitudes and behaviours.[28]

Archaeological Evidence

In his classic study of the ancient monuments of Algeria, Gsell devoted only a brief section to indigenous (pre-Roman) sites and these were almost exclusively funerary structures and rock art.[29] Most subsequent archaeological work on the NAIA period has maintained the primary focus on funerary monuments, following the fundamental typological studies of Gabriel Camps.[30] There are, in truth, some amazing structures, notably the Numidian and Mauretanian "royal" mausolea, with manifest Hellenistic influence, as at Medracen, *Thugga*, Tombeau de la Chretienne,[31] but we should also be aware there were monumental Maghribian and Saharan funerary traditions at play.[32]

24. Camps 1955; Christol 1988; Euzennat 1986; Frézouls 1980; 1981; Hamdoune 2018; Laporte 2003.
25. Fentress 1982a for a similar argument.
26. Laporte 2014 on Kasr el-Kaoua (Ammi-Moussa); Mattingly and Hayes 1992; Mattingly et al. 2013b on fortified farms in general.
27. Hamdoune 2018, 64; Merrills 2022, 319–21; Modéran 2003, 12, 17–18; cf. Fenwick 2020, 33 on the Arabic distinction between *al-barbar*, "the Berbers," and the *Afariq*, Latin-speaking and often town-dwellers: "These homogenizing labels disguise a great deal of variety, as we shall see, but it is clear that differences between 'Byzantine Africa' and 'Berber Africa' posed substantial challenges to the Umayyads and Abbasids."
28. Mattingly 2011a, 214–15 on the constraints on an individual's ability to choose how to define his or her identity in the eyes of others in a colonial situation.
29. Gsell 1901a, 1–54.
30. Camps 1961; 1995b; Camps and Camps-Fabrer 1964. Sanmartí 2022, 53–56.
31. Coarelli and Thébert 1988; Kuttner 2013; Quinn 2013; Rakob 1979; 1983.
32. Camps 1961; 1986a; 1995b; Gatto et al. 2019a; Mattingly 2003a, 195–205; Reygasse 1950. See also the wide-ranging PhD thesis by Moodie 2019

Some groups of distinctive monuments seem to reflect changing attitudes to funerary commemoration and to increasing hierarchisation within these societies. Punic subterranean chamber tombs related to the Libyphoenician *emporia* at one time dominated discussion (Figs. 3.6, 4.3b),[33] but there has been an increasing recognition of inland variants of monumental tombs (Fig. 4.2). One prominent monument type in northern Tunisia comprises rock-cut funerary chambers that internally were very similar in shape and decoration to the underground Punic tombs, but with the main difference that they were entered through highly visible doors cut in vertical rock faces rather than via shafts. They are known as haouanet (singular hanout), meaning "boutiques," because the rows of doors resemble small shops in the souk.[34] The distribution of the haouanet slightly overlaps with that of the "Punic tombs," with a particular concentration in northern Tunisia (Fig. 4.3b).

A second distinctive type (with many subgroups) is represented by megalithic tombs or dolmens.[35] Unlike in Europe, where these relate to earlier periods of prehistory, these African monuments seem to have been built mainly in the 1st millennium BCE. Typically they comprised small rectangular chambers formed by large vertically set slabs, capped with a large slab (Fig. 4.2a). Access to the funerary chamber in many tombs was from the side, where a cut-out in one of the slabs allowed that to be manipulated as a door, or, in a regional variant known as "zenithal access dolmens," from above (that is by moving the capstone).[36] Some recent work has revealed that the megalithic structures were sometimes enhanced by being placed within low circular enclosing walls or with the addition of lateral walls and other features.[37] However, there is no evidence that the megalithic burial structures were encased in tumuli. Rather, they were intended to be seen in the landscape and to be accessible for further use. It is evident that additional bodies were often added into dolmen tombs.[38] Some complex megalithic monuments in central Tunisia were built in serried rectilinear ranks, as at *Ulules* (Elles) and *Mactaris*.[39]

A third group of common burial types in North Africa are variants of tumuli, essentially mounds of earth or piled stones (Fig. 4.3a).[40] These were clearly distinct from burials in the Punic tradition. A type of tumulus was quite widespread in the hinterland of *Qart Hadasht*.[41] Drum tombs, with a built vertical outer wall, are often referred to as chouchets (stepped structures) and bazinas (flat-topped drum tombs) and constitute a fourth broad category (Fig. 4.2b–c). Although these last types have

33. Fantar 1995; Ben Younès 1995; 2007. Also relevant sections of Chapter 3 above.
34. Ben Younès 2007, 32–35; Camps 1961, 91–110; Ghaki 1999a; Longerstay 1995; 2011; Stone 2007a.
35. Camps 1961, 115–55; 1999; Camps and Camps-Fabrer 1964; Ghaki 2003; Tanda et al. 2009.
36. Camps 1995b, 20–21; Kallala et al. 2017; Sanmartí et al. 2019, 259.
37. Kallala et al. 2017, 14–15, 42–48; Sanmartí et al. 2019; 2020.
38. Krandel Ben-Younès 1993, 186–92; 2002, 112–34; 2013.
39. Camps 1995b, 22–24; Ghaki 1997b.
40. Camps 1961, 65–91; Peyras 1991, 215–34; Stone 2016b.
41. Ferchiou 1987.

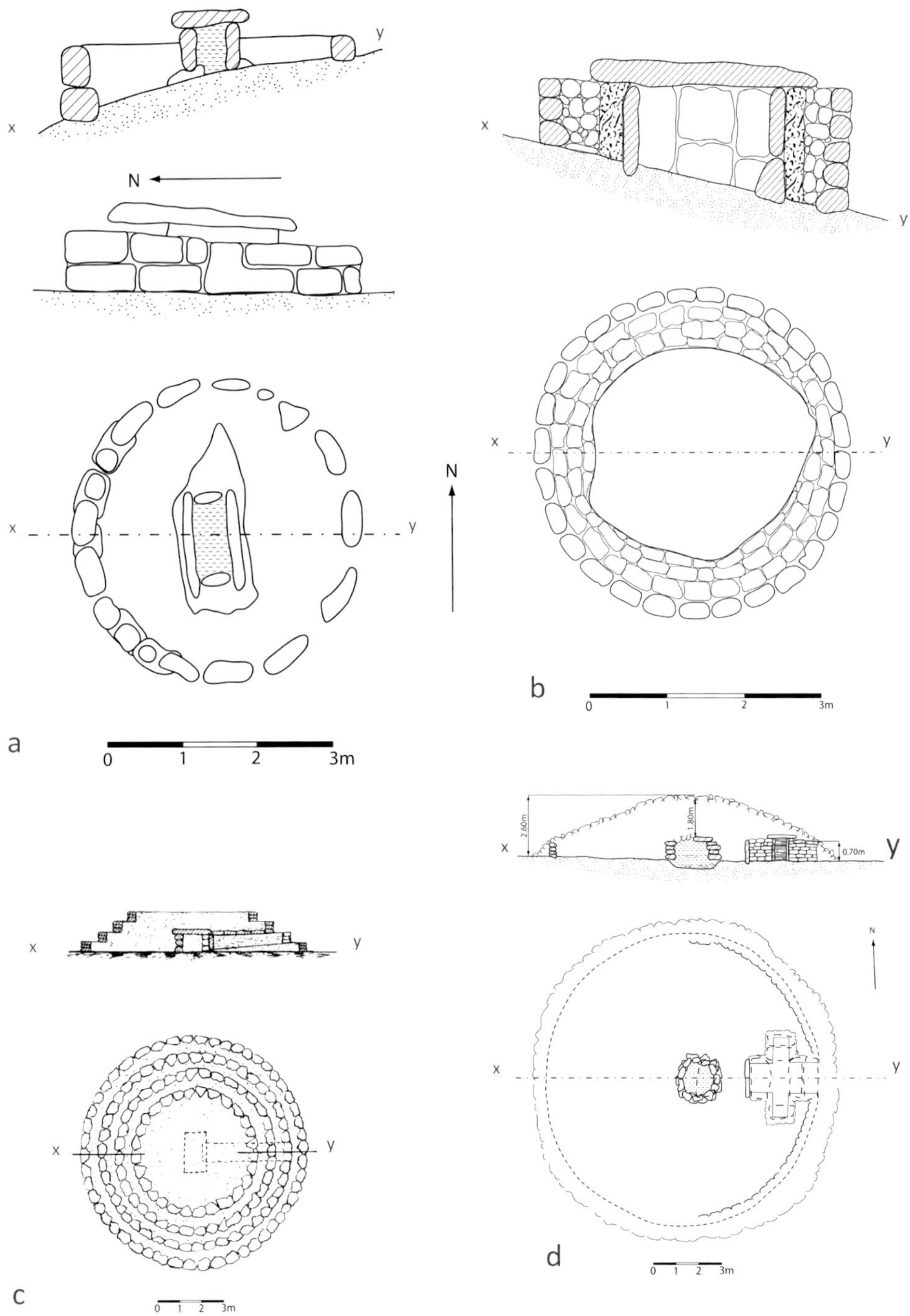

Figure 4.2. Some of the main types of NAIA tombs in Numidian Maghrib. a) Dolmen. b) Bazina/drum tomb. c) Chouchet/stepped tomb. d) Tumulus with funerary chapel (author's montage from Camps 1961; Gatto et al. 2019).

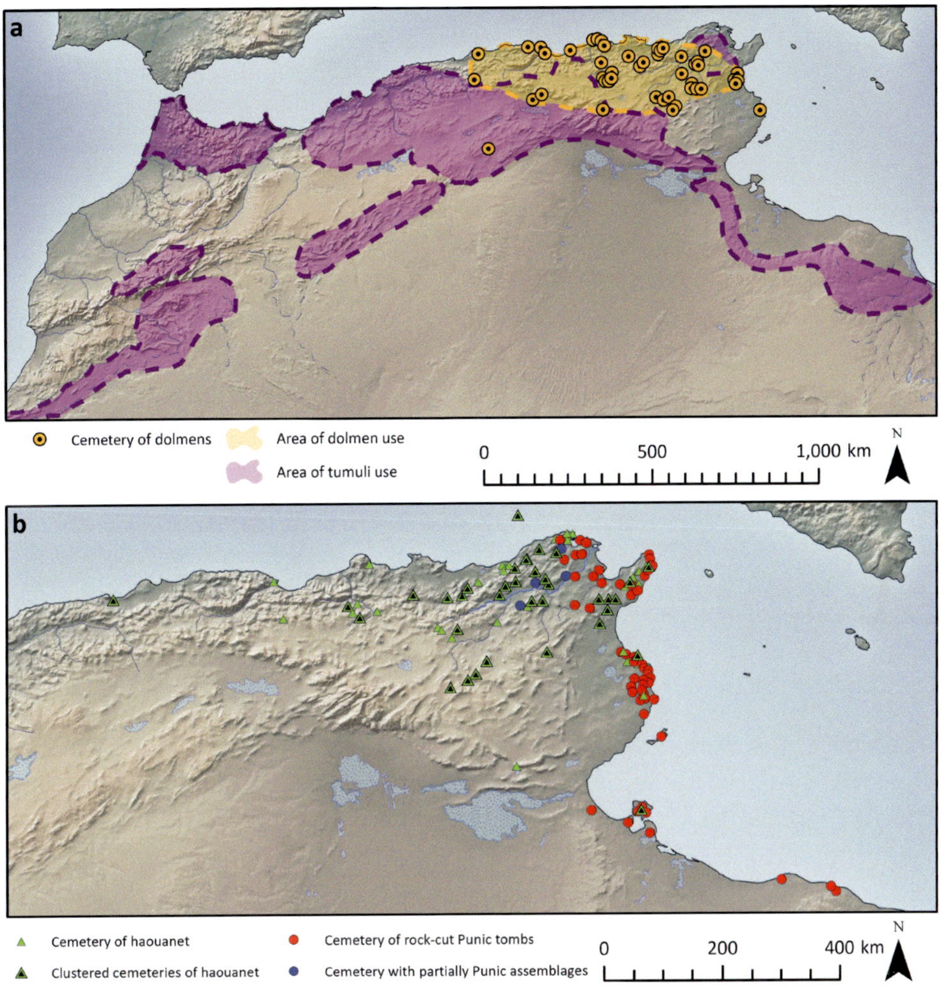

Figure 4.3. Distributions of main North African Iron Age tomb types. a) Megalithic/dolmen tombs and tumuli/drum tombs (where distributions overlap, the predominant type is shaded and the other marked by dashed lines). b) Haouanet and rock-cut "Punic" tombs (Martin Sterry with author, from various sources including Camps 1999; Stone 2007a/b).

strong Saharan associations, they are sometimes also found at Maghribian sites and some well-dressed masonry examples dating to the latter centuries BCE have been discovered at key Numidian centres (discussed below).

Dating of both haouanet and megalithic tombs is not very precise as the vast majority have been robbed, and few have been subject to scientific excavation or radiocarbon dating. The architectural and painted decoration of certain of the haouanet suggests

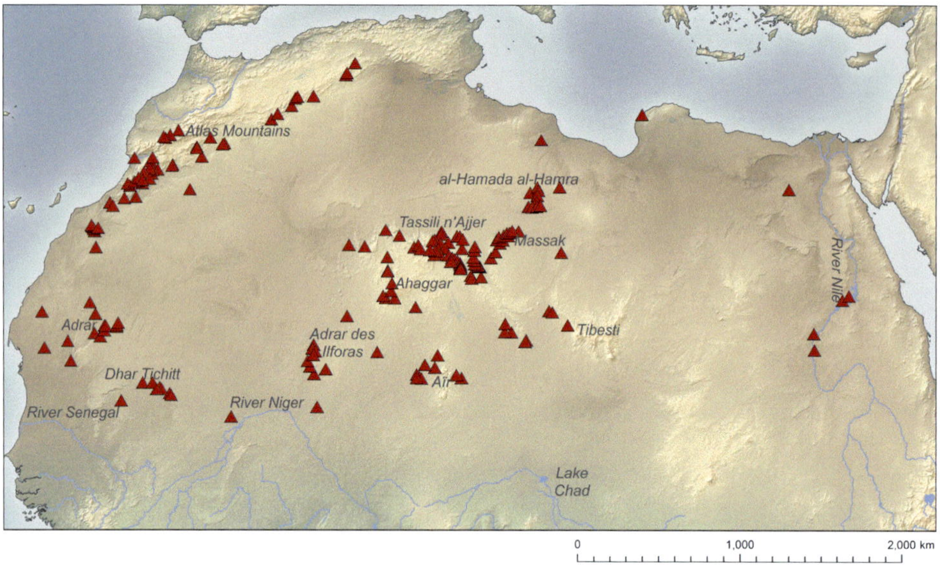

Figure 4.4. Distribution of Saharan rock art featuring horses and/or chariots (Martin Sterry from Mattingly et al. 2017a, 23).

that some at least were made in the latter centuries BCE, and some Roman-era finds also imply continued use into the early centuries CE.[42] The distributions of these tomb types are distinct but overlapping spatially and chronologically (Fig. 4.3). There has inevitably been discussion about the extent to which these monument types may have had a relation with the main population groups of the Maghrib.[43] The dolmen tombs in particular appear to have a strong correlation with the Numidian population group known as the *Massyli* (see below).

There was further evolution of the NAIA monumental burial tradition during Roman times. For instance, distinctive large cairns with a space built into the east side of the tumulus are plausibly interpreted as allowing rites related to the ancestor cult to be performed close to the central cist (Fig. 4.2d). This type was widely distributed along the Saharan margins.[44]

Another prominent source of evidence relates to rock engravings and paintings from both the Maghrib and the Sahara. Two particularly common themes comprise mounted cavalrymen and depictions of horse-drawn chariots, leading to the identification of NAIA imagery as a Horse (Caballine) Phase within the broader

42. Stone 2007a, 70–71; Longerstay 2011.
43. Camps 1993b; 1995b; Stone 2007b.
44. Bokbot 2019, 328–31; Camps 1984; 1986a; 1995a. Some of the funerary chapels were decorated with painted images, with new discoveries of such artwork in the Wadi Draa.

spectrum of North African rock art.[45] The image of the mounted warrior in particular had a long lifespan and broad geographical salience. This provides a strong echo of frequent allusions in the ancient sources to the skill and resilience of North African cavalry and the scale of horse-breeding in the region.[46] An interesting aspect of the distribution of Caballine rock art (Fig. 4.4) is that it is closely aligned with evidence of inscriptions in the ancient Libyan alphabets both in the Sahara and Maghrib.[47] However, both these categories of evidence are often discussed in isolation and seldom with reference to other types of data relating to religion, funerary practices, and settlements (but see Chapter 11).[48]

NAIA settlement is very poorly investigated at present. There are a number of reasons for this and many consequences. Of the suspected early settlement sites in *Numidia* and *Mauretania* we have frustratingly little to go on. This is in part because of their often deep burial beneath Roman-era successors. The lack of relevant excavations has impeded our ability to date closely the characteristic handmade pottery forms prevalent in periods before the wide dissemination of late Punic and Roman wares.[49] While that is now starting to change, a consequence of limited knowledge of diagnostic pottery is that the sedentary settlements (urban and rural) of the NAIA have remained a major blind spot. Many Roman towns may have had pre-Roman origins, but there has been little appetite for excavating beneath the substantial structures of Roman sites to look into this. Scientific dating is another key to advancing our understanding in the absence of closely diagnostic artefacts (that is, Mediterranean imports) in the lowest levels of these sites. Many Numidian sites have only been identifiable by the presence of Punic or Roman "imports," and these imports often significantly post-dated initial activity or are extremely rare in areas where contacts with Libyphoenician settlements were minimal.

There are some substantial hillfort sites in Algeria and Tunisia that are not overlain by Roman remains, but dating of occupation of these proto-urban sites remains imprecise.[50] As a result, the relative lack of identified permanent settlements has in the past encouraged the belief that most Numidians lived in tents or huts—the *mapalia* of our literary sources—which would leave little trace archaeologically.

Another major gap in our evidence of NAIA societies relates to palaeoenvironmental data that can inform us of their lifeways. Given the dearth of excavations of settlement sites, it is no surprise that detailed information derived from

45. Barnett 2019a; 2019b; Camps and Gast 1982; Di Lernia and Zampetti 2008; Gauthier and Gauthier 2011; 2015; Lutz and Lutz 1995.
46. On the introduction and importance of horses in Maghribian and Saharan societies, Bokbot et al. 2021; Camps and Chaker 1993; Daumas 1968; Pezzoli 1995.
47. Barnett 2019a; Biagetti et al. 2012; Gauthier and Gauthier 2011.
48. But compare the approach in Sterry and Mattingly 2020a.
49. See pioneer work by Camps 1961, 211–416. See now Bokbot 2020; Callegarin et al. 2016b; Ghaki 1999b; Kallala et al. 2017; Sghaïer and Dammak-Latrach 2020.
50. Ferchiou 1990a; 1990b; 1994. Cf. also Fentress 2006 on pre-Roman proto-urban origins.

analysis of botanical and faunal remains is largely lacking. This sort of evidence has the potential, of course, to transform the debate about the supposed nomadic tendencies of the indigenous "tribes."

Despite the above-mentioned constraints, some important advances in recent years have transformed our knowledge of the archaeological realities of these societies and now require a paradigm shift in our interpretation of the NAIA societies. Three crucial questions can be raised regarding the autochthonous communities of the NAIA with regard to their active role in the making of Africa in the Roman era. The first concerns the date of appearance of sedentary settlements, and most notably of larger nucleated settlements of proto-urban form. The second, related to the first, is the earliest evidence for agriculture and for subsequent phases of agricultural expansion or intensification. The third aspect involves the dating of specific stages of important technological advances that can also be linked to the expansion of agriculture, notably the development of metallurgy providing superior weapons of war and tools for cultivation, harvesting, and for constructing irrigation systems.[51] The existence of metallurgy in North Africa prior to the arrival of Phoenician settlers needs reviewing.[52] The supposed absence of these three elements (sedentary settlement/urbanism, agriculture, and metallurgy) are the keystones of the orthodox interpretation of paternalistic incomers jump-starting social developments in Africa. If we can demonstrate that the first adoption of agriculture, substantial availability of metal tools, and the initial steps towards urbanism predated and/or ran in parallel with Phoenician/Greek or Roman colonial ventures in Africa, then we have a very different and more balanced starting position for considering the question of who made Africa.[53]

The *Numidae*

By the late 3rd century BCE it is clear from the ancient sources that Rome was dealing with not only the powerful Carthaginian state but also with emergent indigenous kingdoms, *Numidia* and *Mauretania*.[54] *Numidia* was evidently the result of the merger of two peoples, the *Masaesyli* and the *Massyli*, most emphatically under the long rule of an extraordinary king called Massinissa from the late 3rd to the

51. Duckworth et al. 2020b, 18–28.
52. Cf. Greene 1997, 157: "The best appraisal of the people encountered by the founders of Carthage is that they were probably ceramic Neolithic farmers and herders clustered in villages or camping in tents and possessing no knowledge of metal or of writing. The Stone Age prehistory of the Maghrib is well understood into the third millennium, but there is no evidence for a native 'Bronze Age' in North Africa."
53. Mattingly 2016 for a first rehearsal of some of these ideas.
54. Aït Amara 2013; Ardeleanu 2021; Bridoux 2006; Camps 1960; Gsell 1927a; 1927b; Hachi and Kherbouche 2017; Horn and Rüger 1979; Lancel 2003; Lassère 2015, 47–63; Sennequier and Colonia 2003. Jallet-Huant 2006 for a popular rehashing of the legends.

mid-2nd century BCE (Fig. 4.1).[55] The *Masaesyli* heartlands stretched eastwards for hundreds of kilometres from a main centre at *Siga* in western Algeria. The *Massyli* were evidently primarily centred in eastern Algeria and western Tunisia, with the fortified site of *Cirta* perhaps close to their initial western limits. People of similar character, and described as *Afri* in the sources, occupied the immediate hinterland of *Qart Hadasht* and came under Carthaginian rule at quite an early date.

As noted already, there has long been a tendency for modern commentators to present these Libyan population groupings as "tribes," even where the ancient terms used could have much broader connotations.[56] The ancient sources encourage this sort of automatic default judgement by the contradictory way in which they speak of the Numidian and Mauretanian kings, let alone the secondary peoples associated with these blocks. Strabo, for instance alluded at one point to the agriculture and towns of the *Numidae* (17.3.9–13), yet almost immediately (17.3.14) explained that *Qart Hadasht* had "gained possession of all that part of *Libya* that men can live in without living a nomadic life." He gave Massinissa credit for introducing towns and agriculture to *Numidia* (17.3.15), while in the same section noting the paradoxical fact that the Numidians chose to live a wandering and migratory life in a land "blessed by nature," allegedly because of their failure to rid the land of wild beasts and due to their warlike tendencies. Both Sallust and Strabo identified a (false) etymological link between the name *Numidae* and the Greek word for nomads, with Strabo describing it as their "special designation" (17.3.15; cf. Sallust *BJ* 18). However, there are also numerous allusions in the accounts of the Numidian kingdom to the existence of fortified centres. Since the siege and capture of these strongpoints was a key feature of the late 2nd-century BCE Jugurthan war, we can hardly ignore their existence. But the same accounts also place stress on the non-urban character of some settlements characterised by "huts" (*mapalia*), and again it is a moot point which of these images has lingered with ancient and modern readers (Sallust *BJ* 18; 46).

Sallust (*BJ* 90) explained Rome's periodic difficulties in supplying their troops with cereals during the Jugurthan war as being due to the fact that "the Numidians apply themselves more to pastoralism than agriculture, and had conveyed, by the king's order, whatever grain had been raised into fortified places." One suspects that the shortage was due more to the latter than the former cause. A further element of misrepresentation of the *Numidae* reported in Sallust (BJ 18–19) linked their origin to Persian and Medean elements of the army of Hercules, though he attributed responsibility to an account in Punic by the Numidian king Hiempsal. These

55. Camps 1960 still remains a fundamental starting point for analysing the process of ethnogenesis, but see now the important new overview of Ardeleanu 2021. On the Masaesyli and Massyli, see Desanges 1962; 1980b, 145–46, 335–36.

56. For an example of this tendency to take too literally the words of the sources, see Luisi 1994, 1–9.

imagined "incomers" allegedly intermingled with the local Africans (by implication contributing the more civilised elements of their society).[57]

The account of the *Numidae* in Pliny (*NH* 5.2) is remarkable for its brevity and its misdirection:

> At the river *Ampsaga Numidia* begins, a country rendered illustrious by the fame of Massinissa. By the Greeks ... the Numidians received the name of "*Nomades*" from their frequent changes of pasturage; upon which occasions they were accustomed to carry their *mapalia*, or in other words, their houses, upon wagons ... This country produces nothing remarkable except its marble and wild beasts.

Such comments might suggest that Massinissa and his successors were "kings" of little more than war-bands, but this does not really fit with the account of the Jugurthan war, for instance, where the Romans encountered a landscape rich in grain and studded with well-defended towns (Sallust *BJ* 46 and 54).[58] The Numidian kings had substantial armies, including troops of elephants (Sallust *BJ* 29), and on occasion showed the ability to confront and beat Roman armies in pitched battles as well as in ambushes and surprise attacks. They could withstand sieges for considerable periods and also prosecute siege-works of their own (*BJ* 56–57). Jugurtha was eventually outmanned by the Romans, after a war that lasted for seven years. He was plainly no petty chief who could be rolled over with ease.

Our sources give us fairly detailed information on the dynastic links of the Numidian kings. A key event during the Second Punic War, was the tussle for power between Syphax, leader of the *Masaesyli*, and Massinissa of the *Massyli*. Syphax had initially gained the upper hand over Massinissa's father, Gaia, and seized control of the combined territory of the two population blocks, moving his centre of power to *Cirta* (Livy 29.29.5).[59] Though overshadowed by the younger Massinissa, who brought about his sudden downfall, Syphax is a fascinating character, and much of what Massinissa later enacted was to an extent already presaged in the kingdom of Syphax. He rather than Massinissa appears to have been the first to unite the *Masaesyli* and the *Massyli*, with his power extending from a western capital at *Siga* near the *Mulucha* river to an eastern capital at *Cirta* on the *Ampsaga* river. In exploiting a privileged relationship with the Romans after their victory over *Qart Hadasht* in 202 BCE, Massinissa undoubtedly took the united kingdom of the Numidians to new heights, but it is clear in the sources that the *Masaesyli* and *Massyli* were already by the 220s BCE sizeable kingdoms. Syphax in particular stands out as a sophisticated and successful ruler of a powerful kingdom, playing a shrewd political game at different times with Carthaginian and Roman allegiances.

57. Morstein-Marx 2001.
58. Lassère 2015, 87–95.
59. Lassère 2015, 48–53.

Massinissa initially had the worse of the contest with Syphax, being driven into exile in the southern Gaetulian zone of Tripolitania. His victory over Syphax was in some respects a surprise and owed much to the decisive alliance the younger man eventually struck with Scipio Africanus.

Three sons of Massinissa (Micipsa, Gulussa, and Mastanabal) initially divided the kingdom after his death in 148 BCE, though the kingdom was again united after about 140 BCE under Micipsa. The next generation of rulers (and rival claimants) came from the sons of Micipsa and Mastanabal, with Jugurtha, son of Mastanabal, initially prevailing over the sons of Micipsa, but after his death the rule passing to the sons and grandsons of his younger brother Gauda. The last Numidian king, Juba I was deposed by Julius Caesar in 46 BCE after backing the wrong side in the civil war.

The earliest coins of the Numidian kings are striking for their sophistication and developed iconography. Syphax was the first to issue coins in the late 3rd century BCE, featuring a bearded portrait head, presumably of himself, and on the reverse a man with a spear on a galloping or prancing horse (reminiscent of the mounted rider iconography of the NAIA). Some coins have a Punic legend "*HMMLKT*" ("ruler of the kingdom").[60] Massinissa's first coin issues are thought to be only slightly later and again depict a bearded portrait and on the reverse a riderless horse, modelled on Carthaginian issues.[61] Some coins also feature a sceptre as a symbol of royal power, and Massinissa's name in Punic.[62]

As we shall see, there is archaeological evidence to support the more generous evaluation of the Numidian kingdom as a sophisticated state that embraced a wide range of Hellenistic/Punic culture.[63] Why does that not come through more clearly in the literary accounts? The answer surely lies in the repeated and exaggerated emphasis on desert features and nomadic lifestyles. For instance, after suffering a defeat, we are informed that Jugurtha had withdrawn "into the deserts of the interior" only for him to reappear in quick response to attack a Roman force at *Sicca*, a town that is c.200 km from the edge of the pre-desert, let alone the full desert (*BJ* 56). Similarly, Sallust makes much of two daring Roman campaigns against Numidian "desert" strongpoints, *Thala* and *Capsa* (*BJ* 75–76, 89–91). While these sites certainly lie in the semi-arid Tunisian high steppe, and *Capsa* is at the edge of the pre-desert as defined by the 150 mm rainfall isohyet line, the Roman escapades were made far more dramatic by exaggeratedly transposing them into a much more hostile environment. For readers of Sallust's account, two of the most memorable incidents were thus used to give the false impression that the Numidians were desert-dwelling.

---

60. Mazard 1955, 18–20.
61. The carefully groomed thrusting beards of the Numidian kings remind me of the pugnacious and charismatic Indian cricket captain Virat Kohli.
62. Mazard 1955, 30–43.
63. Sennequier and Colonia 2003, 81–113; Horn and Rüger 1979; Kuttner 2013; Quinn 2013; Tahar 2005.

There is then a clear disconnect between different aspects of the same literary sources when they refer to the Numidians, on the one hand hinting at complexity, but continually returning to images and vocabulary that reinforce an impression of primitive society. Leaving to one side for the moment the early evolution of Numidian society, what are the principal indicators that by the late 1st millennium BCE the Numidian kingdom was an important polity? As described in the sources, the overall territorial extent of the Numidian kingdom was vast, stretching more than 1,000 km from the *Mulucha* (Mouloya) river in Morocco (that separated it from the kingdom of the *Mauri*) to the *fossa regia* ditch (that delineated it from Carthaginian territory) in Tunisia. The territory of the *Masaesyli* at its maximum extent was c.150,000 km^2 and that of the *Massyli* c.80,000 km^2, comparable in size to the great Meso-American early states and 50 to 100 times larger than the average city states of Greece.[64] That fact alone should alert us to the danger of underestimating the capabilities and structural sophistication of this polity.

The Numidian kingdom also demonstrates many other markers of a civilised and complex state. For a start, their leaders were not isolated from the broader developments of Mediterranean society. Syphax married a high-born Carthaginian, and Massinissa had campaigned with the Carthaginian armies in Spain. Later kings and princes were recognised by Rome as client rulers.[65] It is unsurprising that by the late 3rd century BCE, Numidian society was influenced by aspects of Punic and Hellenistic culture. Punic inscriptions have been found at a number of Numidian sites—most famously the bilingual Punic/Libyan text of 139 BCE from *Thugga* that reveals Punic influence, but also some distinctive local aspects of personal styling and urban titulature.[66] Coinage was adopted by the Numidian kings, following Punic models.[67] Monumental architecture in dressed stone appeared at a number of sites, especially for grandiose funerary monuments (Fig. 4.5a–b).[68] A detailed examination of the forum area at *Thugga* has recently recognised considerable evidence of Numidian monumental structures that preceded the Roman-era public buildings.[69] There is also evidence for the use of well-dressed and ornately decorated masonry in religious buildings, as in the structure erected at a high holy place at the quarry at *Simitthu*, adorned with images of arms and armour (Figs. 4.5c; cf. Fig. 8.13).[70] The Numidian kingdom came to be a formidable military power and, as Carthaginian

64. Sanmartí et al. 2020, 440. On Greek *poleis*, see Hansen and Nielsen 2004, 1319
65. Sennequier and Colonia 2003, 81–113.
66. Gsell 1927a, 133–35. He describes the urban organisation as "assez analogue mais non pas empruntée à celle des ville puniques" (133). See Quinn 2013 for a thorough discussion.
67. Alexandropolous 2000; Mazard 1955.
68. Quinn 2013; Rakob 1979 on monumental tombs. On Hellenistic architecture more broadly in North Africa, see Ferchiou 1989a. For some reconstruction views, see Laronde and Golvin 2001, 54–73.
69. Aounallah and Golvin 2016, 29–74; Saint-Amans 2004, 35–54.
70. Kuttner 2013, 228–48; Rakob 1994 on "panoply monuments" at Chemtou and Kbor Klib.

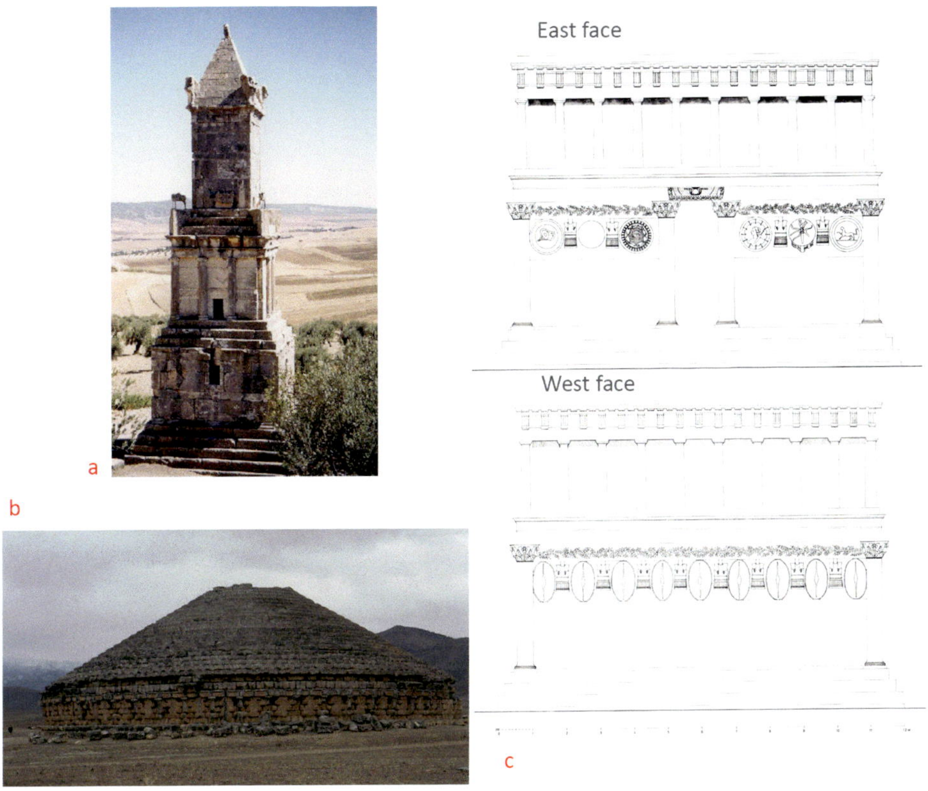

Figure 4.5. Numidian royal architecture. a) Mausoleum at *Thugga*. b) Medracen tomb. c) *Simitthu* monument (a–b: Author photos; c: Author montage after Horn and Rüger 1979, 121).

power waned after the Second Punic War, was able to increase its territory in the *Bagrada* valley and the Tunisian Tell at the expense of *Qart Hadasht*.[71] It is worth noting that there were no precocious polities of comparable territorial scale, sophistication, and power at this time in large parts of temperate Europe (France, Britain, Germany, the Balkans). Even in southern Europe, the scale of most polities was much smaller—with a few notable exceptions, like Rome, Athens, and Macedon.

Given the huge extent of the kingdom of the Numidians, it is important to consider to what extent this represented the union of broadly related ethnic groups. Recent linguistic research into the Berber/Amazigh language group has identified a number of phases of language evolution, suggesting successive phases of separation across the north Sahara and Maghrib.[72] What Chris Ehret calls Proto-Amazigh

71. Lassère 2015, 70–73.
72. Ehret 2019; Fentress 2019 for a crucial series of maps giving visual (and chronological) meaning to Ehret's models.

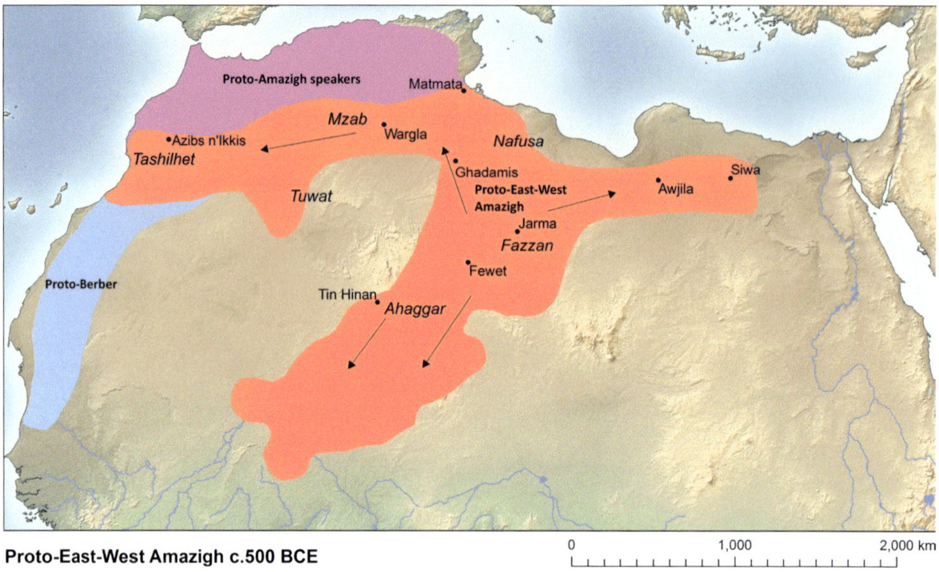

Figure 4.6. Distribution of the Proto-East-West Amazigh language group by around 500 BCE (adapted from Fentress 2019, 509, showing her interpretation of Ehret 2019).

appears to have achieved its main distribution across the Maghrib in the early 1st millennium BCE and seems to be the language group that will have marked out the *Numidae* and the *Mauri* from the *Gaetuli* and the *Garamantes*, who seem instead (according to Ehret) to have spoken a dialect called Proto-East-West Amazigh by around 500 BCE (Fig. 4.6).[73] This is important as it implies greater social affinity of the peoples of the Maghrib proper and some linguistic distance between them and the Saharan peoples, including those of the pre-desert zone.

Thugga (Dougga) is known to have been a fully constituted urban community on the basis of bilingual Punic/Libyan texts of the 2nd century BCE, with tantalising traces of late Numidian religious buildings around the forum area and a number of impressive mausolea and drum tombs.[74] Diodorus Siculus (20.57.4) described it as a proper town in the 4th century BCE. The existence of at least 36 towns in Africa whose magistrates followed the Punic pattern of magistracies (*sufetes*) is another indication of pre-Roman urban organisation.[75] While 11 of these were Libyphoenician *emporia* or sites in Cap Bon (*Qart Hadasht*, *Curubis*, *Chul*, *Lepcis Magna*, *Oea*, *Ruspae*, *Sabratha*, *Themetra*, *Thinissut*, *Utica*, *Vina*) and another

73. Fentress 2019, 504–09, figs. 16.3 and 16.4. The theory needs to be tested against the evidence of observed differences in Libyan inscriptions, Galand 2005.

74. Aounallah and Golvin 2016, 25–74; Aounallah et al. 2020a.

75. Belkahia and di Vita-Evrard 1995.

16 were from the core Carthaginian territory in north-eastern Tunisia (Hr Aioune, *Abbir*, *Apisa Maius*, *Apisa Minus*, *Aradi*, *Avita Bibba*, *Biracsaccar*, *Gales*, *Limisa*, *Siagu*, *Sucubi*, *Tepelte*, *Thaca* (*Civitas*), *Thapphugabensis*, *Thibica*, *Thuburbo Maius*), nine examples are known from Numidian or other deep inland towns (*Althiburos*, *Calama*, *Capsa*, *Cirta*, *Gadiaufala*, *Mactaris*, *Masculula*, *Thuburnica*, *Thugga*).[76] But this sort of evidence does not help us resolve the question of the date at which urbanisation occurred or the morphological form of these early sites. As recently as 2000, Mahjoubi stated: "Unfortunately, there is no evidence surviving of either the town planning or the architecture of these Numidian cities."[77]

Althiburos and Urban Development among the *Numidae*

A remarkable Spanish–Tunisian project led by Joan Sanmartí Grego and Nabil Kallala at the Numidian and Roman town of *Althiburos* (western Tunisia) has provided a new and radically different perspective on early Numidian society and urbanisation.[78] The town is known for its relatively well-preserved but modest Roman ruins,[79] though a neo-Punic text referring to magistracies (*sufetes*) on the Punic model indicates pre-Roman origins for the site. It sits on a peninsula within a tight bend in a steeply scarped wadi (Figs. 4.7–4.8, cf. also Fig. 8.4).[80] The settlement was set back in a valley penetrating into the Massif du Ksour of the southern edge of the extensive rolling upland plain of Zouarine. The high ground of the massif to the south of the town was studded with megalithic tombs of NAIA date and a c.2 km-long low wall in that direction seems to have served as a sort of symbolic boundary a similar distance from the settlement (Fig. 4.7).[81] While it is too slight for a defensive function (c.1.2–1.5 m wide and of negligible height), it may well have had some sacred or boundary-marking function.

By excavating deep trenches in two areas beneath and between the Roman remains, where most past excavators have tended to stop, this project has exposed a c.6 m-deep sequence of pre-Roman buildings and occupation levels that have been well dated using AMS (radiocarbon) determinations on single fruits or short-lived crops, in addition to stratified pottery finds. Although the relatively small size

76. Belkahia and di Vita-Evrard 1995, 271.
77. Mahjoubi 2000, 21: "Il ne reste malheureusement pas des souvenirs de l'urbanisme ni de l'architecture de ces cités numides." For other reviews of the evidence for pre-Roman urbanism before the recent advances in evidence, see Camps 1994a. Quinn 2009 remained confident that there was no inland urbanisation prior to the 4th century BCE.
78. Kallala and Sanmartí 2011; Kallala et al. 2016; 2017; Sanmartí et al. 2012.
79. Ennaïfer 1976; Kallala and Sanmartí 2011, 9–28.
80. Ennaïfer 1976, 27; Sanmartí et al. 2020, 448.
81. Kallala et al. 2017, 53–58 on the "grande mur" to south of the town.

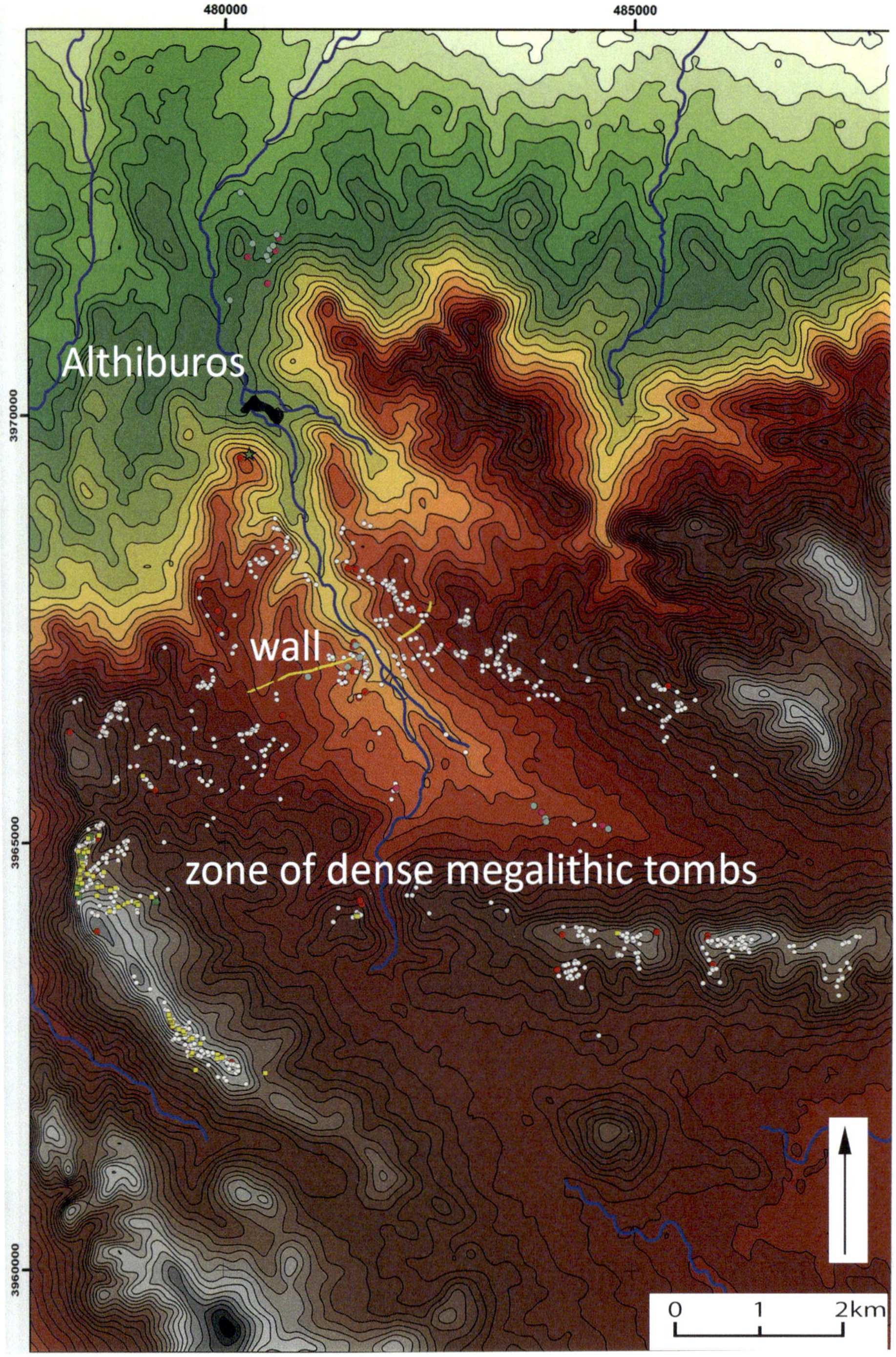

Figure 4.7. The topographic setting of *Althiburos*: settlement, southern boundary wall, and surrounding dolmen tombs (dots) (from Kallala et al. 2017, 91).

of the trenches (and the even more restricted area excavated to the deepest depths) inevitably resulted in rather incomplete building plans, the structural evidence uncovered is striking.[82] Three broad phases of 1st-millennium BCE occupation were identified, designated the *Numide Ancien* (with three subphases: NA1, NA2, NA3; broadly 10th, 9th, 8th centuries BCE), the *Numide Moyen* (NM, 7th–5th century BCE), and the *Numide Recent* (NR1, 4th to mid-2nd century BCE; and NR2, mid-2nd to late 1st century BCE).[83] While some might object to the use of the term "Numidian" for cultural phases many centuries before the Numidian state came into existence, the cultural continuities in the deeply stratified sequence justify the term, though with the proviso that we must think of the initial phases as is some sense proto-Numidian.

A major surprise has been the identification at the very lowest levels of more or less rectangular stone-footed buildings dating back to the 10th–9th centuries BCE, associated with evidence for cultivation of a range of cereals, legumes, and viticulture from the beginning of occupation, and with the addition of the olive by the late 8th century if not before.[84] The earliest buildings had broad wall footings constructed in short and slightly irregular segments.[85] Later buildings were evidently more regular and complex, but even the early-phase structures are far from the imagined *mapalia* huts of the sources.[86] There is also firm evidence for ironworking by the 8th century, and the nature of the archaeological structures and deposits strongly supports the view that this was a sedentary settlement from the outset.[87] The early date for local metallurgy is particularly important in that it again contradicts the presumed primacy of Phoenician technological know-how.[88] The Early Numidian phase lasted into the early 7th century, when there may have

---

82. Kallala and Sanmartí 2011, 45–110 (zone 1) and 153–262 (zone 2); Kallala et al. 2016, 13–47 (Numidian architecture).
83. Kallala and Sanmartí 2011, 31–38 on the chronological divisions and key dating evidence for the phases; Sanmartí et al. 2012, 30–31 for discussion and table of radiocarbon date from the early Numidian levels.
84. Kallala and Sanmartí 2011, 31–32, 70–73, 184–86; Kallala et al. 2016, 13–19, for detail of the early Numidian structures excavated; Sanmartí et al. 2020, 448–61 for a succinct summary. These aspects will be further discussed at the appropriate place in Chapters 8 and 10.
85. Kallala et al. 2016, 15, 19–23; Sanmartí et al. 2020, 453.
86. For photographs of Numidian wall construction, see Kallala and Sanmartí 2011, 97–99, 222–35; 2016, 15–19, 36.
87. Kallala and Sanmartí 2011, 34; Sanmartí et al. 2012, 33 (8th-century metallurgy).
88. For a perfect example of the collision of prior assumptions and new evidence, see Johnston and Kaufman 2019, 411: "The impact of Carthaginian activities would have been even stronger in North Africa itself, where local indigenous cultures . . . had in essence a Neolithic basket of technologies before Phoenician contact, with no known metallurgical technology. The influx of new technologies combined with protracted culture contact changed these local societies profoundly during the North African Iron Age. The earliest known iron implements and ferrous slags are found—somewhat surprisingly—at the inland site of *Althiburos*, in late ninth- and eighth-century BCE contexts."

been a slight hiatus, before a Mid Numidian revival of activity and the construction of new suites of buildings in the 6th century. The site is believed to have had a fully urban character by the 5th century BCE at latest, with increasing evidence of contact with *Qart Hadasht* at this time. There was a further distinct episode of building in the latter centuries BCE, the Late Numidian phase, linked again with close contacts with *Qart Hadasht* and then Rome. The first evidence of urban defences probably relates to the 4th century BCE, though earlier defences could have existed outside the excavated areas.[89]

What of the economic base at *Althiburos*? There is evidence of grazing animals, notably sheep and cattle, being kept by the population from earliest times.[90] The typology of handmade pottery from the site offers both the chance to recognise and date other sites of the Numidian era, but also supports the view that these people were essentially sedentary from the earliest phases of occupation. Pastoral peoples do not generally have so wide a range of pottery forms.[91] However, the most dramatic evidence relates to agriculture, which is radiocarbon-dated at *Althiburos* to the very start of the 1st millennium BCE, and the agricultural component of the economy was consistent through all the Numidian phases (Table 4.1).[92]

As discussed in Chapter 1, it is not clear when or where agriculture became established in Mediterranean North Africa. Though there are some precocious occurrences in Neolithic contexts in Morocco,[93] it is quite possible that a number of separate areas had begun to incorporate plant cultivation into their lifestyle by the 2nd millennium BCE.[94] The traditional technologies of ploughs in the Maghrib shows some correlation with the basic ethnic groups of *Mauri* and *Numidae* being distinct from *Gaetuli*.[95] Of potentially greater significance, though, is the fact that the material at *Althiburos* predates the establishment of Phoenician *emporia* on the North African coast, so an endogenous explanation for its spread within the Maghrib now seems probable. *Althiburos* was a substantial sedentary (agro-pastoral) farming settlement from the beginning of the 1st millennium BCE, with its well-developed agriculture (including viticulture and probably olive

---

89. Kallala et al. 2016, 23–25, 39 (pl. 1.4); Sanmartí et al. 2020, 454–55.
90. Kallala et al. 2016, 421–48.
91. Kallala and Sanmartí 2011, 111–51 (catalogue of ceramic finds from zone 1), 263–391 (zone 2), 407–10 (zone 3); Kallala et al. 2016, 49–84 (typology of pre-Roman wheel-made pottery); 85–140 (typology of handmade wares).
92. Kallala et al. 2016, 449–90 (botanical remains); 491–515 (charcoal); 517–27 (phytoliths and spheroliths); 529–31 (pollen).
93. Zapata et al. 2013.
94. As discussed in Chapter 1 above, Broodbank and Lucarini 2019, 247 suggest separate introductions in north Morocco and in Tunisia, where the proximity to Iberia, Sardinia, Italy, and Sicily may have facilitated transfers of cultivars. Early spread from Egypt along the Mediterranean coastal zone seems to be ruled out by the lack of evidence for cultivars in late Neolithic levels in the Haua Fteah cave in Libya, Barker et al. 2012.
95. Camps 1986b.

Table 4.1. Main cultivated plants exploited at *Althiburos* (NA = "Numide Ancien") (after Kallala et al. 2016).

Cultivated plant	Common name	Major cultivar	Phase	First occurrence	Origin
Triticum aestivum/ durum	Bread wheat/ Durum wheat	*	Alth-NA1	1020–810 calBCE	Mediterranean
Triticum dicoccum	Emmer wheat	*	Alth-NA1	1020–810 calBCE	Mediterranean
Triticum cf spleta	Spelt wheat		Alth-NA3	1020–810 calBCE	Mediterranean
Hordeum vulgare	Barley	*	Alth-NA1	1020–810 calBCE	Mediterranean
Panicum miliaceum	Millet	*	Alth-NA1	1020–810 calBCE	Mediterranean
Vitis vinifera	Grape vine	*	Alth-NA1	1020–810 calBCE	Mediterranean
Ficus carica	Fig tree	*	Alth-NA1	1020–810 calBCE	Mediterranean
Lens culinaris	Lentil	*	Alth-NA1	1020–810 calBCE	Mediterranean
Vicia faba	Faba bean		Alth-NA1	1020–810 calBCE	Mediterranean
Linum cf usitatissimum	Flax		Alth-NA1	1020–810 calBCE	Mediterranean
Setaria italica	Foxtail millet		Alth-NA2	910–820 calBCE	Mediterranean
Pisum sativum	Pea	*	Alth-NA2	910–820 calBCE	Mediterranean
Punica granatum	Pomegranate		Alth-NA2	910–820 calBCE	Mediterranean
Olea europaea	Olive	*	Alth-NA3	790–760 calBCE	Mediterranean
Secale cereale	Cereal rye		Alth-Med	Medieval	Mediterranean
Avena sativa	Oats		Alth-Med	Medieval	Mediterranean

cultivation) predating the archaeological date for the foundation of *Qart Hadasht* in the late 9th century BCE. The *Althiburos* discoveries make it clear from the nature of the crop package involved that cultivation was already well established in the Maghrib many centuries ahead of the wider dissemination of Libyphoenician sites in Africa.[96] It is not easy to distinguish between remains of bread and durum wheat, and in the early phases this is perhaps more likely to represent evidence of bread wheat (*Triticum aestivum*), but in general the agricultural package was quite an evolved one (the apparently slightly later introduction of the olive may be due to the sample size from early levels).[97] This is key evidence to contradict the long-held belief that the agriculture was only introduced and promoted by Phoenician, Greek, and Roman "colonists."[98] Agricultural development is thus not attributable

96. Although the evidence for metalworking is quite limited in the lowest levels of the site, the excavators believed that metal artefacts were in use and possibly produced at the site from its earliest phases, Kallala et al. 2016, 391.
97. Pelling 2013a, 479. I am grateful to Lisa Fentress for discussion on the conflation of durum and bread wheat in the reporting of early botanical remains from North Africa.
98. Mattingly 2016.

to the direct stimulus of the agencies most commonly credited: *Qart Hadasht*, Massinissa, and Rome—though that is not to deny that those later connections gave further impetus to these trends.[99] The material culture includes some Punic material, but not from the very earliest levels. If there was a Phoenician "Prince Charming" in this story, Numidian civilisation was awake and out of bed by the time he showed up.

Another element of the work at *Althiburos* has concerned the funerary environment, producing a detailed record of c.1,000 megalithic tombs that cluster in the landscape of the town (Fig. 4.7).[100] Though only four of these burials have been excavated and only two scientifically dated,[101] the evidence firmly points to their construction being primarily associated with the early phases of development of the "Numidian" town. As noted above, the megalithic tombs of the eastern Maghrib have a broad distribution that seems to associate them with the people we can later identify as the *Numidae*. What is now becoming clearer is that an important element of this distribution is a pattern of dense clustering of such burials around urban centres.[102] For example, other clusters have been noted around the Roman period towns of *Mididi*, *Bagat*, *Mactaris*, *Ulules*, *Bulla Regia*, and *Thucca Terebentina*, where we may now confidently predict NAIA precursors.[103] The landscape around *Althiburos* was undoubtedly "busy" in the pre-Roman period, and the combined evidence of the excavations and survey clearly demonstrates that this was a zone of both intensive sedentary agriculture and pastoral exploitation.[104]

However, the true significance of *Althiburos* is not its exceptionalism, but its ordinariness. It was not the Numidian capital at any point, it represents just one site among many Numidian centres that are recorded in our sources for the latter centuries BCE.[105] The demonstration that this site was a centre of sedentary agricultural people, practising advanced metallurgy from early in the 1st millennium BCE, rather than a much later development that emulated the spread of Punic/Libyphoenician urbanisation, agriculture, and technology, thus represents a major

99. Ben Younès 2016 for similar reflections on pre-Phoenician cultural connections between Libyans of coastal areas and those of the interior.
100. Kallala and Sanmartí 2011, 393–99; Kallala et al. 2014a (for excavated tombs); 2017, 34–53 (excavation of tombs); 9–33 (background to survey and typology); 143–304 (catalogue of tombs and structures); 59–142 (for overall survey and analysis); Sanmartí et al. 2015; 2019 (for wider reflection on Numidian burial rites).
101. Kallala et al. 2017, 12 for dates of 700–400 calBC and 780–410 calBC for two tombs at *Althiburos*, and 790–480 calBC and 670–400 calBC for two others from *Mididi*.
102. Kallala et al. 2017, 88–102 for distribution maps.
103. The point was made by Camps 1993b and 1995b, but is now reinforced through more focused studies and surveys. See, for instance, Ben Baaziz 2000; Krandel-Ben Younès 2013; M'Charek et al. 2008; Tanda et al. 2009, 301–07.
104. Kallala et al. 2008; 2014b.
105. See Sanmartí et al. 2020 for wider reflections on Numidian urbanisation and state formation.

revision to established models.[106] Other recent discoveries demonstrate that it was far from a lone Numidian urban centre.

Althiburos lies towards the west of a distinctive zone designated the *chora Tusca* by Appian (*Libyca* 68), "*RST TSKT*" in a Punic text erected under King Micipsa (128–127 BCE), and *pagus Thuscae* in the 2nd century CE.[107] The inscription of Micipsa is a boundary marker, testifying to land survey in pre-Roman times, while Appian mentioned 50 *poleis* in this area, and the inscription relating to the *pagus Thuscae et Gunzuzi* indicated there were 64 urban communities (*civitates*) falling within its boundaries (*AE* 1963, 96).[108] Some previous interpretations have assumed that the urban centres of this region, possession of which was disputed between the Numidian kings and *Qart Hadasht* in the latter centuries BCE, were Punic foundations.[109] Though he admitted the Numidian origin, Desanges was sceptical of the urban character of these sites:

> In Numidia, these agglomerations were probably only stop-overs of nomads or temporary markets, where the number of tents outweighed actual buildings.[110]

The *Althiburos* discoveries open a new possibility for understanding the early Roman urban organisation of this zone, in that the 64 towns (of which *Mactaris* appears to have been the most important) can in fact be seen as the end product of a long process of urbanisation and sedentary agriculture in this region of the Numidian kingdom, with origins in the early 1st millennium BCE.

Can this idea of widespread early Numidian (proto-)urbanism be supported by archaeological evidence from other centres? Similar deep sondages below the forum at *Simitthu* (Chemtou) were begun in the late 1970s, but only in recent years revisited and better recorded. These have revealed substantial late Numidian tombs and, close by, a deep sequence of buildings constructed primarily in mud-brick erected on stone footings.[111] There were at least four phases predating a horizon dated by imported Italian black gloss pottery of the 2nd century BCE. This implies a similar sequence to that recorded at *Althiburos*, and this is now confirmed by

106. Quinn 2009, 268–71 for a recent restatement of the view that there was no Numidian urbanisation or agriculture before 4th century BC.
107. M'Charek 1999; Picard et al. 1963.
108. *L'Année épigraphique*, 1963. Of these, it is thought 50 towns related to the *pagus Thuscae* and 14 to the *pagus Gunzuzi*, believed to be territory on the other side of the *fossa regia*, Picard et al. 1963, 127–28.
109. Picard et al. 1963, 129: "Ces villes existaient au milieu du IIe siècle av. J.-C. On peut croire qu'elles furent fondées par les Carthaginois pendant le temps qu'ils possédèrent le pays." Cf. also Manfredi 2003.
110. Desanges 1980b, 327: "En Numidie, ces agglomérations devaient souvent n'être que des relais de nomads ou des marchés, où le nombre des tentes l'emportait sur celui des bâtiments." Cf. also Desanges 1980a.
111. Khanoussi and von Rummel 2012; von Rummel 2014, 127–28.

radiocarbon dates of the 8th century BCE from the lowest levels.[112] Also from *Simitthu*, the architecture of the Hellenistic-era temple above the Roman quarries is a further reminder about the sophistication of later Numidian society (Fig. 4.5b).[113]

At *Thugga*, the great "royal" mausoleum and Punic inscriptions (including the famous bilingual Libyan/Punic texts) have long indicated the early origins of the site.[114] Excavations in the forum area have almost certainly identified the remains of temple of Massinissa in the Numidian *agora* area and, south of the House of the Trifolium, there were further Numidian buildings of the latter centuries BCE overlying some 2nd-millennium BCE burials.[115] Excavations on the north side of the city have found evidence of another mausoleum and a large pre-Roman cemetery and religious area dating from the early 3rd century BCE onwards.[116] Important assemblages of both local handmade wares and wheel-made imported material have been recovered in these excavations and promise better chronological control on the local Numidian handmade series.[117]

Recent excavations at *Zama Regia*, though not yet published, have also apparently revealed further evidence of early urbanism. Future excavations below other Roman-Numidian towns will thus no doubt amplify this picture of widespread urban development at a far earlier date than previously imagined and provide additional evidence that this went alongside the spread of Numidian agriculture. At *Musti*, an old excavation evidently reached Numidian levels dated to the 3rd century BCE, though the published details are scant.[118] *Cirta* has long been known to have pre-Roman structures associated with its extraordinary fortress site (Fig. 4.8e), including an early tophet (late 3rd century BCE) confirming the importance indicated by the literary sources.[119] In the light of these various excavations, it is apparent that many urban centres in north-western Tunisia and north-eastern Algeria had Numidian origins. We can identify even more candidates by using proxy indications, drawing confidence from these examples.

The literary and epigraphic evidence is full of clues, once one looks beyond the nonsensical insistence on wandering pastoralists. *Cirta* and *Zama* were described as eastern Numidian capitals, along with *Iol* and *Siga* on the Algerian coast further

112. Von Rummel et al. 2016, 101.
113. Rakob 1994.
114. Ghaki 1997a.
115. Golvin and Khanoussi 2005, 29–74 (Numidian *agora*); Khanoussi et al. 2004; Ritter and Von Rummel 2015 (House of Trifolium).
116. Aounallah et al. 2020a; 2020c.
117. Sghaïer and Dammak-Latrach 2020.
118. Ferchiou 1986a.
119. Benseddik 2012; Berthier 1980; 1981; Berthier and Charlier 1955. Many of the users of the tophet had semitic names, hinting at a resident alien element in the community, but some names were Libyan and it seems illogical to suppose that the cult was not being followed also by Numidians (McCarty 2017, 399).

west, while four cities were named as *Regia*, suggesting royal connection: *Bulla Regia*, *Hippo Regius*, *Thimida Regia*, and *Zama Regia*.[120] We can add in the evidence from the inland towns with suffetal magistrates (*Gadiaufala*, *Gales*, *Limisa*, *Masculula*, *Thugga*) and a range of other Numidian sites (including some coastal sites often assumed to be Punic foundations) where the literary testimony attests an urban presence prior to the 1st century BCE: *Calama*, *Camarata*, *Capsa*, *Gunugu*, *Icosium*, *Lares*, *Macomades*, *Mactaris*, *Madauros*, *Musti*, *Naragarra*, *Regiae*, *Rusicade*, *Saldae*, *Sicca*, *Simitthu*, *Suthul*, *Thabraca*, *Thaenae*, *Thagura*, *Thala*, *Timigi*, *Tisidium*, *Vaga*, *Zucchabar*.[121] I have already alluded to the epigraphic evidence relating to the 64 towns of *pagus Thuscae* and *Gunzuzi*, which occupied an area of c.80 (west–east) × 30–40 km (north–south) of the Tunisian Dorsal centred on *Mactaris*. A reference in Appian (*Punica* 3) to hundreds of Libyan cities ready to revolt against *Qart Hadasht* when Regulus invaded North Africa in 256 BCE has often been dismissed as hyperbole, but takes on a different significance when the possibility of such an advanced level of urbanisation is recognised.

Tuning back to the archaeology, there are tophets or sanctuaries of Baal/Saturn reported at quite a few Numidian inland towns, though many are presumed to postdate the Roman conquest: *Althiburos*, *Bagat*, *Bulla Regia*, *Cirta*, *Sicca*, *Furnos Maius*, Henchir el-Hami, *Mactaris*, *Magota*, *Maraci*, *Mididi*, *Simitthu*, *Thibilis*, *Thignica*, *Thuburnica*, *Thubursicu Numidarum*, *Thubursicu Bure*, *Tiddis*.[122] The predominance of Libyan toponyms is striking among the towns of "Roman Africa" and there are literally hundreds more sites that are potential candidates for nucleated Numidian settlements that went on to be urban settlements under Rome.

Another approach is to recognise that the vast majority of towns in the Numidian landscape were sited for defensive reasons on hilltops or on promontories between dry river courses, and this is in fact one of the key characteristics of large numbers of African towns.[123] Three examples from the *pagus Thuscae* and two from further west will serve as representative examples of the "wadi promontory spur" type, with *Althiburos* the type site, since its early Numidian origins are now demonstrated (Fig. 4.8). It occupied a defensible spur of land between two wadis, looking out to the north towards plainlands and protected by flanking hills. The Roman town eventually spilled out across a larger area,[124] but the early settlement appears to have been located on this narrow promontory c.500 × 120 m (6 ha). The characteristic elements here are the relatively small size and the location on a narrow defensible

120. Bénabou 1976, 406.
121. Bénabou 1976, 405–08.
122. D'Andrea 2014.
123. Ferchiou 1990a; 1990b, 1995b, 1998a; 2004a; 2004b; 2004c; Mattingly 2016.
124. Kallala and Sanmartí 2011, 10 suggest 28 ha, but that appears to include a lot of steep scarp and some suburban structures. Even at the peak of the Roman era, the urban core does not appear to have been much more than 12 ha.

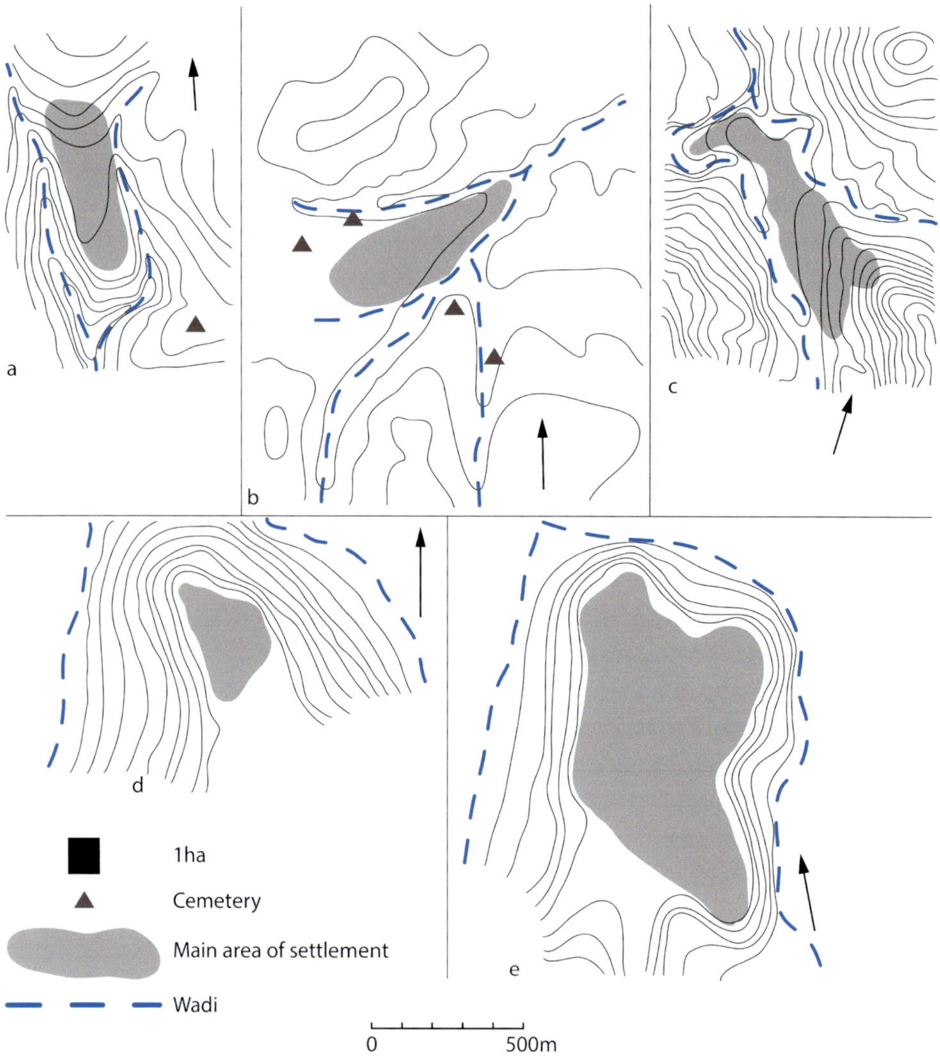

Figure 4.8. The wadi promontory spur type of proto-urban settlement. a) *Mididi*. b) *Bagat*. c) *Althiburos*. d) *Cuicul* e) *Cirta* (Mike Hawkes, from author's roughs).

spur, with dry streams constituting a substantial moat around much of the perimeter. The small Roman town of *Bagat* (Henchir Ghayadha), near *Zama Regia*, is another good example of the type.[125] The small walled site (8 ha only) sits on a defensible spur of land between two converging wadis. The urban core is surrounded by an extensive set of cemeteries, covering at least 25 ha and incorporating pre-Roman megalithic tombs and bazina monuments. There was a suburban sanctuary of Baal

125. M'Charek et al. 2008.

Hammon, later elaborated with a temple of Saturn, and Saturn stelae were also recovered in relation to one of the northern cemeteries. *Mididi* is another example of this same sort of setting, and although the Roman town eventually spread across c.30 ha, the original Numidian core presumably lay within the c.5 ha area on the top of the prominent plateau. Here again there was a cemetery of megalithic dolmens to the south of the site and numerous stelae to Baal Hammon and Saturn, including 18 Neo-Punic texts.[126] There were many other examples of this sort of topographic siting, perhaps most dramatically the sheer cliffs and steep escarpments of *Cirta* (Constantine) and *Cuicul* (Djemila), the latter normally considered a Roman foundation for a late 1st-century CE *colonia* (Fig. 4.8d, cf. Fig. 8.12).[127]

A second type of Numidian fortified settlement utilised "hilltop sites," sometimes with steep drops on one or more sides. Examples of the "hilltop fortress" include *Bulla Mensa* (Kalaat Senane), *Thala*, *Thugga*, *Tiddis* (Fig. 8.5–8.6), and *Uchi Maius*, with consequences for the layout of the Roman-era towns that followed.[128] Some of the larger Numidian centres occupied positions at the edge of plateau areas, where the land dropped away in at least one direction. Examples of "plateau-edge sites" include *Bulla Regia*, *Mactaris*, *Sicca Veneria*, *Zama Regia*.[129] There are also some examples of "low-lying settlements," often by rivers (*Simitthu*) or in mountain passes (*Capsa*).[130] A further factor in determining the locations of Numidian urban centres was evidently proximity to springs.[131]

Another clue to pre-Roman origins concerns extensive funerary zones of dolmens, haouanet, or Libyan tumuli and drum tombs in the immediate vicinity of later Roman settlements. The correlation is again very strong in the *pagus Thuscae* area, as at *Althiburos*, *Bagat*, *Mactaris*, *Mididi*, *Thucca Terebentina*, *Ulules*.[132] Similar patterns involving both dolmens and haouanet clustered by urban centres have been observed by Jean Peyras in the north-east Tunisian Tell.[133] Tumuli and bazinas are prominent in the landscape of the hinterland of *Qart Hadasht*, showing a strong Libyan presence on those lands.[134] This sort of evidence can be combined with the distribution of Libyan inscriptions, which are now being recognised in

126. Ben Baaziz 2000, 213–59.
127. Benseddik 2012 (*Cirta*); Février and Blanchard-Lemée 2019, 15 for a contour plan of *Cuicul*. The presence of a Libyan inscription from *Cuicul* is a further hint at its origins as a Numidian stronghold, Ghaki 1995, 102.
128. Berthier 1981 (Kalaat Senane); 2000 (*Tiddis*); Khanoussi and Mastiino 1997 (*Uchi Maius*); Khanoussi and Maurin 2002 (*Thugga*). See also Ferchiou 2004c for a similar but small site, Henchir Bou Nader.
129. Ferjaoui 2004 (*Zama Regia*); Montali 2015, 346–47 (*Bulla*).
130. Borderau 1907; Rakob 1993; Von Rummel et al. 2013.
131. Ferchiou 1998a.
132. Ben Baaziz 2000; Camps 1973a; 1995b; Kallala et al. 2017; Tanda et al. 2009.
133. Peyras 1991, 213–18.
134. Ferchiou 1987; Stone 2016b.

greater numbers around Roman-era urban settlements and again may be a clue to early origins (cf. Fig. 11.5).[135]

Table 4.2 summarises some of this evidence for a range of potential Numidian urban centres (plus a small number of settlements in the Gaetulian zone to the south). The data are far from complete, and further investigation will no doubt reveal additional markers at many of these sites and of other sites that can be added to the list. I offer it as a starting point on which we can build.[136] The sites fall into a number of groups (Fig. 4.9): there is a core distribution in north-eastern Algeria and north-western Tunisia that corresponds with the projected heartlands of the *Massyli*; and a thinner distribution in central and western Algeria that relates to the *Masaesyli*. In the north-eastern Tell and the lower *Bagrada* and *Miliane* valleys, the distribution relates to the *Afri* and overlaps with the westward expansion of the Carthaginian territory (*pertica*). The conventional narrative of the *chora/pagus Thuscae* is that it was the result of Carthaginian urban and agricultural expansion deep into the hinterland, with Massinissa later wresting control away from *Qart Hadasht* in the 2nd century BCE. The new evidence suggests a different scenario—that this was essentially a Numidian expansion south of the core Massylian territory, that later came under Carthaginian domination, but was reclaimed by the Numidian kingdom. In a similar way, much of the early urban development in the north-east Tell and lower *Bagrada* valley may have been originally Numidian, linking to the tumuli and haouanet cemeteries in the landscape. It is striking that these sorts of tombs are absent in the closest hinterland of *Qart Hadasht*, where more traditionally Punic forms predominate, but that the wider expansion of Carthaginian territory did not see a more general spread of Punic burial types. The urban and agricultural development of the lands between the early Phoenician centres at *Utica* and *Qart Hadasht* thus appear to be more plausibly linked to early "Numidian" developments coming under Carthaginian authority, as the power of *Qart Hadasht* grew.[137] The *pagus Gunzuzi* appears to have been another area of Numidian towns to the north-east of the *pagus Thuscae* and across the *fossa regia* dividing Carthaginian and Numidian territory.[138] It was probably also one of the three *pagi* (*Muxsi*, *Gususi*, and *Zeugei*) in Carthaginian territory named in an inscription from *Utica*.[139]

These *pagi* and others that are mentioned in the early Roman period thus appear to have been predominantly Numidian/Libyan districts, whose control had been contested between *Qart Hadasht* and the Numidian state in the latter centuries BCE. South of the *pagus Thuscae* was another region that appears to

135. For the evidence, Camps 1978; Chabot 1940; Rebuffat 2013. For distribution maps, Ghaki 1995.

136. The data are built on works cited in the above section, plus my own visits to some sites and Google Earth investigation of others.

137. Peyras 1991.

138. M'Charek 1999.

139. *ILAf* 2422; Picard et al. 1963, 127;

have been known as *Gamonia* and that extended approximately from Kairouan to the modern Algerian border.[140] This was evidently a border zone between *Numidae* and *Gaetuli*. It is evident that there were some potential early urban centres to the south of the eastern Numidian core territory (sites like *Theveste*, *Thala*, *Capsa*), whether outposts of Numidian power or precocious Gaetulian urban centres. It is notable that most of the sites shown in Figure 4.9 were located in the zone of the Maghrib that receives in excess of 400 mm of rainfall annually.

Table 4.2. List of locations (mainly Roman-era towns) with possible evidence for Numidian proto-urban origins (Pre-R occ. = pre-Roman occupation; FP site = fortified promontory or hilltop site; stelae = Tophet/Saturn stelae; "Royal" archit = "Royal" mausoleum or other Numidian monumental architecture; Cemy = **D**olmen/**H**anouet/**B**azina cemetery; Punic epig. = Punic inscriptions; Libyan epig. = Libyan inscriptions; Latoin lit. or epig. = Latin source refs or inscriptions).

Ancient name	**Modern name**	**Pre-R occ.**	**FP site**	**Stelae**	**'Royal' archit.**	**Cemy**	**Punic epig.**	**Libyan epig.**	**Latin lit. or epig.**
?	Henchir el-Hami (region of el-Kef)			*			*		
?	Bir Meraktit							*	
Althiburos	Henchir Medina	*	*	*		D		*	*
Ascururm	Ascous							*	
Assuras	Zanfour							*	
Autipsida	Ain M'dhoja					D		*	
Auzia	Sour el-Ghozlan							*	
Bagat	Henchir Ghayadha	*	*	*		D	*	*	
Belalis Maior	Henchir el-Faour			*					
Biha Bilta	Henchir Behia					H			
Bulla Mensa?	Kalaat Senane		*			DH			
Bulla Regia	Hammam Derradj	*	*	*		DH			*
Calama	Guelma						*	*	*
Camarata	?								*
Capsa	Gafsa								*
Chiniava	Henchir Gueriba		*			H			
Chullu	Collo					D			
Chusira	Kesra		*	*		D	*		
Cirta	Constantine	*	*	*	*	DH	*	*	*
Cuicul	Djemila		*					*	

(Continued)

140. M'Charek 1999, 158–76.

Table 4.2. *(Continued)*

Ancient name	**Modern name**	**Pre-R occ.**	**FP site**	**Stelae**	**'Royal' archit.**	**Cemy**	**Punic epig.**	**Libyan epig.**	**Latin lit. or epig.**
Furnos Maius	Ain Fourna		*	*					
Gadiaufala	Ksar Sbahi		*						*
Gales	Henchir Kharrouba								*
Gunugu	Gouraya	*							*
Hippo Regius	Annaba	*	?	*				*	*
Icosium	Algiers	*		*		D			*
Iol	Cherchel	*		*	*		*		*
Iomnium	Tigzirt			*					
Lares	Lorbeus								*
Limisa	Ksar Lemsa							*	*
Macomades	Henchir el-Mergueb								
Mactaris	Maktar			*		D	*	*	
Madauros	Mdaourouch							*	
Magota	Maghraoua		*	*		D	*	*	
Maraci	Ksar Toual Zammeul			*					
Masculula	Henchir Guergour								*
Membressa	Mejez el-Bab							*	
Mididi	Henchir Mided	*	*	*		D	*	*	
Milev	Mila			*				*	
Musti	Henchir Mist	*						*	*
Muzuca	Henchir Khachoun							*	
Naragarra	Sakiet Sidi Youssef								*
Neferis	Hr Bou Baker		*					*	
Numluli	Henchir el-Matria		*						
Onellaba	Borj bou Lares		*					*	
Oppidum Materense	Mateur			*					
Oppidum Novum	Ain Defla							*	
[*Civitas*] *Popthensis*	Ksiba Mraoui		*	*			*	*	

Table 4.2. *(Continued)*

Ancient name	Modern name	Pre-R occ.	FP site	Stelae	'Royal' archit.	Cemy	Punic epig.	Libyan epig.	Latin lit. or epig.
Portus Magnus	Bethioua			*					
Regiae	?								*
Rusicade	Skikda			*					*
Rusippisir	Taksebt			*					
Rusucurru	Dellys			*					
Saldae	Bougie			*					*
Sicca Veneria	Le Kef		*			D		*	*
Siga	Takembrit		*						*
Sigus	Sigus		*	*		D	*	*	
Sila	Bordj-El-Ksar					D			
Simitthu	Chemtou	*		*	*	DB		*	*
Suas	Chaouach		*			DH			
Sululos	Bir el-Hech		*						
Sustrii	Henchir el-Ergueia		*					*	
Suthul	?								*
Suttua (pagus Suttuensis)	Henchir Chett							*	
Thabarbusis	Ain Nechma			*					
Thabraca	Tabarka					H			*
Thaenae	Henchir Thina								*
Thagaste	Souk Ahras		*	*				*	
Thagura	Taoura							*	*
Thala	Thala		*			D			*
Theveste	Tebessa							*	*?
Thibaris	Henchir Thibar			*					
Thibilis	Announa		*	*					
Thigibba	Henchir Zouakra			*		D			
Thigibba Bure	Djebba		*			D			
Thignica	Ain Tonga		*	*					
Thimida Bure	Kouchbatia		*			D			
Thimida Regia	La Mohammadia?			*					*
Thuburbo Maius	Henchir Kasbat			*					
Thuburnica	Sidi Ali Bel Kassem			*				*	

(Continued)

Table 4.2. *(Continued)*

Ancient name	Modern name	Pre-R occ.	FP site	Stelae	'Royal' archit.	Cemy	Punic epig.	Libyan epig.	Latin lit. or epig.
Thubursicu Bure	Teboursouk		*	*		D	*	*	
Thubursicu Numidarum	Khamissa		*	*				*	*
Thuccabori	Toukabeur		*			H			
Thucca Terebentina	Henchir Dougga					D			
Thugga	Dougga	*	*	*	*	DHB	*	*	*
Thunusuda	Borj Hellal		*					*	
Tiddis	El-Kheneg		*	*		B			
Timigi	?								*
Tipasa	Tipasa	*		*		H		*	*
Tisidium	?								*
Uccula	Henchir Douirat		*			H			
Uchi Maius	Henchir Douamis		*						*
Ulules	Elles		*	*		D		*	
Ureu	Bordj Ourau		*			H			
Urusi	Henchir Soudga		*					*	
Uzali Sar...	Henchir Jall	*	*			DH			
Uzappa	Ksour Abdelmalek						*	*	
Uzalis	Oudjiel			*				*	
Vaga	Beja ez Zit								*
Vasampus	Sidi Abdulla?							*	
Zama Regia	Jama	*	*	*	*				*
Zucchabar	?								*

The east coast of Tunisia (*Byzacium*) has more convincing evidence for Libyphoenician urbanism, but the development of the hinterland also seems to have involved Libyan communities with three Libyan *civitates* (*Gurza*, *Uzita*, and *Cynasyn*) combined in a *pagus Gurzensis*.[141] I shall return to north-west Libya (Tripolitania) in the next chapter. Along the north coast of *Numidia*, we have seen in chapter 3 that the evidence for Phoenician settlement is not entirely convincing

141. *CIL* 8.68; Ghaddab 2020; Picard et al. 1963, 127.

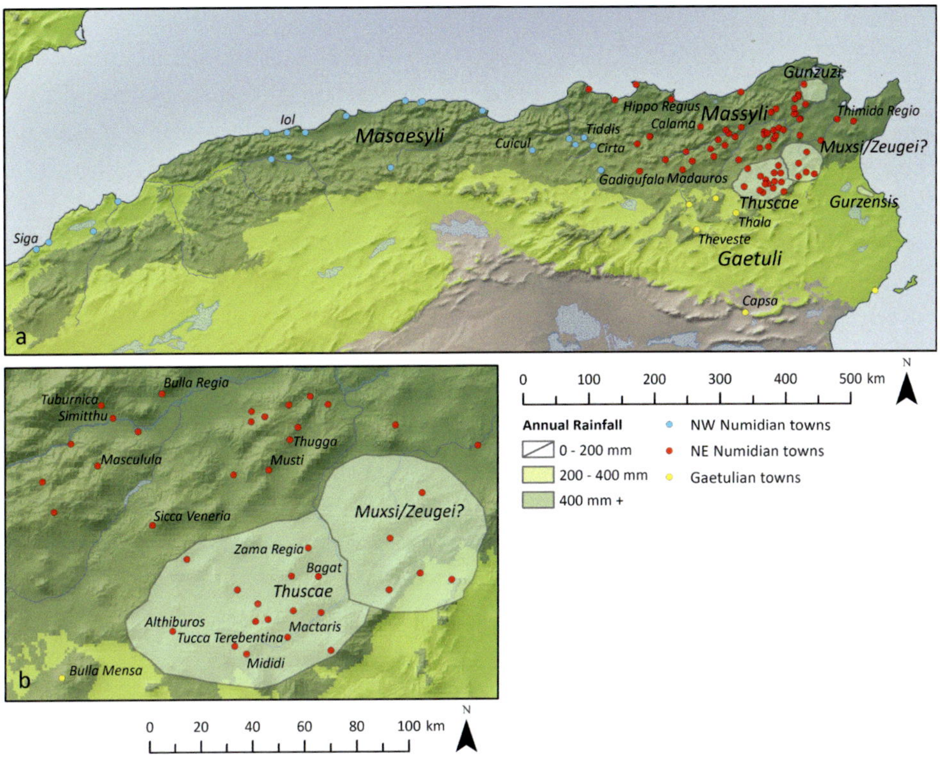

Figure 4.9. Distribution of Numidian and related proto-urban sites. a) Overall map of sites identified in Table 4.2, with hypothetical *pagi* boundaries and notional assignment to different population groups. b) Detail of *Pagus Thuscae* area (Martin Sterry, from author's rough).

at many of the sites traditionally postulated as *emporia*, and some of these locations are in fact known to have royal associations for the Numidian monarchy (*Siga*, *Iol*). That these sites were somewhat hybrid in cultural character is evident from the diversity of the burial practices (megalithic dolmens and haouanet are rare close to the seaboard). At any rate, as an agricultural and urban society, the Numidian peoples may have played a much larger role in the development of such sites than traditionally allowed. The *emporia* were not just staging posts along the African coast or entry points into Africa for Punic and other merchants, but also portals out to the Mediterranean world for the emerging Numidian society.

In combination, these indications strongly support a more generous reading of the indications in the literary sources and a different model of Numidian urbanisation. While urbanism was particularly flourishing by the latter centuries BCE, it can be argued that this built on a much older tradition of sedentary settlement and agrarian economy. Our default assumption now must be that other sites mentioned as "Numidian" centres in the later centuries BCE are also likely to have originated as sedentary nucleated settlements in the early 1st millennium BCE.

These sites may initially have been villages in terms of scale and sophistication, but it is now clear that they were on a pathway to urbanisation long before the rise of Massinissa. Indeed the potential numbers and wealth of these sorts of agricultural settlements in the Tunisian Tell were presumably a prime reason for the rise in the power of the *Massyli* in that region. The recent excavations have radically transformed our view of the sophistication of Massylian society in the early 1st millennium BCE. The emergence of state-level society in the last centuries BCE was not a sudden revolution, but the outcome of a long process of socio-economic transformation that ran in parallel with that of the coastal settlements of the Libyphoenicians or the settlements of *Afri* in the Carthaginian territory in north-east Tunisia.[142]

In cultural terms, it is hard to deny some profound influences on Numidian society from *Qart Hadasht*.[143] The Punic written script and language is attested at a number of Numidian sites, most notably in the great bilingual texts from *Thugga*, but Punic/Libyan bilinguals are also known from *Mactaris* and *Sigus*, for example. In general, Neo-Punic texts have been recorded more commonly at Numidian sites than Punic ones (which are rare), suggesting the wider uptake of Punic was relatively late in pre-Roman times.[144] However, as is clear from the references to spoken Punic in Saint Augustine's writing, the longevity of Punic in the Numidian heartlands was astonishing.[145] Commentary on the bilinguals from *Thugga* and what they reveal about Numidian municipal organisation has changed radically as understanding of the ancient Libyan script has improved. From an initial view that the titles of urban offices derived closely from Carthaginian practice, it is now evident that the Numidian titulature reflects local preoccupations and innovations to a much greater extent than previously thought.[146] While some terms relate to the upper organisation of society (king: "GLD"; chiefs of the 100/wise men/elders: "MWṢN"), other titles are plausibly linked to Libyan words/titles for specialist roles related to the major construction projects of the late Numidian era: chief of 50/head of construction ("GLDMṢK"); architect/builder ("MṢṢKW"); inspector of works ("GẒB"); supervisor of the works ("GLDGMYL").[147]

---

142. Sanmartí et al. 2020 for a sophisticated discussion on the nature of Numidian state formation and what it encompassed. See also Altaweel and Squitieri 2018 for parallel developments in Near Eastern societies and reflections on how this led on to incorporation in megastates and empires.
143. Krandel-Ben Younès 2002 for a detailed summary of multiple strands of evidence.
144. Ghaki 1995, 106; Rebuffat 2013.
145. Lepelley 2005a for the most thorough review of the textual evidence. On the other hand, it is equally remarkable how little evidence there is for spoken Libyan language in the written sources, Lengrand 2005.
146. For the initial views linking titles more closely with Punic organisational structures, see Février 1965.
147. Camps 1994a, after Chaker 1986; Ghaki 1997a. The reference to a possible council of elders provides an echo of long tradition in Berber societies, Shaw 1991b.

The great ashlar masonry tombs of the Numidian kingdom fall into several types.[148] Most are tower tombs (turriform), with a pyramidical uppermost section, as in the reconstructed monument at *Thugga* or the As Soumaa mausoleum at Al Kroub near *Cirta* (and intervisible from that city).[149] There is also an example of a tower tomb with hexagonal ground plan and concave sides, Beni Rhenane by *Siga* (with parallels from Libyphoenician *Sabratha* and Henchir Bourgou in Tripolitania).[150] There are also two great masonry tumuli: the Tombeau de la Chretienne (Kbor ar Roumia), intervisible from the city of *Tipasa* on the coast; and the Medracen in the Aurès plains, far from any known early Numidian centre.[151] There are also some panoply monuments with relief decoration of weaponry and shields in a Hellenistic tradition, notably at *Simitthu* and Kbor Klib, the latter close to *Zama Regia* and potentially a monument commemorating from a Numidian perspective the site of the battle of *Zama*.[152] The largest of the tombs are over 30 m tall: Kbor ar Roumia is 64 m diameter and 33 m tall, the Medracen 59 m diameter. The dating of these various monuments (and their possible association with various royal personages) has been much debated. Pomponius Mela (1.31) confirmed the royal association of Kbor ar Roumia. For many of the monuments, the dating evidence suggests a range of options across the 3rd–1st centuries BCE and the interconnection of the *Numidae* with a wider Hellenistic world.[153] It is probably less important that we can connect individual monuments with known individuals as opposed to the recognition that Numidian society possessed the technical competence, the ambition, and the wherewithal to construct such extraordinary monuments at this time.

The cult of Baal and Tinnit was widespread in eastern Numidian lands (though much less so among the western *Numidae*) and this was reinforced in the Roman period in the continued worship of Baal as Saturn in the same territory.[154] At the al-Hofra tophet by *Cirta*, the diversity of worshippers reflected a particularly cosmopolitan community at the Numidian capital, with a very high use of Punic language, but also evidence of Greeks and Italians.[155] More typical of the Numidian Baal/Tinnit cult centres are the sanctuaries investigated at *Althiburos*, Henchir el-Hami

148. Quinn 2013, 183–86 for a brief summary. See also bibliography referred to in note 31 above.
149. A second but slightly smaller turriform mausoleum has now been identified at *Thugga* as well. Aounallah et al. 2020a.
150. Di Vita 2015a; Ferchiou in Fentress et al. 2009, 107–28.
151. Though the argument advanced here for greater advances in Numidian urbanisation might suggest that the isolation of the Medracen far from the nearest town may be worth revisiting—especially in relation to the Gaetulian centre of Ichoukkane, south of Timgad. See Fentress 1979, 32, 39.
152. Kuttner 2013; Rakob 1994; Ross 2005 (for linkage with battle of *Zama*).
153. Hellenistic influences: Coarelli and Thébert 1988; Kuttner 2013; Quinn 2013. Fentress, pers. comm. is doubtful about the reliability of a supposedly earlier radiocarbon date of the Medracen (Camps 1973b).
154. D'Andrea 2014 for an up-to-date gazetteer, building on Leglay 1961; 1966a; 1966b.
155. McCarty 2017; 2019; See also Berthier and Charlier 1955 (al-Hofra, *Cirta*); Bertrandy and Sznycer 1987; Camps 1994a.

and *Thugga*, with more anepigraphic stelae but also evidence of long-continuing observance of sacrificial rites into the Roman period.[156] The transition from the cult of Baal and Tinnit to Saturn and Caelestis in the Roman period has been often remarked on. I shall return to this in Chapter 11. What I want to insist on at this point, though, is that just as the Punic language was widely adopted in a multilingual society, the scale of practice of the Baal/Tinnit cult demonstrates that it was a key element of the religious identity of the Numidians.[157] That has major implications, not just for how the cult developed in North Africa differently to its practice elsewhere in the Phoenician/Punic worlds, but also for how we may discern difference between the Numidians and other autochthonous peoples of the Maghrib in antiquity and the legacy of this in Roman provincial societies.

Funerary practices among the *Numidae* were quite varied, as already alluded to above—though given that the dating of many monument types is extremely uncertain, we cannot exclude the possibility that the diversity represents change over time.[158] Some of the megalithic tombs appear to be quite early within the 1st millennium BCE, but the tradition was still continuing down to late Numidian times, and even in the Roman era there was activity around some of the tombs.[159] The general consensus is that most of the tombs postdate the 5th century BCE, but there is a danger of circularity since dating often relies on diagnostic grave goods, which are rare to non-existent before that time. Relatively few radiocarbon determinations have been done and these may be compromised by sampling on secondary or later interventions.[160] The larger tombs were certainly designed to accommodate multiple interments, and the complex processes of reopening the tombs and adding additional bodies and material often involved disturbance and even removal of prior material.[161] Bodies were commonly laid on the side and red ochre was often present. These features have also been noted at some "Punic" burials nearer the coast, but they appear to relate to African traditions.[162]

The haouanet are another distinctive category of tomb—though much less is known of their contents, as their visibility in the landscape has led to them being

156. Aounallah et al. 2020c (*Thugga*). Ferjaoui 2007 (Henchir el-Hami); Kallala et al. 2018 (*Althiburos*).
157. Krandel-Ben Younès 2002, 152–282. See McCarty 2017, 395–96 for the important argument that this was not simply an adoption of Phoenician cult, but a conscious reinvention of the 1st-century BCE Numidians.
158. Ben Younès and Krandel-Ben Younès 2014; Krandel-Ben Younès 2002, 21–151 (see also Krandel-Ben Younès 1988; 1993 for the development of her thinking).
159. Camps 1961, 146–48 suggested that megalithic dolmens are 1st millennium but before main Punic contacts; Ghaki 2003; Krandel-Ben Younès 2002, 148–51 suggests most postdate 500 BCE.
160. For *Althiburos*, Kallala et al. 2014a; 2017, 38 (tomb SP370005, continued Roman use), 41 (tomb 647, 700–400 calBCE), 42 (tomb 42, later centuries BCE), 43–48 (tomb 53, construction 6th–5th century BC but continued modification and use into early Roman imperial period), 49–51 (tomb 2nd–1st century BCE).
161. Aounallah et al. 2020a; Krandel-Ben Younès 1993, 86–92; Ghaki 1997b.
162. Ben Younès and Krandel-Ben Younès 2014, 157–68; Krandel-Ben Younès 2002, 112–34; Tanda et al. 2009, 303–06.

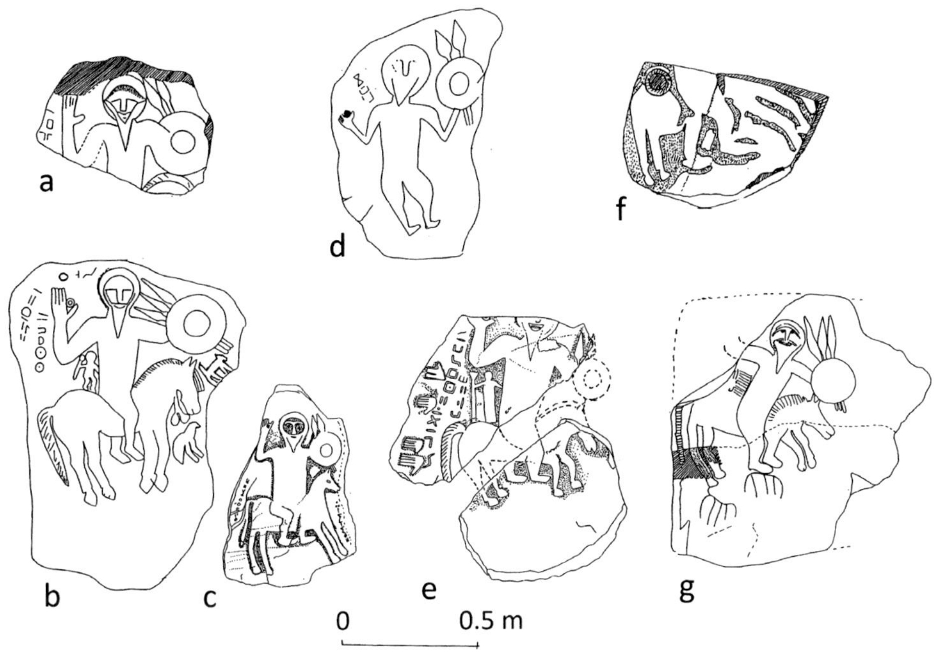

Figure 4.10. Horse and rider stelae from Algeria. a) Thensaouth. b) Abizar. c–d) Souama. e) Bou Djemaa. f) Thala Gala. g) Cheurfa (author's montage from Laporte 1992, 394–95).

robbed. However, the rock-cut chambers, often with niches, columns, and painted decoration (including people, animals, and geometric designs) are a rich source of information. The earliest dating of these tombs remains uncertain, but the period of construction certainly continued late in the 1st millennium BCE.[163] While they imitate some aspects of the coastal tombs of broadly Punic types, there are also significant differences in their morphology and elaboration.

Attempts to narrowly interpret the different tomb types (dolmens, haouanet, tumuli/bazinas) in terms of broad ethnic groups are hazardous as the distributions are overlapping. However, the heartlands of the eastern *Numidae* do seem to match well with the distribution of the dolmen burials (Fig. 4.3). Another way of thinking about this variability, though, is that it reflects diverse influences within and upon Numidian society (Punic, Maghribian, Saharan).[164] It is also probable that the range of tombs reflects the impact of broader cultural changes during the 1st millennium BCE, with the spread of urbanism and agriculture.

A final point to make about Numidian civilisation is that it was very much a horse culture. That is to say, the rearing, owning, and riding of horses were crucial aspects

163. Stone 2007a; 2007b for an excellent English summary of both the tombs and their landscape context. On the interior decoration see, inter alia, Camps 1992a; Camps and Longerstay 2000; Ghaki 1999a; Longerstay 1995; 2011.

164. Cf. Camps 1961; Stone 2007a; 2007b.

of wealth, power, and status in Maghribian society. The proficiency of Numidian and Moorish horsemen in battle was celebrated, and in fact the Numidians provided the bulk of the Carthaginian cavalry wings in many wars.[165] Leadership and power were very much bound up with the image of the armed horseman (often bearing a small circular shield and three short spears)—whether featuring on the coins of Numidian kings or on the extraordinary stelae of the Kabylie area of northern Algeria (Fig. 4.10).[166] We shall also encounter horse imagery recurrently in relation to the *Mauri* and the desert peoples. No doubt it was one of the things that helped unite the different elements of these societies, both the sedentary farmers and the pastoral groups who also occupied parts of the landscape.

The *Mauri*

There is less direct evidence for the evolution of the Mauretanian kingdom in the western Maghrib.[167] However, the *Mauri* can be recognised to have been relatively closely related to the *Numidae* in that they seem to belong to the same linguistic branch of the Berber language tree as the *Numidae*.[168] When the Mauretanian kingdom under the rule of Juba II became a key client state of Rome in the late 1st century BCE, its territory was expanded to include the lands of the western *Numidae* (*Masaesyli*).[169]

Strabo (*Geography* 17.3.2) located on the North African side of the Straits of Gibraltar the people "whom the Greeks call Maurusians, and the Romans and the natives *Mauri*—a large and prosperous *ethnos*."[170] Pliny (*NH* 5.17) identified the *Mauri* as the principal people of *Mauretania Tingitana*, though noting that by his day their numbers had been diminished by war to a few clans (*ad paucas familas*).[171] Ptolemy (*Geography* 4.1–2) perhaps implied something similar when he listed the *Maurenses* and the *Masaesyli* as just two among many minor peoples of *Mauretania*. The same stereotypes that were applied to the *Numidae* were also linked to the *Mauri* in the ancient sources. Strabo (*Geography* 17.3.7) hinted at the contradiction in his account when he stated: "Although most of the country inhabited by the Maurusians is so fertile, yet even to this time most of the people persist in living a nomadic life."

165. Ait Amara 2013.
166. Coins and horses: Alexandropolous 2000; Mazard 1955. Stelae from Algeria: Camps et al. 1999; Février 1979; Laporte 1992; Rebuffat 2013.
167. For overviews, see, inter alia, Coltelloni-Trannoy 1997; 2010; Lassère 2015, 47–48; Sennequier and Colonia 2003, 139–47.
168. Ehret 2019; Fentress 2019.
169. Coltelloni-Trannoy 1997; 2011a; Gsell 1928a, 156–57, 199–200; 210–12.
170. *Ethnos* is translated in the Loeb edition as "tribe."
171. Desanges 1962, 35–36; 1980b, 144–45.

As a starting proposition, it seems reasonable to suggest that the *Mauri*, *Masaesyli*, and *Massyli* of the early 1st millennium BCE were broadly similar societies, with a mix of sedentary farmers and pastoral groups, a shared language (or at any rate closely related dialects), a strong emphasis on cavalry warfare and advanced pyrotechnologies including metalworking, and increasingly more sophisticated pottery production over time. All three of these peoples were distinct from the peoples who lived to their south, generally known as *Gaetuli* and almost certainly belonging to a different linguistic branch. Initially, the name *Mauri* seems to have been limited to the inhabitants of the far western extremity of the Maghrib, broadly the area of northern Morocco. The origins of their name are not certain, though it evidently came from the local population, rather than being externally imposed (Strabo 17.3.2). Some scholars have suggested a connection with the toponym later applied to the Aurès mountain, making them potentially "people of the mountains" or perhaps "people of the mountainous region"[172]—a reference that would be very applicable to their initial heartlands in the plainlands of modern Morocco encircled by the Atlas ranges to the south and the Rif region to east. The *Mulucha* river that marked the ancient divide between *Mauri* and the *Masaesyli* essentially takes its waters from the eastern flank of the Rif.

Pliny (*NH* 5.17) confirmed the *Masaesyli* as the nearest neighbours of the *Mauri* and there is a suggestion in Livy (24.49.5) that some of the *Mauri* were vassals of Syphax. However, between the late 2nd century BCE and early 1st century CE the Mauretanian kingdom was extended at certain moments to the east of the *Mulucha* encompassing parts of the territory of the *Masaesyli*.[173] As a result of these extensions, the *Mauri* were in Roman times associated with a much broader sweep of territory encompassed by the Mauretanian provinces. Further change occurred by late antiquity, when the *Mauri* were synonymous not only with the western Maghrib but also with the peoples bordering the more settled territories of the eastern Maghrib and Syrtica as well.[174] For the moment, it is the earlier *Mauri* of northern Morocco that we shall focus on.

Given the lack of hard evidence on the early stages of their evolution in the 1st millennium BCE, it is instructive to reflect on the parallelism with the rise of the Numidian kings in the last centuries BCE. The *Mauri* are mentioned in relation to Carthaginian history from the mid-5th century.[175] There is a first reference to an unnamed king of the *Mauri* as early as the mid-4th century BCE (Justin 21.4.7).

172. Lassère 2015, 47.

173. Coltelloni-Trannoy 1997.

174. Desanges 1980b, 145: "Il devait désigner par la suite, au déclin de la romanité, tous les africains restées en dehors de la romanisation"; Hamdoune 2018, 153–426; Merrills 2022; Modéran 2003, 445–540.

175. Gsell 1927a, 91; Justin 19.2.4 (mid-5th century, war with Mauri); Diodorus 13.80.3 (late 5th century, *Qart Hadasht* recruiting troops from allied Mauri).

Around the time that Massinissa was gaining his ascendancy in *Numidia* in the late 3rd century BCE, we hear of a king of the *Mauri*, Baga. The details of a dynastic line are sketchy down to the later 2nd century, when a ruler called Bocchus took power, ruling till around 80 BCE and succeeded by two surviving sons, Bogud and Sosus Mastanesosus, with the latter's sons (Bogud and Bocchus the younger) succeeding him around 43 BCE. Following the death of the younger Bocchus in 33 BCE, control of the Mauretanian territory seems to have passed to Rome for eight years, before Augustus installed Juba II, son of the last king of independent *Numidia*, as client king of *Mauretania*. He ruled from 25 BCE to 23 CE, being succeeded by his son Ptolemy, who was eventually assassinated on the orders of Caligula c.40 CE—leading to the formal annexation of the kingdom and formation of Rome's Mauretanian provinces.[176]

Juba II in particular stands out among the Berber kings as an extraordinary cosmopolitan individual—educated at Rome and married off to the daughter of Cleopatra and Mark Antony, he made his capital at *Iol* a testament to his Hellenistic and Roman attachments and acquired a reputation as a scholarly king—authoring many works on a huge range of subjects.[177] Mostly written in Greek, his literary works sadly survive only in fragments that were quoted by later authors, such as Plutarch or Pliny the Elder, but he was recognised as "the most learned of kings" and "among the most polymathic Greek scholars" (Plutarch, *Sertorius* 9.5; *Caesar* 55.2). While the specific external influences are apparent here, what can easily be missed is the extent to which his achievements and his wealth were founded on a long-established, economically developed, well-organised and populous kingdom. Even in his literary exploits, Juba II was following in a tradition dating back to his grandfather, Hiempsal of *Numidia* (Sallust, *Jugurtha* 17), and exploited the fact that Rome had handed over parts of the Carthaginian state library to their Numidian allies at the fall of *Qart Hadasht*.[178]

Archaeological Evidence for the Mauri

As discussed in the previous chapter, the ancient sources strongly emphasise the contribution of "Phoenicians" or "Carthaginians" to the development of Morocco in the 1st millennium BCE. Pseudo-Skylax (111.9) says this explicitly: "As many townships or trading towns as have been written in *Libye*, from the Syrtis beside Hesperides as far as the Pillars of Herakles in *Libye*, are all of the *Karchedonai*

176. On the Mauretanian dynasty see, Coltelloni-Trannoy 1997, 9–14; 2010; Desanges 1989a; Gsell 1927b, 91.
177. Gsell 1928b, 251–76; Roller 2003, 163–82 for a detailed discussion of his literary outputs.
178. Roller 2003, 27.

[Carthaginians]." Beyond the Pillars of Herakles down the Atlantic coast of Africa, the Phoenician traders were equally evident as dominant players (112.1–12).[179] Strabo (*Geography* 17.3.2) likewise mentions the *Emporicus* Gulf south of *Lixus*/*Tingi*, containing "settlements of Phoenician merchants." These sources have led many modern scholars to ascribe any sites with evidence of imports of the 1st millennium BCE to "Phoenician" settlers.[180] As related in the previous chapter, this has started to be challenged recently.[181] Another dominant discourse of recent date, focused on Iberian influences in the "Circle of the Straits,"[182] is also being re-evaluated.[183]

This section will assess the evidence of funerary monuments and sedentary settlement for an improved understanding of the *Mauri* (Fig. 4.11). The most striking monuments of the 1st millennium BCE are funerary in nature and are mostly located in the plainlands of north-western Morocco, rather than in the mountainous periphery.[184] A number of these funerary monuments are of very substantial scale and are suggestive of the emergence of strongly hierarchical aspects of society during the 1st millennium BCE.[185] For example, the Mzora tumulus was c.6 m high and >50 m in diameter, with a ring of standing stones marking its outer edge.[186] The dating of the monument remains contentious, but is considered to potentially be as early as the 4th century BCE.[187] It is plausibly identified with the ancient tomb "excavated" on the orders of the rebel Roman commander Sertorius in the 1st century BCE.[188] Mzora lies away from the coast and between the major sites of *Zilil* and *Lixus*. Some of the other major tombs were situated close to sites that later emerged as major Roman centres, as in the case of Sidi Jari (40 m diameter) near *Lixus*, or Sidi Slimane (47 m diameter, with an elaborate rectangular stone funerary chamber at its centre) c.8 km south of Rirha (see below).[189] Both these and others that are more remotely located, Papi has argued should be seen in relation to the emergence of large chieftainships, denoted by the names of peoples mentioned in the sources of the later 1st millennium BCE.[190] Rare imports among reported grave goods from the major tombs allow a few to be dated approximatively—Sidi Slimane to the 3rd or more likely early 2nd century BCE and the Lalla Momouna

179. Shipley 2011, 85–87 with discussion 200–10.
180. Carcopino 1944; see also discussion in Chapter 3.
181. Bokbot 1991; 2020; Papi 2014; 2019.
182. Coltelloni-Trannoy et al. 2016.
183. Papi 2016.
184. Though the largest tumulus of all, at around 100 m diameter has been recorded near Taza: Bokbot 2020, 492.
185. Bokbot 2019; 2020; Papi 2019; Souville 1973.
186. Camps 1961, 76–78; Bokbot 2020, 491.
187. Gozalbes Cravioto 2006; 2018; Papi 2019, 294.
188. Gozalbes Cravioto 2018, 10.
189. On Sidi Jari, Souville 1973, 39; on Sidi Slimane, Bokbot 2020, 492–93; Callegarin et al. 2016b, 85–90, 117–19; Camps 1961, 196–99.
190. Papi 2019, 283–85, 289–93.

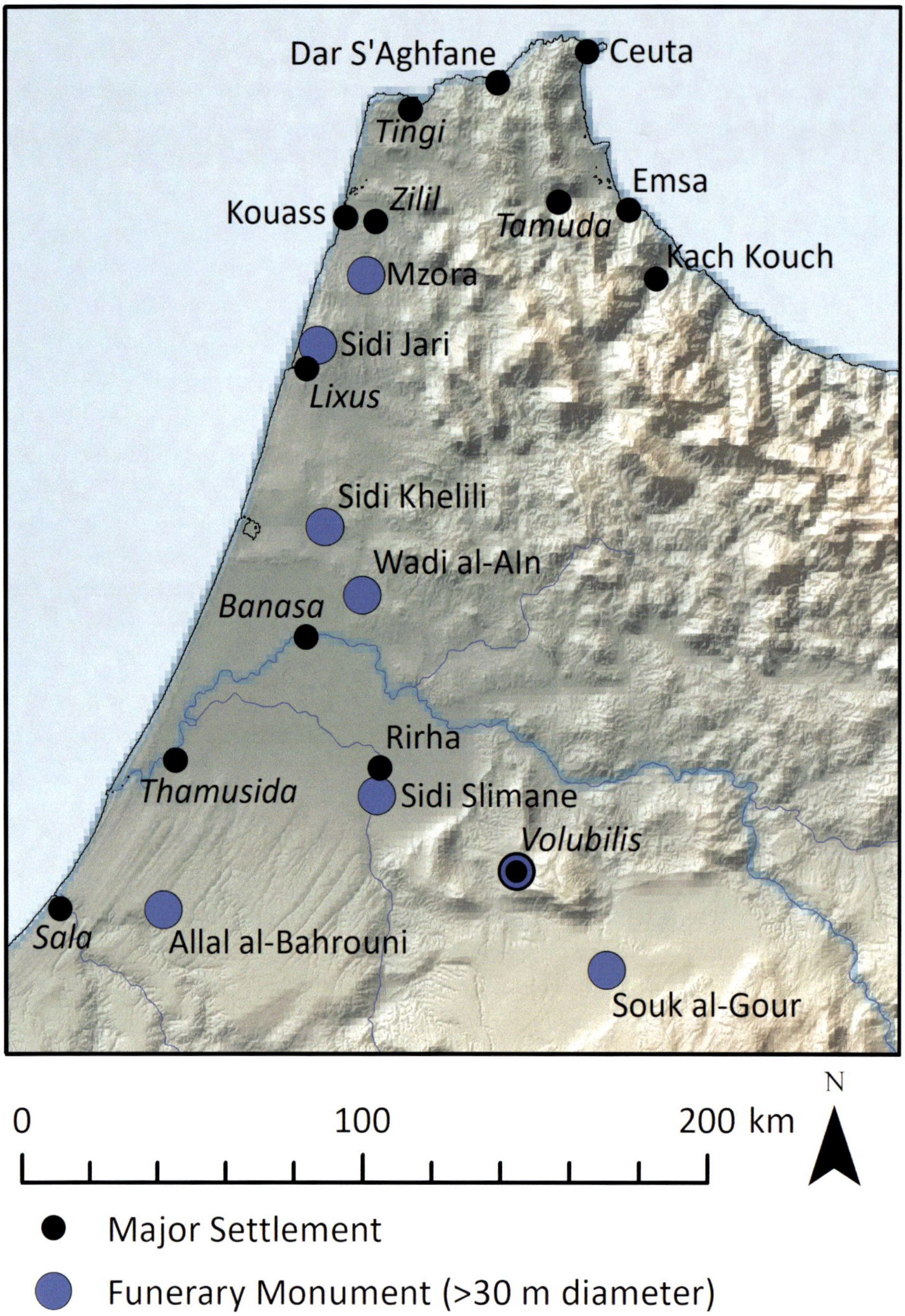

Figure 4.11. Principal north Moroccan Iron Age funerary monuments and settlements discussed (Martin Sterry from author's rough, after Papi 2019, 284 with additions).

(between *Lixus* and *Banasa*) to the 5th-3rd centuries BCE.[191] The larger monuments easily bear comparison with the scale of the major Numidian tombs (Tombeau de la Chrétienne, Medracen), and the late antique tombs of Mauretania including both the great stepped monument of more Saharan type (bazina) of al-Gour (south-east of *Volubilis*) and the "royal" monuments known as Djeddar.[192] They certainly represented a conspicuous investment of communal labour and far exceed in scale the typical tumuli and minor burials of this period. Youssef Bokbot associates the display manifest in the tombs with a growth in chiefly power and authority.

Within the wider landscape there were many smaller-scale tumuli and dense cemeteries of east–west aligned trapezoidal cist graves constructed of stone slabs, in which individuals were generally laid on their left side in an extended position.[193] Although the dating of many of the burials is uncertain, a focus on the middle centuries of the 1st millennium BCE is reasonable. The form of burials and their orientation, the deposition of the body on its side, the coating of the body with red ochre, and the nature of associated finds, including things like handmade pottery and ostrich eggshell, all differentiate these burials from contemporary "Phoenician" practices.[194] Although the rural cemeteries of the mid–late 1st millennium BCE in the hinterland of *Tingi* have long been recognised as not straightforwardly "Phoenician," a more careful analysis would minimise the external influences and prioritise the local.[195] The cemeteries of Ain Dahlia al-Kabira and Djebila also provide some evidence of contemporary agriculture in the form of charred wheat seeds and pulses.[196] The dense spread of these cemeteries from as early as the 6th century BCE can thus to some extent be seen as a proxy indication of growth of early sedentary agriculture in the rural landscapes of the *Mauri*.[197]

In the same way that it can now be demonstrated for *Numidia* can we also see indications of early development of sedentary nucleated/proto-urban settlements? For a long time, despite finds of some unusual imports at later urban settlements, there was little overall consideration of the earliest activity and the scale of the early towns remains difficult to assess in most cases. At *Volubilis*, however, a few architectural fragments and Punic inscriptions seem to predate the provincial-era town, and

191. Callegarin et al. 2016b, 90, 117–19; Papi 2019.
192. Laporte 2005; Papi 2019, 294, fig. 9.6. On the dating of al-Gour and the Djeddar monuments, see Fentress 2019, 513–14.
193. Papi 2019, 286–304 for detailed discussion of cemeteries (including grave goods) of Ain Dahlia Kabira and Djebila 1.
194. Papi 2019, 305–06.
195. Papi 2019, 286–87 with references to earlier work.
196. Papi 2019, 301–02.
197. As noted in Chapter 1, the initial evidence for domesticated plants from Morocco is unusually precocious from a number of sites of 6th or 5th millennium calBC date. See Ballouche and Marinval 2003; Morales Mateos et al. 2013; Peña-Chocarro et al. 2011.

there are buried structures that certainly go back several centuries BCE.[198] Emanuele Papi has recently argued for the identification of 1st-millennium BCE activity at a total of 19 major sites in Morocco: six coastal sites with 8th–6th century BCE activity (Melilla, Sidi Driss, Kach Kouch, *Lixus*, Rabat, and Mogador), plus a further 12 with evidence from the 6th–4th centuries BCE (including coastal sites at Ras Kebdana, Emsa, Sidi Abdesalem del Behar, Ceuta, Tangier, Kouass, *Zilil*, and inland sites, albeit some on navigable rivers, at *Tamuda*, Azib Slaoui, *Banasa*, *Thamusida*, and Rirha), and *Volubilis* from the 3rd–2nd centuries BCE. Other recent surveys give slightly variant lists and dates, but what is beyond doubt now is that there are a substantial number of sites beyond those previously identified as Phoenician *emporia* where 1st-millennium BCE sedentary settlement can be demonstrated.[199]

Once again the picture is complicated by the extent to which these have in the past been interpreted as purely Punic initiatives.[200] This is somewhat harder to contest in relation to the coastal settlements, but, as in the Numidian case, many of the key locations were inland settlements. Papi's group of 19 sites can in fact be divided into two distinct groups. The first is a series of locations along the north-east coast of Tingitana, between Ceuta (ancient *Septem*) and Ras Kebdana at the mouth of the *Mulucha* river. *Tamuda* is an inland site at a key topographic point on a route linking this coastline with *Tingi* through the mountains and its origins certainly predate the Roman period.[201] An additional site of 1st-millennium BCE date has been identified at Kach Kouch on the Wadi Laou in north-east Morocco.[202] The site was quite small (only about 40 m in diameter), naturally defended by its location on the end of a spur above the valley a few kilometres inland from the sea. The structural traces were somewhat vestigial (mainly hearths, pits, and some burials), but the site produced both imported wheel-made vessels and local handmade wares, with a suspected date of the 9th–6th centuries BCE. Kach Kouch potentially represents a wider class of indigenous settlement that interacted with the coastal sites where ships could anchor.

Tingitana proper is constituted by the thin triangular zone of plains and low hills with its corners marked by *Tingi*, *Sala* (Rabat), and *Volubilis* (Fig. 4.11). Within this zone, six of the sites with 1st-millennium BCE evidence correspond to later Roman towns (*Tingi*, *Zilil*, *Lixus*, *Banasa*, *Sala*, *Volubilis*), and *Thamusida* was later the site of a major Roman fort and river harbour. The navigability of the ancient rivers allowed access to sites some way from the actual coastline—such as *Thamusida*, *Lixus*, *Sala* (Chella/Rabat), and *Banasa*.[203]

198. *Volubilis*: Jodin 1987. Also Papi 2014. Mugnai 2018.
199. Papi 2014; 2019; See also Callegarin et al. 2016b, 121–22; Mederos Martín 2019;
200. Bokbot 2020.
201. Bernal Casasola et al. 2018.
202. Bokbot 2020, 484–87; Bokbot and Onrubia-Pintado 1995.
203. Mederos Martín 2019, 630.

The older view of Punic/Phoenician settlement along the Moroccan coasts emphasised the maritime outlook of sites, prioritising the best harbours and defensible sites like offshore islands.[204] Yet a striking aspect of the accumulating archaeological data is that even sites well inland and up-river reveal very early interconnections with Mediterranean trade. For instance the earliest pottery identified at *Sala* and *Banasa* is of late 7th- or 6th-century date, while *Thamusida* has 6th-century material.[205] Although at one time presented as "Punic" sites, the increasing recognition of local pottery, much handmade, has highlighted the possibility that these centres related primarily to the "proto" *Mauri*.[206] In any event, in combination with the contextualising of the long-known funerary monuments, this suggests that the indigenous contribution to the development of these sites must have been much more significant than commonly acknowledged.[207] The identification of other Moroccan coastal sites with the *Mauri*, like Kouass, *Tingi*, *Lixus*, *Sala*, and Azib Slaoui must now be given serious consideration.

For sites that were further inland, the same arguments apply. *Zilil*, *Tamuda*, and *Volubilis* have strong evidence of pre-Roman development,[208] but the most striking picture comes from a site that was only a secondary settlement in the Roman era. The exemplary publication of work carried out between 2005 and 2012 at the crucial site of Rirha is having much the same impact for Morocco as the *Althiburos* project has had for the Eastern Maghrib.[209] This site occupied a prominent promontory site (c.11 ha) in a sharp bend in the Wadi Beht in the Gharb plain, in many ways very similar to the location of *Althiburos* (Fig. 4.12b).

The site is extremely deeply stratified with up to 9 m of deposits above the subsoil, imposing challenges to and limitations on how much of the lowest levels could be accessed.[210] Prior excavations in 1955 had identified pre-Roman activity, but had only a limited understanding of the complexities of the mud-brick structures and dated them to no earlier than the early 2nd century BCE. The initial occupation is now pushed back to at least the second half of the 5th century BCE (though there is an unstratified sherd of a late 7th- to mid-6th-century amphora) and continued through much of the Roman era, with a final Islamic phase. The results of the investigation of Mauretanian levels and features are of particular importance.[211] The depth of the excavations means we have no sense of the plan of buildings at the lowest levels, but from the start of the site's occupation (Early "Mauretanian")

204. Cintas 1954.
205. Mederos Martín 2019, 630.
206. *Banasa*: Arharbi et al. 2001; Arharbi and Lenoir 2004; Girard 1984; Lenoir 1996; Thamusida: Akerraz et al. 2009; Papi 2014, 212–13.
207. Bokbot 2020.
208. Bernal Casasola et al. 2018; Jodin 1987; Papi 2014, 208, 213–17.
209. Callegarin et al. 2016a; 2016b; 2016c; 2016d.
210. Callegarin et al. 2016b, 11–22.
211. Callegarin et al. 2016b.

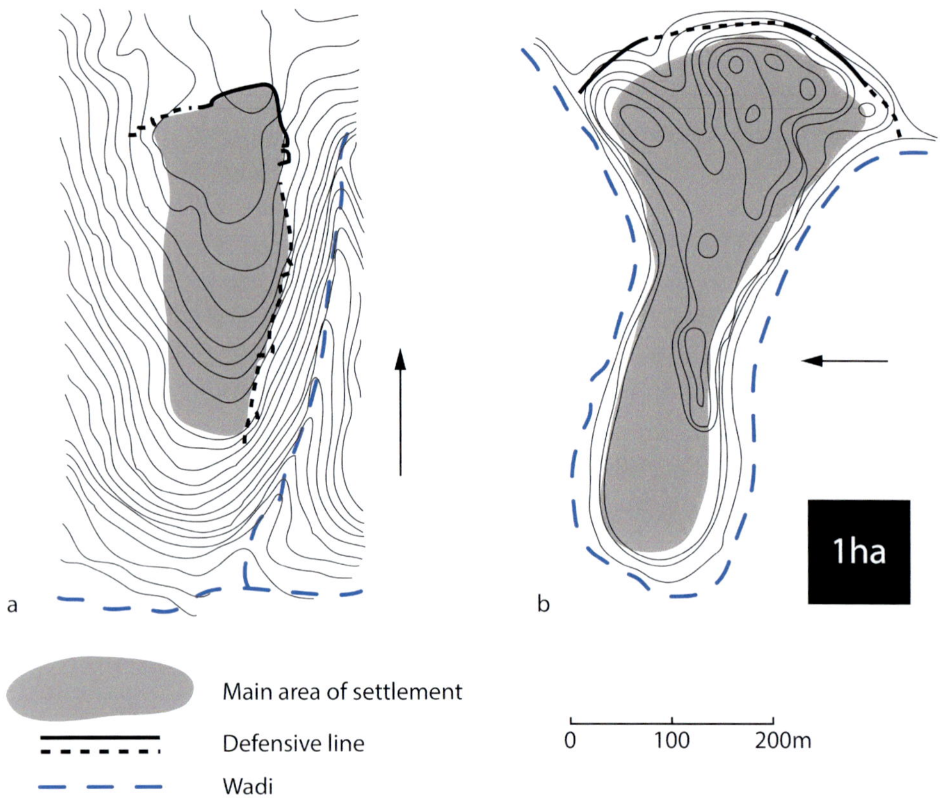

Figure 4.12. Proto-urban Mauretanian settlements. a) *Volubilis*. b) Rirha (Mike Hawkes, from author's rough based on: a) Euzennat 1989, 204; and b) Callegarin 2016a, 14).

these appear to have been built structures using mud-brick. A radiocarbon date on an animal bone from the lowest level provides a calibrated date focused on the 7th–5th century BCE. Both wheel-made and handmade pottery were found at the lowest levels, with some identified imports of 5th-century date.[212] By the Mid or Late "Mauretanian" phases, the buildings were certainly multiroomed rectilinear buildings.[213] The mud-brick architecture of the Mauretanian levels is among the earliest attested in North Africa and is sophisticated.[214] Overall, the structural evidence supports the idea that Rirha was a proto-urban centre of the Mauretanian kingdom, potentially the site known in Roman times as *Gilda* (though the nearby settlement of Domaine du Beht is another contender). With *Volubilis* 35 km to the

212. Callegarin et al. 2016b, 19–25 for the dating evidence. It is a pity that relatively few radiocarbon dates were obtained and none by AMS dating of annual crops.

213. Callegarin et al. 2016b, 25–44, with some of the later buildings combining mud-brick with stone footings.

214. Callegarin et al. 2016b, 46–84.

south-east and the "lost" city of *Babbat* (later *Babba Campestris*) also somewhere in this region, Rirha is thus part of a cluster of inland "urban" sites.[215]

The original topography of *Volubilis* was very similar to Rirha, with settlement focused on a narrow tongue of land with steep scarps on three sides and surviving traces of a rough coursed enceinte wall above the Wadi Fertassa (Fig. 4.12a).[216] Both these sites correspond with the Numidian "wadi promontory spur" type.

From its first occupation, Rirha was linked to cultivation of cereals and vines, olives, pulses, and other cultivated plants and fruit trees were added before the Roman-era occupation (Table 4.3).[217] The site clearly occupied an intensively cultivated landscape. Microscopic examination of mud-bricks has revealed cereal chaff and other fragments from primary threshing and winnowing activity, so there is not the least doubt that the cereals being consumed at the site were cultivated locally.[218] The fact that there is less impressive evidence of olive and vine cultivation, and in general a narrower range of cultivated plants than at *Althiburos*, should not surprise us since the Gharb plain is prime cereal land.[219] However, the differences between the two agricultural packages are sufficiently broad to suggest that they do represent separate developments of agricultural capacity in the Maghrib, as Broodbank and Lucarini predicted.[220]

The Mauretanian identity of the site's inhabitants is supported by a number of indicators. The great tumulus of Sidi Slimane lies c.6.5 km to the south and 1.3 km from another nucleated settlement that has also yielded evidence of both Mauretanian and Roman occupation, Domaine du Beht.[221] A stele engraved on both sides with Libyan texts was found 30 m from Sidi Slimane—perhaps referring to two sons of the same father—and almost certainly can be linked to the burial of two individuals in the main chamber of the tomb. The fact that they were accompanied in the outer corridor of the burial structure by two further individuals may hint at sacrifice accompanying the burial of the two elite individuals. As noted above, the tomb is a typical monument that seems characteristic of the rise of Mauretanian princes and high rulers. The Rirha excavations have produced a further Libyan text engraved on an amphora sherd of probable 1st century BCE date[222]

215. Callegarin et al. 2016b, 123–24; Papi 2014; Rebuffat 1967b.
216. Euzennat 1989, 201–10.
217. See Callegarin et al. 2016a, 25–109 for a detailed presentation of botanical, palynological, and anthracological results.
218. Callegarin et al. 2016b, 80–84.
219. My Table 4.3 is a simplified presentation after Callegarin et al. 2016a, 56–92. The only early attestation of olive is as wood, with olive stones only present, and still in small quantity, from the Late Mauretanian period.
220. Broodbank and Lucarini 2019, 245.
221. Callegarin et al. 2016b, 119, 147–49 for finds from Domaine du Beht.
222. Callegarin et al. 2016b, 90–95. Unfortunately, the ostracon was discovered in a disturbed context and must be considered unstratified.

Table 4.3. Cultivated crops attested at Rirha (after Callegarin et al. 2016a).

Cultivated plant	Common name	Major cultivar	Phase	First occurrence	Origin
Triticum aestivum/ durum	Bread wheat/ Durum wheat	*	Early Mauret	5th–4th c BCE	Mediterranean
Triticum dicoccum	Emmer wheat		Early Mauret	5th–4th c BCE	Mediterranean
Hordeum vulgare	Barley	*	Early Mauret	5th–4th c BCE	Mediterranean
Panicum miliaceum	Millet		Late Mauret	1st c BCE–1st c CE	Mediterranean
Vitis vinifera	Grape vine		Mid Mauret	3rd–2nd c BCE	Mediterranean
Olea europaea	Olive		Early Mauret	5th–4th c BCE	Mediterranean
Ficus carica	Fig		Early Mauret	5th–4th c BCE	Mediterranean
Ceratonia siliqua	Carob tree		Early Mauret	5th–4th c BCE	Mediterranean
Vicia faba	Faba bean		Mid–Late Mauret	3rd c BCE–1st c CE	Mediterranean
Pisum sativum	Pea		Mid Mauret	3rd–2nd c BCE	Mediterranean
Linum cf *usitatissimum*	Flax	*	Mid Mauret	3rd–2nd c BCE	Mediterranean
Sinapis sp	Mustard		Early Mauret	5th–4th c BCE	Mediterranean

and three neo-Punic texts also on potsherds (two are list-like documents and the third a simple name graffito).[223] The neo-Punic texts come from the very late 1st century BCE or early 1st century CE—so the very end of the Mauretanian period. Although the translation of the longer texts is unclear, it appears to contain a number of Libyan personal names. A further interesting insight into cultural identity, as well as economic orientation, concerns the 15 Numidian and 31 Mauretanian coins (including six issues of the city of *Babbat*) recovered there.

It is interesting that the major Moroccan sites with such coin finds also include coins and other material produced at other Moroccan sites discussed already in relation to "Punic colonisation" and *Mauri* (*Tamuda*, *Tingi*, *Zilil*, *Lixus*, *Thamusida*, *Banasa*, *Sala*, *Volubilis*).[224] Rirha was a consumption centre for some rare imported

223. Callegarin et al. 2016b, 95–103.
224. Callegarin et al. 2016b, 103–12.

pottery finds, including amphorae, but also for a wide assemblage of regional wheel-made and handmade pottery, essentially very similar to material produced at *Banasa*, but some locally made also, to judge by finds of waster sherds. As at *Banasa*, some forms were decorated with painted geometric designs (especially triangles and lattices).[225] Another striking find from Rirha, though again sadly unstratified, was a small sculpted terracotta head of a bearded male of distinctive appearance—a good candidate for an autochthonous artistic style of representation.[226]

Rirha is significant in that it gives us a window on the world of the *Mauri* in the second half of the 1st millennium BCE.[227] What is revealed is a sedentary, indeed proto-urban, agricultural society, which was actively engaged in trading with a wider Mediterranean and Iberian world. Like *Althiburos*, we should not consider this an outlier, and we can now strongly support the idea of Mauretanian origins of all the major urban sites and several of the locations where major Roman bases were placed. Indeed, Rirha plausibly provides a good demonstration of the capabilities and achievements of Moorish society before the coming of Rome, and that these results would be replicated and amplified by excavations beneath the more substantial Roman ruins at many of the key centres, or by a more wide-ranging exploration of the NAIA archaeology. This also has implications for how we may visualise the social organisation of some of the localised peoples of the provincial territory, such as the *Zegrenses* at *Banasa* under Roman rule. In the past there has been a tendency to consider them as a "tribal" people only just undergoing sedentarisation, rather than an established element of the urban community at *Banasa* and occupying a potentially long-established sedentary farmed landscape.[228]

The kingdom of the *Mauri*, at least while it was confined to northern Morocco prior to the addition of the lands of the *Masaesyli*, was much smaller than that of the *Numidae*. There were thus fewer major settlement sites both in the NAIA and Roman era. As noted, like the Numidian sites discussed earlier, Rirha, *Lixus*, *Sala*, *Volubilis*, *Zilil*, and Kouass all used hilltop or escarpment locations to some degree. However, we might also note that the coastal and riverine settlements at *Thamusida*, *Thamuda*, and *Banasa* all occupied low terrace positions adjacent to navigable rivers, and *Tingi* and Ceuta are truly coastal sites. Even in pre-Roman times, there were thus different locational types at play in Mauretanian urbanism.

The cultural separation of the two parts of the enlarged Mauretanian kingdom (reflected also in the Roman provincial structure) was a long-term consequence of the fact that the mountainous intermediate zone was occupied by people who were differentiated from the *Mauri*.[229]

225. Callegarin et al. 2016b, 119–25, 157–71 for illustrations of the pottery assemblage.
226. Callegarin et al. 2016b, 112–15.
227. Callegarin et al. 2016b, 117–28 for final conclusions on the Mauretanian phase.
228. Euzennat 1974; Shaw 2014, 536–37; Sherwin-White 1973.
229. Hamdoune 2011; Coltelloni-Trannoy 2011a; Rebuffat 2011a, 86.

The Roman and Islamic geographies of Morocco were both structured around a bifurcation of two routes, one broadly running closer to the west coast from *Tingi*/Tangiers to *Sala*/Rabat, and the other more inland from *Tingi*/Tangiers to *Volubilis*/Meknes/Fez. In the Islamic era, both routes also extended much further to the south across the Atlas ranges and linked to Saharan trade. The new evidence presented above suggests that the political geography of the Roman and Islamic eras was in fact already hardwired in the landscape and peoples of the western Maghrib in the NAIA.

Conclusions

> The history of Numidia and Mauretania before the Roman conquest was, in short, very similar to that of Berber Africa in the Middle Ages. It is the same confusion, the same monotonous and costly sequence of plots, of murders, revolts, wars, collapses; the same mixture of mud and blood; the same inability, on the part of the masters, to organise the cogs of the government machine.[230]

Gsell's final verdict on the Numidian and Mauretanian kingdoms was damning. In emphasising a fatal failure of the successors of Massinissa to build on the foundations he had laid, he echoed a familiar trope of the French colonial government of Algeria and Tunisia on the lack of capacity among Berber populations for settled and well-organised society. This statement also patently contradicts much of the detailed work in volumes V and VI of his great history of North Africa (which, to be fair, was well ahead of its time in rebutting many of the cruder assumptions of colonial ideology—such as an absence of agriculture and sedentary settlement before Punic and Roman examples). Here we see the power of imperial discourse at work and how it twists the established facts to fit a predetermined assumption. This is not to deny that the history of these kingdoms was not marked by plots, murders, revolts, wars, and sundry other crises. The same could, of course, be said of the Roman and Carthaginian states as well, without also entailing similar indictment of the underlying lack of capacity of the state to govern or the solidity of its social and economic base.

As illustrated at numerous points, the ancient sources are a distorting mirror through which to assess pre-Roman Africa, especially if no correcting testimony is introduced from archaeology. However, a careful evaluation of the available material has established that the *Numidae* and *Mauri* came to comprise sophisticated kingdoms, with urban centres, and large-scale sedentary agricultural production alongside the traditionally highlighted pastoral and stock-raising elements of their

---

230. Gsell 1927a, 167: "L'histoire de la Numidie et de la Maurétanie avant la conquête romaine fut, en somme, très semblable à celle de l'Afrique berbère au moyen âge, C'est la même confusion, la même suite monotone et rebuttante, de complots, de meutres, de révoltes, de guerres, d'effondrements; le même mélange de boue et sang; la même incapacité, de la part des maîtres, d'organiser les rouages de la machine gouvernmentale."

population. In order to account for the discrepancy between the *topoi* of barbarians that the sources also relayed, much emphasis was placed on the role of a few exceptional individuals—rulers like Massinissa and Juba II—who were able temporarily to raise these societies to higher things, with less competent leaders sparking collapse and degeneration.

The story of the incorporation of the kingdoms into the Roman provincial territory entailed further literary deceit. In place of the well-organised states of *Mauretania* and *Numidia* (once their kings were forcibly removed), the Roman sources reverted to talking about "tribal" peoples—closely echoed and amplified by modern scholarship. This was in part a reflection of the pattern of Rome's fractionalising of defeated enemies into regional subgroupings, which served as the building blocks for semi-autonomous local government in the provincial structures. However, for the core areas of *Numidia* (between *Cirta* and *Thugga*) and *Mauretania* (between *Tingi*, *Sala*, and *Volubilis*) we have seen that these people were already urbanised and included substantial numbers of sedentary cultivators. While proto-urbanism was perhaps less extensive among the *Masaesyli*, it is evidently traceable at many of the early Roman urban centres of *Mauretania Caesariensis*.[231] Even on the periphery of these kingdoms, pastoral groups had had long contact with sedentary society.

From the evidence presented above, it is apparent that both *Qart Hadasht* and Rome encountered a well-developed agricultural landscape in northern Tunisia, northern Algeria, and northern Morocco, based around numerous towns, hamlets, and fortified settlements. This landscape was not a sudden manifestation of the last centuries BCE, but had been evolving steadily for hundreds of years. While it is apparent that Punic and wider Mediterranean cultural innovations had a profound influence on certain aspects of life for the autochthonous polities discussed in this chapter, it is also important to recognise that cultural flows also moved in the opposite direction, and the active Amazigh populations contributed in multiple ways to the shape of what we recognise as NAIA and "Punic" culture.[232]

Finally, the high level of political, social, and cultural development achieved by *Numidae* and *Mauri* by the latter centuries BCE must be stressed in order to combat the colonial discourse that sought to reinvent the people of the Maghrib exclusively as "tribal" societies following the annexation of the kingdoms by Rome.[233] Nonetheless, beyond the precocious states of the northern Maghrib, there were communities—the peoples described as *Gaetuli* in the sources—whose societies seem to have been differently constructed. It is time to turn to them in the following chapter, with further challenges to our starting assumptions.

---

231. Laporte 2011, 114–15.
232. Ben Younès and Krandel-Ben Younès 2014; Morel 2003 for finds of obsidian tools, handmade pottery, and ochre in Carthaginian burials.
233. Hamdoune 2018; Ibba 2011b.

Chapter 5

GAETULI OF THE PRE-DESERT AND *GARAMANTES* OF THE SAHARA

Introduction

In this chapter, I turn my attention to the peoples of the Sahara and its pre-desert and steppic margins in North Africa (Fig. 5.1), starting with the *Gaetuli*, a general term used to describe the peoples bordering the Roman provinces in the pre-desert landscapes. In the first section, I review and comment on how they have been presented in the ancient sources and interpreted in the orthodox historiography of "Roman Africa." I then move further out into the desert to look at an important case study from the central Sahara, relating to the people known as the *Garamantes*. As a result of intensive archaeological research, they provide the most detailed window on the world of the ancient Saharan peoples.[1] The final section of the chapter returns to the *Gaetuli* more broadly and seeks to re-evaluate their lifestyles, their pre-Roman development, and their significance.

After the demonstration in the previous chapter that the archaeology of the Maghribian NAIA peoples does not match the conventional stereotypes of nomadic barbarians, there is further revisionism to come here. The Sahara now emerges as a much more important influence on the story of Africa in the Roman Empire, with rather more varied and different contributions from its peoples and cultures to those commonly assumed.[2]

The *Gaetuli*

If the *Numidae* and *Mauri* struggled in Roman writings to get a proper evaluation of their society and level of civilisation, what chance the Gaetulian peoples who bordered the two kingdoms to the south and who were uniformly presented in

1. Mattingly 2003a; 2007a; 2010a; 2013a. Cf. also Liverani 2006; Mori 2013.
2. This chapter draws significantly on the main results of the Trans-SAHARA project, which I directed with European Research Council funding from 2011–2017, see Duckworth et al. 2020a; Gatto et al. 2019a; Mattingly et al. 2017; Sterry and Mattingly 2020a.

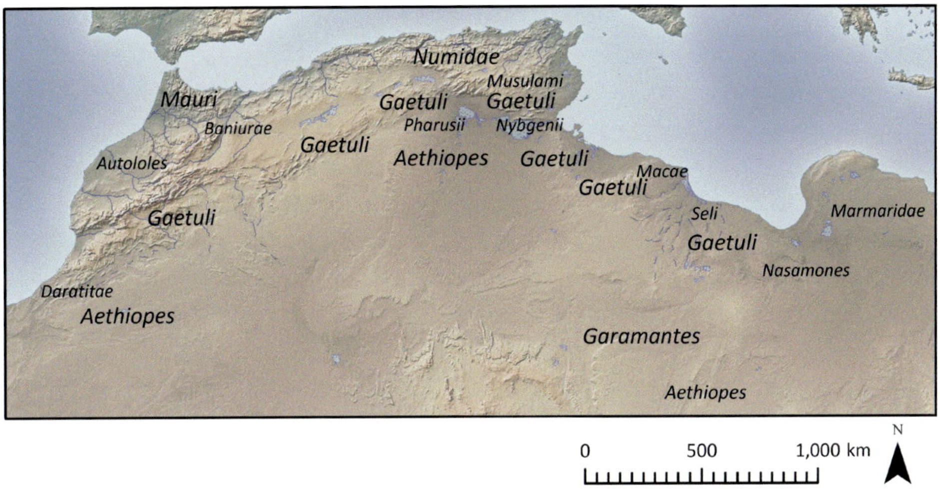

Figure 5.1. Location of the main peoples of the northern Sahara and its pre-desert and steppic margins. Names in smaller font represent subgroups mentioned in the text (Martin Sterry, from author's rough).

terms of their nomadic, warlike, and primitive ways? For Sallust (*BJ* 18), "Africa was originally occupied by the *Gaetuli* and Libyans, rude and uncivilised tribes, who subsisted on the flesh of wild animals, or, like cattle, on the herbage of the soil. They were controlled neither by customs, laws, nor the authority of any ruler; they wandered about, without fixed habitations, and slept in the abodes to which night drove them." Strabo concurred (17.3.19): [the *Gaetuli*] "are very simple in their modes of life and in their dress. The men have many wives and many children and in other respects are like the nomadic Arabians ... horse breeding is followed with such exceptional interest that the number of colts each year amounts to 100,000." Their lands from the Atlantic to the Greater Syrtes were characterised as "barren and arid" (17.3.23). At the time Strabo was writing, the *Gaetuli* to a large extent still lay outside the territory directly controlled by Rome: "the whole of the coast on our sea is subject and the rest of the country is uninhabited or else inhabited only in a wretched or nomadic fashion" (17.3.24). Sallust (*BJ* 80) emphasised their remoteness and isolation: "After the loss of *Thala*, thinking no place sufficiently secure against Metellus, Jugurtha fled ... into the country of the *Gaetuli*, a people savage and uncivilised, and, at that period, unacquainted with even the name of Rome."

The ethnicity and identity of the *Gaetuli* and the geographic specificity of *Gaetulia* has been much discussed.[3] The references to *Gaetuli* in the ancient sources span a vast space from the Atlantic to the Greater Syrtes (a distance of more than

3. Desanges 1962, s.v. "Gétules"; 1964b; 1980a; 1980b, 142–46; 1998; 2001; Fentress 1982a; Hamdoune 2018, 63–64, 69–70; Leveau 2018, 91–93.

3,000 km), with a general indication that these peoples lay to the south of the *Mauri*, *Numidae*, and Libyphoenician populations. Strabo (17.3.2) noted that the great east–west ranges of *Maurusia*—the Atlas and the Tell—were inhabited "first by the Maurusians (*Mauri*) but deep in the interior by the largest of the Libyan peoples (*ethnos*), who are called the *Gaetuli*." Mela (1.21–23) described the *Gaetuli* as "a numerous and diverse people living between the maritime facade and the desert." Indeed, for Gsell, the main criterion for distinguishing the *Gaetuli* was that they comprised the diverse populations bordering the lands of the kingdoms (that is, the distinction was mainly political).[4] Camps has argued that the difference was more to do with lifestyle, recognising the early development of (and greater suitability of land and climate for) agriculture in the Maghrib, with the *Gaetuli* being inhabitants of desert and steppic landscapes.[5] Indeed, many of the features that he uses to give a geographical definition to the *Numidae* and *Mauri* by the same token identify the *Gaetuli* with the lands beyond.[6] As we have seen above, the sources emphasise the harshness and desertic nature of their homelands. In my early work on the *Gaetuli*, I argued that the term represented a high level of latent confederation, based on extended kinship links.[7] Like Desanges, I recognised that many of the ethnic names in the sources were in effect subgroups of the people also referred to as *Gaetuli*.[8] A refinement to the argument is now possible, following the recognition that there was a linguistic division between the Amazigh peoples of the Maghrib and desert regions (Fig. 4.6).[9] This has major implications for our understanding of the NAIA situation and for the relations between *Mauri* and *Numidae* on the one hand and their southern neighbours on the other. Although political boundaries and limits of authority might shift over time or be permeable to movement of people (whether short-term transhumance or long-term migration), the linguistic difference will have defined identity.[10]

If we look in detail at the indications of the sources, running from west to east, we can identify the broad locational limits of Gaetulian peoples.[11] By the 1st century CE they were present in the southern part of *Mauretania Tingitana*, having apparently displaced *Mauri* there (Pliny, *NH* 5.17). Gaetulian peoples listed there included

4. Gsell 1927a, 109–112, thought the name originated as a tribal ethnic, but eventually achieved a much wider and more generalised application.
5. Camps 1960, 156.
6. Camps 1999, especially 57–69 for his maps.
7. Mattingly 1995, 17–33.
8. Desanges 1980b, 344–46; Mattingly 1995, 29–33.
9. Ehret 2019; Fentress 2019, 509–10 for the explicit recognition of the *Gaetuli* with the southern language bloc, Proto-East-West Amazigh.
10. For a general introduction to issues of migration in a Saharan context, see Mattingly et al. 2019a. For arguments relating to a renewed phase of Saharan population movements, see Fentress 2019; Fentress and Wilson 2016.
11. Desanges 1999b for a detailed review of the limits of *tota Getulia*.

the *Autololes* and the *Baniurae*, with the former inhabiting the coastal districts south of *Sala* and stretching south towards the High Atlas and Mogador (Pliny, *NH* 5.5; cf also 5.9),[12] while the latter were people of eastern *Tingitana*, perhaps of the mountainous interface between the two Mauretanian provinces.[13] Indeed, part of the explanation for the long-term difficulty of creating a unified Mauretanian province is that there appears to have been a deep northward penetration of Gaetulian peoples towards the Mediterranean along the *Mulucha* river.[14]

Pliny (*NH* 5.10) also referred to *Gaetuli* of the river *Darat* (Wadi Draa).[15] In western Algeria, the *Gaetuli* appear to have been the predominant groups in the high plains to the south of the Tell and in the Saharan Atlas to the south.[16] Transhumance and long-range movements were evidently part of the picture here. Further east, the northern limits of *Gaetulia* lay relatively close to Numidian *Cirta*, since Sittius seized Gaetulian *oppida* nearby (Caesar, *Bell Af.* 25.3), and a group called the *Pharusii* are attested by Strabo (17.3.7) to have periodically travelled out of the desert as far as *Cirta*.[17] In the Roman era, a prefect was appointed to supervise a group of six Gaetulian peoples located within "*Numidia*" (in this context, the region south of *Cirta*).[18] Another indication of the northern limits concerns the town of *Madauros*, on the grounds that its most famous son, Apuleius (*Apologia* 24.1) described himself as semi-Numidian, semi-Gaetulian.[19] Thus, at certain times or in specific conditions of exploitation, it appears Gaetulian lands included the high plains and Aurès mountains. The people known as the *Musulami* can plausibly be identified as *Gaetuli* and their territory extended in a triangular belt between *Madauros*, *Thala*, and *Theveste* (Tebessa).[20] Gaetulian peoples are also linked with the oasis zones of southern Tunisia, with the lesser Syrtes, the Libyan coastal hinterland, and with the Greater Syrtes.[21]

The southern limits of the *Gaetuli* are harder to determine. The ancient sources generally indicate that to the south of the *Gaetuli* lay Black Africans, *Aethiopes*,

12. The region south of *Sala* was characterised with considerable exaggeration by Philostratus 5.5.1 as "uninhabited desert."
13. Desanges 1980b, 146–47; cf. Hamdoune 1993; 2018; Rebuffat 2001; 2011.
14. Hamdoune 2018 does not comment on this salient explicitly, but recognises that many of the key ancient peoples who occupied this region, including the *Bavares*, were probably Gaetulian.
15. Desanges 1980b, 117.
16. Hamdoune 2018, 76–77 identifies the Mauretanian *Bavares* as a Gaetulian "tribe" occupying territory running from the Tafilalt region of Morocco to the Chott el-Hodna in Algeria.
17. Desanges 1964b; 1999b.
18. *CIL* 5.5267: "*praefectus nationum Gaetulicarum sex quae sunt in Numidia.*"
19. Briand-Ponsart 2002; Stone 2014a.
20. Desanges 1980b, 331–32, 344–45; Shaw 2014 for identifying the *Musulami* as *Gaetuli*. Camps 1960, 155–56 thought otherwise, but the arguments for seeing them as *Numidae* are weak, and the implications of his own geographical studies (1999b) suggest otherwise—see further discussion in Chapter 6.
21. Desanges 1980b, 343–44; Mattingly 1995, 26–28.

and Pliny explicitly placed the dividing line at the river *Nigris* (*NH* 5.30), identified by Desanges with the Wadi Jedi in Algeria.[22] However, this is another instance where geographical realities are in danger of being distorted by the highly schematic thinking of the ancients, being driven by a model of progressive descent into decadent barbarism with distance from the Mediterranean. In that racist model, we might expect to see an evolutionary regression from north to south of, for example, *Libyphoenices*, *Numidae*, *Gaetuli*, *Aethiopes*, and that is broadly what the sources present.[23] That things were actually more complicated is clear from several references to *Gaetuli*, with names that indicate varying degrees of darker skin colour—the *Erebidae*, *Melanogaetuli*, *Nigritae*, and the Aethiopian *Daratitae*, as well as some lighter-skinned Aethiopians, such as the *Leucoaethiopes*.[24] While the geographical allusions to *Aethiopes* are often imprecise, it is clear that Black Africans were a significant presence in the northern Sahara in antiquity and are not simply the result of the medieval and modern slave trade transporting people northwards from sub-Saharan regions.[25] The *Nigritae* and the *Pharusii* were described by Pliny (*NH* 5.43) as *Aethiopes* and lying above (that is, south of) the *Gaetuli*, separated from them by a region of deserts; yet in other contexts both groups are mentioned operating in the Gaetulian zone (Pliny, *NH* 5.39; Strabo, *Geography* 17.3.7).[26] When Mela (3.104) mentions *Nigritae* and *Gaetuli* nomads south of *Mauretania*, was he reflecting a genuine ethnic difference, or a perceptual one between darker- and lighter-skinned desert populations?

The late Neolithic population of the Sahara appears to have been largely of Black Africans, with evidence of migration of some Mediterranean Africans (Amazigh) into the Sahara after the last major climatic change c.3000 BCE. Intermixing between these incomers and the original populations is to be expected and will have been augmented by a pre-Islamic commencement in Saharan trade and especially slaving.[27] Indeed, there is now increasing archaeological evidence to attest to the presence of "Berbers," Black Africans, and mixed-race individuals in the oases from Classical times.[28] The likelihood is that many *Gaetuli* groups were already mixed populations by the time Rome was in regular contact with the Sahara. For

22. Desanges 1980b, 346–49;
23. Desanges 1999b for the schematic approach to North Africa in the sources based on latitude; Mattingly 2011a, 34–37 for an analysis of the discourse of progressive barbarisation present in such accounts.
24. Desanges 1976; 1978a; 1980b, 346–49; 2010. See also Gsell 1913, 233–304 for a detailed synthesis of the ancient sources.
25. Gsell 1913, 293–94 notes the strong correlation of Black Africans with the oases of the northern Sahara, without exploring the possibility that these populations were of ancient origins, like the oases. On iconography of Black Africans in the Mediterranean, see Desanges 1976; Snowden 1970; Van Wyk Smith 2009, 281–378.
26. Desanges 1980b, 346–37, 452–54.
27. On Saharan trade, see now Mattingly et al. 2017a; Fentress 2011.
28. Gatto et al. 2019b.

this reason, I shall not give separate consideration to *Aethiopes*, but I shall argue that some at least of the Gaetulian peoples (and the *Garamantes*) were quite diverse in appearance and included people of varying degrees of skin colour reflecting genetic and ethnic complexity.[29] At all events, Black Africans were very much part of the story of Africa under Rome.

The ancient sources and most modern commentators are agreed on the pastoral orientation of the *Gaetuli*. Drawing his authority from various sources, Gsell stated that:

> These natives were almost all nomads. Besides, a good part of the regions which belonged to them hardly allowed any other kind of existence ... The necessities of their pastoral life and, undoubtedly still more, their taste for looting, brought them in contact with their neighbours to the north.[30]

This sort of statement is little changed, even in the most recent overviews.[31]

> [The *Gaetuli* were] nomadic pastoralists or semi-nomads, they had little contact with cities, to the point that we tend to think today that the term *Gaetuli* denoted nomadic Libyan peoples, a way of life more than a true ethnic group.[32]

The testimony of the sources is unequivocal on the nomadic tendencies of the *Gaetuli*. Sallust (*Jugurtha* 19.5) stated that "beyond Numidia dwell the *Gaetuli*, some of whom live in huts, while others, more barbarous, as nomads." Mela (3.104) linked the *Gaetuli* with the *Nigritae* "who wander as nomads here and there" along the southern borders of *Mauretania*, echoed also in Orosius (*adv. pag.* 6.21). Pastoral lifestyles are well attested at all periods of history in North Africa and the Sahara, and it is not really a question of whether there were pastoralists in the NAIA and Roman eras, but rather of how many and how invariable this pattern was.[33] Since

29. Gsell 1913, 294, 300–02; cf. Desanges 1999a, 215–27, 229–38 for two papers on the identity of the *Aethiopes* and their relations to other Saharan peoples (including his strong presumption that *Garamantes* were at least in part Black Africans).
30. Gsell 1927a, 112: "Ces indigènes étaient presque tous des nomads. Du reste, une bonne partie des régions qui leur appartient ne comportaient guère d'autre genre d'existence ... Les nécessités de leur vie pastorale et, sans doute plus encore, le goût du pillage devaient les mettre en relations avec leurs voisins du nords."
31. Hamdoune 2018, 63, while recognising that there are signs of sedentarisation and proto-urban sites in the case of the *Musulami*, argued that pastoralism and transhumance, more than nomadism, remained of particular importance to them; Lassère 2015, 60–61 emphasises their disdaining of cultivation and passion for hunting and raiding on horseback.
32. Briand-Ponsart and Hugoniot 2006, 23: "[des Gétules] ... pasteurs nomades ou semi-nomades, ils entrainent peu en contact avec les cités, à tel point qu'on a tendance à penser aujourd'hui que le terme Gétule désignait les peoples libyens nomades, un genre de vie plus qu'un véritable ethnie."
33. Devallet 2003; 2010; Trousset 1982b; 2012b for more nuanced discussions of the nature of North African pastoralists.

the Gaetulian lands bordered those of the *Numidae* and *Mauri*, where we have already seen that sedentary habitation and agriculture had become well established during the 1st millennium BCE, there is certainly reason enough to carefully interrogate the evidence for the lifestyle of the most closely adjoining Gaetulian peoples. We might expect some impact on their subsistence patterns and strategies over time. In the next section on the *Garamantes*, I shall demonstrate that Saharan oases originated in the NAIA and our default assumption now should be that oasis formation may have begun in other parts of the Sahara in pre-Roman times.[34]

In later antiquity the *Gaetuli* disappeared from the sources, apart from some anachronistic listings, being replaced by people described as *Mauri Mazices* or simply *Mazices*.[35] Although the term *Mazices* appears originally to have been applied to a people of the eastern Sahara, and *Mauri* had previously indicated those of the north-west Maghrib, by late antiquity these terms had gained a wider application in relation to the peoples of the mountainous and desert margins of the Maghrib, in much the same way as the *Gaetuli* earlier.[36]

The *Garamantes*

This archaeological case study concerns fieldwork in the central Sahara of southern Libya. A Libyan people known from the time of Herodotus (4.183–85) as the *Garamantes* lived here in a zone that was already hyper-arid desert before the 1st millennium BCE.[37] The *Garamantes* can be associated with three major bands of oases in the central Sahara: the Wadi ash-Shati to the north, the Wadi al-Ajal in the centre, and the Wadi Barjuj/Murzuq/Hufra depression to the south (Fig. 5.2). There are also some smaller isolated clusters to south-west, south-east, and north-east. The Wadi al-Ajal was the heartland territory and will be the main focus of attention here. There were also Garamantian sites in the southerly oasis belt around Murzuq and the northern valley of Wadi ash-Shati and a few outlying sites near Ghat, Sabha, and Wadi Hikma.[38]

34. Sterry and Mattingly 2020a for a thorough overview of the evidence, backed up by c.2,000 radiocarbon dates.
35. See, for example, *Expositio totius mundi et gentium* 62: "Deinde post Africae omnem regionem adiacet et deserta maxima in austri partibus ubi aiunt in minima parte ipsius deserti habitare barbarorum pravam gentem quae sic vocatur Mazicum et Aethiopum." ("Then beyond Africa, the neighbouring countries and the great deserts to the east, where in the smallest part dwells a perverse race of barbarians called *Mazices* and *Aethiopes*."
36. Hamdoune 2018, 76–78; Modéran 2010. The possibility of a new wave of Berber migration in late antiquity is discussed by Fentress 2019; Fentress and Wilson 2016.
37. See Mattingly and Sterry 2020a 8–12 for a discussion of climate change.
38. Mattingly et al. 2020a for a detailed summary of the evidence from all these regions.

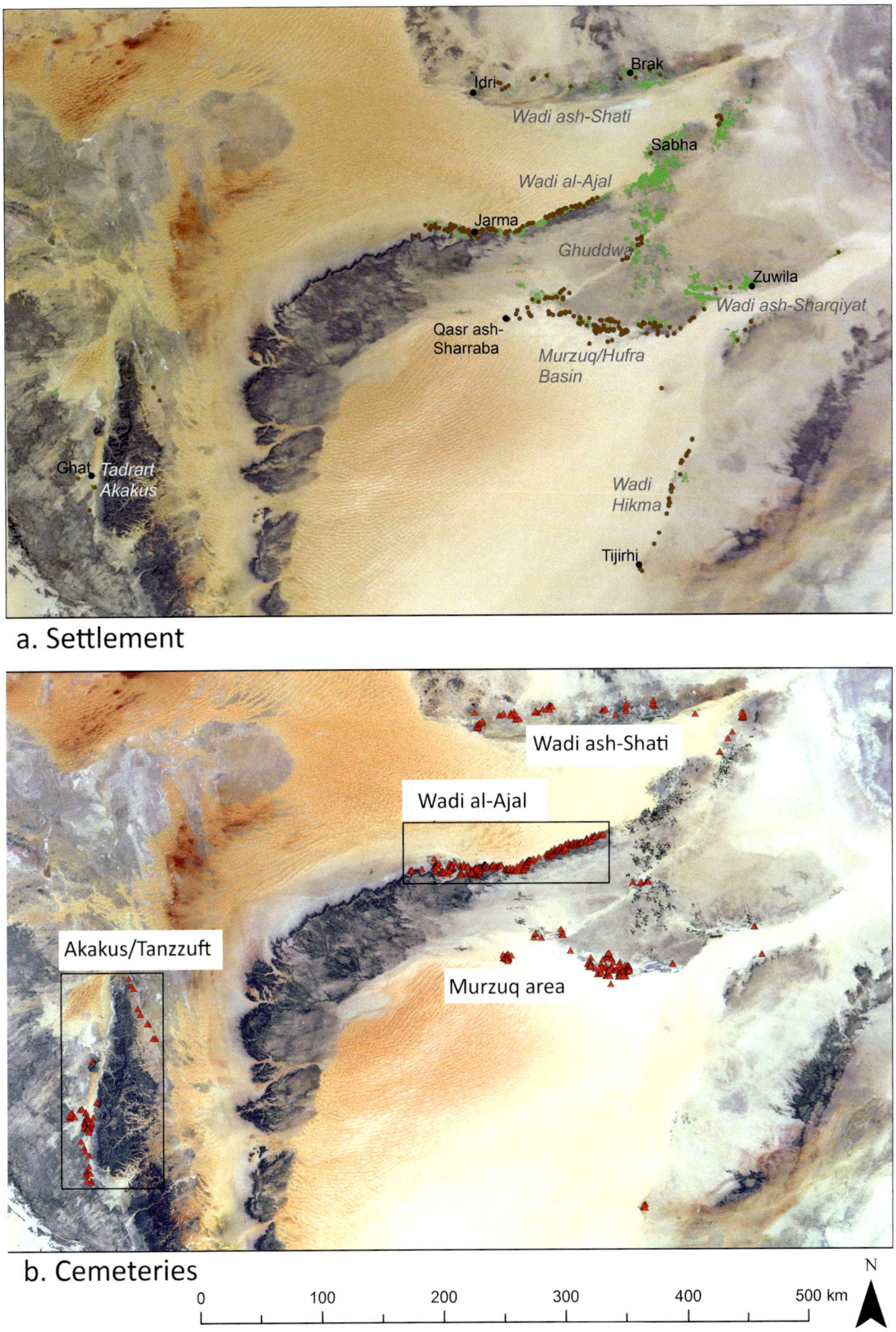

Figure 5.2. The heartlands of the *Garamantes*. a) Distribution of oasis settlements. b) Distribution of cemeteries (Martin Sterry, from Gatto et al. 2019, 11).

The Greco-Roman writers made a few fleeting allusions to cultivation, but the much more pronounced emphasis in the sources was on the nomadic and uncivilised tendencies of the *Garamantes*, their warlike disposition, and propensity for raiding.[39] They were synonymous in Latin literature with the desert wastes and primitive social development, as is clear in Lucian's description:

> Who could live in a land so savage and barren and consumed by drought? ... Only the *Garamantes* live on its borders, a lightly clad, agile tribe who dwell in tents and live mainly by hunting. (*Dipsades* 2)

The epithets used in our Classical sources to describe the *Garamantes* were almost universally negative or designed to highlight the threat they posed to civilised life: black, cruel, devious, fierce, given to brigandage, hut-dwelling, indomitable, lawless, light-armed, lightly clad, miserable, naked, numerous, outermost, panting, promiscuous, receivers of stolen booty, savage, scattered, tent-dwelling.[40] An interesting point is that the ancient writers do not explicitly describe the *Garamantes* as "nomadic," though the assumption has often been made by modern commentators that the *Garamantes* were part of the broad category of desert nomads described by Herodotus (4.186) and Strabo (17.3.19). However, while Herodotus (4.183) mentioned the herding of fabulous long-horned cattle by the *Garamantes*, in the same passage he also described them as cultivating salty ground by spreading humic material and confirmed the existence of date-palm oases in Garamantian lands (4.182–183):

> *Augila* is also inhabited, and it is here that the *Nasamones* come for their date harvest. Again at the same distance to the west is a salt hill and spring, just as before, with date palms of the fruit bearing kind, as in the other oases. Here live the *Garamantes*, a very numerous people, who spread soil over the salt to sow their seed in.[41]

Despite this early attestation of Garamantian oasis cultivators, the later sources largely ignored this aspect of Garamantian society and have been followed by modern commentators.[42] The subject index of Desanges's great study on Pliny's account of Africa in his *Natural History* reflects this distortion in both ancient and modern framing—there are entries for *deserta*, *ferae*, *harenae*, *solitudinum horror*, *scorpiones*, and *serpentes*, but nothing on oases or palms.[43] Two major recent studies

39. Mattingly 2003a, 76–79 on the literary references to the *Garamantes*; 2011a, 34–37 on progressive barbarisation concept.
40. Mattingly 2003a, 86.
41. Adapted from the Penguin Classics translation, 2003 (translated by de Sélincourt).
42. But note Strabo, *Geography* 17.3.23, on *Augila*: "this region resembles Ammon, being productive of palm trees and also well supplied with water."
43. Desanges 1980b, 495–97.

of the literary sources on the *Garamantes* (and other ancient Libyans) have taken little account of the counter-indications of agriculture and sedentary lifestyle, privileging the traditional view of them as raiders and nomads.[44]

As with the *Gaetuli*, ancient historians have thus tended to categorise them as a nomadic or semi-nomadic group:

> The southern boundaries of the province were fluid. One can hardly draw a distinction between protection of Roman interests and intimidation of semi-nomadic tribes ... Balbus a friend and loyal lieutenant of Augustus and a man experienced in Africa, drove deeply into the territory of the *Garamantes*, the restive Berber people who dwelled south of the Roman province ... The intimidation took immediate effect. Two decades passed with no evidence of trouble from nomadic or semi-nomadic tribes on the fringes of the province.[45]

The Archaeology of the Garamantes

The archaeological picture of the *Garamantes* could not be more different.[46] It is now clear that, like the *Numidae*, their society included a significant number of sedentary people who from the early 1st millennium BCE—despite a hostile desert environment—practised advanced irrigated agriculture of cereals, dates, vines, and a range of fruit trees, and lived in permanent and well-defended settlements. By c.400 BCE these settlements were taking on an increasingly proto-urban form. The nature of Garamantian society is perhaps best illustrated by a few direct examples from my work, which has involved excavation at the Garamantian capital at Jarma, and survey and excavation of other settlements, cemeteries, and irrigation works (Fig. 5.2).[47] Initial work on the Garamantian heartlands was drawn to the extensive and impressive funerary landscape of the Wadi al-Ajal.[48] Huge numbers of tombs were visible on the lower slopes of steep escarpments that marked the southern edge of the Wadi al-Ajal, most comprising mound cairns, corbelled cairns, and various types of drum and stepped tombs of distinctive Saharan types, but also shaft

44. Colin 2000 devotes 47 pages to a detailed discussion of nomadism (40–86), but just five to agriculture and sedentarism (115–19), concluding that there were three predominant activities of the desert peoples (in descending order of importance): nomadism, raiding, and agriculture (221–23), elsewhere dismissing evidence for Saharan trade in a few pages (45–47). Luisi 1994 has a chapter on the "Garamanti genti indomita di razziatori" (21–34), but is entirely uncritical of the literary tradition and ignorant of the archaeological evidence.
45. Gruen 1996, 167; echoed also in Whittaker 1996, 592–95.
46. For a handy summary account, see Mattingly 2022. My work followed up pioneering work by Daniels 1968; 1970; 1989 and the more problematic interventions of Ayoub 1967; 1968.
47. The major reports on this work are Mattingly 2003a; 2007a; 2010a; 2013a. For summary accounts, see Mattingly 2006c; 2011b; Mattingly et al. 2020a.
48. Mattingly et al. 2019b. Cf. also González Rodríguez 2014.

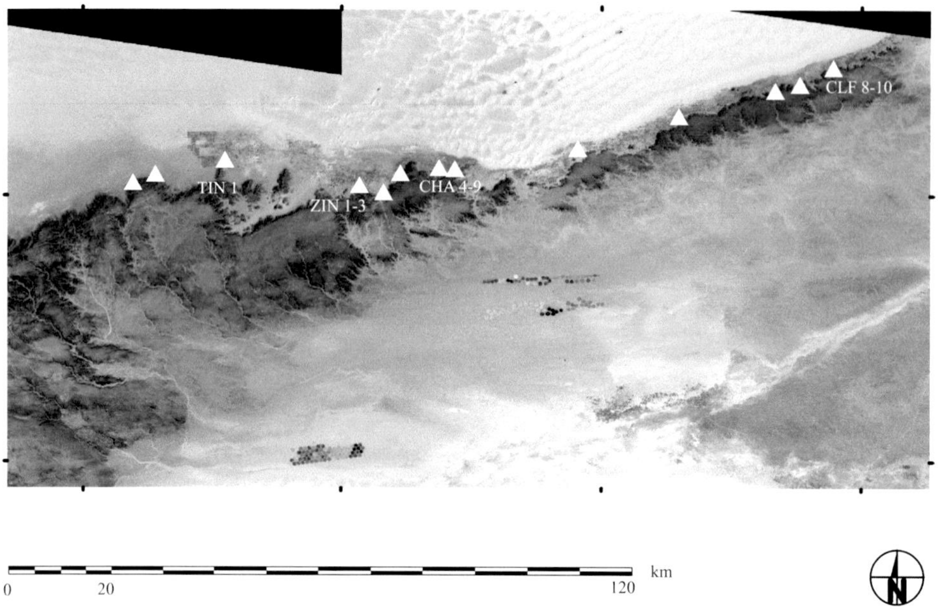

Figure 5.3. Early Garamantian hillfort settlements (1st millennium BCE) (from Mattingly 2010a, 85).

burials that lacked significant superstructure, and (rare) pyramids and mausolea.[49] Estimates of the total number of visible burials have gradually increased with more intensive survey. The first Italian archaeologists produced a figure of 60,000, which Charles Daniels felt needed to be doubled to 120,000.[50] However, my own work has revealed that numbers of tombs on the escarpments were even higher that Daniels recognised (11,000 recorded along just 10 km of the escarpment), and there is also now more evidence of additional cemeteries in the oasis zone in the centre of the valley. The fact that early investigators saw little evidence for associated settlement initially encouraged the view that these were the tombs of mobile pastoralists, despite the fact that the tombs clustered densely along the margins of the bands of oasis in Fazzan.

But what of settlement? In the late Neolithic period the peoples of the central Sahara had inhabited ephemeral campsites as they followed available grazing with their flocks and herds or hunted the still abundant wild fauna. There is no evidence for cultivation, though more intensive exploitation of gathered plants is evident. Some of the larger campsites were located at lakes and other permanent water sources, and these could be quite extensive, perhaps marking repeated visits over many years. In upland areas, some rock shelters were also regularly used, but again

49. Mattingly 2003a, 187–217; Mattingly et al. 2019b, 57–64.
50. Daniels 1989, 49; Pace et al. 1951, 210–12.

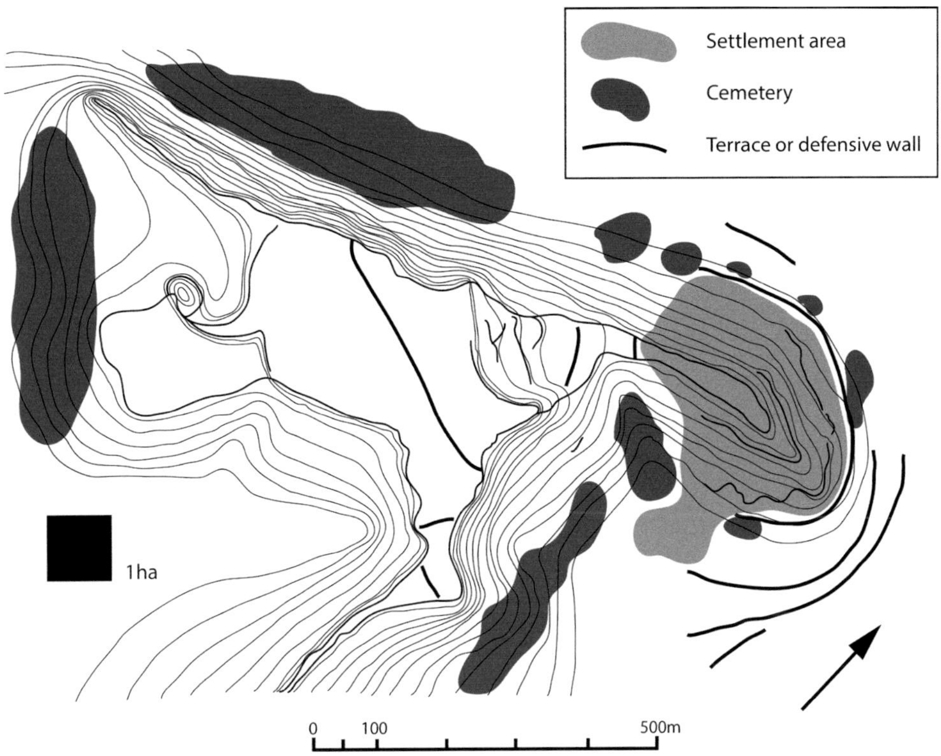

Figure 5.4. Plan of Zinkekra in its full proto-urban development (Mike Hawkes, from author's rough after Mattingly 2010a).

for seasonal occupancy. There was a lack of defensive features at these sites, and structures were evidently impermanent.[51]

The recent fieldwork has dramatically refined our knowledge of Garamantian settlement. From about 1000 BCE the people who we later call *Garamantes* began to construct new types of fortified settlements on prominent rocky spurs of the Wadi al-Ajal, with Zinkekra the type site (Figs. 5.3–5.4).[52] The initial buildings were small oval huts with mud walls founded on uncoursed drystone foundations. The associated finds strongly suggest that from the outset occupation was sedentary and year-round. The material culture on these sites is similar to the final Late Pastoral Neolithic, involving handmade pottery, stone tools, grinding stones, and ostrich eggshell beads. This suggests some overlap in the population with the pre-existing Late Pastoral communities despite hints of new Berber-speaking arrivals. The Early Garamantian period is defined as 1000–500 BCE and activity at this early date has been confirmed by numerous radiocarbon dates.[53]

51. Cremaschi and Di Lernia 1998, 37–44; Di Lernia and Zampetti 2008.
52. Daniels 1968; Mattingly 2010a, 19–84.
53. Mattingly et al. 2018, 210–11; 2020a, 59–69.

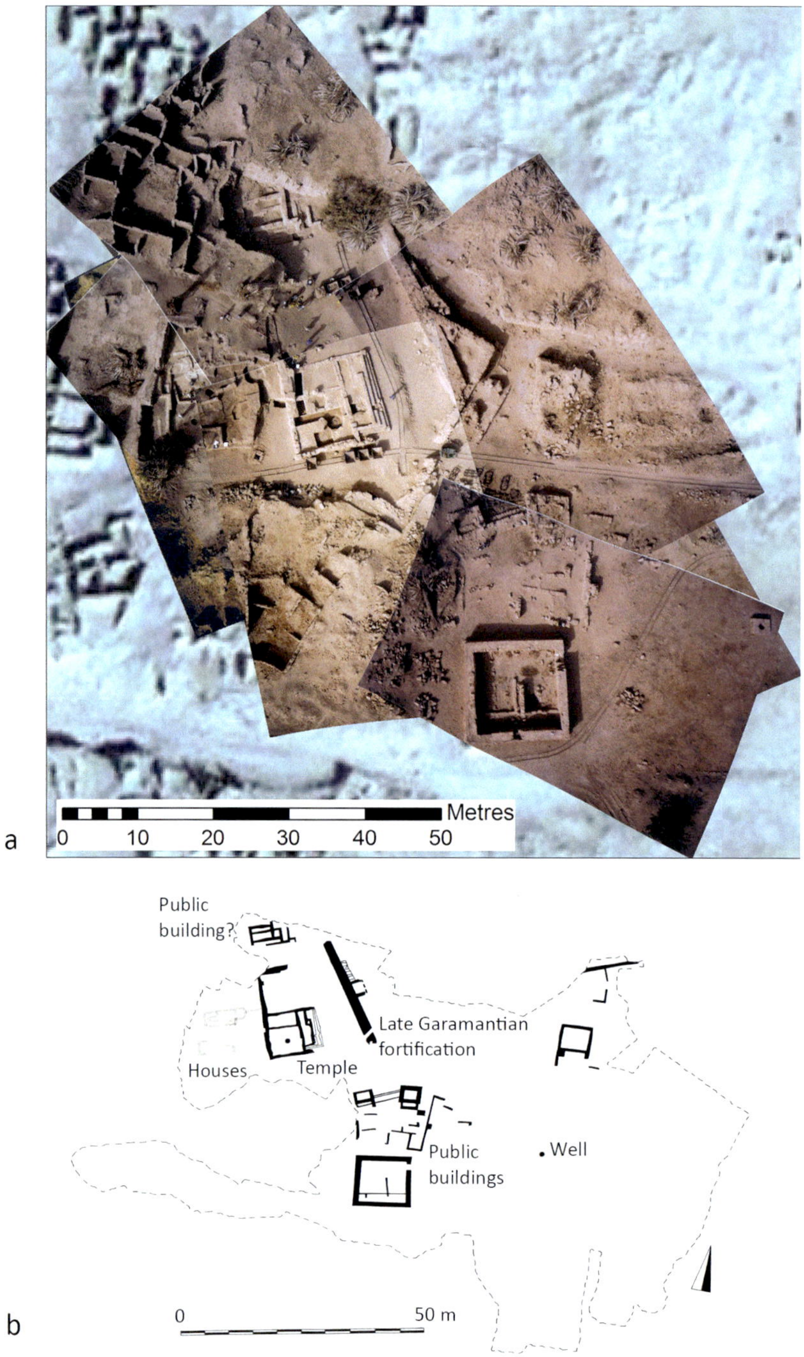

Figure 5.5. a) Photomontage and b) plan of central area of Classic-era *Garama*, showing stone buildings (from Mattingly 2013a, 70).

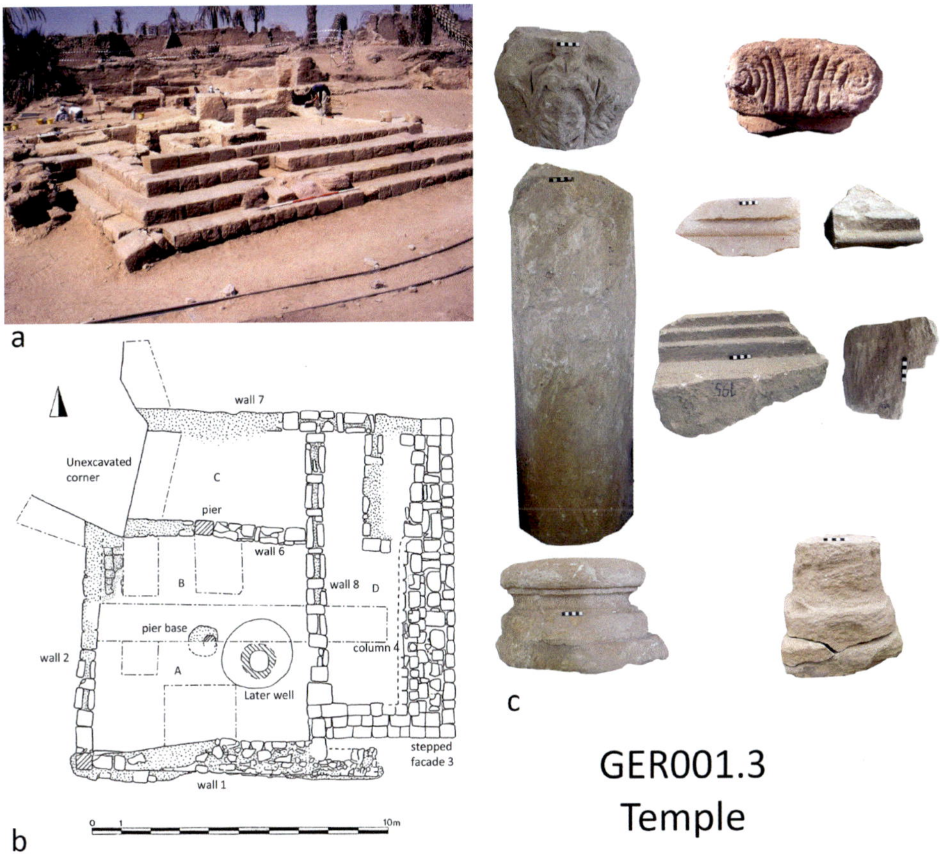

Figure 5.6. Temple at *Garama* (GER001.3). a) General view. b) Plan. c) Montage of architectural elements (author's montage, after Mattingly 2013a).

From about 500 BCE the natural defences of Zinkekra hill were being supplemented by the construction of walls protecting the settlement. Buildings were not only on the small upper plateau but were terraced into the steep scarps. In the final occupation phase, dating to the last centuries BCE, the dwellings became more complex and more rectilinear, and there was the first use of sun-dried mud-bricks. During this Proto-urban Garamantian phase (500–1 BCE) there commenced a move away from the hillfort sites in favour of the establishment of new settlements in the valley centre.[54]

Garama (Jarma), the Garamantian capital, was one such valley-centre site, though the Garamantian levels are here overlain by the ruins of a sequence of later towns. In the 1960s some large-scale soundings were made at the centre of the site by Mohamed Ayoub, exposing some significant Garamantian structures, but

54. Mattingly et al. 2010, 123–210; 2018, 211–13.

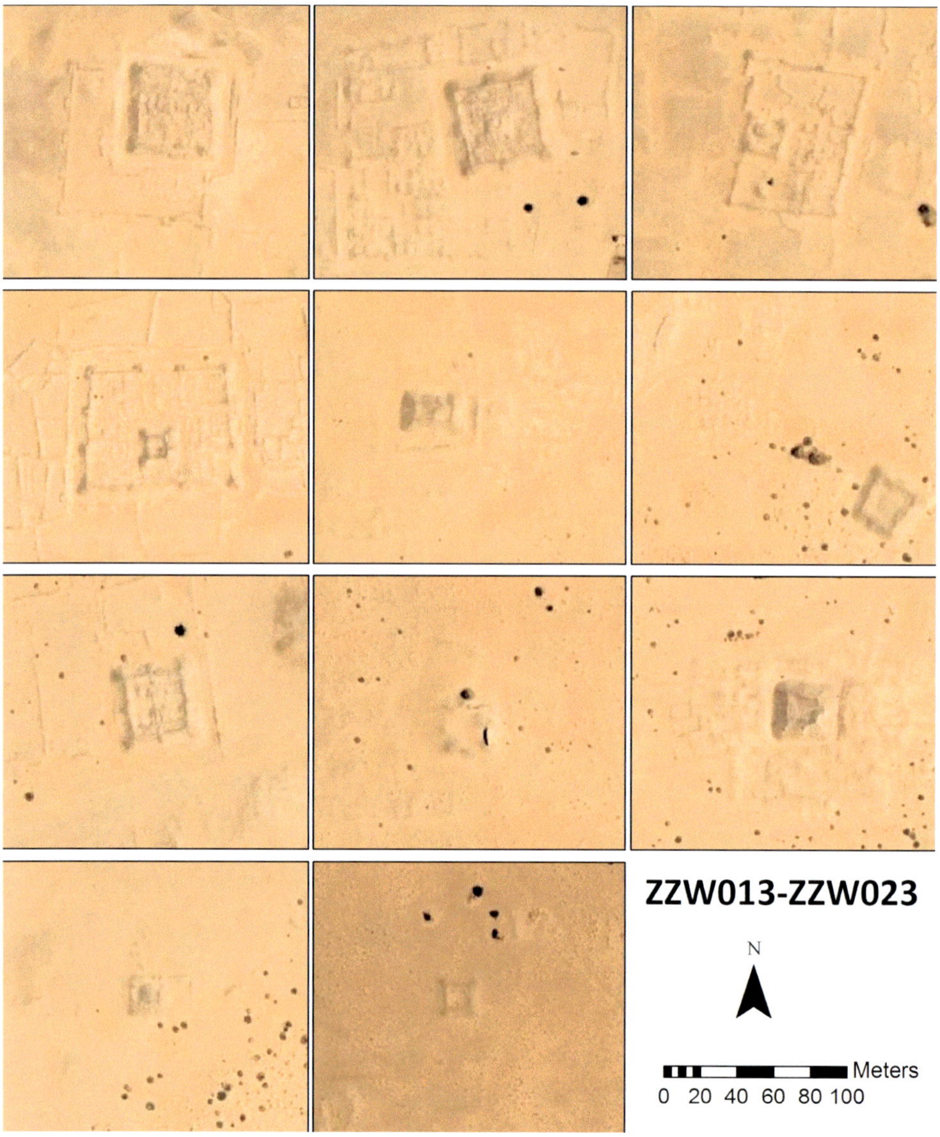

Figure 5.7. Typical Late Garamantian fortified villages (*qsur*) from the Zizaw area, east of Murzuq (from Sterry and Mattingly 2020a, 81; imagery: Google, DigitalGlobe).

the lack of adequate recording and publication left many questions unanswered.[55] My excavations at Jarma from 1997–2001 documented an extraordinary urban sequence running from its foundation in c.400 BCE to c.1935 CE. The most impressive architecture uncovered by myself and Ayoub corresponds with the Classic Garamantian phase, broadly 1–300 CE, when the settlement was ornamented with

55. Mattingly 2013a, 67–115.

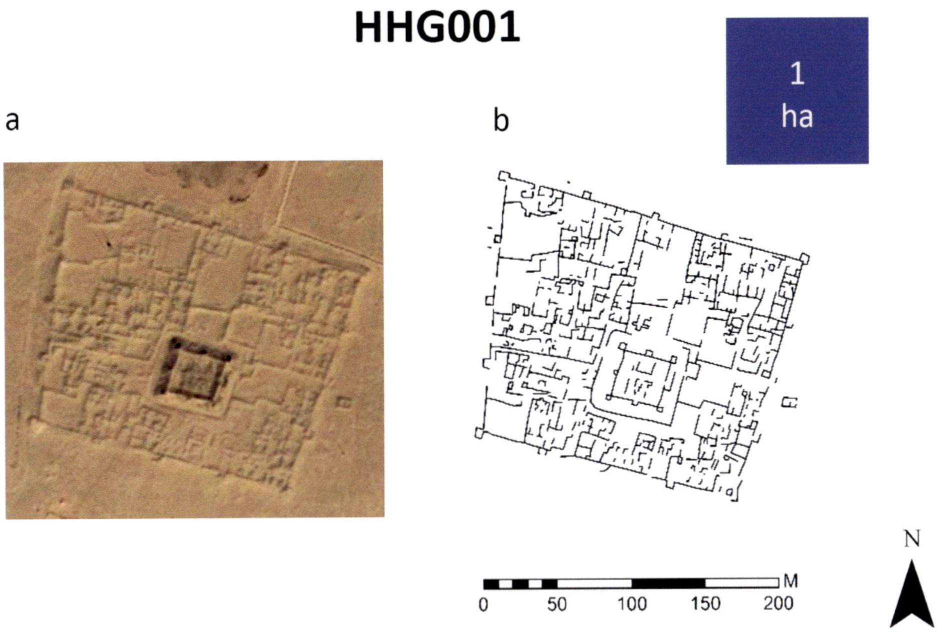

Figure 5.8. HHG001, a Late Garamantian fortified village near Murzuq. a) Satellite image (imagery: Google, DigitalGlobe). b) Plan (from Sterry and Mattingly 2020a, 81).

stone-footed buildings, including a temple featuring ashlar-quality masonry and architectural decoration of Mediterranean inspiration (Figs. 5.5–5.6).[56] There were ten phases of construction recognised. As at *Althiburos*, the use of AMS dating and detailed study of material culture and palaeoeconomic markers have transformed our understanding of the origins and economy of the site.[57] *Garama* may have been a site of exceptional importance, but other Garamantian settlements of the Classic period are also notable for their architectural sophistication, their semi-planned nature, their density in the landscape, and their scale.

The Late Garamantian period (300–700 CE) is notable for an increasingly defensive aspect at Garamantian sites, frequently marked by the construction of fort or castle-like structures (s. *qasr*, pl. *qsur*) at the centre of settlements. The fortified character of the villages east of Murzuq is particularly striking (Fig. 5.7) and AMS dates from a good sample of these sites have confirmed the Classic and Late Garamantian date suggested by surface finds of imported Roman pottery.[58] The *qsur* vary in size from c.20–40 m^2, mostly with rectangular or circular projecting towers at their corners and gates. Some examples, such as HHG001, had substantial outer enceintes (Fig. 5.8), again with corner and interval towers along their sides. In

56. Mattingly 2013a, 267–93.
57. Mattingly 2013a, 125–34; Mattingly et al. 2018, 213–15.
58. Mattingly et al. 2018, 215–19; 2020a, 58–69.

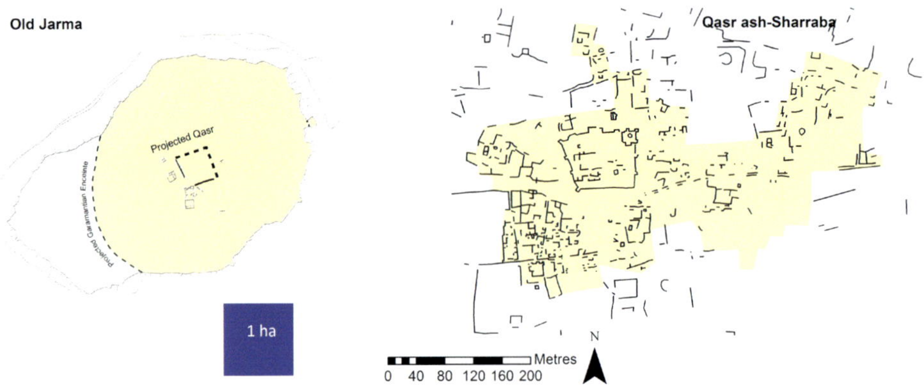

Figure 5.9. Garamantian urban centres. a) *Garama* (Old Jarma). b) Qasr ash-Sharraba (from Sterry and Mattingly 2020a, 79).

terms of layout and appearance, such structures would not have looked out of place in the Roman military zone at this time, a point I shall return to in Chapter 6. The surrounding settlement structures, generally 1–3 ha in extent, often show a high degree of regularity and orderly planned layouts.

The largest Garamantian sites, such as Jarma and Qasr ash-Sharraba, though only 10–18 ha in area, were urban in scale and functional characteristics (Fig. 5.9).[59] While some aspects of Garamantian settlement have been known for some time,[60] what has become increasingly apparent in the last few years is that the settlement system merits the appellation "urban" from the latter centuries BCE onwards, and the dense nexus of permanently settled villages does not at all conform with the negative testimony of the ancient sources.

The overall numbers and densities of Garamantian-era settlements are a compelling demonstration of the potential size of the desert-dwelling population (Fig. 5.2a). When I started my work on the *Garamantes*, only a handful of settlements had been identified, largely through the work of Daniels between 1957 and 1977.[61] Subsequently, in a 25 km section of the Wadi al-Ajal centred on Jarma we have recorded no less than 50 certain or suspected Garamantian villages or hamlets. Allowing for the different survey intensities in other parts of the 150 km long wadi (and the very high site density in the areas we have surveyed in most detail), the total Garamantian settlements must have significantly exceeded the 125 villages identified to date for the entire Wadi al-Ajal. In a 100 km sector of the Murzuq depression to the south we have recorded more than 90 settlement sites, though

59. Mattingly and MacDonald 2013; Mattingly and Sterry 2013; Sterry and Mattingly 2020c.

60. Daniels 1989.

61. This is reflected in my map of the Garamantian region in the Barrington Atlas (Mattingly 2000b), completed just as I was starting work in the region in the late 1990s.

the foundation of these seems to be a few centuries later in general than for those in the Wadi al-Ajal.[62] Extensive survey in the Wadi ash-Shati has so far identified 15 Garamantian settlements, many with associated *qsur*, though again the total distribution of Garamantian burials would suggest that more sites remain to be discovered.[63] The outlying oases of Fazzan have generally yielded only small numbers of settlements (though again this is probably due to low survey intensity): Ghuddwa, 6; Ubari lakes, 1; Sabha area, 7; Wadi Tannzuft, 7; Wadi Hikma, 17; Wadi Barjuj, 4. Overall, that gives a minimum of over 270 nucleated sites. Allowing for the still preliminary nature of research in many areas, it is probable that the total Garamantian settlements will have exceeded 350–400 (and applying the higher site density figures from the best-surveyed areas would suggest a total of nearer 1,000).[64] By way of comparison, in the early modern period the region had a total population of 34,000 spread between 150 villages and hamlets and various pastoral groups.[65] Although not all the Garamantian settlements were occupied contemporaneously, of course, these figures do at the least give a sense of scale of the ancient population, which must have numbered in the tens of thousands (and arguably 50–100,000 at its peak in the Classic period).[66]

Reconsideration of the economy and lifestyle also confounds our expectations. As demonstrated already, many ancient historians and Classical archaeologists still struggle to escape from the traditional mindset and persist in referring to the nomadic character of the *Garamantes*.[67] Archaeology tells us something different. Although livestock was evidently penned alongside the simple dwellings on Zinkekra, the abundant botanical remains from the earliest levels at that site provide unequivocal evidence for the adoption of agriculture between 980–670 calBCE.[68] The possibility that the origins of central Saharan agriculture were even earlier is suggested by a date stone found in a burial c.400 km south-west of Jarma that has been dated to c.1200 calBCE.[69]

Botanical and palynological evidence relating to the *Garamantes* has been well published, but its significance needs emphasising here (Table 5.1).[70] There were three phases of crop introductions to Garamantian Fazzan. The "agricultural

62. Mattingly 2013a, 530–34.
63. Mattingly et al. 2020a, 84–89.
64. Mattingly 2013a, 538–42 for detailed settlement modelling and demographic calculations.
65. Despois 1946; Scarin 1934; Mattingly 2013a, 529–31, 534–42.
66. Mattingly 2003a, 351; 2013a, 538–42.
67. Bénabou 1976, 102: "Le recul des Garamantes ... marque incontestablement le premier grand succès dans la lutte contre les nomads du Sahara"; Briand-Ponsart and Hugoniot 2006: "Les grands tribus nomads ... les Nasamons, ... les Maces ou les Garamantes"; Camps 2007, 119: "les *Garamantes*, peuple nomade"; Corbier and Griesheimer 2005: "... les Garamantes. Le légat Valerius Festus mit en fuite ces nomads"
68. Van der Veen and Westley 2010; Pelling 2013a.
69. Di Lernia and Manzi 2002, 179 (date stone with date of 1200 calBC).
70. Pelling 2013a; 2013b; van der Veen 1995; van der Veen and Westley 2010.

Table 5.1. Main cultivated plants exploited by the *Garamantes* (after Pelling 2013a/b; van der Veen 2010).

Cultivated plant	Common name	Major cultivar	Site	First occurrence	Possible Origin
Phoenix datilifera	Date palm	*	Zinkekra	980–670 calBCE	Egypt, Mediterranean
Triticum aestivum	Bread wheat	*	Zinkekra	980–670 calBCE	Egypt, Mediterranean
Triticum dicoccum	Emmer wheat		Zinkekra	980–670 calBCE	Egypt, Mediterranean
Hordeum vulgare	Barley	*	Zinkekra	980–670 calBCE	Egypt, Mediterranean
Vitis vinifera	Grape vine	*	Zinkekra	980–670 calBCE	Egypt, Mediterranean
Ficus carica	Fig tree	*	Zinkekra	980–670 calBCE	Egypt, Mediterranean
Gossypium	Cotton	*	Jarma	416–320 calBCE	Sub-Saharan
Sorghum bicolor	Sorghum	*	Jarma	390–110 calBCE	Sub-Saharan
Pennisetum glaucum	Pearl Millet	*	Jarma	360–40 calBCE	Sub-Saharan
Punica granatum	Pomegranate		Jarma	49–183 calCE	Mediterranean
Prunus amydalis	Almond		Jarma	183–353 calCE	Mediterranean
Olea europaea	Olive		Jarma	183–353 calCE	Mediterranean
Pisum sativum	Pea		Jarma	183–353 calCE	Mediterranean
Triticum durum	Durum wheat		Jarma	183–860 calCE	Mediterranean
Vicia faba	Faba bean		Jarma	353–860 calCE	Mediterranean
Lens culinaris	Lentil		Jarma	860–1093 calCE	Mediterranean

package" attested at Zinkekra early in the 1st millennium BCE can be characterised as Mediterranean/Nilotic, ultimately derived from Near Eastern domestication of the date palm, emmer and bread wheat, barley, the fig tree, and the grapevine.[71] Later, another group of plants of probable Mediterranean origin were added (durum wheat, almond, olive, pomegranate, pulses), first appearing at Jarma in the early centuries CE. There is a third group of agricultural innovations involving sub-Saharan cultivars, with the introduction of pearl millet, sorghum, and cotton. Although not attested in abundance until the early centuries CE, these are persistently present in levels dating to the later 1st millennium BCE.

The natural vegetation record suggests a marked decrease in water availability in the Late Pastoral phase (last millennia BCE) and comprises species well adapted

71. Pelling 2013a; 2013b; van der Veen 1995; 2010; van der Veen and Westley 2010.

to hyper-arid conditions.[72] The cultivated crops, on the other hand, all require significant amounts of water to be cultivated, demonstrating that this must have been irrigated (i.e. oasis) agriculture. Moreover, the sudden uptake of cultivation of an evolved "crop package," rather than a gradual domestication of locally available plants, highlights the fact that this involved technological transfer from outside the region. Given that Fazzan is 1,000 km from the Mediterranean and over 2,000 km from the Nile, it is apparent that when agriculture was first practised in the central Sahara it was dependent on a range of technologies and knowledge whose ultimate origin was external. The clearest hints of where the initial package came from all point to the oases of the Western Egyptian Desert, where sedentary settlements and cultivation commenced during the 3rd or 2nd millennia BCE.[73]

However, the distance between the suspected source and the central Sahara strongly suggests that oasis cultivation in the latter area was not the result of a single one-off migration out of the Egyptian Western Desert area, but rather the end result of a gradual spread of oasis cultivation (and cultivators) into and between a series of pre-existing Saharan *refugia* and populations.[74] Rather than attributing all credit for oasis formation to the migration of external agents, then, we should recognise that the pioneering oases almost certainly also involved much more local actors, drawn from the Late Pastoral societies. However, the early stages of agriculture in the Saharan case study did not preclude further introductions over time. The sub-Saharan additions to the initial "agricultural package" by the latter centuries BCE are particularly interesting as they potentially indicate a different direction of technological movement and that the Garamantes were active agents in improving their cultivation regime, not simply reliant on what came along a diffusionist route from the east.[75] The alternative explanation is that they reached Fazzan directly from the Lake Chad area.[76] This is highly significant as it shows that not all agricultural innovations had the same point of origin. Finally, at the height of Garamantian trading contacts with the Roman Empire in the early centuries CE, additional Mediterranean crops, including a range of pulses not present in the initial agricultural phase, made their appearance.

The range of crops cultivated is interesting because it represents a developed agricultural package that was imported to the central Sahara long before any contact with Rome or even *Qart Hadasht*. Garamantian agriculture continued to

72. Mercuri et al. 1998; Pelling 2013a, 484–6; van der Veen and Westley 2010, 515–16.
73. Mattingly et al. 2020a; 2020c.
74. Mattingly et al. 2018, 206–08. Cf. also the general introduction on *refugia* by Purdue et al. 2018b.
75. Pelling 2013a, 478–84; 2013b, 841–52. See Liverani 2020 for an account that emphasises east–west diffusion.
76. Although there have been suggestions that these crops could have travelled north along the Nile valley and then reached Fazzan from the east along the oasis trail from the Western Desert (Wild et al. 2007; 2011), the available chronological indices suggest their presence in the central Sahara may be earlier than in Egypt.

develop in dynamic ways in later phases with the addition of the highlighted sub-Saharan crops to the earlier repertoire. Of particular interest is the cultivation of cotton, possibly as early as the 4th century BCE and certainly strongly attested by the 3rd–6th century CE.[77]

The farming technologies used by the *Garamantes* were very different from those of early agriculturalists in the Maghrib, with all cultivation in the central Sahara dependent on irrigation from groundwater sources. The agricultural and technological package appears to have been imported in the 1st millennium BCE from outside the region, and the most likely origin point for Saharan agriculture was in the arid environment of the Western Desert of Egypt, where the early development of oases dates to the 3rd or 2nd millennium BCE.[78] Initially, Garamantian irrigation may have involved springs and wells, but by the latter centuries BCE they were making use of underground water channels known as foggaras.[79] The archaeological evidence for these features is particularly striking, and the labour inputs in construction and maintenance imposed a considerable burden on Garamantian society. The foggara technology again can be traced back to the Egyptian oases, where it appears to have been introduced by the Persians in the 5th century BCE. We now have a radiocarbon date from the mud-brick lining of a foggara shaft in the Wadi al-Ajal of 390–207 calBCE, corresponding to the phase when Garamantian settlements spread to the valley floor from the escarpment hillforts and dramatically increased in numbers.[80] The wadi valley-floor settlements seem in general to have been unfortified at this date, perhaps reflecting a growth in centralised power within society. This expansion of Garamantian oasis settlements also long-preceded contact with Rome.

A third element of interest concerns craft activity at the Garamantian settlements. There is evidence of metallurgy in this area of the Sahara during the 1st millennium BCE, and by the Classic Garamantian period this was sophisticated and large-scale at some sites. There is also evidence that the *Garamantes* were engaged in substantial working of semi-precious stones, notably carnelian and turquoise amazonite, from the Proto-urban phase. High-quality textiles were also produced at Garamantian settlements. These developments reflect not simply self-sufficiency but artisanal specialisation and the emergence of a significant manufacturing capacity in Garamantian society that seems to have been utilised in trans-Saharan trading networks.[81]

The abundance of Mediterranean trade goods now attested in Garamantian oases is testimony to the fact that the *Garamantes* controlled access to things that

77. Pelling 2013a, 476–77, 482–83; 2013b, 847.
78. Mattingly et al. 2020c.
79. Sterry et al. 2022; Wilson 2006a; 2009a; Wilson and Mattingly 2003; Wilson et al. 2020.
80. OxA-26746, 2243±26 BP.
81. Mattingly 2010a, 523–30; 2013a, 511–21, 525–29, 530–34.

Mediterranean societies desired and valued. There is some evidence to indicate that the *Garamantes* also maintained trading relationships with communities south of the Sahara.[82] The most likely cargoes of significant value on the Saharan trade networks included, in no particular order: metals (including gold), enslaved people, ivory, textiles, beads and semi-precious stones like carnelian, agricultural staples (such as dates and grain), and salt. The *Garamantes* seem to have had access to all of these and in the case of textiles manufactured fine-quality products, not just in wool but also in cotton.[83]

Like the Numidians, then, the *Garamantes* provide a corrective to the orthodox view of African societies encountered by Rome. Both these societies were highly sedentarised from early in the 1st millennium BCE, developing village-based settlement patterns that would evolve in the course of time to urban status. Both societies were agricultural from an early date and arguably even before Phoenician or Roman colonial ventures got under way in Africa. There is evidence of an early development of craft production and trade networks, revealing that these people were not simply producers of raw materials and food for "more advanced" colonial societies. In sum, what we seem to be witnessing is a long process of socio-economic development that started early in the 1st millennium BCE and led to state formation by the latter centuries BCE.[84]

The *Gaetuli* and Other Early Oasis Communities

There are a number of significant implications from the new evidence about the *Garamantes*. It is now clear that 1,000 km south of the Mediterranean in the central Sahara there existed a sophisticated desert kingdom, both urbanised and agricultural. But what lay between the *Garamantes* and the other areas of precocious agriculture in *Numidia*, *Mauretania*, and the Libyphoenician developments? This Gaetulian zone is, of course, the area of the map where generations of scholars have placed their nomads, albeit in more recent times often recategorised as transhumant pastoralists. As we have seen, they follow the ancient sources closely in making this characterisation. It is a classic example of a *terra nullius* colonialist

82. Sub-Saharan contacts: Fentress 2011; MacDonald 2011; Magnavita 2013; 2017; Mattingly 2017, 22–29. See also the further discussion of Saharan trade in Chapter 6.

83. Mattingly 2017; Wilson 2012a; 2017.

84. Liverani 2006; 2007; Mattingly and Sterry 2020a, 27–30; 2020b, 711–18 for a summary of the arguments in favour of recognising the *Garamantes* as a state. Despite their default assumptions about desert "tribes," the evidence of developed Garamantian society has found support in Hamdoune 2018, 77: "un véritable état organisé, tel celui des *Garamantes*"; Lassère 2015, 61: "L'état des *Garamantes* qui mérite bien ce titre." But note also the counter views of Scheele 2020, with response in Mattingly and Sterry 2020b.

mentality: the empty landscape that was ill-used before the arrival of an imperial power to people it and invigorate it.[85] Geographical studies of the economic trajectory of this same region in more recent periods reveal the existence there of numerous oases.[86] Could this have been the same in Roman times and earlier? Although the possibility of oases is occasionally mentioned in the scholarly literature, the implications of this have tended to be lost in the face of default judgements of the poor level of NAIA socio-economic development in the pre-desert and desert zone. In this section I shall draw together the evidence of early oasis development in this broad zone and suggest that a re-evaluation of the overall significance of sedentary agriculturalists in the make-up of Gaetulian society is needed.

At first glance, we are hampered by a critical lack of modern archaeological research at most of these locations. However, there are actually strong hints in our ancient sources that something more may have been going on. Similarly, the archaeological record of Roman remains and activity in some of the oases could potentially mark the point when the oases become visible to us as opposed to when the oases were first created.[87]

As already noted, Herodotus (4.182–83) explicitly mentioned a line of oasis communities linking the *Garamantes* with the Western Egyptian Desert, including the oracular centre at *Ammon* (Siwa). In the Western Egyptian Desert, the earliest oases date back to the 3rd millennium BCE, especially in the Kharga and Dakhla depressions. It is logical that intermediate locations on the main route heading west, like *Ammon*, al-Jiarabub, and *Augila* (Awjila), predated the first oases in Fazzan, and archaeological evidence confirms activity in the 1st millennium BCE (Fig. 5.10a).[88] The Awjila oasis cluster was evidently associated with the *Nasamones* people (Herodotus 4.182), as probably were other minor oases known to the south of the Syrtic coastline (Fig. 5.10b).[89] The *Nasamones* are not generally treated as a Gaetulian people, but their location is equivalent to those of the *Gaetuli* further west, and they may well have been a significant offshoot (like the *Garamantes*) of the same broad grouping.[90]

There is thus no doubt, then, that early oases were widely spread in the eastern Sahara by the 1st millennium BCE, but can we identify evidence for oasis development so early to the north, north-west, and west of the *Garamantes*? My account will follow a broadly east-to-west arc along the Roman military sectors from Tripolitania to the Atlantic, with occasional forays further south into the Sahara.

---

85. Gosden 2004, 114–52, Mattingly 2011a, 30–37, on *terra nullius* colonialist mentalities.
86. Capot Rey 1953; Despois and Raynal 1967; Laureano 1991.
87. The section below closely follows a region-by-region survey in Sterry and Mattingly 2020a, 112–276.
88. Mattingly et al. 2020c, 112–46; Boozer 2020, 147–86.
89. Mattingly et al. 2020c, 127–30 for the detailed evidence.
90. Desanges 1962, 152–54; 1980b, 269–71.

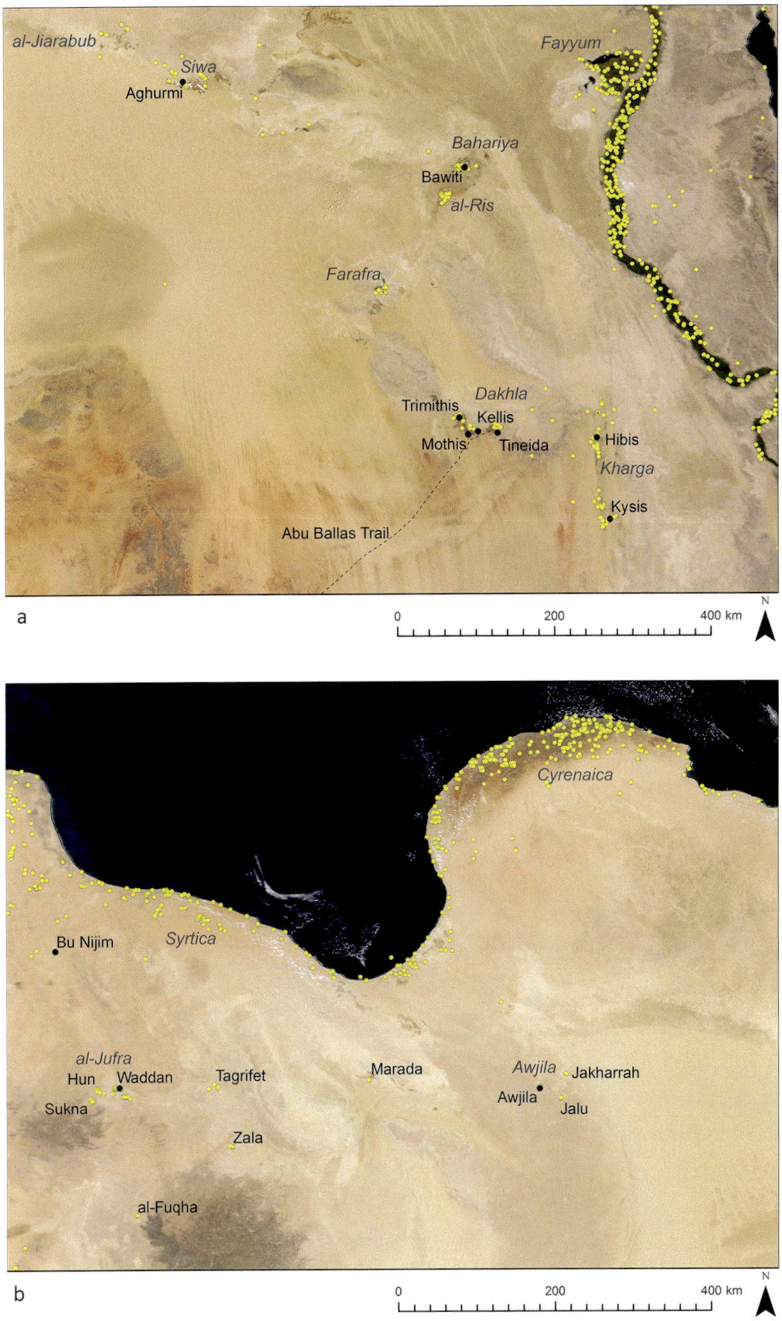

Figure 5.10. Early oases of the eastern Sahara. a) Egyptian Western Desert sites. b) Syrtica (from Sterry and Mattingly 2020a; 113–14).

As established above, the ancient peoples of this broad zone at the end of the 1st millennium BCE were generally known as *Gaetuli*.

Between the *Garamantes* and the Mediterranean there are several clusters of oases, of which the most significant is the al-Jufra group. A number of important early sites, including several of urban scale, have recently been identified on satellite imagery, and some of these certainly date to the Roman or late antique era (if not earlier). Foggara irrigation technology has also been identified, matching the Garamantian evidence to the south.[91] The most plausible interpretation is that these oases were already in existence in the 1st millennium BCE.

A second group of oasis sites in Tripolitania coincide with Roman garrison points (Fig. 5.11): *Gholaia* (Bu Nijim), *Myd[...]* (al-Qurrayyat/Gheriat al-Garbia), al-Qurrayyat ash-Sharqiya, Mizda, *Cidamus* (Ghadamis), *Tillibari* (Remada), *Talalati* (Ras al-Ain), *Auru* (Ain al-Auenia), *Thenadassa* (Ain Wif).[92] It is possible, of course, that Roman forts and fortlets were placed at strategic locations where water was available and that over time oases sprung up to support the garrison communities. However, an alternative possibility is that oasis development preceded military intervention—I shall return to this issue after discussing more of the military zone. *Cidamus* (Ghadamis) exploited an abundant spring in a barren desert area. Limited investigation of the NAIA and Roman phases of the oasis has revealed Roman pottery, stone architectural elements, some Latin inscriptions (including an indication of a period of Roman military occupation), and a series of monumental late Roman tombs (designed for multiple interments) with a distinctive Libyan iconography in their sculptural decoration.[93] However, there are strong additional pointers to its origin as an oasis in the 1st millennium BCE, as it was a target of the desert campaign of Cornelius Balbus in 20 BCE (Pliny *NH* 5.35–36), 200 years before the extension of the Roman garrison deployment to this remote location. Pliny's account of the triumph of Balbus has generated much discussion about the list of toponyms he mentions being paraded on placards in Rome, but it is generally agreed that two groups of *oppida* were mentioned, one in the Libyan desert, the other in Algeria, some way to the west (see below).[94] Given the certainty of ancient origins for the oases of Garamantian Fazzan, it seems likely that *Cidamus* and the other *oppida* mentioned were also oasis settlements.

91. Mattingly et al. 2018, 220–21; Mattingly et al. 2020c, 130–37.
92. Mattingly et al. 2020c; 2020b, 188–200.
93. For archaeological evidence of Roman-era tombs, Latin inscriptions, and related features at the oasis, see Corò 1956; Mattingly and Sterry 2010; Mattingly et al. 2020b, 195–98; Mercier 1953.
94. Desanges 1957; 1978a, 189–213; 1980b, 387–412; Mattingly 1995, 70–73; 2003a, 83. See now the excellent discussion by Merrills 2016 on the "peculiar choreography" of the Roman triumphal procession in Rome, which introduced a wide range of diverse locations, peoples, and natural features alongside the "headline" victories in order to enhance the perception of the scale of conquest.

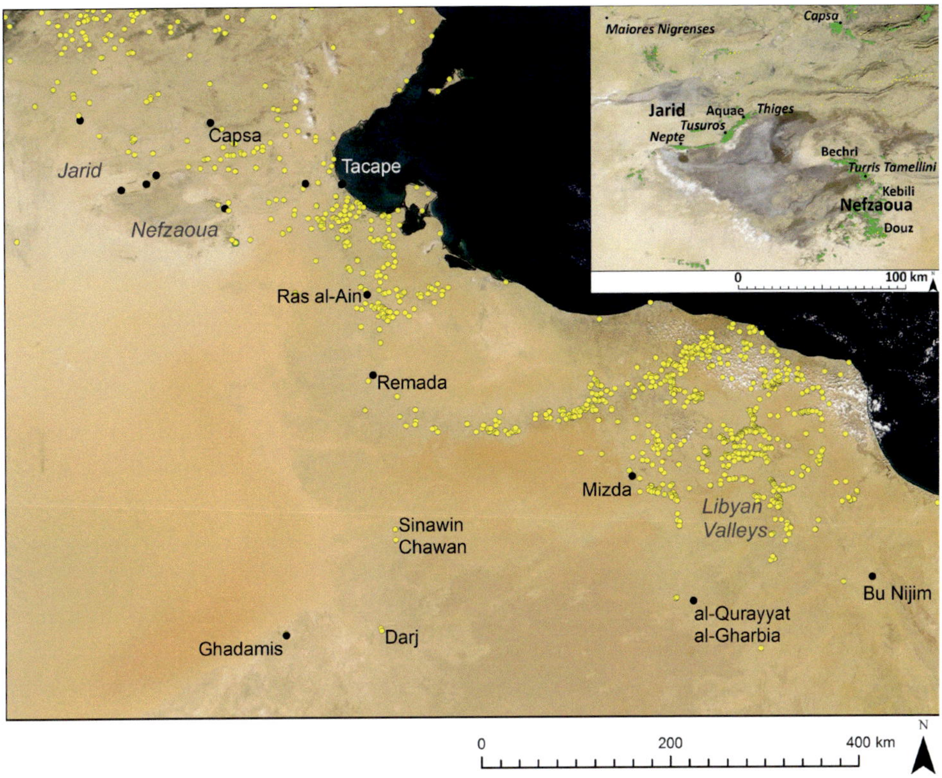

Figure 5.11. Early oases of Tripolitania, with inset detail of Nefzaoua and Jarid oases (from Sterry and Mattingly 2020a, 191, 202).

Several other minor oases between either *Cidamus* or the *Garamantes* and the coast have produced Roman pottery and evidence of fortifications, some of which appear to be indigenous in nature.[95]

The southern shore of the Lesser Syrtes has a system of springs that feed coastal oases. The most famous of these was *Tacape* (Gabes). *Tacape* controlled another *passage obligé* through the coastal plain. There is no suggestion in Pliny's famous account of the oasis here (*NH* 18.188) that its creation was due to Roman initiative. Rather there is much marvelling at the extraordinary productivity of the alien oasis agriculture, where palms, fruit trees, and cereals/legumes formed several distinct layers of cultivation.[96] Inland from *Tacape* there was a Roman spa site on a hot spring at *Aquae Tacapitanae* that again fed an important oasis cluster.[97]

A number of the coastal sites, including sites on Jerba, have already been referred to in Chapter 3 in the context of Libyphoenician *emporia*, but the Libyan

95. Mattingly et al. 2020b, 198–99; Rebuffat 1972a, 323–24.
96. Mattingly et al. 2020b, 206–07; Trousset 1986a,173–76; 1987a.
97. Mattingly et al. 2020b, 207–08; Trousset 1974, 17–18.

part of that relationship merits revisiting, if we now recognise that these Libyan peoples were *Gaetuli* and that they may already have been adopting agriculture and sedentary settlement prior to the arrival of any outsiders. On Jerba, for instance, the clear evidence of external contacts at coastal Ghizène and *Meninx* are not dated before the 6th or 4th centuries BCE. At the inland site of Henchir Bourgou, finds of basket-impressed handmade pottery from the very earliest levels are dated to the 8th century BCE and suggest initial Libyan sedentarisation on the island.[98] This pottery has been found on other sites on Jerba (Henchir Tawrirt) and the nearby mainland (*Gigthis*, *Zitha*, and el-Menaguib, Tatouine).[99] The timber and rammed earth buildings at Henchir Bourgou look like semi-permanent occupation and clearly predated the 5th-century levels with the earliest imported wares—that might be taken to indicate the start of the Libyphoenician phase.[100] I thus argue that along the Tripolitanian coastal zone the *Libyphoenices* incorporated Gaetulian peoples who were already on the path towards sedentary settlement prior to the start of substantial maritime contacts. Henchir Bourgou is currently under more detailed examination and is likely to emerge as a key site in the Gaetulian zone. By the latter centuries BCE it seems to have been a substantial centre (growing from c.5 to 20 ha in area), with a monumental Hellenistic turriform mausoleum, one of a cluster of imposing mausolea on Jerba of pre-Roman date.[101] In the Roman era, a Gaetulian people, the *Cinithi*, were explicitly connected with the town of *Gigthis*, on the mainland facing Jerba. The picture that is starting to emerge suggests that this inclusion of *Gaetuli* groups was not some Roman administrative afterthought, but rather an essential element of the first urbanisation starting in the 1st millennium BCE.

A strong case can be made for the existence of other oasis towns in southern Tunisia by the late 1st millennium BCE. Sallust (*BJ* 89) attested to the existence of a strongly fortified oasis town at *Capsa* (Gafsa) in the late 2nd century BCE, situating the town in a stereotypical desert landscape infested with wild beasts: "except the parts adjoining the walls, all the surrounding country is waste and uncultivated, destitute of water, and infested with serpents, whose fierceness, like that of other wild animals, is aggravated by want of food." The success of Marius's surprise attack in the early morning was due to the fact that a large proportion of the town's population had gone outside the gates, evidently into their gardens in the oasis (*BJ* 91). The Roman town at *Capsa* was centred on two natural springs that watered both the town and the oasis.[102]

98. Ben Tahar 2018; Ben Tahar et al. 2020, 103–04; 2022.
99. Ben Tahar 2016.
100. Ben Tahar 2018.
101. Ben Tahar et al. 2020, 98–101 (overall survey); 2022; Ferchiou in Fentress et al. 2009, 107–28; Werriemi 1985; 1995b.
102. Mattingly et al. 2020b, 208–09.

The wider regional significance of *Capsa* has rarely been mentioned, but is relevant here. It controlled an important passage through east–west mountain ranges and in the French colonial period was recognised as the key site for the control of the Jarid, the oasis zone on the north-west side of the Chott Jarid.[103]

When the Roman garrison deployment was extended into the area of the Chott Jarid in the 1st century CE, there again appear to have been oases already in place that Roman roads were directed to, and where Roman fortifications were constructed to watch over the local communities that in some cases gained recognition as urban centres. The oases around the chott are fed by abundant natural artesian springs and were thus prime candidates for early development (Fig. 5.11, insert).[104] Telmine in the Nefzaoua group on the south side of the Chott Jarid/Chott Fjaj was recognised under Trajan as the *civitas* centre of the Gaetulian *Nybgenii* people and promoted to *municipium* status under Hadrian, when its name became *Turris Tamalleni*.[105] About 12 other oases in the Nefzaoua group have produced evidence of Roman-period activity.[106] On the opposite side of the Chott Jarid, within the large Jarid oasis at least three oasis centres *Thusuros* (Tozeur), *Nefta* (Nepte), and *Thiges* (Guebbah) were accorded Roman urban status, while Kriz and al-Hamma also have clear evidence of Roman-era structures.[107] Proceeding westwards into Algeria there are further oases at the mouths of valleys issuing from the southern flank of the Aurès mountains, with oasis irrigation in part based on seasonal flow down these wadis (Fig. 5.12).[108] Roman forts or Roman-era communities have been recognised at or very close by several oasis locations: *Speculum* (Chebika), *Nigrenses Maiores* (Henchir Besseriani and Negrine).[109]

To the west again lay another important group of oases, known as the Ziban. Irrigation here is part based on the existence of artesian springs and part on seasonal floodwaters carried down the major wadis, including the Wadi Jedi—generally identified as the *Nigris* river mentioned by Pliny (*NH* 5.30) as marking the boundary between *Gaetuli* and *Aethiopes*.[110] A Roman fort at *Thabudeos* (Sidi Okba) marks the eastern edge of the Ziban, with the modern *chef lieu* at Biskra, ancient *Viscera* (again the site of a Roman fort). Just south of the Wadi Jedi to the west of *Viscera* was another fort, *Gemellae* (al-Kasbat), closely linked to the

103. Borderau 1907, 177 described *Capsa* as the "key to the Jarid"; Trousset 1986a.
104. Martel 1965; Moreau 1947; Trousset 1987a; 1995b; 2012a.
105. Desanges et al. 2010, 274–75; Di Stefano 2004; Mattingly et al. 2020b, 202–04; Trousset 1974, 43–46. On the possible links between *Nybgenii* and the group later known as Arzuges, see Desanges 1989b; Trousset 2011.
106. Mattingly et al. 2020b, 201–06; Trousset 1974, 42–50;.
107. Desanges et al. 2010, 187; 275; Mattingly et al. 2020b, 209–11; Trousset 1986a; 1986b; 1987a; 1995b.
108. Birebent 1962, 118–21.
109. Laporte and Dupuis 2011; Mattingly et al. 2020b, 211–13; Trousset 1978a; 1980b.
110. Desanges 1980b, 346–49.

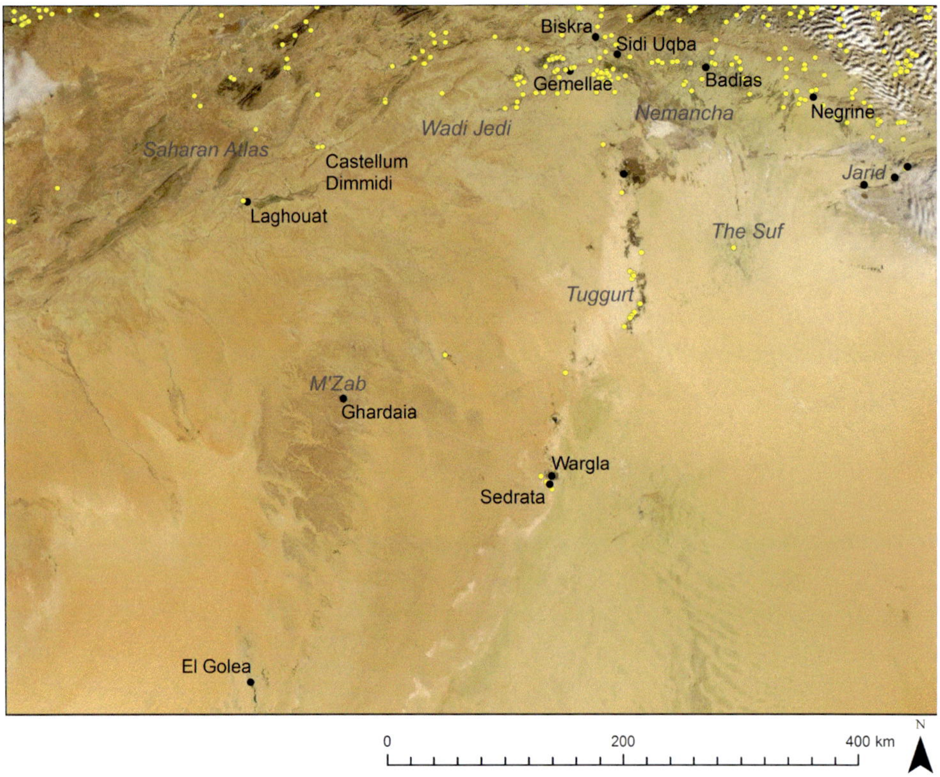

Figure 5.12. Early oases development south of the Aurès, Wadi Jedi, and Saharan Atlas regions (from Sterry and Mattingly 2020a, 213).

Mlili oasis.[111] All three of these locations appear to correspond to locations or people mentioned in the triumph of Cornelius Balbus in 20 BCE (*oppida* of *Tabudium* and *Miglis Gemella, Viscera natio*).[112] Evidence from Roman-era activity has been noted in 14 separate oasis villages in the Ziban, including some stone structures.

There are additional sites where Roman military activity is attested at oases in the military zone both north and west of the Ziban, in the area up to the Chott el-Hodna and in the Saharan Atlas and Ouled Nail mountains.[113] The most south-westerly Roman outpost on the upper Wadi Jedi was at *Castellum Dimmidi* (Messaad), itself a minor oasis. Laghouat, 80 km further south-west, is another important oasis on the upper Wadi Jedi, but also lies at the end of a key route through the Saharan Atlas, leading towards the Roman military posts in *Mauretania*.

111. Fentress 1979; Mattingly et al. 2020b, 214–16; Trousset 1977a.
112. Desanges 1980b, 400–04.
113. Mattingly et al. 2020b, 216–18 for the detail. See also Faure and Leveau 2015.

It is another candidate for precocious development. Orthodox interpretations of Roman military expeditions and interventions in the Saharan Atlas region, moving out beyond the main Roman garrisons, have tended to emphasise the control of montagnard pastoral communities, but in light of the growing evidence for early oasis development along the desert edge, it is worth exploring the possibility that part of the challenge to Rome lay in populous oasis communities as well.[114]

To the south of the Wadi Jedi, there are further groups of Saharan oases, whose pre-Islamic origins are not certainly established, though finds of Roman coins at several of these locations are suggestive.[115] Tuggurt and the Wadi Rhir form an important north–south aligned group of oases, with the most northerly oasis within 50 km of the Roman *limes*. These oases are again fed by natural artesian springs and would be good candidates for early development, though no incontrovertible evidence of Roman activity has been found. On the other hand, Sidi Okba in the mid-7th century contemplated campaigning southwards, which suggests that there were active communities in the pre-Islamic period.[116] The Wargla and the M'zab oases lie further out into the Sahara to the south and south-west of Tuggurt. Their main period of importance was in the medieval era, but further investigation is needed in view of the existence of hydraulic resources at all these oasis locations that were similar to the conditions encountered at the oases of the garrison zone to their north. In the next chapter, I shall further consider the implications that the Wadi Jedi marked some sort of division point among the desert peoples.

In many of the examples looked at above, Roman garrison points coincide with locations where oases came to flourish. The *topos* of "nomadic *Gaetuli*" has blinded us to the possibility that many of these oases were already established by the time Rome arrived on the scene. Rather than seeing the appearance of agriculture and oases in the military zone as a Roman achievement, can we accept instead a different scenario in which Roman deployments were shaped by autochthonous developments? The development of oases was the *sine qua non* for supporting substantial bodies of people on a year-round basis. So which scenario is more plausible? That Rome was responsible for founding oases around sites where its army established forts? Or that Rome posted desert garrisons at water points, where pre-existing oases required supervision but could also help sustain the troops?[117]

There are further small oases to the south of the Mauretanian provinces along the south side of the Saharan Atlas in the c.450 km stretch from Laghouat to Figuig, though the interposition of the High Plains between the Atlas and Algerian Tell ranges and the Saharan Atlas increased the distance between the Roman forts

---

114. Faure and Leveau 2015; Leveau 2018; Morizot 1999.
115. Mattingly et al. 2020b, 218 for references.
116. Mattingly et al. 2020b, 218–20.
117. Mattingly et al. 2020b, 223–28 for an expansion of this argument; cf. Trousset 1986a/b, for pioneering work on the early oases.

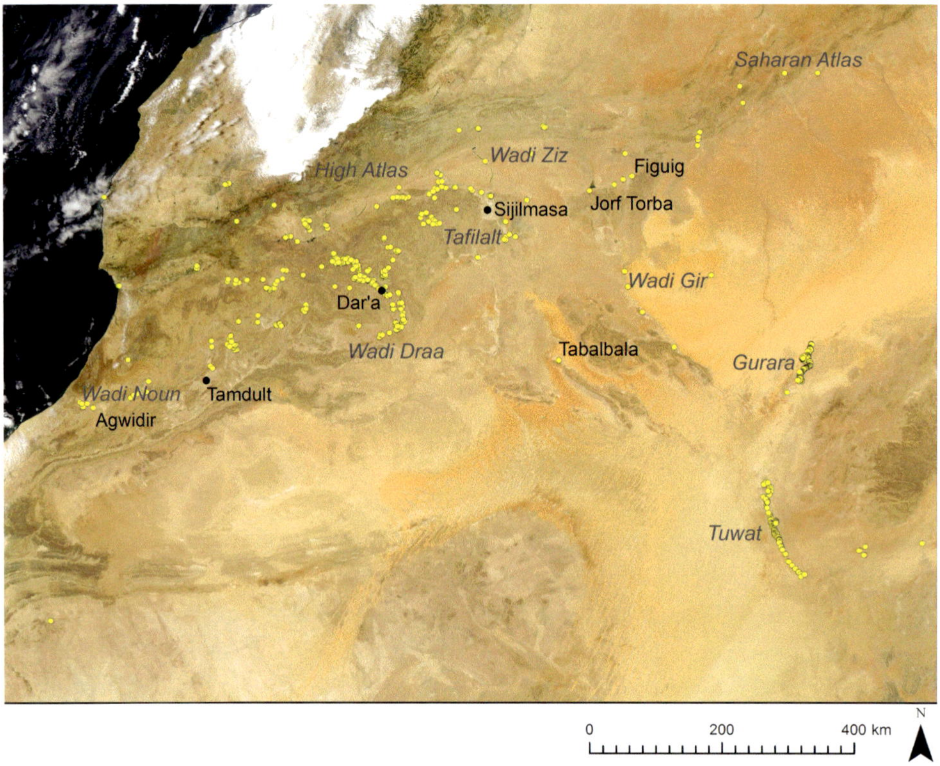

Figure 5.13. Early oasis development among the *Gaetuli* of the west (from Sterry and Mattingly 2020a, 241).

and possible oasis locations. Around Figuig, there is a dense cluster of small oases along a key route over the Saharan Atlas towards the coast at Oran, passing by the westernmost forts of *Mauretania Caesariensis* (*Numerus Syrorum* and *Pomaria*).[118] Foggara irrigation systems are associated with most of these oases, though specific evidence of Roman contacts have not been reported—but these sites lie 250 km south of the Roman provincial territory.

Just to the west of Figuig is the Wadi Gir, almost certainly the *Ger* of the ancient sources, which carried seasonal floodwaters from the Atlas range deep into the Sahara, ultimately feeding the groundwater table of the oasis of Tuwat (Fig. 5.13).[119] There are certainly candidates along the Gir for ancient oasis sites, and human activity is also demonstrated by extensive cemeteries of traditional Saharan tombs.[120] A notable example is the necropolis of Jorf Torba, with its famous painted and engraved images of horses and people. These slabs were

118. Sterry et al. 2020, 252.
119. Sterry et al. 2020, 240–41, 249–50, 252–54.
120. Bokbot 2003; 2019; Bokbot et al. 2008.

evidently placed as an aspect of ancestor worship in funerary chapels attached to the east side of substantial NAIA tumuli of typical Saharan type.[121] These late antique tombs with funerary chapels are a particular feature of the pre-Saharan zone in western Algeria and Morocco and it can be argued present an interesting window on the world of the *Gaetuli*.[122] The people who built and commemorated ancestors in them are generally assumed to have been horse-rearing pastoralists.[123] However, in fact the locations of most known examples of this type of tomb coincide with oasis zones.

The two major oases of southern Morocco are the Tafilalt and the Wadi Draa, and there is increasing evidence from both locations for pre-Islamic origins of oasis agriculture, albeit not before the early centuries CE.[124] Once again, radiocarbon dating of sites and botanical remains have transformed the picture.[125] Further paintings have been found in funerary chapel tombs in the Wadi Draa, in a context that relates them to agricultural-focused settlement. This increases the probability that the similar tombs at Jorf Torba and in the Tafilalt were also related to early oasis communities.[126] Survey work in the Middle Draa Valley has recorded more than 50 settlement sites and 5,600 tombs of NAIA date (Fig. 5.14; cf. also Fig. 10.5 below). The settlement sites located so far are mostly hillforts on the steep escarpments flanking the river valley, where a 150 km long oasis is fed by diversion of water from the river Draa, which until recent dam construction flowed perennially. A smaller number of settlements directly adjacent to or within the oasis have been located and are expected to be more numerous, but they are much more difficult to identify beneath the palimpsest oasis landscape. The Tafilalt has been less explored for NAIA activity, with most attention focused on its great medieval capital, Sijilmasa, but there are some very strong hints at a similar pattern of development as now observed in the Draa. The same types of pre-Islamic burials cluster densely around the oasis, along with several hillforts associated with rock art of chariots and horses, and handmade pottery.[127]

If oasis formation was underway in the early 1st millennium CE at the latest in the pre-desert areas of Morocco and Algeria, then it is also probable that similar changes were occurring to the south too. The outlying oases in both regions, like Tabalbala, Tuwat, Gurara, Tidikelt, and In Salah have numerous foggara irrigation systems and fortified villages of very similar form to the *qsur* of Late Garamantian Fazzan.[128] In the

121. Camps 1984; 1986a; 1995a; Lihoreau 1993; Reygasse 1950, 104–08; Sterry et al. 2020, 254.
122. Bokbot 2019, 328–31.
123. Camps 1986a, 163 attributed the paintings to the *Gaetuli*, whom he described as "nomadic herders and redoubtable horsemen of the northern and western Sahara during the first centuries CE."
124. Mattingly et al. 2017b; 2019c; Sterry et al. 2020, 254–63.
125. Mattingly et al. 2017b, 147–49; 2018, 221–24; Sterry et al. 2020, 242–47.
126. Bokbot 2019; Sterry et al. 2020, 254.
127. Sterry et al. 2020, 254–57.
128. Sterry et al. 2020, 265–69.

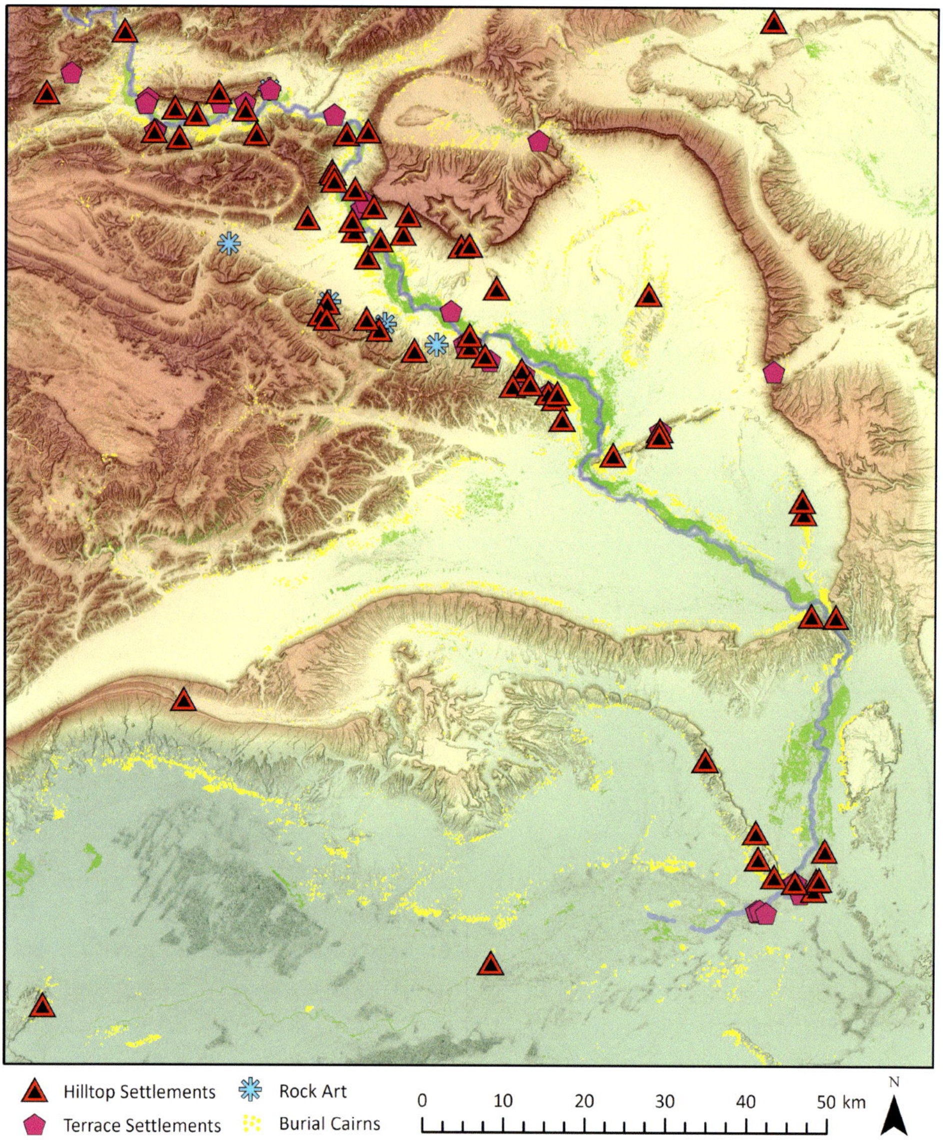

Figure 5.14. The NAIA settlement and funerary monuments (small yellow dots) of the Wadi Draa, southern Morocco (with modern oasis indicated by green shading) (Martin Sterry for OasCiv Project).

absence of any scientific dates from these oases, the presumption hitherto has been that this represents medieval development, but the essential similarity with the now firmly dated Garamantian examples must raise a question as to whether the origins of the undoubted Islamic oasis culture of the Algerian Sahara were earlier.

Looking even further to the south, there are also hints of sedentary development and oasis development in the rarer ecological niches of the southern desert landscapes from al-Kufra and Tibesti, Kawar, the Ahaggar and Aïr massifs, and the Adrar des Ilforas.[129] The late antique burial at Tin Hinan in the Ahaggar is associated by myth with a pastoral Tuareg faction, but can now be read as relating to a group who had oasis connections (dates and grain were found in the tomb).[130] There are many uncertainties in the data, but the overall picture provides compelling evidence that the Sahara was a much more connected space in the NAIA than has been commonly recognised.

The picture outlined here is not entirely out of line with what we may draw from the admittedly confused and confusing account of interior Africa in Ptolemy (*Geography* 4.6). Ptolemy's geographical knowledge was partial, to say the least, but he did have some more detailed information relating to itineraries to Garamantian lands (*Geography* 1.8–11). The problem is that he has clearly tried to join the dots between features reported in different contexts, leading to a condensing of space between, say, the *Garamantes* and the river *Gir* in western Algeria. What is apparent from his account is that he was aware of a number of significant wadis in the Sahara, where at least seasonally there was water—*Daras*, *Gir*, and *Nigris* (Draa, Gir/Saouara, Jedi)—and that some of these flowed into seasonal lakes (chotts). He specifically mentions a number of Gaetulian and Aethiopian peoples from *Gaetulia* and *Libya* and then lists 46 sites, 43 described as "town" and three as "*metropolis*," many in specific relation to the wadi systems. The toponyms are recognisably "Berber," though most are not identifiable with places known in other sources or modern toponyms. The three *metropolis* sites are of obvious interest, not least as they include *Garama*, capital of the *Garamantes*, along with sites called *Nigira* and *Gira* and thus related to the *Nigris* and *Gir*. Were there then two other oasis centres of sufficient scale and development to stand comparison with the Garamantian capital? It seems most logical that, regardless of the exact geographical locations, Ptolemy's portrayal of the Sahara was describing a region studded with oases and with a mix of pastoral and sedentary populations.[131] Finally, it is worth bearing in mind that Ptolemy's information on the *Gir* may well have derived from the Roman campaigns across the Atlas in the early 40s CE (Pliny, *NH* 5.14; Dio, *Histories* 60.9).[132] Notwithstanding the fact that the currently limited scientific dating from the Draa suggests that oasis development in the western Sahara took off only in the 1st millennium CE, these indications in Ptolemy and Pliny might suggest that it had begun earlier.

Some *Gaetuli* groups were noted in the literary sources close to the Atlantic coast and the *Syrtes*. In the latter area, as already noted, there were small coastal

129. Sterry and Mattingly 2020b.
130. Camps 1997; Sterry and Mattingly 2020b, 311.
131. Sterry et al. 2020, 249 for a discussion of these issues in relation to Morocco.
132. Sterry et al. 2020, 241, 249.

oases and these may have been developed quite early. The lifeways of these groups were somewhat different to other *Gaetuli*, with a focus on marine resources, including the production of purple dye and salt fish. Pseudo-Skylax (110.3), for instance, mentions fish-salting areas west of *Sabratha* (*Taricheiai*), and the archaeological evidence from the Libyphoenician sites along the coast indicates involvement with such processes. In a similar way, Gaetulian peoples down the Atlantic coast of Morocco can be equated with coastal communities exploiting shellfish for purple production, as hinted at by Pliny (*NH* 5.12–13)[133] but now confirmed by discovery of an indigenous site with 1st-millennium BCE purple production at Foum Asca on the Moroccan coast north of the Wadi Noun.[134]

So far I have focused on oasis development among the *Gaetuli* groups. Another category of substantial indigenous settlement that is well attested across the Maghrib is the hillfort, and many examples are known from the "transhumance" zone of pre-desert and high steppe, though there has been little attempt to explain how these sites fitted into the transhumant migration patterns. In the absence of excavation at these sites it is no doubt speculative to suggest that, as in examples of the *Garamantes* and Wadi Draa, they may be markers of a society in transition between pastoralism and mixed farming, including an element of agriculture. However, they represent some sort of social evolution in ancient Libyan societies that was most likely underway during the 1st millennium BCE. Further work on this class of sites is urgently required. Hillforts have been recorded in several Gaetulian areas (Fig. 5.15). I have already mentioned the NAIA settlements of the Wadi Draa (Fig. 5.15a–f). Jean Marion also recorded an important group close to Oujda in the northward salient of Gaetulian territory that separates the two Mauretanian provinces.[135] An air photograph shows that an imposing site at al-Krozbet in Algeria lay very close to a Roman fort near the al-Kantara pass (Fig. 5.15k) and the site certainly continued in occupation into the Roman era.[136] Pierre Morizot has published a number of similar type from the Aurès ranges.[137] The work of the UNESCO Libyan Valleys Survey in the Libyan pre-desert recorded quite a number of hillforts whose origins are believed to extend back to pre-Roman times (Fig. 5.15b–j).[138] The majority of these sites were under 1 ha in area, with relatively simple habitation units, though there are signs of increasing sophistication of construction and plan over time. Some of these sites at least were still in occupation in late Roman times.

133. Desanges 1980b, 127–30; Hamdoune 2018,
134. Onrubia Pintado et al. 2016. Rebuffat 1974b for some other evidence along the coastal region south-west of Rabat.
135. Marion 1957; 1959.
136. Baradez 1949a, 251 (photo), 253; Mattingly 1995, 46 (plan); Mattingly et al. 2013a, 75 (locational plan)
137. Morizot 1997; 2003, 71–74.
138. Barker et al. 1996a, 116–18; 1996b, 263–64, 310–14; Mattingly 1995, 42–48.

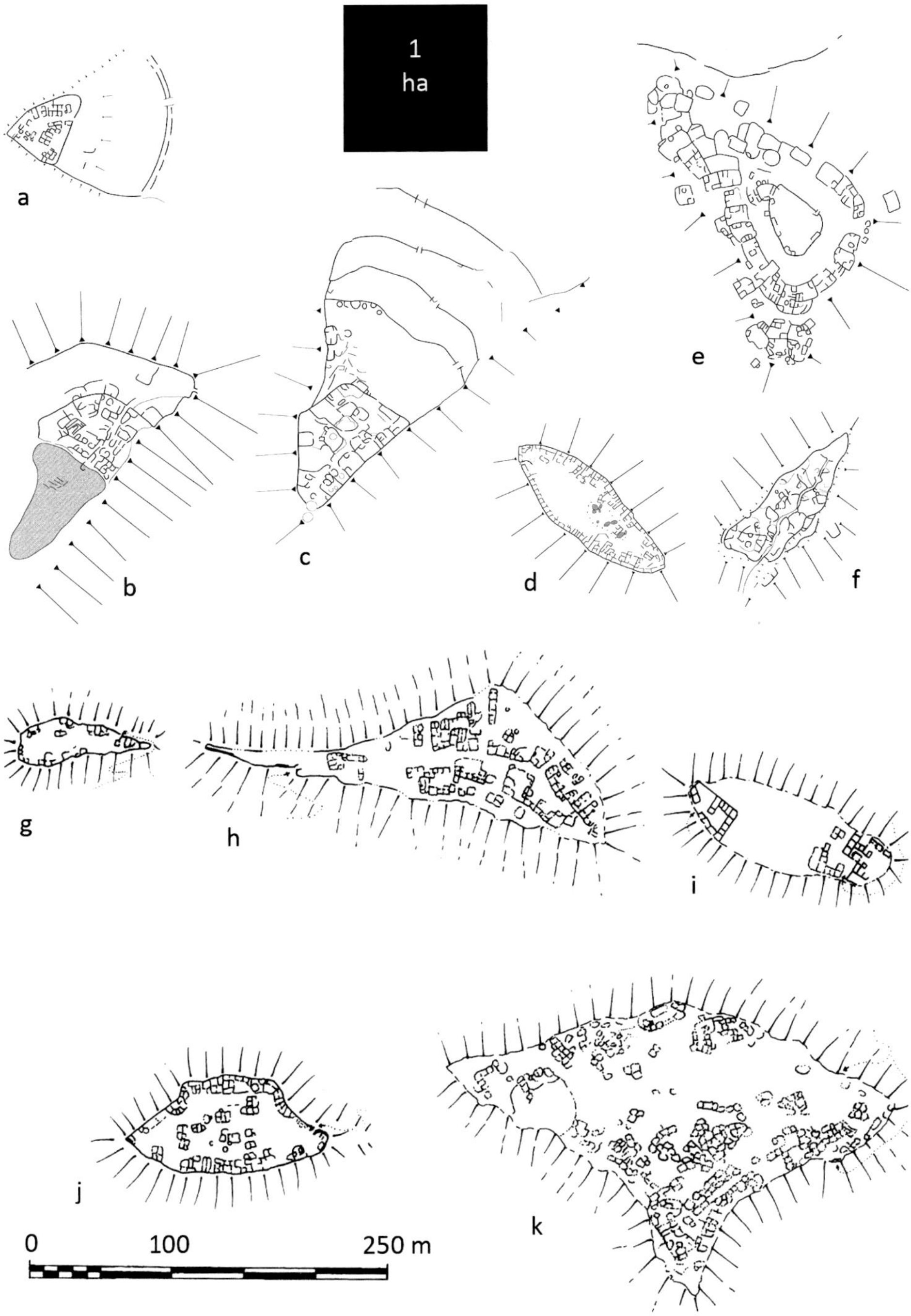

Figure 5.15. Gaetulian hillforts. a–f) Moroccan pre-desert (Wadi Draa). g–j) Tripolitanian pre-desert. k) Algerian pre-desert (author's montage after Mattingly et al. 2017b, 154; Mattingly 1995, 46).

Other Evidence of a Gaetulian Cultural *Koine*

Just as the *Numidae* and the *Mauri* can to some extent be associated with distinctive and somewhat regionalised funerary traditions, so the peoples of the Sahara and its northern margins seem to have shared some commonalities of burial tradition and style of monuments, while also displaying regional difference.[139] Terms such as *bazina* and *chouchet* are often used to describe various styles of monument, and in general the modern scholarly categories can be confusing.[140] In my work I have preferred to use descriptive language to define the categories. In fieldwork in southern Morocco and southern Libya, my projects have encountered remarkably similar types of monument, significant alignments and orientations, and similar treatment of the body and cultural practices, such as the use of red ochre in funerary rituals.[141] The most common types of pre-Islamic funerary monuments in the Sahara comprise circular tumuli of varied size (Fig. 5.16). Typically these are low mounds of piled stone over a burial laid on the surface or placed in a shallow pit or a built cist structure, generally centrally placed.[142] In the NAIA such tombs were mostly designed to accommodate a single burial, whereas in the late Neolithic age they had typically accommodated multiple burials.[143]

In both Morocco and Libya, some of the NAIA cairns were built up to a greater height (up to 3 m), commonly involving more careful selection and placement of construction materials, to create a corbelled superstructure.[144] A third predominant and widespread type was the drum cairn or drum tomb, with a low vertical wall defining the perimeter of the monument and often with a flat or slightly domed upper surface.[145] A further category comprised a range of stepped constructions.[146] These are arguably the most widespread Saharan types and can be found between Morocco and Libya, Algeria and Niger. A peculiarity of the *Garamantes* is that in addition to a long tradition of these sorts of monuments in the 1st millennium BCE, they added further innovative types and shapes in the 1st millennium CE.

139. Sterry et al. 2019, 527–31 for a summary of the ideas of a funerary *koine* in the Sahara.
140. For the classic exposition, see Camps 1961, (with region-by-region bibliographical essay, 573–605); see also Mattingly 2003a, 188–89 for the confusing terminology of chouchet, bazina, etc.
141. For Libya, see Mattingly 2003a, 187–204; 2007a; 2010a; Mattingly et al. 2019b; for Morocco, Mattingly et al. 2017b, 149–53; 2019c, 76–78.
142. For a range of examples, see Camps 1961, 65–76; Clarke and Brooks 2019, 344–49; Mattingly 2003a, 196–98; Mattingly et al. 2017b, 149–51; 2019b, 58 (types 1a, 1c, 1d); Mori 2013, 204–08; Paris 1995; Reygasse 1950, 32–62.
143. Di Lernia and Manzi 2002.
144. For example, see Bokbot 2019, 331–32; Camps 1961, 186–87; Mattingly 2003a, 197–98; Mattingly et al. 2017b, 151 (type 4); 2019b, 57–58 (type 1b).
145. For example, see Bokbot 2019, 331–32; Camps 1961, 166–72; Clarke and Brooks 2019, 349–50; Mattingly 2003a, 198–99; Mattingly et al. 2017b, 149–151 (type 3); 2019b, 55–60 (type 3: differentiating between drum cairns (3a) and drum tombs (3b) in terms of the height of the perimeter wall and/or the quality of its construction); Mori 2013, 204–07.
146. For example, see Camps 1961, 163–66; Clarke and Brooks 2019, 351; Mattingly 2003a, 199–201; Mattingly et al. 2017b, 149–151 (type 3); 2019b, 59, 61 (type 5).

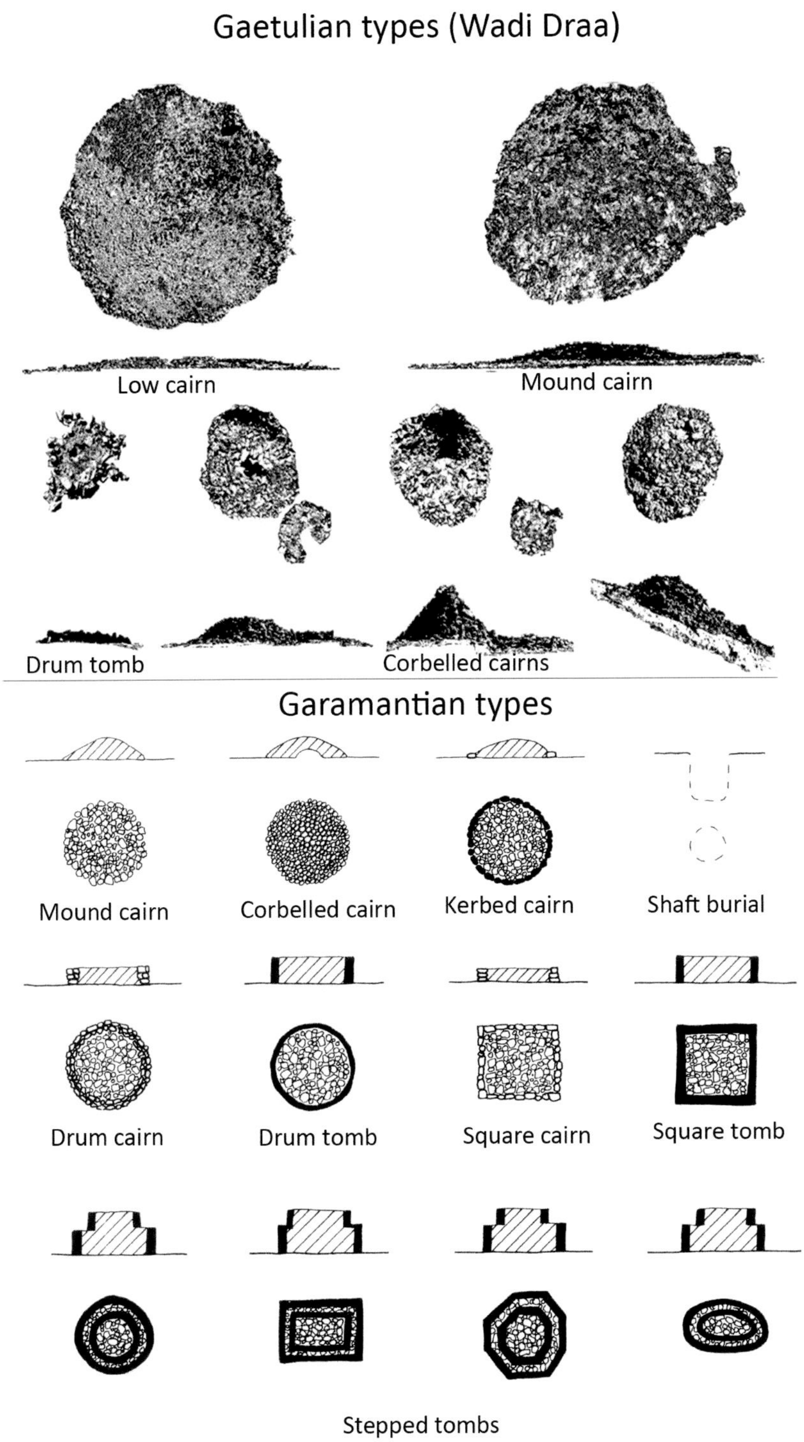

Figure 5.16. Typical forms of Saharan Iron Age burial monument. a) *Gaetuli* of Wadi Draa. b) *Garamantes* of Wadi al-Ajal (author's montage after Mattingly et al. 2017b, 151; Mattingly 2003a, 197).

Large cemeteries of conjoined shaft burials, creating a honeycomb effect, is one example of this.[147] More striking was the Garamantian uptake of rectangular and square forms of monument, alongside the traditional Saharan emphasis on circular form and the construction of mud-brick pyramids and stone mausolea, the latter imitative of Mediterranean traditions.[148]

The body of the deceased was quite commonly wrapped in a shroud of leather or textile and placed on the left or right side in a flexed position. It is not uncommon to find traces of red staining on the bones, evidently the result of ochre being deposited on the corpse. Grave goods tend to be relatively few, with the exception of occasional beads and amulets, though again the *Garamantes* are a significant outlier in the Classic and Late periods, when a large volume of Mediterranean imports along with local handmade wares, textiles, and beadwork were included in burials relating to different social levels. Funerary furniture is sometimes encountered, often placed on the east side of tombs and comprising stelae, offering tables or receptacles, small built altars, funerary enclosures, and in the most elaborate cases funerary chapels. There are echoes of these Saharan burial rites in the Libyphoenician centres and in Roman times as well. Many of these features seem to relate to the sun or to ancestors. For example, in the Garamantian heartlands, most burials had an east–west orientation of either surface features or orientation of the body below, with stelae and offering tables (and sometimes funerary enclosures) mainly on the east side (but sometimes alternatively to the west).[149] As already noted above, near the Moroccan oases, some of the larger NAIA tumuli had more developed funerary chapels built into their east side, providing crawl spaces in which descendants could approach close to the tomb chamber in the centre of the mound. Some of these funerary chapels were decorated with paintings, including images that seem to evoke family relations.[150]

Further evidence of a possible cultural *koine* in the Sahara concerns Libyan inscriptions, and rock engravings and paintings of horses, mounted warriors, and chariot images, which are very widespread, not only in the Gaetulian zone but further south as well.[151] Although the imagery of warriors on horseback bearing circular shields and spears also bears comparison to the tradition among the *Numidae* and *Mauri* further north, the Saharan repertoire follows its own visual code (Fig. 5.17).[152] The imagery of chariots is widespread across the Sahara and has

147. Mattingly 2003a, 197–98; Mattingly et al. 2019b, 58, 60 (type 2).
148. Mattingly 2003a, 189–94, 197, 200; Mattingly et al. 2019b, 59–61 (type 4 rectangular, pyramids, and mausolea)
149. Mattingly 2003a, 210–34; Mattingly et al. 2019b, 81–100.
150. Bokbot 2019, 322–31.
151. Barnett 2019a, 58–65 (dating), 104–06 (horses), 131–41 (armed men), 146–51 (chariots); 160–66 (Libyan inscriptions), 230–31 (distribution in Garamantian heartlands of Wadi al-Ajal); Camps 1989; 1991; Camps and Gast 1982; Dupuy 1995; Gauthier and Gauthier 2011; 2015; Lutz and Lutz 1995. See also Aghouli-Zaha 2006; Biagetti et al. 2012; Le Quellec 2011 on Libyan inscriptions from the Sahara.
152. Bokbot et al. 2021.

Figure 5.17. Saharan imagery of mounted warriors and chariots. a–b) Chariot imagery from Tadrart Akakus, Libya. c) Horseman from Akakus. d–e) Garamantian heartlands, Wadi al Ajal. f–j) Gaetulian horsemen, Wadi Draa (all photos: author).

sometimes been overgeneralised as evidence of Garamantian influence—in fact it makes better sense if we see horses and chariots as having been equally associated with a wide range of the Gaetulian peoples, who were also opening up the Sahara for oasis settlement and trade in the 1st millennium BCE and early 1st millennium CE. The warlike propensity of the *Gaetuli* was of course alluded to by the sources, and we also hear of them serving under Carthaginian, Numidian, Mauretanian, and, later, Roman commanders. The scale of Saharan horse-breeding mentioned by Strabo (17.3.23), 100,000 colts a year, though possibly inflated, seems more reasonable when the possibility of larger development of the Saharan population at this time is appreciated.

Saharan Trade

The identification of pre-Islamic trans-Saharan trade, for long a point of deep controversy, is now better supported by scientific evidence, providing a "smoking gun" argument for trade.[153] There is a visibility issue with Saharan trade, due to its being based on organics and perishables (textiles, enslaved people, salt, leather goods, oasis produce) and exotic valuables (gold, other metals, ivory), none of which are well represented in archaeological deposits (though significantly all are attested in finds from Garamantian Fazzan).[154] Liverani's arguments for the early beginnings of this trade—associating it with the oasis route that is central to the Herodotean account of the Sahara (4.181–84)—emphasise the essential interconnectedness of oasis formation and the establishment of networks of trading contacts.[155] The *Garamantes* provide a particular (and perhaps unrepresentative) perspective on Saharan trade with the Roman Empire due to their high consumption of Mediterranean goods. The large volumes of Roman cook wares, table wares and fine wares, amphorae (primarily used for transporting wine and olive oil), vessel glass, metalwork, and metals represent organised and sustained trade, and cannot be explained as the result of the short-term results of Roman subsidies or gift-exchange outside the Empire.[156] These goods were not restricted to the centre of Garamantian power at Jarma, but widespread across both funerary and settlement sites, and in different zones of the Garamantian oases.[157] While the volume of Roman material found at other Saharan locations is smaller, it is widespread.[158] However, the *Garamantes*

153. Mattingly 2017; Mattingly et al. 2017c 433–38, for the broad debate.
154. Mattingly 2010a, 523–30; Mattingly 2017; Wilson 2012a; 2017.
155. Liverani 2000; 2006, 445–56. On the early development of desert "roads" Förster and Reimer 2013; Rebuffat 1970c; 1970d;
156. Mattingly 2017; Mattingly and Cole 2017; Leitch et al. 2017.
157. Leitch et al. 2017, 326–33 for maps illustrating distributions for a number of commodities.
158. Mauny 1956; 1978a; Salama 1981, for a record of other finds of Roman material culture from the Sahara. The material is thin outside the Garamantian heartlands, but wide-spread.

were perhaps exceptional in their engagement with Roman material culture, and it is important to remember that at all times the staples of Saharan trade have been organic or perishable materials (enslaved people, textiles and finished garments, leatherwork, wild beasts, horses, camels, salt, oasis crops), or luxury goods (gold, silver, copper alloys, ivory, semi-precious stones) and thus leave little trace in normal archaeological deposits.[159] Further interesting conclusions about Garamantian trade are that it depended on Garamantian control of separate trading networks to north and south, and that the Garamantian manufacturing capacity of a number of key materials (textiles, carnelian, and, later, glass beads) facilitated this. Trade is in fact an essential adjunct of the oasis economy; because the start-up and running costs of irrigated agriculture are so high, the enterprise can easily become unsustainable without the additional income sources that trade brings.[160] This too has implications for the relations between the oases of the northern Sahara and the Roman provinces, to which I shall return in Chapter 12.

Some Overall Conclusions on the NAIA

The level of archaeological investigation of both oasis and hillfort settlements of the NAIA remains minimal, but the evidence I have gathered together is highly suggestive. The combined evidence of a degree of sedentarisation among the *Garamantes* and the *Gaetuli* is now substantial and compelling. The implications of this new vision of the Africa that Rome encountered are considerable in historical terms alone. This does not, of course, mean that there were no pastoral groups in these societies. On the contrary, I am absolutely certain that pastoralists were at all times an important part of the Saharan societies. A crucial difference of my perspective is that I see transhumant groups as operating not with some supposed antipathy for cultivators, but being closely interrelated both with sedentary farming communities in the desert oases and with other sedentary groups at the northern ends of their transhumance routes. Hillforts are another important category of sites whose distribution needs to be more fully mapped and whose development and social function investigated, especially as they may allow us to date and establish stages in the semi- or full sedentarisation of pastoral groups, starting in the 1st millennium BCE.

We now have to take account of a more diverse and mixed economic basis for these societies, with the agricultural production of oases allowing an incremental

159. Mattingly 2017, 24–29 for discussion and a table.

160. Mattingly et al. 2017c; Scheele 2010; 2017; Sterry and Mattingly 2020c, 350–51. The availability of slave labour, whether linked to trade or raiding, was also a probable important consideration, Fentress 2011; Wilson 2012a.

step-up in Saharan populations. Our perspective on Rome's early attempts to extend her control of the southern zone is very different if we accept that the military disposition was attempting to control and dominate *both* mobile people *and* oasis communities. The manpower resources of oasis communities should not be underestimated, especially if, as I suspect, they were confederated or allied with more mobile elements in the intervening desert spaces.

A further important observation is that the evolution of oases represented not an instant of change, but rather a gradual and dynamic process spread across thousands of years, beginning in the Western Egyptian Desert in the 3rd millennium BCE and still continuing in the Islamic era well into the 2nd millennium CE. Rome's relationship with the desert and steppic peoples was thus from the outset either dealing with mixed communities of sedentary oasis-dwellers and pastoral groups, with strong symbiotic relations between them, or with pastoral communities where some degree of sedentarism was starting to get underway or was latent.[161]

The nature of the agricultural package adopted by the *Garamantes* was subtly but clearly distinct from that of the *Numidae*, revealed by the work at *Althiburos* or the *Mauri* as represented at Rirha, demarcating the Saharan agricultural revolution from the Maghribian one (compare Tables 4.1, 4.3 and 5.1).[162] On the other hand, that is not to imply that the *Garamantes* were the ultimate origin for an agricultural diffusion from the central Sahara to the regions to the west. The nature of the hydrological regimes encountered across the Sahara are very varied, from perennial rivers (Wadi Draa, the Nile and the Niger) to seasonal floods in wadis (Wadi Gir, Wadi Ziz, other oases along the Atlasian and Aurès mountain fronts), artesian springs, other natural springs from a high watertable, balance wells into elevated groundwater, deeper wells, underground channels (foggaras), groundwater catchments, and so on.[163] The nature of the crops grown will also tend to vary in relation to the nature, quantity, and security of the water supply. In modern Morocco, one can observe these differences from one oasis to the next and even within different zones of a single oasis.[164]

The crucial argument for the purposes of this book is that in many parts of the Sahara, oases were already in existence at the point of first contact with Rome, and in other areas it is likely that there was experimentation, with cultivation being adventitiously added to the lifeways of groups that remained primarily pastoral—for instance, with the scratch cultivation of cereals after rains.

161. Mattingly and Sterry 2020a, 5–24; Sterry and Mattingly 2020b, 330–43 for a summary discussion of the key issues of ancient Saharan sedentarisation.
162. See Duckworth et al. 2020b, 19–24 for a detailed development of this argument.
163. Mattingly and Sterry 2020a, 12–17 with map on p. 16.
164. Future work on a wider array of Saharan oasis environments will no doubt show something of this diversity.

There is a strong model in Moroccan history of the confrontation of two zones, the *Bilad al-Mahkzan* (the land of order) and the *Bilad as-Siba* (the land of disorder), in which the rich agricultural lands of the former have been periodically (indeed recurrently) overrun by the people from the latter.[165] However, the almost invariable sequel to the overthrow of the established order has been that the people from the deserts have created new dynasties to replace those they had defeated. If nothing else, this shows the dangers of underestimating the communities at the margins of Maghribian history. Far from being a sparsely inhabited space of nomadic pastoralists, the ancient Sahara was, within its ecological limits, a reservoir of people, food, horses, and horsemen. The lack of acknowledgement of the oasis-dwelling component—and the importance of these people to the overall Gaetulian demography—continues to limit many studies of the "tribal situation" in North Africa, no matter how well deployed the primary sources of texts and inscriptions.[166]

Furthermore, there is also an important question to ask about the urban characteristics of the largest and most successful of the oasis settlements. The detailed evidence from the *Garamantes* demonstrates a strong hierarchy of sites in terms of scale and function. Within their own terms, there are strong arguments for recognising these as examples of a distinctively Saharan form of urbanisation.[167] Once again, we need to recognise that this was a separate and distinctive urban tradition from that developed in the northern Maghrib among *Mauri* and *Numidae*. These diverse African traditions of urbanisation need to be taken account of alongside the Libyphoenician examples when we consider the urban developments under Rome (Fig. 5.18).

Another of the main conclusions from this introductory section is that the story of Africa in the Roman era needs to be told in relation to a broad geographical and chronological frame, recognising that there were some fundamental differences in terms of climate, environment, population groups, languages, and culture across time. However, it can also be argued that there were some important continuities too, and one of the purposes of this introduction has been to establish something of the character of regions and peoples of North Africa and to argue that these distinctions had long-term salience in the story of Africa and Rome.

I have illustrated that primarily with reference to two specific markers of ancient civilisation that are normally attributed to exogenous influences: urbanisation

165. Sterry et al. 2020, 249–50.

166. Hamdoune 2018 is an exemplary study in many ways and presents the key textual material in impressive detail, but at no point is there a recognition that the people occupying the spaces where oases later existed were other than pastoralists in Roman times. See, for example, p. 75 on "une remontée temporaire de pasteurs depuis le Tafilalet jusqu'à la Moulouya, une movement aussi puissant que temporaire."

167. Mattingly and MacDonald 2013; Mattingly and Sterry 2013; Sterry and Mattingly 2020b, 243–51.

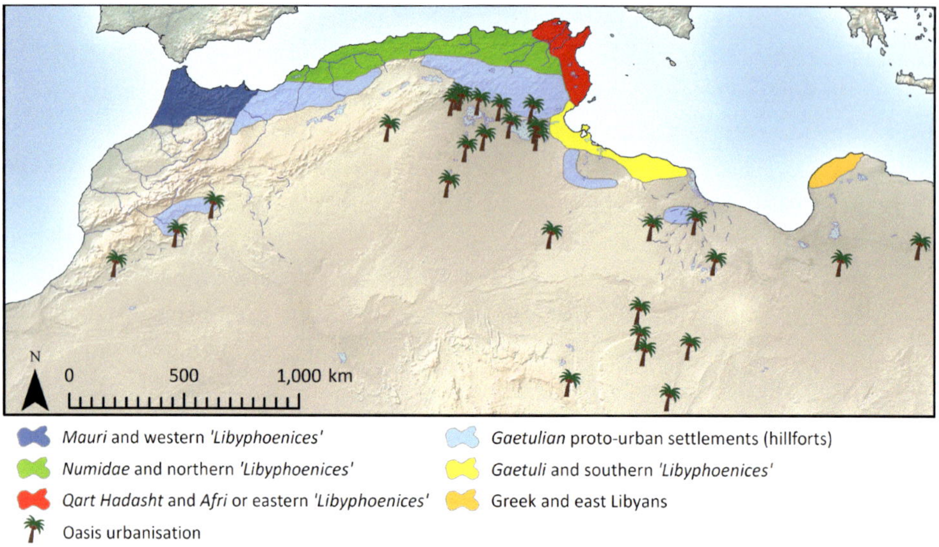

Figure 5.18. Different pathways to urbanisation in North Africa (Martin Sterry, from author's rough).

and agriculture. The importance of Libyphoenician sites in the urbanisation in Africa has long been recognised, but I also suggest that it has been overemphasised in the absence of evidence pertaining to contemporary purely autochthonous developments. When towns did start to appear in the deep Carthaginian hinterland and in neighbouring areas of Numidia, this has been assumed to have been driven by Punic models and inspiration. The new evidence I have presented necessitates a re-evaluation of the significance and early origins of towns in North Africa, recognising that there were a number of separate paths to urbanisation (Fig. 5.18).

In addition, though, it is now clear that later urbanisation in the southern parts of the Roman provinces also built on pre-existing oasis communities. In place of an empty desert, with a few scattered nomad bands, I argue that by the time Augustus began to extend the southern boundary of Rome's African province, there was an already well-developed (and spreading) zone of oasis communities inhabiting nucleated settlements, cultivating date palms and a range of other crops.[168] The date palm was adopted as a strong symbol of Carthaginian identity not only because of the punning similarity between the Greek words for "Phoenician" and "date palm" but also, I suggest, for the simple reason that it expressed Carthaginian territorial

168. This argument is not in itself new—Pol Trousset published some remarkably perceptive studies in the 1980s on this issue (1986a; 1987b), and my own earlier work on the African military deployment (Mattingly 1995, 41–49) emphasised the potential significance of oasis communities—but the evidence on the ground has hitherto been meagre.

claims in North Africa more widely—a landscape that was already studded with palm oases in the 1st millennium BCE.[169]

Similarly, the expansion of agriculture in Maghrib and Sahara during the 1st millennium BCE is no longer tied to the idea of it being a Phoenician and Greek introduction as part of their colonial ventures. Rather than diffusion from a single point of first introduction, we also seem to have separate adaptations and transmissions in different parts of North Africa, and some of this activity certainly predates the first colonial settlements on the Mediterranean littoral. However, for the desert at least, this was not *in situ* domestication but an imported package. The agricultural package of the *Garamantes* is different in crucial respects to the first steps towards domestication of Saharan plants, evident in the Late Neolithic era, when certain grasses appear in fodder deposits in caves in the Akakus mountains.[170] On the other hand, it diverges from the evidence of the adoption of agriculture in the Maghrib in the early first millennium BCE, as demonstrated at the site of *Althiburos* in central Tunisia and Rirha in Morocco.[171] The different composition of the Maghribian and Saharan agricultural packages in the first millennium BCE is a strong indicator of their probable separate pathways of technological transfer. Broadly, we may characterise *Althiburos* and Rirha as adaptations of a Mediterranean package and Fazzan as a Saharan one. Although there is some overlap in the range of crops, the differences are also significant, with the date palm, the limited range of cultivated trees, and delayed appearance of pulses in Fazzan contrasting with the high presence of pulses and greater development of arboriculture at an earlier date at *Althiburos.*

Accepting indigenous agency in things like developing urbanisation and agriculture is a lot more straightforward once we fully recognise the scale and sophistication of the autochthonous societies. First, we have to deconstruct and clear aside the crude stereotypes and *topoi* of both ancient and modern writings on the "barbarian other." Indeed, a striking aspect of the 1st millennium BCE was the emergence of *Mauri* and *Numidae* states covering a large area of the Maghrib alongside the burgeoning power of *Qart Hadasht*, whose African territory was centred on modern Tunisia, and of *Cyrene* in east Libya. To the south of all of these lay the Gaetulian and other societies of the Sahara.

Under Rome, the former kingdom of *Mauretania* was largely replicated in the provinces of *Mauretania Tingitana* and *Caesariensis* (and later *Sitifensis*). Part of the former Numidian kingdom was continued as the eponymous province and part was added in to *Africa Proconsularis*, which had absorbed the main zone of Carthaginian and Libyphoenician cities, while the Cyrenaican territory was established as a separate province linked to Crete and the Greek-speaking East Mediterranean world.

---

169. Cherif 2006.
170. Castelletti et al. 1999; Mercuri 1999; Mercuri et al. 1998.
171. Callegarin et al. 2016a, 45–109; López and Cantero 2016.

The development of Saharan societies continued apace, with oasis development spreading west from the central Sahara among the Gaetulian societies.

In the early Islamic period, these same broad divisions are still reflected in the sources, with the region divided between *Maghrib al-Aqsa* (equivalent to *Mauretania*), *Maghrib al-Awsat* (eastern *Mauretania* and *Numidia*), *Ifriqiya* (*Africa Proconsularis*), and *Barqa* (*Cyrenaica*).[172] The Sahara (*Bilad as-Siba*) was also seen as a land of opportunity by the Islamic invaders and was soon connected into new trading networks.

I have argued for a linguistic difference and distance between the Libyan population groups of the Maghrib (*Mauri* and *Numidae*) and the peoples of the steppe, pre-desert, and Saharan regions to the south (*Gaetuli*, *Aethiopes*, and *Garamantes*). Recent linguistic studies of the evolution and spread of Saharan and Maghribian linguistic groups, especially those associated with Berber dialects, correlate quite closely with phases of development of Saharan oasis societies and the sedentary agricultural settlements of *Numidia* like *Althiburos*.[173] But while "Berbers" were undoubtedly part of Garamantian society, studies of Garamantian skeletal remains clearly indicate a more mixed population including Black Africans in all probability of both Saharan and sub-Saharan origins.[174] Similarly, the material remains on the early Garamantian site of Zinkekra include lithic tools that associate strongly with the Late Pastoral tradition. This seems to be evidence in favour of the sort of integrationist and cyclical model of the spread of agriculture in northern Europe advocated by Gron and Sørensen.[175]

The cultural encounters between Rome and the broad blocks of Africans identified were from the start diverse and differentiated one from the other. Some of the interaction involved groups who were to a degree representative of earlier settlers from outside the region. The Libyphoenician cities of the coastal territories had well-developed settlements and farming systems on a Mediterranean model, tied into Mediterranean trade and cultural networks, though we have also seen that the inputs of local African groups to these communities may have been substantial. Things were inevitably complicated further by the settlement in Africa of Roman veterans and other immigrants. In revising the view of the makings of "Roman Africa," I have redressed the balance between endogenous and exogenous factors, so as, in other words, to explore more carefully an emic approach alongside the more conventional etic emphasis.

I have concentrated in Chapters 4 and 5 on the African components. The Numidians and Mauretanians (and indigenous Libyans in Libyphoenician

172. Fenwick 2020, 3.
173. Ehret 2019; Fentress 2019.
174. Power et al. 2019, 148–54.
175. Gron and Sørensen 2018.

territory) were developing urbanisation, agriculture, and trading economies in parallel during the 1st millennium BCE. Although it is clear that both *Numidae* and *Mauri* were profoundly influenced by aspects of Punic culture, the extent of this was visibly different. There is evidence that both groups adopted Punic as an elite language of communication and written authority, though it is clear that Libyan dialects remained predominant within their territories. They were early adopters of Mediterranean architectural innovations and other cultural paraphernalia. However, in religious practices there were some sharp divisions, with the Baal/Tinnit cult widely adopted in Numidian territory, but almost entirely absent in western Mauretania. When integrated into the Roman provinces, they strongly associated with certain aspects of Roman culture—such as Latinising the names of their major deities, erecting Latin tombstones, and ornamenting their many towns with Roman civic amenities, though it appears that Numidian cultural traits also endured. There are numerous instances in the Roman onomastics from Africa of individuals' names evoking *Mauri*, *Numidae*, and *Gaetuli* identities.[176]

Ancient Saharan identities under Rome appear to have differed considerably from those in the north of the Roman provinces, and I shall argue below that this in part follows on from pre-Roman cultural differences between *Gaetuli* and *Numidae/Mauri*. This probably reflects not only a degree of cultural distance from early times between the Libyan peoples of the Maghrib and *Gaetuli*, but also plausibly the presence of "Aethiopian" elements within the oases.[177]

One of the arguments I shall develop in the rest of this book is that the populations of these varied zones had pronounced cultural differences, including different languages (or at least dialects) that recurrently resurfaced and worked against the long-term unification of the entire zone, either by Rome or the Islamic caliphate (and the successor Islamic dynasties of the Maghrib). In other words, the distinctions between the *Mauri* and the *Numidae* mattered, as did their mutual differences from the *Gaetuli*, while a Gaetulian would have recognised their own cultural distance from a Garamantian. There were also important cultural distinctions pertaining to the Libyphoenician centres, reflecting the diversity of the Libyan components. The extent to which the North African populations engaged with Latin (and/or Greek in Cyrenaica) was to some extent context specific—fundamental in the Roman army, in city affairs and Christianity, but of varying penetration in rural districts and in the religious and funerary spheres. Other languages were incorporated into the epigraphic habit in various parts of North Africa, reflecting the mixed heritage. Libyan texts are common in some areas, but almost absent in others. The same is

176. Coltelloni-Trannoy 2011a, 105.

177. See Power et al. 2019; Ricci et al. 2019 for the mixed ethnicities of the Garamantian population based on osteological and other analyses.

true of Punic/Neo-Punic and the so-called Latino-Punic texts. One of the problems with the homogenising tendencies of Romanisation theory is that it inevitably creates an unrepresentative *average* from such diverse societies. In my approach, the differences are more important than the broad similarities, allowing us to see the emergence of discrepant identities. That is what I shall now tackle in the rest of this book.

Part 3: The Military Community

Chapter 6

ARS MILITARIS

Pacifying, Protecting, Policing, Posturing?

Introduction

On 1 July 128, after inspecting their manoeuvres close to the legionary fortress at *Lambaesis*, the emperor Hadrian addressed his "very own *legio III Augusta*" and other units of the provincial garrison. The emperor evidently enjoyed "playing at soldiers" and military governors more routinely did this sort of thing, one imagines, both as a way of keeping troops up to the mark and as a means of renewing the close bond between the emperor/Empire and its armies.[1] Uniquely, the speech that Hadrian gave that day has been substantially preserved. It tells us much about both Hadrian, the first ruling emperor to visit North Africa, and the military community in Africa. Hadrian was careful to deliver his speech in a direct style of Latin that would be clear and comprehensible to the soldiers.[2]

> Your commander has himself told me on your behalf of numerous factors that would have excused you in my judgement [absence of a cohort serving with the Proconsul of *Africa*, reinforcements sent from the legion to another province, the dispersed nature of African garrison outposts, recent changes of legionary base] ... but you have not been dilatory in any respect at all.[3]

It was engraved on a stone monument on the main military parade ground to the west of the legionary fortress so that Hadrian could continue to engage the attention of the community of soldiers long after his visit.[4] However, the speech also makes it clear that the military community was not a single homogeneous body. Hadrian's words reflected the hierarchical nature of the military community, led by its officer corps and with some units notably more elite than others, as indicated

1. Birley 1997 for a detailed biography of Hadrian.
2. Campbell 1984, 74–80; cf. Birley 1997, 203–14; Opper 2008, 85–87.
3. *ILS* 2487, 9133–35. Translation after Campbell 1994, 18–20. For most recent commentary on the text, see Le Bohec 2003; Speidel 2006.
4. Le Bohec 2003.

by his comments on the cavalry *ala*: "the beauty of their horses and the splendour of their equipment are in keeping with their pay."

One of the most interesting things about the speech is that it did not continue as a simple paean of praise, though Hadrian was careful to refer positively to his legate, Q. Fabius Catullinus, to the auxiliary prefects and to the centurions. He directed specific comments at each of the different groups of troops he had inspected, with the strongest praise reserved for the legionary cavalry and an auxiliary *ala*.

> To the legionary cavalry. Military manoeuvres have their own rules so to speak and if anything is added or taken away from them the drill is made either less effective or more difficult. Indeed the more complications are added the less impressive it appears. Of the difficult manoeuvres, you have completed the most difficult of all, throwing the javelin while wearing metal corslets.
>
> To the *ala I Pannoniorum*. You did everything in order. You filled the plain with your exercises, you threw your javelins with style … Just now you mounted your horses agilely and yesterday you did it swiftly. If anything had been lacking in your performance I should have noted it, if anything had been obviously bad I should have mentioned it, but throughout the entire manoeuvres you satisfied me uniformly … I grant you a donative.

Hadrian showed himself an aficionado of military manoeuvres and mixes complimentary phrases with more critical comment, and when the judgement was more neutral he was a master at damning with faint praise. This was particularly evident with the less elite units of the garrison, including two *cohortes equitata*.

> [T]his manoeuvre … has the appearance of real warfare and trains you in such a way that I can congratulate you. Cornelianus your prefect has performed his duties satisfactorily. However, the riding manoeuvres do not win my approval ... The cavalryman should ride out from cover and engage in pursuit [cautiously, for if he cannot] see where he is going or if he cannot rein in his horse when he wishes, he will surely be exposed to hidden traps … It is difficult for cavalry attached to a cohort to win approval even on their own, and more difficult still for them not to incur criticism when following on a manoeuvre by an *ala* … But, despite the heat, you avoided any boredom by doing energetically what had to be done.

The main emphasis in the speech was on the work of the cavalry contingents present, but when auxiliary infantry were mentioned it was in the context of showing their constructional skills in the speedy erection of defences.

> [Defences which] others take several days to finish, you completed in one. You have built a wall, a considerable construction ... with large, heavy and irregular stones. You dug a ditch straight through hard and rough gravel and have made it smooth by levelling. When the work was approved, you entered camp quickly, got your rations and weapons and followed the cavalry ... hailing them with a great shout when they returned.

The overall impression one derives from Hadrian's speech is that the army had been asked to showcase for imperial scrutiny its strength in cavalry and in construction of defences. The first was perhaps inevitable since the African peoples watched over by the garrison were renowned for their light cavalry. The message was that Rome's imperial forces were well armed and well trained in cavalry warfare and were not to be messed with. The reward for the army's excellent display in wall-building may well have been the announcement of Hadrian's plan to erect linear barriers in select locations in the African theatre in emulation of his great schemes in Britain and Germany.

• • •

The military community, built around Rome's substantial and widely distributed standing armies, was the chief instrument of the Empire. In the 19th-century European tradition, the Roman army was seen very much as the protective shield of provincial populations and the guarantor of the Pax Romana. In the more extreme postcolonial versions, the Roman army was a brutal and repressive force.[5] The truth probably lies between these two extremes, but it is important that we recognise that the scale of Roman military expenditure, year on year, was extraordinary for a pre-modern state (around HS 700,000,000 in the mid-2nd century).[6] This was upwards of 70% of total imperial revenues and, once imperial expansion slowed and one-off bounties of conquest were removed, the logical corollary of this is that the army had to play an important role in enabling the Empire to exact its required budgetary resources. The "imperial economy" that evolved to meet this need was based around a group of interlinked mechanisms: census and supervision of subject populations, land survey and division, tax extraction, exploitation of natural resources, and the extraordinary supply systems of the city of Rome and the provincial garrisons (see further, Chapter 12).[7] In the absence of a large civil branch of colonial government, the Roman army played a big role in delivering these varied aspects of provincial governance that went far beyond its evident martial purpose. In the end, we must recognise that the garrisons in North Africa, as in

5. Campbell 2002; Le Bohec 2000.
6. Mattingly 2011a, 132–38.
7. Mattingly 2011a, 138–45.

other provinces, impacted in a wide range of ways on the lives of both neighbours and provincials. Africa was an important chapter in the story of Roman imperialism and proved to be a lucrative addition to the Empire, vital for its contribution to the food supply of the city of Rome.[8] The garrisons based there were responsible not only for enforcing Rome's authority, but also for projecting power to secure compliance. In the areas of highest troop density especially, the garrison represented a long-term imposition on and challenge to traditional socio-economic relations. How we choose to interpret the perception of these situations by provincials reflects the underlying discourses of colonialism I discussed in Chapter 2, on a spectrum between "protective shield" and "repressive army of occupation."

In this chapter, I explore the historical and topographical contexts of the Roman military deployment in North Africa, with particular focus on the varied roles played by the army.[9] Specifically, I review the acts of conquest and pacification by which martial opponents were defeated and territory added to the provinces. Second, I look at changing patterns of garrison deployment and the development of a deep zone of military infrastructure. This goes beyond the protection of the provinces (and in particular its towns and sedentary farmers) from raids from beyond the "frontier"; security also concerned internal revolts and brigandage. The traditional focus on "frontiers" distracts attention from the wide geographical sphere of garrison operations. Moving beyond traditional dichotomies concerning pastoralists and sedentary populations, I examine the army's broader responsibilities to police everyone living in the military zone as well as peoples from outside the directly controlled territory, conducting censuses, surveying land, and collecting taxes and customs dues. In Chapter 7, I then turn to the cultural impacts of the military community, contesting a common view that soldiers were in some ways ambassadors of "Romanisation" and instead arguing that the military was above all interested in promoting (and posturing) a particular understanding of what it meant to be Roman that was specific to itself.

The Accident of Empire: War, Conquest, and Revolt

Warfare and armed conflict were recurrent themes of Rome's relationship with North Africa, albeit that there were also prolonged periods of relative peace.[10] All empires depend on the projection of power over subject territories and, though

8. Garnsey 1978; Harris 1979 (for Republican background); Whittaker 1996; 1997; 2000; Woolf 1992a.
9. For a good summary account, see Faure 2022. The definitive modern study of the Roman army in Africa is by Le Bohec 1989a; 1989b, updating the classic work of Cagnat 1913. The military installations are much less well studied than in many provinces of the empire; see Mattingly et al. 2013a; Reddé 2014, for short introductions. For summaries of recent epigraphic-focused work see, inter alia, Rosignol and Dana 2020. For bibliographic surveys, see Le Bohec 1979; 1990; 1991; Guédon 2018a.
10. See Coltelloni-Trannoy and Le Bohec 2014 (High Empire); Fields 2010.

force is a finite resource, power is often advertised through displays of force.[11] Conflict in colonial situations can arise through a number of scenarios: planned aggression to expand territory or to pre-emptively strike against potential enemies, autonomous decisions by outside groups to attack the Empire (particularly at times of perceived internal turmoil, as when civil wars occurred), and what may be seen as unintended consequences of the imperial situation, such as unauthorised raiding or abuses of power by the Roman garrison forces. To put this another way, there were intentional acts of the imperial power, high-level resistance to imperial power by kingdoms and peoples who felt threatened by it (or perceived opportunity to profit from its temporary weakness), and systemic violence that was born out of the deep power inequalities inherent in colonialism. In particular, transgressive individual acts of brutality or extortion by imperial servants could result in spontaneous resistance and rebellion.[12]

The military history of Rome in Africa was arguably a product of all three of these. In part, territorial acquisitions were an "accidental" by-product of larger power struggles (with *Qart Hadasht* or in the civil war of the 40s BCE). There are also moments where it looks like there was an officially sanctioned plan to embark on wars of aggrandisement (both territorial and hegemonic) and outbreaks of violence when Rome appears to have been caught unawares by the opportunism of local groups.[13] Some of the campaigns appear to have been little more than glorified raids, perhaps stimulated as much by the soldiers desire for booty as official strategy. Finally, there were no constants in the martial relations at the outer edges of empire: power relations were prone to shift, but were delicately balanced on both sides by perceptions of threat, calculations of advantage, and what individuals saw they could get away with in terms of both oppression and resistance.[14]

In this section, I review the diverse and evolving patterns of military action, but do not attempt to provide a comprehensive narrative (cf. Appendix 1).[15] The main focus will be on the province of *Africa* (including *Numidia* and *Tripolitana*), but with analysis also of the Mauretanian provinces (Fig. 6.1).[16] The military disposition

11. Luttwak 1976, 195–200 for a discussion of the differences and dependencies between power and force.
12. For all that the colonialist discourse has centred on imperial response to incessant indigenous raids, the operation of colonial violence against North African peoples was not necessarily measured and proportionate. Although Roman sources endeavoured to blame unrest on the wilful tendencies of the barbarian "other," there is ample evidence that Rome's actions directly provoked many acts of resistance and revolt, especially when the Roman aggression went beyond what was centrally sanctioned, Dyson 1971; 1975; Shaw 2000.
13. Champion 2004; Harris 1979; 1984.
14. See further discussion of colonial and indigenous strategies in Mattingly 2014a, 25–30.
15. Le Bohec 2014a; 2014b.
16. For the Numidian sector, the standard work is now Guédon 2018a; see also Fentress 1979; 1985; for Tripolitania, Mattingly 1995 and Trousset 1974; for the Mauretanian provinces, see Benseddik 1986; Callegarin 2018; Euzennat 1989; Hamdoune 2018; Malvolta 1986; Rebuffat 1987a; 1999.

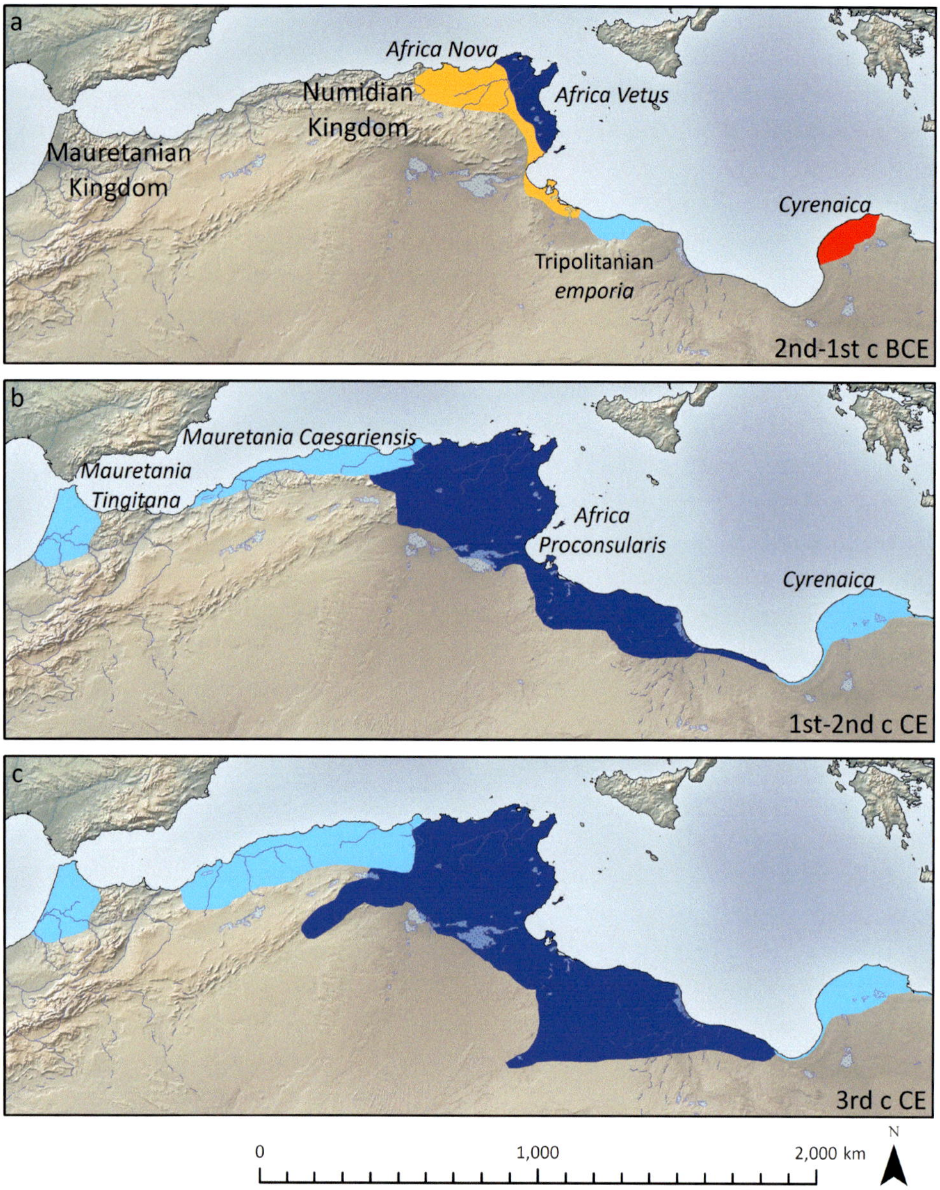

Figure 6.1. The stages of Roman annexation. a) 2nd–1st centuries BCE (showing separate additions of *Africa Vetus*, *Africa Nova*, Tripolitanian *emporia*, and *Cyrenaica*). b) 1st–2nd centuries CE (showing addition of Mauretanian provinces and growth of *Africa* and *Cyrenaica*). c) 3rd century CE (showing maximum growth in Severan period) (Martin Sterry, from author's roughs).

in *Cyrenaica* and *Marmarica* is too poorly known to justify much attention here.[17] *Africa* was governed by a proconsul selected by the Senate and was unusual among the senatorial provinces in having a substantial military deployment including legionary troops. Between 46 BCE and 40 CE there was quite a lot of active campaigning, and while the *princeps* could no doubt mostly rely on his views being reflected in the Senate's choice of proconsul, there were several occasions when direct appointment seems to have been made by the emperor to deal with particular military situations. From c.40 CE the command of the troops was separated from the proconsul and vested entirely with the legionary legate, appointed directly by the emperor. This reflects a paradox of the Roman Empire, where the army as the main instrument of power in the provinces became a double-edged sword. Military success for the emperor's appointed representative could threaten the position of the *princeps,* leading to opportunities for military glory becoming more carefully controlled than under the Republic.

Qart Hadasht

The acquisition of lands in North Africa appears a classic instance of "accidental imperialism" in that it was the battle with *Qart Hadasht* for Mediterranean hegemony that brought Roman armies to Africa for the first time rather than a specific expansionist aim.[18] Rome's first imperative in the 3rd century BCE was to counter the burgeoning power of *Qart Hadasht* overseas, in Sicily, Sardinia, Spain, and (under the extraordinary command of Hannibal) in Italy itself. In the process, Rome turned itself into a naval force to be reckoned with and, as a consequence of its eventual victory, an imperial power with substantial overseas territories. Even the Third Punic War was driven by a desire to prevent a resurgence of Carthaginian power.

The first Roman campaigning in Africa occurred in the First Punic War, when a substantial force under the command of M. Atilius Regulus landed on Cap Bon (Appian 8.3; Polybius 1.29–36). Though ultimately forced to withdraw after a defeat, the campaign of Regulus had revealed that Carthaginian territory was vulnerable to attack (something already exposed by the 4th-century campaign of Agathocles). The imposing defences of *Qart Hadasht* itself had been wisely avoided by Regulus. The First Punic War led to the loss of Punic territory in Sardinia and Sicily, but also to a refocusing of Carthaginian power in metal-rich Iberia, leading in a generation to a further clash with Rome. Towards the end of the Second Punic War, a Roman

17. For *Cyrenaica*, see Goodchild 1976; Guédon 2018a, 88–90 Laronde 2009. For reflections on the military deployments between Tripolitania and Egypt, see Reddé 2014; 2018.
18. For the Punic Wars, see now Hoyos 2011. Also Gsell 1918b; Lassère 2015, 65–78; le Bohec 1996.

expeditionary force was sent into Africa in a successful attempt to get Hannibal to leave Italy. A crucial moment in the campaign came when Rome aided the young Numidian prince Massinissa to overthrow the pro-Carthaginian king Syphax. In 202 Scipio Africanus came face to face with Rome's long-term nemesis, Hannibal, in a great pitched battle near the Numidian eastern capital of *Zama*. With the substantial assistance of Massinissa's cavalry, Rome prevailed. This was a "winner takes all" battle, involving on Hannibal's side the unprecedented number of 80 battle-trained elephants. Rome was able to impose crippling terms on *Qart Hadasht*, but did not take any territory for herself in Africa, though Massinissa's kingdom was enabled to grow with Roman support and encouragement over the next decades. The loss suffered by *Qart Hadasht* of rich agricultural lands in the disputed borders between its own and Numidian territory, and also tribute that came from the *emporia* of Tripolitania, further weakened *Qart Hadasht*, so that when the Third Punic War eventually came in 149 BCE it took the form of an epic but ultimately fatal siege of the city itself, which fell in 146 BCE. The sack and total destruction of *Qart Hadasht*, accompanied by the mass slaughter and enslavement of its population, also impacted on other Libyphoenician cities. Those that had remained loyal to *Qart Hadasht* to the end lost territory and some may even have shared the extreme fate of *Qart Hadasht*'s citizens. Rome effectively annexed the Carthaginian territory, turning much of the land into *ager publicus*. Those cities who had defected to Rome from the Carthaginian cause were treated favourably, retaining lands. With Massinissa having died in 148 BCE and being succeeded by his son Micipsa, the Numidian kingdom's gains since the Second Punic War were now solidified in the treaty between the kingdom and Rome.

Numidia

Once *Qart Hadasht* was defeated, Rome's warfare in North Africa was henceforth focused on the Numidian, Mauretanian, and Gaetulian, Garamantian, and Marmarican peoples. As we have seen these comprised a diverse range of montagnard, plains dwellers, desert, and pre-desert groups. What united them was the horse and horse-based warfare, covering a spectrum from large-scale organised campaigns to raiding.[19] It is important to emphasise that the royal armies of the Numidian and Mauretanian kingdoms were not bands of disorganised horsemen, but presented a wider range of martial capabilities. For instance, both Jugurtha and Juba I had access to war elephants, and infantry contingents are also frequently mentioned.

19. Aït Amara 2013; Coltelloni-Trannoy 2011b; 2014; Gsell 1927a, 142–52; Krimi 2014.

The predominance of light cavalry across the Maghrib and Sahara in antiquity meant that the nature of war and raids often depended on rapid movements on horseback. Pitched battles with large infantry forces engaged were rarer and the superiority of the indigenous cavalry forces meant that defeats in such battles did not necessarily result in the sort of routs that end wars, as the defeated cavalry force could often beat a retreat. A recurrent feature of the wars and revolts in Africa was the ability of the local forces to withdraw following defeats and regroup to fight another day, out of easy range of Roman follow-up action. The Romans continued to place strong reliance on their infantry strength, where the heavier armour and tactical discipline of the legions could generally be relied on to defeat lighter-armoured infantry. But Roman victories also depended on augmenting cavalry support for the infantry (often from other North African peoples) and developing greater capacity for rapid cavalry raids of their own. Large infantry forces marching through enemy territory could also inflict significant collateral damage to the fixed resources of enemies—settlements, livestock, crops, and gardens. Such attritional tactics were often resorted to by Rome in order to bring an elusive and mobile enemy to battle. As established in Part 2, in addition to the stereotypical pastoral groups, North African societies included many sedentary elements with fixed assets to protect. The Romans also excelled in siege warfare, as is illustrated by the account of the storming of Numidian citadels in the Jugurthan War.[20]

The destruction of *Qart Hadasht* in 146 BCE created a new situation, one that the Roman state appeared not to have thought through very much in advance, in which Rome assumed responsibility for Carthaginian territory in North Africa, evidently demarcated from Rome's Numidian ally by a linear ditch, the *fossa regia* (Fig. 6.1a; 6.15).[21] Though a vast amount of land had fallen into Roman hands in northern and eastern Tunisia, there is little sign initially of major Roman efforts at land survey or colonisation of the initial African province (later known as *Africa Vetus*).[22] The *fossa* ran from near *Thabraca* (Tabarka) on the north coast of Tunisia to *Thaenae* (just south of Sfax on the east coast) and, as the name implies, it was an attempt (presumably by Massinissa) to fix the boundary of the king's territory, rather than of Carthaginian lands. It is clear that the boundary between *Qart Hadasht* and Numidia had moved forward and back at different points, depending on the balance of power between the two states, and the *fossa regia* appears to have been instituted to demarcate Numidian repossession of lands in the eastern Tell and upper *Bagrada* valley. Although details of its exact course remain disputed (and

20. Berthier 1981, 74–76.
21. Abda 2013; Ferchiou 1998b. Traces of a potential second linear ditch suggest the linear course may have been redefined on different occasions, Ferchiou 1986c.
22. Gargola 2017; Lassère 2015, 47–112 (history of Roman conquest down to Augustus); Quinn 2004; 2009.

this is largely known from the discovery of later Roman boundary stones related to a resurvey in the 70s CE), its function appears to have been as a boundary marker rather than a defensive or fortified line.[23]

Rome's relationship with the neighbouring Numidian kingdom was initially more reactive than proactive. This policy was exposed by a succession dispute between Numidian princes, sparking the so-called Jugurthan war that ran from 111–105 BCE.[24] Jugurtha was arguably the most ambitious and ruthless of the princes. Having served with the Roman army in Spain in the 130s, he was initially encouraged by his Roman friends in his hopes to succeed his uncle Micipsa as sole ruler (Sallust, *BJ* 8.1). However, when Micipsa died in 118, the division of the kingdom between Jugurtha and Micipsa's two sons, Hiempsal and Adherbal, led quickly to internecine strife between them, with Hiempsal killed and Adherbal fleeing to Roman territory.[25] Further attempts at Roman mediation, reinstating Adherbal in Massylian territory and relegating Jugurtha to the western (Masaesylian) kingdom were undone when Jugurtha again attacked Adherbal in 112 BCE, storming his capital at *Cirta*. The massacre of Roman merchants who had been assisting in the defence of *Cirta* provoked Roman military retaliation.

The war proved more difficult to resolve than expected, despite the investment of huge resources of military manpower (the first commander was sent with four legions and a large number of auxiliary troops). This force of 40,000 men soon entered Numidian territory and started to storm towns (Sallust, *BJ* 28.7).[26] Jugurtha's initial tactic was to sue for peace, as logically what he most wanted was for Rome to recognise the new situation of the kingdom united under his rule, and he was prepared to make substantial reparations (and pay bribes) to achieve that, including providing Rome with cash payment, cattle, horses, and 30 elephants (Sallust, *BJ* 29.5–6). Unfortunately for him, factional politics in Rome saw the deal rejected and the war renewed. Jugurtha then practised delaying tactics and strategic withdrawals, and his stronghold of *Suthul* withstood a Roman siege, before a night attack on the Roman camp of the Roman *praetor* Aulus Albinus brought a first stunning victory (*BJ* 36–42). The new consul sent to Africa in 109 was Q. Caecilius Metellus and, after a careful advance into the upper *Bagrada* and its tributaries, he won a hard-fought pitched battle in the *Muthul* (Mellegue) valley (*BJ* 46–53). When Jugurtha withdrew and started raising a new army, Metellus increased the severity of his tactics—burning villages, massacring and enslaving populations. However, the strongest Numidian towns, like *Zama*, could not be subdued by siege, and Jugurtha

23. For traces of the *fossa regia*, see, inter alia, Abda 2013; Abid 2014; di Vita-Evrard 1986; Ferchiou 1986b; 1998b;

24. For accounts of the causes and events of the war, see, inter alia, Berthier 1981; Lassère 2015, 86–92; Paul 1984.

25. On the build-up to the war, see Sallust, *BJ* 5–35.

26. Lassère 2015, 89.

continued to inflict damage on Roman forces through ambushes and sieges. As the war dragged on, Rome engaged the Libyphoenician *emporia* of Tripolitania as allies. The failure of Metellus to win a decisive victory led to his replacement by C. Marius in 107 and he prosecuted the war with renewed vigour, capturing *Cirta* and *Capsa* at opposite ends of the territory controlled by Jugurtha. Victory was eventually achieved when Bocchus, the Mauretanian king (and father-in-law of Jugurtha), was persuaded to deliver up Jugurtha to the Romans.

While the war with Jugurtha did not lead to the annexation of the kingdom (that Republican reluctance to take on the responsibility of extra territory again), Rome's next approved client king, Gauda, was obliged to allow the settlement of some groups of Roman and Gaetulian veterans in eastern *Numidia*. The course of the war had obliged Rome to campaign into hitherto unknown areas of the African continent and led to tighter bonds being drawn with the Mauretanian kingdom, with some Gaetulian peoples who served as allies for Marius and the free Libyphoenician cities of Tripolitania significantly widening the ambit of Roman power (Sallust, *BJ* 77, 88).[27] Although our sources recurrently default to emphasising the guerrilla and skirmishing tactics of Jugurtha, a close reading of the account of the war suggests a different appreciation of the military resources and capabilities of the Numidian kingdom. He was able to assemble substantial armies, involving both infantry and cavalry forces, and to deploy war elephants in battle. Numidian cities were fortified to withstand siege from an experienced power like Rome, and Jugurtha had his own ability to besiege Roman positions. Rome's advantage in heavy infantry imposed its own logic on the character of the war, with Rome mostly making cautious advances and Jugurtha taking advantage of the deep hinterland of his kingdom to move his treasure around (and mostly keep it safely out of reach) and, after experiencing defeats, to avoid pitched battle by tactical withdrawal. On the Roman side, the alliances with *Gaetuli* and the Mauretanian kingdom were crucial to countering the Numidian cavalry superiority and widening the geographical frame of the conflict. Indeed, it required the Mauretanian king's betrayal of Jugurtha, favouring his developing alliance with Rome over kinship, to end a war that had been proving intractable for Rome.

The annexation of the Numidian kingdom, when it came in 46 BCE, was not a premeditated assault on a lucrative asset but rather Caesar's punishment for Juba I having backed the wrong side in the Roman civil war.[28] Caesar's victory was surprising for its scale and completeness, when his encircled and outnumbered army trounced the combined forces of the Pompeians and Juba at the battle of *Thapsus*. The impact of defeat for Juba was compounded by the near simultaneous attack on the Numidian heartlands by an Italian military adventurer allied with Caesar,

27. Lassère 2015, 90; Mattingly 1995, 51.
28. On the incremental uplift of Roman militarisation in Africa from Caesar and Augustus, Hinard 1991; Hobson 2016.

P. Sittius, seizing the key city of *Cirta*. When *Zama* closed its gates on him in his retreat, Juba killed himself and left the fate of his kingdom in Caesar's hands.

The eastern lands of the *Massyli* were essentially converted into a new Roman province, *Africa Nova*, but Caesar's settlement left a large swathe of western Numidian territory under the control of the Mauretanian client king, who also undertook to regulate the neighbouring Gaetulian peoples. An important territorial enclave around *Cirta* was presented to the Italian military adventurer P. Sittius in recognition of his services. Most of the Libyphoenician towns along the African coast were allowed to continue as nominally free towns under Roman suzerainty, though a number were singled out for fines or other punishment having supported the Republican forces.

Given the record of Numidian resilience in the Jugurthan war, the suddenness of the collapse of the Numidian state may seem surprising. However, the world had changed around the kingdom. The decapitation of the kingdom at the death of its unchallenged ruler (and with his son soon an effective hostage at the court of Augustus) was one factor. In due course, Juba's heir would be inserted into the vacant Mauretanian kingship, strengthening the client kingdom bonds there. The defensive advantage of *Numidia*'s deep hinterland territory was no longer so apparent in 46 BCE. By the very fact of its penetration by Roman armies, settlers, merchants, and adventurers, it was less immediately daunting, and at this date there were already groups of Roman colonists embedded in Numidian towns in the east. The incorporation of *Numidia* west of the *Ampsaga* river into the Mauretanian kingdom shortened the depth of the hinterland, and Caesar and Augustus were both active in establishing further groups of colonists in Mauretanian centres. The Roman enclave established around *Cirta* by Sittius also meant that any revolt of Massylian territory would have been, from the start, enveloped by Rome and its allies. That is not to say there was no resistance to the Roman takeover of *Numidia*; rather the nature of the dismantling of the kingdom made large-scale revolt difficult, especially in the absence of a plausible claimant to the lost throne. From the perspective of a Numidian peasant, the king's tribute became Roman taxation and the king's lands became *ager publicus* or imperial estates. Rome's approach to the provincialisation of the Numidian population was to divide and rule, with separate settlements made with localised communities relating to land, taxation, and so on.

The Gaetulian Wars

The first clear evidence for a more aggressive Roman policy linked to targeted expansion of its African territories came under Augustus.[29] Prior to this time, Rome had effectively annexed the Carthaginian heartlands and incorporated

29. See Guédon 2018a, 43–66; Lassère 2015, 113–30; Le Bohec 1989a, 337–43; Roddaz 2004.

the southern Libyphoenician *emporia* of Tripolitania, along with the northern and eastern lands of the *Numidae*. The creation of *Africa Nova* had now brought Rome into direct contact with the *Gaetuli* peoples and this initiated a prolonged phase that we might characterise as the Gaetulian Wars. The unification of the two African provinces, at some point between 40–36 BCE, created the conditions for a more unified approach to further expansion.[30] There were triumphs celebrated *ex Africa* in 34, 33/32, 28, 21, and 19 BCE.[31] With the exception of the last of these campaigns, the sources are silent on the location and scope of the military actions involved. However, the fact that they met the formal requirements for the award of triumphs (5,000+ enemy dead and action to end a war) suggests these were significant campaigns.[32] It is likely from subsequent events that the main focus of these actions was the lands of the Gaetulian peoples beyond the initial limits of *Africa Nova*.[33] The triumph of 19 BCE related to a celebrated campaign in 20 BCE, when the proconsul L. Cornelius Balbus evidently launched a two-pronged assault against desert peoples well in advance of provincial territory in southern Libya and Algeria, bringing the name of the *Garamantes* to public prominence in Rome.[34] The long-range nature of the campaigns suggests that Roman aggression rather than African raiding lay behind the warfare at this time, echoing expeditions well beyond imperial territory to *Arabia* by Aelius Gallus in 26–25 BCE and far up the Nile against the Meroitic kingdom by P. Petronius between 25–22 BCE.[35] In order to be operating in the specific Garamantian and Gaetulian theatres by 20 BCE, some substantial population groups in the zone between *Capsa* and *Theveste* and the important oasis populations of the Jarid, Nefzaoua, and *Tacape* region surely will have had to be subdued at an earlier date. These "lost" conflicts, presumably corresponding with some of the recorded triumphs between 34–21 BCE, were the first phases of the "Gaetulian wars," which were to last into the reign of Tiberius.

Most scholarly explanations of these wars accept the fundamental logic of the Roman imperial discourse about only fighting defensive wars and blame the bellicose inclinations of nomadic or semi-nomadic bands. Transhumant pastoralism had been a traditional mode of life in the pre-desert steppe lands of southern

30. Fishwick 1993; Hobson 2016.
31. Dio, *History* 49.5 (Statilius Taurus, 34 BCE); *CIL* 1[2] *Fasti Consularis* p. 77 (L. Cornificius, 33/32 BCE); *CIL* 1[2] *Fasti Consularis* p. 50 (L. Autronius Paetus, 28 BCE; *CIL* 1[2] *Fasti Consularis* p. 50, 76–77 (Sempronius Atratinus, 21 BCE); *CIL* 1[2] *Fasti Consularis* p. 50 and Pliny, *NH* 5.36–37 (L. Cornelius Balbus, 19 BCE). M. Acilius Glabrio is also thought to have been awarded a triumph around 25 BCE, Le Bohec 1989a, 338.
32. *Inscriptiones Italicae* 13.1. On the Roman triumph, see Beard 2007.
33. Guédon 2018a, 44–47; Le Bohec 1989a, 338–39 both suggest some of the pre-27 BCE campaigning may have related to events surrounding Octavian establishing his power in succession to Lepidus, but recognise that the campaigns of the 20s BCE related to problems with Gaetulian and Garamantian "semi-nomades" initiating raids against Roman territory during the civil wars.
34. Desanges 1957; 1980b.
35. Guédon 2018a, 54; Kirkwan 1971; Roddaz 2004; Pliny, *NH* 6.157–59; Strabo 16.4.22–24.

Tunisia and northern Libya. There are double listings of names of a number of peoples by Ptolemy close to the Mediterranean and deeper in the desert, suggesting such migration ranges for some peoples (all the more plausible if the southern locations were oasis-focused).[36] This also echoes the passage in Herodotus (*Histories* 4.172) about the annual migration of the *Nasamones* from the Syrtic coast to the oasis of *Augila* for the date harvest. This example also reminds us, as we have seen in the previous chapter, that the Gaetulian lands were more densely populated than once recognised, including substantial numbers of oasis cultivators alongside more mobile elements, and that migration *to* as well as *from* the desert might be important.

This necessitates a re-evaluation of Rome's imperial interests and approach in the Gaetulian region. Seasonal migrations of transhumant pastoralists have rightly been recognised as a key issue, but trade with oasis communities in a range of commodities (dates and other crops, salt, manufactured goods, wild beasts, ivory, gold, enslaved people) needs also to be recognised as a possible motivation. When the first Islamic armies campaigned west from Egypt in the 640s CE, they almost immediately split their column into two branches, one focused on the rich Roman cities of *Libya* and *Tripolitana*, the other probing into the Libyan desert to establish suzerainty and extract tribute from the oases that controlled the Saharan trade routes.[37] The sizeable populations of the oases also magnified the threat of the Gaetulian peoples for Rome. Control of the activities of northward seasonal migrations of herders depended to some extent on the demonstration that the affiliated oasis centres were in range of and vulnerable to Roman attacks. It is thus unlikely that the initial Roman campaigns were aimed at territorial acquisition, but it is highly plausible that Rome was proactive in exerting its hegemonic claim to power over remote locations and people. This is what is implied in Virgil's famous inclusion of the *Garamantes* within the *imperium sine fine* of the Augustan age (*Aeneid* 1.278–79).[38] It was not a territorial claim, but one that recognised the geographical extent of treaty relations and the projection of Roman power far beyond core territory. This was normally the result of direct experience of Roman force operating far in advance of the expanding Empire's provincial core.

The campaign of Cornelius Balbus in 20 BCE is an important illustration of this principle in action because of the greater information we have on its targets and achievements. There is fairly general agreement nowadays that several areas

36. Mattingly 1995, 30–31 relating to Ptolemy, *Geography* 4.3.6, 4.6.6 (*Akhaemenis/Akhaemae; Astakoures/Astakouri; Dolopes/Dolopes; Eropaei/Oreipaei; Nigitimi/Nigitimae; Nybgenii/ Nugbenitae).*
37. Mattingly et al. 2015.
38. Mattingly 1992 for some reflections on the difference between hegemonic and territorial empire in the early Principate.

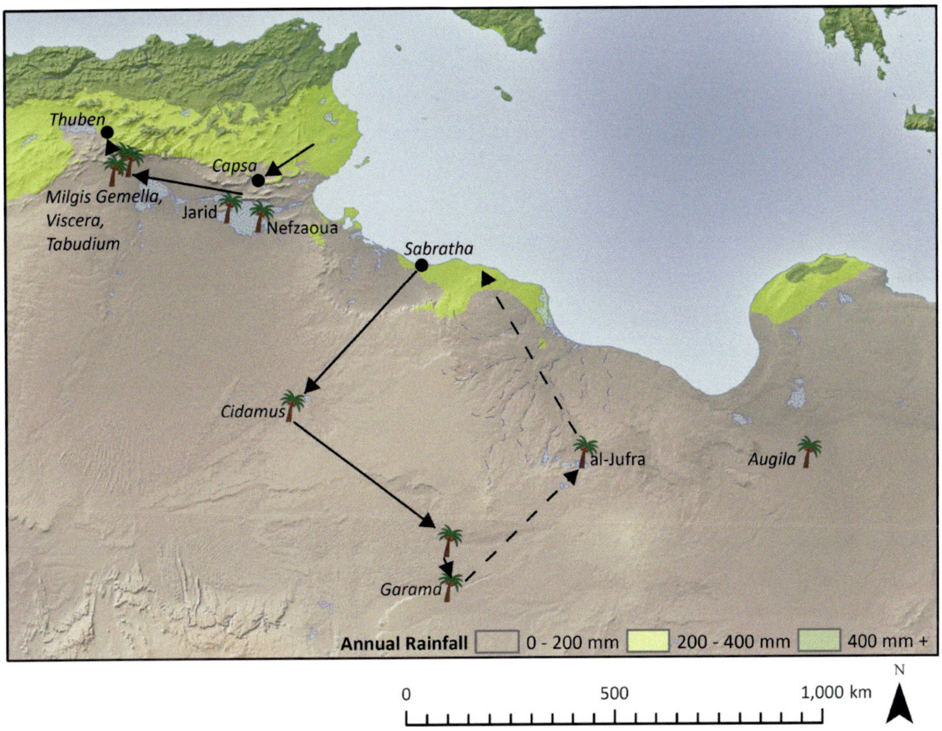

Figure 6.2. Hypothetical reconstruction of the campaigns of Cornelius Balbus against *Garamantes* and *Gaetuli* c.20 BCE, and other key locations relating to Augustan/Tiberian campaigning. The oases of Jarid and Nefzaoua are not mentioned in relation to Balbus and these important locations must have been subdued in prior campaigns (Martin Sterry, from author's rough).

were targeted by two separate Roman columns. One group of toponyms and names relate to the main assault on *Cidamus* (Ghadamis) and *Garama* (Jarma), while the closest parallels for a second group are to be found in a dense cluster of desert locations in Algeria (Fig. 6.2). Pliny (*NH* 5.35) indicates that the campaign to *Cidamus* and *Garama* set off from *Sabratha*. From *Cidamus* there is a difficult route across the Hamada al-Hamra and the Ubari sand sea to reach the Garamantian capital at *Garama*. The column may then have followed a more direct route back to the north, probably via the al-Jufra oasis group.[39] To reach the *oppida* of *Tabudium* and *Miglis Gemella* and *Viscera natio* (all names to be equated with the Algerian Ziban oasis group), the campaign probably passed via *Capsa* and headed south-west to pass along the southern flank of the Aurès mountains, with a possible exploration up the eastern Aurès flank towards the Hodna plains (*Thuben*). The distance

39. Mattingly 2003a, 79–83; Mattingly et al. 2020c, 130–37; Merrills 2016.

between the two theatres makes it practically impossible to think of this as a continuous action involving a single column. The fact that there is no reference in the list of names recorded by Pliny as featuring in the triumphal procession that can be related to places identifiable with either the Jarid or the Nefzaoua oases supports the view that the populations of those oasis had already been subjugated in an earlier campaign, opening the way for the deeper penetration of the desert zone by Balbus. The campaigns of the 30s–20s BCE thus probably aimed at defeating Libyan peoples, imposing Roman suzerainty over still remote population centres, and establishing a basis for future understandings regarding Gaetulian movement into Roman-controlled territory whether to exploit traditional grazing rights, to provide labour, or to trade.

A generation later, it is possible that the situation was changing, with an increasing emphasis on the establishment of advanced military bases and on the imposition of tributary terms or formal annexation of new territory. This seems to be implied by the outbreak of serious revolts in 3 BCE–6 CE.[40] This revolt seems to have been sparked by the murder of the proconsul of *Africa* by the *Nasamones*.[41] A second phase of the revolt in 3 CE involved the *Cinithi*, a people of western Tripolitania, though evidence of a direct threat to *Lepcis Magna* suggests it was more widespread in the hinterland of the Tripolitanian cities.[42] There is evidence to suggest that the *Marmaridae* and the *Garamantes* were also involved in the east and south, and the *Gaetuli* bordering on the territory of Mauretania to the west.[43] What was at issue during the Augustan period was a sustained attempt to impose Rome's suzerainty on widespread groupings and ultimately to incorporate some of those closest to Roman territory within the province. It thus seems more likely that the rebellion encompassed many *Gaetuli* groupings and other desert peoples like the *Garamantes*, spread across a large territorial extent from *Mauretania* to the Greater Syrtic gulf.

There was a further phase of extensive Gaetulian war in 17–24 CE, this latter rebellion led by Tacfarinas.[44] Tiqfarin, to give him his African name,[45] was a deserter from the Roman army, but also a chief of the *Musulami* people, whose core territory can be reconstructed with some degree of precision from boundary markers erected under Trajan (Fig. 10.9 below). The *Musulami* have sometimes been identified as *Numidae* because Tiqfarin is referred to by Tacitus as a "Numidian" chief and the rebels as "Numidians," though this seems a geographical

40. On the second Augustan Gaetulian war, see Guédon 2018a, 61–66; Le Bohec 1989a, 339.
41. Desanges 1969; Mattingly 1995, 51–52.
42. Dio 55.28.1–4; Orosius 6.21.18; Velleius Paterculus 2.6.
43. Desanges 1964b; Mattingly 1995, 52, 69–73. Cf. Florus 2.31.
44. On the revolt of Tacfarinas, see Guédon 2018a, 67–78; Lassère 1982b; Vanacker 2015; Woolf 2014.
45. Here I follow the suggestion for the African form of the name of Tacfarinas of Lafrenz Samuels 2010, 31–36.

and historical anachronism or simply a misunderstanding.[46] Tacitus did not use the ethnic name *Gaetuli* in his *Annals* and the simplest explanation is that he had incorrectly subsumed *Gaetuli* with *Numidae*. All the other evidence points to the fact that the *Musulami* were *Gaetuli*.[47]

Most modern accounts of the Gaetulian wars still present the *Gaetuli* as essentially nomadic or semi-nomadic populations and thus find the prime causes of the wars in the assumed bellicosity of such people when confronted by growing sedentarisation of the landscape and an imperial power that set new controls and limits on their seasonal movements and migrations.[48] Much emphasis has been placed by these modern commentators on the construction of a road in 14 CE from *Tacape* to *Ammaedara* (the *castra hiberna* of the *legio III Augusta*).[49] Without wishing to dismiss the impact of such an action and the physical erection of milestones along it, it is more useful to reflect on its wider implications for Roman policy and intervention at this time. *Ammaedara* lay in Musulamian territory and this may well have been a Roman military garrison centre for a while—perhaps since the end of the preceding phase of rebellion. The road implies a greater permanence to the Roman military presence and a next step on the way to incorporation of this region into provincial structures, including clarity about landholding, taxation, and other impositions (such as military recruitment). The *Musulami* lands lay some way to the north of the oasis belt, at the northern edge of Gaetulian lands where they bordered Numidian territory. It is also evident that urbanisation and sedentarisation were already underway before Roman times—at centres such as *Capsa*, *Thala*, and *Theveste*.[50] Similarly, hillforts in and near the Aurès, such as Ichoukkane, Kalaat Senane, and al-Krozbet, are all candidates for Gaetulian centres, though at times perhaps falling under Numidian control.[51] In any event, it seems reasonable to argue that the *Gaetuli* were not simply pastoralists.

Tiqfarin/Tacfarinas is a member of a select band of serious rebels against Rome across the Empire, including the likes of Sacrovir and Florus in Gaul, Arminius and Civilis in Germany, Caratacus and Boudica in Britain.[52] These were all people who had initially enjoyed a seemingly close relationship with Rome; one might even say they had been "groomed" for imperial service. With all these "rebels" something happened to destroy this relationship and turn Rome's close associates into

46. The prolonged revolt must have felt to the Romans in part like a replay of the Jugurthan war and Tacitus may have wanted to play that up, see Lassère 2015, 131.
47. Desanges 1980b, 344–45; Guédon 2018a, 64; Laporte and M'Charek 2010; Shaw 2014. Compare Lassère 2015, 131–34 and Le Bohec 1989a, 344 who too readily accepts the "Numidian" identification, which contradicts the indications of where the main action of the war took place.
48. Lassère 1982b; 2015, 131–32; Syme 1951; Vanacker 2014; 2015.
49. On the milestone evidence of the road construction, see Le Bouef 1905; Naddari 2014.
50. Guédon 2018a, 65; Laporte and M'Charek 2010.
51. See discussion on hillforts in Chapter 5.
52. Mattingly 2011a, 75–93; Whittaker 1996, 593.

desperate opponents. That "something" appears in several of these cases to have been the unveiling of Rome's plans for the incorporation of new territories into the Empire. Only at that point perhaps did the full extent of what was to be lost become clear to these people. In Britain, the resistance to the Claudian invasion was led by the kingdom (and its leading princes) of southern Britain that had enjoyed the closest and most privileged relationship with Rome in the preceding generation. They had most to lose and most cause to feel aggrieved that their hopes and expectations of the relationship should be overturned. A generation later, it was the widow of one of the most loyal client kings of the post-conquest phase, Boudica, who led the outraged reaction to a brutally executed annexation of her people's lands, rape and violence directed at the royal household, and seizure of the royal assets. Similarly, Jugurtha, though clearly wishing to develop his status as a client king, was transformed into an enemy by Roman *real politik* as much as his own assault on co-monarchs.

Like these others, Tiqfarin/Tacfarinas had perhaps at one time seemed destined for advancement under Rome. It is likely that the first military victory of Rome over his people the *Musulami* had come a few decades before during the 30s–20s BCE. Rome commonly required that the sons of chiefs be sent to Rome as *obsides* for education (effectively these were hostages for good behaviour) as part of the treaty arrangements after such victories. Perhaps Tiqfarin had been one of those. He certainly served in the Roman auxiliaries—another standard instrument of pacification of conquered people in the Empire was direct recruitment of their manpower. He was labelled as a deserter from the auxiliaries at the outbreak of the revolt, though the reason for this rejection of duty to Rome is not specified. Given that he became leader of a widespread revolt, it is likely that he was more than the opportunistic brigand that the Roman sources depict him as. His defection from the army may have been a direct consequence of what had happened to his people and other Gaetulian groups between 14–17 CE. Land was probably at the heart of the revolt: when Tiqfarin tried to negotiate a settlement in 23 CE, he offered Tiberius a choice between giving land to him and his followers, or facing unremitting warfare across Gaetulian lands. While Tacitus claims Tiberius was outraged to have a brigand demanding land from him, it is equally possible that some sort of agreement over Gaetulian lands had been presented by Rome to the Gaetulian leaders immediately prior to the outbreak of the revolt, perhaps in the context of formal incorporation of their territory into the province. A second implication is that the settlement offered then was nowhere near as generous as leaders like Tiqfarin had expected and this was a prime cause of the revolt.[53]

Tacitus is somewhat unhelpful in describing the main events of the revolt. Tiqfarin was a "deserter and brigand," his followers "vagabonds and marauders."

53. For similar conclusions, see Guédon 2018a, 76–77.

The rebels were seriously defeated in a first pitched battle with Roman forces in 17 CE and afterwards reverted to a more hit-and-run style, which Tacitus characterised as "nomadic." However, at least two of these attacks involved frontal assaults or sieges of Roman forts or defended settlements. The success of the rebels in destroying Roman settlements and in carrying off considerable property is a repeated feature of the accounts. The theatre of the war was evidently very wide, going far beyond the *Musulami*, and this suggests that the circumstances that lay behind the revolt were not limited to just that one Gaetulian people, but more generally impacting on others (or with the wide perception of the possibility of a similar fate awaiting them). This is certainly true of the *Cinithi*, who were evidently the people of the Lesser Syrtes coastal region extending from north of *Tacape* to the neighbourhood of the island of Jerba. One of the sequels of the end of the war was a major programme of land survey and territorial delimitation in southern Tunisia, impacting on the lands of the *Musulami*, *Cinithi*, and *Nybgenii* and establishing new boundaries for urban *territoria*, like *Tacape* and *Capsa* (further discussed in Chapter 10).[54] The death of Tiqfarin was not the end of Musulamian revolt, as they rose again in 45 CE, though the paucity of sources deny us the detail (Dio 60.9; Aurelius Victor 4.2).[55]

The *Garamantes* evidently played only a subsidiary role in Tiqfarin's war, but were sufficiently aware of Rome's capability for revenge that they sent peace envoys to Rome in 24 CE. They were embroiled in conflict with Rome again in 69 CE, when during the succession crisis following the death of Nero, they opportunistically took the side of *Oea* in a territorial dispute with *Lepcis Magna*. Their siege of *Lepcis* was only lifted by the arrival of Roman auxiliaries—presumably a flying squad of cavalry—and the legionary legate then undertook a campaign to their heartlands in 70 CE. There were further desert expeditions later in the Flavian period, but these appear to have been more attempts to develop a collaborative relationship with the *Garamantes*, including accompanying their king on a slave-raiding expedition several months travel to the south of *Garama*.[56]

While the relationship with the *Garamantes* appears to have been generally peaceful thereafter—no doubt carefully regulated by treaties—there was periodic trouble with other desert groups—as indicated by events early in the reign of Septimius Severus, when there was evidently conflict in the region.[57] A mid-3rd-century inscription explicitly alludes to "barbarian" raiders, though this seems to be a reference to a chronic irritation rather than an acute threat.

54. Guédon 2018a, 77–78; Mrabet 2014; Trousset 1978; 2004.
55. Guédon 2018a, 77;Le Bohec 1989a, 349.
56. Guédon 2018a, 78–82; Mattingly 2003a, 82–85.
57. Birley 1988a.

Stéphanie Guédon recognises a "borderland solidarity" in the face of Roman authority, citing the sometimes close relation between *Gaetuli*, *Garamantes*, *Nasamones*, and *Marmaridae* peoples.[58] The potential for the new geopolitical realities of an expanding imperial power to have a transformative effect on neighbouring peoples has long been recognised in anthropology and archaeology.[59] The Gaetulian and Garamantian wars of the early Principate seem to betoken higher levels of co-operation in the face of a common threat across the varied population groups of the northern Sahara and pre-desert zones.[60] In late antiquity a new threat emerged in the shape of the *Austuriani* and *Laguatan*, evidently a large confederation of desert peoples, which seems to have encompassed many of the previous Gaetulian groups. The sources also describe them as *Mauri*, in the later sense of that term, meaning Libyan people who were outside the provincialised structures and cultural norms.[61]

Through the late 1st and 2nd century, the expansion of provincial territory appears to have advanced in gradual steps (Fig. 6.1b). However, there is clear evidence for a further concerted phase of extension of provincial territory in the early 3rd century, relating to the Tripolitanian pre-desert and the Saharan Atlas ranges to south-west of the 2nd-century territorial limits of *Africa*, and also coinciding with an advance of the Mauretanian deployment.[62] There is some evidence for 2nd-century expeditions into the Saharan Atlas ranges (*CIL* 8.21567 from al-Agueneb),[63] but it is clear that this was consolidated under Septimius Severus, presumably following some major campaigning (Fig. 6.1c).[64] A native of *Lepcis Magna*, he was also only the second emperor to visit Africa during his reign.

The later history of warfare in *Africa* was in part related to support for the Mauretanian provinces to the west (see below) and in part a story of self-inflicted wounds, such as the suppression by the *legio III Augusta* in 238 of the revolt that aimed to make emperors of the proconsul Gordian and his son (Gordian I and II), but led to their deaths instead.[65] The legion was cashiered soon after, when, in a twist, the grandson who had remained safe at Rome became Gordian III. The consequential reorganisation of the garrison arrangements was accompanied by some

58. Guédon 2018a, 82–92; cf. also Mattingly 1995, 19–25 on hierarchy and confederation of African peoples in opposition to Rome.
59. Mattingly 1992; Whitehead 1992.
60. Mattingly 1992, 50–57; 1995, 68–73.
61. Mattingly 1983; 1995, 176–80; Modéran 2003. See now Merrills 2019 for an excellent analysis of the ethnographic underpinnings of the *Laguatan* peoples, suggesting that the citation of ethnic names in Corippus echoes reports of Roman triumphs.
62. Le Bohec 1989a, 391–401.
63. Le Bohec 1989a, 380.
64. Faure and Leveau 2015; Le Bohec 1989a, 392.93.
65. Le Bohec 1986; 2004.

signs of increased raiding, as at the Tripolitanian outpost of Gasr Duib.[66] Another proconsul, Sabinianus, revolted in 240. A revolt by *Mauri* in 253–60 impacted *Mauretania* and *Numidia* and required joint action by the different provincial forces. In the late 290s Maximian was the third and last ruling emperor to visit Africa in person, campaigning in both *Mauretania* and *Tripolitana*, though scant detail of the enemy is known.[67] During the civil wars 310–11, Domitius Alexander briefly declared himself emperor in Africa, before being defeated near *Cirta*.[68]

There was a more serious incursion of external people, the *Austuriani*, impacting *Tripolitana* in the 360s, though the larger scandal was the failure of the *comes Africae* Romanus to take effective countermeasures.[69] In the 370s, a major revolt focused on the family of Firmus, a Moorish leader and a high-ranking Roman official, impacted on both *Numidia* and *Mauretania*. There was a sequel involving Gildo, the brother of Firmus in the 390s, when as *comes Africae* he cut the grain supply to Rome.[70] Again, in the aftermath of the internal troubles, there are reports of more *Austuriani* invasions of *Tripolitana* and *Cyrenaica* and further internal troubles in *Mauretania* and *Numidia*. In 429, following further internal discord between the *comes* Boniface and the imperial court, the Vandals invaded North Africa from Spain and started the dismantling of the Roman provinces.[71]

Mauretania and Mauri

The annexation of the Mauretanian kingdom was much longer delayed than its Numidian neighbours. Indeed, the fall of Juba I allowed the Mauretanian client kingdom to consolidate its authority over the western part of the Numidian kingdom and over the neighbouring Gaetulian groups—probably those of the High Plains, the Saharan Atlas, and the Aurès. As previously noted, this expanded Mauretanian kingdom fell into two distinct parts: a western territory comprising the mountain-encircled plainlands of north-western Morocco; and, some distance to the east, the ranges of the coastal Tell and the Chelif valley in Algeria. Between the two, the terrain was broken and less well watered, much of it occupied by montagnard and pastoral groups of *Gaetuli*, with some possible oasis developments to the south. The Mauretanian control of the entire region and its diverse peoples was probably of varying authority and reach. In 49 BCE the kingdom was divided

66. *IRT* 880: "preserved the area distinguished as the frontier district of *Tentheis*, and the road along it, from the attacks of barbarians"; Mattingly 1991; 1995, 81–83.
67. Hamdoune 2010a.
68. Lassère 2015, 541.
69. Lassère 2015, 630–40; Modéran 2003, 279–81.
70. Lengrand 1994; Modéran 1989.
71. On the Vandals, see Merrills 2004; Merrills and Miles 2010; Modéran 2014.

between two princes, Bogud and Bocchus II, but after Bogud's death (again due to taking the wrong side in Roman civil war), it was reunited under the sole authority of Bocchus, who also took over an extended western Numidian territory in 46 BCE. After his death in 33 BCE, the kingdom seems to have been put into an interregnum state under Roman control for eight years until Augustus installed Juba II, the Rome-educated son of Juba I, as a trusted client king.

Juba was provided with a suitably cosmopolitan wife in Cleopatra Selene, daughter of Cleopatra and Mark Antony, and ruled until 23 CE, when he was succeeded by his son Ptolemy I. Ptolemy was assassinated by order of Caligula in 40 CE, leading to the annexation of the kingdom.[72] This was contested by the *Mauri*, led by one of Ptolemy's freedmen, Aedemon (Dio, *History* 60.8.6, 60.9.1; Pliny, *NH* 5.11).[73] In the absence of a suitable heir to the kingdom and with Roman colonial deductions already attached to various Mauretanian towns, resistance to the Roman takeover does not appear to have been long-lived, though our sources for this period are very deficient. However, in a second and potentially more challenging phase of war, Roman generals crossed the High Atlas and campaigned in the desert against a local chief, Salabos.[74] One way of reading the events would be to see the first phase of the war as the securing of the core territory of the kingdom of the *Mauri*, and the second phase as a necessary attempt to impose Rome's authority over Gaetulian peoples of the mountains and the desert beyond. This action may well have started in the Gaetulian salient between the two parts of the kingdom, but then followed the *Gaetuli* over mountain passes into the northern Sahara. As suggested in the previous chapter, it is quite likely that the first oases were already appearing in the valleys of the Wadis Draa, Ziz, Rheris, and Gir, but these were in any event occupied by Gaetulian groups of varying degrees of mobility.

The Roman provincial structure for *Mauretania* recognised the topographical and sociological challenge of the divided kingdom, by settling on two separate provinces, *Mauretania Tingitana* (west) and *Mauretania Caesariensis* (east). The *Gaetuli*/*Mauri* peoples were a recurrent security issue by reason of proximity and autonomy both outside and within imperial territory, though there were regular attempts to control their activities through treaty arrangements. For instance, there were marginal groups among the *Mauri* peoples, especially in the mountainous enclaves of the coastal Tell, such as the Kabylie ranges. Over time the term *Mauri* came to cover all the Libyan groups who lay outside the more settled provincial areas, encompassing both Gaetulian and Mauretanian/Masaesylian elements.[75] The extent to which periodic raids and brigandage tipped over into full-blown warfare

72. On Ptolemy's death and the take-over of the kingdom, see Aït Amara 2014; Coltelloni-Trannoy 1997, 55–65; Hamdoune 2018, 125–29.
73. For an exploration of the African context of the resistance to Roman takeover, see Vanacker 2013.
74. De la Chapelle 1934, for the trans-Atlas campaigns.
75. Hamdoune 2018, 123–47; cf. Bénabou 1976, 250–51; Rachet 1970.

or revolt is now much debated. However, it is apparent that some of the military action of the mid-2nd century was on a significant and prolonged scale. The 140s and early 150s CE saw repeated reinforcements being required for the Mauretanian garrisons—in a military diploma of 152 CE troops drawn from no less than 12 cavalry *alae* from five provinces were involved.[76] Tombstones attest two soldiers from the *cohors IV Sygambrorum* killed in battle by "barbarians."[77] Legionary reinforcements were also brought in at times via *Africa* and from other provinces.[78]

The long-term military history of the Mauretanian provinces suggests that the principal threats were as much inside as outside the provincial territory.[79] The potential for the mountains, high plains, and desert oases to support large population reservoirs mean that we need to move beyond a view of small and scattered nomadic tribes posing an intermediate threat of raids. The depth and difficulty of the landscape beyond the borders of Roman territory hampered Rome's ability to dominate peoples far beyond the core provincial territory. As we shall see, this led to different configurations of the garrison deployment in an effort to find the best solution. The civil zone in the Mauretanian provinces was compressed and intermingled with the military in a way that is somewhat different to the situation in *Africa*. There is a particularly rich epigraphic record of both revolts/wars and chiefs and prefects of a range of powerful Gaetulian and Moorish peoples (*Baquates*, *Bavares*, *Fraxinenses*, *Isaflensium*, *Mazices*, *Quinquegentanei*).[80]

In the later Roman period, the advancement of Moorish officers in imperial service had important consequences for the region. The family of Flavius Nubel appears to have had extensive estates in the Chelif and Soummam valleys and between the Mitijien and Kabylie ranges in the 4th century. Nubel was long identified with the commander of the *equitum armigerorum iuniorum*, but that *praepositus* now appears to be a homonym.[81] Ammianus Marcellinus (29.5) described Nubel as being "powerful as a king among the Moorish peoples." Nubel's extensive family included several sons who held military or quasi-military roles (Firmus, Sammac, Gildo, Mascezel, Mazuca) and a daughter, Cyria, who also played her part in the revolt that ensued when Nubel died in 370. The *comes Africae* Romanus promoted the succession of Sammac over his siblings and when Sammac was killed, Firmus was implicated (shades of Jugurtha here).[82] Firmus declared himself

76. Birley 2020, 324. See also Speidel 1975.
77. Kasdi and Slimani 2020; new inscriptions mention soldiers' fates: *a barb(aris) | inter<f>(ectus)* and *interfec(to) in bello*.
78. Speidel 1982.
79. Laporte 2011, 130–31.
80. Hamdoune 2018, 81–199; Lengrand 1999.
81. Lassère 2015, 638 n8.
82. For the events of the revolt, Ammianus Marcellinus 29.5; Hamdoune 2018, 201–13; Laporte 2004b; Lassère 2015, 641–43; Lengrand 1994.

king of *Mauretania*, winning over some military units and 12 Moorish *gentes* to his cause, requiring a four-year campaign led by the *magister equitum* Theodosius to reconquer the territory, ending with the death of Firmus and one of his brothers. The main action of the war took place within eastern *Mauretania Caesariensis*. Although often presented as a confrontation between "Romanised" Africa and "tribal" Africa,[83] one could view this equally as a conflict between powerful rivals for military powers and authority under Rome. This is even more apparent in the sequel in the 390s, when Gildo, having risen to be *comes Africae* before he revolted against the Empire, was eventually defeated in battle by a Roman army led by another of his brothers, Mascezel.[84] The family of Nubel may not match our expectations of elite Romano-Africans under the Romanisation paradigm, but nor were they "barbarian outsiders." As Andy Blackhurst puts it, the question is whether they were rebels or players.[85] Their ownership of large estates in the key agricultural zones of the province shows that they were well integrated into the provincial elite and they clearly had close associations with the Roman military dispositions. My solution to the conundrum they present is to suggest they were associated with the military community, which, as in other parts of the Empire in the 4th century, was undergoing profound identity changes, with the incorporation of former "barbarian" groups.[86]

Marmaridae and Cyrenaica

The *Nasamones* and the *Marmaridae* were the main peoples bordering *Cyrenaica*, and probably were to some degree equivalent to the *Gaetuli* further west. Although Herodotus (*History* 4.186–91) characterised all the peoples close to the African coast west of Egypt as nomadic until he came to *Lacus Tritonis* (the Chott Jarid in southern Tunisia), this evidence is contradicted in his own account by the references to oases and to the date palms that were cultivated there, by the *Nasamones* among others. There is increasing archaeological evidence for precocious oasis development in the northern Sahara; *Marmaridae* and *Nasamones* both seem to have had links with the oasis cultivators, even if also in part comprising pastoral groups operating in the spaces between. The *Nasamones* and *Marmaridae* were at times a target for military action from either *Cyrenaica* or *Africa*. The Nasamonian murder of a proconsul in 3 BCE[87] had a near sequel under Domitian when the Roman legionary legate, Cn. Suellius Flaccus, suffered a severe reverse in 85–86,

83. Lengrand 1999.
84. Hamdoune 2018, 211–13; Lassère 2015, 645–47.
85. Blackhurst 2004. The answer is surely they were both at different moments.
86. Potter 2004, 448–59.
87. Desanges 1969.

but was able to retrieve the situation as the *Nasamones* pillaged his camp instead of pursuing their advantage (Zonaras 11.19; Eusebius, *Chron.* A86).[88] The description of the nature of the eventual victory ("He attacked them and annihilated them, even destroying all the non-combatants") led Domitian to claim to have "exterminated" the people, though some at least seem to have survived.[89] In later antiquity the *Nasamones* were probably subsumed into the *Ausuriani/Austuriani* and *Laguatan* groups whose heartlands seem to have lain in the oases south of the Syrtic gulf.

Different Types of Wars, Revolts, and Raiding Activity

In this section I have described a number of different types of military encounter between Rome and African peoples. It is important to recognise the variability of these actions and of the underlying situations that led to them. We also need to be sceptical of the framing of the account of conflict in the surviving ancient sources. There are some serious biases and *topoi* on show. Nonetheless, it is possible to see that Rome used force to establish its power over neighbouring peoples as well as to attempt the conquest of territory. Revolts against Rome—which are commonly presented as perverse resistance to the benefits of Roman civilisation—need to be understood as, in part at least, a logical response to Roman aggression or imposition of imperial structures on people hitherto autonomous or semi-autonomous. In addition, we should not underestimate the capacity of the Roman army to foment unrest in the frontier regions as an unintended consequence of its normal activities and even more so through its sometimes transgressive use of power.

The expansion of territory continued through the 1st to early 3rd centuries CE not as a smooth progression but in fits and starts. This was accompanied by the development of the infrastructure of empire—construction of roads, the establishment of garrison points, massive centuriation and land delimitation schemes, the promotion of sedentarisation, and recognition of civil administrative units based on towns.[90] The growth of an African equestrian class, founded on military command as an entry point to wider careers in imperial service, forged a strong engagement with the imperial project in some communities. However, the long-term effects of the presence of the Roman army in North Africa varied region by region. It is a moot point whether it was endemic resistance in *Mauretania Caesariensis* which necessitated a heavier garrison presence there, or whether the size of the

88. Le Bohec 1989a, 354.
89. Shaw 2000, 379.
90. On roads, see the updated edition of Salama's classic map, Desanges et al. 2010. On centuriation see, Caillemer and Chevalier 1959; Trousset 1977b; 1978; 1997a.

garrison stationed there also contributed to prolonged unrest. In the next section, I turn to the development of the garrison deployment over time and the emergence of demarcated boundaries.

Garrison Deployment

The infrastructure of the Roman army is exceptionally well studied across the Empire's provinces, though North Africa lags far behind the European provinces in terms of accumulated data.[91] The methodical and engineered advance of the army on campaign is well attested in literary sources and by discoveries of temporary marching camps in provinces like Britain. Few are as yet recorded in Africa, though scrutiny of high-resolution imagery will no doubt add to the tally.[92] Similarly, impressive siege works have been recorded in other provinces and must have had their counterparts in North Africa at sites known to have been besieged by Rome.[93] In campaigning phases, the army often constructed large bases to serve as winter quarters for the battle groups as well as specialist supply depots.[94] But most archaeological attention has focused on the fortresses, forts, and smaller installations developed to house the garrison troops post-conquest. By the later 1st century CE these installations were becoming more standardised, with the elite citizen infantry (*legiones*) (generally 5,000–6,000 strong) housed in large fortresses separate from the forts designed for non-citizen (auxiliary) units, generally 500–1,000 strong, comprising lighter-armed infantry (*cohortes*), cavalry (*alae*), or a mixture of the two (*cohortes equitatae*), though, as we shall see, the evidence suggests that in reality units might be split between two or more bases.

There are two particular problems with the archaeology of Roman forts in North Africa: first, there is an overall lack of well-excavated sites; and second, there is a tendency for the available epigraphic documentation to constrain interpretation of the individual site history.[95] At some sites, a unit of garrison is known from chance epigraphic discovery, but in many instances this will not reflect the full story of the military occupation, which often involved a succession of units in garrison. For many identified Roman forts in Africa we have no idea what troops were present in garrison. In relation to many postulated smaller outposts, it is not even certain that the military interpretation is correct.[96] Moreover, the epigraphic evidence relating

91. Mattingly et al. 2013a; Ployer et al. 2019; Reddé 2014.
92. For an example from Syrtica of two superimposed marching camps, see Lequesne et al. 2010, 20–21.
93. Roman siegeworks have not been identified from North Africa, though might be expected at a number of naturally fortified locations, such as Kalaat Senane, Berthier 1981, 74.
94. *Ammaedara* was evidently first constructed as a *castra hiberna*, *CIL* 8.10018.
95. For studies of Roman forts across North Africa, see, inter alia, Daniels 1987; Fentress 1979; Lenoir 2011; Mattingly et al. 2013a; Rebuffat 1975e; 1982a; 1993.
96. Lenoir 2011; Mattingly 1989a; Mattingly et al. 2013b.

to the garrison composition tends to be heavily biased to those sites that have seen most extensive excavation (*Lambaesis*, *Gholaia*, *Gemellae*).[97] Study of finds assemblages from military sites is generally poor, making difficult the dating of occupation in the absence of epigraphic testimony.[98] Future excavations or chance discoveries may well add to the numbers of known units, or lead to significant revisions to the dates of establishment or abandonment of sectors of the "frontier."[99]

Were there Frontiers in Africa under Rome?

The description of the garrison deployments and the elements of linear barriers presented below raises important questions about what we mean by terms such as the Roman *limes/limites*. Roman frontier studies is a well-established subfield of the discipline, but one that carries a fair share of colonialist baggage, not least in its title. The very idea of "frontiers" is rife with anachronistic assumptions, and the early history of the investigation of Roman frontiers was very much influenced by modern colonial ideas about territorial borders and lines on maps.[100] This is not to say that Rome had no concept of territorial borders—indeed Rome is rightly celebrated for the extent to which all manner of boundaries were surveyed and demarcated in the landscape—but it is also evident that Rome's concept of its Empire was more fluid, and extended to peoples controlled through treaty agreements. The modern connotations of frontiers emphasise the linear demarcation of territory, whereas even with the most imposing Roman linear barriers, like Hadrian's Wall or the Antonine Wall in Britain, their correlation with provincial boundaries was ambiguous. It is clear that Roman garrisons controlled territory some way in advance of the British walls and there was also a deep hinterland studded with garrison posts behind them. The emphasis in the literature on "Roman frontiers" also focuses attention on the outward-facing relationships.

In recent decades, the Roman *limites* have come increasingly to be recognised as broad zones rather than frontier lines and to have been highly contingent on (or responsive to) environmental factors and involving complex stories of sedentarisation and economic development.[101] The recognition of the depth of the frontier zone and of the range of impacts that arose from the military deployment is

97. For surveys of forts in Numidia and Tripolitania, Daniels 1987, 237–60; Fentress 1979, 83–108; Lenoir 2011, 151–228; Mackensen 2021b.
98. Guéry 1986 for a rare exception.
99. For a series of progressive updates on work on the African *limites* down to 1990, see Euzennat 1972; 1977a; 1977b; 1986; 1990. For specific work on Tripolitania and *Mauretania Tingitana*, see Rebuffat 1969b; 1971b; 1972a; 1977b; 1977c; 1979; 1980a; 1987a; 1999.
100. For a good summary of traditional views, see Mann 1974. Compare now Breeze 2011; Ployer et al. 2019; Reddé 2014.
101. Guédon 2018a, 191–219; Leveau 1995; Rebuffat 1999; Trousset 1976; 1980a; 1984a; 1986b; 2004; Whittaker 1994, 31–97.

vital for the proper understanding of the military community in North Africa. For this reason, in what follows I shall use the terminology of "security zones" to a greater extent than "frontiers."[102] Borderlands are very ambiguous cultural spaces, often marked by distinct forms of hybridity, and are central to studies of colonial systems.[103] But the term "frontier" perhaps focuses us too much on what divided colonial territory from what lay beyond (in terms of land/people) and makes those external relations all important, rather than also considering the internal complexities of life alongside garrisons.

As we shall see, in North Africa the deployments reflect more than "defence in depth." The Mauretanian provinces were fundamentally highly militarised in their entirety, rather than divisible into civil and military zones. The security zones of *Numidia* and *Tripolitana* were also extremely deep—a traveller might take a week or more to pass through. Such large territories under effective military supervision or oversight presented challenges to the numerical strength of the garrison and it is no surprise to hear of incidents of brigandage, such as the assault by bandits on a military surveyor, Nonius Datus, in the Babors range.[104]

The infrastructure of linear "frontier" systems is a key focus of Roman army studies.[105] Most impressive were the linear barriers, like Hadrian's Wall in Britain or the palisades, earthworks, and walls of the German frontier, with a complex associated infrastructure of gates, watch towers, fortlets, connecting roads, and so on. North Africa has revealed evidence of a number of impressive barriers, but the level of investigation of both barriers and associated features remains very limited.[106]

The Roman military deployments in North Africa need to be considered as a series of separate security zones rather than as a single system. In part, this reflects the provincial structures, but it also relates to the radically varied topographic setting, from the mountains of *Mauretania* to the desert margins of *Numidia* and *Tripolitana*. Because of the large distances covered by the Roman provinces and the importance of horses in the societies confronting Rome, cavalry units were an essential element of the African garrisons. But it is also true that Roman infantry troops could constrain the activities of mobile Libyan people by controlling important fixed points in the landscape, such as mountain passes, major water sources (oases, desert wells), or access to pastures or agricultural lands.

---

102. With thanks to Bruce Hitchner for his helpful discussion of my initial use of terminology and the suggestion of the phrase "security zone" in place of "frontier."
103. Naum 2010 for an interesting review of the colonial context of frontiers and the hybrid "Third Space" that often results.
104. *CIL* 8.2728; Hamdoune 2018, 124 for this and other examples.
105. Napoli 1997.
106. Baradez 1949a; Guédon 2018a, 123–33.

Africa (including Numidia and Tripolitana)

The large armies involved in the initial Roman conquests of *Qart Hadasht* and *Numidia* (20,000–40,000) appear to have been succeeded by much smaller armies of long-term occupation, despite a large increase in provincial territory between the 1st century BCE and the early 3rd century CE. The relatively small size of the garrison has often been adduced to demonstrate the economy of force achieved in *Africa* compared to some of the European provinces. In addition to the *legio III Augusta*, a total of only eight to 13 auxiliary units are known from the province across several centuries (Table 6.1). The impression from the epigraphic evidence is that the garrison was never larger than about 10–12,000 men. A striking aspect of the list of auxiliary units is the high proportion that involved a cavalry component, probably necessitated by the local strength in this regard. The evidence for the outstationing of substantial numbers of the *III Augusta* troops in the late 2nd and 3rd centuries CE certainly supports the view that the auxiliary forces were not adequate to man all the known forts and the troops had to be thinly spread. It also emphasises the role of the garrison as a police force rather than a defence against a sustained external military threat.

However, due to the lack of excavation and research in the garrison regions in recent decades, the current strength listing of the garrison is probably a significant underestimate. Even allowing for several phases of garrison deployment, there seem to be more forts than known units to occupy them. Fentress counted 42 forts and fortlets of different periods in her overview of the Numidian garrison (1 legionary fortress, 17 forts, 6 fortlets, 2 outposts, 16 late Roman forts and fortlets)[107] and my own work on Tripolitania recorded a total of 38 fortifications (8 forts, 12 fortlets, 10 smaller outposts, along with 8 fortlets of late Roman type).[108] In a recent review of the evidence, and making use of newly available high-resolution satellite imagery, upwards of 140 forts and fortlets were identified, covering the entire military zone from *Numidia* to *Tripolitana* (an increase of 75% over the previous total).[109] This includes a number of forts whose existence is pretty certain, but whose precise identification on the ground has not been possible (such as Mizda and Zintan in Tripolitania),[110] but also many sites where no inscriptions have ever been recovered and thus the dating and garrison unit are unknown. Additional unidentified forts are likely in many sectors, especially those of short-lived occupation at sites with subsequent urban growth. In consequence,

107. Fentress 1979,
108. Mattingly 1995, 90–106, 192–94.
109. The work was carried out with Martin Sterry and is reported on in Mattingly et al. 2013a.
110. On these sites, whose existence was predicted in Mattingly 1995, see Mackensen 2012; Schimmer 2012.

Table 6.1. Military units attested in *Africa* in High Empire (after Le Bohec 1989a; 1989b).

Period	***Legiones* (temporary detachments)**	***Alae***	**Auxiliary units:** **C = *cohors*,** **C *eq* = mixed unit,** **N = *numerus***	**Minimum number of troops?**
Julio-Claudian period	*Leg III Augusta* *(Leg IX Hispana)*	*Ala I Pannoniorum* *Ala Siliana*	*C eq II Thracum* *C eq VII Lusitana* *C XV*	8,500
End 1st century	*Leg III Augusta*	*Ala I Pannoniorum* *Ala Flavia*	*C eq I Chalcidenorum* *C eq I Flavia* *C eq II Thracum* *C eq VII Lusitana* *C eq VI Commagenorum* *C II Afrorum (?)*	10,000
2nd century	*Leg III Augusta* *(Leg VI Ferrata)* *(Leg VII Gemina)* *(Leg III Gallica)*	*Ala I Pannoniorum* *Ala [..] Pa…* *Ala Flavia*	*C eq I Chalcidenorum* *C eq I Flavia* *C eq II Hispanorum* *C eq II Thracum* *C eq VII Lusitana* *C eq VI Commagenorum* *C II Afrorum* *C II Hamiorum* *C I Afrorum* *N Palmyrenorum*	12,000
3rd century	*Leg III Augusta* (238–253 CE cashiered)	*Ala I Pannoniorum* *Ala Flavia*	*C eq VI Commagenorum* *C eq VIII Fida* *C eq I Flavia* *C II Afrorum* *C II Hamiorum* *C I Syrorum* *C II Maurorum* *N Hemesenorum* *N Palmyrenorum*	11,000

our knowledge of the chronology and spatial extent of the garrison deployment in its different phases is very patchy compared with other *limites* of the Empire.[111] It seems certain that there were additional military installations beyond those that are well known and can be dated and assigned to specific units. This need not in itself be an argument in favour of a drastically larger provincial garrison, if units were from an early date regularly subdivided between two or more posts.[112] With a few localised exceptions we lack knowledge of the smallest outposts, signalling towers, and watchtowers.[113]

111. For summaries of the African garrison evolution, see Fentress 1979; Guédon 2018a, 99–136.
112. As seems to have been the case in Britain in the late 1st century, Mattingly 2006a, 153–54.
113. Rebuffat 1978; Trousset 1990. See now Schmid et al. 2019.

PHASE 1: THE AUGUSTAN EXPANSION AND AFTER

The early military deployment in Africa was not conceived in terms of a frontier, but was essentially a concentration of forces at key winter and summer bases. Little is known of the initial deployment in consolidating Roman control of either *Africa Vetus* or the Numidian lands of *Africa Nova*, though parallels with other provinces and a few tantalising hints are all we have to go on.[114] To describe deployments before the Flavian period as "systems" or "frontiers" is really to misconstrue the nature of Roman control in the late Republic and early Principate, which seems to have been more tactical than strategic.[115] We might think of the early army in terms of a number of distinct battle groups (comprising legionary vexillations and assigned auxiliary support units) placed so as to able to respond to threats from different sectors and to engage in campaigns when sanctioned.[116]

Can we find any evidence to support the view that the African legion may have been subdivided into vexillations and brigaded with other troops in the early phase of garrisoning? In this regard it is interesting to note that both the *legio III Augusta* and the *ala I Pannoniorum* are attested at *Ammaedara*.[117] Although the exact location of the fortress at *Ammaedara* is unknown, the logical topographical location appears to be far too small to have been full legionary size (a legionary fortress requires c.20 ha).[118] However, a vexillation fortress of c.9 ha would fit on the platform defined by wadi gullies at the heart of the later town (Fig. 6.3). The construction of the road between *Ammaedara*, *Capsa*, and *Tacape* was thus not a frontier line, but probably a connecting link between three key bases, with each representing a winter camp for battalions that were probably expected to have spent summers campaigning or operating well in advance of it. *Capsa*, for instance, was the key position from which to dominate the Jarid and Nefzaoua oases. There were some smaller garrison points established in the war against Tiqfarin, some manned by soldiers and others by veterans, but these were not intended as a defensive screen so much as a means of countering the attacks. While a garrison was also based at the provincial capital, *Karthago* (and an urban cohort was eventually based there), the division of military responsibility between the legate and the governor meant that it was to become less significant in *Africa* than the equivalent forces in *Mauretania*.[119]

114. Le Bohec 1989a, 340–43, 356–60. See also Baroni 2020 for an interpretation of epigraphic hints at garrison around *Cirta*.
115. Faure and Leveau 2015, 132–34; Guédon 2018a, 37–41; Isaac 1990; Luttwak 1976, 51–126; Trousset 1980a; 1984a. Cf. Jones and Mattingly 1990, 88–129 for a comparative case study from Britain, demonstrating the evolution of the idea of the frontier.
116. For British parallels for vexillation fortresses, see Jones and Mattingly 1990, 88–97; Mattingly 2006a, 132–46.
117. Le Bohec 1989b, 34.
118. Mackensen 2000.
119. Duval et al. 1984; Ricci 2011, 494–96, noting that the urban cohort seems to have evolved particular responsibilities for the security and protection of the grain supply through *Karthago*, including firefighting, rather than a frontline fighting role.

Figure 6.3. Satellite image showing the probable extent and position of a vexillation fortress buried beneath the centre of the town of *Ammaedara* (Haidra) (Martin Sterry, from author's rough, Image copyright CNES/Airbus/Google).

PHASE 2: FLAVIAN–HADRIANIC CONSOLIDATION

The late 1st and early 2nd century saw substantial reorganisation of Roman troop deployments, with garrisons being moved forward into more advanced positions, both in the Aurès mountains and beyond into the pre-desert, and with more evidence now of separate brigading of units at key locations. The construction of roads and the delimitation of land assigned to urban and autochthonous communities created a new spatial infrastructure of peripheral Roman territory, gradually coalescing as recognisable security systems.[120] In the Flavian period, the legionary fortress was advanced from *Ammaedara* to *Theveste*, perhaps in order to reunite the unit in a single fortress from a series of vexillation fortresses.[121] Around the same time, an auxiliary fort was established at *Lambaesis*, a precursor to the eventual move forward of the main legionary base under Trajan.[122] This c.24 ha legionary fortress at *Lambaesis* was extensively excavated in the late 19th and early 20th

120. Fentress 1979; Le Bohec 1995.
121. Guédon 2018a, 101.
122. Fentress 1979, 94–96; Janon 1973;1977.

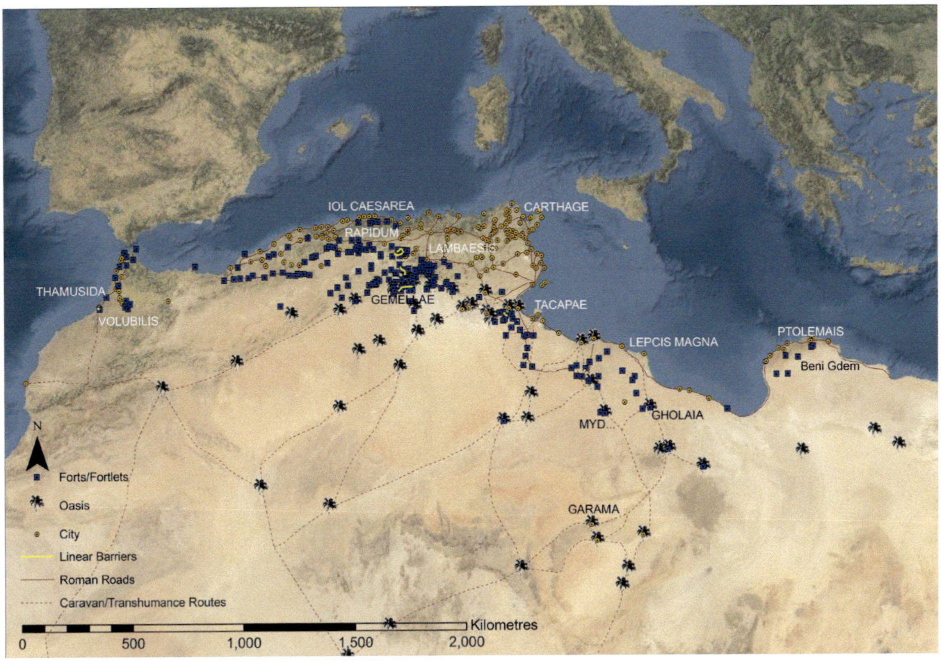

Figure 6.4. The developed state of the North African security zones (from Mattingly et al. 2013a, 40).

centuries (in part using the labour of French political prisoners held in the large penitentiary that was established across part of the site).[123] This was the point as well when Roman forts and roads were established south of the Aurès (Fig. 6.4).[124] The fort of *Nigrenses Maiores* (Besseriani) is the best preserved of the Trajanic forts, though has been little excavated.[125]

The reign of Hadrian consolidated the shape of the Numidian garrison deployment, with the legionary base in a withdrawn position on the Aurès high plains, some forts and outposts along the key passes, and access routes and an outer screen of auxiliary forts along a road south of the Aurès mountains in the pre-desert (Fig. 6.5). It is likely that construction of the linear barriers, collectively known as the *fossatum Africae*, commenced at this time, though they may have been elaborated over a long time period down to late Roman times. The Hadrianic fort of *Gemellae* was established for the *ala I Pannoniorum* (whom we encountered at the start of the chapter being inspected by Hadrian).[126] Jean Baradez's excavations of

123. Cagnat 1913, 450–515; Guédon 2018a, 101–03; Le Bohec 1989a, 407–244. On the story behind the excavations, Effros 2018, 139–67.

124. Fentress 1979, 108–14; Guédon 2018a, 103–07; Le Bohec 1989a,425–35.

125. Laporte and Dupuis 2011 (the site is sometimes known as *Ad Maiores*).

126. Baradez 1949b; 1966a“ 1966b; Le Bohec 1989b, 33–36; Leschi 1949; Trousset 1977a.

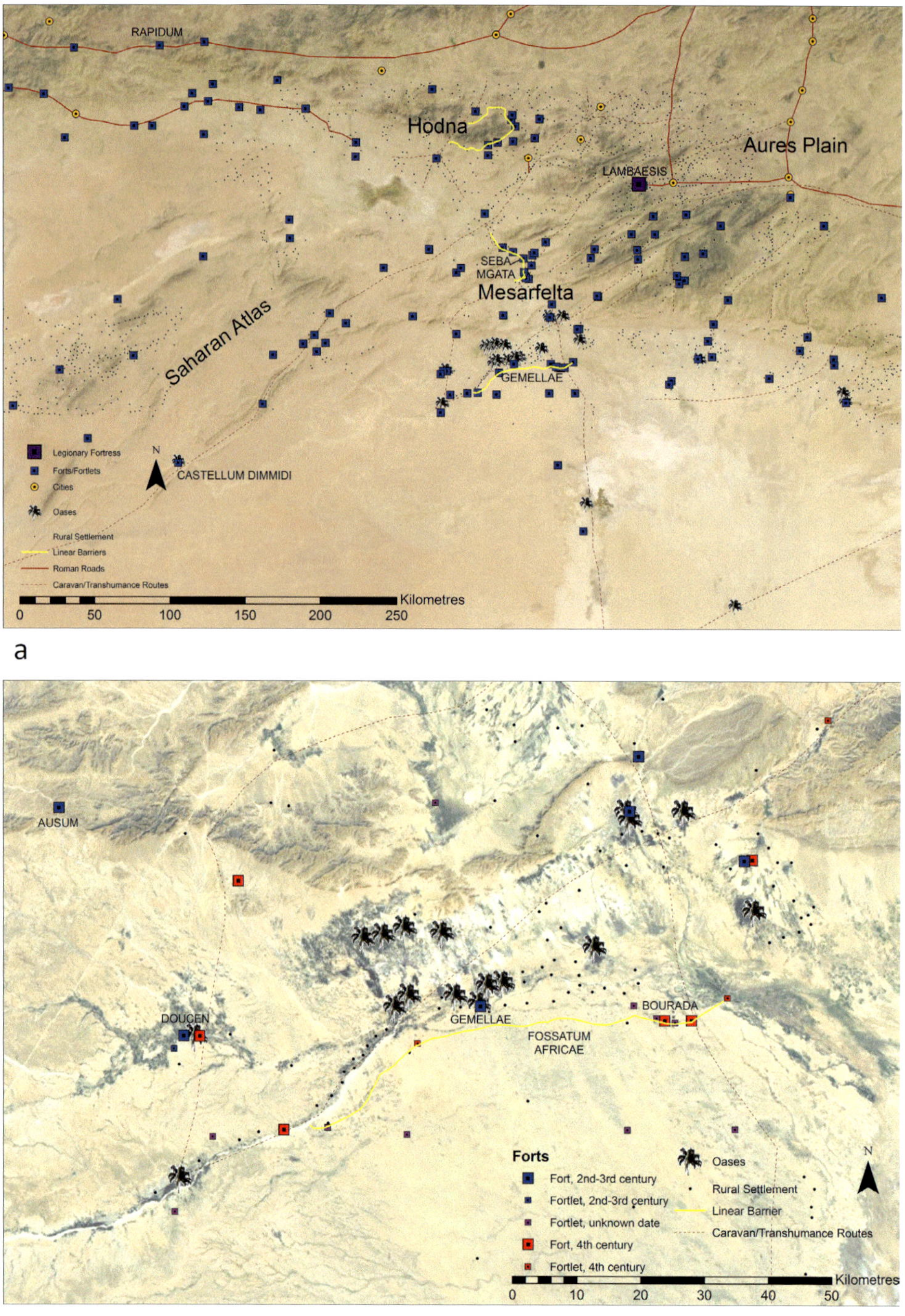

Figure 6.5. The Numidian security zone. a) Sectors of the *fossatum Africae* in *Numidia* (from Mattingly et al. 2013a, 76). b) Detail of the *Gemellae* sector (from Mattingly et al. 2013a, 74).

the baths, amphitheatre, and headquarters building were only partially published but nonetheless make this the best known fort site in the Numidian sector.[127] To the east, the development of the military deployment in Tripolitania is not well established, due to lack of excavation at many sites, but there are signs that a network of forts at key oases and water points was taking shape during the 2nd century, as at *Bezereos*, *Tillibari*, and perhaps also *Thenteos* and Mizda (Figs. 6.6, 6.9).[128]

In terms of the Gaetulian peoples within the Numidian security zone, we should draw a distinction between two broad groups. On the one hand there were upland peoples of the Aurès mountains and the fertile plains to the north, who seem to have been partly sedentarised in pre-Roman times, with occupation in fortified promontory and hilltop sites (similar to the early Numidian settlements).[129] The second group concerned the oasis centres of the Ziban and Nemencha.[130] The movement of pastoral groups between these two broad zones can also be assumed to have been part of the security situation.

PHASE 3: SEVERAN OUTPOSTING

There were apparent advances of the military deployment in the reign of Septimius Severus, echoed also by a major reorganisation in *Mauretania Caesariensis* (see below).[131] In southern Numidia, a network of outposts was pushed out far to the south-west of the Hadrianic garrison posts into the mountains of the Ouled Nail and the Saharan Atlas.[132] Traditional interpretations have tended to emphasise the "nomadic" nature of people from this area, but more recent evaluations suggests that substantial sedentary groups were also settled in the mountains and their major valleys.[133] The establishment of distant outposts here seems less to do with controlling seasonal movements of pastoralists than with supervision of oasis and sedentary populations around and within the mountains. In Tripolitania (Fig. 6.6), oasis outposts were also created at *Cidamus* (Ghadamis), *Castra Madensia/Myd...* (al-Qurrayyat al-Garbia/Gheriat al-Garbia), and *Gholaia* (Bu Nijim/Bu Njem).[134] Again, the purpose of these advances seems to have been to establish supervision of

127. Baradez 1949a; 1949b; 1966a; 1966b; Fentress 1979, 83–84; Trousset 1977a.
128. Guédon 2018a, 108–11; Le Bohec 1989a, 437–44; Mackensen 2010a (*Tisavar*); Mattingly 1995, 79–83; Trousset 1974, 75–133.
129. Fentress 1979, 28–36, 39 (with map on p. 29); Morizot 1997.
130. Mattingly et al. 2020b, 211–16.
131. On 3rd-century changes linked to provincial reorganisation, see Dupuis 2017.
132. Faure and Leveau 2015; Fentress 1979, 114–17; Guédon 2018a, 111–12; Le Bohec 1989a, 435–37.
133. Faure and Leveau 2015, 134–38.
134. For older views, see Cagnat 1914b; Goodchild 1954a; Gsell 1933. See now Guédon 2018a, 112–2; Mackensen 2021a for the definitive publication of recent work in German; also 2010b; 2011; 2012; 2016; 2021b, 131–41 for the *castra Madensia* identification; Mattingly 1995, 95–97; Rebuffat 1989; Trousset 1974; Welsby 1983; 1988; 1990. For the broader context of Severan activity in *Africa*, see Cordovana 2007.

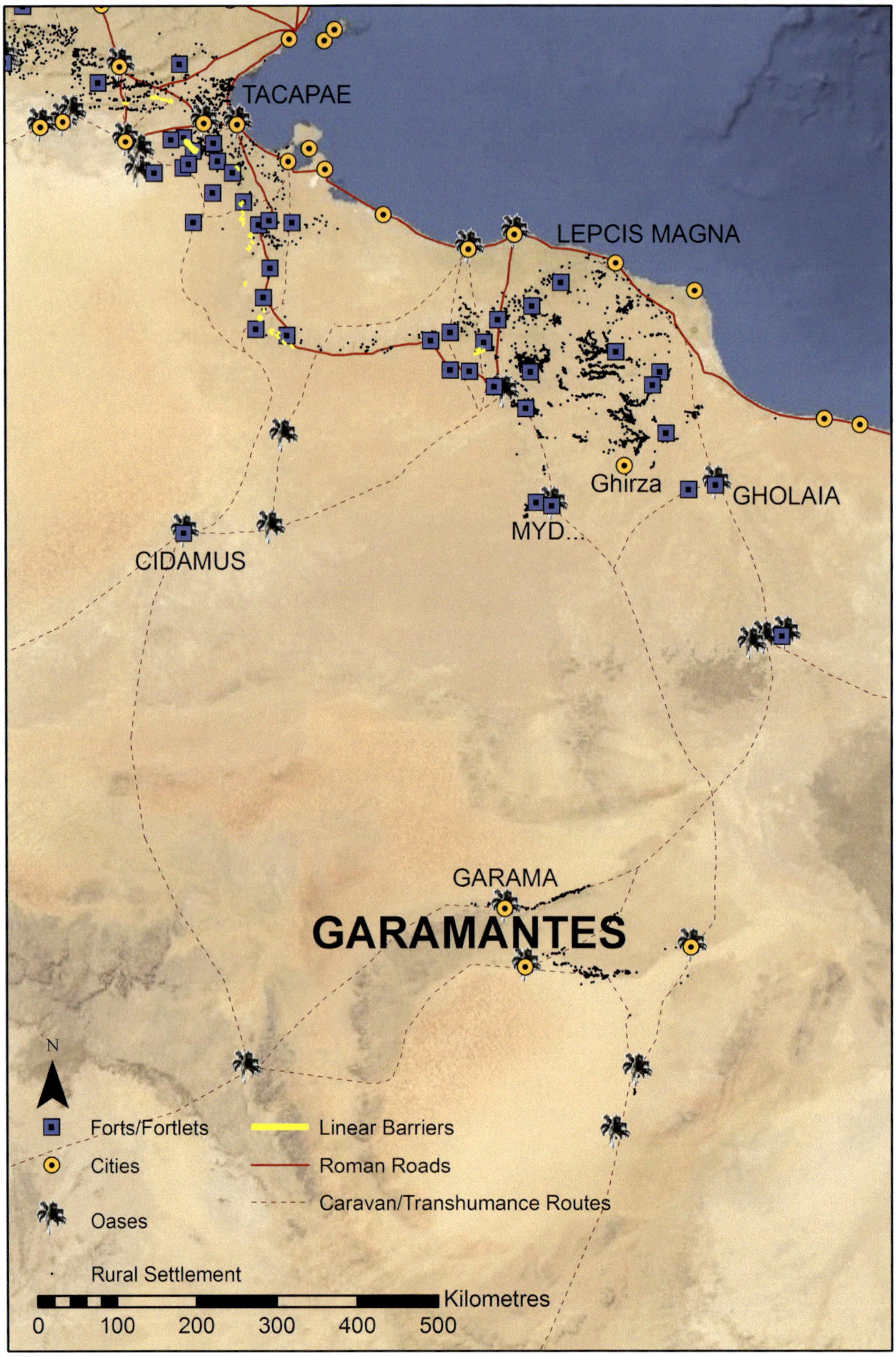

Figure 6.6. Garrison deployment in Tripolitania and the *Garamantes* (from Mattingly et al. 2013a, 48).

already established oases and to gain greater control of the main routes to the south towards the *Garamantes*.[135] The extensive excavations at Bu Nijim in the 1960s–1970s are of particular importance, not only for the richness of detail on the layout of the fort[136] and a mass of epigraphic documentation,[137] including ink documents on potsherds (ostraca) that provide a unique insight into garrison life.[138] Survey and excavation at the near contemporary fort of al-Qurrayyat al-Garbia has also been of huge importance in illustrating the scale of fort defences and other aspects of garrison life in the Tripolitanian pre-desert.[139] The Severan advances were evidently achieved, in the absence of evidence for a major augmentation in garrison strength, by outstationing substantial numbers of the legionary troops of the *III Augusta,* increased units of irregular auxiliary units (*numeri*), and subdivision of units across multiple installations.[140]

Some of the detail in my reconstruction is necessarily speculative or hypothetical, but I think the overall patterns suggested represent a good fit with the available evidence and our knowledge of Roman military deployments elsewhere. But what was the underlying tactical and strategic rationale for the changing pattern of deployment? How far is it possible to relate this to indigenous threat? How far was this due to the imperial imperative of imposing order and control over a broad militarised zone?

Linear Barriers on the African limites

The role of the discontinuous segments of linear barrier in the various military sectors in *Africa* needs discussion. The existence of three (or possibly) four long linear obstacles (*fossata*) was made famous by the work of Baradez, though the lack of adequate follow-up investigation on the ground hampers understanding today (Fig. 6.5).[141] In addition there are shorter elements (sometimes referred to in modern literature as *clausurae*) often blocking mountain passes or controlling access corridors through hilly terrain in southern Tunisia and north-west Libya.[142] The longer sectors of *fossatum* are described in turn.

135. Mattingly et al. 2020b, 188–201.
136. Rebuffat 1967a; 1970a; 1970b; 1975b; 1977a; 1989; 1992b.
137. Rebuffat 1973a; 1973b; 1973c; 1985a; 1985b; 1985c; 1987b; 1988a; 1988b; 1990b.
138. Guédon 2018a, 205–08; Marichal 1979; 1992; Rebuffat and Marichal 1973.
139. Mackensen 2010b; 2011; 2012; 2021a; Mattingly 1995, 92–95; Welsby 1983; 1988; 1990.
140. Le Bohec 1989a, 392–94 for evidence of multiple vexillations of legionaries.
141. Baradez 1949a for the original aerial surveys; Cf. inter alia for general discussions Daniels 1987, 242–46; Fentress 1979, 111–14; Guédon 2018a, 123–33; Le Bohec 1989a, 370–71, 425–30; Mattingly et al. 2013a, 72–76; Napoli 1997, 64–72, 96–119; 408–12, 457–60; Trousset 1998a; 2004, 82–88.
142. Mattingly 1995, 106–15; Mattingly et al. 2013a, 76–80

THE HODNA SECTOR(S)

The traces of the Bou Taleb *fossatum* appear to encircle the Hodna mountain range (total length c.90 km), though, in the absence of detailed survey of the remains, alternative interpretations are possible.[143] For instance, it is feasible that these represent two separate phases of earthworks to north and south of the range. At any rate, there appears to be significantly higher agricultural development to the north of the Bou Taleb range than to the south.[144] They also lie close to what were probably the southern boundaries of the late Roman province of *Mauretania Sitifensis*, though have not been seriously considered in relation to its limits.[145]

THE *MESARFELTA* SECTOR

This was the main sector presented in Baradez's famous book on the *fossatum*, evidently running c.50 km from near the town of *Tubunae* (Tobna) to *Mesarfelta*. The *Mesarfelta* section was particularly well preserved, running along the west flank of a key north–south corridor, with numerous towers and some gates attached to the barrier. The forts were positioned slightly to the east of the barrier along the military road. Much of the barrier consisted of a bank and ditch, but in places it was built as a drystone wall without ditch (Fig. 6.7c).

THE *GEMELLAE* SECTOR

To the south of the substantial seasonal watercourse, the Wadi Jedi, a running ditch and bank extends from west to east for at least 60 km (Fig. 6.7a–b). Again, it is regularly provided with towers and twin-tower gate houses along its length (though the claim by Baradez that these were at mile intervals has never been substantiated). Baradez printed few images of it. The major Hadrianic fort at Gemellae lay a few kilometres to the rear of the barrier and there were further forts close to the east and west ends of the barrier.

THE (NON-EXISTENT) *NIGRENSES MAIORES* SECTOR

Baradez also reported seeing a further stretch of *fossatum* at the end of a single reconnaissance flight near the fort of *Nigrenses Maiores*,[146] though Trousset has subsequently questioned whether this was perhaps a misinterpretation of the traces

143. Baradez 1949a, 85–92, but note that Baradez only made two brief flights over this sector. Cf. Soyer 1976, 146–48, 161. According to Aibeche 2014, 511, the *fossatum* of Bou Taleb comprised a double-faced wall, with other phases using orthostatic slabs and a rubble infill.
144. Soyer 1976, 146 notes that extensive Roman-era land divisions are concentrated to the north of Bou Taleb; Aibeche 2014 has recently published a late-antique inscription from a small *quadriburgus* (c.68 × 57 m) situated near the west end of the northern stretch of linear barrier, mentioning repair to walls.
145. Laporte 1999.
146. Baradez 1949a, 109–11. It is confidently mapped in the Barrington Atlas, following Baradez, Fentress 2000b.

Figure 6.7. Montage of views of the *fossatum Africae*. a) Remains of a double-tower gateway across the *Gemellae fossatum*, with ditch and bank visible to left of the standing figure. b) The ditch and bank of the barrier. c) Stone wall in the *Mesarfelta* sector (all photos: author).

of the military road.[147] No features of linear barrier have been identified on the ground and this "sector" must currently be discounted, though it is conceivable that some shorter elements of barrier may have been erected in the valleys running back up through the Aurès and Nemencha mountains, following the pattern of the *clausurae* further east and south-east (see below).

As regards the identified elements of *fossatum*, the barrier was in places constructed as a wall, but more commonly as a running bank and ditch, with watch-towers and gates attached to the linear element (Figs. 6.7–6.8). In the absence of excavation of any of the associated towers and gates, the earliest construction date is very speculative. Baradez advanced arguments for some of the Numidian elements

147. Trousset 1980b, 135–39.

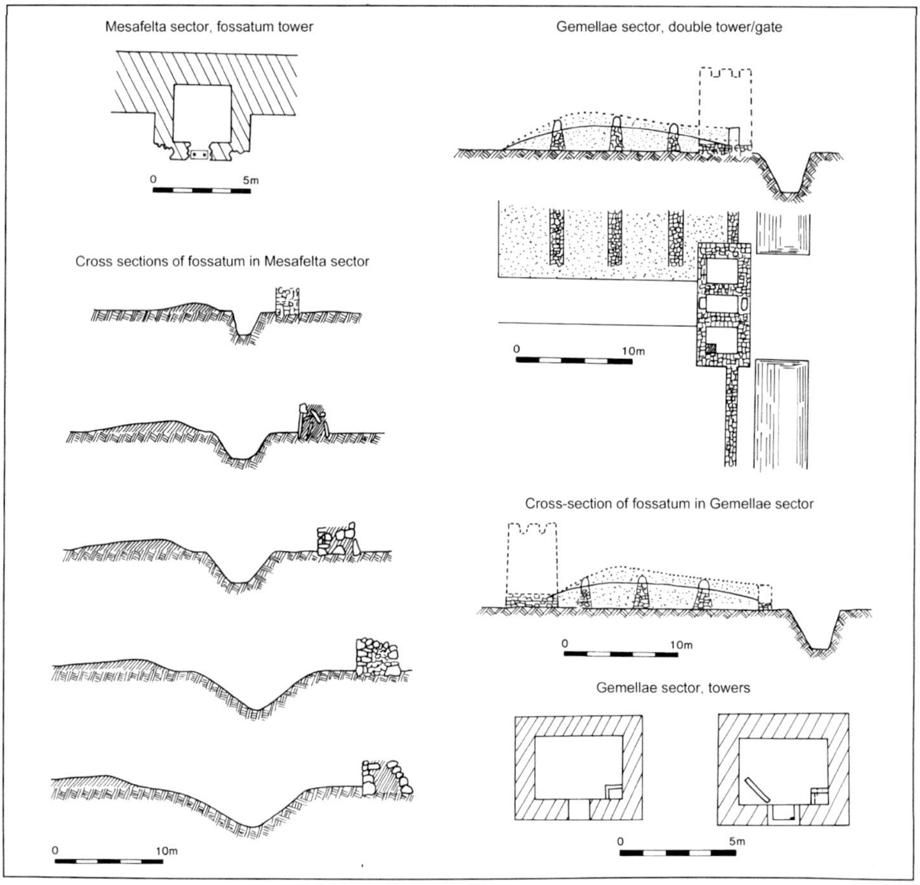

Figure 6.8. Features of the *fossatum Africae* (montage from Mattingly et al. 2013a, 72, after Daniels 1987).

being Hadrianic, and that still seems the most likely explanation for the initial barriers.[148] Roman pottery is certainly associated with these structures, spanning the 2nd to 4th centuries or slightly later. A 4th-century coin has been found in relation to a *fossatum* tower.[149] The combined evidence suggests construction, maintenance, and rebuilds over a prolonged timeframe, a view supported also by the structural diversity of these linear barriers.

THE JABAL TEBAGA SECTOR AND OTHER MINOR BARRIERS (*CLAUSURAE*)

Pol Trousset brought to wider notice the existence of a series of shorter barriers, sometimes described as *clausurae*, in southern Tunisia, and over the years there has

148. Baradez 1967.

149. Daniels 1987, 264; Jones and Mattingly 1980.

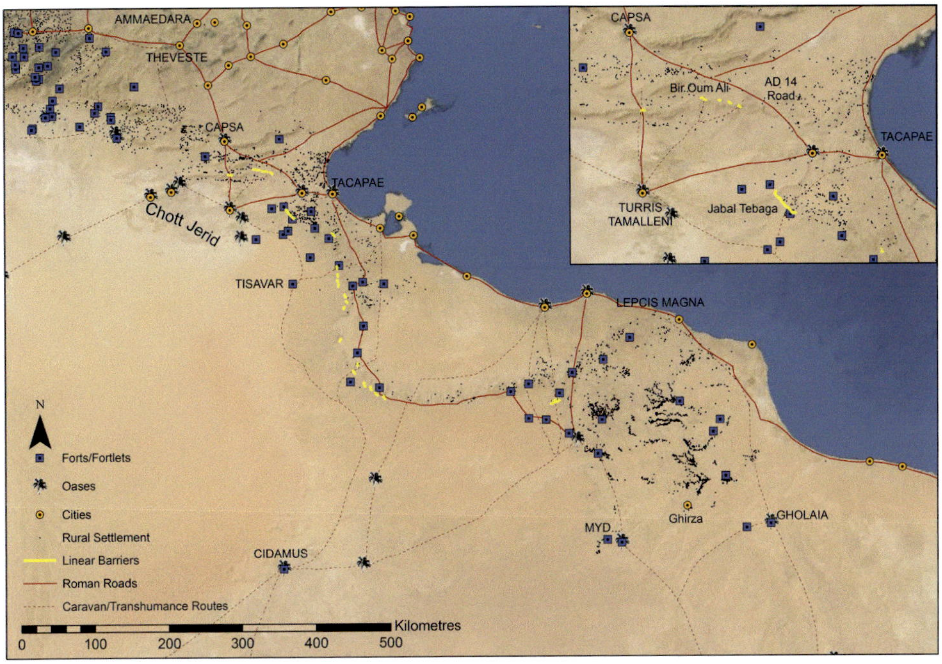

Figure 6.9. Map of *clausurae* in Tripolitania (from Mattingly 2013a, 80).

been a steady increase in their numbers.[150] Most of the Tripolitanian *clausurae* were quite short, none exceeding 17 km in length and the shortest just a few hundred metres. Three groups can be defined (Fig. 6.9): a series north of the Chott Jarid/ Fejej (seemingly close to the boundary between the territory of *Capsa* to the north and *Turris Tamalleni* to the south); a second to the south of the Jabal Tebaga, controlling access between the Dahar and the Jafara coastal plain; and third, a Libyan outlier at Hadd Hajar controlling access from the Libyan Sahara towards the agricultural zone of the Jabal Gharian.[151] The middle group comprises, in addition to one lengthy monument (the Tebaga *clausura*), at least 15 shorter obstacles erected in narrow mountain passes or across traditional routeways between desert and sown (Fig. 6.9). The most extraordinary of these *clausurae* structurally is the Bir Oum Ali masonry wall, which still stands in places to over 3 m high (Fig. 6.10a–b). Gates flanked by double towers (Fig. 6.10d, f) appear to have been a feature of some, but not all, of the *clausurae* (Bir Oum Ali, Tebaga, Wadi Skiffa, Hadd Hajar).[152]

---

150. Brogan 1980; Mattingly 1995, 106–15; Mattingly and Jones 1986; Mattingly et al. 2013a, 76–80; Napoli 1997; Trousset 1984b; 1997b; 1998a.
151. Mattingly 1995, 106–13; Mattingly et al. 2013a, 76–80 (based on remote sensing work by Martin Sterry); Trousset 1997b.
152. Mattingly 1995, 109, 111–12 for plans of gates.

Figure 6.10. Montage of view of *clausurae* in Tripolitania. a–b) The wall of Bir Oum Ali. c) The Tebaga bank and ditch. d) Tunisian policeman by the ruins of the Tebaga gate. e–f) Skiffa *clausura* with detail of its gate (all photos: author).

Cutting across a key routeway from the Dahar towards the Tunisian coastal plain, the Tebaga *clausura* extends for 17 km. This was the Tebaga corridor up which General Montgomery sent his tank column to turn the Mareth line of German defence at the coast.[153] The barrier was situated close to what seems to have been the division between the territory of *Turris Tamalleni* to west and *Tacape* to east (see below, Fig. 10.10). Across the centre of the plain it consisted of a c.4 m wide ditch and 4 m bank, revetted front and back by drystone walling of large blocks. The original height is difficult to estimate, but it stands in places even today to c.2 m height. There were a few towers attached to the barrier, or on closely adjacent hilltops, and a single gateway situated on a low but pronounced hillock towards the southern end of the corridor (Fig. 6.10c–d).

As regards the dating of the *clausurae*, the Tebaga gate reused blocks from an earlier mausoleum in what was evidently a late remodelling (perhaps 3rd- or 4th-century), though it also yielded a 2nd-century lamp form. The Bir Oum Ali gate has some pottery that should be 2nd- or 3rd-century in date. Trousset favours a Severan date overall on the grounds that military deployment only appears fully fledged at that point, but given the gaps in knowledge of early sites and the structural variability of the various barriers, a spread of dates seems more plausible, across several centuries.[154]

The important point to stress about all these linear elements is that they do not seem to have marked the limits of the Empire—that is, the frontier in a modern sense. But there is a close coincidence with some demarcation between urban authorities within the provincial structure (*Turris Tamalleni* and *Capsa* to the north and *Tacape* to the east). Along with the more southerly barriers, they also mark to some extent points of sharp transition from pre-desert lands to zones of rain-fed agriculture. The provision of gates shows that they were intended as control points in relation to movement (of people, animals, goods), not impenetrable barriers. Overall, these features seem less about protecting the province than about facilitating policing. The interpretation of the *fossata* and shorter linear elements as effective points of control in relation to the movement of transhumant pastoralists has been commonly accepted since Pol Trousset and I both published work on them in the 1980s.[155] What has changed in my perception is a clearer sense that part of what made these filtering mechanisms workable was precisely the fact that Roman authority extended over oasis cultivators in the zone *in advance of* the dry-farmed lands and to whom the mobile pastoral groups were closely linked. Trade (and

153. While filming part of a BBC documentary in 2012 at the linear barrier at Tebaga, my eyes were opened by the military historian Dan Snow (the main UK presenter on the film) to the extensive debris of the battle that took place around the Roman barrier in 1942.

154. Mattingly 1995, 114–15; Napoli 1997, 440–46; Trousset 2004, 86.

155. On the function of the barriers, see discussion in Guédon 2018a, 161–85, 127–33; Mattingly 1995, 113–14; Mattingly and Jones 1986; Trousset 1980a; 2004, 86–88; contra older ideas of the barriers as a hard defence against nomadic raids, Guéy 1939. For environmentally focused discussions of the Roman "frontier," see Cordovana 2012; Leveau 1995; 2018; Trousset 1984a; 1986b.

control of trade) beyond Roman territory with oasis communities also needs to be considered anew following my reappraisal of the scale of Roman trade with the *Garamantes*. The potential that the garrison zone was connected with communities deep in the Sahara has significant implications for the interpretation of the Roman infrastructure.

Figure 6.9 combines available settlement data for the security zones from *Numidia* to *Tripolitana*, incorporating information from the *Atlas archéologique* maps, survey data from the Libyan Valleys Survey, and new satellite image analysis by Martin Sterry to reveal how the Roman garrison deployment relates to the ecological transition from the desert to the sown. Sedentary cultivation extended into the oases to the south and west, but the linear barriers in many locations were erected at points of sharp transition. The linear barriers made it easier to regulate movements between a more extensive cultivated zone and pre-desert pastures, to supervise labour migrants, to tax pastoral production, and to exact customs dues on the trade with the oases and more distant parts of the trans-Saharan zone. The involvement of the garrison in collection of customs and in other fiscal roles is indicated by a number of pieces of evidence from Africa.[156] The key point here is that the Roman army was not making particular distinctions between those who were subjects of Rome and those who were considered external to the Empire. The margins of Roman territory were somewhat fuzzy and shifting over time, of course, but what was important about the location of the linear barriers was that they were positioned to allow policing and economic exploitation of everyone living and passing through the military zone. Unlike traditional presentations of the frontier as a hard line drawn in relation to external "tribal groups," this was the reality of what the army bases meant to civilian settlement (and vice versa) in a densely occupied security zone.

Types of Fort and Units of Garrison

Figure 6.11 brings together a selection of fort plans from North African sites, primarily from *Numidia* and Tripolitania, but including some examples from the Mauretanian provinces (*Rapidum*, *Thamusida*, *Tamuda*).

In general, the layout and accommodation of the North African fort should reflect the nature of the unit it was designed for. In practice, things seem to have been more complicated, and there is increasing evidence of parts of units being outstationed across two or more forts. An interesting aspect of fort design in North Africa is that many forts were at the smaller end of the size range attested in

156. France 2015, 123, 130–31 (customs tariffs). See also *CIL* 8.18224 (*Lambaesis*); *AE* 1980, 954 (*Calceus Herculis*) for soldiers with responsibility for markets and weights and measures.

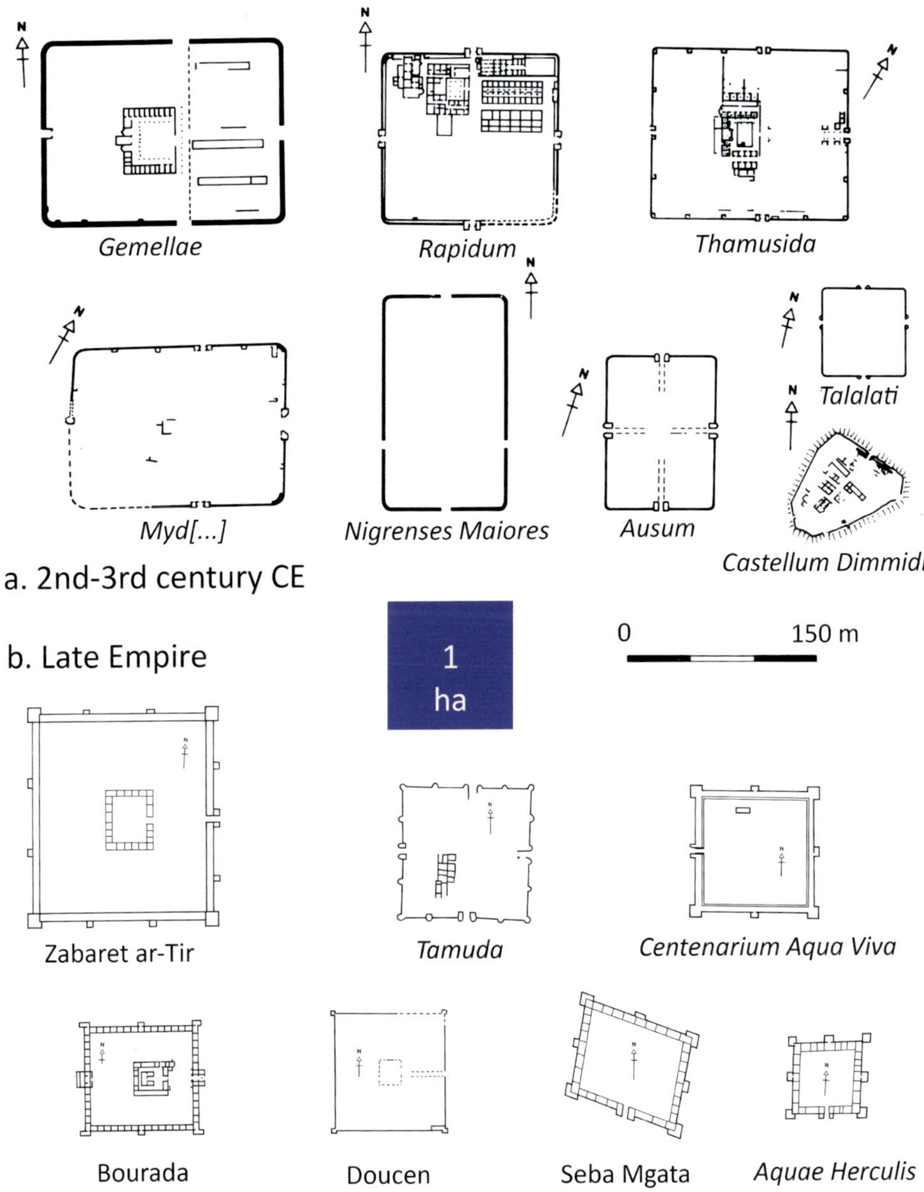

Figure 6.11. Selection of plans of Roman forts from Africa. a) 2nd–3rd centuries. b) Late Empire (author's montage from Mattingly et al. 2013a, 68, 82, after Daniels 1987).

other Roman provinces, with many sites of 1 ha or less in internal area (Fig. 6.11). Although the sample of well-recorded sites is small, this is certainly suggestive of forts often being designed for only a portion of a standard auxiliary unit (as listed in Tables 6.1–6.6), with the unit's roster being split across two or more sites in many cases. As in more recent eras, colonial garrison posts were probably not always kept fully up to strength either, the trade-off being between the extent of terrain covered and concentration of sufficient forces to be able to deal with insurrection or attack. The late imperial forts followed a similar pattern, with relatively few larger bases of over 1 ha in area and more frequent smaller forts, suitable to accommodate only low hundreds of men.

There were some basic design modifications over time. Roman forts in the early Principate were not really designed to withstand sustained sieges, though their walls were intended, of course, to provide some protection to the garrison against attack and to project an image of imperial power. Later forts tended to have higher walls, with more prominent projecting towers (commonly referred to as the *quadriburgus* type). But it is also apparent that some earlier forts continued to be occupied with little or no modification to their defences. It is possible that the smaller the garrison actually installed at a location, the more importance was attached to the improved defensive features offered by the *quadriburgi*. They were certainly designed to look like strongpoints to discourage attack in much the same way that the outposts of the French foreign legion or the Italians in the Libyan desert projected a sense of greater power than was the reality of the relatively small garrisons quartered there. As noted, the relative shortage of auxiliary units in *Numidia* resulted in the need to outstation legionary troops in places like *Gholaia*, *Myd[...]*, *Cidamus*, and *Bezereos*, and there is also evidence of forts having troops distributed in smaller outposts in their area.[157] Future work on Roman forts in North Africa needs to focus on these aspects more, rather than assume a neat correlation between a specific unit attested epigraphically and a single location.

The Mauretanian Security Zones

The successive phases of garrison deployment in *Mauretania Caesariensis* strongly reflect the peculiar topography of the Algerian Tell (Fig. 6.12).[158] As described in Chapter 1, the abrupt coastal ranges provide a dramatic backdrop to small coastal plains. From the river *Ampsaga* westwards, the Grand Kabylie, the Atlas Mitijien, and the Dahra allow relatively few straightforward south–north passageways, and a second line of ranges to the south of and roughly parallel with the first accentuates this mountainous screen: again moving from east to west, the Lesser Kabylie, the Bibans, Titteri, Ouarsenis, Frenda, Saida Daya, and Tlemcem ranges. Between the two ranges there are two river systems: the *Sava*, which flows west to east to the coast at *Saldae*; and the *Chulimath* (Chelif) runs east to west to the Mediterranean near Quiza. The major zone of good agricultural land falls along the Chelif valley

157. Mattingly 1995, 79–88 on outstationing of troops in Tripolitania.
158. Benseddik 1999; Laporte 2011; Lawless 1978; Salama 1977.

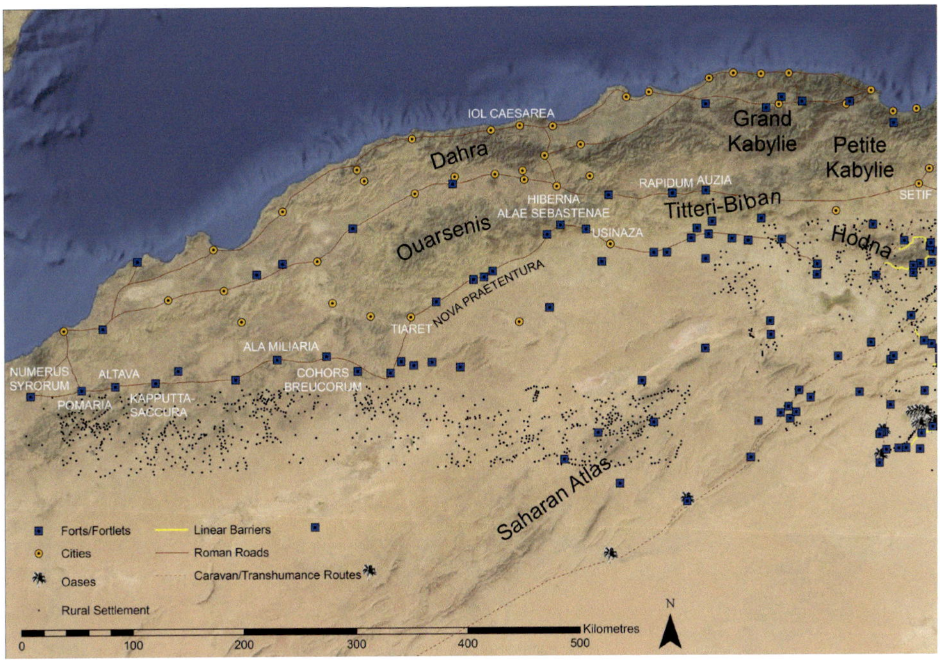

Figure 6.12. The military deployment in *Mauretania Caesariensis* (from Mattingly et al. 2013a, 64).

and the bulk of the known early forts are located there (or just across the watershed) and across the upper *Sava* valley, through the Bibans and towards the boundary with *Africa* near the east end of the Hodna mountains.

Almost nothing is known about the earliest troop deployments in the 1st century CE, though there is evidence for the presence of soldiers at *Iol Caesarea*, where the governor was based. Indeed, a substantial garrison appears to have been maintained there in all phases of the province's existence. By the mid-2nd century, a number of forts can be identified in relation to a first phase of garrison deployment: *Auzia, Rapidum, Thanaramusa Castra, [Zucchabar, Manliana], Oppidum Novum, Tigava Castra, [Castellum Tingitanum, Gadaum Castra, Ballene Praesidium, Castra Nova], Praesidium Sufative.*[159] This was very much focused on the Chelif valley and other positions controlling passes through the mountains or linking routes towards *Africa*. *Rapidum* is the most extensively excavated fort.[160]

159. Not all of these inland sites have produced dated inscriptions of the 2nd century, or certain archaeological evidence of a fort (though some names are very suggestive), but their position suggests pre-3rd-century origins. See Benseddik 1999; Le Bohec 1999, 124; Salama 1977. Names in square brackets are considered less certainly to have been Roman forts by Le Bohec, though some of these are suggestive.

160. Laporte 1989. For other forts, see Lenoir 2011, 229–49.

One of the functions of the forts in the Chelif valley may have been supervision of urban centres of *Masaesyli/Mauri*.

In a second phase of development, garrison posts were advanced 60–80 km to the south beyond the second set of mountain ranges (though by no means all of the original forts were abandoned). A new road was constructed in 198 CE running along the northern edge of the high plains at the point where it meets the mountain front, indicated by milestones and dedications of the successive procuratorial governors C. Octavius Pudens and P. Aelius Peregrinus Rogatus. Sometimes referred to as the *nova praetentura* after an ambiguous phrase on the milestones, this has at times been portrayed as a "frontier line" of c.600 km length, bristling with forts at fairly regular intervals. However, subsequent evaluations have decreased the number of certain military posts and it is now thought unlikely that this was developed in a single phase.[161] A number of forts are certain, whether from the toponyms based on unit names or by remains identified on the ground, but evidence is more equivocal at some of the following: [Zabi], *Aras*, [Grimidi, Ain Touta], Kherba des Oulled Hellal, Derrag, [Ain Toukria, *Columnata*], Aioun Sbiba, *Cohors Breucorum*, *Ala Milliaria*, Lucu, *Kaputtasaccura*, *Altava*, *Pomaria*, *Numerus Syrorum*.[162] In addition, a small number of other forts have been identified on the roads uniting the two main east–west lines (*Tatilti* and *Aquae Sirenses*) or between the northern line and the coast (Ain Oum Dib, *Sertei*, *Quiza*).[163]

The initial impression from maps of two successive "frontier" lines is deceptive. The 2nd-century deployment focused on the protection and oversight of the main agricultural and urbanised areas of the central valleys and the coastal plains, but also controlled the main access ways from the high plains into provincial territory and allowed supervision of the main mountain massifs within the province. In addition to the garrison at *Iol Caesarea* (which appears to have constituted a substantial reserve of troops), there is also evidence of troops being periodically present at the other major coastal city of *Thapsus*, though no forts have been identified at either site.[164] Thus, despite the appearance of an advanced "frontier line" to the south in the 3rd century, in reality a significant number of more northerly bases also seem to have been retained, and the deployment has the appearance of a deep security zone, looking inwards to the mountainous enclaves as well as outward to the high plains to the south.[165] The military zone was coextensive with the

161. For the maximal view, see Salama 1977 (47 forts); for the minimal view Benseddik 1999 (15); Le Bohec 1999, 124–25 (17).

162. Benseddik 1999, 94–98; Le Bohec 1999, 124–25. Names in square brackets are considered less certainly Roman forts by Le Bohec.

163. Le Bohec 1999, 126. On *Tatilti*, base of the *cohors IV Sygambrorum*, see now Kasdi and Slimani 2020.

164. Le Bohec 1999, 126–27.

165. Hamdoune 2018, 55–61.

Table 6.2. Military units attested in *Mauretania Caesariensis* in High Empire (after Le Bohec 1999).

Period	*Alae*	Auxiliary units: C = *cohors*, C *eq* = mixed unit, N = *numerus*	Min number of troops?
2nd c. CE	*Ala I Augusta Parthorum* *Ala exploratorum Pomariensium* *Ala I Claudia Kapitoniana* *Ala milliaria (I Nerviana Augusta pf)* *Ala II Thracum Augusta pf* *Ala Pia Gemina Sebastena*	*C II Breucorum* *C eq II Brittonum* *C I Corsorum c R* *C VI Delmatarum* *C VII Delmatarum* *C Aelia Expedita* *C II Gallorum* *C I Flavia Hispanorum* *C eq I Flavia Musulamiorum* *C Nurritanorum* *C I Pannoniorum* *C II Sardorum* *C I Aelia singularium* *C IV Sygambrorum* *C I Augusta Nerviana Velox* *N Gaesatorum* *N Syrorum sagittariorum* *Singulares praesidis* *Classiarii*	c.5,000 cavalry and 6,000 infantry (not necessarily all present at same time)

provincial territory and the character of the province was thus highly militarised. Almost all the attested wars and revolts documented epigraphically appear to have been concentrated inside the *nova praetentura*.[166]

Because of the limitations with the documentation relating to many of the attested units, it is difficult to discuss the composition of the garrison over time (Table 6.2). A single discharge diploma of 107 CE indicates an overall strength of two *alae* and ten *cohortes* at that date.[167] It is possible that the number of cavalry, including both *alae* and *numeri*, was increased over time, especially given the attested warfare in the mid-2nd century. The larger number of forts necessitated by the creation of the *nova praetentura* in the 3rd century would also favour an increased number of troops overall, though subdivision of units between multiple bases again needs to be considered a probability. Over time, it appears that the number of Moorish ethnic troops in the garrison increased, creating complexities in the relationship between garrison and the "enemies of Rome"—who now frequently came from the same ethnic groups.[168]

166. Laporte 2011, 130–37. Cf. also Hamdoune 2018, 134–47, 201–13.
167. Hamdoune 2018, 55–56.
168. Hamdoune 2018; 2020.

Mauretania Tingitana

The widespread disposition of forts within *Mauretania Tingitana* again attests to the profound military character of the entire province (Fig. 6.13). There were forts in the north and the south of the province and along the two main roads running down the spine of the territory.[169] From north to south, the 17 known forts of the high Empire are: Ain Daliya, *Tamuda*, *Tabernae*, Souiyar/*ad Novas*, el-Mers, el-Khanayez, *Frigidae*, Souk el-Arba/*Vopisciana*, *Banasa*, *Thamusida*, *Sala*, Khedis, Fouarat, Sidi Said (*Babba*?), Sidi Moussa Bou Fri (*Ulpia*?), *Tocolosida*, and Ain Schkor.[170] Some of these were evidently quite small (<1 ha), which is suggestive of subdivision of units in garrison. However, from the ample diploma evidence relating to the Tingitanian garrison, we know that in the late 1st to mid-2nd century, there were generally around 5 *alae* and 10 or 11 *cohortes*, a total garrison of c.8,000 troops, of which c.3,000 were cavalry (Table 6.3).[171] There was no frontier per se, rather a generalised distribution of garrison posts *throughout* the province, with a number of forts alongside or very close to many of the main urban centres (*Babba*?, *Banasa*, *Sala*, *Tamuda*, *Thamusida*, *Volubilis*, *Vopisciana*). *Tamuda* and *Thamusida* are the two best investigated forts.[172] Several of these sites had been important pre-Roman population centres, so the function of the forts may have been involved in both supervision and protection of urban centres and their associated agricultural territories. A second group of the forts were accompanied by large garrison settlements of semi-urban character (*Ad Novas*, *Tocolosida*). The group of four forts in the region of *Volubilis* in the upper reaches of Wadi Beth and its tributary valleys (Sidi Said (*Babba*?), Sidi Moussa Bou Fri, *Tocolosida*, and Ain Schkor) has been described as the *limes* of *Volubilis*, but with the understanding of a localised "security zone" rather than a "frontier line."[173]

About 5–6 km south of *Sala* (Rabat) there is a 10.5 km long linear barrier, cutting across the coastal plain between the ocean and a point where it met a prominent southward bend of the Wadi Bou Regeg in hilly terrain (Fig. 6.14).[174] The obstacle comprised a ditch (either a steep-sided V-shaped ditch or a flat-bottomed ditch of c.4 m breadth by 2 m depth, with an earthen embankment on its north side and possibly a c.1 m thick wall constructed on the south side of the ditch.

169. See Akerraz 2012 for recent overview; also Euzennat 1989; Rebuffat 1998; 1999.
170. Recent work is adding additional sites, notably in the northern part of the province and these appear to be not simply of late Roman date, see Martorella 2021.
171. Hamdoune 2018, 53–55. For the evidence of diplomas, see RMD 1–4; Roxan 1973.
172. Akerraz and Papi 2008; Bernal Casasola et al. 2013; 2018; Callu et al. 1965; Gliozzo et al. 2009; Hallier et al 1970; Marion and Rebuffat 1977; Papi et al. 2013; Rebuffat 1972b. For studies of other sites, see also Lenoir 2011, 251–78; Rebuffat 1975d;
173. Euzennat 1989, 175–292
174. On the "seguia Faraoun," see Euzennat 1989, 128–73; Rebuffat 1980c; 1981.

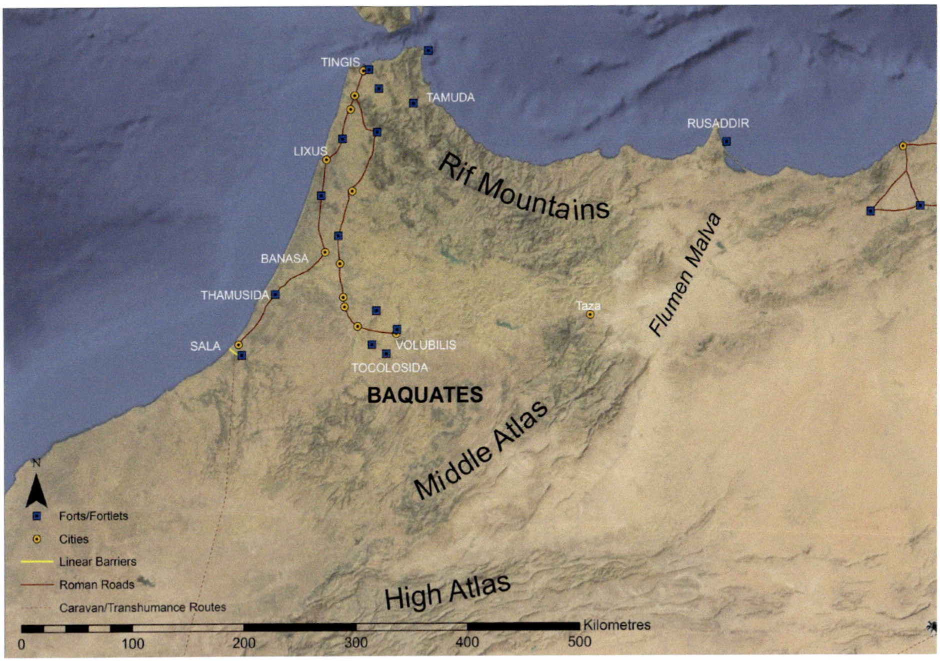

Figure 6.13. The military deployment in *Mauretania Tingitana* (from Mattingly et al. 2013a, 60).

However, this wall is not attested in all locations where excavations have been carried out, and in one place at least it appears to relate to a larger series of walls forming a building that extended back across the ditch. It is thus possible that the traces of wall noted by Maurice Euzennat relate to a secondary phase of the barrier or to secondary structures, potentially post-dating the abandonment of the linear

Table 6.3. Military units attested in *Mauretania Tingitana* in High Empire.

Period	*Alae*	Auxiliary units: C = *cohors*, *C eq* = mixed unit, *N* = *numerus*	Min number of troops?
c. 152 CE	*Ala I Augusta Gallorum* *Ala Gemelliana* *Ala I (Flavia Gallorum)* *Tauriana victrix cR* *Ala III Asturum pf cR* *Ala I Hamiorum Syrorum sagittariorum*	*C I Ituraeorum cR* *C V Delmatarum* *C II Hispana Unsconium cR* *C eq IV Gallorum cR* *C I Asturum et Callaeorum cR* *C eq mill. II Syrorum sagittariorum* *C III Asturum pf cR* *C II Hispanorum cR* *C I Lemavorum cR* *C III Gallorum felix* *C IV Tungrorum*	c.2,500 cavalry and 5,500 infantry

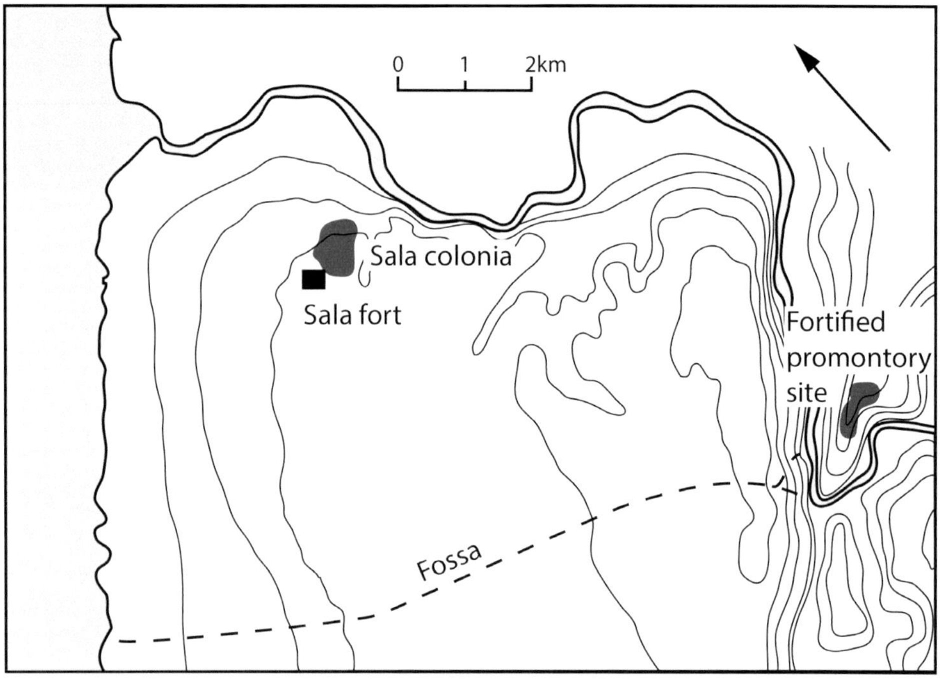

Figure 6.14. The linear barrier south of *Sala* (Mike Hawkes, after Euzennat 1989, fp 153).

barrier in its original form.[175] The available dating evidence suggests that the barrier was created in the late 1st or early 2nd century CE and abandoned at the latest by the mid-3rd century. The barrier effectively controlled movement up the coastal plain, though it could also be seen as demarcating the southern limits of the urban *territorium*. However, a military function seems most likely, given the presence of a fort adjacent to the city of *Sala*.[176] The *Antonine Itinerary* (3.2; 7.4) indicates a further military outpost 16 Roman miles south of *Sala* and beyond this linear barrier; the (unlocated) *exploratio quae ad Mercurios dicitur* demonstrates that once again the linear barrier did not mark a "frontier" in that direction. A well-known inscription (IAM_{lat} 307) of 144 CE from *Sala* mentions the actions of M. Sulpicius Felix, securing the territory of *Sala* against barbarian raids, probably relating to fortification of the city and the addition or strengthening of the linear barrier. No gates in the wall have been identified (and indeed much of the linear barrier has now been lost to the modern development of Rabat, but it seems assured that there was at least one such controlled passage, in the manner of the Tripolitanian *clausurae*. In any event, the fortifications around *Sala* did not form the western end of a grand system covering the 110 km separating this area from *Volubilis*. Roman

175. Euzennat 1989, 135–45 on the supposed "fortin" structure linked to the wall.
176. Euzennat 1989, 159–67.

communications between the two garrison sectors ran much more to the north, in the Sebou valley and the garrison installations close to both cities were in effect isolated security sectors.[177]

The Late Roman Deployment in North Africa

The problems encountered in reconstructing the High Empire garrison deployments are even more acute for the late Roman period. Although there are some striking examples of new forms of fortification with higher walls and projecting gate and angle towers, the *quadriburgi*, these are by no means a ubiquitous feature, and it seems that many of the older forts and outposts continued to be occupied without structural modification.[178] The detailed listings provided by the *Notitia Dignitatum* are difficult to interpret because of the varied dates of compilation of the information in different parts.[179] In *Africa/Numidia*, the later deployment was based around a field army under the control of the *comes Africae*, with regional garrison districts (*limites*) commanded by *praepositi* (Table 6.4).[180]

The overall size of the garrison was probably similar in late Roman times to the earlier deployment if the now lower-grade troops of the *limitanei* are included, but the field army now perhaps contained a larger number of cavalry. *Tripolitana*, under command of its own *dux*, was also organised by individual *limes* sectors commanded by *praepositi* (in Table 6.4, *Occ* 31, the overlaps with the list of the *comes Africae Occ* 25 probably reflect different dates of composition and the periodic need of the *comes* to exert direct control over the *limitanei*, as under Romanus in the 360s). Some of the difficulties in attempts to reconstruct this as a frontier system again run into the problem than not all these *limes* sectors were necessarily at the extreme periphery of Roman territory. With our broader understanding of "security zones" established for the earlier period, we might expect some at least of the *limites* to be well within provincial territory.

The system of *praepositi limites* continued into *Mauretania Sitifensis* and *Caesariensis*, under overall control of the *praeses provinciae Mauretaniae et Caesariensis* (Table 6.5).[181] The overlap between this list and that of the *comes Africae* perhaps reflects the fact that during the periods of revolt, the nearest field army troops were those of the *comes*, who would also have taken temporary control of the *limitanei*.

---

177. Euzennat 1989, 173.
178. On North African *quadriburgi*, see Baradez 1949a, 9–12, 88, 122–29, 221–23, 279–88; Daniels 1987, 260–63; Lenoir 2011; Leschi 1943; Mattingly et al. 2013a, 82; 2013b.
179. For discussions of the late Roman army in North Africa and the *Notitia*, see, inter alia, Briand-Ponsart and Hugoniot 2006, 300–18; Le Bohec 2004; Matthews 1976;
180. Fentress 1979, 119–21; Matthews 1976, Mattingly 1995 187–93; Rebuffat 1988b.
181. Matthews 1976.

Table 6.4. Late Roman field army units and garrison sectors in the *Notitia Dignitatum*: a) *Comes Africae* and *Dux Tripolitanae.*

Notitia Dignitat.	Limes sector	Main base
	Intra Africam cum uiro spectabili comite Africae:	
Occ. 7	12 *Comitatenses* (Infantry legions): *Celtae iuniores; Armigeri propugnatores seniores; Armigeri propugnatores iuniores; Secundani Italiciani; Cimbriani; Primani; Secundani; Tertiani; Constantiniani; Constantiaci; Tertio Augustani; Fortenses.*	Some including *Tertio Augustani* perhaps still at *Lambaesis*
Occ. 7	19 *Vexillationes* (cavalry units): *Equites stablesiani Italiciani; Equites scutarii seniores; Equites stablesiani seniores; Equites Marcomanni; Equites armigeri seniores; Equites clibanarii; Equites sagittarii Parthi seniores; Equites cetrati seniores; Equites primo sagittarii; Equites secundo sagittarii; Equites tertio sagittarii; Equites quarto sagittarii; Equites Parthi sagittarii iuniores; Equites cetrati iuniores; Equites promoti iuniores; Equites sagittarii iuniores; Equites Honoriani iuniores; Equites scutarii iuniores scolae secundae; Equites armigeri iuniores.*	?
Occ. 25	***Sub dispositione viri spectabilis comitis Africae***	
	Praepositus limitis Thamallensis	*Turris Tamalleni* (Telmine)
	Praepositus limitis Montensis in castris Leptitanis/Neptitanis	*Nepte* (Nefta)
	Praepositus limitis Bazensis	*Badias* (Badis)
	Praepositus limitis Gemellensis	*Gemellae* (al-Kasbat)
	Praepositus limitis Tubuniensis	*Thubunae* (Tobna)
	Praepositus limitis Zabensis	*Zabi* (Bechilga) (MS)
	Praepositus limitis Tubusubditani	*Tubusuptu*? (MC)
	Praepositus limitis Thamallomensis	*Thamallula*? (Tocqueville) (MS)
	Praepositus limitis Balaretensis	?
	Praepositus limitis Columnatensis	*Columnata* (Sidi Hosni) (MC)
	Praepositus limitis Tablatensis	*Talalati* (Ras el-Ain)?
	Praepositus limitis Caputcellensis	*Caput Cilani*? (MC)
	Praepositus limitis Secundaeforum in castris Tillibanensibus	*Tillibari* (Remada)
	Praepositus limitis Taugensis	?
	Praepositus limitis Bidensis	*Bida* (MC)
	Praepositus limitis Badensis	*Badias* (Badis)?

Table 6.4. *(Continued)*

Occ. 31	***Sub dispositione viri spectabilis ducis provinciae Tripolitanae***	
	Praepositus limitis Talalatensis	*Talalati* (Ras el-Ain)
	Praepositus limitis Tenthettani	*Thenteos* (Zintan)
	Praepositus limitis Bizerentane	*Bezereos* (Henchir Rhilane)
	Praepositus limitis Tillibarensis	*Tillibari* (Remada)
	Praepositus limitis Madensis	*Castra Madensia/Myd...* (al-Qurrayyat al-Garbia)?
	Praepositus limitis Maccomadensis	*Macomades* (Sirte)
	Praepositus limitis Tintiberitani	?
	Praepositus limitis Bubensis	?
	Praepositus limitis Mamucensis	?
	Praepositus limitis Balensis	?
	Praepositus limitis Varensis	?
	Milites Fortenses in castris Leptitanis	*Lepcis Magna*?
	Milites Munifices in castris Madensibus	*Castra Madensia/Myd...* (al-Qurrayyat al-Garbia)?
	Praepositus limitis Sarcitani	*Secedi* (unknown location E Tripolitania)?

Table 6.5. Late Roman garrison sectors in the *Notitia Dignitatum*: b) *Praeses Mauretaniae.*

Notitia Dignitatum	Limes sector	Main base
Occ. 30	*Sub dispositione viri spectabilis ducis et praesidis provinciae Mauretaniae et Caesariensis*	
	Praepositus limitis Columnatensis	*Columnata*? (Sidi Hosni)
	Praepositus limitis Vidensis	*Bida* (Bide)
	Praepositus limitis inferioris	Chelif valley?
	Praepositus limitis Fortensis.	?
	Praepositus limitis Muticitani	?
	Praepositus limitis Audiensis	Auzia?
	Praepositus limitis Caputcellensis	*Caput Cilani*
	Praepositus limitis Augustensis	?

In contrast, the *comes Tingitaniae* commanded a handful of field army units as well as a list of units that appear a more direct inheritance of the earlier auxiliary deployment, some units still in the forts they had occupied earlier (Table 6.6). The different style of presentation may be more apparent than real, as there are indications from the other sectors that the *limitanei* in garrison were, in part at least,

Table 6.6. Late Roman garrison sectors in the *Notitia Dignitatum*: c) *Comes Tingitanae.*

Notitia Dignitatum	Troops available to *comes Tingitanae*	Main base
Occ. 7	***cum uiro spectabili comite***	
	Comitatenses (field army units) *Mauri tonantes seniores, Mauri tonantes iuniores, Constantiniani, Septimani iuniores*	?
Occ. 26	***sub dispositione viri spectabilis comitis Tingitaniae***	
	Limitanei	
	Praefectus alae Herculeae, Tamuco	*Tamuda* (Tetouan) or *Thamusida* (Sidi Ali)?
	Tribunus cohortis secundae Hispanorum, Duga	?
	Tribunus cohortis primae Herculeae, Aulucos	?
	Tribunus cohortis primae Ityraeorum, Castrabarensis	?
	Tribunus cohortis ...., Sala.	*Sala* (Rabat)
	Tribunus cohortis Pacatianensis, Pacatiana	?
	Tribunus cohortis tertiae Asturum, Tabernas	*Tabernae* (Lalla Jilaliya)
	Tribunus cohortis Friglensis, Friglas	*Frigidae* (Hazib al-Harrak)

formed around the core of earlier auxiliary units (for instance, the *Secundaeforum in castris Tillibanensibus* are surely to be identified with the *cohors II Afrorum* known at *Tillibari* (Remada) at an earlier date.[182]

There is a strong degree of overlap in the nomenclature of the *limes* sectors of the late garrison and known forts in earlier phases of development. Thus, cumulatively the evidence suggests that the late arrangements to a large extent were founded on earlier security sectors, with many of the earlier forts and outposts still in occupation. It was long believed that the Severan advanced posts of the Tripolitanian garrison posts had all been abandoned by the late 3rd century (when Bu Nijim certainly was relinquished) and that the security zone there was largely stripped of regular garrisons in the 4th century, instead becoming focused on a network of small fortified sites occupied by solder militia.[183] However, recent excavations by Michael Mackensen at al-Qurrayyat al-Garbia require a rethink, as both structural and epigraphic evidence demonstrate a regarrisoning of that fort after a gap in occupation from c.280 to c.360 CE.[184] The discovery that the ancient name

182. Le Bohec 1989b, 67–69.
183. Goodchild 1949; 1950a; Ward-Perkins and Goodchild 1949 for the classic expressions of the theory. For rebuttals, see Mattingly 1989a; 1995.
184. Mackensen 2012, 57–58.

for al-Qurrayyat al-Garbia was *Myd[...]* also invites correlation with the *castra Madensia* and the late Roman *limes Madensis.*[185] In the light of this evidence, it can be suggested that the *Notitia* listings of garrisons for *Tripolitana* and *Numidia* do broadly reflect 4th-century continuity of and contiguity with the early security system. The fort at al-Qurrayyat remained in military use into the early 5th century. There is also evidence from Tripolitania that the late system of *limes* sectors under command of *praepositi* had begun in the mid-3rd century, during the period when the *legio III* was disbanded.[186]

It was at one time believed that the forts of western *Caesariensis* had all been abandoned, but an inscription (*CIL* 8.9834) of Honorius and Theodosius from *Altava* suggests that some parts at least of the western security zone remained in operation.[187] The military withdrawal from parts of southern *Tingitana* also appears less clear-cut than it once did, though some retrenchment towards the north and west appears to have occurred.[188] The abandonment of the south-western expansion of the Numidian security zone into the Saharan Atlas in the 4th century is less controversial.[189]

The construction of new style *quadriburgi* and the fact that some towers on the *fossatum* were evidently still in use (see below) suggests that observation and control of the security zone remained an important function.[190] Some at least of the late *limites* were concerned with movement into and out of the provincial territory.

The same thing is demonstrated in Augustine's famous correspondence with Publicola, concerning migrant Libyan workers crossing from the desert into provincial territory under licence.[191] Publicola was evidently a landowner in western *Tripolitana*, anxious about the pagan oaths sworn by migrant labour recruited from the desert people known as the *Arzugi* and whether these were sufficient to guarantee the security of his lands.

> Among the *Arzugi* (*in Arzugibus*), from what I have heard, the barbarians (*barbari*) have the custom of taking an oath before the decurion who commands the *limes*, or before the tribune, and they swear by their demons. Those who enter into engagements with such people to perform baggage transports or landowners and farmers who

185. Mackensen 2021b for an updated and detailed analysis of the late Roman frontier disposition in *Tripolitana*.
186. Mattingly 1991; Rebuffat 1988b.
187. Cf. Courtois 1955; Salama 1966.
188. Euzennat 1989, for general lack of occupation in southern forts beyond mid-3rd century; but see now Akkeraz and Papi 2008 for some activity into the 4th or 5th centuries at *Thamusida*. Callegarin 2018; Villaverde Vega 2001 for overviews.
189. Faure and Leveau 2015, 124–27; Fentress 1979, 117–19.
190. Fentress 1979, 104–08; Mattingly 1995, 192–95.
191. St Augustine, *Letters* 93.8.46–47. See discussion in Ellefi 2016, 54–58; Guédon 2018a, 167–68; Lepelley 2002.

> contract them to protect crops are used to welcoming them as trustworthy people on the basis of the decurion having sent a letter. Similarly, the travellers who have to cross the country taking them as guides do the same ... If I sent someone to the *Arzugi*, would he be allowed to receive this deadly oath from the barbarians?[192]

A more fundamental question to ask in relation to these security sectors is what triggered higher levels of confederation against Rome's African provinces after centuries of more or less successful divide and rule by Rome? The *Austuriani* and *Laguatan* of the 4th and 5th centuries (synonymous with different phases of the most significant of the desert coalitions) are now generally recognised to have been built up around the peoples of the Syrtic oases and pasture lands (especially the people known in earlier times as the *Nasamones*). But we lack adequate understanding of why relations with the desert peoples broke down at this time, especially if, like the *Garamantes*, they had been engaged for centuries in treaty relations and trade with the Empire. The evidence from the Garamantian heartlands of Fazzan certainly indicates a lower volume of imports in late Roman times than earlier, but not a full cessation. Many of the objects that were getting through were of similar type to the earlier imports—Roman glass, tableware, cookware, flagons, lamps, wine amphorae, and so on, and some of these artefacts were very high-quality goods. One plausible conclusion is that the profits of trade with the Roman Empire were greatly reduced and now more concentrated at high elite levels within the desert societies. If this also coincided with increased restrictions on movement of seasonal labour and transhumant groups from the desert into provincial territory, the impact on the lifestyle of oasis and pastoral communities could have been devastating. Such a scenario may be suggested by the events connected with the Austurian invasion of *Tripolitana* in the 360s, when a Libyan chief called Stachao was executed by Rome after being arrested within the province on suspicion of spying and inciting trouble. This suggests that relationships between Rome and the desert peoples had been becoming progressively strained, but that also there were efforts afoot to consolidate the resentment into concerted action involving people both outside and inside Rome's security zone.

The reoccupation of the oasis of al-Qurrayyat is an indication of Rome trying to re-establish some initiative in relation to the desert peoples. However, a crucial factor in the late Roman crises with the *Austuriani* and *Laguatan* raids was the fact that the Roman elite field army units were brigaded far from Tripolitania, and Rome no longer seems to have launched major retaliatory strikes against the oases beyond provincial territory.

For the most part, between these early and late periods of more concerted opposition and war in the security zone, Roman surveillance seems to have been

---

192. The loose translation here is based on Lepelley 2002, 81.

relatively efficiently achieved. The forts, even when widely dispersed across the Maghrib, were the focal points in Roman protection of the province. Roman power could be projected and protected, provided these garrison units were well trained and armed. Unsurprisingly, there was a strong cavalry component in the garrison, essential for rapid communication across long distances, but also as a counter to the traditional Libyan strength in equine cavalry.[193] However, there are also indications, particularly in *Mauretania Caesariensis*, that some of the leading members of the military community of the security zone were recruited from local peoples and that through their local power at times they may have contributed to the late Roman unrest. In Tripolitania and the Mauretanian provinces, one can question whether late Roman "gamekeepers" sometimes turned "poachers."

Some Conclusions on the Garrison Patterns

In Chapters 2 and 5 I argued that past scholarship has overestimated the nomad threat and underestimated the numbers of people living as sedentary farmers in oases in the northern Saharan fringe. In all probability, Rome's security arrangements were a response to *multiple* factors: taking account of the existence of substantial sedentary mountain and oasis communities; the regular transhumance movements of pastoral groups; and periodic larger and more bellicose coalitions of desert and mountain peoples against Roman interests. This has major implications for our understanding of the operation and objectives of Rome's garrison forces. The major incidents of confederated opposition to Rome occurred in three key phases: the formative stages of the 1st centuries BCE/CE; in the mid-2nd century (especially in *Mauretania*); and in the declining years of the 4th and 5th century. In the first case, higher levels of confederation were probably triggered by indigenous perceptions of Roman aggression and threats to their autonomy and lands. Most explanations of later unrest seek to understand widespread resistance both inside and outside the Mauretanian provinces as localised antipathy to Roman power, but the major outbreak corresponds to an era of increased Roman campaigning or expeditions into the Saharan Atlas to the south. In late antiquity, the emergence of new and powerful "Moorish" and "Libyan" groups beyond (and then within) the security zone has been variously explained as building on long-present groups (as suggested by Modéran) or on some level of migration of population (as argued by Wilson and Fentress in a recent paper).[194] I suspect the truth was actually a bit of both.

193. Aït Amara 2013; Coltelloni-Trannoy 2011b; Hamdoune 2005.
194. Modéran 2003,123–30; Fentress and Wilson 2016; cf. also Mattingly 1983; 1995, 173–80; Merrills 2018.

Table 6.7. Wars, revolts, unrest in North Africa from 150 BCE to 450 CE.

Date	*Africa*	*Numidia*	*Tripolitana*	*Mauretania Caesariensis*	*Mauretania Tingitana*
150–126	Y		Y		
125–101	Y	Y	Y	Y	
100–76	Y				Y
75–51					
50–25	Y	Y	Y	Y	Y
25–1 BCE	Y	Y	Y		
1–25 CE	Y	Y	Y	Y	
26–50	Y	Y		Y	Y
51–75	Y	Y	Y	Y	Y
76–100		Y	Y	Y	Y
101–125		Y		Y	
126–150				Y	Y
151–175				Y	
176–200			?		
201–225			Y		
226–250	Y	Y	Y	Y	Y
251–275				Y	
276–300			Y	Y	
301–325					
326–350				Y	
351–375		Y	Y	Y	
376–400	Y	Y			
401–425	Y		Y		
426–450	Y	Y	Y	Y	

While it is true that the Pax Romana of the High Empire was achieved with great economy of force in North Africa, this was no *Asia Minor*, where the garrison was negligible by the 2nd century CE. It is also appropriate to reflect on the functional integrity of the Pax Romana in the security regions of the African provinces. Looking at the late 1st century BCE to the mid-5th century CE in generational blocks, Table 6.7 suggests that there were periodic and persistent ruptures in some sectors. While it is important to recognise that this was not a state of near constant war or implacable opposition to Rome, such episodic breakdowns of imperial authority is an expected element of colonial encounters.[195]

195. For a more maximal list of revolts, see Bénabou 1976, 250–51. Cf. Hamdoune 2018, 123–49. On the recurrent and structural nature of colonial resistance, see now Gopal 2019.

The structural inequalities of colonialism will always generate unrest and dissatisfaction in some sectors of societies. The continued maintenance of military garrisons responsible for security both within and beyond the notional borders of Roman power created systemic effects due to transgressive behaviours of individual soldiers and officials. While major wars and revolts may have been comparatively rare, Roman rule in Africa was permeated by a recurrent sense of insecurity.

The long-term presence of Roman troops had a profound impact on large parts of the Maghrib and its Saharan fringe. The assimilation of different groups of indigenous peoples progressed on various timescales and to diverse levels. The *Libyphoenices* and the eastern *Massyli* were relatively soon free of garrisons. However, the *Gaetuli* and western *Numidae* (*Masaesyli*) and *Mauri* territories remained more closely supervised throughout the Roman period. It is too simplistic to ascribe this to the harsher environments that these groups occupied—as we have seen, mountain enclaves and desert margins were densely settled in places. Nor is it satisfactory to ascribe this to the underlying social condition of these populations. In part at least, we must understand the patterns of unrest as a local consequence of long-maintained military governance, with all the power inequalities such security systems engender. In this context it is important to note that the revolts came as often as not from within the provincial territory, which the garrisons supervised just as much as they attempted to control the behaviours and movements of groups living outside. Supervising annual movements of transhumant groups certainly seems to be a plausible explanation for some of the linear barriers. The demographic impacts of Roman conquest must have been large, especially in the early years of subjugation: deaths and serious injuries in war and revolts, collateral damage against civilian settlements, enslavement of captured enemies, enforced recruitment of African manpower into Roman armies. Some veterans no doubt returned to their home region after service with a different outlook on the Roman Empire, and from the 2nd century the Roman army in Africa was largely recruited from within the African provinces (and especially the growing military community there).

The Roman project was built on a sequence of linked processes: pacification, provincialisation, promotion of sedentary agriculture, protection of key assets, policing the security zones, and procuring tax and other resources from those living in these militarised zones and beyond. The cultural impact of the army is very evident in the material record of the zone and it is easy to read this as a simple gauge of the success of the Roman project. I revisit this theme in Chapter 7, with a slightly more sceptical understanding of the mechanics of imperialism, challenging the idea of the army as key agents of Romanisation. But before I get to that, we need to understand more about the work of the Roman garrisons.

The Work of the Army

Having established the parameters of armed conflict, the size and approximate distribution of the garrison, and the presence of elements of linear barriers, in this section I consider the work of the army and how this changed with the evolution of the security zones. Most accounts of the Roman army in Africa focus on the martial and policing aspects of the garrison, seeing it in dichotomous terms as an unequal confrontation between paternalistic state and "barbarous peoples."[196] Beyond that, there is also ample evidence for a wider set of roles involving diplomatic networks in advance of Roman territory, carrying out a census of conquered peoples, surveying and delimiting land (including reassigning its ownership and use), recruiting manpower for service in the armies of North Africa and elsewhere, support for taxation and customs exaction, supervision (of local peoples, markets, labour movements), protection of the grain supply of Rome, involvement in extractive industries (metals, marble), and a wide range of activities related to the supply and maintenance of the garrisons. All the North African provinces were garrisoned territories, and the presence of the troops was essentially to facilitate the smooth functioning of imperial rule and the exaction of the resources needed to meet the bottom-line costs of empire.

Protection of provincials from external threats was a secondary (and discontinuous) benefit, and in the Roman Empire the threat to provincials from civil war was often greater than external enemies. As argued above, the security zones were not constructed simply to face outwards; the deployments were also about internal social control and intimidation through displays of Roman force and power. The density of garrison varied, of course, but because of military involvement in the security of the grain supply, the shadow of the army was visible even in districts of Africa that were far removed from the edge of Roman territory. Day-to-day tasks related to the display of force were varied: construction work, patrols and policing, holding exercises (as during Hadrian's visit), the maintenance of wide networks of bases (even if not always fully manned), and the surveillance of routes and water points.[197]

Census, Supervision, Military Recruitment, Land Survey, Settlement

I have already noted the danger of revolt in the generation or two following conquest of a people by Rome. A prime reason for this concerned the intrusive nature of the processes that followed imposition of treaty relations, especially if territorial

196. For more extreme views of the early 20th-century colonial era, see, inter alia, Cagnat 1913; Guéy 1939; Rachet 1970. But more recent accounts still reflect the same models of Roman military power pitted against intractable "tribal" resistance: Bénabou 1976, 67–251; Corbier and Griesheimer 2005, 35–75; Géroudet and Ménard 2005, 150–56 ("Rome face au monde des tribus"). Cf. Leveau 2014; also Bertrandy and Coltelloni-Trannoy 2005, 41–76 for a good bibliographic overview.

197. Rebuffat 1982a.

annexation had occurred. I have characterised these processes as the imposition of an "imperial economy" on conquered territory and peoples.[198] The elements of this imperial economy (primarily census, land survey, taxation, exploitation of natural resources, and imperial supply systems) are often somewhat hidden in the surviving historical record, and the evidence pertaining to them will at best be highly fragmentary. Nonetheless, in "colonial" contexts such tools are commonplace and often vested in the military garrison, which thus plays a key role in the incorporation of peoples into provincial structures of governance and taxation.[199] My analysis primarily reflects early Roman arrangements, but even in later Roman times similar control of knowledge of provincial territory and people was fundamental to imperial rule.

Knowledge is power, and the first requirement of Rome was to document and quantify subdued peoples, meaning significant army involvement in census-taking. The census was essentially imperial stock-taking to establish a quantitative basis regarding numbers of people, their livelihood, lands held, of what quality, numbers of animals, and natural resources of the region. The census also could serve as a basis for future taxation levels, recruitment of troops for the army, and compulsory service.[200]

Closely linked to the census was land survey. Land was both a valuable asset of Rome's colonial rule and a principal lever to employ with conquered populations to secure compliance.[201] Most commonly, Rome initially claimed the territory of its defeated enemies, though subsequent agreements could be made to return some or most of it to local control, subject to good behaviour. Land could be used to both punish and reward (elements of) local communities. An under-remarked aspect of Roman land surveys is that there was often a significant time lag between conquest of territory and the formal placement of boundary stones marking long-term arrangements. A generation (or several) of Roman-imposed uncertainty seems to have been commonplace; for instance, the *Musulami*, first conquered by Augustus and a key player in several revolts against Rome (3 BCE– 6 CE, 17–25 and 47 CE), had to wait to the early 2nd century for their now much reduced territory to be formally surveyed, with the delimitation of their lands spread across the period 100/103–116 CE.[202] This sort of deferred land settlement seems to have been used as a deliberate lever of Roman colonialism.

Roman imperialism in Africa was written on the landscape. The vast centuriation schemes imposed on the territory seized to form *Africa Vetus* are a stark witness to the scale of Roman land-delimitation and reassignment (Fig. 6.15). These

198. Mattingly 2011a, 125–45.
199. Given 2004, 49–50.
200. Mattingly 2011a, 141–42.
201. Peyras 1986; 1999; 2005a; 2005b.
202. Bénabou 1976, 437–38, with table; Fentress 1979, 72–75.

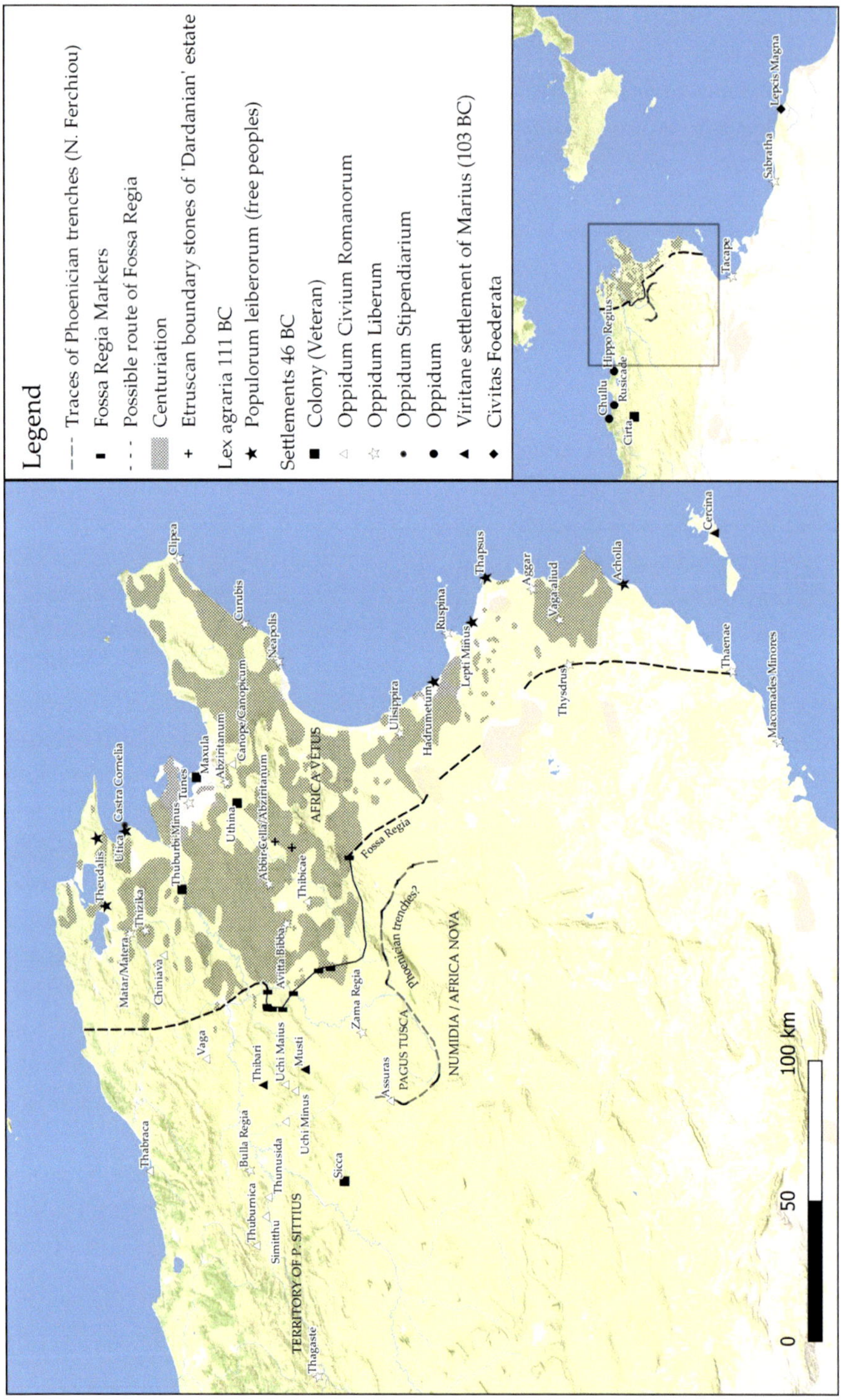

Figure 6.15. The main centuriation and other land survey schemes relating to *Africa Vetus*. (from Hobson 2022, 102).

largest centuriation schemes were carried out by military personnel in *Africa Vetus*, in the heartlands of the former *territorium* of *Qart Hadasht*, probably in the later 2nd century BCE and secondly in *Byzacium* in the reign of Augustus.[203] A reinterpretation of two long-known inscriptions in the latter region now suggests that the Centre-East centuriation was carried out in the reign of Augustus, presumably by the *legio III Augusta*.[204] The Roman grid specifically excluded the lands of a number of Libyphoenician independent cities (*oppida libera*), which retained their own distinctive land division systems (*Hadrumetum*, *Ulizippira*, *Ruspina*, *Leptiminus*).[205] However, the Centre-East survey did include the lands of a number of indigenous settlements (*oppida stipendaria*), now lumped together as the *Pagus Gurzensis*.

Centuriation involved the redrawing of land boundaries on a grand scale and established a simple system for the quantification and reassignment of landholding. Many peasants probably remained in the same district, but Roman centuriation will have changed the basis of their right to land and its usage, the precise location and dimension of land accessible to them, and above all the overall owner. Even where Rome did not enact new gridded physical land divisions, the passage of military survey teams was used to delimit and measure land that was associated with a people. There is a large volume of epigraphic testimony to the assignation of boundaries of named peoples, especially in the Gaetulian zone (Table 6.8).[206] Sometimes the boundary stones record their territorial limits in relation to imperial estates or urban communities, reflecting the complex mosaic that emerged as a result of the conquest. A particularly notable act of *delimitatio* was carried out in southern Tunisia in 29–30 CE, following the end of Tiqfarin's revolt. Starting close to the legionary fortress at *Ammaedara*, army surveyors created a vast virtual grid, only developed on the ground in the area between *Capsa* and *Tacape*, though even there not imprinted on the landscape as a true centuriation.[207] Boundary stones were erected at key points in the grid system and these seem to have then served as a basis on which lands ascribed to the cities of *Tacape* and *Capsa* were delimitated from those of the *Nybgenii* people, whose main centre was the oasis town of *Turris Tamalleni* (Telmine, Nefzaoua).[208] The work begun in the 20s CE was followed up at several other points where concerted survey work appears to have taken place, notably under the Flavian Emperors and Trajan (see Fig. 10.10). The

203. Hobson 2015a, 36–42; see also fuller discussion in Chapter 10 below.
204. Ghaddab 2020.
205. Ghaddab 2020, 88–97; Peyras 1999; 2005b; Ouni and Peyras 2002.
206. Trousset 2001.
207. Trousset 1978; 1997c for the classic study.
208. For a consideration of the relationship between the *Nybgenii* and the late antique *Arzuges* in the same region, see, inter alia, Desanges 1989b; Ellefi 2016; Trousset 2011.

Table 6.8. Delimitation of lands of African peoples.

People	Date (CE)	Under authority of	Designation of lands surveyed	References
Suburbures and *Nicives*	80/81	Legate Tullius Pomponianus Capito	Lands allocated to two peoples from *ager publicus* near *Cirta*	*AE* 1957, 175; *AE* 1969/1970, 669; Dupuis 1999; Lancel 1955
Suburbures	116/117	Legate T. Sabinorum Barbarum	*Fines adsignati* to people	*ILS* 9380–31
Suppenses and *Vofricenses*	80/81 Hadrian	Legate	Boundary (*terminus*) between lands of two peoples (*nationes*)	*AE* 1942/1943, 35
Muducivvii and *Zamucii*	87	Legate	Boundary (*terminus*) between lands of two peoples (*nationes*)	*IRT* 854
Capsitani, Nybgenii, Tacapitani	29–30 c.105	*Leg III Aug* and Proconsul C. Vibius Marsus. Resurvey under Trajan	Delimitation of lands of *Nybgenii* from those assigned to two cities	*CIL* 8.22786a-m, 22787–88. *ILT* 68–71, 73–74. Trousset 1978; 1997c
Musulami	100/103 104/105 116 138	Legate L. Munatius Gallus Legate Minicius Natalis Legate Acilius Strabo Clodius Nummus	*Musulami* territory defined with respect to veteran settlement (*Ammaedara* and *Theveste*), other towns (*Madaurus*), imperial and private estates and the *Tisibenses*	*CIL* 8.10667/16692, 23246, 28073a/b; *ILAlg* 2828–29, 2939, 2939bis, 2978, 2988–89; *ILT* 1653 Latest finds: M'Charek 2008; Naddari 2008.
Numidae	137	Procurator Mauretania Caesariensis	Boundaries set (*fines assignati*)	*CIL* 8.8813–14
Zimiges and *Igilgilitani*	128	Procurator Mauretania Caesariensis	Boundary fixed between two peoples	*CIL* 8.8369
Pagus Gurzensis	11–6/5 BCE	Proconsul Africa	Centre-East Centuriation and creation of *pagus Gurzensis* involving lands of *Gurza, Uzita,* and *Cynasyn*	*AE* 1955, 40; *CIL* 8.68 = *ILS* 6095
Musuni	?	?	Boundary between *Musuni* of *Sufetula* and a private estate	Khanoussi 2008; 2010 for boundary stone

final settlement of Musulamian lands was made under Trajan almost a century after their great revolt under Tiqfarin (Fig. 10.9).[209]

In *Africa Nova*, there seems to have been little centuriation, but extensive land survey activity, as is evident from, *inter alia*, the Flavian resurvey of the *fossa regia* and numerous boundary stones relating to the *pagus Thuscae et Gunzuzi*, imperial estates, private estates, and civic territories (most of these, of course, based on pre-Roman urban centres).[210] While we do not always know who was responsible for undertaking the surveys underlying the boundary arrangements, it is likely that many such works were ultimately founded on delimitation work by the *legio III Augusta*.

Another great surveying and engineering task commonly undertaken by the army as part of the creation of imperial infrastructure related to road building. This was certainly the case with the major provincial arteries (*Capsa–Ammaedara*, *Karthago–Theveste*, *Karthago–Hippo*, *Hippo–Theveste*, *Theveste–Lambaesis*, *Rusicade–Cirta*, *Hippo–Cirta*).[211] Road construction in North Africa varied in quality, and in the more arid areas they were sometimes little more than earth trackways marked with milestones.[212] But in mountainous or wetter parts of the Maghrib they were certainly carefully surveyed, involving engineered ascents and descents, and crossings of rivers and wadis were sometimes provided with stone bridges. However, whether a built structure or a surveyed line marked on the landscape, the initial creation of a Roman road was in itself a territorial claim. In agricultural zones it meant someone giving up land to accommodate the new road, and in pastoral areas it created a new geography of communication and control. As noted already, the construction of the road from *Tacape* to *Ammaedara* is often seen as the prime cause of the revolt led by Tiqfarin. I argued above that the road should be seen as a symptom of a wider Roman programme of census, survey, and road and fort building in Gaetulian territory rather than the instigating episode of the revolt ("un conflit routier").[213]

Supervision of conquered peoples was a necessary sequel to military victory. With peoples living beyond directly controlled Roman territory, diplomatic means were employed, as illustrated by the famous altars of peace from *Volubilis* (Fig. 6.16) recording long-term relations (and regular renewals) between Rome and the *Baquates* (sometimes confederated also with the *Bavares* or *Macennites* in the

209. On survey of Musulamian lands, see now Ben Abdullah 1992; Kallala 2004; Laporte and M'Charek 2010; M'Charek 2008; Naddari 2008.
210. M'Charek 1999; 2008.
211. Fentress 1979, 164–66, with listing of dated constructions of the army in *Africa/Numidia*.
212. Mrabet 2008 notes, however, the discovery of a section of built gravel and pebble road in southern Tunisia.
213. Lassère 1982b.

PRO SALVTE IMPE
RATORIS CAESARIS
M. AVRELI ANTONINI
AVG ARMENIACI
MEDICI PARTHICI
GERMANICI MAX
EPIDIVS QVADRATVS
PROC EIVS CONLOCVT
CVM VCMETIO PRIN
CIPE GENTIVM MA
CENNITVM ET BAQVA
TIVM

To the health of the emperor M. Aurelius Antoninus Augustus Armeniacus Parthicus Germanicus Maximus, Epidius Quadratus the emperor's procurator, held a council [to confirm the peace] with Ucmetius, the overall leader (princeps gentium) of the Macennites and Baquates peoples

(*IAM*$_{LAT}$ 384)

Figure 6.16. One of the "altars of peace" (*IAM*$_{lat}$ 384) from the forum of *Volubilis* (photo: N. Mugnai).

documentation).[214] The precise reason why it was felt necessary to make a public display of these treaty relations at *Volubilis* escape us, but the absence of equivalent inscriptions elsewhere in no way precludes the extensive use of diplomatic measures, as is implicit in Rome's relations with the *Garamantes*, for instance.[215] For African peoples under direct rule, a common method of control in the post-conquest phase appears to have been the use of "tribal (or, better, "ethnic") prefects" (*praefecti gentis*), often serving soldiers or officers.[216] In time, the role of "ethnic prefect" also became assigned to civilians within local urban communities. Some of the appointments appear to have been for multiple groups, as in the case of L. Calpurnius Fabatus, *praefectus nationum Gaetulicarurm sex quae sunt in Numidia* (*CIL* 5.5267) or T. Claudius Pollio, *praefectus gentium* in Africa (*CIL* 6.31032). But others were linked to a specific group, and it is no surprise to find some of the names here corresponding with groups that had been prominent in the Gaetulian wars and revolts: the *Musulami* (*CIL* 8.5351) and the *Cinithi* (*CIL* 8.10500). Both types of oversight imply an intrusive level of external supervision and potential interference.

A different scenario is suggested by the employment of the term *principes gentis*.[217] Most of the chiefs of the (external) *Baquates* were designated in this way,

214. Hamdoune 2014, 422–23, 437; 2018, 117–21; Shaw 1987; Vanacker 2013.
215. Mattingly 1992; 1995.
216. Bénabou 1976, 448–57, with table; Christol 2010; Lepelley 2001, 305–17; Leveau 1973; 2015.
217. Bénabou 1976, 457–69; Rebuffat 1995a.

and the *principes* who were recognised within the provinces were thus individuals perceived to hold pre-eminent status within their communities, whether through continuation of pre-Roman traditions or through Roman favour to individuals of high status who proved useful to the Roman colonial project. A prime example of the latter is the *Tabula Banasitana*, a bronze tablet on which were transcribed imperial letters (the last of 177 CE) confirming the award of Roman citizenship to two Juliani of the *Zegrenses*; the second (probably the son of the first) was Aurelius Julianus, the *princeps gentis Zegrensium*.[218] It is generally assumed that the *Zegrenses* were a people of eastern Morocco, on the periphery of the province along the Wadi Ouerrha, a tributary of the Sebou, but the discovery of the tablet at *Banasa* further to the west on the Sebou has led some to place them in the immediate hinterland of the city.[219] On the model of some other urban-based cases of enfranchised *principes gentis* in Africa,[220] it is surely more likely that Aurelius Julianus was already dwelling in the city and operating his authority from there.[221] Christine Hamdoune saw the roles of *praefectus* and *princeps* of a *gens* as largely synonymous terms, rather than recognising the former as relating to external supervision and the latter as self-regulation. It is also possible to imagine differing levels of autonomy allowed to a *princeps* within the province (like the *Zegrenses*) compared with one dwelling outside (*Baquates*).[222] In any event, variance in powers accorded to *praefecti* and *principes* would be consistent with Roman differential treatment of defeated enemies according to their individual merits:

> Certain peoples, with pertinacity, have waged war against the Romans, others having once experienced Roman military valour, have kept the peace, others who have encountered Rome's good faith and justice, declared their submission to Rome and frequently took up arms against their enemies. That is why each people has received a legal settlement according to merit: it would not have been just if those who had so frequently broken the peace and committed perjury and taken the initiative in making war, were seen to be offered the same guarantees as loyal peoples. (Siculus Flaccus, *De condicionibus agrorum* 7–8.)

The implications of this statement for the understanding of the impact of Roman imperialism are profound. The timing of land survey and legal settlement, the nature of supervision of communities, the legal settlement of lands and tax were all

218. Hamdoune 2018, 66–68; Seston and Euzennat 1971; Sherwin White 1973.
219. Rebuffat 2011a.
220. L. Memmius Pacatus of the *Cinithi*, based at *Gigthis CIL* 8.22729, Florus Chanaris and A. Larcius Macrinus of the *Numidae* at *Thubursicu Numidarum* (*CIL* 8.4884; *ILAlg* 1 1297, 1341). Bénabou 1976, 459–62.
221. The implications of this are discussed further in Chapter 9.
222. Hamdoune 2014; 2018, 119–21.

Figure 6.17. Moorish cavalry in action in the Dacian wars, as depicted on Trajan's Column (photo: author).

contingent on behaviour and degrees of compliance. Treatment of African peoples was thus varied (as were the settlements eventually negotiated) and their experience of empire was highly discrepant in consequence. Long-term military supervision of external peoples lay at one end of a very broad spectrum of outcomes.

Recruitment of military manpower from subdued peoples was a favoured Roman tactic for diminishing the possibility of revolt and for exploiting a key resource of the Empire.[223] Such arrangements might represent a one-off levy or a recurrent requirement until a more long-term taxation settlement was made.[224] There is a total of at least 28 auxiliary regiments (c.13–15,000 men) raised in Africa known in other provinces of the Empire. This includes 6 *alae* of *Afri* and *Gaetuli* and 21 *cohortes* (at least 4 *equitata*) of *Afri, Cirtenses, Cisipadenses, Gaetuli, Mauri, Musulami Numidae,* plus 2 miscellaneous units (*vexil. Afri* and *equites Afri*).[225] In addition, from the mid-2nd century onwards at least 6 less regular cavalry *numeri Maurorum* are attested in *Britannia* and *Dacia* (Fig. 6.17).[226] In this context *Afri* was probably a shorthand for a mix of various peoples dispatched from the province of *Africa,* but the importance of the population blocks I have emphasised in Chapters 4 and 5 is also reflected in the individual references to *Mauri, Numidae,* and *Gaetuli.* Although he recognises the anachronistic implications of the term, Yann Le Bohec terms these ethnic units "collaborators in the Roman order," which misses the often non-voluntary nature of such recruitment.[227] On the other hand, there is no doubt that in time those recruits will have been highly likely to associate

223. Christol 2020, for some consideration of the supervision and juridical controls of such recruits.
224. Haynes 2001; 2013.
225. Le Bohec 1989a, 508–15, including table; cf. also Hamdoune 1999; 2005; Lassère 1988; 1991; 1994. There are also some units of "Cyrenaican" origin.
226. Christol 2020; Hamdoune 2005, 251–52.
227. Le Bohec 1989a, 512.

with the Roman military community. In addition, there is abundant evidence of individuals from the African provinces serving in a variety of units elsewhere in the Empire.[228] Many of these (c.100 of about 170 instances) were Roman citizens recruited into the legions in the 1st and early 2nd centuries, drawing particularly on the descendants of Roman colonists.

By the 2nd century, continuing recruitment from African peoples seems mainly to have been focused on servicing the needs of replenishing the ranks of the legion and auxiliary units in the African provinces.[229] However, the composition of the late Roman field armies reveals a renewed wave of recruitment, especially of African cavalry.[230] *Equites Mauri Illyriciani* are mentioned several times in the *Notitia Dignitatum* (*Orient* 32.18, 33.26, 34.21, 35.17, 37.17) along with a *cuneus equitum Maurorum scutariorum* (*Orient* 31.23), and there were four different groups of *equites Mauri* in the western Empire (*Occ.* 33.13, 34.23, 7.164, 7.177). The three periods of high recruitment for ethnic African units to serve overseas in the Empire thus correspond with moments of elevated military activity—the Gaetulian wars of the 1st century CE, the *Mauri* revolts in the mid-2nd, and more widespread "Moorish" problems in the 4th century.

A final point to note, though, is that alongside the burden of recruitment of soldiers, conquered peoples may also have been obliged to furnish horses as remounts for the army, and other pack animals needed for supply work. The large distances and difficult mountain and desert terrain encompassed by the African provinces created a heavy dependence on control of or access to large numbers of pack animals and horses. Desert warfare, raiding, and counter-patrolling were heavily dependent on horses and to some extent camels. Wheeled traffic was not absent, but was probably most prominent in connecting the grain-producing areas with the coastal export ports.

228. Le Bohec 1989a, 508–12.

229. See notably Le Bohec 1989a, 517–30; cf. Lassère 1977.

230. Hamdoune 2005, 253; Speidel 1993.

Chapter 7

MILITARY IDENTITIES IN ACTION

The Military Community

The Roman armies have often been presented as great champions of *Romanitas* in the provinces.[1] However, their cultural impact was disproportionate to the actual numbers of troops in Africa. This was because the army was both a major creator and consumer of material culture that is seen today as emblematic of Rome. Their practices were also often exaggeratedly "Roman," as in the use of Latin epigraphy to underscore every aspect of life and death, or the religious calendar and broad pantheon of gods embraced.[2] Nor were the soldiers in this alone. The military bases of the Roman army were often accompanied by the growth alongside them of civil settlements, commonly described as *canabae* and *vici* in Roman army studies (Fig. 7.1). Some of these became chartered towns in time, even while the Roman fort remained in occupation embedded in the core of the settlement. In the majority of cases we do not know the exact status of what can be very extensive sites, and I prefer to refer to them as "garrison settlements," reflecting the fact that even where formal civic status was accorded, their cultural character was profoundly influenced by the military, in much the same way as garrison towns have tended to be distinctive among urban communities in other time periods.[3]

In previous work on Britain, I have observed how the garrison settlements there participated in and contributed to the cultural coherence of the military community.[4] In other words, the divisions between soldiers and civilians *within* such settlements were less significant than the cultural gap between the overall population of garrison settlements and the wider rural population (especially in the security zones) or the urban populations of the core provincial territories. The distinctive identity projection of the military community was in part intended to emphasise and reinforce such differences and create "cultural distance" between the agents of

1. Groslambert 2009b, 62 describes the army as a "machine" diffusing Roman civilisation.
2. Goldsworthy and Haynes 1999; James 1999b; 2001b.
3. One thinks of towns like Aldershot or Catterick in Britain, or West Point in the USA.
4. Mattingly 2006a, 170–76. On how material culture differs at garrison settlements from contemporary sites, see the fundamental work of Cool 2002; Cool and Baxter 2002; Cool and Philo 1998.

Figure 7.1. General view of the garrison settlement of *Rapidum*, *Mauretania Caesariensis* (photo: author).

empire and subject populations.[5] Roman traits were often closely circumscribed in spatial terms by proximity to the army and while it is certainly likely that African people were being continuously recruited to the army or absorbed into the garrison settlements, there were nonetheless significant differences in the behaviours and cultural preferences of the military community when compared to indigenous settlements in the security zones.[6] In Britain, for instance, the military community seems to have created cultural "biospheres" around their bases, rather than propagating a Roman identity that was embraced more broadly within society in and beyond the military zone. In the rest of this chapter I examine whether the same holds true for *Africa*.[7]

A first question to address is how different were people in the army from civilians? It is certainly clear that African recruitment for the garrisons was already extremely high by the mid-2nd century CE. Nonetheless, as in Britain, it seems that the army had a strong sense of its collective identity, based on shared working structures, the use of camp Latin as the language of command and records, religious

5. Mattingly 2006a, 199–224; 2011a, 221–23.
6. How to interpret this sort of difference underpinned the argument between Fentress and Shaw discussed in the next section.
7. Guédon 2018a, 247–74 makes some interesting observations about the push and pull effects of military and indigenous cultural behaviours in the military zone.

behaviour, and so on. Interestingly, the African identity markers of soldiers tended to be de-emphasised during and to some extent even after service. We also need to recognise that not all recruits *ex Africa* related to African ethnic groups.

Another point to make about the military community is that it effectively encompassed other groups of imperial agents in provincial government, the governors' staff and procuratorial support (including imperial-owned enslaved people and freedmen, and also individuals involved in the *annona*)—all of whom worked closely with soldiers. It also included individuals born in the African provinces who travelled to other parts of the Empire to participate in imperial service as soldiers, equestrians, and senators. A unifying characteristic of all these different people is that their sense of identity was powerfully shaped by their position within complex status hierarchies linked to their specific roles (past and present) in the Roman imperial project, often defined by well-developed *cursus honorem* pathways.[8] Even with this expanded view of the membership of the military community, it is clear that it contributed only a small percentage of the overall population of the African provinces. If for the mid-2nd century CE we assume an overall population of 5–10 million, the total figure for the army, dependents, and other occupants of garrison settlements, individuals involved in colonial governance (and their families) are unlikely to have exceeded 200,000 (2–4%).[9] However, in the archaeological and epigraphical record, the military community is far more prominent than its size might suggest. In this chapter, I mainly focus on the soldiery and their dependents, but I want to emphasise this broader definition of their community, which extended across into other areas of the governing order. It is not possible to do justice to the full complexity of military identity and cultural behaviours in a single chapter. Rather I provide a few key examples to show how we can read this evidence not as a general spread of Roman culture, but as illustrative of something that was more exclusive to just one small sector of society.

The Soldiery

In the 1st century BCE and early 1st century CE, the majority of troops in Africa came from overseas. Some soldiers on retirement were given land in Africa, initially in quite ad hoc ways (as in the case of the Marian veterans settled

8. For example, see Pflaum 1978; 1982, on the equestrian career paths.
9. Population figures are notoriously difficult to estimate, but Corbier and Griesheimer 2005, 103 suggest 5 million for the urban population alone. As we shall see in Chapters 9 to 10, advances in knowledge of rural population levels now favour the larger estimate, as Lassère 2015, 275 concedes that the majority of the overall population was rural. Frier 2000, 812–814 provides estimates of population for all provinces of the Empire in 14 and 164 CE, suggesting figures for Africa of 3.9 million and 7.1 million respectively (including Cyrenaica and the Maghribian provinces).

around the upper *Bagrada* valley, or the followers of Sittius around *Cirta*), but from the time of Augustus onwards often in more premeditated ways.[10] This involved the foundation of colonies or the assignment of groups of veteran colonists to already existing population centres. Now that we know more about the scale and nature of Mauretanian and Numidian pre-Roman urbanisation, the latter scenario is recognised as being more the norm for many of the African veteran settlements—that is, veteran settlement often essentially involved embedding small deductions of veterans within existing towns, effectively creating two groups of differing status.[11] Caesar is thought to have settled up to 25,000 of his veterans in Africa, as did Augustus, making a total of c.50,000 in a little over two generations.[12] The distribution of veterans was concentrated in certain cities, and they were almost absent in others, with profound implications for subsequent social development.[13]

In 1983 Brent Shaw and Lisa Fentress crossed swords in a disagreement about the impact of the army in the Numidian landscape.[14] Fentress emphasised the profound changes brought about by the army; Shaw argued for broad continuities of society and minimal impact. I think both were correct in different ways, in that this academic spat is a perfect example of discrepant identity in action. Once we disassociate the army from a "policy" of Romanisation, it is perfectly obvious why there is less impact of the military culture away from the hotspots of army bases and veteran settlements. Since the army was an agent of imperial rule, land redistribution, taxation, and colonisation, it is understandable why there was little voluntary association of the population of the security zone with its cultural package, with the exception of those who chose or were obliged to live within garrison settlements. Parts of the Aurès plains are notable for the concentration of veteran settlement and imperial property, triggering major cultural impacts with a colonial flavour, whereas more indigenous cultural patterns are observable in many of the remoter valleys in the massif.[15]

Over time the percentage of new soldiers recruited from the descendants of veterans in Africa grew. Additionally, while African ethnic regiments continued to be raised from population groups with martial traditions, as provinces became more settled they were now sometimes used in Africa rather than be deployed overseas.

10. Chausa Sáez 1997; Lassère 1977, 143–233.
11. Briand-Ponsart 2005a.
12. McMullen 2000, 30–35; but NB Corbier and Griesheimer 2005, 100–101 have a lower estimate of the number of Caesarian and Augustan deductions (between 20–30,000).
13. Chausa Sáez 1997; Dupuis 1991; Lassère 1977, 285–89.
14. Fentress 1983; Shaw 1983b.
15. Fentress 1979, 124–44; Morizot 1991; 1993; 1997 has noted the cultural divergence between veteran settlements and indigenous settlements in his detailed work on the Aurès zone in the Roman period.

Table 7.1. Army recruitment in North Africa. The left-hand columns show the percentage of troops recruited to the Roman army in Africa from overseas (Italy/other provinces) and from within Africa. The right-hand columns show the percentages of the overall total that came from different African provinces/regions and from garrison settlements (*castris*) (data from Le Bohec 1989a).

Recruitment	Overseas	Africa	Total	*Procos*	*Byz*	*Trip*	*Numid Cirt*	*Numid mil*	*castris*
117–161 CE	41	59	100	24	13	2	2	3	14
161–192 CE	5	95	100	37	18	2	9	8	20
193–238 CE	5	96	100	23	16	1	11	9	36
Totals	16	84	100	24	15	2	8	7	28

The exceptional epigraphic record from Africa illustrates in detail the switch in recruiting emphasis from outside to inside the province (Table 7.1).[16]

A couple of caveats should be noted. First, while the growth of veteran colonies and other towns with substantial Roman citizen populations in Africa is clear, military recruitment was not evenly representative of these communities. In fact, the vast bulk of legionary recruits in the early 2nd century came from a limited number of *coloniae* or other centres of veteran settlement like *Lambaesis* (Table 7.2). The top 14 recruiting nodes included active military bases (*ex castris*), provincial capitals (where troops were garrisoned), and major regional administrative centres (*Karthago*, *Cirta*, *Hadrumetum*), sites that were or had been legionary fortresses or had received veteran settlement (*Ammaedara*, *Cillium*, *Lambaesis*, *Theveste*, *Thamugadi*, *Sicca Veneria*, *Utica*), or towns where there was a continuing military presence for some other reason (the marble quarries at *Simitthu*). The area of the Cirtan Confederation, where Sittius had settled his veterans in the 40s BCE was another long-term focus for military recruitment, with a recent study identifying over 100 military personnel (including 5 centurions, 27 ranking officers, 40 soldiers and 30 veterans).[17] The presence of troops, veterans, and their descendants, or Roman administrative officials who were regularly accompanied by troops or who may have played a role in recruitment, gave these particular urban centres a distinctive association with the military community. The two sites that stand out in Table 7.2 as having less connection with the military community are *Thysdrus* and *Leptiminus*, though both at times hosted elements of imperial administration.

16. See in particular the forensic analysis of the epigraphic data by Lassère 1977, 633–643; Le Bohec 1989a; 1989b; note also the important onomastic study of Lassère 1980 on the list of nearly 300 named legionaries from the fort of *Bezereos* in the later 2nd century.

17. Bertrandy 2009.

Table 7.2. Detailed breakdown of main settlements providing army recruits within *Africa* (data from Le Bohec 1989a). Under **status** column, c = *colonia*; m = *municipium*. MC in final column indicates site associated with military community.

African recruitment		**Legionaries**			***Auxilia***	**Total**	
	Status	**1st CE**	**2nd CE**	**3rd CE**			
ex castris			61	188		249	MC
Karthago	c	2	73	52	50	177	MC
Cirta	c	9	8	43	8	68	MC
Theveste	c		10	29	7	46	MC
Hadrumetum	m/c		17	13	10	40	MC?
Thamugadi	c		7	24	2	33	MC
Utica	m/c	2	3	6	18	29	MC
Ammaedara	c		15	7	4	26	MC
Thysdrus	m/c		5	7	10	22	
Sicca Veneria	c		3	12	2	17	MC
Lambaesis	m/c		2	7	5	14	MC
Simitthu	c		1	12	1	14	MC
Cillium	m/c			12	1	13	MC?
Leptiminus	c		1		9	10	
6 sites with 6–9		0	13	24	8	45	5 MC
55 sites with 1–4		1	39	53	21	114	7 MC

The recruiting bias towards towns with close connections with the military community must at least in part be that they were seen as a source of the right sort of recruit—potentially towns that maintained a distinctive military atmosphere in the way that major garrison towns do to this day, with many young men growing up in a profoundly militaristic culture, where service in the army was a common and expected choice for able-bodied young men. Intending recruits for the army may also have gravitated towards such towns in the hope of getting preferment in terms of choice of unit. Although another 61 sites are known to have contributed recruits to the Roman army, in 55 of these cases the known recruits number less than 5, and 12 of the sites can also be associated with the military community. Overall, the percentage of the known recruits that came from sites associated with the military community is >86%.

Auxiliary recruitment is harder to track in detail, as ethnic unit names came to have less meaning, and numbers were made up from more local sources of peoples of the perceived right martial spirit. This does not mean that all overseas recruiting had ended, as has long been recognised from the evidence of a number of Syrian units in the African garrison, who maintained the worship of some specifically Syrian gods into the 3rd century.[18]

Soldiers, veterans, and their close family were more commonly commemorated on tombstones than civilians in the provinces, in part because of the provisions of funerary clubs within regiments and in part because such memorialisation was a key aspect of military behaviour and identity (Fig. 7.2).[19] Military funerary monuments often took on distinctive forms, with four main types recognised: MI, tombstones (simple slabs, often with a rounded or gabled top); MII, funerary altars or *cippi*; MIII, *cupula* tombs (with distinctive half-barrel shape); MIV, (much rarer) mausolea.[20] Although overlapping chronologically, type MI was primarily of 1st- to early 2nd-century date, type MII of 2nd–early 3rd-century, type MIII mainly 3rd-century. The altar and *cupula* types were by far the most commonly attested.[21]

Epigraphically and iconographically, military community tombstones tend to stand out from civil ones in a number of ways. A typical funerary text for a soldier, after acknowledging the shades of the dead (*DM* or *DMS*), named the individual, gave their rank and unit of service, age, and (if a death in service) the number of years served, plus a reference to their family member or heir responsible for the tombstone. For wives and children of, and enslaved people owned by, soldiers and veterans, the link was often explicitly made to the named soldier and their unit. Funerary texts for more senior officers were generally more elaborate and might include additional details of their career postings to multiple units.

Military tombstones were more likely to be accompanied by iconographic representations of the deceased, often in military garb appropriate to their role and grade. Across the Empire, tombstones of cavalrymen commonly depicted images of the horse and rider charging over the fallen body of a barbarian enemy.[22] In North Africa, with its strong martial associations with horses, such scenes are unsurprisingly common, but also accompanied by other equine iconography such as unridden horses with grooms.[23] Le Bohec identified four main groups of military tombstone imagery from North Africa:[24] RI, individual portraits; RII, standing figures (images of soldiers with arms and armour, sacrifice at altars, associated with scenes of funerary banquets and with families); RIII, equestrian imagery; RIV, diverse objects (often individual items of military equipment or decorations).

18. Carcopino 1933; Le Bohec 1989b, 120–40 for detailed dossier relating to the *numerus Palmyrenorum Sagittariorum*. See also Le Bohec 1987.

19. Hope 2001.

20. Le Bohec 1989a, 83–92.

21. Le Bohec 1989a, 88–92.

22. Haynes 2013, 371–74 making the point that the cavalry *auxilia*, largely recruited from "barbarian" peoples, were effectively distancing themselves from their roots with such memorials; see also Kramer 2014.

23. Le Bohec 1989b, 44–48.

24. Le Bohec 1989a, 92–106.

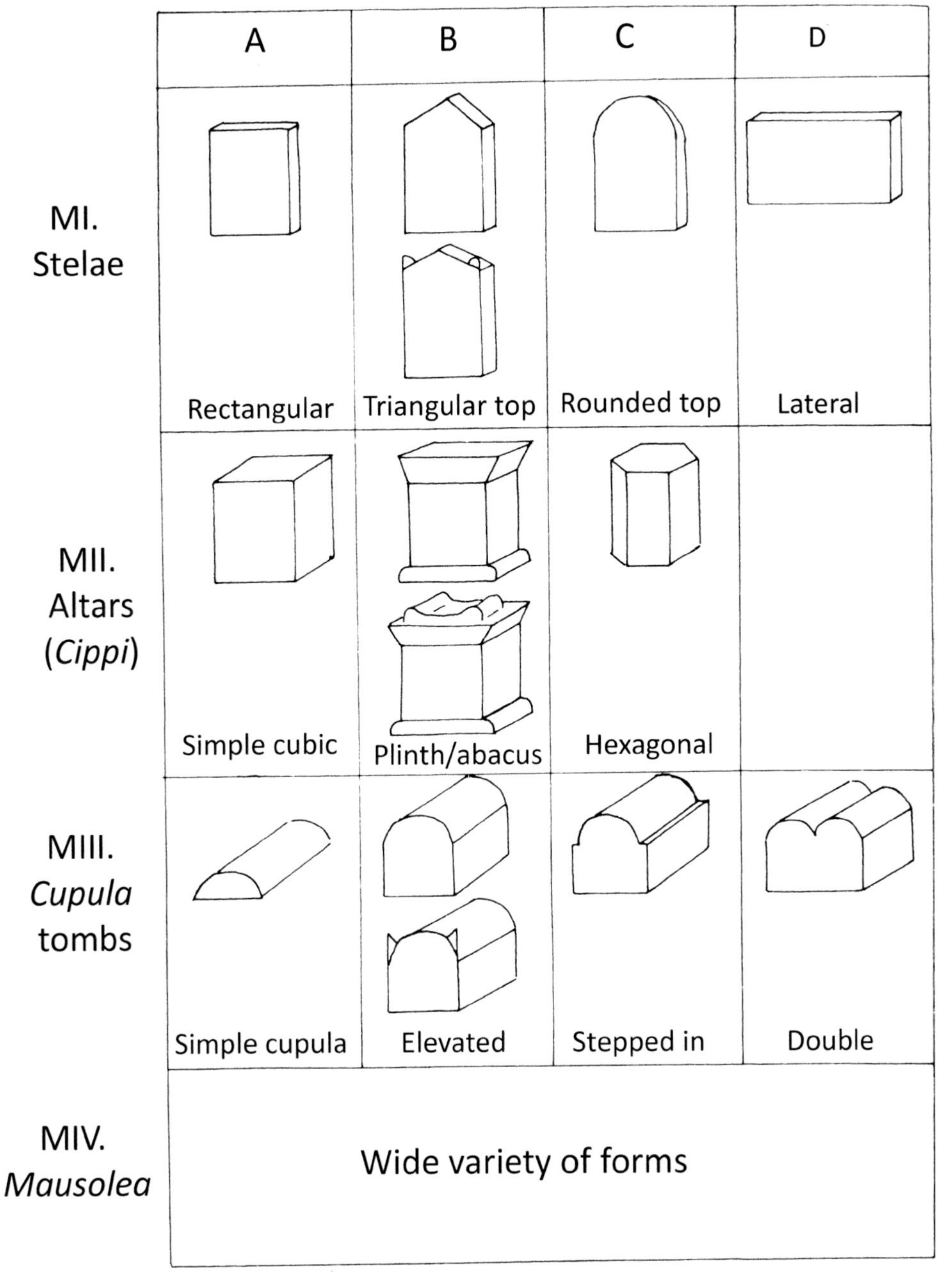

Figure 7.2. Typology of Roman (commonly military) tombstones and funerary monuments from North Africa (author's montage after Le Bohec 1989a, 85).

Of the 55 examples collected by Le Bohec, the majority were of type RI (32), with 9 examples of RII, 11 of RIII, and 3 of RIV.[25] The occurrence of imagery was much more common among officers, higher-grade troops, and veterans than the lower rank infantry. In combination, the choice of monument type (reflecting also an underlying set of common funerary practices), the use of distinctive iconography when this could be afforded and the ubiquitous formulaic inscriptions will have given the cemeteries of the military community a distinctive look that at a glance differentiated them from normal civic or rural communities. Whatever their origins, most soldiers and their families emphasised above all their adherence to the military community.

The tombstone data confirm in a number of ways the coherence of the military community, encompassing both serving and retired soldiers, with their dependants, as well as other civilians living in the garrison settlements. David Cherry's analyses of the marriage patterns detectable in 3,436 funerary texts from the security zones of *Mauretania Caesariensis* and *Numidia* are highly revealing, though not always precisely in the way he imagined.[26] The primary categories into which he divided the material were Romanised/un-Romanised, soldier/civilian and male/female. On the first of these, his judgement of what constituted being Romanised is rather subjective—essentially it comes down to naming styles. For Cherry, the un-Romanised were those with African names or a single Latinised African name or auxiliary soldiers.[27] The last of these seems particularly contentious, and on the issue of African names, the family of Nubel in 4th-century Mauretania was full of African personal names, but was undoubtedly deeply engaged with aspects of Roman culture.[28] In place of Cherry's ascription of epitaphs to military or civilian categories (defined by mention or not of military service), a better starting point would perhaps be to reflect on the extent to which the inscriptions can be assigned to the military community, the urban community, and rural communities.[29] A large percentage overall of the tombstones catalogued by Cherry related to sites with clear associations with the military community: garrison settlements (e.g. *Auzia*, Bir Oum Ali, *Calceus Herculis*, *Lambaesis*, *Mesarfelta*, *Rapidum*, *Zarai*), military *coloniae* (*Ammaedara*, *Theveste*, *Thamugadi*), and veteran settlements (*Casae*, *Diana Veteranorum*, *Verecunda*). A relatively small number came from rural sites, and some at least of these reveal a connection with former soldiers (Ksar Seriana, *CIL* 8. 4375; Ksur el-Ghennaya, *CIL* 8.4310). In consequence, I think our default assumption should be that the similarity in cultural behaviour exhibited by both

25. Le Bohec 1989a, 105–06.
26. Cherry 1998, 119–40, 162–224 (for the full epigraphic catalogue).
27. Cherry 1998, 116.
28. Hamdoune 2018, 166–71.
29. For similarly flawed analysis of military and civilian tombstones from Britain, see Adams and Tobler 2007; with alternative analysis and conclusions in Mattingly 2008.

tombstones identified with soldiers and by those that are not explicitly military but that are at garrison settlements is indicative of a collective sense of identity. In any case, while a soldier's identity was extremely likely to be advertised on a tombstone commemorating their own life, it was perhaps more optional on a tombstone erected to their deceased wife. Also, it is possible that further into retirement, a veteran's military link was less specifically alluded to.

What Cherry's corpus of inscriptions from the Roman security zones does reveal is a similar preference for men and women at garrison settlements to have Roman-styled nomenclature and to marry individuals with similar naming practices. There are strikingly few instances of men with Latinised names marrying women with solely African names, and this is true for soldiers and other men present in the settlements.[30] Equally rare are women with Roman-style names married to men with African names. In fact the exceptions to the general pattern amount to just 15/707 epitaphs (2%). A deviation from this pattern considered by Cherry is the body of material from the urban site of *Thubursicu Numidarum*, where c.13% of epitaphs related to these sorts of "mixed" marriages based on nomenclature. Several conclusions may be drawn from this I think. The first is that the military community's practices (funerary commemoration, naming, marriage) all stand out as distinctive from that of an urban community that was not specifically influenced by the military community. Within the military community, serving soldiers, veterans, and civilians closely associated with them followed broadly the same patterns of behaviour as one another, with differences largely due to wealth. In conclusion, the evidence shows a strong behavioural attachment to Roman styles of naming and the adoption of Latinised versions of African names where these were maintained, often as *cognomina*. Just as African recruits into the army might have their names Latinised on enlistment, or be given a new "Roman" name, so too in marriage and death it seems that women associated with the military community preferentially had or took on such naming practices. Finally, many tombstones clearly reflect the existence of wills, through the mention of heirs. Again, this was a practice that was underwritten in the army and promulgated more widely in the military community. While there are undoubtedly some tombstones from the security zone from people who did not identify with the military community, it is my contention that they were a distinct minority and that they revealed differences in their identity presentation that marked them as not being with the military community. As an example of this, we might note the greater predominance of Libyan names, the use of Punic language, and non-military iconography on funerary monuments in Tripolitania (to which I shall return in Chapter 11).[31]

30. Cherry 1998, 119–31.
31. Mattingly 1987b; 1995, 162–67.

A different perspective on the primacy of the military identity in the case of a former soldier of indigenous descent is given by a bilingual funerary inscription from the town of *Thullium* (Kef Beni Fredj in north-east Algeria). This probably 2nd-century CE tombstone commemorates a veteran with Libyan roots, C. Iulius Gaetulus (Fig. 7.3).[32] This is one of a number of bilingual texts from an area where there is a dense cluster of Libyan inscriptions. The Latin text of the tombstone of Iulius Gaetulus records that he was a decorated veteran, though his unit is not specified, and that he had been appointed a perpetual *flamen* at his home town of *Thullium*. There are some key differences between the Libyan and Latin texts, which were not direct translations of each other. The Latin text conveys the "African" identity of the veteran by his assigned cognomen G(a)etulus. However, *Thullium* was far from the Gaetulian territory (or even assumed northern settlements of Gaetulians under Marius); indeed, this was a Massylian zone (where in Roman times the local people were known as *Misiciri*), and this may suggest that the cognomen was imposed rather than self-selected—as was sometimes the case with recruits into the Roman army who had non-Roman names.[33] The Libyan text in fact presents a completely different identity for the veteran, plausibly naming him as "KTi son of MSWLT of the subgroup S'RMMi of the MSKRI people" (or "Keti son of Maswalat of the subgroup *Saremmi* of the *Misiciri*").[34] It is also possible that Keti's father was commemorated in another text, only in Libyan, from the same cemetery, suggesting that he too had served as a Roman soldier.[35]

What I would suggest here is that the inscriptions in memory of Keti were not a straightforward bilingual text, but presented two alternative social identities for the individual. For those who could read Latin, the service to the Empire would be the clear emphasis; for the Libyan-speaking community, there was a hidden transcript

32. *CIL* 8.5209/*RIL* 146/*ILAf* 132; Rebuffat 2005. Shaw 2021 is a detailed and perceptive discussion with much in common with my analysis below.

33. For an Egyptian from the Fayum called Apion, who was renamed Antonius Maximus on enlistment, see *Select Papyri* 112; Campbell 1994. Cf. Gascou 1970 for an onomastic study of the cognomen Gaetulus in Africa. Shaw 2021, 75–77 suggests that he was the descendant of an African who served under and was enfranchised by Julius Caesar. In that case we would have to account for at least 150 years and several generations of his family having borne Roman citizenship. A possible alternative would be that Gaetulus was the first generation to be enfranchised and that his army name was translated into his *tria nomina*.

34. Cf Shaw 2021, 60–62 for texts and translations. One wonders if the phonetic resemblance between Keti's name and *Gaetuli* was a factor in the choice of a cognomen by the recruiting officer that was otherwise probably ethnically inappropriate.

35. Shaw 2021, 68, n.28: RIL 148 "MSWLT W GPNYM S'RRMi MSWi MNKDi," "Maswalat son of GPNYM from the (subgroup of the) S'RRMi, servant/soldier of the emperor." If this man was the father of Keti, it is singular that he did not record his assumed Roman citizen status (if he was, as Shaw suggests, already a remote descendant of a soldier of Caesar). It is also of note that Keti's Latin text does not express his filiation, which might be expected if his father was also a C. Iulius. It is, of course, possible that Maswalat had been discharged from the army prematurely and thus was not enfranchised. At any event, the area appears to have been one that the Roman army targeted for ethnic recruits, Shaw 2021, 75–77.

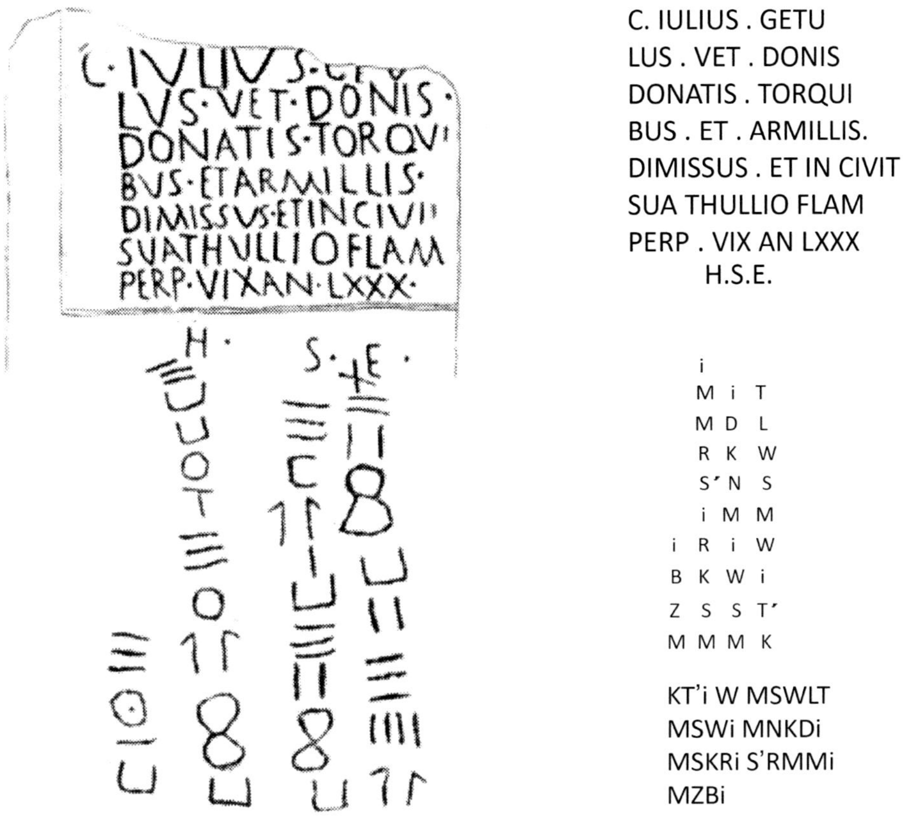

Figure 7.3. Tombstone of C. Iulius Gaetulus of *Thullium* (author's montage after Rebuffat 2005, 224).

more focused on the African specificities. This also suggests that when they moved away from the military community, ex-soldiers did not always maintain their military identity in the same way as when they remained resident in a garrison settlement. The *Thullium* text is an interesting example of the discrepant identity or hybridity that could result.

The Garrison Settlements

In this section I use a few examples to illustrate just how the military community differed from civilian communities in terms of projecting a distinctive identity.[36] There was a broad spectrum of garrison settlements associated with military bases

36. Groslambert 2009b sees the distinctiveness of the cultural reference points but chooses to express it in terms of a conventional Romanisation narrative.

in North Africa, in terms of their scale and urban characteristics.[37] Several examples of garrison settlements alongside forts from *Numidia* (*Gemellae* and *Nigrenses Maiores*) and Mauretania Caesariensis (*Rapidum*) went on to acquire formal urban status (Fig. 7.4), but they also stand out as a somewhat distinctive form of urbanism in the African provinces (to which I return in the next chapter).[38] At *Gemellae* and *Nigrenses Maiores*, the fort sat at the centre of the garrison settlement, and the roads approaching its four entrances defined the layout of the peripheral structures. Although the settlements appear relatively regularly laid out, they were both surrounded by oddly shaped outer wall circuits. In the case of *Rapidum*, the town developed to the south-west and west of the fort and was both externally protected by a polygonal circuit and subdivided internally into a series of units by additional major walls, some studded with towers.

The establishment of new nucleated sites in the security zones extended beyond the growth of garrison settlements, and in a few cases we can detect the hand of the state; for instance, in the establishment of numerous veteran and other settlements (*vici*) on imperial land in the Aurès plain and *castella* in the region round *Sitifis*, which will have had a strong connection with the wider military community.[39] Another dramatic example concerns the site of *Usinaza* (Saneg) on the *nova praetentura* in *Mauretania Caesariensis*, where the discovery of an inscription in 1990 proved to be the missing half of a long-known text that had been previously taken to imply the foundation of a fort.[40] The key phrase in this inscription of c.202–203 CE mentions the movement of people on the orders of the procuratorial governor of *Caesariensis* from *Africa* to occupy a new *oppidum* at *Usinaza*. The governor, Aelius Peregrinus, was the known founder of a number of forts elsewhere on the *nova praetentura*, so it seems reasonable to assume that the new settlement, though apparently civil in nature, was also strongly aligned with the military community and with the broader issue of security.[41] This is another example where some specific groups of civilians in the security zone seem to have had a close relationship with the military community, differentiating them from the local rural populations.

37. For examples from *Mauretania Tingitana*, see Akerraz and Papi 2008, 34–35 (*Thamusida*); Bernal Casasola et al. 2013 (*Thamuda*); Euzennat 1989, 71, 242–47 (*Thamusida*, *Tocolosida*); for *Mauretania Caesariensis*, Laporte 1989; 2004a; 2009 (Grimidi, Tarmount, *Rapidum*, *Auzia*); for *Numidia*, Daniels 1987 (*Gemellae*, al-Ghara); Laporte 2004a (al-Ghara); Le Bohec 1989a, 430–36 (*Nigrenses Maiores*, *Gemellae*, al-Ghara); for *Tripolitana*, Mattingly 1995, 92, 134–37 (*Tillibari*, *Gholaia*, *Myd[...]*, *Talalati*); Rebuffat 1975a, 165–87 (*Gholaia*).

38. Daniels 1987, 258–59 (*Gemellae* and *Nigrenses Maiores*); Laporte 1989, 11–29, 99–146, 205–92 (*Rapidum*); Laporte and Dupuis 2011 (*Nigrenses Maiores*); Trousset 1977a (*Gemellae*).

39. Fentress 1979, 134–44.

40. Benseddik 1992; The key part of the text reads: *populis nouis ex Africa inlatis oppid[u]m Vsinazensem per I P(ublium) Aelium Peregrinum proc(uratorem).*

41. Benseddik 1999, 100 comments on the strategic purpose and “intention colonisatrice” of the foundation of Usinaza. Cf. also Euzennat 1995b; Laporte 2009; Laporte 2011, 123–24.

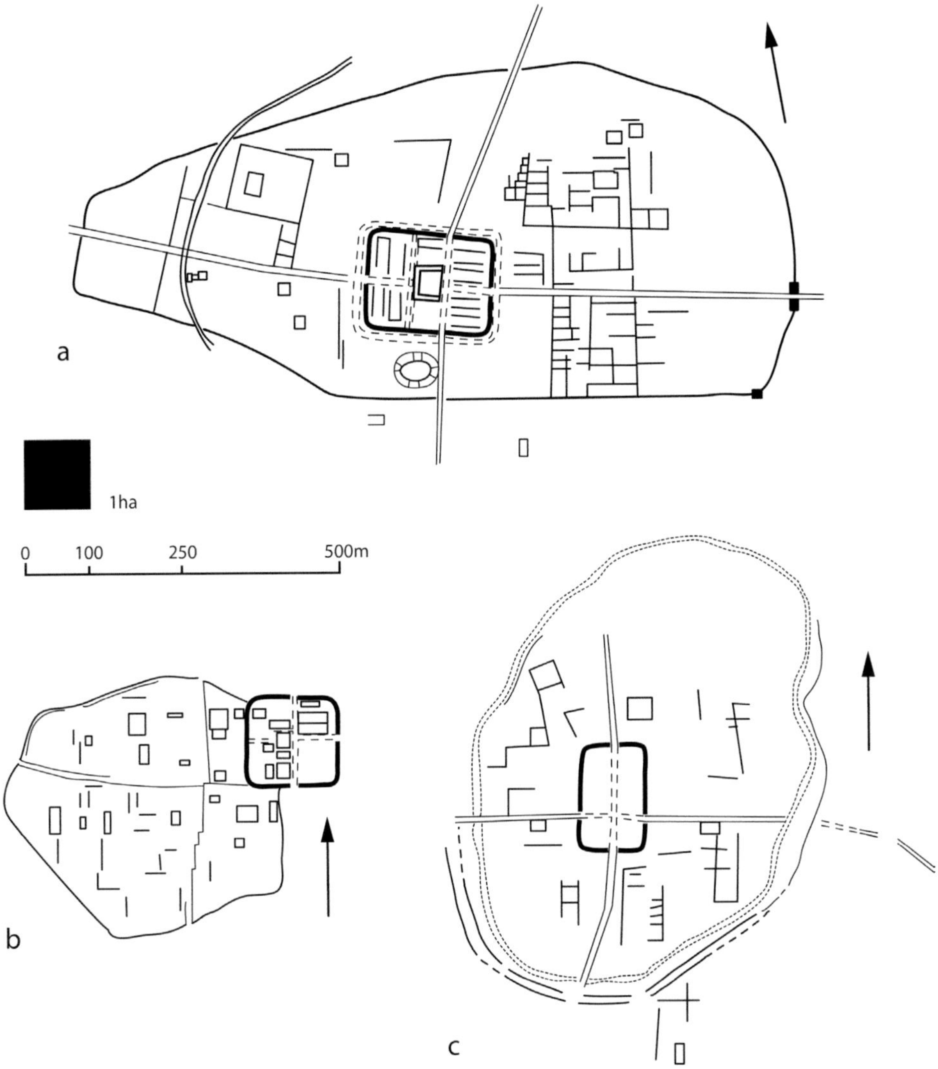

Figure 7.4. Comparative plans of walled garrison settlements that achieved municipal status. a) *Gemellae*. b) *Rapidum*. c) *Nigrenses Maiores* (M. Hawkes, from author's rough).

The Legionary Base: Lambaesis

The most extraordinary military site in North Africa was the legionary base at *Lambaesis* in the Aurès plain.[42] There was a complex and long-term sequence of military occupation at the site. There are three separate military enceintes (Fig. 7.5): a) a fort (148 × 120 m) established in 81 CE on an elevated platform

42. On Lambaesis, see Cagnat 1913, 441–519; Groslambert 2011; Janon 1973; 1977; 2005; Le Bohec 1989a, 407–24; 2008.

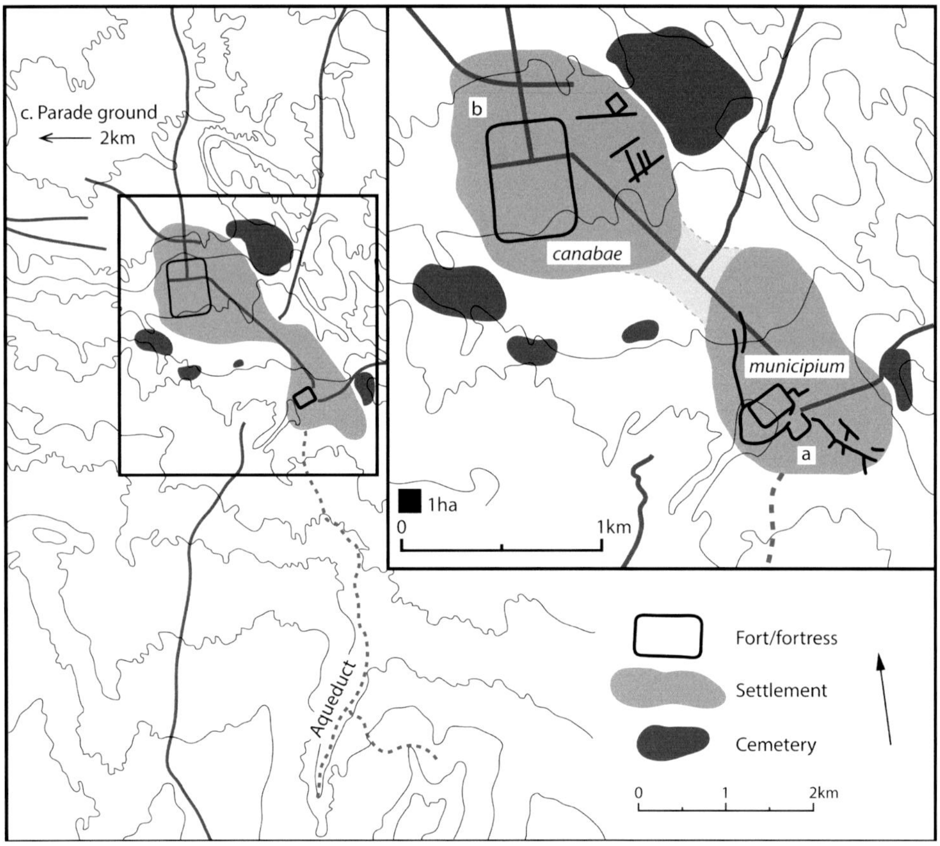

Figure 7.5. The complex garrison settlement at *Lambaesis*. a) 81 CE fort and *municipium*. b) Legionary fortress and *canabae*. c) Direction of parade ground (Mike Hawkes, from author's rough, after Janon 1977).

between two wadi courses; b) the Trajanic legionary fortress (500 × 500 m) built on lower ground just over 1 km to the north-west of a); c) the large parade ground (200 × 300 m) a few kilometres west of the fortress (where the inscription of Hadrian was found on a centrally placed monument almost certainly marking the site of the manoeuvres he supervised). Militarily speaking, the complex of installations was dominated by the legionary fortress, with a notional garrison of 5–6,000 men. It was surrounded by buildings of the *canabae*, extending to east and west up to parallel wadis running south-east to north-west). The legionary amphitheatre lay in the eastern part of the *canabae*. The main legionary cemeteries were initially to the north (I) and north-east (II), though there were further cemeteries to the south (IV) and south-east (III) and on the south-east side of the upper town. Analysis of the rich epigraphic haul from these cemeteries suggests that cemetery III was the earliest, with cemeteries I and II slightly later, after the foundation of the fortress, and cemetery IV becoming the most active zone in the 3rd century. Cemetery I had a larger percentage of officers buried in it, whereas lower ranks predominated in cemeteries III and IV and veterans were more strongly represented in cemetery II.[43]

The 1st-century fort appears to have remained occupied by a cavalry force alongside the fortress down to the 240s at least. A substantial garrison settlement also grew up around the early fort, and this nucleated settlement was granted municipal status and became the governor's seat when the province of *Numidia* was created in the Severan period. A major sanctuary of Aesculapius and other gods was built at the town, impinging on the fort defences, so was clearly an officially sanctioned development (unsurprisingly, given its relation to the health of the garrison). The relative social and legal status of the various bits of this archaeological landscape have been debated, and the exact limits of town and *canabae* are uncertain—indeed, the two may have eventually merged together rather than being clearly demarcated zones of settlement.[44] I think the associations with army and governor are everywhere apparent, and the differences between fort, fortress, *canabae*, and town are far less significant than the differences between the totality here and most other sites in the region. As the base of the largest unit (the legion), at least one element of auxiliary garrison, and the headquarters of the military commander in Africa (later provincial governor of *Numidia*), it is apparent why *Lambaesis* was a honeypot site for soldiers, Roman citizens, foreigners, other imperial officials, and so on. While there were undoubtedly Africans here, their identity markers are much less in evidence. The close proximity of a number of other veteran settlements (*Thamugadi, Verecunda, Casae, Diana Veteranorum*) gave a very military aspect to the western end of the Aurès plain.[45]

While traditional studies of onomastics have tended to focus more on the soldiery,[46] recent work has also highlighted the important evidence from this site for the composition of the civilian community at *Lambaesis*.[47] For instance, over 1,800 civilians are named on inscriptions, of whom about 86% appear to have been Roman citizens. Both in numerical terms and the numbers of citizens, this is a substantial and unusual sample from a single location—far more than from other sites in *Numidia*. We need to be cautious about drawing broader conclusions about Roman society in North Africa from this sort of evidence. *Lambaesis* was by no means a typical site—the presence of the garrison and being a centre of provincial government from the early 3rd century were factors that also shaped the civilian community that lived alongside. There were more foreigners here than at the

43. Le Bohec 1989a, 107–10. Cf. Dondin-Payre 2010.
44. Benseddik 2003, 172; Groslambert 2011; Janon 1973.
45. Fentress 1979, 132–44.
46. Le Bohec 1989a, 117–332; cf. Lassère 1977, 75–289.
47. Cherry 1998; Groslambert 2009b, 59–60; 2011, 61–72.

average African town, and the proportion of citizens was consistently high well before Roman citizen rights were more generally extended, due to the settlement of veterans and traders. Cherry's study of the marital relations attested to in the funerary inscriptions from garrison settlements in general demonstrates a strong trend for men with Roman-style names to marry women with Roman-style nomenclature (whether citizens or not). *Lambaesis* was probably unusual in the numbers of citizen-status women present at the settlement in the 2nd century, and certainly the pattern noted from other Numidian sites by Cherry is more varied.[48] His conclusion that the Roman army operated as a "distinct and separate society" within North Africa appears justified on this evidence and fits with what we know of the operation of the military community elsewhere.[49]

The Garrison Settlement at Gholaia

The fort of *Gholaia* (Bu Nijim) in Libya controlled a small oasis on the desert route about 200 km south from *Lepcis Magna* towards the land of the *Garamantes*. It is currently the most extensively excavated garrison site and can also be set within a detailed local landscape (Figs. 7.6; 12.8).[50] Its significance is enhanced further by the remarkable epigraphic records there. Inscriptions on stone record with precision many of the key events in the history of the fort, its construction and repair, and the religious life of the garrison.[51] The fort was founded by a detachment (*vexillatio*) of the *legio III Augusta* commanded by a legionary centurion on 24 January 201, with its bath complex completed in 202. Part of the vexillation was then absent for a period, its return to the fort celebrated in a text of 205.[52] The south gate was repaired in 222[53] and the legionary presence is attested down to 238, in the last years accompanied by an auxiliary component (*numerus collatus*). After 238, when *legio III Augusta* was disbanded following its part in the suppression of the Gordian revolt, it seems likely that the *Gholaia* garrison was simply rebranded as a *vexillatio Golensis*. In the 240s CE we have the first evidence of a new command structure, with the appearance of a *praepositus limitis Tripolitanae*—the first indication of the transformation towards the late Roman security arrangements of multiple regional *limites* detailed in the *Notitia Dignitatum*.[54] From the last phase of the

48. Cherry 1998, 101–40. Cf. James 1999b.
49. Cherry 1998, 133.
50. For the excavation reports, see Rebuffat 1967a; 1970a; 1970b; 1975b; 1977a. Overall summeries of discoveries, Rebuffat 1977b; 1985b; 1989; 2000.
51. Speidel 1988.
52. Rebuffat 1973b.
53. Adams 1999; Rebuffat 1985c.
54. Rebuffat 1985b; 1988b.

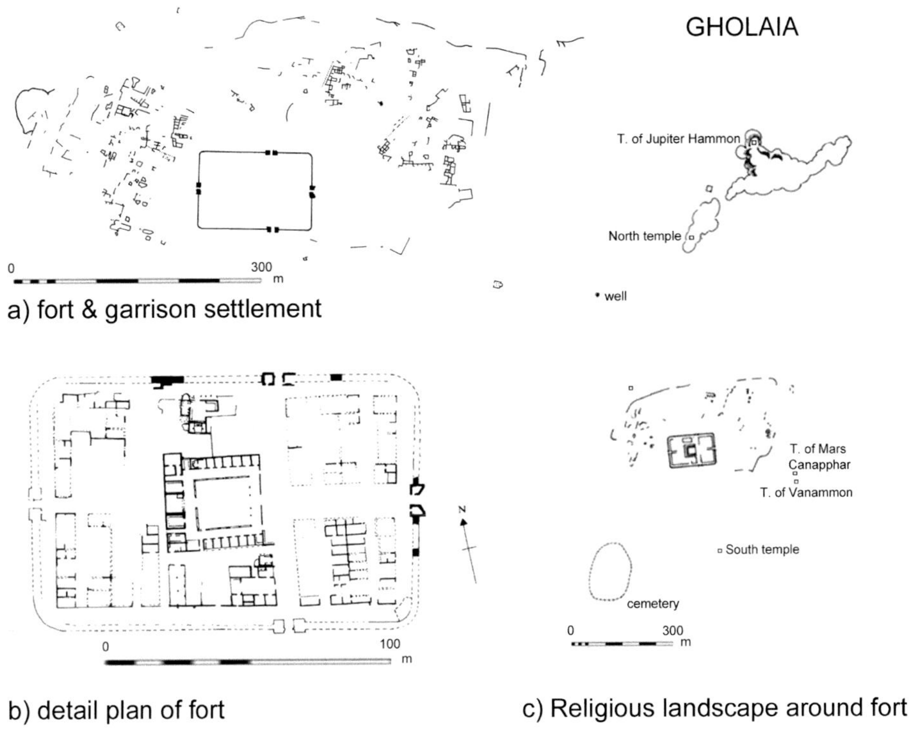

Figure 7.6. The garrison settlement of *Gholaia*. a) Plan of fort and garrison settlement. b) Plan of fort. c) Religious landscape around fort (from Mattingly 2013a, 88).

fort's occupation 253–259 come a remarkable series of documents written in ink on potsherds (ostraca).[55] The last document from the site dates to 259 and final withdrawal seems to have occurred by 263, though some "squatter" activity in the fort and associated settlement is attested into the 4th century.

The layout of the 1.28 ha fort is plainly visible beneath the engulfing sand dunes, though the plan reveals that a cardinal surveying error led to the fort constructors placing the north and south gates at different distances from the east defences, leading to a skewed alignment of the principal internal buildings (Fig. 7.6b; 7.7). The main excavated buildings are spread across the central range: the headquarters complex, the commanding officer's house, two store buildings, and the baths. The barrack accommodation is sufficient for c.480 legionaries and perhaps 64–128 cavalry, though the epigraphic evidence suggests that actual numbers of troops present were frequently well below this. The presence of troopers from the *cohors VIII Fida* are attested alongside the *vexillatio* at *Gholaia* in the 250s, and a mounted component is likely to have been the norm at such an isolated site.

55. Marichal 1992.

Figure 7.7. Aerial photograph of fort of *Gholaia*, with north to left (original photo ULVS, from Mattingly 1995, pl. 8).

Around the fort a sizeable garrison settlement of 10 ha grew up (Fig. 7.6a).[56] Although one building in the settlement yielded a series of Libyan inscriptions,[57] the overriding impression is that this was a settlement dominated by Latin culture and focused on servicing the needs of the fort at its centre. There was also a nearby oasis zone to the north-west and a rectangular enclosure to the north, which can plausibly be identified as the location of the *statio camellariorum* mentioned in the ostraca (Fig. 12.8). A series of small temples have been identified on the low hills surrounding the fort (Fig. 7.6c and below) and the cemetery of the garrison community lay to the south-west, along with a huge rubbish midden.

The epigraphic corpus from *Gholaia* sheds indirect light on the recruitment pattern for the army. The *cognomina* include 11% that are certainly Punic or African, and 45% of the Latin ones also had African affinities. Over half the *nomina* relate to Iulius and Aurelius, and these suggest that many of the soldiers had been recruited in Africa between 222–249 CE. It also seems probable that some at least were

56. Mattingly 1995, 134–35.
57. Rebuffat 1975a.

recruited from indigenous communities and received Roman-style names for the first time on enlistment, rather than inheriting them from veteran fathers. Further support for this idea is given by Jim Adams' analysis of the linguistic competence in Latin of these soldiers.[58]

The ostraca were almost all written in Latin, albeit showing variable levels of grammatical precision, and detailing the relationship between the army and indigenous farmers—who made regular deliveries of foodstuffs to the garrison. Although there is at least one ostracon in Latino-Punic (and the fort may have been laid out in multiples of the Punic cubit), the predominant cultural elements in the army were Roman and based on the daily use of Latin as the lingua franca of army life.[59] It was not just the level of Latinity that made the army stand out, it was the way that the use of Latin was enshrined in day-to-day behaviours—the fort administration and command, letters and reports, religious dedications, funerary practices, and so on. As Adams has emphasised, the Latinity of the troops was of poor quality, but he disagrees with Marichal that this might be interpreted as evidence for a pidgin or creole form of Latin.[60] His careful study demonstrates clearly that this was a vulgar form of Latin, with many of the mistakes in syntax and grammar attributable to learners' errors by individuals whose first language was probably Punic or Libyan.[61] The consistency with which some mistakes were produced is an indication that this was not simply a problem of limited literacy, but reflected the vulgar spoken patterns of Latin in the garrison community.[62] Nonetheless, Latin was undoubtedly spoken by the troops and was a defining characteristic of the military community.[63] The fort and garrison settlement at *Gholaia* was not only a Latin hotspot in a rural landscape with very different linguistic preferences, but this was also a place where social practices and cultural reference points would have seemed very alien to many inhabitants of the pre-desert region. The short distance between the garrison settlement and the oasis and well (which we can assume predated the arrival of the army) was a deliberate choice in setting the community apart. The same phenomenon can also be remarked at *Gemellae* and *Nigrenses Maiores*, where the Roman forts and towns were situated a kilometre or so to the south of the pre-existing oasis communities.

Other differences are evident in the cultural behaviours on display. Although incompletely published, the pottery from Bu Nijim (and al-Qurrayyat) reflect

58. Adams 1994.
59. Rebuffat 1985b; Marichal 1992, 240 for Punic influences and documents. Recently discovered ostraca from the fort of al-Qurrayyat al-Garbia in Tripolitania were written in the Punic language using the Latin alphabet, Ziegler and Mackensen 2014.
60. Marichal 1992, 18–48 on the writing (script) and language of the tablets.
61. Adams 1994, especially 89–103
62. Adams 1994, 103–112.
63. Adams 1994; cf Marichal 1992, 46–114; Rebuffat and Marichal 1973.

differences from the pre-desert farming communities, with far more amphorae, reflecting higher consumption of things like olive oil, wine, and fish sauce.[64] For example, the cemetery at *Gholaia* differed in significant ways from the usual Libyan burial rites of the pre-desert zone. Small cremation burials under regular stepped markers aligned in serried ranks contrasted with the normal regional pattern of crouched inhumation beneath cairn tombs.[65] Tombstones with Latin texts are extremely rare in the Tripolitanian pre-desert outside of the known military bases. In eastern Tripolitania, for example, only two other Latin tombstones are known.[66] Most of the non-military funerary inscriptions from the western Tripolitanian security zone overall came from mausolea, and a large percentage of these seem to have been located in close proximity to the *limes* road or to military installations. The more common phenomenon of Latino-Punic funerary texts in eastern Tripolitania will be discussed in Chapter 11. Here I simply observe that the burial practices and behaviours of the military community at *Gholaia* differed fundamentally from the civilian populations in the pre-desert zone.

Religion and the Military Community

Lambaesis and Numidia

The list of gods worshipped at *Lambaesis* is one of the longest from any site in Africa and presents an impressive pantheon of Roman and Eastern divinities along with key North African cults, many with chthonic undertones (Table 7.3).[67] As is clear in the second part of the table, other military sites from the Aurès region and from the security zone individually have yielded many fewer religious inscriptions, but cumulatively strongly echo the religious pattern at *Lambaesis*.[68] The military influence at all the sites where these texts have been recovered has not been stressed as much as it might be. My argument is that sites associated with the military community tended to present a religious identity that was *sui generis*. There was a strong emphasis on the Roman pantheon, on healing cults like Aesculapius and Hygeia, as well as a clear engagement with cults originating in the East or Alexandria but achieving a global reach under Rome. There is overlap with urban

64. Bu Nijim: Rebuffat 1970a; 1970b; 1975b; 1997: al-Qurrayyat: Weber and Schmid 2012. Pre-desert zone in general: Dore 1996; Leitch et al. 2018; Leone 2017; Mattingly 2013b.
65. Barker et al. 1996a, 142–45, for regional burial types.
66. See fuller discussion in Chapter 11.
67. Benseddik 2009; 2014; Cadotte 2007; Groslambert 2011, 73–101; Hilali 2016; Leglay 1971.
68. Benseddik 2009. The list of other sites includes forts and other military outposts of the security region, Roman colonies, and known veteran settlements or sites where significant concentrations of army veterans have been noted.

Table 7.3. Gods and goddesses attested at *Lambaesis*, other military sites, and rural settlements in the Numidian security zone.

Location	Greco-Roman Gods/Cults	Oriental/Egyptian Cults	Romano-African Cults
Lambaesis	Aesculapius, Apollo, Aquae Sinuessanae, Bona Dea, Diana, Disciplina, Fortuna, Fortuna Redux, genius castrorum, genius centuriae, genius coloniae Cirta, genius coloniae Lambesis, genius domus, genius legionis, genius loci, genius populi Lamb., genius praetorii, genius sanctus provinciae, genius scholae, genius tabularii, genius tribunicialis, genius vici, Hercules, Hygeia, Ianus pater, Iuno, Iupiter (incl IOM, I. Iuno Minerva, I. Valens), Mars, Mars Gradius, Mercurius, Mercurius Silvanus, Minerva, Numen Aquae, Nutrix, Nymphae, Salus, Silvanus, Silvanus castrensis, Silvanus pegasianus, Victoria	Cybele, Hierobol, Isis, Iupiter Dolichenus, Iupiter Heliopolis, Malagbel, Mithra, Serapis, Sol Invictus	Caelestis, Cereres, Dea Africa, Dii Mauri, Frugifer, Liber Pater, Neptune, Pluto, Saturnus
Other forts, urban sites with military or veteran connections	Aesculapius, Apollo, Aquae Bona Dea, Concordia, Diana, Dii Campestres, Dii Conservatores, Dii Fautores, Dii Iuvantes, Fortuna, genii, genius coloniae, genius exercitus, genius loci, genius pacis, genius patriae, genius ordinis, genius populi, genius vici, Hercules, Hygeia, Ianus pater, Iuno, Iuno Concordia, Iupiter, Iupiter (incl IOM, I. Iuno Minerva, I. Stator, I. Victor), Mars, Mercurius, Mercurius Augustus, Mercurius Silvanus, Minerva, Momenta, Nymphae, Pegasus, Silvanus, Sol, Venus, Victoria, Victoria Auggg	Cybele, Magna Idaea, Iorchobol, Iupiter Serapis, Malagbel, Mater Deum, Mithra, Serapis, Sol Augustus, Sol Invictus	Caelestis, Ceres, Cillenius deus patrius, Dea Africa, Dea patria, Draco, Frugifer, Liber Pater, Mercurius Vazaivitanus, Neptunus, Pluto, Saturnus
Other sites in Aurès			Frugifer, Neptunus, Pluto, Saturnus

religious practices in other parts of North Africa, of course, but the overall religious behaviours and polytheistic range of the military community distinguished garrison settlements from civilian ones.[69]

If we turn to the third category of sites in the table, consisting of non-military urban and rural settlement in the Aurès and pre-desert regions, two things are evident. First, there is far less evidence of epigraphic-based religious behaviour at these sites; and second, when gods are evoked, these were African cults represented in syncretised form as Saturn, Pluto, Neptune. This difference goes beyond issues about the epigraphic habit as it relates to key religious preferences and the behaviours involved in the practice of religion. A further point of interest is, as Le Bohec observed, that the overall numbers of epigraphic dedications to Saturn and to other key Romano-African cults is extremely low across both the military and rural communities in the Aurès and security zone. As was argued in Chapters 5 and 6, the security zones in general corresponded with *tota Gaetulia*. The distribution of Saturn stelae is very much synonymous with the territory of the eastern *Numidae*, and to the degree that we can trace the extension of the Saturn cult into the Gaetulian territory it seems almost entirely explicable in terms of its practice within the military community. Saturn stelae have been found at some military sites (*Calceus Herculis*, *Lambaesis*, *Mascula*) and other settlements strongly associated with the military community (*Ammaedara*, *Lambafundi*, *Nicivibus*, *Thamugadi*, *Theveste*).[70]

Gods at Gholaia and in the Tripolitanian Pre-desert

In addition to several shrines to key Roman divinities within the main buildings of the fort at Bu Nijim, the peripheral landscape around *Gholaia* is marked by five small temples, representing loci of worship of Libyan cults (Fig. 7.6c).[71] The spatial placement of these temples to Libyan desert gods on the periphery of the military settlement at *Gholaia* is interesting. Similar discoveries have also been made close to the fort at al-Qurrayyat al-Garbia, where five probable temples or shrines to unknown gods have been identified.[72] There is a near complete lack of Latin religious texts from the pre-desert zone outside of these military sites.[73]

One of the most revealing epigraphic finds from *Gholaia* contains a reference to the consecration of an *ara cerei* (a candle altar) honouring *IOM* and the imperial

69. Mattingly 2011a, 241–45.
70. Leglay 1966a; McCarty 2010c.
71. Brouquier-Reddé 1992a; 1992b; Rebuffat 1990b.
72. Barker et al. 1996b, 98–100; Mackensen 2012, 53–54.
73. Barker et al. 1996a, 141–43. In eastern Tripolitania, the only Latin rural dedications are *IRT* 888 (Iupiter), *IRT* 905 (Mercury).

Table 7.4. The religious affiliations of the Tripolitanian security zone.

	Phoenician or Libyan cults	Syncretised cults	Classical cults	Eastern Cults
Gholaia Military community	Vanammon	Mars Canaphar Iupiter Hammon Genius Gholaiae	Fortuna, Imperial Cult, IOM, Salus	IOM Dolichenus, Sol Hieroboulos, Sol Invictus
Pre-desert Rural communities	Ancestor cults, [Gurzil, Mastiman?, Sinifer?]	Iupiter [Hammon?],	Mercury	[Christianity]

household on 3 May 236 or 238, one of a possible seven occurrences of such altars being erected at military sites in Africa on 3 May, which marked the final day of the festival of Flora, who had associations with bees and beeswax.[74] This, thus, seems to be a military tie-in with the classic Roman calendar and is reminiscent of the discovery of an actual copy of the calendar at *Dura-Europos*. It emphasises the striking adherence of the Roman army to the minutiae of Roman state religion, also indicated by dedications to Iupiter Optimus Maximus and to the imperial cult. But alongside this we also see a high level of engagement with local gods in syncretised form (Iupiter Hammon and Mars Canaphar are known from inscriptions dedicated by military personnel) and with a group of Eastern cults popular with the army. By way of contrast, the lack of epigraphic testimony from rural settlements in the security zone concerning the names of the gods worshipped is very striking (Table 7.4).

Here again, we see a marked disjunction between the practices of the military community and the civilian populations who lived around and interacted with the soldiers. By and large, Libyans who delivered agricultural supplies to the fort, or lived for a time in the garrison settlement, or participated in Saharan trade passing by the fort, do not seem to have worshipped in visible ways at the Bu Nijim temples, nor introduced the cultural practices of the army into their home settlements (see further Chapter 11). Despite the fact that some of the gods worshipped were local cults (Ammon/Hammon, Canaphar, Vanammon), in their syncretised forms they were subjected to a degree of transformation.[75] As Jane Webster has observed regarding religious syncretisation in Britain, explicit name-pairing of local and Roman gods was most commonly due to members of the military community. Name-pairing of gods was rare in Britain among autochthonous groups.[76] Syncretism in the military

74. Rebuffat 1982b; 1988a.
75. For older views on syncretism, see Leglay 1971; Picard 1954; to some extent this view still prevails today in Cadotte 2007.
76. Webster 1997a; 1997b.

zone can thus to some extent be seen as the military marking the subordination of local gods by Roman ones, just as local peoples had been subjugated. In propitiating the local gods and the spirits of the place (*genius loci*), the soldiers were taking precautions to ensure that these deities protected their water supply, desert journeys, and the general health and well-being of the garrison community. The religious practices of the *Gaetuli* were in general very differently expressed in terms of behaviours, architecture, and epigraphic testimony, as we shall see in Chapter 11.

The epigraphic evidence from other small forts elsewhere in the militarised zone is generally less comprehensive, though *Rapidum* in *Mauretania Caesariensis* has a number of inscriptions, statues and relief carvings, and temple remains.[77] The evidence attests to the worship of Africa, Ceres, Caelestis, Deus Patrius, Dii Mauri, Aesculapius (or at any rate a healing god), Fortune, a *genius loci*, Hygeia, Iupiter, Mercury, Priapus, Saturn, Silvanus, and Victory. With a few nods to local gods, this is a fairly typical assemblage of state cults.

Literary Pretensions: The Poetic Centurions of *Gholaia*

Two of the most remarkable inscriptions from *Gholaia* were acrostic poems written by legionary centurions in charge of the garrison at different moments in the life of the fort.[78] The first text was composed by the centurion responsible for the building of the baths in 202 CE. This 18-line poem is an acrostic disguising the name of Q. Avidius Quintianus and celebrating the relief that the baths offered from the scorching sun and winds of the desert (Table 7.5).[79]

The second inscription was erected by a centurion in command of a legionary detachment at the fort in 222 CE (Table 7.6). This records the reconstruction of the south gate of the fort (Fig. 7.8)—but the inscription is singular in several respects. It was found not by the gate, but in the fort baths. The reason for this unusual placement is clear when the form of the text is considered—it is a 33-line acrostic poem in Latin verse in which the name of the dedicator is revealed by the first letters of each line (though the poet/dedicator took no chances on this, by pointing out the cipher in the last line of the poem).

The poem is full of imagery of sweaty legionaries exerting themselves rebuilding the gate to a state of great magnificence. It was evidently composed in emulation of the rather better poetic effort of Avidius Quintianus. The literary ambitions of the two *Gholaia* centurions are extraordinarily interesting.[80]

---

77. Laporte 1989, 169–88.
78. Adams 1999; Rebuffat 1985c.
79. See detailed discussion in Adams 1999; Lavagnani 1928; Rebuffat 1987b.
80. Adams 1999, 113–34; Rebuffat 1985c; 1987; 1995b.

Table 7.5. *IRT* 918–919: The poem of Q. Avidius Quintianus (text and translation after Adams 1999, 110–11).

Quaesii multum quot memoriae trader	I have sought much what to hand down to posterity
Agens prae cunctos in hac castra milites	acting in command of all the soldiers in this fort
Votum communem proque reditu exercitu	and (what) common vow, for the return of the army
Inter priores et futuros reddere	to render up among previous and future (vows?).
Dum quaero mecum digna diuom nomina	While seeking privately worthy names of gods
Inueni tandem nomen et numen deae	I found at last the divine name of a goddess,
Votis perennem quem dicare in hoc loco	To whom to consecrate, everlastingly in vows, in this place.
Salutis igitur quandium cultores sient	Therefore, as long as there should be worshippers of Salus I have
Qua potui sanxi nomen et cunctis dedi	sanctified (her) name in the way I could, and I have given to all
Veras salutis lymphas tantis ignibus	the true waters of safety, amid such fires
In istis semper harenacis collibus	in those always sandy dunes
Nutantis austri solis flammas feruidas	of the south wind causing to shimmer the fiery flames of the sun
Tranquille ut nando delenirent corpora	so that by bathing peacefully they might soothe their bodies
Ita tu qui sentis magnam facti gratiam	And so you who feel great gratitude for (this) deed
Aestuantis animae fucilari spiritum	that the spirit of your burning soul is revived
Noli pigere laudem uoce reddere	do not be reluctant to render genuine praise with your voice
Veram qui uoluit esse te sanum tibi	(of him) who wanted you to be healthy for your own benefit
Set protestare uel salutis gratia	but bear witness even for the sake of Salus.

They were by no means unique, as two veterans prominent in the town of *Cillium* (Kasserine) erected mausolea on which not only their prior military service was commemorated, but also lengthy poems.[81] The architectural splendour of the Kasserine mausolea, decked out with statues and extensive Latin texts that put on record the careers of the deceased, make even more explicit the performative context of such behaviours. Lengthy verse poems on funerary monuments and other buildings were a feature of African society and are perhaps surprisingly common in the garrisoned regions and among the military community.[82]

What is particularly striking about M. Porcius Iasucthan is that his cognomen points to an origin in one of the security zones of Africa. The same man appears to have been transferred at a later stage of his career to Britain, to join *legio XX Valeria Victrix*, and made a dedication to the Dii Mauri at *Lambaesis*.[83] In every other respect he appears a model Roman soldier who has shed almost all traces

81. *CIL* 8.211–216 (Flavii) and 8.217–218 (Petronii); Lassère et al. 1993, 65–71 for the texts. Hitchner 1995a, for a perceptive discussion.

82. See Hamdoune 2016.

83. *CIL* 8.2638; Le Bohec 1989a, 181.

Table 7.6. The poem of M. Porcius Iasucthan (text and translation Adams 1999, 111–12. See also Rebuffat 1995b).

Imp caes M Aurelio Antonino pio felici aug sacerdoti amplissimo pontifici maximo trib pot v cos iiii p p et	In honour of imp. Caes. M. Aurelius Antoninus pius felix augustus, priest supreme, pontifex maximus, with tribunician power for the fifth time, consul for the fourth time, pater patriae and
M Aurelio Alexandro nobilissimo caes d n Antonini aug fil aug	of M. Aurelius Alexander, most noble Caesar, son of our master Antoninus augustus, augustus (himself)
Flauius Sossianus u e uice praesidis Numidiae per uexillationem	Flavius Sossianus, uir egregius, vice praeses of Numidia, through the uexillatio
leg iii Aug p u Antoninianae deuotissimi numini eorum	of the Legion III Augusta pia, uictrix, antoniniana, (all) devoted to their divinity
Portam uetustate conlabsam lapidi quadrato arco curuato restituit	restored the gate which had collapsed through age, by means of squared stone in a curved arch
Omnes praeteriti cuius labore uitabant	The labour of which (thing) all (our) predecessors avoided
Rigido uigore iuuenum tertia augustani fecerunt	(that), with firm vigour of the warriors, the third Augustans did
Creto consilio hortante parato magistro	by fixed design, encouraged by Paratus (?) the magister
Iuncta uirtus militum paucorum uelocitas ingens	linked (were?) the valour of a few soldiers (and) vast speed
Usui compendio lapides de longe adtractos chamulco	for use, by a saving of effort, stones drawn from afar by traction engine
Sub arcata militum uirtus funib cannabinis strictis	under the arches, the valour of the soldiers, with hempen ropes drawn tight
Iam nunc contendunt fieri cito milites omnes	now all the soldiers strive that it be quickly done
Arta uirtute sua opera aeternale fecerunt	by extreme(?) valour they did their eternal work
Subsequentes stipendiis antecessorum onestia bona sumebant	following upon the service of their predecessors they acquired honourable advantage (?)
Urguente tempore hiemis necumqua cessauerunt	with the period of winter pressing they never ceased
Celerius excelsae turres quater diuisae cum uoce militum a terra uenerunt	quickly the lofty towers, divided into four (stages?), came from the earth to the accompaniment of the voice of the soldiers
Torrens uirtus leg III Aug p u	the rushing valour of the Legion III Augusta pia victrix
Haec ut fierent milites omnes sibi zelum tradebant	that this should be done all the soldiers handed zeal to themselves
Animaduertentes quod priores sibi uestigia fecissent	noticing that their predecessors had made traces for them
Nunc et ipsi titulis suis uirtutis deuotionis ornauerunt	now they too adorned with their own marks (?) of valour (and?) loyalty
Contendentes si amplius esset athuc opera fecissent	eager that, if there were more, they should as well have done the work
Ex numero militum quidam amplius uoluntatem suam dederit	of the body of soldiers, one gave his enthusiasm more
Necumquam operam suam erupi exhibuerunt	never did they allow their work to be broken off
Tantus fuit eis zelus magna uir	so great was their zeal, and great
Laetis temporibus honoribus	in happy times honours
Effecta opera gaudet aeterna militum uirtus	the eternal valour of the soldiers rejoices in the completed work
Gemma ut auro cluditur sic castram porta decorat	As a jewel is set in gold, so the gate decorates the fort
Florida tertia Augusta legio cum magna uirtute	The flourishing Third Legion Augusta with great valour
Curauit faciendum deuotionis suae honorem	saw to it that it paid the honour of its obedience/loyalty
Muneri quoque dictatores strenue cesserunt	to the task as well the “dictators” strenuously devoted themselves (?)
Animosos duo contemnentes residuum turpis oppresserat	?
Capita uersorum relegens adgnosce curantem	reading the start of the verses, identify him who saw to it

Figure 7.8. Gates and towers at *Gholaia*. a) Lyon's painting of the well-preserved north gate in 1820. b) Graffito from the fort showing its tall gate and angle towers (from Mattingly et al. 2013a, 44, 86).

of his African identity in favour of the corporate values of the Roman military. The attempted literary emulation of his predecessor Quintianus (who probably originated in Italy) shows all too clearly the aspirational nature of military culture, where getting on was as much about linguistic abilities as physical brawn. However, the range of literate practice at *Gholaia* also reminds us of a key dimension of mastery of Latin. This was far from a perfect world of model Romans. While centurions composed (or commissioned) lengthy poems, some of the soldiers under their direct command struggled to write even simple reports using standardised formulaic model documents. Just as we saw in Hadrian's comments on his African troops, the military community operated in very hierarchical ways in which rank, status, pay, and education were often openly on display to reinforce social structure that in turn reflected very mixed levels of attainment and engagement with the Roman project.

Social Convergence in the Security Zones

My main contention in this chapter is that in the initial phases of garrison deployment the military community held itself aloof from local communities, using cultural behaviour and practice to reinforce its own identity and to create social distance. Initially, one suspects, the feeling was probably mutual, with indigenous populations living under military supervision keeping their distance too—socially and culturally—as far as that was physically allowed to them. However, over the long term, some degree of social convergence was almost inevitable, and over time we can also detect signs of African cultural resurgence in the security zones. I want to finish with a few late Roman and late antique examples to illustrate this.

There are obvious reasons why the Roman military will have been viewed initially as an alien occupying force: the painful process of conquest and "pacification," the loss of control of land and resources, the restrictions on free movement and assembly, the power inequalities that military rule created. As the army became more regionally embedded, there was increased local recruitment (even if this preferentially drew on garrison settlements and towns with a particular affiliation with the army, such as veteran colonies). The amenities at garrison settlements were somewhat different to normal towns—there was more emphasis on functional buildings. While there were often multiple temples, these were often quite small-scale rather than monumental. Baths and amphitheatres were the most common form of entertainment structures.[84]

The use of *praefecti gentium* and *principes gentium* also served to create new networks of power and patronage in society in and beyond the security zones, especially if Roman subsidies and gifts were part of the deal for keeping the peace. Prefects were initially serving military officers, but later the role was invested in civilians, who seem to have belonged to the upper echelon of the relevant people.[85] Regardless of the pre-Roman level of sedentary farming in different parts of the security zones, there is clear evidence that sedentarisation increased under Roman rule, and both outsiders and locals seem to have participated in the creation of estates, emphasising enhanced inequalities of wealth within society in the security zones.[86] There are indications that, in some security sectors, some degree of policing and local control was delegated to high-ranking individuals in rural society, often styled *praefecti gentium* and *reges* in late sources.[87] The increasingly fortified nature of rural buildings in the security zones has often been remarked on, though with varied interpretations. At one time these were seen as either an intensive defence in depth by the military or as deliberate settlements of soldier-farmers by the Roman state, but more recently they have tended to be interpreted as prestige buildings of local elites.[88] The form of these fortified structures can be recognised to imitate to a greater or lesser extent the architecture of genuine military installations (towers,

84. Baradez 1966a; 1966b; Laporte 1989.
85. Hamdoune 2018, 110–21; see also discussion in Chapter 6.
86. Baradez 1957; Birebent 1962; Soyer 1976.
87. Hamdoune 2018.
88. For older views, see Goodchild 1976. For more recent discussion, Mattingly 1989a; 2014b; Mattingly and Hayes 1992; Mattingly et al. 2013b.

Table 7.7. The inscription of the *Praesidium Sammacis (Ighzer Amokrane, M'Lakou, AE 1901, 50).*

*Praesidium aeternae firmat prudentia paci**S*** ***R**em quoque Romanam fida tutat undique dextr**A*** ***A**mni praepositum firmans munimine monte**M*** ***E** cuius nomen vocitavit nomine Petra**M*** ***D**enique finitimae gentes deponere bell**A*** ***I**n tua concurrunt cupientes foedera, Samma**C*** ***U**t virtus comitata fidem concordet in omn**I*** ***M**unere Romuleis semper sociata triumphi**S***
By this fortress, his Prudence affirms the eternity of peace From his faithful right, he [Sammac] protects from all attack that which is Roman he strengthens the mountain which commands the river by the fort, which he named Petra, from the name of the mountain. And here the peoples who around about want to lay down their arms and run to solicit your alliance, Sammac, so that valour in harness with fidelity agrees with it in all the duties, she who has always been allied to the triumphs of the sons of Romulus

outposts, and fortlets),[89] and in a few cases at least we can recognise that there was a genuine delegation of paramilitary powers to the occupant. This is most notably the case with the *praesidium* (fort) or *praedium* (estate) of Sammac near the Kabylie on a low hillock on the right bank of the Wadi Soummam (Table 7.7).[90]

The duality (or ambiguity) of the relationship between military function and agricultural domain is captured in the use of both terms in the inscription and the left-hand acrostic, but the text is clear about the quasi-military role played by Sammac in relation to the neighbouring peoples, as is also apparent in the description of the site in Ammianus Marcellinus (29.5.13).[91] Recent excavations at the site have emphasised its luxurious and agricultural aspect rather than its fortifications,[92] but other contemporary fortified estate centres in Mauretania reveal a characteristic cross-shaped layout, as at Ksar al-Kaoua (Ammi Moussa), Ksar Djerane, Ksar Khabaand Ksar Sedaja.[93] These sites also combine sturdy defensive features with luxurious internal layouts.[94] Several of these fortified estate centres had to be reduced during the campaigns of Theodosius against Firmus.[95]

89. Mackensen 2009; 2010a; Mattingly 1995, 98–106, 192–94; Mattingly et al. 2013b for an attempt at typology; Rushworth 2015.
90. Hamdoune 2018, 167–69; Lengrand 1992; Matthews 1976, 175–76.
91. Hamdoune 2018, 172.
92. Boukhenouf et al. 2017. See also Duval 1986 for the conventional view of how to reconstruct such fortified villas.
93. Hamdoune 2018, 174–77; Laporte 2014.
94. Laporte 2014 (for a detailed study of Ksar al-Kaoua).
95. Laporte 2014, 498–99.

Another strong contender for a site with a special relationship with the Roman authorities and the Roman security arrangements is the village of Ghirza in Tripolitania. The settlement comprises over 40 buildings, many of them fortified, including two vast complexes that are of unprecedented scale in the pre-desert.[96] The epigraphy and iconography from the monumental tombs in two cemeteries associated with Ghirza reveal the identity of the elite families in the settlement to have been Libyco-Roman. The adoption of Roman *nomina* alongside Libyan *cognomina* and the use of Latin in some of the funerary texts suggests a closer than usual relationship between the settlement and the Roman state, and the tombs are full of imagery reflecting the exercise of delegated military and social power.[97]

The classic style of late Roman fort (the *quadriburgus*), with prominent external bastion towers at the corners and along the outer walls, also seems to have impacted on rural architecture more generally in late Roman times. A valid question in relation to Figure 7.9 is which of the sites featured were formally military sites in the late Roman period? The answer is that we do not know for sure: none of the sites is particularly large and all lie in areas of civil settlements. Ksar Graouch (60 km east of Gafsa) has sometimes been interpreted as Byzantine in date; Bularkan lies at a strategic crossroads in the Libyan pre-desert, and Benia Guedah Ceder just 1.1 km from the gateway through the Tebaga *clausura*.[98] We may also note the comparisons with the sites illustrated in Figures 5.7 and 5.8, which are late Garamantian fortified villages lying 500 km outside the Roman Empire.[99] An unintended consequence of the creation of the garrison posts was that civilians in the security zone and neighbours of the Empire were increasingly likely to construct sites that mimicked the outward form of Roman military architecture.[100] Wider identities become entangled in such processes, and we need more work on the fate of the Roman military deployment precisely because it seems to underlie to some degree the emergence of new power structures and states in the late and post-Roman period.

A further example concerns a series of inscriptions from a remote pre-desert location to the west of Ghirza, where a cemetery of atypical cremation burials was discovered in relation with a series of engraved Latino-Punic stelae, some of which mention the Latin title of *tribunus*. A strong case can be made for associating these burials with the occupants of a dense cluster of fortified farms in the Bir Scedua basin c.12 km to the north.[101] As with Ghirza, this looks a strong contender for some

96. Barker et al. 1996a, 133–34; 1996b, 118–20; Brogan and Smith 1984; Mattingly 1995, 197–200.
97. Barker et al. 1996a, 338–42; Mattingly 1995, 206–07; 1999; 2003b.
98. Barker et al. 1996a, 173–75, 178 (Md3, Gasr Bularkan); Trousset 1974, 134 (Benia Guedah Ceder)..
99. Mattingly et al. 2020a, 80–81.
100. Rushworth 2015; Smith 1971 for divergent views on the difference between *centenaria* and *castra*.
101. Goodchild 1954d; cf. Barker et al. 1996a, 144, 341; 1996b, 78–80. On the Bir Scedua *gsur*, see Barker et al. 1996b, 43–55.

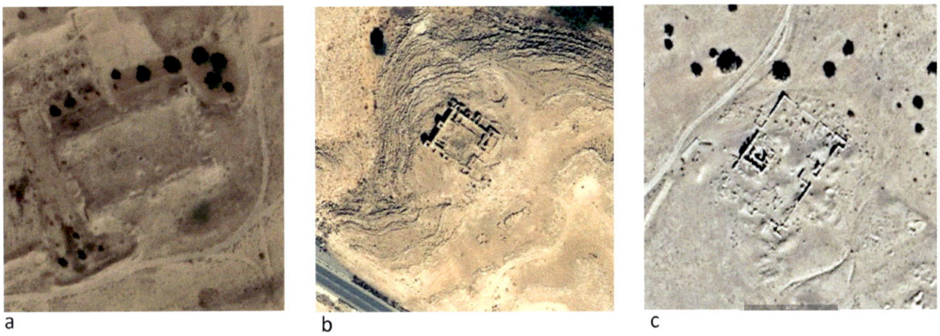

Figure 7.9. Military or civil *quadriburgi*? a) Ksar Graouch, Tunisia. b) Gasr Bularkan, Wadi Merdum, Libya. c) Henchir Benia Guedah Ceder, Tunisia (Martin Sterry montage, images: Google, DigitalGlobe).

elements of military control having been formally delegated by Rome to a prominent Libyan elite landholding group.

Similarly, when the Roman Empire in Africa collapsed in the face of the Vandal invasion, the old military commands based on regional *limites* seem to have formed the basis for a number of the sub-Roman Berber kingdoms that came into being. This is illustrated, for instance, by the *Altava* inscription of one of these kings, Masuna, who was using an old Roman fort and garrison settlement as his base. The text is remarkable in that it reveals Roman titles, the Latin language, and some Roman nomenclature continuing in this ex-security zone long after the effective end of Roman rule (the inscription dates to the early years of the 6th century).

> For the health and safety of Masuna, king of the Moorish peoples and the Romans, the fort has been constructed by Masgivin, prefect of Safar. Idier, procurator at *Castra Severiana*, who Masuna assigned to *Altava*, and Maximus, procurator at *Altava*, achieved the work in the year 469 of the provinces.[102]

This is either a case of a descendant of the military garrison carrying on as an effective warlord, or of a newcomer modelling power on the most potent regional structure available (the use of Latin suggests the former possibility, as Rushworth has argued).[103] It shows the longevity of the military community in this region through the maintenance of some of its core behaviours and institutions and the continued occupation of its forts.

---

102. *CIL* 8.9835: *Pro sal(ute) et incol(umitate) reg(is) Masunae gent(ium)/ Maur(orum) et Romanor(um). Castra edific(atum) a Mas/giuni pref(ecto) de Safar. Iider proc(urator) Cast/ ra Severian(a) quem Masuna Altava posuit/ et Maxim(us) proc(urator) Alt(ava) perfec(erunt) (anno) pr(ovinciarum) CCCCLXVIIII*; Camps 1984, 192–97; Hamdoune 2018, 343–48.

103. Rushworth 2000; 2004.

An indication of the political significance of these late antique kingdoms is provided by the remarkable series of 13 great stepped tombs known as Djedar near Tiaret in western Algeria.[104] The location is close to the *nova praetentura* of the Roman security zone and the fort of Ain Sbiba, some 200 km east of *Altava*. The tombs fall into two main groups, A–C and D–M. Oriented towards the east, they had a square plan, but rose as low stepped pyramids above the base. The largest (F) was a square of 46 m side (with an estimated original elevation of 18.5 m), but several others are 30 m square or more (A, C, J)—containing multiple internal chambers accessed by long entrance corridors. Fragmentary Latin inscriptions link them with the Latinate world of the *Altava* text.[105]

In later antiquity, while some things like the use of Latin and Roman military titles were maintained, the African reference points of the former military communities became much more overt. Although Fentress and Wilson have noted the fact that the Djedar tombs are profoundly influenced by Saharan forms and suggest an association with a new migration of Saharan peoples into the region,[106] in many respects they reflect long-term cultural preferences of the *Gaetuli*. In any event, they mark a shift of the cultural balance of power within the military community of the Roman security zone, from more Roman to more indigenous forms of cultural expression.

104. Kadra 1983; Laporte 2005. Dating: Camps 1984; 1995d; Fentress 2019, 513–14.
105. Laporte 2005, 351–54 (A), 358–60 (B), 364–66 (C); Rushworth 2000.
106. Fentress and Wilson 2016.

Part 4: The Urban Communities

Chapter 8

DIFFERENT TOWNS AND VARIED TRAJECTORIES

Introduction: An Urban Society

It is widely acknowledged that the Roman Empire was "a world of cities," notwithstanding the fact that the vast majority of the population lived in the countryside. Towns were crucial to governance, the administration of law, tax collection, manufacturing and market activity, religious and social activity, entertainment and other lifestyle facilities, and the emergence of distinctive forms of consumerism. Ancient urbanism is also a central feature of the foundation myths of Western civilisation (and as such something we need to deconstruct carefully).[1]

The urban achievements of "Roman Africa" have been widely acclaimed.[2] Towns are in many ways the fundamentals of modern study of the African provinces. The figures suggested for the number of cities vary, but in late Roman times something in the order of 500 is a widely cited benchmark for the African provinces overall and 200 for *Africa* alone (excluding *Tripolitana*, *Byzacena*, *Numidia*, and the Mauretanian provinces).[3] The archaeology of the 19th and 20th centuries set the pattern through a preponderant emphasis on exposing the remains of long-abandoned towns for the greater glory of the modern colonial projects.[4] At the same time, the colonial regimes were also major despoilers and obliterators of ancient sites in the interests of swift modern development, especially at coastal ports and key strategic

1. As Woolf 2020 has shown, there were multiple lines of ancient urbanism in the Mediterranean zone and the story is not one of smooth, progressive evolution. Many of his sceptical judgements about the Roman cities find echoes in my account below, though I encountered his book at a late stage in writing these pages.
2. Bertrandy and Coltelloni-Trannoy 2005, 77–94; Briand-Ponsart and Hugoniot 2006, 91–140, 348–74; Corbier and Griesheimer 2005, 371–417; Ibba and Traina 2006, 104–20; Lassère 2015, 367–400; Le Bohec 2005a, 109–31, 207–22; Picard 1990, 155–97. The main focus of many historical accounts is on the status of towns within an urban hierarchy, their monumentalisation, and the detailed knowledge of the elite families and religious practices discernible through the epigraphic record.
3. Lepelley 1981, 121–39 for the most comprehensive attempt at a list based on urban status; Hobson 2020 for a classification that mixes different legal statuses, but that includes about 1,000 sites that span the urban spectrum from *megalopolis* to road station; Picard 1990, 26–27, 56; Wilson 2011, 183.
4. Balice 2010; Mattingly 2011a, 50–57; Mattingly and Hitchner 1995, 179–87; McCarty 2018; Munzi 2001; 2004; 2012.

locations, resulting in a potentially biased sample.[5] The overall syntheses of the city in Africa are now somewhat dated or still focus on the same traditional themes and the same major examples.[6] Two recent projects have generated important data on the North African cities, especially on their size and potential populations (on which more below).[7] Some of the most interesting work of synthesis has concerned changes in the nature of the city in late Roman times.[8]

With well-preserved architectural elements, monumental complexes suited for restoration, and an abundance of mosaics, statuary, and inscriptions, the Roman town in Africa was a godsend for modern imperialists seeking inspiration and justification. They are amazing and beautiful places to visit—my own first encounter with *Lepcis Magna* was life-changing.[9] Most studies of the African provinces have made the towns the primary focus; some have never got further than the urban centres. To a large extent, this is a reflection on the archaeological, iconographical, and epigraphical realities. However, the resulting picture of Roman towns in Africa is potentially problematic in a number of ways. First, it presents a somewhat pristine spectacle of urban success and conformity to Roman norms, with a strong focus on the public monuments and elite housing. Second, visitors are encouraged to marvel at the "Roman" achievement in Africa, with the deserted aspect of the romantic ruins also highlighted to evoke the decline and fall of civilisation in post-Roman times. Since the late antique and post-Roman levels were commonly shovelled away without record in order to quickly expose the monumental structures and mosaics of the High Empire, the apparent rapid collapse of urban civilisation is at least in part an artefact of the modern colonial discourse, making assumptions appear real.[10] Third, the quality of most of the earliest excavations was poor: large work gangs with varying levels of supervision were tasked with clearing areas of

5. Effros 2018; Greenhalgh 2014. Many of the most extensively excavated sites were in relatively remote rural locations and, as we shall see, the harbour cities are less well understood from colonial-era excavations.
6. For overview studies of North Africa towns, see Bullo 2002; Cagnat 1909; Mahjoubi 2000; Romanelli 1970; Sears 2011; Toutain 1895; 1912. See also Laurence et al. 2011 for an attempt at placing the African cities in the west Mediterranean context. Scheding 2019 is an important new study that takes some similar approaches to those advocated in this chapter, but which appeared too late to be fully integrated here. See also the important summary chapters by Dufton and Fentress 2022; Scheding 2020; Stone 2020.
7. The Oxford Roman Economy Project has frequently discussed North African towns; see, inter alia, Wilson 2011. The Empire of 2000 Cities ERC-funded project at Leiden has re-evaluated the information on a large number of urban sites, see now Hobson 2020 for an important new synthesis.
8. Fenwick 2019; Leone 2007a; 2013b; Potter 1995; Sears 2007.
9. Mattingly 2019 for the autobiographical details.
10. For rare examples of the recording of late antique levels that illustrate how much has been lost elsewhere, see Benseddik and Potter 1993 (*Caesarea*); Mahjoubi 1978 (*Belalis Maior*); Mohamedi et al. 1991 (*Sitifis*); Stirling et al. 2001 (*Leptiminus*); Ward-Perkins et al. 1986 (*Ptolemais*). For up-to-date discussions on transitions into Islamic era, see Bockmann et al. 2019; Fenwick 2020; Leone 2007a; 2013b.

the ruins down to solid floors and walls. Finds were very much secondary, with the important exceptions of inscriptions, architectural elements (which were generally carefully collected for potential future restoration), items of statuary, and mosaics. Intact portable items (metals, pottery/ceramic, glass, coins) were routinely collected, though not always very accurately located spatially. For pottery and glass, museum-quality specimens tended to be acquired through rapid and poorly recorded "treasure hunts" in cemeteries, which paid little attention to the human remains or to the associations of grave markers and subsurface features. Such practices were very much of their era and are highlighted here primarily because of the consequences for our overall knowledge.

While the major monuments and artworks recovered are of undeniable importance, it leaves us with a problem akin to interpreting the story of the world based only on dinosaur bones and ignoring mammalian and other species. We have some extensive plans of Roman cities (or substantial quarters of them), but far less chronological understanding of their evolution and phasing. This is compounded by the fact that a large number of major excavations of the colonial era were never published in any adequate fashion. Astonishingly, as late as the 1950s relatively few cities had a monographic publication, and for many sites the best summary account was a scholarly guidebook.[11] Of course, a huge amount of publication had taken the form of preliminary articles in a wide range of journals, both international and more local, but in a subject where the monograph has become established as the "gold standard" for reporting excavations, the relative scarcity of such works from more than 150 years of intensive activity is striking.[12] For dating major public buildings, inscriptions can come to our rescue, but the epigraphic record is fragmentary and the urban story involves more than just urban promotions and acts of civic benevolence (euergetism) by leading citizens. Towns were important centres of population, markets and economic activity, consumption, religion, local jurisdiction, and cultural and identity expression. I sketch out some of the key elements and infrastructure of the urban community in this chapter and turn to its identity and behavioural choices in Chapter 9.

There is a greater awareness today that the urban civilisation of Africa in the Roman Empire was a rich amalgam of cultural influences, Roman, Punic, and Libyan and not simply a colonial imposition.[13] But there is still a tendency to aggregate all

11. For sites with monographic reports, the key early exemplars were *Thamugadi*—Ballu 1897; 1903; 1911; Boeswillwald et al. 1892–1904; *Madauros*, *Thubursicu Numidarum*, *Thibilis*—Gsell and Joly 1914; 1918; 1922; *Lepcis Magna*: Romanelli 1925. *Mactaris* is an example of a site with a published report, Picard et al. 1977, but where there has been a continuing lack of an overview study; though see now M'charek 1986. Examples of important sites where the "monographic" study was essentially a guidebook summary include: *Cuicul*, Ballu 1926; Leschi 1953; *Thugga*, Poinssot 1958.
12. For the site of Thugga, the key publications were long in articles only, Poinssot 1919 or in extended guidebook, Poinssot 1958.
13. See the balanced synthesis of Wilson 2020.

the evidence together to illustrate the false paradigm of Romanisation.[14] Part of the problem is that our image of Roman urbanism in Africa is constructed around a series of spectacular sites and monuments—let us call these "The Usual Suspects"—with not enough questioning by writers and readers of just *how* these were typical of the broader class of urban sites. A recent book[15] on *The Cities of Roman Africa* illustrates the tendency in its choice of plans and photographs: three sites provided 60% of the visual images of African towns, and the book only featured 17 towns in total from the c.500. If we add in seven other recent books on "Roman Africa" (Table 8.1), from a list of 39 cities, just 6 sites provide c.57%, and the top 10 accounts for 71% of all the images of towns featured.[16] The tendency is even more apparent if one analyses the coffee table books of images of the architectural and artistic jewels of North African archaeology.[17] While the exact composition of the "top 10" may vary across different books, there is a large gap between the pool of around 30 highly illustrated cities and the overall total of urban sites. This is a crude analysis, but it makes the point that our vision of what the North African town was like is shaped disproportionately by a limited number of sites.

A specific problem with the emphasis on commonalities under the Romanisation paradigm is that it commonly elides over points of divergence from perceived Roman norms. As an example of this, it is interesting to scrutinise reconstruction drawings of Roman towns in North Africa to see how far they are supported by the evidence on the ground. A particularly misleading aspect is the tendency to show large numbers of buildings with tile roofs, in the manner of Italian cities.[18] My personal experience is that tile roofs were comparatively rare in Africa; for instance, field survey at *Leptiminus* revealed a very light scatter of tile fragments across the urban core, consistent with prestige public buildings like temples having tiled roofs, but suggesting that domestic buildings were primarily flat-roofed, not dissimilar to more recent vernacular architecture in the Maghrib.[19] I suggest that not all African towns looked like Italian Roman centres, and not all of them looked the same as

14. On the different understandings of what is meant by Romanisation, see discussion in Chapter 2.
15. Sears 2011. His 71 illustrations feature *Lepcis Magna* 23 times, *Karthago* 11 times, *Thugga* 9 times, *Thamugadi* 3 times, Kerkouane, *Sufetula*, *Lambaesis*, *Oea*, *Cyrene*, *Thuburbo Maius*, *Thysdrus*, *Cuicul* twice each, with a small group (mostly predictable names like *Sabratha*, *Caesarea*, *Volubilis*, *Theveste*, *Gigthis*) just once.
16. Table 8.1 combines information from Sears 2011 with analysis of Briand-Ponsart and Hugoniot 2006; Corbier and Griesheimer 2005; Géroudet and Ménard 2005; Ibba and Traina 2006; Lassère 2015; Le Bohec 2005a; Picard 1990. Of the other textbooks published since 2005, Bertrandy and Coltelloni-Trannoy 2005 and Prévot et al. 2006 have no photographs or plans of individual sites.
17. See, for example, Baratte 2012 (top ten sites provide 79% of illustrations); Laronde and Golvin 2001 (top ten, 75%).
18. See, for example, Golvin's illustrations in Laronde and Golvin 2001 for images of *Karthago* and *Thugga*. His images of predominantly flat-roofed domestic buildings at *Lepcis* and Kerkouane seem more plausible.
19. Stone et al. 2011a, 168–70, 476.

Table 8.1. The "Usual Suspects." Illustrations of North African cities in recent text books.

Site	Picard 1990	Corbier & Griesheimer 2005	Le Bohec 2005a	Briand-Ponsart & Hugoniot 2006	Géroudet & Ménard 2005	Ibba & Traina 2006	Sears 2011	Lassère 2015	Total
Lepcis Magna			1		4	1	23	2	31
Karthago	2	3		2		1	11	6	25
Thamugadi	1	4	6		1		3	9	24
Thugga			5	1		1	9		16
Thysdrus	4				1		2	5	12
Cuicul	1	3		2	2		2	1	11
Clipea								8	8
Iol Caesarea	1		1			1	1	4	8
Theveste		2		2			1	3	8
Sitifis		2					1	2	5
Sufetula		1	1				2	1	5
Hippo		2						2	4
Pupput		4							4
Thabraca								4	4
Tipasa		1						3	4
Volubilis			1		1	1	1		4
Ammaedara			2					1	3
Bulla Regia	1		2						3
Mactaris	3								3
Acholla	2								2
Cyrene							2		2
Lambaesis							2		2
Oea							2		2
Simitthu								2	2
Thelepte								2	2
Thuburbo Maius							2		2
Tiddis								2	2
Cillium		1							1
Cirta								1	1
Gigthis							1		1
Hadrumetum								1	1
Madauros								1	1
Rusicade								1	1
Sabratha			1						1

(Continued)

Table 8.1. *(Continued)*

Site	Picard 1990	Corbier & Griesheimer 2005	Le Bohec 2005a	Briand-Ponsart & Hugoniot 2006	Géroudet & Ménard 2005	Ibba & Traina 2006	Sears 2011	Lassère 2015	Total
Thicnica								1	1
Uthina								1	1
Utica								1	1
Uzalis								1	1
Vaga								1	1

each other. We need to investigate this evidence of difference and diversity more closely in relation to the physical traces from each site.

The unusual prominence of some sites over others in publications on "Roman Africa" has much to do with preservation. The imposing bulk of the *Thysdrus* (El Djem) amphitheatre still dominates the skyline in modern times. Another factor is the history of excavation and research. The site of *Thamugadi* (Timgad), for instance, was very extensively excavated during the colonial era and was one of the few to see significant publication.[20] During the colonial era, many other cities saw extensive clearance excavations of key monuments or urban quarters, coupled with major reconstruction programmes on the more significant exposed monuments.[21] It is fair enough to say that "we work with what we have," but more consideration could be given to the typicality of specific sites and monuments, or the extent to which expectations are still shaped by colonial discourse. Roman archaeology was to some extent subordinated to the architectural study of the major urban monuments.[22] In Libya, Italian archaeologists were particularly active.[23] French epigraphers and archaeologists dominated much of the Maghrib, though Spanish researchers also played an important role in northern Morocco.[24]

While the strength of the contributions of Maghribian scholars will be very evident in my footnotes below, foreign teams have continued to be involved in the postcolonial work at many urban sites. In Libya, the Italian Missions of various

20. Ballu 1897; 1903; 1911; Boeswillwald et al. 1892–1904; Lassus 1969; 1981.
21. See, for instance, Poinssot 1919 for a major early excavation in the forum area at *Thugga*.
22. Ferchiou 1975; Gros 1996.
23. See many volumes on individual monuments and classes of artworks in the *Monografie di Archeologia Libica* series. Note also Balice 2010, for the explicitly colonial context of the early excavations.
24. Babelon et al. 1893/1913; Dondin-Payre 1988; Gsell 1901a; 1901b; 1911; Salama 1999b.

universities have dominated urban archaeology at *Cyrene*, *Lepcis Magna*, and *Sabratha*.[25] Work by British, French, and Polish foreign missions has also been important in research at Libya's Classical cities in the east (*Apollonia*, *Berenice*, *Euesperides*, *Ptolemais*, *Tocra*) and west (*Lepcis Magna* and *Sabratha*).[26] Work by Libyan archaeologists on the cities and their suburbs is also to be noted, but has tended to be smaller in scale.[27]

In Tunisia, both because of Mhamed Fantar's extensive excavations and its premature abandonment as a settlement, Punic Kerkouane has achieved particular scholarly prominence (out of proportion to its ancient political importance).[28] Important collaborations between Tunisia's national heritage agency (INP) and French teams have been developed off the back of earlier colonial-era investigations: in the High Steppe area at *Ammaedara* and *Sufetula*,[29] in the upper *Bagrada* valley at *Bulla Regia*,[30] or the Roman colony of *Uthina* in the lower Miliane valley.[31] German–Tunisian teams have become more prominent in recent decades, for instance through exemplary work at the marble quarry town of *Simitthu* (Chemtou).[32] *Thugga* has emerged as a particular focus for intensive investigation by Tunisian colleagues with several international groups, improving publication of its monuments and the voluminous epigraphic records, with correspondingly high-quality data from the rural landscape too.[33] Italian and Spanish teams have also had joint projects with the INP at *Uchi Maius* and *Althiburos* respectively.[34] *Karthago* is particularly notable for the scale of excavations carried out by multiple international teams, though not all the work has been fully published.[35] Tunisian

25. See, inter alia, Bianchi Bandinelli et al. 1966; Bonacasa and Ensoli 2000; De Miro and Polito 2005; Di Vita 2010a; 2015a; 2015b; 2017; Di Vita et al. 1999; Fabricotti and Menozzi 2006; Gasperini and Marengo 2007; Luni 2006; 2010; 2014; Stucchi 1976; Stucchi and Luni 1987.
26. For Cyrenaican cities, see, for example, Goodchild 1976; Jaworski and Misiewicz 2015; Lloyd 1977; Lloyd et al. 1998; Michel 2013; 2015; Wilson 2005; 2006b; Zelazowski 2012. For Tripolitania, see, Jones 1989b; Kenrick 1986; Mattingly 1995, 116–37; Ward-Perkins 1993.
27. For example, Abdrbba 2018 on suburbs.
28. Fantar 1984; 1985; 1986.
29. *Ammaedara*: Baratte and Duval 1974; Baratte et al. 1999; Ben Abdallah 1996; Ben Abdallah and Naddari 2013; Duval 1975; 1982a; *Sufetula*: Duval 1971; 1973; 1982b; 1990; Duval and Baratte 1973.
30. *Bulla Regia*: Beschaouch et al. 1977; 1983; Broise and Thébert 1993.
31. Ben Hassen and Maurin 1998; 2004.
32. Khanoussi and von Rummel 2012; Rakob 1993; 1994; 2005.
33. Aounallah and Golvin 2016; Aounallah and Maurin 2013; Golvin and Khanoussi 2005; Khanoussi, M. and Maurin, L. 1997; 2000; 2002; Khanoussi and Strocka 2002; Ritter and Von Rummel 2015; Saint Amans 2004; Stutz 2007.
34. *Uchi Maius*: Khanoussi and Mastino 1997; Ibba 2001; Vismara 2007; *Althiburos*: Kallala and Sanmartí 2011; Kallala et al. 2016; 2018 (following earlier work of Ennaifer 1976).
35. On the great UNESCO excavation programme initiated in the 1970s, see Ennabli 1992; 2020; Humphrey 1980a. For rare examples of detailed publication of excavation results, including a wide range of artefact types and palaeoeconomic and environmental data, see Humphrey 1976b; 1977; 1978a; 1978b; 1980b; 1981; 1982; 1988. See also the important but still incomplete series of Fulford and Peacock1984; 1994; Hurst 1994; 1999; Hurst and Roskams 1984.

researchers with American and German colleagues have recently been making major advances in knowledge in southern Tunisia and especially on the island of Jerba.[36] At *Leptiminus*, *Meninx*, and *Segermes* archaeologists have deployed intensive field survey methods to the study of the ancient city, with groundbreaking work in terms of expanding knowledge of the growth and shrinkage of sites across time, suburban economic activity, and relations with the immediate hinterland.[37] The use of geophysical survey techniques at these and other sites has proved another important tool for expanding knowledge of large areas, given the unfeasibility of excavations on the same scale as the destructive clearances of the colonial era.[38]

In Algeria, the nature of archaeological work changed dramatically after independence, with much more restrictive access for foreign teams. Much of the urban research has focused on back-log publication, as at *Cuicul*, *Tiddis*, and *Tipasa*.[39] Two urban sites where some renewed fieldwork has been possible are also among the best published, *Caesarea* and *Lambaesis*.[40] The latter is of course an important military settlement as well as a town, and the archive-based publication of old excavations at *Rapidum* is a key example of a Mauretanian garrison settlement.[41]

The post-independence pattern in Morocco has been similar to Tunisia, with continuing engagement of foreign missions, notably French in the south and Spanish in the north, but also Italian.[42] Of the cities of *Tingitana*, little is known of *Tingi*, buried beneath modern Tangiers, but *Volubilis* and *Lixus* have seen substantial publications.[43] Despite extensive excavations at *Banasa*, *Sala*, and *Zilil*, the state of publication on those sites leaves many questions still unclear.[44]

---

36. Ben Tahar 2014; 2018; Fentress et al. 2009; Ritter and Ben Tahar 2020.
37. *Leptiminus*: Ben Lazreg and Mattingly 1992; Ben Lazreg et al. 2006; 2021; Ben Younès and Sghaïer 2018; Stirling et al. 2000; Stone et al. 2011a; *Meninx*: Fentress et al. 2009, 133–76; Ritter and Ben Tahar 2020; Ritter et al. 2018; *Segermes*: Dietz et al. 1995a; 1995b.
38. *Leptiminus*: Stone et al. 2011a, 91–120; *Meninx*: Fentress et al. 2009, 16–37, 153–57; Ritter et al. 2018; *Simitthu*: von Rummel and Schöne 2013; von Rummel et al. 2013. Cf. also a Moroccan example from *Banasa*, Lenoir 1996.
39. *Cuicul*: Février 1978; Février and Blanchard-Lemée 2019; *Tiddis*: Berthier 2000; *Tipasa*: Lancel 1970 (a summary account).
40. *Caesarea*: Benseddik and Potter 1993; Leveau 1984; Potter 1995; *Lambaesis*: Duval 1995; Janon 2005.
41. Laporte 1989. For other discussions of urban settlements in *Mauretania Caesariensis*, see Hamdoune 2015; 2018, 47–51; Laporte 2009.
42. Mugnai 2018, 37–54 for an excellent summary of the major individuals and teams active pre- and post-independence.
43. *Lixus*: Aranegui Gascó 2001; 2005; Aranegui Gascó and Hassini 2010; Mugnai 2018, 155–70; Ponsich 1981; *Volubilis*: Étienne 1960; Euzennat 1989, 200–39; Jodin 1987; Morestin 1980; Mugnai 2018, 81–110; Panetier 2002; Thouvenot 1958. On post-Roman *Volubilis* see now, Fentress and Limane 2018; Fenwick 2020, 72–74.
44. Mugnai 2018, 48–49 for the evidence and the problems, 11–54 on *Banasa* and *Sala*. See also Chatelain 1931; Lenoir 1996; 2005; Thouvenot 1941. Brouquier-Reddé has been leading an important project in recent decades looking at the temples in *Mauretania Tingitana*, with important results, see for example in Baratte et al. 2018. For the smaller and less "Roman" site of Rirha, see Chapter 4 above and Callegarin et al. 2016a-d.

North Africa has long been a key theatre for ancient mosaic studies, with urban excavations providing many of the most stunning finds.[45] Important work has been done in locating these finds within their architectural setting, in the process improving our knowledge of the urban plan of a number of poorly published sites.[46] This links with a strong research interest in elite houses and their broader architectural and decorative embellishment.[47]

It may seem self-evident that our picture of urban life and *Romanitas* is very much framed around elite lifestyles and identity. It is all too easy to construct a stereotype of aristocratic culture and values around the globalised high culture of Empire (marble, mosaics, wall paintings, Classical allusions, statuary, luxurious dining suites, public amenities for leisure and entertainment, and so on). Less commonly has the question been asked how non-elite lives fitted into this picture. These individuals made up the majority of the urban population and it is surely mistaken to assume that they lived their lives in pale imitation of elite behaviours and desires. The cultural footprint of these people was probably very different.

The inequalities of evidence from Africa are considerable—the wealth of epigraphic data is both a blessing and a curse, and the same can be said for the architectural and artistic treasures that have been uncovered in profusion. These can be readily inflated to cover up deficiencies in our knowledge of ordinary material culture from urban sites. The remarkable analysis of house assemblages at *Trimithis* in the Daklah oasis in Egypt by Anna Boozer shows what can be achieved when sites are excavated and published in full detail.[48] Two very different contemporary households have been revealed by her: one belonging to a town councillor and rather oriented to globalised Roman culture; the other less well-to-do and much more involved with Egyptian and Greek cultural behaviours. The identities presented by these two contemporary households were thus distinctive and full of social significance. This is the sort of work that is needed in Africa, but that cannot easily be reconstructed from the archaeological data presently available.

In Chapters 3 to 5 I explored the changing picture of early urbanism in North Africa, with much greater emphasis now on Numidian, Mauretanian, and Saharan proto-urbanism to put alongside the Greek, Libyphoenician, and Roman "colonial" cities.[49] A key aspect of this work has been that it has looked beyond the "usual

45. Among other major site publications, see for *Acholla*: Gozlan 1992; Gozlan and Jeddi 2001; *Bulla Regia*: Hanoune 1980; *Caesarea*: Ferdi 2005; *Clipea*: Lassère and Slim 2010; *Cuicul*: Blanchard-Lemée 1975; Février and Blanchard-Lemée 2019; *Thamugadi*: Germain 1969. For larger overviews, see Ben Abed and Soren 1987; Blanchard-Lemée et al. 1996; Dunbabin 1978.

46. See the detailed survey work of the Corpus des Mosaïques de la Tunisie at: *Utica*, CMT I.1–I.3; *Thuburbo Maius* and nearby sites, CMT I.1–II.4; *Thysdrus*, CMT III.1; *Karthago*, CMT IV.1. 1973–1999.

47. Carucci 2007; Ghedini and Bullo 2003; Rebuffat 1969a; 1974a; Stutz 2007; Thébert 1987.

48. Boozer 2012.

49. See also Ardeleanu 2015; Mattingly 2016.

suspects" and recognised that Roman towns in Africa were not in fact identical, or even necessarily points on a single spectrum. The great diversity of urban forms has been previously acknowledged, of course, but the implications have not been followed through.[50] However, we now must be challenged to think about urbanisation as following a number of different trajectories, wherein the variance is as important to our understanding as recognising the commonalities that the traditional Romanisation model has focused on. This requires us above all to consider the variability of the urban populations, ethnically, culturally, socially.

In one of the fundamental works on "Roman Africa", published in 1977, Jean-Marie Lassère asked: *ubique populus*? His answer, drawn on over 700 pages of detailed epigraphic and demographic analysis, was that the picture was far more mixed than the early French colonial studies had imagined, with Africans contributing in vast numbers to the complexity and success of the Roman imperial project. While he traced the impacts of veterans and foreign migrants in the construction of *Africa*, he adduced more fully than ever before the impressive evidence of Africans taking on Latin names and playing significant roles in their communities.[51] The book was in some ways a riposte to the early stages of postcolonial debate about resistance to Rome, in that it repositioned the conventional notion of what Romanisation had achieved:

> What then is "Roman" Africa? … A handful of more or less pure Italians, a few diverse provincials, a good number of hybrid half-bloods, and a lot of pure Romanised Africans: these are the Roman citizens in an African city who attract to them the masses of Libyans from the surrounding country.[52]

Despite the extraordinary value of his demographic analysis, the cosy consensus that the demographic and cultural mix in Africa can best be understood via the positive paradigm of Romanisation needs to be challenged. After 35 further years of postcolonial debate, it is perhaps time to insist on more attention being paid to an additional question to Lassère's original: *cui bono*? Romanisation theory is not well suited to addressing this question (or the related issue of who lost out) as it tends to conflate everything around an idealised average. Imperial systems are all about winners and losers, and with social inequalities widening under Rome, the latter almost certainly outnumbered the former. To understand the nature of inequalities in such systems, we need to be more explicit about who benefited and the extent to which they are representative of specific groups rather than of society as a whole.

50. Le Bohec 2005a, 116; Maurin and Peyras 1990, 126: "nos cites étonnent par leur diversité."
51. Lassère 1977, 647–62 for his conclusions.
52. Lassère 1977, 660: "Qu'est ce alors que l'Afrique "romain'? … Une poignée d'Italiens plus ou moins pure, quelques provinciaux divers, bon nombre de demi-sang hybrids, et beaucoup de pur africaines romanisés: voilà quels sont, dans une ville africaine, les citoyens romains qui attirent vers eux la masse des Libyens du plat pays.."

In this book, I review the evidence in relation to several broad groups of people: the indigenous societies, the military communities, and the urban and rural communities. In what follows I again seek to counteract the homogenising tendencies of the Romanisation paradigm, in favour of an approach that highlights aspects of heterogeneity and difference between distinct types of both towns and townspeople. I shall argue not only that urban communities differed one from the next in ways that require explanations more complicated than the availability of resources, but also that these varied forms of urban expression had profound social meanings and were widely employed to create and sustain feelings of superiority or difference, as well as strong local or communal identities.

The Names, Numbers, and Legal Statuses of Towns

How many towns were there in Africa under Rome? The often cited range of 400–600 reflects the varied drawing of boundaries (chronological and geographical).[53] A lot depends on how we define towns, of course, and in the context of the Roman Empire there is a tendency to fall back on questions of legal status, since local government and law was to some extent devolved to and enacted through urban centres with defined constitutions. Here, of course, we are overdependent on the epigraphic evidence, whether through large dossiers from excavated sites or the chance survivals at many unexcavated ones. What is clear is that the number of administratively functional towns grew under Rome, peaking in the 4th century, with many promotions to *municipium* and *colonia* rank of sites that in the 1st or 2nd century may have been little more than large villages. The 571 bishoprics in *Africa*, *Numidia*, and *Tripolitana* in 411 CE is a useful indicator, though complicated by Catholic/Donatist duplication and the rural location of some bishops; though balancing that, by no means all towns were bishoprics (see Fig. 11.11). The recent revision of Pierre Salama's map of eastern *Numidia*, *Africa*, and *Tripolitana* contains over 360 places whose ancient name is known and in total more than 600 substantial settlements (towns, garrison settlements, road stations, and small towns).[54] The overwhelming majority of these towns had African toponyms, another reason to take seriously the pre-Roman roots of the settlement pattern. There were numerous additional urban settlements in western *Numidia*, the Mauretanian provinces, and in *Cyrenaica*. The idea of *Cyrenaica* as a *Pentapolis*

53. Lepelley 1981 provides the fullest list, but many sites are poorly known archeologically, and discoveries of inscriptions continue to allow the identification of new towns; see, for example, Beschaouch 1974; 1975; 1976; 1983; Bourgida-M'Charek 2004. For overviews of newly discovered toponyms, see Aounallah and Ben Romdhane 2015; Desanges 1990; Desanges *et al.* 2010.

54. Desanges et al. 2010.

was a fiction by the 2nd century CE, with at least seven major towns (*Apollonia*, *Barce*, *Berenice*, *Cyrene*, *Hadrianopolis*, *Ptolemais*, *Taucheira*) and numerous small towns, some of quite large extent.[55] For *Mauretania Caesariensis* and *Sitifensis*, the garrison settlements were an important component of the overall urban picture (there were at least 30 centres with bishoprics, with at least 16 of these garrison settlements).[56] In *Tingitana* also, of nine main urban centres, at least four had a garrison alongside. There are thus some important contrasts between the scale and extent of urbanisation in the Mauretanian provinces and *Africa*.[57]

The absolute numbers of towns at any given moment are perhaps less important than the general picture that North Africa overall was an area of the Empire that came to have an extraordinary density of urban centres.

There is an interesting correlation between the high number of urban centres and the figure of 516 *populi* quoted by Pliny (*NH* 5.29–30) for the province of *Africa* in the early 1st century CE. Analysis of Pliny's account has suggested that this number derived from data contained in official records held at Rome (the *Formula provinciae Africae*), relating mainly to the situation in either the time of Caesar or Augustus. Pliny listed 6 *coloniae*, 15 *oppida civium Romanorum*, 1 *oppidum Latinum*, 1 *oppidum stipendiarium*, 30 *oppida libera*, and 463 other "peoples" (comprising not simply *civitates* but also larger units, *nationes*).[58] The structure of the list reminds us of the strongly hierarchical nature of Roman urban organisation, with varying obligations and privileges at each level.[59] Whereas the 463 other *populi* have often been assumed to be pastoral "tribes," the implication of the new evidence for Numidian and Gaetulian urbanism discussed in Chapters 4 and 5 makes it more likely that the majority of Pliny's *populi* were associated with nucleated centres of some sort, whether oasis, fortified village, or Numidian town or other urban/proto-urban status. The exact point at which such settlements became legally constituted towns is often unclear from the extant evidence (and some perhaps never did). But it is important to recognise that the process of establishment of civil government was often lengthy, with various forms of interim status and administrative arrangements. This is implicit in Pliny's list, which seriously underrepresents what we might recognise as "urban." One of the mechanisms used to manage the numerous Numidian towns was the *pagus*, both in the sense of a large administrative division covering multiple centres, such as the *pagus Thuscae et Gunzuzi* or the *pagus Gurzensis*, and in the more restrictive

55. Mattingly 2000d; 2000e. For the small towns and larger villages, see Stucchi 1975; Ward-Perkins and Goodchild 2003.
56. Hamdoune 2018, 295–305, 361–90.
57. Lepelley 1998b, 104–12.
58. Desanges 1980b, 276–349. Cf. Shaw 1981d.
59. The literature on different urban status levels and dates of promotion is huge; see, for example, Chastagnol 1990; Gascou 1972; 1982a.

sense of a subordinate urban community, as, for instance, within the territory (*pertica*) of *Karthago* or the Cirtan Confederation.[60] The larger *pagi*, the Cirtan Confederation, and the *pertica* of *Karthago* were thus major entities allowing the initial supervision of multiple Numidian urban centres prior to them being accorded full and independent status, though they had a continuing life beyond the point that individual urban status was granted to constituent elements. Another mechanism was the ascription of a group of Roman citizens, whether veterans or other settlers, to pre-existing urban centres, creating effective double communities, with some built-in inequalities between the citizens and the African component populations. This process had started with Marian veteran settlements in the *Muthul* (Mellegue) valley, but was extended in Caesarian and Augustan veteran settlements (including those of Sittius around *Cirta* which foreshadowed the Cirtan Confederation).[61] Coupled with major land surveys and centuriation, these double communities heralded the Roman targeting of the prime agricultural landscapes of the *Bagrada* and *Muthul* valleys in the late 1st century BCE and 1st century CE. As we shall see, these townscapes, while retaining some aspects of their pre-Roman origins, were put on a different trajectory of urbanisation under Rome to many other parts of *Africa*.

Africa is one of seven main urban hotspots in the Roman Empire, the others being Italy, Greece, *Asia Minor*, the Levant, the Nile Delta, and southwestern Spain (Fig. 8.1).[62] What all of those areas share is the fact that Roman urbanism built on already well-established local urban traditions. If we compare the success of Roman urbanism in regions of low pre-Roman urbanism and proto-urbanism, like northern Gaul and Britain, the difference in numbers, density, and status promotions of towns is very striking.[63] So densely packed were towns in northern Tunisia, for instance, that it has been estimated that the average territory of a city was only in the order of 80 km^2, which does not seem the most efficient way for Rome to have divided the landscape into administrative units.[64] The possibility that the dense urban pattern that emerged over time was as much due to pre-Roman development as to Roman initiative has rarely been considered, though it was acknowledged by the ancient sources (Strabo, *Geography* 17.3.15). What I am suggesting is that the hundreds of Roman-era towns in Africa were made possible by the fact that a similarly large number of sedentary nucleated settlements already existed and these urban and proto-urban sites were already widely disseminated, even in the steppe

60. Aounallah 2010a; 2010b; Aounallah and Maurin 2008; 2013; Bernard 2014; Christol and Mokni 2017; Gascou 1983; 1984; Picard et al. 1963.
61. Gascou 1983; Maurin 1995.
62. See de Ligt and Bintliff 2020; Hanson 2016; Russell 2013.
63. On urban densities across Roman provinces, see Bekker-Nielsen 1989; Hanson 2016; Russell 2013, 66.
64. Picard 1990, 56.

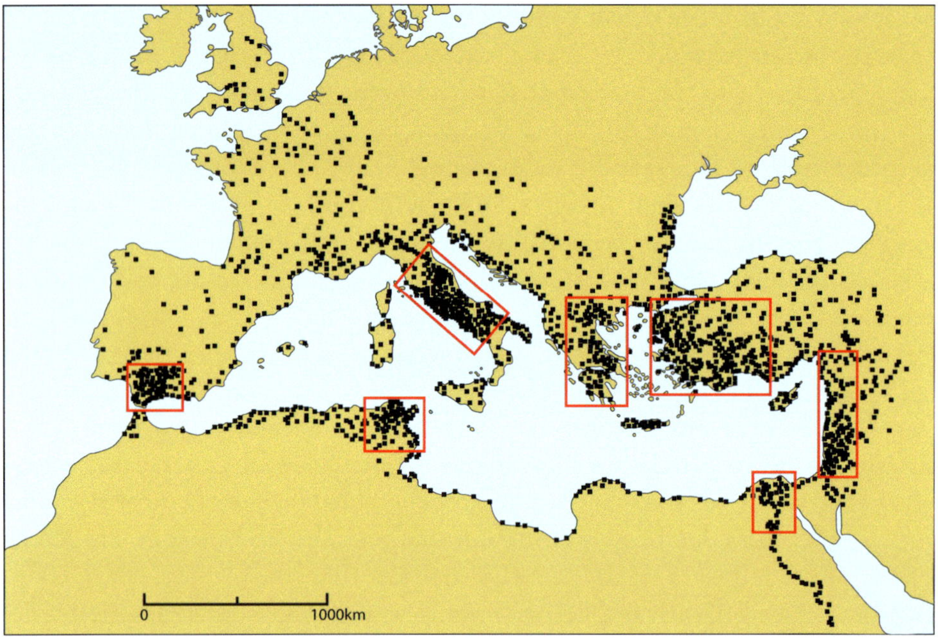

Figure 8.1. Distribution of urban centres in the Roman Empire: rectangles highlight areas of highest density (Mike Hawkes, from author's rough following Russell 2013, fig. 3.8).

and pre-desert areas (compare Fig. 4.9 with Fig. 8.2). This also presupposes strong pre-Roman traditions about urban living within African societies, and we might expect these to have some bearing on the patterns of urban life that emerged.

Whatever the exact date of the information drawn on by Pliny, the data were soon to be superseded by further urban developments, through promotions and changes of urban status. The question of urban status has been a major focus of scholarship on North Africa, notably through the work of Gascou on the early centuries CE[65] and Lepelley on late Roman times.[66] It must be emphasised that the data are very incomplete, due to the vagaries of epigraphic discoveries and lack of excavation at many sites. We also need to recognise that the process of urban promotion did not follow a predictable pattern. It was dependent on the ability of urban elites to petition and the power and interest of any patron they had, as much as it related to the size and importance of the settlement. The numbers of towns in particular categories must therefore be recognised as minimum figures that may need revising significantly upward as new epigraphic discoveries occur. Matthew Hobson's analysis has identified a total of c.240–250 settlements that we can demonstrate

65. Gascou 1972; 1982a; 1982b; 2003; cf. also Briand-Ponsart 2005b; Chastagnol 1990; Ibba 2020; Jacques 1991.
66. Lepelley 1979; 1981.

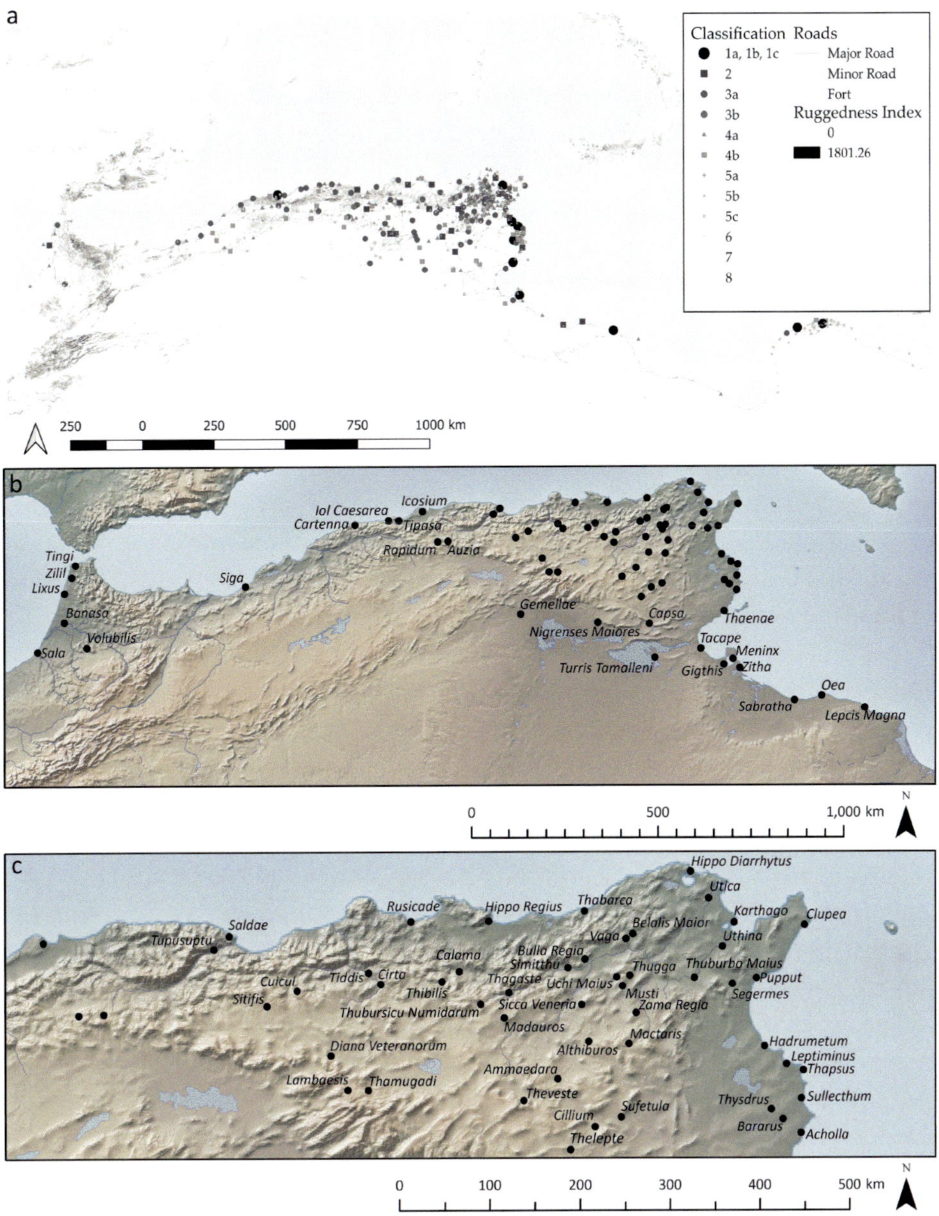

Figure 8.2. Distribution of main urban centres in Africa. a) All sites in Hobson's classification. b–c) Key towns mentioned in chapter (map a) from Hobson 2020; b–c) Martin Sterry, from author's rough).

received a formal urban charter of some sort (of which 89 were *coloniae* and 131 *municipia*).[67] Of the *coloniae*, 39 were veteran colonies (30 established under Caesar or Augustus) and 50 were honorary grants of colonial status to peregrine communities, with promotion mainly achieved in the 2nd or 3rd century CE. The scale of colonial promotions is unparalleled in the western Empire.[68] With the exception of a handful of pre-Claudian Roman *municipia*, the municipal charters mainly ascribed Latin status. There are a few examples in the Flavian period, but the vast majority of African promotions of this type occurred in the 2nd and, even more so, 3rd centuries, with a few additions in the early 4th century. There were numerous peregrine self-governing communities below the level of chartered cities, though explicit reference to their status as *civitates* is sometimes lacking, and the status is inferred from the adoption of Roman institutional forms such as magistrates.[69] Hobson lists 61 sites in this category.[70] A large number of "urban" sites in Tunisia and Algeria have not yielded an inscription indicating a particular urban status, but even some quite small sites seem to have made it to chartered town rank in the late 3rd and 4th centuries, so it is not appropriate to make assumptions about the status of these unknowns on the basis of size or monumentality.

Moving beyond the issue of juridical status, how are we best to categorise the corpus of urban sites? A prime point of difficulty is that there is no obvious census point (nor the possibility with the available data) at which to compare different towns. Many text book presentations rely on only a small number of case studies or combine details from a number of discrete examples to furnish a composite pen-picture of a "typical" Roman city in Africa. Both are potentially highly misleading in relation to the wider group of urban stories. On the other hand, Silvia Bullo presented 26 detailed case studies in her important survey of towns and clearly demonstrated (but did not really explain) extreme heterogeneity.[71] Hobson has attempted to use a combination of urban status, monumentality, and size to define six broad classes of town with two further categories of nucleated settlement that represent a rural continuum (with a number of subcategories at the different levels, as summarised in Table 8.2).[72] This uses a large dataset of over 1,000 sites from the Atlantic to Cyrenaica and is based on a careful evaluation of site

67. Hobson 2020, 287–88, 289–90 (charts and map). The difference in numbers here is due to the fact that we know some towns were chartered, but not their exact status, and some towns were sequentially both a *municipium* and a *colonia*. For comparison, Lepelley 1979, 129 counted 58 *coloniae*, 97 *municipia*, 2 *castella*, 9 *civitates* or *respublicae*, 41 communities of unknown status for a total of 207 for pre-Severan times in an area comprising most of *Africa* and *Numidia*.

68. Hobson 2020, 288.

69. Urban magistracies is another important area of epigraphic research, see inter alia, Gascou 1972; 1984; 1990; 1998;

70. Hobson 2020, 291.

71. Bullo 2002, 59–212.

72. Hobson 2020, 298 (table), 313–15 (with site listings by type).

Table 8.2. Hobson's categorisations of urban sites, with predominant recorded municipal status of sites included (PC = provincial capital, VC = veteran colony, C = honorary colony, M = *municipium*, O = other civil status—normally *civitas* or *oppidum liberum*, GS = garrison settlement, RS = road station, RA = rural agglomeration, estate village, etc.).

Hobson class	**Size (ha)**	**Predominant Status**	**Monumentality and other descriptive characteristics**	**Number of examples**
1	>100	*Colonia, municipium*	Exceptionally large cities with extensive suite of public monuments and high civic status	10 (1 VC, 6 C, 1 PC, 2 unknown but probable C)
2	50–99.99	*Colonia, municipium, oppidum liberum*	Very large cities with quite extensive suite of public monuments and high civic status	19 (10 VC, 8 C, 1 O)
3a	20–49.99	*Colonia, municipium*	Medium size and quite extensive suite of public monuments and high civic status	71 (12 VC, 23 C, 33 M, 2 O and 1 uncertain)
3b	50–99.99	*Uncertain*	Few major monuments but large size	3 (status unknown)
4a	<20	*Colonia, municipium, civitas*	Few to quite extensive suite of major monuments	122 (15 VC, 13 C, 68 M, 6 O, 1 GS and 19 status unknown)
4b	20–49.99	*Civitas,* garrison settlement	Medium size, but comparatively few major monuments	49 (1 PC, 1 M, 11 O, 2 GS, 34 status unknown)
5	<20	*Civitas, castellum, pagus,* garrison settlement	Some—few major monuments	171 (57 O, 8 GS, 106 status unknown but including *castelli*, *pagi*, and road stations, etc)
6	10–19.99	*Civitas, pagus,* garrison settlement, aggglomeration, road station	Small agglomerations with limited monumentality and mostly low status, but with some sites that attained civic status	203 (5 O, 7 GS, 191 status unknown including *castelli*, *pagi*, road stations and estate centres)
7	5–9.99	Primarily rural nucleated settlements, some road stations	Little to no monumentality in very small agglomerations	190
8	1–4.99	Primarily rural nucleated settlements, some road stations	Limited monumentality	210
			Total	**1048**

size through satellite image analysis and direct measurement from plans. However, the limitations with this method of categorisation are apparent in that size/monumentality/status do not neatly map against each other. It is nonetheless useful as a way of showing something of the range of urban sites and the disparity within status type in terms of size and monumentality. There were some huge cities, like *Karthago* and *Lepcis Magna* (measuring several hundred ha in area), but the typical town was vastly smaller. Only *Cyrene* of the ten largest sites was situated inland (and then only about 17 km from the sea). About half the Group 2 sites were also coastal (Libyphoenician) settlements, and many of the largest inland sites were veteran colonies or strongly associated with the military community (*Ammaedara*, *Lambaesis*, *Thelepte*, *Theveste*, *Thamugadi*, *Uthina*). Table 8.2 also reveals some of the problems of the approach, in that some sites of higher urban status, whose true size and monumental aspect is masked by modern development, appear some way down the hierarchy. On the other hand, it also shows that we cannot assume that all high status sites were uniformly larger and more monumentally developed than *civitas* centres and garrison settlements. Properly constituted urban centres are to be found through categories 1–6, though with a smaller proportion at level 6, where larger numbers of proto-urban types are represented (garrison settlements, *castelli*, *pagi*, *vici*, road stations, and rural agglomerations, such as estate centres). Categories 5 and 6 contain quite a number of sites of urban appearance, but whose ancient name is not known.

An alternative way of thinking about the Roman-era urban centres in Africa is to focus on their location, their relation to pre-Roman traditions and population groups, and to consider the sites with the closest affinity with the military community as a distinct grouping (here I include garrison settlements, provincial capitals, veteran colonies, and cities with veteran attachments). Lassère was thinking on similar lines when he broke his analysis down into three sections: coastal cities, agricultural cities of the hinterland, and towns associated with the army.[73] I develop this analysis further later in the chapter.

The indication of size is important for assessing population. Andrew Wilson has recently estimated that in only about 60 of c.600 towns in Africa did the population exceed 5,000, with the implication that the remaining c.540 had relatively small populations, perhaps averaging 2,000 people.[74] Nonetheless, even on this minimum view the urban population of Africa overall will have exceeded 2 million, one of the highest returns after Italy. Hobson produced a slightly different list of sites over 50 ha in area (for which populations of over 10,000 seem plausible).[75] In Table 8.3 I combine sites in Hobson's and Wilson's lists for about 50 towns with

73. Lassère 2015, 370–74 (port cities), 374–78 (agricultural towns), 378–80 (military towns).

74. Wilson 2011, 183–84. Cf. the earlier attempt by Duncan-Jones 1963.

75. Hobson 2020, 313.

Table 8.3. Types of urban settlements, size and estimated population for selected cities (Key: African = *Numidae* or *Mauri* town; Libyph = Libyphoenician town; Oasis = Oasis town; Veteran = Veteran settlement in colonia or municipium; Dual = Dual community of Roman citizens and African people; Garrison = Garrison Settlement).

Name	*African*	Libyph	Oasis	Veteran	Dual	Garrison	Max size (ha)	Popul (after Wilson 2011)
Karthago		*		*			450	300,000
Lepcis Magna		*					452	90,000
Hadrumetum		*					155	31,000
Thysdrus	*	*		*				45,000
Iol Caesarea	*	*				*	318	63,000
Cyrene		Greek					123	
Ptolemais		Greek					217	
Tocra		Greek					40	
Cirta	*			*				30,000
Tingi	?	*						
Volubilis	*						40	
Cartenna		*						
Tipasa		*					55	
Icosium		*						
Rusicade		*						
Tubusuptu	?			*				
Sitifis	?			*				5,000+
Cuicul	*			*			15	5,000+
Calama		*		*				5,000+
Thubursicu Numidarum	*			*			60	5,000+
Hippo Regius		*			*		60	5,000+
Thagaste	*							5,000+
Madauros	*			*				5,000+
Theveste	*			*		*	56	5,000+
Diana Veteranorum				*				5,000+
Lambaesis				*		*	100	5,000+
Thamugadi				*			50	5,000+
Thabraca		*		*				5,000+
Hippo Diarrhytus		*		*				5,000+
Utica		*		*	*		80	5,000+

(Continued)

Table 8.3. *(Continued)*

Name	*African*	Libyph	Oasis	Veteran	Dual	Garrison	Max size (ha)	Popul (after Wilson 2011)
Sicca Veneria	*			*				5,000+
Bulla Regia	*						31	5,000+
Simitthu	*			*		*		5,000+
Thuburnica	*			*				5,000+
Ammaedara				*		*	61	5,000+
Thubursicu Bure	*			*				5,000+
Thugga	*				*		25	5,000+
Althiburos	*							5,000+
Mactaris	*							5,000+
Uthina				*			120	5,000+
Thuburbo Maius	*						25	5,000+
Leptiminus		*					38	5,000+
Sullecthum		*						5,000+
Thapsus		*					39	5,000+
Acholla		*						5,000+
Thaenae		*						5,000+
Cillium	?			*?	*?	?	31	5,000+
Sufetula					*?	?	38	5,000+
Ksar el-Guellal							53	5,000+
Thelepte				*			180	5,000+
Gigthis		*						5,000+
Meninx		*					30	5,000+
Sabratha		*					35	5,000+
Oea		*						5,000+

postulated 5,000 plus populations. There are, of course, many uncertainties relating to origins, status, and size/population, but the table makes allowance for changes of status and arguably contains most of the key sites that shape the orthodox view of Roman towns in Africa. The dominance of certain categories of town within the overall corpus of African urbanism is clearly visible. Roman veteran colonies and Libyphoenician towns, especially the harbour centres, are particularly notable in this list. The Libyphoenician towns split fairly evenly between those that flourished as indigenous centres under Rome and those that were refounded as Roman colonies, but where we assume a considerable element of the original population remained alongside veterans and other Roman citizen settlers. Of the pre-Roman

Table 8.4. Urban population (following Wilson 2011).

Name	Population in 1000s (after Wilson 2011)	Percentage
Two very large towns (*Karthago* and *Lepcis*)	390	19.10%
Five other 100 ha+ towns (*Hadrumetum, Iol Caesarea, Thysdrus, Cyrene, Ptolemais*)	194	9.46%
50 towns with ave 7,500 population	375	18.34%
543 sites with 2,000 ave population	1,086	53.10%
Total urban population	2,045	100.00%

Numidae centres, the majority of those that achieved prominence in the Roman era were ones where some degree of Roman colonial settlement had taken place, whether refounded as veteran *coloniae* or with settler deductions added to continuing indigenous communities. Garrison settlements and veteran deductions were also significant factors at towns in southern and western *Numidia*. There are comparatively few inland towns in the list that achieved prominence without some form of colonial intervention and none of the oasis centres feature here. The vast majority of the rest of the urban centres belonged to these underrepresented categories. The urban trajectories of my different types of town were thus varied, and the most successful towns in terms of adhesion to Roman cosmopolitan norms were not representative of the majority of sites.

Table 8.4 follows Wilson's distribution of urban population and suggests that almost half the urban population was concentrated in the largest 10% of urban sites (and 20% in the two largest cities). The other c.90% of the urban sites accounted for the remaining 53% of urban population. The urban experience at either end of this spectrum of towns will have been very different. Hobson's longer list of medium-sized towns would increase the overall urban population somewhat, but not change the unequal distribution between the largest group and the rest.

Urban Competition and Emulation

What made a town recognisably so for ancient Mediterranean peoples? There is no universal answer, though in the Roman period such baseline expectations were perhaps closer to being fulfilled than at some other periods of history. Lassère saw urban identity being closely linked to specific monuments; he highlighted the forum, basilica, and temple as symbolising civic and social functions at its centre.[76] The commonalities in Roman architectural models across provinces are well

76. Lassère 2015, 382, with n. 90.

appreciated, and North African examples feature prominently in many general studies of Roman architecture.[77]

With rare exceptions, the Roman state did not provide the funds for urban building programmes, and it is clear that the income streams available to city councils were somewhat limited.[78] The alternative was for private individuals to either fund a project entirely or to subscribe to a scheme. This encouraged a spirit of public benefaction or euergetism within elite society, and the traditional models of urbanisation in "Roman Africa" have tended to present urban development primarily in terms of competition for honour and status. Such strategies of emulation were focused on perceived Roman norms and sometimes linked to periods of public office-holding.[79] As in many other Roman provinces, there is some strong evidence in support of this view.[80] The embellishment of towns also extended to public artworks, notably statuary and relief sculpture, which at the upper end of a broad spectrum might closely follow imperial trends.[81]

The hierarchical structure of towns within the provincial structure, with different statuses associated with varying levels of privileges and burdens, was also a significant incentive for communities to seek urban promotion to a higher rank. The story of the promotion of *Lepcis Magna* to *municipium* in the Flavian period and *colonia* under Trajan, following an intensive campaign of investment in Roman-style civic amenities from the reign of Augustus, will serve as one example among many. But this case also reminds us that promotion was often a slow and far from automatic process, especially in the early Principate.[82] Investment made in the urban fabric in one generation might not bring a reward until two or three generations later. As such, the initial monumentalisation of towns can rarely have been undertaken in the expectation of swift reward for the investment of local capital.

The costs of monumentalising towns were significant and not without risk for communities that sought to invest (Table 8.5).[83] Earthquakes were a recurrent threat in the Mediterranean, even if the idea of widespread devastation has sometimes

77. Barton 1989; Gros 1996; 2002; MacDonald 1982; Ward-Perkins 1981; Yegül and Favro 2018. For an excellent synthesis of the North African evidence, see Mugnai 2022.
78. Duncan-Jones 1985 for a clear discussion of who paid for urban buildings, drawing on African examples. Cf. Rebuffat 2012a on city walls. For a fundamental survey of public building activity in North Africa, see Jouffroy 1986. See also the interesting articles by Dufton 2019 and Dupuis 1992 on the social strategies behind gentrification.
79. On urbanisation (sometimes elided with town planning) in North Africa, see inter alia Bullo 2002, 213–29; Février 1982; 1990, 9–48; Groslambert 2009a; Ward-Perkins 1982; Wilson 2020; Younes 2012.
80. See the numerous indications of building costs donated by individuals from North Africa, Duncan-Jones 1982, 63–119. Also Jouffroy 1986.
81. Baratte and Chaisemartin 2018; Hurlet 2000. Février 1971 was ahead of his time in choosing a much wider representation of styles and qualities in his survey of urban art.
82. Mattingly 1995, 116–20. Cf. Cooley 2012, 250–85; Di Vita et al. 1999, 50–87. See further Chapter 9 below.
83. The table is adapted and expanded from MacMullen 1974, 142–45.

Table 8.5. Typical costs for suite of public buildings in High Empire (after MacMullen 1974).

Structure	**Cost (HS)**
Theatre	400,000
Curia	100,000
Basilica	120,000
Macellum	100,000
Library	400,000
Baths	400,000
Baths	400,000
Baths	400,000
Large temple	100,000
Small temple	60,000
Small temple	60,000
Small temple	60,000
Decorated fountain (nymphaeum)	50,000
Decorated fountain (nymphaeum)	50,000
Decorated fountain (nymphaeum)	50,000
Gymnasium	150,000
Monumental arch	40,000
Forum paving & porticoes	200,000
30 statues @ HS 5,000 each	150,000
Amphitheatre	1,000,000
Aqueduct	2,000,000
Roads/sewers	2,000,000
Racetrack/circus	1,000,000
Total	**9,290,000**

been overplayed.[84] Given the huge cost of a full suite of civic amenities, it is also likely that the scale of capital investment to the main donors outweighed the return that may have accrued to their descendants who some time later obtained Roman citizen rights. Dio Chrysostom's struggle to keep his fellow citizens of *Prusa* in *Asia Minor* engaged with his goal of gaining urban promotion on the back of a programme of civic renewal is a good illustration of how such vanity projects could create divisions within a community.[85] This supports the view that it was more

84. Di Vita 1990; Rebuffat 1980b.
85. Dio Chrysostom, *Orations* 40; 45; 47; 48.

often competition between elite families within cities that drove euergetism and investment in public building, rather than competition between communities.

Despite the financial and social constraints on unbridled investment in urban embellishment, there is still some expectation in modern scholarship that the African provincial towns were uniformly focused on such monumentalism. We can, of course, demonstrate exceptionally well-appointed cities from our list of the usual suspects, but how typical were they? Let us consider the distribution of some key urban entertainment facilities (Table 8.6).[86] The presence of forum/basilica complexes or Classical style temples might also be thought important markers of urban status, but identification of the former is somewhat more dependent on the state of excavation or on chance epigraphic finds.[87] Temples are pretty ubiquitous at urban sites, though a large number are known primarily from inscriptions, and without clearer association between temple form (possible for only a relatively small sample of sites) the relevance to urban standing is not clear-cut.[88] For example, a recent study has dismantled the conventional view that *capitolia* (temples to Iupiter, Iuno, and Minerva) were a key feature of Roman towns across the provinces, especially *colonia* and other "showcase" towns. All the same, the 36 certain or probable examples from Africa constitutes 59% of all those mapped Empire-wide by Quinn and Wilson (and Italy's 13 examples represent another 21%). The distribution in North Africa is skewed towards *Africa* and *Numidia* with few in the Mauretanian provinces, and (though dependent to some extent on epigraphic discoveries) they are nowhere near as ubiquitous as we might imagine at the huge numbers of veteran and honorary colonies—the types of towns generally identified as being most likely to invest in such a "Roman" monument. There are other unexplained peculiarities. Where they did appear, construction was often not synchronous with the urban foundation or attainment of higher urban status, nor were they all centrally located within the townscape.[89]

Despite a commonly held view on the commonality of theatres and amphitheatres in North Africa,[90] these structures are in fact attested at only about 10%

86. Table 8.6 is compiled with data from Desanges et al. 2010; Humphrey 1986; Lassère 2015; Sear 2006; Slim 1984 and sundry other sources.
87. Fora and basilica complexes have been much discussed, Ammar 1994; Ben Baaziz 1987; Benseddik and Potter 1986; Euzennat and Hallier 1986; Février 1982, 342–45; Gros 1994; 2014; Kenrick 1986; Lenoir et al. 1987; Livadiotti and Rocco 2018; Ward-Perkins 1993.
88. On North African temple architecture, see inter alia Aiosa 2013; Aounallah and Golvin 2016; Baratte et al. 2018; Blanc-Bijon 2008; Brouquier-Reddé 1992a; 1992b; Di Vita and Livadiotti 2005; Eingartner 2005; Golvin and Khanoussi 2005; Joly and Tomasello 1984; Kenrick 1986; Morestin 1980; Saint Amans 2004; Tomasello 2011.
89. Quinn and Wilson 2013. Cf. older views of Barton 1982; Kallala 1992.
90. Lassère 2015, 393: "Il y a des théâtres à peu près dans toutes les villes, un peu à l'initiative d'Auguste qui a voyait, comme on l'a dit, le meilleur instrument de la diffusion de la culture romaine." Cf. 394: "L'amphithéâtre ... En Afrique, on en retrouvé un peu partout." See also Montali 2018.

Table 8.6. Towns from African provinces with evidence for a range of urban amenities. NB There are hundreds of other sites that have yielded no evidence for any of these supposedly key urban features. Status indicates highest known rank: VC = veteran colony, C = *colonia*, M = *municipium*, O = other (*pagus*, *civitas* or *oppidum*).

Name	Status (VC/C/M/O)	Capitolium	Theatre	Amphitheatre	Circus	Baths	Aqueduct
Abbir Maius	M			*			
Abthungi	M	*					
Acholla	C		*	*			
Agbia	M			*			
Agger	C		*				
Althiburos	M	*	*				
Ammaedara	VC		*	?			
Apollonia (Cyr)	PC		*			*	
Assuras	VC		*				
Auzia	C				*		
Banasa (MT)	VC					*	
Bararus	M		*	*			
Belalis Maior	C	*				*	
Bulla Regia	C		*	*		*	
Calama (N)	C		*			*	
Capsa	C		T or A	A or T		*	
Carpis	VC			*			*
Cartenna (MC)	VC						
Cillium	C		*			*	*
Cincari	M	*		?			
Cirta (N)	VC/PC	*	*				*
Clipea	VC						
Cuicul (N)	VC?		*			*	
Curubis	VC		*	?			*
Cyrene (Cyr)	C		*	A/T	*	*	*
Diana Veteranorum (N)	M						*
Furnos Minus	M		*				*
Gemellae (N)	M			*			
Gigthis (T)	M					*	

(Continued)

Table 8.6. *(Continued)*

Name	Status (VC/C/M/O)	Capitolium	Theatre	Amphitheatre	Circus	Baths	Aqueduct
Giufi	M		*				
Gori	O			*			
Gurza (B)	O		*				
Hadrumetum (B)	C/PC		*	*	*	*	*
Hippo Diarrhytus	VC						
Hippo Regius	C		*	?		*	
Icosium (MC)	C						
Iol Caesarea (MC)	C/PC	*	*	*	*	*	*
Karthago	VC/PC	*	*	*	*	*	*
Lambaesis (N)	C/PC	*		*		*	
Lepcis Magna (T)	C/PC		*	*	*	*	*
Leptiminus (B)	C		*	*		*	*
Limisa (B)	M		*				
Lixus (MT)	C		* TA	* TA		*	
Macomades (N)	M					*	
Mactaris (B)	C			*		*	*
Madauros	VC	*	*			*	
Membressa	O?			?			
Meninx (T)	M/C?			*		*	*
Mididi (B)	O					*	
Missua	O		*			*	
Municipium Aurelium Commodianum …	M			*			
Musti	M						
Nara (B)	?			*			
Numuli	M	*	*				
Oea (T)	C			?			
Pheradi Maius (B)	C			*		*	
Popthi?	O		*			*	
Ptolemais (Cyr)	PC		*	*		*	*

Table 8.6. *(Continued)*

Name	Status (VC/C/M/O)	Capitolium	Theatre	Amphitheatre	Circus	Baths	Aqueduct
Pupput (B)	C	*		*			
Rusicade (N)	C		*	*		*	*
Ruspina (B)	O					*	
Sabratha (T)	C		*	*		*	*
Sala (MT)	C	*				*	
Saldae (MC)	VC				*		*
Segermes (B)	M	*				*	
Seressi	M		*	*		*	
Sicca Veneria	VC		*	*			
Simitthu	VC		*	*		*	*
Sitifis (MS)	VC/PC		*	*	*	*	
Sufes (B)	C					*	
Sufetula (B)	C		*	*		*	
Sullecthum (B)	O						
Sutunurca	O		*				
Taucheira (Cyr)	C					*	
Thabraca	VC					*	
Thaenae (B)	C			*		*	
Thagaste	M		*	?		*	
Thamugadi (N)	VC	*	*			*	*
Thapsus (B)	C			*			
Thelepte (B)	VC		*			*	
Theveste	VC	*	*	*			*
Thibaris	M		*	*			
Thibilis (N)	M						
Thignica	M		*	*		*	
Thimissua	O			*			
Thisica	C			*			
Thuburbo Maius	C	*	*	*		*	
Thuburbo Minus	VC			*			
Thuburnica	VC			?		*	*
Thubursicu Bure	C		*				

(Continued)

Table 8.6. *(Continued)*

Name	Status (VC/ C/M/ O)	Capitolium	Theatre	Amphitheatre	Circus	Baths	Aqueduct
Thubursicu Numidarum (N)	C	*	*			*	
Thugga	C	*	*		*	*	*
Thunigaba	O		?				
Thysdrus	C		*	*	*	*	*
Tiddis (N)	O					*	
Tigava Castra (MC)	?			*			
Tingi (MT)	C						
Tipasa (MC)	C		*	*		*	*
Tuburnuc	M					*	
Tubusuptu (MC)	C						
Tuccador	M?			?			
Tunes	O		*				
Uchi Maius	C			*			*
Ucubis	M	*	*				*
Ulissipira (B)	M		*	*			
Uppena	C			?			
Uthina	VC		*	*		*	*
Utica	C		*	*	*	*	
Uzalis	C	*	*				
Uzappa	M						
Vaga (B)	O			?		*	
Vallis	C		*				*
Vazi Sarara	O					*	
Vicus Augusti (B)	O		*			*	
Vina	M		*	?			
Volubilis (MT)	C	*				*	*
Zama Regia	C						*
Zitha (T)	M						

of towns in *Africa*, and even adding examples from *Numidia*, *Mauretania*, and *Cyrenaica* does not much change the picture.[91] The best-preserved examples of theatres contribute richly to our understanding of the spread of the architectural form in the provinces.[92] The city of *Cyrene* had no fewer than five theatre structures, including an *odeion* and two theatres specifically linked to suburban sanctuaries.[93] In other provinces, communities that could not afford both a theatre and amphitheatre sometimes chose to adapt the plan of the theatre to accommodate amphitheatral spectacles; examples of this sort of practice are attested at *Lixus*, *Iol Caesarea*, and *Cyrene*. The Mauretanian provinces have to date yielded traces of only five theatres, five amphitheatres, and four circuses (and the total includes the theatre/amphitheatre hybrid at *Lixus* and several structures known only from inscriptions, at *Auzia*, *Sitifis*, and *Saldae*).[94] It is certainly possible that further examples remain undiscovered or unrecognised, but these are among the largest and most diagnostic of urban monuments, and their non-identification at hundreds of the lesser urban centres is surely significant. Circuses were even rarer, and it was generally a mark of particular esteem for a town to possess one.[95] Public baths were among the most ubiquitous urban amenities (and among the most recognisable traces), common to large and small towns alike, though differing in scale of ornamentation in light of local resources.[96] Yvon Thébert lists 139 major baths in North Africa,[97] still well short of the overall number of towns, especially given that the largest towns often had multiple baths complexes—summer and winter baths were common, and *Thamugadi*, with an abundant spring, had 14, including five large complexes.[98] Aqueducts are less commonly reported as a monument class, but when the source lay at any distance across undulating terrain they were among the most expensive civil works to construct

91. On amphitheatres in general, see Bomgardner 2000; Golvin 1988; Lachaux 1977; on theatres see Sear 2006. Lachaux 1977, 15 listed 25 theatres and 21 amphitheatres (with 9 and 10 respectively known only by epigraphic data), and 14 sites with both; Sear 2006, 271–301 lists 48 examples of theatres in *Africa Proconsularis* (14 known only from epigraphic evidence) and 5 examples in *Numidia*; Slim 1984 lists 34 certain and 4 possible amphitheatres for Tunisia. Montali 2015, 323–535 provides a full gazetteer of 58 sites where amphitheatres have been postulated in *Africa* (but only 40 represented by structural evidence) See also Maggi 1998 (*Africa*); Pichot 2008 (*Mauretania*)
92. For theatres, see inter alia: *Lepcis Magna*, Caputo 1987; *Sabratha*, Di Vita et al. 1999, 164–81. For amphitheatres, see: *Karthago*, Bomgardner 1989; Montali 2015, 356–65; *Thysdrus*, Montali 2015, 484–507; Slim 1986; 1988; *Lepcis*, Montali 2015, 383–94; Ricciardini 2018; *Sabratha*, Di Vita et al. 1999, 148, 150; Montali 2015; *Theveste*, Lequement 1979; *Uthina*, Ben Hassen and Maurin 2004, 117–80; Montali 2015, 516–28.
93. Kenrick 2013.
94. Pichot 2008.
95. Humphrey 1986.
96. Bartoccini 1929; Bonacasa 2018; Broise and Thébert 1993; Thébert 2003; cf. Nielsen 1990; Yegül 1992.
97. Thébert 2003, 728–29.
98. Blas de Roblès et al. 2019, 186–214.

(Table 8.5).[99] Many Numidian cities had been sited to take advantage of freshwater springs, and the continued occupation of these sites in the Roman period reflected the crucial importance of water. Rainwater storage in cisterns also remained essential for urban water supply at many African cities.[100] Fountains and nymphaea were not just for display but were vital for domestic water supply for many inhabitants.[101]

There are 19 examples of Italian-style purpose-built market buildings in the African provinces (*Ammaedara*; *Auzia*—the only Mauretanian example; *Bulla Regia*; *Cuicul*; *Gigthis*; *Hippo Regius*; *Lambaesis*; *Lepcis Magna*; *Mactaris*; *Madauros*; *Meninx*; *municipium Aurelium Commodum*; *Neferis*; *Thamugadi*; *Thibilis*; *Thignica*; *Thubursicu Numidarum*; *Thugga*).[102] Even allowing for some additional unexcavated examples, this seems a very small sample, given the scale of 19th-century clearance at many sites. It demonstrates that not all "Roman" architectural styles travelled as widely as others. Monumental fountains (*nymphaea*) are attested at 51 cities, though here a further limitation may have been the dependence on an abundant aqueduct or spring source for the town.[103] A notable class of monument, with around 90 examples known across North Africa, was the monumental arch, evolving from simple arches over a key access road, to substantial free-standing monuments with ornate columnar facades, to great four-way structures at key road junctions.[104]

Town walls were generally rare in *Africa* and *Byzacena*, though as noted already, many sites had developed from earlier fortified settlements (whether Numidian or Libyphoenician). The provision of urban defences was much more common in the main military provinces (*Mauretania Tingitana*, *Caesariensis*, *Sitifensis*, *Numidia*, and *Tripolitana*) and not only for garrison settlements.[105] The major towns in *Cyrenaica* all seem to have been provided with walls.[106] By late antiquity, *Karthago* had a large-scale defensive wall circuit, and many other towns in *Africa* and *Byzacena* contained defended compounds built within the townscape—these

99. Aqueducts: Argou et al. 1992; Boucher 1983; Brouquier-Reddé and Hurlet 2018; Hodge 1991. For North African specifics, see Euzennat 1992; Gsell 1901a, 247–60; Leveau 2012; 2013; Leveau and Paillet 1976; Rakob 1974 (*Karthago*); Romanelli 1970, 215–29; Shaw 1991a; Wilson 1997; 1998; 2001b.

100. Hallier 1987; Wilson 1998; 2001b.

101. Tomasello 2011.

102. Hamdoune 2009.

103. Aupert 1974, 90–104; Lamare 2019, for discussion of towns with *nymphaea*.

104. Blonce 2008, lists 87 examples; see also 2014; Jouffroy 1986, 402, lists 74 of 1st-3rd-century date; Mazzili 2016, 207–86, documents c.200 arches, gates and tetrapylon monuments from *Mauretania Tingitana* to *Cyrenaica* (but includes some military examples in the count). For illustrations of different types of arches, see Gsell 1901a, 155–85; Guéry and Hallier 1998; Romanelli 1970, 131–45.

105. Daniels1983; Déroche and Leclant 2012; Leveau 1985b.

106. Kenrick 2013.

are commonly referred to as "fortresses" or "fortins byzantines." While some were undoubtedly features of the Byzantine reoccupation, they occur in such numbers as to suggest that many of these fortifications were local initiatives in times of increasing insecurity.[107] Urban defences is an area requiring much more work in general.

The 100-plus sites included in Table 8.6 include those with the clearest evidence of monumentalisation under Rome relating to key markers; but in comparison with the overall spectrum of urban sites known in Africa (cf. Table 8.2), it is apparent that the majority of towns were not nearly so impressively developed. Few centres, outside the largest and most important cities, had anything like the full suite of key urban amenities (and we must assume in any case that the development of such facilities was spread over a long period).[108]

Different Types of Town and Varied Urban Trajectories

I have argued that towns in Africa had varied origins and inspirations, and these urban societies were incorporated into the Empire at various moments and under different circumstances. The colonial context within which the Roman-era urbanism occurred also means that we have to allow for varying degrees of state interference and dictat in certain cases—what Elizabeth Fentress memorably describes as "coercive urbanisation."[109] It should not surprise us that the subsequent trajectory of urbanism was not uniform across these groups.

Another issue that needs to be borne in mind is the progressive and dynamic nature of the urbanisation process. Urban development at many sites between 146 BCE–50 CE was radically different to what was achieved between 50–250 CE. A traveller in Africa in the mid-1st century CE would have had a very different experience of the nature and achievements of urbanism in Africa in comparison to someone making the same journey a century later. Much variation would also have been encountered depending on the itinerary of the journey—a key argument here is that different sorts of urban centres would have been encountered along the coast, up the *Bagrada* valley, into the High Aurès plains, along the frontier, and into the desert. What is needed is a more nuanced view of urbanism, not an "average" picture that conflates time and space and aggregates together different social and cultural groupings. This in part relates to regional differences, but a key argument here is also to recognise that underlying the regional patterning there were

107. Pringle 1981; Trousset 1985. See sites descriptions in Desanges et al. 2010 for multiple reference to "fortin" at urban sites.

108. See Stone 2014b; 2016a for similar conclusions on harbour towns, with the same sort of discrepancy between the largest ports (often provincial capitals) where we can see huge investment on facilities, and lesser ports where major development and investment often came later.

109. Fentress 2021.

also deeply ingrained social differences in urbanisation. In the next sections, I shall illustrate some of the variation in urban planning and layout across a range of different types of urban centre.

Karthago as Provincial Capital and Portal to Another World

Many studies of "Roman Africa" have made *Karthago* the centrepiece of the urban story, whereas I have deliberately separated *Karthago* out from the general discussion that follows. I have done this not because I think *Karthago* unimportant, but rather because both its Punic and Roman history and trajectory were so exceptional. Also, in terms of its archaeological investigation, this is not only the most intensively excavated site, but also the one that has seen the highest level of "modern" urban excavation, involving close attention to stratigraphy and the fullest array of finds reporting and palaeoeconomic sampling.[110] Thus it is not easy to compare *Karthago* with other urban centres.

In some respects *Karthago* is a point of departure rather than a way in to "Roman Africa." In a world of many different varieties of cities, *Karthago* was something altogether exceptional. It was by a considerable margin the largest city in Africa (Fig. 8.3). Wilson estimates the population at c.300,000, compared to the next largest, *Lepcis Magna*, at 90,000.[111] As already noted the vast majority of Africa's postulated 600 towns had populations that were below 5,000. The urban amenities at *Karthago* were all on a gigantic scale, emphasising the magnitude and power of the Empire that lay beyond.[112] The nature of public religion there was also far more focused on the Roman religious calendar and state cults, with evidence of engagement with African cults generally much lower.[113] As the pre-eminent centre of Christianity in North Africa, with an extraordinary number of churches and burials, *Karthago* is also of fundamental importance for studies of early Christianity more broadly (Fig. 8.3). Much of the evidence we have on Roman *Karthago* speaks above all of its exceptionality.

As a major harbour city, *Karthago* was the portal to the wider Roman world, and, more than most towns in Africa, it was an artificially created and uniquely constituted cosmopolitan urban community, involving a disproportionate number of individuals linked to the imperial administration, to itinerant lifestyles, and coming from diverse geographic origins.[114] The story of the Roman conquest

110. See for instance, Ennabli 1992; 2020 (an impressive "gazetteer" of all the main monuments and excavations); Pedley 1980.
111. Wilson 2011, 184.
112. Ennabli 2020.
113. Rives 1995, 17–172 contrasts *Karthago* with *Thugga* in this respect.
114. Carlsen, J. 2020a/b; Santangelo 2008.

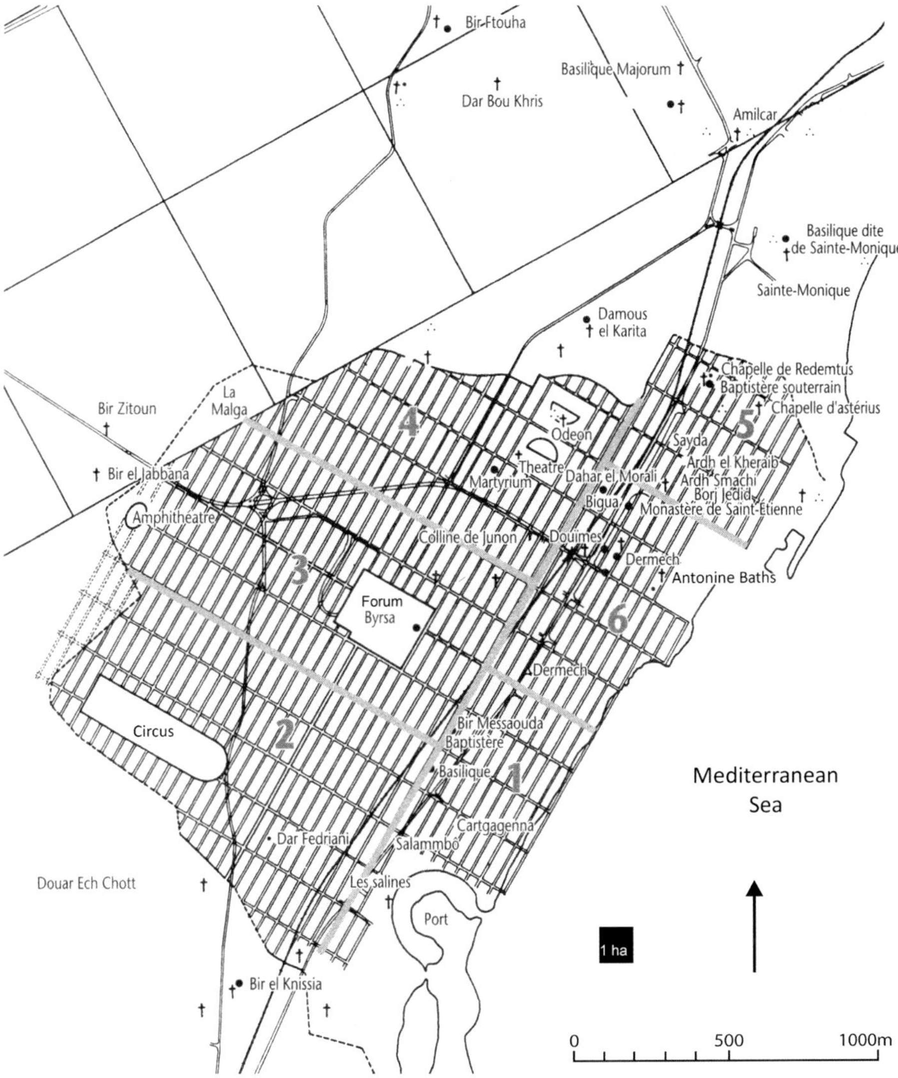

Figure 8.3. *Karthago* as a Christian city, showing its six ecclesiastical subdivisions (modified by author from Corbier and Griesheimer 2005, 278).

and refounding of *Karthago* is, needless to say, of huge significance to our understanding of the Roman Empire, but the colonial discourse that surrounds this city can also overshadow our attempts to make sense of the wider story of Africa and Africans in the Roman Empire. The circumstances of the sack of *Qart Hadasht* and the slaughter and enslavement of its population in 146 BCE marked a caesura with the past.[115] Its subsequent refoundations and repopulation with settlers from outside

115. Lancel 1992; 1995; Miles 2010; Warmington 1969.

Africa in the 120s, the 40s, and again in the 20s BCE was also different to most other early "colonies," which tended to build on pre-existing population centres. Finally its roles as provincial capital and a focal point in Rome's food supply made it central to the Roman imperial project in Africa. The imperial governor was based there along with numerous financial officials (including many imperially owned enslaved people and freedmen).[116] The huge territory (*pertica*) assigned to the city, involving administrative and economic dominance over more than 80 other urban centres, ensured that the wealth of *Karthago* far surpassed other African towns. The permanent establishment of the provincial council and an urban cohort were other distinguishing features. As the most important port, the city also had a very cosmopolitan transient population. All together these features made *Karthago* the largest and richest city, the most impressive in terms of its monuments, the most Roman in cultural character, the most intimately engaged with the functioning of the Roman Empire. It simply stands apart from the other urban centres.

Group 1. Pre-Roman Foundations

Numidian and Mauretanian Towns

Because many Roman towns in North Africa were undefended until late Roman times (if even then), it is easy to overlook the fact that there was nonetheless an important priority given to defensible topographic positions in the initial location of many of these sites. As demonstrated in Chapter 4, the most dramatic of the pre-Roman Numidian centres were perched hillfort sites, above dramatic cliffs and gorges, such as *Bulla Mensa* (Kalaat Senane), *Cirta*, *Cuicul*, or *Tiddis*. Indeed, a key urban characteristic of the NAIA development in the Maghreb was the emphasis on such defensive positions.

The urban character of these smaller urban centres, some of which seem to have been initially designated as *castella*, is only gradually coming into clearer view.[117] Even in mid to late Roman times, many of these sites had quite an irregular layout, lacked some of the normal urban structures we are led to expect of Roman towns and were of very small size. Henchir Bou Nader is a good example at the bottom end of the spectrum and, because it did not develop Roman urban characteristics and later reworking of the site was more limited, its features are revealing of the group.[118] The site utilised a series of wadi channels to provide natural ditches

116. Bockmann 2022; Carlsen 2022.
117. Aounallah 2010a for a discussion of the relationship between *pagi*, *castella* and *civitates* in northern Tunisia.
118. Ferchiou 2004c.

around three sites of the low platform on which it sat. The natural defences were enhanced by a series of enceintes, enclosing just over 1 ha. In miniature, this site probably gives us a good impression of what many of the Numidian nucleated settlements encountered by *Qart Hadasht* and Rome looked like, making the most of defensive positions provided by deeply incised wadis.

The small town of *Bagat* (Henchir Ghayadha), near *Zama Regia*, is a slightly larger example of the Numidian promontory location type (see Fig. 4.8b).[119] Leaving aside the uncertain question of its legal status under Rome, the site has urban characteristics that are illustrative of both Roman and African urbanism. The core of the town contains limited traces of monumental constructions around a central rectangular space (forum?), probably the locality of a known temple of Tellus.[120] The urban core is surrounded by extensive cemeteries and a suburban sanctuary of Saturn. Saturn stelae were also recovered in relation to one of the northern cemeteries. In late Roman times *Bagat* appears to have been seat of a bishopric.[121] Survey at the site has turned up Libyan, Neo-Punic and Latin inscriptions, reflecting the diverse cultural influences and identities at play.[122]

The site of *Althiburos* represents a more developed version of this, with the core of the Roman-era town still occupying the tongue of land between the wadi gullies, but with the limited monumentalisation and urban development extending beyond those limits over time (Fig. 8.4). The major public buildings here were still relatively modest (a forum, two Classical style temples, an *Aesculapium*, a theatre, two arches), with the lanes and building alignments varying according to the constrained topographic setting.[123] *Mididi* is a third example of this same type and like a number of these sorts of sites, the restricted fortified promontory was not ideally suited for the development of the subsequent "Roman" townscape.

The same sort of variation is illustrated in three sites within the *pertica* of *Karthago* looked at by Ferchiou.[124] *Sulules* (20 ha) and Henchir Debbik (14 ha) were both eventually *municipia* in the Severan era, but the ruins suggest little monumentalisation took place at either, and they seem to have lacked the major amenities, like theatres and amphitheatres. The status of the third site, *Seressi*, is unknown, though it too probably attained chartered status at some point. This was evidently a larger town (between 20–30 ha) and altogether better appointed—perhaps indicating that it was a *municipium*—with theatre, amphitheatre, baths, four arches, and so on.

119. M'Charek et al. 2008.
120. M'Charek et al. 2008, 118–19; *CIL* 8.23712.
121. M'Charek et al. 2008, 116–17 point out that the site was one of the urban centres within the *Pagus Thuscae* (see Picard et al. 1963), and another equally small urban centre of this group, *Cuttilula*, was eventually promoted to *municipium* rank.
122. M'Charek et al. 2008, 145–61, 169–227 on the stelae, Libyan, neo-Punic, and Latin texts.
123. Kallala and Sanmartí 2011; Kallala et al. 2016; Sanmartí et al. 2020.
124. Ferchiou 2004a.

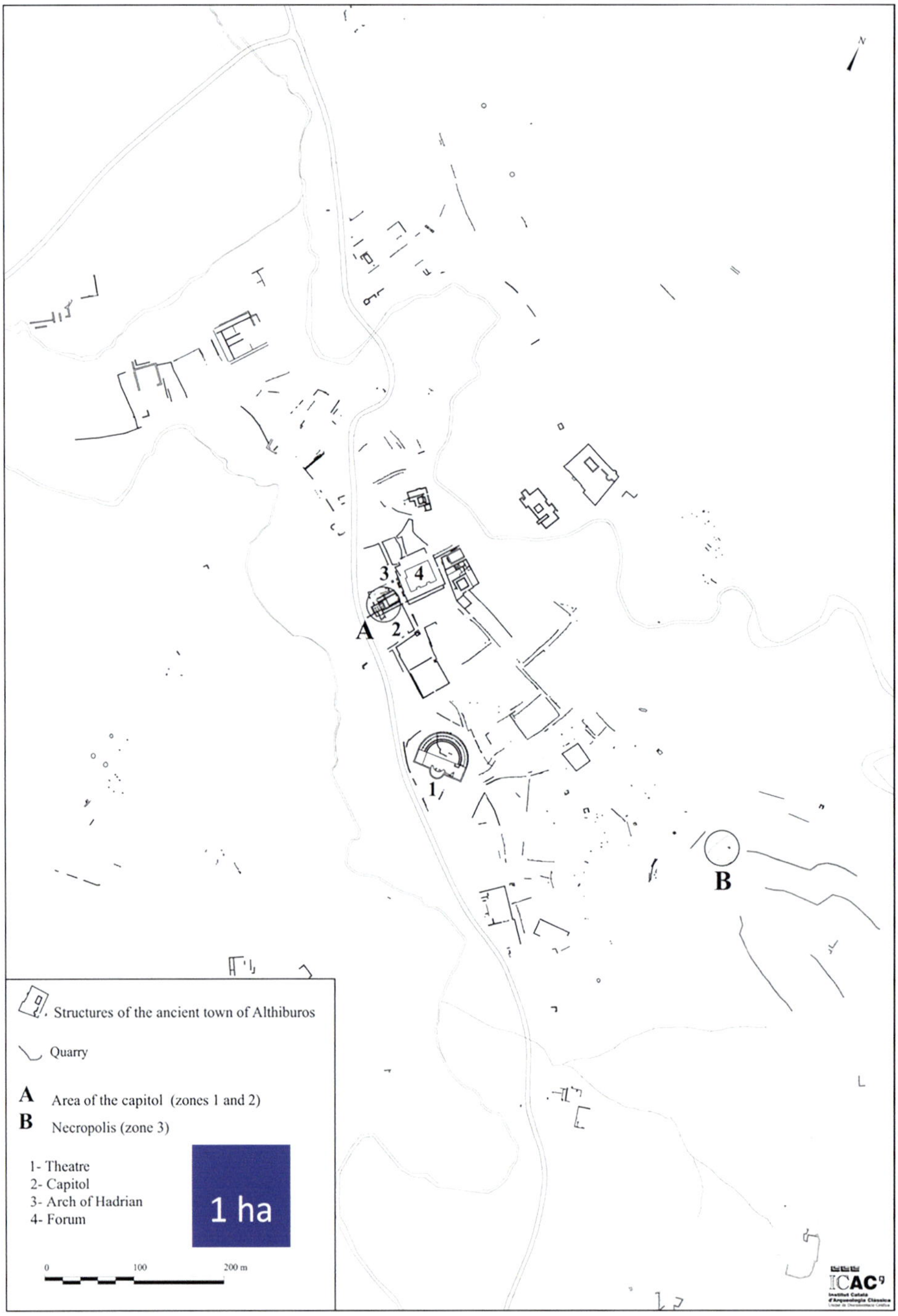

Figure 8.4. Plan of *Althiburos* (from Kallala and Sanmartí 2011, f.p. 25).

At a number of the major early Numidian towns, we have evidence of Roman direct intervention post-conquest, compromising their independent development under Roman rule. As will be explored in more detail in the next main section, Roman veteran colonies or veteran deductions or citizen *conventus* were imposed at some previously prominent centres, such as at *Cirta*, *Simitthu*, and *Sicca*. It is increasingly clear that the normal Roman approach to establishing colonies and settling veterans in North Africa involved the creation of dual communities by planting deductions at already established Numidian, Mauretanian, or Libyphoenician settlements. This followed the practice already established under Marius in the upper *Bagrada* valley.[125] A distinction thus needs to be made between Numidian sites, where we have evidence of significant veteran or Roman citizen settlement in the late 1st century BCE or early 1st century CE, and sites that evolved more independently. The latter tended to develop Roman suites of public buildings more slowly than the former and obtained urban promotion only gradually. For example, in the old eastern Numidian heartlands this suggests some measure of colonial differentiation operated between centres with dual communities and those whose populations remained essentially Numidian.

Thugga is a good example of the former category (see also Chapter 9 for discussion of its monumental development). Yet, in plan, what we see in essence is a hilltop and hillslope settlement, with steep escarpments on two sides and highly irregular and meandering internal roads, with buildings following multiple different alignments. The superimposition onto this maze of lanes of numerous rectilinear monumental buildings during the Roman era (Fig. 8.5) is all the more striking because of the difficulties of alignment that this presented. While this has often been celebrated as a great success story of "Romanisation," a more pessimistic reading of the architectural transformations is possible.[126] It is also interesting to note that while Roman-style temples and religious structures are packed into the urban core around the forum, some of the most significant sanctuaries (to Numidian deities syncretised with Roman gods) were suburban and situated among the cemetery zones. The significance of these chthonic Numidian cults in the Roman world is discussed further in Chapters 9 and 11.

In the area of the Cirtan Confederation, from the 46 BCE settlement by Sittius onwards Roman colonists had dominated the major urban centres and were present in smaller numbers in many long-established Numidian centres. *Tiddis* (also known as *Castellum Tidditanorum*) was by origin a Numidian fortified centre of c.12 ha area within its rampart walls, perched above deep gorges (Fig. 8.6).[127] Although it eventually gained urban status, its fundamental character was shaped

125. Aounallah 2010a; Maurin 1995.

126. Fentress 2021.

127. Berthier 2000; Blas de Roblès et al. 2019, 138–51.

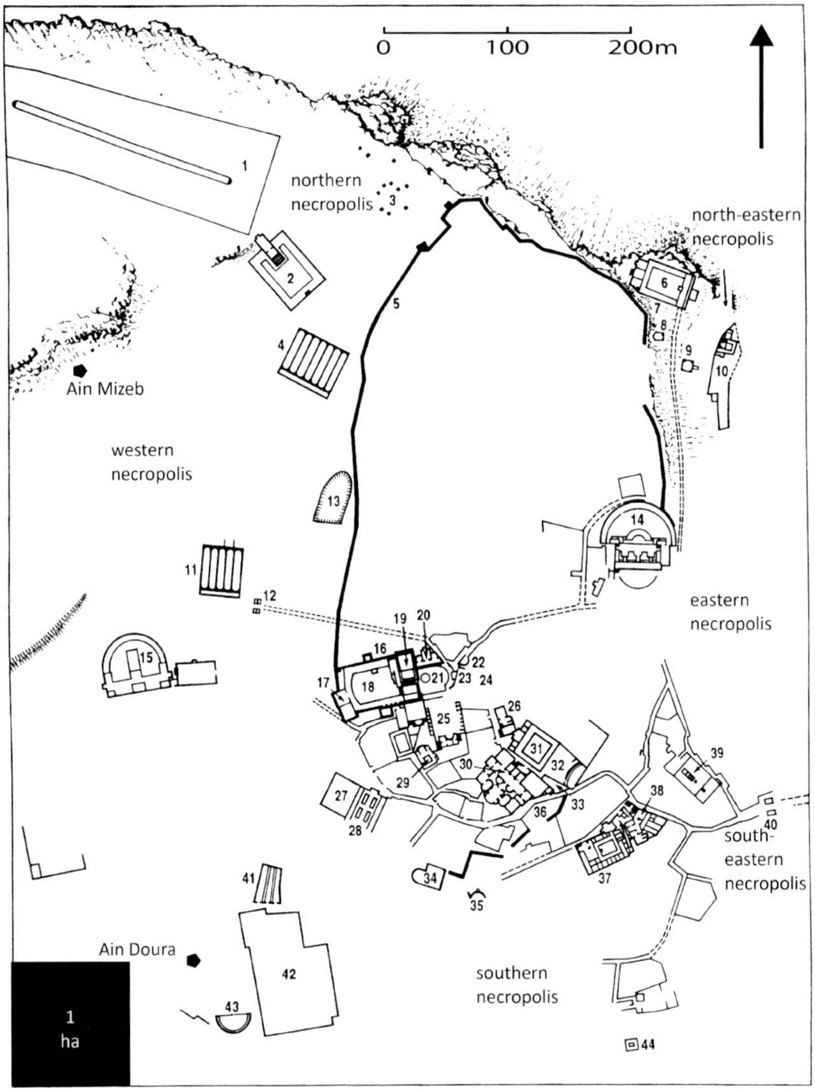

1. Circus; 2. T of Minerva; 3. Dolmens; 4. Cisterns; 5. Late Antique enceinte; 6. T of Saturn; 7. T of Neptune; 8. T (anon); 9. Christian hypogeum; 10. Church; 11. Cisterns; 12. Arch of Severus Alexander; 13. Amphitheatre?; 14. Theatre; 15. T of Caelestis; 16. Byzantine fortress; 17. T of Saturn?/Curia?; 18. Forum; 19. Capitolium; 20. T of Mercury; 21. Square of Wind Rose; 22. Shrine of Augustan piety; 23. T of Fortuna?; 24. Mosque; 25. Market; 26. T A; 27. T of German Victory of Caracalla; 28. Dar Lachhab; 29. T of Tellus; 30. Licinian Baths; 31. T of Concord; 32. Auditorium; 33. T (anon); 34. T of Minerva; 35. Nymphaeum; 36. H of Labyrinth; 37. H of Trifolium; 38. Baths of Cyclops; 39. T of Pluto; 40. Arch of Septimius Severus; 41. Cisterns; 42. Baths of Ain Doura; 43. Public latrines; 44. Libyco-Punic mausoleum.

Figure 8.5. Plan of *Thugga* (modified by author, after Khanoussi and Maurin 2000).

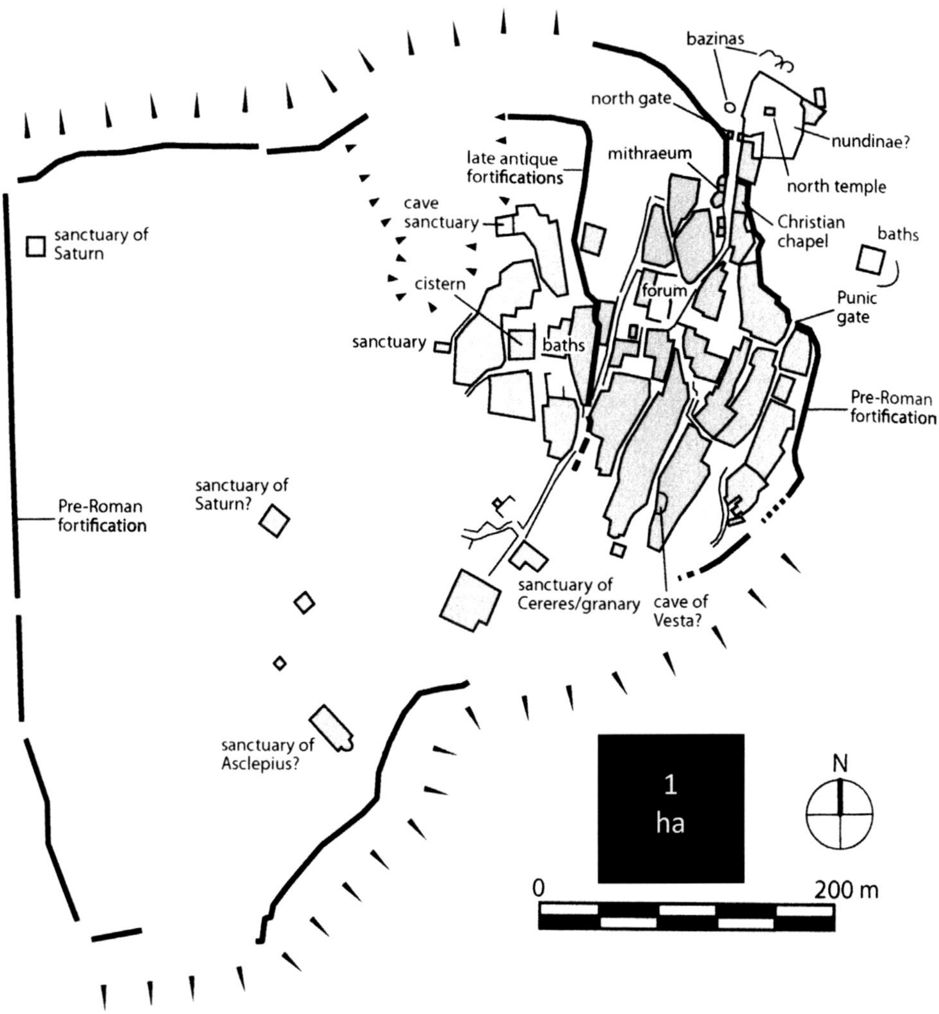

Figure 8.6. Plan of *Tiddis* (from Dufton and Fentress 2022, 194).

by its topography and pre-Roman past, with narrow lanes following the contours or stepped down the hillslope. The majority of the excavated quarter comprises densely packed, simple domestic structures and workshops (including pottery production and fullers), with only a single wealthy *domus* identified. A sanctuary of Baal/Saturn was located on the summit of the hill. The forum was a very small (30 × 10 m) public square and anomalous in its attenuated design. Elsewhere in the town, there were a couple of simple arches, a temple of Fortuna, a sanctuary of Cereres, a possible temple of Aesculapius and a couple of other small temples, a *Mithraeum*, and a small and a medium-sized bath complex. The contrast with the much more expansive monumentalisation of the similar topography at *Thugga* is striking. We

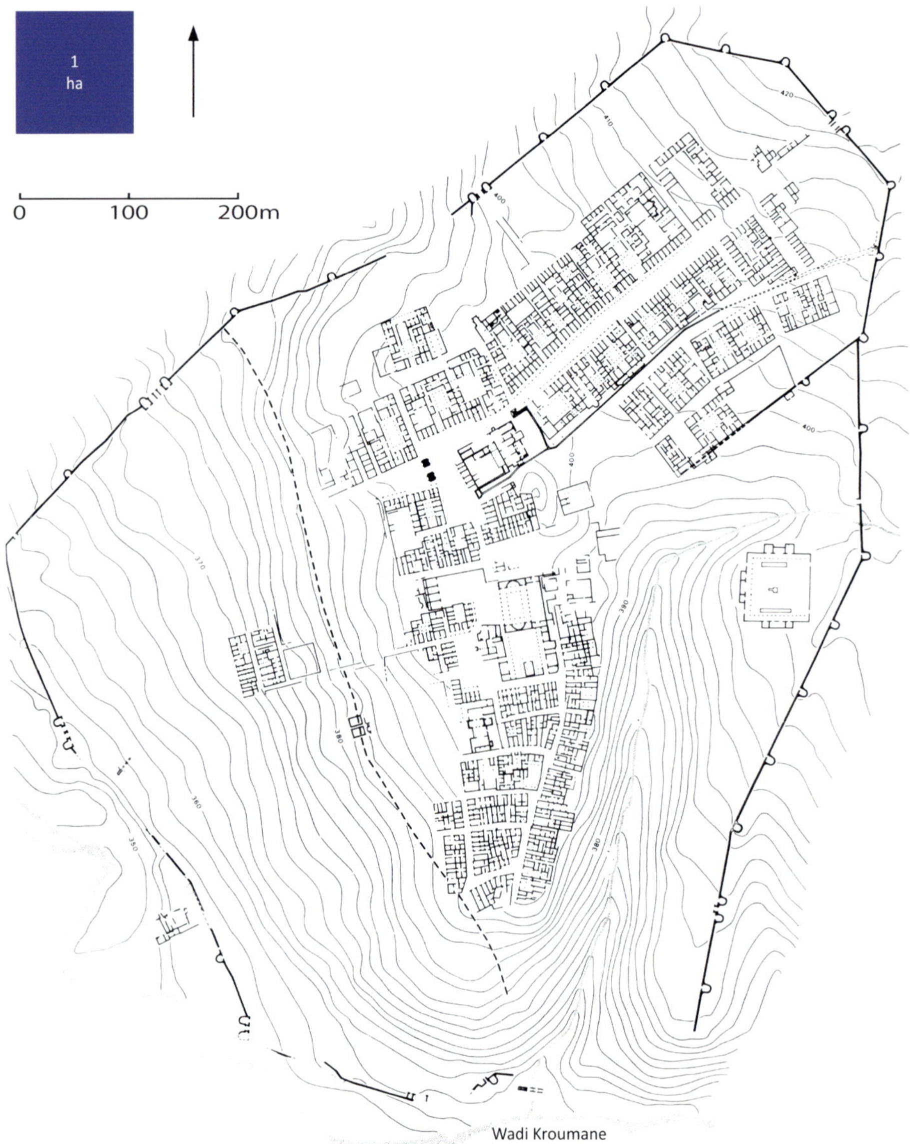

Figure 8.7. The evolved urban plan of *Volubilis* (adapted from Euzennat 1989, 213).

might note that Q. Lollius Urbicus, Prefect at Rome and the man who initiated construction of the Antonine Wall in Scotland, came from this area (he is honoured by a statue as patron of *Tiddis* and constructed a monumental ashlar drum tomb for his family within 3 km of the town, presumably where they had a large estate). Here more than at any other site, perhaps, one experiences a compromise urbanism, sprung from an already established African tradition in contact with new Roman models.

In *Mauretania Tingitana* there were evident urban continuities with Mauretanian centres, such as *Babba*, *Banasa*, Rirha, *Sala*, and *Volubilis*. The Roman veteran colony implanted at *Babba* has not been certainly located, though the Mauretanian coins issues of the town indicate its pre-Roman importance.[128] *Banasa* was another site where veteran colonists were assigned to an already established urban centre. Most interesting, though, are the plans of Mauretanian Rirha, *Sala*, and *Volubilis*, which all exploited classic promontory locations (cf. Fig. 4.12).[129] The growth of *Volubilis* beyond its original Mauretanian core promontory settlement is very clear in the developed urban plan, even with the superimposition of areas of gridded layout and Roman-style buildings (Fig. 8.7). The site was eventually enclosed by an expansive wall circuit, but a substantial part of the internal area of the town was terraced down quite steep scarps.

There are significant implications if the Mauretanian *coloniae* were in effect double communities combining Roman settlers and indigenous communities together. They highlight the strong affinities between Mauretanian and Numidian urbanism. The peregrine element of the urban community at *Banasa* may have been the *Zegrenses*, known from the *Tabula Banasitana*, a bronze inscription detailing the award of Roman citizenship to two men called Julianus. They were probably father and son, and the younger man was designated *princeps gentium Zegrensium*.[130] As the tablet was recovered in excavations at *Banasa* it is plausible that they were already urban-dwelling. Although both their wives had African names, their children had Latin names.

Libyphoenician Towns

There is a general view that the Libyphoenician coastal towns that had been dependent on *Qart Hadasht* were favourably treated after 146 BCE. The reality was perhaps more mixed, with many of the Tunisian *emporia* losing some land to the Roman state, though most escaped the total confiscation and destruction visited on *Qart Hadasht* itself. *Utica*, though allowed to remain a free city initially, became the first centre of imperial administration, which must have significantly changed the character of the town.[131] Some Punic centres in the Cap Bon area were

128. *Babba*, see Callegarin et al. 2016b, 108–12.
129. Rirha: Callegarin et al. 2016a, 14; *Sala* and *Volubilis*, after Euzennat 1989, 166, 204, 213.
130. Seston and Euzennat 1972; Sherwin-White 1973. For an English translation, see Levick 1985, 163–64.
131. For *Utica*, see Ben Jerbania et al. 2019; Chelbi 1996. For the legacy of *Qart Hadasht* after Punic wars, see Hobson 2019a.

destroyed and later refounded as veteran colonies, such as *Clipea* and *Neapolis*. On the other hand, the Tripolitanian cities had alliances with Rome from the time of the Jugurthan war if not earlier and were granted free city status. Caesar's 46 BCE victory in the civil war for control of Africa compromised some of the towns that had supported (or at any rate not opposed) the Pompeian forces. Some of Caesar's penalties were probably quite short-lived, and most of the cities of *Byzacium* and Tripolitania, for instance, seem to have flourished. By the reign of Augustus, several of the *emporia* had been allowed to mint coins, and the monumentalisation of some cities, like *Lepcis Magna*, was underway, though the paucity of archaeological or epigraphic evidence for 1st-century CE development at most sites makes it difficult to assess how typical *Lepcis Magna* was.[132]

As we saw in Chapter 3, the evidence for the size of the pre-Roman Libyphoenician *emporia* is limited. The available indications at *Lepcis Magna, Sabratha*, and *Leptiminus* suggest substantially less extensive Libyphoenician settlements than their Roman successor towns, amounting to 10–12 ha at most. Roman-era *Lepcis Magna* was abnormally large at 425 ha within an outer earthwork (Fig. 8.8), but the presence of extensive funerary features inside that earthwork show that the built-up urban core was considerably smaller, though even its late Roman walls enclosed 130 ha. *Sabratha* (core of c.40 ha and including suburban spread over 100 ha) and *Oea* (c.50 ha) were also substantial towns.

Both at *Leptiminus* and at *Meninx* on Jerba, intensive survey has revealed the importance of suburban activity at these coastal sites. At *Leptiminus,* the early to mid-Roman town core grew from c.24 to 45 ha in area, with a zone of dense manufacturing activity spread between the suburban cemeteries adding a further 100 ha to the wider townscape.[133] At *Meninx* the urban core was at least 30 ha by the later 1st century CE and the full extent of the city and its suburban zone, where lots of productive industry is attested, was c.140 ha.[134] The progressive expansion of a number of these sites, such as *Lepcis Magna* and *Sabratha*, saw new quarters laid out in a regular gridded alignment, though with successive phases taking slightly different orientations (Fig. 8.8). Initial survey at *Meninx* had assumed the same sort of regular gridded layout, but recent geophysical survey has revealed a much more complicated picture, with some significant irregularities in relation to the road layout as the site spread extensively along the coastline (Fig. 8.9).[135]

---

132. See Chapter 9 for discussion of early urban embellishment at *Lepcis*. Mugnai 2021 provides an interesting perspective on how this monumental centre was experienced by its citizens and visitors.
133. Stone et al. 2011c, 121–4.
134. Fentress et al. 2009, 131–76; Ritter and Ben Tahar 2020; Ritter et al. 2018.
135. Cf. Fentress et al. 2009, 134 (fig. 10.3); Ritter and Ben Tahar 2020; Ritter et al. 2018.

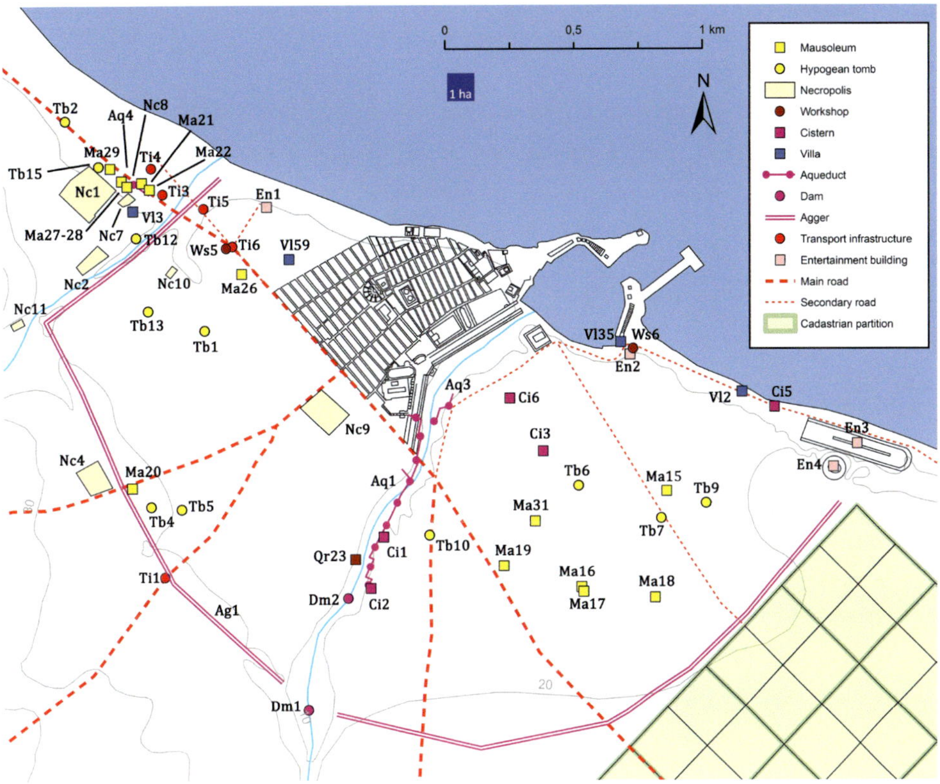

Figure 8.8. Plan of *Lepcis Magna*, showing cemeteries and other features of the *suburbium* (from Zocchi 2018a, 215).

In general, the harbour cities grew to much more substantial size than inland cities in the Roman period. There is ample evidence to show the involvement of the harbour cities in making fish sauce and salt fish, in purple dye production, and in large-scale amphora manufacture for fish products, oil, and wine.[136] There was massive investment in harbour facilities at these towns, especially along the shallow shoreline of the Lesser Syrtes gulf, in order to improve access for sea-going shipping.[137] Warehousing was another prerequisite of these commercial cities.[138] The

136. On fish processing, see Mattingly et al. 2011; Morère 2014 (on linked salt production); Slim et al. 1999; 2004; Trousset 1992; Wilson 2002a. On amphora production, Bonifay 2004, 8–44; Hobson 2015a, 103–42; Mrabet and Remesal Rodríguez 2007; Peacock et al. 1989; 1990; Stirling et al. 2000; Stone 2010. Purple dye manufacture, see Chebbi 2010; Drine 2007; Wilson 2002a. On urban production and economic growth, Hitchner 1993a; Hobson 2015b; Stone and Mattingly 2011; Wilson 2002b.

137. On a particular North African type of harbour feature, the jetty with platform, see Stone 2014b; 2016a.

138. Martorella 2020; Zocchi 2018a.

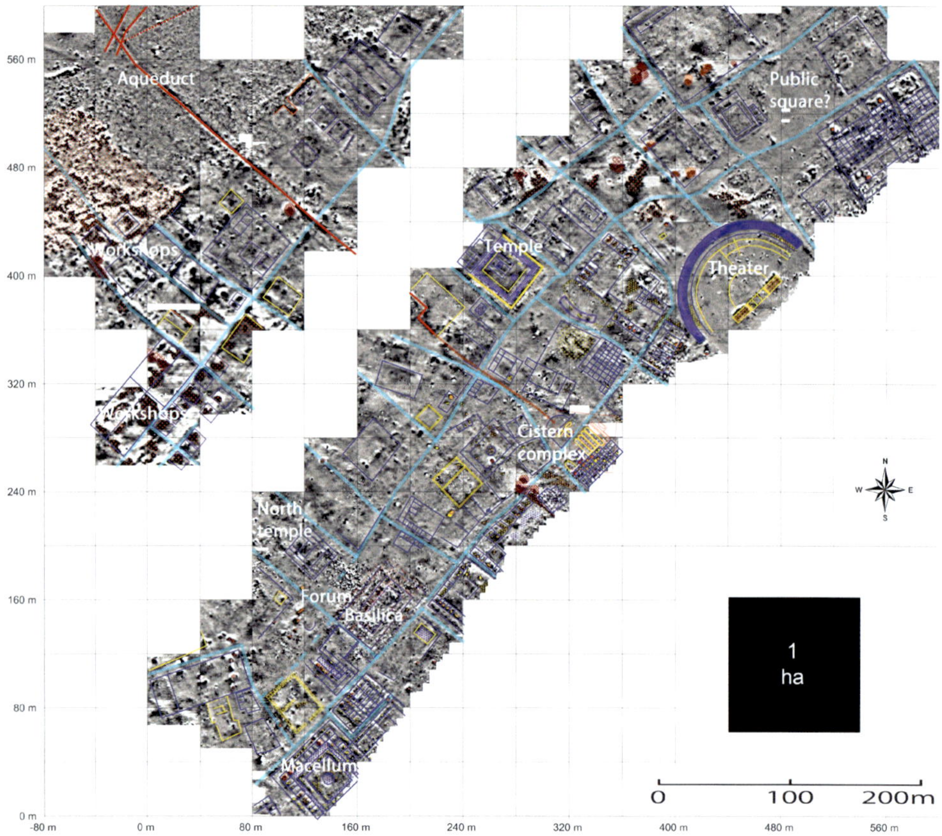

Figure 8.9. Plan of *Meninx* based on geophysical survey (from Ritter and Ben Tahar 2020, 121; plan: J. Fassbinder, S. Ritter).

expansion of these cities and their urban topography was significantly impacted by this commercial and productive orientation. The same was true, to a slightly lesser extent, of the harbour cities of northern Algeria and Morocco.[139]

Because of the wealth generated through trade, the old Libyphoenician harbour towns both in Tripolitania and *Byzacena* were among the most precocious in terms of their monumentalisation in the 1st and early 2nd centuries CE.[140] They were also among the first towns to receive honorary promotion in urban status in the later 1st century and early 2nd century CE. These towns also featured prominently among the African centres contributing people to the equestrian and senatorial order in the 2nd century. While at some sites, communities of foreign merchants

139. Papi 2007.

140. For other Libyphoenician centres of coastal *Byzacena*, see Foucher 1964 (*Hadrumetum*); Kaabia 2019; Nacef 2015 (*Sullecthum*); Younes 1999 (*Thapsus*).

existed from an early date and may have been significant actors within the urban community, other towns like the Tripolitanian cities appear to have been much less welcoming to outsiders, as most famously demonstrated by the prosecution of Apuleius by his Tripolitanian in-laws.[141] There is a paradox in the archaeology of *Lepcis*, as we shall see—it is both one of the most Roman towns of Africa and at the same time one of the sites that illustrates most clearly the continuing strength of regional identity and local tradition.

Oasis Towns

In Chapter 5, I argued that we need to take more account of the possible existence of numerous pre-Roman urban and proto-urban oases communities, relating to different traditions of urbanisation.[142] Some of these locations were later garrisoned by Roman army units, but many evolved into Roman urban centres, specifically designated as *civitas* centres for African *gentes*, like the *Nybgenii* at *Turris Tamalleni* (Telmine). The urban centre there was recognised by the Flavians and promoted to *municipium* rank under Hadrian.

But what did an oasis *municipium* look like? It is noteworthy that there are precious few examples of oasis towns or monuments in the tables earlier in the chapter. The archaeological evidence is tantalisingly sparse and this may in part relate to the intensive redevelopment of oases over time.[143] The village of Telmine, where two inscriptions referring to the *municipium* were found, is generally agreed to have been the site of *Turris Tamalleni* (Fig. 8.10). The eastern part of the village of Telmine sits on a prominent mound (perhaps the relic of a large artesian spring mound), round the foot of which runs a modern ring-road. The evidence for Roman construction at Telmine has come from the area of the mound, including a spring basin near its top and numerous Classical capitals and columns, evidently deriving from several ancient buildings. Pol Trousset recorded 22 column shaft fragments (including 2 marble and 1 fluted), 22 capitals (14 Ionic and 7 Corinthian, 1 late type in marble), and 15 column bases of diverse types.[144] The area within the annular modern road stands above the level of the surrounding oasis gardens and plausibly represents the ancient footprint of the town, within a wall or moated circuit. The area of the town would in this case be only 7–8 ha—seemingly small for a settlement accorded *municipium* status, but paralleled by similar-sized sites in the Numidian heartlands. Another possibility, however, is that the *municipium* in

141. Bradley, 2000, 227–33.
142. Mattingly and Sterry 2020a; Sterry and Mattingly 2020a; 2020c.
143. As is very apparent at Garamantian Jarma, Mattingly 2013a.
144. Eleffi 2015; Trousset 1974, 43–46; 2011, 211–13.

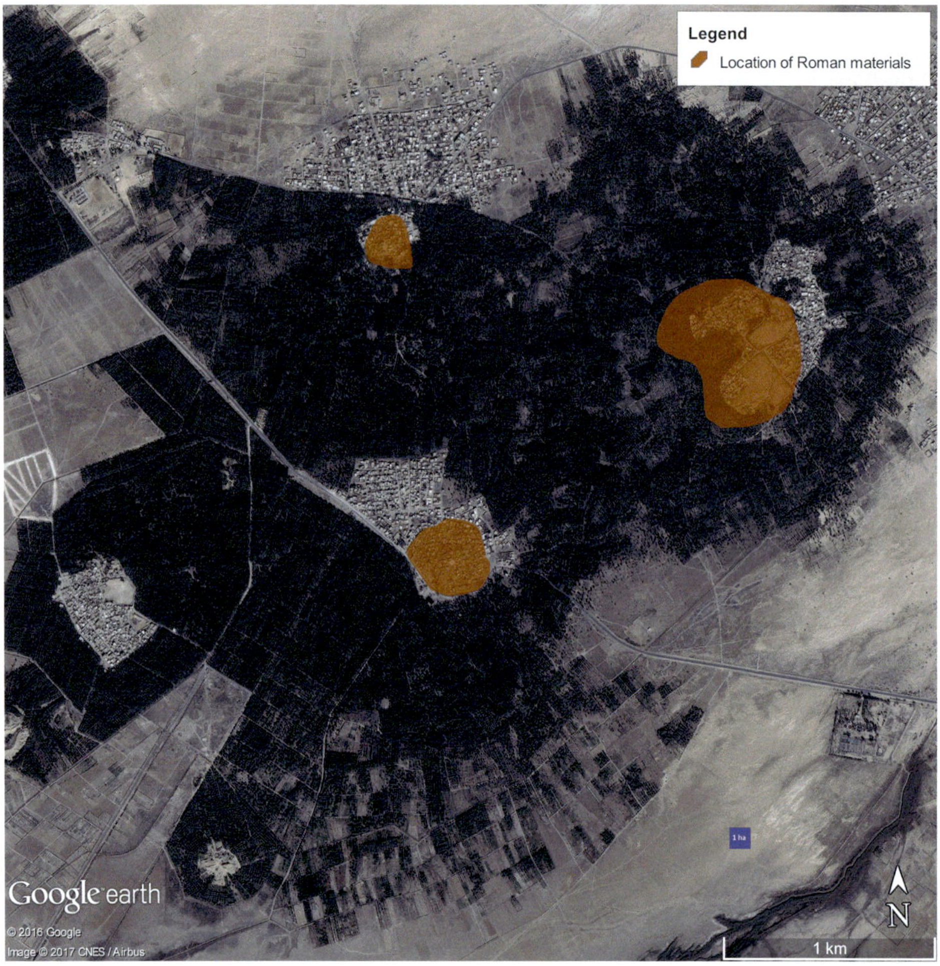

Figure 8.10. Roman remains in the oasis of Telmine relating to the *municipium Turris Tamalleni* (author annotation on satellite image: Google, DigitalGlobe).

fact designated the combined community of several closely adjacent oasis villages here, as there are also Roman remains in a number of the neighbouring oases in the Nefzaoua group (Fig. 8.10).[145]

The nearby coastal town of *Tacape* (Gabes) is something of a mystery, since despite eventually being made an honorary *colonia*, remarkably scant traces of its structural footprint have ever been located. The main clues again suggest several distinct foci within the Gabes oasis.[146] It thus seems likely that these oasis towns

145. Mattingly et al. 2020b, 202–04.

146. Hilaire 1900; Mattingly et al. 2020b, 207; Montezun 1885.

had a very different look in terms of layout and monumentalisation compared to the towns of northern Tunisia and north-eastern Algeria.

The evidence of other oasis towns suggests that this may not be unreasonable, as oasis towns rarely achieve a large footprint and are often made up of multiple subunits of village-like scale. The Garamantian capital at Jarma, for instance, is thought to have not exceeded 9.5 ha and had several minor satellite settlements close by.[147] Early modern Ghadamis covered only c.11 ha. Another Garamantian urban settlement, Qasr ash-Sharraba has yielded the most complete plan of one of these early desert towns, and at c.15 ha it is one of the largest settlements recorded, though this includes a substantial fort-like compound at its centre (Fig. 5.9).[148] Both *Cidamus* and *Garama* featured decorative Mediterranean architectural schemes in their buildings. If this was possible in the central Sahara, what should we expect of oasis towns recognised by Rome within the provincial territory? The archaeological investigation of one of the Tunisian oasis towns is an urgent priority if we are to advance our understanding of such sites. But my strong prediction is that oasis towns in *Africa Proconsularis* and *Numidia* were not all that well provided with urban amenities, were generally small in overall area and probably mainly constructed in less durable materials like mud-brick.

Group 2. Colonial Towns

A number of different types of towns had a more or less colonial character—that is to say, they were settlements with a stronger than normal association with the imperial project, often comprising communities or subgroups who enjoyed privileged status, lower taxes, and enhanced legal rights. There were reasons why these sorts of towns might be expected to associate strongly with Roman urban norms and to have been early adopters of Roman-style amenities.

Veteran Colonies and Other New Foundations and Refoundations

The North African veteran colonies comprise a significant minority among the cities. The exact number may never be known because of gaps in the epigraphic evidence, though we might note that the list and map given by Ramsey MacMullen, identifying more than 20 Caesarian/Augustan foundations between *Cirta* and the Syrtic gulf, include some dubious examples.[149] Veteran settlements

147. Mattingly 2010a, 123–60; 2013a, 525–29.

148. Mattingly et al. 2020a, 78–79.

149. MacMullen 2000, 32–33 includes, for instance, *Hadrumetum*, *Thuburbo Maius*, *Thapsus*. See Gascou 1972; also Briand-Ponsart 2005b for a recent summary.

were a heterogeneous group, varying from the extraordinary ad hoc settlement of the veterans of P. Sittius around *Cirta* after 46 BCE, based on four colonies and a vast territory,[150] to numerous deductions of veterans placed by Marius or Caesar in villages and smaller nucleated centres (*castella*) within the old Carthaginian territory. Later colonies were founded under the Flavians (*Ammaedara*, *Madauros*), Nerva, and Trajan (*Sitifis*, *Cuicul*, and *Thamugadi*). *Thelepte* also appears to have been a 2nd-century veteran colony.[151] We should not necessarily imagine these centres as being entirely formed around a large ex-legionary deduction—the veterans may have in most instances been combined with other civilian groups. The total number of ex-soldiers settled in Africa is uncertain, but the number of colonies and other smaller settlements where veteran deductions are attested indicates that these must have involved in excess of 50,000 men—the largest numbers were settled in the several generations after 46 BCE. The redistribution of land to these men, and the higher status of the veterans as Roman citizens, will have had significant implications for their relationship with indigenous Africans in the vicinity. A significant number of the early colonies were in effect refoundations of pre-existing towns that had either been sacked or, more likely, were still occupied by communities that were singled out to have a veteran contingent imposed on them. Thus we find the Libyphoenician coastal sites of *Hippo Diarrhytus*, *Utica*, *Clipea*, *Curubis*, *Neapolis*, with a second significant group of inland sites such as *Maxula* and *Uthina*. A third group involved refoundations or veteran impositions at Numidian towns like *Musti*, *Simitthu*, *Cirta*, *Sicca*, *Thuburnica*, *Assuras*, *Zama Regia*. At most of these sites, the colonists were installed alongside Africans and Libyphoenicians, who had lower status and fewer privileges (legal and fiscal).[152] We might expect such sites to both engage with Roman urban norms and to reflect a degree of cultural hybridity.

In terms of urban form, our mental picture of a Roman veteran colony probably tends automatically towards the plan of *Thamugadi* (Fig. 8.11), with the striking checker-board layout of its original core zone.[153] From their extreme regularity of plan, a number of other towns appear to have been new foundations in the late 1st century CE, though their initial status is unclear, and recent

150. Bernard 2014.

151. On the significance of the Flavian era for the reinvigoration of the Roman urban project in North Africa, see Leglay 1968a; Lepelley 2005b.

152. The mixture of Roman colonists and *negotiatores*, some with links to central Italy, and Africans at *Simitthu* is evident in a detailed study of 65 funerary texts, but with the Roman citizens standing out from non-citizens, see Ardeleanu et al. 2019.

153. *Karthago* was another example of a Roman colony with a regular gridded layout, but as noted by Le Bohec 2005a, 116, "Timgad et Carthage constituaient non pas deux exemples mais deux exceptions."

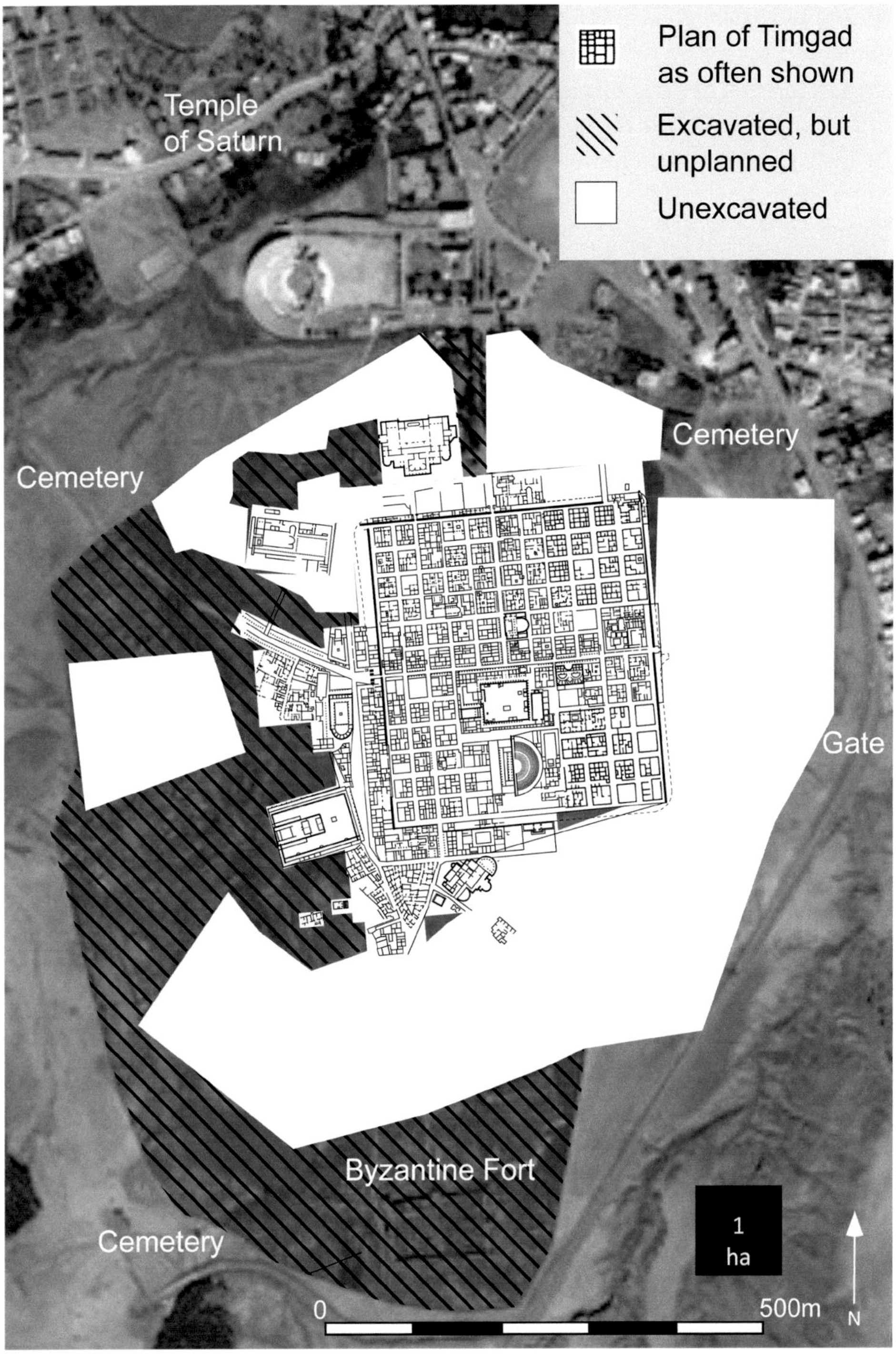

Figure 8.11. Plan of veteran *colonia* of *Thamugadi* (from Stone 2021).

epigraphic discoveries at *Sufetula*, for instance, hint at the involvement of local people.[154] At nearby *Cillium* we have some evidence that veterans were prominent in the first generations of the town's existence.[155] But these "typical" Roman orthogonal town plans are not common in the overall African context. The reality may have been rather different, especially where colonies were superimposed on existing towns. *Uthina* provides a contrasting picture to the checkerboard layout of *Thamugadi*. Although provided with an excellent range of amenities (theatre, amphitheatre, baths, aqueduct, forum, and *capitolium*, and so on), at *Uthina* different quarters are variously aligned.[156] The veteran colony at *Cuicul*—closely contemporary with *Thamugadi*—is even more unusual (Fig. 8.12). Notwithstanding aspects of regularity in the layout of its streets and monuments, the overall plan reflects the constraints of a narrow peninsular and several phases of expansion. The topographic location of the site is that of a Numidian fortified promontory site between wadi gorges, like *Bagat* and *Althiburos*. The original walled settlement here, prior to its expansion in the 3rd century, covered only c.4 ha, a very small area for a major Roman town.[157] Although there is no excavated evidence for pre-Roman origins, beyond a local Libyan inscription, the use of a typical Numidian urban location suggests this was a small colonial imposition on an existing population centre.[158]

Simitthu is an even more unusual site, in that an early Numidian urban centre built in a low-lying riverside position to west and south-west of the marble quarries was developed by Rome and reinforced by a colonial deduction (Fig. 8.13). The town eventually achieved a fair degree of monumentalisation, including provision of a forum complex, theatre, amphitheatre, Roman-style temples and some well-planned extensions to the urban road grid to the north. There was also a major bridge with sophisticated water mills built on the river. But overall, the urban facilities are haphazard, wrapped like a crescent around the western end of the quarry outcrops that dominate the urban landscape here. Although there were some important temples within the town, several long-term sanctuaries to Numidian gods were located on Jabal Chimtu. We should note also the ominous presence of a large military compound on the north side of the quarries for the supervision of production and housing of a partially slave-labour force.[159] This was a town

154. Khanoussi 2008; 2010.
155. Lassère et al. 1993.
156. Ben Hassen and Maurin 2004, 51–91. Cf. Ben Hassen and Maurin 1998, for some fine reconstruction images.
157. See Février and Blanchard-Lemée 2019, 15 for contoured plan.
158. The recognition of an underlying Numidian urbanisation changes our perspective on the overall development of the town.
159. Rakob 1993; 1994; 2005; von Rummel 2014; von Rummel and Schöne 2013; von Rummel et al. 2013.

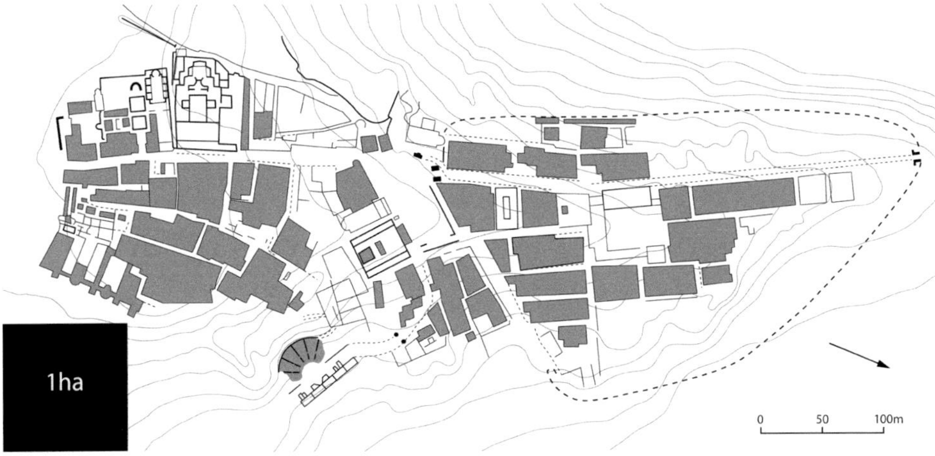

Figure 8.12. Plan of *colonia* of *Cuicul* (Mike Hawkes, after Février and Blanchard-Lemée 2019, 15).

with a number of distinct cultural elements at play—colonists, Numidians, migrant quarry workers (free and enslaved), and soldiers and an imperial bureaucracy associated with the quarry exploitation.

Dual Communities

In addition to the formally constituted *coloniae* and *municipia*, there were other locations with significant numbers of Roman citizens living alongside Africans. This was particularly common in the Carthaginian *pertica*, where small groups of veterans had initially been distributed between villages and administered from *Karthago*, but where over time they seem to have become part of growing urban communities, as at *Uchi Maius*, *Musti*, and *Thugga*.[160] The existence of large imperial estates in this area meant that the chief tenants (*conductores*) from these domains were also significant players in the region's towns. The Roman citizens within these dual communities had higher status and rights, even while the towns lacked urban charters. As these towns gained promotions and Roman chartered status, it was still the families who had held Roman citizenship longest (and who may have had larger opportunities to accumulate lands) who tended to dominate. The archaeology of *Thugga* provides the clearest evidence of how this sort of dual settlement operated (Fig. 8.5). There is no evidence that the two communities lived segregated from each other within the townscape, though some zoning in funerary areas is possible.[161] *Thugga* is often presented in the literature as a

160. Ben Ahaba 2012; Gascou 1982c; 1984; Khanoussi and Mastino 1997; 2012; Poinssot 1962.
161. Aounallah et al. 2020b; Khanoussi and Maurin 2002, 77–78. See also Scheding 2019.

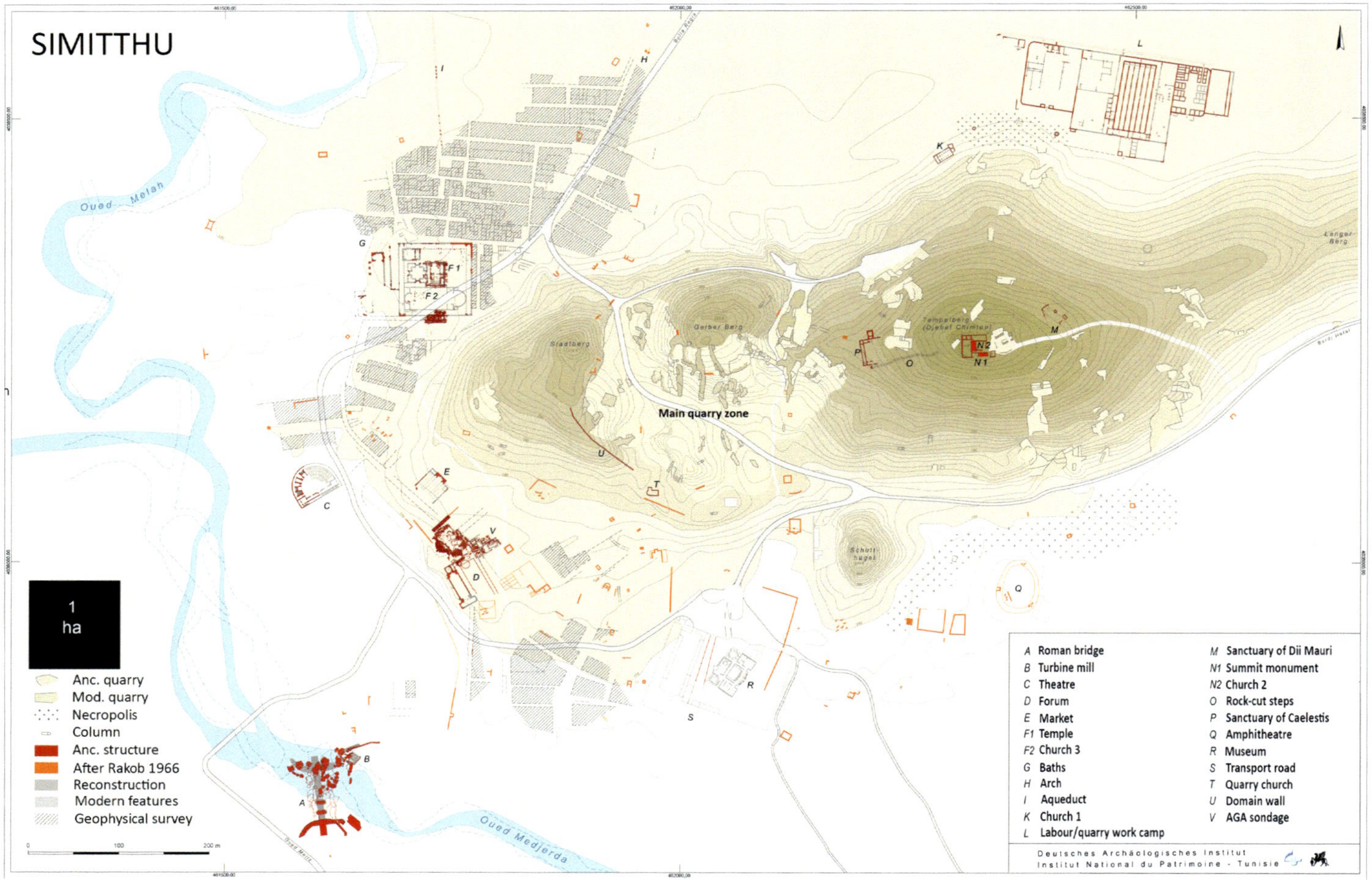

Figure 8.13. Plan of *colonia* of *Simitthu* and the marble quarry workings (from von Rummel et al. 2016, 102).

relatively small and irregular town that reached its apogee comparatively late. However, with a built up core of c.20 ha and a suite of public buildings that included a theatre, a circus, a possible amphitheatre, and two major bath complexes, it stands out from many of the other towns of the *Numidae* and the Carthaginian *pertica*.

Garrison Settlements

The idea of a defined group of garrison settlements was introduced in Chapter 7. Although they represent a relatively small fraction of sites in relation to the totality of urban centres, this was another important group with a distinctive cultural character. The garrison town par excellence was *Lambaesis*, comprising in effect both the *canabae* immediately adjacent to the legionary fortress and the higher town to the south-east. A number of the garrison settlements around auxiliary forts achieved urban promotion to become chartered Roman towns. *Gemellae* and *Nigrenses Maiores* in *Numidia*, and *Auzia* and *Rapidum* in *Mauretania Caesariensis* are among prominent examples that gained *municipium* status (Fig. 7.4). The Numidian examples were constructed close to oasis settlements, but the focal architecture of the forts made these towns very different to the normal oasis centres of the zone. *Nigrenses Maiores* has yielded evidence of two monumental arches and *Gemellae* possessed an amphitheatre, but there was little else at either site to parallel the urban amenities familiar from towns in northern Tunisia.[162] Regardless of the urban status attested at these sites, the character of the urban environment here was evidently very different to other urban centres described so far. Again, a proper investigation of one of these garrison towns is needed for us to understand better how they functioned as urban centres and how identity was represented in material culture, architecture, and behaviour.

162. Mattingly et al. 2013a, 66, 88; 2020b, 225–27.

Chapter 9

EXPLORING URBAN IDENTITIES

Introduction

> The Empire was then made up of a multitude of identical cities from which emerged universal social classes and which served as the basis for a system of common institutions, which were increasingly perfected over time. Of all the western provinces—apart from Italy—Africa is where this biological transformation of the human environment had the greatest success.[1]

In the previous chapter I have demonstrated the falsity of the idea of a world of "all-alike cities," as suggested in the quote above. The subject of this chapter is the cultural variability of these urban communities, resulting in rather heterogeneous markers of urban identity across North Africa's towns—contrasting markedly with the situation imagined by Picard and others working within the Romanisation paradigm. This parallels my work on Britain in the Roman Empire, where I have demonstrated that Roman garrison settlements, veteran *coloniae*, and provincial capitals followed a very different cultural engagement with the urban form and urban behaviours when compared with the *civitas* centres of the indigenous British peoples.[2] To give just one example of this, there is a distinct imbalance in Britain in the adoption of the tradition of erecting tombstones for the dead.[3] While tombstones were very common at forts and garrison settlements, and exist at the towns most closely associated with the military community, they are almost entirely unattested at *civitas* towns, and the rare exceptions there are most often attributable to foreigners or people with an association with the army or with provincial bureaucracy. It might be tempting to write this off as an accident of survival or of lack of local resources at the time when the epigraphic habit was at its strongest in Britain, but the significant investment in British towns in 2nd-century mosaics

1. Picard 1990, 26: "L'Empire est alors formé d'une multitude de cites toutes pareilles d'où sortent des classes sociales universalles et qui servent de base à un système d'institutions communes, de plus en plus perfectionnées. L'Afrique est, de toutes les provinces occidentales—l'Italie mise à part—celle où cette transformation biologique du milieu humaines a connu le plus grand succès."
2. Mattingly 2006a; 2011a, 219–36.
3. Mattingly 2008.

is an indication that this absence of tombstones was more plausibly the result of a strongly expressed cultural preference among different "Roman" behaviours.

The epigraphic evidence from Africa is very different, of course, and civil tombstones certainly existed in very large numbers in many places. However, they were not uniformly present across all urban sites, and I think that future studies could engage with the diverse patterning. The epigraphic habit was socially contingent and the urban elite (the curial class) have left the fullest account of their actions and identities, though the contribution to urban life and development of a broader urban community needs also to be considered.[4] Urban communities addressed not only the monumental and epigraphic aspects of Roman urbanism, but also the legal and social connotations.[5] Taking this further, the possibility that there were similar variations in the consumption of a range of supposedly Roman cultural practices is worth exploring in the different sorts of urban settings identified in the previous chapter. In the compass of this chapter, I can only sketch a few initial ideas, but I hope that the material relating to religious practices, burial rites and funerary practices, and linguistic preferences will be suggestive of the potential for a larger study of this sort. A key point is that identity mattered hugely in Romano-African societies and not simply in terms of how far people took on "Roman" behaviours, names, and the Latin language, and we neglect evidence of cultural continuities from African communities at our peril.

> The traditional aristocracy ... in any case disappears before our eyes and plays no cultural role. The Punic aristocracy disappeared in 146 BCE after seeing the decline of the port of Carthage ... The Numidian or Moorish aristocracy is almost unknown to us ... contact with an agrarian economy may have led to difficulties, impoverishment and decadence ... Romanisation of Libyans was normal in the region of the coastal cities, closest to the classical world, and close to other urban foci.[6]

There is a clear contradiction between that passage and another in the same book where Lassère presents the funerary inscription of Plancina, from *Sicca Veneria*. She was mourned by her husband Q. Arruntius Mascel (the *cognomen* attests his African identity). The metrical Latin funerary inscription on a large altar-type *cippus* suggests a date in the 2nd–3rd century CE, and many of the idealised

4. On the urban elite, see, for instance, Belkahia Karoui 2009. See the interesting reflections of popular engagement in urban life of Magalhães de Oliveira 2012.

5. Belkahia Karoui 2014.

6. Lassère 2005b, 146: "L'aristocratie traditionelle ... ne joue aucune rôle culturel. L'aristocratie punique a disparu en 146 av. J.-C.; après avoir vu le decline du port du Carthage ... L'aristocratie numide ou maure est à peu près inconnu de nous ... le contact avec une économie agraire a pu entrainer des difficultés, l'appauvrissement et la decadence ... La romanisation des Libyens apparaît normale dans les regions côtières, proches du monde classique, ou au voisinage des cités qui sont des centres de rayonnement."

attributes of Plancina mentioned in the inscription recalled Roman norms—good mother, good wife, honourable woman. So far, so Roman, but the hybrid identity at play is reflected by the fact that, though she appears to be from a Roman citizen family (and probably the same woman as the Maria Plancina referred to in another text, *ILT* 1633), her full Roman names are not given here. More importantly, she is referred to as "highest ranking of the Numidian women" (*Numidarum prima mulierum*), of "royal lineage" (*genere regio*), "more honourable than other women."[7] The last comment might be seen as an attempt to claim greater honour among women beyond the already mentioned Numidian women, specifically Roman colonist families settled alongside the Numidians at *Sicca*. Lassère tried to turn Plancina into the daughter of a Gaetulian *princeps gentis*, but the allusion to her being a Numidian woman, her domicile at a Numidian town, *Sicca*, and the twice repeated insistence on her royal descent, favours the view that her family really did cherish the memory of their royal roots long after Rome's dissolution of the Numidian kingdom. If the inscription dates to the later 2nd century CE (as seems most plausible) then she was born more than 150 years after the fall of Juba I. This seems a direct example of the long-continuing importance of Numidian aristocratic status in some Roman-era urban communities. A somewhat parallel example concerns a man who identified himself before the Roman governor Zenophilus in 320 CE as "a teacher of Roman literature, a Latin grammarian. My father is a decurion here in the city of *Constantina*, my grandfather was a soldier who served in the *comitatus*, and my family origin is descended from Moorish blood."[8] We shall see how the same long-held remembrance of local identity was true for the Libyphoenician elite of *Lepcis Magna* below.

In this chapter, I mainly focus on linguistic practices, on religion and funerary traditions, and what they reveal about the diversity of urban identity. In a similar way it ought to be possible to analyse Roman-period art and other material culture as representative of diverse and divergent practices. High-end cosmopolitan artworks there certainly were, though again these are most abundant in the cities with the greatest engagement in the architectural programmes of the Empire.[9] Most attention has focused on the extraordinarily accomplished statuary and relief sculptures in marble, and the vibrant mosaics.[10] However, more rustic-style artworks, seemingly addressing a different sort of aesthetic and function in urban

7. Lassère 2005c, 43–44.
8. *Gesta apud Zenophilum*, l = *CSEL* 26, 185. Shaw 2014, 537 for translation and discussion.
9. Février 1971; 1976a; Hurlet 2000; Picard 1982; Salcedo 1996. Zanker 1988 remains the classic discussion of how art served discourses of power within Empire, though cf. Scott and Webster 2003, for discussion of the need to pay more attention to the more "provincial" and less accomplished artworks, which have an important story to tell.
10. Inter alia, Bartoccini 1929 (statuary from *Lepcis* baths); Landwehr 1993; 2000; 2006; 2008 (Caesarea—including much fine sculpture from the Mauretanian kingdom period also); Squarciapino 1974 (Severan forum at *Lepcis*).

society, have been less analysed for their social significance.[11] Hopefully, this lacuna can be filled by future studies.

The lives of the urban poor are mostly inaccessible for us due to the nature of the evidence available, though there are occasional reminders of hidden horrors—as in the discovery of the human remains of an enslaved female prostitute, Adultera, who was still wearing an inscribed metal collar when her body was dumped in the courtyard of the Temple of Apollo at *Bulla Regia*.[12] Between the richest and poorest and most oppressed in society there was a huge spectrum of social experience.

Languages and Identity

The sort of urban diversity presented so far—due to regionalism, to origins, and to economic orientation—is also reflected in cultural differences.[13] To illustrate the principle, I first use the example of languages in the urban communities. A large percentage of the urban community in Africa was probably at least bilingual,[14] though the bulk of the epigraphic evidence emphasises above all the Latinity of society. There is a tendency to assume that this evidence represents commonality and homogeneity,[15] but the linguistic mix was highly varied across the province and we need to be careful about imposing conclusions from one particular city onto others as a general rule.[16]

Latin

Latin was by far the most prevalent language group epigraphically if we use the relative size of corpora of Latin, Greek, Punic, and Libyan inscriptions from Africa. However, it was not always or everywhere thus, and one of the remarkable aspects of the huge epigraphic dossier is the way in which we can track linguistic change over time. Bearing in mind the fact that the urban evidence is skewed towards the cities that were more closely engaged with the Roman colonial project, there is also a danger that the ubiquity of Latin is overrepresented in the epigraphic dossier accumulated. Excavation has tended to gravitate towards sites with the largest

11. See below on Saturn stelae. For discussion of the sort of cultural issues relating to the independent artistic traditions of Iron Age societies, see Garrow and Gosden 2012.
12. Leone 1996; Trimble 2016, 457 (*Adultera meretrix (sum). Tene quia fugivi de Bulla R(e)g(ia).* "I am Adultera, a prostitute. Hold me because I have fled from *Bulla Regia*."
13. As also noted by Ibba et al. 2011; Scheding 2019; Stone 2020.
14. On bilingualism and multilingualism, see Adams 2003; Mullen 2013; Mullen and James 2012.
15. Baratte 2012, 72: "Le Latin est assimilé par la plupart, on voit bien, à regarder les inscriptions.'
16. On the linguistic mix in Africa, see Lengrand 2005.

numbers of Latin inscriptions and the highest engagement with Roman monumentality. Once again, this raises questions about the representativeness of the "usual suspects" within a broader spectrum of urban communities.

Greek

Greek was always a minority language in African towns, but was learned and shown off by many wealthy families, keen to reveal their sense of belonging to the cultural elite of the Empire. The cultural value of Greek was already recognised in the Numidian and Mauretanian kingdoms—as references to the learning of Massinissa's son Mastanabal and later to Juba II demonstrate.[17] Greek was also a sharp weapon to be wielded against those in provincial society who had not made the educational investment. This is perhaps clearest in the story of the trial of Apuleius (as documented in his *Apologia*) at *Sabratha* in the 150s CE, where he repeatedly emphasised his own education and cultural identity as a Roman, unfavourably contrasting the "rustic" and ill-educated nature of his Tripolitanian adversaries in court.[18] Although he does allude to his African identity, Apuleius clearly belonged to a cosmopolitan Mediterranean set of "intellectual Romans." There were also Greek traders and Jewish groups (who often communicated in Greek) operating in various African cities from early times.[19] Finally, of course, *Cyrenaica* was a Greek-speaking province, though with evidence of Libyan, Latin, and Punic alongside.[20]

Punic

Punic was more widely disseminated in North Africa than simply in the territories of *Karthago* and the Libyphoenician cities. In Chapters 3 and 4, I showed how the "Phoenician identity" of many sites in *Mauretania*—primarily based on the literary tradition of Punic foundation or some Punic inscriptions—is now complicated by the evidence for Mauretanian and Numidian urbanisation and the profound engagement of these communities with Punic culture. Punic bilingual texts at *Thugga* and the reputation of Hiempsal's "Punic books" are good illustrations of the functional use of written Punic in the kingdoms.[21] The strong evidence of neo-Punic inscriptions at *Lepcis Magna* up to and beyond the general acquisition of citizenship with its

17. Coltelloni-Trannoy 2005b; Gsell 1927b, 90–92; Lengrand 2005, 120.
18. Briand-Ponsart 2002; Pavis d'Escurac 1974; Stone 2014a; Ward 1968.
19. For example, Várhelyi and Bagnall 2009 (Greek commercial ostraca from *Meninx*, with reference to others known from *Sabratha* and *Lepcis*); Le Bohec 2021; Stern 2007 (on Jews).
20. See now *IRCyr* 2020.
21. Lengrand 2005, 120–21.

promotion to *colonia* rank indicates that Punic continued as a living language long afterwards.[22] One of the aristocratic accusers of Apuleius in the 150s allegedly spoke "nothing but Punic" (*Apologia* 98.8), while the sister of Septimius Severus was reputed to scarcely speak Latin—a source of great shame for the emperor, who evidently had her sent back to *Lepcis* from Rome (*Historia Augusta, Septimius Severus* 1.4, 15.7).[23] These were elite families, which suggests that many people lower down society in Tripolitania will have had limited Latin even in the late 2nd century. Tripolitania was probably quite an extreme case in that it was a region that was spared any significant level of colonisation or settlement from outside. This is also hinted at by the recently published amphitheatre excavations at *Lepcis Magna*, where in addition to a number of blocks of seating inscribed in Latin with distinguished family names, perhaps indicating reserved areas, there were also hundreds of Punic and even some Libyan characters in similar positions on both vertical and horizontal faces of the seating steps.[24] The interpretation of the neo-Punic and Libyan texts is ambiguous, but many seem also to relate to marking out areas of seating rather than being simply quarry signs or casual graffiti. The implication is that the mass of the people needed such directions in neo-Punic. A similar phenomenon has also been noted in the amphitheatre at Sabratha, though with less abundant surviving evidence.[25]

Northern Tunisia was to some extent a more Latin-dominated landscape, though even there the letters of Augustine make it clear that Punic survived in pockets (St Augustine, *Letters* 108.5.14; 209).[26] Many of the c.600 stone neo-Punic inscriptions of Roman date from this area were funerary or religious in nature (especially related to the cult of Baal/Saturn), but there is some interesting use in public building and euergetism.[27]

Libyan

Libyan is the most difficult language to evidence in urban contexts, though it was present. Astonishingly, St Augustine makes no reference to its continued existence as the spoken vernacular in large parts of the Maghrib.[28] It is hard to explain, but

22. On Punic inscriptions from Tripolitania, see the important work of Levi Della Vida (1927; 1935; 1949; 1951; 1964a; 1964b; 1965), leading up to the publication of the *IPT* corpus. For the later continuing tradition of Punic language using Latin letters, see Jongeling 2008; Jongeling and Kerr 2005; Kerr 2007; Levi della Vida 1963; Wilson 2012b.
23. Mattingly 1995, 160–61.
24. Ricciardi 2018, 213–57 (Latin and some Greek), 263–316 (Punic and Libyan).
25. Montali 2015, 185–210 with 20 Latin texts, but 31 separately inscribed neo-Punic (or Libyan) characters.
26. Lepelley 2003; 2005a. For a discussion of mixed language usage in late antique *Mauretania*, see Merrills 2017b.
27. Jongeling 2008, for a major collection of texts.
28. Lengrand 2005, 124.

the fact that the vast majority of toponyms, including names of cities, were Libyan (Berber) is the clearest indication of its importance.[29] It was, perhaps, more predominantly a spoken language of the countryside. The area south of *Hippo Regius* is notable for the concentration of Libyan inscriptions, related both to rural and urban sites.[30] For some reason in this one region, the use of Libyan script was deemed an important identity marker by some individuals and extended to the use of Latin/Libyan bilingual tombstones. There are plenty of indications of Libyan speakers in the overall epigraphic record. Mansour Ghaki's catalogue of Libyan inscriptions from the Maghrib includes examples from 34 known towns in *Africa*, 4 in *Mauretania Caesariensis*, and 6 from *Tingitana*. Now that this is recognised as a phenomenon of Roman towns, further examples are being recorded.[31] There is an assumption that most of the extant Libyan inscriptions should be dated relatively early in the Roman period and that the practice diminished over time in favour of wider adoption of Latin. However, this remains to be demonstrated, and I would note that there is evidence of late-Roman Libyan texts from Ghirza and from various desert communities I have worked on in Libya and Morocco demonstrating that at least at the fringes of the provinces an inscribing tradition persisted among Libyan communities.

Libyans are also possible to spot by their distinctive nomenclature in the Latin epigraphy, at least at sites where we have a large onomastic sample prior to the general acquisition of Roman citizenship.[32] But even after changes in personal nomenclature as citizens, the choices can reflect Libyan affinities. There are several individuals from *Lepcis*, for example, with the *cognomen* Gaetulicus, which presumably indicated a more overtly Libyan identity (and confirms my suggestion that the Libyan component of Libyphoenician cities in that region were *Gaetuli* groups).[33] An interesting point is that this also operated in the other direction, with Latin personal names appearing in translation in Libyan texts.[34] As noted in Chapters 4 and 5, the form of spoken Libyan probably had many local variants, but there are strong linguistic arguments for seeing a more profound division between "Numidian" (spanning Mauretanian and Numidian societies) and "Gaetulian" Libyan of the montagnard, steppic, and desert peoples. In terms of the inscriptional evidence, there are at least three major variants of ancient Libyan script known: eastern, western and Saharan.[35] I would equate these with the fundamental divisions I have

29. Mercier 1924; Desanges 1990; Aounallah and Ben Romdhane 2015.
30. Camps 1994c; 1999, 44–46, 58–59.
31. Ghaki 1995; cf. also Rebuffat 2013.
32. Mattingly 1987b; Millar 1968. On Libyan personal nomenclature in epigraphic and ancient sources, see the long list in Camps 1993a; 2003; also Chaker 2013a.
33. Gascou 1970; Rebuffat 2005.
34. Ait Kaci 2012.
35. Chaker 2003, 267–70.

identified in earlier chapters—the *Numidae*, *Mauri*, and *Gaetuli/Garamantes*, with the first two being regional dialects of Proto-Amazigh, and the desert peoples incorporating regional dialects of Proto-East-West Amazigh.[36] In other words, we should think in terms of two major Libyan language groups being present in Africa in the Roman Empire. This may give us a new clue as to what Apuleius meant when he described himself as "semi-Numidian, semi-Gaetulian" (*seminumidam et semigaetulum*).[37] It was not simply that his hometown *Madauros* lay at the border between Numidian and Gaetulian lands (*sitam Numidiae et Gaetuliae in ipso confinio*), but perhaps an indication that his parents came from families who still spoke different Libyan dialects alongside Latin, and who recognised their ultimate heredity on opposite sides of a Libyan ethnic divide.

Linguistic competence, literacy, and multilingualism undoubtedly varied across urban society, and we should not expect the same situation to have applied everywhere. A first step to understanding this complexity may be to identify hotspots of Latinity within the overall urban community, reflecting on how those cities and their populations sought to express their identity in a particularly distinctive way compared to others.

Onomastics and Toponomics

Proper names are a window into a society's identity. The richness of the source material from North Africa has made this a privileged and highly specialised field of research in which I hesitate to venture. The predominance of indigenous toponyms in "Roman" Africa has long been recognised, and this can be seen as a general characteristic of the Roman Empire at large.[38] On the other hand it also adds weight to the idea that these were not empty and unsettled landscapes when the Romans arrived on the scene, but ones where rivers, mountains, promontories, and other natural features had well-established names alongside sedentary settlements. Analysis of the toponyms from Africa reveals that for *Africa* and *Tripolitana*, >85% of 322 toponyms were of African origin; for northern *Numidia*, *Mauretania Sitifensis*, and eastern *Mauretania Caesariensis* the totals were 60–78% of 45, 43, and 40 toponyms; for southern *Numidia* (the frontier zone) and *Mauretania Tingitana* the total was 55–60% of 57 and 22 toponyms. Finally, for the far western end of *Mauretania Caesariensis*, 51% of 41 toponyms were local.[39] Several points arise from

36. This is a development of an important argument made by Fentress 2019, 503–12.
37. Apuleius, *Apologia* 24.1; cf. Bradley 2000; Mattiaci 2014; Shaw 2014, 530–32; Stone 2014a.
38. Jones and Mattingly 1990, 37–42 for discussion of Romano-British place-name evidence; see also Rivet 1980.
39. Camps 1994b; Laporte 2011, 25–27.

this. First, the highest number of urban toponyms relates to the Massylian eastern Numidian territory and the Libyphoenician coastlands of Tunisia and Libya. The lowest number relates to the limited urban development of *Tingitana*, and together with western *Caesariensis* and *Numidia Militaris*, these were areas of high military activity. Many of the Latin toponyms or hybrid toponyms concern Roman forts or road stations. Latin toponyms and elements were thus more a feature of the military community and were more common in areas of lower-density pre-Roman sedentary settlement.

While civic epigraphy might dress up a place name with honorific mentions of status or emperors (*CIL* 8.26582: *colonia Licinia Septimia Aurelia Alexandriana Thuggensis*), the core Libyan toponym remained, and presumably it was this element (*Thugga* in the example) that served in day-to-day parlance. Even in cases where Rome imposed a more Italian pronunciation, as in the case of *Leptis Magna* in Latin literature and on Italian inscriptions mentioning the city, in Africa the spelling was always *Lepcis Magna*, reflecting the original Punic form "*LPQY*".[40]

The evidence regarding personal names is more complicated due to the practice of people adopting Roman-style names on attaining Roman citizenship. Enlistment in the Roman army and enslavement were two other routes by which people might have their birth names changed. Despite a steady increase in Roman citizens, through the enfranchisement of auxiliary veteran soldiers, manumission, and individual, group, and communal extensions of citizen rights—often linked to urban promotion—there were still many people with African or Punic names at the start of the 3rd century CE. The general extension of Roman citizenship under the *constitutio Antoniniana* was not as far reaching in Africa as in some provinces, in that it seems to have left out significant groups in the security regions—in terms of our analysis, these were mainly *Gaetuli*.[41] Recognisably African names remained common in the onomastics throughout the later Roman period.

Careful work over many decades on the onomastics of "Roman Africa" have also revealed the presence of an unusually high occurrence of Latin *cognomina* that seem to have connections to pre-Roman nomenclature.[42] There were a number of distinct processes by which autochthonous names might be transformed in written script into Latin ones:

Transliteration: a Punic or Libyan name was expressed in Latin letters, involving the interpolation or interpretation of vowel sounds not present in the Punic or Libyan original written form. Example: *Hannibal* or (*Annobal*) from "*HNBL*".

40. Amadasi Guzzo in Ricciardi 2018, 263.
41. Hamdoune 2018, 63–64.
42. Dondin-Payre 2012 provides a succinct and insightful account of the development of onomastic studies.

Latinisation: a Punic or Libyan name was modified to reflect Latin norms. Example, *Annobal Tapapius Rufus from* "*HNBL TBHPY*".

Translation: using Latin or Greek equivalents of elements of the original name. Examples, *Donatus* or *Datus* or *Diodorus* for *Muttunbaal* ("gift of god), *Felix* or *Agathopus* for *Namp* (Punic for "good fortune."[43]

Assonance: choice of a similar sounding name (but of different meaning) in Latin to indigenous original. Examples, *Aemilius* for *Himilis*, *Amicus* for *Amilcar*.[44]

Further complications and strategies can be observed in relation to the choice of Roman citizen names, which tended to see the more complete disappearance of recognisably ethnic elements (transliteration and Latinisation). In some instances, individuals appear to have used different nomenclature in different social groupings, expressed through bilingual inscriptions, as in the case of a stone basin dedicated to Apollo from *Oea* by someone who styled himself as "Aurellius son of Epagrius" in the Latin and "Abdmelqart son of Mutunbal" in the Punic version.[45] For people granted citizenship, there was considerable scope for name selection, especially in the choice of *cognomen*. Apart from the use of translation and assonance as described above, high-status individuals might also choose to adopt a *cognomen* from a high-ranking patron or a famous Roman with local/African connections. Anthony Birley lists more than 40 examples of *cognomina* known at *Lepcis Magna* that echoed those of former proconsuls of Africa or prominent relatives.[46] Perhaps unsurprisingly, given the importance of the Saturn cult (derived from Punic Baal) in northern and coastal parts of *Africa*, Saturninus became the most commonly attested *cognomen* there.[47] Another interesting trend is the apparent creation of *gentilicia* from urban toponyms, thus Aradius, Capsius, Cercinius, Leptius,[48] or native peoples, thus Gaetulus, Gaetulicus.[49]

The specific African associations of certain Latin names are only apparent by large-scale analysis of names from different provinces, but while certainty of interpretation is impossible in every individual case, the overall patterns seem clearly to show these four different naming strategies in action, sometimes in combination

43. The African preponderance of Latin names ending in -atus (Donatus, Rogatus, Expectatus, etc.) was noted early on in Roman onomastic studies and despite Le Bohec 2005b, which tried to cast doubt on the statistical validity of these supposed "African" names, the association still seems valid, Lassère 2012.
44. Dondin-Payre 2005a, 157–59. Cf. also Birley 1988b for a detailed case study focused on names at *Lepcis Magna*.
45. *IRT* 229; *IPT* 5b; Wilson 2012b, 301–02.
46. Birley 1988b, 4–9.
47. Birley 1988b, 2.
48. Lassère 2005a.
49. Gascou 1970.

in a single individual's name, with the option of having multiple *gentilicia* allowing ample scope for discrepant identity references. The most obvious point of reference is the corpus of Punic personal names, made accessible through the large volume of Punic inscriptions (tombstones and religious stelae).[50] However, there is also a growing body of almost 1,000 Libyan personal names known from the literary sources and epigraphy.[51] The potential Libyan connotations of a number of seemingly Latin names at *Lepcis* also needs to be recognised—Geta at *Lepcis* possibly derived from *Gaetuli*, and Macer from *Macae*, for example.[52]

For French colonial-era scholars, the changes in naming practice were seen as a victory of top down "Romanisation" and the imposition of colonial norms. More recently, scholars like Marcel Bénabou have depicted the name choices in terms of passive resistance.[53] The systematic work of Lassère stands out as a key contribution on which others are now building more subtle versions of the Romanisation model.[54] As Monique Dondin-Payre observes, rather than the subject peoples having taken foreign names in their conqueror's language as one might at first assume, "[i]n fact, the vanquished have kept their names, adapting them to the language of the victors, without constraint and without the latter perceiving this attachment as a challenge."[55] To some degree, the changes in naming practices are to be expected in an imperial situation, where higher status attached to Roman citizenship, and Roman citizenship carried with it new codes of nomenclature. We must be careful not to assume ethnic identity aligned with the identity associations of specific names—there are plenty of Punic names in "Libyan" and "Numidian" dominated settlements, for instance,[56] and Libyan names crop up in "Punic" contexts, reminding us that these were Libyphoenician societies. But nor was this a one-way street with no U-turns or deviations possible from Libyan to Punic to Roman, as has sometimes been suggested on the basis of documents like the list of the *iuvenes* from *Mactaris*, where we can see generational changes in naming practice within a community.[57] What is most striking is the way that, within the urban context, pre-Roman traditions persisted more or less explicitly and were accommodated.

50. Amadasi Guzzo 1983; 1986; 2003; Benz 1972; Half 1964; Jongeling 1994; 2008; Jongeling and Kerr 2005.
51. Camps 1993a; 2003.
52. Birley 1988b, 5 (Macer), 15–16 (Geta, noting *IRT* 649: M Pomponius Geta Chirit, son of M Pomponeius Gaetulicus).
53. Cf. Bénabou 1976, 491–578; Pflaum 1978, 315–24; Toutain 1895, 167–96.
54. Lassère 1977; 1980; 2005a; 2005b. Cf. inter alia, Dondin-Payre 2004; Khanoussi and Maurin 2002.
55. Dondin-Payre 2005a, 159: "En fait, les vaincus ont conservé leurs noms, les adaptant à la langue des vainqueurs, sans contraine et sans que ceux-ci ne ressentent cet attachment comme un défi."
56. Ferjaoui 1995 notes that names in neo-Punic texts relating to mausoleum construction linked "Libyan" men with "Punic" women, but this may well be a naming fashion in Numidian and Gaetulian societies, rather than a reflection of intermarriage patterns between these groups and Libyphoenician groups.
57. Picard 1957, 77–95; cf. Lassère 2015, 249.

The persistence of Libyan and Punic names, and of Latin name forms that were their equivalents, is above all a reflection of the continued presence of a much more varied language pool and the related cultural memories.

Monumentalism, Bilingualism, and Multilingualism

The diversity of the urban communities is perhaps best illustrated by the varied record of monumentalism in the provincial cities. One of the interesting points to emerge from the discussion so far concerns the inequalities present in bilingualism and multilingualism within the Roman Empire. Of the five predominant languages spoken in the Maghrib from *Mauretania* to *Africa* (Latin, Greek, Punic, "Numidian," "Gaetulian"), the Roman Empire massively distorted the pattern of written communication in favour of Latin. This is perhaps not surprising in itself, but it does highlight why deviations from the use of Latin are important to investigate. At some towns, Latin was the more or less invariable choice of language for public building dedication, reflecting the strong presence of Roman citizens and Roman institutions from an early date (as at the colony of *Thamugadi*).[58]

A first issue concerns the production of genuine bilingual texts in cities—that is, texts conveying more or less the same information in different languages. The overall distribution of bilingual inscriptions is quite thin, but encompasses 5 examples of Libyan/Punic texts (2 from *Thugga*, 1 each from Mechta des Beni Oukden, *Sigus*, and *Lixus*), 5 examples of Libyan/neo-Punic (from *Mactaris*, *Thubisicu Bure*, *Thunusuda*, *Calama*, and Aïn el-Kebech), 15 Libyan/Latin texts (all funerary), and neo-Punic/Latin (24 examples). There are also 3 known trilinguals (Latin/Greek/neo-Punic).[59] There are also 3 texts written using the Greek script but the Punic language, and more than 70 using the Latin script and Punic language.[60] The *Thugga* Punic/Libyan texts, composed in the decades after the destruction of *Qart Hadasht*, reveal the emergence of independent Numidian urban institutions.[61]

Over a century later at *Lepcis Magna*, neo-Punic remained an essential component of bilingual texts, but now sat alongside Latin (Fig. 9.1 and Table 9.1).[62] There are also a number of Greek inscriptions and Latin/Greek bilinguals and 3 trilingual

58. Briand-Ponsart 2003; Duncan-Jones 1985; Dupuis 1991.
59. Numbers derived from Jongeling 2008 cited by Wilson 2012b, 269–71. See also Ghaki 1995; Marcy 1936; Rebuffat 2005 for the Libyan texts.
60. Jongeling and Kerr 2005; Kerr 2007; Wilson 2012b, 269.
61. Camps 1994a; Ghaki 1997a.
62. See the key texts in *IPT* and *IRT*, with extended discussion in Wilson 2012b, who provides full texts and translations of all languages, allowing detailed comparisons, in contrast with the generally separate publication in the Latin and Punic corpora. For some related discussions of this important corpora of material, see Amadasi Guzzo 1983; 1986; 2003; Sznycer 2003. There are interesting observations on the texts and buildings they ornamented in Mugnai 2022.

Figure 9.1. Neo-Punic and Latin bilingual inscription from theatre at *Lepcis Magna* (photo: author).

texts (Latin/neo-Punic/Greek) from *Lepcis*.[63] The group of 9 Latin/neo-Punic bilingual and 3 trilingual texts from *Lepcis* represent one aspect of a strong tradition of neo-Punic inscriptions (with 126 examples from the region), though this compares with c.1,000 Latin texts from eastern Tripolitania alone.[64] The linguistic diversity at the city and the cross-linguistic translations find a striking echo in a table of measurements from the city's marker that allowed conversion from Punic cubits into Roman feet and other Mediterranean systems.[65]

This remarkable body of civil inscriptions reveals the key role of the local Libyphoenician elite in the monumentalisation of the city from the 1st century BCE onwards.[66] One of the most striking aspects of the onomastic analysis of the epigraphy from *Lepcis* is how few settler families from outside the locality can be

63. See *IPT* 12–13, 16; *IRT* 481 654–655, trilinguals; *IRT* 264, 282, bilingual Latin/Greek; *IRT* 265, 293, 310–310a, 311–14, Greek.
64. Figures again from Wilson 2012b, 272.
65. Joppolo 1967.
66. For discussions of the development of *Lepcis*, see Cooley 2012, 250–85; di Vita 1982, 516–37; di Vita et al. 1999, 44–145; Mattingly 1995; Quinn 2010; 2018, 154–59; Wilson 2012b.

Table 9.1. *Lepcis Magna* building record. NB This list is based on the surviving inscriptions and main archaeological remains. There are other buildings for which no inscription survives.

Date	Donor	Building	Language	IRT/IPT #
1st century BCE?	Hadrubal son of K[...] son of Bodashtart	Statue to Shadrapa and Melkashtart in Old Forum	Hybrid Punic/neo-Punic style	*IPT* 31; Wilson 2012b, 272–74
8 BCE	Annobal Tapapius Rufus	Market	Latin & neo-Punic	*IPT* 21/*IRT* 319; Wilson 2012b, 274–78.
1 CE	Annobal Tapapius Rufus	Theatre	Latin/neo-Punic	*IPT* 24/*IRT* 321–323; Wilson 2012b, 278–81.
12	Iddibal Caphada Aemilius	*Chalcidicum*	Latin	*IRT* 324a-c; Wilson 2012b, 381–82.
14–19	Unknown donor, when *sufetes* were B'LYTN S'TRNYN (Saturninus) son of HN' (Hanno) and BDMLQRT TBHPY (Taphapi) son of BDMLQRT	Temple of Rome and Augustus and statuary in Old Forum	Neo-Punic	*IPT* 22; Wilson 2012b, 282–84.
Tiberian period?	Caecilius Diodorus (the *cognomen* suggests translation of Punic Muttunbaal)	Temple to Augustus (found at Ras el-Hammam to SW of city, but perhaps reused from *Lepcis*	Latin/Greek/neo-Punic trilingual	*IPT* 16; *IRT* 481; Wilson 2012b, 284–86.
29–30	Vibius Marsius (*Procos Af*)	Arch of Augusta Salutaris	Latin	*IRT* 308
35–36	Revenues from lands restored to town	Paving of streets	Latin	*IRT* 330–331
35–36	Suphunibal, adorner of her city, wife of Annobal Ruso.	Shrine to Ceres Augusta in theatre	Latin	*IRT* 269
43	Iddibal Tapapius	Shrine to Dii Augusti	Latin	*IRT* 273
54	Caius Anno/G'Y BN HN' (in name of his grandson Caius Phelyssam son of Macer, grandson of Caius Anno), work overseen by adopted son, Baliton/Balitho Commodus, son of Anno Macer	Paving and porticoes of Old Forum	Latin/neo-Punic, Latin	*IPT* 26/*IRT* 338, 615; Wilson 2012b, 287–90

(Continued)

Table 9.1. *(Continued)*

Date	Donor	Building	Language	IRT/IPT #
50s	Unknown	Civic *basilica*		
56	Town?	Amphitheatre		Di Vita-Evrard 1965
62	Ithymbal Sabinus Tapapius & town	Harbour colonnade	Latin & neo-Punic	*IPT* 23/*IRT* 341
Later 1st century	HMLKT DRYDS, descendant of Hanno,	Temple near harbour	Neo-Punic	*IPT* 32
72	Iddibal son of Balsillec, grandson of Annobal, great grandson of Asmun	Magna Mater (HS200,000)	Latin	*IRT* 300
77–78?	Town? Dedicated by Proconsul and Patron, C. Paccius Africanus	Arch (celebrating promotion to *municipium* status)	Latin	*IRT* 342
83	Unknown. Dedicated by Proconsul and Patron, L. Nonius Asprenas	Large (15 m + frontage) unknown building near market	Latin	*IRT* 346
Later 1st century?	Boncarth/Bodmelqart, son of Muthumbal Sydby, acting as IIIvir, but supplementing funds from fines with own cash	Statue of Shadrapa/Liber Pater in market (62 *denarii* from fines and 53 from Boncarth)	Latin/neo-Punic	*IPT* 25; *IRT* 294; Wilson 2012b, 292–93.
Later 1st century?	Series of stone seats paid for from (market?) fines and contributions under a series of aediles, Candidus and Donatus: 'DNB'L son of Annobal SDŠMR 'DYMN and Anno son of 'RŠM YGM'K.	Set of stone seats (original location unknown, later reused in Hadrianic baths)	Neo-Punic	*IPT* 17.1–3; Wilson 2012b, 294–95.
Later 1st century	Ytnbal son of Arish Tapapius Sabinus set [this] up to his maternal aunt Arishat, daughter of Ytnbal	Building in memory of aunt	Neo-Punic	*IPT* 23

Table 9.1. *(Continued)*

Date	Donor	Building	Language	IRT/IPT #
Later 1st century?	Caius Sossius	Statue of Neptune in market	Latin/neo-Punic	*IPT* 30; *IRT* 305; Wilson 2012b, 293.
92	Ti Claudius Sestius son of Ti Claudius Sestius	Improvements in theatre	Latin/neo-Punic, Latin	*IPT* 27; *IRT* 318, 347; Wilson 2012b, 296–99.
93–94	Unknown	Flavian temple	Latin	*IRT* 348
Reign of Domitian	Unknown individual	Temple of Iupiter Dolichenus by harbour	Latin/neo-Punic	*IPT 9; IRT* 349a). Wilson 2012b, 295–96.
Late 1st century?	a) Laelianus (L'YLY'N') b) Sextus the son of Diodorus (SKST' BN DYDR') c) Servius Sulpicius Plautus (SRWY SLPQY PL'WT')	Individual columns or colonnades (engraved on column shaft)	Neo-Punic	*IPT* 69, 73, 74; Wilson 2012b, 291–92
Late 1st or early 2nd century?	Q'NDD (Candidus) son of Q'NDD son of HN (Hanno) son of BDMLQRT (Bodmelqart)	*Exhedra* and *porticus* of temple of El near amphitheatre	Neo-Punic	*IPT 18*
Trajanic?	Unknown	Curia		
101–102	[....] Severus son of Marcus	Works on *basilica maioris, thermae*	Latin	*IRT* 352
Trajanic?	Unknown (subject of later restoration by L. Volusius Bassus Cerealis cv)	*Basilica/forum*	Latin	*IRT* 543
109	Town (*pecunia publica*)	Arch (celebrating promotion to honorary *colonia* status)	Latin	*IRT* 353 (cf. 523, 537)
2nd century?	Marcus Vipsanius Clemens, marble-merchant, under the administration of Quintus Servilius Candidus	Dedication to gods of *Lepcis* (temple of Liber Pater)	Latin	*IRT* 275
120	Q. Servilius Candidus	Aqueduct & public fountains	Latin	*IRT* 357–359

(Continued)

Table 9.1. *(Continued)*

Date	Donor	Building	Language	IRT/IPT #
127/139-	Town?	Hadrianic Baths	Latin	*IRT* 361, 545
128-	Aemilia Iou[ina]	Building opposite the *chalcidicum*	Latin	*IRT* 363
136–137	Town	Some marble adornment of theatre	Latin	*IRT* 372
152–53	Calpurnia Honesta	Temple in Old Forum area	Latin	*IRT* 370
145	Marcius Vitalis & Iunius Galba donated to public funds	Rebuilding of stage backdrop in theatre (HS 500,000)	Latin	*IRT* 533–534
162	Town?	Circus (monumental form)		Di Vita-Evrard 1965
pre-197	P. Septimius Geta (heir to his deceased sister)	Silver statue of Septimia Polla, daughter of L. Septimius Severus (HS 100,000+)	Latin	*IRT* 607
173–74	Dedicated by C. Septimius Severus (Procos Africa) and L. Septimius Severus (legate), funds for project from will of C. Avilius Castus	Arch of Marcus Aurelius (HS 120,000)	Latin	*AE* 1967, 536
pre-180	Unknown	Shrine of Apollo (HS 272,500)		*IRT* 707
Late 2nd century	Unknown	Hunting Baths		
196-	[...] Rusonianus	Major repairs in *frigidarium* of Hadrianic baths, marble, and statuary adornments	Latin	*IRT* 396

Table 9.1. *(Continued)*

Date	Donor	Building	Language	IRT/IPT #
203	Granting of *Ius Italicum* status			
209–216	L. Septimius Severus & Caracalla (emperors)	Severan forum, basilica, colonnaded street, nymphaeum, harbour improvements	Latin	*IRT* 427–428
3rd century	Unknown	*Serapaeum*	Latin	IRT 311
3rd century	Plautius Lupus	Repairs and marble and mosaic ornamentation of baths (& games and paid for chariot statue group in his honour)	Latin	*IRT* 601
317–323	Town with support of governors (Laenatius Romulus) and city curator	Basilica, market, curia, walls, and other restoration	Latin	*IRT* 467–468, 580
355–360	Flavius Archontius Nilus, governor and patron honoured for his benefaction	Rebuilding of city walls	Latin	*IRT* 562–563
4th century	Flavius Nepotianus, governor	Work on city walls	Latin	*IRT* 565

identified—these include, most notably, the Sicilian banker T. Herennius (a victim of Verres in the mid-1st century BCE) and the "Fulvii Lepcitani."[67] Urban finances included market fines, and these were deployed with top-ups from the pockets of the junior magistrates for minor projects (statues or public benches). Some of the larger schemes like the amphitheatre, circus, the public baths, and honorific arches may have been public projects, to which a larger number of citizens contributed, as well as drawing on any available city funds, but the recurrent major contributions of the city's leading families to urban monumentalisation are very evident in Table 9.1. We might also note the paving of the city's streets under imperial supervision in the mid-30s CE (*IRT* 330a/b, 331) using revenues from lands restored to *Lepcis*, presumably in the aftermath of Tiqfarin's revolt.

In the initial stages, there were relatively few Latin loan words, though some direct transcription of imperial titulature into Punic (for example, "*Q'YSR 'WGSTS P'MT*" for *Caesar Augustus Imperator* in *IPT* 31). More commonly, the neo-Punic texts offered translations of original Latin formulas, but some of the phrasing in the Latin text was also a direct translation of Punic expressions that were not present in standard Roman civil epigraphy (for example, *IRT* 321, *ornator patriae* and *amator concordiae*), strongly hinting at the continued local predominance of Punic over Latin as the language of public discourse.[68] In a similar way, we can see the varied and changing handling of personal names with transliteration (Punic to Latin and vice versa; for example, *IRT* 319 Muttun/*MTN*; *IPT* 21 *'WGSTS*/Augustus), Latinisation (Annobal Tapapius Rufus in *IRT* 319), translation (Diodorus for Muttunbaal in *IRT* 481 and *IPT* 91), and assonance (Macer for *M'QR* in *IRT* 338).[69] Even after the acquisition of Roman citizenship, local notables were rendering their Roman names in a transliterated form of traditional filiation (*IPT* 18, *Q'NDD* (Candidus) son of *Q'NDD* son of *HN'* (Hanno) son of *BDMLQRT*). The bilingual texts are rarely exact translations, and the Punic texts often differ from the Latin ones by omitting the imperial titulature or detail of the Roman official who had attended a building's inauguration, and focus instead on the generosity of the individual who had donated funds and their filiation. Sometimes the lack of equivalences in Punic for Latin technical or legal terms involves lengthy periphrasis (*IPT* 38):

> Caius, son of Anno, in the name of Caius, son of his son Macer, had the columns and the place repaired and he had the forum paved according to their work, at his own

67. Birley 1988b, 3, 11–12; Thompson 1971. On Herennius, see Rebuffat 1986b; on the Fulvii Lepcitani, Romanelli 1981, 157–60.
68. See, for example, *IRT* 221 "Annobal Tapapius Rufus, son of Himilcho, adorner of his country, lover of concord, flamen, sufete, in charge of sacred things, saw to the construction at his own expense and also dedicated it."
69. Birley 1988b, 5 for the argument that Macer is an assonance of either a Punic name related to Melqart, or a Libyan name perhaps related to the *Macae*, rather than the latter being a transliteration into Punic of Latin Macer ("lean").

> expense. Baliton Commodus *who entered as a son among the sons with Macer, the son of Caius, through the means of a document concerning the affairs of the house of Caius,* the son of Anno, had it made and completed it.

Here the clumsy italicised passage is required to convey the sense of the adoption of Baliton Commodus in the will of Caius (*testamento adoptatus*).[70]

One of the striking aspects of the list in Table 9.1 is the lack of standardisation of epigraphic practice in the city in the 1st century CE, with some euergistic acts being commemorated in a bilingual text on the same block or blocks, others in separate Latin and Punic texts erected in different places, and others by just Latin texts alone. When bilingual texts were erected, they were frequently not exact translations but rather gave different emphases for discrete audiences (though by the late 1st century CE the translations were becoming more literal and more commonly the Punic following established Latin norms). From quite early in the sequence, the Latin texts were given greater prominence on the buildings, with added emphasis in terms of larger letters or bronze inlay (as in *IRT* 338). This is unsurprising, as many of these buildings were dedicated in ceremonies involving high Roman officials, commonly the provincial governor, so were very much part of an imperial negotiation between city and Empire. Such emphases became more pronounced over time, but it is also true that for four generations after the acquisition of its Italian-style market and theatre, the leading citizens of *Lepcis* still presented a public identity that was both Latinate and Punic. However, by the end of the 1st century CE, monumental bilingual texts were much rarer, and the use of neo-Punic for such texts seems to have been definitively ended by the honorific promotion of the city to *colonia* status in 109 CE. Public inscriptions were henceforth in Latin alone, though epigraphic habits were still constructed differently in the domestic sphere, as we shall see.

Because the nomenclature of the city's population changed with acquisition of citizenship, there is an apparent break in continuity between the old dominant families and the later donors of public buildings, but this is clearly illusory. Indeed, the probable link between Q. Servilius Candidus (*IRT* 357–359) and the family of the man referred to as "*Q'NDD*" (*IPT* 17.1; 18) demonstrates the links between the Roman citizens and the old Libyphoenician aristocracy. The family of the future emperor L. Septimius Severus was also of this group, as is made plain by comments in the the ancient sources on his heritage.[71]

After 109 CE the civic epigraphy more closely adhered to Latin norms of expression. As we shall see, there is strong circumstantial evidence that Punic remained

70. Wilson 2012b, 288–89.

71. Birley 1988a for a detailed biography and overview of his ancestral roots.

an important vernacular language long after this. There are, for instance, a few rare transliterations of Punic in Latin characters at *Lepcis* (so-called Latino-Punic texts), including brickstamps for the Hadrianic baths and three tombstones.[72] More significantly, the amphitheatre has numerous neo-Punic letters and short inscriptions carved on the seating. They indicate the long continuation of a Punic substrate beneath the Latinate surface of Roman *Lepcis Magna*. The early 3rd-century period marked both a high point and, to some extent, the beginning of the decline of the city, as the rise of L. Septimius Severus tightened the links of the city's elite with Rome, but the end of his dynasty undoubtedly had serious consequences for the region.[73]

An interesting aspect of the spread of Latin at *Lepcis* is that it seems to have been adopted at different rates for different types of epigraphic act. For instance, the non-synchronicity of adoption and abandonment of linguistic practice in the epigraphy at *Lepcis* is very striking. The first use of Latin was for public inscriptions in the Augustan period, especially dedications of major building works, or in official pronouncements or commemorations, such as texts relating to the end of Tiqfarin's war or the use of revenues from lands returned to productive use after the war. During this period, funerary texts continued to be in neo-Punic script on the cinerary urns. Only in the Flavian era did the first Latin funerary inscriptions appear on the outside of tombs and graves, though Punic remained the language of commemoration within tombs for longer; though from the early 2nd century CE, Latin and Punic were used together on urns. I shall return to this in discussing burial rites later in the chapter.[74]

Latin/Neo-Punic Bilingualism in Other Parts of Africa

There is other evidence from Tripolitania for the extensive use of neo-Punic continuing into the Roman era. At *Sabratha*, there are two building inscriptions in neo-Punic, and a bilingually inscribed stone basin dedicated to Baal/Saturn by a man with Libyan names: Iunatan or Iurathan, son of Ogodar or Agiadar.[75] From *Oea*, there are two similar stone basins with bilingual inscriptions, and other neo-Punic texts are known.[76]

Among a larger corpus of neo-Punic funerary and religious stelae, Karel Jongeling lists only nine neo-Punic building inscriptions from elsewhere in

72. Kerr 2007, Lepcis Magna LP 1; Wilson 2012b, 307–09 (brickstamp); *IRT* 671; 826–82 (tombstones).
73. Cordovana 2007; Mattingly 1995, 155.
74. Fontana 2001, 165–71.
75. *IPT* 1–2; Jongeling 2008: 48–49 (Sabratha N16); Wilson 2012b, 299–300. Cf. Di Vita-Evrard 2003, 298–300.
76. Wilson 2012b, 300–02.

North Africa.[77] One cluster of sites lay in the Numidian heartland zone of the Dorsal around *Mactaris* (texts from *Mactaris*, *Althiburos*, and *Mididi*) and two others came from the broader Carthaginian hinterland in northern Tunisia (*Thinissut* and *Thuburbo Maius*).

The survey of the Rohia area of the Tunisian Dorsal has found evidence of mixed linguistic practice between urban centres and between town and countryside.[78] The vast bulk of the inscriptions came from the urban centres, and the picture is even more pronounced if we note that a few unusual rural sites account for the bulk of the non-urban material (sanctuaries and larger cemeteries, perhaps related to a major estate). The most notable urban centre of the region (*Mididi*) has produced four times more evidence than the other five urban-scale settlements put together. Neo-Punic inscriptions indicate that inscribing habits were present before Latin was established at a date after the fall of *Qart Hadasht*. The Libyan inscriptions are undated, but appear to show a degree of Libyan emulation of the epigraphic habit, though always a minority of the material. We might note that the occurrence of inscriptions here is probably in inverse relation to the importance of the spoken languages in this region, where Libyan probably predominated, then Punic, then Latin.

In general, Libyan does not seem to have been used much for monumental dedications (with the notable exceptions of the *Thugga* temple and mausoleum texts).[79] It is encountered most commonly in contexts where the use concerned funerary commemoration or religious acts. There are only 15 Libyan/Latin bilinguals and all of them are funerary in nature, coming from a particular region around the town of *Thullium* to south of *Hippo Regius*.[80] The tombstone of the veteran C. Iulius Getulus at *Thullium*, already alluded to in Chapter 7, shows how the Latin text played on both his decorated military career and his subsequent civic standing (*flamen perpetuus* at *Thullium*) (Fig. 7.3 above).

> *(Latin text roughly translated as)* Here lies C. Iulius Getulus, a veteran awarded military honours, discharged and settled in his home town of *Thullium*, where he was a perpetual priest (*flamen*), he lived 80 years.[81]

---

77. Jongeling 2008, from *Thinissut*, *Thuburbo Maius*; *Mactaris* (× 3), *Mididi*, *Althiburos* (bilingual, Latin-neo-Punic); Aïn Youssef (Algeria, bilingual, Latin–neo-Punic). See also Jongeling and Kerr 2005.
78. Ben Baaziz 2000.
79. Ghaki 1997a.
80. Rebuffat 2005; 2007; 2013; Wilson 2012b, 271: *RIL* 85 = *CIL* 8.17317; *RIL* 145 = *CIL* 8.5218, 17933, *ILAf* 138; *RIL* 146 = *CIL* 8.5209, *ILAf* 137; *RIL* 147 = *CIL* 8.17396 = 5225a, *ILAf* 153; *RIL* 150 = *CIL* 8.5216, *ILAf* 141; *RIL* 151 = *CIL* 8.5220 + 17395, *ILAf* 147; *RIL* 182 = *ILAf* 152; *RIL* 193 = *ILAf* 145; *RIL* 252 = *ILAf* 156; *RIL* 288 = *CIL* 8.17320, *ILAf* 169; *RIL* 289 = *CIL* 8.17319, *ILAf* 168; *RIL* 510; *RIL* 665 = *ILAf* 468; *RIL* 844; *RIL* 906. See the excellent discussions in Shaw 2014; 2021.
81. *CIL* 8.5209 = *ILAf* 137 = *RIL* 146. Rebuffat 2005, 194; Shaw 2021: (Latin) *C. Iulius Get/ulus vet(eranus) donis/ donates torque/bus et armillis/ dismissus et in civit(ate)/ sua Thullio flam(en)/ perpet(uus) vix(it) an(nis) lxxx/h.s.e.*

> *(Libyan text translated as)* Keti son of MSWLT imperial servant (soldier) of the *Misiciri* people sub-fraction S'RMMi priest (MZBi).[82]

The differences apparent in the Libyan text (despite some uncertainties of translation) once again highlight the hidden transcripts and code-switching involved in the different modes of literate communication. Different names and traditional Libyan filiation are revealed in the Libyan text—interestingly, the *cognomen* Getulus, which was possibly given to him at the time of his army recruitment, works as an assonance on his given name Keti. The nature of his imperial service is somewhat disguised in both texts—but this is someone who had left the military community long before his death (allegedly aged 80), returning to his people in an urban and rural context, so no mention of unit or rank is given for his local audience. Even his urban credentials were somewhat minimised in favour of his ethnic association with the *Misiciri* people. This seems to me a perfect example of discrepant identity in action, where the life of a single man can be presented in such contrasting ways and identity presentation subtly altered to suit different audiences. The Latin text on its own could be read as a simple case of successful integration into Roman life, but the associated Libyan inscription reveals the fundamental flaws of the Romanisation concept. This is someone who, when he chose, could be both Roman and Libyan, both soldier and civilian.

The monumental evolution of *Thugga* can be traced in detail thanks to the good preservation of many structures, the extent of excavation, abundant epigraphy, and the painstaking research and publication of all the material (Table 9.2, with Fig. 8.5).[83] There are clear indications of an established Numidian tradition of major urban construction at *Thugga*, with a number of monuments erected in the area later occupied by the Roman forum, to which a series of Libyan or Libyan-Punic bilingual texts probably related.[84] The subsequent story was very different to that of *Lepcis Magna* in that by the 1st century CE the civic set-up was a double community of a native *civitas* and a *pagus* of Roman citizens, subsidiary to the *colonia* of *Karthago*.[85] Building projects were financed by a wider range of actors: external patrons (generally associated with *Karthago*), Roman citizens from the more privileged *pagus* community, members of a family with long-term links to management of a local imperial estate (the Gabini), wealthy freedmen from *Karthago*; but there are also some individuals with Numidian onomastic links from

82. Rebuffat 2005, 203; Shaw 2021.
83. See, notably, Aounallah and Golvin 2016; Golvin and Khanoussi 2005; Khanoussi and Maurin 1997; 2000; Saint Amans 2004.
84. Aounallah and Golvin 2016, 29–74.
85. Aounallah and Golvin 2016, 354, 454–56 concluding that there was no physical demarcation of urban zone between the two communities of *civitas* and *pagus*.

Table 9.2. *Thugga* (Dougga) building record. NB This list is based on the surviving inscriptions. There are other buildings for which no inscription survives.

Date	Donor	Status	Building (cost where known)	Inscription reference
2nd century BCE	People of *Thugga*	Work overseen by various named individuals	Monument for Massinissa	*RIL* 2
2nd–1st centuries BCE	People of *Thugga*	Work overseen by various named individuals	Unknown monuments (possibly relating to remains of Numidian temples in agora area)	*RIL 3 and 4*
Tiberius	Anon		Temple of Caesar and initial layout of forum?	*ILAf* 558; *DFH* 23
36/37 CE	L. Postumius Chius, with his sons Firmus and Rufus	Citizen of *Karthago*, patron of *pagus*	Paving of forum and adjoining square by Temple of Caesar, erection of altar of Caesar, *aedes* of Saturn and arch	*ILAf* 558; *DFH* 23
late 30s	M. Licinius Tyrannus	Freedman and patron of *pagus*	Temple and statues restored, new Temple of Ceres	*AE* 1969–70, 651, 648; *DFH* 25
	Licinia Prisca	Freedwoman, *flamen*, wife of Licinius Tyrannus	Temple of Venus Concordia	*AE* 1969–70, 650; *DFH* 26
40	C. Caesetius Perpetuus, with sons Honoratus and Perpetuus	Magistrate of *Karthago*, patron of *pagus*	Arch	*ILAf* 520; *DFH* 24
33–44	C. Pomponius Restitutus	Dedication of monument by patron of *pagus* from *Karthago*	Temple of Unknown divinity	*CIL* 8.26475; *DFH* 68
48/49	Iulius Venustus, son of Thinoba, with wife Gabinia Felicula and son Faustus	Members of native *civitas.* Dedication by patron from *Karthago*	Monument to Augustus	*DFH* 46
54	M. Licinius Rufus	Equestrian, *flamen perpetuus* at *Karthago*, patron of *pagus* and *civitas*	Market and small temple	*AE* 1969–70, 652, 649; *DFH* 69

(*Continued*)

Table 9.2. *(Continued)*

Date	Donor	Status	Building (cost where known)	Inscription reference
Flavian era	Rufinus son of Rufus son of Nimlilis	Member of *civitas*, but structure dedicated by magistrate from *Karthago*	Small structure in forum area	*AE* 1991, 1666a-b; *DFH* 3
Hadrian	A. Gabinius Datus and M. Gabinius Bassus	Leading family of region with some relation to *conductores* of imperial estates, citizens of *Karthago*, *flamen*, patrons of *pagus* and *civitas*	Temples of Concord, Frugifer, Liber Pater (HS 50,000)	*CIL* 8.26467–70; *DFH* 27–28
	Q. Maedius Severus, with daughter Maedia Lentula	Father was patron of *pagus* and *civitas* and daughter *flamen perpetuus*	Temple of Fortuna (HS 70,000)	*CIL* 8.26471; *DFH* 136
Hadrianic?	[.] Pompeius Rogatus (bequest of brother C. Pompeius Nahanus)	Brothers from *civitas*	Temple of Pietas (HS 30,000)	*CIL* 8.26493; *DFH* 30
Antoninus	Q. Gabinius Felix Faustinianus, with children Gabinius Datus and Gabinia Processa	Patron of *pagus*	Portico round forum	*ILAf* 521; *DFH* 29
	Iulia Paula Laenatiana		Temple of Minerva	*ILAf* 518, 522; *CIL* 8.26525
M. Aurelius	*Pagus* granted right to receive legacies, and native *civitas* also with improved rights)			*ILS* 9399; *CIL* 8.26534; 26528; *DFH* 51
166/169	L. Marcius Simplex and son L. Marcius Simplex Regillianus	*Iudex* at Rome, citizen of *Karthago*	Capitoline temple	*DFH* 31–32, *cf.* 83
168/69	P. Marcius Quadratus	Brother of Marcius Simplex, citizen of *Karthago*	Theatre	*ILS* 9364; *DFH* 33
	L. Calpurnius Aris,also in name of his father Faustinus, his son Faustinus and children of his brother Nahanus	*Flamen perpetuus* from leading family of *civitas*	Anonymous temple (HS 100,000) and games and other public donations	*CIL* 8.26527; Aounallah and Golvin 2016, 461

Table 9.2. *(Continued)*

Date	Donor	Status	Building (cost where known)	Inscription reference
Commodus	Q. Pacuvius Saturus with wife Nahania Victoria and brother M. Pacuvius Felix	*Augur* and *flamen perpetuus /flaminica perpetua* at *Karthago*, patronage given separately to *pagus* and *civitas*	Place of the Winds, Temple of Mercury and public funds for *civitas* (HS 145,000 total)	*ILAf* 516; *CIL* 8.2648226484; *DFH* 34
	Q. Pacuvius Saturus with wife Nahania Victoria	*Augur* and *flamen perpetuus /flaminica perpetua* at *Karthago*	Portico of market (part of the above-mentioned scheme)	*CIL* 8.26530, 26533; *ILAf* 523
	L. Octavius Victor Roscianus		Anonymous temple	*CIL* 8.26500
180s	*Civitas Aurelia Thugga*	Dedicated by proconsul	Aqueduct (7 miles) & baths	*DFH* 36
Severus 194–195	L. Octavius Victor Roscianus		Temple of Saturn (HS 100,000+)	*CIL* 8.26498; *DFH* 38
	Municipium, following promotion of town to		Erection of arch to emperor	*CIL* 8.26539; *DFH* 10
	Asicia Victoria	*Flaminica perpetua*	Decoration of tribunal (HS 20,000)	*CIL* 8.26593; *ILAf* 534
Caracalla 214	Gabinia Hermiona		Temple of Victory of Caracalla (HS 100,000) and land for circus	*DFH* 39
Severus Alexander	*Municipium* of *Thugga*		Circus	*CIL* 8.26549–50; *DFH* 15
	Municipium of *Thugga*		Arch (thanks for tax break)	*CIL* 8.26460
	A. Vitellius Privatus		Unspecified building within territory (Ain al-Ksar)	*CIL* 8.26548

(Continued)

Table 9.2. *(Continued)*

Date	Donor	Status	Building (cost where known)	Inscription reference
222–224	*Municipium* of *Thugga*		Restoration of Temple of Fortuna	*CIL* 8.26547; *ILAf* 528; Aounallah and Golvin 2016, 386–88
	Q. Gabinius Rufus Felix Beatianus with parents		Temple of Caelestis	*CIL* 8.26557/62
Gallienus	Promotion of town to *colonia* rank			*DFH* 62
	Colonia of *Thugga?*		Licinian baths	*ILT* 1500
261	Botria Fortunata	*Flaminica perpetua*	Temple of Tellus	*ILAf* 530; *DFH* 40
264	Anon	Equestrian	W portico of forum and cash sum	*CIL* 8.26559; *ILT* 1416; *DFH* 163–168
268/305	*Colonia* of *Thugga*		Temple of Sol Augusto	*DFH* 41
290s	Anon individual, with Papirius Balbius Honoratus and heirs of Sergius Firmus Iunianus	Anon was *clarissimus vir*	Temple of Genius Patriae	*CIL* 8.26472; *DFH* 139
298	*Colonia* of *Thugga*		Portico for Temple of Mater Deum	*ILAf* 531; *DFH* 134
375–383	[..]dius Honoratianus	*Flamen perpetuus*	Restoration of Licinian baths	*DFH* 42
376/377	L. Napotius Felix	*Flamen perpetuus*	Restoration of aqueduct and nymphaea	*DFH* 43
401–500	Exupius		Portico of church	*DFH* 45

the *civitas* community.[86] The Gabini were particularly active donors as patrons of the community between the early 2nd and early 3rd centuries—porticoes in the forum, temples of Concord, Frugifer, Liber Pater, Neptune, Caracalla's German Victory, the Sanctuary of Caelestis, and donation of land for the construction of the circus.[87] Larger projects were also funded by the town as it rose in status and increased its scope for generating income, and by public subscription. Both men and women were involved in the individual acts of euergetism, and it is clear that the existence of the different constituencies in (and around) the town to some extent fed the competition between them for such public displays.[88] Quite a few of the local benefactions appear to have been in fulfilment of payment of the fees (*summae honorem*) for office-holding, notably the flaminate. Among the local families attested, several appear as benefactors recurrently. Benefactors also often associated their children and other close relatives with their acts of largesse to put their names in the public eye.[89] The behaviour of euergetism in most towns was focused on a small number of families and it was not so evident everywhere. For an inland town, *Thugga* was one of the most impressively monumentalised by the mid-3rd century CE and this despite its lack of chartered urban status until its recognition as a *municipium* under Septimius Severus. On the other hand, it was much more dependent on private donors than a town like *Thamugadi*, where many of the basic amenities appear to have been built with military support and many of the later buildings were publicly funded, though this was again in part through the *summae honorariae*, which it benefited from over a longer period due to its direct foundation as a veteran *colonia*.[90]

Religion: Urban Gods and Identity

In Chapter 7 I argued that there were considerable differences between the religious practices of the military and civilian communities that were not closely associated with the army. Closer scrutiny of urban practices reveals considerably more internal diversity across different types of urban community. Many factors affected religious outlook and behaviours, including pre-existing locally dominant cults and divinities, the ease of reception of new gods and religious ideas, the presence of

86. Duncan-Jones 1985, 29–31. *Uchi Maius* is another nearby town that shows a similar pattern of external intervention of notable people from *Karthago* in its monumentalisation in early Roman Empire, Khanoussi and Mastino 2012.
87. Khanoussi and Maurin 2000, 76–80.
88. On women as donors of public buildings, see Waldherr 2003. On women in Africa under Rome, see Benseddik 2017; Ladjimi Sebai 2011.
89. Sterrett-Krause 2012.
90. Briand-Ponsart 2003; Duncan Jones 1985, 31–32. See also, Hellström 2020; Scheding 2019.

outsiders within the community, and the evolution of new structures of organisation such as the imperial cult or religious associations.[91]

The Provincial Capital: Karthago

For the reasons outlined in Chapter 9, *Karthago* was far from typical of North African urban centres. This was certainly true of its religious outlook, where practice and form were most shaped by external factors.[92] The erasure of the pre-existing Carthaginian metropolis and its population in 146 BCE created unique conditions for the implantation of a foreign city peopled for the most part by Roman citizen migrants. While the popularity of the Saturn cult at *Karthago* should alert us to the fact that over time the city's population was strongly reinforced by Africans, the basis of public religion was staunchly Roman.[93] The public cult of the city (*sacra publica*) reflected the very close ties between the citizens and Rome, with at its centre many of the key gods, goddesses, and cults of Rome (for instance, Iupiter Optimus Maximus, Iuno, Minerva, Mars, Venus, Concordia, Magna Mater, Ceres, Tellus).[94] The prominence of the cult of Caelestis was an acknowledgement of the prior importance of her Punic equivalent Tinnit at *Qart Hadasht*, but it also represented a Roman annexation of the goddess to serve the needs of the new colony.[95] As the provincial capital of *Africa*, the presence of the gubernatorial staff will have further shaped the city's religious calendar on that of Rome, with state officials officiating at many key ceremonies. The many varied manifestations of "imperial cult" were sharply focused here, not least because this was one of the prime functions of the provincial assembly (*concilium provinciae*), meaning that "emperor worship" was promulgated on two levels, as part of both public and provincial cults.[96] Finally, as a great seaport, the early presence of various "Eastern" mystery cults (Isis, Serapis, Mithras) and the monotheistic Christian and Jewish religions is not a surprise.[97]

Cosmopolitan Libyphoenician Centres (Lepcis Magna and Tripolitania)

The closest parallel to *Karthago* for the breadth of engagement with Roman religion in a broad sense was *Lepcis Magna*. Table 9.3 summarises the evidence for religious activity in all the Tripolitanian cities, though the vast majority are attested at *Lepcis*

91. Bel-Faida 2008; Rives 1995.
92. Rives 1995 provides a detailed overall study of religion at *Karthago*.
93. Rives 1995, 209–211 recognising the Saturn cult as lacking official standing in the city and as an "ethnic African cult."
94. Rives 1995, 17–99 on the nature of public religion.
95. Rives 1995, 65–72.
96. Rives 1995, 85–96.
97. Rives 1995, 261–73.

Table 9.3. Religious activity in the Tripolitanian former Libyphoenician coastal cities.

	Phoenician or Libyan cults	**Classical cults**	**Eastern Cults**
Urban community	Milk'ashtart, Shadrapa, El Qone Aras, Baal-Hammon, Tinnit	Amor, Apollo, Caelestis, Cereres, Concord, Di Augusti, Di Inferi et Superi, Dioscuri, Esculapius, Fortuna, Genius coloniae, Genius municipiae, Hercules, Imperial cult, Iuno, Iupiter, Liber, Liber Pater, Mars, Mercury, Minerva, Nemesis, Neptune, Rome and Augustus, Silvanus, Saturn, Venus	Christianity, Judaism, IOM Dolichenus, Isis, Magna Mater, Mithras, Serapis

Magna. The list is at first sight an impressive endorsement of the engagement of the *Lepcitani* with Roman cults. How representative was this eclectic mixture of African towns in general? Few cities have produced as rich an epigraphic haul as *Lepcis*, of course, and it is worth reflecting that *Lepcis* had an atypical urban profile.

It had one of the largest urban footprints of any town and, at its peak, probably the second largest population after *Karthago*. The rapid evolution of the town under Augustus and the Julio-Claudian emperors is almost unparalleled in the rest of *Africa*. The dates of its promotions to *municipium* and *colonia* status were also precocious for a city that had not received a deduction of veterans or citizen settlers. The elevation of the Lepcitanian Septimius Severus to emperor gave rise to a further extraordinary phase of development in the early 3rd century, backed by imperial largesse. So, while *Lepcis* is certainly interesting, it is, like *Karthago*, somewhat exceptional in its urban development.

At the same time, we also need to recognise that some of the names in the list had considerably more resonance locally than others, reflected in the number of dedications and the scale of monuments vowed. As in Tripolitania more generally, the cult of Baal Hammon/Saturn was nowhere near as important as in northern *Africa Proconsularis*. Tophets or sanctuaries of Baal Hammon/Saturn and Tinnit/Caelestis have been located (or posited from finds of stelae) at *Tacape*, *Gigthis*, *Meninx*, *Zitha*, *Sabratha*, and *Oea*, and though not located at *Lepcis*, it seems inconceivable that the site lacked one.[98] There is comparatively little evidence from the Tripolitanian cities of later worship of Saturn and Caelestis.[99] Thus, although present, the worship of Baal and Tinnit at the Tripolitanian cities appears much less central than in other parts of the province of *Africa*.

Instead, at *Lepcis* there was a continuing emphasis on different Libyphoenician tutelary gods, even as late as the 3rd century CE. The Phoenician cults of Milk'ashtart (Melqart) and Shadrapa were equated with Roman Hercules and Liber Pater (Dionysus). Both were worshipped in the Old Forum alongside the new temple of Rome and Augustus.[100] When Septimius Severus initiated work on the magnificent new forum/basilica complex, he had the framing pilasters in the apses of the basilica decorated with imagery evoking these two divinities. The correlation of the forum's imposing temple with an unlocated temple of Hercules and Liber Pater built under Severus, that was negatively remarked on by Dio because of its cost (and is often assumed to have been in Rome), remains an attractive possibility.[101] Hercules and Liber Pater were also built into the architectural framing of the Hadrianic baths, with separate shrines at opposite ends of the *palaestra*.[102]

While some of the religious architecture at *Lepcis* plainly reflects the adoption of Roman models, as in the Temple of Rome and Augustus, there were other temple complexes that seem to follow Punic models.[103] Similarly, at *Sabratha* there were both pedimental temples of conventional Roman design (the *capitolium*, Antonine and East Forum temples) and others of more distinctly Libyphoenician aspect (South Forum temple and Temple of Hercules).[104]

Numidian Towns

The numerous towns of Numidian origin were not culturally uniform in their Roman manifestation. One group we might highlight comprises towns with a significant Roman colonial dimension, whether due to refoundation as Roman colonies, to the deduction of veteran or citizen groups to sit alongside a native *civitas*,

98. De Miro and Polito 2005; Di Vita 2015a, 157–58, 184–85, 300, 462–64; Drine 1991; 2002; Krimi 2005; Zocchi 2018a, 53.
99. See Brouquier-Reddé 1992a; Cadotte 2007, 23–111.
100. Di Vita and Livadiotti 2005.
101. Dio 76.16.3; Birley 1988a, 150–51; Mattingly 1995, 121.
102. *IRT* 288, 297. I am grateful to Emily Drummond for bringing this to my attention.
103. Brouquier-Reddé 1992a; 1992b.
104. Eingartner 2005; Kenrick 1986;

or towns that lay within the *pertica* of *Karthago*. I have already noted that these sites saw faster and more extensive monumentalisation and urban promotion than the bulk of Numidian market towns. However, a common feature of many of these sites, in religious terms, was a strong adherence to the Saturn/Caelestis (Baal/Tinnit) cults. *Thugga* is an example of the former group, with a well-explored religious landscape, where we can appreciate the range and scale of religious monuments.[105] As already noted, the nature of the donors in the monumentalisation of the centre was quite distinct from *Lepcis Magna*, involving some local Numidian families but, more prominently, Roman citizens and citizens of *Karthago*, individuals associated with the large neighbouring imperial estates—with the competitive interactions between these groups an important dynamic.[106] The *capitolium* on the forum is one of the most striking Roman monuments in North Africa. But there is a strong sense of religious dualism between the distinctive engagement with new architectural settings and traditional African gods (albeit dressed up with Roman names—Saturn, Neptune, Caelestis, Mercury, and so on). The religious landscape at *Thugga* can in part be perceived as a "Roman" monumental core and an "African" periphery, with major sanctuaries to the chthonic cults (notably Saturn and Caelestis) interspersed with the cemetery zone around the town.

The majority of inland towns in Africa had a much reduced range of divinities than the more cosmopolitan centres mentioned so far, and epigraphic attestations generally related to a smaller subset of the syncretised African cults. The idea of religious syncretism (commonly understood as an *interpretatio Romana*) is generally seen as a fundamental aspect of religion in the Roman provinces.[107] However, it is often considered in an uncritical way as a universal and homogenous process by which native gods were readily equated with Roman ones. However, the power imbalances in a colonial society need to be considered as part of what shaped religious choices and behaviours.[108] The Romanisation paradigm has directed our thinking about religion towards the idea of greater conformity with Roman practices elsewhere and to a somewhat monolithic concept of "Romano-African religion." I argue that, on the contrary, we need to recognise the probability of extreme heterogeneity of practices (effectively creating multiple Romano-African religions). Even where Roman names for the divine were adopted, we also need to carefully reflect on the extent to which underlying practices of transaction with divine forces were transformed. Religion was one of the most crucial areas for identity expression and also one where traditional beliefs and behaviours might continue to evolve

105. Saint Amans 2004.
106. Christol 2014; de Vos 1997; Duncan-Jones 1985; Khanoussi and Maurin 1997; 2000.
107. Hauschild et al. 2007; Leglay 1975; 1984; McCarty 2016; 2022; Picard 1954; Rives 2007, 142–48.
108. For a series of very important discussion (and post-colonial theorising) of the *interpretatio Romana* and syncretism in Roman provincial societies, see Webster 1995; 1997a; 1997b; 1999; 2001. See also Février 1976b.

alongside imported novelties. A major problem with the evidence is that it is so focused on epigraphic attestations of cults. Because of the history of excavation, we have precious little detail on the actualities of cult practice at temples and other religious sites across North Africa. In any case, we should not assume that every inscription mentioning Mars or Minerva or Iupiter represents the same or similar religious actions. The more logical interpretation is that different individuals or groups in society at large shaped their behaviour according to regionally or socially constituted norms in which pre-Roman practices remained of importance for subject peoples.

The importance of religious practices in reinforcing group identity is also demonstrated by inscriptions commemorating communal dedications and acts.[109] Minority groups were often keen to distinguish themselves in this way, as in the case of a self-identifying association of Roman citizen merchants at *Thinissut*.[110]

Cadotte's study of religious syncretism in Africa is extremely important for mapping the overall patterns of religious dedication for a wide array of cults.[111] It is apparent from his maps that there was a strong urban emphasis for most of the divinities that were worshipped by a Roman divine name. However, in many cases, one suspects that there was an African cult underlying it (Saturn, Caelestis, Hercules, Pluto, Liber Pater, Aesculapius, and Neptune). In North Africa, these divinities seem to have had particular associations with chthonic forces, and their distribution may be read as more reflective of the religious interests of the wider rural population in this region. What is most striking is the broad similarity for many different gods of Cadotte's mapped distributions, with a strong geographical emphasis on northern and eastern Tunisia and northern Algeria, with occasional outliers in the Aurès military zone. The level of evidence from the High Steppe region, for instance, is far lower—despite the significant scale of excavations at *Sufetula*, for instance—and southern Tunisia is a virtual blank. The distributions appear to be primarily related to the pre-Roman eastern *Numidae* (*Massyli*) and the Libyphoenician coastal region of *Africa Vetus*. Moreover, as we saw in the case of *Thugga*, many of the temples to these chthonic gods were located in *suburban* locations around towns, emphasising connections with the rural community. For these reasons, I postpone full discussion of Saturn worship and the other chthonic cults until Chapter 11 and discuss the urban and rural evidence together there.

The Gaetulian zone to the south, with the exception of the Tripolitanian cities, appears to have been a different religious world. If we exclude the evidence associated with the military community from the Numidian garrisoned zone and the Mauretanian (western *Numidae*/*Masaesyli* and *Mauri*) areas, those regions too seem to be very distinct in terms of their religious behaviours.

109. Bel Faida 2008.

110. *AE* 1978, 836: *cives romani qui Thinissut negociator.*

111. Cadotte 2007.

Towns Associated with the Military Community

As discussed already in Chapter 7, the military community had its own preferences and practices in religious matters. The multiplicity of divinities worshipped in the garrison settlements at *Lambaesis*, for instance, was extremely diverse. The dominance of individuals associated with the military and the governor of *Numidia* require us to consider the civic complex as being to a large extent military in outlook. *Lambaesis* is one of a group of urban centres west of *Theveste* on the Aurès High Plains with a much higher representation of military veterans. There is a distinctive alignment of these urban centres with aspects of the military identity revealed at *Lambaesis* and the garrison settlements of the frontier. The religious panoply and behaviours of these sites are quite distinctive from normal towns of the African provinces, and the military community employed syncretism in a way that was distinctive to civilians. For the military, syncretism was not a happy marriage of Roman and native gods, but a way of representing the subordination of local gods to Roman ones, just as the people of the security zones were required to recognise Roman suzerainty.[112] Nonetheless, within settlements like *Lambaesis* or *Thamugadi* levels of literate communication with the divine still varied considerably, depending on the nature of the cult. Compared to the overall volume of funerary inscriptions from these two sites, only a small proportion of the many Saturn stelae were inscribed (at *Lambaesis* 9/130 and *Thamugadi* 4/134), indicating that this was not due to low levels of literacy, but to an active behavioural choice.[113]

Funerary Practices and Identity

In this section, I review another important area of varied urban behaviours, that of funerary practice. After first discussing some of the inherent biases in the epigraphic evidence, I then turn to the wider archaeological picture of funerary practices, linking them back to the pre-Roman societies of select areas to reveal the significant local variations in behaviours.

Tombstones and Funerary Inscriptions

The c.18,000 funerary texts from Africa offer an abundance of data on the urban populations. This total represents 42% of the total from the western Empire (and Italy accounts for another 37%), indicating an adoption of this form of funerary

---

112. Webster 1997b.
113. Kerr 2007, xi.

commemoration at a far higher level than in the other western provinces.[114] The vast majority of these have come from towns, in which I include the combined garrison settlement (legionary fortress, *canabae*, and town) at *Lambaesis*. Rural finds make up a relatively small percentage. However, as Lassère long ago demonstrated, there were considerable differences in styles of funerary monument and epigraphic practice over time. Though these provide a relative dating framework, it is clear that there was variation between different urban and military contexts.[115] More work is needed on the less Roman artistic style of some funerary monuments, which at some urban centres resemble the rustic images of the Saturn stelae.[116]

One of the most notable assemblages is from the town of *Thugga*, where 1,525 tombstones are known from the town's cemeteries, and a further 92 (c.6% of the overall total) from its postulated territory.[117] This one medium-sized town and its territory has thus yielded c.9% of the total funerary epitaphs known from Africa and c.4% of all those known from the western Empire. There has been some debate about whether this sort of assemblage is useful for modelling wider social and demographic patterns in the Empire as a whole, and my view is that we need to recognise the fundamentally localised nature of many of the identity strategies at play.[118]

The vast majority of the *Thugga* funerary texts were recorded away from their original context, but some *in situ* finds allow a few comments on the development of the cemetery zones to be made.[119] The earliest tombstones came from the north (where pre-Roman dolmens are still visible) and west cemeteries, while the southern cemetery around the Libyco-Punic mausoleum and the north-east cemetery around the Temple of Saturn saw their main Roman development in the Antonine era and later (Fig. 8.4).

The vast majority of tombstones were simple unadorned stelae bearing only a short funerary text, though there were c.200 more elaborate *cippi* (funerary altars) and 10 texts from mausolea, evidently relating to groups in society who sought to show off perceived status or identity differences in more extravagant ways. As already noted, *Thugga* was evidently a dual community for the 1st–2nd centuries CE, comprising Roman citizens from a *pagus* and an indigenous *civitas*.[120] The first group appears to be much more prominent in the funerary record than we might

114. Khanoussi and Maurin 2002, 84.
115. Lassère 1973, 7–152 for a detailed study of *Karthago*, *Thugga*, and the military zone. See also Le Bohec 1989a, 84–106.
116. Ben Abdallah 1999b (*Bisica*); Ben Baziz 2000, 321–30 (Rohia region); M'Charek-Bourghida 1997 (area of Bargou).
117. See the exemplary *Thugga* publication of Khanoussi and Maurin 2002 . Cf. Ben Abdallah et al. 2013, for a similar overview of *Ammaedara*.
118. Khanoussi and Maurin 2002, 84–90.
119. Lassère 1973, 71.
120. Beschaouch 2011.

expect, though this most likely relates to differences in funerary behaviours than a demographic imbalance favouring the Roman citizen group. There are 1,000 Roman citizens named in the funerary inscriptions (c.63% men), compared to c.300 individuals identified as autochthonous based on the form of names (of which 54% were men).[121] The Roman citizens seem to have been responsible for the majority of the *cippi* and mausolea dedications.

There is a small number of funerary poems (13 from the town and 6 from the territory), all commemorating Roman citizens where the name of the deceased is preserved. Most funerary texts at *Thugga* were very simple, giving the bare minimum of onomastic and age information, and little indication of origin, status, and occupation. Mentions of Roman tribes are rare (16 examples), as are mentions of employment or profession. Two of the rare exceptions were military veterans.[122] More surprisingly, there are few indications of local status markers, such as priesthoods or magistracies—even where we are probably dealing with the tombstone of an individual known from a dedication in the town to have been the donor of a public building. Affectionate epithets (*coniunx optimus*, *filius carissimus*, and so on) were also rare here (only 100 examples outside the poems). The adoption of the practice of erecting Latin texts to the dead at *Thugga* is not, therefore, quite the standardised and normative Roman behaviour one might at first imagine. Members of the peregrine *civitas* are identifiable because of the distinctive ways they recorded names and filiation. The naming practices they employed (and were commemorated under) involved in simple form using a Latinised *nomen* alone, a *nomen* and indication of filiation, a *nomen* and double filiation, or double names (generally two *cognomina*).[123] There are other peculiarities in the case of locals who had acquired Roman citizenship, where the *cognomen* sometimes appeared before the *nomen*.[124] These divergences in naming practices between Roman citizens and *Numidae* at *Thugga* reflected specific cultural choices pertaining to identity. The emphasis on family name and filiation was a clear continuation of pre-Roman ways of indicating social belonging and commemorating identity within the Numidian community. The differences also suggest long-maintained social distinctions within the combined population of the town.[125]

All in all, there seems to have been a calculated set of differences at *Thugga* between the epigraphic habits of the *pagus* citizens and the indigenous community of the *civitas*. Even when citizenship was extended to the latter, they did not

121. Khanoussi and Maurin 2002, 7–78.
122. Khanoussi and Maurin 2002, 64.
123. Khanoussi and Maurin 2002, 79–82.
124. Khanoussi and Maurin 2002, 82.
125. Khanoussi and Maurin 2002, 84: "Les romains du *pagus* ont certes constitué un modèle pour les pérégrins de la *civitas*, mais tout laisse croire qu'il a existé une hiérarchie séparant ceux-ci des nouveaux parvenus issus de la *civitas*."

simply copy the conventional form of Latin nomenclature. The general lack of engraved images on the tombstones is also interesting, not least because there was a parallel stelae tradition linked to the Saturn cult at *Thugga* (with 450 known stelae), including many Tinnit symbols, crescents, bulls, rams, palms, caducei, and eight with anthropomorphic figures.[126] The choice not to engrave images on tombstones must have been deliberate. Conversely, most of the Saturn stelae were anepigraphic, but of the 15 with Latin texts, eight recorded either *tria nomina* or *praenomen* and *nomen*. This again might point to different preferences and practices in religious behaviour among the Roman citizen inhabitants and the indigenous Africans at *Thugga*. Over time, with individual grants of citizen status to Africans and later the *constitutio antoniniana*, these differences may have narrowed somewhat, at least at the upper end of the social scale. But the evidence does suggest that the different branches of the dual community behaved differently and expressed identity in distinctive ways in their use of epigraphic and votive habits, and that these discrepancies will have been very evident to and have had social impact on people in the town.

Wider comparisons with the larger African corpus of tombstones are needed, but I would make a couple of initial observations. Soldiers and other members of the military community often used the medium of inscribing tombstones in a rather different way to urban communities like that at *Thugga*. Status and hierarchy were of prime importance in the army, and indications of military rank and specialisation were frequently provided on tombstones. As most soldiers served away from their place of origin, indications of home town or homeland were also often given greater importance. These habits were adopted or mimicked by the civilians associated with the military community. In urban communities in general, the most likely individuals or groups to include additional information about their origin or status were Roman citizens present in largely non-citizen communities,[127] foreigners and outsiders, enslaved people and freedmen, or distinctive religious minorities like Jews.[128] However, Karen Stern's analysis of the evidence of Jewish communities in North Africa suggests that their identity was not entirely alien to other groups within the African provinces—indeed, there was overlap with the sort of naming practices employed by other Romano-Africans, and in general the identity construction of such groups reflected their engagement with the African context in which they lived. Tombstones (and the associated funerary rites that might well advertise difference in specific practice)

126. McCarty 2010, 432–35.

127. The significance of Roman citizenship as a stimulus for funerary commemoration is stressed by Meyer 1990.

128. On Roman citizens, see Inglebert 2002b. On Jews in Africa, see Iancu and Lassère 1985; Stern 2007.

were an excellent way for different groups to assert their varied identity. It would be fascinating to compare the epigraphic evidence from tombstones with a detailed knowledge of the burials they accompanied and the material culture deposited therein. Sadly, that information is rarely available to us in individual burials, let alone for an extensive cemetery area.[129] However, cemetery excavations in themselves can yield excellent markers of varied past behaviours, and it is to these I now turn.

Varied Burial Practices

Most towns had extensive burial grounds on the periphery of the urban core, sometimes extending along roads running away from the settlement, in other cases substantial parts of the *suburbium* were taken up with cemetery enclosures, though with the foci of such activity moving over time (Fig. 9.2).[130] Though many cemetery zones were targeted for the retrieval of inscriptions in the colonial period,[131] the lack of attention to the skeletal remains and the more general focus of excavation work on the monumental centres of Roman towns in Africa, has left cemeteries under-investigated and, in many cases, subject to progressive degradation through modern development around archaeological areas. Where cemetery excavations took place in the colonial period, these amounted to little more than treasure hunts for museum specimens, mostly targeting artefact-rich cremation burials of early imperial date and with scant detail recorded of the burial type, associated human remains, finds groups, indications of ritual followed, and so on.[132] Christian burials in churches and catacombs, accompanied by funerary mosaics, were another area of interest, with the mosaics the prime focus.[133]

The archaeological categorisation of cemetery zones around North African towns is, as a result, fairly poor and skewed to a small number of better excavated and published sites, such as *Iol*, *Karthago*, *Leptiminus*, *Pupput*, *Sitifis*, *Tiddis*, and *Tipasa*.[134] The number of published cemeteries that combine detailed description of structural,

129. Aounallah et al. 2020b.
130. *Leptiminus* provides detailed evidence, Stone et al. 2011c, 174–88 (figure from p. 174).
131. Stone and Stirling 2007b for a good introductory survey.
132. For the pillaging of the main *Leptiminus* cremation cemetery, Ben Lazreg and Mattingly 1992, 27–30.
133. For Christian funerary mosaics discovered at *Leptiminus*, see Ben Lazreg and Mattingly 1992, 17–24. For African Christian mosaics and other burials more generally, see Duval 1976; 1995; Yasin 2009.
134. *Iol*: Leveau 1976; 1983; *Karthago*: Delattre 1898; Ennabli 1992, 183–87, 131–34; Gauckler 1895; MacKinnon 2007a, 205–08; Stone and Stirling 2007b, 9–10; Raqqada: Mahjoubi et al. 1970; *Sitifis*: Guéry 1985; *Tiddis*: Février 1970; *Tipasa*: Baradez 1961; 1968; Bouchenaki 1975; Lancel 1970.

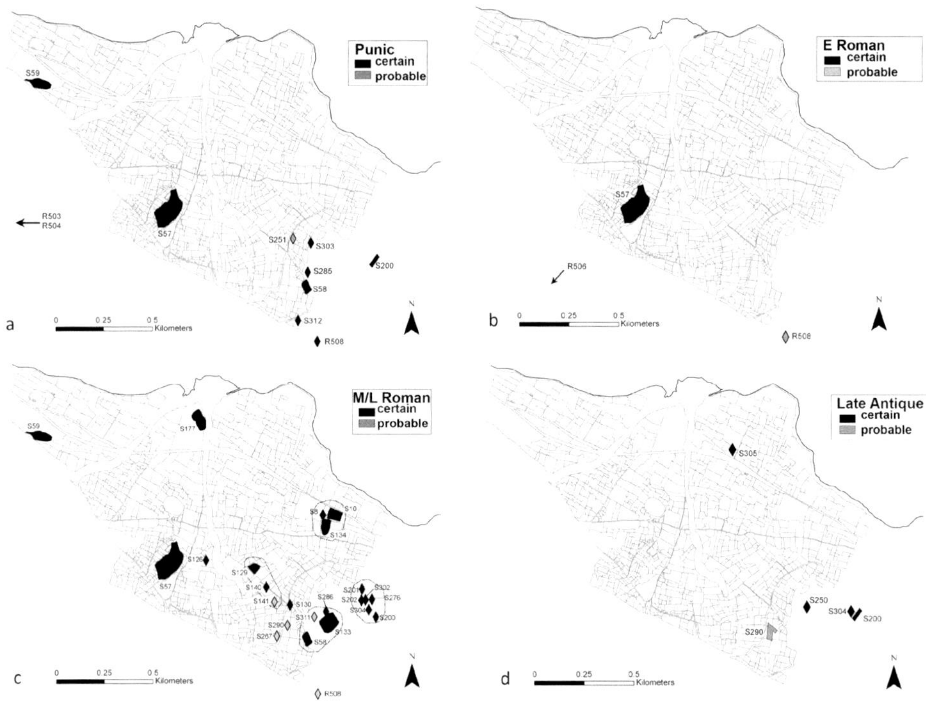

Figure 9.2. Cemetery zones at *Leptiminus* (from Stone et al. 2011a, 179–85).

skeletal, and artefactual data remains minuscule.[135] Full examination of skeletal elements remains rare or summarily dealt with.[136] *Karthago* provides an unusually detailed data set across time, social hierarchy, and with important epigraphic comparative material.[137] A series of excavations at *Leptiminus* provides one of the largest comparative data sets, albeit limited to late Roman inhumations.[138] Cutting-edge scientific approaches like aDNA and stable isotope analysis, to inform on genetic background, diet, and geographical origins of population, are in their infancy in Africa, but could revolutionise our understanding of the demographic mixture.[139]

135. See for instance, *Karthago*: Humphrey 1988, 218–84; Norman 2002; 2003; Norman and Haeckl 1993; *Lepcis Magna*: Musso et al. 1997; 1998; 2010; 2014; Zocchi 2018a, 66–128; *Leptiminus*: Ben Lazreg and Mattingly 1992; Ben Lazreg et al. 2021; Stirling et al. 2001; Stone et al. 2011a; *Pupput*: Ben Abed-Ben Khader and Griesheimer 2004; For a full survey of human anthropology reports from North Africa, see MacKinnon 2007a: 2007b; 2007c, 12–13. Some early work on human remains in the colonial era, especially craniometric analysis, was also underpinned by racist assumptions, see Pace et al. 1951.
136. See for, example, Bailet 2004, an 11-page report on the cremated material from *Pupput*.
137. Kilgore and Jurmain 1988; Stevens 1995; Walth 2005; Walth and Miller 1993, with further references in MacKinnon 2007c.
138. Meiklejohn 2000; Osborne 1992; Osborne and Stirling 1992; Rife 2001; Walth 2001; Walth and Mattingly 2001.
139. Keenleyside et al. 2009; Power et al. 2019.

North Africa was impacted by globalised trends in funerary practices in the wider Empire—broadly, there is a well-known early pattern in the western provinces of cremation burial, giving way progressively to more widespread inhumation by the early 3rd century. At the same time, in part under the influence of the rise of Christianity, grave goods that had been relatively common in the early Roman period (including things like coins, figurines, small pots, glassware, lamps, brooches, and other jewellery items) became rare or absent. Christianity also led to a shift into common west–east alignments of graves, from more random layouts.[140] The extent to which all parts of the African provinces were affected by these changes (and at what dates) is much less clear.[141] The late Roman period certainly saw significant changes, with the creation of specifically Christian cemeteries and an increase of intra-urban burials.[142]

Michael MacKinnon has provided a useful synthesis of what we know about the Romano-African society from osteological remains.[143] The skeletal analyses have inevitably favoured the later Roman period inhumations over earlier cremated remains (though North Africa was not uniform in following a cremation-to-inhumation switch). An extended supine body position predominated, but there were certainly exceptions of burials laid on the side (notably the left side) in flexed position, recalling pre-Roman African traditions. Despite the Christian preference for west–east alignment with head to west, this is less common in the overall data set than a pagan north–south orientation with head to north or south. The predominance of these alignments confirms that both pagan and Christian cemetery areas in the Roman period were well laid out and regulated spaces, though it is not uncommon to see some variance in individual cemeteries as graves were dug as space allowed.[144] There appears to be an imbalance between adult males and females (with the former between 1.2–3 times more common in the excavated burials), which raises some interesting questions regarding the lives of women, pre-adult mortality rates, and infanticide.[145] Some cemeteries have revealed an unusual age profile and seem to have been predominantly reserved for children, as in an example from *Thysdrus*, and Site 250 at *Leptiminus*.[146] The overall age profile in North African cemeteries reflects expected patterns of high

140. Jones 1987; Morris 1992.
141. For pre-Roman background, see relevant parts of Chapters 3, 4, and 5. For Roman overview studies and collections of papers, see Stone and Stirling 2007a; Trousset 1995a.
142. Duval 1995; Leone 2007b for an important survey of the evidence.
143. MacKinnon 2007a, 220–32.
144. Stirling et al. 2001, 159–62 for site 10 at Leptiminus, where 54% were oriented east–west, and 46% north–south; with head to south: 41%; west: 40%; north: 17%; and east: 2%.
145. MacKinnon 2007a, 222.
146. Slim, L. 1984; Rife 2001.

infant mortality (30–50% of skeletons relate to sub-adults) and relatively constrained life expectancy across society.[147]

Notwithstanding their splendid monuments, ancient towns were notoriously unhealthy places to inhabit, and relatively few individuals lived to what we would today consider old age (despite the inflated numbers that occur more commonly in the epigraphic commemorations).[148] Beyond the danger from pathogens, palaeopathological analyses remind us of some of the constraints on life. Signs of stress in both adults and children are evident in the relative commonality of conditions such as cribra orbitalia and enamel hypoplasia, potentially signs of malaria or anaemia and nutritional deficiencies.[149] Dental calculus, caries, abscesses, and loss of teeth were also commonplace, as were indications of degenerative osteoarthritis at levels far in advance of modern society for specific age groups. These data provide a useful corrective to the tendency to present a rose-tinted view of "Roman Africa" as a universal golden age. Overall mortality rates were high, and many members of society displayed signs of stress and wear and tear on their bodies.

Discussions of funerary rites, including the shift from cremation to inhumation in North Africa, are hampered by the relatively limited quantity and quality of the data set.[150] Not all regions started in the same place. In the latter centuries BC, Punic centres of the western Mediterranean were predominantly using cremation, as at *Qart Hadasht*.[151] However, at other Libyphoenician cities, where primary use of cremation focused on child offerings to Baal/Tinnit, adults continued to be mainly inhumed. There seems to have been a rapid shift from the late 1st century BC to more adults being cremated and interred in funerary chambers in specialised ash urns that differed from those of the tophet.[152] Libyphoenician cities were subsequently early adopters of inhumation from the early 2nd century CE. The story was possibly different in the Numidian and Moorish areas, where inhumation had been the predominant pre-Roman rite and seems to have remained so into the early Roman period in places, though cremations are attested in 1st century BC contexts at a few sites.[153] The point here is that while scholarly attention has generally focused on major external stimulated changes, such as the rise of the epigraphic habit or the more extensive use of cremation in the late 1st century BC to 2nd century CE, the

147. For an incisive overview of modelling of ancient demography, see Frier 2000. MacKinnon 2007a, 223 for the sub-adult mortality rate.
148. On the health risks of ancient city life, Harper 2017; Scobie 1986. On epigraphic age inflation, see Meyer 1990; Suder 1984; 1985.
149. MacKinnon 2007a, 225–26.
150. Février 1982; Février and Guéry 1980. Cf. Lassère 1995 for an epigraphic-focused approach to funerary rites.
151. Ben Younès 2007; Ben Younès and Krandel-Ben Younès 2014; Gomez Bellard 2014.
152. Examples of sites with limited evidence of cremation in Punic tombs, *Leptiminus*, Ben Younès, H. and Sghaïer 2018, 35–40; at *Lepcis Magna*, Zocchi 2018a, 109–11.
153. Ben Younès and Krandel-Ben Younès 2014; Krandel-Ben Younès 2002

autochthonous elements of the hybrid and diverse cultural traditions that emerged also merit much closer attention.[154] The inhuming traditions of North Africa were very diverse, including extended supine burials and flexed burials laid on the side (the traditional Saharan form), and there are other aspects revealing a persistent influence of autochthonous traditions, such as the common inclusion of red ochre in burials.[155]

Another interesting theme relates to the monumentalisation of death, most impressively with the spread of a "mausoleum culture" in the African provinces. Already present in the pre-Roman landscapes of Libyphoenician and Numidian regions, distinctive tower, temple/*aedicula*, and obelisk mausolea became much more abundant in the Roman era.[156] Jennifer Moore attests over 340 in Tunisia alone, and Julia Nikolaus has recently catalogued 140 for Tripolitania.[157] While these seem to have been primarily a feature of rural landscapes, erected as memorial monuments and places of worship on the estates of the landed elite, there is growing evidence that these occurred in larger numbers in suburban areas and in urban cemeteries. For instance, Andrea Zocchi has recorded 36 (the majority not included in Nikolaus' total) in the near hinterland of the single city of *Lepcis Magna*, with at least 13 associated with urban cemeteries.[158] The *Leptiminus* excavation work located at least three mausolea in the cemeteries that had all been demolished to below ground level and were thus invisible through survey.[159] The larger than anticipated numbers at these two sites suggest that urban mausolea may have been a more common phenomenon than Moore acknowledges.[160] However, she is surely correct in seeing the wide distribution of mausolea as representing something with strong links in indigenous rural societies.[161] I shall return to the rural dimension of mausoleum culture in Chapter 11.

There is great potential to use funerary data if it is of sufficient quality for evaluating issues of varied and changing identity. It can also highlight locational shifts in urban funerary practices, as demonstrated by the *Leptiminus* survey, for instance. Of particular interest is the overlap of Roman-era practices with pre-Roman traditions. The Spanish–Tunisian team working at *Althiburos* excavated a dolmen

154. Stone and Stirling 2007b, 12–23 for similar views.
155. Ben Younès and Sghaïer 2018, 39; Gatto et al. 2019a; Mattingly 2007b.
156. Di Vita 2015a, 303–54 for *Sabratha* mausoleum B.
157. Moore 2007; Nikolaus 2016; 2017. For descriptions of 67 examples in Algeria, Gsell 1901b, 54–99. See also Bentivogli 2004; Ferchiou 1995a; 2001; Werriemi 2003.
158. Zocchi 2018a, 88–94.
159. Stirling et al. 2001, 141–46; 397–414; Stone et al. 2011c, 185–86.
160. Moore 2007, 94: "Most mausolea in Africa Proconsularis were apparently situated on private estates, not in cemeteries [...] They were not accessible as burial structures located in the immediate vicinity of a town."
161. Moore 2007, 100–3.

burial immediately south of the town.[162] This was part of a group of more than 100 megalith monuments within the southern cemetery area, and while anomalous in a Roman urban context, the concentration and density are explicable in relation to the Numidian town that lay beneath the Roman-era one. Despite the robbed state of the dolmen, it was demonstrated that the tomb was a collective monument and contained traces of at least 15 individuals having been buried within it over a period of time. These may well have been family monuments, and when new interments were made, the bones of the previous burial were piled respectfully against the rear wall of the tomb. The pottery present spanned several centuries, terminating in the early 1st century CE. This shows continuation of ritual behaviours focused on NAIA tombs into the early Roman period, and this is supported by the presence of several Roman inhumation graves that were dug around the dolmen. The funerary rite employed (inhumation rather than cremation), the relative lack of associated grave goods, and the lack of tombstones contrasts with a contemporary (early Roman) cremation cemetery with Punic-style stelae on the north side of the city. This raises the possibility that not only were the earlier Numidian megalithic monuments incorporated into a Roman-era cemetery area, but that two identity groups within the town, one more Numidian, the other more "Punic," chose to differentiate themselves from each other by choosing different forms of burial rite and styles of memorialisation.[163]

The wider work at *Althiburos* has added 11 new Libyan inscriptions associated with the megalith funerary landscape, dated stylistically to the 1st century BCE rather than earlier, and potentially extending into the Roman period if we accept that such traditions could continue alongside Latin styles of commemoration.[164] From my point of view, this looks like another example of discrepant identity in action—perhaps with a Numidian identity group continuing to use the southern cemetery, and a more Punic- or Roman-influenced group the northern cemetery. The other point we might take from this demonstration of a close association between a major dolmen cemetery and an early nucleated sedentary settlement is that the known distribution map of such tombs and cemeteries may give us clues as to the location of a number of other early Numidian villages and towns, beyond the list of names we can derive from the ancient sources.[165]

A second example of the Roman afterlife of the megalith tradition concerns the excavation of a tomb complex at *Mactaris*. The "nouveau megalithe" was a complex of well-built chambers.[166] There were multiple inhumations in each chamber, with

162. Kallala and Sanmartí 2011, 393–410; Sanmartí et al. 2012, 27–29, 38–40.
163. Kallala and Sanmarti 2011, 393–405; Sanmartí et al. 2012, 38–40.
164. Kallala et al. 2017, 365–72.
165. This point was previously made by Camps 1995b, 28, but as demonstrated in Chapter 4 is reinforced by new data.
166. Ghaki 1997a.

up to 40 individuals recorded along with hundreds of pottery vessels, including local handmade forms along with Punic and Roman imports. The date range covers the last centuries BCE and the 1st century CE, so this form of collective burial monument continued in use during the first 150 years that *Mactaris* was incorporated into the African province. The bodies appear to have been laid on the right side in the traditional Numidian ritual and there were also indications of ochre being spread on the burial and the chamber.

In a similar way, the cemeteries associated with the town of *Bagat* (Henchir Ghayadha) reveal a great diversity in monument type: dolmen and some bazina monuments in the NAIA (and perhaps continuing into the early Roman period); individual inhumations continuing the Numidian rite and accompanied by neo-Punic, Latin, and possibly Libyan tombstones; a columbarium with cremations and Latin inscriptions; and later Roman inhumations with Latin tombstones.[167] This could be the result of sequential evolution, but it is also possible that elements of burial tradition were heterogeneous, relating to different status or identity groups contemporaneously.

Some funerary monuments had a very regional distribution. In North Africa, a common burial monument of the 2nd–3rd centuries CE was the so-called *cupula* type: a half-barrel-shaped structure, varying between 1 and 2.5 m in length, produced either from a solid stone block or with mortared masonry coated with plaster. Lea Stirling's important study of this class of monument traces the origins earlier and the last use later, but identifies the mid-Roman period as the *koine* of the *cupula* tomb.[168] She makes an important functional observation about the suitability of the *cupula* monument as a cover for both *in situ* cremations and inhumations, and the type spans the changeover from the former rite to the latter rite in Africa.[169] However, the overall distribution of the *cupula* type is peculiar (Fig. 9.3). It was far from ubiquitous in Africa and shows both unusual concentrations and unexpected gaps in the distribution, as is evident from Lassère's 1973 study.[170] Subsequent to his work, further *cupula* cemeteries have been excavated at other coastal sites in Tunisia, notably *Pupput*, *Leptiminus*, *Lepcis Magna*, and *Sullecthum*, increasing the evidence for the adoption of the type in the Libyphoenician zone. There are outliers also at coastal and military sites in *Mauretania*, but the four densest concentrations of *cupula* tombs are at Libyphoenician coastal sites, in the area of the Cirtan confederation, in the Aurès region focused on *Lambaesis*, and in the High Steppe region around *Ammaedara* and *Theveste*. The type was certainly one of the forms favoured by the military community, as is evident from the examples at *Lambaesis*,

167. M'Charek et al. 2008.
168. Stirling 2007, 119–22.
169. Stirling 2007, 123–29.
170. Lassère 1973, 125 for map.

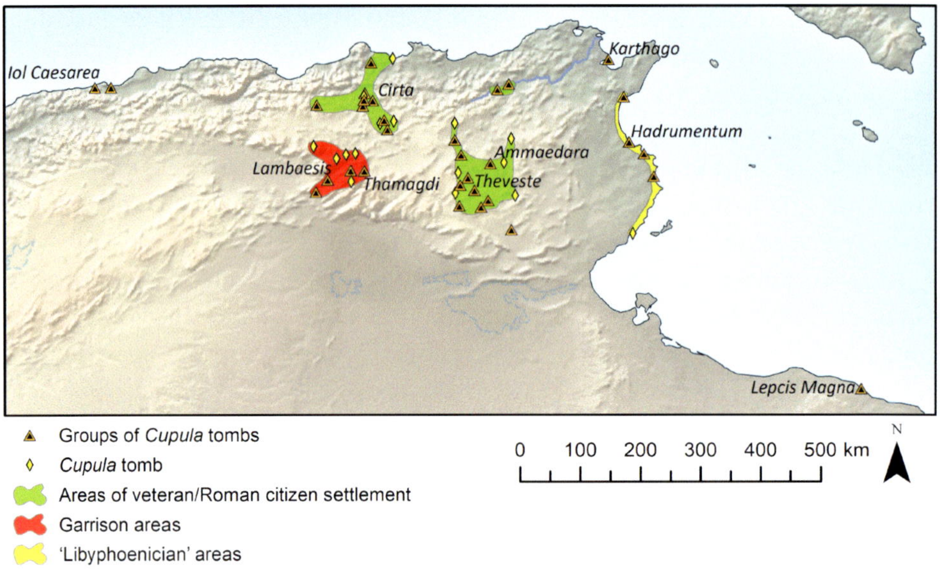

Figure 9.3. Distribution of *cupula* tombs in North Africa (Martin Sterry from author's rough after Lassère 1973, with additions).

Ad Calceum Hercules, and other military sites, but it also seems to have been popular in veteran colonies like *Ammaedara*, *Cuicul*, *Thamugadi*, and other centres with a high proportion of Roman citizens, including veterans, from an early date (such as *Cirta* and its region). The only examples in the *Bagrada* valley come from *Simitthu*, a Roman colony with an ongoing military presence at the imperial quarries, and nearby *Bulla Regia*. The type is not otherwise attested at *Thugga* or the vast majority of other *Numidae* sites or in the Carthaginian *pertica*. This again looks like a deliberate cultural choice, reflecting different emphases in portraying identity.

The stone *cupulae* often had integral inscriptions, so provide a rare link between texts and burial type. The inscriptions indicate *cupulae* were mainly constructed for soldiers, veterans, enslaved people, and freedmen, with a few rare examples of more notable individuals (members of the curial class, educated individuals, a priest and priestess, even a couple of equestrians). This suggests that in general the *cupula* type was one more widely used below the upper elite level of society (who favoured more elaborate monuments like mausolea). However, it is clear from the excavations at *Pupput* and *Leptiminus* that between the *cupula* burials there were many less substantial burials—beneath amphorae, tiles, and simple stone slabs, or in uncovered grave cuts. It is likely that the *cupula* was a monument type favoured at some towns by those who could afford a permanent surface grave marker and a memorial inscription, and that it was designed to show off that degree of status.

In Gaetulian lands to the south, little is known about the form of urban cemeteries away from military bases or coastal towns. Cemeteries associated with forts at *Nigrenses Maiores* and *Gholaia* both had *cupulae*, though there are also some very large drum tombs (bazinas) at the former site.[171] A rare exception is Kedouat Johala by Kebili (*ad Templum*?) in the Nefzaoua, where a number of *cupulae* and slab-covered cremations accompanied with offering tables were found within a funerary enclosure. The dating appears to be late Roman, well beyond the normal range for cremation burials in Africa and probably reflecting a highly local variation in rite.[172] On the other hand, late Roman burials at *Cidamus* associated with the mausolea there, and evidently designed for locals, were inhumations in elongated, slab-covered *loculi*. The burials within the mausolea there appear to have been multiple inhumations.

The town of *Leptiminus* offers a rare insight into the long-term shifts in funerary zones and burial rites, both through extensive survey and focused excavation (Fig. 9.2).[173] In the Punic period, there were subterranean funerary chambers of Punic-type cut into a series of low rocky eminences to east, west, and south of the town. These inhumation burials were accompanied by a range of burial goods, though most of these tombs have been robbed long ago. In the early Roman period, most of these cemetery zones were evidently abandoned in favour of a very intensive cremation cemetery overlying part of the southern Punic necropolis (Henchir Methkal). The access shafts of the earlier Punic burials were buried beneath a thick accumulation of ash (up to 1 m deep), evidently the result of individual *bustum* pits, over which funerary pyres were lit. These cremation burials were accompanied by abundant grave goods: pottery, lamps, glass, coins, beads, terracotta masks and statuettes, hairpins.[174] By the 2nd century, new cemeteries were being established in the suburban zones, containing a mixture of cremations and, increasingly, inhumations beneath *cupulae*. A number of mausolea were also constructed at this time, often in special funerary enclosures, within which secondary burials of simpler type were also introduced. Grave goods were generally rare in these inhumations, even before they took on an east–west and probably Christian orientation. In one important mid-imperial cemetery on the Dahar Slima ridge to the east of the town, there was a fashion for constructing *hypogea* for inhumations, somewhat reminiscent of the earlier Libyphoenician

171. *Nigrenses Maiores*: Laporte and Dupuis 2011, 54–56 (drum tombs), 87–88 (*cupulae*). Bu Njem: personal observation. Fentress and Wilson 2016, 44–49 link the bazinas with late antique migration of desert peoples.

172. Trousset 1974, 47–48.

173. Ben Lazreg and Mattingly 1992; 17–30, 177–252, 260–300, 304–24; 311–33; Ben Lazreg et al. 2006; Ben Younès, H. and Sghaïer 2018; Stirling et al. 2001, 107–214; Stone et al. 2011c, 174–87.

174. Stone et al. 2011c, 179–82.

tradition, as well as at least one mausoleum.[175] These were surrounded by a dense infill of contemporary *cupula* tombs and other surface markers, as well as simpler burial types. The burials were a mix of cremations and inhumations with an interesting variation in funerary ritual evident in *cupulae* constructed over the two types. Cremations were provided with libation pipes between the ceramic vessel containing the ash and bone, and the exterior of the surface monument, while inhumation burials lacked libation tubes but regularly had offering tables attached to the side of the *cupula*.[176] In the late Roman period, Christian burials became an important category, including mosaic covered graves in an urban church and a catacomb below the Dahar Slima cemetery.[177] Differences in contemporary burial types in the same cemetery most likely denoted social status. Similarly, the placement of burials in close proximity to other monuments within special enclosures may indicate family or social relations. It is probable, though hard to prove conclusively, that some of the observed distinctions in burial rite and funerary practice may have related to specific groups within the urban community expressing their identity through variations in burial practice (as is certainly the case by the time we get to the Christian community). Unfortunately, we lack the epigraphic data from these cemeteries to shed light on social status, as most funerary texts were marble plaques and only small fragments survived the post-Roman limekilns.[178]

A clear example of specialised funerary areas for a self-identifying group can be found at *Karthago*, where a series of cemetery areas at Bir el-Jebbana and Bir es-Zeitoun are known collectively as the cemetery of the *officiales* because of the preponderance of imperial slaves and imperial freedmen associated with the Roman administration.[179] The earliest burials were marked by grave stelae, but most of the later tombs here were *cippi* (altar-like monuments mainly in plastered masonry, with inscribed marble plaques attached). Across at least three centuries the cemeteries seem to have maintained their prime focus on imperial servants, with densely packed burial monuments and a rapidly rising ground surface, such that there are multiple levels of monuments at Bir es-Zeitoun. The situation is exceptional, but is indicative of the ways in which a small but cohesive social grouping could present a consistent picture of its version of Roman identity that effectively distanced itself from other inhabitants of *Karthago*.

An interesting aspect of the urban mausolea at the Libyphoenician cities is that they came into competition with another elite burial tradition at these sites, the

175. Ben Lazreg et al. 2006; 2021; Stone et al. 2011c, 181–87 and gazetteer S304.
176. Ben Lazreg et al. 2006, 352.
177. Ben Lazreg 2002; Ben Lazreg et al. 2006.
178. See Aounallah et al. 2007.
179. Carlsen 2020a; 2020b; Lassère 1973, 25–57; Stirling 2007, 127–29.

subterranean familial vault (*hypogea*), often ornately decorated with painted scenes in the late Hellenistic period, but continuing into the early centuries CE.[180] A funerary enclosure with ritual dining facilities close to Sabratha at Sidret al-Balik was also ornately decorated with wall paintings, emphasising the long-term importance of rituals of the dead.[181] At *Lepcis Magna* the distribution and chronology of these subterranean tombs overlaps with that of mausolea, with the latter eventually supplanting the former, though they seem to have co-existed for a period, and there are a few hybrid examples where a mausolea seems to have been specifically linked to an adjacent *hypogea* (Fig. 8.8 for the distribution).[182]

In an important series of articles, Luisa Musso, Ginette Di Vita-Evrard, and Sergio Fontana have illustrated the cultural complexity of funerary practice in *hypogea* at *Lepcis*.[183] The pre-Roman tradition in Tripolitania included the use of subterranean *hypogea* for multiple burials, and free-standing tower and obelisk mausolea in the Punic tradition. Excavations at *Lepcis* have shown a diversity of Roman burial and commemorative practices. Initially, many burials continued to be made in specially constructed *hypogea* of Libyphoenician type. By the mid-imperial period, as at *Leptiminus*, larger suburban cemetery zones were developing around the *hypogea*, involving an array of surface markers such as *cupula* tombs and simpler burials beneath tiles and amphorae. The funerary archaeology in the early Roman period, though, looks to have followed very different trajectories at *Leptiminus* and *Lepcis Magna*.

The *hypogea* type of burial at *Lepcis* is well illustrated by a double-chambered example at Gelda, c.2.5 km south-west of *Lepcis* (Fig. 9.4).[184] The two funerary chambers were each constructed with ten niches for cinerary urns, with a wide bench running round the walls in front of the niches for the placement of other grave goods. One of the chambers had been completely cleared in antiquity, but the other contained 11 cremations and three inhumations, evidently deposited between the Flavian period and the mid-2nd century.[185] The burial rite followed, the tomb contents and the epigraphic indications on the cinerary urns provide a remarkable record of a society in cultural transition. The family seems to have been from the very top level of Lepcitanian society, as indicated by the quality of the burial

180. Publications on some of the finest painted tombs are conveniently gathered in Di Vita 2015b, 567–594 (*Sabratha*: Tomb of Gorgon and Tomb of "defunto eroizzato"/deceased hero); 2015a, 363–92; 2015b, 625–628, (Gargaresh/Tripoli: Tomb of Adam and Eve, Tomb of Aelia Arisuth, with her impressive white turban); 2015b, 873–90 (Janzur: Tomb of the Mysteries).

181. Di Vita 2015b, 622–26, 859–72.

182. Zocchi 2018a, 67–82, 87–108.

183. Di Vita-Evrard et al. 1995; 1996; 1997; Faraj et al. 1996; Fontana 2001; Musso et al. 1996; Zocchi 2018a, 66–81.

184. Di Vita-Evrard et al. 1995; 1996.

185. Di Vita-Evrard et al. 1996, 87–97

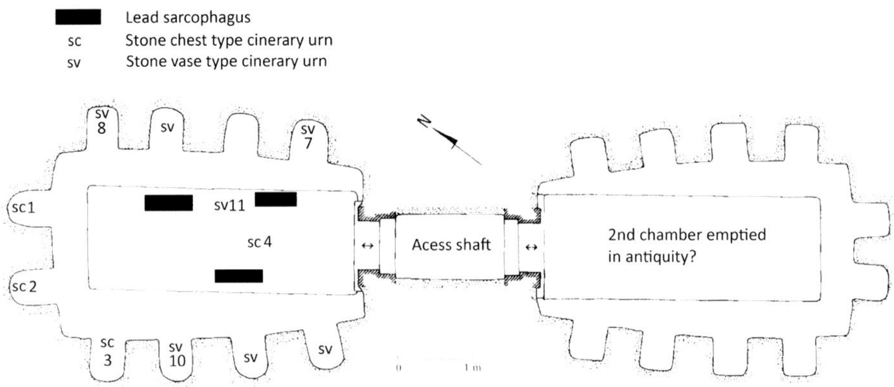

Figure 9.4. The Gasr Gelda *hypogeum* tomb near *Lepcis Magna*. Numbers correspond with those of individual urns in Table 9.4 (adapted from from Di Vita-Evrard et al. 1995, 155, 159).

monument, the best of the ash urns, and associated grave goods, including fragments of two folding stools. Two types of cinerary urn were used: the earlier form was a gabled stone chest (SC); the later type a stone vase (SV), some plain, some with elaborate vegetal decorative motifs.[186] The original placement of some (but not all) can be reconstructed (Fig. 9.4), with the stone chests 1 and 2 directly facing the door seemingly the earliest to be deposited.

Most of the urns carried engraved inscriptions, the earlier examples in neo-Punic script, the later ones in Latin characters. The urns contained ash and burnt fragments of lamps, glass perfume flasks, and other vessels that had been placed with the body on funerary couches.[187] Additional ash, with matching bone and fragments of these artefacts, was included in 10 of the 18 amphorae deposited in the chamber. Eight coins were retrieved between the urns and the amphorae, another from one of the inhumations, and a further 10 from the chamber. Two small amphorae had painted Tinnit symbols between palms and caduceus symbols. There were also numerous unburnt ceramic and glass vessels deposited in the tomb. In total, 24 open glass forms and 17 closed glass vessels were identified, along with 11 Italian sigillata dishes and cups, 1 African Red Slip ware (ARS) askos, 2 eastern sigillata vessels, 3 thin-walled ware vessels, 2 lamps, 22 flagons, and 3 other coarse ware vessels. Some of the open vessels had *in situ* animal bones representing evidence of sacrifice or funerary feast at the tomb. In addition to the 2 folding chairs, there were at least 14 iron strigils and 2 bronze lanterns. The

186. Di Vita-Evrard et al. 1996, 89–97.
187. Di Vita-Evrard et al. 1996, 112–25 for the finds assemblage.

3 lead sarcophagi lacked inscriptions, but seem to have been accompanied by moulded plaster heads of the deceased.[188]

A tentative family tree has been constructed, spanning three or possibly four generations of a single family; though, as the authors admit, alternative reconstructions would be possible if the tomb was originally built for a group of brothers, rather than the descendants of a particular individual.[189] Considerable interest lies in the naming practices observed on the ash chests and urns. Two of the ash chests had neo-Punic inscriptions on, but evidently related to individuals who already at that time possessed Roman citizenship, Publius Flavius Proculus Iaton and [Publius Flavius] Iustus Iaton, transliterated into neo-Punic.[190] The final element is evidently a peregrine name added to the *tria nomina*. The third ash chest bore the name Flavia Amothmic Nysfur in Latin. The vase urns all had inscriptions in Latin letters, but though (seemingly) dealing with Roman citizens, the form of names did not generally respect the expected form of presentation of *tria nomina* (see Table 9.4). The vase urns represented an innovation of the Flavian period and probably derived from Roman models, though several were of clear local manufacture. Overall, this fascinating assemblage shows a family of early adopters at work, taking on Roman citizenship and Roman names, but maintaining onomastic practices in the tomb that evoked earlier identity markers in Punic and Libyan society. This family was also quick to switch to coffined inhumation and plaster portrait busts from the mid-2nd century.

Of c.200 inscribed urns known from burials near *Lepcis* only c.10% used the Latin naming system properly.[191] The majority of these hypogeal burials evidently related to the elite class, though one of the cremation urns in a tomb discovered near Homs in the 1990s bore a surprisingly lengthy epitaph to Secundus, *actor* of Q. Servilius Candidus, the latter evidently the same man who provided *Lepcis* with its aqueduct. The high-status features of the tomb and its burials fully reflect the power and wealth of the Servilii family.[192] The Gelda tomb reveals a mix of Latin, Punic, and Libyan names, and even the Latin names sometimes reflect the Libyan heritage of an individual, as in the case of Flaminia Gaetulia mentioned in Table 9.4. There are few young children represented in the hundreds of cremations

---

188. Di Vita-Evrard et al. 1996, 97–101. Zocchi 2018b, 340–49 provides a wider study of finds from *hypogea* around *Lepcis*. Most of the amphorae were for wine, and the importance of wine in funerary rituals is also emphasised by frequency of flagons and cups. Lamps and unguentaria, both glass and ceramic, were also common finds.
189. Di Vita-Evrard et al. 1995, 172–77; 1996, 129–32.
190. Di Vita-Evrard et al. 1995, 157: *PWBLY PL'WY PRQL YT/NN/T* and *YHST' YT/NN/T*
191. Fontana 2001, 167.
192. Faraj et al. 1996. The tomb contained a mix of two cremations and two inhumations in a *hypogeum* originally designed for seven cremations. There was an accompanying assemblage of 3 ARS forms, a thin-walled ware vessel, 5 flagons, 7 other coarse ware vessels, 2 lamps, 3 amphorae, 4 glass vessels and fragments of 4 other forms, a bronze mirror, and a coin.

Table 9.4. Nomenclature on funerary urns from *hypogea* of the Flavii, *Lepcis Magna*.

Urn number	Urn type (SC = chest; SV = vase)	Form on urn	Reconstructed name?
1 (Neo-Punic)	SC	PWBLY PL'WY PRQL YT/NN/T	Publius Flavius Proculus Iaton
2 (Neo-Punic)	SC	YHST' YT/NN/T	(Publius Flavius) Iustus Iaton
3	SC	FLAVIA AMOTH/ MIC NYSFUR	Flavia Amothmic Nysfur
4	SC	No inscribed name—perhaps originally painted	
5	SV	C. FLAVI PROCULI	C. Flavius Proculus
6	SV	NAMGYDDE	(?) Namgyddus
7	SV	C. F. PROCUIL BYDBA/LIS F	C. Flavius Proculus, son of Bydbal
8	SV	PROCUL	(C. Flavius?) Proculus
9	SV	CANDIDE	(?) Candidus (or Candida?)
10	SV	M. F. IUSTI	M. Flavius Iustus
11	SV	FLAMINIAE GAETULIAE	Flaminia Gaetulia

from *Lepcis*, and on the ash chests female names are much less common than male ones (33:67). Both these anomalies may reflect continuation of pre-Roman cultural traits. Although no tophet has yet been discovered at *Lepcis*, the existence of one seems extremely likely from the near absence of child cremations in the *hypogea*.[193] A final point about the hypogeal burials is that they continued in use even after the switch to inhumation, and the fact that the inhumations were inserted into the *hypogea* alongside the existing ash urns, which were moved to one side, but not cleared out completely, suggests continuity of family use.

The contrast between building dedications from within the city where *tria nomina* were generally used by prominent *Lepcitani* from the late 1st century CE and funerary texts on mausolea, evidently for people of the same sort of elevated social status, is striking. The man commemorated on the Qasr Duirat mausoleum, C. Marius Boccius Zurgem, has a distinctly Libyan extra *cognomen*, and this pattern echoes other examples.[194] These Libyan or Libyphoenician lineage groups seem to

193. Fontana 2001, 167, 169. A tophet has been discovered to the south-west of the city at Messalata, but is too remote to have been the main tophet for *Lepcis*.

194. *IRT* 729 (Qasr Duirat); Fontana 2001, 168–69, citing Q. Domitius Camillus Nysim (*IRT* 692); Q. Caecilius Cerialis Phiscon (*IRT* 673); C. Calpurnius Tracachalus Dosiedes (*IRT* 677).

have remained of high significance for the first generation of so after acquisition of Roman citizen status.

Reflecting back on the pattern of monumental inscriptions at *Lepcis*, it is apparent that the uptake of Latin and the last neo-Punic inscriptions was not synchronous across all social contexts at *Lepcis*. Public inscriptions were the first to change, followed by funerary inscriptions, and finally by names inscribed on the urns within tombs. In other words, the Libyphoenician elite adopted Latin much sooner and more completely in the public sphere than in the domestic sphere. The funerary landscape at *Lepcis* thus reveals a rather different world to the monumental urban core and the world of public inscriptions, statues, and mosaics.

What we have encountered in this chapter is evidence of wildly differing cultural behaviours and identity formulations beneath the apparently still waters of the Roman pond. Such displays were, for the most part, not incompatible with Roman rule and were not primarily about resistance to Rome among the urban communities. However, they do testify to the very different ways of engaging with Rome and to the discrepant identities that could result. Much more work remains to be done, especially when we have more evidence on things like urban foodways and food production and consumption at urban sites.[195]

195. MacKinnon 2010; 2017.

Part 5: The Rural Communities

Chapter 10

DIFFERENT LANDSCAPES, DIFFERENT WORLDS

Introduction

This section concerns the peoples of the countryside and the ways in which rural communities were differentiated from one another and from the military community and urban dwellers. I also explore the evidence for change in rural production. A first proposition is that cultural differences were large between rural populations and urban or military groups. Past work on "Roman Africa" has tended to undervalue and underemphasise the rural populace.[1] For Tunisia and Algeria, at least, this is not for want of a basic knowledge of the density of Roman sites in the landscape, as the colonial-era *brigades topographiques* were spectacularly efficient at mapping this.[2] Richard Goodchild's research in Libya initiated recording of rural sites in both west and east, though subsequently work has progressed further in Tripolitania.[3] National mapping and systematic survey was less developed in colonial-era Morocco, though reviving in recent years (Table 10.1).[4] Scale of mapping and range of sites to be included are two big problems affecting many attempts to present key data on Roman provincial landscapes in map form. Typically these have concentrated on places for which an ancient toponym is known or that were evidently at the more "Roman" end of the site spectrum (towns, forts, aqueducts, roads). The areas of the landscape occupied by ancient peoples are generally illustrated by large capital letters across blank space, rather than in relation to settlement patterns. These maps, immensely valuable as they are, provide us with a very top-down view of provincial society,

---

1. For example, Lassère 2015, 425–93 does provide a lengthy region-by-region survey, but one that makes only sporadic use of the rural surveys and other archaeological data. Some modern accounts make no detailed mention of the archaeological survey data when discussing agriculture and rural society, primarily describing rural society and the economy in terms of literary sources and epigraphic evidence: Briand-Ponsart and Hugoniot 2006, 178–23; Ibba and Traiana 2006, 120–33; Le Bohec 2005a, 137–47; Prévot et al. 2006, 78–99.
2. See the sheets of the *AAA* (Gsell 1911); and *AAT* (Babelon et al. 1892–1913).
3. Goodchild 1950c; 1952; 1954b; 1954c; 1976.
4. Cf. Luquet 1964; 1966; 1975; Ponsich 1964a; 1964b; 1966; Souville 1973. The new *Carte Archéologique du Maroc antique* series is being published in a series of fascicules, Rebuffat 2011b; 2012b; Rebuffat and Limane 2011.

and in fact, because of their slanted emphasis, can be said to map "Roman Africa" rather better than Africa in the Roman world. At the small scale of such maps—typically 1:500,000 to 1:1,000,000 m—representing rural settlement in a meaningful way is a big challenge; in the collaborative Barrington Atlas project, it was a point of strong contention and varied practice between contributors, as a quick survey of the relevant map sheets will reveal. The national mapping series dealing with ancient sites, such as the AAA and AAT were generally at 1:100,000 or 1:200,000 m scale (with a limited number of sheets of the AAT at 1:50,000) allowing much closer resolution, but the incomplete coverage of these series inhibits attempts to stich the maps together digitally to generate overviews.[5]

While it is undeniably useful to be able to accurately locate the many toponyms known in ancient sources and inscriptions cartographically, this leaves a lot of gaps in our understanding. Most obviously this concerns the sources of wealth on which the urban centres were built, or the nature of settlement in the security zones that helped shape the garrison deployment. In a future of zoomable digital maps and data layers that can be turned on and off, the next generation of mapping will hopefully allow us to look more closely at the rural landscapes.[6]

With rare exceptions, work on the rural landscapes has been essentially survey-focused work, albeit allowing a remarkable level of detail about site morphology to be recorded, especially in areas where rural sites are well preserved in the modern landscape. Excavations of rural sites remain uncommon, especially of non-luxury productive structures: a large villa close to *Segermes* with olive and wine pressing facilities,[7] the al-Amud farm in the Libyan Valleys,[8] and a Byzantine farmstead in the territory of *Thugga*[9] provide a few random snapshots, but many more such excavations are needed to reveal the cultural variability of such sites. Excavations of late Roman fortified farms have been equally rare, though these types of site are crucial to understanding changes in society.[10]

However, despite the dearth of excavated sites, in the last few decades field surveys have started to reveal more about the variety of rural settlements and their

5. iDAI website (https://arachne.dainst.org/) for online editions of *AAA* (https://arachne.dainst.org/entity/2127777) and *AAT* (https://arachne.dainst.org/entity/2183927).
6. Lapierre 2012; Lapierre and Briand-Ponsart 2017; Lapierre et al. 2015 reports on "project AFRICA," involving the digitisation of Salama's map within a GIS environment covering Algeria and Tunisia. So far this has focused on incorporating the traditional markers of towns, roads, forts, with a particular focus on accurate positioning of milestones and centuriation boundary markers. The "Empire of 2000 cities" project (Hobson 2020) is another GIS-focused project that again focused on urban settlements and other larger settlements.
7. Ghalia 2005.
8. Barker and Jones 1984, 13–18, 20–22; Barker et al. 1996a; 1996b.
9. de Vos and Maurina 2019.
10. Anselmino 1989; Barker et al. 1991; Brogan and Smith 1984; Mattingly et al. 2013b; Munzi et al. 2014; Welsby 1992.

Table 10.1. Mapping "Roman Africa" at small scales.

Map	Reference	Scale	Principal sites mapped
Tabula Imperii Romani, Lepcis Magna; Cyrene	Goodchild 1954b; 1954c	1:1,000,000	Towns, harbours, aqueducts, roads, milestones and road stations, villages, forts and military installations, temples, mausolea, villas, fortified farms, other major farms
Les voies romaines de l'Afrique du nord	Salama 1951; 1999a	1:1,500,000 (*Karthago* hinterland at 1:500,000)	Roman roads, towns and major settlements linked to roads, military bases
Carte des routes et des villes de l'est de l'Africa	Desanges et al. 2010	1:500,000	Towns, roads, forts and military works, other Roman locality (mainly road stations, but includes some rural sites).
Barrington Atlas of the Greek and Roman World (W *Mauretania Caesariensis, Numidia, Tripolitana, Garama, Syrtica, Cyrene,*	Africa maps by: Fentress 2000b; Mattingly 2000a; 2000b; 2000c; 2000d; 2000e; Potter 2000a.	1:1,000,000	Towns, other major settlements, major roads, centuriated landscape, mines, Roman military sites, rural monuments, major rural settlements
Barrington Atlas of the Greek and Roman World (*Mauretania Tingitana, Iol Caesarea, Cirta, Carthago, Theveste-Hadrumetum*)	Africa maps by: Euzennat 2000; Fentress 2000a; Hitchner 2000a; 2000b; Potter 2000b.	1:500,000	Towns, other major settlements, major roads, centuriated landscape, mines, Roman military sites, rural monuments, major rural settlements

relative date spans (Fig. 10.1). Of particular importance has been the rise of intensive and systematic field survey, designed to record a cross section of all types of rural sites and structures, often applying interdisciplinary techniques to contextualise regional settlement patterns in their broader environmental and palaeoeconomic setting.[11] Foreign initiated surveys have increasingly been complemented by Maghrebian researchers, in part linked to revived national mapping programmes.[12]

11. For overviews of Roman landscapes in Africa, De Vos Raaijmakers 2022; Dossey 2010; Fentress and Docter 2008; Février 1990, 75–109; Leveau 1990; 1993; Leone and Mattingly 2002; Mattingly 1997c; Mattingly and Barker 2005; Mattingly and Hitchner 1995, 189–96; Stone 2004; 2020. For a useful bibliographical overview down to the mid-1990s, Vismara 1998.
12. For the Tunisian national mapping project, Ben Baaziz, 2005; 2015 (with important index of toponyms from 34 completed sheets). For details of c.70 sheets in various stages of preparation for publication, see bibliography reference for *CNSAMH* and the Institut national du patrimoine website. See also Dabbaghi et al. 2004, for the IPAMED project, which sought to develop the results in a digital format.

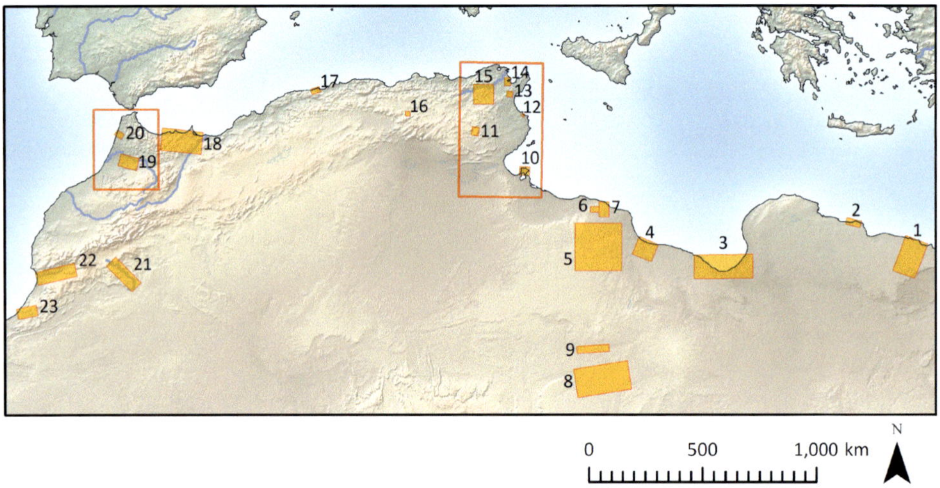

Figure 10.1. Location of main survey projects in North Africa. 1. Eastern Marmarica Survey; 2. Western Marmarica Survey; 3. Shell Sirtica; 4. ULVS Sirtica; 5. ULVS Pre-desert; 6. Jabal Tarhuna; 7. *Lepcis*; 8. Fazzan; 9. Wadi ash-Shati; 10. Jerba; 11. Kasserine; 12. *Leptiminus*; 13. *Segermes*; 14. Carthage; 15. *Thugga*; 16. *Diana Veteranorum*; 17. *Caesarea*; 18. Rif; 19. Sebou valley; 20. Loukkos valley; 21. Middle Draa; 22. Wadi Sous; 23. Wadi Noun. Open rectangles indicate areas of Tunisian and Moroccan national mapping programmes (Martin Sterry from author's rough).

Sadok Ben Baaziz was the architect of the Tunisian mapping programme, which has achieved not only impressive scientific results in the series of maps and gazetteers produced, but has also resulted in a cultural shift by engaging many other young researchers in this form of archaeology.[13] I shall be drawing on some of their remarkable results here. One of the problems with all the national mapping programmes (both of the colonial era and more recently) is the tendency for these initiatives to run out of steam before completion.

In this chapter, after first reviewing some of the legal aspects of landholding under the Roman Empire, I document the state of knowledge of the Roman-period landscapes of North Africa. Here I will attempt to redress the imbalance in traditional accounts that has prioritised the most exceptional epigraphic or textual evidence, but made less of the frequently reported rural discoveries of things like inscribed tombstones or engraved stelae.[14] As we shall see, there is a substantial volume of data on rural settlements and productive activity to support discussion of

13. Capacity building in the technical skill sets of satellite image analysis, GIS, and rapid field recording methods is a priority across the region, supported by initiatives like the Endangered Archaeology of the Middle East and North Africa Project, Hobson 2019b.

14. Lassère 1998 for an epigraphic-focused account on key texts. Note the importance, though, of minor epigraphic finds such as reported in Ben Baaziz 2000, 64–74, 111–21.

the ancient economy. The material to hand is sparser in relation to reconstructing how these societies engaged with Rome and how identities were presented, though I hope to demonstrate in Chapter 11 that some of the gaps are in themselves quite revealing about rural attitudes.

From Western Egypt to Morocco: The Rise of Survey Archaeology

One of the most striking aspects of the rural surveys in North Africa is how they reveal the evolution of farming systems that were well adapted to desert or hyper-arid conditions. Starting in the east along the Marmarican coast toward Egypt, there is growing evidence of extensive settlement and pottery production.[15] The rural landscapes of *Cyrenaica* are perhaps the least intensively explored of all of North Africa, though the region's numerous village settlements have been noted, especially in study related to Christian churches, and a series of Libyan PhD students have recently turned to aspects of rural Cyrenaica.[16]

Moving westwards, the desert landscapes along the Syrtic gulf have been explored by several survey projects, revealing details of a mixed farming and certainly semi-sedentarised peoples.[17] In Tripolitania, the Libyan Valleys Survey revealed the remarkable landscapes of Romano-Libyan floodwater farming regimes (Fig. 10.2).[18] This has been complemented by work in the hilly hinterland country of the Jabal Tarhuna[19] and around *Lepcis Magna*.[20] Western Tripolitania has seen extensive survey for the national mapping programme as well as the systematic work on Jerba.[21] To the south of Tripolitania, the exploration of the desert landscapes of the *Garamantes* is now well advanced, allowing for greater appreciation of sedentary oasis cultivation (see Chapter 5).[22] The late Garamantian rural landscape

15. Eastern Marmarica Survey: Rieger 2017; Rieger and Möller 2011; Rieger et al. 2012; Western Marmarica Survey: Hulin et al. 2009; 2010.
16. *Cyrenaica*: Goodchild 1976; Ward-Perkins and Goodchild 2003. For a series of PhD theses exploring aspects of the rural landscape and history, see Abdelhamed 2018 (ancient sources, inscriptions); Buzaian 2022 (oil and wine production); Emrage 2015 (fortified farms); Hesein 2015 (minor ports and pottery production sites).
17. Shell Syrtica: Lequesne et al. 2010; ULVS Syrtica: Longerstay 1999; Rebuffat 1988c; Reddé 1985; 1988.
18. ULVS: Barker et al. 1996a; 1996b; see also numerous articles in *Libyan Studies*; Sheldrick 2016; 2021 (for an up-to-date synthesis). For broader evaluation of the farming of desert lands, Mattingly 2014b; Sterry and Mattingly 2020a.
19. Jabal Tarhuna: Ahmed 2019, following up earlier work by Mattingly 1988a; 1988b; Oates 1953; 1954.
20. *Lepcis Magna*: Cifani et al. 2003; Felici et al. 2006; Fontana et al. 1996; Munzi 2010; Munzi et al. 2004; 2010; 2016; Zocchi 2018a, 139–75, 211–224 for a good summary of the data.
21. Jerba: Fentress et al. 2009; national mapping: Mrabet 1996; 2011.
22. Garamantian Fazzan: Mattingly 2003a; 2007a; 2010a; 2013a; Mattingly et al. 2020a (including the Wadi ash-Shati area surveyed by Merlo). Cf. Mattingly et al. 2020b for the oasis belt running from Libya to Algeria. For survey of NAIA/historic tombs of the Nefzaoua oasis zone, see now Monaco et al. 2020.

Figure 10.2. Typical wadi farming landscape of the Libyan Valleys (from Barker et al. 1996a, 202).

was an extensive oasis zone, studded with fortified villages whose architecture evoked the form of late Roman *quadriburgi* from the Roman garrison zone far to the north (Fig. 10.3).[23]

Within central and northern Tunisia, the extensive survey in the colonial tradition[24] and for the national mapping programme is complemented by a number of

23. Sterry and Mattingly 2011; 2013.
24. For example, the extremely useful study of the Tunisian Tell by Peyras 1991, but which totally lacks site plans. Other surveys that demonstrated the potential for more intensive survey in the well-preserved archaeological landscapes of the Tunisian High steppe included Addyman 1962; Addyman and Simpson 1966; Barbery and Delhoume 1982. Note also the many important observations of Ferchiou 1986b; 1989c S; 1990a; 1990b; 1990c; 1994; 1995b; 1998a.

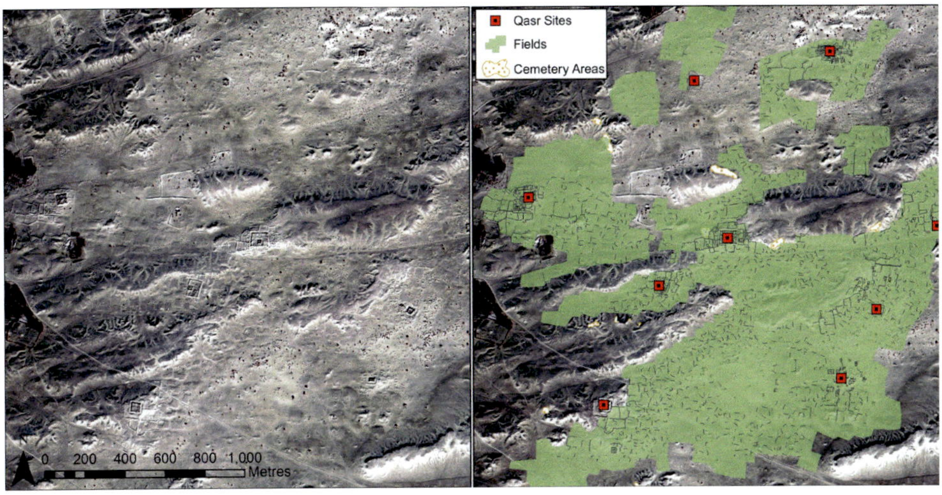

Figure 10.3. Abandoned late Garamantian oasis landscape in Zizaw area of Fazzan (Martin Sterry for Trans-Sahara Project).

intensive surveys: Kasserine,[25] *Leptiminus*,[26] *Segermes*,[27] *Thugga*.[28] The potential for exceptional surface preservation is well illustrated by the Kasserine survey, where Figure 10.4 presents a detailed survey of a 3.5 sq km area containing ten presses at four major farms, in a landscape that also featured numerous farmsteads, cemeteries and other burials, terrace walls, and so on. There have been notable individual contributions by a number of Tunisian archaeologists, going beyond the extensive work of the national mapping programme.[29] Work on the immediate hinterland of *Karthago* has not been fully published.[30] There has also been some very extensive surveys, with a specific focus on coastal features and pottery production sites in Tunisia.[31]

Much less work has been done in Algeria beyond the extraordinary survey by Philippe Leveau in the hinterland of *Caesarea*, the still largely unpublished work by

25. Kasserine: Hitchner 1988; 1989; 1990.
26. *Leptiminus*: Stone and Carr 2011; Stone et al. 2011b. For other rural survey in the Sahel, see Ben Baaziz 1999.
27. *Segermes*: Dietz et al. 1995a; 1995b; Ørsted et al. 2000.
28. *Thugga*: de Vos 2000; 2004; 2013; de Vos and Attoui 2013; 2015; de Vos and Maurina 2019; de Vos et al. 2013.
29. See, for example, work in the: Tunisian Dorsal, Ben Baaziz 1985; 1990; 2000; 2003a; 2003b; Sehili 2009; 2010; Sahel, Annabi 1988; 1993; Ben Baaziz 1988; Gafsa region, Ben Baaziz 1991; 1993; Brahmi 2017; Wadi Sejnane, Ghalia 1992.
30. Greene 1992; cf. Sycamore and Buchanan 2016. See also Ennabli 2020, 380–99.
31. Coastal survey: Slim et al. 2004; Pottery production: Jerray 2015; 2016; Mrabet and Remesal Rodriguez 2007; Nacef 2015; Peacock et al. 1989; 1990.

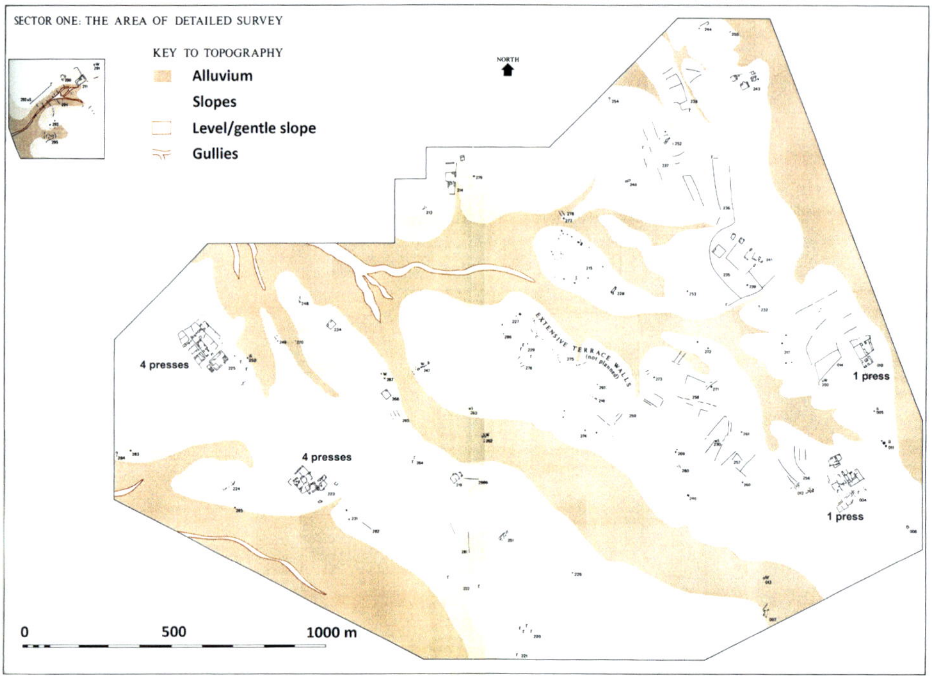

Figure 10.4. High Steppe landscape in the Kasserine area (from Hitchner 1990, f.p. 258).

Mariette de Vos in the hinterland of Annaba, and a curtailed project around *Diana Veteranorum* by Lisa Fentress, following poorly published prospection of villages with churches by André Berthier.[32] Leveau has compiled a detailed regional case study for the Nemencha area, and Pierre Morizot has made important contributions based on analysis of air photographs and satellite imagery in the Aurès and Saharan Atlas.[33] A number of Algerian researchers are also now carrying out extensive survey of rural sites in several districts.[34]

In Morocco, the main colonial-era archaeological effort had focused on the towns, but some collation of other settlement was made.[35] There has been continuing limited survey in the environs of *Volubilis*.[36] Larger-scale investigations include an extensive survey of the Sebou basin in the south of the country.[37] The Rharb

32. *Caesarea*: Leveau 1984; *Diana Veteranorum*: Berthier 1943; Fentress 2013b; Fentress et al. 1991. Other work in *Mauretania Caesariensis*: Laporte 1974; 1985; Leveau 1975; 1977b.
33. Aurès and Nemencha: Dupuis and Morizot 1992; Leveau 1977a; 2020b; Morizot 1979; 1991; 1993; 1997; Nasraoui 2005; Saharan Atlas: Morizot 1999; cf. Leveau 2018.
34. Hodna region: Aibeche 2014; Slimani 2015; Slimani and Kherbouche 2018. Cf. also Soyer 1973; 1976.
35. Early regional overviews were published in *Bulletin d'Archéologique Marocaine* 5 and 6 (1964, 1966).
36. Akerraz and Lenoir 1990, 219–29.
37. Akerraz et al. 1995; Rebuffat 1986a; 2012b; Rebuffat and Limane 2011.

plain to the south of the Sebou river is potentially a key resource in terms of alluvial soils, but also prone to flood and marshlands. The Loukkos valley in the hinterland of *Lixus* is another valley where there again appears to have been considerable alluviation since antiquity, with most surviving settlements recorded in survey on the flanks of the valley.[38] Survey has also been conducted in the mountainous coastal region of the Rif and in the extra-provincial lands of eastern Morocco around Oujda and along the Atlantic coast.[39] Across the Atlas mountains, survey has recently been conducted in the Draa valley, producing significant new evidence of NAIA burials and sedentary settlement (both hillforts and oasis terrace sites) contemporary with the Roman Empire (Fig. 10.5).[40] Other surveys in the Wadi Noun and Wadi Sous have added some limited information on pre-Islamic activity.

Overall, our picture of rural settlement across North Africa has been much enhanced across the last 40 years—there is no major region about which we are wholly uninformed now. Although some parts of Algeria are still rather inadequately surveyed in modern times, the colonial era *Atlas archéologique de l'Algérie* remains an invaluable resource.[41] Despite the dearth of excavation, the surface preservation of sites and rural equipment is often considerably better than in the European provinces of the Roman world, revealing many details of site plan and overall settlement extent that are not visible in European plough-zone archaeology.[42] The associated farming features—irrigation systems, terraces, field boundaries, cisterns, dams, etc.—are also in many areas still legible in the "fossilised agricultural landscape."[43]

Several issues need to be considered in relation to our data. First, it is a well-known phenomenon of field survey that the more intensive and systematic the nature of the work, the greater the density of sites will be recorded, with the range of site types also extended to smaller rural settlements and structures, as well as the larger villages, estate centres, and major farms, which tend to be the main focus of extensive work.[44]

The dating frameworks underlying the regional settlement distributions evidenced by the survey projects above vary massively. Only for the more intensive

38. Akerraz and Collins-Elliott 2017.
39. Rif: Akerraz et al. 2019; Alaoui et al. 2004; Bokbot and Onrubia-Pintado 1995; Coletti 2018; Vismara 2014; Oujda: Boudouhou 2015; Marion 1957; 1959; Atlantic coast south of provincial boundaries, Rebuffat 1974b..
40. Wadi Draa: Mattingly et al. 2017b; 2018; 2019c; Sterry et al. 2020. See also discussion of the Draa in Chapter 5.
41. Gsell 1911.
42. A classic example is olive oil production, on which more will be said below.
43. The quote is from Hitchner 1995b, 133. On hydraulic features in North African farming, see, inter alia, Barker et al. 1996a; Ben Ouezdou and Trousset 2009; Birebent 1962; Euzennat 1992; Hitchner 1995b; 1995c; Ibba and Mastino 2011a; Leveau 2009a; Meuret 1996; Mrabet 2003a; Pavis d'Escurac 1980; Reddé 2012; Shaw 1982; 1984; Trousset 1986a; 1987b.
44. Stone 2004, 137–37 charts this in relation to North African surveys—showing that modern intensive surveys tend to record ten times more sites in terms of density.

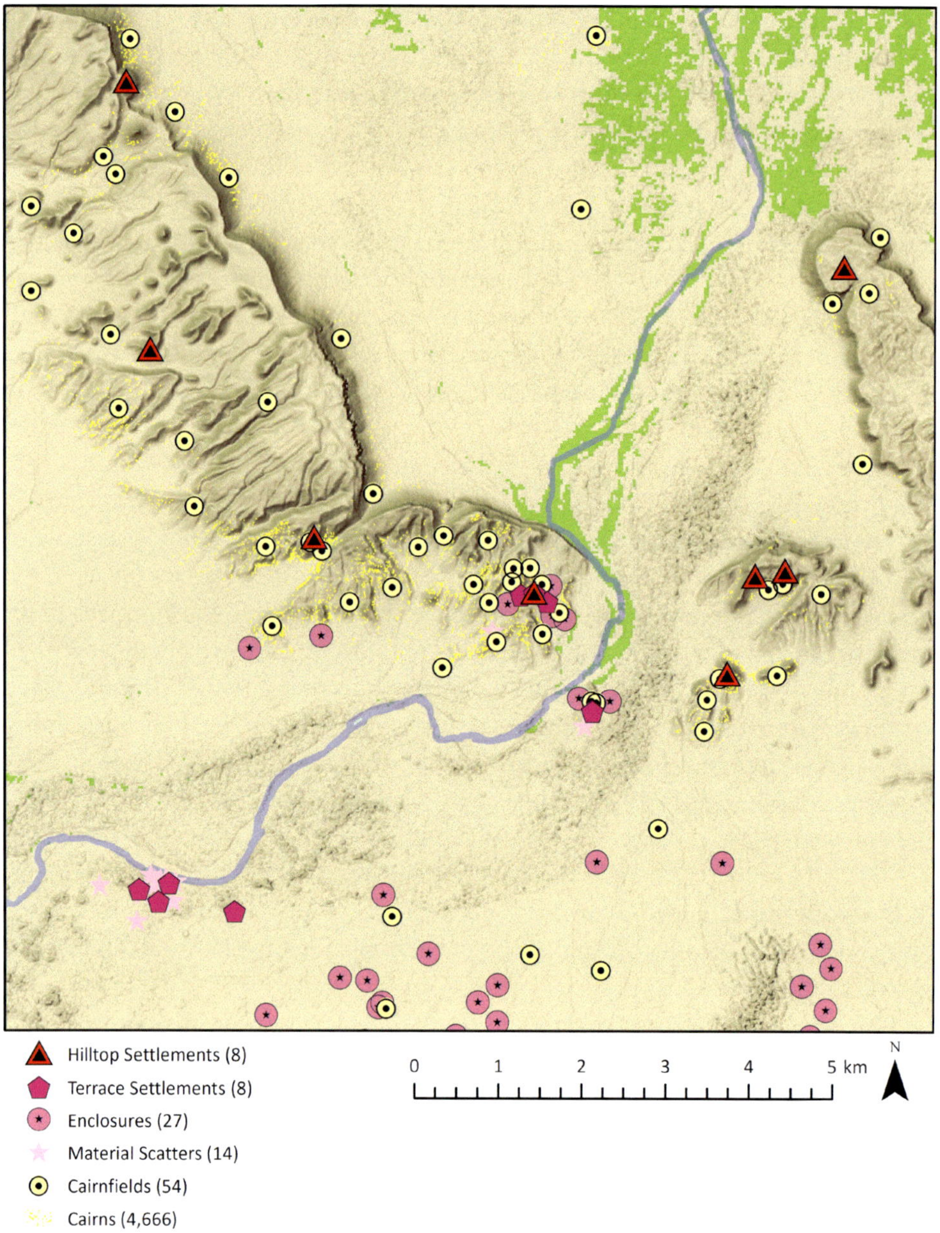

Figure 10.5. NAIA landscape at Foum Larjam in the Wadi Draa, Morocco (Martin Sterry for OasCiv project).

surveys, with systematic collection and detailed study of surface pottery and other artefacts, is it possible to model growth and shrinkage of site numbers across time. Many of the more extensive surveys lack chronological data beyond a general recognition of "Roman" characteristics. Even with surveys where pottery is reported, there are a number of limitations in the dating evidence to consider.[45] It is a truism in field survey that pots do not equal people, though the assumption is still often made that the periods of most abundant diagnostic ceramics were the times of peak population and rural settlement. However, there are a number of inherent biases in survey dating evidence. For example, there are potential issues if only diagnostic fine wares have been used, as coarse ware pottery may tell a different story. Indeed, for many parts of the Maghrib and Sahara there are no such studies of handmade and coarse pottery. There are also questions about the extent to which the surface pottery provides an accurate reflection of all phases of site occupation. Settlement in periods when there was less access to diagnostic pottery may appear far less active, rather than necessarily being ones of lesser activity. Black gloss pottery of the late centuries BCE generally occurs in very small quantity on African surveys and then mainly in relatively close proximity to the coastal zone. In numerical terms it is dwarfed by the volumes of later red slipped wares, especially those of African production.

There are several potential factors to account for this. In a number of field surveys in North Africa, surface finds have been found to over-emphasise certain phases of the site's occupation, with much less material of early phases. This is most clearly evident at *Leptiminus*, where the pottery assemblage from the urban survey of a city occupied from the 5th century BCE to late antiquity was heavily skewed to the 2nd–4th centuries CE, a period of high local pottery manufacture.[46] While the late antique period at this site saw genuine contraction, there is little doubt that the dearth of early material also relates to its deeper burial below the reach of shallow modern cultivation. For many of the best-preserved rural sites, modern cultivation tends to avoid the stony remains of ancient farms, meaning that the associated surface pottery at such sites is predominantly material relating to the later phases of occupation. In European field survey archaeology, deep ploughing has often impacted on all levels of buried sites providing a better cross section of diagnostic material.[47]

Another issue with African field survey is that the volume of pottery collected for any given period may reflect issues of ceramic supply. That is, the relative abundance of locally or regionally produced pottery of higher quality (the diagnostic wares) is not uniform, and ceramic consumption, especially in the countryside, may rise and fall dramatically in relation to variance in supply. Comparative analysis has established an annual consumption curve for African Red Slip ware (ARS)

45. For a key discussion about the levels of inference that connect the material recovered in survey to the original depositional contexts, see the classic discussion by Haselgrove 1985. For general discussions of these sorts of interpretative issues, see papers in Alcock and Cherry 2004; Francovich et al. 2000.

46. Stone et al. 2011b, 84–87.

47. Some of the issues are discussed in Mattingly 2011c, 76–79.

and highlights two broad peaks in production volume: the late 1st to early 3rd centuries CE and the late 4th to mid-6th centuries CE.[48] Individual field surveys in North Africa and elsewhere deviate from this normative curve, clearly indicating localised patterns of consumption.[49] Both the *Segermes* and *Thugga* surveys, for instance, reveal very high occurrence of late antique red slip wares of local production.[50] For the *Thugga* area, while 67–70% of sites had pottery indicating Vandal or Byzantine activity, only 25–30% had evidence of early or mid-Roman pottery (note that the late antique phases are not included in Fig. 10.15).[51] Dossey has argued that this boom in late ceramics may indicate increased prosperity or enhanced access to consumer markets for peasant families in late Roman and late antique times.[52] However, even in the late period, pottery was especially well disseminated in areas of the countryside close to where it was being produced (as noted at *Thugga* and *Segermes*), presumably because it was affordable and local markets operated efficiently. The fact that the boom in sherd counts for late ARS does not occur in all surveys demonstrates that pottery supply is an important issue underlying our data.

Beyond the lack of chronological resolution in much of the data, modelling past rural population on the survey evidence is also difficult because of uncertainties regarding what proportion of the ancient site universe has been recorded, with survey practitioners varying in their confidence in the completeness of the recovery rates.[53] The amount of mountain and desert terrain in North Africa renders futile any attempt to model population density per square kilometre, but it is very striking that both in the prime agricultural landscapes and even in the arid pre-desert margins, the recorded site densities are comparable to the levels of the most intensively cultivated zones of the north Mediterranean countries. Indeed, one of the things that most struck the modern colonial archaeologists in many parts of the Maghrib was how far the evidence of Roman-era rural settlement exceeded expectations formed from the 19th- and early 20th-century landscape. This agricultural boom in antiquity has conventionally been presented as a fundamentally Roman achievement, based on the erroneous belief in limited pre-Roman sedentary agriculture away from the coast—views that we have seen in Chapters 4 and 5 can now be effectively challenged.[54] However, although we must now start by recognising that pre-Roman rural society was much further

48. Fentress and Perkins 1988; Fentress et al. 2004.
49. Well documented in Fentress et al. 2004, 150–53.
50. *Segermes:* John Lund in Dietz et al. 1995b, 447–629; *Thugga*: Andreoli and Polla 2019, 149–244; De Vos and Attoui 2013, 9–17; Polla 2011.
51. De Vos 2013, 163–66.
52. Dossey 2010, 55–87.
53. See the discussion between Fentress 2009b and Mattingly 2009 on this point, specifically in relation to the systematically acquired data set from Jerba.
54. See Barker et al. 1996a; Shaw 1984; 1991a for some important discussions of the autochthonous contributions to hydrological developments.

developed that once believed, it must also be acknowledged that the Roman period in North Africa saw major changes compared to pre-Roman times.

One aspect was a greater spread of sedentary farming into marginal landscapes, including some where there had been no or limited fixed settlement in pre-Roman times. This was accompanied by increased agricultural specialisation in certain crops. Whereas in a more subsistence-based farming economy we might expect to see a rough balance between different core crops of the Mediterranean zone (grains, olives, vines, pulses and legumes, a variety of fruit trees, and so on), Africa in the Roman Empire stands out for the extent to which some regions seem to have specialised in grain cultivation or olive production or wine production, in each case linked to long-range export markets (whether linked to the imperial economy or wider markets). These changes cannot be divorced from the overarching imperial context in which they occurred.[55] The evidence of olive mills and presses for wine and olive oil production is particularly abundant and numerically impressive (see also Fig. 12.1 below).[56] Differences in the regional technologies and the scale of production are visible in the archaeological data.[57] The apparent modern inversion of peak olive oil production between the Tunisian High Steppe and the coastal Sahel (where the main modern plantations are) has often been remarked on.[58] In Roman times, the Sahel had a relatively low density of press finds compared to the Steppe. This may in part reflect a greater Roman emphasis in the Sahel on cereal production, but it is also probable that the finds of press elements are rarer there due to the greater intensity of medieval and early modern cultivation compared to the High Steppe, making archaeological remains less distinct in the landscape.

For olive oil production in particular there is convincing evidence that production increased in the Roman era, in terms of the size and working capacity of individual presses, the scale of oil production sites, and the provincial volume of production. The extent of change represented genuine economic growth, not simply increased production to meet the needs of an uplift in local population (Fig. 10.6).[59] Of particular interest is the fact that the scale of the press structures was increased

55. Mattingly 2011a, 144–45.
56. For overall summaries, see Ahmed 2019; Ben Baaziz 1990; Brun 2003; 2004; Camps-Fabrer 1953; Hobson 2015a, 63–102; Laporte et al. 2013; Leveau 2005; 2011; Mattingly 1988b; 1996a; Sehili 2018; Sehili and Ben Baaziz 2011; Vismara 2007, 19–62.
57. On overall questions of scale, see Hobson 2015a, 76–80; Mattingly 1988c; 1993; 1996c; Mattingly and Hitchner 1993. For regional specificities, see for Cyrenaica: Buzaian 2018; eastern Tripolitania: Ahmed 2019; Mattingly 1988a; 1988c; western Tripolitania: Drine 1999; Mrabet 1997; 2003b; Tunisian High Steppe: Hitchner 1990; Hitchner and Mattingly 1991; Mattingly 1988b; Sehili 2008a; 2008b; 2009; Tunisian Sahel: Ben Baaziz 1999; Tunisian Dorsal: Ben Baaziz 2000; 2003b; Upper *Bagrada* region: De Vos 2007; 2013; Vismara 2007; The Aurès: Morizot 1993; *Mauretania Caesariensis*: Laporte 1985; Leveau 1984; 1985; *Mauretania Tingitana*: Akerraz and Lenoir 1982; Bigi 2019.
58. Ben Baaziz 1999, 45–46; Hobson 2015a, 80–89.
59. Mattingly 1988a; 1988b; Hitchner 1993a; Hobson 2015a, 99–102.

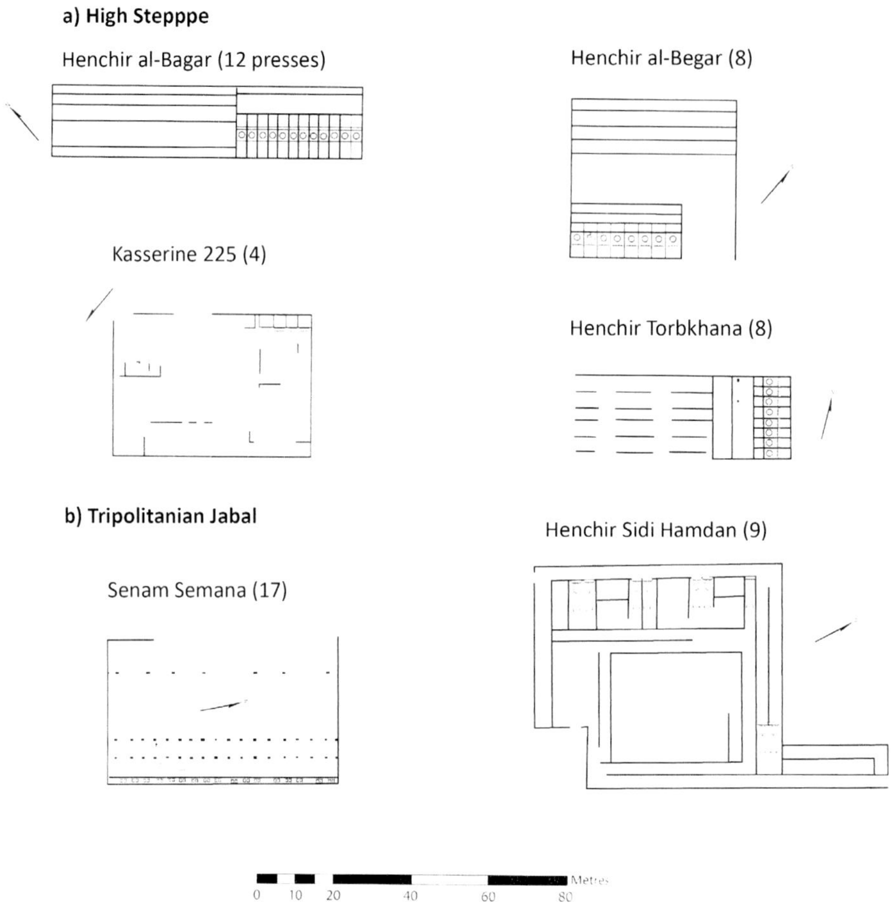

Figure 10.6. Comparative plans of large-scale Roman era oileries. a) From Tunisian High Steppe. b) From Tripolitanian Jabal (author's montage from Hobson 2015a, 92 and 100).

in some regions, pushing the basic lever and windlass technology to new limits (see Fig. 10.12 below). While all presses are an indicator of surplus-oriented production, another innovation was the construction of mass production facilities (oileries) with banks of presses. This is one of the most important indicators of crop specialisation, focused on high-volume surplus production. While olive oil production was widespread in North Africa, the distribution of large oileries (with five and more presses) is more regionally limited.[60] Interestingly, the primary evidence for oilery production units lay in the Gaetulian zone of the Tunisian High Steppe and the Libyan Jabal Tarhuna (though in the latter case within the expanded *territoria* of

60. On oileries, see Ahmed 2019, 19, 41, 52–54, 72, 77, 81–84; Brun 2004, 190–95; Hobson 2015a, 89–102; Sehili 2008a; 2009; 2018.

the Libyphoenician coastal cities). One explanation for this may concern the nature of landholding in the Gaetulian lands and the less developed pre-Roman agrarian landscape, facilitating the creation of large and specialised estates.

It is increasingly clear from the evidence of presses and amphorae production that African wine was also produced on a considerable scale in some regions for export.[61] Though olive and wine presses are very similar, in some areas we can detect structural distinctions between olive oil and wine presses (Cyrenaica, northern Tripolitania).[62] The presence or absence of mills, and size and arrangement of vats within press rooms, can be additional discriminators, though the dearth of excavation is a problem in this regard. Although it seems counter-intuitive, given the possibility of tainting the taste, that a single press structure might be used for both oil and wine production sequentially following their separate harvest seasons, in some remote areas this does seem to have occurred. Jean-Pierre Brun has rightly commented that the press at the al-Amud farm excavated by the Libyan Valleys Survey looks like a wine press with adjacent treading floor, but the production of oil at the site seems equally assured given the abundant botanical evidence of olive cultivation and the arrangement of a series of small vats for settling oil alongside the main vat.[63] Some of the wine production facilities could also reach a spectacular scale, as in the case of Kherbet Agoub in *Mauretania Sitifensis*, which contained at least 11 presses and 10 treading floors in a single building (c.45 × 30 m).[64]

Imperial (Dis)Possession: Occupation and Disposal of Land and Associated Rights

A crucial aspect of the study of the rural communities is the recognition of the different ways in which colonial power impacted on such groups. The circumstances of Rome's conquest of *Africa* were particularly dramatic and unusual in the overall context of the Empire.[65] The defeat and destruction of *Qart Hadasht* in 146 BCE led to massive land confiscation on the part of Rome in northern Tunisia. Although this land was designated Carthaginian, much of it was occupied by sedentary cultivators (*Afri* in the sources), effectively the equivalents living under Carthaginian dominion of the *Numidae* extending to the west.[66] This is a graphic example of

61. On wine presses and production, see Brun 2003; 2004; 2018; Hobson 2015a, Lequement 1980; Leschi 1947; Leveau 2005; Rebuffat and Gabbard 1988. On wine amphorae, see Hobson 2015a, 115–17; Mattingly et al 2011, 240–50.
62. Ahmed 2019, 103–04; 133–34; Buzaian 2018, 46–49, 249.
63. Brun 2004, 195–96; cf. Barker and Jones 1984.
64. Brun 2004, 233–36.
65. See Chapter 6.
66. Ben Romdhane 2017.

the principle of what I term "imperial possession": seizure by the Roman state of a rich portfolio of land to be subsequently disposed of. Although there were numerous settlements and a large Libyphoenician and African population living on Carthaginian lands at the time of conquest, the circumstances of victory meant that Rome took over a subservient peasantry, rather than thousands of independent landowners. This is evident in the sequel, with the centuriation of a total of c.16,000 km^2 of land (Fig. 10.7).[67]

There were three major zones of centuriation in Tunisia: a northern area of 12,500 km^2 with an alignment of 29° west of north; a centre-eastern area of 2,500 km^2 and an alignment of 37–38° west of north; and a south-eastern area of c.1,000 km^2 between the towns of *Thaenae* and *Acholla* with an alignment of 61° 30′ west of north.[68] This represents the greatest single disposal and reallocation of lands in any province of the Roman Empire, and the Agrarian Law of 111 BCE makes it clear that the process of the first centuriation in northern Tunisia was well under way by the late 2nd century BCE.[69] The two other main centuriation schemes in Tunisia are most likely later in date, and the most recent assessment of the centre-east scheme in northern *Byzacium* suggests an Augustan date for that. The south-east centuriation in southern *Byzacium* appears later still, though still perhaps in the reign of Augustus.[70] As Matthew Hobson has observed, all the big centuriation schemes seem to fall within *Africa Vetus*, as defined by the *fossa regia*, though the course of this enigmatic boundary ditch is very poorly known away from the central sector where Flavian resurvey took place.[71] It is perfectly plausible that the centuriation of *Byzacium* occurred after the formation of *Africa Nova* in 46 BCE or indeed the amalgamation of the two provinces. The legal status of the territory seized in 146 BCE seems to have been different to the subsequent settlement after the defeat of Juba in 46, where confiscation of Numidian lands was less total. However, though manifested in different ways, as I shall explain further below, the land disposals following the conquest of both *Africa Vetus* and *Africa Nova* appear to have been on a very considerable scale, with significant impacts on established communities.

The process was taken further in several stages. Firstly, one of the outcomes of the Jugurthan war appears to have been the establishment by Marius of veteran contingents (including both Roman citizens and Gaetulian units) beyond the *fossa regia* at

67. Caillemer and Chevallier 1959; Dilke 1971, 151–58; Peyras 1986. See now Hobson 2015a, 35–49 for an archaeologically informed discussion of the legal and historical texts relating to land allocation in Africa.
68. Saumagne 1929; Caillemer and Chevallier 1959; Dilke 1971; Trousset 1997a.
69. For the Agrarian Law, see Crawford 1996, 113–80. For recent discussion, see De Ligt 2007a; 2007b; 2008; contra Quinn 2003.
70. Ghaddab 2020, for the new dating of the Centre-East centuriation between 19–6 BCE.
71. Ferchiou 1998b.

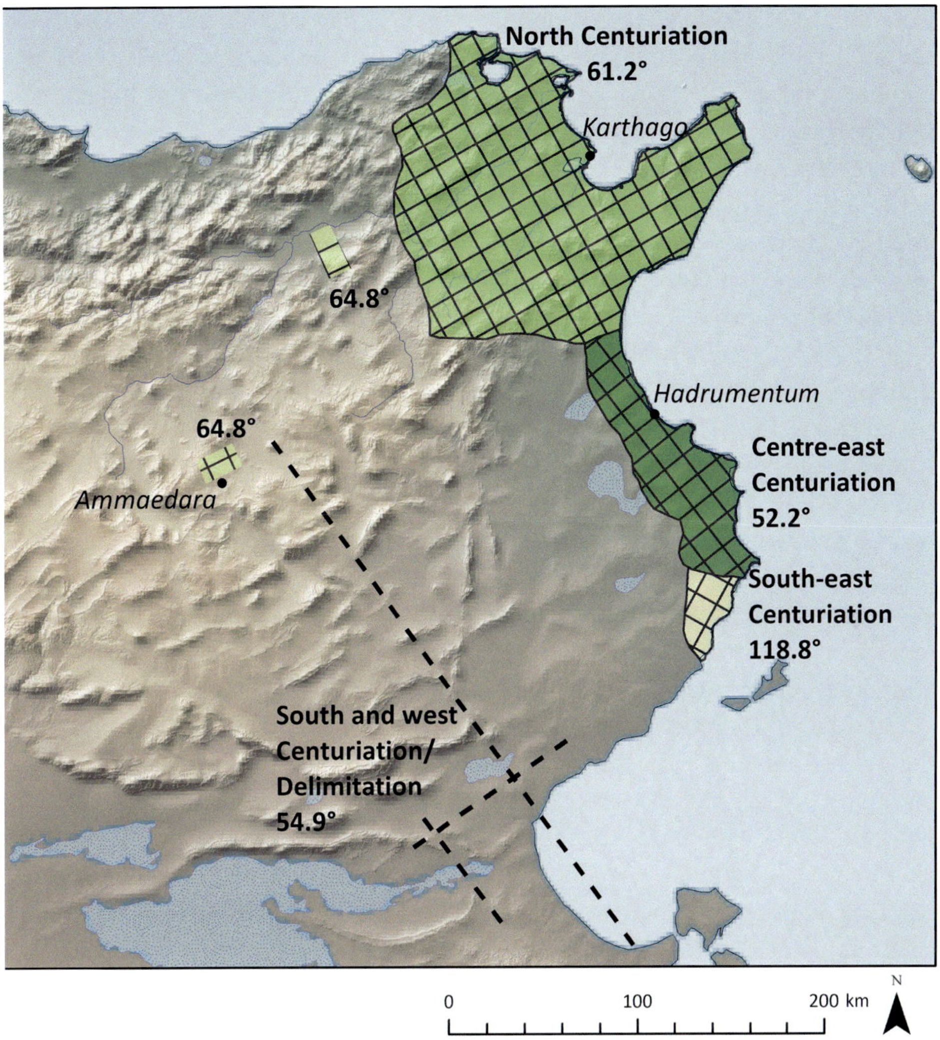

Figure 10.7. The major centuriation schemes in Tunisia (Martin Sterry, after author's rough).

Numidian centres like *Uchi Maius*, *Musti*, *Thibaris*, and *Thuburnica*.[72] Caesar's defeat of Juba I and his annexation of the Numidian kingdom brought another vast area of territory under Roman control. The award of a huge block of land and several major settlements around *Cirta* to one of his prominent lieutenants, P. Sittius, had profound consequences for that region. The former Numidian royal estates incorporated in

72. The account of Aurelius Victor (*de Vir. Illus.*, 73) has often been doubted, but new evidence from *Uchi Maius* is broadly supporting informal deductions of colonists in this area; see ben Kacha 2012, 170; Hobson 2015a, 44–48.

the province of *Africa Nova* were another major resource for potential land disposals, and large estates seem to have been established in the *Bagrada* valley area by a number of senatorial families (later to be turned into imperial estates).[73] Again there was likely continuity of a dependent rural labour force on these lands, but a major rupture in the overall ownership and control of land.

Both under Caesar and Augustus, the land bounty in *Africa* started to be drawn upon in a more substantial way. The existence of a large volume of confiscated land in *Africa* made it a favoured terrain for the foundation of veteran colonies or the addition of veteran colonists to existing communities.[74] By the end of Augustus's reign there were numerous *coloniae* or *municipia* with Roman citizen settler communities, as well as smaller groups of colonists enrolled in rural *pagi* and attached to indigenous towns. All of the settler groups must have involved assignation of land rights to new people. The Libyphoenician coastal *emporia* were mostly treated respectfully, though the size of some *territoria* may have been reduced. This could be seen as the function of the centre-east centuriation, which wrapped around and delimited field divisions on different alignments related to towns like *Hadrumetum*, *Leptiminus*, and *Thapsus* (Fig. 10.8).[75] A few favoured communities were permitted to control far larger territories, of which *Lepcis Magna* is the most notable example, with profound consequences for its hinterland.[76]

The key point I want to stress is that the story of Africa under Rome was largely determined by the varied disposal of these confiscated lands (and of subsequent additions). In legal terms, several different types of land rights were recognised by Rome, with the picture becoming more complex over time and often a separation between absolute ownership of the land and its usufruct. The period from 146 BCE to the end of the 1st century CE was a time of significant and often traumatic upheaval in prior patterns of land ownership and land rights in large parts of *Africa*.[77] Land essentially fell into ten main categories:

1) *Ager publicus*—land confiscated from *Qart Hadasht*, other Libyphoenician cities, and the Numidian royal house. The state benefited through rents and dues on these lands, but could periodically donate or sell off parts of the portfolio.
2) Lands granted to certain free cities, notably the Libyphoenician *emporia*—though subject to revision as a condition of good behaviour or due to subsequent change in urban status.
3) Lands given to the descendants of Massinissa in 146 BCE, but reverting to Rome in 46 BCE.

73. Hobson 2015a, 54–56.
74. Ferchiou 1980.
75. Ghaddab 2020; Ouni and Peyras 2002; Peyras 1999.
76. Di Vita-Evrard 1979; Mattingly 1995, 138–41.
77. Romanelli 1974; Picard 1990, 47.

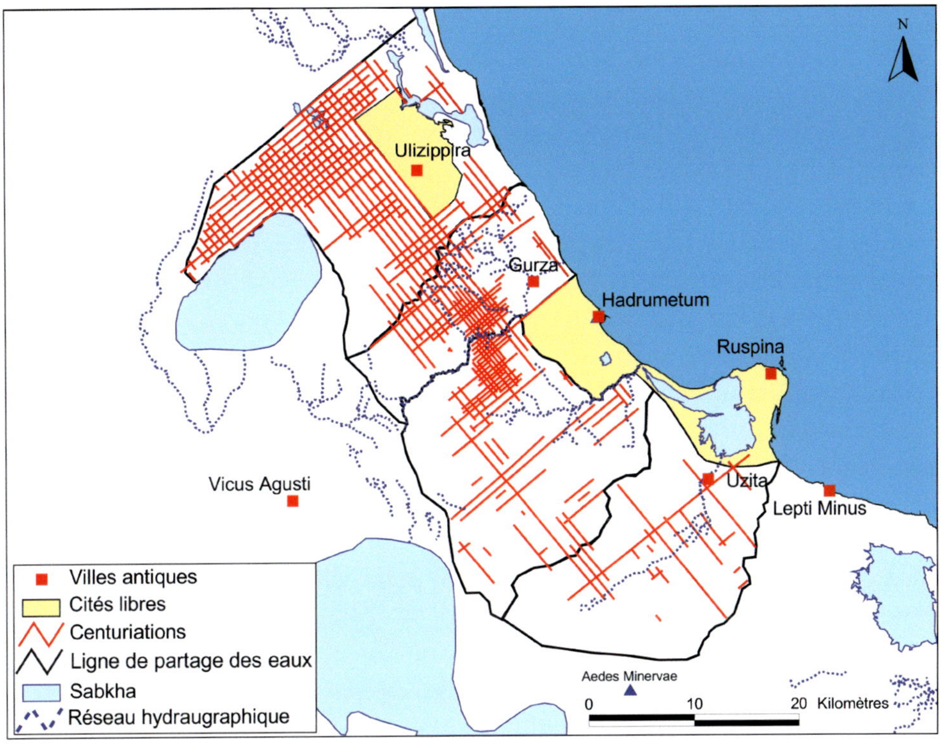

Figure 10.8. The centre-east centuriation with differently aligned land division schemes of Libyphoenician cities (from Ghaddab 2020, 82).

4) Lands allotted to colonists in regular packages.
5) *Ager privatus vectigalis*, lands that were sold off to private individuals, whether Africans or outsiders, subject to taxation.
6) Imperial estates built up over time as part of spoils of victories, confiscations, and inheritance.
7) Lands that were allocated to urban entities recognised by Rome, as the civil zone of the province expanded.
8) Lands that were allocated to non-urban communities as part of a process of land delimitation. Some of these supposed "tribal reserves" in fact probably contained urban centres and agricultural lands already, but certainly in some cases these may have included range lands of transhumant groups.
9) There were also no doubt sacred lands, associated with specific cults and sanctuaries, a form of landholding that took on a new significance with the rise of the Christian church in late antiquity.
10) Land that was subject to military jurisdiction (this might include broad swathes of territory during the conquest phase, but even after formal settlement of lands for subject peoples, military bases continued to have assigned territories).

A problem for Rome was all that these categories of lands were already occupied and exploited economically before the conquest, and whatever the legal principles of land allocation and land sale, the reality was that new owners or chief tenants were liable to find the situation on the ground more complicated, with established communities effectively sitting tenants. The Roman settlement seems to have made use of pre-existing Carthaginian subdivisions of its huge territory, and a series of these *pagi* continued to have significance long into the Roman period. These were probably the ultimate origin of *Zeugitana* and *Byzacena*. For instance, in the Dorsal round *Mactaris*, the jurisdiction of the *pagus Thusca* and *pagus Gunzuzi* covered numerous small towns and *castella*.[78] Similarly the *pagus Gurzensis*, encompassing at least three Libyan communities, was absorbed into the centre-east centuriation.[79]

The mosaic pattern of landholding was made more complicated by the further expansion of the provinces into the steppe and pre-desert zones, with consequent delimitation of Gaetulian groups and annexations of territory from particularly intransigent peoples. A good example is the case of the *Musulami*, whose lands were defined by boundary stones in the early 2nd century CE (Fig. 10.9). From the extant boundary markers, these lands were evidently located between the upper Wadi Mellegue basin between *Madauros* and *Thala*. The boundary stones indicate the delimitation of lands assigned to the *Musulami* in relation to a number of Roman veteran settlements, *Madauros*, *Theveste*, and *Ammaedara*, evidently involving some loss of territory to these Roman colonies. Other boundary stones also indicate the existence in this landscape of imperial and private estates, including a very large senatorial estate known as the *saltus Beguensis*, which lies c. 40 km to the east. Another senatorial estate existed near *Thala*, again established in what was probably once Musulamian territory.[80] Figure 10.9 presents a hypothetical model of how this sort of land settlement might have impacted on the *Musulami*. They still occupied a large part of the Wadi Mellegue basin under Roman rule, though the evidence suggests that the historic lands of the *Musulami* had once been much more extensive. We do not know the exact size of the various imperial and private estates established here or precisely how much land was allocated to the colonies (though our boundary stones give some clues). The point is that such arrangements were highly intrusive and cumulatively may have resulted in a 50% or more reduction in the lands of the *Musulami*. These instances suggest that the fixing of African people in the landscape by the Roman authorities often involved significant losses of their land to imperial and wealthy estates.

The great Tiberian delimitation of Gaetulian lands in southern Tunisia is another good example of the impact of Roman land surveys.[81] The *limitatio* is sometimes

78. Picard 1990, 27–28;Picard et al. 1963; M'Charek 1999.
79. Ghaddab 2020.
80. Kallala 2003.
81. Decramer 2002; Decramer et al. 2002; Lapierre et al. 2015; Trousset 1978; 1997c.

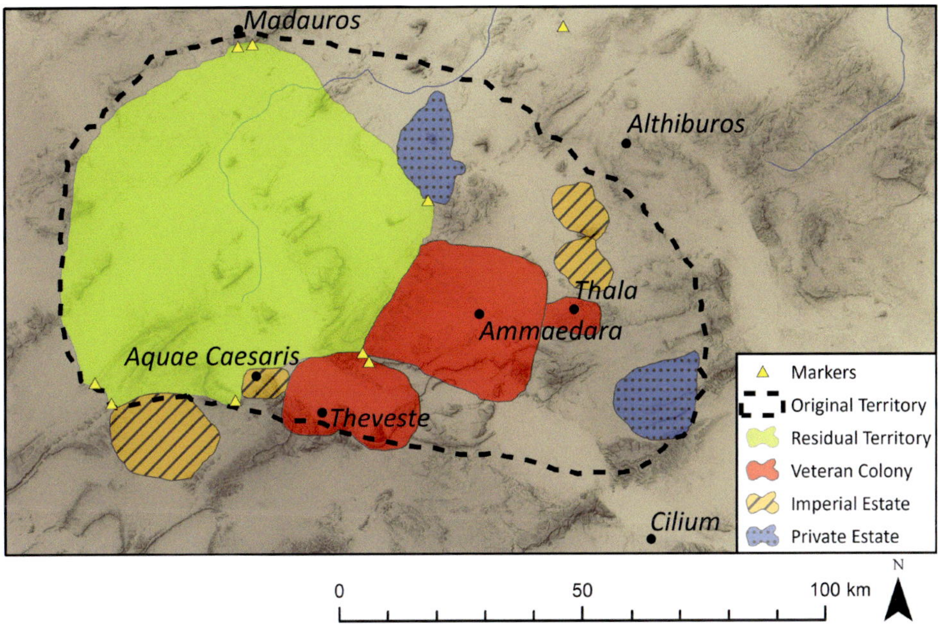

Figure 10.9. Hypothetical territory of the *Musulami* as demarcated by boundary stones in relation to other forms of land ownership (Martin Sterry from author's rough).

described as the "great centuriation" in that notionally it covers an area of 260 × 120 km (31,200 km^2),[82] but it was not in fact a formal centuriation scheme and most of that larger area was not surveyed in detail. The origin point of the survey was close to the legionary fortress of *Ammaedara*, with a baseline orientated 144.5° that was carried c.250 km before an outline grid was laid out in a zone broadly covering the territories of the towns of *Capsa*, *Tacape*, and the *Nybgenii* people, with almost 40 boundary markers known from this survey of steppic and pre-desert landscapes (Fig. 10.10). The initial layout dates to 29–30 CE, but the grid was reused under Trajan, with eight survey stones evidently marking the boundaries between the territories of the *Tacapitani* and *Nybgenii*, and the *Capsitani* and *Nybgenii*.[83] It is clear that this scheme lacked the fine detail of land divisions to allow assignation of individual properties that characterises the true centuriation schemes.[84] It also created a framework within which further sedentarisation and land development took place.[85]

In a number of previously published papers, I have identified a variety of different landscapes of imperialism in North Africa.[86] My point was that all the

82. Lapierre et al. 2015, 125.
83. Lapierre et al. 2015, 128–29; Trousset 2001; 2011.
84. Compare Trousset 1977b for the extraordinary detail visible in the centre-east system.
85. Mrabet 1996; 1997; 2011.
86. Mattingly 1997c; 1998.

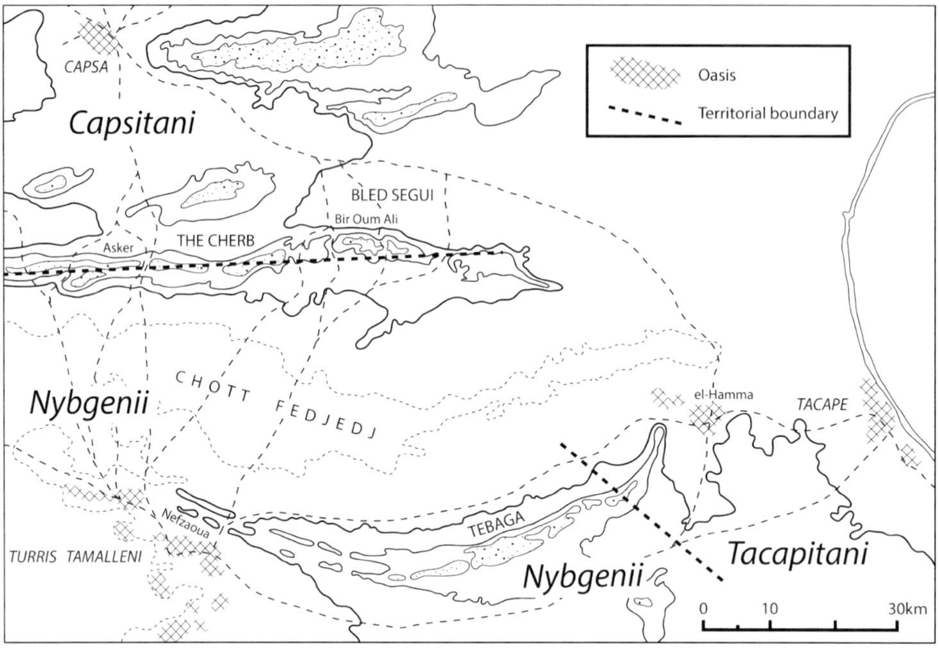

Figure 10.10. The delimitation of territory of *Tacapitani*, *Nybgenii*, and *Capsitani* following the survey of 29–30 CE (Mike Hawkes, after Mattingly 1995, 108).

landscapes reflected the varied impact and experience of colonial rule. This is most evident in areas of visible rupture, as in the centuriated landscapes. However, even areas of strong continuity with past land use and settlement forms must be seen as the result of a negotiation between local populations and the imperial power.

Different Rural Trajectories

Many parts of the African landscape were substantially altered during the Roman period, though there were profound regional differences in the patterns that emerged. Field survey data reveal how settlement was structured and, in combination with air photographic or satellite imagery or epigraphic finds, shed light on both form and process of land allocation and land survey. I am going to divide my examples into two broad groups, but the case studies will reveal considerable internal diversity within these.

Group 1. Intensification and Specialisation

Extensive areas of North Africa already had a well-established agricultural regime prior to the Roman conquest. In Chapters 3 to 5 I highlighted the importance of the agricultural lands of *Qart Hadasht* and the Libyphoenician coastal *emporia*, but also pointed out the new evidence of precocious agricultural development at inland Numidian sites like *Althiburos*. My Group 1 case studies thus involve the land subject to these groups prior to the Roman era. A common feature of many of these areas is the evidence of an intensification and specialisation in farming during the Roman period, though this seems to have been achieved by different means and at different rates in the various cases.[87]

As noted already, the fully centuriated landscapes in *Africa* fall almost entirely within the presumed boundary of the *fossa regia*, the ditch that marked the limits of the original province. It is plausible to suggest that the northern alignment represents the territory directly controlled by *Qart Hadasht* in 146 BCE, while the eastern centuriation blocks involved lands under the general control of the Libyphoenician *emporia* and related African populations in *Byzacium*. In total, this centuriated landscape probably represented land seized by the Roman state in 146 BCE. The dates at which these schemes were carried out are uncertain, but given their huge scale, the work must have been spread across many years. It seems probable that the northern surveys originated well before Caesar established *Africa Nova*, though the infilling of detail within the outline grids may have continued over many years into the Principate. The almost total lack of centuriation in Numidian territory annexed as *Africa Nova* presumably indicates very different conditions of incorporation of that area into the Empire. There were some extremely large estates created out of the conquered Numidian territory and some evidence of localised centuriation in relation to a number of Roman veteran colonies, like *Ammaedara*. The Cirtan Confederation is another area where we should expect, from the nature of its incorporation into Empire, the existence of very large estates for the benefit of leading colonist families.[88]

COLONISTS, THE *PERTICA* OF *KARTHAGO*, VETERAN SETTLEMENTS

The core territory (*pertica*) of *Karthago* represented the largest contiguous bloc of land confiscated by the Roman state. This area was systematically resurveyed into a centuriated landscape, indicating considerable upheaval of land ownership and land-use rights. Centuriation is sometimes portrayed as a tool of land development in the Roman Empire—opening the way for the exploitation of previously underutilised rural zones. However, in *Africa*, the large northern centuriated zone coincided with a region that we know to have been very agriculturally developed in the pre-Roman period. Thus, an alternative view is that centuriation often marked a traumatic caesura with past systems of land use and land rights. The cost of such surveys was only justified in cases where the Roman state had seized substantial quantities of land and there was no intention to return the majority of it in parcels to the original possessors. Between the late 2nd century BCE and the early

87. Hobson 2015a; Stone 1997.

88. Bertandy 1991, 163–66 for a list of known estates, with supporting evidence.

1st century CE, northern Tunisia was the prime reservoir of unallocated land in the Roman Empire, and it is no surprise that significant numbers of veteran colonists were settled there under Caesar and Augustus. Some were in new settlements (like *Uthina*), some in "refoundations" of earlier settlements (like *Clipea*), and others comprised small groups of citizens inserted into existing communities (as at *Thugga*, *Uchi Maius*). The issue of control of the land was a powerful lever in Rome's relations with the many nucleated settlements of the *pertica* (villages, small towns, and towns) and the reward for good behaviour might be the eventual return of larger amounts of land to these communities. In addition there is evidence that some of the land was disposed of as private estates, often purchased by people from outside the region with capital and influence. This is indicated by the references in the Agrarian Law of 111 BCE to land sales.[89]

THE LANDS OF LIBYPHOENICIAN TOWNS

The Libyphoenician *emporia* of the Tunisian and Libyan coastline were spared the catastrophic penalties of destruction and enslavement inflicted on *Qart Hadasht*. Most were recognised as *oppida libera* by the later 1st century BCE, though some were punished for support of the Pompeian forces against Caesar. Several towns also hosted powerful *conventus* of Roman citizens (*Utica*, *Hadrumetum*, *Leptiminus*, *Thapsus*), which may also have impinged on the autonomy of the Libyphoenician elites.[90] However, the extent of Roman centuriation systems in eastern *Byzacium* indicates a large amount of land confiscation by the Roman state, probably effective from 146 BCE. Satellite image analysis has demonstrated that many of the Tunisian Libyphoenician harbour towns had core *territoria* that were differently aligned to the extensive centuriation systems of eastern Tunisia.[91] The relatively small scale of these defined *territoria* suggests that the degree of autonomy allowed here was circumscribed. The massive scale of the encircling Roman centuriation systems surely represents considerable loss of territory that had once been under direct or indirect control of these coastal sites. The creation of the Roman centuriated landscapes here also effectively blocked expansion of the agricultural land of coastal settlements other than through mechanisms controlled by Rome.

The Libyphoenician towns in Libya (*Sabratha*, *Oea*, *Lepcis Magna*) appear to have been treated very differently in that there was no overall centuriation scheme (so no large-scale land confiscation) in the hinterland, and the evidence of 1st-century CE boundary stones reveals that they controlled very large *territoria* (in excess of 3,500 km^2 in the case of *Lepcis Magna*).[92] There is evidence of intensive

89. Crawford 1996, 147–52. Though the text is fragmentary, the existence of land sales is clear.
90. Le Bohec 2005a, 32.
91. Ghaddab 2020; Ouni and Peyras 2002.
92. Ahmed 2019, 16–17; Di Vita-Evrard 1979; Mattingly 1995, 140–41. For a figure of 3,530 km^2 for the *territorium*, see the latest calculation by Ahmed 2019, 61.

development of specialised olive oil and to a lesser extent wine production in the hinterland of *Lepcis*, but recent work has also revealed significant differences between parts of the territory: relating to an area immediately adjacent to the city, the coastal area more generally, the near hinterland and the deeper hinterland of the Jabal Tarhuna (Fig. 10.11).[93] The recognition of a c.13.5 km^2 area of centuriated land (based on 12 × 12 *actus* units) to the south-east of *Lepcis Magna* covers only a small fraction of this *territorium* and appears to have been an area of distinctive character from the rest.[94] This was a strip of irrigated cultivation (effectively a coastal oasis), and its proximity to the city may have favoured its intensive exploitation as market gardens and orchards. The interpretation of this is intriguing, but the use of Roman measurements in the surveyed area and the correspondence with the approach line of the early 2nd-century aqueduct suggests a connection with the promotion to *colonia* status in 109 CE. The land survey is not epigraphically attested, but seems to indicate a revision of land allocation in standard blocks of what may have been city land in this prime irrigated area. The centuriated block lacks evidence of the sorts of farms and villas found elsewhere in the territory and may have been worked directly from the city.

Elsewhere on the Tripolitanian seaboard, there is impressive evidence for luxury coastal villas of palatial aspect, with stunning mosaics of circus and amphitheatral spectacle emphasising the links with the urban elite, as at Silin and Zliten.[95] The majority of rural buildings in the near hinterland zone were more functional, though some can be differentiated as villas by their more impressive size, architectural and decorative embellishment, and the presence of baths. Close to the city, while press elements are common on rural sites, evidence of multiple presses is modest.[96] In the Jabal Tarhuna, some 50–60 km inland, there is the greatest concentration from North Africa of massive monumental presses in multiple production units.[97] Some of the press uprights (*arbores*) stood over 4 m high, with press beams of over 10 m in length (Fig. 10.12). The largest oilery, Senam Semana, accommodated 17 massive presses in a single range (Fig. 10.6).[98] Recent survey by Mftah Ahmed has revealed some evidence for mosaics, marble, and baths at a number of these estate centres.[99] Many of the large oileries were connected with amphora production also, and in many cases the stamps on the amphora can be

93. On survey of the territory of *Lepcis*, see, inter alia: Cifani et al. 2003; Felici et al. 2006; Fontana et al. 1996; Munzi 2010; Munzi et al. 2004; 2010; 2016; Zocchi 2018a, 139–75, 211–224.
94. Zocchi 2018b, 57–63.
95. Aurigemma 1926; Di Vita 1966; Musso 1997; Picard 1985; Salza Prina Ricotti 1971.
96. Zocchi 2018a, 139–75. Of 48 sites with evidence of presses, 3 had three presses, 15 two presses and 30 just one (p. 167).
97. Ahmed 2019 (for most detailed and authoritative discussion); Hobson 2015a, 95–99; Mattingly 1995, 138–44.
98. On the size of presses, Mattingly 1988c; 1993. On Senam Semana, Ahmed 2019, 54, 82.
99. Ahmed 2019, 58–59.

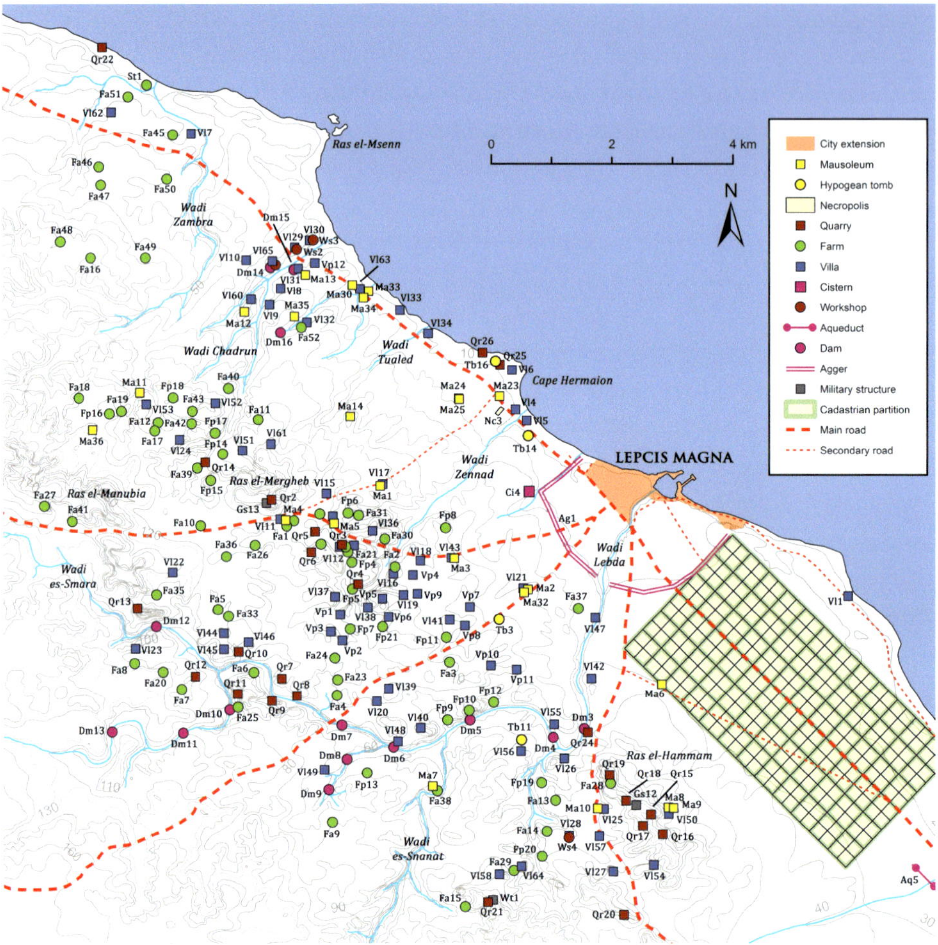

Figure 10.11. Settlement in the hinterland of *Lepcis Magna* in the 2nd–3rd century CE (after Zocchi 2018a, 216).

linked to the leading families at *Lepcis Magna* who by the late 2nd and early 3rd century had achieved senatorial status at Rome.[100] Dating evidence from a range of surveys reveals the earliest rural development in the hinterland closer to *Lepcis* in the 4th–3rd centuries BCE. In the Jabal, there is pre-Roman evidence at a number of sites from the 2nd–1st centuries BCE.[101] What the evidence suggests is an initial intensive development of the territory close to *Lepcis*, where competition between elite landowners was a limiting factor on the scale of rural estates, followed by

100. Ahmed 2019, 146–71 (amphora production); Mattingly 1988a, 31–36, links with senatorial families).

101. Ahmed 2019, 61–69; Zocchi 2018a, 158–60.

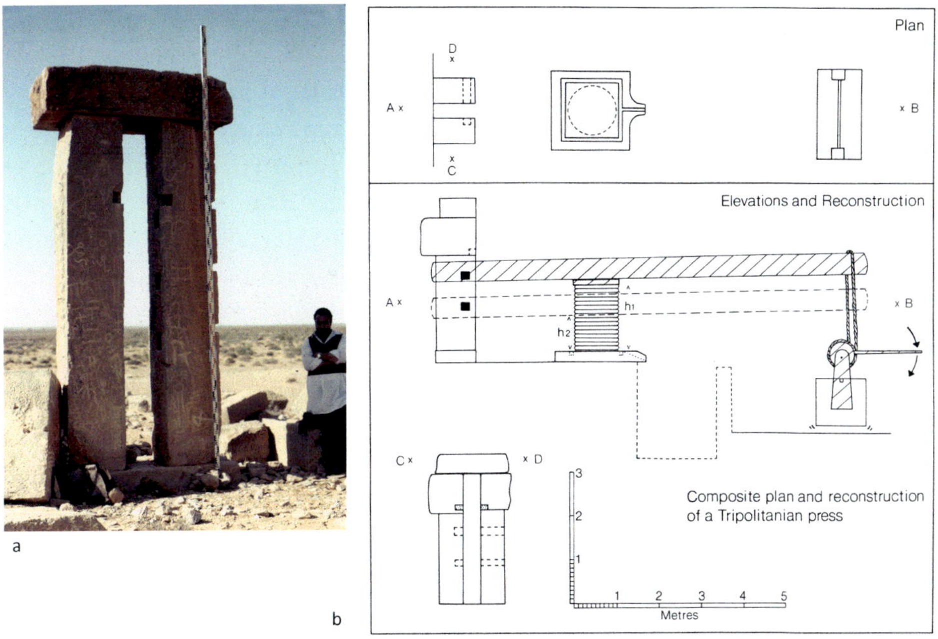

Figure 10.12. Massive presses from Tripolitania. a) Monolithic stone press uprights. b) Reconstruction in plan and elevation of press (from Mattingly 1995).

an expansion of the territory into the Jabal in the latter centuries BCE, at the expense of Gaetulian groups, with the Lepcitanian elite carving out some large estates, alongside a range of smaller farms that presumably related to sedentarised Gaetulian people. A notable feature of the Lepcitanian story was the near total absence of Roman colonists and incomers.

IOL CAESAREA IN MAURETANIA CAESARIENSIS

Iol Caesarea has a claim to be both a Libyphoenician *emporion* and a Numidian/ Mauretanian town in the pre-Roman period. Leveau's pioneering survey of its territory remains a landmark study of the Mauretanian landscape.[102] Within a 500 km^2 hinterland zone, he located 241 sites, including c.60–70 villas or estate centres that stood out in terms of size and evidence of capital investment in processing capacity, notably olive presses, several in oilery type facilities. Although oil production here appears to have been less intensive than in the case of *Lepcis Magna*, it was evidently an important factor in the region's economy. The varied size of settlement and the existence of small farms and villages alongside

102. Leveau 1984. See also Leveau 1985a; 1993.

the villas reflects a hierarchy of settlement and the presence of smaller landowners and tenants alongside the estates. Dating evidence is somewhat problematic, especially for the pre-Roman period when rural expansion had surely begun in relation to the early town. However, the 2nd–4th centuries CE appear to have marked the highpoint for rural settlement. Towards the southern fringes of Leveau's survey area, villas disappeared in the landscape and were evidently replaced by nucleated villages (agglomerations), perhaps reflecting an underlying *Numidae/Mauri* tradition of settlement characterised by Roman sources as *castella* (Fig. 10.13).

OWNERS, CHIEF TENANTS (*CONDUCTORES*), AND SHARECROPPERS (*COLONI*) OF LARGE ESTATES

There is good epigraphic evidence for the existence of extremely large estates in several regions of *Africa*. Pliny the Elder (*NH* 18.35) famously remarked that half of *Africa* was owned by six proprietors put to death by Nero, when their lands became imperial estates). A similar message is conveyed by Agennius Urbicus

> disputes between communities and private individuals ... often occur in the provinces, especially in Africa, where private individuals have estates no less extensive than the territory belonging to communities. Indeed many estates are bigger than (urban) territories. Moreover, private individuals have on their estates a substantial population and villages scattered around their villa rather like *municipia*.[103]

The situation revealed by these sources represented a significant shift in Roman exploitation of African land. The initial phase of colonisation had focused on allocation of many standardised and smallish plots to discharged veterans, with mechanisms in place to control future sales or amalgamation of plots. The massive land grant from Caesar to Sittius, and others by Augustus to his key supporters in *Africa*, created a new sort of land market.[104] It is no surprise that the largest estates should be attested outside the centuriated zone on Numidian lands brought into *Africa Nova*. As well as gifting land in this region, it is also possible that the Julio-Claudian emperors made some large blocks of land available for purchase by senators and other capital-rich outsiders.

The most coherent reconstruction of such a landscape can be made in the vicinity of *Thugga*, where the combination of an unusually abundant rural epigraphy and detailed field survey permits identification of a number of private estates on the

103. Campbell 2000, 42–43.
104. De Vos 2013, 183 notes that most of the estate owners around *Thugga* were promoted from equestrian to senatorial status by Augustus, and the prime movers in investment in *Africa* thus seem to have been "new men."

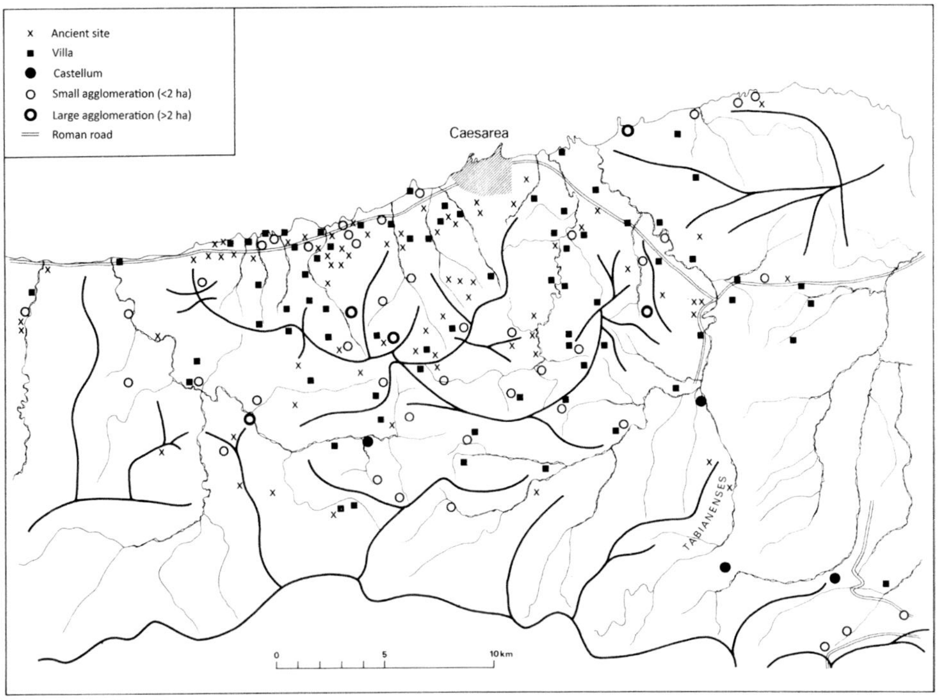

Figure 10.13. Settlement distribution in Mauretanian coastal hinterland of *Caesarea* (adapted from Leveau 1984, 482).

ground, alongside the huge estates taken into imperial control during the 1st century CE (Fig. 10.14).[105] As in the case of the *Musulami*, we can see the impact here of the colonial takeover, leading to substantial parts of the landscape being incorporated into private and imperial estates, to the detriment of the many Numidian towns and villages of this area (cf. Fig. 10.15a). An interesting aspect of the estates around *Thugga* is that some of the largest of these seem to have been started by former proconsuls of Octavian/Augustus and Tiberius: T. Statilius Taurus, L. Caninius Gallus, L. Aelius Lamia, and C. Rubellius Blandus.[106] That is quite revealing about the colonial "opportunities" for some well-placed outsiders. Their descendants are assumed to be among the six *possessores* who according to Pliny (*NH* 18.35) were disposed of for owning "half the farmland in *Africa*."[107] For long, the organisation of the imperial estates that resulted from Nero's land grab was only known from the remarkable series of inscriptions relating to the rights and obligations of the chief

105. De Vos 1997; 2013, 183–200 for detailed discussion.

106. De Vos 2013, 146–47 (Taurus); 183–84 (Blandus, Caninius, Lamia). The 3,600 ha estate of Statilius Taurus was the basis of the later *saltus Neronianus*, De Vos and Maurina 2019, 5–9.

107. Kehoe 1988, 11; Lassère 2015, 147.

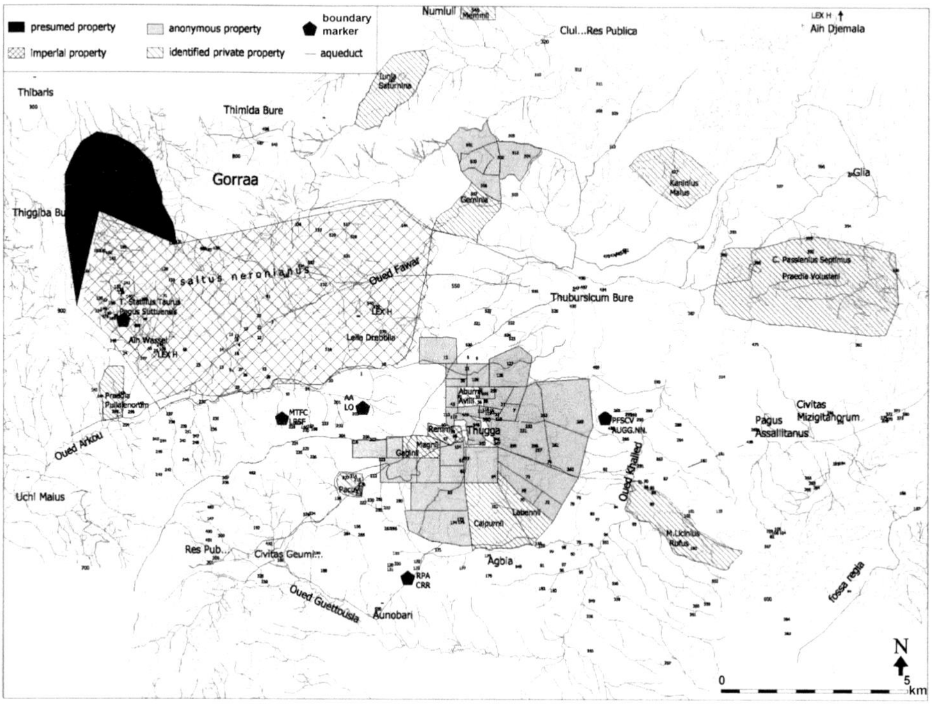

Figure 10.14. Evidence of private and imperial estates near *Thugga* (from de Vos 2013, 148, based on mapping by Redha Attoui).

tenants (*conductores*) and subtenants (*coloni*).[108] Although the region lay outside the northern centuriated zone, this had clearly been a carefully surveyed landscape, as references in the inscriptions to land-division terms shows, backed up by an abundance of boundary markers demarcating different sorts of land ownership in the landscape (imperial *saltus*, senatorial estate, other private estate, urban community, other rural community).

A number of the private estates attested around *Thugga* can unsurprisingly also be linked to some of the major families known from the city's civic epigraphy and acts of euergetism there (as discussed in Chapter 9). As already noted, this area saw a significant influx of outsiders in the late 1st century BCE and 1st century CE, and these veterans and Roman citizens also seem to have carved out estates, though on a less extensive scale than the senators under Augustus. For example, the estate of the Passieni (10 km^2) and M. Licinius Rufus (2.5 km^2).[109]

108. Kehoe 1988; cf. also 2007; 2015. For recent discoveries and renewed discussions of the texts, see de Vos 2000, 35 and figs. 57.1–58.8; González Bordas 2017; González Bordas and France 2017.

109. De Vos 2013, 193–93; cf. Khanoussi and Maurin 2000; 2002.

Building on a shadowy 1st-century CE *lex Manciana*, the *lex Hadriana de rudibus agris* set out the rights and responsibilities of the chief tenants (*conductores*) and share-cropping tenants (*coloni*) on the imperial estates near *Thugga*. The *conductores* paid a fixed lease for the estate, generally of five-year duration and renewable, and their interests were primarily to maximise production in the short term. The *lex Hadriana* was designed to encourage the *coloni* to make a long-term commitment to increasing production, which was in the emperor's interest, as it would allow the rate paid by the *conductores* for the main leases to rise over time. The law enshrined a separation between ownership of the land and the use (*usus proprius*) of whatever was placed upon it (buildings, orchards, and other crops). The *usus proprius* was granted in perpetuity to *coloni* who brought into production uncultivated areas of the estate in return for specified proportions of their yields, principally in grain, olive oil, and wine (a third after threshing/pressing). The required level of investment shows that the *coloni* were not poor peasants but farmers with resources and a mentality focused on surplus production.[110] Since the tenant's investment might be in olive orchards, vineyards, and the processing facilities, their capital stake in the *usus proprius* was considerable, and measures of relief from rent/tax were included for establishing olive orchards, for instance, that could take ten or more years to enter full production. The rights were hereditable and saleable, providing incentives to *coloni* to think long-term. However, if land was left uncultivated for two successive years it reverted to the estate.

Because the measures were designed to encourage intensification of production on the estates, we are less well informed about the regular tenancy arrangements, though it is likely that normative tenancy was on a similar basis, and part of the purpose of inscribing the law in relation to uncultivated land being brought into cultivation was precisely to confirm that the same levels of rents and obligations were due on such land.[111] On imperial estates, *coloni* were obliged to provide a certain number of days of labour and use of draught animals for the chief tenant (*conductor*), and there were periodic resentments about the potential for abuses in relation to this by the *conductores*.[112] Thinking back to my models of imperialism presented in Table 2.1, the evidence of rules, incentives for specific types of action, and complaints of abuses and measures taken to address these illustrates the interactions of imperial policy, local reaction, systemic interference, and rebalancing actions.

There are also some references to the Mancian tenure applying to private estates, including the Vandalic date "Albertini tablets" found near the steppic border

110. Kehoe 1988 71–72. For a range of views on the status of *coloni*, see Kolendo 1991; Lenski 2017; Vera 1988; 1987; Whittaker 1978a.

111. Kehoe 1988, 55.

112. Kehoe 1988, 146–53; 2013, 40–41 on the dynamic tension between *conductor* and *coloni*.

between Tunisia and Algeria.[113] In view of the new evidence for extensive pre-Roman agricultural development in *Africa*, it seems quite probable that the form of share cropping attested in the imperial estate inscriptions built on established tenurial practices rather than imposing something alien. There is no clear model for the Mancian tenure outside *Africa*, increasing the probability of an endogenous origin of this form of share-cropping.

The *Thugga* survey work by Mariette de Vos and her team (1994–2008) covered an area of 371 km^2 of rich agricultural landscape, with its productivity boosted in places by complex irrigation works.[114] Although not all the nucleated centres were promoted to full urban status until a relatively late date, the region eventually contained nine sites of recognised urban status (thus, an average city territory of only c.40 km^2 even before allowing for the private and imperial estates) and 15 "clustered settlements" (Fig. 10.15).[115] The spectacular growth of rural settlement right through the Roman era (Fig. 10.15b–d) clearly built on the existence of a large number of Numidian nucleated (proto-urban and urban) centres (Fig. 10.15a). The density of larger settlements here would have allowed many individuals to travel to rural farms each day from those centres, though the survey still located 636 rural settlements. The large imperial estate (*saltus Neronianus*) just to the north-west of *Thugga* occupied a block of c.9 × 4 km, so around 36 km^2 (cf. Fig. 10.14).[116] The survey has revealed much about the archaeological similarities between the imperial estate area and other parts of the landscape.

There are plenty of indications of capital investment in farm buildings of substantial form (often employing ashlar blocks in construction and well-dressed blocks for press elements, specialised mills, and so on) and cisterns.[117] One of the practical implications of the epigraphic evidence is that the tenant farmers needed access to processing facilities for grain (threshing floors) and oil and wine production (mills and presses). Ownership of one's own press guaranteed timely processing of the harvest and could bring a potentially lucrative return—hence the plethora of presses (at least 335) in the *Thugga* region, rather than a single large facility for the whole estate.[118] The overwhelming majority of the presses were at rural sites, rather than the urban centres; 82 sites had just a single press, while 24 sites had a double press, and 5 a triple press facility—there were none of the really large oileries that typify the High Steppe region to the south. Some of the nucleated sites had

113. Hitchner 1995b; Mattingly 1989b; Whittaker 1978a.
114. De Vos 2013, 186–87.
115. De Vos 2013, 144.
116. De Vos 2013, 148; cf. Picard 1990, 63, who estimated the overall area of imperial estates in Africa at c.1,500 sq km.
117. De Vos 2013, 152–83.
118. De Vos 2013, 184–88 with calculation (185–86) of return to farmer from a single olive press equivalent to ten years' wages for an agricultural labourer. It is not certain however what proportion of the presses in this region were for oil production as opposed to wine, and the rarity of milling equipment suggests that wine making was significant.

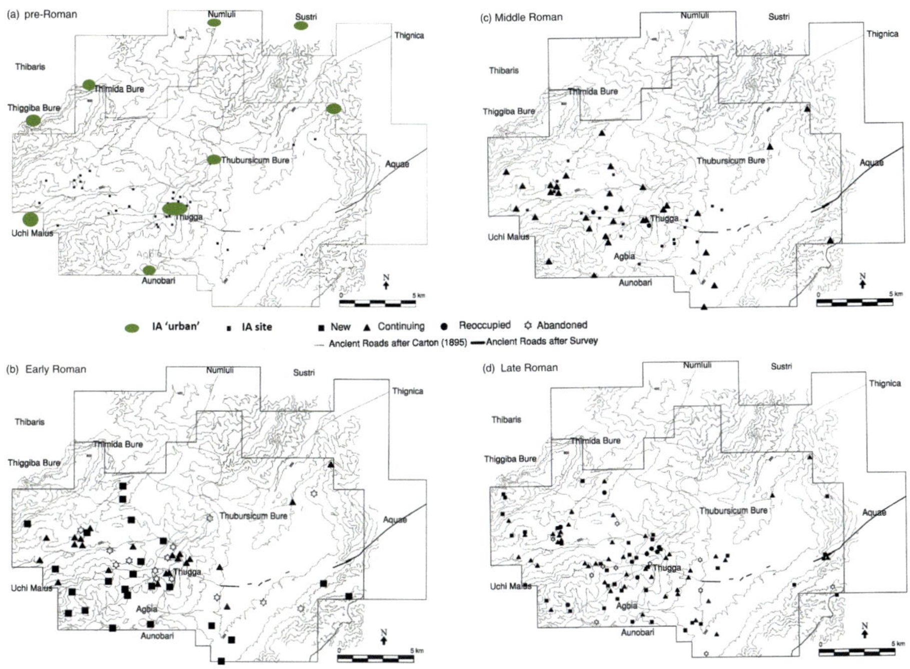

Figure 10.15. Rural settlement in the *Thugga* area. a) Pre-Roman. b) Early Roman. c) Mid Roman. d) Late Roman (from De Vos 2013, 164–65; mapping by Silvia Polla and Redha Attoui).

several individual presses in different buildings.[119] The *conductores* may have tried to extract extra profit by processing the crops of *coloni* (as suggested by a number of the two- or three-press buildings occurring at nucleated sites on the imperial estate), but the survey evidence suggests that in general the *coloni* preferred to invest in their own independent arrangements.

Excavation at the site of Ain Wassel, find-spot of one of the copies of the *lex Hadriana* on the *saltus Neronianus*, examined one building in a small cluster of at least ten structures (c.1 ha area). This turned out to be a Byzantine rebuild of a late Roman agricultural building housing an olive press. From the residual pottery recovered it is evident that the site extended further back in time, but the excavated sequence only relates to the late antique phases. The longevity of the activity at Ain Wassel is striking, but it is unfortunate not to have more direct evidence (ceramic, material cultural, architectural, botanical, faunal) relating to the heyday of the imperial estate.[120]

119. De Vos 2013, 154–56, 159–60 (for rare examples of sites with multiple presses).
120. De Vos and Maurina 2019, especially 56–148 for the stratigraphic report.

There are a number of other examples where the combination of epigraphy and archaeology enables us to perceive heavy capital investment in the development of landed estates. The *fundus Aufidianus* in northern Tunisia, was close to the town of *Biha Bilta*.[121] The anonymous *conductor* of this estate that had fallen into disrepair was commemorated in a funerary text (*AE* 1975, 883) for his improvement and investment in the land (planting olive trees, an orchard, a vineyard) and facilities (a well and cistern). As a chief tenant, theoretically on a short and fixed lease, a *conductor* was not normally incentivised to make long-term investments in improving the productivity of an estate. However, sometimes the association between an agent and an estate could be long-maintained—Flavius Caecilias Primus was *custodus* and *actor* of the *fundus Glebonianus*, where he was eulogised for being responsible for "all the new tree plantings."[122] The emphasis on increasing olives and vines is reminiscent of a shorter text (*ILTun* 243) in a funerary mosaic of a certain Dion, who is celebrated for having apparently planted 4,000 trees.[123] Similarly, the self-glorifying poem (*CIL* 8. 21, 212) on the mausoleum of T. Flavius Secundus at *Cillium*, recorded that he had been the first to introduce viticulture to the region, presumably at the time of setting up the estate on his discharge from the army.

Another good example of an excessively large estate concerns the *saltus Beguensis*, owned by the senator L. Africanus, who in the 2nd century CE petitioned for the right to be able to hold a periodic market there.[124] Recent survey of the locality from which the *saltus Beguensis* inscription came by Sehili has revealed that there were in fact two estate centres c.1.5 km apart at Henchir al-Begar (Fig. 10.7). Each comprised a substantial nucleated settlement area, the first 19 ha and the second 14.5 ha in area, both centred on an olive oil factory, with a combined total of 20 presses in the oilery buildings, and traces of further presses and a massive circular water reservoir in the surrounding settlement.[125] Boundary stones marking divisions between two estates have been found nearby, so the likely explanation is that there were two massive estates side by side here, both carved out of what had originally been Musulamian lands.[126] We might note the urban scale of these settlements, which were akin to "agrovilles."[127] Another example of a village estate

121. Leveau 1978b; Peyras 1975; Stone 1998, 106.
122. De Vos and Porena 2020.
123. Stone 1998, 106.
124. *CIL* 8.270 = 23246; Shaw 1981a.
125. Sehili 2008b; 2009, 379–90. The urban scale of these sites is paralleled by other examples surveyed by Sehili, see 2009, 374–406 for overall discussion. See also Hobson 2015a, 89–90.
126. Sehili 2008b, 94–95, 106 (map) for the boundary stones between Q.A.F (Q Anicius Faustus?) and CMP (C Memmius Placidius?). This would suggest a 3rd-century date for the boundary stones and a change of senatorial owner—Anicius Faustus was legate of the *III Augusta* 197–201 CE. Sehili also argues for extensive imperial estates in this region.
127. Cf. Hitchner 1990, for the site of Ksar el-Guellal, with more than 20 individual presses, and proposition of the term agroville.

centre is the site of Henchir al-Gousset between *Thelepte* and *Theveste*, with a press building of impressive construction housing a bank of six presses at the heart of a 19 ha settlement.[128] In contrast to the *Thugga* area, the concentration of productive capacity in centralised facilities suggests a very high degree of specialisation and a desire on the part of the absentee owner to retain oversight of the oil production of the tenants. The scale of olive oil production attested in the High Steppe area (and in the neighbouring Dorsal) indicates a significant growth in production during the Roman period, in part stimulated by the massive capital investment in major estates, but evidently emulated also at many smaller sites.

Group 2. Areas of Sedentarisation and Control

My second group of case studies relates to areas where agriculture was less well established in pre-Roman times and where the Roman period often marked a substantial extension of sedentary farming. This is primarily the story of the lands of the *Gaetuli*, peoples of desert, pre-desert, and steppe. The traditional presentation of this transformation has been in terms of a binary opposition between Roman sedentary farmers and African pastoral peoples who had to be subdued and obliged to settle down to agriculture, or who had their transhumance routes closely circumscribed under Rome. There is a serious danger with such models that they overlook the extent of pre-Roman cultivation and presume virgin and largely empty landscapes where there was in fact already considerable complexity and cultivation going on. As explained in Chapter 5, for instance, there has been a consistent underestimation of the extent and importance of oasis agriculture in the pre-Roman period in Africa. This has major implications for our understanding of the process of increased sedentarisation under Rome.

THE AURÈS

The mountain-hemmed plainlands of the Aurès represent a rather different context for the intensification of sedentary farming. The land quality and climate are better than the Tunisian steppe and pre-desert, but less suited for cereal cultivation than northern Tunisia. We suffer from a chronic lack of archaeological data on rural settlement in this area in pre-Roman times. The major "Numidian" tomb, known as the Medracen, and many NAIA tombs are important indicators that this landscape was by no means empty of people and wealth in the latter centuries BCE.[129] It would certainly not be a surprise if future work identified pre-Roman

128. Brun 2004, 228–29; Hermassi 2003, 83–90.

129. Fentress 1979, 61–75.

agriculture in the Aurès region. Parts of the Aurès zone developed a significant capacity for olive oil and/or wine production, though the lack of excavated sites is again a frustration.[130] It is also possible that the rich plains provided another key resource for the Numidian kingdom, and later the Roman Empire, in the form of pasture lands for horse-rearing. The Aurès zone reveals a significant imprint of military colonisation and imperial estates, suggesting that substantial areas of land were confiscated by Rome and subsequently used for settling veteran communities (as noted in Chapter 7), but we cannot exclude growth of African settlements in the region alongside them, something that would be interesting to look at archaeologically.

OASIS CULTIVATORS

The mechanics of oasis agriculture were new to Rome when encountered in Africa for the first time, at coastal centres such as *Tacape* and *Oea*, or the inland pre-desert oasis of *Capsa*. Pliny's account of the oasis of *Tacape* emphasises the extraordinary fecundity of the oasis, with its several layers of planting and its multiple harvests from small gardens.[131] Land prices in the oasis were accordingly shockingly high.[132] I have argued that oasis cultivation was already well-established along the northern edge of the Sahara by the latter centuries BCE. The pastoral peoples reported by Rome as occupying the arid parts of Africa were closely linked in many cases to these oasis cultivators—as was certainly the case, for instance, with the *Nasamones* of the Libyan Syrtic desert.[133] The oasis of *Cidamus* is a further instance of an isolated sedentary community that must have had close and reciprocal relations with pastoral groups exploiting the surrounding Saharan landscapes.[134] An interesting aspect of Roman irrigation technology in the broad "frontier" zone is that it came to embrace the underground irrigation channel (foggara)—a distinctly Saharan/Garamantian tradition.[135]

TRANSFORMATION OF PASTORAL PEOPLES

Our most detailed evidence for the development of sedentary farming in zones that were not intensively cultivated in pre-Roman times comes from the Tunisian High Steppe and the Tunisian and Libyan pre-desert zones, including Syrtica. The mechanics of the transformation were different in each case.

---

130. Morizot 1991; 1993.
131. Pliny *NH* 18.188–89; Trousset 1986a, 173–76; 1987a.
132. Pliny *NH* 18.188–89; Trousset 1986a, 175–76 for the calculation that land at *Tacape* cost 40,000 HS per ha or 1 denarius per m^2.
133. Mattingly et al. 2020c, 127–30.
134. Desanges 1980a, 389–90; Mattingly et al. 2020b, 195–206.
135. Wilson 2005; 2006a; 2009a; Wilson et al. 2020.

The *Musuni Regiani* were a people of the High Steppe whose territory was long suspected to have been impinged on by the foundation of the towns of *Sufetula*, *Cillium*, and *Thelepte*. The recent discovery of a boundary stone near *Sufetula* now shows that the city was known as the *municipium Sufetulensium Musuniorum*, indicating that the *Musuni* were formally attached to the town.[136] Military (or veteran) origins for *Cillium*, *Sufetula*, and *Thelepte* have been suspected in the past and, though the new discovery reminds us that the pre-Roman occupants of the land also had to be fitted into the settlement system, it still seems that there was an important element of military personnel among the early settlers at some of these sites. At *Cillium*, for instance, there were at least two elite families descended from retired soldiers and, as noted above, one of them boasted on his tomb that he had been the first to introduce proper vineyards to the region. That does not mean that the zone was uncultivated in pre-Roman times, though it suggests that there was significant intensification and specialisation under Rome. The territory of the *Musuni*, as in the case of the *Musulami*, may have been squeezed between lands made available to other settlers in the new towns and private estates, but there is no evident distinction to be drawn from the archaeological evidence to identify a "tribal reserve," leading to the conclusion that the *Musuni* followed similar sedentary farming practices in the Roman period. The regional settlement hierarchy includes agrovilles, large estates, and a range of smaller farms and farmsteads.[137] The model here seems to be one of Roman colonists and veterans playing a role in establishing specialised sedentary farming in the High Steppe landscape, but the scale of investment in specialised production facilities, represented by the numerous olive and wine presses, indicate that the local population groups were also deeply implicated in this landscape transformation. However, Bruce Hitchner's work also suggests that pastoralism remained active and important even within the area of intensive oleoculture and viticulture.[138]

The *Nybgenii* were the people of the Nefzaoua oases in southern Tunisia and the desert plain known as the Dahar that stretches away to the south down the east side of the Grand Erg Oriental. There are indications in the ancient sources that this people comprised both oasis cultivators and transhumant pastoralists.[139] The Roman limits imposed on the *Nybgenii* can be established with some precision from inscriptions related to the land survey (*limitatio*) carried out by Vibius Marsus and the *legio III Augusta* in 29 CE and then renewed under Trajan across a vast area of southern Tunisia. The Trajanic boundary markers delimited the lands

136. Khanoussi 2008; 2010.

137. Hitchner 1988; 1989; 1990; 1993b; cf. Sehili 2009.

138. Hitchner 1994.

139. Ptolemy ascribed two separate locations to the *Nybgenii*, and the most logical interpretation of this is that he was attempting to convey the reality of a people with fixed bases in the oases and a transhumant range for pastoral elements. Ptolemy 4.3.6; 4.6.6; Mattingly 1995, 28–31.

of the *Nybgenii* from the territory of neighbouring urban communities to north-west (*Capsa*) and east (*Tacape*). The series of linear barriers in the mountain ranges north of the Chotts appear to correspond closely with the dividing line between the lands of the *Nybgenii* and the *Capsitani*, and the longer barrier of the Jabal Tebaga, with that between them and the *Tacapitanae*. These linear barriers also coincide with points in the landscape where there is sharp transition even today between cultivated land and desert.

The picture of Roman-era settlement on either side of the Tunisian linear barriers is quite complicated. The Nybgenian side of these control lines was notably less intensively covered with Roman-era settlement, though there were evidently some sedentary farms built in these marginal landscapes. But more importantly, the lands to the north of *Nybgenii* territory now appear to have been much more densely populated than at one time believed. In the Bled Segui plain to the south-east of *Capsa* (Fig. 10.16), recent satellite image analysis has revealed a significant number of village-scale settlements, some at least of which appear to have been built up around fortlets or fortified compounds. This looks like a fairly intensive programme of settlement and intensification of land use, with implications for the potential northern range lands of the *Nybgenii*. The linear barriers were permeable in that the routes through them were controlled by gates. A plausible scenario here is that transhumant elements of the *Nybgenii* had their automatic right to move far to the north with their flocks circumscribed by the fixing of new land boundaries and that this was henceforth controlled and regulated. The more fertile plain-lands to the north were also now more intensively cultivated, with some suspected involvement of the military community, but almost certainly (given the intensive nature of settlement) with increased sedentarisation of Gaetulian peoples. The same situation seems to have applied to the entire security zone along the south side of the Aurès mountains and continuing in the Wadi Jedi area, where there seems to have been a major expansion of cultivated area beyond the pre-existing oasis centres.[140] Traditionally explained as land reclaimed by soldier farmers (*limitanei*), this seems to betoken a much broader level of sedentarisation in local society in the lee of the advanced Roman garrison posts.[141] Nonetheless, the character of the rural society in proximity to the many of the garrison posts in Algeria appears to have been a good deal more Latin-literate than comparable areas of Tripolitania. For example, there are a number of late antique documents relating to these societies—the Vandal-era Albertini tablets, Byzantine and Vandal ostraca—that demonstrate a continuation of Roman systems of documenting land sales, production of oil and

140. Baradez 1949a, 147–48; 1957; Birebent 1962; Rouvillois-Brigol 1986 for the field systems. Leschi 1948 for an inscription that shows direct state involvement in land assignation.

141. Guédon 2018a, 194–201.

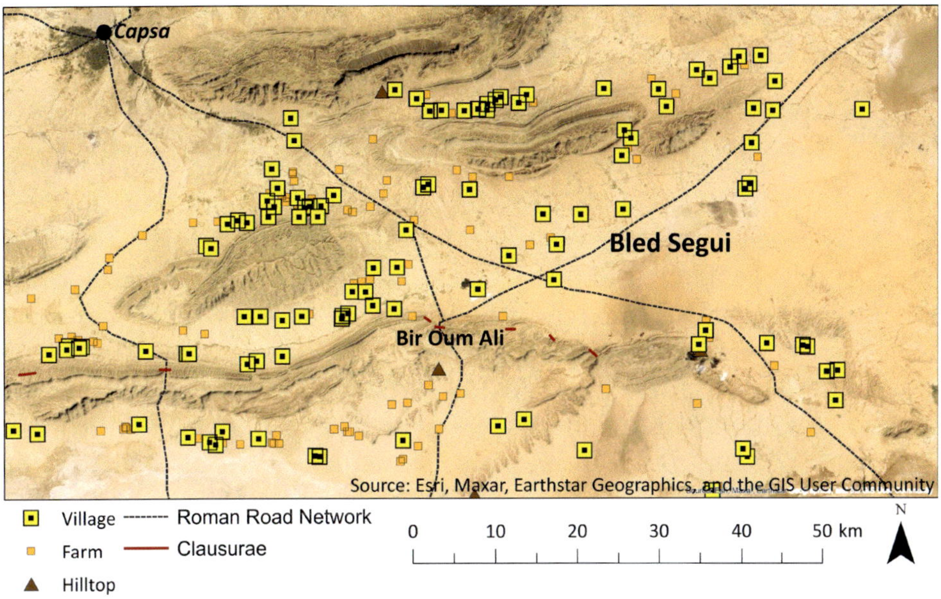

Figure 10.16. Map of villages and other Roman settlements in the Bled Segui (Martin Sterry for Trans-Sahara Project).

grain, the making of wills, and so on.[142] There are clear similarities with a recently reported dossier of 4th-century wooden tablets, probably from this same area near the Algeria/Tunisian border.[143]

The *Macae* of the Tripolitanian pre-desert are believed to have been a largely pastoral people prior to the Roman era. The UNESCO Libyan Valleys project surveyed a large part of their heartlands.[144] There were a number of oases on the fringes of this zone (at Mizda, al-Qurrayyat, Bu Nijim, and so on), but hillfort sites of suspected early date have also been identified (see Fig. 5.15g–j).[145] The occupation of hillforts is in itself interesting as it implies at least fixed-based transhumance if not some degree of sedentary occupation. In the absence of excavation at the hillforts or radiocarbon dates, their first occupation must remain uncertain. Like

142. Albertini tablets: Courtois et al. 1952; Leveau 2020b; Mattingly 1989b; Wilson forthcoming; Ostraca from southern region: Ast 2016; Laporte and Dupuis 2011, 61–62, 90–91; Leveau 2020b; *AE* 1967, 588–592;

143. Rothenhöfer and Blänsdorf 2016 for an initial publication; also *AE* 2016, 2029–2036. This seems to relate to a large archive of tablets (the "Sfez Collection") of dubious provenance that came on the antiquities market in 2016–2017. The tablets (seemingly a collection of wills and sales documents) were written in Latin, but recorded Latin, Punic, and Libyan names and toponyms, with a number of indicators of an origin in the pre-desert region running from Algeria to Libya.

144. Barker et al. 1996a; 1996b; Sheldrick 2016.

145. Barker et al. 1996a, 116–18.

other pre-desert settlements they have produced no diagnostic pottery finds earlier than the later 1st century CE, but is this evidence of absence or simply absence of evidence?

The results of surveys along the pre-desert wadis and in Syrtica demonstrate a significant growth in sedentary farms from the late 1st century CE and that these sites were tied into regional trade networks (Fig. 10.17).[146] The architecture of the larger farms parallels the small-to-medium olive farms of the *territoria* of the coastal cities to the north, while many of the smaller farms with enclosures and ranges of rooms along one side seem to take their inspiration from tents and pastoral stock pens.[147] The most plausible interpretation of the evidence is that these farms represent the settlements of sedentarised *Macae* groupings.[148] The farming in this pre-desert area was based on floodwater irrigation systems, harnessing run-off in the floors of the dry rivers (wadis) after spasmodic rains to irrigate the alluvium in the valley bottom. Catchment walls, terrace walls, and field boundary walls guided and spread the waters, making use of sluice gates and spillways. The irrigation technologies employed here were distinctive to the pre-desert environment and again suggest local expertise was fundamental to the evolution of farming here (Fig. 10.2).[149] We shall see in Chapter 11 that there is evidence of cultural hybridity within these communities. The wadi cultivation encompassed a classic range of Mediterranean crops (grain, olives, vines, fruit trees, legumes), though such farming would have been impossible without the run-off irrigation.[150]

Settlement congregated strongly along the margins of the wadis. From an early stage the sedentary farming systems seem to have been quite hierarchically organised, with local wadi systems dominated by one or more elite sites, rather than being initially based on an egalitarian allotment of land.[151] There is no doubt in this case that the local Libyan people were being sedentarised and brought into the market-oriented economic sphere of the Empire. Nonetheless, the disproportionate advantage given to select individuals in society hints that colonial politics underlay the development to some extent.

The sedentarisation of the *Macae* is mirrored in a less emphatic style in the evidence from their Syrtic neighbours, the *Seli* and the *Nasamones*. In western Syrtica, although there was an increase of sedentary settlement linked to similar systems of wadi farming, the typology of sites seems to be missing the upper echelon settlements

146. Barker et al. 1996a, 147–58 for the dating evidence
147. Barker et al. 1996a, 120–24; Liverani 2006, 396–97.
148. Barker et al. 1996a, 321–24; Grahame 1998. Kerr 2007, ix rather implausibly proposes that the pre-desert farmers were Libyphoenician colonists; though the Punic cultural influences cannot be denied, the overriding character is Libyan, as we shall see in Chapter 11.
149. Barker et al. 1996a, 191–226. Cf. Ibba and Mastino 2011a; Leveau 2009a; Shaw 1984; 1991a.
150. Barker et al. 1996a, 227–63.
151. Mattingly 2011a, 162, 166 for an attempt to model this.

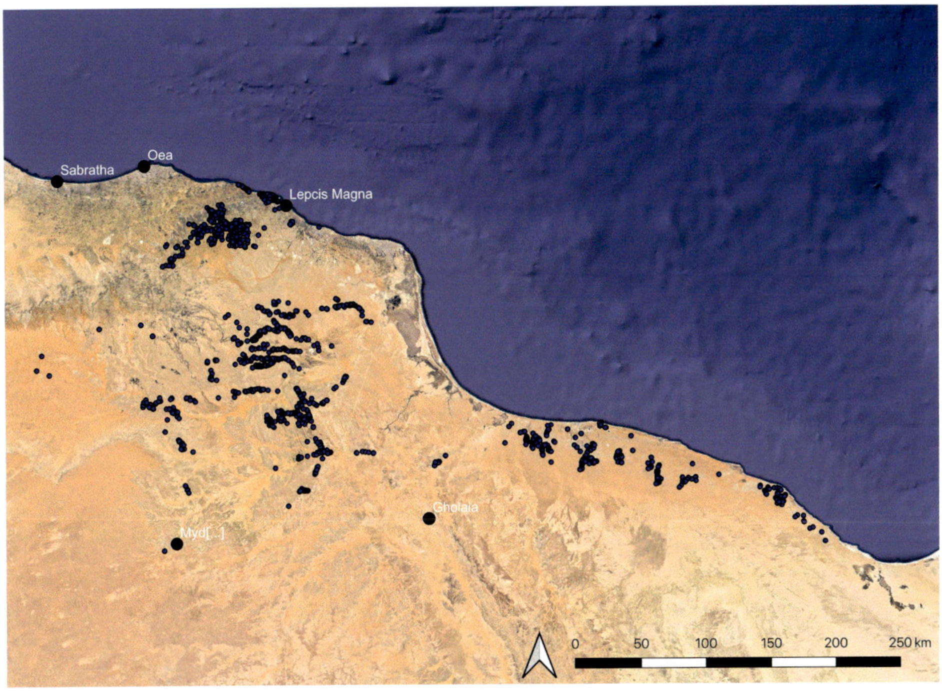

Figure 10.17. Distribution of Roman-era settlement in Tripolitania and Syrtica, showing significant advance of sedentary farming (from Sheldrick 2021).

that we encountered in the *Macae* region, and animals also seem to have remained a more significant element of the economy.[152] In the eastern part of Syrtica, there were some distinctive site types, including elongated buildings, and less emphasis on wadi farming.[153] The former groups probably can be related to the *Seli* and the latter to the *Nasamones*, who also maintained oases settlements around *Augila*. These peoples appear to have remained more pastoral and mobile in outlook.

Some Conclusions

The rural landscapes of North Africa were highly productive in the Roman era, belying the contemporary reputation of the region as an underpopulated and arid environment. Several colonial-era myths can be debunked. The rural boom time is not attributable to some climatic amelioration.[154] Nor was it the product of exogenous

152. Fakroun 2004; Longerstay 1999; Rebuffat 1988c; Reddé 1985; 1988.
153. Lequesne et al. 2010.
154. For detailed discussion of climatic and environmental evidence, Davis 2007; Leveau 2009a; 2018.

technology and know-how that permitted the greening of the landscapes. In the final analysis, it depended to a great extent on local and long-developed knowledge of crops and hydrological resources. However, the patterns of development (and of underdevelopment) that we can see archaeologically reflect the underlying imperial exploitation of North Africa and this was far from uniform in its effects. The new opportunities of landholding under Rome and of access to the globalised markets of the Roman world were unequal within provincial society, and a small minority of actors benefitted disproportionally. The rural poor were always in the majority and exploited through rental and labour requirements to a greater or lesser extent.[155] Late Roman measures to prevent the colonate abandoning their lands (*Cod. Th.* 5.17.1; 2.24.2) also link to wider evidence of repressive force and resistance.[156] In the next chapter, I turn to the nature of rural society and how the rural population, winners and losers, expressed their cultural identities.

155. Hobson 2015a, 143–62; Leveau 1978a; Sirago 1987; 1990. Mattingly 1997c, 130–35 reflected on *Africa* as a "landscape of opportunity," the "opportunity" being framed as a favourable contrast to *Achaia*, but the scope for exploitation and resistance in *Africa* was also noted.

156. Hobson 2015a, 158–59; Shaw 2011.

Chapter 11

EXPRESSIONS OF RURAL IDENTITIES

The Rural Majority

Despite the high density of urban settlement in some regions, the vast majority of the ancient population of North Africa lived in the countryside. The rural surveys reported in the previous chapter have confirmed region by region that the Roman era marked a peak period of ancient North African populations. Nonetheless, putting a precise figure on the rural population is fraught with uncertainty. Bruce Frier's estimate for 14 CE gave an overall population of the Maghrib and *Cyrenaica* of 3.9 million, with the figures reaching 7.1 million by the 160s CE.[1] With the peak urban population likely to have exceeded 2 million, these overall figures may need revising upward. If we assume that the rural population amounted to at least 75% of the total population by the mid-2nd century that gives us a rough estimate of 8 million. Rural populations included some of the poorest in society, who were also those least invested in the Roman project and the norms of Roman culture.

This chapter concerns the make-up of the rural populations and how they expressed their cultural identities. While at one level they can be related to the broad groupings repeatedly referred to in this book (*Libyphoenices*, *Afri*, *Numidae*, *Mauri*, *Gaetuli*, and Roman settlers and their descendants), rural dwellers differed in important respects from the military and urban communities already discussed. For instance, as we shall see, the evidence of religious practices is strikingly different to the well-documented epigraphic behaviours of soldiers and townspeople.

A key proposition is that rural communities were very heterogeneous socially and culturally, and were represented by a wide spectrum of internal identity markers. The most visible were the social elite, who constructed architecturally imposing farms or villas, which were sometimes ornamented with sumptuous mosaics and wall paintings.[2] Some of their dead were honoured with elaborate mausolea and Latin epitaphs. But it is all too easy to mistake this sort of evidence for a general trend, which it patently was not. In reality, rural communities were representative

1. Frier 2000, 812–14.
2. See, for instance, Duval 1986; Precheur-Canonge 1962; Rind 2009; Wilson, R. 2018 for idealised "elite" images of rural life.

of the inequalities of empire. The visible wealth of the few was generally the product of the labour of countless others whose opportunities in life were severely limited by birth, by lack of capital, by access to land, and by the burden of rents, customary dues, and taxes owed to the rich and the state.[3] This is not to deny some possibilities for social mobility. Much has been made in studies of "Roman Africa" of the celebrated life of the "Mactar harvester," who rose from being a landless labourer, to rural gangmaster, to landowner and town councillor.[4]

> I was born into a poor dwelling, of a poor father, who had no property or household. From the time of my birth, I lived in the country looking after my business; there was no time off in the countryside and none for me at any time. And when the time of year had brought forth the grain ready for harvest, then I was the first reaper of the stalks. When the sickle-bearing gangs of men had made their way to the fields, whether heading for the "Nomads of *Cirta*" or the "Fields of Iupiter," as harvester I preceded them all, first into the fields, leaving the packed bands behind my back. I reaped 12 harvests under the raging sun, and afterwards became a work gang leader instead of a labourer. I led the gangs of harvesters for 11 years and our band cut down the Numidian fields. This effort and my frugal lifestyle brought success and made me master of a household and gained me a house, and my home itself lacks nothing. My life gained the rewards of office: I was myself enrolled among the conscript councillors. Elected decurion, I had a seat in the order's temple and, starting out as a humble country boy, I too became censor. I produced children and saw them grow into young men and saw their children too. In accord with my services in life, I have enjoyed years of fame, which no bitter tongue has hurt with any reproach. People, learn to pass your lives without giving reason for reproach. The man who has lived without deceit has earned meeting his death in such a manner.[5]

A different sort of biography is represented by T. Flavius Secundus of *Cillium*. He was a retired soldier turned pioneer farmer and climbed further up in social standing as a result of his investments and innovations. A lengthy poem engraved on his elaborate tower mausoleum on his estate near Kasserine claimed he was:

> First to introduce the gifts of Bacchus in abundance, planted the first vines in rows, brought into production land by streams of running water.[6]

In the cases of the harvester and the soldier, we might note their social rewards were the fruits of 23–25 years of hard graft. Both these individuals were exceptions

3. Hobson 2015a, 13–29 for an elegant theoretical presentation of the argument about colonial inequality. See also Shaw 2013a.
4. *CIL* 8.11824/*ILS* 7457. Picard 1970; Shaw 2013a, 281–98; Stone 1998.
5. *CIL* 8.11824; translation adapted from Parkin and Pomeroy 2007, 39–40.
6. *CIL* 8.211, 212; Hitchner 1995a; Lassère et al. 1993.

Figure 11.1. The countryside as viewed by the urban elite. a) The *Dominus Iulius* mosaic, *Karthago*. b) Villa mosaic, *Thabraca* (photos: author from Bardo Museum, Tunis).

to the more general rules that more often than not hampered social mobility. The idea of social and economic progress it relates also links with the *topos* of the "good farmer," which recurs a number of times in the epigraphic and literary record of "Roman Africa."[7] It echoed the colonialist discourse, ancient and modern, of a barren land brought to fruition by Rome and the hard work of these good farmers, creating a "privileged and relatively happy zone."[8]

In a similar way, there are a number of famous artworks reflecting an idealised elite view of the countryside, where estates were organised for their comfort and enrichment.[9] The *Dominus Iulius* mosaic (Fig. 11.1a), excavated in a rich house at *Karthago*, depicts the rural estate of Iulius, who approaches his architecturally elaborate villa on horseback from the left in the central band.[10] The domes of a bathhouse can be seen behind the main façade. To the right we see a hunting expedition departing, representing one of the key leisure pursuits available there. In the lower and upper registers the seasons of the year are represented in terms of what they offered to the lord and his lady. In spring (lower left) the lady of the house is attended by a female servant (probably servile) with her jewellery box, while a man approaches with a box of roses. Summer (top right) is evoked by a field of ripened wheat and by flocks of sheep and goats; autumn (bottom right) by the grape harvest, while the lord is presented with a scroll addressed to "Dominus Iulius" by a man carrying two storks. Finally, in winter (top left) we see the olive harvest in full swing, while the centrally placed and seated *domina* once again receives offerings

7. Stone 1998.
8. Albertini et al. 1955, 81: "Dans le monde antique, où la vie en générale n'était ni douce ni facile, l'Afrique était une zone privilege et relativement heureux."
9. Blanchard-Lemée et al. 1996, 167–88; Rind 2009 for mosaics depicting rural estates.
10. Dunbabin 1999, 118–20.

of produce of the land from servile people or tenants. The villa is thus depicted as a perfect world of pleasure, rest, and profit for the elite owners. There are many other mosaic and fresco representations of rural life that evoke a similarly idealised vision.[11] The *Thabraca* mosaic (Fig. 11.1b) shows an architecturally elaborate main building surrounded by ancillary structures and neatly trellised vines interspersed with olive trees. The multiple buildings here are perhaps representative of a nucleated, village-scale estate centre.

Not all land owners were men, of course, and Africa provides numerous instances of powerful women estate owners.[12] Pudentilla of *Oea*, for example, was a millionaire with extensive estates. She had been widowed and was placed under pressure to remarry within her extended family group, not because she was unable to manage her estates successfully, but because her family wanted to keep the wealth within the clan.

The colonial paradigm of the *bonus agricola* would not have been recognised by the majority in the countryside. In many areas, the origins of agriculture were already ancient, and good husbandry was as likely to be seen as a continuation of established tradition as a product of colonial innovation. The imperial context exacerbated inequalities and selectively opened opportunity to individuals or groups who were seen as more integral to the colonial project—veteran colonists, Roman citizens with capital to invest in land, local notables who had shown themselves amenable to brokering the political integration of their peoples into provincial structures.

The traditional model of Romanisation is at its weakest in the face of the cultural diversity and mixed messages put out by such structurally unequal communities. The notion of discrepant identities has particular value in these contexts, though the available data are somewhat unsatisfactory. Nonetheless, I hope my analysis will make a case for prioritising the rural communities in future agendas of study.

Who were the rural population? We have seen in earlier chapters that some were incomers—veterans and surplus population from Italy and other parts of the Empire—who were allocated lands from the African portfolio that Rome had acquired in war. But they were always in a small minority overall.[13] Enslaved people were another potential group of outsiders, though in comparison to Italy there is not much evidence of estates dependent on slave labour in Africa. Pudentilla, evidently had something like 400 enslaved people, presumably mostly rural-based (*Apologia* 87.7, 93.4), but that part of Tripolitania may have been fairly exceptional

11. Aurigemma 1960; 1962; Ben Abed and Soren 1987; Blanchard-Lemée et al. 1996, 167–88; Dunbabin 1999, 117–20; Precheur-Canonge 1962; Rind 2009.
12. For general studies of women in ancient North Africa, see Benseddik 2017; Ladjimi Sebai 2011. For female estate owners, Sehili 2002, with a dossier of 25 attested from literary and epigraphic sources. For women in urban contexts, Waldherr 2003.
13. On the modern colonial era exaggeration of ancient Gallic migrants in Africa, Dondin-Payre 2006; cf. Leglay 1962.

in this regard.[14] Enslaved people were certainly traded across the Empire's borders as well as taken in wars against rebellious subjects and neighbours of Rome long after the initial wars of conquest.[15] Along with textiles, enslaved people were listed as the main export of *Mauretania Caesariensis* (*Expositio Totius Mundi et Gentium* 505).[16] It would be far too simplistic to argue that most Black Africans attested within the African provinces were enslaved people (or their descendants), as we know that the Gaetulian populations were already mixed in pre-Roman times, and it is therefore probable that many dark skinned people lived as free inhabitants within the provinces, especially in the oases.

It is also important to recognise that important components of the rural population were mobile at all times and in all places. As well as pastoral groups with approved grazing rights that might involve them in medium-range transhumance, there was a flow of casual labour and traders through the security zones. Seasonal labour was a key element of rural business—especially when there were large cereal, grape, and olive harvests to bring in and process. Note that the harvester from *Mactaris* started as just such an itinerant reaper. The people described as *circumcelliones* in the late sources, with a bad reputation for rural violence during the Donatist schism, are almost certainly to be identified with this underprivileged, mobile, and easily roused labour pool.[17]

The bulk of the rural population across North Africa was drawn from the NAIA peoples. There have been previous discussions of the Amazigh/Roman interaction in North Africa, but these sometimes end up producing binary oppositions of civilised and uncivilised, which are not helpful in a postcolonial age.[18] I think we can recognise both regional and chronological diversity, with different groups still active in broadly the same zones they had occupied before: *Libyphoenices* and *Afri* near the coasts, *Numidae* in the area of the ancient eastern Numidian kingdom, *Mauri* in the western Numidian kingdom and Mauretanian kingdom, *Gaetuli* along the military security zones from Atlantic to Greater Syrtes, *Marmaridae* in the desert margins of *Cyrenaica*, and *Garamantes* to south of Tripolitania. The distinctive styles of rural architecture in Roman North Africa spoke to the regional past as much as to the Roman present.[19] This chapter will illustrate the long-term significance of these distinctions.

14. Carlsen 1991 on servile status bailiffs on African estates; Garnsey 1978, 235–37; Ibba 2012; Lenski 2017.
15. Fentress 2011. Augustine, *Letters* 199, mentions that his knowledge of barbarian peoples derived from individuals from those countries who had been captured and traded as slaves; see also Lepelley 2005c, 36–38.
16. Fentress 2013b, 332–33;
17. On this interpretation of the circumcellions, see Shaw 2011, 630–50.
18. See, inter alia, Bénabou 1976; Brett and Fentress 1996; Camps 2007; Fentress 1983; 2006; Fentress and Wilson 2016; Morizot 2013; 2015; Shaw 1983b; 1991b.
19. Fentress et al. 2009, 87–91 (Punic); Fentress 2000c (Berber); Sheldrick 2016 (Gaetulian).

These different groups engaged with the realities of life as subjects of the Roman Empire in many varied ways. Roman material culture, social behaviours, and legal and economic structures all had an impact on people's lives and identity choices. We have seen how identity projections that prioritised Roman norms were employed by the military community and some sectors of urban society to differentiate themselves from others in society. To a lesser extent, we can see this also in rural societies, generally among the elite who chose to flaunt their wealth, status, and education in ways that illustrated their position within Roman colonial structures. But it was also in the rural community that tradition, regionalism, and cultural memory remained strongest and where alternative identity construction was most diverse.[20] Hybridity and ambiguity of identity were also important factors. To give just one brief example, in *Mauretania Caesariensis* there was an ancient tradition of representing important individuals as mounted warriors brandishing spears (cf. Fig. 4.10). The long afterlife of this iconographic theme can be recognised in the style adopted for "Roman" tombstones in the area, whether in a Roman military context (Fig. 11.2a) or from the Kabylie region (Fig. 11.2b–e).[21] The hybridity of imagery passing from Moorish tradition to Roman and vice versa is fascinating.

The family of Firmus, encountered as a 4th-century rebel in Chapter 6, came from this half-and-half world, consolidating their social power and wealth through imperial service and engagement with, inter alia, poetic Latin inscriptions and ownership of large agricultural estates. Yet at the same time, they retained sufficient standing among the less advantaged peoples in the region to mount a sustained challenge to Roman authority as acknowledged rulers of Moorish peoples.[22]

Many aspects of rural identity are difficult for us to access, due to the dearth of evidence available on diet and the social structures around consumption of food and drink, material culture choices, the organisation of domestic versus productive space, and household religious practices. However, there are suggestive hints that cultural choices were not entirely driven by external models. For instance, if we look at the evolution of African Red Slip ware (ARS) production and consumption, it is clear that over time these moved from being influenced by forms and types and vessels produced elsewhere, to disseminating innovative African forms of vessels to other parts of the Mediterranean. These changes in ceramic forms and fashions are, of course, also manifest in the cities, but as the majority of the population was rural, it seems reasonable to infer that the underlying social behaviours of food preparation and consumption dating back to the NAIA played a significant part in the nature of Roman-period developments. Put simply, African ceramics innovated as well as imitated. Furthermore, adoptions of Roman ideas from elsewhere

20. Belkahia et al. 2016.
21. Camps et al. 1999; Laporte 1992; Hamdoune 2005, 243–60; 2018, 158–66.
22. Hamdoune 2018, 155–99 for the most detailed overview.

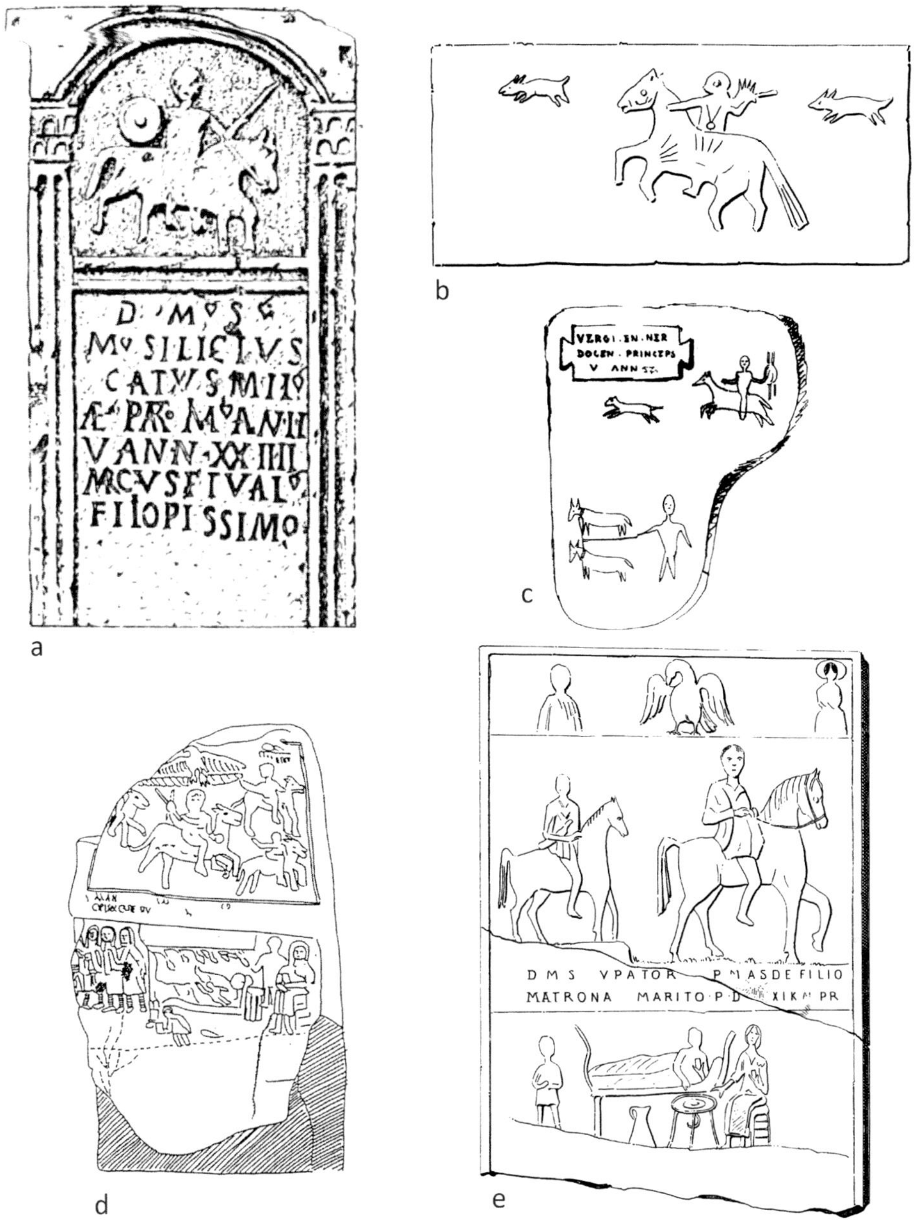

Figure 11.2. The afterlife of Moorish horsemen. a) Military tombstone with traditional Moorish circular shield and spear from *Portus Magnus* (*CIL* 8.21629). b) Stele from Khelouch. c) Tombstone from Touja. d) Tombstone from *Castellum Tulei*. e) Tombstone from Taouga (author's montage after Hamdoune 2005, 259; 2018, 162, 164; Laporte 1992, 415–16).

were often adaptations. To give an example relating to wine consumption, early Roman fine wares included an extensive range of small cups suited to this purpose. However, these forms were much less common in Africa than elsewhere, and some evidence suggests an African preference for drinking wine in larger bowls. Imports of Roman fine wares deposited in Garamantian tombs include numerous examples of the Dragendorff 18 footed bowl (13–15 cm in diameter) but very few cups (Dragendorff 24/25, 27).[23] A mosaic from *Thugga* shows men of presumed servile status pouring wine from amphorae into similarly sized medium bowls rather than cups.[24] When ARS production got fully underway, it eschewed small cups, but had plenty of small to medium bowl forms that could have been used for wine drinking.

Another example of local predilections in foodways concerns the move away from multiple smaller dishes to large platters and large shallow dishes, in both cook wares and serving vessels. Discussion of Roman dining has tended to take a very top-down view of dining-room architecture, with an early focus on rectangular couches (and small tables with individual servings) in the traditional *triclinium*, to a late Roman emphasis on curved communal couches (*stibadia*).[25] Both of these dining-room arrangements can be traced in the architecture of elite Roman houses in Africa,[26] but how did ordinary people eat? Is it possible that the shift from more isolated to more communal dining arrangements in late Roman times actually reflects a transformation of elite and urban dining to more closely reflect communal eating habits of African society more generally? An interesting paper by John Hawthorne demonstrated (by volumetric analysis) that the average size of ARS vessel forms increased over time from the late 1st to mid-3rd century and then remained fairly stable into late antiquity. These seem to clearly relate to an emphasis on communal eating, and the diameter of the largest dishes (such as Hayes 50, in excess of 0.5 m) clearly can contain enough food for a group of four to six people.[27] Nicholas Hudson has developed Hawthorne's idea to demonstrate that by late antiquity this was a generalised phenomenon of the Roman world, but Africa has as good a claim as anywhere to be the originator of such habits.[28] As most houses did not have specialised dining rooms, the probable scenario for eating such meals would be for small groups of people sitting on the floor around a dish, in much the

23. Mattingly 2010a, 313–17 for a cemetery with 50 examples of Dragendorff 18 and just 3 in total of cups Dragendorff 24/25 and 27.
24. Blanchard-Lemée et al. 1996, 76–77. The significance of the "wine bowls" also noted by Dossey 2010, 46–47.
25. Ellis 1997.
26. Carucci 2007; Ghedini and Bullo 2003.
27. Hawthorne 1997, especially 30–33, though note that on 33–36 he linked the increase in vessel size to the growth of Christianity, rather than pre-existing tendencies in African society. Dossey 2010 also notes the important increase in large vessels in rural food consumption during the Roman era as a distinctive phenomenon.
28. Hudson 2010.

same way that traditional meals are still consumed in rural communities across much of the Maghrib and northern Sahara.

Interestingly, from the early Numidian levels onwards at *Althiburos*, there is a strong presence of flat handmade cooking dishes of large diameters, with a capacity to have fed a family group or more—described in the publication as "tajines" and clearly in the same tradition as the modern functional class of vessels that serves both for cooking and serving food.[29] In Garamantian society, while much cooking was evidently done in large casserole-style pots, there was another common type of shallow flat dish (*doka*) that could have been used for serving food, and again there are large diameter versions of this.[30] In the present underdeveloped state of knowledge of the NAIA ceramic repertoire elsewhere, these can stand as suggestive examples. "Tagine culture" and "Couscous culture" can thus be argued to have been an integral part of African society in the NAIA and Roman period and, through the export of ARS, also to have been shared later on with other Mediterranean regions.[31] A group of people huddled round a large dish on the floor was in all probability the sort of meal that a late Roman local magistrate was sharing with his workmen when he was interrupted by visitors.[32] Food remains an understudied aspect of society in Africa under Rome, and is a prime area where we might expect diverse regional and social identities to stand out.[33]

Languages and Identity

The diversity of rural communities in Africa (including much migration due to the imperial context) will have given rise to a great deal of cultural complexity to layer on top of the pre-Roman background distinctions. How might we attempt to track this diversity? A starting point is to look at languages and linguistic practices, though this evidence will always be slanted towards the literate sector of rural society—probably always a small minority and at a more elite level. Nonetheless, some interesting pointers do emerge.

Northern Tunisia provides some significant examples of a very high engagement with Latin, even among rural communities. There was a much higher prevalence of Latin inscriptions and, in the case of the lengthy legal texts that describe the world of the imperial estates, the landscape was literally studded with iterations of

29. Kallala et al. 2016, 90–92, 114–116 (for illustrations). These dishes varied in size from 0.24–0.48 m diameter.
30. Leone 2013a, 364; Mattingly 2007a, 417–19, diameters from 0.24 to 0.44 m. The lack of evidence for burning on underside makes them more likely a serving dish than one used for cooking.
31. Hudson 2010, 676–92; Willett 2012.
32. Birley 1987, 30–31.
33. Déroche and Zink 2016.

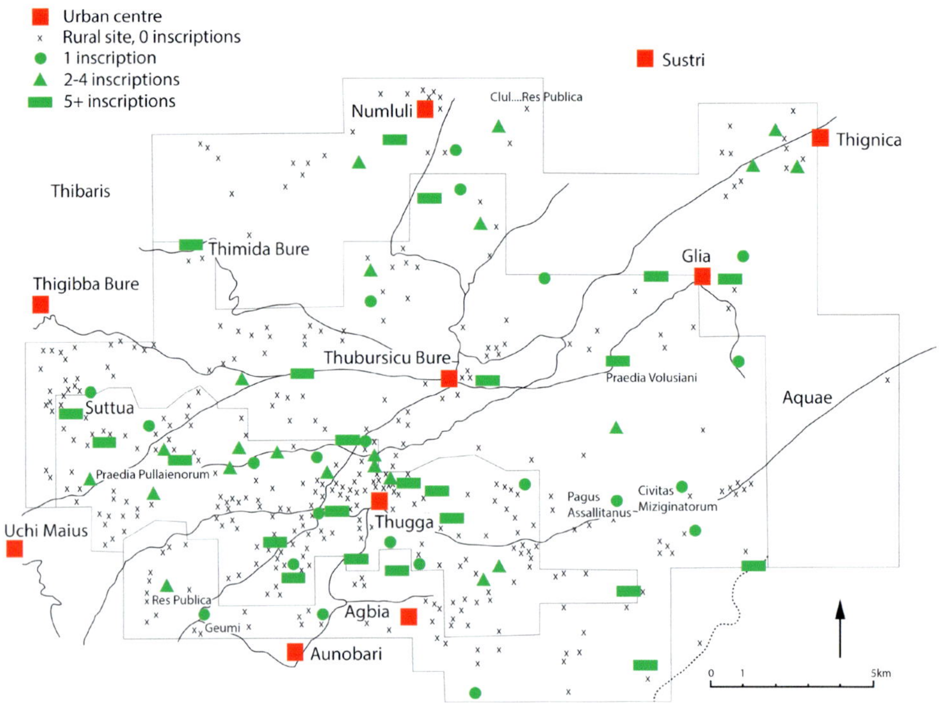

Figure 11.3. Rural inscriptions around *Thugga* (Mike Hawkes, from author's rough based on data in De Vos and Attoui 2013).

the law. This landscape was also dominated by physical boundary markers, setting in stone the *termini* between different forms of land ownership: imperial estates, private landowners, urban lands, lands ascribed to non-urban peoples, and so on.[34] The rural territory related to the town of *Thugga* (estimated at c.80 km^2 beyond the suburban limits of the town) has produced 92 Latin inscriptions, the vast majority tombstones, and this is a clear indication of an unusual level of engagement with Latin epigraphy by the rural population in this highly urbanised area (Fig. 11.3).[35]

Other rural communities were much less engaged with the epigraphic habit and with Latin in particular. In Chapter 9 I reviewed the continuing importance of Punic and Libyan in urban communities, and the tendency was even more pronounced with the rural communities in some regions. An important point to note is that even people with Latinised names sometimes chose to write them in the Libyan alphabet.[36]

One of the most remarkable features about Tripolitania was the region's linguistic diversity as it was manifested in the epigraphic record (Fig. 11.4). While a few

34. De Vos 2013, 183–87. Cf. Christol 2014.
35. Khanoussi and Maurin 2002, 37–38.
36. Aït Kaci 2012; Rebuffat 2005.

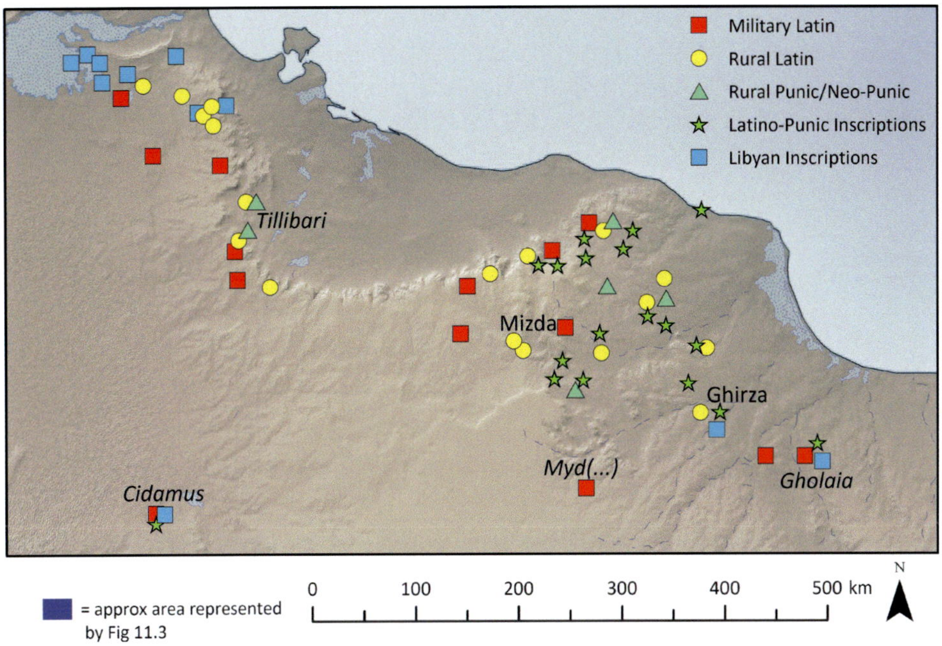

Figure 11.4. Finds of rural inscriptions in Tripolitania (Martin Sterry, from author's rough).

rural inscriptions relate to domestic buildings, often fortified in the late Roman period, the major use of epigraphy appears to have been in funerary contexts, with a dearth of normative Roman religious epigraphy. The disparity between the rural epigraphic habit here compared with the tiny territory of *Thugga* is striking—the latter has yielded more than double the number of Latin rural texts and from c.0.04% of the area of Tripolitania.

Socially contingent linguistic preferences are a recurrent pattern across the pre-desert communities of Tripolitania, though there are clear differences between western and eastern regions, in large part related to the great salient of wadi farming in the eastern Tripolitanian pre-desert. In southern Tunisia, by contrast, there is less evidence of Punic language in rural districts. With a few exceptions, such as two neo-Punic texts on mausolea from the region of Tatahouine,[37] the overwhelming majority of rural inscriptions were either Latin funerary texts (mainly from mausolea, rather than tombstones—see further below) or Libyan inscriptions, the latter mainly from the arid Dahar plain rather than the agricultural lands of the Jabal and coastal zones. Most of the Latin and Punic inscriptions in western Tripolitania lie within a narrow band along the military *limes* road. The pattern in rural eastern Tripolitania was rather different, with larger numbers of neo-Punic

37. Trousset 1974, 107 (Tatahouine) and 113 (al-Amrouni)

Table 11.1. Rural inscriptions from Tripolitania (Note: The totals for Latin texts do not include milestones, garrison settlements, or the late antique Christian cemeteries of Ain Zara and en-Ngila close to Tripoli. Many Latin inscriptions in *IRT* have been here reclassified as Latino-Punic, following Kerr 2007; the Latino-Punic total includes 12 texts from catacombs at Sirte, 2 of unknown provenance and 3 from suburban cemeteries of *Lepcis Magna*.)

Region	Latin	Punic/Neo-Punic	Latino Punic	Libyan
Eastern Tripolitania	27	6	68	60
Western Tripolitania	13	3		20
Total	40	9	68	80

and Latino-Punic inscriptions (the latter especially indicating the longevity of a spoken Punic dialect in the countryside) and proportionally fewer Latin texts, though there is an important group of texts from the mausolea at Ghirza.[38] Table 11.1 reflects the regional differences between east and west Tripolitania and shows the surprising minority engagement with Latin in rural landscapes there compared to Punic and Libyan. This patterning seems to be the result of specific cultural preferences and choices, rather than illiteracy and ignorance of Roman norms.

To focus on eastern Tripolitania for the moment, comparatively few Latin texts have been found outside the towns and military community. There are rural examples of neo-Punic texts, but in general these are more frequent closer to the Libyphoenician coastal cities. Most notable is the dedication of the *Ammonium* of Ras al-Haddagia in the Jabal Tarhuna,

> To the Lord Ammon: this divine statue of a bull and the sanctuary of his rooms and the porticoes which has built and consecrated, in the year of the proconsul in the land of the Libyans Lucius Aelius Lamia, NKSP son of Shasidwasan, the son of NMRR, who is among the sons of Masankaw, at his own expense completely.

The reference to the Proconsul Aelius Lamia dates this to 17–19 CE and, as Andrew Wilson notes, the periphrasis "in the land of the Libyans" for "*provincia Africae*" shows the interplay of bilingual translation here, as at 1st-century CE *Lepcis Magna*.[39] It is interesting to note that the dedicant was a Gaetulian (of the *Macae*?), expressing his lineage in a typically Libyan way. The massive mausoleum at nearby Gasr Doga also originally bore a neo-Punic text of similar type.[40] Another cemetery in

38. On Latino-Punic inscriptions, see Kerr 2007. When first encountered, these were wrongly classed as Latino-Libyan by Goodchild 1950b.
39. *IPT* 76; Wilson 2012b, 286.
40. Bigi et al. 2009, 37–39.

the Jabal, at Saniet al-Crema, yielded a fragmentary bilingual Latin/neo-Punic text, again to an individual with a Libyan cognomen.[41] Several early mausolea in the pre-desert area also bore Punic texts, relating to people of distinctive Libyan lineages, with less commonly Punic names.[42]

> The tomb in absolute ownership, which Masawkan made for his father Yamrur, son of Gatit of the M.s.li and for his mother Zut, daughter of Gatidan/Ganidan the T.g.l.bi/N.g.l.bi and for his son and for his wife Asliyat daughter of Yankdassan, son of Siyuk of the T.g.l.bi/N.g.l.bi. O woe that there are four. The tomb was made at his expense and during his life and the lives of his sons Arisham and Iosdan.[43]

These inscriptions attest to Punic-speaking Libyan people in the Tripolitanian hinterland, who mainly went by Libyan names, but with occasional Phoenician or semitic examples incorporated alongside. This practice went on throughout the Roman period, and regular Latin inscriptions remained extremely rare in the countryside, apart from in the context of the Roman army. The compilers of *Inscriptions of Roman Tripolitania* in the 1950s had to struggle with many puzzling inscriptions that appeared to be in Latin letters, but defied translation as such. These are now understood to be Latino-Punic texts, transcribing the long-surviving local Punic vernacular in Latin script.[44] Of currently published inscriptions in Latin letters from the pre-desert region, 79% are of Latino-Punic type: that is, engraved in Latin letters but expressing the local Punic language. Personal nomenclature is dominated by Libyan onomastics, though there are some Punic and occasional Latinised names.[45] In addition, there are a number of Libyan written texts, which still defy modern attempts to read them in full.

Ghirza is a key mid-to-late Roman site in the Libyan desert and one of the few to have been excavated on any scale.[46] It is notable for its elaborate *aedicula*/temple tombs decorated with many relief carvings.[47] Several of the funerary texts at Ghirza are in Latin and record people with Roman first names (Marcus, Marcia) but Libyan *cognomina* (Chullam, Fydel, Maccurasan, Mathlich, Metusan, Nasif, Nimira, Thesylgum, Varnychsin).[48] These Latin texts are the longest and have attracted most attention. They detail the construction

41. *IPT* 80: *MSQ[N]*; *IRT* 860: *D M Flabi[..] Mysu[ca]n vixit a XL.*
42. *IPT* 77–79 (al-Amud), 81 (Bir Gebira). For the sites, see Barker et al. 1996b, 165–67, 183.
43. *IPT* 77; Mattingly 1995, 163–65 for reconstruction of the family trees).
44. Reynolds and Ward-Perkins 1952; the material has been reviewed by Kerr 2007. See also the online edition of *IRT2021*.
45. Mattingly 1995, 160–68, 205–09.
46. Brogan and Smith 1984; Barker et al. 1996a/b; Mattingly 1995, 206–07; 1999; 2011a.
47. Brogan and Smith 1984, 119–203; Mattingly 2011a, 247–53.
48. *IRT* 898–900, Brogan and Smith 1984, 260–262, nos 1–4, 6; online version *IRT2021*, *IRT* 994.

of tombs to parents by their children and, in some cases, the cost of the monuments, including food for the workmen employed.

> Of M(archius) Nasif and M(archia) Mathlich, mother; the Marchii Nimira and Fydel, their sons, had this built for their dear parents. (*IRT* 899, Tomb NA)

> Marchius Fydel and Flavia Thesylgum, father and mother of Marchius Metusan who had this memorial made for them, and have reckoned that there was spent on this, in coin [·· ? ··] thousand *folles* and in addition the food for the workmen. May my sons and grandsons read (this) in good fortune and build others like it. (*IRT* 900, Tomb NB)[49]

> Marchius Chullam and Varnychsin, father and mother of the Marchii Nimmira and [?M]accurasan, who had this memorial built for them. We paid out in reckoning for these things, in coin on salaries a total of forty-five thousand six hundred *folles*, in addition to the food for the workmen. May their sons and grandsons visit it happily. (*IRT* 898, Tomb NC)

A fourth Latin text, found in association with tomb A in the north cemetery, commemorated a sacrifice described by the Latin religious term *parentalia*, but clearly relating to something quite distinctive to the Libyan context as it involved the slaughter of 51 bulls and 38 goats.[50]

There are also at least three texts on the Ghirza tombs in Latino-Punic.[51] The most complete of these was almost certainly dealing with the same types of monument (described in very similar terms to the Latin texts) and even the same families whose relationships are recorded in the Latin texts; it eschews the Latin first names and used only the Libyan cognomina (Nasif, Thualath).[52] This looks like a statement of a different sort of identity on the part of some members of the community who were foregrounding their Punic and Libyan culture ahead of their affinity with Roman ways. The majority of the Ghirza tombs have no inscriptions at all—does this represent lack of access to literate stonecutters, or diminishing relevance in identity displays of inscribed commemoration in the later years of the settlement?

---

49. Translations here and below adapted from 2021 online version of *IRT*.
50. *IRT* 994: *sacrificia parentaliorum tauros n(umero) LI quinquaginta e[t unum] capros [n(umero)] [XX]XVIII tri[ginta o]ct[o...]* ("The following [---] commemorator of the M[..]nei is Mon[.]san, son of Voc[.]is; he set up for all his ?family ?for whom [---] the day of his victories he presented the sacrificial animals of the parentalia, bulls to the number of 51, goats to the number of 38 [---]"). See also Brogan and Smith 1984, 262, n. 6. For discussion, see Mattingly 2011a, 265.
51. *IRT* 901; Brogan and Smith 1984, 262, no. 5, 7; Kerr 2007, 142–144, Ghirza LP 1–3.
52. Kerr, 2007, 142 (Ghirza LP 1): "The memorial which made Thualath, daughter of Hasif, which she made for her parents." *IRT* 901; Brogan and Smith 1984, 262–63.

There are also some 36 ancient Libyan inscriptions from the settlement and tombs at Ghirza, including a notable set on 5 altars and other religious paraphernalia (1 or 2 bowls) in a temple there.[53] These texts have often been overlooked in discussions of the site, which have sought to play up its "Roman" affinities, but their numbers, their centrality to religious practices, their distribution on both the main tombs (3 examples) and buildings of the settlement (13), all suggest Libyan was the primary language of Ghirza's community. Interestingly, the temple yielded no Latin or Latino-Punic texts, showing how literate practices related not solely to linguistic abilities, but also depended on social context and choices about the use of a particular writing system in one context or another. Brogan also recorded 13 Libyan texts from other pre-desert sites and tombs (Wadis Umm al-Agerem, Bir Schedua (2), Gheslan (2), Gasr al-Gebab (2), al-Qurrayyat al-Garbia, Khanafes (2), Shetaf, Sofeggin, Tininai),[54] Rebuffat reported 11 Libyan graffiti in a building in the garrison settlement at *Gholaia*,[55] and there are at least another 20 Libyan inscriptions known from western Tripolitania.[56] This total of 80 ancient Libyan inscriptions for Tripolitania echoes finds of numerous Libyan texts in the Garamantian heartlands to the south of Tripolitania, showing that there was a widespread Libyan epigraphic tradition, even if most texts were relatively short and difficult to make sense of.[57]

The broad differences in engagement with the epigraphic habit between urban, rural, and military sites in Tripolitania can be expressed in simplified tabular form (Table 11.2). There were evidently significant divergences in broad patterns of cultural behaviour between the three groups, with the army and the urban community closer to each other in the extent of their engagement with Latin and with metropolitan Roman cultural norms. There remain some signal differences between these town-dwellers and the military community, and the rural community had little in common with either group.

Although much religious practice appears to have been anepigraphic, it is interesting that funerary rites (perhaps linked to the ancestor cult) took on Latin and Latino-Punic expression, while cultic altars and other cultic objects from the temple at Ghirza were engraved, if at all, with Libyan characters. Finally, although Latin and Latino-Punic became the main languages of inscriptions in the region overall by the 2nd century CE, Punic and Libyan must have remained important spoken languages by sectors of the community in all three of my broad communities.

53. Brogan and Smith 1984, 250–57. Fentress and Wilson 2016, 52, 57–59 argue for a late reintroduction of the Libyan script there, though on rather slight circumstantial grounds.

54. Brogan and Smith 1984, 252, 257. Cf. also Brogan 1975.

55. Rebuffat 1992b.

56. Ghaki 1995, 95–97.

57. For Garamantian Libyan inscriptions, see Barnett 2019a, 161–66; Daniels 1975; Mattingly 2010a, 348–50; 2013a, 517–18.

Table 11.2. Comparisons of the epigraphic habit across the military, urban, and rural communities in Tripolitania (covers inscribed altars; Baal/Saturn stelae; Latin, Punic (including Neo-Punic), Latino-Punic and Libyan inscriptions).

	Altars	Stelae	Tombstones	Latin epig.	Punic epig.	Latino-Punic epig.	Libyan epig.
Military community	Many	Rare	Many	Many	Rare	Rare	Some
Urban community	Many	Some	Many	Many	Many	Rare	Rare
Rural communities	Rare	Rare	Rare	Rare	Some	Many	Many

Another example of distinctive regional linguistic profile comes from an area only c.50 km west of *Thugga* and contrasts with the high emphasis on Latin in the latter district. St Augustine, the bishop of *Hippo Regius*, is often quoted for his comments about the continuing vitality of Punic as a spoken language in the hinterland of that city, though there is a dearth of epigraphic evidence to support it.[58] What we do find, though, is an extraordinary concentration of Libyan inscriptions, including some examples of bilinguals or Latin/Libyan combinations (this corresponds with the densest cluster on Fig. 11.5). No bilingual examples are certainly dated later than the 3rd century CE, and while some of these occur in urban cemeteries, many are rural.[59] The cluster is a unique memorial to a Libyan epigraphic habit maintained by an ethnic group, and it reminds us that in rural districts Libyan was probably the most widespread spoken language.

Figure 11.5 summarises the evidence for the distribution of Libyan inscriptions across North Africa. The lack of systematic records in many areas means this is a drastic underrepresentation, though for many parts of the Sahara where the tradition of inscribing in Libyan script (*tifinagh*) has continued to the modern populations, I have concentrated on examples of certain antiquity only.[60] It is a sobering reminder nonetheless of the ubiquitous presence of the Libyan languages across the Roman provinces, challenging our normative response to the volume of Latin inscriptions. The density in the former Massylian and Masaesylian territories of the Maghrib is of particular note.

One of the interesting points about both the Libyan texts from south of *Hippo* and the Latino-Punic texts from Tripolitania is that the choice of written language highlighted a non-Roman aspect of identity, which was not only exclusive to those in society who had the ability to read it, but also effectively imposed distance between this group and literate people who lacked linguistic understanding of Libyan or Punic. The fact that a few inscriptions in rural Tripolitania were also

58. Lepelley 2003; 2005a. For the distribution of Punic and neo-Punic inscriptions in the hinterland, see Février 1990, 116.
59. Camps 1994c; 1996; Chabot 1940; Février 1990, 114–20; Ghaki 1995; Rebuffat 2005; 2013;
60. See Barnett 2019a; Biagetti et al. 2012; 2015.

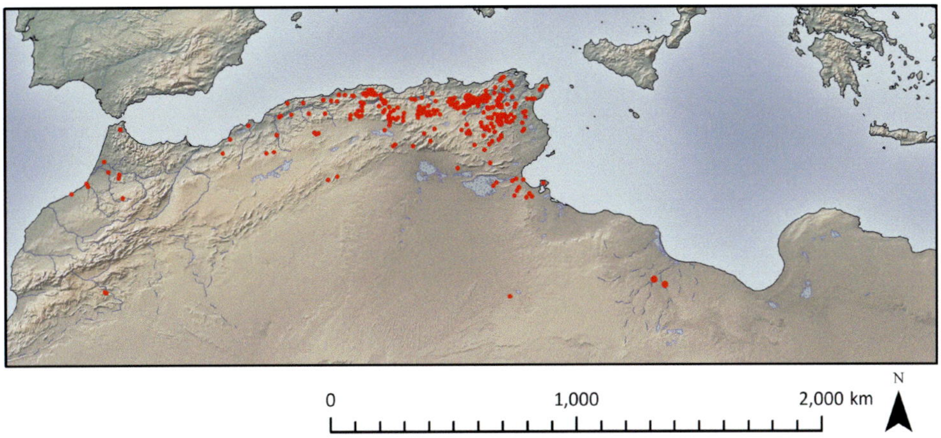

Figure 11.5. Generalised distribution of Libyan inscriptions across North Africa (Martin Sterry, from author's rough based on Camps 1999; Ghaki 1995).

in Latin, or bilingual in the case of the Libyan texts in the hinterland of *Hippo*, does not alter the fact that the majority linguistic choice reflected a non-Latinate identity. Much more work is needed on Libyan inscriptions—one has the sense that the scholarly priority accorded to Latin texts has inhibited systematic recording of the Libyan epigraphy, though there has been a resurgence of interest in recent years.[61]

Rural sites occasionally yield up informal written documents, such as ink writing on pottery sherds (ostraca) or wooden tablets. A recent listing of known examples from North Africa shows a strong association with port cities and with military bases.[62] There are nonetheless a number of documents that have been found at rural locations or that plainly related to Roman estates. These occur in multiple languages: (neo-)Punic: Cussabat; Greek: *Lepcis Magna*; Latin: Henchir Bou Gornine, Ksar Koutine, Albertini tablets, the Sfez collection, Bir Trouch, Henchir al-Maize, Henchir Khanefi, Henchir al-Abiod, Henchir Tuta; Latino-Punic: Wadi al-Amud.[63] One striking aspect of such discoveries in Africa is that the vast majority are of late Roman, Vandal, or Byzantine date. This may be a bias in the admittedly small sample, but one also wonders whether the spread of Christianity in rural districts may have also influenced the greater production of such documents, testifying to contracts, sales, inventories, and perhaps rudimentary accounts.[64] These are what Leslie Dossey calls "textual communities," whereby the disruption of traditional power structures and the rise of the Christian church opened new pathways for

61. Galand 1989; 2005; Ghaki 1995; Rebuffat 2013.
62. Várhelyi and Bagnall 2009, 343–44.
63. Most sites referred to by Várhelyi and Bagnall 2009; for the Sfez collection, see Rothenhöfer and Blänsdorf 2016.
64. Courtois et al. 1952; cf. Conant 2012b.

rural communities to participate in literate acts.[65] Nonetheless, it should not surprise us to find documentary records related to rural production at earlier dates associated with major estate centres, nor for that matter with farms in the security zone that were involved in supply arrangements with the Roman garrisons, as attested by ostraca from the fort of *Gholaia* (Bu Nijim). While, the overall epigraphic picture from rural districts is thin regardless of the language, there was clearly some significant regional differentiation.

Rural Gods and Identity

The starting point for my discussion is Alain Cadotte's collation of the known dedications of different cults in North Africa, documenting a range of cults with helpful distribution maps.[66] His interpretative framework rests on the twin pillars of *interpretatio Romana* (syncretism) and Romanisation, which he sees as working in parallel with each other: Religious syncretism is presented as an "inevitable phenomenon" of the Roman world, because polytheistic religions were by their nature particularly assimilative.[67] The co-association of divinities in rival pagan pantheons may seem very straightforward when framed in this way, but postcolonial theorisation has suggested greater complexity of practice.[68] Cadotte seems to assume that syncretism is always present, and always in the same way, when a Roman god is named in an inscription in North Africa. His language also imputes that syncretism indicates the dominance of Roman gods over local ones and the active employment of syncretism as a tool of Roman social control (this is very old style Romanisation).[69] He is correct to emphasise the strong evidence for the continuing worship of local gods under the cover of Latin names, but by imposing such an old-fashioned and limited interpretative framework, he fails to ask important questions about what his distribution maps actually reveal about regional and ethnic differences in religious practice.

Ever since Marcel Bénabou's masterly argument about religious resistance to Rome, the importance of Libyan and Punic gods in the pantheon of Africa under Rome has been widely acknowledged.[70] It is clear that for many Roman cults there were at least two distinctive types of occurrence in Africa: one following official or external Roman norms of making dedications to a Roman god, with all its signifiers

65. Dossey 2010, 174.
66. Cadotte 2007.
67. Cadotte 2007, 1–10. Cf. also Leglay 1975; 1991.
68. Webster 1997a; 1997b. For North Africa, see notably the subtle overview analyses of McCarty 2016; 2022; Shaw 2013b.
69. These same issues are picked up in a review by Dondin-Payre 2009.
70. Bénabou 1976, 261–380. On the pre-Roman background, see also Lipiński1995; Shaw 2013b.

and attributes; and the other involving the worship of local divinities that had been linked by name with a Roman god. In many of the latter cases, the specific qualities, attributes, and areas of action were rather different to the traditional Roman cult.[71] Rural religion was particularly likely to reflect the second type of association, leading to what Bénabou terms the "Africanisation" of Roman cults.[72] In this respect, the pagan Roman interlude marks one among multiple moments of religious non-conformism in North Africa, Christianity and Islam included.[73] The repeated periods of imperial rule over the region to some extent favoured the emergence of religious revitalisation movements or non-conformist religious practices, especially among rural populations. Rural observance of Roman state religion was much rarer, and exceptions are always instructive. A concentration of dedications to the imperial cult among the villages (*castella*) near *Sitifis*, for example, can be explained by the fact that these were made by *coloni* on imperial estates there.[74] This illustrates the fact that rural religion was not always conservative and unchanging, but rather that religious practices were sometimes a key area of social change and discrepant identities within colonial territory.

One of the unusual aspects of *Africa* when compared to *Gallia* or *Britannia* is that there seems to have been a high level of uptake of Latin names for local gods (in line with the higher engagement with the epigraphic habit in general).[75] Thinly disguised as Roman divine equivalents in epigraphy and iconography, the core attributes of these divinities reflect an African penchant for chthonic forces, and a prevailing interest in fertility, fecundity, weather, the seasons, desert routes, and water. Saturn, Caelestis, Neptune, Mercury, for example, had very distinctive specificities in Africa.[76] However, is it correct to talk of a simple syncretism of Punic-Libyan gods to Roman ones? Did this lead to a standardised Romano-African religious package?

I want to suggest first of all that there are grounds for making a broad distinction between the religious practices and beliefs of rural communities in the northern and southern parts of *Africa*/Tripolitania. To some extent this corresponds with the old cultural division between *Numidae* and *Gaetuli*, emphasising once again the long-term significance of that distinction. For this reason I divide my comments below between the Numidian/Mauretanian and Gaetulian zones.

Much of what we know of the Libyan gods relies on their apparent syncretism with Roman counterparts (see Table 11.3). However, at first sight, the syncretism

71. Bénabou 1976, 331–33.
72. Bénabou 1976, 331–75.
73. Webster 1999 for druidism in Britain and Gaul as a revitalisation movement. See McCarty 2013; 2017; 2019 for the Roman-era Saturn cult in inland North Africa as an "invented tradition."
74. Stone 2008.
75. Cadotte 2007, 9.
76. See, inter alia, Bénabou 1976; Cadotte 2007; Leglay 1966b; Shaw 2013b, 236–39, 246–49.

Table 11.3. Correlations of Roman and Punico-Libyan gods.

Punic/Libyan divinity	Roman equivalent	Attributes/powers	Reference
Baal Hammon	Saturn	Sun/moon, sky, weather, seasons, fertility, fecundity, human prosperity, supreme god	Bénabou 1976, 370–75; Cadotte 2007, 25–63
Tinnit	Iuno, Caelestis (sometimes Iuno Caelestis)	Female agricultural deity, nursemaid of Saturn	Bénabou 1976, 362–69; Cadotte 2007, 65–111
Baal Addir	Mercury, Silvanus (sometimes Mercury Silvanus is assimilated)	Trade (less common in Africa), olive production, agricultural production in general, woods and forests	Bénabou 1976, 341–47; Cadotte 2007, 113–64
Shadrapa	Liber Pater	Wine, agriculture	Bénabou 1976, 351–56; Cadotte 2007, 253–81
Melqart, Milk'ashtart	Hercules	Protector of routes	Bénabou 1976; Cadotte 2007, 283–305
Hadad, Canaphar and others	Mars	War, horses, agriculture	Bénabou 1976, 347–51
Chthonic deities	Neptune, Pluto	Underworld, water	Bénabou 1976, 356–59; Cadotte 2007, 307–24, 325–41
Chthonic fertility deities	Cereres	Underworld, fertility	Bénabou 1976; Cadotte 2007, 343–61
Celestial powers	Sol, Luna	Annual cycle	Bénabou 1976; Cadotte 2007, 362–84
Eshmoun	Aesculapius, Apollo	Healing cults	Bénabou 1976, 359–62; Benseddik 2014; Cadotte 2007, 165–200
Ashtart, Astarte	Venus, Fortuna	Fortune, protector of cities	Bénabou 1976; Cadotte 2007, 201–52
Ammon	Iupiter Ammon	Supreme god of desert communities, desert routes and travel, sun, human protector, oracular cult.	Bénabou 1976, 334–38

attested epigraphically or iconographically tends to take us back to Phoenician gods rather than African ones—though it must be noted that our knowledge of the African pantheon is more limited. Nonetheless, drawing on a wide variety of sources, Camps was able to name and briefly describe 50 African gods, spanning across the Moorish, Numidian, and Gaetulian zones. The inscribed relief

Macurtam Macurgum Vihinam Bonchor Varsissima Matilam Iunam

Figure 11.6. The *Vaga* relief of Libyan gods (author's adapted version after Corbier and Griesheimer 2005, 112).

from near the town of *Vaga* (Fig. 11.6) lists seven gods (Macurtam, Macurgum, Vihinam, Bonchor, Varsissima, Matilam and Iunam) with a rather mixed iconography of Roman and local symbolism (*CIL* 8.14394).[77] The date palms visible to rear reference the African context (though *Vaga* is well north of the oasis zone). The specific attributes of the gods allow us to identify at either end of the line two figures equated with Libyan horsemen gods/Dioscuri (Macurtam and Iunam). Given the importance of the horse in North African society and warfare, and in historic era rock art, for instance, it is no surprise that there should be horseman gods in the local pantheon. The second figure from the left (Macurgum) was evidently a healer, being associated with a scroll and the healing staff of Aesculapius—suggesting that the dense cluster of evidence for "Aesculapius" in the east *Numidae* heartlands related to a local god.[78] In the centre of the group sits a possibly pre-eminent male god, Bonchor, holding a club. He is flanked by two female divinities (Vihinam and Varsissima), plausibly with links to fertility. The final god Matilam is shown sacrificing a ram. The Vaga relief thus shows that there were African equivalents available for at least some of the Roman and Punic pantheon.

77. Benseddik 2003; Camps 1954; 1995c; *AE* 1948, no. 114: *Macvrtam Macvrgvm Vihinam Bonchor Varsissima Matilam Ivnam/ M Aemilivs Ianvarivs et Q Aelivs Felix de svo fecervnt et dedicrv/.*

78. Benseddik 2003; 2014; Camps 1995c. The distribution of all North African evidence for Aesculapius correlates strongly with the eastern Maghrib and the Libyphoenician cities, with rare occurrences in Roman *Numidia* and *Mauretania* (especially the Gaetulian zone) mainly related to the garrison community.

Another example concerns a temple at *Magifa* (Hr Matkides near the Algerian/Tunisia frontier north of *Theveste*) that evidently featured statues of the gods Masiden, Thililva, Suggan, Iesdan and Masiddica.[79] This is in the Gaetulian zone, but in a sector with a strong impact of veteran settlement, so the precise local significance of these gods is not certain. The imbalances in the epigraphic evidence—there are virtually no other references to these cults—may be highly misleading. From *Simitthu* comes a relief carving of another local pantheon of eight unnamed divinities, of which one was female.[80] It is quite possible that worship of these sorts of cults continued to be conducted largely through non-epigraphic practices at locations that may not have been particularly monumental. Some of the same people who made Roman-style dedications at temples to gods and emperors in the Roman pantheon within the towns may have found it no contradiction in another part of their religious identity to engage in different (non-epigraphic) ways with old gods at suburban and rural sanctuaries.

In some locations we also find dedications and relief sculptures pertaining to African cults, expressed as a collectivity of "Dii Mauri."[81] In total there are 20 inscriptions that refer to the Dii Mauri.[82] There is an interesting difference between the dedicants to African gods, in that more than 80% of those honouring the Dii Mauri were members of the military community, while more than 80% of dedicants to individually named Libyan deities were civilians.[83] That reflects interesting differences in engagement with non-syncretised gods, with imperial agents tending to approach them via blanket appeals to local gods and spirits, in contrast to more personalised civilian acts. It is also likely that the epigraphic evidence we have represents the tip of a substantial iceberg of non-epigraphic religious practices involving the local gods. This is particularly apparent if we consider the distribution of the known inscriptions[84]—almost all come from the areas of North Africa where the epigraphic habit was strongest (the same zone of the north-eastern Maghrib that features strongly on Cadotte's maps of "Roman cults" or from garrison settlements in *Tripolitana*, *Numidia*, and *Mauretania*). The traditional understanding of the Dii Mauri has been that they were predominantly gods of the peoples on the fringes of the provinces and beyond. There must have been a vast amount of religious behaviour in those regions that is simply invisible

79. Camps 1995c; *CIL* 8.16749/ *ILAlg* 1, 2977: *Diis Magifae Avg Q T Politicvs simvlacra deorvm n v/ Masidenis et Thililvae et Sugganis et Iesdanis et Masiddice et templvm /a fondamentis ex sva pecvnia fecit ex HS VIII n itq capiti viso ipsis atpetentibvs cum /suis omnibvs usla bbmb/.* To judge from the low price (HS 8,000) for temple and images of the five gods, this was quite a small rural shrine.

80. Lassère 2015, 3.

81. Bénabou 1976, 309–330; Camps 1954; 1995c; Fentress 1978.

82. Camps 1995c for the lists of both Dii Mauri inscriptions and the 50 individual gods.

83. Camps 1995c for table.

84. Camps 1995c fig. 2.

epigraphically. I also think that this formulation is too black and white—a classic Romanisation opposition between civilised and barbarian—and on the available evidence I think we need to accept that there was a more substantial engagement with such gods within the provinces as well, even if the form of worship continued to be traditional, and epigraphic commemoration of transactions and iconographic representation the exception rather than the norm. Much rural religious practice was no doubt aimed at local gods with African names but is masked by variations in the epigraphic habit.

The Saturn Cult

Since Marcel Leglay's magisterial studies, the popularity of the Saturn cult in the Roman period has been seen as a strong element of continuity with pre-Roman tradition. African Saturn is generally understood to have been the Roman-era manifestation of the Punic cult of Baal Hammon, a chthonic deity with a sacrificial ritual linked to immolation of infants and the deposit of the remains in sacred spaces known as tophets. Bénabou went further in seeing the Saturn cult as a key element of religious resistance to Roman rule. However, recent studies by Matthew McCarty suggest further complexity of interpretation.[85] While the ultimate origins of the cult are much debated, McCarty has argued persuasively that the eventual popularity of Baal among the *Numidae* and other northern Libyan groups post-dates the destruction of *Qart Hadasht* in 146 BCE. Thousands of stelae associated with the Baal/Saturn cult have been found at more than 100 locations, but the dating of only a few sites (*Carthage*, *Utica*, *Hadrumetum*, and *Cirta*) goes back as early as the 2nd century BCE and most are considerably later (Fig. 11.7a). In other words, the integration of African elements with a semitic cult occurred *after* Rome replaced *Qart Hadasht* as the regional superpower, and its practice spread especially during the period when Rome incorporated the *Numidae* into the Empire.[86] The Saturn cult, despite its Punic origins, might thus be seen as an "invented tradition," primarily as a revitalisation cult as part of the response of African and Libyphoenician populations to incorporation into the Roman Empire.

The overall geographic extent of the Baal Hammon/Saturn cult is very striking in its density and zonal coverage (Fig. 11.7). There was limited uptake of the African Saturn cult outside the northern regions of *Africa* and *Numidia*, with the sparse Mauretanian dedications essentially relating to connections with the military community there. The cult does not appear to have made much impact on the Moorish population at large. The overwhelming majority of dedications

85. Bénabou 1976, 370–75; Leglay 1961; 1966a/b; McCarty forthcoming b.
86. McCarty 2022, 289–93. See also McCarty 2010a; 2017; 2019; 2021; forthcoming b.

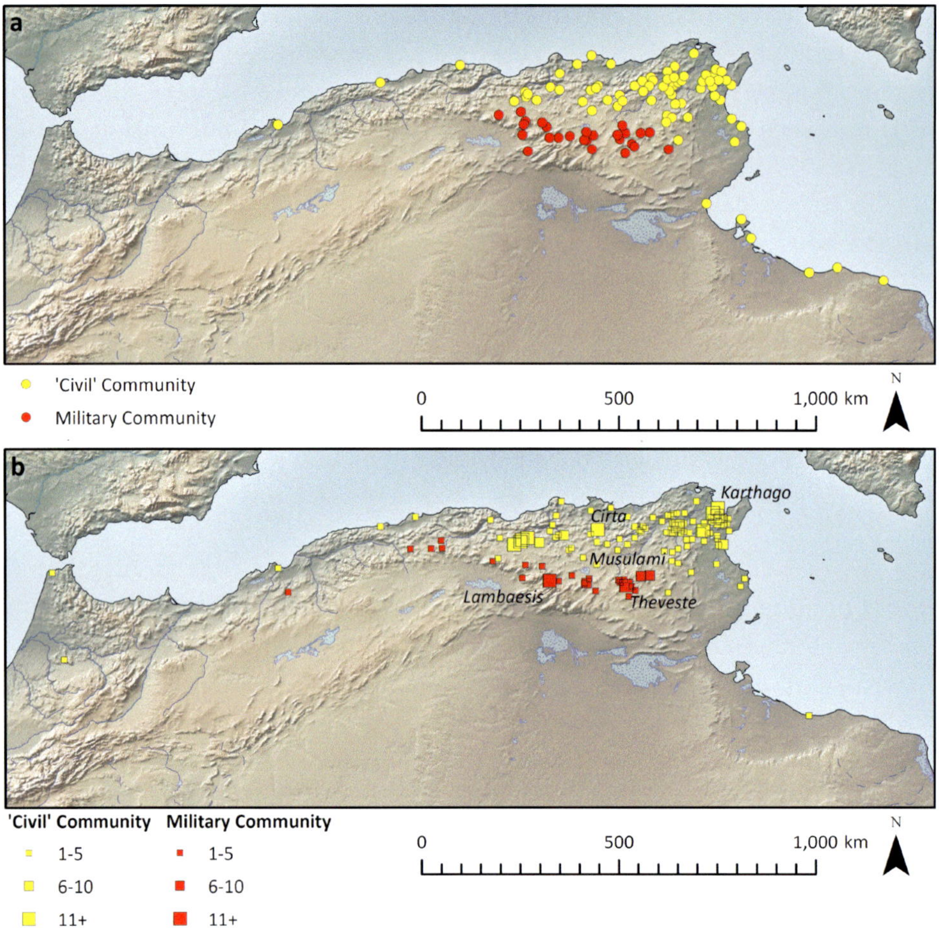

Figure 11.7. Distribution of Saturn cult in *Mauretania* and *Africa*. a) Saturn temples and stelae/statues. (Martin Sterry, after Leglay 1961, 1966a/b; McCarty 2019.) b) Saturn inscriptions (Martin Sterry, after Cadotte 2007).

to Saturn and of votive stelae associated with the cult (both inscribed and uninscribed) emphasise a close association with the *pertica* of *Karthago*, with the area of the eastern Libyphoenician centres, and with the lands of the eastern Numidian (Massylian) kingdom (Fig. 11.7). Remarkably similar distributions also apply to a range of other "Roman" gods that seem to equate with African chthonic deities. These were all areas which had a strong engagement with Punic language and culture in the pre-Roman period. There are some indications that parts of the distribution were shaped by colonial infrastructures. For example, McCarty has pointed to a concentration of Saturn sanctuary sites along the roads from *Karthago* to *Theveste* and *Theveste* to *Cuicul*, focused on a number of key centres related to the military community.[87] The concentration of evidence for the Saturn cult in the Aurès mountain region, nominally part of the Gaetulian zone, appears primarily associated with military bases and veteran settlements there. However, south of the Aurès the cult is poorly represented, even at forts in the pre-desert zone.

Although some tophet sites are known on Jerba and the adjacent mainland of western Tripolitania and near *Lepcis*, *Sabratha*, and *Oea* in eastern Tripolitania, there is the general lack of evidence from the southern parts of *Africa* and *Numidia* or the Mauretanias. In broad terms, therefore, I argue that the Saturn cult was strongly identified with the eastern *Numidae* and the eastern Punic/Libyphoenician communities, while the *Gaetuli* communities disassociated from the cult. For example, there is an interesting hole in the distribution maps of both Saturn stelae and Saturn inscriptions in the area north of *Ammaedara* and *Theveste*, corresponding with the territory of the *Musulami*—a further indication to my mind that the *Musulami* were *Gaetuli* rather than *Numidae* (Fig. 11.7). The limited evidence for tophets in Tripolitania, and their absence away from the major Libyphoenician cities there, is interesting in that in other respects there was a strong regional connection with Punic culture. Here, then, the link between Libyphoenician identity and Baal/Saturn, so strong in north and central Tunisia, seems to break down, but as I have argued, the southern Libyphoenician cities involved the *Gaetuli* peoples and, with rare exceptions, these groups diverged in their religious outlook from the *Numidae*. This geographically constrained religious landscape is also apparent in relation to a broader and frequently linked group of chthonic deities favoured by the *Numidae* and eastern *Libyphoenices*.[88] Neptune is another example of a cult popular in Numidian inland locations that links to a pre-Roman divinity.[89]

Saturn sanctuaries and stelae fields are commonly associated with urban centres, but I suggest that to some extent the cult may more appropriately be thought of as one of the rural populace. The "urban" association can be questioned firstly in terms of the precise location of Saturn sanctuaries at towns. Saturn stelae and temples were, in fact, generally erected in *suburban* locations, close to the cemetery zones, and linked with funerary rituals and practices. In a more general way, suburban temples were also focused on the African chthonic cults, reflecting their rural roots and primary focus on rural issues like weather, crop fertility and productivity, and water.[90] The female divinity, Tinnit/Caelestis, and other chthonic deities were often closely linked with Baal/Saturn.

---

87. McCarty 2010b; 2010c; forthcoming b.
88. The rural sanctuary of Henchir el-Hami stands in as the best example of Saturn sanctuary. Ferjaoui 2007, 88–111 reveals that a range of cults were worshipped along the prime focus on Baal Hammon/Saturn: a fertility goddess, the Dioscuri, Sol and Luna, Hercules.
89. Ben Baaziz 1996; Hamdoune 2010b. Cf. Cadotte 2007.
90. Rossignoli 1994 on peri-urban temples.

The Saturn/Tinnit stelae were highly varied in form. Early examples show distinct Punic influences and symbolism, and the occasional use of Punic/neo-Punic inscriptions invoking standard formulae.[91] The Tinnit symbol, a simplified female figure shown with arms upraised in the "orant" pose, is especially common in the pre-Roman material, but persisted also in the Roman era, along with solar and lunar symbols. In the Roman period, the repertoire became far wider, though continuing to evoke traditional themes of fertility, with the grandest examples featuring several registers of superimposed detail and some use of Latin inscriptions. Stylistically, even when occurring at urban sanctuaries, Saturn stelae tend to have a rather rustic appearance.[92] The iconographic repertoire included things like the crescents, solar discs, rosettes, Tinnit symbols, triangles, caduceus, cornucopia, laurel wreaths, incense burners, sacred stones (bétyles), flowers, crops, palm trees, livestock, doves, the hand, along with images of people. Some of the most flamboyant examples, with developed Latin epigraphy and with iconographic representations of individuals in Roman togas, can be associated with potentially atypical subgroups of devotees, notably members of the military community at sites like *Thamugadi*, *Nicivibus*, (N'Gaous) and *Lambiridi*.[93] However, many examples, and particularly those from the rural tophets, were much simpler and in general anepigraphic in nature. Overall, what is most striking about the Saturn cult is its absolute heterogeneity, and it is inappropriate to see the most developed stelae (as at N'Gaous) as in any way paradigmatic of behaviours followed at other sites.

Much of the iconography seems to allude to fertility and fecundity—matters of prime concern to farmers—as emphasised by images of crops (cereals, grapes), herds and flocks (cattle, sheep, and goats), cornucopia, astral symbols, palms, wreaths, the *caduceus*, doves, flowers, and so on.[94] Saturn was certainly the predominant cult, but it is clear that not all stelae at tophets/sanctuaries of Saturn were related to Saturn exclusively. A number of sites provide iconographic or epigraphic evidence of a range of African male and female gods, and some at least of the dedications presumably relate to these secondary divinities. At the rural shrine of *Thinissut*, where the sole explicit Latin inscription names Saturn, the sanctuary consisted of multiple sections and shrines (also attested by a neo-Punic text that refers to the dedication of two *mqdsm* or holy places). Equally revealing is the distribution of ten terracotta statues in different areas of the sanctuary, including a nursing female and another female figure standing on a lion's back. Considering

91. McCarty 2010a; forthcoming b.
92. Leglay 1966a; McCarty forthcoming (extensive presentation of sites); Ben Abdallah 1999a; Ben Baaziz 2000, 321–29 (area of *Mididi*); Ben Hassan and Ferjaoui 2008 (*Thignica*); Fantar et al. 2015 (*Mactaris*)Ferjaoui 1993b (*Cusira*); 2007, 124–61 (Henchir el-Hami); Kallala et al. 2018 (*Althiburos*); Moore 1999 (Ghorfa).
93. McCarty 2010b; 2010c (military community); forthcoming a (N'Gaous).
94. Ferjaoui 2007, 104–09.

the extent of the engagement with the epigraphic habit in other areas of life, it is very striking that in rural districts the practice of religion commonly involved non-epigraphic behaviours. From the Dorsal area of Rohia and Sraa Ouertane (close to southern *Numidae* towns of *Mididi* and *Tucca*), Ben Baaziz has recorded over 250 inscribed or figural stelae (including both religious stelae and tombstones, with some crossover in iconography between the two), with 97 of these (c. 40%) from rural contexts. Only 134 stelae were inscribed in Latin, 25 in neo-Punic and 9 in Libyan, with 87 anepigraphic.[95] Some of the religious stelae featuring bunches of grapes can be associated with Caelestis/Tinnit.

Many stelae and tophet sites have also been discovered in rural contexts or associated with smaller nucleated centres. In rural contexts, anepigraphic religious stelae were by far the majority, and cemetery areas generally were unmarked by inscriptions. Given the other evidence for expansion of the epigraphic habit under Rome, this counter-indication is surely of significance and underlines the fact that these cults were primarily seen as African, not Roman.[96] It also supports the notion that the practitioners of the Saturn cult were primarily from the lower social orders rather than the imperial (governing staff, army officers, senatorial/equestrian families) or municipal elites.[97]

A sanctuary of Saturn was sometimes little more than an enclosure for cremation of the sacrificial victim and ritual burial of the ashes, over time leading to the development of stelae fields and in some cases to the physical placement of temple structures.[98] The practice of the Saturn cult was not necessarily everywhere the same or followed in the same manner by all adherents and the point is well illustrated by the significant differences in spatial architecture at Saturn temples at *Thinissut* (rural community) and *Thamugadi* (linked to military community), suggesting somewhat different sorts of devotional practices at each location.[99] As noted already, the immense variation in iconographic programmes on the so-called Saturn stelae also hint at differing practices or emphases.

There has been a long debate about the realities of child sacrifice in the Carthaginian period, but a tendency to assume that by the Roman era, sacrifices were based on sheep or goats. The excavation of the rural sanctuary of Henchir al-Hami has challenged many of these assumptions and demonstrated just how little we really know about such sites and the religious practices associated with them.[100]

95. Ben Baaziz 2000, 321–29.
96. Ferjaoui 1993b; Moore 1999 notes that only 11/40+ stelae were inscribed and that Latin texts follow the formulae of earlier Punic ones.
97. Shaw 2013b, 248 and n. 52 ("Of the more than 1,400 dedicators to Saturn, at an absolute maximum there are only 30 who might have had any formal link with the Roman imperial order").
98. McCarty 2022, 294–95.
99. *Thinissut*: Dridi and Sebai 2008. *Thamugadi*: Leglay 1966a.
100. Ferjaoui 2007.

This site, lying between *Musti* and *Zama Regia*, was extensively excavated in the 1990s, revealing a temple and sacred area that reportedly covered c.20 hectares (the excavated area is c.0.15 ha). The sacred area comprised lines of socles and broken stelae that had been erected over dense deposits of pottery vessels with cremated bone and a range of votive offerings.[101] It was evidently in use from the 1st century BCE to the 2nd century CE, with the temple and structures to the north continuing much later. The iconography and limited epigraphy of the stelae show that the main cult was Saturn/Baal Hammon, but with an important representation of a Libyan fertility goddess, the "Dioscuri," "Sol" and "Luna," and "Hercules."[102] Apart from three neo-Punic texts, the bulk of the stelae were uninscribed.

The urn and stelae field comprised the larger area, where complex ritual behaviours were carried out involving the "sacrifice" of children, young kids or lambs, doves or other birds, their cremation, deposition of ash in an urn, and erection of a stele commemorating the sacrificial deal with the divine. Four types of "sacrifice" were made here: two types of blood sacrifice (human and animal/bird); botanical (as implicit in stelae iconography of pine cones, ears of wheat, bunches of grapes); and perfume offerings (indicated by thousands of broken unguentaria). The first two types relate to the cremated offerings. Of 322 votive vessels excavated, the contents of 268 were examined osteologically revealing a surprising pattern, with 67% containing perinatal or infant human bone, 5% had a mixture of human and ovicaprine bones, 4% mixed human and bird bones, 23% ovicaprine bones, and 1% just bird bones.[103] Far from being replaced by animal substitutes in Roman times, children continued to be offered up to Saturn/Baal Hammon, though some scholars argue that these were neonates or young infants who had died before being brought for immolation.[104] Animal and bird remains do suggest that some degree of sacrificial substitution was going on, but cases where a human baby was involved predominated through all periods of the site down to its end by the 4th century CE. Thus, though the hardline sacrificial demands of the cult may have been partially moderated by some worshippers through the expedient of substitute sacrifices, this was evidently not a universal development. Even at a military community settlement like *Lambafundi* where the cult is attested (and we might expect to see evidence of a "Roman" accommodation away from human sacrifice occurring), 2nd-century CE urns associated with stelae depicting children in a "Roman" style continued to contain infant bones.[105]

101. Ferjaoui 2007, 17–75.
102. Ferjaoui 2007, 88–111
103. Ferjaoui 2007, 97–101: some 150 urns had human bone only, 9 had mixed human and ovicaprine bone, 11 had bird and human, 51 had ovicaprine only, 3 had bird bones.
104. Ferjaoui 2007, 101.
105. McCarty 2022, 293.

Two factors strongly suggest that the "sacrificed" babies are not accountable as simply the remains of stillborn or early perinatal natural deaths that were offered to the gods. First, Tertullian (*Apologia* 9.2.3) specifically mentions the continuing practice of child sacrifice in the later 2nd century CE:

> Throughout Africa, infants were openly sacrificed to the god Saturn up to the proconsulship of Tiberius [sic] who had the priests set out, crucified alive on crosses, on the same trees of the sacred area, in the shadows of which they had committed their crimes. I have my own father as a witness to this fact. He was among the soldiers who served the proconsul in this task. Even to the present day, this same sacred crime is still being perpetrated, although in secret.

The reference to Tertullian's father implies that the last attempted suppression of the practice was around the mid-2nd century CE. If the practice did continue after that "in secret," one imagines it did so primarily in remote rural sanctuaries.[106] A continuing "official" disapproval of and distaste for the Saturn cult into the early 3rd century is implied by an incident detailed in the *Passio Sanctarum Perpetuae et Felicitatis* (18.4): "And when they [Perpetua and her companions] were led to the gate of the arena, they were forced to put on new clothing, the men that of the priests of Saturn, the women that of the priestesses of Ceres."[107] Although the Roman official who tried to enforce this further humiliation on the Christians eventually relented, the incident sheds an interesting light on his regard for the Saturn Cult (and Ceres here may well stand in for Tinnit), in that the intention appears to have been to expose the prisoners to the beasts wearing this garb. By that date, of course, Christianity was starting to usurp the position of the Saturn cult as the popular religion of the underprivileged African subjects of Empire and attracting the same sort of sporadic attempts at repression by the Roman state.

My second argument relates to the religious geography of the Saturn cult in North Africa. The sharp boundary around the region where the cult was most practised in Roman times (as revealed by Fig. 11.7) suggests that there was some behavioural limitation to its spread. Reflecting on the underlying social geography of my map, it appears that Saturn worship linked to child sacrifice was something that the Libyphoenicians and eastern *Numidae* had bought in to (with some uptake also focused on the garrison settlements of the security zones), but it was fundamentally alien to the beliefs and practices of *Gaetuli*, western *Numidae*, and *Mauri*. Had the cult under Rome been entirely neutralised of its more hardline cultural behaviour, one might expect it to have spread more widely in North Africa.

---

106. Shaw 2013b, 242 for text and discussion of Tertullian.
107. Van Beek 1936. Translation here by Brent Shaw, with thanks to him and Bruce Hitchner for interesting discussion of the passage's significance.

Far from the sympathetic Romanisation imagined by Leglay and Cadotte, one can posit that the Saturn cult evolved as a divisive element in Romano-African society, requiring discrepant behaviours in the urban religious spaces (which looked more to standard Roman cult) and the suburban sanctuaries of chthonic and dark deities, which looked out to the countryside and served up the propitiatory offerings required to secure divine help with human, animal, and plant fertility, with weather and, especially, rainfall.

Religion and the Peoples of the Wider Maghrib and Maghribian Coastal Zones

Across the Maghrib there is some evidence of other types of sanctuary sites. For example, above the quarry at *Simitthu*, the suburban Numidian high holy place was surrounded by hundreds of open-air relief carvings cut into the living rock. Cave sites are another prominent locale for religious activity in North Africa. At one cave in the Jabal Taya near *Thibilis*, Roman urban magistrates recorded annual pilgrimages to sacrifice to a god called Bacax. Near *Cirta*, painted and inscribed inscriptions to Giddaba have been found in a rock shelter at Jabal Chettaba.[108] Such acts are most visible to us when urban dwellers travelled into the countryside to sacrifice at such informal sites and left an epigraphic attestation of the activity. A huge amount of religious practice in rural areas undoubtedly remains hidden in that it did not entail Latin epigraphic acts.

The only claimed example of a Saturn temple in *Mauretania Tingitana* is Temple B, located in the suburbs of *Volubilis*. The site has yielded fragments of more than 826 votive stelae, most with single figures (though a small number have two or three people) executed in a very simplified frontal style.[109] However, the lack of inscriptions and the unusual iconography of the stelae make it highly unlikely that this was a temple of Saturn. The images clearly represent devotees of the cult, and Henri Morestin identified five main variant poses relating to making offerings, invocations, salutations, images of fecundity, and meditations.[110] Although showing some similarities with conventional Saturn stelae, the distance from the nearest certain Saturn sanctuary and distinctive aspects of the repertoire suggest that we may be dealing with a different and decidedly local chthonic divinity, perhaps Aulisua.[111] The *Mauri* thus cannot on present evidence be said to have embraced the Saturn cult, but rather had their own chthonic god(s).

---

108. Shaw 2013b, 238. For the inscriptions, see *ILAlg* 2.2, 407–21 (nos. 4502–85); *ILAlg* 2.3, 968–76 (nos. 8907–70)
109. Morestin 1980.
110. Morestin 1980, 78–85. Note also there is no evidence here for associated child sacrifice/cremation.
111. Brouquier-Reddé et al. 1999.

*Religion and the Peoples of the Desert Zones (*Gaetuli *and* Garamantes*)*

While conventional epigraphic sources leave us uncertain about many details of the religion of the desert peoples, my account below will identify three prominent strands: animism, zoomorphism, and ancestor cult. Animism is strongly present in the Maghrib and Sahara, with myriad spirits of place associated with natural features (springs, water pools, hills, mountains, passes, trees, caves and rock shelters, and so on). This animism is reflected in the marking-out of special places in the landscape in all phases of Saharan rock art by concentrated clusters of imagery. The late-phase images of Saharan rock art featuring horses and camels and Libyan inscriptions continue to occupy many of the same topographic locations as the Late Pastoral imagery (which had arguably been seeking divine assistance with the climatic shift that marked the end of the green Sahara).[112] In the Islamic era, the tradition is echoed by the prominence accorded to *jinns*—spirits that needed placating.[113] Much of the rock art imagery appears to relate to themes of human and animal fertility, hunting, occasionally martial combat—all things that human communities may have sought divine assistance with.[114] So our first clue to the religious practices of the pre-desert and desert peoples lies with the late rock art and informal Libyan inscriptions that decorate so many rock surfaces.

Zoomorphism is clearly another element of Late Neolithic rock art, with many images of animal-headed theomorphs suggesting a deep Saharan tradition for such practices prior to its transferance to the Egyptian Nilotic civilisations.[115] This chimes with other evidence. The *Gaetuli* peoples of Tripolitania seem to have worshipped desert divinities, such as Ammon, Sinifer or Canaphar, Vanammon, and Gurzil, though two of these are known only from military dedicants at *Gholaia*, and Gurzil is only attested in literary references. The zoomorphic tradition is illustrated by Ammon often being represented as ram-headed, and Gurzil evidently a bull-headed god.

Another aspect of zoomorphism may relate to the significance of depictions of animals in rock art, on funerary monuments within the Roman provinces, and in horse and camel figurines from a Garamantian temple.[116] In particular, the plentiful Iron Age rock art of horses and riders is suggestive that there was some sort of generalised horse cult (see Figs. 5.17 and 11.8–11.9 below for examples).[117]

The ancient sources allude to ancestor worship among the desert peoples, specifically mentioning the practice of sleeping at the tombs of significant ancestors

112. Barnett 2019a, 197–277; Mattingly 2003a, 317–19.
113. Barnett 2019a, 276–77.
114. Mattingly 2003a, 302–05.
115. Lutz and Lutz 1995, 145–64.
116. Bokbot et al. 2021, 179–83; Mattingly 2013a, 517–18.
117. Bokbot et al. 2021.

to experience revelatory dreams.[118] As we shall see, there is abundant evidence to demonstrate the realities of this sort of practice, and to some extent the spirits of the ancestors can be seen to fulfil a similar role among the *Gaetuli* to the chthonic gods of the *Numidae*.

Very few rural temples have been identified in rural Tripolitania, though there is epigraphic or literary evidence for six temples to Ammon (or Iupiter Ammon) from the region including the examples known at *Gholaia*, *Arae Philaenorum*, Breviglieri, Zaviet at-Maghuib (15 km west of Misurata), Tininai, and *Ad Amonem* (24 km west of *Sabratha*).[119] There were likely more *Ammonia*, though these have proved difficult to identify archaeologically because they were often architecturally simple structures and were not necessarily associated with epigraphic practices. Ammon was evidently an important cult for desert travellers, and the three temples attested on the coastal road indicate this fact for a major transport route; and it is unsurprising to find a temple of Iupiter Hammon at *Gholaia*, where one dedication makes explicit connection with the safe return of the unit from a desert expedition. The use-life of the temple seems to have extended beyond the abandonment of the fort.[120] It is probable that one of the temples at the fort of *Myd[...]* (al-Qurrayyat), of unknown dedication, was likewise an *Ammonium* marking an important stage on another desert route south to the land of the *Garamantes*. At the Garamantian capital at *Garama*, a monumental building plausibly identified as a temple again seems likely to have been associated with Ammon.[121] This might suggest that *Ammonia* were more likely a feature of the oasis towns, provincial road stations, and caravan stopovers (including the garrison points of the security zone), rather than of rural settlement more generally.

The UNESCO Libyan Valleys Survey, which surveyed thousands of pre-desert rural settlements, identified only three structures in total that appeared to have been temples or shrines (Tininai, Wadi Mimoun, and Ghirza).[122] Overall, there is a distinct lack of identified rural temples in the Gaetulian zone, despite a large number of known settlement sites. The Romano-Libyan village of Ghirza in the Libyan pre-desert can probably be identified as the main cult centre of the Libyan god Gurzil, the bull-headed progeny of Ammon mentioned by Corippus. The similarity of the name, associations with bull sacrifice in inscriptions and relief sculpture, and the existence at this location of the largest pre-desert temple associated with numerous miniature altars inscribed with Libyan inscriptions are strongly suggestive of the interpretation. The temple at Ghirza was excavated by Brogan and Smith,

118. Libyan ancestor worship: Herodotus, *Histories* 4.172; Mela, *de situ orbis* 1.8.45.
119. Brouquier-Reddé 1992a, 121–23.
120. Rebuffat 1990b; 1992b.
121. Mattingly 2013a.
122. Barker et al. 1996b, 118–19 (Ghirza), 225, 228 (Mimoun), 305 (Tininai). See also Brogan and Smith 1984, 80–92, 243–51, for the Ghirza temple.

revealing a structure of Semitic form. It is striking that while Ghirza has yielded Latin and Latino-Punic inscriptions from its tombs, the only epigraphic practice attested at the temple involved the Libyan script on crude stone altars, at least two of which also featured an individual with arms raised in the orant pose.[123]

It is interesting, for instance, to note that figural relief carving on funerary monuments marks an important exception to the general low engagement with Roman iconographic practices in Gaetulian lands. This is most evident in the creation of numerous mausolea in the pre-desert zone in general and at Ghirza in particular. A key element of what seems to have been going on at Ghirza related to a Libyan ancestor cult and the translation of familial rituals into communal power using an expanded iconographic repertoire. The significance of mausoleum culture in the various rural communities of North Africa merits further reflection.[124] I shall also argue that something similar was occurring in western Algeria and Morocco, linking back to the image of the mounted warrior.[125]

The apparent lack of religious activity among the rural communities in Mauretanian and Gaetulian landscapes, as evident in Cadotte's maps (e.g. Figs. 11.7), cannot be a true representation of those societies. The most plausible conclusion is that their religious activities were differently expressed, but it is also no doubt due to the dearth of relevant archaeological investigation. The distribution of Saharan "horse-phase" rock art, generally dated to the 1st millennia BCE/CE, offers one window on this world (see Fig. 4.4). The Garamantian heartlands stand out in the east, and recent research in the far west, in the Wadi Draa near Foum Chenna, provides an important type site of a potential open-air sanctuary associated with a NAIA settlement site dating to the early to mid-1st millennium CE. This small settlement is notable for the huge concentration of incised rock art along its entrance path, its main alleyway, on blocks in the walls of the houses and enclosures, and in huge numbers in an open area of bare rock plateau at the top end of the sloping site—where the engravings are particularly clustered on two rough oval "enclosures" of large boulders, but also cover many horizontal bare rock surfaces (Figs. 11.8–9). In total, there were at least 756 images of horses identified (234 with riders). Some of the scenes contained multiple horses in a distinctive and naturalistic fashion, while others reduced the horses to a few schematic lines (and it is likely that a significant proportion of the 273 unidentified quadrupeds were also intended as schematic horse representations). The dense concentration of horse imagery and the huge range in quality of execution indicates a long-lived ritual practice of repetitive acts of engraving at this location (cf. Figs. 5.16f–j and 11.9).

123. Brogan and Smith 1984, 243–48. Frustratingly the drawings do not show the position of the Libyan inscriptions and orant figures (cf. plate 139).

124. See Moore 2007.

125. Bokbot et al. 2021.

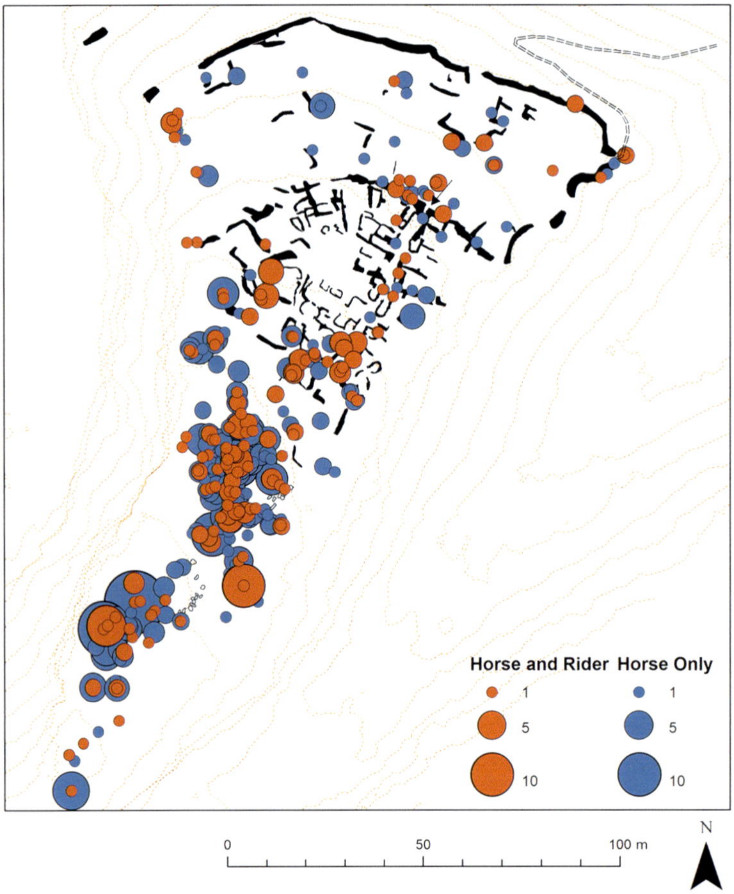

Figure 11.8. Distribution of horse imagery at a hillfort site (TIN015) in the Wadi Draa. The concentration of hundreds of individual engraved horses (many with riders), especially on an open "sacred" area of the fortified hilltop, was evidently contemporary with the settlement and appears most likely to have had a religious function (from Bokbot et al. 2021, 175).

While we cannot know the exact reason for the engravings and what the people responsible hoped to gain by the act, this does look like a form of devotional communication with a divine power.

In summary, the *Gaetuli* seem to have had little need for formal temples or epigraphic communication with their gods in Latin in the manner of some of the *Numidae*. Particularly striking is the failure of the Saturn cult to spread across Gaetulian lands alongside increased urbanisation and sedentarisation. As already observed, the only attestations of the African Saturn cult in the Gaetulian zone can be related to either the military community (and people closely associated with it) or the Libyphoenician coastal towns. The same is true of the *Mauri* to the west.

a

b

Figure 11.9. Two examples of horse imagery from TIN015 in the Wadi Draa. a) Hunting scene with two horsemen approaching a pair of ostriches. b) A complex scene of massed horsemen around some larger than life standing figures (from Bokbot et al. 2021, 170).

Table 11.4. Religious practices in ancient North Africa compared (Anthrop images = Anthropomorhic images of gods; Maus = Mausolea).

	Temple type	Saturn stelae	Anthrop images	Altars	Maus	Ancestor cult	Christianity
Military community	Classical/ army types	Some	Many	Many	Rare	Rare	Initially rare, main focus at garrison settlements
Urban community	Classical/ Phoenician	Many	Many	Many	Some	Rare	Common
Rural communities	Few, most of Saturn in north, most of Ammon in south	Many in north, rare in south	Some in north, rare in south	Rare	Many	Common, especially in south	Common in Maghrib, rarer in desert

It is perhaps asking the wrong question to focus on what it was about Gaetulian and Moorish societies that made them ill-disposed towards this key African cult. An alternative approach is to consider what it was about this cult of the north-eastern Maghrib that inhibited its spread to neighbouring regions. It is certainly clear that the eastern *Numidae* had a very different set of cultural affiliations in the pre-Roman period, but that does not seem an adequate explanation. However, if at the heart of Baal/Tinnit worship was a practice of infanticide or child sacrifice to placate chthonic deities and this continued to some degree into the Roman period, one can see that the uptake of the religion was quite probably constrained by issues of social taboo in neighbouring societies.

In general the rural zones of North Africa always seem to have followed distinctive pathways of religious behaviour compared to the military community and the towns (Table 11.4). By and large, epigraphic communication with the gods was limited, especially in the southern Gaetulian regions, though the worship of Saturn/ Baal Hammon and associated deities often involved figural stelae in the northern rural districts.

Mausolea Culture, Funerary Practices, and Identity

While rural survey has started to fill in the detail of Roman rural settlement, the contemporary Roman-period cemeteries remain relatively poorly known, apart from where they contain inscriptions.[126] There are great geographical disparities in

126. Lassère 1973; 1995; Ferchiou 1995a.

the occurrence of funerary inscriptions as "entire regions of the province did not see fit to use writing to perpetuate the memory of the deceased with an epitaph."[127] This can only partially be explained in terms of availability of suitable stone for the making of tombstones.[128] For instance, as noted, the small territory of *Thugga* has produced 92 funerary inscriptions from rural sites, which we might compare with a tiny handful known from the territories of *Sufetula* and *Cillium*.[129] There was also tremendous regional variability in the types of funerary monuments encountered, though again the detail is tantalisingly incomplete.[130] It is no surprise that the rural monuments we know most about were the most monumental or the most frequently inscribed.

There are well over 500 known mausolea across Libya, Tunisia, and Algeria.[131] While some have been recorded at sites associated with the military community, and there is an important group associated with urban communities, the vast majority appears to have comprised rural monuments, many erected on estates. Some of the most impressive mausoleum inscriptions relate to the military community, notably featuring veterans. Another group can be identified as monuments commemorating prominent citizens and landowners.[132] But we need to be careful not to explain the wider occurrence of mausolea simply in relation to the social values of high-status individuals seeking to express their *Romanitas*. Rather than talking of mausolea as symptomatic of Romanisation in Africa or as a unitary phenomenon,[133] we might reflect on differences within the mausoleum culture, noting varying emphases between the military, urban, and rural communities. As we shall see, there are also some significant divergences within the rural community in different regions that raise questions about the social significance and associated funerary and, indeed, religious behaviours.

The existence of a pre-Roman mausoleum tradition in Africa has been demonstrated both in relation to the Libyphoenician *emporia* (as at *Sabratha*), the Carthaginian *pertica* (Ksar Chenane), and the Numidian kingdom (*Thugga*, *Siga*, Es Soumaa).[134] In the Numidian case, it is suspected that many of the early tombs related to members of the royal lineage following Syphax and Massinissa, though specific associations with individual monuments are difficult to prove. The royal

127. Ferchiou 1995a, 136: "des régions entières de la province n'ont pas jugé bon de recourir à l'écriture pour perpétuer le souvenir des défunts par une épitaphe."
128. Lassère 1995, 104–05. The detail of this regional variation merits drawing out further.
129. Khanoussi and Maurin 2002, 84; cf. Hitchner 1990, 240–42 recorded four cemeteries, a number of burials being marked by simple stone grave markers, but only three inscribed.
130. Ferchiou 1995a, 124–29; Stone and Stirling 2007b, 8–14.
131. Barker et al. 1996a, 144–48; Ferchiou 1995a; 2001; Gsell 1901b, 54–99; Moore 2007, 73–88; Nikolaus 2016, 199–205.
132. Bentivogli 2004; Ferchiou 1995a, 114–15.
133. Bentivogli 2004.
134. Moore 2007, 78–80.

associations of tower mausolea in North Africa could easily be overstated, as most early Roman examples seem to relate to local notables of less exclusive status. As with Saturn stelae, however, the Roman conquest of Africa seems to have sparked a spread and intensification of mausoleum culture. While there are undoubtedly prominent cases of retired veterans staking a claim for posterity with ostentatious monuments (as with the Flavii and Petronii at *Cillium*, Iulius Dexter of Bir Oum Ali between *Theveste* and *Thelepte*, Anniolenus Faustus near *Madauros*, Anneus Balbus at *Thuburnica*),[135] these represent a very small minority of our examples. As Jennifer Moore observes, a number of characteristics of the African mausolea certainly appears to relate to a non-Roman tradition. For example, the majority of mausolea, where orientation of the monument has been recorded, faced approximately east—a ritually significant orientation in African religion.[136] The cockerel placed on top of the tomb of the Flavii at *Cillium* was a calculated and striking juxtaposition of an African cultural marker on this epigraphically most Roman of monuments.[137] Paintings of mausolea associated with the image of the cockerel from the walls of haouanet tombs reveal the pre-Roman symbolism.[138]

Mausolea in "Roman Africa" followed two predominant models: the tower and temple types, with the latter becoming progressively more popular as time went on. While the tower type reflected the pre-Roman tradition, the temple type again hints at a religious function of some of these monuments, a point also highlighted in some of the funerary inscriptions. For example, many monuments appear to have been formally dedicated in the same way a temple would have been, and the Flavian mausoleum at *Cillium* was explicitly referred to as a "new temple," rather than simply a tomb to the head of the family.[139]

Moore has queried whether there is actually solid evidence to demonstrate an explicit religious and sacred use of the Tunisian mausolea, but the robbed state and lack of modern excavation in and around these monuments impede full consideration of this.[140] Certainly, the evidence from Tripolitania is more explicit on this score and seems to attest regular ritual activity at the tombs. As discussed above, the tradition of ancestor worship was a strong tendency in pre-Roman African societies, and one that was generally linked to powerful and charismatic individuals, in a similar way to the concept of *baraka* that underlies medieval and early modern maraboutic monuments.[141] While it is true that some of the mausolea appear to

135. Bentivogli 2004, 425–33.
136. Moore 2007, 90 n. 49; cf. on Saharan burial orientations, Mattingly 2003a, 218–19, 226–27; Mattingly et al. 2019b, 81–83.
137. Lassère et al. 1993, 235–50.
138. Camps 1992a; Longerstay 1995, 48.
139. Moore 2007, 91–92; *CIL* 8.213 line 4: *non monimenta patri, sed nova templa.*
140. Moore 2007, 90–96.
141. Mattingly 2011a, 262–67.

be exercises in measuring status, wealth, and worth in material form—the bigger the monument, the longer the engraved poem, etc.—it is also worth considering the possibility that the construction of monumental tombs in Roman Africa also served to house powerful ancestral forces to watch over families and communities. There has been a very long tradition of tombs of powerful or charismatic individuals becoming foci for acts of devotion—from the Numidian kings to the marabout monuments of the Islamic era.[142] The mausoleum culture thus seems to fit in to a very long-term pattern in Africa. Some mausolea were constructed by the person destined to be the first individual to be placed within the monument; others were the work of the descendants and beneficiaries. Tombs on rural estates may also have had a geospatial function, in that the Roman period marked a time of significant reallocation and reorientation of landholding. Such visible monuments were a means both of articulating new ownership rights and of creating fresh loci wherein ancestral forces could dwell in support of translocated families.

The ornamentation of the mausolea varied considerably. Most of the central and northern Tunisian tombs were ashlar constructions involving architectural attachments, such as engaged pilasters, columns, architrave, and, occasionally, decorative frieze blocks. Free-standing statuary and portraits of the deceased were evidently quite common features, but many of the northern examples were comparatively lacking in other relief sculpture. By contrast, the southern Tunisian and Libyan examples were much more elaborately decorated with relief sculpture, though much of it is in a very rustic regional style. A few tombs stand out for the quality of their sculpture and refined architecture (al-Amrouni, Beni Guedal, Tigi), but they were more likely special commissions rather than tombs for outsiders.

In the area covered by Trousset's study of the western *limes Tripolitanus* in southern Tunisia, a total of 35 mausolea is known from 21 locations, with over half having evidence of relief sculpture (Fig. 11.10).[143] These cover a range of scenes, some of which are paralleled in Roman funerary iconography: Orpheus and Euridice, two birds drinking from a chalice, pine cones, fish, Hercules and Alcestis, representations of the deceased, sphinx, rosettes, and so on. Others seem to echo the more regional preoccupations of reliefs from eastern Tripolitania: scenes of ploughing, hunting, bucrania, desert wildlife, and fortified farms. The distribution of the mausolea can be closely related to the zone where sedentary farms developed in a region under some degree of military supervision. Study of the inscriptions reveals that many of the dedicants were of Libyan origin, though in the process of acquiring Latin names and the Latin epigraphic habit. The al-Amrouni tomb is one of the most famous examples, bearing inscriptions in Latin and neo-Punic commemorating a certain Q. Apuleus Maxssimus (*sic*), son of Iuzale, grandson of Iurathe,

142. Camps 1984; 1986a.

143. Trousset 1974, supplemented by my own observations on some sites.

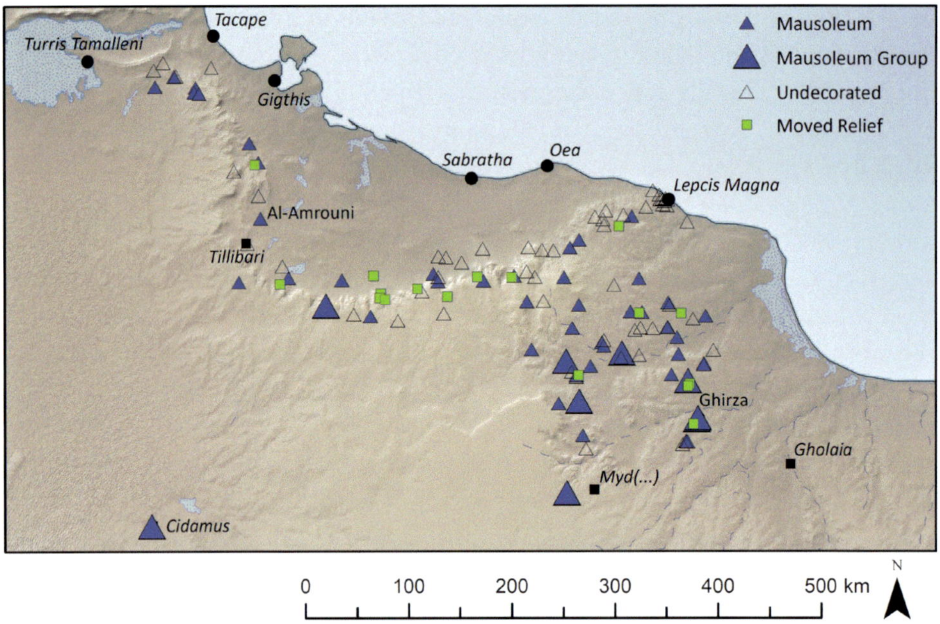

Figure 11.10. Distribution of mausolea with relief sculpture in *Tripolitana* (Martin Sterry, from author's rough based on Nikolaus 2017).

and husband of Thanubra. His sons were Q. Apuleus Pudens, Q. Apuleus Severus, and Q. Apuleus Maxsimus, whose African roots would have been much harder to detect. To complicate matters further, the mausoleum of Apuleus Maxssimus senior had a second funerary text engraved in neo-Punic script.[144] Other Latinised Libyans include L. Domitius Tellulus and Miha Vasari at Henchir Khrebita,[145] L. Domitius Aumura and Arelia Tammassa, L. Domitius Masculus and Mallia[...] from Henchir Oum el Abbes.[146] A neo-Punic text from Tatahouine commemorated Poltakan, son of Massoulat, habitant of *Thagi*, son of Madar.[147]

The UNESCO Libyan Valleys Survey recorded more than 50 mausolea, of which many carried relief sculpture. A number of other important examples are known from the Jabal zone to the north of the pre-desert and in the vicinity of the coastal cities, though the decoration of the last group tends to be of higher quality, but with a concomitant reduction in the range of relief sculpture. The tombs from close to the coast tend to feature only busts and statues of the deceased.

144. Mattingly 1995, 167 – note the two variant spellings of Maximus. The neo-Punic text should indicate that the construction be dated no later than the 2nd century rather than the 3rd as sometimes proposed, Trousset 1974, 110–13. Ferchiou 1989b; Lassère 2005b, 146–47.

145. Trousset 1974, 84; *ILT* 51.

146. Trousset 1974, 85; *ILT* 52, 54.

147. Trousset 1974, 107.

Again, we need to be careful not to assume a common set of motivations behind these diverse groups of tombs.

I have previously argued that the funerary iconography from the most important mausolea group at Ghirza and the ritual structure of the cemeteries can be related to a regionally significant ancestor cult that went beyond the immediate community living at the settlement.[148] There is comparatively little imagery that is explicitly linked to Classical mythology or to the norms of Roman funerary symbolism.[149] The style of the carving is distinctively "provincial," but differences in status and social roles are conveyed by deliberate distortions of scale of figures and through things like dress.[150] The key themes relate to local power, and the fecundity of the landscape in terms of crops and beasts for hunting. The emphasis on agricultural scenes (ploughing, sowing, reaping, threshing, winnowing) are often described as representations of "daily life," though it is recognised that we lack parallels for much of this imagery in funerary art elsewhere.[151] In addition to the 12 relief panels from six tombs at Ghirza, Julia Nikolaus noted 22 other agricultural relief sculptures from Tripolitania, making this one of the most common themes in mausoleum decor.[152] There are other scenes that find no parallels in Roman funerary art and clearly evoke local power and prestige—chieftain scenes, fights with semi-naked "barbarians," possible execution scenes. The dress and headwear of the figures, especially the larger elite figures, consistently defy easy parallel in contemporary urban fashions.[153] Rather than emulating Roman monuments as a means of evoking a Roman identity, the pre-desert mausolea builders thus seem to have adapted Mediterranean architectural and sculptural styles to follow local Libyan agendas of identity presentation.[154] In this context it is surely significant that mausolea also appeared outside provincial territory, for instance in the heartlands of the *Garamantes* (where they were not used as burial monuments, but appear to have served as focal "temples" within cemetery areas) and at the oasis of *Cidamus*.[155]

There is a significant contrast between the Tripolitanian pre-desert mausoleum tradition and those of coastal Tripolitania and northern Tunisia. Mausolea in those northern zones generally lacked elaborate figurative relief sculpture. In the *Numidae* zone we might note that while most mausolea were unadorned, some of

148. On Ghirza, see Mattingly 1999; 2003b (also in 2011a); Nikolaus 2016; 2017. Cf. also Brogan and Smith 1984, 215–26; Fontana 1997.

149. Note, though, the tendency to try and interpret the imagery in conventional Roman terms, Brogan and Smith 1984.

150. Audley-Miller 2012; Zanker 2008.

151. On the agricultural scenes, Brogan 1965; Brogan and Smith 1984, 220–21; Mattingly 2011a, 259–60; Nikolaus 2016, 209; Zanker 2008, 217.

152. Nikolaus 2016, 209–211.

153. Audley-Miller 2012; Nikolaus 2017, 194–202.

154. Nikolaus 2017, 223–26.

155. Mattingly 2003a, 189–92; 2010a, 370–71; Mattingly and Sterry 2010.

the same iconographic themes and the rustic artistic style of carving characterised the Saturn stelae. Where there seems to be specific crossover between Gaetulian mausoleum sculpture and *Numidae* Saturn stelae imagery includes themes of agricultural and pastoral fertility and productivity, imagery of palms, vines, cereals, birds, sacrifice, and the orant pose. One way to look at this is to assume that this imagery relating to fertility and fecundity served much the same religious purpose in each zone, with ancestral gods in the Gaetulian zone thus fulfilling the role of the chthonic gods in eastern Numidia. It is interesting that the only overtly divine figures featuring on the Tripolitanian mausolea are Hercules and Orpheus, key interlocutors with the Underworld. In conclusion, I argue that by presenting chthonic forces with the hopes and fears of rural communities regarding crop and animal fertility, mausolea attained a much higher religious significance in the Gaetulian regions than they had in the Libyphoenician and Numidian zones to the north, where the Saturn cult fulfilled a similar role. The ancestor cult was also present in those northern regions, and was a key part of mausoleum culture throughout North Africa, but was secondary to a more formalised paganism built around a set of chthonic gods. The paucity of temples and the lack of penetration of Romano-African cults in the Gaetulian zone that is so evident in Cadotte's maps can thus be seen to be due to the higher importance of religious practices around funerary monuments of significant ancestors, which had the same status as temples and, in the case of mausolea, often evoked temple or *aedicula* architecture.[156]

The Libyan Valleys Survey also recorded in some detail a number of cemeteries, both monumental ones and those comprising only simpler burial types.[157] What is striking about the dossier is the extreme variability in the features recorded, albeit lacking chronological precision in the absence of excavation (and this, of course, might account for some of the variance). But there were clearly different traditions represented in the same cemetery spaces, such as circular cairn tombs and rectangular grave structures formed with slabs. There is evidence for both cremation and inhumation, with both extended and flexed presentation. The social implications of this are not clear; however, the seemingly isolated mausolea were often surrounded, at a slight distance, by clusters of simpler monuments and markers, and thus sometimes served as focal points of extended funerary landscapes.[158] The architectural and behavioural gulf between mausolea with inscriptions and relief carvings and these other burials was large. In societies that paid particular honour to significant and powerful ancestors, the presence of these extraordinary structures seems more credibly associated with ancestor cult than with notions of being Roman.

156. Nikolaus 2016, 206–08.
157. Barker et al. 1996a, 142–47; 1996b, 20–25, 33–38, 45–46, 50, 78–79, 119–20, 152–53, 165–67, 171–73, 178, 200–05, 220–21, 225–27, 261–64, 280, 283, 287–88. For Libyan burials at Ghirza, see also Brogan and Smith 1984, 100–26.
158. Ray and Nikolaus 2019.

Christianity and Late Antique Paganism

Christianity, like urbanism, appears a remarkable aspect of the North African provinces, especially in the coastal regions and in the interior of *Mauretania Caesariensis*, *Mauretania Sitifensis*, *Numidia*, *Zeugitana*, *Byzacena*, coastal *Tripolitana*, and *Cyrenaica*. The spread was intensified and complicated by sectarian discord between Catholics and so-called "Donatists" in the 4th and early 5th centuries, though that lies beyond my scope in this book.[159] Overall there were more bishops in late Roman *Africa*, *Numidia*, and *Byzacena* (534) than Gaul (115), Italy (242), and *Asia* (349), in part because African bishoprics were not limited to the main urban centres, but also existed in some villages and rural estates (Fig. 11.11).[160] An alternative suggestion is that the spread of bishoprics mapped onto structural units of African "communities" that had a long tradition from the proto-urban NAIA settlements onwards, via the 516 *populi* of Pliny. Not all of these became urban entities under Rome, but as I have argued in this chapter, local identities remained strong. Like the Saturn cult, early Christianity was in essence a non-conformist religion, antithetical to key aspects of the Roman state religion—which no doubt was part of its attraction. It was also especially strong initially in rural and smaller urbanised communities far from the more "Roman" cities. The distribution of bishops, with a particularly strong concentration in the north-eastern Maghrib, shows the success of Christianity in supplanting Saturn and the other chthonic gods of that region. But it is also clear from the wider dispersal into Gaetulian and Moorish lands that Christianity was a bit more successful than Saturn in spreading beyond that core zone. The idea that Christianity attracted adherents not just for its salvationist aspects, but also because of its non-conformist relationship with the Empire, is an attractive one. It also helps explain the 4th century Donatist schism as in part a battle between pragmatists, who wanted to embrace the opportunities of imperial approval and support, and dissidents who sought to maintain the older spirit of independence and non-cooperation.

Some of our best evidence regarding the rural communities relates to later antiquity and, in particular, to the epigraphically habituated Christian groups, supported by a rich body of literary sources. Despite the wealth of evidence, different visions of late antique rural society abound: wealthier and more vocal peasants, a collapse of agriculture in some areas, dysfunctional and divided communities, a shrinking "Roman" core increasingly terrorised by the Moorish fringes of

159. See the evocative account of the attendant "sacred violence" in Shaw 2011.

160. Dossey 2010, 125. I must thank David Stone for inspiring my follow-up comment on Dossey's explanation of the phenomenon.

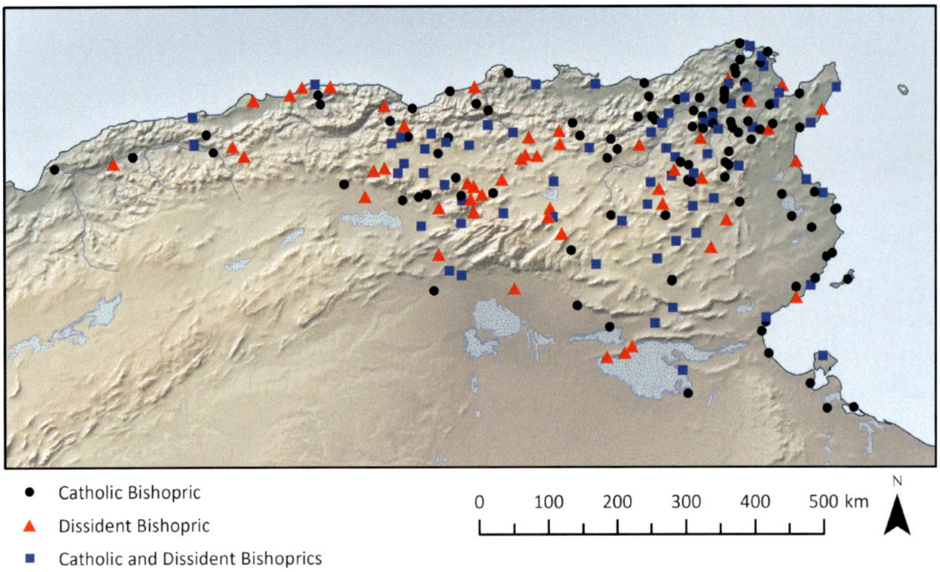

Figure 11.11. Distribution of Catholic and dissident bishoprics in North Africa (Martin Sterry, after Shaw 2011).

mountain and desert.[161] There are also large debates about the impacts of migration of the Vandals[162] and Libyan desert peoples, like the *Laguatan*, in late antiquity.[163]

What I want to highlight briefly, is that while rural churches and even rural bishoprics abounded in most regions of North Africa, they were more concentrated in *Numidia* and *Mauretania*, the old *Numidae* or *Mauri* heartlands, where settlement had traditionally featured many village-scale settlements (*castella*).[164] There are some churches in *Numidia Militaris* in connection with garrison or veteran settlements in the Aurès plains and in the Gaetulian High Steppe zone.[165] More generally, bishoprics in the Gaetulian zone coincided with a few of the southern oasis centres (in the Jarid and Nefzaoua) and in relation to garrison settlements, as at *Nigrenses Maiores*, *Badias*, *Thabudeos*, *Vescera*, *Gemellae*, *Mesarfelta*, *Tubunae*, *Ala Miliaria*, *Altava*, and *Pomaria*.[166]

161. See the overviews of, inter alia, Conant 2012a; Courtois 1955; Decret 1996; Dossey 2010; Frend 1971; 1978; Lancel 2005; Modéran 2003; Shaw 2011.
162. Lepelley 2005b; Merrills 2004; Merrills and Miles 2010; Modéran 2014.
163. Felici et al. 2006; Fentress and Wilson 2016; Mattingly 1995; Modéran 2003.
164. *Numidia*: Berthier 1943; *Mauretania*: Hamdoune 2018, 215–62 (Christianity in countryside); 295–314 (discussion and catalogue of late antique bishoprics); 431–71 (collation of epigraphic and other evidence of Christianity). Cf. also *Cyrenaica*: Ward-Perkins and Goodchild 2003.
165. High Steppe: Baratte et al. 2014; Bejaoui 1995; 1998; 2015.
166. Churches and bishoprics at garrison settlements: Hamdoune 2018, 234, 389; Shaw 2011, maps 2b and 2c.

Figure 11.12. Late antique ancestor worship scene from Jorf Torba, western Algeria (Mike Hawkes, from Bokbot 2019, 330).

Other parts of the Gaetulian zone, and especially its desert fringes, appear to have remained more steadfastly pagan into late antiquity. The Libyan Valleys Survey found only two churches in a region of 75,000 km^2, and the heyday of the pagan site of Ghirza was in the 4th century.[167] It is striking how the reluctant and thin adoption of Christianity in Gaetulian zones beyond the garrison settlements echoes the earlier divergence of religious behaviours between the peoples of the northern Maghrib and the Gaetulian south.

At the other end of the Maghrib, in western Algeria and southern Morocco, there is a series of large tumulus burials, notable for the construction of elaborate subterranean funerary chapels in their eastern edges.[168] The most famous examples of these tombs excavated at Jorf Torba were found to contain engraved and painted panels in the funerary chapels, depicting horses, horses and rider, a range of other animals, and some family groups (Fig. 11.12).[169] A late Roman or antique date appears most likely, and most of the known examples lay outside Roman territory. Camps recognised the function of the chapels as being intimately linked to the practice of the ancestor cult in that their subterranean crawl spaces allowed the living to approach close to the resting place of a powerful ancestor, to experience revelatory dreams or visions. The imagery related to key aspects of animal fertility (horses and foals) and communication between the living and the

167. Barker et al. 1996a, 337–38.
168. Bokbot 2019; Camps 1984; 1986a.
169. Camps 1995a; Lihoreau 1993.

dead—human figures are generally shown in the orant pose. However, because of what he interpreted as crucifixes held by female figures in one scene, Camps suggested this Gaetulian community had been converted to Christianity. This is hard to square with the evident pagan context of the rituals observed here, and an alternative explanation can be advanced for the supposed crosses. These are, more plausibly, distaffs with spindle whorl, representing a key female attribute to match the spears held by the male figures. Although the artistic style of the paintings and engravings shows familiarity with Roman artworks and techniques, the detail of the costumes of the figures clearly evokes a local tradition of textile and clothing production. Once again, then, we have evidence of the strength of a pagan ancestor cult among the *Gaetuli* (or whatever their late Roman descendants called themselves).[170]

Water Cultures

Another fruitful area for examining fundamental differences between rural communities concerns their relationship with water. Here again I want to draw a distinction between the northern Maghribian populations (*Numidae*, *Mauri*, and various groups of colonial incomers), who were predominantly dry farmers, and the *Gaetuli* and *Garamantes*, whose cultivation was in varying degrees dependent on irrigation strategies. This is obviously driven in part by climate, local hydrological and environmental conditions, in part by the availability of technology and know-how. But the exploitation of scarce water resources in the desert margins will inevitably take on deep cultural significance, as is evident from studies of more recent irrigating communities in the Sahara. The modern colonial projects took a deep interest in the ancient evidence for irrigation and water management features, by and large seeing this as the key to Rome's success in making Africa green.[171] This is another area, of course, where the traditional emphasis on exogenous invention and passive reception by the supposedly "primitive" pastoralists of the deserts is unhelpful. As Brent Shaw observed long ago, the fundamental technological knowledge of irrigation strategies was more likely to have developed among the peoples living in the environments where it was most required, rather than those coming to Africa from better-watered regions of the Mediterranean or inhabiting the parts of

170. My excavations of a group of chapel tombs at Foum Larjam in the Wadi Draa in 2016 and 2021 have yielded an import dossier of new paintings relating to the ancestor cult and will be the subject of a future publication.

171. Birebent 1962; Gauckler 1900/1912. The traditional colonialist interpretation of hydraulic technology was later somewhat modified in Euzennat 1992, who saw the major Roman contribution to be not technology but the conditions of peace. See also the critique of the colonial discourse on water technologies in Shaw 1984, 124–29.

the Maghrib with the highest rainfall.[172] It is true, of course, that the variable nature of Mediterranean climate has tended to make all its farmers mindful of water conservation and good management. In the northern Maghrib, springs were more commonly exploited to sustain settlements rather than for agriculture, and NAIA centres were already being sited to take advantage of such water sources. Roman aqueducts marked a logical conclusion to such projects, not a radical innovation.[173]

Frontinus (*de controv agrorum* 2) recognised that regional preoccupations with water differed significantly when he commented that:

> In Italy a pretty big dispute may flare up in order to keep off flood water. But in Africa the same issue is handled quite differently. Since that is a very dry area, they have no dispute on this score unless someone has stopped rain water flowing on their land. They make embankments and catch and retain the rain water, so that it may be used on the spot rather than flow away.[174]

This is a clear reference to the sort of floodwater farming that is best evidenced archaeologically in the UNESCO Libyan Valleys work (Figs. 1.11, 10.2) or the Kasserine survey (Fig. 10.4).[175] Farming concentrated on the floors of wadis, within which walls, sluice gates, and spillways controlled the flow of seasonal flash floods. Water was also "harvested" by long walls on the plateau areas flanking the wadis, directing rain water into particular sectors of the field systems. It is easy to see how disputes might arise in such systems between neighbours over the extent to which a particular water catchment zone was monopolised by one farmer over another. Floodwater farming was essential in much of *Tripolitana* (including the Syrtic coastland wadis) and south/south-west *Byzacium*, and along the southern and eastern flanks of the Aurès. As noted, these were areas of evidently enhanced sedentarisation under Rome, but the specificities of the floodwater farming technology would suggest it was building on something that was potentially already underway to some extent in the later 1st millennium BCE. The earliest floodwater farming development should perhaps be looked for nearer the Tripolitanian coast with the Gaetulian Libyphoenicians.

The floodwater farming of the Libyan Valleys consisted mainly of basic run-off, in which the fields in the wadi beds were irrigated by directing and controlling the flow of seasonal flash floods in the wadis—spreading the water and slowing its progress so the soil got a good soaking. The technology was a little different to the south of the Aurès and Nemencha mountains in Algeria, where the volume of water coming down the wadis and exiting the mountain front was larger and

172. Shaw 1984; 1991b.
173. Shaw 1991b; Slim 1992.
174. Translation from Dilke 1971, 65.
175. ULVS: Barker et al. 1996a, 191–225; Mattingly and Barker 2005; Kasserine: Hitchner 1990; 1995c.

flooding events more regular. As well as cultivating the wadi beds in the path of the water flow, here resources were also invested in diversion dams and canal systems designed to spread the flood across adjacent terraces. This created large fan-like areas of cultivation, essentially flood-fed oases.[176] The farming systems recorded in the Albertini tablets at the eastern end of the Nemenchas were almost certainly of this flood-diversion type, with references to "*aquaria*" most plausibly understood in reference to the main diversion canals that provided boundaries of many of the properties mentioned in the tablets.[177]

Floodwater farming is largely distinct from the groundwater irrigation systems that supported the evolution of most oases. An exception to this rule concerns some of the oases of the Moroccan Sahara, which derive their water from seasonal (or, in the case of the Draa, perennial) rivers flowing off the Atlas and Anti Atlas ranges.[178] However, most Saharan oases depended on natural springs (the most abundant being the artesian springs of the Jarid and Nefzaoua), foggaras (the underground irrigation channels we encountered in discussion of the *Garamantes* in Chapter 5), or wells. All forms of irrigation dependent on groundwater sources are very labour-intensive and costly to establish and maintain, with the water gained a precious and highly regulated commodity. Water rights tend to be well defined and quite specific in these sorts of oasis communities, since the labour to construct systems often depends on communal efforts. The systems devised by communities to allocate shares of the available water reflect this.

A key decision about how to divide irrigation water from a perennial spring concerns whether to use units of time or units of volume. One of the most famous of Latin inscriptions from North Africa concerns the management of an irrigation scheme at *Lamasba* (Aïn Merwana) in the Bellezma valley just west of the Aurès plain (*CIL* 8.18587/4440; *ILS* 5793).[179] *Lamasba* lies towards the northern end of the Gaetulian zone, but in a region of substantial veteran settlement, and this may be of relevance to the erection of the inscription. The surviving part of this substantial text represents perhaps only a fifth of the original inscription that presented in detail the irrigation rights of a large number of property owners. The reason the arrangements were "published" in such permanent form was the result

176. Birebent 1962 for detailed studies of these systems. Field systems recorded in the *limes* zone to east and south-east of the Aurès were similar, Baradez 1949a; 1957.

177. For the Albertini tablets, see Courtois et al. 1952. A forthcoming article by Andrew Wilson argues that the term referred to waterwheel lifting apparatus, but this seems inherently unlikely in the case of streams that flowed only seasonally. To my mind, references to "*aquaria de flumine ascendente*" (TAlb IV) and "*aquaria qui de torrente lebat*" (TAlb XV) link the use of the *aquaria* to a stream that was elevated or in flood, and that seems the more obvious and technologically more suited interpretation.

178. Sterry et al. 2020, 240–63

179. The definitive version of the text is published by de Pachtere 1908. For commentaries, see Meuret 1996; Shaw 1982.

of a local dispute that had necessitated a commission being appointed to review water rights at *Lamasba*. Although endlessly discussed by philologists and ancient historians, much of what was at issue remains uncertain simply because it details a very Saharan approach to water division. However, the basic outline is not in doubt. The irrigation related to a perennial spring (*aqua Claudia* must be Aïn Merwana), since the allocations imply a constant state of flow through the winter months, and the units of allocation were measured in multiples of half-hour blocks.[180] A main channel (*matrix*) seems to have carried the water to a series of terraces (*scalae*) on which were the individual field-units, associated with named individual landholders. The allocation of water was not made in relation to the area of individual fields, but to something represented by the letter K (most probably denoting trees).[181] The number of trees would provide a good approximation for land area if these terraces were essentially planted with olives and fruit trees but with other crops intercultivated. The system seems to have operated by the opening and closing of sluice gates along the main distribution channel and within each of the terrace areas sequentially for designated periods of time, presumably controlled by a water clock device that measured 30-minute intervals. The closest parallels lie, in all probability, in the traditional water division arrangements at oases like those of the Jarid or Ghadamis.[182]

What may have brought the operation of the customary system into dispute could have been a cultural clash between part of the local population who fully accepted such an allocation system and others who had challenged it or who were trying to undermine its allocation principles to gain unfair advantage. There were clearly some large discrepancies in the amount of land held by individuals in the surviving text, with the largest holdings 10 to 25 times the area of the smallest, and 12 families controlling about 75% of the irrigated land.[183] It is certainly conceivable that these dominant landholders included military veterans who originated from outside the region, and who were effectively trying to undermine the fairness of the water allocation scheme for self-advantage and through lack of sensitivity of the cultural principles that underlay it. The commission seems to have essentially accepted the local allocation system based on time units, and the record on stone was designed to make concrete the allocations.

180. Shaw 1982 remains the best account of much of this, though I like Meuret's (1996) explanation of a particularly puzzling aspect of the document, which describes two types of water from the same source: *aquae ascendens* (AqA) and *aquae descendens* (AqD). He suggests that in the AqD phases, the outflow from the header tank exceeded the inflow volume, gradually drawing down the water level, necessitating a reduction of outflow by means of a sluice to allow the water level within the header tank to build up again (AqA).

181. Shaw 1982, 82–87.

182. Jarid: Trousset 1986a; 1987b; Ghadamis: Eldblom 1968. See also Mattingly et al. 2020b.

183. Shaw 1982, 69.

Oasis communities with access to springs or foggaras followed similar principles of allocation of water by units of time or volume (the latter determined by sluice structures with standard apertures).[184] The details of allocation may have been written in some cases, but would normally be on impermanent materials. But a common feature of such systems is that the allocation principles were well established and understood in the community, so the practice of distribution functioned smoothly and irregularities of procedure could be challenged.

It is possible that these diverse water cultures of North Africa can also help us understand some of the religious differences identified in the previous sections. In the northern Maghrib, average annual rainfall figures would suggest that dry farming was practicable, but the big danger for farmers was the unequal spread of rainfall within and between years. This was something that was hard for farming communities to control except through direct appeals to the chthonic gods that were believed to govern the weather, rain, and fertility. The seriousness of the negotiation is indicated by the practice of child sacrifice in the Baal/Saturn cult.

On the other hand, for the *Gaetuli* communities, the problem required both an appeal to divine forces and practical inputs by human communities to create and maintain irrigation systems. For pre-desert floodwaters, it was still important that chthonic forces brought rain to the locality when it was needed, but the floodwater systems were marked in the landscape by walls built by the labour of past generations and were often under the surveillance of the tombs of ancestors. In this case, the connection between living community and the investment in irrigation infrastructure by the forebears perhaps favoured an appeal directed through ancestor veneration.

Irrigated oasis communities may have had concerns around the maintenance of water flow from springs and the level of water tables feeding wells and foggaras, but the most immediate threats to the oasis generally came from failure of or damage to the distribution systems (wells, foggaras, and canals). Again, it seems plausible that the ancestors who had created this infrastructure were deemed well placed to protect the interests of descendant communities. In both of the Saharan irrigation cultures, ancestor worship was thus a logical corollary of the human investment in irrigated technologies that sustained life. More conventional deities existed too, but these were more related to the spheres of warfare and desert travel.

In any event, there seem to be some grounds for differentiating between the "water culture" of the peoples of the Maghrib and the Sahara.

---

184. Sterry and Mattingly 2020a, 12–17; 2022; Wilson et al. 2020, 69–99.

Conclusions

The countryside is where we find the most ambiguous cultural engagement with the Roman Empire. Certainly, there were some privileged groups who advertised their relationship with the Empire, variously through use of Latin inscriptions, cosmopolitan elite material culture of the Empire, Roman citizen nomenclature, or reference to parallel membership of military or urban communities. It was also where Libyan and Punic culture endured most strongly, where Punic and Libyan gods in loosely syncretised forms were preferentially worshipped, and where provincial art was at its most idiosyncratic in terms of style, iconography, and meaning. In such landscapes, the value of investigating discrepant identities is readily apparent.

Part 6: Some Final Themes

Chapter 12

DIFFERENT ECONOMIES

Introduction: Economic Discrepancies

The main focus of this book has been on the cultural nonconformities that resulted from the imperial experience of Africa under Rome, in part built on deep historic differences, but also accentuated and changed by the colonial situations. In this chapter, I reflect on some of the economic discrepancies that also typifies a region under imperial rule. North Africa is generally viewed as a great economic success story under Rome—indeed, a veritable boom seems to be indicated by the scale and style of urban monumentalisation. However, as in other areas of the story of Africa under Rome, there is greater complexity here and a lack of a uniform outcome.

In my previous work on other provinces, I have argued that we can identify three basic types of economic systems operating in tandem in the Roman Empire.[1] The *imperial economy* relates to a series of mechanisms used by the Roman state to deal with the complex issues of managing and exploiting the Empire's resources and supplying key state actors (the emperor's household, the army, and administrators/governors) and the city of Rome. The blunt impacts of Roman conquest in terms of booty seized and enslavement of the defeated could have powerful initial effects, but the imperial economy was much more about the detailed arrangements that underpinned subsequent colonial government. Knowledge was key to extracting resources from the provinces; and Rome, like other imperial powers, engaged in extensive information-gathering exercises of conquered territory and peoples (land-survey, the census). This in turn supported measures like large-scale land redistribution and taxation in coin or kind, including customs dues. Imperial and state ownership of property (and rents therefrom) was another important sphere of the imperial economy, as too was the monopolisation of key resources (metals, decorative building stone, etc.). In times of war especially, Rome also resorted to requisition and compulsory purchase of what it needed logistically. Treaties with conquered or defeated enemies often included coercive measures to extract manpower (compulsory recruits for the army to serve in other regions). The other side of the imperial economy was the huge cost of empire: paying the army, supplying

1. See in particular Mattingly 2006a, 491–502; 2006b, 295–97; 2011a, 125–45.

and maintaining widespread garrisons, building the infrastructure of the security zones, supporting the building programmes and benefactions of emperors. The major imperial supply system known as the *annona* encompassed both military and other aspects of imperial redistribution, but most notably was organised around extraordinary arrangements to supply the city of Rome (and later other imperial centres) and the Roman army. Large volumes of essential materials were moved around the Empire under the umbrella of the imperial economy.

I define the *extra-provincial economy* as trade and other economic activity extending between different provincial territories or going beyond the limits of the Empire to neighbouring peoples. In principle, this was free trade, conducted by private individuals rather than state agents, though the patterns of interprovincial movement of goods were often coincident with or influenced by the main supply lines of imperial redistribution systems. Trade in the Mediterranean boomed in the Roman era, in part at least because of the economic opportunities that the existence of the Empire created. Rome did not have its own merchant fleet and relied instead on subcontracts with traders to move key imperial resources like metals, grain, olive oil, and wine. However, the overall patterns of material culture distribution reflect a profound globalisation and economic connectedness of the Roman world. The capital investments to develop the extra-provincial economy and the spending of profits accrued from it are very evident in North Africa.

Nonetheless, much economic activity of the Roman world was essentially at the local level, what I define as the *provincial economy*. Most goods that changed hands under the provincial economy travelled relatively short distances from where they were produced, because as low cost essentials they were vulnerable to transport costs or the tariffs that operated at provincial boundaries. The provincial economy covers a range of activities at varying levels of economic sophistication, from more embedded economies to evolved local markets. Again, the spread of monetisation and the impacts of taxation had a part to play in bringing change to these areas.

In reality, these were overlapping spheres of activity, rather than exclusive models, but the relative importance of the three concepts in different regions and across my three broad communities (military, urban, rural) resulted in significantly different outcomes and outlooks. In what follows, I blend some observations of the economic interactions of the three communities with reflections on the importance of the imperial economy in particular.[2] There is continuing debate about the nature of the Roman economy (laissez-faire or regulated), its capacity for growth, and its structural underpinnings.[3] It certainly does not appear to have been homogenous in its operation, though regional groupings of provinces may sometimes have followed similar trajectories.[4] The story of the economy merits a book to itself, but

2. Leveau 1978a, 89–92 also recognised the significant colonial dimension of the African economy.
3. Erdkamp et al. 2015; Scheidel et al. 2007.
4. Lepelley 2005b.

I restrict myself to a few examples to indicate the way that the imperial power also impinged on other areas of rural, urban, and military production. Cumulatively, there is impressive evidence of African exports to Rome and the wider Empire, though discriminating between materials that moved as part of the imperial economy and those that were due to free market trade is not always easy.[5]

The Rural Economy

While the evidence of agricultural intensification in Africa under Roman rule is uneven, the aggregated impact of rural change is hard to deny.[6] Older views of a precipitant overall decline in the rural landscape and productivity in late Roman times have been countered by the accumulation of archaeological data and a more critical view of the sources.[7] A recurrent theme of Chapter 10 was an intensification of rural production in the Roman period and, in the more marginal zones, increased sedentarisation of the Gaetulian peoples, though in many instances building on pockets of pre-existing agriculture in oases and other environmentally favourable niches. I have argued previously, from the evidence of much enhanced oil (and wine) production, that this went beyond mere population growth and in fact represented real growth in the African economy (Fig. 12.1 for an overall distribution map of olive and/or wine presses in North Africa).[8] However, as is also apparent from the detailed evidence, the patterns of intensification, specialisation, and upscaling of production capacity cannot be easily separated from the colonial context in which they occurred. Rome had a huge impact on the regional economies, both by direct mechanisms, such as land redistribution (associated with the emergence of large estates and resource appropriation through the *annona* system), taxes, customs, and share-cropping rents, or indirect mechanisms, such as opening up of "global" markets to African producers. Like growth, economic contraction, when it occurred, was also highly regionalised within the African landscapes.

Rural Markets

The main markets were attached to the many urban centres, but North Africa undoubtedly had many additional rural markets, especially in areas of lower urban density. Periodic markets (*nundinae*) provided not only opportunities to buy/sell

5. For an overview of North African exports, see Tran 2005.
6. Cf. De Vos Raaijmakers 2022; Deman 1975; Haywood 1938; Lassère 1979; Thompson 1982.
7. Dossey 2010; Lepelley 1967.
8. Mattingly 1988b; also Hitchner 1993a; Hobson 2015a; 2015b. For a contrary view and response, see Scheidel 2009; Wilson 2009c.

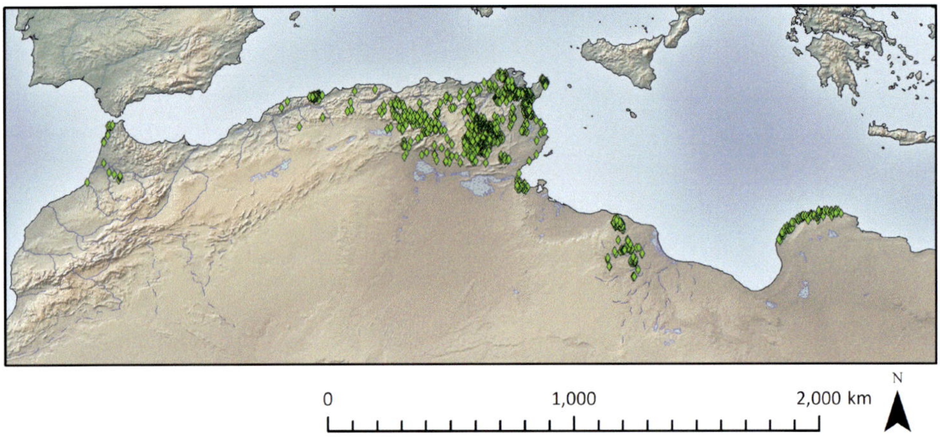

Figure 12.1. Overall distribution of olive and wine presses from North Africa (Martin Sterry, from data in Ahmed 2019; Barker et al. 1996a; Bigi 2019; Buzaian 2022; Camps-Fabrer 1953; Hobson 2015a; Mattingly 1988b).

or exchange commodities, but also served as convenient labour markets for people seeking either workers or casual work. An important inscription from a senatorial estate at Henchir al-Begar between *Cillium* and *Thala* shows that it was necessary to obtain senatorial approval in Rome for the setting up of such a periodic market.[9] Two points are worth noting here. First, the right to hold a market was a restricted one in the Roman provinces and had to be petitioned for. Second, some individuals were better positioned in society and in relation to the provincial governor to make successful requests. The estate of Henchir al-Begar was undoubtedly one of the largest of the High Steppe, to judge by its olive processing facilities and the large area covered by its main settlements (Fig. 10.6). While markets in North Africa under Rome were thus notionally free, they were not independent of all colonial oversight and control, and were a likely conduit through which the imperial economy might at times operate to source required goods and services.

The Grain Supply, Olive Oil, Wine, and the Annona

In reviewing the survey data in Chapter 10, the most visible archaeological markers of the rural economy have been the stone elements of the distinctive mills and presses used in olive oil production (with presses of similar types also in use for wine production). However, *Africa* had a particular reputation as the breadbasket of Rome, allegedly (Josephus, *Bellum Judaicum* 11.16) contributing 18 million

9. Shaw 1979b; 1981a. Cf. more recent discussions by Chaouali 2003; Fentress 2007.

modii (117–126,000 tonnes) of grain each year. Our most direct evidence for grain production relates to literary and epigraphic data.[10] From these we learn not only of the generation of a substantial surplus of grain in the African provinces, but the evolution of a sophisticated infrastructure of well-made roads and bridges, a fleet of massive four-wheeled wagons, warehousing and harbour infrastructure, and a staff to oversee and document all aspects of the collection, transport, storage, and shipping of the essential commodity.[11] However, the archaeological correlates for all this remain slight.

The main grain-producing area was northern Tunisia, with the imperial estates in the vicinity of *Thugga* at the heart of it, but also extending into the Dorsal region around *Sicca*.[12] The rolling landscapes around *Thugga*, with frequent hillslopes, are not really suited for strict monoculture—with the imperial estate inscriptions attesting that olives and vines were part of their production. However, the numbers of presses recorded in the *Thugga* survey (c.335 in 371 km^2 surveyed) are significantly higher than might have been expected previously.[13] In regions suited to it, as in the area of the *Villa Magna/Mappalia Siga* (Henchir Mettich), cultivation of vines was also encouraged.[14] Nonetheless, grain was at the heart of the business of the estates in the upper *Bagrada* valley and its tributaries, though the dearth of excavation work has left their granaries and threshing floors unexposed.[15] An interesting and distinctive regional architectural find from five sites in the *Thugga* survey is a huge combined kerbstone and door pivot, designed to prevent the large wagons from damaging the farm doors, and thus provides proxy evidence of the vehicles that moved grain from the production area to the port at *Karthago*.[16] The systematic stock-taking and quality-control sampling of the grain en route to Rome is well illustrated by evidence from Africa, Egypt, and Rome.[17] There is equivalent evidence for regulation (counting and weighing) of olive oil consignments from *Karthago* in late antique times, with the strong presumption that this was a continuation of an earlier *annona* system.[18]

While olive oil and wine were not initially part of the free distribution of foodstuffs at Rome, they were nonetheless both essential commodities that the emperors needed to ensure there were adequate and affordable supplies for the city. There

10. Christol 1994; de Romanis 2003; Pavis d'Escurac 1976; Picard 1956; Rickman 1980; Sirks 1991; Tengstrom 1974.
11. Codex Theodosianus 8.5; Rickman 1980, 120–21, 231–35. Cf. also de Romanis 2003.
12. Rickman 1980, 108–12.
13. De Vos 2013, 152–56; for landscape views, see, for example, De Vos and Attoui 2013, 215–18; De Vos and Maurina 2019, 3, 7.
14. De Vos 2013, 172; *CIL* 8.25902.
15. Saidi 1980 for a study of the plainlands of the upper Medjerda.
16. De Vos 2013, 188–189 (examples from sites 21, 31, 175, 378, 570).
17. Rickman 1980,120–55.
18. Peña 1998.

is good evidence that *annona* officials were engaged in obtaining supplies in Spain and Africa, and making arrangements with private shippers for the movement of such cargoes to Rome.[19] Under Antoninus Pius there was certainly at least one experiment with free donations of oil and wine along with grain to the populace (HA, *Antoninus Pius* 8.11). The addition of an olive oil dole to the *annona* supply for the population of Rome under Septimius Severus (HA, *Septimius Severus* 18.3) was made possible by a deal under which his home town of *Lepcis Magna* undertook to supply oil in lieu of other taxes.[20] A close association also existed in parts of the Mauretanian provinces between agricultural production and the food supply of Rome, though the evidence of direct *annona* arrangements is less clear-cut.[21]

Some Other Key Products of African Economies

While the countryside was the engine room of the economic well-being of the African provinces, a number of other commodities can be highlighted.

Marine Products

The Atlantic coast of Africa and the southern shore of the Mediterranean has always been a favoured zone for the exploitation of marine produce, and there is abundant evidence to demonstrate this for the Roman period. Annual blue fish migrations (tuna, herring, mackerel, gilt sardines) into the Mediterranean through the straits of Gibraltar have followed the currents along the African littoral, and the arrival of such a bounty of cheap protein has traditionally been exploited by coastal communities.[22] The shallow seas off the eastern coast of Tunisia are favoured spawning grounds of many of these fish, and a substantial seasonal fishing industry has existed there in most periods of history (Fig. 12.2).[23] Fish were sometimes salted whole, but much of the harvest could be rotted down in deep tanks to produce pungent fish sauces (*salsamenta*).[24] Although some of the production was centred

19. Aldrete and Mattingly 1999 for a survey of the evidence of the *annona* for Rome. *Annona* officials involved with olive oil procurement in the 2nd century include C. Iunius Flavianus (*CIL* 6.1620) and Sextus Iulius Possessor *CIL* 2.1180).
20. Mattingly 1988a.
21. Papi and Martorella 2007.
22. Mattingly et al. 2011, 206–07; Slim et al. 2004, 45.
23. Ben Lazreg et al. 1995; Slim et al. 2004; Trousset 1998b; cf. also Mattingly et al. 2011, 205–14; Wilson 2002a; 2002b.
24. Curtis 1991; Marzano 2013 for general studies on fish products in the ancient Mediterranean. Ponsich 1988b, 95–102 for a good account and photographs of traditional tuna fishing in the Straits of Gibraltar area.

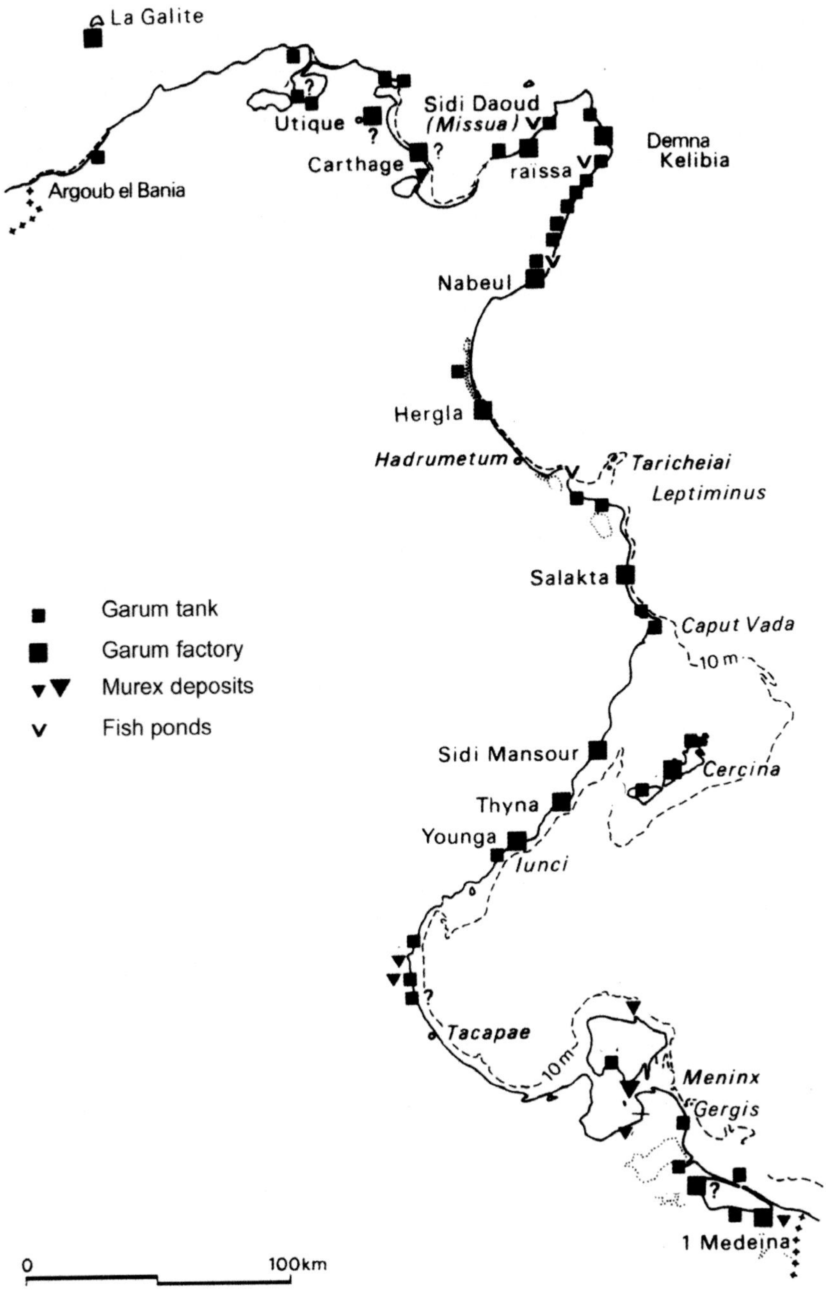

Figure 12.2. Location of fish salting and processing sites along the African coast (from Stone et al. 2011a, 208).

on coastal towns, much of it was strung out along the littoral between the major centres. There was also a significant density of fish processing on either sides of the straits of Gibraltar in southern Spain and Morocco.[25] Although relatively few of the fish salting sites have been excavated, their characteristic rows of deep mortar-lined vats have been recorded in many locations.[26] The globalised Roman Mediterranean offered extensive opportunities to export to Rome and many other areas less well provided in marine products by nature. Inland North Africa was, of course, another large potential market.

A further marine product that was extensively exploited in the Roman period, building on pre-Roman beginnings, was purple dye.[27] With its imperial connotations, purple production was a commodity subject to imperial oversight.[28]

These marine productions were both rural- and urban-based. The largest-scale facilities seem to have been urban or closely situated near a major port. The opportunity of accessing Roman world trading networks encouraged investment and up-scaling of production capacity, linked to the investment in improved harbour facilities at coastal cities like *Leptiminus* or *Meninx*.[29]

Quarrying and Mining

State intervention in the economy also affected the exploitation of decorative stone (especially marble) and metals, in both of which Rome took a keen interest and, with the more valuable materials, operated a monopoly.[30] For the former, there is the abundant evidence now available from the quarries of *giallo antico* at *Simitthu* (Chemtou). Exploitation had commenced under the Numidian kings, with the expansion of the quarry workings in Roman times now documented in fine detail.[31] Although the town adjacent to the west of the quarry workings was clearly significantly involved in the enterprise, the long-maintained military/prison camp and production facility on the north side of the quarries emphasises coercive state control (Fig. 8.13).[32] Further inland marble quarries are known at Ain Smara near *Cirta* and at *Calama*, as well as along the Algerian coast at Cap de Garde and

25. Cerri 2007; Ponsich 1988b; Ponsich and Tarradell 1965; Trakadas 2015; 2018.
26. For excavations at Cotta and *Lixus* in Morocco, see Ponsich 1988b,102–68; for Nabeul, Slim et al. 1999.
27. Chebbi 2010; Drine 2007; Wilson 2002a; 2002b.
28. Várhelyi and Bagnall 2009, 342, with references to imperial control of purple production at *Girba/Meninx*.
29. Stone 2016a.
30. On imperial interests in quarrying and mining, see Hirt 2010; Russell 2013, 38–52.
31. Ardealanu 2018; Rakob 1993.
32. Rakob 2005.

Filfilla, though these have been less explored archaeologically.[33] Pliny (*NH* 5.22) mentioned marble as one of the few notable products from Africa (paired with wild beasts). Many other quarries are known that supplied the great urban expansion with building stone.[34]

For mining exploitation in North Africa, we are much less well informed, though there were clearly Roman-era workings of many of the principal ore deposits of copper, silver/lead and iron, with more limited gold deposits.[35] Semi-precious stones were another type of natural resource that was widely exploited by Rome and, given the desert locations of many of the major sources of gems, was an important element of trade with people like the *Garamantes* and *Nasamones*.[36] Red carnelians were much used in the Roman Empire for decorative signet ring stones, and according to Pliny (*NH* 37.92) North Africa was second only to India as a source.[37]

The Slave Market and Wild Beasts

Another area that was distinctly influenced by the imperial economy was the slave market. In the early centuries of Roman expansion in North Africa, wars and revolts provided ample opportunities for enslaving elements of defeated peoples as part of the spoils of victories. It is, of course, impossible to evaluate the demographic impact of this, but for some of Rome's most persistent or recalcitrant enemies of the early Empire, such as the *Musulami*, one imagines it was considerable, especially when combined with enforced conscription of manpower into the Roman *auxilia*. In the longer term, slave trading certainly operated across the provincial borders with peoples like the *Garamantes*.[38] Individuals inside the province with *cognomina* related to the *Garamantes* or enslaved people referred to as "Garamantian" were probably black-skinned, with the *Garamantes* (themselves a very mixed ethnic society) seizing people from neighbouring regions of the Sahara and sub-Sahara and trading them northwards.[39] Similar patterns of slave trading (and slave raiding in the interests of Rome, but carried out by African intermediaries) were probably a feature of Rome's security zones. The late antique *Expositio*

33. Braemar 1986; Tourbal 1995, 58 (map), 60.
34. Russell 2013, 66–71; Slim et al. 2004 (for coastal quarries).
35. Gsell 1928c; Tourbal 1995; on iron exploitation, see also Schrüfer-Kolb 2011, 450–53.
36. Géroudet 1995 for a review African gemstones mentioned in Pliny's *Natural History*.
37. Gliozzo et al. 2014; Mattingly 2017, 24–29. Géroudet 1995, 49 notes the different terms used by Pliny for carnelian—variously Carthaginian stones, Garamantian carbuncles, Nasamonian stones, Syrtican stones.
38. Fentress 2011; Mattingly 2017, 27–29.
39. See also Desanges 1978a; 1999a, 229–38; 239–47.

a b

Figure 12.3. Arena *venationes* (wild beast hunts). a) In a mosaic from *Hadrumetum*. b) A wall painting from *Lepcis Magna* (photos: author).

totius mundi et gentium (62) specifies that enslaved people and textiles were exports from *Mauretania* and the combination may well be a reference to Saharan trade.[40]

North Africa was renowned for its wild beasts, especially the ferocious ones that were much prized by Roman magistrates putting on displays in the amphitheatres across the Empire.[41] The capture and transport of such valuable commodities was a well-organised and potentially lucrative undertaking (Fig. 12.3). As agriculture became more and more extensive within the Maghrib, so the hunting had to penetrate further into the mountainous enclaves and the desert regions.

Pottery Production

There are several distinct types of pottery production to consider. All parts of North Africa had needs of everyday wares, whether handmade or wheel-made, and these were mainly fulfilled by local or regional producers.[42] More significant from an economic perspective were the manufacturers of amphorae and of fine wares (in a range of red gloss finishes) and lamps, though it is generally recognised that pottery serves as a proxy for trade in other sorts of commodities, rather

40. See Chapter 5 and Mattingly et al. 2017a for arguments regarding Sahara trade.
41. Bertrandy 1987; various papers in Blanc-Bijon et al. 2021.
42. Most conveniently summarised in Bonifay 2004, with excellent maps and form series. For recent summaries of multiple strands of evidence, see Ben Tahar 2020; Bonifay 2022; Hobson 2015a, 103–42.

than an intrinsically valuable commercial good.[43] Both internal and external (Mediterranean and Saharan) patterns of distribution of African ceramics need to be considered.[44]

Although amphorae were not the only containers used in Roman times for the transport of liquid products, their peak production period very much matches the height of Roman globalisation in the early centuries CE.[45] Amphora production relates most clearly to Africa's trading and imperial supply relations, as the vessels were containers for three main categories of mass exports: olive oil, wine, and salt fish/fish sauces. At one time, it was commonly assumed from the evident prominence of olive presses in the landscape that the majority of African amphorae were oil containers.[46] However, more detailed study of amphora morphology, organic residue analyses, and the recovery of some forms with fish remains inside or traces of pitch linings (which are unsuitable with olive oil but commonly used with wine) suggest that this picture needs substantial revision (Fig. 12.4 for a summary chart).[47]

At *Leptiminus*, where the intensive surface survey allowed detailed quantification of amphora rim types, we can distinguish two main clusters of mid-Roman amphorae): Group 1 (essentially variants of the Africana I series with average capacity of c. 44 litres) were used for olive oil and made up c.37% of the total; Group 2 (variants of the Africana II series with average capacity of 64 litres) were used for fish products and wine, and comprised 31.5%. This suggests that numerically olive oil amphorae were marginally more important, but if the larger capacity of the Group 2 amphorae is factored in, then volumetrically combined exports of fish products and wine exceeded olive oil at this port.[48]

The concentration of North African amphora production for the most part close to or at the coastal harbours demonstrates the export focus of these ceramics, though some of the large wine amphorae were certainly used at African wineries for fermenting the must, in place of the more usual *dolia* found on European sites (Fig. 12.5, showing some of the main types produced in different locations).[49] Coupled with the investment in improving harbour facilities, including frequent construction of artificial moles to give greater access to seagoing ships in shallow seas, it is hard to deny a very significant rise on the export

43. Carandini 1983.
44. On internal consumption, see Bonifay 2013; Dossey 2010; on Saharan trade, see Leitch et al. 2017; Mattingly 2013b; on Mediterranean trade, see Bonifay 2004; 2018; Malfitana and Bonifay 2016, 403–39 (for a detailed Sicilian study).
45. Bevan 2014, 394 for a figure summarising diversity in amphora shape, contents, and chronology.
46. Peacock et al. 1989; 1990; Zevi and Tchernia 1969.
47. Bonifay 2004, 471–75; 2007; 2021 for most recent updates, though noting that much more organic residue analysis is needed; Stone 2010; Stone et al. 2011a (for *Leptiminus* amphorae).
48. Mattingly et al. 2011, 240–50.
49. Brun 2004, 202–04.

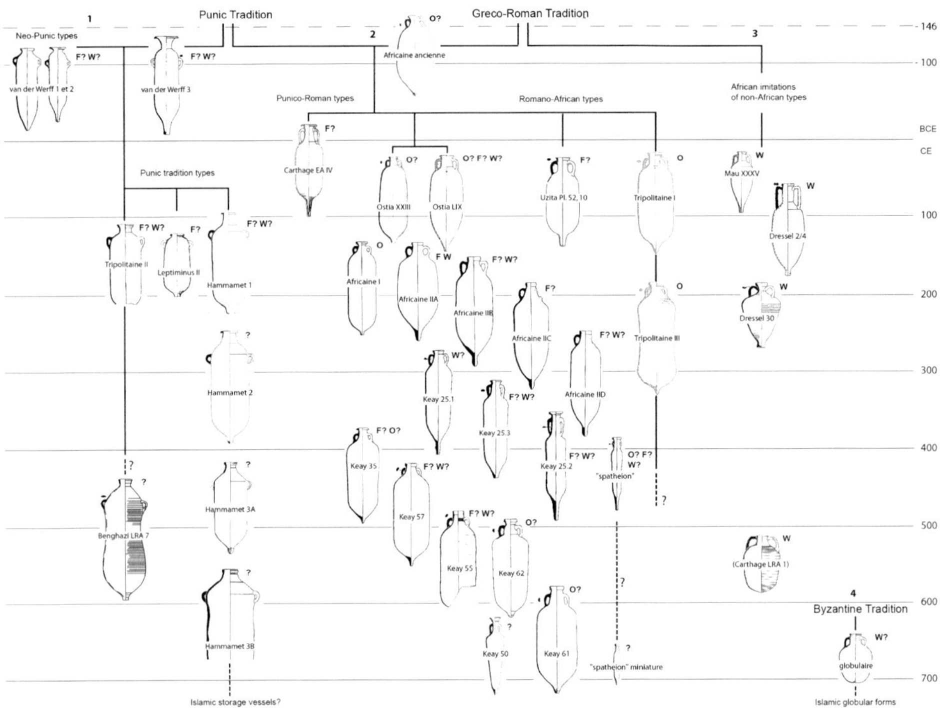

Figure 12.4. North African amphora production, linked to oil and wine/fish sauce exports where possible (O = olive oil; W = wine; F = fish products) (after Bonifay 2004, 88, with additions).

capacity of North Africa.[50] What is now clearly demonstrated is that North Africa exported substantial volumes of olive oil, wine, and various fish products, all of which were significant contributors to the regional economies.

North African fine wares are generally referred to as African Red Slip (ARS), but came in a series of distinct fabrics denoting regions of production (Fig. 12.5).[51] The A fabric group is generally assumed to have been produced in northern Tunisia, but no kiln sites have been firmly identified. The production sites of the late Roman D fabrics that are characteristic of northern ARS did not follow on from A ware production at the same locations. Of the two main variants of D, D1 can be related to the lower Medjerda valley, and D2 to the lower Siliane valley. There is a third D variant from Sidi Khalifa and near Nabeul on the eastern coast. C wares mainly originated in central Tunisia in the region west and south-west of Kairouan and north of *Sufetula*. There were further inland variants in southern Tunisia that are less

50. Stone 2014b; 2016a.

51. On the main fabrics and forms, see Bonifay 2004, 45–65; Hayes 1972; Mackensen 1998; Mackensen and Schneider 2002.

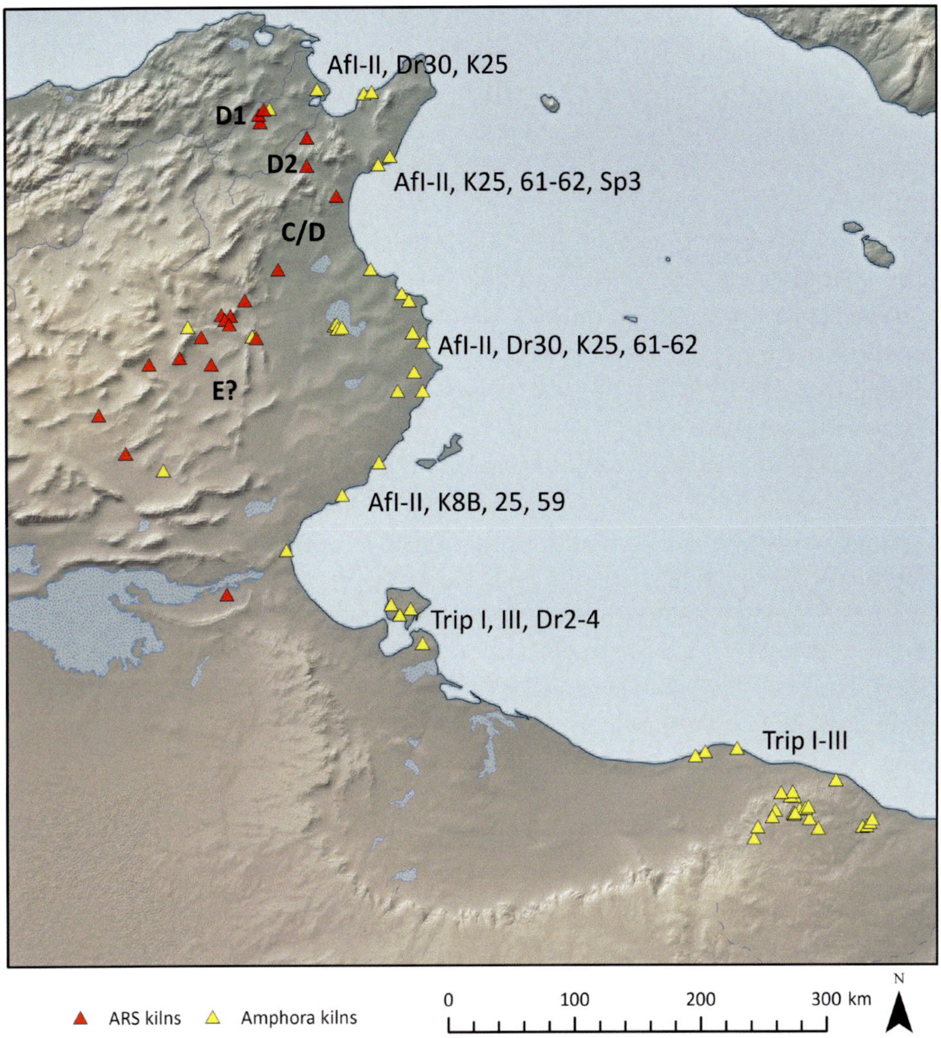

Figure 12.5. Main production centres of African amphorae and fine wares. For amphorae, numbers in main typological series are indicated as follows: Af = Africana; Dr = Dressel; K = Keay; Sp = Spatheion; Trip = Tripolitana (Martin Sterry, from author's rough after Hobson 2015a, 104, 120).

well known at present, including E fabrics. Regional productions are sometimes recognised by separate classifications, as in the case of Tripolitanian Red Slip (TRS).[52]

Lamps were produced at most of the main fine ware production sites. There are also a number of cook wares that mark an intermediate range of wares, often with just one slip-coated surface. Some of the later forms of ARS were quite elaborately

52. Hayes 1972, 304–09.

decorated with stamped motifs or moulded figures.[53] Although most of the red slip pottery was not intrinsically valuable, it achieved a phenomenally wide distribution in North Africa and the Mediterranean, in part, no doubt, by piggybacking a ride with shipments of other cargoes out of African ports (grain, oil, wine, fish sauces, marble, beasts, textiles, and so on).[54] The export affiliation of A and D wares may have been closest with grain, as many of the largest known production sites lay in Northern Tunisia, as at al-Mahrine in the lower Medjerda valley, or *Uthina* in the lower Siliane valley.[55] The C wares originate from a region bordering on the major zone of olive oil production in the High Steppe. Cook wares seem to have been produced at many of the same production sites that made the fine wares, but also at additional coastal production sites, which perhaps explains their unusually wide distribution outside Africa.[56]

Much of our knowledge of African pottery exports relates to consumption centres. Unfortunately, studies of Mediterranean shipwrecks are biased towards the hotspots of Mediterranean leisure diving, with relatively little underwater archaeology having been done along the Maghribian coasts.[57] The main shipping routes between Africa and Rome were open sea routes where limited exploration has been possible, though with some important discoveries of undisturbed wrecks on the Skerki bank, between Tunisia and Sicily.[58] Such discoveries have the potential to illuminate the relationship between the different sorts of African production and cargo compositions.

Urban Economic Diversity

In Chapter 8 I noted the significant morphological differences between different categories of towns in Africa and this also in part translates into economic distinctiveness.[59] For instance, many of the so-called Libyphoenician coastal cities became large harbour towns under Rome, with evidence of enhanced urban manufacturing, though much more research on such industry and workshops is needed.[60] Africa had a very long coastline along which harbour sites were at a premium. The pre-Roman development of coastal anchorages was well advanced and further investment saw improved facilities at many sites in the Roman period. A boom in the

53. Mackensen 2019.
54. Bonifay 2004, 445–85 on the diffusion of African pottery and its meaning in terms of commerce and economic growth. Cf. also Carandini 1970; 1983; Fentress et al. 2004.
55. Mackensen 1993; Mackensen and Schneider 2002.
56. As at *Leptiminus*, Bonifay 2004, 66–71; Stone et al. 2011a,
57. Mattingly 2006b, 293–94 ("Riviera effect"); Parker 1992; Wilson 2009b, 219–29.
58. McCann and Freed 1994; McCann and Olesen 2004.
59. Stone 2013a.
60. Amraoui 2018; 2020; Brun and Leguilloux 2004; Wilson 2001a; 2002b; Wilson and Flohr 2016,

volume of shipping and exports from African ports is reflected in the archaeology of many of these sites—whether represented by the impressive standing remains of *Lepcis Magna*, or the surface carpet of mosaic and marble fragments at a site like *Leptiminus*. The *Leptiminus* survey provided a vivid picture of a coastal town that was a major centre of manufacturing focused on export markets. The production of olive oil, wine and fish sauce amphorae in particular hint at the major sources of the city's wealth (Fig. 12.6). A similar picture emerges also from the survey of *Meninx* on Jerba, with amphora production supplemented there by purple dye manufacture. These coastal producer/commercial cities diverge significantly from the consumer city model of ancient urbanism.[61] At these major harbour sites, the urban manufacturing reflects the importance of overseas trade. While the imperial economy may have helped structure the commercial networks, and no doubt accounted for some exports, it was the products exported as part of the extra-provincial economy that one suspects generated the greatest profits for these communities.

By contrast, some inland towns in Africa display less impressive signs of wealth accumulation, monumentalisation, or manufacturing activity. A good example in this context is the town of *Segermes*, which at most covers c.20 ha including suburban structures. The core area of development does not seem to have much exceeded 7 ha. The Danish–Tunisian investigation of the site, saw little evidence of monumental ornamentation beyond the forum and capitol complex at its heart.[62]

One consequence of the eventual density of urban sites in Africa was that many had quite restricted *territoria*, and, as noted earlier, some late promotions to chartered status appear to have been dressing up large villages as towns. The disparities in wealth between the curial class of such small sites and the major harbour cities or the owners of the largest rural estates were as significant as their ability to access the economic opportunities of empire. The elite of small towns were rather closer, one suspects, to the less wealthy members of their communities than were cosmopolitan intellectuals like Apuleius or the mega-rich of *Lepcis Magna*. A good example is the early 4th-century magistrate Alfius Caecilianus of *Abthungi*. His testimony regarding the events of Diocletian's persecution of 303 CE reveals that he ate with his workmen and spoke a rather informal and ungrammatical Latin (he was probably a tailor or weaver by trade).[63]

More work on the manufacturing and productive economy of inland towns, following the preliminary work of Amraoui, Fentress, and Wilson is needed.[64] Although urban manufacturing at inland towns was more likely of local significance (serving the provincial economy), we should be aware that textile production may

61. Whittaker 1995; Mattingly et al. 2001.
62. Dietz et al. 1995a; 1995b; Ørsted 1992; Ørsted et al 2000. For other inland towns of northern Tunisia, see Ferchiou 1995b; 2004b; Maurin and Peyras 1990; Peyras 1991; Peyras and Maurin 1974.
63. Birley 1987, 30–31.
64. Amraoui 2017; 2018; Fentress 1990; 2013b; Wilson 2001a.

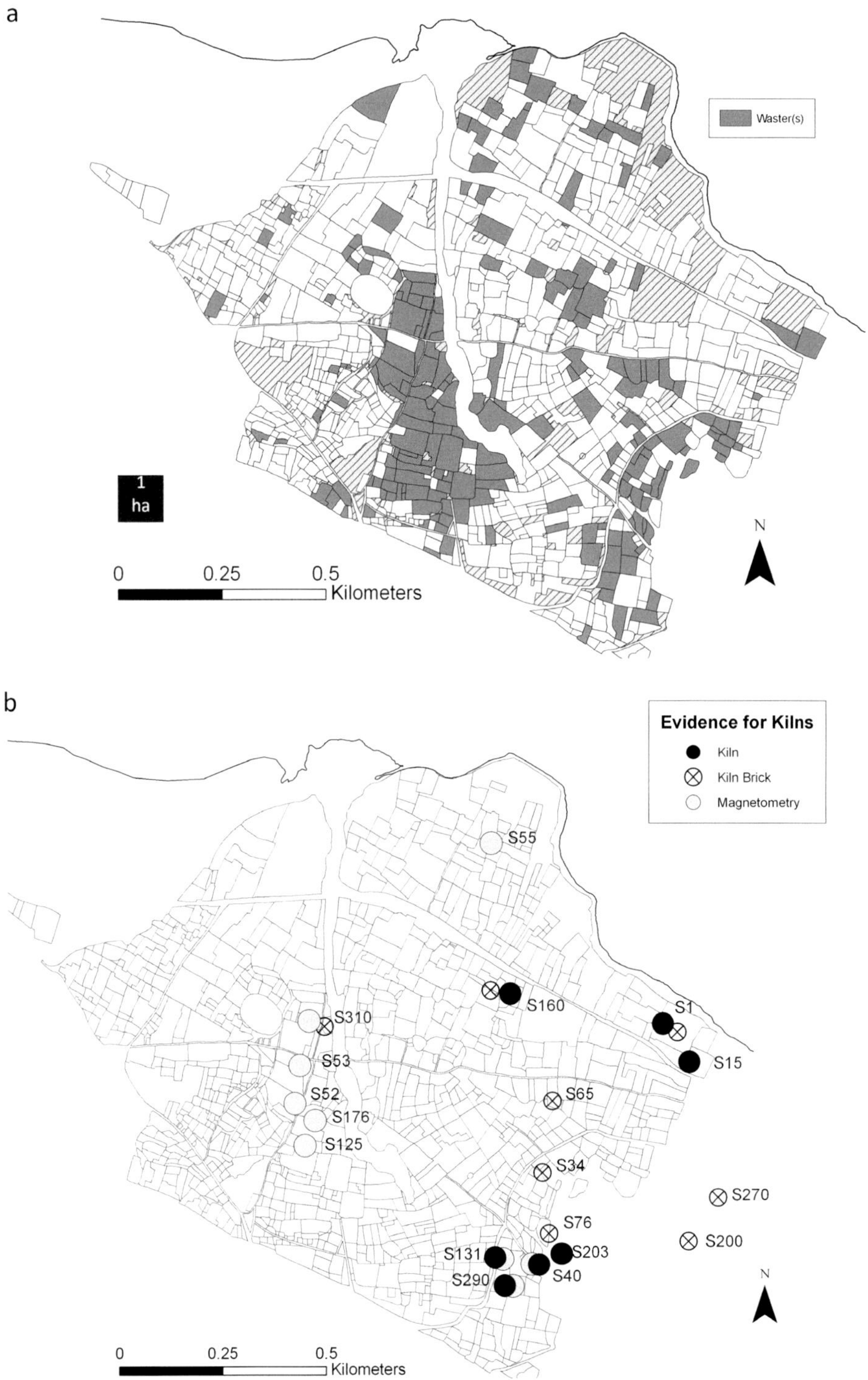

Figure 12.6. Pottery production in the suburban zone of *Leptiminus* (from Stone et al. 2011a, 225).

well have been an important component of the economy of some inland and oasis towns, with links to the imperial economy (military supply) or extra-provincial trade.[65] The commonality of agrarian processing facilities within towns, notably presses for oil and wine, also suggests that there was an important category of town in Africa that was predominantly focused on processing rural production.[66]

Overall, the evidence from town and country in Africa reveals very different economic experiences and outcomes of Roman rule, with, at one end of the spectrum, unprecedented wealth and opportunities to profit from the Empire, but at the other, vastly increased inequality and colonial exploitation. The popularity of revitalisation religious movements like the cult of Saturn and salvationist Christianity should remind us that the lived condition of the majority under Roman rule was far from heaven on earth.

Military Supply and Other Economic Impacts of the Garrisons

Supplying the Garrisons

An obvious aspect of the economic impact of Roman garrisons concerned the means by which they met their own logistical needs.[67] Garrisons needed supplying with many things: water and food (including grains, legumes, fruits, domestic animals for meat, salt, honey, herbs and spices, drinks such as wine and beer); construction materials for forts, outposts, internal buildings; fuel for cooking, heating, and pyrotechnical activities; textiles, leather, clothing and arms/armour/equipment; metals and metal artefacts; wood and basketry products; pottery and glassware; riding and pack animals, and other transport related materials like carts; leisure activities (covering a broad spectrum of goods and services like drinking, prostitution, gambling/gaming, hunting); literate equipment (stone cutters and appropriate local stone, wooden tablets, pottery ostraca, papyri, ink, styli, sealing materials); people (recruits for the ranks, slaves, women, traders, craftspeople and service specialists); coinage and money systems for transacting business. The consumption footprint of the garrison was large in comparison to the overall numbers of troops, not least because the military community encompassed a wide range of civilians who lived with and alongside the troops.[68] Establishing a legionary fortress was equivalent to creating a major town, even a small fort was equivalent to a large village or small

65. Amraoui 2020, 128–36; Guédon 2018a; Wilson 2001a.
66. Bigi 2019; Vismara 2007.
67. See further the excellent analysis of Guédon 2018a, 179–246. Also Davies 1987; Erdkamp 2002; Whittaker 1994, 98–131; 2004.
68. Mattingly 2006a, 191–94 for comparable situation in Britain.

town. Cumulatively, the military communities created around garrison posts were numerous and had large economic impacts at the regional level. The supply of the garrison community was a complex operation and quite distinct from the market mechanisms that supplied the rural population of the surrounding zone—as is evident, for instance, in the significant divergence between pottery assemblages registered by the UNESCO Libyan Valleys Survey and those recorded at the forts at *Gholaia* and *castra Madensia*.[69]

Rare documents such as the *Vindolanda* tablets or papyri from Egypt give us glimpses of the complexity surrounding the web of transactions involved in such supply systems. From Libya we have another important dossier, the ostraca from Bu Nijim (with a few recently published examples from al-Qurrayyat al-Garbia also).[70] It must be acknowledged that if we did not have these documents we would struggle to detect (or at any rate fully account for) the transactions they attest to in the archaeological record. This is in part due to a major lacuna in the archaeological data concerning botanical and faunal analyses from military sites.[71]

One of the main conclusions we can draw from the windows into day-to-day practices that such ostraca provide is that the Roman army regularly made use of long range contracts or purchases for some elements of their supply needs. It is also apparent that serving soldiers fulfilled specialised roles in the supply of food and other materials for the garrison.[72] The most important Bu Nijim ostraca dealing with military supply in the mid-3rd century CE, relate to consignments of food obtained for the garrison by named soldiers who were operating at a distance from the fort. A typical document (Bu Njem 79) tells us about such a transaction:

> To Octavius Festus, my decurion and *praepositus*, Aemilius Aemilianus, soldier, sends greetings. I am sending to you, sir, by the camel-driver Macargus, two *siddipia* of wheat which make 24 (*modii*). In the year of the consuls after Thuscus and Bassus [259 CE]. [second hand] Received 21 January [259 CE][73]

Apart from grain, the ostraca also mention liquid commodities, most likely olive oil, but, perhaps significantly, not dates. These do not appear to be supplies from oasis farmers (though I argue below that oasis farmers may also have contributed to provisioning). The most plausible explanation, recognised by all commentators

69. Cf. Dore 1996; Leone 2017; Mackensen 2021a, 155–214.
70. Guédon 2018a, 167–78; Marichal 1992; Rebuffat and Marichal 1973. For the new material from al-Qurrayyat al-Garbia, written in local Punic using a Latin cursive script, see Ziegler and Mackensen 2014.
71. Though see now Morales and Mackensen 2020.
72. For comparable documentation from *Vindolanda*, see *Tab Vind* II, 343.
73. All references to ostraca in the numbered "Bu Njem" series are to Marichal 1992 (see 99–106 for discussion of food supply).

on the ostraca, is that Aemilius Aemilianus was operating in the pre-desert zone to the north-west of Bu Nijim, where the UNESCO Libyan Valleys Survey demonstrated the vitality of floodwater farming systems and dense sedentary agricultural communities, as at the famous site of Ghirza—from where we also have images of small camel caravans.[74]

The amounts of produce mentioned in these ostraca are in a variety of named local measures, with equivalents in *modii* for wheat or *urnae/libra* for liquid goods. Although some of the documents were fragmentary, and thus aspects of the reconstruction is hypothetical, several different Libyan terms were evidently equivalents to a unit of c.105 litres and the significance of this demands attention. The dry weight of wheat (c.0.79 kg per litre) and barley (c.0.60 kg per litre) is known, so 105 litres would weigh 63 kg (barley) or 83 kg (wheat). The carrying capacity of a camel is approximately 150–200 kg with the load normally split in two parts, either side of the hump.

The logic of this, as Robert Marichal, the original editor of the ostraca, recognised, is that grain units of 105 l capacity (*sidippia*, *selesua*, *sbitualis*) had a probable relationship to a camel-load, especially for wheat, where two of these units would make a load of 166 kg (and wheat is the more probable grain involved here).[75] Other local units appear to be fractions (¼, ½ or ¾) of a unit equivalent to 105 litres. In Table 12.1 I have taken this argument a bit further by developing Marichal's analysis to include an indication of how many camels and/or different animals may have been involved in the transport of the attested consignments. The 105 l units seem to equate to the contents of one panier or a loading of olive oil in skins or amphorae (with double this volume normally carried together as a camel-load).[76]

An interesting observation is that many of the quantities in the list do not correspond to what we might expect in terms of a given number of camels each with a load equivalent to 2 × 105 litres of grain or olive oil. Assuming the basic idea of camel-loads is right, then either some animals were carrying only part-loads, or the small convoys contained a mix of different animals alongside camels. In favour of this latter possibility, the subunits of the standard 105 litre volume might be equated with different-sized packs and thus different animals. In Table 12.1 I have also indicated the appropriate number of animals needed if all the goods were carried by camels and, in the final column, an indication of how this might also have been accommodated by using a mix of camels, mules, and donkeys. Stéphanie Guédon has argued that because the Bu Nijim supply documents mention camels, and other documents relating to the Garamantes only refer to donkeys, that this suggests that camels were used only in relation to military supply, and Saharan trade

74. Barker et al 1996a; 1996b; Mattingly 1995, f.p. 173 for image of Ghirza small camel caravan.
75. Marichal 1992, 100–02.
76. On carrying capacity of pack animals, see Mattingly et al. 2021.

Table 12.1. The Bu Nijim (Bu Njem) ostraca and camel-loads.

Ostracon (Bu Njem no.)	Camel-driver	Units in local measure	Equivalence in libra (lib), *modii* (mod) or *urnae* (urn)	Equivalence in litres (kg)	Equivalence of 1 local unit in litres (kg)	Potential number of camels	Potential use of other draft animal (c=camel, m=mule, d=donkey)
75	?	?	530+ libra	200+ l (173.5+ kg)	? + weight of jars	1 (× 173,5 kg)	1 c
76	Iddibalis	7.5 *selesua*	90 mod	787.5 l (622 kg)	105 litres (83 kg)	4 (× 155.5 kg)	3 c, 1 m? (3 × 166 + 1 × 124 kg)
77	Iassuchtan	9 *sbitualis*	108 mod	945 l (746.5 kg)	105 litres (83 kg)	5 (× 149.31)	4 c, 1 m (4 × 166 + 1 × 133 kg)
79	Macargus	2 *siddipia*	24 mod	210 l (166 kg)	105 litres (83 kg)	1 (× 166 kg)	1 c
81	Glareus	2.5 *ašgatui*	30 mod	262.5 (207 kg)	105 litres (83 kg)	2 (× 102.5 kg)	1 c, 1 d (1 × 166 + 1 × 36.5 kg)
80	Fezinis fil.	7 (?)	63 mod	551.25 l (435.5 kg)	78.75 litres (62.2 kg)	3 (× 145 kg)	2 c, 1 m (2 × 166 + 113 kg)
78	Iaremaban	20 *iśidarim[.]s*	60 mod	525 l (414.75 kg)	26.25 litres (kg)	3 (× 138 kg)	2 c, 2 d (2 × 166+ 1 × 41 kg)
88	Macarcus	4 *in.s..*	16 urn	210 l (186.7 kg of olive oil)	52.5 litres (46.7 kg) + weight of amphorae	1 (× 187 kg)	2 m (× 93 kg)

depended at this time on donkeys.[77] I think this is a case of an inadequate amount of evidence. One of the problems with the Bu Nijim ostraca is that we have a relatively small sample of the total documentation that must once have existed, and we should be cautious about concluding that it provides a complete picture. That the Garamantes had camels is demonstrated, for instance, by the fact that excavations at *Garama* have yielded clay figurines of camels in levels contemporary with the Bu Nijim ostraca.[78]

In ostracon Bu Njem 79, relating to Macargus, we can see that the driver was operating with a single camel to transport the load. All the consignments that we know of seem to have involved between one and five animals. This does not seem the most efficient way to source and transport supplies to the fort, but in the absence of mention of payments to the farmers and drivers, we may speculate that Aemilius Aemilianus was progressing estate by estate and collecting a stipulated surplus contribution of so many camel or other animal pack-loads of oil or grain from the pre-desert farmers. Bu Njem 75 mentions a *procurator* and what appears to be a consignment of oil "*dedi ad usus m[ilitum...]*," which suggests a somewhat different supply mechanism, perhaps bringing olive oil from further north in Tripolitania, though again in quite small quantities.

The Roman garrison also had important economic relationships with pastoral peoples of the security zones. Under Rome it is clear that transhumance routes became more circumscribed, water and grazing rights were defined and recorded in stone, and pastoral migration was closely supervised and economically exploited by the Empire. Pastoralists were highly important to the economy of ancient Africa and contributed in a number of ways.[79] They provided primary and secondary animal products to many sedentary communities, both rural and urban. Animals were essential for traction and transport, and the horse had long-term significance as the specialised weapon of North African warfare. Meat was probably a secondary consideration for many in the population, with its dietary consumption more focused on social elites, sacrifices, and feast days. But the consumption of leather and wool will have been on a significant scale. Large numbers of livestock are not always welcome around agricultural crops, but after harvest the grazing on the stubble in exchange for manuring of the ground is one of the most important pastoral/sedentary interactions.[80] Pastoral groups who arrived in an agricultural area on a predictable seasonal cycle that coincided with peak labour need in the farming cycle could provide vital support for sedentary labour especially at harvest time. Finally, pastoralists were the people with specialised

77. Guédon 2018a,173–74.
78. Mattingly 2013a, 427, 518.
79. Leveau 1988.
80. Whittaker 1978a remains a classic statement of the case.

livestock and equipment, as well as the experience of long-range desert travel. Overland trade in the peripheral parts of the province and beyond, deep into the Sahara, will have relied on them.

Saharan Trade beyond the Provinces

At different times, there has been more or less confidence in the existence and significance of trans-Saharan trade in antiquity. I must confess to having been a sceptic up to the mid-1990s, but my investigations of the *Garamantes* have caused me to revise my opinion.[81] Andrew Wilson has reviewed the evidence for and against trans-Saharan trade and proposed some interesting ideas about its evolution over time.[82] However, he has also advanced a view that rather than thinking of trans-Saharan trade as fundamentally a targeted long-range exchange system, we should instead conceive of it more as a series of short- or medium-range interlocking subsystems. In this view, we might expect there to be a close correlation between the supply of civilian and military markets in the security zones with the evidence of what travelled out beyond. In fact, there appear to be some important distinctions between what was traded with the *Garamantes* and the goods moved as part of the supply mechanisms for the garrisons in Tripolitania and for the civil community in the pre-desert zone.[83] The logical implication of this is that different pottery supply mechanisms served each of these markets, rather than, say, pre-desert communities piggybacking on military supply (or vice versa), or trade beyond Roman territory representing a subset of the material that was regularly traded to the pre-desert peoples and forts of the security zone. There are, of course, some similarities in the pottery assemblages in the three groups of site; this is to be expected, since they shared similar access to imports from overseas via the coastal harbours and to the major pottery production centres of northern Tripolitania.

The best indicator of a substantial volume of Saharan trade relates to Roman goods imported to Garamantian sites across 1,000 km of desert trails. If only small quantities were found, limited to a few elite structures or burials, one might argue that this was not the result of trade at all, but explicable in terms of diplomatic exchanges between Rome and the *Garamantes*. However, the volume and range of Roman material culture found in Fazzan are extraordinary in scope and scale.[84]

81. Cf. Mattingly 1995, 155–57; Mattingly 2017.
82. Wilson 2012a; 2017. Cf. also Liverani 2006, 445–56. Despite some interesting analyses of trends over time, the article by Broekaert and Vanacker 2019 is problematic—notwithstanding the wealth of evidence now published on the *Garamantes* (some of which they cite), their starting premise is that they were a semi-nomadic people.
83. Barker et al. 1996b (for John Dore's pottery type series); Bonifay 2017; Leone 2017; Leitch et al. 2017; Mackensen 2021a, 163, 172–73, 191–92; Mattingly 2013b.
84. Leitch et al. 2017; also finds assemblages reported in Mattingly 2010a; 2013a.

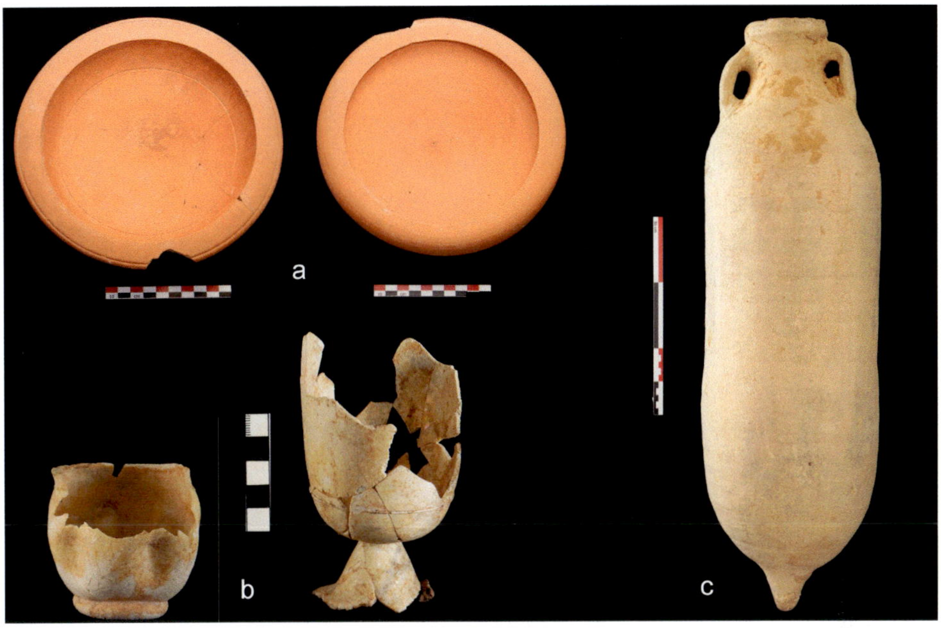

Figure 12.7. Roman imports into the Garamantian heartlands. a) African red slip dishes. b) Glass beaker and goblet. c) Wine amphora (photos: Toby Savage for Desert Migrations Project).

Roman fine pottery, glass, and amphorae are the main consumer durables that stand in as markers for no doubt more wide-ranging exchanges. They occur in abundance in Garamantian burials—most heavily concentrated in tombs of elite type, where multiple fine ware vessels, together with lamps, flagons, amphorae, and multiple glass vessels have been found (Fig. 12.7).[85] However, even relatively simple burial monuments of the 1st to 4th centuries CE contain one or more Roman imports. More than 180 amphorae have been recovered from around 200 excavated Garamantian burials. With a total number of burials of Garamantian date of around 240,000, and perhaps half of those relating to the period when most imports arrived, this sample suggests a trade of, say, 120,000 amphorae across a 500-year period, which corresponds to an average of 240 per year or 120 pack animals if carried in pairs.

The use of heavy amphorae for transporting oil and wine on desert trails merits some further comment, as lighter and less breakable alternatives existed in the form of animal-skin containers. There is evidence from *Karthago* and the Tunisian Sahel, for instance, of considerable use of skins in the transport of olive oil from

85. Mattingly 2010a, 222–98 for the rich assemblages in tombs at the Saniat Bin Huwaydi cemetery.

the African hinterland to the coastal export harbours.[86] The necessity of Saharan caravans to transport large volumes of water, best done in animal-skin bags, may have been a factor favouring a clear demarcation between skin and ceramic containers. Alternatively, it is possible that larger volumes of oil and wine were moved in a combination of skins and amphorae, with only the latter being visible archaeologically. A simple consideration of the numerous intact amphorae recovered from Garamantian burials shows that these came in three main size modules: small, medium, and large, which logically link to the varied carrying capacities of different pack animals. A pair of small amphorae could easily have been carried by donkey, a pair of medium ones by horse (or more likely mule), and the largest ones only by camels.[87]

It is also apparent from excavations at Garamantian settlement sites that the amphora-borne products were used and disposed of in Garamantian day-to-day life. The amount of imported Roman pottery at *Garama*, the Garamantian capital (about 2,500 sherds) is also impressive when the relatively small area of the excavations is taken into account. The absolute minimum number of individual (MNI) vessels present would be 100 from 1/600th of the area of the site, giving a rule-of-thumb figure of 60,000 vessels for *Garama* alone (say 120/year over 500 years). Roman pottery is a common occurrence at hundreds of other Garamantian settlement sites in Fazzan. This certainly implies imports for domestic use on a commensurate scale to the funerary material, so perhaps we should double the above estimate for number of pack animals for amphorae alone (so 240 pack animals per year). The transport of table wares and glass is much more difficult to equate with pack-loads, as in order to be carried safely on rough trails, pottery and glass will have needed careful wrapping and padding—perhaps using things like straw or textiles. Among other notable imports, we might note the Roman hydraulic cement, hypocaust bricks, and flue tiles used to construct a Roman-style bath house at *Garama*. Even if not on a grand scale, the construction of that one building is likely to have required a substantial caravan to transport materials (if just 10 tonnes of materials were transported, a minimum of 50 camels would have been required, plus additional animals, of course, to carry food and water to support the caravan on the march).

Estimating total numbers of pack animals and numbers of caravans per year from this sort of data is plainly very uncertain, but from these pointers the average number of animals for annual caravans carrying all manner of goods south

86. Marlière and Torres Costa 2007; Peña 1998.

87. Mattingly et al. 2021, 186–87. Perhaps of greatest interest is the fact that the amphorae found in Fazzan were often abnormally sized variants of types that are known in different standard size modules in Mediterranean trade. That demonstrates that the amphorae producers were manufacturing special consignments of vessels for the Saharan trade.

could easily have been in three figures; and following practice from other phases of Saharan trade, when caravans were rarely below 30 animals or above 100, this would suggest multiple separate groups each year. Some periods no doubt had more frequent or larger caravans.

The Bu Nijim ostraca provide some important supporting evidence for the existence of caravans specifically destined for the *Garamantes*. There are references to a *statio camellariorum* in the ostraca, and though its function and precise identification on the ground are debated, the most plausible interpretation is that this was the equivalent of a caravanserai.[88] Studies of the Silk Road trade running through Palmyra, for instance, have identified a number of examples of what these structures might look like—a large rectangular walled compound for shelter and the feeding and watering of animals, with numerous small rooms around the periphery for housing merchants.[89] Structures of this type are known in the suburbs of *Lepcis Magna*, and though they could also have been warehouses for stockpiling olive oil and other regional produce awaiting export to overseas markets, it is just as plausible that they were the terminal bases for the Saharan trade—where goods were stockpiled and pack animals assembled prior to departure and brought to at the end of their return journey.[90] The reference to the *statio camellariorum* in the ostraca suggest it was at, or very close to, the Bu Nijim fort, as day duties for soldiers include a work detail *ad camellos*. A problem here is that the main focus of archaeological investigation at Bu Nijim has been on the fort and its associated garrison settlement, and while it is possible the *statio* comprised a sector of the garrison settlement directly around the fort, there may be more logical alternatives. If we look at the wider context of the fort at Bu Nijim, it lay less than 1 km from a small oasis and the location of a number of important wells (Fig. 12.8). A short distance north of the main well and oasis, there is a large subrectangular enclosure of c.65 × 57 m. It is not dateable and could relate to any phase of Saharan trade, but it is at least a good candidate for the *statio camellariorum* and situated where we might expect it—in close association with a major well where pack animals could be watered and accommodated.[91]

The hundreds of pack animals I estimated above to have travelled to Fazzan annually must also have carried return cargoes. Clearly, this was not the equivalent of the Silk Road or the Red Sea trade with India in terms of volume or value, though its organisation shares some characteristic features. It seems reasonable to argue that Saharan trade was in the second tier of external trade in the Empire. The

88. Guédon 2010, 157; 2018a, 173–78. Cf. Marichal 1992, 73–75, 112–13, with references to *ad camellos* in Bu Njem 3, 4, 9, 42, and to a *statio camellariorum*, Bu Njem 5.
89. Degeorge 2001.
90. Zocchi 2018a, 190–97 for a recent overview of these structures.
91. The enclosure was first noted on the high resolution satellite imagery now available via Google Earth.

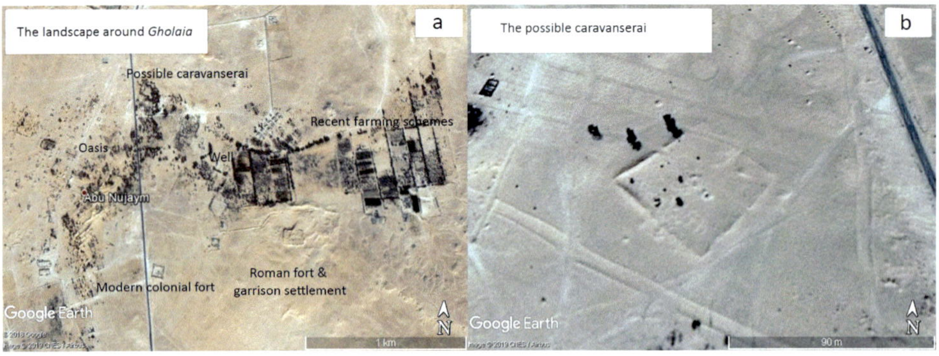

Figure 12.8. The fort, garrison settlement, oasis, and possible *statio camellariorum* by the well at *Gholaia* (author's interpretation of Google, DigitalGlobe image).

fact that Roman goods did not move beyond Fazzan in any great quantity indicates that the *Garamantes* had other things to exchange with trading partners further to the south and south-west. There are some obvious possibilities for products desired by (and taxable by) Rome—in part derived from what we know of other periods of trans-Saharan trade, notably gold, enslaved people, ivory, wild beasts, and salts (including natron), but that is far from all. The agricultural produce of the oasis itself—especially dates and grains—were clearly of high potential value. Pliny the Elder devotes quite a bit of attention to date varieties and the marvels of oasis productivity (*NH* 13.111). I noted in Chapter 5 evidence of manufacturing capacity in Garamantian society. We also know from Pliny (*NH* 37.92; 37.104) that the *Garamantes* were a major source of supply for the Roman Empire of carnelian—second only to India, perhaps—and fieldwork has produced plenty of evidence of carnelian working on Garamantian sites in the Wadi al-Ajal, even though the most likely sources were hundreds of kilometres away. The Roman Empire's main interest may have been in cabochons for signet rings, and the *Garamantes* were certainly skilled enough to have prefabricated these as blanks, rather than simply have exported raw lumps of carnelian. They also manufactured well-cut and polished carnelian beads in large quantities, both for internal use and potentially for Saharan trading networks.[92]

The *Garamantes* had ready access to iron sources in the Wadi ash-Shati area of northern Fazzan, but other metal mines were more distant, and they will have needed to acquire raw materials through trade. Some of this came from the Roman world. Scientific analysis of copper alloys from Garamantian sites has suggested

92. In the commodities of Garamantian trade with Rome, see Mattingly 2017; Wilson 2017. On potential traces of Garamantian trade with West Africa, see Fentress 2011; MacDonald 2011; Magnavita 2013; 2017.

that artefacts (especially brass) manufactured in the Mediterranean were being recycled or remelted to produce locally made artefacts or small bar ingots that were perfectly adapted as trading material for use further along Saharan trails. It is interesting that the majority of the recorded silver *denarii* in Fazzan have turned up at a metalworking site, suggesting they may have been intended for recycling of their silver content there (there is no evidence that the *Garamantes* used coins as money). At the same site, a lot of glass cullet is also suggestive of glass working, with finds from other Garamantian sites indicating glass bead production from the carefully sorted cullet.[93]

Finds of textile equipment, like loom weights and spindle whorls, as well as distinctive fragments of textiles in Garamantian burials, attest to a large-volume and high-quality textile manufacturing capacity in the Garamantian oases.[94] Although unheralded in most accounts of historic Saharan trade, close examination of detailed descriptions of cargoes indicates that textiles and garments were, in most periods, one of the most important commodities in terms of volume. The relative weight, foldability, and durability of textiles made them ideal for desert carriage on pack animals. They could also serve as packaging for more delicate items. They were also universally needed on all parts of the trading networks—everyone requires garments, and even in the central Sahara, thick woollen cloaks are welcome on cold winter evenings or early mornings. Garments or textiles that were otherwise not locally available could command a premium price in such market. The *Garamantes* were producing cotton, probably from about 400 BCE, but in larger volume from the early centuries CE. Such textiles or made-up garments would have had a high value in both the Mediterranean and the south-western markets of the Niger Bend.[95] The overall manufacturing capacity of Garamantian sites and their access to other commodities of value, like enslaved people, gold, and ivory, suggests that supervision and customs control of the Saharan trade was an important task of the advanced Roman garrisons at *Gholaia*, *Myd[...]*, and *Cidamus*.

Border Economies

Both Roman army supply and trade beyond the limits of the Empire were important economic drivers. What did the people of the security zones and beyond have to offer Rome in economic terms? The evidence of a wider spread of precocious oasis farming in the central and northern Sahara and its substantial growth through the Roman era is important here. The *Gaetuli* clearly shared much in common with the

93. On Garamantian metallurgy and glass working, see Duckworth et al. 2020a; Schrüfer-Kolb 2007.
94. Mattingly and Cole 2017.
95. Magnavita 2020.

Garamantes in terms of early oasis development, and the advance of Roman forts into the full desert environment becomes much more comprehensible if they were placed at established water points, where oases already existed, with a double function of oversight of these communities and Saharan trade. Many Roman buildings in the fort and garrison settlement at Bu Nijim (*Gholaia*) used trunks of mature palm trees in their superstructure, confirming that the oasis was well established when the fort was founded, rather than the oasis being developed subsequently. Similar correlations with oases can be made for many other desert garrison posts—*Myd[...]*, *Cidamus*, Mizda, *Tillibari*, *Nigrenses Maiores*, *Badias*, *Thabudeos*, *Viscera*, *Gemellae*. These oases were going concerns when the military deployment reached them; the forts were placed both to supervise these established sedentary communities and to be able to draw on them for food supplies and other needs. The oasis communities were well placed to deliver a range of foodstuffs, including some domestic animals like chickens. As noted, the Bu Nijim ostraca also evidence collection of what appear to be some sort of tribute in grain and oil from farmers in the pre-desert zone at some distance from the fort. However, it is likely that the forts also acquired food supplies from the oasis communities; as these were more adjacent to the forts, the transactions may not have generated the same documentary trail as those involving the pre-desert wadi farms (ostraca like Bu Njem 79 were ultimately a fraud check to ensure that farmers did deliver what they had agreed with the requisitioning soldier at a distance from the base). The use of date palm wood in construction at Bu Nijim, and an ostracon (Bu Njem 71) reference to *Garamantes* accompanying a donkey transport of a small volume of barley to the fort, hint at the important role played also by oases communities in sustaining the garrisons. Interestingly, botanical analysis from al-Qurrayyat al-Garbia of both Roman and post-Roman levels reveals a dramatic decline in grain consumption after the end of the Roman phase, suggesting that in the earlier period the garrison was dependent on supply of grain from a distance, with the small al-Qurrayyat al-Garbia oasis mainly focused on dates and fruits.[96]

Larger volumes of meat could have been sourced from sheep/goat-herding pastoral groups moving between the oases. Interestingly, Strabo (17.3.19) mentions horse-breeding as a major preoccupation of the desert peoples, and given the importance of cavalry in the Roman garrison, the supply of remounts will have provided another area of economic interaction. The heavy water-dependence of horses makes it likely that their breeding was, in part at least, based around oasis communities, not solely in the hands of mobile pastoral groups. On the other hand, though camels had been present since the late first millennium BCE, their importance in Saharan transport clearly increased in late antiquity—perhaps in part due to the reduction over time of the non-renewable water table, resulting in greater

96. Morales and Mackensen 2020, 217.

distances between abundant wells on the trails. Because of the greater hardiness of the camel, mobile pastoral groups were more likely eventually to have become specialised camel-raisers than the oasis communities.

Another aspect of the transborder relations of Rome may have been to create or sustain a slave market. There are strong reasons for believing this was a key aspect of the Garamantian dealings with other Saharan and sub-Saharan peoples.[97] While slave-taking may already have been a feature among these societies in pre-Roman times, it is likely that this became more pronounced under Rome. Similarly, organised hunting for wild beasts from the peripheral landscapes of the African provinces for the supply of the arenas of the Roman world was undoubtedly a specialised area of economic activity, perhaps at times under the supervision of the army, but more often, one suspects, of freelance experts.[98] Provision of enslaved people and wild beasts from outside the Empire were certainly two economic "opportunities of empire" promoted by the presence of the garrison for indigenous groups to fulfil.

The importance of Garamantian textile production has been alluded to and ethnographic studies of more recent oasis communities in the Sahara show that textile production has often been a significant subsidiary economic activity of these communities—another way of balancing the books in labour-intensive irrigated agriculture. In an interesting series of studies, Guédon has reinterpreted a famous document of the African military zone, the *Zarai* customs tariff.[99]

The list of commodities in the *Zarai* tariff fell under a number of customs laws:

Lex capitularis: Slaves, horses, mules, donkeys, pigs, piglets, sheep and goats, kids and lambs, cattle;
Lex vestis peregrinae: Woollen cloaks, tunics, blankets, mantles, other African garments;
Lex coriaria: Animal hides (finished and hair-covered); sheepskins, goatskins (pliable and rough), glue, sponges;
Lex portus maximi: Beasts of burden, amphorae (wine, garum, etc.?), dates, figs, peas, nuts, resin, pitch, alum, iron.[100]

The range of commodities includes items that must have been sourced inside the province (amphorae, sponges) and a number that more likely came from outside (enslaved people, dates). The range of animal products is surely indicative that pastoral people were involved at some level in the trade and exchange indicated. There

97. Fentress 2011 for the most explicit argument.
98. Faure and Leveau 2015, 126 for discussion of the possibility that the mysterious expedition celebrated by a Roman army group deep in to the Saharan Atlas at el-Agueneb was a lion hunt.
99. *Zarai*: *CIL* 8.4508; Guédon 2014; 2017, 259–66; 2018a, 238–40; Cf. also France 2014; 2015. For a more fragmentary text from *Lambaesis*, see Cagnat 1914a; *AE* 1914, n. 234; *CIL* 8.18352. For English text, Fentress 1979, 208–09.
100. *Zarai*: France 2014; Guédon 2014; 2017, 259–66; 2018a, 238–40; Trousset 2003. *Lambaesis*; Cagnat 1914a.

are also a number of other staples of Saharan trade here—such as textiles, garments, and leather goods.[101] The document has, at different times, been seen as marking tariffs on goods moving along the "frontier" of *Numidia*, or between *Numidia* and *Mauretania Caesariensis* or passing out of the Empire.[102] The alternative option, that goods of value were also entering the Empire, here has not been given much credence—largely because of the assumed underdevelopment of Gaetulian society, and despite the fact that the tariff includes a reference to dates and numerous items of livestock, leather, and skins. A peculiarity of the document, evidently drawn up following the removal of a cohort that had been based at *Zarai*, is that it makes no explicit reference to cereals and olive oil (the two products that we have direct evidence of in the Bu Nijim ostraca). The main purpose of the customs law was perhaps to establish a new basis for trade (removing previous immunity from tariffs for goods intended for military supply). In that case, the absence of oil and cereals might suggest that they had been sourced by non-commercial arrangements, similar to what the Bu Nijim ostraca reveal about these sorts of supplies.

Guédon focused on the section of the *Zarai* tariff dealing with textiles and has drawn attention to the use of two adjectives—*peregrinus* and *afer*—evidently to describe textiles of provincial and external origin (Table 12.2). Being aware of the new evidence of Garamantian textile production, she suggested that we might have a record here of Garamantian textiles/garments crossing the "frontier"—though *Zarai* is a very long way to the north and west of Fazzan.[103] That seems an improbable and unnecessary detour for Garamantian textiles to take. However, there are other alternatives that fit better. The Algerian Sahara, only a little to the south of *Zarai*, contained several groups of oases that lay on both sides of the *fossatum Africae*—so perhaps both within the province and exterior to it. Saharan manufacturing and trade is thus likely to have been a part of the *raison d'être* of this zone. It seems very likely that textiles from these oases were integral to the exchange networks recorded at *Zarai*, and the distinction between foreign and local was registered in different levels of customs dues.

The context of the Roman military deployment in the North African desert sectors looks very different when we reconstitute the oases and sedentary populations alongside the long-recognised pastoral elements of the *Gaetuli*. This was not just a question of political and military control—though in some respects the fixed lifestyle and assets of oasis farmers made them easier to supervise than their mobile pastoral counterparts. At the same time, the cumulatively large populations of numerous oases—whether inside or outside the Roman provinces—provided

101. On the staples of trans-Saharan trade, see Mattingly et al. 2017a.

102. For key earlier studies of the tariff, see Darmon 1964; Trousset 2003. For an English translation of the text (and a fragmentary parallel text from *Lambaesis*), see Fentress 1979, 208–09.

103. Guédon 2017, 266.

Table 12.2. The section of the *Zarai* tariff dealing with textiles (from Guédon 2017, 261).

Lex uestis peregrinae,	Tariff for foreign fabric:
abollam cenatori(a)m X IS,	Dinner mantles 1.5 denari
tunicam ternariam X IS,	Ternary tunic: 1.5 denari
lodicem S,	Blanket: 1 quinarius
sagum purpurium X I,	Purple cloak: 1 denarius
cetera uestisafra in singulas lacinias (S?)	Other African cloths, per piece: 1 quinarius?

potentially greater threats to the Pax Romana than the conventional vision of a "nomad threat." On the other hand, the army's economic interactions with the communities both in the security zones and beyond, if balanced and reciprocal, may have contributed to peaceful conditions for extended periods from the late 1st to late 3rd centuries CE.

Nonetheless, there was undoubtedly an exploitative aspect to the economic relationships between the Roman army and civilians of the security zones. When we recognise that the *Gaetuli* spanned across territory both directly and indirectly controlled by Rome, ideas of defending a provincial "sown landscape" against desert raiders seem less plausible than those that depict a Roman occupation that imposed close supervision and obligations on both those inside and outside the Empire. However, unlike in northern Britain, say, where the economic impacts on British peoples seem to have been particularly heavy due to the density of the garrison posts, the smaller size of the Roman army in Africa perhaps created some opportunities also for some *Gaetuli* and *Garamantes*. Fewer troops to support logically meant less economic burden imposed on local groups. The best demonstration of this more favourable outcome lies in positive markers of generation of wealth in several sectors, from the farmers of the Libyan pre-desert to the heartlands of the *Garamantes*. I suggest this was in part the result of relationships that promoted trading, not raiding.

Chapter 13

AFRICAN AGENCY

African Novelty

> Always something new out of Africa (Pliny, *NH* 8.42)[1]

The meaning of Pliny the Elder's reflection of an earlier Greek sentiment seems a good point to end this book with. This comment can be read in various ways, but I think it underscores a prime argument of my book: that we should not underestimate the extent to which Africans contributed to the prosperity of the African provinces and to the richly varied culture that flourished there. It also highlights the impact of Africa and Africans within the Roman Empire. By the 2nd century CE there were increasing numbers of senators who originated from North African cities and not just from settler families or from the largest and most cosmopolitan towns.[2] L. Septimius Severus (with his family) was not the only one to aspire to the purple; his immediate predecessor Pertinax and his rival Clodius Albinus are both thought to have been from Africa. Moreover, Septimius Severus certainly came from a Libyphoenician family, rather than being the descendant of Roman settlers.[3] In place of the 19th-century view that North African peoples were wholly dependent on ancient colonising powers for their acquisition of the trappings of civilisation (urbanisation, agriculture, literacy, and the arts), there is now plenty of evidence to suggest that the Africans were much more active agents in the process of the spread of sedentarisation, urbanisation, agriculture, and civilisation in the Maghrib and northern Sahara. The emphasis on indigenous agency is commonplace in many European provinces of the Roman Empire, but due to the long-term impact of modern colonialist discourse it is less developed in North African studies.[4] A first objective of this book has been to explore the concepts of innovation and social agency in relation to the various groups that made up the ancient population of North Africa. It should be apparent by now that a radical reappraisal

1. *Semper aliquid novi Africam adferre*. Desanges 1999a, iv for a discussion of the passage.
2. Ifie 1998 lists senators from more than 50 African cities, including not only Roman colonies but also many other Libyphoenician and *Numidae* towns, with a few also from the Gaetulian zone.
3. Birley 1988a, 212–20; Mattingly 1995, 54–55, 58.
4. Mattingly 2011a, 43–72.

is required of some of our starting assumptions about the autochthonous contributions to Africa in the Roman Empire.

One of my underlying themes in this book has been that the stories of "Roman Africa" and "Africa in the Roman Empire" are not at all the same thing.[5] The traditional agenda of study has been constructed around the former approach and is less suited to addressing all aspects of the latter. "Roman Africa" privileges the Roman side of the story and the false prioritisation of outside invention and innovation (political, cultural, social, economic). "Africa in the Roman Empire" is more open to the bottom-up contributions and to the hybrid mix in all these spheres. Searching for and evaluating the African elements and context is also an essential rebalancing step towards decolonising our subject.

So What Is New in My Vision for "Out of Africa"?

I end with some thoughts arising from writing this book about a new agenda for study of Africa in the Roman Empire. This is not meant to imply that work under the established traditions of study should be abandoned—I hope the value of the accumulated data is evident from my referencing of and engagement with them. However, as I argued in Chapter 2 and consistently through this book, we need to update the theoretical underpinnings of the subject, and to work harder to decolonise the language of scholarly debate, and to promote methods that are now commonplace in archaeology elsewhere. Some of the best recent work has done precisely this, with transformative impacts on our knowledge and understanding (as, for instance, in studies on *Althiburos* or *Thugga*). A decolonised and modernised archaeology of Africa in the Roman world is a practical proposition and one better suited to the post-Arab Spring world.

The NAIA Period Shaped Africa in the Roman Empire

My first proposal is that we need to develop a much better knowledge of the archaeology of the North African Iron Age (NAIA). Nonetheless, recent developments and a re-evaluation of older data allowed me to recognise (in Chapters 3 to 5) the pre-Roman and pre-Phoenician origins of urbanisation, sedentarisation, and agriculture in Africa. In a nutshell, *Africa* became one of the most densely urbanised and richest provinces in the Empire because it was a densely occupied zone of sedentary farming long before Rome.[6] The *Numidae* and the *Mauri* of the northern

5. Mattingly 2006a for similar arguments applied to Britain.
6. This argument was at the core of the research and development of the Jerome lectures and this book—for a first published development, see Mattingly 2016.

Maghrib were embarked on a proto-urban path from the early 1st millennium BCE, linked in places to a fully developed agricultural regime. The contemporary Saharan peoples, notably the *Garamantes*, but also some of the *Gaetuli* peoples, were also becoming sedentarised at oasis locations, where irrigated cultivation of a package of crops was again well established in the early 1st millennium BCE. Two of the traditionally claimed distinctions of "Roman Africa"—urbanisation and agriculture—thus were underway far earlier that commonly recognised, and the indigenous contributions to the growth of towns and agricultural production by Roman times now need re-evaluating. The extent to which pre-Roman concepts of urbanism shaped the later developments has not been given much thought hitherto. But as is clear from my examination of many plans, the influence of the pre-Roman topographic settings on hilltops and steep-scarped promontories was an important factor at many inland sites. Chapter 8 showed how it is possible to look beyond the most rigidly gridded layouts and the monumental "usual suspects" to arrive at a more nuanced understanding of the spectrum of urban stories in Africa in the Roman Empire.

The cultural footprints of the *Libyphoenices*, *Numidae*, *Mauri*, and *Gaetuli* were also long-enduring, even under the globalising impact of Rome's imperial civilisation. Knowledge of the long-term survivals of Libyan and Punic language and culture are essential for understanding Africa in the Roman Empire, just as modern notions of about "Roman" culture have created our image of "Roman Africa." This theme has featured importantly in Chapters 7, 9, and 11. What I hope to have demonstrated is the long-enduring impact of the fundamental cultural and ethnic divisions of the NAIA era on the lived experience of people in the Roman period.

Discrepant Identity

I hope that the foregoing chapters have demonstrated sufficiently the failings of the Romanisation paradigm and convinced many readers that alternative approaches should be explored instead. Romanisation biases our perspective in favour of a top-down view of society, with a simplistic emphasis on degrees of similarity within and between provinces. More problematically, it is not an ancient term but a direct product of the modern colonial discourse and thus fundamentally antithetical to a modern agenda that seeks to decolonise the discipline of Classical studies.

Hybridity and discrepant identity provide a dynamic alternative to Romanisation.[7] The aggregated *homogeneity* at the core of Romanisation theory is heavily slanted towards elite consumption and behaviours on the one hand, towards the

7. For a fuller articulation of the theoretical basis of discrepant identity, see Mattingly 2011a, 203–45; 2014a.

Roman army on the other. Urban communities also tend to have a different material culture baseline to rural ones. Rather than elide these differences in presenting an overall view of things like "Romano-African" religion, art, funerary practices, literacy, and so on, I have chosen to explore the *heterogeneity* of such practices across three broad "communities": military, urban, and rural. What this means is that we should look for evidence of a plurality of religions, artistic styles and practices, burial rites, and so on, and seek to interrogate the undoubtedly complex social significance of such distinctions. The picture is further complicated by changes over time and by regional variations (in part informed by cultural memory and local traditions). Discrepant identity also recognises that individual and group affiliations were not fixed but dynamic and context specific, allowing for diverse identity presentations for different audiences and for code-switching.

North Africa in antiquity was a polyglot world, with multiple cultural influences. Despite its long coastline, for long periods of its history, the networks and relationships have been as often with the desert as the Mediterranean. Libyan identities (and languages/dialects) varied, and I have argued in particular for a significant difference between the main blocs of north Maghribian peoples and those of the high plains and desert landscapes to the south. Breaking up the idea of ancient "Amazigh identity" in this way makes much better sense of the evidence than assuming an overall commonality of indigenous Africans.[8] Perceptions of different levels of adoption (and even the apparent rejection) of the trappings of *Romanitas* have traditionally been interpreted as due to environmental determinism or social backwardness. An alternative approach, recognising that change is present in all parts of the landscape, is to explore more carefully the imperial entanglements of each region and ethnic grouping, as sketched out in Chapters 7 and 11 in particular.

THE MILITARY COMMUNITY

A country that has endured the experience of modern colonial rule will inevitably have a less optimistic perspective on past imperial systems.[9] In North Africa this is exacerbated by the extent to which agendas were hijacked in the service of modern colonial discourse. The close association between serving colonial army officers and the early exploration of the Roman military deployment is one of the starkest examples of this.[10] For obvious reasons, the Roman army has thus not been a priority area of study for the post-independence Maghribian countries. Yet to have a rounded view of the story of the Roman provinces, we need to engage with the

8. Brett and Fentress 1996; Fentress 2019.
9. Mattingly 2011a, 11 for a map that contrasts the largely "colonising" modern European territories of the former Roman Empire with the modern "colonised" regions of the Middle East and North Africa.
10. Dondin-Payre 2005b; Effros 2018.

evidence of the Empire's coercive systems and assess the role played by the garrison.[11] The Roman security zones and the *Gaetuli* (and the later *Mauri*) peoples had a long-term and complex relationship, and any renewed study of these needs to integrate investigation of both garrison and garrisoned. As I demonstrated in Chapter 6, the garrison was not particularly large by the standards of the Empire, especially given the territorial extent covered by its forts, linear barriers, and other installations. But that does not mean its *impacts* were not significant across multiple areas: the conquest and occupation of territory; suppression of revolts; survey and census of land and people to facilitate taxation and resource extraction; policing of movement and markets; supervision of rural communities and peoples; recruitment of manpower; and a high consumption of horses and pack animals. In Chapter 7 we saw that, although the army increasingly recruited locally among African peoples over time, in cultural terms the military community was bound together in distinctive ways that distanced it from neighbouring civilian groups. The epigraphic habit, religious and funerary practices, and engagement with Roman material culture served to differentiate the military community from others in society.

THE URBAN COMMUNITY

As explored in Chapter 8, urban communities were much more diverse than the most celebrated examples indicate.[12] On the one hand, it is routine to discuss the hundreds of urban centres as representing one of the great triumphs of "Roman Africa." On the other hand, our mental images of towns are dominated by a small number of the most spectacular sites, creating a false expectation that the majority followed the same model.[13] In fact, as we have seen, most of the inland towns were quite small in area and population, with more basic amenities or monuments, and varying engagement with the epigraphic habit and the more specifically Roman religious aspects (emperor worship, the Capitoline Triad, etc.). Many local centres evolved out of nucleated settlements of the *Afri* and *Numidae*, but some only obtained full urban status in the 3rd or 4th centuries. Some of the largest towns developed from the Libyphoenician *emporia* along the coastlines (though here more recognition to the Liby- contribution to their earliest evolution is warranted). The commercial and productive economy of these sites and their harbour links to the wider Mediterranean world made them prosperous and cosmopolitan in feel—though, as we saw even in the case study of *Lepcis Magna*, there was still a long-term imprint of pre-Roman culture. Garrison settlements were a quite distinctive category of town formed around or close by active military bases, like *Lambaesis* or *Gemellae*.

11. It is worth restating that Guédon 2018a is the key starting point for future work.
12. Bullo 2002 is far from alone in not fully differentiating between the various types of urban centre, or reflecting on what lay behind this variability.
13. Though see Scheding 2019 for some promising moves in a new direction.

Although urbanisation was strongest among the *Libyphoenices*, *Numidae*, and *Mauri*, it is apparent that the *Gaetuli* peoples also saw urban development in parts of their territories. We know extremely little about oasis towns in the south, but the tantalising hints that survive strongly suggest they were very different again, perhaps multifocal, within zones of oasis gardens, and perhaps with much more limited areas given over to public space and monumental buildings. Distinct from the early oases, there were other nucleated settlements and towns in the Gaetulian High Steppe and pre-desert landscapes, to some extent building on pre-Roman hillforts, but undoubtedly reflecting enhanced levels of sedentarisation under Rome. The overall urban density in the Gaetulian zone was less high than in the lands of the eastern *Numidae*, and in places it never amounted to much more than proto-urban hillforts and villages. Nonetheless, these were far from the nomadic wastelands of the 19th-century imagination.

In Chapter 9 I demonstrated that the cultural orientation of towns, as visible through archaeology, reflected the aspirations and investments of their elite citizenry above all. But once again, there was a huge variance across time and space. It is unsurprising that the major harbour cities, like *Karthago*, *Lepcis Magna*, *Hadrumetum*, *Iol Caesarea*, became cosmopolitan hubs, not only with suites of large-scale public amenities, but also a wealth of marble statuary and mosaic art. Nor is it unexpected to find that the leading citizens of other harbour cities (for example, *Sabratha*, *Leptiminus*, *Hippo Regius*, *Tipasa*) invested competitively in emulation of these role models. Some of the cities in the hinterland zone also pursued urban promotion and monumentalisation through euergistic competition (*Thugga*, *Thamugadi*, *Cuicul*). Many of the most prominent were those with early Roman citizen adjuncts to pre-existing centres or veteran settlements, though there are elements of these situations that seem more coercive than opportunistic. The cultural character of a large percentage of the overall urban dossier was less overtly "Roman," with a more limited range of urban monuments and a more African religious orientation.

THE RURAL COMMUNITY

The traditional focus of studies of the rural landscapes of "Roman Africa" has been the existence of substantial estates of the emperor and elite families, studded by luxurious country villas and mausolea proclaiming high "Roman" status. However, as I have demonstrated in Chapters 10 and 11, rural communities also followed regionally diverse development trajectories and cultural paths. These related to differing past histories and cultural reference points, as well as varying relationships with the Roman Empire. We must not forget that Africa was essentially conquered and subdued territory of a Mediterranean empire, whose primary interest was the maintenance and glorification of itself. The consequences of this colonial status were especially profound in rural districts, where Rome could (and frequently did) redefine property and territorial boundaries, redistribute land, and take into imperial possession key resources like mines and marble quarries. Archaeologically, the great centuriation schemes of *Africa* are the most visible features of these imperial landscapes, but it is worth interrogating the evidence from every zone to understand how the imperial relationships changed, shaped, and transformed society.

For instance, from the evidence of their rural hinterlands, we can perceive differences in Rome's treatment of the Libyphoenician cities. The demarcation of crowded agricultural lands in the area of the eastern *Numidae* and the Carthaginian *pertica* also distorted the underlying patterns through the growth of massive private estates and imperial *saltus*. This was an area of higher external settlement and deliberate placement of groups of Roman citizens at Numidian centres, resulting in a more Latinate culture, though with sharp boundaries, for instance, with the majority Libyan-speaking communities to the west.

The challenges of the arid nature of the Roman security zones in general was exacerbated for its autochthonous population by the intrusive power and interference of the military community. Across all these landscapes, inequality increased or became embedded in land distribution arrangements under Rome. Land was the great lever of Roman imperialism and its destiny post conquest was both (or alternatively) carrot or stick for subject peoples, with the outcome dependent on their behavioural spectrum from compliant to resistant.[14]

There is plenty of evidence of the socio-economic advance of Africans across many regions, as is clear in the onomastics. Individual subjects of colonial societies have a wide array of strategies to choose from between flight and fight, and an element of accommodation with the imperial power was necessary to secure the basic necessities of life within the province. What is interesting to see in places like *Mauretania* or *Tripolitana* is the way that local (often African) elites used the iconography and literary practices of Rome to enhance their local status, but often in ways that differed from normative Roman behaviours, or that represented a fusion of local tradition with Roman modes of artistic or literate expression.

What Are We Missing?

While new discoveries are accruing all the time, there remain huge lacunae in our knowledge of Africa in the Roman Empire.[15] Some things apply across all three of my putative communities: notably, a general lack of really detailed stratigraphic

14. The principle of Rome making differential settlements is well captured by Siculus Flaccus, *De condicionibus agrorum* 7–8, discussed in Chapter 6.

15. See also Stone 2022 for a somewhat similar analysis of the priorities for new research methods and more scientific approaches in North African archaeology.

excavation, linked to full analysis and publication of finds assemblages and related scientific studies that are increasingly commonplace in the archaeology of other regions or periods. Palaeoeconomic studies, most specifically linked to the analysis of botanical and faunal remains, can contribute a detailed picture of diet and of differences across communities and regions.[16] Household archaeology needs to move beyond architectural and artistic discussion of elite mansions and consider a wider range of houses studied as social units with complex artefactal assemblages. Such studies can provide badly needed quantified data to test further the ideas about discrepant identities outlined in this book. Petrographical and archaeometric analysis of North African pottery, as pioneered and championed by Michel Bonifay and Claudio Capelli, or organic residue analysis of pottery vessels used for transport of liquid commodities or cooking pots are other priority areas.[17] Aerial photography has been heavily restricted across most of the region, despite some pioneering use in the earlier 20th century for mapping Roman centuriated landscapes and identifying elements of the Roman military deployment.[18] Archaeologists have shown ingenuity in obtaining low-level photos using kites and now drones, while the greater availability of high-resolution satellite imagery in recent years is a game-changer.[19]

How could archaeology expand knowledge of the security zones? It would be really helpful to have improved dating schema, especially for the linear barriers (*fossata* and *clausura*). However, the prime desideratum is for integrated programmes of research that would address both the military infrastructure and neighbouring indigenous settlements. This would allow fuller comprehension of the similarities and differences between the military community and the broader community of the security zone—covering things like diet, material culture consumption, epigraphic and iconographic engagement, religious practices. It would be particularly interesting to do isotopic and aDNA work to determine if perceived cultural differences in, say, the early 3rd century CE essentially equated to a single locally derived population split across the two types of site. For indigenous civil sites, it would be interesting to see how their economic orientation was impacted by the presence of the garrison.

Finally, as with my work on the *Garamantes* of southern Libya or the *Darae* of south Morocco, we need more complementary studies of the peoples who

---

16. Fothergill et al. 2020; Van der Veen 1995.
17. Bonifay 2007; 2021 for the still limited organic residue analysis of amphorae and an appeal for greater focus on this in future. For an exemplary dossier of archaeometric studies, see various authors in *Antiquités africaines* (2018), 149–84. For a focused group of papers covering multiple approaches to pottery, see the section on North African pottery co-ordinated by M. Bonifay and C. Panella in D'Alessio and Marchetti 2020, 213–440.
18. Jones 1989a.
19. Barker et al. 1996a, 33–34, 116, 122, 354; Bokbot et al. forthcoming; Rayne 2017a; Sterry and Mattingly 2011.

lived beyond the limits of empire.[20] These desert societies have been significantly underestimated in the story of "Roman Africa," but they were the key extraprovincial actors in the parallel tale of Africa's wider engagement with the Roman Empire, involving war, raiding, diplomacy, and different kinds of trade providing the Empire with things it needed or valued (enslaved people, gold and other metals, ivory, wild beasts, textiles, leather goods, precious stones, dates, and other oasis produce).

What is missing in our knowledge of urban sites? While it will always be nice for Classical archaeologists to excavate another theatre or set of baths or a house with stunning mosaics, the knowledge returns from successive examples of well-known types of site are to some degree limited. Despite colonial-era large clearance excavations, we are also not so well informed about the sub-elite-level housing, shops, and workshops that must have made up a large part of the townscape. Intensive sampling of botanical and faunal remains is essential to address questions relating to foodways.[21] Studies and full publication of a wide range of material culture collected through stratigraphic excavation would start to fill another significant *lacuna*.[22]

As the scale of modern excavation cannot hope to match the large clearance operations of the colonial era, our best way to acquire new evidence relating to issues of urban layout and overall plan is geophysical survey, building on the outstanding results achieved at a number of sites already (see, for example, Figs. 8.9, 8.13). The origins of urbanism at Libyphoenician *emporia*, *Numidae*/*Mauri* inland settlements, and Gaetulian oasis centres also require much more investigation to fill out our knowledge of the organisational principles of such sites and how this may have influenced Roman-era planning and development. Similarly, the late antique and early Islamic transitions were routinely shovelled away with minimal record in older excavations, but need addressing if we want to improve understanding of how Africa in the Roman word led on to *Ifriqiya* in the Islamic world.[23] More work on cemeteries and larger-scale skeletal analysis, coupled with the newer techniques of aDNA, isotope analysis, dental calculus, and so on would transform our understanding about population mobility and demography in general, as well as helping us compare ethnic identity with cultural identity. Studies of religious structures that go beyond the architectural, iconographical, and epigraphical aspects are needed to develop understanding of the African specificities of ritual behaviours.

---

20. See Sterry and Mattingly 2020a.
21. See MacKinnon 2010; 2017 for a useful model based on work at *Karthago*. Also Fothergill et al. 2020; Van der Veen 1995.
22. Integrated study of all types of material culture evidence is essential for sophisticated examination of identity. See the notable work in Britain by Cool 2002; 2004; 2006; Cool and Baxter 2002; Cool and Philo 1998; Crummy 1983; Eckardt and Crummy 2008.
23. Fenwick 2020.

For rural communities, fundamentally we need a massive expansion of excavation of multiperiod settlements across different regions and at all levels of society, to inform us not only of the domestic architecture, productive practices, and consumption habits of these communities, but also about diet, health, technology, economic orientation of production, religious behaviours, burial rites, and so on. The lack of modern excavations of the great wineries and oileries—literally manufactories on a quasi-industrial scale—is a really surprising omission given the part that olive oil and wine played in the ancient economy and in the generation of the wealth of Africa under Rome. A well-presented excavation of an oilery site, for instance, could be a fantastic and informative visitor attraction for tourists and North Africans alike, celebrating the technological sophistication and economic dominance of African production.

Survey archaeology also needs to be pursued vigorously, as the evidence is now under increasing threat through the processes of modernity and development. In the last decades, the landscapes have been transformed by massive expansion of settlements, changes in farming practice and intensity of cultivation, and big infrastructure projects, especially the construction of new roads. Despite the advances in this time in field survey in parts of the Maghrib, there remain huge regions where little has been recorded on the ground, and analysis of satellite images demonstrates that the once well-preserved landscapes are vanishing at an alarming rate.[24]

Finally, it needs stressing that time is not on our side for recovering the data that will fully enable new agendas to flourish. The pace of damage and destruction of the heritage of the NAIA and Roman eras is accelerating, especially beyond the confines of the generally better protected World Heritage Sites (and even some of those are facing significant encroachment). Perhaps the greatest challenge for the next generation of archaeologists in North Africa is that to expand the discipline in the ways suggested will mean eschewing to some extent the distraction of the great "honeypot" urban sites.

Looking Back

This book is the result of many journeys, physical and intellectual, across more than 40 years of engagement with North African archaeology. My travels have taken me from the Nile to the Atlantic, into most micro-regions of the Maghrib and the Mediterranean zones of east and west Libya, then deep into the Libyan Sahara and across the Moroccan High Atlas.[25] My work has involved research in all

24. Rayne et al. 2017a; 2017b for the work of the EAMENA project documenting threats through the use of satellite imagery.
25. See Mattingly 2019 for some biographical background on this.

three of the communities I focus on in this book. As a student, my first enthusiasm was for the Roman "frontiers," but I soon found my real métier in rural survey, through work on the UNESCO Libyan Valleys Survey and the Kasserine projects. Interests in urban archaeology took me to *Euesperides* in *Cyrenaica* and *Leptiminus* in Tunisia. But perhaps the most important epiphany came when I followed in the footsteps of Charles Daniels and travelled south of the Roman Empire to work on the *Garamantes* of Libyan Fazzan.[26] In confronting the mismatch between the Greco-Roman literature pertaining to this people and the archaeological reality, I was forced to think about my understanding of the Roman Empire in a new way. Working on the minutiae of Garamantian daily life also helped me look at the Roman Empire through their eyes and re-evaluate what an empire like Rome represented to its subjects and its neighbours.[27] A subsequent project, focused on the trans-Saharan zone overall, has enabled me to situate the *Garamantes* in their broader context, further underlining the significance of the desert in the long-term story of North Africa and the Roman Empire.[28]

This personal biography is relevant, as I have deliberately chosen to write this book, like my other recent treatments of Roman imperialism, in a personal voice and at times with a polemical edge. I am aware that some of the views expressed run counter to cherished orthodoxies in the field, but I hope that readers will have found my broad observations stimulating, as well as challenging. I cannot claim to have all the answers, and in many areas discussed, the evidence is rather limited, ambiguous, or potentially unrepresentative. However, the ultimate aims of this book have been to advance a decolonised approach to ancient North Africa and to set out some new ideas about how to read and interpret the past. I cannot change my personal history and educational background (as a white man growing up in England in the twilight years and aftermath of empire),[29] but I have tried to demonstrate the necessity and value of exploring my unconscious biases, considering alternative perspectives, and of deconstructing the orthodox agendas that I was first educated in. In approaching conventional topics from different angles, I hope I have made a strong case for decolonising our approaches to the study of ancient Africa. But I have also tried to show how even the data collected in the modern colonial era under the worst colonialist agendas can still be given new life and relevance. I have tried to represent as wide a range of approaches and views in the bibliography cited precisely so that interested readers can follow up with more detailed

26. Mattingly 2003a; 2007a; 2010a; 2013a.
27. In parallel, the 1990s also saw me engage more fully with postcolonial theory, Mattingly 1996a; 1997a.
28. Duckworth et al. 2020a; Gatto et al. 2019a; Mattingly et al. 2017a; Sterry and Mattingly 2020a.
29. Sanghera 2021 provides an excruciating account of growing up in Britain with its toxic imperial nostalgia permeating many areas of education, culture, and society.

research on the wide range of topics alluded to. In no way do I consider this book the last word, but rather I hope it will be a springboard for future research, while casting new light on the broad state of knowledge at this point in time.

Finally, I hope that both sympathetic readers and critics will recognise that the book has brought "something new out of Africa" and that its core ideas are important ones to engage with.

Appendix 1

CHRONOLOGICAL TABLE

Date	Events relevant to North Africa	Date	Roman World	Date	Cultural and technological landmarks in Africa
c.3000 BCE	Last major climatic change in Sahara, start of current hyper-arid phase			7th mill BCE	Arrival of domesticated cattle in Sahara
1101	Phoenician foundation of *Utica* (high chronology)			2nd mill BCE	Arrival of domesticated horses
c.1000	Proto-urban settlements at *Althiburos* (Maghrib), Henchir Bourgou (Jerba), and Zinkekra (Sahara)			1st mill BCE	Agriculture and urbanism; arrival of domesticated camel
814	Phoenician foundation of city of *Qart Hadasht* (low chronology)	753 BCE	Legendary foundation of city of Rome	Early 1st mill BCE	Earliest metallurgy attested in North Africa
675–650	Traditional date for foundation of Cyrene by Greek colonists				
c.630	Libyphoenician *emporium* at *Lepcis Magna* established				
c.515	Attempted establishment of Greek colony in Tripolitania rebuffed by Libyans			6th–5th c	Carthaginian political and cultural hegemony established among Libyphoenician *emporia*
c.509, 384, 306, 279	Treaties between *Qart Hadasht* and Rome	509	Establishment of Roman Republic	Late 4th c	Pseudo-Skylax description of the African coast and harbours

Date	Events relevant to North Africa	Date	Roman World	Date	Cultural and technological landmarks in Africa
310–307	Expeditions of Agathokles of Syracuse in N Africa			End 4th c	*Periplus* of Hanno down Atlantic coast
264–241	First Punic War		Mainly fought in Sicily and at sea, but 256 expedition of Regulus into Africa		
Mid-3rd c	First reference to kings of *Mauri*, *Masaesyli*, and *Massyli*	241–238	Rome takes Carthaginian territory in Sicily, Sardinia, and Corsica		
c.220–203	Syphax king of *Masaesyli* and ousts Gaia as king of *Massyli* in 212/211	237–221	Hamilcar Barca revives Carthaginian fortunes in Spain, succeeded in command by Hasdrubal and Hannibal Barca		
218–201	Second Punic War (Hannibalic)		Mainly fought in Italy and Spain, final battle in Africa at *Zama* in 202, with Carthaginian surrender 201		
206	Death of Gaia, father of Massinissa—various rival claimants to succession	205	Massinissa ally of Rome		
203	Defeat of Syphax by Rome and Massinissa				
203–148	Massinissa, king of united *Numidae*. Progressive extension of Numidian kingdom at expense of *Qart Hadasht* and Tripolitanian *emporia*			c.185	Publius Terentius Afer born. Taken as an enslaved child to Rome, he became one of greatest Roman playwrights (commonly known as Terence)

Date	Events relevant to North Africa	Date	Roman World	Date	Cultural and technological landmarks in Africa
149–146	Third Punic War—siege and destruction of *Qart Hadasht*. Establishment of Roman province of *Africa Vetus*	146	Sack of Corinth	c.146	Voyage of Polybius down Atlantic coast of Africa
139–118	Sole reign of Numidian king, Micipsa				
123–121	Foundation of a Roman colony *Karthago* on site of destroyed *Qart Hadasht* (further deductions of colonists in c.44 and 29)	123–122	Tribunate of Gaius Gracchus	120s	Northern centuriation scheme initiated?
118–111	Conflict between heirs to Micipsa; ends with Jugurtha seizing power and massacre of Italian merchants at *Cirta* in 112				
111–105	War between Rome and Jugurtha; after ineffectual campaigns of Metellus (109–108), eventual victory of C. Marius (108–105)	108 104	Senators accused of taking Jugurtha's bribes investigated. Jugurtha killed in prison in Rome	111	*Lex Thoria*: agrarian law relating to centuriated *ager publicus* in *Africa*
103	*Lex Apuleia* grants lands in *Africa* to veterans of Marius	91–88	Social War in Italy		
78	*Cyrenaica* inherited from last king and provincialised	78	Death of Sulla		
60–46	Reign of Juba I in *Numidia*	59	First consulship of Julius Caesar		
49–46	Roman civil war extends to *Africa*	49–46	Roman civil war between Caesar and Pompey.		

Date	Events relevant to North Africa	Date	Roman World	Date	Cultural and technological landmarks in Africa
49	Death of Mastanesosus, king of *Mauri*, division of kingdom between Bogud and Bocchus II				
46	Defeat of Juba I by Caesar and annexation of kingdom as *Africa Nova* (separated from *Africa Vetus* by *fossa regia*); "*Leptis*" fined 3m pounds of olive oil by Caesar; Cirtan Confederation established under P. Sittius	46	Cato the Younger commits suicide after battle of *Thapsus*; Caesar dictator at Rome till assassination in 44; *Africa* under control of Lepidus during the Triumvirate in 43		
c.40	Unification of two provinces as *Africa Proconsularis*, with Senatorial governor				
38	Bocchus II reunites Mauretanian kingdom	44	Renewed period of civil wars in Rome		
33–25	Death of Bocchus, *Mauretania* adminsistered by Rome	31	Victory of Octavian (later Augustus) over Mark Antony and annexation of Egypt as Roman province. Inauguration of Roman Principate		
26	Cirtan Confederation reamalgamated into province of *Africa*				
25	Juba II (son of Juba I of Numidia) after education in Rome becomes client king of reconstituted Mauretanian kingdom	31 BCE – 69 CE	Julio-Claudian dynasty at Rome		
20s BCE – 24 CE	Period of extended Gaetulian Wars (and revolts)			19	Appearance of Virgil's *Aeneid*

Date	Events relevant to North Africa	Date	Roman World	Date	Cultural and technological landmarks in Africa
22, 20	Campaigns against *Gaetuli* and *Garamantes* (L. Sempronius Aratinus and L. Cornelius Balbus)	19	Triumph of Cornelius Balbus is last by a private citizen at Rome	c.20–10 BCE	Central Centuriation scheme carried out in *Byzacium*
1–6 CE	Further wars with *Gaetuli* and *Marmaridae* (C. Cornelius Lentulus Cossus and Q. Sulpicius Quirinus)				
6	First evidence of *legio III Augusta* at *Ammaedara*				
15–16	Construction of road from *Tacapae* to legionary base at *Ammaedara* through lands of Gaetulian *Musulami*	14	Succession of Tiberius after death of Augustus		
17–24	Revolt of Tiqfarin (Tacfarinas) against Rome. *Mauri* and *Garamantes* later join revolt; final victory achieved by P. Cornelius Dolabella				
23–40	After death of Juba II, son Ptolemy king of *Mauretania*	37	Death of Tiberius and succession of Gaius (Caligula)	27–30	Land delimitation in southern Tunisia round Chott Fjej (territory of *Nybgeni*)
37–39	Separation of military authority in *Africa* from Proconsul (henceforth rests with legate of *legio III Augusta*)	40 41	Assassination of Ptolemy by Caligula leads to annexation of *Mauretania*. Assassination of Caligula and accession of Claudius		

Date	Events relevant to North Africa	Date	Roman World	Date	Cultural and technological landmarks in Africa
40–41	Campaigns in *Mauretania*, in Atlas Mountains, and to south by Suetonius Paullinus and Hosidius Geta.				
c.43	Division of *Mauretania* into two provinces (*M Caesariensis* and *M Tingitana*) governed by procurators	54	Death of Claudius, accession of Nero		
68	L. Clodius Macer, legate of *III Augusta* rebels against Nero, but killed by Procurator Trebonius Gerucianus. Next legate puts to death Proconsul Calpurnius Piso	68 66–71	Death of Nero; Year of the Four Emperors, civil war. Jewish revolt in *Judaea*	60s	Nero sends an expedition up the Nile into *Nubia*
69–70	*Mauretania* and *Africa* embroiled in civil war—attack on *Lepcis Magna* by *Garamantes*	69	Accession of Vespasian, Flavian dynasty 69–96		
70	Expedition of Valerius Festus to Garamantian heartlands	c.77	Pliny the Elder's account of North Africa in his *Natural History*	70s	*Lex Manciana*: new regulations of land on imperial estates in *Africa*; new wave of land surveys and delimitation relating to indigenous peoples
70s	Move of main base of *legio III Augusta* from *Ammaedara* to *Theveste*	79	Pliny the Elder dies investigating the eruption of Mount Vesuvius	71–73 c.78	First *concilium* of priests of imperial cult at *Karthago*. P. Annius Florus born, perhaps at *Cirta*

Date	Events relevant to North Africa	Date	Roman World	Date	Cultural and technological landmarks in Africa
86	Revolt of *Nasamones* and campaign of Suellius Flaccus			90s	Expedition of Julius Maternus to land of *Agisymba* (Lake Chad?) with king of *Garamantes*
96–106	Veteran colonies of *Sitifis*, *Cuicul* and *Thamugadi* founded; honorary colony status given to *Lepcis Magna*, *Hadrumetum*			100–117	Further delimitation of lands of African peoples
105	Advance of forts south of Aurès mountains	97	Accession of Trajan; Antonine dynasty to 192	100	Successful prosecution of former African Proconsul Marius Priscus
c.117	Installation of *legio III Augusta* at *Lambaesis*			c.105	Birth of Fronto at *Cirta*, later tutor of Marcus Aurelius
110–114	Trouble in *M Tingitana* with *Mauri* and *Gaetuli*			107	Tacitus completes *Histories*
117	Significant damage from Jewish revolt in *Cyrenaica*	117–118	Death of Trajan, Hadrian becomes emperor; Lusius Quietus from Mauretania, one of Trajan's lading generals, put to death; Jewish revolt in Eastern provinces	115–117	Henchir Mettich inscription (*consuetudo manciana*) and Ain al-Jemala inscription (*lex Hadriana de rudibus agris*) from imperial estates
118–123	Trouble with *Mauri* and *Gaetuli* in *Mauretania*			121–125	Tacitus completes *Annales*
126	Fort established at *Gemellae* near Wadi Jedi; first phase of linear barrier (*fossatum Africae*) may date to this period	120s	Hadrian's Wall built in Britain	c.125	Birth of Apuleius of *Madauros*

Date	Events relevant to North Africa	Date	Roman World	Date	Cultural and technological landmarks in Africa
128	Hadrian's visit to Africa: *Karthago*, *Theveste*, *Lambaesis*, and *Mauretania Caeariensis*	131–135	Bar Kochba's Jewish revolt	128	Hadrian's discourse to troops at *Lambaesis* engraved on memorial
140–280s	Series of treaties between Rome and the *Baquates* (also *Bavares* and *Macenites*) recorded at *Volubilis* in *Mauretania Tingitana*	137 160	Accession of Antoninus Pius; Antoninus Pius celebrates victory over *Mauri*		
140s–160s	Major rebuilding schemes at *Karthago* including Antonine baths and aqueduct			138	Granting of market (*nundinae*) to *saltus Beguensis* estate
139–143	Troubles with *Mauri* and *Gaetuli*, decree from *Sala* (144) in *M. Tingitana* honouring governor M. Sulpicius Felix for fortifying town and repulsing raids			140s 145 155/160	Ptolemy compiles his *Geography* Birth of Septimius Severus at *Lepcis Magna* Birth of Tertullian
150s	*Sabratha* and *Oea* become honorary colonies	160	Accession of Marcus Aurelius and Lucius Verus	158	Apuleius delivers his defence (*Apologia*) against witchcraft charge at *Oea*
171–171	Raid on *Iberia* (S Spain) by *Mauri*	166	Major outbreak of plague impacts Roman Empire	165–177	*Tabula Banasitana* records citizenship grant to Zegrensian notable in *Mauretania Tingitana*
174	Roman military expedition to Saharan Atlas and Jabal Amour				
174	L. Septimius Severus, Proconsul of *Africa*				

Date	Events relevant to North Africa	Date	Roman World	Date	Cultural and technological landmarks in Africa
180	First attestation of Christianity and first African Christian martyrs (from *Scilli*)			180–183	Petition of *coloni* of *saltus Burunitanus* to Commodus seeking redress of grievances against *conductor* of imperial estate
193–211	Reign of Septimius Severus—the African emperor	192	Assassination of Commodus sparks civil war (lasts till 197); Severan dynasty 193–235. Two other short-lived emperors, Pertinax and Clodius Albinus also of African origin?	197	Tertullian, *Apologeticus*
197	Creation of province of Numidia, governed by legate of *legio III*	197–205	Another Lepcitanian, C. Fulvius Plautianus, Praetorian Prefect and son-in-law of Septimius Severus until executed		
201	Foundation of desert outpost fort at *Gholaia* (Bu Nijim) and other oases in Tripolitania. Advance of garrison in *Numidia* and *Mauretania* (*nova praetentura*) also.			202	*Lex de portu Zarai*: customs tariff document
202–203	Visit of Septimius Severus to *Africa*; arch erected at *Lepcis Magna*	c.203	Addition of African olive oil to the *annona* distributions at Rome	203	Award of *Ius Italicum* status to *Karthago*, *Utica*, and *Lepcis Magna*
203	Martyrdoms of Perpetua, Felicita, and Saturus in amphitheatre at *Karthago*, and of Guddene nearby				

Date	Events relevant to North Africa	Date	Roman World	Date	Cultural and technological landmarks in Africa
202–203? 203–208	Campaigning in Africa? *Numidia* now separated off as a distinct province from *Africa* (Proconsularis)	211 212	Succession of Caracalla and Geta (soon eliminated); *Constitutio Antoniniana* (mass extension of Roman citizenship across Empire)	217–221	*Lamasba* water regulation inscription
217–18	M. Oppelius Macrinus, from *M Caesariensis*, Praetorian Prefect and briefly becomes emperor after assassination of Caracalla.				
227, 235	Further possible revolts of *Mauri*	235	End of Severan dynasty and start of mid-3rd c imperial instability	205–245	The African Minucius Felix writes defence of Christianity
238	*Legio III Augusta* dissolved by Gordian III after its involvement in putting down pretenders Gordian I/II at *Thysdrus*, where procurator had been lynched by mob	240 250	Accession of Gordian III; Revolt of Sabinianus at *Karthago* crushed by *procurator* of *Mauretania Caesariensis*; Edict of Decius on sacrifice—initiates new phase of Christian persecution	246	Cyprian becomes bishop at *Karthago*—his defence of Christianity and Letters are influential in development of Church in Africa
253	Reconstitution of *legio III*, following further revolts of *Mauri*	252–253	Another major outbreak of plague impacts Africa	250s	Main period of extant ostraca from *Gholaia* (Bu Nijim) fort; abandonment of fort by 263
256	First Council of *Karthago* attended by 87 African bishops			251	Cyprian, *The Unity of the Christian Church*

Date	Events relevant to North Africa	Date	Roman World	Date	Cultural and technological landmarks in Africa
257–258	M. Cornelius Octavinus (governor *M Caesariensis*) given extraordinary command as *dux* of *Africa, Numidia,* and *Mauretania.* Inscription of 259 from *Lambaesis* records victory of C. Macrianus Decianus (legate of *Numidia*) over *Bavares Fraxines* and *Quinquegentanei*			c.250	Arnobius, another important defender of Christianity and critic of paganism, born at *Sicca Veneria*
258	Martydom of Cyprian and other African Christians	258	General persecution of Christians initiated by Valerian. After capture of Valerian by Persians, Gallienus issued edict of toleration of Christians		
268	Trouble with peoples of *Marmarica*			c.270	Harvester of *Mactar* inscription
280s	Partial reduction in size of *Mauretania Tingitana*, revolts of Moorish *Bavares* and *Quinquegentanei*				
290	T. Aurelius Litua defeats *Barbari Transtagnenses* and *Quinquegentiani* in *Mauretania*				
297	Emperor Maximian campaigns against *Quinquegentanei* and *Laguatan*	296–305	The Tetrarchy	296/297	*Karthago* mint established

Date	Events relevant to North Africa	Date	Roman World	Date	Cultural and technological landmarks in Africa
301–303	Subdivision of provinces: *Africa* (becomes *Byzacena*, *Tripolitana*, *Zeugitana*), *Numidia* (*N Cirtensis* and *N Militana*) and *Mauretania* (*M Caesariensis* and *M Sitifensis*). A shrunken *M Tingitana* attached to *Hispania*	296–303	*Cyrenaica* reorganised as part of the Diocese of Orient into two provinces: *Libya Superior* (*Pentapolis*) and *Libya Inferior* (*Marmarica*)		
303–304	Numerous Christian martyrs and compromised clergy in Africa	303–305	Great Persecution of Christians across Roman Empire (edicts of toleration in 311, 313)	311	Start of Donatist schism when Donatus leads Christian group refusing to recognise rehabilitation of priests who compromised during persecution
308	Usurpation of Vicar of *Africa*, Domitius Alexander, defeated and killed 310/311	306–312	End of Tetrarchic arrangements leads to renewed period of political unrest and civil war, culminating with victory of Constantine I over Maxentius at Rome	310–320	Lactantius, an African Christian follower of Arnobius, *De mortibus persecutorum*
314 316	First condemnation of Donatists by church councils. Constantine recognises Caecilianus as legitimate bishop of *Karthago*	312	Constantine furthers legitimation of Christianity; restoration of church property and rights	312	City of *Cirta* becomes *Constantina*
325	Supremacy of bishop of Karthago over Christians in Africa recognised	324	Foundation of Constantinople	c.320	Birth of Optatus of *Milev*
340	Start of Circoncellion unrest	337	Death of Constantine I	c.330	Sextus Aurelius Victor born in Africa, later author of *Liber de Caesaribus*

Date	Events relevant to North Africa	Date	Roman World	Date	Cultural and technological landmarks in Africa
347–348	Council of *Karthago* and exile of Donatus				
350–352	African Diocese breaks away in support of usurpation of Magnentius			354	Birth of Augustine at *Thagaste*
363–366	Raids of *Austuriani* (*Laguatan*) on *Tripolitana comes Africae* Romanus accused by *Lepcitani* of dilatory action and corruption	365	Year of great earthquake (or series of major seismic events) impacting on N Africa	363	The Album of *Thamugadi*—long inscription listing people with municipal offices and responsibilities
370–375	Rebellion of Firmus, ended by Count Theodosius (who also executed at *Karthago* in 376), Sammac (brother of Firmus) continues revolt briefly			c.367	Optatus of *Milev* writes anti-Donatist critique
375	Eventual condemnation of Romanus	378	Disastrous defeat of Roman army by Visigoths at *Hadrianople*		
385–398	Gildo, brother of Firmus, *comes et magister utriusque militia per Africam*. Exploits control of food supply for Rome in disputes with emperor	380	Edict of Theodosius establishes Christianity as state religion of Rome	395	Augustine ordained bishop of *Hippo Regius*
397–398	Revolt of Gildo ends in his defeat and death near *Ammaedara*—another brother Mascezel served with Stilicho against Gildo			401	Augustine, *Confessions*

Date	Events relevant to North Africa	Date	Roman World	Date	Cultural and technological landmarks in Africa
409, 413	Insubordination and insurrection of *comes Africae* Heraclian ends in his assassination at *Karthago*	410	Sack of Rome by Alaric and Goths	c.405–413	Letters of Synesius, Bishop of *Ptolemais* in *Cyrenaica*, many dealing with conditions in province, raids of *Ausuriani* (*Laguatan*)
411	Conference of *Karthago* and final condemnation of Donatism in 412				
427–428	Insurrection of *comes Africae* Boniface and campaigns of Gallia Placidia against him in Africa; Boniface appeals to Vandals for help				
429	Invasion of North Africa by Vandals from *S Hispania*			426	Augustine, *City of God*
430	Boniface defeated in battle by Vandals and death of Augustine during Vandal siege of *Hippo*, which became Gaiseric's capital after capture in 431	435	Gaiseric recognised by treaty with Rome, with capital of his kingdom at *Hippo*		
439	Fall of *Karthago* to Vandal kingdom	442	New treaty with Rome, recognising more extensive territory of Vandal kingdom		
455	Vandals complete assimilation of *Numidia* and *Tripolitana*	455	Vandals attack city of Rome		
479–484	Persecution of Catholics by Arian Vandals under Huneric	476	Fall of Western Roman Empire		
484	Revolt of people of Aurès against Vandal rule			493–496	Date of Albertini tablets

Date	Events relevant to North Africa	Date	Roman World	Date	Cultural and technological landmarks in Africa
529	Raids of *Laguatan* and allies against Vandal kingdom				
532	Revolt of Pudentius in *Tripolitana* against Vandal rule				
533	Byzantine reconquest of *Africa* under command of Belisarius	527–565	Reign of Justinian	551	Procopius, *History of the Wars*
534–539	Revolts and resistance of *Mauri* to Byzantine control				
544–548	Major revolt of *Laguatan* in *Tripolitana* and *Byzacena*; victory of John Troglita			549–550	Corippus, *Iohannids*
568–590s	Sequence of further revolts in *Africa* and *Mauretania*				
640s	First Arab campaigns versus Cyrenaica, *Tripolitana* and *Byzacena*				
660s	Campaigns of Sidi Uqba into Sahara and across Maghrib				
670	Foundation of Kairouan				
681–682	Sidi Uqba campaign in Morocco, but killed in S Algeria on return				
698	Final capture of *Karthago* by Arabs, defeat of Arab army by Berbers led by Kahina				
c.702	Death of Kahina				
711	Surrender of last Byzantine outpost in Africa at *Septem* (Ceuta)				

BIBLIOGRAPHY

AAA = Gsell 1911.

AAT = Babelon et al. 1892–1913.

Abda, H. 2013. *Fossa regia: une frontière culturelle? Contribution à la géographie historique.* Saarbrücken: Presses Académiques Francophones.

Abdelhamed, M.H.H. 2018. *The Economic Condition of the Main Cyrenaican Cities (North-Eastern Libya) from the Hellenistic to the Mid-Roman Period: Textual Analysis.* Unpublished PhD thesis, University of Leicester.

Abdrbba, M.O.M. 2018. *Outside the Walls: Cyrene's Suburban Zone between the Greek and Roman Eras.* Unpublished PhD thesis, University of Leicester.

Abid, H. 2014. Le tracé de la Fossa Regia dans la vallée de l'oued Siliana. Précisions et réflexions. In Briand-Ponsart 2014, 401–18.

Abulafia, D. 2011. *The Great Sea: A Human History of the Mediterranean.* Penguin: London.

Adams, J.N. 1994. Latin and Punic in contact? The case of the Bu Njem ostraca. *Journal of Roman Studies* 84: 87–112.

Adams, J.N. 1999. The poets of Bu Njem: Language, culture and the centurionate. *Journal of Roman Studies* 89: 109–34.

Adams, J.N. 2003. *Bilingualism and the Latin Language.* Cambridge: Cambridge University Press.

Adams, G.W. and Tobler, R. 2007. *Romano-British Tombstones between the 1st and 3rd Centuries. Epigraphy, Gender and Familial Relations.* British Archaeological Reports, British Series B437. Oxford: Archaeopress.

Addyman, P. 1962. The archaeology of the Sbeitla area: Interim report. *Brathay Exploration Group Annual Report 1962*, 60–77.

Addyman, P. and Simpson, W.G. 1966. Archaeology of the Sbeitla area: Second interim report. *Brathay Exploration Group Annual Report 1966*, 153–70.

AE = *L'Année épigraphique.* 1888–present. Paris: Presses Universitaires de France.

Aghali-Zakara, M. 2006. Langues, écritures libyco-berbères et liens culturels saharo-séhéliens. In M.H. Fantar 2006, 11–30.

Ahmed, M.A.M. 2019. *Rural Settlement and Economic Activity: Olive Oil, Wine and Amphorae Production on the Tarhuna Plateau during the Roman Period.* London: Society for Libyan Studies.

Aibeche, Y. 2014. Une nouvelle trace de l'occupation byzantine au sud de la Maurétanie Sitifienne. In Briand-Ponsart 2014, 509–22.

Aiosa, S. 2013. *Il tempio di Ercole a Sabratha. Architettura e contesto urbano.* Rome: L'Erma di Bretschneider.

Aït Amara, O. 2013. *Numides et Maures au combat. États et armées en Afrique du Nord jusqu'à l'époque de Juba I*[er]. Ortacesus: Sandhi.

Aït Amara, O. 2014. La conquête de la Maurétanie (39–42). In Coltelloni-Trannoy and Le Bohec 2014, 69–83.

Aït Kaci, A. 2007. Recherche sur l'ancêtre des alphabets libyco-berbères. *Libyan Studies* 38: 13–37.

Aït Kaci, A. 2012. Ajouter 'tira 2004 ttf' et la carte. Noms latins en graphie libyque. In Corda and Mastino 2012, 11–20.

Akerraz, A. and Lenoir, E. 1990. Volubilis et son territoire. In *L'Afrique dans l'Occident romain* 1990, 213–29.

Akerraz, A. and Lenoir, M. 1982. Les huileries de Volubilis. *Bulletin d'Archéologie Marocaine* 14: 69–101.

Akerraz, A. 2012. Les fortifications de la Maurétanie Tingitane. In Déroche and Leclant 2012, 75–96.

Akerraz, A. and Collins-Elliott, S.A. 2017. Gardens of the Hesperides: The rural archaeology of the Loukkos Valley. Interim report on the 2016 season. Fasti Online Documents & Research: Archaeological Survey Series 5. http://www.fastionline.org/docs/FOLDER-sur-2017-5.pdf.

Akerraz, A. and Papi, E. 2008. *Sidi Ali Ben Ahmed – Thamusida, vol. 1: I contesti*. Rome: Edizioni Quasar.

Akerraz, A., Brouquier-Reddé, V. and Lenoir, E. 1995. Nouvelles découvertes dans le bassin du Sebou. 1. L'occupation antique de la plaine du Gharb. In Trousset 1995c, 235–97.

Akerraz, A., el Khayari, A and Papi, E. 2009. L'habitat maurétano-punique de Sidi Ali ben Ahmed – Thamusida (Maroc). In S. Helas and D. Marzoli (eds), *Phönizisches und punisches Städtewesen*, 147–70. Mainz: Verlag Philipp von Zabern.

Akerraz, A. Siraj, A. and Vismara, C. 2019. *Carte archéologique du Maroc. Le Rif côtier. Recherches archéologiques maroc-italiennes 2000–2005*. Rabat: Institut National des Sciences de l'Archéologie et du Patrimoine.

Akkari Werriemi, J. 1985. Un témoinage spectaculaire sur la présence libyco-punique dans l'ile de Jerba: Le mausolée de Henchir Bourgou. *Reppal* 1: 189–96.

Akkari Werriemi, J. 1995a. Le nécropole libyco-punique de Ghizene (Djerba- Tunisie). *Africa* 13: 51–74.

Akkari Werriemi, J. 1995b. Note préliminaire sur deux tombes phenico-puniques à Aggar au nord-ouest de Djerba (Tunisie). *Africa* 13: 77–82.

Akkari Werriemi, J. 2003. Sépultures monumentales d'époque romaine à Djerba (Tunisie): Le mausolée temple de Henchir Ghardaya. *Africa: Séances scientifiques* 1: 163–99.

Alaoui, M.K., Siraj, A. and Vismara, C. 2004. Recherches archéologiques maroc-italiennes dans le Rif. *L'Africa romana* 15: 567–604.

Albertini, E. 1950. *L'Afrique romaine*. Algiers: Imprimerie Officielle.

Albertini, E., Marcais, G., Yver, G. and Prigent, E. 1955. *L'Afrique du Nord francaise dans l'histoire*. Lyon/Paris: Editions Archat.

Alcock, S.E. and Cherry, J.F. (eds). 2004. *Side-by-Side Survey: Comparative Regional Studies in the Mediterranean World*. Oxford: Oxbow Books.

Alcock, S.E., D'Altroy, T.N., Morrison, K.D. and Sinopoli, C.M. (eds). 2001. *Empires: Perspectives from Archaeology and History*. Cambridge: Cambridge University Press.

Aldrete, G.S. and Mattingly, D.J. 1999. Feeding the city: The organization, operation, and scale of the supply system for Rome. In D.S. Potter and D.J. Mattingly (eds), *Life, Death, and Entertainment in Ancient Rome*, 171–204. Ann Arbor: University of Michigan Press.

Alexandropoulos, J. 2000. *Les monnaies de l'Afrique antique: 400 av. J.-C. – 40 ap. J.-C.* Toulouse: Presses universitaires du Mirail.

Allen, M.G., Lodwick, L., Brindle, T., Fulford, M. and Smith, A.T. 2017. *The Rural Economy of Roman Britain. New Visions of the Countryside of Roman Britain, vol. 2*. Britannia Monograph Series 30. London: Society for the Promotion of Roman Studies.

Altaweel, M. and Squitieri, A. 2018. *Revolutionizing a World: From Small States to Universalism in the Pre-Islamic Near East.* London: UCL Press.

Amadasi Guzzo, M.G. 1983. Una grande famiglia di Lepcis in rapporto con la ristrutturazione urbanistica della città (I sec. A.C. – I sec. D.C.). In *Architecture et société: De l'archaïsme grec à la fin de la République* (Actes du Colloque international organisé par le Centre national de la recherche scientifique et l'École française de Rome, Rome 2–4 décembre 1980), 377–85.

Amadasi Guzzo M.G. 1986. L'onomastica nelle iscrizioni puniche tripolitane. *Rivista di studi fenici* 14, 21–51.

Amadasi Guzzo, M.G. 2002. Le iscrizioni del tofet: osservazioni sulle espressioni di offerta. In C.G. Wagner and L.A. Ruiz Cabrero (eds), *El Molk como concepto del Sacrificio Punico y Hebreo y el final del Dios Moloch*, 93–119. Madrid: Centro de Estudios Fenicios y Punicos.

Amadasi Guzzo, M.G. 2003. Le plurilinguisme dans l'onomastique personnelle à l'époque néopunique. *Antiquités africaines* 38–39: 281–88.

Amadasi Guzzo, M.G. 2008. Il tofet. Osservazioni di un'epigrafista. *Scienze dell'Antichità* 14: 347–62.

Ammar, S.I. 1994. Réflexions comparatives sur quelques programmes d'urbanisme en Tunisie antique: l'aménagement des fora (du Ier au IIIe siècle de notre ère). *L'Africa romana* 10(1): 445–62.

Amouretti, M.-C. and Brun, J.-P. (eds). 1993. *La production du vin et de l'huile en Méditerranée.* Paris: De Boccard.

Amraoui, T. 2017. *L'artisanat dans les cités antiques de l'Algérie (Ier siècle avant notre ère–VIIe siècle après notre ère).* Oxford: Archaeopress.

Amraoui, T. 2018. L'évolution de l'urbanisme en Afrique et l'implantation des ateliers entre le Ier s. avant notre ère et la fin de l'Antiquité. Approche chronologique et spatiale à travers le cas de quelques villes antiques d'Algérie. *Antiquités africaines* 54: 95–114.

Amraoui, T. 2020. Crafts in Roman North Africa: Technical transfer and permanence through grain mills and fullonicae. In Duckworth et al. 2020a, 115–42.

Anderson, B. 1991. *Imagined Communities: Reflections on the Origin and Spread of Nationalism.* London and New York: Verso.

Ando, C. 2016. Colonialism, colonization: Roman perspectives. In D.L. Selden and P. Vasunia (eds), *The Oxford Handbook of the Literatures of the Roman Empire*, 1–31. Oxford: Oxford University Press.

Andreoli, M and Polla, S. 2019. La ceramica domestica. In de Vos Raaijmakers and Maurina 2019, 149–244.

Annabi, M.K. 1988. Prospection archéologique dans la région de Sousse. *Bulletin des travaux de l'Institut National de l'Art et l'Archéologie* 2: 17–31.

Annabi, M.K. 1993. Archéologie du paysage à oued Cherita. *Bulletin des travaux de l'Institut National de l'Art et l'Archéologie* 4 (1989) [1993]: 7–28.

Anselmino, L. 1989. *Il castellum del Nador. Storia di una fattoria tra Tipasa e Caesarea (I-VI sec d.C)*. Rome: L'Erma di Bretschneider.

Aounallah, S. 2010a. *Pagus, castellum et civitas: Études d'épigraphie et d'histoire sur le village et la cité en Afrique romaine*. Paris: de Boccard.

Aounallah, S. 2010b. Le *pagus* en Afrique romaine. *L'Africa romana* 18(2): 1615–30.

Aounallah, S. and Ben Romdhane, H. 2015. La toponymie de l'Afrique du Nord antique (bilan des recherches depuis 1990). In Mrabet 2015, 223–39.

Aounallah, S. and Golvin, J.-C. (ed). 2016. *Dougga: Études d'architecture religieuse, 2. Les sanctuaires du forum, du centre de l'agglomération et de la Grande rue courbe*. Bordeaux: Ausonius.

Aounallah, S. and Maurin, L. 2008. *Pagus et civitas Siviritani*: une nouvelle "commune double" dans la *pertica* de Carthage. *Zeitschrift für Papyrologie und Epigraphik* 167: 227–50.

Aounallah S. and Maurin L. 2013. Remarques sur la topographie rurale et urbaine du *pagus* et de la *ciuitas* de *Thugga* (Dougga, Tunisie). In I. Pimouguet-Pédarros, M. Clavel-Levêque and F. Ouachour (eds), *Hommes, cultures et paysages: de l'Antiquité à la période moderne. Mélanges offerts à Jean Peyras*, 27–55. Enquêtes et documents 44. Rennes: Presses universitaires de Rennes.

Aounallah, S., Ben Abdulla, Z.B. and Hurlet, F. 2007. Inscriptions latines du Musée de Sousse: Lamta, *Lepti(s) Minus*. *Africa* 21: 151–66.

Aounallah, S. and Brouquier-Reddé, V. 2020. Dougga, la périphérie nord (résultats des campagnes 2017–2019). Introduction au dossier. *Antiquités africaines* 56: 175–81.

Aounallah, S. and Mastino A. (eds). 2020. *L'Epigrafia del Nord Africa: Novità, riletture, nuove sintesi*. Faenza: Fratelli Lega Editori.

Aounallah, S., Brouquier-Reddé, V., Abidi, H., Artu, J., Ben Slimane, H., Maligorne, Y., Poupon, F., Sghaïer, Y. and Touj, F. 2020a. Architecture et pratiques funéraires préromaines dans la nécropole du Nord-Ouest à Dougga. *Antiquités africaines* 56: 183–205.

Aounallah, S., Brouquier-Reddé, V., Bonifay, M., Chérif, A., Hadded, F., Larminat, S. de, Mukai, T. and Poupon, F. 2020b. L'ensemble funéraire romain de la nécropole du Nord-Ouest à Dougga. *Antiquités africaines* 56: 221–44.

Aounallah, S., Brouquier-Reddé, V., Abidi, H., Ben Romdhane, H., Bonifay, M., Hadded, F., Hafiane Nouri, S., de Larminat, S., Mukai, T., Poupon, F. and Zech-Matterne, V. 2020c. L'aire sacrée de Baal Hammon – Saturne à Dougga. *Antiquités africaines* 56: 245–73.

Appiah, K.A. 2016. There is no such thing as western civilisation. *The Guardian*. 9 November 2016. https://www.theguardian.com/world/2016/nov/09/western-civilisation-appiah-reith-lecture.

APT = *Atlas préhistorique de la Tunisie*. Rome: INAA/EFR. All at scale of 1:200,000.

Aranegui Gascó, C. (ed). 2001. *Lixus: Colonia fenicia y ciudad púnico-mauritana, Anotaciones sobre su ocupación medieval*. Sagvntvm Extra 4. Valencia: Universitat de Valencia.

Aranegui Gascó, C. (ed). 2005. *Lixus-2: Ladera sur. Excavaiones arqueólogicas Marroco-Españolas en la colonia fenicia. Campañas 2000–2003*. Sagvntvm Extra 6. Valencia: Universitat de Valencia.

Aranegui Gascó, C. and Hassini, H. (eds). 2010. *Lixus-3. Área suroeste del sector monumental (Cámaras Montalbán) 2005–2009*. Sagvntvm Extra 8.Valencia: Universitat de Valencia.

Ardeleanu, S. 2015. Au-delà du couple "continuités et ruptures": Problèmes de périodisation en Numidie entre le 2e siècle av. J.-C. et la fin du 1er siècle ap. J.-C. *L'Africa romana* 20: 581–90.

Ardeleanu, S. 2018. *Giallo antico* in context. Distribution, use and commercial actors according to new stratigraphic data from the western Mediterranean (2nd c. BC – 1st c. AD). In D. Matetić Poljak and K. Marasović (eds), *ASMOSIA XI: Interdisciplinary Studies on Ancient Stone*, 155–65. Proceedings of the XI ASMOSIA conference, Split 18–22 May 2015. Split: University of Split.

Ardeleanu, S. 2021. *Numidia Romana? Die Auswirkungen der römischen Präsenz in Numidien (2. Jh. V. Chr. - 1. Jh. N. Chr.)*. Archäologische Forschungen 38. Wiesbaden: Reichert Verlag.

Ardeleanu, S., Chaouali, M., Eck, W. and von Rummel, P. 2019. Die frühkaiserzeitlichen Grabsteine aus Simitthus (Chimtou). Stilistisch-epigraphische Analyse und urbaner Kontext. *Archäologischer Anzeiger* 2019(1): 277–322.

Argoud, G., Marangou, L., Panayotopoulos, V., and Villain-Gandossi, C. 1992. *L'eau et les hommes en Méditerranée et en Mer Noire dans l'Antiquité: De l'époque mycénienne au règne de Justinien*. Athens: CNRS.

Arharbi, R. 2003. L'occupation du littoral du Maroc à l'époque pré-romaine. In C. Gaultier-Kurhan (ed), *Patrimoine culturel marocain*, 57–102. Paris: Maisonneuve & Larose.

Arharbi, R. and Lenoir, E. 2004. Les niveaux préromains à Banasa. *Bulletin d'Archéologie Marocaine* 20: 220–70.

Arharbi, R., Kermovant, A. and Lenoir, E. 2001. *Iulia Valentia Banasa*: De la découverte du site aux recherches récentes. In *Actes des 1ères Journées Nationales d'Archéologie et du Patrimoine. 2 Archéologie préislamique, (Rabat 1–4 juillet 1998)*, 147–68. Rabat: Société Marocaine d'Archéologie et du Patrimoine.

Ashcroft, B., Griffiths, G. and Tiffin, H. 1995. *The Post-Colonial Studies Reader*. London: Routledge.

Ashcroft, B., Griffiths, G. and Tiffin, H. 1998. *Key Concepts in Post-Colonial Studies*. London: Routledge.

Ast, R., 2016. Latin ostraca from Vandal North Africa. In J.-L. Fournet and A. Papaconstantinou (eds), *Mélanges Jean Gascou: Textes et études papyrologiques*, 7–32. Paris: Association des Amis du Centre d'Histoire et Civilisation de Byzance.

Atalay, S. 2006. Indigenous archaeology as decolonizing practice. *American Indian Quarterly* 30(3–4): 280–310.

Atalay, S.L. 2007. Global application of Indigenous archaeology: Community based participatory research in Turkey. *Archaeologies: Journal of the World Archaeological Congress* 3(3): 249–70.

Atlas centuriations = Caillemer, A. and Chevallier, R. 1959. *Atlas des centuriations romaines de Tunisie*. Paris: Institut géographique national.

Aubet, M.E. 2001. *The Phoenicians and the West: Politics, Colonies and Trade*, 2nd edition. Cambridge: Cambridge University Press.

Audley-Miller, L. 2012. Dressed to impress: The tomb sculpture of Ghirza in Tripolitania. In M. Caroll and J.P. Wild (eds), *Dressing the Dead in Classical Antiquity*, 99–114. Stroud: Amberley Publishing.

Aupert, P. 1974. *Le nymphée de Tipasa et les numphées et "septizonia" nord-africains*. CEFR 16. Rome: École française de Rome.

Aurenche, O. (ed). 1984. *Nomades et sédentaires: Perspectives ethnoarchéologiques*. Paris: Éditions Recherche sur les Civilisations.

Aurigemma, S. 1926. *I Mosaici di Zliten.* Rome: Societa editrice d'arte illustrata.

Aurigemma, S. 1960. *L'Italia in Africa, vol. 1: Mosaici.* Rome: Istituto Poligraphico dello stato.

Aurigemma, S. 1962. *L'Italia in Africa, vol. 2: Le Pitture.* Rome: Istituto Poligraphico dello stato.

Ayoub, M.S. 1967. *Excavations in Germa between 1962 and 1966.* Tripoli: Ministry of Education.

Ayoub, M.S. 1968. *Excavations in Germa (Fezzan). Cemetery of Saniat Ben-Howidy.* Tripoli: Ministry of Tourism and Antiquities, Department of Antiquities, Southern Governorates Controllery.

Babelon, E., Cagnat, R. and Reinach, S. 1892–1913. *Atlas archéologique de la Tunisie.* Paris: Ministère de la guerre/E. Leroux.

Bailet, P. 2004. La fouille et l'étude anthropologique des tombes à crémation de la nécropole de Pupput: Résultats préliminaires et perspectives. In Ben Abed and Griesheimer 2004, 73–83.

Balice, M. 2010. *Libia. Gli scavi italiani 1922–1937: Restauro, riconstruzione o propaganda?* Rome: L'Erma di Bretschneider.

Ball, W. 2000. *Rome in the East: The Transformation of an Empire.* London: Routledge.

Ballouche, A. and Marinval, P. 2003. Données palynologiques et carpologiques sur la domestication des plantes et l'agriculture dans le Néolithique ancien du Maroc septentrional (site de Kaf I el-Ghar). *Révue d'Archéometrie* 27: 49–54.

Ballu, A. 1897. *Les ruines de Timgad (antique Thamugadi).* Paris: E. Leroux.

Ballu, A. 1903. *Les ruines de Timgad, antique Thamugadi: Nouvelles découvertes.* Paris: E. Leroux.

Ballu, A. 1911. *Les ruines de Timgad: Sept années de découvertes (1903–1910).* Paris: Neurdein Frères.

Ballu, A. 1926. *Ruines de Djemila (antique Cuicul).* Paris: Carbonel.

Baradez, J. 1949a. *Vue aérienne de l'organisation romaine dans le sud-Algérien: Fossatum Africae.* Paris: Arts et Métiers Graphiques.

Baradez, J. 1949b. Gemellae: Un camp d'Hadrien et une ville des confins sahariens aujord'hui ensélevis sous les sables. *Revue Africaine* 93: 5–24.

Baradez, J. 1957. Travaux d'hydrauliques romains révélés par photographies aériennes dans une région aujord'hui steppienne. In *Actes du 79e Congrès National des Sociétés Savants, Alger 1954*, 273–75. Paris: Imprimerie nationale.

Baradez, J. 1961. Nouvelles fouilles à Tipasa: Nécropole païenne occidentale sous la maison des fresques. *Libyca* 9: 7–48.

Baradez, J. 1966a. Deux amphithéâtres inédits du "limes" de Numidie: Gemellae et Mesarfelta. In *Mélanges d'archéologie, d'épigraphie et d'histoire offerts à Jérome Carcopino*, 55–63. Paris: Hachette.

Baradez, J. 1966b. Les thermes légionnaires de Gemellae. In *Corolla memoriae Erich Swoboda dedicata*, 14–22. Cologne: Böhlau.

Baradez, J. 1967. Compléments inédits au "Fossatum Africae". In *Studien zu den Militärgrenzen Roms: Vorträge des 6. Internationalen Limeskongress in Süddeutschland*, 200–10. Cologne: Graz.

Baradez, J. 1968. Les nécropoles de Tipasa: Tombes du cimetière occidental côtier. *Antiquités Africaines* 2: 77–93.

Baratte, F. 2012. *L'Afrique romaine: Tripolitaine et Tunisie.* Mainz: Verlag Phillip von Zabern.

Baratte, F. and Chaisemartin, N. de. 2018. North Africa. In E.A. Friedland, M.G. Sobocinski and E.K. Gazda (eds), *The Oxford Handbook of Roman Sculpture*, 504–21. Oxford/New York: Oxford University Press.

Baratte, F and Duval, N. 1974. *Les ruines de Sufetula: Sbeitla*. Tunis: Société tunisienne de diffusion.

Baratte, F., Bejaoui, F. and Ben Abdallah, Z.B. 1999. *Recherches archéologiques à Haïdra: Miscellanea 2*. CEFR 17/2. Rome: École française de Rome.

Baratte, F., Béjaoui, F., Duval, N., Berraho, S., Gui, I. and Jacquest, H. 2014. *Basiliques chrétiennes de l'Afrique du Nord: 2 – Monuments de la Tunisie*. Bordeaux: Ausonius.

Baratte, F., Brouquier-Reddé, V. and Rocca, E. (eds). 2018. *Du culte aux sanctuaires. L'architecture religieuse dans l'Afrique romaine et byzantine*. Orient & Méditerranée 25. Paris: Boccard.

Barbery, J. and Delhoume, J.-P. 1982. La voie romaine de piedmont Sufetula-Masclianae (Djebel Mrhila, Tunisie centrale). *Antiquités africaines* 18: 27–43.

Baring, E. 1910. *Ancient and Modern Imperialism*. New York: Longmans, Green and Co.

Barker, G.W. 2006. *The Agricultural Revolution in Prehistory. Why Did Foragers Become Farmers?* Oxford: Oxford University Press.

Barker, G.W. 2019. Libyan landscapes in history and prehistory. *Libyan Studies* 50: 9–20.

Barker, G.W. and Gilbertson, D. (eds). 2000. *The Archaeology of Drylands: Living at the Margin*. London: Routledge.

Barker, G.W. and Jones, B. 1984. The UNESO Libyan Valleys Survey VI: Investigations of a Romano-Libyan farm, part 1. *Libyan Studies* 15: 1–44.

Barker, G.W., Lloyd, J.A. and Reynolds, J. 1985. *Cyrenaica in Antiquity*. British Archaeological Reports International Series S236. Oxford: BAR Publishing.

Barker, G.W., Gilbertson, D.D., Jones, G.D.B., Welsby, D. and Wakely, J. 1991. UNESCO Libyan Valley Survey XXIII: The 1989 season. *Libyan Studies* 22: 31–60.

Barker, G.W., Gilbertson, D, Jones, B. and Mattingly, D. 1996a. *Farming the Desert: The UNESCO Libyan Valleys Archaeological Survey, vol. 1: Synthesis*. (Editor G. Barker). Paris: UNESCO.

Barker, G.W., Gilbertson, D, Jones, B. and Mattingly, D. 1996b. *Farming the Desert: The UNESCO Libyan Valleys Archaeological Survey, vol. 2: Gazetteer and Pottery*. (Editor D.J. Mattingly). Paris: UNESCO.

Barker G., Bennett, P., Farr, L., Hill, E., Hunt, C., Lucarini, G., Morales, J., Mutri, G., Prendergast, A., Pryor, A., Rabett, R., Reynolds, T., Spry-Marques, P. and Twati, M. 2012. The Cyrenaican Prehistory Project 2012: The fifth season of investigations of the Haua Fteah cave. *Libyan Studies* 43: 115–136.

Barnett, T. 2019a. *An Engraved Landscape: Rock Carvings in the Wadi al-Ajal, Libya, vol. 1: Synthesis*. London: Society for Libyan Studies.

Barnett, T. 2019b. *An Engraved Landscape: Rock Carvings in the Wadi al-Ajal, Libya, vol. 2: Gazetteer*. London: Society for Libyan Studies.

Baroni' A.-F. 2020. Mobilité des unités et 'dislocation' de la documentation: L'exemple des auxiliaires attestés en Numidie septentrionale au Ier s. ap. J.-C. *Antiquités africaines* 56: 303–21.

Barth, F. (ed). 1969. *Ethnic Groups and Boundaries: The Social Organization of Ethnic Difference*. Boston: Little, Brown.

Bartoccini, R. 1929. *Le Terme di Leptis (Leptis Magna)*. Bergamo: Istituto italiano d'arti grafiche.

Barton, I.M. 1972. *Africa in the Roman Empire*. Accra: Ghana Universities Press.

Barton, I.M. 1982. Capitoline temples in Italy and the provinces (especially Africa). In H. Temporini (ed), *Aufstieg und Niedergang der römischen Welt: Principat, vol. 12/1: Teilband Künste*, 259–352. Berlin: De Gruyter.

Barton, I.M. (ed). 1989. *Roman Public Buildings*. Exeter Studies in History 20. Exeter: Exeter University Press.

Bates, O. 1970. *The Eastern Libyans*. London: Cass.

Bauduin, P., Gazeau, V. and Modéran, Y. (eds). 2008. *Identité et ethnicité: Concepts, débats historiographes, exemples (IIIe – XIIe siècle)*. Caen: Presses universitares de Caen.

Bazzana, A. and Bocoum, H. (eds). 2004. *Du nord au sud du Sahara: Cinquante ans d'archéologie française en Afrique du ouest et au Maghreb: Bilan et perspectives*. Paris: Éditions Sepia.

Beard, M. 2007. *The Roman Triumph*. Cambridge, MA: Belknapp Press.

Bejaoui, F. 1995. Une église d'époque vandale à Henchir el Gousset (région de Thelepte-Tunisie). *Africa* 13: 101–22.

Bejaoui, F. 1998. Une nouvelle église de la région de Sufetula (Sbeïtla): Ksar El Guellal. *Africa* 16: 1–14.

Bejaoui, F. (ed). 2001. *Histoire des Hautes Steppes: Antiquité–Moyen Âge. Actes du colloque de Sbeitla, sessions 1998 et 1999*. Tunis: INP.

Bejaoui, F. (ed). 2003. *Histoire des Hautes Steppes Antiquité–Moyen Age. Actes du colloque de Sbeitla 2001*. Tunis: INP.

Bejaoui, F. (ed). 2006. *Actes du 4ème colloque international sur l'histoire des steppes tunisiennes*. Tunis: INP.

Bejaoui, F. (ed). 2008. *Actes du 5ème colloque international sur l'histoire des steppes tunisiennes*. Tunis: INP.

Bejaoui, F. (ed). 2010. *Actes du 6ème colloque international sur l'histoire des steppes tunisiennes*. Tunis: INP.

Bejaoui, F. 2015. *Les hautes steppes tunisiennes: Témoignages archéologiques chrétiens*. Tunis: INP.

Bekker-Nielsen, T. 1989. *The Geography of Power: Studies in the Urbanization of Roman North-West Europe*. British Archaeological Reports International Series S477. Oxford: BAR Publishing.

Bel Faida, A. 2008. Place de collèges, associations et collectivités dans la vie réligieuse de l'Afrique antique: Témoignages épigraphiques. In Blanc-Bijon 2008, 163–75.

Belkahia, S. and Di Vita-Evrard, G. 1995. Magistratures autochtones dans les cités pérégrines de l'Afrique proconsulaire. In Trousset 1995a, 255–74.

Belkahia Karoui, T. 2009. *Élites des cités de "Byzacène" du Ier au IVème siècles ap. J.-C.* Tunis: Éditions CPU.

Belkahia Karoui, T. 2014. La libertas municipale en Afrique et ses défenseurs. In Briand-Ponsard 2014, 205–41.

Belkahia, T., Ben Abid, L. and Gharbi, M. (eds). 2016. *Identités et territoires dans le Maghreb antique. Actes du colloque international organisé à Tunis (29–30 novembre 2013)*. Tunis.

Belvedere, O. and Bergemann, J. (eds). 2021. *Imperium Romanum: Romanization between Colonization and Globalization*. Palermo: Palermo University Press.

Ben Abdallah, Z.B. 1986. *Catalogue des inscription latines païennes du musée du Bardo*. CEFR 92. Rome: École française de Rome.

Ben Abdallah, Z.B. 1992. Du côté d'*Ammaedara* (Haïdra): *Musulamii* et *Musunii Regiani*. *Antiquités africaines* 28: 139–45.

Ben Abdallah, Z.B. 1996. Ammaedara (Haïdra) sous le Haut-Empire: Aspects historiques et topographiques. *Africa* 14: 65–101.

Ben Abdallah, Z.B. 1999a. Sur une collection d'antiques (steles à Saturne et épitaphes figurées). *Africa* 17: 11–24.

Ben Abdallah, Z.B. 1999b. Un cippe funéraire de Bisica (Afrique Proconsulaire). *Africa* 17: 25–30.

Ben Abdallah, Z.B. and Ladjimi-Sebaï, L. 1983. *Index onomastique des inscriptions latines de la Tunisie: Suivie de l'index onomastique des inscriptions latines d'Afrique*. Paris: CNRS Éditions.

Ben Abdallah, Z.B., Ibba, A. and Naddari L. (eds). 2013. *Mourir à* Ammaedara*: Épitaphes latines païennes inédites d'*Ammaedara *(Haïdra) et sa region*. Studi di storia antica e di archeologia 11. Ortacesus: Sandhi.

Ben Abed, A. and Soren, D. (eds). 1987. *Carthage: A Mosaic of Ancient Tunisia*. New York: Norton.

Ben Abed, A. and Griesheimer, M. (eds). 2004. *La nécropole romaine de Pupput*. CEFR 323. Rome: École française de Rome.

Ben Akacha, W. 2012. L'histoire municipale d'*Uchi Maius*: Un essai de reconstruction. *Antiquités africaines* 46–48: 169–83.

Ben Baaziz, S. 1985. L'occupation humaine dans le plaine de Rohia et le Sraa Ouertane dans l'Antiquité. *Histoire et archéologie de l'Afrique du Nord. Actes du IIIe Colloque international*, 289–300. Paris: Éditions du CTHS.

Ben Baaziz, S. 1987. Les forum romains en Tunisie: Essai de bilan. In *Los foros romanos de las provincias occidentales. Actas de la Mesa Redonda celebrada en Valencia 1986*, 221–36. Madrid: Ministerio de Cultura.

Ben Baaziz, S. 1988. Les sites antiques de la région de Sidi el Hani. *Bulletin des travaux de l'Institut National de l'art et l'archéologie* 2: 7–15.

Ben Baaziz, S. 1990. Les huileries de la Tunisie antique. *Cahiers de Tunisie* 43(155–156): 39–64.

Ben Baaziz, S. 1991. Les sites archéologiques de la région de Gafsa. In CTHS Strasbourg 1991, 535–48

Ben Baaziz, S. 1993. Prospection archéologique de la région d'el Meknassi. *Bulletin des travaux de l'Institut National de l'art et l'archéologie* 4 (1989) [1993]: 29–39.

Ben Baaziz, S. 1996. Les temples de Neptune en Afrique romaine. *Africa* 14: 103–11.

Ben Baaziz, S. 1999. Les etablissements ruraux du Sahel antique. In Mrabet 1999, 31–50.

Ben Baaziz, S. 2000. *Rohia et le Sraa Ouertane dans l'antiquité*. Tunis: Ministère de la culture.

Ben Baaziz, S. 2003a. Les fermes rurales fortifiées de la Dorsale méridionales à l'epoque romaine. In Bejaoui 2003, 49–80.

Ben Baaziz, S. 2003b. Les huileries antiques de la dorsale tunisienne (Thala et Ksar Tlili). In Bost et al. 2003, 203–14.

Ben Baaziz, S. 2005. La carte archéologique de la Tunisie. Bilan de la recherche archéologique sur l'occupation du sol. In Mrabet 2005, 7–42.

Ben Baaziz, S. 2015. La toponomie dans la carte archéologique. In Mrabet 2015, 203–22.

Ben Hassen, H. and Ferjaoui, A. 2008. Nouvelles stèles votives provenant d'Aïn Tounga et la question de localisation du sanctuaire de Ba'al Hammon Saturne. *Reppal* 14: 5–14

Ben Hassen, H. and Maurin, L. 1998. *Oudhna (Uthina). La rédecouverte d'une ville antique de Tunisie*. Paris: INP/Ausonius.

Ben Hassen, H. and Maurin, L. 2004. *Oudhna (Uthina): Colonie des vétérans de la XIIIe légion: Histoire, urbanisme, fouilles et mise en valeur des monuments*. Paris: INP/Ausonius.

Ben Jerbania, I. and Redissi, T. 2014. Utique et la Méditerranée centrale à la fin du IXe s. et au VIIIe s. av. J.-C.: Les enseignements de la céramique grecque géometrique. *Rivista di Studi Fenici* 42(2): 177–204.

Ben Jerbania, I., Dufton, J.A., Fentress, E. and Russell, B. 2019. Utica's urban centre from Augustus to the Antonines, *Journal of Roman Archaeology* 32: 66–96.

Ben Lazreg, N. 2002. Roman and early Christian burial complex at Leptiminus: first notice. *Journal of Roman Archaeology* 15: 336–45.

Ben Lazreg, N. and Mattingly, D.J. 1992. *Leptiminus (Lamta): A Roman Port City in Tunisia. Report no. 1.* JRA supplement 4. Portsmouth, RI: Journal of Roman Archaeology.

Ben Lazreg, N., Bonifay, M., Drine, A.and Trousset, P. 1995. Production et commercialisation des *salsamenta* de l'Afrique ancienne. In Trousset 1995c, 103–42.

Ben Lazreg, N., Stevens, S., Stirling, L. and Moore, J. 2006. Roman and early Christian burial complex at Leptiminus (Lamta): second notice. *Journal of Roman Archaeology* 19: 347–67.

Ben Lazreg, N., Stirling, L.M. and Moore, J.P. (eds). 2021. *Leptiminus (Lamta) Report No. 4. The East Cemetery: Stratigraphy, Ceramics, Non-Ceramic Finds and Bio-Archaeological Studies.* JRA supplement 110. Portsmouth RI: Journal of Roman Archaeology.

Ben Ouezdou, H. and Trousset, P. 2009. Aménagements hydrauliques dans le sud-est tunisien. In V. Bridoux (ed), *Contrôle et distribution de l'eau dans le Maghreb antique et médiéval*, 1–18. CEFR 426. Rome: École française de Rome.

Ben Romdhane, H. 2017. Les *Afri* et leurs territoires à l'époque romaine. In Mrabet 2017a, 103–16.

Ben Tahar, S. 2004. Quelques réflexions sur les autochtones de Gigthis à l'époque punique. *Reppal* 13: 45–59.

Ben Tahar, S. 2014. Le site punique de Ghizène (Jerba): Premiers resultats des fouilles 2008–2009. *Römische Mitteilungen* 120: 59–97.

Ben Tahar, S. 2016. Henchir Tawrirt (Jerba). Une site libyque aux origines protohistoriques. *Antiquités africaines* 52: 9–52.

Ben Tahar, S. 2018. Henchir Bourgou (Jerba) à la lumière des nouvelles recherches archéologiques. *Römische Mitteilungen* 124: 311–51.

Ben Tahar, S. 2020. La céramique africaine à la lumière des dernières recherches archéologiques et archéométriques: Bilan. In D'Alessio and Marchetti 2020, 239–54.

Ben Tahar. S., von Rummel, P., Ritter, S., Aoudi, M., Dinies, M., Fassbinder, J., Mansel, K., Möller, H., Mukai, T., Peters, J., Reichmuth, S. and Trixl, S. 2020. Henchir Bourgou (Djerba), Tunesien. Die Arbeiten der Jahre 2017 bis 2019. *e-Forschungsberichte* 2020.1: 97–108.

Ben Tahar, S., von Rummel, P., Mansel, K., Möller, H., Mukai, T., Lappi, T., Peters, J., Trixl, S., Aoudi, M., Dinies, M. and Büchner, S. 2022. Henchir Bourgou (Djerba, Tunesien): Stratigraphie und Fundvorlage einer Sondage im Zentrum der antiken Siedlung (8. Jh. V. Chr. –2. Jh. N. Chr.). *Archäologischer Anzeiger* 2021(2), 1–178.

Ben Younès, H. 1981. *La présence punique au Sahel.* Unpublished PhD thesis, Université de Tunis.

Ben Younès, H. 1985. Rapport sur la campagne de fouilles effectuée dans la grande nécropole punique de la région de Mahdia: octobre–novembre 1982. *Reppal* 1: 23–61.

Ben Younès, H. 1995. L'architecture funéraire punique au Sahel. État et perspectives. In Trousset 1995a, 73–90.

Ben Younès, H. 1996. Le Sahel et l'île de Djerba: Les charactérisiques de l'architecture funéraire punique. *Africa* 14: 7–12.

Ben Younès, H. 1997. Découvertes de deux nouveaux éléments dans le mobilier de la tombe à la cuirasse de Ksour-Essaf au Sahel tunisien. *Reppal* 10: 35–40.

Ben Younès, H. 1999. Le Sahel préromain, pays des Libyphoeniciens. In Mrabet 1999, 11–20.

Ben Younès, H. 2007. Interculturality and the Punic funerary world. In Stone and Stirling 2007a, 32–42.

Ben Younès, H. 2013. Le Sahel préromain. Quelle urbanisation. In *Urbanisme et architecture en Méditerranée antique et médiévale à travers les sources archéologiques et littéraires*, 111–19. Tunis: Institut Supérieur des Sciences Humaines de Tunis.

Ben Younès, H. 2016. Un itinéraire matériel et immatériel préphénicien entre le Sahel et la région de Tébessa. In Mrabet 2016, 129–38.

Ben Younès, H. and Krandel-Ben Younès, A. 2014. Punic identity in North Africa: The funerary world. In Quinn and Vella 2014, 148–68.

Ben Younès, H. and Sghaïer, Y. 2018. *Lepti Minus (Lamta): Une expression de la culture libyphénicienne: Les nécropoles puniques, la céramique*. Tunis: INP.

Bénabou, M. 1976. *La résistance africaine à la romanisation*. Paris: Maspero.

Bénabou, M. 1977. Tacfarinas, insurgé berbère contre la colonisation romaine. In *Les Africains* 7: 293–313. Paris: Éditions Jeune Afrique.

Bénabou, M. 1978a. Les Romains ont-ils conquis l'Afrique? *Annales. Economies, sociétés, civilisations* 33(1): 83–8.

Bénabou, M. 1978b. Quelques paradoxes sur l'Afrique romaine, son histoire et ses historiens. In M. Galley (ed), *Actes du 2e congrès international. D'étude des cultures de la Méditerranée occidentale, vol. 2*, 139–44. Alger: Société Nationale d'Edition et de Diffusion.

Bénabou, M. 1980. L'imperialisme et l'Afrique du Nord: Le modèle romain. In D. Nordman and J.-P. Raison (eds), *Sciences de l'homme et conquête coloniale. Constitution et usage des sciences humaines en Afrique XIXe–XXe siècles*, 15–22. Paris: Presses de l'école normale superieure.

Bénabou, M. 1981. L'Afrique et la culture romaine: Le problème des survivances. *Cahiers de Tunisie* 29(117): 9–21.

Bénabou, M. 1982. Les survivances préromaines en Afrique romain. In Wells 1982, 13–27.

Bénabou, M. 2004. Entre l'histoire et l'ouvroir. Noé arrachant lui-même son manteau. *L'Inactuel* 12: 135–43.

Bénichou-Safar, H. 1982. *Les tombes puniques de Carthage. Topographie, structures, inscriptions et rites funéraires*. Paris: Éditions du CNRS.

Bénichou-Safar, H. 1995. Tophets et nécropoles puniques. In Trousset 1995a, 91–102.

Bénichou-Safar, H. 2004. *Le tophet de Salammbô à Carthage: Essai de reconstitution*. CEFR 342. Rome: École française de Rome.

Bennett, P., Wilson, A., Buzaian, A. and Kattenberg, A. 2004. The effects of recent storms on the exposed coastline of Tocra. *Libyan Studies* 35: 113–22.

Benseddik, N. 1982. *Les troupes auxiliaires de l'armée romaine en Maurétanie Césarienne sous le Haut-Empire*. Algiers: SNED.

Benseddik, N. 1986. "Limes" – Mauretania Caesariensis. In E. De Ruggiero (ed), *Dizionario Epigrafico di Antichità Romane, vol. 4*, fasc. 43.2–3 (1376), 47–67.

Benseddik, N. 1992. *Vsinaza* (Saneg): Un nouveau témoignage de l'activité de P. Aelius Peregrinus sur la *praetentura* sévèrienne. *L'Africa romana* 9(1): 425–37.

Benseddik, N. 1999. Septime Sévère, *P. Aelius Peregrinus Rogatus* et le *limes* de Maurétanie Césarienne. In Lepelley and Dupuis 1999, 89–110.

Benseddik, N. 2003. *Lambaesis* (Lambèse): Un camp, un sanctuaire, mais où était la ville? In Khanoussi 2003, 165–79.

Benseddik, N. 2003. À propos du bas-relief de Béja: Recherches sur les cultes guérisseurs au Maghreb. In Bazzana and Bocoum 2004, 183–88.

Benseddik, N. 2009. Les dieux de la Numidie militaire. In Groslambert 2009a, 239–85.

Benseddik, N. 2012. *Cirta-Constantina et son territoire.* Paris: Errance.

Benseddik, N. 2014. *Esculape et Hygie en Afrique. 1. Recherches sur les cultes guérisseurs; 2. Textes et images* Paris: AIBL.

Benseddik, N. 2017. *Femmes en Afrique ancienne.* Bordeaux: Ausonius.

Benseddik, N. and Bel Faïda, A. 2015. *Bibliographie de l'Algérie antique.* Collection Mémoires du CNRA, 2. Algiers: CNRA.

Benseddik, N. and Laporte, J.-P. 2016. Les *Bavares transtagnenses*, peuple de Maurétanie césarienne. In C. Wolff and P. Faure (eds), *Les auxiliaires de l'armée romaine: Des alliés aux fédérés*, 409–19. Lyon: CEROR.

Benseddik, N. and Potter, T. 1986. *Fouilles du Forum de Cherchel. Rapport préliminaire.* 4e supplément au Bulletin d'Archéologie Algérienne. Alger: Ministère de la culture et du tourisme.

Benseddik, N. and Potter, T. 1993. *Fouilles du Forum de Cherchel 1977–1981.* Alger: Agence Nationale d'Archéologie et de Protection des Sites et Monuments Historiques.

Bentivogli, V. 2004. Ai confine dell'Impero: Mausolei e romanizzazione del Nord Africa. *L'Africa romana* 15: 421–38.

Benz F.L. 1972. *Personal Names in the Phoenician and Punic Inscriptions.* Studia Pohl 8. Rome: G&B Press.

Bernal Casasola, D., Raissouni, B., Verdugo, J. and Zouak, M. (ed). 2013. Tamuda. *Cronosecuencia de la ciudad mauritana y del* castellum *romano.* Tétouan-Cadiz: Museo Arqueológico de Tetuán.

Bernal Casasola, D., Bustamante-Álvarez, M., Díaz Rodríguez, J.J., Expósito Álvarez, J.A. and Moujoud, T. 2018. *Tamuda* revisitada. De la primera destrucción ¿sertoriana? Al foso del *castellum* (2014–2018). *Antiquités africaines* 54: 53–84.

Bernard, G. 2014. Le lien de *contributio* entre colonies et communautés de citoyens romains dans les provinces africaines. Réflexions sur les colonies de la confédération cirtéene et sur la *contributio* entre *Icosium* et *Ilici*. In Briand-Ponsart 2014, 65–80.

Berque, J. 1953. Qu'est-ce qu'une "tribu" nord-africaine? In *Eventail de l'histoire vivante: Hommage à Lucien Febvre*, 261–80. Paris: Armand Colin.

Bernus, E. 2006. Le dromadaire, le cheval et l'âne: Usages et symboles chez les Touaregs. In M.H. Fantar 2006, 45–54.

Berry, J. and Laurence, R. (eds). 1998. *Cultural Identity in the Roman Empire.* London: Routledge.

Berthier, A. 1943. *Les vestiges du Christianisme antique dans la Numidie centrale.* Algiers: Maison Carrée.

Berthier, A. 1956. Les bazinas de Tiddis. *Libyca* 4: 147–53.

Berthier, A. 1968. Nicibes et Suburbures. Nomades ou sédentaires? *Bulletin d'Archéologie Algérienne* 3: 293–300.

Berthier, A. 1980. Un habitat punique à Constantine. *Antiquités africaines* 16: 13–26.

Berthier, A. 1981. *La Numidie: Rome et le Maghreb.* Paris: Picard.

Berthier, A. 2000. *Tiddis: Cité antique de Numidie.* Paris: de Boccard.

Berthier, A. and Charlier, R. 1955. *Le sanctuaire punique d'el-Hofra à Constantine.* Paris: Arts et métiers graphiques.

Bertrandy, F. 1987. Remarques sur le commerce des bêtes sauvages entre l'Afrique du Nord et l'Italie (IIe s. av. J.-C. – IVe s. ap. J.-C.). *Mélanges de l'Ecole française de Rome: Antiquité* 99: 211–41.

Bertrandy, F. 1991. Notes à propos d'un *fundus* (*CIL*, VIII, 6351) de la région de *Cirta* (Constantine) en Numidie. *Antiquités africaines* 27: 157–66.

Bertrandy, F. 2009. Les Cirtéens dans l'armée romaine d'Afrique. In Groslambert 2009a, 77–101.

Bertrandy, F. and Coltelloni,-Trannoy, M. 2005. *L'Afrique romaine de l'Atlantique à la Tripolitaine 69–439*. Paris: Armand Colin.

Bertrandy, F. and Sznycer, M. 1987. *Les stèles puniques de Constantine au Musée du Louvre*. Paris: Ministère de la culture et de la communication.

Beschaouch, A. 1974. La découverte de trois cités en Afrique Proconsulaire: Alma, Vrev et Asadi. *Comptes rendus des séances de l'Académie des inscriptions et belles-lettres* 1974, 118(2): 219–34.

Beschaouch, A. 1975. A propos de récentes découvertes épigraphiques dans le pays de Carthage. *Comptes rendus des séances de l'Académie des inscriptions et belles-lettres* 1975, 119(1): 101–18.

Beschaouch, A. 1976. Sur la localisation d'Abitina, la cité des célèbres martyrs africains. *Comptes rendus des séances de l'Académie des inscriptions et belles-lettres* 1976, 120(2): 255–66.

Beschaouch, A. 2011. Recherches récentes sur l'histoire municipale de *Thugga*, ville à double communauté civique, en Numidie proconsulaire (Dougga en Tunisie). *Comptes rendus des séances de l'Académie des inscriptions et belles-lettres* 2011, 155(4): 1803–18.

Beschaouch, A., Hanoune, R. and Thébert, Y. 1977. *Les ruines de Bulla Regia*. CEFR 28. Rome: École française de Rome.

Beschaouch, A., Hanoune, R., Khanoussi, M. and Thébert, Y.1983. *Recherches archéologiques franco-tunisiennes à Bulla Regia, I: Miscellanea*. CEFR 28/1. Rome: École française de Rome.

Bevan, A. 2014. Mediterranean containerization. *Current Anthropology* 55(4): 387–418.

Biagetti, S., Ait Kaci, A., Mori, L. and di Lernia, S. 2012. Writing the desert: The "Tifinagh" rock inscriptions of the Tadrart Acacus (southwestern Libya). *Azania: Archaeological Research in Africa* 47(2): 153–74.

Biagetti, S., Aït Kaci, A. and Di Lernia, S. 2015. The "written landscape" of the central Sahara: Recording and digitising the Tifinagh inscriptions in the Tadrart Acacus Mountains. In M. Kominko (ed), *From Dust to Digital: Ten Years of the Endangered Archives Programme*, 1–29. Cambridge: Open Book Publishers.

Bianchi Bandinelli, R., Vergara Caffarelli, E. and Caputo, G. 1966. *The Buried City: Excavations at Leptis Magna*. New York: F.A. Praeger.

Bigi, F., Di Vita-Evrard, G., Fontana, S. and Schingo, G. 2009. The mausoleum of Gasr Doga. *Libyan Studies* 40: 25–46.

Bigi, L. 2019. *Gli oleifici di Volubilis e della Mauretania Tingitana*. Rome: Edizioni Quasar.

Birebent, J. 1962. *Aquae Romanae: Recherches d'hydraulique romaine dans l'Est algérien*. Algiers: Service des antiquites de l'Algérie.

Birley, A.R. 1987. Some notes on the Donatist schism. *Libyan Studies* 18: 29–41.

Birley, A.R. 1988a. *Septimus Severus: The African Emperor*. London: Batsford.

Birley, A.R. 1988b. Names at Lepcis Magna. *Libyan Studies* 19: 1–19.

Birley, A.R. 1997. *Hadrian: The Restless Emperor*. London: Routledge.

Birley, A.R. 2020. Antoninus Pius' Guard Prefect Marcus Gavius Maximus, with an Appendix on new evidence for the *Fasti* of Britain under Antoninus. In D.J. Breeze and W.S.

Hanson (eds), *The Antonine Wall: Papers in Honour of Professor Lawrence Keppie*, 313–31. Oxford: Archaeopress.

Bisi, A.M. 1967. *Le stele puniche*. Rome: Università di Roma.

Bisi, A.M. 1990. *Le terrecotte figurate fenice et puniche in Italia*. Rome: Istituto Poligrafico e Zecca dello stato.

Bisson, J. 1957. *Le Gourara: Étude de géographie humaine*. Memoires de l'Institut de recherches sahariennes 3. Alger: Université d'Alger.

Blackhurst, A. 2004. The house of Nubel: Rebels or players? In Merrills 2004, 59–75.

Blanc-Bijon, V. (ed). 2008. *Lieux de cultes: Aires votives, temples, églises, mosquées*. Études d'Antiquités africaines. Paris: Éditions du CNRS.

Blanc-Bijon, V., Bracco, J.-P., Carre, M.-B., Chaker, S., Lafon, X. and Ouerfelli, M. (eds). 2021. *L'Homme et l'Animal au Maghreb de la Préhistoire au Moyen Âge: Explorations d'une relation complexe. Actes du XIe Colloque international histoire et archéologie de l'Afrique du Nord (Aix- en- Provence, Marseille, 8–14 octobre 2014)*. Aix-en-Provence: Presses universitaires de Provence.

Blanchard-Lemée, M. 1975. *Maisons à mosaïques du quartier central de Djemila (Cuicul)*. Paris: Éditions OPHRYS.

Blanchard-Lemée, M., Ennaïfer, M. and Slim, H. 1996. *Mosaics of Roman Africa: Floor Mosaics from Tunisia*. London: George Braziller

Blas de Roblès, J.-M., Sintes, C. and Kenrick, P. 2019. *Classical Antiquities of Algeria: A Selective Guide*. London: Silphium Press.

Blonce, C. 2008. Le rôle des administrations municipales dans l'érection des arcs monumentaux en Afrique (de la Tingitaine à la Tripolitane du Ier au IVe s. ap. J.-C. In *Le quotidian municipal dans l'Occident romain*, 595–623. Clermont-Ferrand: Press Universitaires Blaise-Pascal.

Blonce, C. 2014. Orner la cité, contrôler le territoire: L'arc monumental comme témoin de l'organisation de l'espace dans les cités de l'Afrique romaine à l'époque impériale. In Briand-Ponsart 2014, 243–62.

Boardman, J. 1999. *The Greeks Overseas: Their Early Colonies and Trade*, 4th edn. London: Thames and Hudson.

Boardman, J. and Hayes, J. 1966. *Excavations at Tocra 1963–1965. The Archaic Deposits*, vol. 1. London: British School of Archaeology at Athens.

Bockmann, R. 2022. African Rome: The city of Carthage from its Roman (re-)foundation to the end of the Byzantine period. In Hitchner 2022a, 119–41.

Bockmann R., Leone, A. and von Rummel, P. (eds). 2019. *Africa – Ifrīqiya. Continuity and Change in North Africa from the Byzantine to the Early Islamic Age*. Palilia 34. Rome: Deutsches Archäologisches Institut Rom.

Bodereau, P. 1907. *La Capsa ancienne. La Gafsa moderne*. Paris: Challamel.

Boeswillwald, E., Cagnat, R. and Ballu, A. 1892–1904. *Timgad: Une cité africaine sous l'empire romain*. 8 vols. Paris: Leroux.

Bokbot, Y. 1991. *Habitats et monuments funéraires du Maroc protohistorique*. Thèse de doctorat en lettres, Université de Provence.

Bokbot, Y. 2003. Tumulus protohistoriques de pré-Sahara marocain: Indices de minorités religieuses. In Khanoussi 2003, 35–45.

Bokbot, Y. 2019. Protohistoric and pre-Islamic funerary archaeology in the Moroccan Pre-Sahara. In Gatto et al. 2019a, 315–40.

Bokbot, Y. 2020. The origins of urbanisation and structured political power in Morocco: Indigenous phenomenon or foreign colonisation? In Sterry and Mattingly 2020a, 476–97.

Bokbot, Y. and Onrubia-Pintado, J. 1995. Substrat autochtone et colonisation phénicienne au Maroc: Nouvelles recherches protohistoriques dans la péninsule tingitane. In CTHS Pau 1995b, 219–31.

Bokbot, Y., Onrubia-Pintado, J., Rodriguez-Rodriguez, A. and Rodriguez-Santana C.G. 2008. Le complexe funéraire et cultuel d'Adrar Zerzem (Anti-Atlas, Maroc): Résultats préliminaires. In Blanc-Bijon 2008, 21–29.

Bokbot, Y., Fenwick, C., Mattingly, D.J., Sheldrick, N. and Sterry, M. 2021. Horses and habitations: Iron Age rock art from hilltop settlements in the Wadi Draa, Morocco. *Journal of African Archaeology* 19(2): 159–86.

Bokbot, Y., Mattingly, D.J. and Sterry, M. Forthcoming. Le projet Moyen Drâa: Resultats des prospections et sondages 2015–18. *Bulletin d'Archéologie Marocaine.*

Bomgardner, D.L. 1989. The Carthage amphitheater: A reappraisal. *American Journal of Archaeology* 93(1): 85–103.

Bomgardner, D.L. 2000. *The Story of the Roman Amphitheatre.* London: Routledge.

Bonacasa, N. and Ensoli, S. 2000. *Cirene.* Milan: Electa.

Bonacasa, R.M.C. 2018. Gli edifici termali di Sabratha. *Libya Antiqua* n.s. 11: 107–62.

Bonifay, M. 2004. *Etudes sur la céramique romaine tardive d'Afrique.* British Archaeological Reports International Series S1301. Oxford: BAR Publishing.

Bonifay, M. 2007. Que transportaient donc les amphores africaines? In Papi 2007, 8–31.

Bonifay, M. 2013. Africa: Patterns of consumption in coastal regions versus inland regions. The ceramic evidence (300–700 A.D.). *Late Antique Archaeology* 10(1): 529–66.

Bonifay, M. 2017. Can we speak of pottery and amphora "import substitution" in inland regions of Roman Africa? In Mattingly et al. 2017a, 341–68.

Bonifay, M. 2018. The distribution of African pottery under the Roman empire: Evidence vs. interpretation. In A.I. Wilson and A. Bowman (eds), *Trade, Commerce, and the State in the Roman World,* 327–52. Oxford Studies on the Roman Economy. Oxford: Oxford University Press.

Bonifay, M. 2021. African amphora contents: An update. In D. Bernal-Casasola, M. Bonfiay, A. Pecci and V. Leitch (eds), *Roman Amphora Contents: Reflecting on the Maritime Trade of Foodstuffs in Antiquity (In honour of Miguel Beltrán Lloris),* 281–97. Oxford: Archaeopress.

Bonifay, M. 2022. African economy: The ceramic evidence. In Hitchner 2022a, 220–32.

Bonnet, C. 1988. *Melqart: Cultes et mythes de l'Héracles tyrien en Méditerranée.* Leuven: Peeters.

Bonnet, C. 1996. *Astarté. Dossier documentaire et perspectives historiques.* Rome: Consiglio Nazionale delle Ricerche.

Bonnet, C. 2004. *I fenici.* Rome: Carocci.

Bonnet, C. 2014. Phoenician identities in Hellenistic times: Strategies and negotiations. In Quinn and Vella 2014, 282–98.

Bonnet, C. and Xella, P. 1995. La religion. In Krings 1995, 316–33.

Boozer, A.L. 2012. Globalizing Mediterranean identities: The overlapping spheres of Egyptian, Greek and Roman worlds at Trimithis. *Journal of Mediterranean Archaeology* 25(2): 93–116.

Boozer, A.L. 2020. The urbanisation of Egypt's Western Desert under Roman rule. In Sterry and Mattingly 2020a, 147–86.

Borca, F. 2004. La percezione del deserto nelle testimonianze letterarie dei Romani. *L'Africa romana* 15: 199–210.

Bost, J.-P., Roddaz, J.-M. and Tassaux, F. (eds). 2003. *Itinéraire de Saintes à Dougga: Mélanges offerts à Louis Maurin*. Bordeaux: Ausonius.

Bouchenaki, M. 1975. *Fouilles de la nécropole occidentale de Tipasa (Matarés) 1968–1972*. Algers: Société nationale d'édition et de diffusion.

Boucher, J.P. (ed). 1983. *Journées d'études sur les aqueducs romains = Tagung über römische Wasserversorgungsanlagen*. Paris: Société d'édition Les Belles Lettres.

Boudouhou, N. 2015. Le territoire entre les deux royaumes de la Maurétanie: Etat de la recherche et bilan des découvertes archéologiques. In Mrabet 2015, 43–54.

Boukhenouf, A., Iaichouchen, O., Azrarak, K and Arif, K. 2017. Aperçu sur la vie rurale antique à travers le site archéologique de Mlakou "antique Petra". In Mrabet 2017b, 209–22.

Bourgida-M'Charek, F. 2004. La découverte d'une nouvelle cité d'Afrique Proconsulaire: Henchir Aïn-Jannet/civitas Totiensium. *L'Africa romana* 15: 1317–1324.

Bowman, A.K. and Wilson, A. (eds). 2009. *Quantifying the Roman Economy: Methods and Problems*. Oxford Studies on the Roman Economy. Oxford, Oxford University Press.

Bowman, A.K. and Wilson, A. (eds). 2011. *Settlement, Urbanization, and Population*. Oxford Studies on the Roman Economy. Oxford: Oxford University Press.

Bowman, A.K. and Wilson, A. (eds). 2013. *The Roman Agricultural Economy: Organization, Investment, and Production*. Oxford Studies on the Roman Economy. Oxford: Oxford University Press.

Bowman, A.K., Champlin, E. and Lintott, A. (eds). 1996. *The Cambridge Ancient History, vol. 10. The Augustan Empire, 43 BC–AD 69*. 2nd edition. Cambridge: Cambridge University Press.

Bowman, A.K., Garnsey, P. and Rathbone, D. (eds). 2000. *The Cambridge Ancient History, vol. 11. The High Empire, A.D. 70–192*. 2nd edition. Cambridge: Cambridge University Press

Bradley, K. 2000. *Romanitas* and the Roman family: The evidence of Apuleius's *Apology*. *Canadian Journal of History* 35(2): 215–40.

Bradley, M. 2010. *Classics and Imperialism in the British Empire*. Oxford: Oxford University Press.

Braemar, F. 1986. Répertoire des gisements de pierres ayant exporté leur production à l'époque romaine. In F. Braemar (ed), *Les ressources minérale et l'histoire de leur exploitation*. Colloque international tenu dans le cadre du 108e Congrès national des sociétés savantes 1983, 287–328.

Brahmi, M. 2017. Notes sur les formes de l'occupation du sol dans une zone frontalière: Le Sud-ouest de la Byzacène. In Mrabet 2017b, 117–46.

Braudel, F. 1972. *The Mediterranean and the Mediterranean World in the Age of Philip II, vol 1*. New York: Harper & Row.

Braudel, F. 1973. *The Mediterranean and the Mediterranean World in the Age of Philip II, vol 2*. New York: Harper & Row.

Braund, D. 1984. *Rome and the Friendly King: The Character of the Client Kingship*. London: Croom Helm.

Breeze, D.J. 2011. *The Frontiers of Imperial Rome*. Barnsley: Pen and Sword.

Brett, M. and Fentress, E.W.B. 1996. *The Berbers*. Oxford: Blackwell.

Briand-Ponsart, C. 2002. La mémoire africaine d'Apulée. In Briand-Ponsart and Crogiez 2002, 59–76.

Briand-Ponsart, C. 2003. Élites et constructions urbaines à Thamugadi au IIe siècle apr. J.-C. In Khanoussi 2003, 181–97.

Briand-Ponsart, C. (ed). 2005a. *Identités et cultures dans l'Algérie antique.* Rouen: Presses universitaires de Rouen et du Havre.

Briand-Ponsart, C. 2005b. Le statut des communautés en Afrique Proconsulaire aux Ier et IIe siècles. In Lafond 2005, 93–116.

Briand-Ponsart, C. 2011. La Numidia ou la difficulté de devenir une province. In Briand-Ponsart and Modéran 2011, 153–8.

Briand-Ponsart, C. (ed). 2014. *Centres de pouvoir et l'organisation de l'espace.* Actes du Xe colloque international sur l'histoire et l'archéologie de l'Afrique du Nord préhistorique, antique et médiévale (Caen, 25–28 mai 2009). Caen: Presses universitares de Caen.

Briand-Ponsart, C. and Crogiez, S. (eds). 2002. *L'Afrique du Nord antique et médiévale: Mémoire, identité et imaginaire.* Rouen: Presses universitares de Rouen et du Havre.

Briand-Ponsart, C. and Hugoniot, C. 2006. *L'Afrique romaine de l'Atlantique à la Tripolitaine 146 av. J.-C. – 533 ap. J.-C.* Paris: Armand Colin

Briand-Ponsart, C. and Modéran, Y. (eds). 2011. *Provinces et identités provinciales dans l'Afrique romaine.* Caen: Presses universitaires de Caen.

Bridoux, V. 2006. *Les royaumes d'Afrique du Nord de la fin de la seconde guerre punique au mort du roi Bocchus II (201–33 av. N. è).* Unpublished PhD thesis, University of Paris.

Bridoux, V. 2014. Numidia and the Punic world. In Quinn and Vella 2014, 180–201.

Bridoux, V. and Kbiri Alaoui, M. 2013. Il sito archeologico di Kouass (Marocco) dall' epoca fenicio-punica al medievo. *Forma Urbis* 18(1): 39–43

Bridoux, V., Kbiri Alaoui, M., Biagi, S., Dridi, H. and Ichkhakh, A. 2011. La mission archéologique franco-marocaine de Kouass au Maroc. *Les nouvelles de l'archéologie* 123: 44–48.

Bridoux, V., Kbiri Alaoui, M., André, N., Clavel, B., Grisoni, E., Hassini, H., Ichkhakh, A, Jullien, T. and Naji, H. 2014. Kouass (Asilah, Maroc): Campagne de fouilles 2013. Chronique des activités archéologiques de l'École française de Rome [online], Maghreb, 23 July 2014. Accessed on 31 March 2020. http://journals.openedition.org/cefr/1236; https://doi.org/10.4000/cefr.1236.

Broekaert, W. and Vanacker, W. 2019. Raiders to traders? Economics of integration among nomadic communities in North Africa. In D. Slootjes and M. Peachin (eds), *Rome and the Worlds beyond its Frontiers*, 96–122. Leiden: Brill.

Brogan, O. 1965. Henschir el-Ausaf by Tigi (Tripolitania) and some related tombs in the Tunisian Gefara. *Libya Antiqua* 2: 47–56.

Brogan, O. 1975. Inscriptions in the Libyan alphabet from Tripolitania, and some notes on the tribes of the region. In Bynon and Bynon 1975, 267–89.

Brogan, O. 1980. Hadd Hajar, a *clausura* in the Tripolitanian Gebel Gharian, south of Asabaa. *Libyan Studies* 11: 45–52.

Brogan, O. and Smith, D.J. 1984. *Ghirza: A Libyan Settlement in the Roman Period.* Libyan Antiquities Series 1, Tripoli: Department of Antiquities.

Broise, H. and Thébert, Y. 1993. *Recherches archéologiques à Bulla Regia, II: Les architectures. 1: Les thermes memmiens.* CEFR 28/2. Rome: École française de Rome.

Broodbank, C. 2013. *The Making of the Middle Sea: A History of the Mediterranean from the Beginning to the Emergence of the Classical World.* London: Thames & Hudson.

Broodbank, C. and Lucarini, G. 2019. The dynamics of Mediterranean Africa, *ca.* 9600–1000 bc: An interpretative synthesis of knowns and unknowns. *Journal of Mediterranean Archaeology* 32(2): 195–267.

Brooks, N., di Lernia, S., Drake, N., Chiapello, I., Legrand, M., Moulin, C. and Prospero, J. 2005. The climate-environment-society nexus in the Sahara from prehistoric times to the present day. *The Journal of North African Studies* 10(3–4): 253–92.

Broughton, T.R.S. 1929. *The Romanization of Africa Proconsularis*. Baltimore: Johns Hopkins.

Brouquier-Reddé, V. 1992a. La place de la Tripolitaine dans la géographie religieuse de l'Afrique du Nord. In CTHS Avignon 1992, 117–23.

Brouquier-Reddé, V. 1992b. *Temples et cultes de Tripolitaine*. Études d'antiquités africaines. Paris: Éditions du CNRS.

Brouquier-Reddé, V. and Hurlet, F. (eds). 2018. *L'eau dans les villes du Maghreb et leur territoire à l'époque romaine*. Bordeaux: Ausonius.

Brouquier-Reddé, V., Ichkhakh, A. and el Khayari, A. 1999. Les stèles votives de Maurétanie Tingitane. Un complément au catalogue du temple B de Volubilis. In Lancel 1999, 343–70.

Brown, S.S. 1991. *Late Carthaginian Child Sacrifice and Sacrificial Monuments in the Mediterranean Context*. Sheffield: JSOT Press.

Brubaker, R. 2004. *Ethnicity without Groups*. Cambridge, MA: Harvard University Press.

Brubaker, R. and Cooper, F. 2000. Beyond "identity". *Theory and Society* 29: 1–47.

Brun, J.-P. 2003. Les pressoirs à vin d'Afrique et de Maurétanie à l'époque romaine. *Africa: Séances scientifiques* 1: 7–30.

Brun, J.-P. 2004. *Archéologie du vin et de l'huile dans l'Empire romain*. Paris: Errance.

Brun, J.-P. 2018. La production du vin en Afrique du Nord durant l'Antiquité. In Sehili et al. 2018, 231–56.

Brun, J.-P. and Leguilloux, M. 2004. Tannerie et parfumerie de l'exemplarité de Pompéi dans la recherche sur l'artisanat antique. *Africa: Séances scientifiques* 2: 37–52.

Buck, D.J. 1984. The role of states in the Eastern Maghreb, 500 BC-AD 500. *The Maghreb Review* 9 (1–2): 1–11.

Buck, D.J. and Mattingly, D.J. (eds). 1985. *Town and Country in Roman Tripolitania. Papers in honour of Olwen Hackett*. British Archaeological Reports International Series S274. Oxford: BAR Publishing.

Bullo, S. 2002. *Provincia Africa. Le città e il territorio dalla caduta di Cartagine a Nerone*. Rome: L'Erma di Bretschneider.

Burbank, J. and Cooper, F. 2010. *Empires in World History: Power and the Politics of Difference*. Princeton: Princeton University Press.

Buzaian, A. 2022. *Ancient Olive Presses and Oil Production in Cyrenaica (North-East Libya)*. London: BILNAS.

Buzaian, A.M. and Lloyd, J.A. 1996. Early urbanism in Cyrenaica: New evidence from Euesperides (Benghazi). *Libyan Studies* 27: 129–52.

Bynon, J. and Bynon, T. (eds). 1975. *Hamito-Semitica*. The Hague: Mouton.

Cabouret, B. (ed). 2005. *L'Afrique romaine de 69 à 439: Romanisation et christianisation*. Questions d'histore. Nantes: Editions du Temps.

Cadotte, A. 2007. *La romanisation des dieux: L'interpretatio romana en Afrique du Nord sous le Haut-Empire*. Religions in the Graeco-Roman World 158. Leiden: Brill.

Cagnat, R. 1909. *Carthage, Timgad, Tébessa et les villes antiques de l'Afrique du Nord*. Paris: H. Laurens.

Cagnat, R. 1913. *L'armée romaine d'Afrique et l'occupation de l'Afrique sous les Empereurs*. 2nd edition. Paris: Imprimerie Nationale.

Cagnat, R. 1914a. A new Roman customs list. *Journal of Roman Studies* 4: 143–46.

Cagnat, R. 1914b. La frontière militaire de la Tripolitaine à l'époque romaine. *Mémoires de l'Institut de France* 39: 77–109.

Cagnat, R. and Merlin, A. 1914/1932. *Atlas archéologique de la Tunisie.* 2nd series, Paris: E. Leroux.

Caillemer, A. and Chevallier, R. 1959. *Atlas des centuriations romaines de Tunisie.* Paris: Institut géographique national.

Callegarin, L. 2018. Négocier la frontière: La fluctuation du limes du Maurétanie tingitaine. In Guédon 2018b, 121–37.

Callegarin, L., Kbiri Alaoui, M., Ichkhakh, A. and Roux, J.-C. (eds). 2016a. *Rirha: Site antique et médiéval du Maroc, vol. 1: Cadre historique et géographique général.* Collection de la Casa de Velázquez 150. Madrid: Casa de Velázquez.

Callegarin, L., Kbiri Alaoui, M., Ichkhakh, A. and Roux, J.-C. (eds). 2016b. *Rirha: Site antique et médiéval du Maroc, vol. 2: Période maurétanienne (Ve siècle av. J.-C. – 40 ap. J.-C.).* Collection de la Casa de Velázquez 151. Madrid: Casa de Velázquez.

Callegarin, L., Kbiri Alaoui, M., Ichkhakh, A. and Roux, J.-C. (eds). 2016c. *Rirha: Site antique et médiéval du Maroc, vol. 3: Période romaine (40 ap. J.-C. – fin du IIIe s. ap. J.-C.)* . Collection de la Casa de Velázquez 152. Madrid: Casa de Velázquez.

Callegarin, L., Kbiri Alaoui, M., Ichkhakh, A. and Roux, J.-C. (eds). 2016d. *Rirha: Site antique et médiéval du Maroc, vol. 4: Période médiévale islamique (IXe–XVe siècle).* Collection de la Casa de Velázquez 153. Madrid: Casa de Velázquez.

Callu, J.-P., Morel, J.-P., Rebuffat, R. and Hallier, G. 1965. *Thamusida: Fouilles du Service des antiquités du Maroc, vol. 1.* Rome: École française de Rome.

Campbell, B. 1984. *The Emperor and the Roman Army 31 BC – AD 235.* Oxford: Clarendon Press.

Campbell, B. 1994. *The Roman Army 31 BC – AD 337. A Sourcebook.* London: Routledge.

Campbell, B. 2000. *The Writings of the Roman Land Surveyors: Introduction, Text, Translations and Commentary.* London: Roman Society Publications.

Campbell, B. 2002. *War and Society in Imperial Rome, 31 BC – AD 284.* London: Routledge.

Camps, G. 1954. L'inscription de Béja et le problème des Dii Mauri. *Revue Africaine* 98: 235–60.

Camps, G. 1955. Les Bavares, peuple de Maurétanie césarienne. *Revue Africaine* 99: 241–88.

Camps, G. 1960. *Aux origines de la Berbérie. Massinissa ou les débuts de l'histoire.* (*Libyca* 8). Algiers: Service des Antiquités.

Camps, G. 1961. *Monuments et rites funéraires protohistoriques: Aux origines de la Berbérie.* Paris: Arts et Métiers graphiques.

Camps, G. 1973a. Une frontière inexpliquée: La limite de la Berbérie orientale de la Protohistoire au Moyen-Age. In *Maghreb et Sahara: Études géographiques offertes à Jean Despois, Acta Geographica,* 39–67.

Camps, G. 1973b. Nouvelles observations sur l'architecture et l'âge du Medracen, mausolée royal de Numidie. *Comptes rendus des séances de l'Académie des inscriptions et belles-lettres* 1973, 117(3): 470–517.

Camps, G. 1978. Recherches sur les plus anciennes inscriptions libyques de l'Afrique du Nord et la Sahara. *Bulletin archéologique du comité des travaux historiques et scientifiques: Afrique du Nord* n.s. 10–11B (1974–5): 143–66.

Camps, G. 1979. Les Numides et la civilisation punique. *Antiquités africaines* 14: 43–53.

Camps, G. 1980. *Berbères. Aux marges de l'histoire.* Toulouse: Éditions des Hespérides.

Camps, G. 1981. L'origine des Berbères. *Les Cahiers du CRESM* 12: 9–33.

Camps, G. 1984. *Rex gentium Maurorum et Romanorum*. Recherches sur les royaumes de Maurétanie des VIe et VIIe siècles. *Antiquités africaines* 20: 183–218.

Camps, G. 1986a. Funerary monuments with attached chapels from the northern Sahara. *African Archaeological Review* 4: 151–64.

Camps, G. 1986b. L'araire berbère. In CTHS Montpellier 1986, 177–84.

Camps, G. 1987a. *Les Berbères. Mémoire et identité.* Paris: Editions Errance.

Camps, G. 1987b. Protohistoire de l'Afrique du Nord: Questions de terminologie et de chronologie. *Reppal* 3: 43–70.

Camps, G. 1989. Les chars sahariens. Images d'une societé aristocratique. *Antiquités africaines* 25: 11–40.

Camps, G. 1991. Chars protohistoriques de l'Afrique du Nord et du Sahara: Engins de guerre ou véhicules de prestige? In CTHS Strasbourg 1991, 267–88.

Camps, G. 1992a. Le coq et la coquille. *Bulletin archéologique du comité des travaux historiques et scientifiques: Afrique du Nord* n.s. 22B: 35–61.

Camps, G. 1992b. Bronze (Âge du). *Encyclopédie Berbère* 11: 1614–26.

Camps, G. 1993a. Liste onomastique Libyque d'après les sources latines. *Reppal* 7–8: 39–73.

Camps, G. 1993b. Réflexions sur l'origine protohistorique des cités en Afrique du Nord. In L. Serra (ed), *La città mediterranea: Eredita antica e apporto arabo-islamico sulle rive del Mediterraneo occidentale e in particolare nel Maghreb.* Atti del Congresso internazionale di Bari, 4–7 maggio 1988, 73–81. Napoli: Istituto universitario orientale.

Camps, G. 1994a. Cité: Les cités numides et maures. *Encyclopédie Berbère* 13: 1980–90.

Camps, G. 1994b. Remarques sur la toponymie de la Maurétanie césarienne occidentale. In Le Bohec 1994, 81–94.

Camps, G. 1994c. "*Punica lingua*" et épigraphie libyque dans la Numidie d'Hippone. *Bulletin archéologique du comité des travaux historiques et scientifiques: Afrique du Nord* n.s. 23B: 33–49.

Camps, G. 1995a. Djorf Torba. *Encyclopédie Berbère* 16: 2477–88.

Camps, G. 1995b. Les nécropoles mégalithiques de l'Afrique du Nord. In Trousset 1995a, 17–31.

Camps, G. 1995c. Dieux africaines et dii mauri. *Encyclopédie Berbère* 15: 2321–40.

Camps, G. 1995d. *Djedar. Encyclopédie Berbère* 16: 2409–22.

Camps, G. 1996. Écriture: Écriture libyque. *Encyclopédie Berbère* 17: 2564–73.

Camps, G. 1997. Tin Hinan et sa légende. À propos du tumulus princier d'Abalessa (Ahaggar, Algérie). *Bulletin archéologique du comité des travaux historiques et scientifiques, Afrique du Nord* 24: 173–95.

Camps, G. 1999. Essais de cartographie culturelle. À propos de la frontière de Numidie et de Maurétanie. In Lepelley and Dupuis 1999, 44–70.

Camps, G. 2003. Liste onomastique libyque. Nouvelle édition. *Antiquités africaines* 38–39: 211–57.

Camps, G. 2007. *Les Berbères: Mémoire et identité.* Revised edition. Arles: Babel.

Camps, G. and Camps-Fabrer, H. 1964. *La nécropole mégalithique du Djebel Mazela à Bou Nouara.* Mémoires du Centre de recherches anthropologiques, préhistoriques et ethnographiques 3. Paris: Arts et métiers graphiques.

Camps, G. and Gast, M. (eds). 1982. *Les chars préhistoriques du Sahara: archéologie et techniques d'attelage.* Aix-en-Provence: Maison de la Méditerranée, Université de Provence.

Camps, G. et Chaker, S. 1993. Cheval. *Encyclopédie Berbère* 12: 1907–11.

Camps, G. and Longerstay, M. 2000. Haouanet. *Encyclopédie Berbère* 22: 3361–87.

Camps, G., Chaker, S. and Laporte, J.-P. 1999. Deux nouvelles stèles kabyles au cavalier. *Bulletin archéologique du comité des travaux historiques et scientifiques: Afrique du Nord* n.s. 25B: 19–32.

Camps-Fabrer, H. 1953. *L'oliver et l'huile dans l'Afrique romaine*. Algiers: Gouvernement Général de l'Algérie.

Capot-Rey, R. 1942. Le nomadisme pastoral dans le Sahara français. *Travaux de l'Institut de Recherches Sahariennes* 1: 63–86.

Capot-Rey, R. 1953. *Le Sahara Français*. L'Afrique blanche française 2. Paris: Presses universitaires.

Caputo, G. 1987. *Il teatro augusteo di Leptis Magna: Scavo e restauro 1937–1951*. Monografie di Archeologia libica 3, Rome: L'Erma di Bretschneider.

Carandini, A. 1970. Produzione agricola e produzione ceramica nell'Africa di età imperiale. *Studi Miscellanei* 15: 97–121.

Carandini, A. 1983. Pottery and the African economy. In P. Garnsey, K. Hopkins and C.R. Whittaker (eds), *Trade in the Ancient Economy*, 145–62. Berkeley and Los Angeles: University of California Press.

Carcopino, J. 1933. Note complémentaire sur les Numeri syriens de la Numidie romaine. *Syria* 14: 20–55.

Carcopino, J. 1944. *Le Maroc antique*. Paris: Gallimard.

Carlsen, J. 1991. Estate management in Roman North Africa. Transformation or continuity? *L'Africa romana* 8: 625–37.

Carlsen, J. 2020a. The necropoleis of the imperial slaves and freedmen in the deathscape of Roman Carthage. In Humphrey 2020, 9–27.

Carlsen, J. 2020b. Epitaphs and the demography of the imperial slaves and freedmen in Roman Carthage. In N. Bargfeldt and J.H. Petersen (eds), *Reflections: Harbour City Deathscapes in Roman Italy and Beyond*, 195–209. Rome: Edizioni Quasar.

Carlsen, J. 2022. Roman imperial administration. In Hitchner 2022a, 142–21.

Carratelli, G.P. (ed). 1996. *The Western Greeks: Classical Civilization in the Western mediterranean*. London: Thames and Hudson.

Carte (Maroc) = *Carte archéologique du Maroc antique*. Rabat: INSAP.

Carte (Tunisie) = CNSAMH

Carter, J.-C. 2006. *Discovering the Greek Countryside at Metaponto*. Ann Arbor: Michigan University Press.

Carter, T.H. 1965. Western Phoenicians at Lepcis Magna. *American Journal of Archaeology* 69(2): 123–32.

Carucci, M. 2007. *The Romano-African Domus: Studies in Space, Decoration, and Function*. British Archaeological Reports, International Series S1731. Oxford: Archaeopress.

Castelletti, L., Castiglioni, E., Cottini, M. and Rottoli, M. 1999. Archaeobotanical analysis of charcoal, wood and seeds. In di Lernia 1999, 131–48.

Catalogue Alaoui 1897–1922 = *Catalogue des musées et collections archéologiques de l'Algérie et de la Tunisie: Musée Alaoui*. 1st supplement 1909, 2nd supplement 1922. Paris: Leroux.

Catani, E. and Marengo, S.M. (eds). 1998. *La Cirenaica in età antica*. Macerata: Istituti editoriali e poligrafici internazionali.

Cerri, L. 2007. Salsamenta dalla *Tingitana*. In Papi 2007, 33–42.

Chabot, J.-B. 1940. *Recueil des inscriptions libyques*. Paris: Imprimerie nationale.

Chaker, S. 1986. A propos de la terminologie libyque des titres et fonctions. *AION: Annali dell'Università degli Studi di Napoli "L'Orientale"* 46(4): 541–62.

Chaker, S. 2003. Variété des usages libyques: variations chronologiques, géographiques et sociales. *Antiquités africaines* 38–39: 267–73.

Chaker, S. 2013a. Onomastique libyco-berberes (Anthroponymie). *Encyclopédie Berbère* 35: 5760–79.

Chaker, S. 2013b. Origine(s) berbère(s): Linguistique et préhistoire. *Encyclopédie Berbère* 35: 5819–44.

Chamoux, F. 1953. *Cyrène sous la monarchie dés Battiades*. Paris: BEFAR.

Champion, C.B. (ed). 2004. *Roman Imperialism: Readings and Sources*. Oxford: Blackwell.

Chaouali, M. 2003. Les *nundinae* dans les grands domaines en Afrique du Nord à l'époque romaine. *Antiquités africaines* 38–39: 375–86.

Chastagnol, A. 1990. Considérations sur les municipes latins du premier siècle apr. J.-C. In *L'Afrique dans l'Occident romain*, 351–65.

Chatelain, L. 1931. *La ville romaine de Sala*. Paris: Moncho.

Chausa Sáez, A. 1997. *Veteranos en el África romana*. Barcelona: Edicions Universitat Barcelona.

Chebbi, N. 2010. Les africains et la pourpre. *L'Africa romana* 18(2): 157–74.

Chelbi, F. 1996. *Utique: la splendide*. Tunis: Institut National du Patrimoine.

Chelbi, F., Maraoui-Telmini, B and Docter, R.F. 2006a. Bilan des fouilles du terrain de Bir Massouda (Carthage): Campagnes 2002 à 2004. *Africa: séances scientifiques* n.s. 3: 207–25.

Chelbi, F., Maraoui Telmini, B and Docter, R.F. 2006b. Découverte d'une nécropole du huitième siècle av. J.-C. à Carthage: Bir Massouda. Rapport préliminaire sur les fouilles de l'Institut Nationale du Patrimoine (Tunis) et l'Université de Gand. *CEDAC Carthage Bulletin* 22: 13–25.

Cherif, A. 2015. Données nouvelles sur l'histoire d'une cité méconnue du Haut-Tell tunisien: La *ciuitas A[---]* / Aïn M'dhoja (région de Makthar). *Antiquités africaines* 51: 45–64.

Cherif, Z. 2006. Le palmier dattier et son image dans l'iconographie carthaginoise. In M.H. Fantar 2006, 67–84.

Cherry, D. 1998. *Frontier and Society in Roman North Africa*. Oxford: Clarendon Press.

Chevallier, R. 1958. Essai de chronologie des centuriations romaines en Tunisie. *Mélanges de l'Ecole Française de Rome* 70: 61–128.

Chifman, C. 1963. *Naissance de la puissance carthaginoise*. Moscow.

Christol, M. 1988. Rome et les tribus indigènes à Maurétanie Tingitane. *L'Africa romana* 5: 305–37.

Christol, M. 1994, Le blé africain et Rome: Remarques sur quelques documents. In *Le ravitaillement en blé de Rome et des centres urbains des débuts de la République jusqu'au Haut-Empire*, Actes du colloque de Naples (14–16 février 1991), 295–304. CEFR 196. Rome: École française de Rome.

Christol, M. 2005. *Regards sur l'Afrique romaine*. Paris: Errance.

Christol, M. 2010. Théveste: Centre administratif à l'époque impériale. *Aouras* 6: 83–101.

Christol, M. 2014. La cité et la domaine impérial: À propos de Thugga. In Briand-Ponsart 2014, 333–48.

Christol, M. 2015. L'Empire romain en Afrique: Aspects et résonances d'un impérialisme. *Cahiers d'histoire* 128: 19–35

Christol, M. 2020. Conflits, tensions et recrutements: Les *Mauri gentiles*. *Antiquités africaines* 56: 293–301.

Christol, M. and Mokni, S. 2017. L'Histoire Naturelle de Pline l'Ancien et la Pertica de Carthage. In S. Mokni and M. Sebaï (eds), *Institutions municipales en Afrique proconsulaire: Sources littéraires, épigraphiques et archéologiques*, 11–28. Sfax: Med Ali éditions.

Cifani, G. and Stoddart, S. (ed). 2012. *Landscape, Ethnicity and Identity in the Archaic Mediterranean Area*. Oxford: Oxbow Books.

Cifani, G., Munzi, M., Felici, F. and Cirelli, E. 2003. Ricerche topografiche nel territorio di Leptis Magna. Rapporto preliminare. In Khanoussi 2003, 395–414.

CIL 2 = Hübner, E. 1869. *Corpus Inscriptionum Latinarum, vol. 2*. Berlin: Berlin-Georg Reimer.

CIL 5 = Mommsen, T. 1872–7. *Corpus Inscriptionum Latinarum, vol. 5*. Berlin: Berlin-Georg Reimer.

CIL 6 = Henzen, W. et al. 1876–2018. *Corpus Inscriptionum Latinarum, vol. 6*. Berlin: Berlin-Georg Reimer.

CIL 8 = Wilmanns, G. et al. 1881–1942. *Corpus Inscriptionum Latinarum, vol. 8 and supplements*. Berlin: Berlin-Georg Reimer.

CIL 16 = Mommsen, T. and Nesselhauf, H. 1936. *Corpus Inscriptionum Latinarum, vol. 16 and supplement*. Berlin: Berlin-Georg Reimer.

Cintas, P. 1954. *Contribution à l'étude de l'expansion carthaginoise au Maroc*. Institut des Hautes-Études Marocaines 56. Paris: Arts et métiers graphiques.

Clarke, J. and Brooks, N. 2019. Burial practices in the western Sahara. In Gatto et al. 2019a, 341–71.

CMT = Corpus des mosaïques de la Tunisie. Tunis: Institut National d'Archéologie et d'Art. CMT I.1 = Alexander, M.A. and Ennaifer, M. et al. 1973. *Utique: Insulae I-II-III*. CMT I.2 = Duliere, C. et al. 1974. *Utique: Les mosaïques in situ en dehors des insulae I-II-III*. CMT I.3 = Alexander, M.A. et al. 1976. *Utique: Les mosaïques sans localisation précise et El Alia*. CMT II.1 = Alexander, M.A. et al. 1980. *Thuburbo Majus: Les mosaïques de la région du forum*. CMT II.2 = Ben Abed, A. et al. 1985. *Thuburbo Majus: Les mosaïques de la région des Grands Thermes*. CMT II.3 = Ben Abed, A. 1987. *Thuburbo Majus: Les mosaïcs dans la région ouest*; CMT II.4 = Alexander, M.A., Ben Abed Ben Khader, A. and Soren, D. 1994. *Thuburbo Majus: Les mosaïcs de la région est; Mise à jour du catalogue de Thuburbo Majus et les environs. Les mosaïques de Aïn Mziger, Bir Chana, Draa ben Jouder et Zaghouan*. CMT III.1 = Duliere, C. and Slim, H. (with contributions by others) 1996. *Thysdrus (El Jem): Quartier du sud-ouest*. IV.1 = Ben Abed Ben Khader, A., Alexander, M.A., Alexander, R., Bairem-Ben Osman, W., Duval, N., Gonosova, A., Kondoleon, C. and Métraux, G. 1999. *Kartago (Carthage): Les mosaïques du parc archéologique des Thermes d'Antonin*.

CNSAMH = *Carte nationale des sites archéologiques et des monuments historiques*. Published sheets of *Carte au 1/50.000* (1998–2020) include: *Kef Abbad 001*; *Bizerte 002*; *Metline 003*; *Cap Negro 004*; *Oued Sejnane 005*; *Tabarka 007*; *Sidi Daoud 008*; *Nefza 010*; *Kelibia 016*; *Tebourba 019*; *Menzel Hor 023*; *Medjaz El Bab 027*; *Bir Mcharga 028*; *Grombalia 029*; *Bou Ficha 036*; *Hammamat 037*; *Enfidha 043*; *Sidi Bou Ali 049*; *Halq El Mejjel 050*; *Sousse 057*; *Kairouan 063*; *Sidi El Hani 064*; *Thala 067*; *Ksar Tlili 068*; *Oued Cherita 072*; *Mahdia 074*; *Jebel Semmama 076*; *El Henchan 089*; *Jebel Mellousi 103*; *Majel el Abbas 109*; *Sidi Aich 110*; *Majpoura 111*; *El Maknassi 112*; *Moularès 117*; *El Sned 119*; *Bou Hedma 120*; *Gabès 147*; *Kettana 157*; *Mareth 158*; *Koutine 169*. Tunis: Institut national du patrimoine. https://inp.rnrt.tn/en/projets/carte-archeologique/

Coarelli, F. and Thébert, Y. 1988. Architecture funéraire et pouvoir: Réflexions sur l'hellénisme numide. *Mélanges de l'Ecole Française de Rome. Antiquité* 100(2): 761–818.

Coletti, C.M. 2018. Risultati e aspetti problematici della ricerca archeologica a Melilla e nel Rif (Marocco settentrionale). *Antiquités africaines* 54: 115–40.

Coletti, C.M. and Guspini, L. 2017. Gli itinerari terrestri della regione del Rif (Marocco settentrionale) tra l'antichità e il medioevo: Un'ipotesi di lavoro in base ai documenti geografici di età moderna. *Antiquités africaines* 53: 129–70.

Colin, F. 2000. *Les peuples libyens de la Cyrénaïque à l'Égypte d'après les sources de l'Antiquité classique*. Brussels: Académie royale de Belgique.

Coltelloni-Trannoy, M. 1997. *Les royaumes de Maurétanie sous Juba II et Ptolémée*. Paris: CNRS Éditions.

Coltelloni-Trannoy, M. 2005a. Rome et les rois "amis et alliés du peuple romain" en Afrique (Ier s. av. J.-C.–Ier s. ap. J.-C.). In Lafond 2005, 117–44.

Coltelloni-Trannoy, M. 2005b. L'usage du grec dans les royaumes et les provinces romaines d'Afrique. In Briand-Ponsart 2005a, 69–117.

Coltelloni-Trannoy, M. 2010. Maurétanie (Royaumes). *Encyclopédie Berbère* 31: 4717–37.

Coltelloni-Trannoy, M. 2011a. La Maurétanie royale et les débuts de la Maurétanie Césarienne. In Briand-Ponsart and Modéran 2011, 87–109.

Coltelloni-Trannoy, M. 2011b. Guerre et circulation des savoirs: Le cas des armées numides. In J.-C. Couvenhes, S. Crouzet and S. Péré-Noguès (eds), *Pratiques et identités culturelles des armées hellénistiques du monde méditerranéen*, 307–35. Hellenistic Warfare 3. Bordeaux: Ausonius.

Coltelloni-Trannoy, M. 2014. Note sur la guerre d'Aedemon: Système d'alliance et composition de l'armée royale. In Coltelloni-Trannoy and Le Bohec 2014, 85–99.

Coltelloni-Trannoy, M. and Le Bohec, Y. (ed). 2014. *La guerre dans l'Afrique romaine sous le Haut-Empire*. Paris: Éditions du CTHS.

Coltelloni-Trannoy, M., Bridoux, V. and Brouquier-Reddé, V. (eds). 2016. *Le Cercle du Détroit dans l'Antiquité: L'héritage de Miguel Taradell. Karthago* 29. Louvain: Peeters.

Conant, J.P. 2004. Literacy and private documentation in Vandal North Africa: The case of the Albertini Tablets. In Merrills 2004, 199–224.

Conant, J.P. 2012a. *Staying Roman: Conquest and Identity in Africa and the Mediterranean 439–700*. Cambridge: Cambridge University Press.

Conant, J.P. 2012b. Public administration, private individuals and the written word in Late Antique North Africa, c.284–700. In W. Brown, M. Costambeys, M. Innes and A. Kosto (eds), *Documentary Culture and the Laity in the Early Middle Ages*, 36–62. Cambridge: Cambridge University Press.

Cool, H.E.M. 2002. An overview of the small finds from Catterick. In P.R. Wilson 2002, Part 2, 24–43.

Cool, H.E.M. 2004. *The Roman Cemetery at Brougham, Cumbria: Excavations 1966–1967*. London: Roman Society Publications.

Cool, H.E.M. 2006. *Eating and Drinking in Roman Britain*. Cambridge: Cambridge University Press.

Cool, H.E.M. and Baxter, M.J. 2002. Exploring Romano-British finds assemblages. *Oxford Journal of Archaeology* 21(4): 365–80.

Cool, H.E.M. and Philo, C. (eds). 1998. *Roman Castleford Excavations 1974–85, vol. 1: The Small Finds*. Wakefield: West Yorkshire Archaeological Services.

Cooley, A.E. 2012. *Cambridge Manual of Latin Epigraphy*. Cambridge: Cambridge University Press.

Corbier, P. and Griesheimer, M. 2005. *L'Afrique romaine 146 av. J.-C. – 439 ap. J.-C.* Paris: Ellipses.

Corda, A.M. and Mastino, A. (eds). 2012. *L'Onomastica Africana: Congresso della Société du Maghreb préhistorique antique et médiéval.* Ortacesus: Sandhi.

Cordovana, O.D. 2007. *Segni e immagini del potere tra antico e tardoantico. I Severi e la provincia* Africa Proconsularis. Catania: Edizioni del Prisma.

Cordovana, O.D. 2012. Historical ecosystems. Roman frontier and economic hinterlands in North Africa. *Historia* 61(4): 458–94.

Corò, F. 1956. Ghadames Archeologica. Storia degli studi, delle esplorazioni e dei risultati su alcuni fra I più tipici antichi monumenti dell'oasi famosa, Libia. *Rivista Trimestrale di Studi Libici* 4(3–4): 3–26.

Courtois, C. 1950. Saint Augustin et la problème de la survivance du Punique. *Revue Africaine* 94: 259–82.

Courtois, C. 1955. *Les Vandales et l'Afrique.* Paris: Art et métiers graphiques.

Courtois, C., Leschi, L., Perrat, C. and Saumagne, C. (eds). 1952. *Tablettes Albertini: Actes privés de l'époque vandale (fin di Ve siècle).* Paris: Arts et métiers graphiques.

Crawford, M.H. 1996. *Roman Statutes, vol. 1.* London: Institute of Classical Studies.

Cremaschi M. 2003. Steps and timing of the desertification during Late Antiquity. The case study of the Tanezzuft oasis (Libyan Sahara). In M. Liverani (ed), *Arid Lands in Roman Times*, 1–14. AZA Monographs 4. Firenze: Edizioni All'Insegna del Giglio.

Cremaschi, M. and Di Lernia, S. (eds). 1998. *Wadi Teshuinat. Palaeoenvironment and Prehistory in South-Western Fezzan (Libyan Sahara). Survey and Excavations in the Tadrart Acacus, Erg Uan Kasa, Messak Sattafet, Edeyen of Murzuq, 1990–1995.* Centro Interuniversitario di Ricerca per le Civiltà e l'Ambiente del Sahara Antico 7. Milan: Edizioni All'Insegna del Giglio.

Cremaschi, M. and Zerboni, A. 2009. Early to Middle Holocene landscape exploitation in a drying environment: Two case studies compared from the central Sahara (SW Fezzan, Libya). *Comptes Rendus Geoscience* 341(8–9): 689–702.

Cremaschi, M. and Zerboni, A. 2011. Human communities in a drying landscape: Holocene climate change and cultural response in the central Sahara. In I.P. Martini and W. Chesworth (eds), *Landscapes and Societies: Selected Cases*, 67–89. New York: Springer.

Crummy, N. 1983. *The Roman Small Finds from Excavations in Colchester 1971–9.* Colchester Archaeological Reports 2. Colchester: Colchester Archaeological Trust.

CTHS Perpignan 1984. *Actes du Ier colloque international sur l'histoire et l'archéologie de l'Afrique du Nord.* 106e Congrès national des sociétés savantes (Perpignan, 1981) = *Bulletin archéologique du comité des travaux historiques et scientifiques*, n.s. 17B. Paris: Éditions du CTHS.

CTHS Grenoble 1985. *Actes du IIe colloque international sur l'histoire et l'archéologie de l'Afrique du Nord.* 108e Congrès national des sociétés savantes (Grenoble, 5–9 avril 1983) = *Bulletin archaéologique du comité des travaux historiques et scientifiques*, n.s. 19B. Paris: Éditions du CTHS.

CTHS Montpellier 1986. *Effet des données géographiques et des variations climatiques sur la civilisation de l'Afrique du Nord depuis l'Antiquité, campagnes et vie rurale, itinéraires traditionnels et voies romaines. Actes du IIIe colloque international sur l'histoire et l'archéologie de l'Afrique du Nord.* 110e Congrès national des sociétés savantes (Montpellier, 1–5 avril 1985). Paris: Éditions du CTHS.

CTHS Strasbourg 1990. *Carthage et son territoire. Actes du IVe colloque international sur l'histoire et l'archéologie de l'Afrique du Nord.* 113e Congrès national des sociétés savantes (Strasbourg, 5–9 avril 1988). Paris: Éditions du CTHS.

CTHS Strasbourg 1991. *L'armée et les affaires militaires. Actes du IVe colloque international sur l'histoire et l'archéologie de l'Afrique du Nord, vol. 2.* 113e Congrès national des sociétés savantes (Strasbourg, 5–9 avril 1988). Paris: Éditions du CTHS.

CTHS Avignon 1992. *Spectacles, vie portuaire, religions. Actes du Ve colloque international sur l'histoire et l'archéologie de l'Afrique du Nord.* 115e Congrès national des sociétés savantes (Avignon, 9–13 avril 1990). Paris: Éditions du CTHS.

CTHS Pau 1995a. *Monuments funéraires, institutions autochtones en Afrique du Nord antique et médiévale. Actes du VIe Colloque international de CTHS, vol. 1.* 118e Congrès national des sociétés historiques et scientifiques (Pau, 1993). Paris: Éditions du CTHS = Trousset 1995a.

CTHS Pau 1995b. *Productions et exportations africaines, actualités archéologiques en Afrique du Nord antique et médiévale. Actes du VIe Colloque international de CTHS, Vol. 2.* 118e Congrès national des sociétés historiques et scientifiques (Pau, 1993). Paris: Éditions du CTHS = Trousset 1995c.

CTHS Nice 1999. *Numismatique, langues, écritures et arts du livre, spécificités des arts figurés.* Actes du VIIe Colloque international sur l'histoire et l'archéologie de l'Afrique du Nord antique et médiévale. 121e Congrès national des sociétés savantes (Nice, 21–31 octobre 1996). Paris: Éditions du CTHS = Lancel 1999.

Curtis, R.I. 1991. *Garum and Salasamenta: Production and Commerce in Materia Medica.* Studies in Ancient Medicine 3. Leiden: Brill.

D'Andrea, B. 2014. *I tofet del Nord Africa dall'età arcaica all'età romana (VIII sec. a.C.–II sec. d.C.).* Pisa/Rome: Fabricio Serra Editore.

Dabbaghi, A., Bejaoui, F. and Ghaki, M. (eds). 2004. *IPAMED – Carte Informatisée du Patrimoine (Projet Euromed Heritage).* Tunis: INP.

D'Alessio, M.T. and Marchetti, C.M. (eds). 2020. *RAC in Rome: Atti della 12[a] Roman Archaeology Conference (2016): Le sessioni di Roma.* Rome: Edizioni Quasar.

Daniels, C.M. 1968. Garamantian excavations: Zinchecra 1965–1967. *Libya Antiqua* 5: 113–94.

Daniels, C.M. 1970. *The Garamantes of Southern Libya.* London: Oleander Press.

Daniels, C. M. 1975. An ancient people of the Libyan Sahara. In Bynon and Bynon 1975, 249–65.

Daniels, C.M. 1983. Town defences in Roman Africa: A tentative historical survey. In J. Maloney and B. Hobley (eds), *Roman Urban Defences in the West*, 5–19. CBA Research Reports 51. London: Council for British Archaeology.

Daniels, C.M. 1987. Africa. In J. Wacher (ed), *The Roman World, Vol. 1*, 223–65. London: Routledge.

Daniels, C.M. 1989. Excavation and fieldwork amongst the Garamantes. *Libyan Studies* 20: 45–61.

Darmon, J-P. 1964. Note sur le tarif de Zaraï. *Cahiers de Tunisie* 12(47): 7–23.

Dauge, Y.-A. 1981. *Le Barbare: Recherche sur la conception romaine de la barbarie et de la civilisation.* Bruxelles: Latomus.

Daumas, E. 1968. *The Horses of the Sahara* (trans. S.M. Ohlendorf) Austin and London: University of Texas.

Daumas, E. 1971. *The Ways of the Desert* (trans. S.M. Ohlendorf) Austin and London: University of Texas.

Davies D.K. 2007. *Resurrecting the Granary of Rome: Environmental History and French Colonial Expansion in North Africa.* Athens, OH: Ohio University Press.

Davies, R.W. 1987. *Service in the Roman Army*. Edinburgh: Edinburgh University Press.

De la Chapelle, F. 1934. L'expedition de Suétonius Paulinus dans le sud-est du Maroc. *Hespéris* 19: 107–24.

De Ligt, L. 2007a. Mancipes, pecunia, praedes and praedia in the epigraphic *Lex agraria* of 111 BC. *Legal History Review* 75: 3–16.

De Ligt, L. 2007b. The problem of *ager privatus vectigalisque* in the epigraphic *Lex agraria. Epigraphica* 69: 87–98.

De Ligt, L. 2008. Provincial *dediticii* in the epigraphic *Lex agraria* of 111 BC? *The Classical Quarterly* 58(1): 356–62.

De Ligt, L. and Bintliff, J. (eds). 2020. *Regional Urban Systems in the Roman World, 150 BCE – 250 CE*. Leiden: Brill.

De Miro, E. 2002. *Leptis Magna*. L'emporio punico e l'impianto romano: Punti fermi di cronologia. *L'Africa romana* 14, 403–14.

De Miro, E. de and Fiorentini, G. 1977. Leptis Magna. La necropoli Greco-Punica sotto il teatro. *Quaderni di Archeologia della Libya* 9: 5–75.

De Miro, E. and Polito, A. 2005. *Leptis Magna. Dieci anni di scavi archeologici nell'area del foro vecchio. I livelli fenici, punici e romani*. Rome: L'Erma di Bretschneider.

De Pachtere, F.G. 1908. Le règlement d'irrigation de Lamasba. *Mélanges de l'Ecole Française de Rome* 28: 373–405.

De Planol, X. (ed). 1973. *Maghreb et Sahara: Études géographiques offertes à Jean Despois*. Paris: Société de Géographie.

De Romanis, F. 2003. Per una storia del tributo granario africano all'annona della Roma imperiale. In B. Marin and C. Virlouvet (eds), *Nourrir les cités de Méditerranée: Antiquité–temps modernes*, 691–738. Aix-en-Provence: MMSH.

De Vos, M. 1997. Gli antichi insediamenti rurali nei dintorni di Dougga e il riciclaggio delle epigrafi. In Khanoussi and Maurin 1997, 201–06.

De Vos, M. (ed). 2000. *Rus Africum: Terra, acqua, olio nell'Africa settentrionale: Scavo e ricognizione nei dintorni di Dougga (alto Tell tunisino)*. Collana Labirinti 50. Trento: Università degli studi di Trento.

De Vos, M. (ed). 2004. *Archeologia del territorio. Metodi materiali prospettive. Medjerda e Adige: Due territori a confronto*. Collana Labirinti 73. Trento: Università degli studi di Trento.

De Vos, M. 2007. L'olio d'oliva per Roma e per il mercato intraregionale. In Papi 2007, 43–58.

De Vos, M. 2013. The rural landscape of Thugga: Farms, presses, mills and transport. In Bowman and Wilson 2013, 143–218.

De Vos Raaijmakers, M. 2022. Rural settlement, land use, and economy. In Hitchner 2022a, 202–19.

De Vos Raaijmakers, M. and Attoui, R. (eds). 2013. *Rus Africum, vol. 1: Le paysage rural antique autour de Dougga et Téboursouk: Cartographie, relevés et chronologie des établissements*. Biblioteca Archaeologica 30. Bari: Edipuglia.

De Vos Raaijmakers, M. and Attoui, R. (eds). 2015. *Rus Africum, vol. 3: La Via a Karthagine Thevestem, ses milliaires et le réseau routier rural de la région de Dougga et Téboursouk*. Biblioteca Archaeologica 37. Bari: Edipuglia.

De Vos Raaijmakers, M. and Maurina, B. (eds). 2019. *Rus Africum, vol. 4: La fattoria Bizantina di Aïn Wassel, Africa Proconsularis (Alto Tell, Tunisia). Lo scavo stratigrafico e I materiali*. Roman Archaeology 58. Oxford: Archaeopress.

De Vos Raaijmakers, M. and Porena, P. 2020. Iscrizione in onore di Flavius Caecilius Primus, amministratore del *fundus Glebonianus* a nord di Thabbora (Proconsolare) nel IV secolo d.C. *Zeitschrift für Papyrologie und Epigraphik* 216: 315–28

De Vos Raaijmakers, M., Attoui, R. and Battisti, A. (eds). 2013. *Rus Africum, vol. 2: Le paysage rural antique autour de Dougga: L'aqueduc Aïn Hammam-Thugga, cartographie et relevés.* Biblioteca Archaeologica 34. Bari: Edipuglia.

Decramer, L.R. 2002. La grande centuriation tunsienne et la voie d'Asprenas. Pour une chronologie des cadastres, routes et limites antique. *Bulletin de la societé nationale des antiquaires de France* 2002: 287–309.

Decramer, L.R., Elhaj, R. Hilton, R. and Plas, A. 2002. Approche géométrique des centuriations romaines. Les nouvelles bornes du Bled Segui. *Histoire et Mesure* 17(1–2): 109–62.

Decret, F. 1996. *Le christianisme en Afrique du Nord ancienne.* Paris: Seuil.

Decret, F. and Fantar, M.H. 1981. *L'Afrique du Nord dans l'antiquité: Histoire et civilisation.* Paris: Payot.

Degeorge, G. 2001. *Palmyre: Métropole caravanière.* Paris: Imprimerie nationale.

Delattre, A.-L. 1898. Les cimetières romains superposés de Carthage (1896). *Revue Archéologique* 33: 82–101, 215–39, 337–49; 34: 240–55, 382–96.

Delpont, E. 2003. *L'Algérie en heritage: Art et histoire.* Arles: Institut du Monde Arabe

Deman, A. 1975. Matériaux et réflexions pour servir à une étude du développement et du sous-développement dans les provinces de l'empire romain. In H. Temporini (ed), *Aufstieg und Niedergang der römischen Welt: Principat, vol. 3: Politische Geschichte (Provinzen und Randvölker: Allgemeines; Britannien, Hispanien, Gallien)*, 3–83. Berlin: De Gruyter.

Demougin, S. and Scheid, J. (eds). 2012. *Colons et colonies dans le monde romain.* CEFR 456. Rome: École française de Rome.

Dench, E. 2005. *Romulus' Asylum: Roman Identities from the Age of Alexander to the Age of Hadrian.* Oxford: Oxford University Press.

Derks, T. and Roymans, N. (eds). 2009. *Ethnic Constructs in Antiquity. The Role of Power and Tradition.* Amsterdam: Amsterdam University Press.

Déroche, F. and Leclant, J. (eds). 2010. *Monuments et cultes funéraires d'Afrique du Nord.* Paris: Académie des Inscriptions et Belles-Lettres.

Déroche, F. and Leclant, J. (eds). 2012. *Enceintes urbaines, sites fortifiés, forteresses d'Afrique du Nord. Actes de la Ve journée d'études nord-africains.* Paris: Académie des Inscriptions et Belles-Lettres.

Déroche, F. and Zink, M. (eds). 2016. *L'alimentation de l'Afrique du Nord de la préhistoire au Moyen Âge. Actes de la VIIe journée d'études nord-africaines.* Paris: Académie des Inscriptions et Belles-Lettres.

Desanges, J. 1957. Le triomphe de Cornelius Balbus (19 av. J.-C.). *Revue Africaine* 101: 5–43.

Desanges, J. 1962. *Catalogue des tribus africaines de l'antiquité classique à l'ouest du Nil.* Dakar: Université de Dakar.

Desanges, J. 1964a. Note sur la datation de l'expedition de Julius Maternus au pays d'*Agisymba. Latomus* 23(4): 713–25.

Desanges, J. 1964b. Les territoires gétules de Juba II. *Revue des Etudes Anciennes* 66: 33–47.

Desanges, J. 1969. Un drame africain sous Auguste: Le meurtre du proconsul L. Cornelius Lentulus par les Nasamons. In J. Bibauw (ed), *Hommages à Marcel Renard, vol. 2*, 197–213. Brussels: Latomus.

Desanges, J. 1976. The iconography of the Black in ancient North Africa. In J. Vercoutter, J. Leclant, F.M. Snowden and J. Desanges, *The Image of the Black in Western Art, vol. 1: From the Pharaohs to the Fall of the Roman Empire*, 246–68. Menil Foundation Collection. New York: William Morrow.

Desanges, J. 1978a. Le peuplement éthiopien à la lisière méridionale de l'Afrique du Nord d'après les témoignages textuels de l'antiquité. In *L'Afrique noire et monde méditerranéen dans l'antiquité*, 29–53. Dakar: Université de Dakar.

Desanges, J. 1978b. *Recherches sur l'activité des méditerranéens aux confins de l'Afrique (VIe siecle av. J.-C.–IVe siècle ap. J.-C.).* CEFR 38. Rome: École française de Rome.

Desanges, J. 1980a. Permanence d'une structure indigène en marge de l'administration romaine: La Numidie traditionelle. *Antiquités africaines* 15: 77–89.

Desanges, J. 1980b. *Pline l'Ancien: Histoire Naturelle, Livre V, 1–46, 1re partie, (L'Afrique du Nord).* Paris: Société d'Éditions les Belles-Lettres.

Desanges, J. 1989a. Hellénisme dans le royaume protégé de Maurétanie, 25 avant J.-C. – 40 après J.-C. *Bulletin archéologique du comité des travaux historiques et scientifiques: Afrique du Nord* n.s. 20–21B: 53–61.

Desanges J. 1989b. Arzuges. *Encyclopédie Berbère* 6: 948–9.

Desanges, J. 1990. La toponymie de l'Afrique du Nord antique. Bilan des recherches depuis 1965. In *L'Afrique dans l'Occident romain*, 251–72.

Desanges J. 1998. Gétules. *Encyclopédie Berbère* 20: 3063–65.

Desanges, J. 1999a. *Toujours Afrique apporte fait nouveau. Scripta minora.* Paris: Éditions de Boccard.

Desanges, J. 1999b. Réflexions sur l'organisation de l'espace selon la latitude dans l'Afrique du Nord antique. In Lepelley and Dupuis 1999, 27–41.

Desanges, J. 2001. De la Marmarique à la Maurétanie. Nouvelles données en matière de mouvements de population. *Antiquités africaines* 37: 85–91.

Desanges J. 2003. Le Sahara dans l'Antiquité: Lien, obstacle ou barrière? In M.H. Fantar (ed), *Le Sahara: Lien entre les peuples et les cultures.* Actes du colloque organisé à Douz, 29–22 décembre 2002, 49-57. Tunis: Université de Tunis El Manar.

Desanges J. 2010, Mélanogétules. *Encyclopédie Berbère* 31: 4855.

Desanges, J., Duval, N., Lepelley, C. and Saint-Amans, S. 2010. *Carte des routes et des cités de l'est de l'*Africa *à la fin de l'antiquité.* Bibliothèque de l'Antiquité Tardive 17. Turnhout: Brepols.

Désiré-Vuillemin, G. 1964. *Le monde libyco-berbère dans l'antiquité.* Paris: Institut pédagogique national.

Despois, J. 1935. *Le Djebel Nefousa (Tripolitaine). Étude géographique.* Paris: Larose.

Despois, J. 1946. *Mission scientifique au Fezzân (1944–1945), vol. 3. Géographie humaine.* Paris: Chevalier.

Despois, J. 1949. *L'Afrique blanche française, vol. 1: L'Afrique du Nord.* 1st edition, Paris: Presses Universitaires de France.

Despois, J. 1955. *La Tunisie orientale: Sahel et Basse Steppe. Étude géographique.* Paris: Presses Universitaires de France.

Despois, J. and Raynal, R. 1967. *Géographie de l'Afrique du Nord-Ouest.* Paris: Payot.

Devallet, G. 2003. *Vagi, palantes Afri*: Quelques observations sur l'image romaine du nomade africain. In Bejaoui 2003, 31–38.

Devallet, G. 2010. Les *solitudines* et le désert des quelques auteurs latins. In Bejaoui 2010, 157–67.

Devisse, J. 1995. Le cheval dans l'histoire de l'Afrique. In Pezzoli 1995, 27–47.

DFH = Khanoussi and Maurin 2000.

Di Lernia, S. (ed). 1999. *The Uan Afuda Cave: Hunter-Gatherer Societies of Central Sahara*. AZA Monographs 1. Firenze: Edizioni All'Insegna del Giglio.

Di Lernia, S. 2013. The emergence and spread of herding in northern Africa: A critical reappraisal. In Mitchell and Lane 2013, 527–40.

Di Lernia, S. and Manzi, G. (eds). 2002. *Sand, Stones, and Bones. The Archaeology of Death in the Wadi Tanezzuft Valley (5000–2000 BP)*. AZA Monographs 3. Firenze: All'Insegna dell Giglio.

Di Lernia, S. and Zampetti, D. 2008. *La Memoria dell'Arte. Le pitture rupestri dell'Acacus tra passato e futuro*. Firenze: Edizioni All'Insegna del Giglio.

Di Stefano, G. 2004. Dai Nibgeni a Turris Tamalleni: Storie di confine lungo il limes Tripolitanus. *L'Africa romana* 15: 355–61.

Di Vita, A. 1966. La villa della "gara delle Nereidi" presso Tagiura: Un contributio alla storia del mosaico romano ed altri recenti scavi e scoperte in Tripolitania. *Libya Antiqua* supplement 2: 11–64.

Di Vita, A. 1969. Le date di fondazione di Leptis e di Sabratha sulla base dell'indagine archeologica e l'eparchia carthaginese d'Africa. In J. Bibauw (ed), *Hommages à Marcel Renard, vol. 3*, 196–202. Brussels: Latomus.

Di Vita, A. 1971. Les emporia de Tripolitaine dans le rayonnement de Carthage et d'Alexandrie: Les mausolées punico-Hellenistiques de Sabratha. In Gadallah 1971, 173–80.

Di Vita, A. 1982. Gli *Emporia* di Tripolitania dall'età di Massinissa a Diocleziano: Un profilo storico-istituzionale. In H. Temporini (ed), *Aufstieg und Niedergang der römischen Welt: Principat, vol. 10/2: Teilband Politische Geschichte (Provinzen und Randvölker: Afrika mit Ägypten [Forts.])*, 515–95. Berlin: De Gruyter.

Di Vita, A. 1983. Architettura e società nelle città di Tripoli fra Massinissa e Augusto: Qualche nota. In *Architecture et société de l'archaïsme grec à la fin de la République romaine*, 355–76. CEFR 66, Rome: École française de Rome.

Di Vita, A. 1990. Sismi, urbanistica e cronologia assoluta. In *L'Afrique dans l'Occident romain*, 425–94.

Di Vita, A. 2010a. L'università di Macerata: Dieci anni di studi e restauri archeologici in Tripolitania (1998–2008). *Libya Antiqua* n.s. 5: 11–23.

Di Vita, A. Culture grecque et tradition locale dans la tombe d'un myste tripolitain de l'époque de Claude. In Déroche and Leclant 2010, 129–49.

Di Vita, A. 2015a/b. *Scritti africani*. 2 vols. Rome: L'Erma di Bretschneider.

Di Vita, A. 2017. *La Tripolitania antica: Scritti inediti*. Rome: L'Erma di Bretschneider.

Di Vita, A. and Livadiotti, M. 2005. *I tre templi del lato nord-ovest del foro vecchio a Leptis Magna*. Rome: L'Erma di Bretschneider.

Di Vita, A., Di Vita-Evrard, G., Bacchielli, L., Golvin, J.-C. and Polidori, R. 1999. *Libya: The Lost Cities of the Roman Empire*. Cologne: Könemann.

Di Vita-Evrard, G. 1965. Les dédicaces de l'amphithéâtre et du cirque de Lepcis. *Libya Antiqua* 2: 29–40.

Di Vita-Evrard, G. 1979. Quatre inscriptions du Djebel Tarhuna: Le territoire de Lepcis Magna. *Quaderni di archeologia della Libya* 10: 67–98.

Di Vita-Evrard, G. 1986. La "Fossa Regia" et les diocèses d'Afrique proconsulaire. *L'Africa romana* 3: 31–58.

Di Vita-Evrard, G. 2003. Sur deux inscriptions votives bilingues de Sabratha et de Lepcis Magna. *Antiquités africaines* 38–39: 297–305.

Di Vita-Evrard, G., Fontana, S. and Musso, L. 1995. Leptis Magna: Une tombe exemplaire du Haut-Empire. In Trousset 1995a, 153–78.

Di Vita-Evrard, G., Fontana, S., Allegni, F.,Munzi, M. and Musso, L. 1996. L'ipogeo dei Flavi a Leptis Magna presso Gasr Gelda. *Libya Antiqua* n.s. 2: 85–133

Di Vita-Evrard, G., Fontana, S. and Munzi, M. 1997. Le necropoli di Leptis Magna, 3: Une tombe hypogée de la nécropole occidentale: Laurentii ou Claudii? *Libya Antiqua* n.s. 3: 119–46.

Díaz-Andreu, M., Lucy, S., Babić, S. and Edwards, D.N. 2005. *The Archaeology of Identity: Approaches to Gender, Age, Status, Ethnicity and Religion.* London: Routledge.

Dietler, M. 2010. *Archaeologies of Colonialism: Consumption, Entanglement, and Violence in Ancient Mediterranean France.* Berkeley: University of California Press.

Dietler, M. and López-Ruiz, C. (eds). 2009. *Colonial Encounters in Ancient Iberia: Phoenician, Greek, and Indigenous Relations.* Chicago: University of Chicago Press.

Dietz, S., L. Ladjimi Sebai and H. Ben Hassen (eds). 1995a/b. *Africa Proconsularis. Regional Studies in the Segermes Valley, Northern Tunesia, vols. 1 and 2: Archeological Fieldwork.* Aarhus: Aarhus University Press.

Dilke, O.A.W. 1971. *The Roman Land Surveyors: An Introduction to the Agrimensores.* Newton Abbot: David and Charles.

Docter, R.F., Chelbi, F., Maraoui Telmini, B., Koens, H., Schmidt, K., Van Neer, W. and Becthold, B. 2003. Carthage Bir Massouda. Preliminary report on the first bilateral excavations of Ghent University and the Institut National du Patrimoine (2002–2003). *BABESCH* 78: 43–70.

Docter, R.F., Niemeyer, H., Nijboer, A. and Van der Plicht, J. 2005. Radiocarbon dates of animal bones in the earliest levels of Carthage. In G. Bartolini and F. Delpino (eds), *Oriente e Occidente: metodi e discipline a confronto. Riflessioni sulla cronologia dell'età del ferro in Italia,* 557–577. Pisa: Istituti Editoriali e Poligrafici Internazionali.

Docter, R., Chelbi, M., Maraoui Telmini, B. 2006. Carthage Bir Massouda. Second preliminary report on the bilateral excavations of Ghent University and the Institut National du Patrimoine (2003–2004). *BABESCH* 81: 37–89.

Docter, R.F., Chelbi, F., Maraoui Telmini, B., Nijboer, A.J., Van der Plicht, J., Van Neer, W., Mansel, K. and Garsallah, S. 2008. New radiocarbon dates from Carthage: Bridging the gap between history and archaeology? In C. Sagona (ed), *Beyond the Homeland: Markers in Phoenician Chronology,* 379–422. Ancient Near Eastern Studies Supplement Series 28. Leuven: Peeters.

Docter, R.F., Boussoffara, R. and Ter Keurs, P. (eds). 2015. *Carthage: Fact and Myth.* Leiden: Sidestone Press.

Dondin-Payre, M. 1988. *Un siècle d'epigraphie classique: Aspects de l'oeuvre des savants français dans les pays du bassin méditerranéen.* Paris: Institut de France.

Dondin-Payre, M. 1991. L'*exercitus Africae* inspiratrice de l'armée française: *Ense et aratro. Antiquités africaines* 27: 141–49.

Dondin-Payre, M. 2002. L'identité de l'Afrique antique à l'épreuve des faits. Avant et après 1830, identité imaginée, identité réelle. In Briand-Ponsart and Crogiez 2002, 181–206.

Dondin-Payre M. 2004. L'évolution de l'onomastique dans les provinces romaines: L'exemple de Dougga. *L'Antiquité Classique* 73: 251–62.

Dondin-Payre, M. 2005a. L'expression onomastique de l'identité autochthone en Afrique du Nord antique. In Briand-Ponsart 2005a, 155–77.

Dondin-Payre, M. 2005b. La découverte de l'Afrique antique: L'influence des acteurs et de l'idéologie sur l'élaboration de l'histoire. In Lafond 2005, 35–48.

Dondin-Payre, M. 2006. Gaulois des Gaules et Gaulois d'Afrique: de la réalité à l'imaginaire; naissance et développement d'un mythe de migration. *L'Africa romana* 16: 857–70.

Dondin-Payre, M. 2009. Review of Alain Cadotte: "La romanisation des dieux. L'*interpretatio romana* en Afrique du Nord sous le Haut-Empire". *L'Antiquité Classique* 78: 426–28.

Dondin-Payre, M. 2010. Archéologie funéraire de Lambèse. In Déroche and Leclant 2010, 83–127.

Dondin-Payre, M. 2012. Romains? Africains? Anthoponymie en Afrique romaine et acculturation. In Corda and Mastino 2012, 57–65.

Dondin-Payre, M. 2020. Les auxiliaires militaires de l'armée d'Afrique héritiers de l'*exercitus Africae*? *Antiquités africaines* 56: 357–64.

Dondin-Payre, M. and Raepsaet-Charlier, M.-T. 2001. *Noms, identités culturelles et romanisation sous le Haut-Empire*. Brussels: Livre Timperman.

Dore, J.N. 1994. Is el-Merj the site of ancient Barqa? Current excavations in context. *Libyan Studies* 25: 265–74.

Dore, J.N. 1996. The UNESCO Libyan Valleys Archaeological Survey: Pottery. In Barker et al. 1996b, 317–89.

Dore, J.N. and Keay, N. 1989. *Excavations at Sabratha 1948–1951, vol 2: The Finds, Part 1: The Amphorae, Coarse Pottery and Building Materials*. London: Society for Libyan Studies.

Dossey, L. 2010. *Peasant and Empire in Christian North Africa*. Berkeley: University of California Press.

Dowler, A. and Galvin, E.R. 2011. *Money, Trade and Trade Routes in Pre-Islamic North Africa*. London: British Museum Press

Doyle, M.W. 1986. *Empires*. New York: Cornell University Press.

Drake, N.A., Blench, R.M., Armitage, S.J., Bristow, C.S. and White, K. 2010. Ancient watercourses and biogeography of the Sahara explain the peopling of the desert. *Proceedings of the National Academy of Sciences* 108(2): 458–62.

Drake, N.A., Lem, R., Armitage, S.J., Breeze, P., Franke, J., El-Hawat, A.S., Salem, M.J., Hounslow, M.W. and White, K. 2018. Reconstructing palaeoclimate and hydrological fluctuations in the Fezzan Basin (southern Libya) since 130 ka: A catchment-based approach. *Quaternary Science Reviews* 200: 376–94.

Dridi, H. and Sebaï, M. 2008. De Tanesmat à Thinissut: Nouvelles observations sur l'amenagement d'un lieu culte africain. In Blanc-Bijon 2008, 101–17.

Drine, A. 1991. Note sur le site de Zitha (Hr. Zian) à Zarzis. *Reppal* 6: 17–30.

Drine, A. 1999. Restes de pressoirs à huile et à vin à Gigthi et à Zarzis. *Africa* 17: 47–68.

Drine, A. 2002. Le sanctuaire de Tala (île de Jerba). *Reppal* 12: 29–38.

Drine, A. 2007. La pourpre de *Meninx*. *Africa* 21: 79–93.

Duckworth, C.N., Cuénod, A. and Mattingly, D.J. (eds). 2020a. *Mobile Technologies in the Ancient Sahara and Beyond*. Cambridge: Cambridge University Press.

Duckworth, C.N., Cuénod, A. and Mattingly, D.J. 2020b. Debating mobile technologies. In Duckworth et al. 2020a, 3–49.

Dufton, J.A. 2019. The architectural and social dynamics of gentrification in Roman North Africa. *American Journal of Archaeology* 123(2): 263–90.

Dufton, J.A. and Fentress, E. 2022. Roman North African urbanism. In Hitchner 2022a, 173–201.

Dunbabin, K.M.D. 1978. *The Mosaics of Roman North Africa: Studies in Icongraphy and Patronage.* Oxford: Clarendon Press.

Dunbabin, K.M.D. 1999. *Mosaics of the Greek and Roman World.* Cambridge: Cambridge University Press.

Duncan-Jones, R.P. 1963. City population in Roman Africa. *Journal of Roman Studies* 53(1–2): 85–90.

Duncan-Jones, R.P. 1982. *The Economy of the Roman Empire: Quantitative Studies.* Cambridge: Cambridge University Press.

Duncan-Jones, R.P. 1985. Who paid for buildings in Roman cities? In F. Grew and B. Hobley (eds), *Roman Urban Topography in Britain and the Western Empire*, 28–33. CBA Research Reports 59. London: Council for British Archaeology.

Dupuis, X. 1991. La participation des vétérans à la vie municipale en Numidie méridionale aux IIe et IIIe siècles. In CTHS Strasbourg 1991, 343–354.

Dupuis, X. 1992. Constructions publiques et vie municipale en Afrique de 244 à 276. *Mélanges de l'Ecole Française de Rome. Antiquité* 104(1): 233–80.

Dupuis, X. 1999. Cuicul, la confédération Cirtéenne et les Suburbures: Des limites ambiguës. In Lepelley and Dupuis 1999, 129–38.

Dupuis, X. 2017. La Numidie de Septime Sévère à Gallien: province ou diocèse de l'Afrique proconsulaire? *Cahiers du Centre Gustave Glotz* 28: 291–308.

Dupuis, X. and Morizot, P. 1992. Une vallée peu connue de l'Aurès occidental: L'oued Fedhala. *L'Africa romana* 9: 365–88.

Dupuy, C. 1995. Bovins montés et chevaux, puis chevaux montés dans l'art rupestre de l'Adrar des Iforas (Mali). In Pezzoli 1995, 105–26.

Duval, N. 1971. *Les basiliques de Sbeitla à deux sanctuaires opposés (basiliques I, II et IV).* Rome: BEFAR.

Duval, N. 1973. *Les églises Africaines à deux absides, vol. 2: Inventaire de monuments – interprétation.* Paris: BEFAR.

Duval, N. 1975. *Recherches archéologiques à Haïdra, 1: Les inscriptions chrétiennes.* CEFR 18/1. Paris: École française de Rome

Duval, N. 1976. *La mosaïque funéraire dans l'art paléochrétien.* Ravenna: Longo.

Duval, N. 1982a. Topographie et urbanisme d'Ammaedara (actuellement Haïdra, Tunisie). In H. Temporini (ed), *Aufstieg und Niedergang der römischen Welt: Principat, vol. 10/2: Teilband Politische Geschichte (Provinzen und Randvölker: Afrika mit Ägypten [Forts.])*, 633–71. Berlin: De Gruyter.

Duval, N. 1982b. L'urbanisme de Sufetula = Sbeitla en Tunisie. In H. Temporini (ed), *Aufstieg und Niedergang der römischen Welt: Principat, vol. 10/2: Teilband Politische Geschichte (Provinzen und Randvölker: Afrika mit Ägypten [Forts.])*, 596–632. Berlin: De Gruyter.

Duval, N. 1986. L'iconographie des "villas africaines" et la vie rurale dans l'Afrique romaine de l'Antiquité Tardive. In CTHS Montpellier 1986, 163–74.

Duval, N. 1990. Sufetula: L'histoire d'une ville romaine de la Haute Steppe à la lumière des recherches récentes. *L'Afrique dans l'Occident romain*, 495–535.

Duval, N. 1995. Les nécropoles chrétiennes d'Afrique du Nord. In Trousset 1995a, 187–206.

Duval, N. and F. Baratte. 1973. *Les ruines de Sufetula-Sbeïtla*. Tunis: Société tunisienne de diffusion.

Duval, N., Lancel, S. and Le Bohec, Y. 1984. Études sur la garnison de Carthage. *Bulletin archéologique du comité des travaux historiques et scientifiques: Afrique du Nord* n.s. 15–16B: 33–89.

Dyson, S.L. 1971. Native revolts in the Roman Empire. *Historia* 20(2–3): 239–74.

Dyson, S. L. 1975. Native revolt patterns in the Roman Empire. In H. Temporini (ed), *Aufstieg und Niedergang der römischen Welt: Principat, vol. 3: Politische Geschichte (Provinzen und Randvölker: Allgemeines; Britannien, Hispanien, Gallien)*, 138–75. Berlin: De Gruyter.

Dyson, S.L. 1993. From new to New Age archaeology: archaeological theory and Classical archaeology—A 1990s perspective. *American Journal of Archaeology* 97(2): 195–206.

Eccleston, S.-M. and Padilla Peralta, D. 2022. Racing the Classics: Ethos and praxis. *American Journal of Philology* 143(2): 199–218.

Eckardt, H. and Crummy, N. 2008. *Styling the Body in Late Iron Age and Roman Britain: A Contextual Approach to Toilet Instruments*. Monographies instrumentum 36. Montagnac: Éditions Monique Mergoil.

Effros, B. 2018. *Incidental Archaeologists: French Officers and the Rediscovery of Roman North Africa*. Cornell and London: Cornell University Press.

Effros, B. and Lai, G. (eds). 2018. *Unmasking Ideology in Imperial and Colonial Archaeology*. Los Angeles: Cotsen Press, UCLA Institute of Archaeology.

Ehret, C. 2019. Berber peoples in the Sahara and North Africa: Linguistic historical proposals. In Gatto et al. 2019a, 464–94.

Eingartner J. 2005. *Templa cum porticibus. Ausstattung und Funktion italischer Tempelbezirke in Nordafrika und ihre Bedeutung für die römische Stadt der Kaiserzeit*. Rahden: Verlag Marie Leidorf

El Khayari, A. 2007. La présence phénicienne au Maroc. *Les Dossiers d'Archéologie* 13: 56–59.

El-Azifi, M.R. 1995. Les nécropoles de la région de Tanger sont-elles phéniciennes? In M.H. Fantar and M. Ghaki (eds), *Actes du IIIe Congrès international des études phéniciennes et puniques (Tunis, 11–16 novembre 1991)*, 401–14. Tunis: Institut National du Patrimoine.

Eldblom, L. 1968. *Structure foncière, organisation et structure sociale: Une étude comparative sur la vie socio-économique dan les trois oasis libyennes de Ghat, Mourzouk et particulièrement Ghadamès*. Lund: Uniksol.

Ellefi, M. 2015. *Turris Tamalleni*: Essai de géographie historique d'une cité du Nefzaoua antique. In Mrabet 2015, 299–315.

Ellefi, M. 2016. *L'Azurgitana: Recherches d'histoire et d'archéologie sur une entité africaine de l'antiquité tardive*. Unpublished PhD thesis, Université de Sousse.

Ellis, S. 1997. Late-antique dining: Architecture, furnishings and behaviour. In R. Laurence and A. Wallace-Hadrill (eds), *Domestic Space in the Roman World: Pompeii and Beyond*, 41–51. JRA supplement 22. Portsmouth RI: Journal of Roman Archaeology.

Elrashedy, F.M. 2002. *Imports of Post-Archaic Greek Pottery into Cyrenaica: From the End of the Archaic to the Beginning of the Hellenistic Period*. British Archaeological Reports, International Series S1022. Oxford: BAR Publishing.

Emberling, G. 1997. Ethnicity in complex societies: Archaeological perspectives. *Journal of Archaeological Research* 5(4): 295–344.

Emrage, A.S.M. 2015. *Roman Fortified Farms (Qsur) and Military Sites in the region of the Wadi al-Kuf, Cyrenaica (Eastern Libya)*. Unpublished PhD thesis, University of Leicester.

Ennabli, A. 1985. Bibliographie d'archéologie et d'histoire ancienne de Tunisie (Carthage excepté) 1957–1979. *CEDAC Bulletin* 5: 33–55.

Ennabli, A. 1992. *Pour sauver Carthage. Exploration et conservation de la cité punique, romain et byzantine*. Paris: UNESCO.

Ennabli, A. 2004. Entre Afrique du Nord antique et Afrique sub-saharienne: Un obstacle infranchisable. In Bazzana and Bocoum 2004: 23–24.

Ennabli, A. 2020. *Carthage: "Les travaux et les jours": Recherches et découvertes, 1831–2016*. Paris: CNRS Éditions.

Ennabli, L. 1975. *Les inscriptions funéraires de Carthage, 1: Les inscriptions funéraires chrétiennes de la basilique dite de Sainte Monique à Carthage*. CEFR 25. Rome: École française de Rome.

Ennabli, L. 1982. *Les inscriptions funéraires de Carthage, 2: La basilique de Mcidfa*. CEFR 62. Rome: École française de Rome.

Ennabli, L. 1991. *Les inscriptions funéraires de Carthage, 3: Carthage intra et extra muros*. CEFR 151. Rome: École française de Rome.

Ennabli, L. 1997. *Carthage: Une métropole chrétienne, du IVe à la fin du VIIe siècle*. Paris: CNRS Éditions.

Ennaïfer, M. 1976. *La cité d'Althiburos et l'édifice des Asclepieia*. Bibliothèque Archéologique 1. Tunis: Institut National d'Archéologie et d'Art.

Erdkamp, P. (ed). 2002. *The Roman Army and the Economy*. Amsterdam: Gieben.

Erdkamp, P., Verboven, K. and Zuiderhoek, A. (eds). 2015. *Ownership and Exploitation of Land and Natural Resources in the Roman World*. Oxford Studies on the Roman Economy. Oxford: Oxford University Press.

Étienne, R. 1960. *Le quartier nord-est de Volubilis*. 2 vols. Paris: de Boccard.

Euzennat, M. 1965. Héritage punique et influences gréco-romaines au Maroc à la veille de la conquête romaine. In *Le rayonnement des civilisations grecque et romaine sur les cultures périphériques*, VIIIème Congrès International d'Archéologie Classique (Paris 1963), 261–78. Paris: de Boccard.

Euzennat, M. 1972. Quatre années de recherches sur la frontière romaine en tunisie méridionale. *Comptes rendus des séances de l'Académie des inscriptions et belles-lettres* 1972, 116(1): 7–27.

Euzennat, M. 1974. Les Zegrenses. In *Mélanges d'histoire ancienne offerts à William Seston*, 175–86. Paris: Boccard.

Euzennat, M. 1977a. Recherches récentes sur la frontière d'Afrique (1964–1974). In *Studien zu den Militärgrenzen Roms II: Vorträge des 10. Internationalen Limeskongresses in der Germania Inferior*, 429–44. Cologne: Rheinland-Verlag.

Euzennat, M. 1977b. Les recherches sur la frontière romaine d'Afrique (1974–1976). In Fitz 1977, 533–43.

Euzennat, M. 1984. Les troubles de Maurétanie. *Comptes rendus des séances de l'Académie des inscriptions et belles-lettres* 1984, 128(2): 372–93.

Euzennat, M. 1986. La frontière d'Afrique 1976–83. In *Akten des 13. Internationalen Limeskongresses (Aalen, 18–25 September 1983)*, 573–83. Stuttgart: Landesdenkmalamt Baden-Württemberg.

Euzennat, M. 1989. *Le limes de Tingitane: La frontière méridionale*. Paris: CNRS Éditions.

Euzennat, M. 1990. La frontière romaine d'Afrique. *Comptes rendus des séances de l'Académie des inscriptions et belles-lettres* 1990, 134(2): 565–80.

Euzennat, M. 1992. Grande et petite hydraulique dans l'Afrique romaine. In Argoud et al. 1992, 75–94.

Euzennat, M. 1995a. Les structures tribales dans l'Afrique préislamique. Un état de la question. In Trousset 1995a, 247–54.

Euzennat, M. 1995b. *Populis novis ex Africa inlatis.* Réflexions sur l'activité de P. Aelius Peregrinus sur la praetentura sévérienne, d'après l'inscription CIL, VIII, 9228. *Bulletin archéologique du comité des travaux historiques et scientifiques: Afrique du Nord* n.s. 24B: 232–34.

Euzennat, M. 2000. Mauretania Tingitana. In Talbert 2000, Map 28 and map-by-map directory, 457–66.

Euzennat, M. and Hallier, G. 1986. Les forums de Tingitane. Observations sur l'influence de l'architecture militaire sur les constructions civiles de l'Occident romain. *Antiquités africaines* 22: 73–103.

Fabbricotti, E. and Menozzi, O. (eds). 2006. *Cirenaica: Studi, scavi e scoperte. Parte I: Nuovi dati da città e territorio.* British Archaeological Reports, International Series S1488. Oxford: Archaeopress.

Fage, J.D. (ed). 1978. *The Cambridge History of Africa, vol. 2: From c.500 BC to AD1050.* Cambridge: Cambridge University Press.

Fakroune, M. 2004. Travaux en Syrtique. Prospection, sauvetage et gestion de patrimoine. In Bazzana and Bocoum 2004, 377–81.

Fantar, M. 2002. *Recherches sur l'architecture funéraire punique au Cap Bon.* Rome: Consiglio Nazionale delle Ricerche.

Fantar, M. 2006. Propos sur la présence du mausolée dans l'architecture funéraire préromaine. In Bejaoui 2006, 23–30.

Fantar, M. 2012. Les ouvrages de défense dans la cité punique de Kerkouane. In Déroche and Leclant 2012, 9–13.

Fantar M.H. 1972. Collections de verres de Tunisie. Le verre à Carthage punique. *Bulletin de l'Association Internationale pour l'Histoire du Verre* 6: 17–27.

Fantar, M.H 1984. *Kerkouane: Cité punique de Cap Bon (Tunisie), vol. 1.* Tunis: Institut national d'archéologie et d'art.

Fantar, M.H 1985. *Kerkouane. Cité punique de Cap Bon (Tunisie), vol. 2: Architecture domestique.* Tunis: Institut national d'archéologie et d'art.

Fantar, M.H. 1986. *Kerkouane. Cité punique de Cap Bon (Tunisie), vol. 3: Sanctuaires et cultes, société, économie.* Tunis: Institut national d'archéologie et d'art.

Fantar, M.H. 1988. Que savons-nous des institutions municipales dans le monde de Carthage. *Reppal* 4: 205–14.

Fantar, M.H. 1990a. Survivances de la civilisation punique en Afrique du Nord. *L'Africa romana* 7: 53–71.

Fantar, M.H. 1990b. Baal Hammon. *Reppal* 5: 67–105.

Fantar, M.H. 1992. L'épigraphie punique et néopunique en Tunisie (1982–1992). *L'Africa romana* 9: 65–72.

Fantar, M.H. 1993a/b. *Carthage. Approche d'une civilisation.* 2 vols. Tunis: Les Éditions de la Méditerranée.

Fantar, M.H. 1995. Nécropoles puniques de Tunisie. In Trousset 1995a, 55–72.

Fantar, M.H. 1997. La vigne et le vin a l'epoque carthaginoise. *Reppal* 10: 41–52.

Fantar, M.H. 1998. *Carthage. The Punic City*. Tunis: Alif.

Fantar, M.H. (ed). 2006. *Le Sahara et l'homme: Un savoir pour un savoir faire*. Tunis: Université de Tunis El Manar.

Fantar, M.H., Sznycer, M. and Bron, F. 2015. *Stèles à inscriptions néopuniques de Maktar, vol. 1*. (Corpus des antiquités phéniciennes et puniques, France 3/Tunisie 1.) Mémoires de l'academie des inscriptions et belles-lettres 51. Paris: de Boccard.

Faraj, M. O., Abd al-Rahman, A. S., Di-Vita-Evrard, G. and Musso, L. 1996. La tomba presso la scuola elementare al-Hadi al-Fergiani a Khoms. *Libya Antiqua* n.s. 2: 135–56.

Faure, P. 2022. The army. In Hitchner 2022a, 152–72.

Faure, P. and Leveau, P. 2015. Les marges de al Numidie romaine à la lumière d'une nouvelle inscription des Monts des Ouled Naïl. *Antiquités africaines* 51: 119–42.

Felici, F., Munzi, M. and Tantillo, I. 2006. Austuriani e Laguatan in Tripolitania. *L'Africa romana* 16(1): 591–687.

Fentress, E.W.B. 1978. Dii Mauri and Dii Patrii. *Latomus* 37(2): 507–16.

Fentress, E.W.B. 1979. *Numidia and the Roman Army: Social, Military and Economic Aspects of the Frontier Zone*. British Archaeological Reports International Series S53. Oxford: BAR Publishing.

Fentress, E.W.B. 1982a. Tribe and faction: The case of the Gaetuli. *Mélanges de l'Ecole Française de Rome. Antiquité* 94(1): 325–34.

Fentress, E.W.B. 1982b. La vendetta del Moro: Recenti richerche sull'Africa romana. *Dialoghi di Archeologia* n.s. 4.1: 107–13.

Fentress, E.W.B. 1983. Forever Berber? *Opus: Rivista internazionale per la storia economica e sociale dell'antichità* 2: 161–75.

Fentress, E.W.B. 1985. "Limes" – Africa. In E. De Ruggiero (ed), *Dizionario Epigrafico di Antichità Romane, vol. 4*, fasc. 43.2–3 (1376): 21–47.

Fentress, E.W.B. 1990. The Economy of an Inland City: Sétif. In *L'Afrique dans l'Occident romain*, 117–28.

Fentress, E.W.B. 2000a. Cirta. In Talbert 2000, Map 31 and map-by-map directory, 483–92.

Fentress, E.W.B. 2000b. Numidia. In Talbert 2000, Map 34 and map-by-map directory, 520–28.

Fentress, E.W.B. 2000c. Social relations and domestic space in the Maghreb. In A. Bazzana and E. Hubert (eds), *Castrum 6: Maisons et espaces domestiques dans le monde méditerranéen au Moyen Âge*, 15–26. CEFR 105/6. Rome: École française de Rome.

Fentress, E.W.B 2006. Romanizing the Berbers. *Past and Present* 190: 3–33.

Fentress, E.W.B. 2007. Where were North African *nundinae* held? In C. Gosden, H. Hamerow, P. de Jersey, and G. Lock (eds), *Communities and Connections: Essays in Honour of Barry Cunliffe*, 125–41. Oxford: Oxford University Press.

Fentress, E.W.B. 2009a. The Punic and Libyan towns of Jerba. In S. Helas and D. Marzoli (eds), *Phönizisches und punisches Städtewesen*, 203–19. Mainz: Verlag Philipp von Zabern.

Fentress, E.W.B. 2009b. Peopling the countryside: Roman demography in the Albegna Valley and Jerba. In Bowman and Wilson 2009, 127–61.

Fentress, E.W.B. 2011. Slavers on chariots. In Dowler and Galvin 2011, 65–71.

Fentress, E.W.B. 2013a. Strangers in the city: Elite communication in the Hellenistic central Mediterranean. In Prag and Quinn 2013, 157–78.

Fentress, E.W.B. 2013b. Diana Veteranorum and the dynamics of an inland economy. *Late Antique Archaeology* 10(1): 315–42.

Fentress, E.W.B. 2019. The archaeological and genetic correlates of Amazigh linguistics. In Gatto et al. 2019a, 495–524.

Fentress, E.W.B. 2021. Coercive urbanism: The Roman impact on North African towns. In Belvedere and Bergemann 2021, 165–78.

Fentress, E.W.B. and Docter, R.F. 2008. North Africa: Rural settlement and agricultural production. In Van Dommelen and Gómez Bellard 2008, 101–28.

Fentress, E.W.B. and Limane, H. (eds). 2018. *Volubilis après Rome: Les fouilles UCL/INSAP, 2000–2005*. Arts and Archaeology of the Islamic World 11. Leiden: Brill.

Fentress, E.W.B. and Perkins, P. 1988. Counting African red slip ware. *L'Africa romana* 5: 205–14.

Fentress, E.W.B. and Wilson, A.I. 2016. The Saharan Berber diaspora and the southern frontiers of Vandal and Byzantine North Africa. In J.P. Conant and S.T. Stevens (eds), *North Africa under Byzantium and Early Islam, ca. 500 – ca. 800*, 41–63. Washington, D.C.: Dumbarton Oaks Research Library and Collection.

Fentress, E.W.B., Aït Kaci, A. and Bounassair, N. 1991. Prospections dans le Belezma: Rapport préliminaire. In *Actes du colloque international sur l'histoire de Sétif (8–10 décembre 1990)*, Bulletin d'archéologie algerienne supplement 7, 107–27. Alger: Agence nationale d'archéologie.

Fentress, E.W.B., Fontana, S., Hitchner, R.B. and Perkins, P. 2004. Accounting for ARS: Fineware and sites in Sicily and Africa. In Alcock and Cherry 2004, 147–62.

Fentress, E.W.B., Drine, A. and Holod, R. 2009. *An Island Through Time: Jerba Studies. 1. The Punic and Roman Periods*. JRA supplement 71. Portsmouth RI: Journal of Roman Archaeology.

Fenwick, C. 2008. Archaeology and the search for authenticity: Colonialist, nationalist and Berberist visions of an Algerian past. In C. Fenwick, M. Wiggins, and D. Wythe (eds), *TRAC 2007: Proceedings of the Seventeenth Annual Theoretical Roman Archaeology Conference*, 75–88. Oxford: Oxbow Books.

Fenwick, C. 2019. The fate of the Classical cities in North Africa in the early Middle Ages. In Bockmann et al. 2019, 137–55.

Fenwick, C. 2020. *Early Islamic North Africa: A New Perspective*. Debates in Archaeology. London: Bloomsbury.

Ferchiou, N. 1975. *Architecture romaine de Tunisie: L'ordre, rhythmes et proportions dans le Tell*. Tunis: Institut national d'archeologie et d'art.

Ferchiou, N. 1980. Remarques sur la politique impériale de colonisation en proconsulaire au cours du premier siècle après J.-C. *Cahiers de Tunisie* 28(113): 9–55.

Ferchiou, N. 1986a. Niveaux numides découverts à Mustis. *Reppal* 2: 277–85.

Ferchiou, N. 1986b. Une zone de petite colonisation romaine à l'époque julio-claudienne: Le centre-ouest de *l'Africa Vetus* (région d'Aradi, Avitina, Dj. Mansour, Siliana). *L'Africa romana* 3: 205–17.

Ferchiou, N. 1986c. Nouvelles données sur un fossé inconnu en Afrique proconsulaire et sur la *Fossa Regia*. In CTHS Montpellier 1986, 351–65.

Ferchiou, N. 1987. Un problème d'éclairage historique: Le cas des tumulus et des bazinas de l'ancien territoire de la Carthage punique. *Reppal* 3: 185–91.

Ferchiou, N. 1989a. *Décor architectonique d'Afrique Proconsulaire (IIIe s. avant J.-C. – Ier s. après J.-C.)*. 2 vols. Tunis: Libr. Archéologique.

Ferchiou, N. 1989b. Le mausolée de Q. Apuleus Maxssimus à El Amrouni. *Papers of the British School at Rome* 57: 47–76.

Ferchiou, N. 1989c. Les environs d'Henchir Tout, hors de courents civilisationnels romano-africains: la problematique d'un paysage humain. *Bulletin des travaux de l'Institut National de l'art et l'archéologie* 3: 7–17.

Ferchiou, N. 1990a. Habitats fortifiés pré-impériaux en Tunisie antique. *Antiquités africaines* 26: 43–86.

Ferchiou, N. 1990b. L'habitat fortifié pré-impérial en Tunisie antique: Aperçus sur la typologie des sites perchés et des sites de versant. In CTHS Strasbourg 1990, 229–52.

Ferchiou, N. 1990c. L'occupation du sol de la province romaine d'Afrique au 1er siècle apr. J.-C.: la petite Syrte et la Djerid. *Cahiers de Tunisie* 155–56: 65–106.

Ferchiou, N. 1994. Le paysage protohistorique et pré-impérial à l'est et au sud de Zaghouan (Tunisie). *Antiquités africaines* 30: 7–55.

Ferchiou, N. 1995a. Architecture funéraire de Tunisie à l'époque romaine. In Trousset 1995a, 111–37.

Ferchiou, N. 1995b. Le paysage pré-impérial dans une zone de contact: Percée de l'oued Kebir sortant de la Dorsale tunisienne pour aborder la plaine de Thuburbo-Maius. *Reppal* 9: 49–62.

Ferchiou, N. 1998a. Aïn Fourna, antique Furnos Maius, ville de confins territoriaux, porte du Haut Tell. *Africa* 16: 31–58.

Ferchiou, N. 1998b. Fossa Regia. *Encyclopédie Berbère* 19: 2897–911.

Ferchiou, N. 2001. Histoire antique et architecture dans le haut steppe en Africa Proconsularis: Recherches préliminaires sur les mausolées de la région de Kasserine. In Bejaoui 2001, 7–22.

Ferchiou, N. 2004a. Recherches sur le cadre géographique et historique de la région de Zama. *Africa: Séances scientifiques* 2: 185–209.

Ferchiou, N. 2004b. Architecture, urbanisme et topographie: À propos de trois villes de l'ancien térritoire de la Cathage punique: *Sululos*, Henchir Debbik, *Seressi*. *Africa: Séances scientifiques* 2: 211–35.

Ferchiou, N. 2004c. L'habitat fortifié numide de l'Henchir Bou Nader (région des Salines, en Tunisie centrale). *Reppal* 13: 135–47.

Ferdi, S. 2005. *Corpus des mosaïques de Cherchel*. Études Antiquités africaines. Paris: Éditions du CNRS.

Ferguson, B. and Whitehead N. (eds). 1992. *War in the Tribal Zone: Expanding States and Indigenous Warfare*. SAR Advanced Seminar Series. Santa Fe: School of American Research Press.

Ferhat, N. and Taveron, M. 2001. *Essai de bibliographie du nord de l'Afrique. Préhistoire et protohistoire*. Paris: L'Harmatton.

Ferjaoui, A. 1993a. *Recherches sur les relations entre l'orient phénicien et Carthage*. Orbis Biblicus et Orientalis. Fribourg/Göttingen: Éditions universitaires/Vandenhoeck & Ruprecht.

Ferjaoui, A. 1993b. Stèles votives et funéraires trouvées à Kesra. *Reppal* 7–8: 127–63.

Ferjaoui, A. 1995. Dédicaces néopuniques d'édifices funéraires. *Reppal* 9: 63–72.

Ferjaoui, A. 2004. Localisation de *Zama Regia* à Jama. *Africa: Séances scientifiques* 2: 173–84.

Ferjaoui, A. 2007. *La sanctuaire de Henchir el-Hami: de Ba'al Hammon au Saturne Africaine 1er s. av J.-C. – IVe s. ap. J.-C.* Tunis: Institut National du Patrimoine.

Ferjaoui, A. (ed). 2010a. *Carthage et les autochtones de son empire du temps de Zama. Hommage à Mhamed Hassine Fantar*. Tunis: Institut National du Patrimoine.

Ferjaoui, A. 2010b. Les relations entre Carthage et l'intérieur de l'Afrique. Le cas de Zama Regia et sa région. In Ferjaoui 2010a, 341–52.

Ferjaoui, A. and Redissi, T. (eds). 2019. *La vie, la mort et la religion dans l'univers phénicien et punique, vol. 3: La mort, la religion*. Actes du VIIe congrès international des études phéniciennes et puniques. Tunis: Institut National du Patrimoine.

Fernández-Götz, M., Maschek, D. and Roymans, N. 2020. The dark side of the Empire: Roman expansionism between object agency and predatory regime. *Antiquity* 94(378): 1630–39.

Février, J. 1965. La constitution municipale de Dougga à l'époque numide. *Mélanges de Carthage: offerts à Charles Saumagne, Cahiers de Byrsa* 10, 85–91. Paris: Geuthner.

Février, P.-A. 1970. La nécropole orientale de Tiddis. *Bulletin d'Archéologie Algérienne* 4: 41–100.

Février, P.-A. 1971. *Art de l'Algérie antique*. Paris: de Boccard.

Février, P.-A. 1976a. Colonisation romaine et forme artistique dans les provinces de la Mediterrané occidentale. In M. Galley (ed), *Actes du 2e congrès international. D'étude des cultures de la Méditerranée occidentale, vol. 1*, 49–102. Alger: Société Nationale d'Edition et de Diffusion.

Février, P.-A. 1976b. Religion et domination dans l'Afrique romaine. *Dialogue d'histoire ancienne* 2: 305–36.

Février, P.-A. 1978. *Djemila*. Alger: Ministère de l'Education nationale, sous-direction des Arts.

Février, P.-A. 1979. L'art funéraire et les images des chefs indigènes dans la Kabylie antique. In *Actes du Ier Congrès d'Histoire et de Civilisation du Maghreb*, 2 vols, 152–69. Tunis: Université de Tunis.

Février, P.-A. 1981. Quelques remarques sur troubles et résistances dans le Maghreb romain. *Cahiers de Tunisie* 29(117): 23–40.

Février, P.-A. 1982. Urbanisation et urbanisme de l'Afrique romaine. In H. Temporini (ed), *Aufstieg und Niedergang der römischen Welt: Principat, vol. 10/2: Teilband Politische Geschichte (Provinzen und Randvölker: Afrika mit Ägypten [Forts.])*, 321–96. Berlin: De Gruyter.

Février, P.-A. 1986. Le monde rural du Maghreb antique: Approches de l'historiographie du XIXe siècle. In CTHS Montpellier 1986, 87–106.

Février, P.-A. 1989. *Approches du Maghreb romain: Pouvoirs, différences et conflits, vol. 1*. Aix-en-Provence: Edisud.

Février, P.-A. 1990. *Approches du Maghreb romain: Pouvoirs, différences et conflits, vol. 2*. Aix-en-Provence: Edisud.

Février, P.-A. 1992. Incinerations et inhumations dans le Maghreb antique. In M. Vidal (ed), *Incinérations et inhumations dans l'Occident romain aux trois premiers siècles de notre ère*, Actes du colloque international, IVème congrès archéologique de Gaule méridionale (Toulouse, 7–10 octobre 1987), 181–89. Toulouse: Association pour la promotion du patrimoine archéologique et historique en Midi-Pyrénées.

Février, P.-A. 1996. *La Méditerranée de Paul-Albert Février*. 2 vols. CEFR 225. Rome: École française de Rome.

Février, P.-A. and Blanchard-Lemée, M. 2019. *L'édifice appelé "Maison de Bacchus" à Djemila*. Paris: CNRS Éditions.

Février, P.-A. and Guéry, R. 1980. Les rites funéraires de la nécropole orientale de Sétif. *Antiquités africaines* 15: 91–124.

Fields, N. 2010. *Roman Conquests: North Africa*. London: Pen and Sword.

Filippo Bondi, S. 2014. Phoenicity, punicities. In Quinn and Vella 2014, 58–68.

Fishwick, D. 1993. On the origins of Africa Proconsularis I: The amalgamation of Africa Vetus and Africa Nova. *Antiquités africaines* 29: 53–62.

Fitz, J. (ed). 1977. *Akten des 11. Internationalen Limeskongresses, (Székesfehérvár 30 August–6 September 1976)*. Budapest: Akadémiai Kiadó.

Flannery, K. and Marcus, J. 2012. *The Creation of Inequality: How Our Prehistoric Ancestors Set the Stage for Monarchy, Slavery, and Empire*. Cambridge, MA: Harvard University Press.

Flügel, C. and Dolenz, H. 2018. Carthage, rue Ibn Chabâat ('quartier Didon'): Le développement urbanistique de la période punique ancienne à la période punique tardive. Rapport préliminaire des fouilles menées par le DAI Rome et l'INP Tunis 2009–2012. *Antiquités africaines* 54: 27–39.

Fontana, S. 1997. Il predeserto tripolitano: Mausolei e rappresentazione del potere. *Libya Antiqua* n.s. 3: 149–67.

Fontana, S. 2001. Leptis Magna: The romanization of a major African city through burial evidence. In Keay and Terrenato 2001, 161–72.

Fontana, S., Munzi, M. and Ricci, G. 1996. Insediamenti agricoli di età ellenistica e romana nell'area dell'uadi Bendar (Leptis Magna). *Libya Antiqua* n.s. 2: 67–75.

Förster, F. and Reimer, H. 2013. *Desert Road Archaeology in Ancient Egypt and Beyond*. Africa Praehistorica 27. Cologne: Heinrich-Barth-Institut.

Fothergill, B.T., Linseele, V. and Valenzuela Lamas, S. 2020. Movement and management of animals in the North and West of Africa from 1000 BC to AD 1000. In Duckworth et al. 2020a, 143–82.

Foucher, L. 1964. *Hadrumetum*. Paris: Presses Universitaires de France.

France, J. 2015. Administration and taxation in the tariff of Zraia (Numidia). In P. Kritzinger, F. Schleicher and T. Stickler (eds), *Studien zum römischen Zollwesen*, 111–40. Duisburg: Wellem Verlag.

France, J. 2014. Normes douanières et réglementation des échanges: Trois questions simples sur le tarif de Zaraï (Numidie). *Antiquités africaines* 50: 93–110.

Francovich, R., Patterson, H. and Barker, G.W. (eds). 2000. *Extracting Meaning From Ploughsoil Assemblages*. Archaeology of Mediterranean Landscapes 5. Oxford: Oxbow Books.

Freeman, P. 2007. *The Best Training Ground for Archaeologists: Francis Haverfield and the Invention of Romano-British Archaeology*. Oxford: Oxbow Books.

Frémeaux, J. 1984. Souvenirs de Rome et présence françois au Maghreb: Essai d'investigation. In Vatin 1984, 29–46.

Frend, W.H.C. 1971. *The Donatist Church*. 2nd edition. Oxford: Oxford University Press.

Frend, W.H.C. 1978. The Christian period in Mediterranean Africa, c.AD 200–700. In Fage 1978, 410–90.

Frey-Kupper, S. 2014. Coins and their use in the Punic Mediterranean: Case studies from Carthage to Italy from the fourth to first century BCE. In Quinn and Vella 2014, 76–10.

Frézouls, E. 1957. Les Baquates et la province romaine de Tingitane. *Bulletin d'Archéologie Marocaine* 2:65–116.

Frézouls, E. 1980. Rome et la Maurétanie tingitane: Un constat d'échec? *Antiquités africaines* 16: 65–93.

Frézouls, E. 1981. La résistance armée en Maurétanie de l'annexation à l'époque sévérienne: Un essai d'appreciation. *Cahiers de Tunisie* 29(117): 41–69.

Frier, B.W. 2000. Demography. In Bowman et al. 2000, 787–816.

Fromentin, E. 2004 (1859). *Between Sea and Sahara: An Orientalist Journey*. London: Tauris.

Fulford, M.G. 1989. To east and west: The Mediterranean trade of Cyrenaica and Tripolitania in antiquity. *Libyan Studies* 20: 169–91.

Fulford, M.G. and Peacock, D.P.S. 1984. *Excavations at Carthage: The British Mission, vol. 1, 2: The Avenue du President Habib Bourguiba, Salammbo: The Pottery and other Ceramic Objects from the Site*. Sheffield: British Academy.

Fulford, M.G. and Peacock, D.P.S. 1994. *Excavations at Carthage: The British Mission, vol. 2, 2: The Circular Harbour, North Side: The Pottery*. British Academy Monographs in Archaeology 5. Oxford: Oxford University Press.

Fulford, M.G. and Tomber, R. (eds). 1994. *Excavations at Sabratha 1948–1951, vol. 2: The Finds, Part 2: The Finewares and Lamps*. London: Society for Libyan Studies.

Fumadó Ortega, I. 2022. Punic Carthage. In Hitchner 2022a, 81–100.

Gadallah, F.F. (ed). 1971. *Libya in History*. Proceedings of a conference held at the faculty of Arts, University of Libya 1968. Benghazi: University of Benghazi.

Gailledrat, E., Dietler, M. and Plana-Mallart, R. (eds). 2018. *The Emporion in the Ancient Western Mediterranean: Trade and Colonial Encounters from the Archaic to the Hellenistic Period*. Mondes anciens series. Montpellier: Presses universitaires de la Méditerranée.

Galand, L. 1989. Les alphabets libyques. *Antiquités africaines* 25: 69–81.

Galand, L. 2005. La libyque en Algérie. In Briand-Ponsart 2005a, 59–68.

Galand, L., Février, J.G. and Vajda, G. 1966. *Inscriptions antiques du Maroc, vol. 1: Inscriptions libyques; Inscriptions puniques et néopunique; Inscriptions hébraïques des sites antiques*. Paris: CNRS Éditions.

Gallet de Santerre, H. and Slim, L. 1983. *Recherches sur les nécropoles puniques de Kerkouane*. Tunis: Institut National d'Archéologie et d'Art.

Gardner, A. 2002. Social identity and the duality of structure in late Roman-period Britain. *Journal of Social Archaeology* 2(3): 323–51.

Gardner, A. (ed). 2004. *Agency Uncovered: Archaeological Perspectives on Social Agency, Power, and Being Human*. London: University College London Press.

Gardner, A. 2013. Thinking about Roman imperialism. Postcolonialism, globalisation and beyond? *Britannia* 44: 1–25.

Gardner, A. 2017. Brexit, boundaries and imperial identities: A comparative view. *Journal of Social Archaeology* 17(1): 3–26.

Gargola, D.J. 2017. Was there a regular *Provincia Africa* in the second century? *Historia* 66(3): 331–61.

Garnsey, P.D.A. 1978. Rome's African Empire under the Principate. In P.D.A. Garnsey and C.R. Whittaker (eds), *Imperialism in the Ancient World*, 223–54. Cambridge: Cambridge University Press.

Garrow, D. and Gosden, C. 2012. *Technologies of Enchantment? Exploring Celtic Art 400 BC to AD 100*. Oxford: Oxford University Press.

Gascou, J. 1970. Le *cognomen Gaetulus, Gaetulicus* en Afrique romaine. *Mélanges de l'Ecole Française de Rome* 82(2): 723–36.

Gascou, J. 1972. *La politique municipale de l'empire romain en Afrique proconsulaire de Trajan à Septime Sévère*. CEFR 8. Paris: École française de Rome.

Gascou, J. 1982a. La politique municipale de Rome en Afrique du Nord, 1: De la mort d'Auguste au début du IIIe siècle. In H. Temporini (ed), *Aufstieg und Niedergang der römischen Welt: Principat, vol. 10/2: Teilband Politische Geschichte (Provinzen und Randvölker: Afrika mit Ägypten [Forts.])*, 136–229. Berlin: De Gruyter.

Gascou, J. 1982b. La politique municipale de Rome en Afrique du Nord, 2: Après la mort de Septime-Sévère. In H. Temporini (ed), *Aufstieg und Niedergang der römischen Welt: Principat, vol. 10/2: Teilband Politische Geschichte (Provinzen und Randvölker: Afrika mit Ägypten [Forts.])*, 230–320. Berlin: De Gruyter.

Gascou, J. 1982c. Les pagi carthaginois. In P.A. Février and P. Leveau (eds), *Villes et campagnes dans l'Empire Romain*, Actes du Colloque organisé à Aix-en-Provence par l'U.E.R. d'Histoire (16 et 17 mai 1980), 139–75. Aix en Provence: Centre Camille Julian.

Gascou, J. 1983. Pagus et castellum dans la Confédération Cirtéenne. *Antiquités africaines* 19: 175–207.

Gascou, J. 1984. Les magistratures de la Confédération Cirtéenne. *Bulletin archéologique du comité des travaux historiques et scientifiques: Afrique du Nord* n.s. 17B: 323–35.

Gascou, J. 1990. La *praefectura iure dicundo* dans les cités de l'Afrique romaine. In *L'Afrique dans l'Occident romain*, 367–80.

Gascou, J. 1998. Remarques sur les *undecimprimi*. *Antiquités africaines* 34: 93–102.

Gascou, J. 2003. Les statuts des villes africaines: Quelques apports dus à des recherches récentes. In Bost et al. 2003, 231–46.

Gasperini, L. and Marengo, S.M. (eds). 2007. *Cirene e la Cirenaica nell'antichità*. Tivoli: Edizioni Tored.

Gatto, M.C., Mattingly, D.J., Ray, N. and Sterry, M. (eds). 2019a. *Burials, Migration and Identity in the Ancient Sahara and Beyond*. Cambridge: Cambridge University Press.

Gatto, M.C., Mori, L. and Zerboni, A. 2019b. Identity markers in south-western Fazzan: Were the people of the Wadi Tanzzuft/Tadrart Akakus region Garamantes? In Gatto et al. 2019a, 108–33.

Gauckler, P. 1895. Découvertes archéologiques en Tunisie. *Mémoires de la Société des Antiquaires* 56: 83–160.

Gauckler, P. 1900/1912. *Enquête sur les installations hydrauliques romaines en Tunisie*. 2 vols, Paris: Imprimerie rapide.

Gauthier, Y. and Gauthier, C. 2011. Des chars et des tifinagh: Étude aréale et corrélations. *Les Cahiers de l'AARS* 15: 91–118.

Gauthier, Y. and Gauthier, C. 2015. Nouvelles figurations de chars sahariens: Technicité et positionnement chronologique relativement au style de Tazina. *Les Cahiers de l'AARS* 18: 5–70.

Gauthier, E.F. 1970. *Sahara. The Great Desert*. New York: Octagon.

Gearon, E. 2011. *The Sahara. A Cultural History*. Oxford: Signal Books.

Geary, P.J. 1988. Ethnic identity as a situational construct in the early middle ages. *Medieval Perspectives* 3: 1–17.

Gellner, E. and Micaud, C. (eds). 1972. *Arabs and Berbers: From Tribe to Nation in North Africa*. London: Duckworth.

Geraghty, R.M. 2007. The impact of globalization in the Roman empire, 200 BC – AD 100. *Journal of Economic History* 67(4): 1036–61.

Germain, S. 1969. *Les mosaïques de Timgad: Étude descriptive et analytique*. Études Antiquités africaines. Paris: Éditions du CNRS.

Géroudet, N. 1995. Le monde minéral africain dans l'*Histoire naturelle* de Pline l'Ancien. In Trousset 1995c, 47–56.

Géroudet, N. and Ménard, H. 2005. *L'Afrique romaine de l'Atlantique à la Tripolitaine (69–439)*. Paris: Belin.

Getachew, A. 2020. Colonialism made the modern world. Let's remake it. *New York Times* [online], 27 July 2020, https://www.nytimes.com/2020/07/27/opinion/sunday/decolonization-statues.html. In print as The slow road to real "decolonization", 2 August 2020.

Ghaddab, R. 2020. Centuriation et statut juridique des environs d'*Hadrumetum* entre la fin de la troisième guerre punique et le règne de Trajan. *Antiquités africaines* 56: 79–100.

Ghaki, M. 1995. La répartition des inscriptions libyques. *Reppal* 9: 93–108.

Ghaki, M. 1997a. Épigraphie libyque et punique à Dougga. In Khanoussi and Maurin 1997, 27–45.

Ghaki, M. 1997b. Le nouveau monument mégalithique de Makthar: Rapport préliminaire. *Reppal* 10: 63–72.

Ghaki, M. 1999a. *Les haouanet de Sidi Mhamed Latrech*. Tunis: INP.

Ghaki, M. 1999b. La céramique modelée du "nouveau mégalithe" de Makhtar. *Reppal* 11: 95–124.

Ghaki, M. 2003. Questions autour du mégalithism en Tunisie. In Khanoussi 2003, 47–63.

Ghalia, T. 1992. Approches du paysage antique de la vallée de l'Oued Sejnane. *Bulletin des travaux de l'Institut National du Patrimoine* 5: 33–57.

Ghalia, T. 2005. La villa romaine de Demna – Wadi Arremel et son environnement: Approche archéologique et projet de valorisation. *Africa: Séances scientifiques* 3: 53–86.

Gharbi, M. 2020. La Petite Syrte à l'époque punique: Une zone des confins? In Guédon 2020, 19–39.

Ghedini, F. and Bullo, S. 2003. *Amplissimae atque ornatissima domus (Aug., civ., II, 20, 26). L'edilizia residenziale nelle città della Tunisia romana*. 2 vols. Rome: Edizioni Quasar.

Giardina, A. and Pesando, F. (eds). 2012a. *Roma Caput Mundi. Una città tra dominio e integrazione*. Milan: Electa.

Giardina, A. and Pesando, F. (eds). 2012b. *Roma Caput Mundi. La mostra*. Milan: Electa.

Giddens, A. 1984. *The Constitution of Society: Outline of a Theory of Structuration*. Cambridge: Polity Press.

Girard, S. 1984. Banasa préromaine. Un état de la question. *Antiquités africaines* 20: 11–93.

Giusti, E. Forthcoming a. Africa and the making of Classical literature: On decolonising Greco-Roman literature syllabi. *Bulletin of the Institute of Classical Studies*: Decolonising Classics in Africa: History, Strategies, Challenges, and Prospects, edited by K. Ackah, M.K.O. Asante and D. van Shoor.

Giusti, E. Forthcoming b. *Haec de Africa*: Rome's imagined Africa and the limits of fiction. In K. Blouin and B. Akrigg, *Handbook of Classics and Postcolonial Theory*, London: Routledge.

Given, M. 2004. *The Archaeology of the Colonized*. London: Routledge.

Gliozzo, E., Turbanti Memmi, T. Akerraz, A. and Papi, E. 2009. *Sidi Ali Ben Ahmed – Thamusida, vol. 2: L'archeometria*. Rome: Edizioni Quasar,

Gliozzo, E., Mattingly, D.J., Cole, F. and Artioli, G. 2014. In the footsteps of Pliny: Tracing the sources of Garamantian carnelian from Fazzan, south-west Libya. *Journal of Archaeological Science* 52: 218–41.

Goff, B. (ed). 2003. *Classics and Colonialism*. London: Duckworth.

Goldsworthy, A. and Haynes, I. (eds). 1999. *The Roman Army as a Community*. JRA supplement 34. Portsmouth, RI: Journal of Roman Archaeology.

Golvin, J.-C. 1988. *L'amphithéâtre romain: Essai sur la théorisation de sa forme et de ses fonctions*. 2 vols. Paris: de Boccard.

Golvin, J.-C. and Khanoussi, M. (eds). 2005. *Dougga: Études d'architecture religieuse: Les sanctuaires des Victoires de Caracalla, de "Pluton" et de Caelestis*. Bordeaux: INP/Ausonius.

Gómez Bellard, C. 2014. Death among the Punics. In Quinn and Vella 2014, 69–75.

Gonzales, A. 1998. La révolte comme acte du brigandage: Tacite et la révolte de *Tacfarinas*. *L'Africa romana* 12(2): 937–58.

González Bordas, H. 2017. Un nouveau regard sur le dossier des grands inscriptions agraire d'Afrique contenant le *sermo procuratorum*. *Cahiers du Centre Gustave Glotz* 28: 213–29.

González Bordas, H. and France, J. 2017. A new edition of the imperial regulation from the Lalla Drebblia site near Dougga (*AE* 2001, 2083). *Journal of Roman Archaeology* 30: 407–28.

González Rodríguez, M. 2014. *Death is Another Country: Mortuary Rituals and Identity in Fazzan, Libya*. Unpublished PhD thesis, University of Leicester.

Goodchild, R.G. 1949. Where archaeology and military training go hand in hand: Roman 'home guard' outposts in Tripolitania. *Illustrated London News* 15 October 1949: 30.

Goodchild, R.G. 1950a. The *limes Tripolitanus* II. *Journal of Roman Studies* 40(1–2): 30–38 = 1976, 35–45.

Goodchild, R.G. 1950b. The Latino-Libyan inscriptions of Tripolitania. *The Antiquaries Journal* 30(3–4): 135–44.

Goodchild, R.G. 1950c. Roman Tripolitania: Reconnaissance in the desert frontier zone. *Geographical Journal* 115(4/6): 161–71 = 1976a, 3–16.

Goodchild, R.G. 1952. Mapping Roman Libya. *Geographical Journal* 118(2): 142–52 = 1976a, 145–54.

Goodchild, R.G. 1954a. Oasis forts of *Legio III Augusta* on the routes to the Fezzan. *Papers of the British School at Rome* 22: 56–68 = 1976a, 46–58.

Goodchild, R.G. 1954b. *Tabula Imperii Romani: Lepcis Magna (sheets H.33 I.33)*. Oxford: Society of Antiquaries.

Goodchild, R.G. 1954c. *Tabula Imperii Romani: Cyrene (sheets H.34 I.34)* Oxford: Society of Antiquaries.

Goodchild, R.G. 1954d. The Romano-Libyan cemetery at Bir ed-Dreder. *Quaderni di Archeologia della Libya* 3: 91–107.

Goodchild, R. G. 1976. *Libyan Studies: Selected Papers of the Late R.G. Goodchild* (edited by J.M. Reynolds). London: Elek.

Gopal, P. 2019. *Insurgent Empire: Anticolonial Resistance and British Dissent*. London: Verso.

Gosden, C. 2004. *Archaeology and Colonialism: Cultural Contact from 5000 BC to the Present*. Cambridge: Cambridge University Press.

Gozlan, S. 1992. *La maison du triomphe de Neptune à Acholla (Botria-Tunisie), vol. 1: Les mosaïques*. Rome: Collection de l'École française de Rome.

Gozlan, S. and Jeddi, N. 2001. *Recherches archéologiques franco-tunisiennes à Acholla (Tunisie): Les mosaïques des maisons du quartier central et les mosaïques éparses*. Rome: Collection de l'École française de Rome.

Gozalbes Cravioto, E. 2006. El monumento protohistórico de Mezora (Arcila, Marruecos). *Archivo de Prehistoria Levantina* 26: 323–48.

Gozalbes Cravioto, E. 2018. El monumento de Mezora (Marruecos). Nuevos datos de las excavaciones (1934–1936) según los informes de César Montalbán. *Antiquités africaines* 54: 9–25.

Grahame, M. 1998. Rome without Romanization: Cultural change in the pre-desert of Tripolitania (first–third centuries AD). *Oxford Journal of Archaeology* 17(1): 93–111.

Greene, J.A. 1992. Une reconnaissance archéologique dans l'arrière-pays de la Carthage antique. In Ennabli 1992. 195–97.

Greene, J.A. 1997. North Africa. In E.M. Meyers (ed), *The Oxford Encyclopedia of Archaeology in the Near East*, 154–64. New York: Oxford University Press.

Greenhalgh, M. 2014. *The Military and Colonial Destruction of the Roman Landscape of North Africa, 1830–1900*. Leiden: Brill.

Gron, K.J. and Sørensen, L. 2018. Cultural and economic negotiation: A new perspective on the Neolithic transition of southern Scandinavia. *Antiquity* 92(364): 958–74.

Gros, P. 1994. Les forums de *Cuicul* et de *Thamugadi*: Ordonnance et functionnement des espaces publics en milieu provincial au IIe siècle après J-C. *Bulletin archéologique du comité des travaux historiques et scientifiques: Afrique du Nord* n.s. 23B: 61–80.

Gros, P. 1996. *L'architecture romaine: du début du IIIe s. av. J.-C. à la fin de Haut-Empire, vol. 1: Les monuments publics*. Paris: Picard.

Gros, P. 2002. *L'architecture romaine du début du IIIe s. av. J.-C. à la fin de Haut-Empire, vol. 2: Maisons, palais, villas et tombeaux*. Paris: Picard.

Gros, P. 2014. La topographie fonctionnelle du centre monumental d'une capitale de province à la fin de IIe siècle après J.-C.: l'exemple de la Carthage antonine. In Briand-Ponsart 2014, 81–103.

Groslambert, A. (ed). 2009a. *Urbanisme et urbanisation en Numidie militaire*. Actes du colloque organisé par l'Université Jean Moulin Lyon, 7–8 mars 2008. Paris: de Boccard.

Groslambert, A. 2009b. Les habitants des villes, des camps et des campagnes en Numidie militaire sous le Haut-Empire romain. In Groslambert 2009a, 57–75.

Groslambert, A. 2011. *Lambèse sous le Haut-Empire (Ier – IIIe siècles): du camp à la cité*. Paris: de Boccard.

Gruen, E.S. 1996. The expansion of the Empire under Augustus. In Bowman et al. 1996, 147–97.

Gsell, S. 1901a. *Les monuments antiques de l'Algérie. I.* Paris: Ancienne Librairie Thorin et fils/ Fontemoing.

Gsell, S. 1901b. *Les monuments antiques de l'Algérie. II.* Paris: Ancienne Librairie Thorin et fils/ Fontemoing.

Gsell, S. 1911. *Atlas archéologique de l'Algérie.* Algiers: A. Jourdan.

Gsell, S. 1913. *Histoire ancienne de l'Afrique du Nord, vol. 1: Les conditions du développement historique, les temps primitifs, la colonisation phénicienne et l'empire de Carthage*. Paris: Hachette.

Gsell, S. 1918a. *Histoire ancienne de l'Afrique du Nord, vol. 2. L'État carthaginois*. Paris: Hachette.

Gsell, S. 1918b. *Histoire ancienne de l'Afrique du Nord, vol. 3. Histoire militaire de Carthage*. Paris: Hachette.

Gsell, S. 1920. *Histoire ancienne de l'Afrique du Nord, vol. 4. La civilisation carthaginoise*. Paris: Hachette.

Gsell, S. 1927a. *Histoire ancienne de l'Afrique du Nord, vol. 5. Les royaumes indigènes: Organisation sociale, politique et économique*. Paris: Hachette.

Gsell, S. 1927b. *Histoire ancienne de l'Afrique du Nord, vol. 6. Les royaumes indigènes: Vie matérielle, intellectuelle et morale*. Paris: Hachette.

Gsell, S. 1928a. *Histoire ancienne de l'Afrique du Nord, vol. 7. La République romaine et les rois indigènes*. Paris: Hachette.

Gsell, S. 1928b. *Histoire ancienne de l'Afrique du Nord, vol. 8. Jules César et l'Afrique – La fin des royaumes indigènes*. Paris: Hachette.

Gsell, S. 1928c. Vieilles exploitations minières dans l'Afrique du Nord. *Hespéris* 8: 1–21 = Gsell 1981, 211–33.

Gsell, S. 1933. La Tripolitaine et le Sahara au IIIe siècle de notre ère. *Mémoires de l'Académie des Inscriptions et Belles-Lettres* 43(1): 149–66 = Gsell 1981, 157–74.

Gsell, S. 1981. *Etudes sur l'Afrique Antique: Scripta varia*. Lille: Diffusion PUL.

Gsell, S. and Joly, C.A. 1914. Khamissa, Mdaourouch, Announa. *Fouilles exécutées par le Service des monuments historiques de l'Algérie, vol. 1:* Khamissa. Alger/Paris: Carbonel/de Boccard.

Gsell, S. and Joly, C.A. 1918. Khamissa, Mdaourouch, Announa. *Fouilles exécutées par le Service des monuments historiques de l'Algérie, vol. 3:* Announa. Alger/Paris: Carbonel/de Boccard.

Gsell, S. and Joly, C.A. 1922. Khamissa, Mdaourouch, Announa. *Fouilles exécutées par le Service des monuments historiques de l'Algérie, vol. 2:* Mdaouroch. Alger/Paris: Carbonel/de Boccard.

Guédon, S. 2010. *Le voyage dans l'Afrique romaine*. Bordeaux: Ausonius.

Guédon, S. (ed). 2012a. *Entre Afrique et Egypte: Relations et échanges entre les espaces du sud de la Méditerranée à l'époque romaine*. Bordeaux: Ausonius.

Guédon, S. 2012b. Voie de mer, voie de terre: Les itinéraires de voyage entre l'Afrique Proconsulaire et l'Egypte romaine à travers les sources écrites. In Guédon 2012a, 45–70.

Guédon, S. 2014. La *lex uestis peregrinae* dans le tarif de Zaraï. *Antiquités Africaines* 50: 111–23.

Guédon, S. 2016. La *statio camellariorum*: Circulation et transports caravaniers dans le corpus des *ostraca* de Bu Njem. *Zeitschrift für Papyrologie und Epigraphik* 197: 249–56.

Guédon, S. 2017. Circulation and trade of textiles in the southern borders of Roman Africa: New hypotheses. In Mattingly et al. 2017a, 259–84.

Guédon, S. 2018a. *La frontière romaine de l'Africa sous le Haut-Empire*. Madrid: Casa de Velázquez.

Guédon, S. (ed). 2018b. *La frontière méridionale du Maghreb: Approches croisées (Antiquité–Moyen Âge)*. La frontière méridionale du Maghreb, vol. 1. Bordeaux: Ausonius.

Guédon, S. (ed). 2020. *Vivre, circuler et échanger sur la bordure septentrionale du Sahara: Anitiquité–époque moderne*. La frontière méridionale du Maghreb, vol. 2. Bordeaux: Ausonius.

Guérin, V. 1862. *Voyage archéologique dans la Régence de Tunis, vol. 1*. Paris: H. Plon.

Guéry, R. 1985. *La nécropole orientale de Sitifis (Sétif, Algérie): Fouilles de 1966–1967*. Études d'Antiquités africaines. Paris: Éditions du CNRS.

Guéry, R. 1986. Chronologie de quelques établissements de la frontière romaine du sud tunisien à partir de la céramique collectée sur les sites. In *Akten des 13. Internationalen Limeskongresses (Aalen, 18–25 September 1983)*, 600–04. Stuttgart: Landesdenkmalamt Baden-Württemberg.

Guéry, R., and G. Hallier. 1998. L'arc municipal de *Bararus municipium* (Rougga, Tunisie). *Antiquités africaines* 34, 121–32.

Guéy, J. 1939. Note sur le *limes* romain de Numidie et le Sahara au IVe siècle. *Mélanges de l'Ecole Française de Rome* 56: 178–248.

Hachi S. and Kherbouche F. 2017. *La Numidie, Massinissa et l'histoire*. Actes du colloque international, Constantine 14–16 mai 2016. = *Libyca* n.s. 2.

Hachid, M. 2000. *Les premiers berbères entre Méditerranée, Tassili et Nil*. Aix-en-Provence: Edisud

Hachid, M. 2003. Le peuplement du Sahara central de la préhistoire à la période paléoberbère. Diversité ethnique et léns culturels. In M. Fantar 2002, 103–34.

Haeussler, R and Webster, E. 2020. Creolage. A bottom-up approach to cultural change in Roman times. *Theoretical Roman Archaeology Journal* 3(1): 5, 1–22.

Hales, S. and Hodos, T. (eds). 2010. *Material Culture and Social Identities in the Ancient World*. Cambridge: Cambridge University Press.

Halff, G. 1964. L'onomastique punique de Carthage. Répertoire et commentaire. *Karthago* 12: 61–145.

Hall, J.M. 1997. *Ethnic Identity in Greek Antiquity*. Cambridge: Cambridge University Press;

Hall, J.M. 2002. *Hellenicity: Between Ethnicity and Culture*. Chicago: Chicago University Press.

Hallier, G. 1987. Les citernes monumentales de *Bararus* (Henchir Rougga) en Byzacène. *Antiquités africaines* 23: 129–48.

Hallier, G., Marion, J. and Rebuffat, R. 1970. *Thamusida: Fouilles du service des antiquités du Maroc. 2*. Rome: École française de Rome.

Hamdoune, C. 1993. Ptolémée et la localisation des tribus de Tingitane. *Mélanges de l'Ecole Française de Rome. Antiquité* 105(1): 241–89.

Hamdoune, C. 1999. *Les* auxilia externa *africains des armées romaines (III*e *siècle av. J.-C. – IV*e *siècle ap. J.-C.)*. Montpellier: Université Paul Valéry.

Hamdoune, C. 2005. Specificité et identité des cavaliers africains de l'armée romaine. In Briand-Ponsart 2005a, 235–60.

Hamdoune, C. 2009. Les *macella* dans les cités de l'Afrique du Nord. *Antiquités africaines* 45: 27–36.

Hamdoune, C. 2010a. L'expédition de Maximien en Afrique. *Antiquités africaines* 46–48: 185–99.

Hamdoune, C. 2010b. Neptune et Mars dans la région des hautes steppes. In Bejaoui 2010, 245–57.

Hamdoune, C. 2011. La Tingitane: Spécificités et identité. In Briand-Ponsart and Modéran 2011, 43–62.

Hamdoune, C. 2014. Les gentes dans l'espace provincial des Maurétanies. In Briand-Ponsart 2014, 419–42.

Hamdoune, C. 2015. De Pline à la *Notitia* de 484: Toponymie et occupation de l'espace dans la moyenne vallée du Cheliff; état de la question. In Mrabet 2015, 55–74.

Hamdoune, C. (ed). 2016. *Parure monumentale et paysage dans la poésie épigraphique de l'Afrique romaine: Recueil de* carmina latina epigraphica. Scripta antiqua 85. Bordeaux: Ausonius.

Hamdoune, C. 2018. *Ad fines Africae Romanae: Les mondes tribaux dans les provinces maurétaniennes*. Scripta antiqua 111. Bordeaux: Ausonius.

Hamdoune, C. 2020. *Auxilia externa* et *gentes* dans les provinces maurétaniennes. *Antiquités africaines* 56: 285–92.

Hanoune, R. 1980. *Recherches archéologiques franco-tunisienennes à Bulla Regia, IV: Les mosaïques*. CEFR 28/4. Rome: École française de Rome.

Hansen, M.H. and Nielsen, T.H. 2004. *An Inventory of Archaic and Classical Poleis*. Oxford: Oxford University Press.

Hanson, J.W. 2016. *An Urban Geography of the Roman World, 100 B.C. to A.D. 300*. Oxford: Oxford University Press.

Harlow, M. and Laurence, R. 2002. *Growing Up and Growing Old in Ancient Rome: A Life Course Approach*. London: Routledge.

Harper, K. 2017. *The Fate of Rome: Climate, Disease, and the End of an Empire*. Princeton: Princeton University Press.

Harris, W.V. 1979. *War and Imperialism in Republican Rome 327–70 BC*. Oxford: Clarendon Press.

Harris, W.V. (ed). 1984. *The Imperialism of Mid-Republican Rome*. Rome: American Academy in Rome.

Harris, W.V. (ed). 2005. *Rethinking the Mediterranean*. Oxford: Oxford University Press.

Hartog, F. 2009. *The Mirror of Herodotus: The Representation of the Other in the Writing of History*. Translated by J. Lloyd. Berkeley: University of California.

Haselgrove, C. 1985. Inference from ploughsoil artefact samples. In C. Haselgrove, M. Millet and I. Smith (eds), *Archaeology from the Ploughsoil: Studies in the Collection and Interpretation of Field Survey Data*, 7–29. Sheffield: J.R. Collis Publications.

Haselgrove, C.C. and Moore, T. (eds). 2007. *The Later Iron Age in Britain and Beyond*. Oxford: Oxbow Books.

Haselgrove, C.C. and Pope, R. (eds). 2007. *The Earlier Iron Age in Britain and Beyond*. Oxford: Oxbow Books.

Hauschild, T., Zillinger, M. and Kottmann, S.L. 2007. Syncretism in the Mediterranean: Universalism, cultural relativism and the issue of the Mediterranean as a cultural area. *History and Anthropology* 18(3): 309–32.

Haverfield, F. 1912. *The Romanization of Roman Britain*. 2nd edition. Oxford: Clarendon Press.

Haverfield, F. and MacDonald, G. 1924. *The Roman Occupation of Britain*. Oxford: Clarendon Press.

Hawthorne, J.W.J. 1997. Post-processual economics: The role of African red slip ware vessel volume in Mediterranean demography. In K. Meadows, C. Lemke and J. Heron (eds), *TRAC 96: Proceedings of the Sixth Annual Theoretical Roman Archaeology Conference*, 29–37. Oxford: Oxbow Books.

Hayes, J.W. 1972. *Late Roman Pottery*. London: British School at Rome.

Haynes, I.P. 2001. The impact of auxiliary recruitment on provincial societies from Augustus to Caracalla. In L. de Blois (ed), *Administration, Prosopography and Appointment Policies in the Roman Empire*, 62–83. Amsterdam: Gieben.

Haynes, I. 2013. *Blood of the Provinces. The Roman* Auxilia *and the Making of the Provincial Society from Augustus to Severus*. Oxford: Oxford University Press.

Haywood, R.M. 1938. Africa. In T. Frank (ed), *An Economic Survey of Ancient Rome, vol. 4*, 1–119. Baltimore: Johns Hopkins University Press.

Hellström, M. 2020. Epigraphy and ambition: Building inscriptions in the hinterland of Carthage. *Journal of Roman Studies* 110: 57–90.

Hermassi, M. 2003. Quelques données sur les vestiges oléicoles autour de Thelepte. In Bejaoui 2003, 81–92.

Herring, E. and Lomas, K. 2009. *Gender Identities in Italy in the First Millennium BC*. British Archaeological Reports, International Series S1983. Oxford: Archaeopress.

Hesein, M.A.H. 2015. *Bridging the Eastern and Western Mediterranean: The Roman Harbour Sites on the Coast of Cyrenaica, North-East of Libya*. Unpublished PhD thesis, University of Leicester.

Heurgon, J. 1969. Inscriptions étrusques de Tunisie. *Comptes rendus des séances de l'Académie des inscriptions et belles-lettres* 1969, 113(4): 526–51.

Hilaire, Capt. 1900. L'emplacement de Tacape. *Bulletin archéologique du comité des travaux historiques et scientifiques* 1900: 115–25.

Hilali, A. 2016. *Armée et religion dans le monde romain: La Legio Tertia Augusta en Afrique.* Paris: Mimésis.

Hinard, F. 1991. La militarisation de l'Afrique sous la République. *Antiquités africaines* 27: 33–38.

Hingley, R. 2000. *Roman Officers and English Gentlemen: The Imperial Origins of Roman Archaeology.* London: Routledge.

Hingley, R. 2005. *Globalizing Roman Culture: Unity, Diversity and Empire.* London: Routledge.

Hingley, R. 2007. Situating a post-colonial Roman Britain. *Journal of Roman Archaeology* 20: 535–40.

Hingley, R. 2008. *The Recovery of Roman Britain 1586–1906: A Colony so Fertile.* Oxford: Oxford University Press.

Hingley, R. 2010. Cultural diversity and unity: Empire and Rome. In Hales and Hodos 2010, 54–75.

Hingley, R. 2021. From colonial discourse to post-colonial theory: Roman archaeology and the province of Britannia. In Belvedere and Bergemann 2021, 181–91.

Hirt, A.M. 2010. *Imperial Mines and Quarries in the Roman World: Organizational Aspects 27 BC–AD 235.* Oxford: Oxford University Press.

Hitchner, R.B. 1988. The Kasserine Archaeological Survey, 1982–1986 (University of Virginia, USA – Institut National d'Archéologie et d'Art de Tunisie). *Antiquités africaines* 24: 7–41.

Hitchner, R.B. 1989: The organization of rural settlement in the Cillium-Thelepte region (Kasserine, central Tunisia). *L'Africa romana* 6, 387–402.

Hitchner, R.B. 1990. The Kasserine Archaeological Survey, 1987. Institut national d'archéologie et d'art de Tunisie – University of Virginia, USA. *Antiquités africaines* 26, 231–60.

Hitchner, R.B. 1993a. Olive production and the the Roman economy: The case for intensive growth. In Amouretti and Brun 1993, 499–508.

Hitchner, R.B. 1993b. The Kasserine archaeological survey 1982–1985. *Africa* 11–12: 158–97.

Hitchner, R.B. 1994. Image and reality: The changing face of pastoralism in the Tunisian High Steppe. In J. Carlsen (ed), *Landuse in the Roman Empire*, 27–43. Analecta Romana Instituti Danici 22. Rome: L'Erma di Bretschneider.

Hitchner, R.B. 1995a. The culture of death and the invention of culture in Roman Africa. *Journal of Roman Archaeology* 8: 493–98.

Hitchner, R.B. 1995b. Historical text and archaeological context in Roman North Africa: The Albertini Tablets and the Kasserine Survey. In D. Small (ed), *Methods in the Mediterranean: Historical and Archaeological Views on Texts and Archaeology*, 124–42. Leiden: Brill.

Hitchner, R.B. 1995c. Irrigation, terraces, dams and aqueducts in the region of Cillium (mod. Kasserine). The role of water works in the development of a Roman-African town and its countryside. In Trousset 1995c, 143–58.

Hitchner, R.B. 2000a. Carthago. In Talbert 2000, Map 32 and map-by-map directory, 493–509.

Hitchner, R.B. 2000b. Theveste-Hadrumentum. In Talbert 2000, Map 33 and map-by-map directory, 510–19.

Hitchner, R.B. 2008. Globalization avant la lettre: Globalization and the history of the Roman empire. *New Global Studies* 2(2) (article 2) http://www.bepress.com/ngs/vol2/iss2/art2.

Hitchner, R.B. (ed). 2022a. *A Companion to North Africa in Antiquity.* Hoboken, NJ: Wiley Blackwell.

Hitchner, R.B. 2022b. The historiography of North Africa in antiquity: An overview. In Hitchner 2022a, 3–8.

Hitchner, R.B. and Mattingly, D.J. 1991. Fruits of Empire. The production of olive oil in Roman Africa. *National Geographic Research and Exploration* 7(1): 36–55.

Hobson, M.S. 2015a. *The North African Boom: Evaluating Economic Growth in the Roman Province of* Africa Proconsularis. JRA supplement 100. Portsmouth, RI: Journal of Roman Archaeology.

Hobson, M.S. 2015b. The African boom: The origins of economic growth in Roman North Africa. In Erdkamp et al. 2015, 207–33.

Hobson, M.S. 2016. Roman imperialism in Africa from the Third Punic War to the battle of Thapsus (146–46 BC). In Mugnai et al. 2016, 103–20.

Hobson, M.S. 2019a. Carthage after the Punic wars and the neo-Punic legacy. In López-Ruiz and Doak 2019, 183–96.

Hobson, M.S. 2019b. EAMENA training in the use of satellite remote sensing and digital technologies in heritage management: Libya and Tunisia workshops 2017–2019. *Libyan Studies* 50: 63–71.

Hobson, M.S. 2020. Roman towns and the settlement hierarchy of ancient North Africa: A bird's-eye view. In de Ligt and Bintliff 2020, 281–323.

Hobson, M.S. 2022. Africa under the Roman Republic. In Hitchner 2022a, 101–15.

Hodge, A.T. (ed). 1991. *Future Currents in Aqueduct Studies*. Leeds: Francis Cairns.

Hodos, T. 2006. *Local Responses to Colonization in the Iron Age Mediterranean*. London: Routledge.

Hodos, T. 2010. Local and global perspectives in the study of social and cultural identities. In Hales and Hodos 2010, 3–31.

Hodos, T., Lane, P., Guerds, A., Lilley, I., Shelach-Lavi, G., Pitts M., Versluys, M. and Stark, M. 2016. *The Routledge Handbook of Archaeology and Globalization*. London: Routledge.

Hoffman, G.L. 2011. Theory and methodology: Study of identities using archaeological evidence from Dura-Europos. In L.R. Brody and G.L. Hoffman (eds), *Dura-Europos: Crossroads of Antiquity*, 45–69. Boston: McMullen Museum of Art.

Hope, V.M. 2001. *Constructing Identity: The Roman Funerary Monuments of Aquileia, Mainz and Nîmes*. British Archaeological Reports, International Series S960. Oxford: Archaeopress.

Horden, P. 2012. Situations both alike? Connectivity, the Mediterranean, the Sahara. In J. McDougall and J. Scheele (eds), *Saharan Frontiers: Space and Mobility in Northwest Africa*, 25–38. Bloomington: Indiana University Press.

Horden, P. and Purcell, N. 2000. *The Corrupting Sea: A Study of Mediterranean History*. Oxford: Blackwell.

Horn, H.G. and Rüger, C.B. 1979. *Die Numider. Reiter un Könige nördlich der Sahara*. Köln: Rheinland-Verlag.

Hoyos, D. 2010. *The Carthaginians*. London: Routledge.

Hoyos, D. (ed). 2011. *A Companion to the Punic Wars*. Malden: Wiley.

Hudson, N.F. 2010. Changing places: The archaeology of the Roman *convivium*. *American Journal of Archaeology* 114(4): 663–95.

Hugoniot, C. 2000. *Rome en Afrique: De la chute de Carthage aux débuts de la conquête arabe*. Paris: Flammarion.

Hulin, L., Timby, J., and Mutri, G. 2009. The Western Marmarica Coastal Survey 2009: Preliminary report. *Libyan Studies* 40: 179–87.

Hulin, L., Timby, J., Muftah, A., and Mutri, G. 2010. Western Marmarica Coastal Survey 2010: Preliminary report. *Libyan Studies* 41: 155–62.

Humphrey, J.H. (ed). 1976a. *Apollonia, the Port of Cyrene: excavations by the University of Michigan. Libya Antiqua* supplement 4. Tripoli: Department of Antiquities.

Humphrey, J.H. (ed). 1976b. *Excavations at Carthage 1975 Conducted by the University of Michigan, vol. 1.* Ann Arbor: Kelsey Museum of Archaeology.

Humphrey, J.H. (ed). 1977. *Excavations at Carthage 1976 Conducted by the University of Michigan, vol. 3.* Ann Arbor: Kelsey Museum of Archaeology.

Humphrey, J.H. (ed). 1978a. *Excavations at Carthage 1975 Conducted by the University of Michigan, vol. 2.* Ann Arbor: Kelsey Museum of Archaeology.

Humphrey, J.H. (ed). 1978b. *Excavations at Carthage 1976 Conducted by the University of Michigan, vol. 4.* Ann Arbor: Kelsey Museum of Archaeology.

Humphrey, J. H. 1980a. Bibliography of the international campaign to save Carthage. In Pedley 1980, 123–52.

Humphrey, J.H. (ed). 1980b. *Excavations at Carthage 1977 Conducted by the University of Michigan, vol. 5.* New Delhi/Ann Arbor: Kelsey Museum of Archaeology.

Humphrey, J.H. (ed). 1981. *Excavations at Carthage 1977 Conducted by the University of Michigan, vol. 6.* New Delhi/Ann Arbor: Kelsey Museum of Archaeology.

Humphrey, J.H. (ed). 1982. *Excavations at Carthage 1978 Conducted by the University of Michigan, vol. 7.* Ann Arbor: Kelsey Museum of Archaeology.

Humphrey, J.H. 1986. *Roman Circuses: Arenas for Chariot Racing.* London: Batsford.

Humphrey, J.H. (ed). 1988. *The Circus and a Byzantine Cemetery at Carthage, vol. 1.* Ann Arbor: University of Michigan Press.

Humphrey, J.H. (ed). 2020. *For the Love of Carthage: Cemeteries, A Bath and the Circus in the Southwest Part of the City; Pottery, Brickstamps and Lamps from Several Sites: The Presence of Saints, and Urban Development in the Pertica Region.* JRA supplement 109. Portsmouth RI: Journal of Roman Archaeology.

Hunt, C.O., Brooks, L., Meneely, J., Brown, D., Buzaian, A. and Barker G. 2011. The Cyrenaican Prehistory Project 2011: Late Holocene environments and human activity from a cave fill in Cyrenaica, Libya. *Libyan Studies* 42: 77–87.

Hurlet, F. 2000. Pouvoir des images, images du pouvoir impérial. La province d'Afrique aux deux premiers siècles de notre ère. *Mélanges de l'Ecole Française de Rome. Antiquité* 112(1): 297–364.

Hurst, H. 1985. The war harbour of Carthage. *Studi Fenici* 2: 603–10.

Hurst, H. 1992. L'ilot de l'Amirauté, le port circulaire et l'avenue Borguiba. In Ennabli 1992, 79–94.

Hurst, H. 1994. *Excavations at Carthage: The British Mission, volume 2, 1: The Circular Harbour, North Side: The Site and Finds other than Pottery.* British Academy Monographs in Archaeology 4. Oxford: Oxford University Press.

Hurst, H. 1999. *The Sanctuary of Tanit at Carthage in the Roman Period: A Reinterpretation.* JRA supplement 30. Portsmouth, RI: Journal of Roman Archaeology.

Hurst, H. and Owen, S. (eds). 2005. *Ancient Colonizations. Analogy, Similarity and Difference.* London: Duckworth.

Hurst, H.R. and Roskams, S.P. 1984. *Excavations at Carthage: The British Mission, vol. 1,1: The Avenue du Président Habib Bourguiba, Salammbo: The Site and Finds other than Pottery.* Sheffield: British Academy.

Huskinson, J. (ed). 2000. *Experiencing Rome: Culture, Identity and Power in the Roman Empire.* London: Routledge.

IAM$_{lat}$ = Euzennat, M., Marion, J., Gascou, J. and De Kisch, Y. 1982. *Inscriptions antiques du Maroc 2. Inscriptions Latines.* Paris: CNRS Éditions.

IAM$_{lat}$*2* = Labory, N. 2003. *Inscriptions antiques du Maroc 2. Inscriptions Latines: supplément.* Paris: CNRS Éditions.

IAM$_{lib}$ = Galand, L. 1966. Inscriptions libyques. In Galand et al. 1966, 2–80.

IAM$_{pun}$ = Février, J.G. 1966. Inscriptions puniques et neopuniques. In Galand et al. 1966, 81–132.

Iancu, C. and Lassère, J.-M. 1985. *Juifs et judaïsme en Afrique du Nord dans l'Antiquité et le Haut Moyen Age.* Montpellier: Université Paul Valéry.

Ibba, A. (ed). 2001. *Uchi Maius 2: Le iscrizioni.* Sassari: Editrice Democratica Sarda.

Ibba, A. (ed). 2011a. *Ex oppidis et mapalibus: Studi sulle città e le campagne dell'Africa romana.* Ortacesus: Sandhi Edizioni.

Ibba, A. 2011b. Roma e le tribù dell'Africa tardo-antica. In Ibba 2011a, 13–51.

Ibba, A. 2012. *L'Africa Mediterranea in età romana (202 a.C. – 442 d.C.).* Roma: Carocci.

Ibba, A. 2020. Statuti e privilegi municipali in Africa: Un aggiornamento. In S. Perea Yébenes and M. Pastor Muñoz (eds), *El norte de África en época romana: Tributum in memoriam Enrique Gozalbes Cravioto*, 145–63. Madrid/Salamanca: Signifer Libros.

Ibba, A. and Mastino, A. 2011a. Utilisation de l'eau en Afrique du Nord dans le passé. In Ibba 2011a, 53–74.

Ibba, A. and Mastino, A. 2011b. La pastorizia nel Nord Africa e in Sardegna in età romana. In Ibba 2011a, 75–99.

Ibba, A. and Traina, G. 2006. *L'Afrique romaine de l'Atlantique à la Tripolitaine (69–439 apr. J.-C.).* Rosny-sur-Bois: Bréal éditions.

Ibba, A., Mastino, A. and Zucca, R. 2011. Communautés urbaines en Afrique méditerranéenne à l'époque romaine. In Ibba 2011a, 137–51.

Ifie, E. 1998. *The Elite of Roman Africa.* Ibadan: End-time Publishing.

ILAf = Cagnat, R., Merlin, A. and Chatelain, L. 1923. *Inscriptions Latines d'Afrique (Tripolitaine, Tunisie, Maroc).* Paris: Institut de France.

ILAlg 1 = Gsell, S. 1922. *Inscriptions Latines de l'Algérie, vol. 1: Inscriptions de la Proconsulaire.* Paris: Edouard Champion.

ILAlg 2.1–3 = Pflaum, H.-G. and Dupuis, X. 1957/1976/2003. *Inscriptions Latines de l'Algérie, vol. 2: Inscriptions de la confédération cirtéene, de Cuicul et de la tribu des Suburbures.* Alger: Société nationale d'édition et de diffusion.

ILS = Dessau, H. (ed). 1892–1916. *Inscriptiones Latinae Selectae.* Berlin: Weidmannsche Verlagsbuchhandlung.

ILT = Merlin, A. (ed). 1944. *Inscriptions Latines de la Tunisie.* Paris, Presses universitaires de France.

Inglebert, H. (ed). 2002a. *Idéologies et valeurs civiques dans le Monde romaine. Hommage à Claude Lepelley.* Paris: Picard.

Inglebert, H. 2002b. Citoyenneté romaine, romanités et identités romains sous l'empire. In Inglebert 2002a, 241–60.

Inglebert, H. 2005. *Histoire de la civilisation romaine.* Paris: Presses universitaires de France.

Insoll, T. (ed). 2007a. *The Archaeology of Identities: A Reader.* Abingdon: Routledge.

Insoll, T. 2007b. Configuring identities in archaeology. In Insoll 2007a, 1–18.

IRCyr2020 = Reynolds, J., Roueché, C. and Bodard, G. 2020. *Inscriptions of Roman Cyrenaica.* Online edition: https://ircyr2020.inslib.kcl.ac.uk/en/.

IPT = Levi Della Vida, G. and Amadasi Guzzo, M. 1987. *Iscrizioni puniche della Tripolitania (1927–1967)*. Rome, L'Erma di Bretschneider.

IRT = Reynolds, J.M. and Ward-Perkins, J.B. 1952. *Inscriptions of Roman Tripolitania*. Rome: British School at Rome. Online version (*IRT2021*): https://irt2021.inslib.kcl.ac.uk/en/.

Isaac, B. 1990. *The Limits of Empire: The Roman Army in the East*. Oxford: Oxford University Press.

Isaac, B. 2004. *The Invention of Racism in Classical Antiquity*. Princeton: Princeton University Press.

Isnard, H. 1971. *Le Maghreb*. Paris: Presses universitaires de France.

Jallet-Huant, M. 2006. *Les rois numides et la conquête de l'Afrique du Nord par les romains*. Chrenton: Presses de Valmy.

James, S. 1999a. *The Atlantic Celts: Ancient People or Modern Invention?* Madison: University of Wisconsin Press.

James, S. 1999b. The community of soldiers: A major identity and centre of power in the Roman Empire. In P. Baker, S. Jundi and R. Witcher (eds), *TRAC 98: Proceedings of the Eighth Annual Theoretical Roman Archaeology Conference*, 14–25. Oxford: Oxbow Books.

James, S. 2001a. Romanization and the peoples of Britain. In Keay and Terrenato 2001, 187–209.

James, S. 2001b. Soldiers and civilians: Identity and interaction in Roman Britain. In James and Millett 2001, 77–89.

James, S. and Millett, M. (eds). 2001. *Britons and Romans: Advancing An Archaeological Agenda*. CBA Research Reports 125. York: Council for British Archaeology.

Janon, M. 1973. Recherches à Lambèse: 1: La ville et les camps; 2: Aquae Lambaesitanae. *Antiquités africaines* 7: 193–254.

Janon, M. 1977. Lambèse et l'occupation militaire de la Numidie méridionale. In *Studien zu den Militärgrenzen Roms II: Vorträge des 10 Internationalen Limeskongresses in der Germania Inferior*, 473–86. Cologne: Rheinland-Verlag.

Janon, M. 2005. *Lambèse: Capitale militaire de l'Afrique romaine*. Ollioules: Les éditions de la Nerthe.

Jacques, F. 1991. Municipia libera de l'Afrique proconsulaire. In *Epigrafia: Actes du colloque de Rome (27–28 maggio 1988) en mémoire de Attilio Degrassi*, 583–606. CEFR 143. Rome: École française de Rome.

Jaworski, P. and Misiewicz, K. (ed). 2015. *Ptolemais in Cyrenaica. Results of Non-Invasive Surveys*. Warsaw: Wydawnictwa Uniwersytetu Warszawskiego.

Jenkins, G.K. and Lewis, R.B. 1963. *Carthaginian Gold and Electrum Coins*. London: Spink.

Jerray, E. 2015. *La production d'amphores en Tripolitaine occidentale: Les ateliers de Zitha et de sa région en Tunisie méridionale*. Unpublished PhD thesis, Aix-Marseille Université.

Jerray, E. 2016. Les ateliers d'amphores de Zítha et le potentiel économique de la Tripolitaine tunísienne. In Mugnai et al. 2016, 157–70.

Jodin, A. 1966. *Mogador: Comptoir phénicien du Maroc atlantique*. Études et Travaux d'Archéologie Marocaine 2. Rabat: Éditions marocaines et internationales.

Jodin, A. 1987. *Volubilis Regia Iubae. Contribution à l'étude des civlisations du Maroc antique préclaudien*. Paris: De Boccard.

Johnson, D.L. 1969. *The Nature of Nomadism: A comparative Study of Pastoral Migrations in South-western Asia and Northern Africa*. Department of Geography Research Paper 118. Chicago: University of Chicago.

Johnson D.L. 1973. *Jabal al-Akhdar, Cyrenaica: An Historical Geography of Settlement and Livelihood*. Department of Geography Research Paper 148. Chicago: University of Chicago.

Johnston, P.A. and Kaufman, B. 2019. Metallurgy and other technologies. In López-Ruiz and Doak 2019, 401–22.

Joly, E. and Tomasello, F. 1984. *Il tempio a divinità ignota di Sabratha*. Rome: L'Erma di Bretschneider.

Jones, G.D.B. 1989a. The development of air photography in North Africa. In D. Kennedy (ed), *Into the Sun: Essays on Air Photography in Archaeology in Honour of Derrick Riley*, 29–47. Sheffield: Department of Archaeology and Prehistory.

Jones, G.D.B. 1989b. Town and city in Tripolitania: Studies in origins and development 1969–89. *Libyan Studies* 20: 91–106.

Jones, G.D.B. and Mattingly, D.J. 1980. Fourth-century manning of the "Fossatum africae". *Britannia* 11: 323–6.

Jones, G.D.B. and Mattingly, D.J. 1990. *An Atlas of Roman Britain*. Oxford: Blackwell.

Jones, R.J.F. 1987. Burial customs of Rome and the provinces. In J. Wacher (ed), *The Roman World, vol.* 2, 812–31. London: Routledge.

Jones, S. 1997. *The Archaeology of Ethnicity: Constructing Identities in the Past and Present*. London: Routledge.

Jongeling, K. 1994. *North-African Names from Latin Sources*. Leiden: Research School CNWS.

Jongeling, K. 2008. *Handbook of Neo-Punic Inscriptions*. Tübingen: Mohr Siebek.

Jongeling, K. and Kerr, R. (eds). 2005. *Late Punic Epigraphy: An Introduction to the Study of Neo-Punic and Latino-Punic Inscriptions*. Tübingen: Mohr Siebek.

Joppolo, G. 1967. La tavola delle unità di misura nel mercato augusteo di Leptis Magna. *Quaderni di Archeologia della Libya* 5: 89–98.

Jordan, D.R. 1996. Notes from Carthage. *Zeitschrift für Papyrologie und Epigraphik* 111: 115–23.

Jouffroy, H. 1986. *La construction publique en Italie et dans l'Afrique Romaine*. Études et travaux 2. Strasbourg: Association pour l'étude de la civilisation romaine.

Julien, C.-A. 1978. *Histoire de l'Afrique du Nord. Des origines à 1830*. Paris: Payot.

Kaabia, R. (ed). 2019. *Sullecthum: Salakta et ses environs à l'époque antique et médiévale*. Actes des journées d'étude sur Ksour Essef. Sousse: Université de Sousse.

Kaddache, M. 1971. *L'Algérie dans l'antiquité*. Algiers: Société nationale d'édition et de diffusion.

Kadra, K.F. 1983. *Les Djedars: monuments funéraires berbères de la région de Frenda*. Alger: Office des Publications Universitaires.

Kallala, N. 1992, Capitoles d'Afrique et statuts municipaux. *Cahiers de Tunisie* 45(159): 185–96.

Kallala, N. 2003. La dédicace d'un sénateur africain retrouvée: Caius Iunius Faustinus Placidus Postumianus (CIL VIII 597 et 11754). In Khanoussi 2003, 381–94.

Kallala, N. 2004. Musulamii et Siccenses. *L'Africa romana* 15: 407–19.

Kallala, N. and Sanmartí, J. 2011. *Althiburos 1: La fouille dans l'aire du capitole et la nécropole méridionale*. Sèrie Documenta 18. Taragona: Institut Català d'Arqueologia Clàssica.

Kallala, N., Sanmartí, J., Belarte, M.C. and Ramon, J. 2008. Recherches sur l'occupation d'Althiburos (région du Kef, Tunisie) et de ses environs à l'époque numide. *Pyrenae* 39(1): 67–113.

Kallala, N., Sanmartí, J., Jornet, R., Belarte, M.C., Canela, J., Chérif, S., Campillo, J., Montanero, D., Miniaoui, S., Bermúdez, X., Fadrique, T., Revilla, V., Ramon, J. and Ben Moussa, M. 2014a. La nécropole mégalithique de la région d'*Althiburos*, dans le massif du Ksour (Gouvernorat du Kef, Tunisie): Fouille de trois monuments. *Antiquités Africaines* 50: 19–60.

Kallala, N., Sanmartí, J., Belarte, M.C., Ramon, J., Ben Moussa, M. and Revilla, V. 2014b. L'occupation du territoire d'*Althiburos* du temps des Numides à la fin e l'Antiquité. In Briand-Ponsart 2014, 179–204.

Kallala, N., Sanmartí, J., Belarte,M.C. (eds). 2016. *Althiburos 2: L'aire du capitole et dans la nécropole méridionale: Études*. Sèrie Documenta 28. Tarragona: Institut Català d'Arqueologia Clàssica.

Kallala, N., Sanmartí, J. and Belarte, M.C. (eds). 2017. *Althiburos 3: La nécropole protohistorique de Althiburos (Massif du Ksour)*. Sèrie Documenta 30. Taragona: Institut Català d'Arqueologia Clàssica.

Kallala, N., Ribichini, S., Botto, M., Fabiani, F. 2018. Le tophet-sanctuaire de Ba'al Hammon-Saturne d'*Althiburos*: De la découverte à la fouille. Résultats préliminaires. In Baratte et al. 2018, 113–34.

Kapuściński, R. 2002. *The Shadow of the Sun: My African Life*. London: Penguin.

Kasdi, Z. and Slimani, S. 2020. Nouvelles données sur la *cohors IV Sygambrorum*. *Antiquités africaines* 56: 335–44.

Keay, S.J. and Terrenato, N. (eds). 2001. *Italy and the West: Comparative Issues in Romanization*. Oxford: Oxbow Books.

Keenleyside, A., Schwarcz, H., Stirling, L. and Ben Lazreg, N. 2009. Stable isotopic evidence for diet in a Roman and late Roman population from Leptiminus, Tunisia. *Journal of Archaeological Science* 36: 51–63.

Kehoe, D.P. 1988. *The Economics of Agriculture on Roman Imperial estates in North Africa*. Hypomnemata 89. Göttingen: Vandenhoeck and Ruprecht.

Kehoe, D.P. 2007. *Law and the Rural Economy in the Roman Empire*. Ann Arbor: University of Michigan Press.

Kehoe, D.P. 2013. The state and production in the Roman agrarian economy. In Bowman and Wilson 2013, 33–53.

Kehoe, D.P. 2015. Property rights over land and economic growth in the Roman empire. In Erdkamp et al. 2015, 88–106.

Kenrick, P.M. 1985. *Excavations at Sidi Khrebish, Benghazi (Berenice) 3.1: The Fine Pottery*. *Libya Antiqua* supplement 5.3. Tripoli: Department of Antiquities.

Kenrick, P.M. 1986. *Excavations at Sabratha 1948–1951: A Report on the Excavations Conducted by Dame Kathleen Kenyon and J. Ward-Perkins*. London: Society for the Promotion of Roman Studies.

Kenrick, P.M. 2009. *Libya Archaeological Guides: Tripolitania*. London: Silphium Press.

Kenrick, P.M. 2013. *Libya Archaeological Guides: Cyrenaica*. London: Silphium Press.

Kerr, R.M. 2007. *Latino-Punic and its Linguistic Environment*. Göttingen: Universiteit Leiden.

Khanoussi, M. (ed). 2003. *Protohistoire, cités de l'Afrique du Nord, fouilles et prospections récentes*, Actes du VIIIe colloque international sur l'histoire et archéologie de l'Afrique du Nord (Tabarka, 8–13 May 2000). Tunis: INP.

Khanoussi, M. 2008. Urbanisme et statut municipal en Afrique Proconsulaire. Le cas de *Sufetula*. In Bejaoui 2008, 73–84.

Khanoussi, M. 2010. Le fait urbain dans les hautes steppes (Tunisie) durant l'antiquité. In Bejaoui 2010, 219–29.

Khanoussi, M. and Mastino, A. 1997. *Uchi Maius 1: Scavi e ricerche epigrafiche in Tunisia*. Sassari: Editrice Democratica Sarda.

Khanoussi, M. and Mastino, A. 2012. *D'Uchi Maius* à Rome … en passant par Pouzzoles. À propos de nouvelles découvertes épigraphiques à Henchir Douamis, en Tunisie. In Demougin and Scheid 2012, 147–77.

Khanoussi, M. and Maurin, L. (eds). 1997. *Dougga (Thugga): Etudes épigraphiques*. Bordeaux: Ausonius.

Khanoussi, M. and Maurin, L. (eds). 2000. *Dougga, fragments d'histoire: Choix d'inscriptions latines éditées, traduites et commentées (1er – IVeme siècles)*. Bordeaux: Ausonius.

Khanoussi, M. and Maurin, L. (eds). 2002. *Mourir à Dougga: Recueil des inscriptions funéraires*. Bordeaux: Ausonius.

Khanoussi M. and Strocka V.M. (ed). 2002. *Thugga 1: Grundlagen und Berichte*. Mainz: Philipp von Zabern.

Khanoussi, M. and von Rummel, P. 2012. Simitthus (Chimtou, Tunesien). Vorbericht über die Aktivitäten 2009–2012. *Mitteilungen des deutschen archäologischen Instituts, Römische Abteilung* 118: 179–222.

Khanoussi, M., Ritter, S. and von Rummel, P. 2004. The German-Tunisian project at Dougga: First results of the excavations south of the Maison du Trifolium. *Antiquités Africaines* 40–41: 43–66.

Kiesling, B. and Isaksen, L. 2014. Anonymous Stadiasmus of the Great Sea. Translation of text from Müller, K. (ed), *Geographi Graeci: Minores, vol. 1* (1855). ToposText project. Available online at: https://topostext.org/work/217.

Kilgore, L., and Jurmain, R. 1988. Analysis of the human skeletal remains. In Humphrey 1988, 257–84.

Kirwan, L.P. 1971. Roman expeditions to the Upper Nile and the Chad-Darfur region. In Gadallah 1971, 253–61.

Ki-Zerbo, J. (ed). 1980. *General History of Africa 1: Methodology and African Prehistory*. London: UNESCO/Heinemann.

Kolendo, J. 1991. *Le colonat en Afrique sous le Haut-Empire*. 2nd edition. Collection de l'Institut des sciences et techiques de l'antiquité 447. Paris: Les Belle Lettres.

Kotula, T. 1976. Les Africains et la domination de Rome. *Dialogue d'histoire ancienne* 2: 337–58.

Kraeling, C.H. 1962. *Ptolemais: City of the Libyan Pentaopolis*. Chicago: Oriental Institute Publications.

Kramer, J.C. 2014. *The Roman Riders: Ethnicity and Iconography on Roman Cavalrymen Tombstones*. Unpublished PhD thesis, Brigham Young University.

Krandel-Ben Younès, A. 1988. Typologie des tombes des nécropoles puniques en pays numide. *Reppal* 4: 1–48.

Krandel-Ben Younès, A. 1993. La nécropole rurale de Thigibba Bure (Djebba). *Reppal* 7–8: 179–288.

Krandel-Ben Younès, A. 2002. *La présence punique en pays Numide*. Tunis: INP.

Krandel-Ben Younès, A. 2013. Les Numides, quelle identité? *Africa* 23: 45–59.

Krimi, H. 2005. Stèles inédites de Gabès. *Africa: Séances scientifiques* 3: 227–37.

Krimi, H. 2014. Montagnards et semi-nomades dans le déclenchment de la guerre et l'instauration de la paix dans la zone du limes tripolitanus. In Coltelloni-Trannoy and Le Bohec 2014, 177–92.

Krings, V. (ed). 1995. *La civilisation phénicienne et punique: Manuel de recherche*. Leiden: Brill.

Kuper, R. and Kröpelin, S. 2006. Climate-controlled Holocene occupation in the Sahara: Motor of Africa's evolution. *Science* 313(5788): 803–87.

Kuttner, A. 2013. Representing Hellenistic Numidia, in Africa and at Rome. In Prag and Quinn 2013, 216–72.

Lachaux, J.-C. 1977. *Les théâtres et amphithéâtres d'Afrique procsonsulaire.* Aix-en-Provence: Édisud.

Ladjimi Sebai, L. 2011. *La femme en Afrique à l'époque romaine (à partir de la documentation épigraphique).* Tunis: INP.

Lafond, Y. (ed). 2005. *L'Afrique romaine: Ier siècle avant J.-C. début Ve siècle après J.-C.* (= *Pallas* 68). Toulouse: Presses universitaires Mirail.

Lafrenz Samuels, K. 2010. *Mobilizing Heritage in the Maghrib: Rights, Development, and Transnational Archaeologies.* Unpublished PhD thesis, Stanford University.

Lafrenz Samuels, K. 2012. Roman archaeology and the making of heritage citizens in Tunisia. In D.M. Totten and K. Lafrenz Samuels (eds), *Making Roman Places: Past and Present.* JRA supplement 89, 159–70. Portsmouth, RI: Journal of Roman Archaeology.

Lafrenz Samuels, K. 2015. Heritage rights and the rhetoric of reality in pre-revolution Tunisia. In K. Lafrenz Samuels and T. Rico (eds), *Heritage Keywords: Rhetoric and Redescription in Cultural Heritage*, 243–58. Boulder: University Press of Colorado.

L'Afrique dans l'Occident romain 1990 = *L'Afrique dans l'Occident romain (Ier siècle av. J.-C.–IVe siècle ap. J.-C.).* Actes du colloque organisé par l'École française de Rome sous le patronage de l'institute national d'archéologie et d'art de Tunis, (Rome, 3–5 décembre 1987). Rome: École française de Rome.

Lamare, N. 2019. *Les fontaines monumentales en Afrique romaine.* CEFR 557. Rome: École française de Rome

Lamirande, E. 1976. Nord-Africains en quête de leur passé: Coups d'oeil sur la période romaine et chrétienne. *Revue de l'Université d'Ottawa* 46: 5–23.

Lancel, S. 1955. Suburbures et Nicibes: Une inscription de Tigisis. *Libyca* 3: 289–98.

Lancel, S. 1965. Tipasitana I: Fouilles dans la nécropole préromaine occidentale de Tipasa (rapport sur les travaux réalisés au cours d'un stage archéologique en juillet 1964). *Bulletin d'Archéologie Algérienne* 1 (1962–1965): 41–74.

Lancel, S. 1968. Tipasitana III: La nécropole préromaine occidentale de Tipasa: Rapport préliminaire (campagnes de 1966 et 1967). *Bulletin d'Archéologie Algérienne* 3: 85–166.

Lancel, S. 1970. Tipasitana IV: La nécropole romaine occidentale de la porte de Césarée: Rapport préliminaire. *Bulletin d'Archéologie Algérienne* 4: 149–266.

Lancel, S. 1983. *Introduction à la connaissance de Carthage: La Colline de Byrsa à l'époque punique.* Paris: Éditions Recherche sur le Civilisations.

Lancel, S. 1990. Problèmes d'urbanisme de la Carthage punique, à la lumière des fouilles anciennes et récentes. In CTHS Strasbourg 1990, 9–30.

Lancel, S. 1992. *Carthage.* Paris: Fayard.

Lancel, S. 1995. *Carthage: A History.* Translated by Nevill, A. Oxford: Blackwell.

Lancel, S. (ed). 1999. *Numismatique, langues, écritures et arts du livre, spécificités des arts figurés.* Actes du VIIe Colloque international sur l'histoire et l'archéologie de l'Afrique du Nord antique et médiévale (Nice, 21–31 octobre 1996). Paris: Éditions du CTHS.

Lancel, S. 2003. *L'Algérie antique: De Massinissa à Saint Augustin.* Paris: Menges.

Lancel, S. (ed). 2005. *Saint Augustin: La Numidie et la societé de son temps*. Scripta antiqua 14. Bordeaux: Ausonius.

Lancel, S. and Morel, J.-P. 1992. La colline de Byrsa: Les vestiges puniques. In Ennabli 1992, 43–68.

Landwehr, C. 1993. *Die Römischen Skulpturen von Caesarea Mauretaniae: Denkmäler aus Stein und Bronze, vol. 1: Idealplastik – weibliche Figuren benannt*. Berlin: Reimer Mann Verlag.

Landwehr, C. 2000. *Die Römischen Skulpturen von Caesarea Mauretaniae: Denkmäler aus Stein und Bronze, vol. 2: Idealplastik – männliche Figuren*. Mainz: Philipp von Zabern.

Landwehr, C. 2006. *Die Römischen Skulpturen von Caesarea Mauretaniae: Denkmäler aus Stein und Bronze, vol. 3: Bacchus und Gefolge, Masken, Fabelwesen, Tiere, Bukranien nicht Bennenbare Figuren*. Mainz: Philipp von Zabern.

Landwehr, C. 2008. *Die Römischen Skulpturen von Caesarea Mauretaniae: Denkmäler aus Stein und Bronze, vol. 4: Porträtplastik, Fragmente von Porträt- oder Idealplastik*. Mainz: Philipp von Zabern.

Lapierre, L. 2012. Initialisation du projet de cartographie de l'Afrique antique – système d'information géographique. *Aouras* 7: 219–36.

Lapierre, L. and Briand-Ponsart, C. 2017. Projet collaborative de cartographie de l'Afrique du Nord antique, AFRICA. In Mrabet 2017b, 293–306.

Lapierre, L., Decramer L.R., Hilton, R. and Alouani, S. 2015. Projet de carthographie de l'Afrique antique sur système d'information géographique (SIG): Études de voies dans leurs environnements antiques. In Mrabet 2015, 119–45.

Laporte, J.-P. 1985. Fermes, huileries et pressoirs de Grande Kabylie. In CTHS Grenoble 1985, 127–46.

Laporte, J.-P. 1989. *Rapidum. Le camp de la cohorte des Sardes en Maurétanie Césarienne*. Sassari: Università degli studi di Sassari.

Laporte, J.-P. 1992. Datation des stèles libyques figurées de Grande Kabylie. *L'Africa romana* 9: 389–423.

Laporte, J.-P. 1999. La limite entre les Maurétanies Césarienne et Sitifienne. In Lepelley and Dupuis 1999, 213–19.

Laporte, J.-P. 2003. Ptolémée et la Maurétanie césariennee. *Comptes rendus des séances de l'Académie des inscriptions et belles-lettres* 2003, 147(1): 171–95.

Laporte, J.-P. 2004a. Trois sites militaries sévériens en Algérie moyenne: Grimidi, Tarmount (Aras), El Gahra. *L'Africa romana* 15: 439–78.

Laporte, J.-P. 2004b. Les armées romaines et la révolte de Firmus en Maurétanie césarienne. In Le Bohec and Wolff 2004, 279–97.

Laporte, J.-P. 2005. Les djedars, monuments funéraires berbères de la région de Frenda et de Tiaret. In Briand-Ponsart 2005a, 321–406.

Laporte, J.-P. 2009. Armée et urbanisme: Quelques sites militaries antiques d'Algérie moyenne (est de la Maurétanie Césarienne, ouest de la Numidie) et leur devenir. In Groslambert 2009, 21–53.

Laporte, J.-P. 2011. Particularités de la province de Maurétanie Césarienne (Algerie central et occidentale). In Briand-Ponsart and Modéran 2011, 111–50.

Laporte, J.-P. 2014. Une maison-forte du IVe siècle: Le Kasr el-Kaoua (Ammi-Moussa, Algérie). In Briand-Ponsart 2014, 469–508.

Laporte, J.-P. 2021. Chasses et captures numides et romaines de fauves africains. In Blanc-Bijon et al. 2021, 297–306.

Laporte, J.-P. and Dupuis, X. 2011. *De Nigrenses Maiores* à Négrine. *Antiquités africaines* 45: 51–102.
Laporte, J.-P. and M'Charek, A. 2010. Musulames. *Encyclopédie Berbère* 32: 5144–55.
Laporte, J.-P., Oulebsir, R., Hamadache, T., Chaker, S. and Brun, J.-P. 2013. Olivier (La culture de l'olivier, de l'Antiquité à la Kabylie contemporaine. *Encyclopédie Berbère* 35: 5730–49.
Laporte, R. 1974. L'habitat rural d'époque romaine en Maurétanie Tingitane. *Rivista storica dell'Antichità* 4: 171–221.
Laronde, A. 1987. *Cyrène et la Libye héllenistique: Libykai Historiai: De l'époque républicaine au principat d'Auguste.* Paris: CNRS Éditions.
Laronde, A. 2009. L'armée romaine en Cyrénaïque. In Groslambert 2009 15–20.
Laronde, A. and Golvin, J.-C. 2001. *L'Afrique antique. Histoire et monuments.* Paris: Tallandier.
Laroui, A. 1970. *L'histoire du Maghreb: Un essai de synthèse.* Paris: Maspero.
Lassère, J.-M. 1973. Recherches sur la chronologie des épitaphes païennes de l'Africa. *Antiquités africaines* 7: 7–152.
Lassère, J.-M. 1977. *Ubique Populus: Peuplement et mouvements de population dans l'Afrique romaine de la chute de Carthage.* Paris: Éditions du CNRS.
Lassère, J.M. 1979. Rome et le "sous-développement" de l'Afrique. *Revue des Etudes Anciennes* 81: 67–104.
Lassère, J.-M. 1980. Remarques onomastiques sur la liste militaire de Vezereos (ILAf 27). In W.S. Hanson and L.J.F. Keppie (eds), *Roman Frontier Studies 1979 XII. Papers presented to the 12th International Congress of Roman Frontier Studies,* 955–75. British Archaeological Reports International Series S71. Oxford: BAR Publications.
Lassère, J.-M. 1982a. L'organisation des contacts de population dans l'Afrique romaine, sous la République et au Haut-Empire. In H. Temporini (ed), *Aufstieg und Niedergang der römischen Welt: Principat, vol. 10/2: Teilband Politische Geschichte (Provinzen und Randvölker: Afrika mit Ägypten [Forts.]),* 397–426. Berlin: De Gruyter.
Lassère, J.-M. 1982b. Un conflit 'routier': Observations sur les causes de la guerre de Tacfarinas. *Antiquités africaines* 18: 11–25.
Lassère, J.-M. 1988. Les Afri et l'armée romaine. *L'Africa romana* 5: 177–88.
Lassère, J.-M. 1991. Le recrutement romain et les Musulames. In CTHS Strasbourg 1991, 299–311
Lassère, J.M. 1994. La cohorte des Gétules. In Le Bohec 1994, 244–53.
Lassère, J.-M. 1995. Nécropoles, monuments et rites funéraires: periode romaine. Bilan épigraphique. In Trousset 1995a, 103–09.
Lassère J.-M. 1998. Épigraphie africaine et paysages ruraux. In A. Rousselle and M.-C. Marandet (eds), *Le paysage rural et ses acteurs,* 65–90. Perpignan: Presses Universitaires de Perpignan.
Lassère, J.-M. 2005a. Onomastica africana XVII/XVIII: Gentilices romains d'origine africaine. In Briand-Ponsart 2005a, 179–92.
Lassere, J.-M. 2005b. Societé et vie sociale. In Cabouret 2005, 144–67.
Lassere, J.-M. 2005c. Choix d'inscriptions relatives à l'histoire de l'Afrique. Traductions avec éléments de commentaire. In Cabouret 2005, 34–73.
Lassère, J.-M. 2012. Onomastica africana XIX sur les cognomina 'traduits'. In Corda and Mastino 2012, 145–49.
Lassère, J.-M. 2015. *Africa, quasi Roma: 256 av. J.-C. – 711 apr. J.-C.* Paris: CNRS Éditions.
Lassère, J.-M. and Slim, H. 2010. *Maisons de Clupea. Exemples de l'architecture domestique dans un port de l'Afrique proconsulaire: Les maisons de l'école de pêche.* Paris: Études d'Antiquités africaines.

Lassère, J.-M. et al. 1993. *Les Flavii de Cillium: Étude architecturale, épigraphique, historique et littéraire du mausolée de Kasserine (CIL VIII, 211–216).* CEFR 169. Rome: École française de Rome.

Lassus, J. 1969. *Visite à Timgad.* Alger: Ministère de l'Education Nationale, Direction des Affaires Culturelles.

Lassus, J. 1981. *La forteresse byzantine de Thamugadi: Fouilles à Timgad 1938–1956, vol. 1.* Paris: CNRS Éditions.

Laubenheimer-Leenhardt, F. 1971. Bibliographie d'archéologie marocaine 1961–1970. *Bulletin d'Archéologie Marocaine* 8: 249–77.

Laureano, P. 1991. *Sahara: Jardin méconnu.* Paris: Larousse.

Laurence, R., Esmonde Cleary, S. and Sears, G. 2011. *The City in the Roman West: c.250 BC–c.AD 250.* Cambridge: Cambridge University Press.

Lavagnini, B. 1928. Il centurione di Bu Ngem (Q. Avidius Quintianus). *Rivista di Filologia e Istruzione Classica* 56: 416–22.

Law. R.C.C. 1978. North Africa in the Hellenistic and Roman periods, 323 BC to AD 305. In Fage 1978, 148–210.

Lawless, R.I. 1972. The concept of *tell* and *sahara* in the Maghreb: A reappraisal. *Transactions of the Institute of British Geographers* 57: 125–37.

Lawless, R.I. 1978. Romanisation et résistance berbère dans la Maurétanie Césarienne (Algérie occidentale). In M. Galley (ed), *Actes du 2e Congrès Int. d'étude des cultures de la Méditerranée occidentale, vol. 2,* 161–67. Alger: Société Nationale d'Edition et de Diffusion.

Le Boeuf, Capt. 1905. La voie romaine de *Tacapes* à *Aquae Tacapitanae. Bulletin archéologique du comité des travaux historiques et scientifiques* 1905: 346–50.

Le Bohec, Y. 1979. *Bibliographie analytique de l'archéologie militaire de l'Afrique du Nord.* Paris.

Le Bohec, Y. 1986. La stratégie de Rome en Afrique de 238–284. In CTHS Montpellier 1986, 377–90.

Le Bohec, Y. 1987. Les syriens dans l'Afrique romaine: civils ou militaires? *Karthago* 21: 81–92.

Le Bohec, Y. 1989a. *La Troisième Légion Auguste.* Paris: Éditions CNRS.

Le Bohec, Y. 1989b. *Les unités auxiliaires de l'armée romaine en Afrique Proconsulaire et Numidie sous le Haut-Empire.* Paris: Éditions CNRS.

Le Bohec, Y. 1990. La recherche bibliographique sur l'Afrique romaine. *L'Africa romana* 7: 1001–08.

Le Bohec, Y. 1991. La recherche récente sur l'armée romaine d'Afrique (1977–1989). *Antiquités africaines* 27: 21–31.

Le Bohec, Y. (ed). 1994. *L'Afrique, la Gaule, la religion à l'époque romaine.* Brussels: Latomus.

Le Bohec, Y. 1995. La frontière militaire de la Numidie, de Trajan à 238. In Rousselle 1995, 119–42.

Le Bohec, Y. 1996. *Histoire militaire des guerres puniques.* Paris: Éditions du Rocher.

Le Bohec, Y. 1999. Frontières et limites militaires de la Maurétanie Césarienne sous le Haut-Empire. In Lepelley and Dupuis 1999, 111–27.

Le Bohec, Y. 2000. *The Imperial Roman Army.* London: Routledge.

Le Bohec, Y. 2003. *Les discours d'Hadrien à l'armée d'Afrique: exercitatio.* Paris: de Boccard.

Le Bohec, Y. 2004. L'armée romaine d'Afrique de Dioclétien à Valentinien I. In Le Bohec and Wolff 2004, 251–65.

Le Bohec, Y. 2005a. *Histoire de l'Afrique romaine: 146 avant J.-C.–439 après J.-C.* Paris: Picard.

Le Bohec, Y. 2005b. L'onomastique de l'Afrique romaine sous le Haut-Empire et les *cognomina* dits "africains". In Lafond 2005, 217–39.

Le Bohec, Y. 2008. L'architecture militaire à Lambèse (Numidie). *Archäologisches Korrespondenzblatt* 38(2): 247–62.

Le Bohec, Y. 2014a. La guerre en Afrique sous le Haut-Empire: Problématique. In Coltelloni-Trannoy and Le Bohec 2014, 13–20.

Le Bohec, Y. 2014b. La guerre en Afrique sous le Haut-Empire: Chronologie. In Coltelloni-Trannoy and Le Bohec 2014, 23–34.

Le Bohec, Y. 2021. *Les Juifs dans l'Afrique romaines*. Saint-Macaire: Memoring.

Le Bohec, Y. and Wolff, C. (eds). 2004. *L'armée romaine de Dioclétien à Valentinien I*[er]. Actes du congrès international de Lyon, 12–14 septembre 2002. Paris: Boccard.

Le Quellec, J.-L. 2006. L'adaptation aux variations climatiques survenues au Sahara central durant l'Holocène. In M.H. Fantar 2006, 109–29.

Le Quellec, J.-L. 2011. Arts rupestres, écritures et protoécritures en Afrique: L'exemple du libyque. *Afriques* [online], Debates and readings. Accessed: 8 April 2020. http://journals.openedition.org/afriques/716.

Le Roux, P. 2004. La romanisation en question. *Annales. Histoire, Sciences Sociales* 59e année, 2: 287–311.

Le Roux, P. 2006. Regarder vers Rome aujourd'hui. *Mélanges de l'Ecole Française de Rome. Antiquité* 118(1): 159–66.

Lee, B.T., Finkelpearl, E. and Graverini, L. (eds). 2014. *Apuleius and Africa*. London: Routledge.

Leglay, M. 1961. *Saturne africain: Monuments, vol 1: Afrique proconsulaire*. Paris: Arts et Métiers Graphiques.

Leglay, M. 1962. *Les Gaulois en Afrique*. Brussels: Latomus.

Leglay, M. 1966a. *Saturne africain: Monuments, vol. 2: Numidie-Mauritanie*. Paris: CNRS Éditions.

Leglay, M. 1966b. *Saturne Africain: Histoire*. BEFAR 205. Paris: De Boccard.

Leglay, M. 1968a. Les Flaviens et l'Afrique. *Mélanges de l'Ecole Française de Rome* 80: 201–46.

Leglay, M. 1968b. A la rechereche d'Icosium. *Antiquités africaines* 2: 7–54.

Leglay, M. 1971. La vie religieuse à Lambèse d'après de nouveaux documents. *Antiquités africaines* 5: 125–53.

Leglay, M. 1975. Les syncrétismes dans l'Afrique ancienne. In F. Dunand and P. Lévêque (eds), *Les syncrétismes dans les religions de l'antiquité*, 123–51. Leiden: Brill.

Leglay, M. 1984. Les religions de l'Afrique romaine au 2e siècle d'après Apulée et les inscriptions. *L'Africa romana* 1: 47–61.

Leglay, M. 1991. Un centre de syncrétisme en Afrique: *Thamughadi* de Numidie. *L'Africa romana* 8: 67–78.

Leigh, M. 2000. Lucan and the Libyan tale. *Journal of Roman Studies* 90: 95–109.

Leitch, V., Duckworth, C., Cuénod, A., Mattingly, D.J., Sterry, M. and Cole, F. 2017. Early Saharan trade: The inorganic evidence. In Mattingly et al. 2017a, 287–340.

Leitch, V., Bonifay, M., Capelli, C. and Mattingly, D.J. 2018. Pre-desert Tripolitania: A new archaeological and archaeometrical examination of red slip ware from the Ghirza excavations and the Libyan Valleys Survey. *Rei Cretariae Romanae Fautorum Acta* 45: 759–64.

Lengrand, D. 1994. L'inscription de *Petra* et la révolte de Firmus. *Bulletin archéologique du comité des travaux historiques et scientifiques: Afrique du Nord* n.s. 23B: 159–70.

Lengrand, D. 1999. Le *limes* intérieur de la *Notitia Dignitatum*: Des barbares dans l'Empire. In Lepelley and Dupuis 1999, 221–40.

Lengrand, D. 2005. Langues en Afrique antique. In Briand-Ponsart 2005a, 119–25.

Lenoir, E. 1996. *Banasa*: Un exemple de prospection géophysique. *L'Africa romana* 11: 1067–72.

Lenoir, E. 2005. La ville romaine de Zilil du Ier au IVe siècle ap. J.-C. In Lafond 2005, 65–76.

Lenoir, M. 2011. *Le camp romain: Proche-Orient et Afrique du Nord.* BEFAR 345. Rome: École française de Rome.

Lenoir, M., Akerraz, A. and Lenoir, E. 1987. Le forum de Volubilis: Eléments du dossier archéologique. In *Los foros romanos de las provincia occidentales.* Actas de la Mesa Retonda celebraia en Valencia 1986, 203–19. Madrid: Ministerio de cultura.

Lenski, N. 2017. Peasant and slave in Late Antique North Africa, c.100–600 CE. In R.L. Testa, *Late Antiquity in Contemporary Debate,* 113–55. Cambridge: Cambridge Scholars Publishing.

Leone, A. 1996. Un'adultera meretrix a Bulla Regia: Alcuni aspetti della città tardoantica. *L'Africa romana* 11: 1371–83.

Leone, A. 2007a. *Changing Townscapes in North Africa from Late Antiquity to the Arab Conquest.* Bari: Edipuglia.

Leone, A. 2007b. Changing urban landscapes: Burials in North African cities from the late antique to Byzantine periods. In Stone and Stirling 2007a, 164–203.

Leone, A. 2013a. Pottery from the FP project excavation in Jarma. In Mattingly 2013, 325–408.

Leone, A. 2013b. *The End of the Pagan City: Religion, Economy, and Urbanism in Late Antique North Africa.* Oxford: Oxford University Press.

Leone, A. 2017. Pottery and trade in north and sub-Saharan Africa during late antiquity. The distribution of North African finewares. In Mattingly et al. 2017a, 369–92.

Leone, A. 2022. Christian North Africa in antiquity. In Hitchner 2022a, 354–72.

Leone, A. and Mattingly, D.J. 2002. Vandal, Byzantine, and Arab rural landscapes in North Africa. In N. Christie (ed), *Landscapes of Change: Rural Evolutions in Late Antiquity and the Early Middle Ages,* 135–62. Aldershot: Ashgate.

Leone, A. and Moussa, F. 2013. Roman Africa and the Sahara. In Mitchell and Lane 2013, 777–88.

Leone, A., Leitch, V. and Mattingly, D.J. 2013. Pottery catalogues. In Mattingly 2013a, 683–706.

Lepelley, C. 1967. Déclin ou stabilité de l'agriculture africaine au Bas-Empire? A propos d'une loi de l'empereur Honorius. *Antiquités africaines* 1: 135–44.

Lepelley, C. 1974. La préfecture de tribu dans l'Afrique du Bas-Empire, *Mélanges d'histoire ancienne offerts à William Seston,* 285–95. Paris: de Boccard.

Lepelley, C. 1979. *Les cités de l'Afrique romaine au Bas-Empire, vol. 1: La permanence d'une civilisation municipals.* Paris: Études Augustiniennes.

Lepelley, C. 1981. *Les cités de l'Afrique romaine au Bas-Empire, vol. 2: Notices d'histoire municipale.* Paris: Études Augustiniennes.

Lepelley, C. (ed). 1998a. *Rome et l'integration de l'Empire (44 av. J.-C. – 260 ap. J.-C.), vol. 2: Apprôches régionales du Haut-Empire romaine.* Paris: Presses universitaires de France.

Lepelley, C. 1998b. L'Afrique. In Lepelley 1998a, 71–112

Lepelley, C. 2001. *Aspects de l'Afrique romaine. Les cités, la vie rurale, le christianisme.* Munera 15. Bari: Edipuglia.

Lepelley, C. 2002. La diabolisation du paganisme et ses conséquences psychologiques: Les angoisses de Publicola, correspondant de saint Augustin. In L. Mary and M. Sot (eds), *Impies et païens entre Antiquité et Moyen Âge*, 81–96. Paris: Picard

Lepelley, C. 2003. L'Afrique et sa diversité vues par Saint Augustin. In Lancel 2003b, 29–43.

Lepelley, C. 2004. The perception of Late Roman Africa: From decolonization to the re-appraisal of Late Antiquity. In C. Straw and R. Lim (eds), *The Past Before Us: The Challenge of Historiographies of Late Antiquity*, 25–32. Bibliothèque de l'Antiquité Tardive 6. Turnhout: Brepols.

Lepelley, C. 2005a. Témoinages de saint Augustin sur l'ampleur et les limites de l'usage de la langue punique dans l'Afrique de son temps. In Briand-Ponsart 2005a, 127–53.

Lepelley, C. 2005b. Deux ruptures dans l'histoire de l'Afrique romaine: Les Flaviens et les Vandales. In Lafond 2005, 49–62.

Lepelley, C. 2005c. L'Afrique et sa diversité vues par saint Augustin. In Lancel 2005, 29–43.

Lepelley, C. and Dupuis, X. (eds). 1999. *Frontières et limites géographiques de l'Afrique du Nord antique. Hommage à Pierre Salama.* Paris: Publications de la Sorbonne.

Lequement, R. 1979. *Fouilles à l'amphithéâtre de Tébessa (1965–1968).* 2e supplément au Bulletin d'Archéologie Algérienne. Alger: Service des Antiquités de l'Algérie.

Lequement, R. 1980. Le vin africain a l'époque impériale. *Antiquités africaines* 16: 185–93.

Le Quesne, C., Basell, L.S. and Sheibani, R. 2010. Archaeology in the Sirte Basin: Preliminary results of mitigation surveys carried out for Shell 2007–2009. *Libyan Studies* 41: 7–32.

Leschi, L. 1942. Rome et les nomades du Sahara central. *Travaux de l'Institut de Recherches Sahariennes* 1: 47–62 = Leschi 1957, 65–74.

Leschi, L. 1943. Le centenarium d'Aqua Viva. *Revue Africaine* 87: 5–22 = Leschi 1957, 47–57.

Leschi, L. 1947. La vigne et le vin dans l'Afrique ancienne. *Bulletin économique et juridique de l'OFALAC*, 101–04 = Leschi 1957, 80–84.

Leschi, L. 1948. Une assignation des terres sous Septime Sévère. *Recueil des notices et mémoires de la Société Archéologique de la province de Constantine* 66: 103–16 = 1957, 75–79.

Leschi, L. 1949. Découvertes épigraphiques dans le camp de Gemellae (El-Kasbat, Algérie). *Comptes rendus des séances de l'Académie des inscriptions et belles-lettres* 1949, 93(3): 220–226 = Leschi 1957, 318–24.

Leschi, L. 1953. *Djemila: antique Cuicul.* Alger: Publications du Gouvernement général de l'Algérie.

Leschi, L. 1957. *Études d'épigraphie d'archéologie et d'histoire africaines.* Paris: Arts et Métiers graphiques.

Leveau, P. 1973. L'aile II des Thraces, la tribu des Mazices et les praefecti gentis en Afrique du Nord. *Antiquités africaines* 7: 153–91.

Leveau P. 1975. Paysanneries antiques du pays Béni-Ménacer: À propos des "ruines romaines de la région de Cherchel (Algérie)". *Bulletin archéologique du comité des travaux historiques et scientifiques: Afrique du Nord* n.s. 8B: 3–26.

Leveau, P. 1976. Une aréa funéraire de la nécropole occidentale de Cherchel. *Bulletin d'Archéologie Algérienne* 5: 73–152.

Leveau, P. 1977a. Une vallée agricole des Nemenchas dans l'antiquité romaine: L'Oued Hallail entre Djeurf et Ain Mdila. *Bulletin archéologique du comité des travaux historiques et scientifiques: Afrique du Nord* n.s. 10–11B: 103–21.

Leveau, P. 1977b. Recherches historiques sur une région montagneuse de Maurétanie Césarienne: Des *Tigava Castra* à la mer. *Mélanges de l'Ecole Française de Rome. Antiquité* 89(1): 257–311.

Leveau, P. 1978a. La situation coloniale de l'Afrique romaine. *Annales. Economies, sociétés, civilisations* 33(1): 89–92.

Leveau, P. 1978b. L'agricola du Biha Bilta. À propos d'une inscription récemment découverte dans la région de Mateur. *Cahiers de Tunisie* 26(101): 7–13.

Leveau, P. 1983. Recherches sur les nécropoles occidentales de Cherchel (Caesarea Mauritaneae), 1880–1961. *Antiquités africaines* 19: 85–173.

Leveau, P. 1984. *Caesarea de Maurétanie: Une ville romaine et ses campagnes.* Rome: École française de Rome.

Leveau, P. 1985a. Pressoirs à huile autour de Caesarea de Maurétanie (Cherchel, Algérie). Problèmes d'interpretation historique. In *Histoire des techniques et sources documentaires: Méthodes d'approche et expérimentation en région méditerranéene,* Aix-en-Provence: Université de Provence, 193–97.

Leveau, P. 1985b. Les enceintes augustéennes d'Afrique à la rencontre de l'archéologie de l'histoire et du droit. In *Les enceintes augustéennes dans l'occident romain (France, Italie, Espagne, Afrique du Nord).* Actes du colloque international de Nîmes: IIIe Congrès archéologique de Gaule méridionale, 9–12 octobre 1985, 151–58. Nîmes: École antique de Nîmes.

Leveau. P. 1986. Occupation du sol, géosytèmes et systèmes sociaux. Rome et ses ennemis des montagnes et du désert dans le Maghreb antique. *Annales. Economies, sociétés, civilisations* 41(6): 1345–58.

Leveau, P. 1988. Le pastoralisme dans l'Afrique antique. In C.R. Whittaker (ed), *Pastoral Economies in Classical Antiquity,* 177–95. Cambridge: Proceedings of the Cambridge Philological Society.

Leveau, P. 1990. L'organisation de l'espace agricole en Afrique à l'époque romaine. In *L'Afrique dans l'Occident romain,* 129–41.

Leveau, P. 1993. L'Afrique. In Leveau et al. 1993, 154–200.

Leveau, P. 1995. Le *limes* d'Afrique à l'épreuve de nouveaux concepts (apport du point de vue systémique à la notion de limite et de frontière. In Rousselle 1995, 57–65.

Leveau, P. 2005. À propos de l'huile et du vin en Afrique romaine ou pourquoi "déromaniser" l'archéologie des campagnes d'Afrique. In Lafond 2005, 77–89.

Leveau, P. 2009a. Les conditions environnementales dans le nord de l'Afrique à l'époque romaine. Contribution historiographique à l'histoire du climat et des relations homme/milieu. In E. Hermon (ed), *Sociétés et climats dans l'Empire romain: Pour une perspective historique et systémique de la gestion des ressources en eau dans l'Empire romain,* 309–48, Naples: Editoriale Scientifica.

Leveau, P. 2009b. Transferts de technologie hydraulique dans l'Afrique romaine. In M. Ben Hassen (ed), *Eau et peuplement au Maghreb durant l'Antiquité et le Moyen Âge,* 117–41. Tunis: Université de Tunis.

Leveau, P. 2011. L'oléiculture en Afrique romaine, une necessaire réévaluation. In *L'olivier en Meditérrannée: Entre histoire et patrimoine,* 57–86. La Manouba: Centre de publication universitaire.

Leveau, P. 2012. D'Alexandrie d'Egypte à Caesarea de Maurétanie: Transfert de technologie hydraulique et diffusion d'un nouveau modèle urbain. In Guédon 2012a, 157–72.

Leveau, P. 2013. Évolution climatique et construction des ouvrages hydrauliques en Afrique romaine. In F. Baratte, C.J. Robin and E. Rocca (eds), *Regards croisés d'orient et d'occident: Les barrages dans l'antiquité tardive*, 125–38. Paris: De Boccard.

Leveau, P. 2014. L'Afrique romaine: Résistance et identité, histoire et mémoire. In S. Ferdi (ed), *L'affirmation de l'identité dans l'Algérie antique et médiévale: Combats et résistances*, 37–59. Algiers: CNRA.

Leveau, P. 2015. *Praefectus gentis* (en Afrique). *Encyclopédie Berbère* 38: 6407–15.

Leveau, P. 2018. Climat, sociétés et environnement aux marges sahariennes du Maghreb: Une approche historiographique. In Guédon 2018b, 19–106.

Leveau, P. 2020a. Lectures coloniales et post-coloniales de l'histoire de l'Afrique romaine. Histoire et constructions mémorielles. *Anabases* 32: 193–209.

Leveau, P. 2020b. L'économie domaniale romaine dans les Némemcha. "Forts byzantins", "salles à auges" L'apport des ostraca aux époques vandal et byzantine. *Bulletin d'Archéologie Algérienne* 8: 221–87.

Leveau, P. 2021. Le climat et l'antiquité tardive: Ses restitutions par les modernes et sa perception par les anciens. *Antiquité Tardive* 29: 81–94.

Leveau,P. 2022. The environment of North Africa. In Hitchner 2022a, 24–38

Leveau, P. and Paillet, J.L. 1976. *L'alimentation en eau de Caesarea de Maurétanie et l'aqueduc de Cherchell*. Paris: Éditions l'Harmattan.

Leveau, P., Sillières, P. and Vallat, J.-P. 1993. *Campagnes de la Méditerranée romaine: Occident*. Paris: Hachette.

Levi Della Vida, G. 1927. Le iscrizioni neopuniche della Tripolitania. *Rivista della Tripolitania* 3 (Libya 1): 91–116.

Levi Della Vida, G. 1935. Due iscrizioni imperiali neopuniche di Leptis Magna. *Africa Italiana* 6: 1–29.

Levi Della Vida, G. 1949. Iscrizioni neopuniche di Tripolitania. *Rendiconti della classe di scienze morali, storiche e filologiche* 8(4): 399–412.

Levi Della Vida, G. 1951. The neo-Punic dedication of the Ammonium at Ras el-Haddagia. (Appendix to Goodchild, R.G. Roman sites on the Tarhuna plateau of Tripolitania.) *Papers of the British School at Rome* 19: 65–68 = Goodchild 1976a, 93–96.

Levi Della Vida, G. 1963. Sulle iscrizioni latino-libiche della Tripolitania. *Oriens Antiquus* 2: 65–94.

Levi Della Vida, G. 1964a. Le iscrizioni neopuniche di wadi el-Amud. *Libya Antiqua* 1: 58–64.

Levi Della Vida, G. 1964b. Ostracon neopunico dalla Tripolitania. *Orientalia* 33: 1–14.

Levi Della Vida, G. 1965. Parerga neopunica. *Oriens Antiquus* 4: 59–72.

Levi Della Vida, G. and Guzzo, A.M. 1987. See *IPT*.

Levick, B. 1985. *The Government of the Roman Empire: A Sourcebook*. 1st edition. London: Croom Helm.

Levtzion, N. and Hopkins, J.F.P. (eds). 1981. *Corpus of Early Arabic Sources for West African History*. Cambridge: Cambridge University Press.

Lézine, A. 1971. Utique: Note d'archéologie punique. *Antiquités africaines* 5: 87–93.

Lichtenberger, A. 2016. "Sea without water": Conceptualizing the Sahara and the Mediterranean. In M. Dabag, D. Haller, N. Jaspert and A. Lichtenberger (eds), *New Horizons: Mediterranean Research in the 21st Century*, 267–83. Paderborn: Ferdinand Schöningh.

Lihoreau, M. 1993. *Djorf Torba: nécropole saharienne antéislamique*. Paris: Karthala.

Linstädter, J., and Kehl, M. 2012. The Holocene archaeological sequence and sedimentological processes at Ifri Oudadane, NE Morocco. *Journal of Archaeological Science* 39: 3306–23.

Lipiński, E. 1995. *Dieux et déeses de l'univers phénicien et punique*. Leuven: Peeters.

Livadiotti, M. and Rocco, G. 2018. *Exornata Aedes. La curia del foro vecchio di Leptis Magna*. Rome: L'Erma di Bretschneider.

Liverani, M. 2000. The Libyan caravan road in Herodotus IV.181–185. *Journal of the Economic and Social History of the Orient* 43(4): 496–520.

Liverani, M. (ed). 2006. *Aghram Nadharif. The Barkat Oasis (Sha'abiya of Ghat, Libyan Sahara) in Garamantian Times*. AZA Monographs 5.Firenze: Edizioni All'Insegna del Giglio.

Liverani, M. 2007. La struttura sociale dei Garamanti in base alle recenti scoperte archeologiche. *Rendiconti dell'Accademia Nazionale dei Lincei, Classe di scienze morali, storiche e filologiche* 9(18): 155–204.

Liverani, M. 2020. Technological innovations transfer through the hyper-arid belt. In Duckworth et al. 2020a, 53–67.

Lloyd, J.A. (ed). 1977. *Excavations at Sidi Khrebish, Benghazi (Berenice) 1: Buildings, coins, inscriptions, architectural decoration. Libya Antiqua* supplement 5.1. Tripoli: Department of Antiquities.

Lloyd, J.A. (ed). 1979. *Excavations at Sidi Khrebish, Benghazi (Berenice) 2: Economic life at Berenice; Sculpture and terracottas; Coarse pottery. Libya Antiqua* supplement 5.2. Tripoli: Department of Antiquities.

Lloyd, J.A., Bennett, P., Buttrey, T.V., Buzaian, A., El Amin, H., Fell, V., Kashbar, G., Morgan, G., Ben Nasser, Y., Roberts, P.C., Wilson, A.I. and Zimi, E. 1998. Excavations at Euesperides (Benghazi): An interim report on the 1998 season. *Libyan Studies* 29: 145–68.

Lloyd, J.A., Buzaian, A., and Coulton, J.J. 1995. Excavations at Euesperides (Benghazi), 1995. *Libyan Studies* 26: 97–100.

Lochin, C. 2021. Images de la chasse: réalités et fiction. In Blanc-Bijon et al. 2021, 307–16.

Longerstay, M. 1995. Les *haouanet*: état de la question. In Trousset 1995a, 33–53.

Longerstay, M. 1999. Prospection archéologique dans cinq vallées de la région syrtique (Libye) et fouille d'un bâtiment antique de la vallée du Wadi Harawah: Rapport préliminaire. *Bulletin archéologique du comité des travaux historiques et scientifiques: Afrique du Nord* n.s. 25: 53–68.

Longerstay, M. 2011. La présence de haouanet définit-elle une identité régionale dans le nord de la Proconsulaire? In Briand-Ponsart and Modéran 2011, 189–200.

López, D. and Cantero, F.J. 2016. Agriculture et alimentation à partir de l'étude des restes de grains et des fruits. In Kallala et al. 2016, 449–90.

López Castro, J.L., Ferjaouib, A., Mederos Martin, A., Martínez Hahnmüllerd, V. and Ben Jerbaniab, I. 2016. La colonización fenicia inicial en el Mediterráneo Central: Nuevas excavaciones arqueológicas en Utica (Túnez). *Trabajos de Prehistoria* 73: 68–89.

López-Ruiz, C. and Doak, B.R. 2019. *The Oxford Handbook of the Phoenician and Punic Mediterranean*. Oxford: Oxford University Press.

Lorcin. P.M.E. 1995. *Imperial Identities: Stereotyping, Prejudice and Race in Colonial Algeria*. London: I.B. Tauris

Lugan, B. 2000. *Histoire de Maroc des origines à nos jours*. Villeneuve: Perrin.

Luisi, A. 1994. *Popoli dell'Africa Mediterranea in età romana*. Bari: Università di Bari.

Luni, M. 2006. Un demi-siècle de recherches archéologiques à Cyrène. *Comptes rendus des séances de l'Académie des Inscriptions et Belles-Lettres* 2006, 150(4): 2173–201.

Luni, M. (ed). 2010. *Cirene nell'anticità*. Rome: L'Erma di Bretschneider.

Luni, M. (ed). 2014. *Cirene greca e romana*. Rome: L'Erma di Bretschneider.

Luquet, A. 1956. Prospection punique de la côte Atlantique du Maroc. *Hespéris* 43: 117–32.

Luquet, A. 1964. Contribution à l'Atlas archéologique du Maroc: Région de Volubilis. *Bulletin d'Archéologie Marocaine* 5: 291–300.

Luquet, A. 1966. Contribution à l'Atlas archéologique du Maroc: Région du Rharb. *Bulletin d'Archéologie Marocaine* 6: 365–75.

Luquet, A. 1975. Contribution a l'Atlas archeologique du Maroc. Le Maroc punique. *Bulletin d'Archéologie Marocaine* 9: 237–306.

Luttwak, E. N. 1976. *The Grand Strategy of the Roman Empire: From the First Century CE to the Third*. Baltimore/London: Johns Hopkins University Press.

Lutz, R. and Lutz, G. 1995. *The Secret of the Desert: The Rock Art of the Messak Settafet and Messak Mellet, Libya*. Innsbruck: Golf Verlag.

Lyons, C.L. and Papadopoulos, J.K. (eds). 2002. *The Archaeology of Colonialism*. Los Angeles: Getty Research Institute.

M'Charek, A. 1986. *Aspects de l'évolution démographique et sociale à Mactaris aux 2e et 3e siècles après J.-C.* Tunis: Université de Tunis.

M'Charek, A. 1999. De Zama à Kairouan: La Thusca et la Gomonia. In Lepelley and Dupuis 1999, 138–83.

M'Charek, A. 2008. L'identification des *Musulamii Magarenses* (ancêtres des "Mager" de la steppe Tunisienne?). In Bejaoui 2008, 141–56.

M'Charek, A., Jaidi, H., Baklouti, H., Sehili, S. et al. 2008. Recherches d'archéologique et d'histoire à Henchir Ghayadha/Bagat? (Tunisie). *Antiquités africaines* 44: 109–265.

M'Charek-Bourghida, F. 1997. Stèles et reliefs inédits de Bargou. *Africa* 15: 17–42.

MacDonald, K.C. 2011. A view from the south: Sub-Saharan evidence for contacts between North Africa, Mauritania and the Niger, 1000 BC – AD 700. In Dowler and Galvin 2011, 72–82.

MacDonald, W.L. 1982. *The Architecture of the Roman World, volume 2: An Urban Appraisal*. Yale: Yale University Press.

MacKendrick, P. 1980. *The North African Stones Speak*. London: Croom Helm.

Mackensen, M. 1993. *Die Spätantiken Sigillata- und Lampentöpfereien von El Mahrine (Nordtunesien): Studien zur Nordafrikanischen Feinkeramik des 4. bis 7. Jahrhunderts*. Munich: C.H. Beck'sche Verlagsbuchehandlung.

Mackensen, M. 1998. Centres of African red slip ware production in Tunisia from the late 5th to the 7th century. In L. Saguì (ed), *Ceramica in Italia: VI–VII secolo*, 23–40. Florence: Edizioni All'Insegna del Giglio.

Mackensen, M. 2000. Les castra hiberna de la legio III Augusta à Ammaedara/Haïdra. *L'Africa romana* 13(2): 1739–59.

Mackensen, M. 2009. Gasr Wames, eine burgusartige Kleinfestung des mittleren 3. Jahrhunderts am tripolitanischen limes Tentheitanus (Libyen). *Germania* 87(1): 75–104.

Mackensen, M. 2010a. Das commoduszeitliche Kleinkastell *Tisavar*/Ksar Rhilane am südtunesichen limes Tripolitanus. *Kölner Jahrb* 43: 451–68.

Mackensen, M. 2010b. Das severische Vexillationskastell Myd(---)/Gheriat el-Garbia am limes Tripolitanus (Libyen). Bericht über die Kampagne 2009. *Mitteilungen des Deutschen Archäologischen Instituts, Römische Abteilung* 116: 363–458.

Mackensen, M. 2011. Das severische Vexillationskastell Myd(---) und die spätantike Besiedlung in Gheriat el-Garbia (Libyen). Bericht über die Kampagne im Frühjahr 2010. *Mitteilungen des Deutschen Archäologischen Instituts, Römische Abteilung* 117: 247–375.

Mackensen, M. 2012. New fieldwork at the Severan fort of Myd(...)/Gheriat el-Garbia on the limes Tripolitanus. *Libyan Studies* 43: 41–60.

Mackensen, M. 2016. Survey and excavation of the German Archaeological Mission at the Roman fort of Myd(---)/Gheriat el-Garbia and its vicinity, 2009/2010. *Libya Antiqua* n.s. 6: 83–102

Mackensen, M. 2019. *Relief- und stempelverzierte nordafrikanische Sigillata des späten 2. bis 6. Jahrhunderts.* Wiesbaden: Ludwig Reichert Verlag.

Mackensen, M. 2021a. *Das severische Vexillationskastell Myd(---) / Gheriat el-Garbia am limes Tripolitanus (Libyen), vol. 1: Forschungsgeschichte, Vermessung, Prospektionen und Funde 2009–2010.* Wiesbaden: Reichert Verlag.

Mackensen, M. 2021b. Observations and results of recent excavations and surveys of late Roman military fortifications in the province of Tripolitana. *Libya Antiqua* n.s. 14: 111–45.

Mackensen, M. and Schneider, G. 2002. Production centres of African red slip ware (3rd–7th c.) in northern and central Tunisia: Archaeological provenance and reference groups based on chemical analysis. *Journal of Roman Archaeology* 15: 121–58.

MacKinnon, M. 2007a. Peopling the mortuary landscape of North Africa: An overview of the human osteological evidence. In Stone and Stirling 2007a, 204–40.

MacKinnon, M. 2007b. State of the discipline: Osteological research in Classical archaeology. *American Journal of Archaeology* 111(3): 473–504.

MacKinnon, M. 2007c. Osteological research in Classical archaeology: Extended bibliography. *American Journal of Archaeology* 111(3) supplemental materials: 1–40.

MacKinnon, M. 2010. "Romanizing" ancient Carthage: Evidence from zooarchaeological remains. In D.V. Campana et al. (eds), *Anthropological Approaches to Zooarchaeology: Colonialism, Complexity and Animal Transformations*, 168–77. Oxford: Oxbow Books.

MacKinnon, M. 2017. Animals, acculturation, and colonization in ancient and Islamic North Africa. In U. Albarella, M. Rizzetto, H. Russ, K. Vickers and S. Viner-Daniels (eds), *The Oxford Handbook of Zooarchaeology*, 466–78. Oxford: Oxford University Press.

MacMullen, R. 1974. *Roman Social Relations 50 BC to AD 284.* Yale: Yale University Press.

MacMullen, R. 2000. *Romanization in the Time of Augustus.* New Haven: Yale University Press.

Magalhães de Oliveira, J.-C. 2012. *Potestas populi: Participation populaire et action collective dans les villes de l'Afrique romaine tardive (vers 300–430 apr. J.-C.).* Turnhout: Brepols.

Maggi, S. 1998. Gli anfiteatri romani della Tunisia, cerniera urbanistica e ideologica tra città e campagna. *L'Africa romana* 12: 275–85.

Magnavita, S. 2013. Initial encounters: Seeking traces of ancient trade connections between West Africa and the wider world. *Afriques* [online] 04/2013. http://afriques.revues.org/1145.

Magnavita, S. 2017. Track and trace: Archaeometric approaches to the study of early trans-Saharan trade. In Mattingly et al. 2017a, 393–413.

Magnavita, S. 2020. The early history of weaving in West Africa: A review of the evidence. In Duckworth et al. 2020a, 183–207.

Mahjoubi, A. 1978. *Recherches d'histoire et d'archéologie à Henchir el-Faouar (Tunisie): La cité des Belalitani Maiores.* Tunis: Université de Tunis.

Mahjoubi, A. 1985. L'urbanisme de l'Afrique antique à l'époque préromaine. *L'Africa romana* 2: 201–11.

Mahjoubi, A. 2000. *Villes et structures urbaines de la province romaine d'Afrique.* Tunis: Centre de publication universitaire.

Mahjoubi, A. and Salama, P. 1981. The Roman and post-Roman period in North Africa. In Mokhtar 1981, 465–512.

Mahjoubi, A., Salomonson, J.W. and Ennabli, A. 1970. *La nécropole romaine de Raqqada.* Tunis: Ministère des affaires culturelles.

Malavolta, M. 1986. "Limes" – Mauretania Caesariensis. In E. De Ruggiero (ed), *Dizionario Epigrafico di Antichità Romane, vol. 4*, fasc 43.2–3 (1376), 67–76.

Malfitana, D. and Bonifay, M. (eds). 2016. *La ceramica africana nella Sicilia romana/La céramique africaine dans la Sicile romaine.* 2 vols. Catania: Istituto per i beni archeologici e monumentali.

Mandouze, A. 1982. *Prosopographie chrétienne du Bas-Empire: Prosopographie de l'Afrique chrétienne (303–533).* Paris: CNRS Éditions.

Manfredi, L.I. 2003. *La politica amministrativa di Cartagine in Africa.* Memoria dell'Accademia Nazionale dei Lincei 9.16. Rome: Accademia nazionale dei Lincei.

Mann, J.C. 1974. The frontiers of the Principate. In H. Temporini (ed), *Aufstieg und Niedergang der römischen Welt: Principat, vol. 1: Politische Geschichte (Allgemeines)*, 508–33. Berlin: De Gruyter.

Manton, L. 1988. *Roman North Africa.* London: Batsford.

Maraoui Telmini, B., Docter, R.F., Bechtold, B., Chelbi, F. and Van de Put, W. 2014. Defining Punic Carthage. In Quinn and Vella 2014, 113–47.

Marcy, G. 1936. *Les inscriptions libyques bilingues de l'Afrique du Nord.* Paris: Imprimerie nationale.

Marichal, R. 1979. Les ostraca de Bu Njem. *Comptes rendus des séances de l'Académie des inscriptions et belles-lettres* 1979, 123(3): 436–52.

Marichal, R. 1992. *Les ostraca de Bu Njem. Libya Antiqua* supplement 7. Tripoli: Grande Jamahira Arabe.

Marion, J. 1957. Les ruines anciennes de la région d'Oujda (dir du Ras Asfour). *Bulletin d'Archéologie Marocaine* 2:117–73.

Marion, J. 1959. L'éperon fortifié de Sidi-Medjahed (Oranie) *Libyca* 7: 27–41.

Marion, J. and Rebuffat, R. 1977. *Thamusida: Fouilles du service des antiquités du Maroc, 3.* CEFR 2/3. Rome: École française de Rome.

Marlière, E. and Torres Costa, J. 2007. Transport et stockage des denrées dans l'Afrique romaine: Le rôle de l'outre et du tonneau. In Mrabet and Remesal Rodríguez 2007, 85–106.

Martel, A. 1965. *Les confins saharo-tripolitains de la Tunisie (1881–1911).* 2 vols. Paris: Presses universitaires de France.

Martínez Sánchez, R.M., Vera Rodriguez, J.-C., Peña-Chocarro, L., Bokbot, Y., Pérez Jordà, G. and Pardo-Gordó, S. 2018. The Middle Neolithic of Morocco's north-western Atlantic strip: New evidence from the El-Khil caves (Tangier). *African Archaeological Review* 35: 417–42.

Martorella, F. 2020. An urban warehouse for foodstuffs in the *Iulia Valentia Banasa* colony (*Mauretania Tingitana*, Morocco). *Antiquités africaines* 56: 61–77.

Martorella, F. 2021. Installazioni militari a nord del fiume Loukkos nella provincia romana della *Mauretania Tingitana* (Marocco): Il campo militare di el Mers alla luce delle nuove indagini magnetiche. *Antiquités africaines* 57: 129–38.

Marzano, A. 2013. *Harvesting the Sea: The Exploitation of Marine Resources in the Roman Mediterranean*. Oxford: Oxford University Press.

Marzoli, D. 2018. Rencontres entre Orient et Occident: Les Phéniciens le long des côtes de la péninsule Ibérique et du Maroc. *Dialogues d'histoire ancienne* 44(1): 225–51.

Marzoli, D. and El Khayari, A. 2010. Vorbericht Mogador (Marokko) 2008. *Deutsches Archäologisches Institut, Madrider Mitteilungen* 51: 61–108.

Marzoli, D. and El Khayari A. 2018. Mogador (Essaouira), Marokko. Ein phönizischer Außenposten an der marokkanischen Atlantikküste. Die Arbeiten der Jahre bis 2018. *e- Forschungsberichte* 2018.1:72–75.

Mastino, A. 1984. La ricerca epigrafica in Tunisia (1973–1983). *L'Africa romana* 1: 72–87.

Mastino, A. 1986. La ricerca epigrafica in Algeria (1973–1985). *L'Africa romana* 3: 113–66.

Mastino, A. 1987. La ricerca epigrafica in Marocco (1973–86). *L'Africa romana* 4: 337–84.

Mastino, A. 2020. Les Syrtes dans l'imaginaire litteraire classique. In Perea Yébenes and Pastor Muñoz 2020, 31–62.

Masturzo, N. 2013. Leptis Magna: Note sulla geografia dell'abitato, tra emporio fenicio e città imperiale. *Mnème. Documenti, culture, storia del Mediterraneo e dell'Oriente Antico* 9: 185–213.

Matthews, J. 1976. Mauretania in Ammianus and the Notitia. In P. Bartholemew and R. Goodburn (eds), *Aspects of the Notitia Dignitatum*, 157–86. British Archaeological Reports International Series S15. Oxford: BAR Publishing.

Mattiaci, S. 2014. Apuleius and *Africitas*. In Lee et al. 2014, 87–111.

Mattingly, D.J. 1983. The Laguatan: A Libyan tribal confederation in the late Roman Empire. *Libyan Studies* 14: 96–108.

Mattingly, D.J. 1987a. New perspectives on the agricultural development of gebel and pre-desert in Roman Tripolitania. *Revue de l'Occident Musulman et de la Méditerranée* 41–42: 45–65.

Mattingly, D.J. 1987b. Libyans and the 'limes': Culture and society in Roman Tripolitania. *Antiquités africaines* 23: 71–94.

Mattingly, D.J. 1988a. The olive boom. Oil surpluses, wealth and power in Roman Tripolitania. *Libyan Studies* 19: 21–41.

Mattingly, D.J. 1988b. Oil for export? A comparison of Libyan, Spanish and Tunisian olive oil production in the Roman empire. *Journal of Roman Archaeology* 1: 33–56.

Mattingly, D.J. 1988c. Megalithic madness and measurement. Or how many olives could an olive press press? *Oxford Journal of Archaeology* 7(2): 177–95.

Mattingly, D.J. 1989a. Farmers and frontiers. Exploiting and defending the countryside of Roman Tripolitania. *Libyan Studies* 20: 135–53

Mattingly, D.J. 1989b. Ancient olive cultivation and the Albertini tablets. *L'Africa romana* 6: 403–15

Mattingly, D.J. 1991. The constructor of Gasr Duib, *Numisius Maximus, Trib(unus Cohortis I Syrorum sagittariorum). Antiquités africaines* 27: 75–82

Mattingly, D.J. 1992. War and peace in Roman Africa: Observations and models of state–tribe interaction. In Ferguson and Whitehead 1992, 31–60.

Mattingly, D.J. 1993. Maximum figures and maximizing strategies of oil production? Further thoughts on the processing capacity of Roman olive presses. In Amouretti and Brun 1993, 483–98.

Mattingly, D.J. 1995. *Tripolitania*. London: Batsford.

Mattingly, D.J. 1996a. From one colonialism to another: imperialism and the Maghreb, in J. Webster and N. Cooper (eds), *Roman Imperialism: Post-colonial perspectives*, 49–69. Leicester: University of Leicester.

Mattingly, D.J. 1996b. First fruit? The olive in the Roman world. In G. Shipley and J. Salmon (eds), *Human Landscapes in Classical Antiquity: Environment and Culture*, 213–53. London: Routledge.

Mattingly, D.J. 1996c. Olive presses in Roman Africa: Technical evolution or stagnation? *L'Africa romana* 11: 577–95

Mattingly, D.J. (ed). 1997a. *Dialogues in Roman Imperialism: Power, Discourse, and Discrepant Experience in the Roman Empire*. JRA supplement 23. Portsmouth, RI: Journal of Roman Archaeology.

Mattingly, D.J. 1997b. Dialogues of power and experience in the Roman Empire. In Mattingly 1997a, 7–26.

Mattingly, D.J. 1997c. Imperialism and territory: Africa, a landscape of opportunity? In Mattingly 1997a, 117–40.

Mattingly, D.J. 1998. Landscapes of imperialism in Roman Tripolitania. *L'Africa romana* 12: 163–79.

Mattingly, D.J. 1999. The art of the unexpected: Ghirza in the Libyan pre-desert. In Lancel 1999, 383–405.

Mattingly, D.J. 2000a. Tripolitana. In Talbert 2000, Map 35 and map-by-map directory, 529–44.

Mattingly, D.J. 2000b. Garama. In Talbert 2000, Map 36 and map-by-map directory, 545–51.

Mattingly, D.J. 2000c. Syrtica. In Talbert 2000, Map 37 and map-by-map directory, 552–57.

Mattingly, D.J. 2000d. Cyrene. In Talbert 2000, Map 38 and map-by-map directory, 558–69.

Mattingly, D.J. 2000e. Ammon. In Talbert 2000, Map 73 and map-by-map directory, 1108–16.

Mattingly, D.J. 2002. Vulgar and weak "Romanization" or time for a paradigm shift? *Journal of Roman Archaeology* 15: 536–40.

Mattingly, D.J. (ed). 2003a. *The Archaeology of Fazzān, vol. 1: Synthesis*. London: Society for Libyan Studies.

Mattingly, D.J. 2003b. Family values: Art and power at Ghirza in the Libyan pre-desert. In Scott and Webster 2003, 153–70.

Mattingly, D.J. 2004a. Nouveaux aperçus sur les Garamantes: Un état saharien? *Antiquités africaines* 37 (2001) [2004]: 45–61.

Mattingly, D.J. 2004b. Being Roman: Expressing identity in a provincial setting. *Journal of Roman Archaeology* 17: 5–25

Mattingly, D.J. 2006a. *An Imperial Possession: Britain in the Roman Empire*. London: Penguin.

Mattingly, D.J. 2006b. The imperial economy. In D.S. Potter, *A Companion to the Roman Empire*, 283–97. London: Blackwell.

Mattingly, D.J. 2006c. The Garamantes: The first Libyan state. In Mattingly et al. 2006, 189–204.

Mattingly, D.J. (ed). 2007a. *The Archaeology of Fazzān, vol. 2: Site Gazetteer, Pottery and Other Survey Finds*. London: Society for Libyan Studies.

Mattingly, D.J. 2007b. The African way of death: Burial rituals beyond the Roman Empire. In Stone and Stirling 2007a, 138–63.

Mattingly, D.J. 2008. Urbanism, epigraphy and identity in the towns of Britain under Roman rule. In H.M. Schellenberg, V.-E. Hirschmann and A. Krieckhaus (eds), *A Roman Miscellany: Essays in Honour of Anthony R. Birley on his Seventieth Birthday*, 53–71. Akanthina 3. Gdańsk/Oxford: Foundation for the Development of Gdańsk University/ Oxbow Books.

Mattingly, D.J. 2009. Peopling ancient landscapes: Potential and problems. In Bowman and Wilson 2009, 163–74.

Mattingly, D.J. (ed). 2010a. *The Archaeology of Fazzān, vol. 3: Excavations of C.M. Daniels*. London: Society for Libyan Studies.

Mattingly, D.J. 2010b. Cultural crossovers: Global and local identities in the Classical world. In Hales and Hodos 2010, 283–95.

Mattingly, D.J. 2011a. *Imperialism, Power and Identity: Experiencing the Roman Empire*. Princeton: Princeton University Press.

Mattingly, D.J. 2011b. The Garamantes of Fazzan: An early Libyan state with trans-Saharan connections. In Dowler and Galvin 2011, 49–60.

Mattingly, D.J. 2011c. Calculating ploughzone demographics: Some insights from arid zone surveys. In Bowman and Wilson 2011, 76–96.

Mattingly, D.J. (ed). 2013a. *The Archaeology of Fazzān, vol. 4: Survey and Excavations at Old Jarma (Ancient Garama) Carried Out by C.M. Daniels (1962–69) and the Fazzān Project (1997–2001)*. London: Society for Libyan Studies.

Mattingly, D.J. 2013b. To south and north: Saharan trade in antiquity. In H. Eckardt and S. Rippon (eds), *Living and Working in the Roman World*, 169–90. JRA supplement 95. Portsmouth RI: Journal of Roman Archaeology.

Mattingly, D.J. 2014a. Identities in the Roman world: Discrepancy, heterogeneity, hybridity, and plurality. In L. Brody and G.L. Hoffmann (eds), *Roman in the Provinces: Art on the Periphery of Empire*, 32–61. Boston: McMullen Museum of Art.

Mattingly, D.J. 2014b. Castles in the desert: Living in Libyan landscapes. In K. Boyle, R.J. Rabett and C.O. Hunt (eds), *Living in the Landscape: Essays in Honour of Graeme Barker*, 299–311. Cambridge: McDonald Institute for Archaeological Research

Mattingly, D.J. 2016. Who shaped Africa? The origins of urbanism and agriculture in Maghreb and Sahara. In Mugnai et al. 2016, 11–25.

Mattingly, D.J. 2017. The Garamantes and the origins of Saharan trade: State of the field and future agendas. In Mattingly et al. 2017a, 1–52.

Mattingly, D.J. 2019. A road less travelled? The Society for Libyan Studies and the landscape archaeology of Libya's early civilisations. *Libyan Studies* 50: 35–46.

Mattingly, D.J. 2022. Beyond barbarians: The Garamantes of the Libyan Sahara. In Hitchner 2022a, 65–80

Mattingly, D.J. and Barker, G.W. 2005. Out of Africa: Approaches to the landscape archaeology of the North Africa desert. In A. Bouet and F. Verdin (eds), *Territoires et paysages de l'âge du fer au Moyen Âge: Mélanges offerts à Philippe Leveau*, 185–96. Bordeaux: Ausonius.

Mattingly, D.J. and Cole, F. 2017. Visible and invisible commodities of trade: The significance of organic materials in Saharan trade. In Mattingly et al. 2017a, 211–30.

Mattingly, D.J. and Hayes, J.W. 1992. Nador and fortified farms in Algeria. *Journal of Roman Archaeology* 5: 408–18.

Mattingly, D.J. and Hitchner, R.B. 1993. Technical specifications for some North African olive presses of Roman date. In Amouretti and Brun 1993, 439–62.

Mattingly, D.J. and Hitchner, R.B. 1995. Roman Africa: An archaeological review. *Journal of Roman Studies* 85: 165–213.

Mattingly, D.J. and Jones, G.D.B. 1986. A new *clausura* in western Tripolitania: Wadi Skiffa south. *Libyan Studies* 17: 87–96.

Mattingly, D.J. and MacDonald, K.C. 2013. Early cities: Africa. In P. Clark (ed), *The Oxford Handbook of Cities in World History*, 66–82. Oxford: Oxford University Press.

Mattingly, D.J. and Sterry, M.S. 2010. *Ghadames Archaeological Survey. Phase 1 Desk-top Report.* Unpublished consultancy report produced for Libyan Department of Antiquities, Ghadames Development Authority, and BP.

Mattingly, D.J. and Sterry, M. 2013. The first towns in the Central Sahara. *Antiquity* 87(366):503–18.

Mattingly, D.J. and Sterry, M. 2020a. Introduction to the themes of sedentarisation, urbanisation and state formation in the ancient Sahara and beyond. In Sterry and Mattingly 2020a, 1–50.

Mattingly, D.J. and Sterry, M. 2020b. State formation in the Sahara and beyond. In Sterry and Mattingly 2020a, 695–721.

Mattingly, D.J. and Stone, D. 2011. Leptiminus: Profile of a town. In Stone et al. 2011a, 272–88.

Mattingly, D.J., Stirling, L., Stone, D. and Ben Lazreg, N. 2001. Leptiminus (Tunisia): A "producer" city? In D.J. Mattingly and J. Salmon (eds), *Economies Beyond Agriculture in the Classical World*, 66–89. London: Routledge.

Mattingly, D.J., Stone, D.L., Stirling, L.M., Moore, J.P., Wilson, A.I., Dore, J.N., and Ben Lazreg, N. 2011. Economy. In Stone et al. 2011a, 205–71.

Mattingly, D.J., McLaren, S., Savage, E., al-Fasatwi, Y. and Gadgood, K. (eds). 2006. *The Libyan Desert: Natural Resources and Cultural Heritage.* London: Society for Libyan Studies.

Mattingly, D.J., Rushworth, A., Sterry, M. and Leitch, V. 2013a. *The African Frontiers*. Frontiers of the Roman Empire (D. Breeze, ed). Edinburgh: Hussar.

Mattingly, D.J., Sterry, M.J. and Leitch, V. 2013b. Fortified farms and defended villages of Late Roman and Late Antique Africa. *Antiquité Tardive* 21: 167–88.

Mattingly, D., Sterry, M.J. and Edwards, D.N. 2015. The origins and development of Zuwīla, Libyan Sahara: An archaeological and historical overview of an ancient oasis town and caravan centre. *Azania: Archaeological Research in Africa* 50(1): 27–75.

Mattingly, D.J., Leitch, V., Duckworth, C.N., Cuénod, A., Sterry, M. and Cole, F. (eds). 2017a. *Trade in the Ancient Sahara and Beyond.* Cambridge: Cambridge University Press and Society for Libyan Studies.

Mattingly, D.J., Bokbot, Y., Sterry, M., Cuénod, A., Fenwick, C., Gatto, M.C., Ray, N., Rayne, L., Janin, K., Lamb, A., Mugnai, N. and Nikolaus, J. 2017b. Long-term history in a Moroccan oasis zone: The Middle Draa Project 2015. *Journal of African Archaeology* 15(2): 141–72.

Mattingly, D.J., Cuénod, A., Duckworth, C., Leitch, V. and Sterry, M. 2017c. Concluding discussion. In Mattingly et al. 2017a, 433–40.

Mattingly, D.J., Sterry, M., al-Haddad, M. and Bokbot, Y. 2018. Beyond the Garamantes: The early development of Saharan oases. In Purdue et al. 2018, 205–28.

Mattingly, D.J., Gatto, M.C., Sterry, M. and Ray, N. 2019a. Introduction: Burials, migration and identity: The view from the Sahara. In Gatto et al. 2019a, 1–50.

Mattingly, D.J., Sterry, M. and Ray, N. 2019b. Dying to be Garamantian: Burial, migration and identity in Fazzan. In Gatto et al. 2019a, 53–107.

Mattingly, D.J., Bokbot, Y. and Sterry, M. 2019c. The Middle Draa Project (Morocco): Results from the survey and trial excavations 2015–18. *Libyan Studies* 50: 73–80

Mattingly, D.J., Merlo, S., Mori, L. and Sterry, M. 2020a. Garamantian oasis settlements in Fazzan. In Sterry and Mattingly 2020a, 53–111.

Mattingly, D.J., Sterry, M., al-Haddad, M. and Trousset, P. 2020b. Pre-Islamic oasis settlements in the northern Sahara. In Sterry and Mattingly 2020a, 187–238.

Mattingly, D.J., Sterry, M., Rayne, L. and al-Haddad, M. 2020c. Pre-Islamic oasis settlements in the eastern Sahara. In Sterry and Mattingly 2020a, 112–46.

Mattingly, D.J., Sterry, M., Fothergill, B.T., Cuénod, A., Duckworth, C. and Leitch, V. 2021. Animal traffic in the Sahara. In Blanc-Bijon et al. 2021, 175–92.

Mauny, R. 1956. Monnaies antiques trouvées en Afrique au sud du 'limes' romain. *Libyca* 4: 249–60.

Mauny, R. 1978a. Trans-Saharan contacts and the Iron Age in West Africa. In Fage 1978, 272–341.

Mauny, R. 1978b. Les contacts terrestres entre Méditerranée et Afrique tropicale occidentale pendant l'antiquité. In *L'Afrique noire et monde Méditerranéen dans l'antiquité*, 122–46. Dakar: Nouvelles éditions africaines.

Maurin, L. 1995. *Pagus Mercurialis Veteranorum Medelitanorum.* Implantations vétéranes dans la vallée de l'oued Miliane. Le dossier épigraphique. *Mélanges de l'Ecole Française de Rome. Antiquité* 107(1): 97–135.

Maurin, L. and Peyras, J. 1990. Romanisation et traditions africaines dans la région de Bir Mcherga. *Cahiers de Tunisie* 43(155–156): 105–48.

Mazard, J. 1955. *Corpus Nummorum Numidiae Mauretaniaeque.* Paris: Arts et métiers graphiques.

Mazzilli, G. 2016. *L'arco di Traiano a Leptis Magna.* Rome: L'Erma di Bretschneider.

McCann, A.M. and Freed, J. 1994. *Deep Water Archaeology: A Late-Roman Ship from Carthage and an Ancient Trade Route near Skerki Bank off Northwest Sicily.* JRA supplement 13. Portsmouth, RI: Journal of Roman Archaeology.

McCann, A.M. and Oleson, J.P. 2004. *Deep-Water Shipwrecks off Skerki Bank: The 1997 Survey.* JRA supplement 58. Portsmouth, RI: Journal of Roman Archaeology.

McCarty, M. M. 2010a. *Votive Stelae, Religion, and Cultural Change in Africa Proconsularis and Numidia 200 BC–AD 300.* Unpublished DPhil thesis, University of Oxford.

McCarty, M.M. 2010b. Réseaux d'idées: Routes romaines et géographie religieuse de l'Afrique du Nord. *L'Africa romana* 18(2): 835–50.

McCarty, M.M. 2010c. Soldiers and stelae: Votive cult and the Roman army in North Africa. *Bollettino di Archeologia Online* 1.

McCarty, M.M. 2011. Representations and the "meaning" of ritual change: The case of Hadrumetum. In A. Chaniotis (ed), *Ritual Dynamics in the Ancient Mediterranean: Agency, Emotion, Gender, Representation*, 203–34. Stuttgart: Franz Steiner Verlag.

McCarty, M.M. 2013. Continuities and contexts. The tophets of Roman imperial-period Africa. *Studi Epigrafici e Linguistici* 29–30: 93–118.

McCarty, M.M. 2016. Gods, masks, and *monstra*: Situational syncretisms in Roman Africa. In S.E. Alcock, M. Egri and J.F. Frakes (eds), *Beyond Boundaries: Connecting Visual Cultures in the Provinces of Ancient Rome*, 266–80. Malibu: Getty Publications.

McCarty, M.M. 2017. Africa Punica? Child sacrifice and other invented traditions in early Roman Africa. *Religion in the Roman Empire* 3(3): 393–428.

McCarty, M.M. 2018. French archaeology and history in the colonial Maghreb: Inheritance, presence, and absence. In Effros and Lai 2018, 359–82.

McCarty, M.M. 2019. The tophet and infant sacrifice. In López-Ruiz and Doak 2019, 310–25.

McCarty, M.M. 2021. Pre-Roman Libyan religion. Colonial ethnography and the problem of religious "survivals". In V. Gasparini and A. Mastino (eds), *Historiography of Religion in Ancient North Africa*, 127–48. Madrid: Universidad Carlos III de Madrid. = *Rivista de Historiografía* 36.

McCarty, M.M. 2022. Transforming religion under the Roman Empire: The case of Africa. In Hitchner 2022a, 285–98.

McCarty, M.M. Forthcoming a. Reconsidering "substitution sacrifice" in Roman Africa: Evidence and the semiotics of ritual efficacy on the N'Gaous stelae. In V. Gasparini (ed), *Lived Religion in Roman North Africa*. Madrid.

McCarty, M.M. Forthcoming b. *Empire and Worship in Roman Africa: Religion, Sacrifice and Image*. Cambridge: Cambridge University Press.

Mederos Martín, A. 2019. North Africa: from the Atlantic to Algeria. In López-Ruiz and Doak 2019, 627–43.

Meiklejohn, C. 2000. Skeletal remains at Leptiminus, 1998–1999. *Echos du Monde Classique / Classical Views* 44, n.s. 19(2): 216–17 [in Stirling et al. 2000].

Mercier, G. 1924. La langue libyenne et la toponomie antique de l'Afrique du Nord. *Journal Asiatique* 205: 189–320.

Mercier, M. 1953. Les idoles de Ghadamès. *Revue Africaine* 97: 17–47.

Mercuri, A.M. 1999. Palynological analysis of the early Holocene sequence. In di Lernia 1999, 149–82.

Mercuri, A.M., Trevisan Grandi, G., Mariotti Lippi, M. and Cremaschi, M. 1998. New pollen data from the Uan Muhuggiag rockshelter (Libyan Sahara, VII–IV millennia BP). In Cremaschi and Di Lernia 1998, 107–24.

Merrills, A.H (ed). 2004. *Vandals, Romans and Berbers: New Perspectives on Late Antique North Africa*. Aldershot: Ashgate.

Merrills, A.H. 2016. African geography in the triumph of Cornelius Balbus. In Mugnai et al. 2016, 121–29.

Merrills, A.H. 2017a. *Roman Geographies of the Nile: From the Late Republic to the Early Empire*. Cambridge: Cambridge University Press.

Merrills, A.H. 2017b. The Moorish kingdoms and the written word: Three "textual communities" in fifth- and sixth-century Mauretania. In E. Screen and C. West (eds), *Writing the Early Medieval West. Studies in Honour of Rosamond McKitterick*, Cambridge: Cambridge University Press, 185–202.

Merrills, A.H. 2018. Invisible men: Mobility and political change on the frontier of late Roman Africa. *Early Medieval Europe* 26(3): 355–90.

Merrills, A.H. 2019. Corippus' Triumphal ethnography: Another look at *Iohannis* II.28–161. *Libyan Studies* 50: 153–63.

Merrills, A.H. 2022. The Byzantine period. In Hitchner 2022a, 391–409.

Merrills, A.H. and Miles, R. 2010. *The Vandals*. Oxford: Wiley Blackwell.

Meskell, L. 2006. *Archaeologies of Identity.* London: Routledge.

Metzler, J. Millett, M., Roymans, N. and Slofstra, J. 1995. *Integration in the Early Roman West: The Role of Culture and Ideology.* Luxembourg: Dossiers d'archéologie du Musée National d'Histoire et D'Art IV.

Meuret, C. 1996. Le règlement de Lamasba: Des tables de conversion appliquées à l'irrigation. *Antiquités africaines* 32: 87–112.

Meyer, E.A. 1990. Explaining the epigraphic habit in the Roman empire: The evidence of epitaphs. *Journal of Roman Studies* 80: 74–96.

Michel, V. 2013. L'activité récente de la Mission archéologique française en Libye pour l'Antiquité. *Antiquités africaines* 49: 219–31.

Michel, V. (ed). 2015. *De Leptis Magna à Derna, de la Tripolitaine à la Cyrénaique: Travaux récents sur la Libye antique.* Paris: Riveneuve editions.

Miles, R. 2010. *Carthage Must Be Destroyed: The Rise and Fall of an Ancient Civilization.* London: Penguin.

Millar, F. 1968. Local cultures in the Roman Empire: Libyan, Punic and Latin in Roman Africa. *Journal of Roman Studies* 58(1–2): 126–34.

Millett, M. 1990. *The Romanization of Britain: An Essay in Archaeological Interpretation.* Cambridge: Cambridge University Press.

Millett, M. 2021. 'Romanization', social centralization and structures of imperial power. In Belvedere and Bergemann 2021, 63–74.

Mitchell, P. and Lane, P. (eds). 2013. *The Oxford Handbook of African Archaeology.* Oxford: Oxford University Press.

Modéran, Y. 1989. Gildon, les Maures et l'Afrique. *Mélanges de l'Ecole Française de Rome. Antiquité* 101(2): 821–872.

Modéran, Y. 2003. *Les Maures et l'Afrique romaine (IVe–VIIe siècle).* BEFAR 314. Rome: École française de Rome.

Modéran, Y. 2010. Mazices, Mazaces. *Encyclopédie Berbère* 31: 4799–810.

Modéran, Y. 2011. La province, troisième patrie? In Briand-Ponsart and Modéran 2011, 9–40.

Modéran, Y. 2014. *Les Vandales et l'Empire romain.* Arles: Éditions Errance.

Mohamedi, A., Benmansour, A., Amamra, A.A. and Fentress, E. 1991. *Fouilles de Sétif 1977–1984).* Bulletin d'archéologie algerienne supplement 5. Alger: Agence nationale d'archéologie.

Mokhtar, G. (ed). 1981. *General History of Africa 2: Ancient Civilisations of Africa.* UNESCO/Heinemann, London:

Monaco, A., Belhouchet, L., Bel Hadj Brahim, H., Ben Fraj, T., Ben Nasr, J., Boussoffara, R., Cancellieri, E., Jnen, M., Lucci, E., Rotunno, R. and di Lernia, S. 2020. Megalithic structures of the northern Sahara (Chott el Jérid, Tunisia). *Cartagine. Studi e Ricerche* 5. https://doi.org/10.13125/caster/4078.

Monlezun, Capt. 1885. Les ruines de Tacape (Gabes). *Bulletin archéologique du comité des travaux historiques et scientifiques* 1885: 126–31.

Monografie di Archeologia Libica. (1948–) Rome: L'Erma di Bretschneider.

Morales, J. and Mackensen, M. 2020. Agriculture and food exchange at the late Roman Fort of Myd(---)/Gheriat el-Garbia (NW Libya): Macro-botanical finds from the German archaeological missions of 2009 and 2010. In Guédon 2020, 203–21.

Montali, G. 2015. *L'Anfiteatro di Sabratha e gli antiteatri dell'Africa Proconsulare.* Rome: L'Erma di Bretschneider.

Montali, G. 2018. Teatri e anfiteatri dell'Africa proconsolare: L'architettura al servizio del potere. Immagine della città e romanizzazione. In *Theatroeideis: l'immagine della città, la città delle immagini*. Atti del convegno internazionale, Bari, 15–19 giugno 2016, vol. 2, 259–80. Rome: Edizioni Quasar.

Moodie, M.R. 2019. *Between the Desert and the Deep: The Lived Experience of the Funerary Landscape of the Ancient Maghreb (4th – 1st millennium BCE)*. Unpublished PhD thesis, University of Edinburgh.

Moore, J.P. 1999. Cultural elasticity in the inscriptions of the so-called 'La Ghorfa' stelae. *Antiquités africaines* 35: 31–37.

Moore, J.P. 2007. The 'mausoleum culture' of Africa Proconsularis. In Stone and Stirling 2007a, 75–109.

Moore, T. 2011. Detribalizing the later prehistoric past: Concepts of tribes in Iron Age and Roman studies. *Journal of Social Archaeology* 11(3): 334–60.

Morales Mateos, J., Pérez-Jordá, G., Peña-Chocarro, L., Zapata, L., Ruíz-Alonso, M., López-Sáez, J.A. and Linstädter, J. 2013. The origins of agriculture in north-west Africa: Macro-botanical remains from Epipalaeolithic and Early Neolithic levels of Ifri Oudadane (Morocco). *Journal of Archaeological Science* 40(6): 2659–69.

Moreau, P. 1947. *Les lacs de sel aux chaos de sable: Le Pays des Nefzaouas*. Tunis: Bascone et Muscat.

Morel, J.-P. 2003. De quelques survivances protohostoriques dans la Carthage Punique. In Khanoussi 2003, 99–114.

Morel, J.-P. 2004. De la Grèce à Rome: Quelques réflexions sur la frontière. *L'Africa romana* 15: 183–97.

Morel, J.-P. 2010. Les tombes puniques de Byrsa à Carthage et leur sort à travers les siècles. In Déroche and Leclant 2010. 47–82.

Morère, N. 2014. Le sel dans l'Afrique ancienne: Ressources et enjeux dans l'emprise du territoire. In Briand-Ponsart 2014, 443–62.

Morestin, H. 1980. *Le Temple B de Volubilis*. Paris: Éditions du CNRS.

Mori L. (ed). 2013. *Life and Death of a Rural Village in Garamantian Times. Archaeological Investigations in the Oasis of Fewet (Libyan Sahara)*. AZA Monographs 6. Firenze: Edizioni All'Insegna del Giglio.

Morizot, P. 1979. Renseignements archéologiques complémentaires sur la vallée de l'oued Mellagou (Aurès). *Bulletin d'Archéologie Algérienne* 7 [1977–79]: 271–88.

Morizot, P. 1991. Économie et société en Numidie méridionale: L'example de l'Aurès. *L'Africa romana* 8: 429–46.

Morizot, P. 1993. L'Aurès et l'olivier. *Antiquités africaines* 29: 177–240.

Morizot, P. 1997. *Archéologie aérienne de l'Aurès*. Paris: Éditions du CTHS.

Morizot, P. 1999. La présence romaine dans le Djebel Amour (Algérie): Apport des images Spot et de la photographie aérienne. In Lepelley and Dupuis 1999, 185–212.

Morizot, P. 2002. Impact de l'armée romaine sur l'économie de l'Afrique. In Erdkamp 2002, 345–74.

Morizot, P. 2003. Les recherches en matière de protohistoire: l'état de la question pour l'Aurès. Indices cartographiques pour le djebel Amour. In Khanoussi 2003, 65–98.

Morizot, P. 2013. Réflexions sur le face-à-face romano-berbère. De la mort de Tacfarinas à l'invasion vandale. In Y. Le Bohec (ed), *La société de l'Afrique romaine = Bulletin archéologique du comité des travaux historiques et scientifiques: Afrique du Nord* n.s. 37: 36–62.

Morizot, P. 2015. *Romains et Berbères face à face*. Arles: Errance.

Morris, I. 1992. *Death-Ritual and Social Structure in Classical Antiquity*. Cambridge: Cambridge University Press.

Morris I. 2003. Mediterraneanization. *Mediterranean Historical Review* 18(2): 30–55

Morstein-Marx, R. 2001. The myth of Numidian origins in Sallust's African excursus (Iugurtha 17.7–18.12). *American Journal of Philology* 122(2): 179–200.

Mosca, P. 2013. The tofet: A place of infant sacrifice? In Xella 2013, 119–36.

Moscati, S. 1963. La questione fenicia. *Rendiconti dell'Accademia nazionale dei Lincei* 8(18): 483–506.

Moscati, S. 1983. *Carthage: Art et Civilisation*. Milan: Jaca.

Moscati, S. 1987. *Il sacrificio punico dei fanciulli: Realtà o invenzione?* Roma: Accademia nazionale dei lincei

Moscati, S. 1988. *The Phoenicians*. Milan: Bompiani.

Moscati, S. 1993. *Nuovi studi sull'identità fenicia*. Rome: Accademia nazionale de Lincei.

Mrabet, A. 1996. Prospection archéologique dans le pays de Mareth: L'occupation du sol dans l'antiquité. *Africa* 14: 133–42.

Mrabet, A. 1997. Huileries et témoins d'activité oléicole antique dans la région de Gabès: Données de la prospection des feuilles: Gabès, Kettana et Mareth. *Africa* 15: 63–76.

Mrabet, A. (ed). 1999. *De Byzacium au Sahel: Itinéraire historique d'une région tunisienne*. Tunis: l'Or du Temps.

Mrabet, A. 2003a. L'irrigation de la plaine d'Augarmi (Ksar Koutine) dans l'antiquité. In Khanoussi 2003, 415–31.

Mrabet, A. 2003b. La frontière sud de la Byzacène: Observations de géographie historique. In Bejaoui 2003, 7–16.

Mrabet, A. (ed). 2005. *De l'occupation du sol en Tunisie pendant l'antiquité*. Sousse: Université de Sousse.

Mrabet, A. 2008. A propos d'un tronçon de voie antique récemment découverte dans le zone du limes tripolitanus. In Bejaoui 2008, 133–40.

Mrabet, A. 2010. A propos de la voie *Tacape-Thelepte* par le sud des Chotts. In Bejaoui 2010, 131–40.

Mrabet, A. 2011. Identité de la Tripolitaine occidentale: De quelques signalements archéologiques. In Briand-Ponsart and Modéran 2011, 221–37.

Mrabet, A. 2014. Le territoire de Tacapes: Essai de delimitation. In Briand-Ponsart 2014, 169–78.

Mrabet, A. (ed). 2015. *Géographie historique du Maghreb antique et médiéval: État des lieux et perspectives de recherches*. Sousse: Université de Sousse.

Mrabet, A. (ed). 2016. *Le réseau routier dans le Maghreb antique et médieval*. Sousse: Université de Sousse.

Mrabet, A. (ed). 2017a. *Le peuplement du Maghreb antique et médiéval*. Sousse: Université de Sousse.

Mrabet, A. (ed). 2017b. *Vie et genres de vie au Maghreb: Antiquité et Moyen Âge*. Sousse: Université de Sousse.

Mrabet, A. and Remesal Rodríguez, J. (eds). 2007. *In Africa et in Hispania: Études sur l'huile africaine*. Collecció Instrumenta 25. Barcelona: Universitat de Barcelona.

Mugnai, N. 2018. *Architectural Decoration and Urban History in Mauretania Tingitana*. Rome: Edizioni Quasar.

Mugnai, N. 2021. A promenade at Lepcis Magna: Experiencing buildings from the Augustan to the Antonine era. *Libyan Studies* 52: 87–118.

Mugnai, N. 2022. Architecture and art. In Hitchner 2022a, 247–84.

Mugnai, N., Nikolaus, J. and Ray, N. (eds). 2016. *De Africa Romaque. Merging Cultures across North Africa*, London: Society for Libyan Studies.

Mullen, A. 2013. The bilingualism of material culture? Thoughts from a linguistic perspective. *HEROM: Journal on Hellenistic and Roman Material Culture* 2: 21–43.

Mullen, A. and James, P. (eds). 2012. *Multilingualism in the Graeco-Roman Worlds*. Cambridge: Cambridge University Press

Munzi, M. 2001. *L'epica del ritorno. Archeologia e politica nella Tripolitania italiana*. Saggi di Storia Antica 17. Rome: L'Erma di Bretschneider.

Munzi, M. 2004. *La decolonizzazione del passato. Archeologia e politica in Libia dall'amministrazione alleata al regno di Idris*. Rome: L'Erma di Bretschneider.

Munzi, M. 2010. Il territorio di Leptis Magna: Insediamenti rurali, strutture produttive e rapporti con la città. In I. Tantillo and F. Bigi (eds), *Leptis Magna: Una città e le sue iscrizioni in epoca tardoromana*, 45–80. Cassino, Università degli Studio di Cassino.

Munzi, M. 2012. Italian archaeologists in colonial Tripolitania. *Libyan Studies* 43: 81–110

Munzi, M., Felici, F., Cifani, G., Citelli, E., Gaudiosi, E., Lucarini, G. and Matoug, J. 2004. A topographic research sample in the territory of Lepcis Magna: Sīlīn. *Libyan Studies* 35: 11–66.

Munzi, M., Felici, F., Cirelli, E., Schingo, G. and Zocchi, A. 2010. Il territorio di *Leptis Magna*: Ricognizioni tra Ras el-Mergheb e Ras el-Hamman (2007). *L'Africa romana* 18(1): 723–46.

Munzi, M., Schirru, G. and Tantillo, I. 2014. *Centenarium*. *Libyan Studies* 45: 49–64.

Munzi, M., Felici, F., Matoug, J., Sjöstrom, I. and Zocchi, A. 2016. The Lepcitanian landscape across the ages: The survey between Ras el-Mergheb and Ras el-Hammam (2007, 2009, 2013). *Libyan Studies* 47: 67–116.

Musso, L. 1997. Leptis Magna e il suo territorio: Suburbio, ville marittime, necropoli, mausolei. In Ministero degli Affari Esteri (ed), *Missioni archeologiche italiane. La ricerca archeologica, antropologica, etnologica*, 203–08. Rome: L'Erma di Bretschneider.

Musso, L., Baldoni, D., G., Felici, F., Fontana, S., Mallegni, F., Masturzo, N., Munzi, M., Pentiricci, M., Severini, F. and Usai, L. 1997. Missione archeologica dell'Università Roma Tre a Leptis Magna, 1996. *Libya Antiqua* n.s. 3: 257–94.

Musso, L., Baldoni, D., Bianchi, B., Cilla, M., Di Vita-Evrard, G., Felici, F., Fontana, S., Mallegni, F., Masturzo, N., Munzi, M. and Usai, L. 1998. Missione archeologica dell'Università Roma Tre a Leptis Magna, 1997. *Libya Antiqua* n.s. 4: 176–218.

Musso, L., Baldoni, D., Bianchi, B., Calì, M.G., Davidde, B., Di Vita-Evrard, G., Munzi, M., Petriaggi, R., Pinna Caboni, B., Ponti, G., and Shebani, R. 2010. Missione archeologica dell'Università Roma Tre, 1998–2007. *Libya Antiqua* n.s. 5: 49–78.

Musso, L., Baldoni, D., Baroni, F., Bessi, B., Bianchi, B., Bruno, M., Buccino, L., Davidde Pietraggi, B., Felici, F., al-Hadad, M., Munzi, M., Petriaggi, R., Shebani, R., Sjöström, I. and Zocchi, A. 2014. Missione archeologica dell'Università Roma Tre (2009–2014). *Libya Antiqua* n.s. 7, 11–54.

Nacef, J. 2015. *La production de la céramique antique dans la région de Salakta et Ksour Essef (Tunisie)*. Oxford: Archaeopress.

Naddari, L. 2008. Entre *coloni* et *Musulamii*: Une opération de délimitation des terres sous Trajan dans la vallée de l'oued Sarrat. In Bejaoui 2008, 157–83.

Naddari, L. 2014. La voie ex castris hiberis-Tacapes. Le Tronçon Ammaedara-Thelepte: Étude d'archéologie et d'épigraphie. In Briand-Ponsart 2014, 349–76.

Napoli, J. 1997. *Recherches sur les fortifications linéaires romaines*. CEFR 229. Rome: École française de Rome.

Napoli, J. 2000. Lecture de Jean Baradez, Fossatum Africae. *L'Africa romana* 13(1): 613–40.

Nasraoui, A. 2005. Les vestiges romains dans l'Aurès profond: Témoins d'un important brassage de cultures romaine et berbère. In Briand-Ponsart 2005a, 293–304.

Naum, M. 2010. Re-emerging frontiers: Postcolonial theory and historical archaeology of the borderlands. *Journal of Archaeological Method and Theory* 17(2): 101–31.

Nicholas, G.P. 2006. Decolonizing the archaeological landscape: The practice and politics of archaeology in British Columbia. *American Indian Quarterly* 30(3–4): 350–80.

Nielsen. I. 1990. *Thermae et Balnea: The Architecture and Cultural History of Roman Public Baths*. Aarhus: Aarhus University Press.

Niemeyer, H.G. 1990. A la recherche de la Carthage archaïque: Premiers résultats des fouilles de l'université de Hambourg en 1986 et 1987. In CTHS Strasbourg 1990, 45–52.

Niemeyer H.G., Rindelaub A. and Schmidt K. 1996. *Karthago. Die alte Handelsmetropole am Mittelmeer. Eine archäologische Grabung* (Veröffentlichungen des Hamburger Museums für Archäologie und die Geschichte Harburgs, Helms-Museum 75), Hamburg: Hamburger Museum.

Niemeyer H.G., Docter R.F., Schmidt K., Bechtold B. (eds). 2007. *Karthago. Die Ergebnisse der Hamburger Grabung unter dem Decumanus Maximus (Hamburger Forschungen zur Archäologie 2)*. Mainz: Philipp von Zabern.

Nikolaus, J. 2016. Beyond Ghirza: Roman-period mausolea in Tripolitania. In Mugnai et al. 2016, 199–214.

Nikolaus, J. 2017. *Roman Funerary Reliefs and North African Identity: A Contextual Investigation of Tripolitanian Mausolea and their Iconography*. Unpublished PhD thesis, University of Leicester.

Norman, N.J. 2002. Death and burial of Roman children: The case of the Yasmina cemetery at Carthage – Part I, setting the stage. *Mortality* 7(3): 302–23.

Norman, N.J. 2003. Death and burial of Roman children: The case of the Yasmina cemetery at Carthage – Part II, The archaeological evidence. *Mortality* 8(1): 36–47.

Norman, N.J., and Haeckl, A.E. 1993. The Yasmina necropolis at Carthage, 1992. *Journal of Roman Archaeology* 6: 238–50.

Oates, D. 1953. The Tripolitanian Gebel: Settlement of the Roman period around Gasr ed-Dauun. *Papers of the British School at Rome* 21: 81–117.

Oates, D. 1954. Ancient settlement in the Tripolitanian Gebel, II: The Berber period. *Papers of the British School at Rome* 22: 91–117.

Onrubia-Pintado, J. 2013. Origines berbères: Néolithisation et berbérisation. *Encyclopédie Berbère* 35: 5845–55.

Onrubia Pintado, J., Bokbot, Y., Hervás Herrera, M.A., García García, L.A., Marchante Ortega, A., Cáceres Gutiérrez, Y., González Marrero, M. del C., de Juan Ares, J., Moreno García, M. and Rodríguez Santana, C.G. 2016. Arqueología de Fum Asaca (Sidi Ifni-Marruecos).

De probable instalación purpuraría gétula a Torre Colonial hispano-canaria. *Anuario de estudios atlánticos* 62: 414–38.

Opper, T. 2008. *Hadrian: Empire and Conflict.* London: British Museum Press.

Ørsted, P. 1992. Town and countryside in Roman Tunisia: A preliminary report on the Tuniso-Danish survey project in the Oued R'mel basis in and around ancient Segermes. *Journal of Roman Archaeology* 5: 69–96.

Ørsted, P., Carlsen, J., Ladjimi Sebaï, L. and Ben Hassen, H. (eds). 2000. *Africa Proconsularis. Regional Studies in the Segermes Valley of Northern Tunisia, vol. 3: Historical Conclusions.* Aarhus: Aarhus University Press.

Osborne, C. 1992. The human skeletal remains from Site 10 (1990). In Ben Lazreg and Mattingly 1992, 267–70.

Osborne, C., and Stirling, L. 1992. Catalogue of Burials (1990). In Ben Lazreg and Mattingly 1992, 271–300.

Osborne, R. 1998. Early Greek colonization? The nature of Greek settlement in the west. In N. Fisher and H. van Wees (eds). *Archaic Greece: New Approaches and New Evidence*, 251–70. London: Duckworth.

Osborne, R. and Cunliffe, B. (eds). 2005. *Mediterranean Urbanization 800–600 BC.* Oxford: Oxford University Press.

Ouni, K. and Peyras, J. 2002. Centuriation et cadastres du centre-est tunisien. In M. Clavel-Lévêque and A. Orejas (edd.). *Atlas historique des cadastres d'Europe* 2, Dossier 9, Tunisie (n.p.). Luxembourg: Office des publications officielles des Communautés européennes.

Pace, P., Sergi, S. and Caputo, G. 1951. Scavi Sahariani. *Monumenti Antichi* 41: 150–549.

Padilla Peralta, D. 2020. Epistemicide: The Roman case. *Classica* 33(2): 151–186.

Padilla Peralta, D. 2021. Anti-race: Anti-racism, whiteness, and the classical imagination. In D. McCoskey (ed), *A Cultural History of Race in Antiquity*, 157–88. London: Bloomsbury.

Pakenham, T. 1992. *The Scramble for Africa.* London: Little, Brown.

Panero, E. 2008. *La Maalga e i porti punici di Cartagine: Una città e il suo territorio dalla fondazione fenicia alla dominazione romana.* Florence: Le Lettere.

Panetier, J.-L. 2002. *Volubilis: Une cité du Maroc antique.* Paris: Maisonneuve et Larose.

Papadopoulos, J.K. 1997. Phantom Euboians. *Journal of Mediterranean Archaeology* 10(2): 191–219.

Papi, E. (ed) 2007. *Supplying Rome and the Empire.* JRA supplement 69. Portsmouth RI: Journal of Roman Archaeology.

Papi, E. 2014. Punic Mauretania? In Quinn and Vella 2014, 202–18.

Papi, E. 2016. L'invention du Círculo de l'Estrecho. In Coltelloni-Trannoy et al. 2016, 105–20.

Papi, E. 2019. Revisiting first millennium BC graves in north-west Morocco. In Gatto et al. 2019a, 281–312.

Papi, E. and Martorella, F. 2007. Il grano della *Tingitana.* In Papi 2007, 85–96.

Papi, E., Camporeale, S. and Akerrraz, A. (eds). 2013. *Sidi Ali Ben Ahmed – Thamusida, vol. 3: I materiali.* Rome: Edizioni Quasar.

Pappa, E. 2009. Reflections on the earliest Phoenician presence in north-west Africa. *Talanta* 40–41: 53–72.

Paribeni, E. 1959. *Catalogo delle sculture de Cirene. Statue e rilievi di carattere religioso.* Rome: L'Erma di Bretschneider.

Paris, F. 1995. Essai de classification des monuments funéraires sahariens. *Bulletin de la Société Préhistorique Française* 92(4): 549–53.

Parker, A.J. 1992. *Ancient Shipwrecks of the Mediterranean and Roman Provinces*. British Archaeological Reports International Series S580. Oxford: BAR Publishing.

Parkin, T. and Pomeroy, A. (eds). 2007. *Roman Social History: A Sourcebook*. London: Routledge.

Parsons, T.H. 2010. *The Rule of Empires: Those Who Built Them, Those Who Endured Them and Why They Always Fall*. Oxford: Oxford University Press.

Paul, G.M. 1984. *A Historical Commentary on Sallust's Bellum Jugurthinum*. Liverpool: Francis Cairns.

Pavis d'Escurac, H. 1974. Pour une étude sociale de l'Apologie d'Apulée. *Antiquités africaines* 8: 89–101.

Pavis-d'Escurac, H. 1976. *La préfecture de l'annone, service administratif impérial d'Auguste à Constantin*. BEFAR 226. Rome: École française de Rome.

Pavis d'Escurac, H. 1980. Irrigation el vie paysanne dans l'Afrique du Nord antique. *Ktèma* 5: 177–91.

Peacock, D.P.S., Bejaoui, F. and Ben Lazreg, N. 1989. Roman amphora production in the Sahel region of Tunisia. In M. Lenoir, D. Manacorda and C. Panella (eds), *Amphores romaines et histoire économique: dix ans de recherche. Actes du colloque (Sienne, 22–24 mai 1986)*, 179–222. CEFR 114. Rome: École française de Rome.

Peacock, D.P.S., Bejaoui, F. and Ben Lazreg, N. 1990. Roman pottery production in central Tunisia. *Journal of Roman Archaeology* 3: 59–84.

Pedley, J. 1980. *New Light on Ancient Carthage*. Ann Arbor: Kelsey Museum.

Pelling, R. 2013a. The archaeobotanical remains. In Mattingly 2013a, 473–94.

Pelling, R. 2013b. Botanical data appendices. In Mattingly 2013a, 841–52.

Peña, J.T. 1998. The mobilization of state olive oil in Roman Africa: The evidence of late 4th-c. *ostraca* from Carthage. In J.T. Peña, J.J. Rossiter, A.I. Wilson and C.M. Wells (eds), *Carthage Papers: The Early Colony's Economy, Water Supply, a Private Bath, and the Mobilization of State Olive Oil*. JRA supplement 28, 117–238. Portsmouth, RI: Journal of Roman Archaeology.

Peña-Chocarro, L., Pérez Jordà, G., Abel Schaad, D., Gibaja Bao, J.F., López-Romero, E., López-Sáez, J.A., Moreno-García, M. and Amani F. 2011. La campaña de excavación 2011 en las cuevas de El Khil (Achakar, Tánger, Marruecos). *Informes y Trabajos: Excavaciones en el exterior 2011* 9: 546–61.

Pennell, C.R. 2000. *Morocco since 1830: A History*. London: Hurst and Company.

Perea Yébenes, S. and Pastor Muñoz, M. (eds). 2020. *El norte de África en época romana: Tributum in memoriam Enrique Gozalbes Cravioto*. Madrid/Salamanca: Signifer Libros.

Perkins, P. and James, P. 2000. *Culture, Identity and Power in the Roman Empire. Block Five: Roman North Africa*. Milton Keynes: Open University.

Perring, D. and Pitts M. 2013. *Alien Cities: Consumption and the Origins of Urbanism in Roman Britain*. London: SpoilHeap Publications.

Peyras, J. 1975. Le *Fundus aufidianus*: Étude d'un grand domaine romain de la région de Mateur, (Tunisie du Nord). *Antiquités africaines* 9: 181–222.

Peyras, J. 1986. Les campagnes de l'Afrique du Nord antique d'après les anciens Gromatici. In CTHS Montpellier 1986, 257–72.

Peyras, J. 1991. *Le Tell nord-est tunisien dans l'Antiquité*. Paris: CNRS Éditions.

Peyras, J. 1999. Statut cadastres des cités libres du centre-est tunisien. In Mrabet 1999, 71–82.

Peyras, J. 2005a. Frontières et écosystèmes. In R. Bedon and E. Hermon (eds), *Concepts, pratiques et enjeux environnementaux dans l'empire romain*, 67–76. Limoges: Presses universitaires de Limoges.

Peyras, J. 2005b. Frontières du principat et arpentage: Sources du droit, qualités des terres, écosystèmes. In R. Bedon and E. Hermon (eds), *Concepts, pratiques et enjeux environnementaux dans l'empire romain*, 107–251. Limoges: Presses universitaires de Limoges.

Peyras, J. and Maurin, J. 1974. *Ureu: municipium uruensium*. Paris: Ophrys.

Peyras, J. and Trousset, P. 1988. Le lac *Tritonis* et les noms anciens du chott el Jérid. *Antiquités africaines* 24: 149–204.

Pezzoli, G. (ed). 1995. *Cavalieri dell'Africa: Storia, iconografia, simbolismo*. Milan: Centro Studi Archeologia Africana.

Pflaum, H.G. 1978. *Afrique Romaine*. Scripta Varia 1. Paris: Harmattan.

Pflaum, H.G. 1982. *Les carrières procuratoriennes équestres sous le Haut-Empire romain: Supplément*. Paris: Geuthner.

Picard, G.C. 1944. *Castellum Dimmidi*. Paris: de Boccard.

Picard, G.C. 1954. *Les religions de l'Afrique antique*. Paris: Plon.

Picard, G.C. 1956. Néron et le blé d'Afrique. *Cahiers du Tunisie* 4: 163–73.

Picard, G.C. 1957. Civitas Mactaritana. *Karthago* 8: 1–156 (whole volume).

Picard, G.C. 1959. La civilisation de l'Afrique romaine. Paris: Librairie Plon.

Picard, G.C. 1974. Les cités sufetales dans l'Afrique romaine. In *Atti del convegno internazionale sul tema: I diritti locali nelle provincie romane con particolare riguardo alle condizioni giuridiche del suolo (Roma 26–28 ottobre 1971)*, 123–33. Rome: Accademia nazionale dei Lincei.

Picard, G.C. 1982. La sculpture dans l'Afrique romaine. *150-Jahr-Feier Deutches Archäologisches Institut Rom, Mitteilungen des Deutschen Archäologischen Instituts, Römische Abteilung* 25: 180–99.

Picard, G.C. 1985. La villa du Taureau à Silin (Tripolitaine). *Comptes rendus des séances de l'Académie des inscriptions et belles-lettres* 1985, 129(1): 227–241.

Picard, G.C. 1990. *La civilisation de l'Afrique romaine*. 2nd edition. Paris: Études Augustiniennes.

Picard, G.C., Bourgeois, A. and Picard, C. 1977. *Recherches archéologiques franco-tunisiennes à Mactar. 1: La maison de Vénus. Stratigraphies et études des pavements*. CEFR 34/1. Rome: École française de Rome.

Picard, G.C., Mahjoubi, A. and Beschaouch, A. 1963. *Pagus Thuscae et Gunzuzi. Comptes rendus des séances de l'Académie des inscriptions et belles-lettres* 1963, 107(2): 124–30.

Picard G.-C., Le Bonniec H. and Mallon J. 1970. Le cippe de Beccut. *Antiquités africaines* 4: 125–64.

Pichot, A. 2008. Théâtres, amphithéâtres et cirques des Maurétanies romaines. *L'Africa romana* 17(1): 261–71.

Pitts, M. 2007. The emperor's new clothes? The utility of identity in Roman archaeology. *American Journal of Archaeology* 111(4): 693–713

Pitts, M. 2008. Globalizing the local in Roman Britain: An anthropological approach to social change. *Journal of Anthropological Archaeology* 27(4): 493–506.

Pitts, M., and Versluys, M.J. (eds). 2015. *Globalisation and the Roman World: World History, Connectivity and Material Culture*. Cambridge: Cambridge University Press.

Ployer, R., Polak, M. and Schmidt, R. 2019. *The Frontiers of the Roman Empire: A Thematic Study and Proposed World Heritage Nomination Strategy*. Vienna: Phoibos Verlag.

Poinssot, C. 1958. *Les ruines de Dougga*. Tunis: Institut national d'archéologie et arts.

Poinssot, C. 1962. *Immunitas perticae Carthaginiensium*. *Comptes rendus des séances de l'Académie des inscriptions et belles-lettres* 1962, 106(1): 55–76.

Poinssot, L. 1919. Les fouilles de Dougga en 1919 et le quartier du Forum. *Nouvelles Archives des Missions Scientifiques et Littéraires* 22: 133–98.

Polla S. 2011. Il paesaggio economico della regione di Dougga (Alto Tell Tunisino): Il dato della ceramica. In R. Attoui (ed), *When Did Antiquity End?* 91–104. British Archaeological Reports International Series S2268. Oxford: Archaeopress.

Ponsich, M. 1964a. Exploitations agricoles romaines de la région de Tanger. *Bulletin d'Archéologie Marocaine* 5: 235–52.

Ponsich, M. 1964b. Contribution à l'Atlas archéologique du Maroc: Région de Tanger. *Bulletin d'Archéologie Marocaine* 5: 253–90.

Ponsich, M. 1966. Contribution a l'Atlas archéologique du Maroc: Région de Lixus. *Bulletin d'Archéologie Marocaine* 6: 377–422.

Ponsich, M. 1967. *Nécropoles phéniciennes de la région de Tanger*. Études et Travaux d'Archéologie Marocaine 3. Tanger: Éditions marocaines et internales.

Ponsich, M. 1969. Influences phéniciennes sur les populations rurales de la région de Tanger. In *Tartessos y sus problemas. V Symposium Internacional de Prehistoria Peninsular*, 173–84. Barcelona: Universidad de Barcelona.

Ponsich, M. 1970a. *Recherches archéologiques à Tanger et dans sa région*. Paris: CNRS Éditions.

Ponsich, M. 1970b. Note préliminaire sur l'industrie de la céramique préromaine en Tingitane (Kouass, région d'Arcila). *Karthago* 15: 77–97.

Ponsich, M. 1981. *Lixus: Le quartier des temples*. Etudes et Travaux d'Archéologie Marocaine 9. Rabat: Musée des antiquités.

Ponsich, M. 1988a. Implantation rurale du Maroc phénicien. *Dossiers Histoire et Archéologie* 132: 84–87.

Ponsich, M. 1988b. *Aceite de oliva y salazones de pescado. Factores geo-económicos de Bética y Tingitania*. Madrid: Editorial Complutense.

Ponsich, M. and Tarradell, M. 1965. *Garum et industries antiques de salaison dans la Mediterranée occidentale*. Paris: Presses Universitaires de France.

Poser, R. 2021. He wants to save Classics from whiteness. Can the field survive? *The New York Times Magazine*. 2 February 2021, 1–13. https://www.nytimes.com/2021/02/02/magazine/classics-greece-rome-whiteness.html.

Potter, D. 2004. *The Roman Empire at Bay, AD 180–395*. London: Routledge.

Potter, T.W. 1995. *Towns in Late Antiquity: Iol Caesarea and its Context*. Sheffield: University of Sheffield.

Potter, T.W. 2000a. Mauretania Caesariensis. In Talbert 2000, Map 29 and map-by-map directory, 467–74.

Potter, T.W. 2000b. Iol Caesarea. In Talbert 2000, Map 30 and map-by-map directory, 475–82.

Power, R.K., Nikita, E., Mattingly, D.J., Lahr, M.M. and O'Connell, T.C. 2019. Human mobility and identity: Variation, diet and migration in relation to the Garamantes of Fazzan. In Gatto et al. 2019a, 134–61.

Prag, J.R.W. and Quinn, J.-C. 2013. *The Hellenistic West: Rethinking the Ancient Mediterranean.* Cambridge: Cambridge University Press.

Prag, J.R.W. 2014. *Phoinix* and *Poenus*: usage in antiquity. In Quinn and Vella 2014, 11–23.

Precheur-Canonge, T. 1962. *La vie rurale en Afrique romaine d'après les mosaïques.* Tunis: Publications de l'Université de Tunis.

Prévot, F. 1984. *Recherches archéologiques franco-tunisiennes à Mactar. 5: Les inscriptions chrétiennes.* CEFR 34/5. Paris: École française de Rome.

Prévot, F., Voisin, J.-L., Blaudeau, P. and Najar, L. 2006. *L'Afrique romaine 69–439.* Tournai: Atlande.

Pringle, D. 1981. *The Defence of Byzantine Africa from Justinian to the Arab Conquest.* British Archaeological Reports International Series S99. Oxford: Archaeopress.

Purcaro Pagano, V. 1976. Le rotte antiche tra la Grecia e la Cirenaica e gli itinerari marittimi e terrestri lungo le coste cirenaiche e della Grande Sirte. *Quaderni di Archeologia della Libya* 8: 285–352.

Purcell, N. 2013. On the significance of East and West in today's "Hellenistic" history: Reflections on symmetrical worlds, reflecting through world symmetries. In Prag and Quinn 2013, 367–90.

Purdue, L., Charbonnier, J. and Khalidi, L. (eds). 2018a. *Des refuges aux oasis: Vivre en milieu aride de la préhistoire à aujourd'hui.* Actes des 38e rencontres internationales d'archéologie et d'histoire d'Antibes, 10–12 octobre 2017. Antibes: Éditions APDCA.

Purdue, L., Charbonnier, J. and Khalidi, L. 2018b. Living in arid environments from prehistoric times to the present day: Approaches to the study of refugia and oases. In Purdue et al. 2018a, 9–32.

Quinn, J.-C. 2003. Roman Africa? *Digressus* Supplement 1, *Romanization?*: 7–34.

Quinn, J.-C. 2004. The role of the 146 settlement in the provincialization of Africa. *L'Africa romana* 15: 1593–1602

Quinn, J.-C. 2009. North Africa. In A. Erskine (ed), *A Companion to Ancient History*, 260–72. Oxford: Blackwell.

Quinn, J.-C. 2010. The reinvention of Lepcis. *Bollettino di Archeologia Online* 1.

Quinn, J.-C. 2011. The Syrtes between East and West. In Dowler and Galvin 2011, 11–20.

Quinn, J.-C. 2013. Monumental power: "Numidian royal architecture" in context. In Prag and Quinn 2013, 179–215.

Quinn, J.-C. 2014. A Carthaginian perspective on the Altars of the Philaeni. In Quinn and Vella 2014, 169–79.

Quinn, J.-C. 2018. *In Search of the Phoenicians.* Princeton: Princeton University Press.

Quinn, J.-C. and Vella, N. (eds). 2014. *The Punic Mediterranean: Identities and Identification from Phoenician Settlement to Roman Rule.* Cambridge: Cambridge University Press.

Quinn, J.-C. and Wilson, A.I. 2013. Capitolia. *Journal of Roman Studies* 103: 117–73.

Rachet, M. 1970. *Rome et les Berbères: Un problème militaire d'Auguste à Dioclétien.* Brussels: Latomus.

Rakob, F. 1974. Das Quellenheiligtum in Zaghouan und die römische Wasserleitung nach Karthago. *Mitteilungen des Deutschen Archaeologischen Instituts*, *Römische Abteilung* 81: 41–89.

Rakob, F. 1979. Numidische königsarchitektur in Nordafrika. In Horn and Ruger 1979, 119–71.

Rakob, F. 1983. Architecture royale numide. In *Architecture et société de l'archaïsme grec à la fin de la Republique romaine*, 325–48. CEFR 66. Rome: École française de Rome.

Rakob, F. 1990. La Carthage archaïque. In CTHS Strasbourg 1990, 31–43.

Rakob, F. (ed). 1991. *Die deutschen Ausgrabungen in Karthago (Karthago 1)*. 2 vols. Mainz: Philipp von Zabern.

Rakob, F. (ed). 1993. *Simitthus 1. Die Steinbrüche und die antike Stadt*. Mainz: Philipp von Zabern.

Rakob, F. (ed). 1994. *Simitthus 2. Der Tempelberg und das römische Lager*. Mainz: Philipp von Zabern.

Rakob, F. (ed). 2005. *Simitthus 3. Militärlager oder Marmorwerkstätten*. Mainz: Philipp von Zabern.

Ramón Torres, J. 1995. *Las ánforas fenicio-púnicas del Mediterráneo central y occidental*. Barcelona: Universidad de Barcelona.

Raven, S. 1993. *Rome in Africa*. 3rd edition. London: Routledge.

Ray, N. and Nikolaus, J. 2019. Buried in the archives: Cemeteries and mausolea in Tripolitania. *Libyan Studies* 50: 93–98.

Rayne, L., Bradbury, J., Mattingly, D.J., Philip, G., Bewley, R., and Wilson, A.I. 2017a. From above and on the ground: Geospatial methods for recording endangered archaeology in the Middle East and North Africa, *Geosciences* 7(4): article 100.

Rayne, L., Sheldrick, N., and Nikolaus, J. 2017b. Endangered archaeology in Libya: Recording damage and destruction. *Libyan Studies* 48: 23–49.

Rebillard, E. 2012. *Christians and Their Many Identities in Late Antiquity, North Africa, 200–450 CE*. Ithaca: Cornell University Press.

Rebuffat, R. 1967a = Rebuffat, R., Deneauve, J. and Hallier, G. 1967. Bu Njem 1967. *Libya Antiqua* 3–4: 49–137.

Rebuffat, R. 1967b. Les erreurs de Pline et la position de *Babba Iulia Campestris*. *Antiquités africaines* 1: 31–57.

Rebuffat, R. 1969a. Maisons à péristyle d'Afrique du Nord: répertoire de plans publiés. *Mélanges de l'Ecole Française de Rome* 81(2): 659–724.

Rebuffat, R. 1969b. Deux ans de recherches dans le sud de la Tripolitaine. *Comptes rendus des séances de l'Académie des inscriptions et belles-lettres* 1969, 113(2): 189–212.

Rebuffat, R. 1970a = Rebuffat, R., Gassend, J.-M., Guéry, R. and Hallier, G. 1970. Bu Njem 1968. *Libya Antiqua* 6–7: 9–105.

Rebuffat, R. 1970b. Bu Njem 1970. *Libya Antiqua* 6–7: 107–65.

Rebuffat, R. 1970c. *Zella* et les routes d'Egypte. *Libya Antiqua* 6–7: 181–87.

Rebuffat, R. 1970d. Routes d'Egypte de la Libya Interieure. *Studi Magrebini* 3: 1–20.

Rebuffat, R. 1971a. Notes sur les confins de la Maurétanie Tingitane et de la Maurétanie Césarienne. *Studi Magrebini* 4: 33–64.

Rebuffat, R. 1971b. Recherches en Tripolitaine du sud. *Revue Archéologique* n.s. 1(1971): 177–84.

Rebuffat, R. 1972a. Nouvelles recherches dans le sud de la Tripolitaine. *Comptes rendus des séances de l'Académie des inscriptions et belles-lettres* 1972, 116(2): 319–39.

Rebuffat, R. 1972b. Les fouilles de Thamusida et leur contribution à l'histoire du Maroc. *Bulletin d'Archéologie Marocaine* 8: 51–65.

Rebuffat, R. 1973a. Les inscriptions des portes du camp de Bu Njem. *Libya Antiqua* 9–10: 99–120.

Rebuffat, R. 1973b. L'arrivée des romains à Bu Njem. *Libya Antiqua* 9–10: 121–34.

Rebuffat, R. 1973c. Gholaia. *Libya Antiqua* 9–10: 135–45.

Rebuffat, R. 1974a. Maisons à péristyle d'Afrique du Nord. Répertoire de plans publiés, 2. *Mélanges de l'Ecole Française de Rome. Antiquité* 86(1): 445–499.

Rebuffat, R. 1974b. Vestiges antiques sur la côte occidentale de l'Afrique au sud de Rabat. *Antiquités africaines* 8: 25–49.

Rebuffat, R. 1975a. Graffiti en libyque de Bu Njem. *Libya Antiqua* 11–12: 165–87.

Rebuffat, R. 1975b. Bu Njem 1971. *Libya Antiqua* 11–12: 189–242.

Rebuffat, R. 1975c. Trois nouvelles campagnes dans le sud de la Tripolitaine. *Comptes rendus des scéances de l'Académie des inscriptions et belles-lettres* 119(4): 495–505.

Rebuffat, R. 1975d. Les principia du camp romain de Lalla Djilaliya (Tabernae). *Bulletin d'Archéologie Marocaine* 9: 359–76.

Rebuffat, R. 1975e. Au delà des camps romains. *Bulletin d'Archéologie Marocaine* 9: 377–408.

Rebuffat, R. 1977a. Bu Njem 1972. *Libya Antiqua* 13–14: 37–77.

Rebuffat, R. 1977b. Dix ans de recherches dans le prédésert de Tripolitaine. *Libya Antiqua* 13–14: 79–91.

Rebuffat, R. 1977c. Une zone militaire et sa vie économique: Le *limes* de Tripolitaine. In *Armées et fiscalité dans le monde antique*, Colloques Nationaux du CNRS 936, 395–419. Paris: CNRS Éditions.

Rebuffat, R. 1978. Végèce et la télégraphe Chappe. *Mélanges de l'Ecole Française de Rome. Antiquité* 90(2): 829–61.

Rebuffat, R. 1979. La frontière romaine en Afrique: Tripolitaine et Tingitaine. *Ktèma. Civilisations de l'Orient, de la Grèce et de Rome antiques* 4: 225–47.

Rebuffat, R. 1980a. A propos du 'limes Tripolitanus'. *Revue Archéologique* n.s. 1(1980): 105–24.

Rebuffat, R. 1980b. Cuicul, le 21 juillet 365. *Antiquités africaines* 15: 309–28.

Rebuffat, R. 1980c. Le fossé romain de Sala. *Bulletin d'Archéologie Marocaine* 12: 237–58.

Rebuffat, R. 1981. L'ouvrage linéaire romain de Rabat (Maroc). *Caesarodunum* 16: 210–22. Bulletin de l'Institut d'Etudes Latines et du centre de recherches A. Piganiol, Actes du colloque: Frontières en Gaule.

Rebuffat, R. 1982a. Au-delà des camps romains d'Afrique mineure: renseignement, contrôle, pénétration. In H. Temporini (ed), *Aufstieg und Niedergang der römischen Welt: Principat, vol. 10/2: Teilband Politische Geschichte (Provinzen und Randvölker: Afrika mit Ägypten [Forts.])*, 474–513. Berlin: De Gruyter.

Rebuffat, R. 1982b. *Ara Cerei. Mélanges de l'Ecole Française de Rome. Antiquité* 94(2): 911–19.

Rebuffat, R. 1982c. Recherches dans le désert de Libye. *Comptes rendus des séances de l'Académie des inscriptions et belles-lettres* 1982, 126(2): 188–99.

Rebuffat, R. 1985a. L'arrivée des romains en Tripolitaine intérieure. *Bulletin archéologique du comité des travaux historiques et scientifiques: Afrique du Nord* n.s. 19B: 249–56.

Rebuffat, R. 1985b. Le 'limes' de Tripolitaine. In Buck and Mattingly 1985, 127–41.

Rebuffat, R. 1985c. Les centurions de *Gholaia*: super et Garamantas et Indos prefert imperium. *L'Africa romana* 2: 225–38.

Rebuffat, R. 1986a. Recherches sur le bassin du Sebou. *Comptes rendus des séances de l'Académie des inscriptions et belles-lettres* 1986, 130(4): 633–61 (including intervention by M. Euzennat: 652–61).

Rebuffat, R. 1986b. Un banquier à *Lepcis Magna*. *L'Africa romana*. 3: 179–187.

Rebuffat, R. 1987a. Implantation militaire romaine en Maurétanie Tingitane. *L'Africa romana* 4: 31–78.

Rebuffat, R. 1987b. Le poème de Q. Avidius Quintianus à la déesse Salus. *Karthago* 21: 93–105.

Rebuffat, R. 1988a. L'inscription de l'Ara Cerei. *Libya Antiqua* 15–16 (1978–79) [1988]: 113–24.

Rebuffat, R. 1988b. L'inscription du limes de Tripolitaine. *Libya Antiqua* 15–16 (1978–79) [1988]: 125–38.

Rebuffat, R. 1988c. Les fermiers du désert. *L'Africa romana* 5: 33–68.

Rebuffat, R. 1989. Notes sur le camp romain de *Gholaia* (Bu Njem). *Libyan Studies* 20: 155–67.

Rebuffat, R. 1990a. Nomadisme et archéologie. In *L'Afrique dans l'Occident romain*, 231–47.

Rebuffat, R. 1990b. Divinités de l'oued Kebir (Tripolitaine). *L'Africa romana* 7: 119–59.

Rebuffat, R. 1990c. Où étaient les *Emporia*? In *Hommages à Maurice Sznycer, vol.* 2: 111–26. = Semitica 38–39, Cahiers publiés par l'Institut d'Etudes sémantiques du ège de France.

Rebuffat, R. 1992a. Compléments au recueil des *Inscriptions Antiques du Maroc. L'Africa romana* 9: 439–502.

Rebuffat, R. 1992b. Bu Njem. *Encyclopédie Berbère* 11: 1626–42.

Rebuffat, R. 1993. Castellum. *Encyclopédie Berbère* 12: 1822–33.

Rebuffat, R. 1995a. L'investiture des chefs de tribus africaines. In *La noblesse romaine et les chefs Barbares du IIIe au VIIe siècle*, Actes du Colloque International organisé par le Musée des Antiquités Nationales et l'URA 880 du CNRS, 23–33. Paris: Association française d'archéologie mérovingienne.

Rebuffat, R. 1995b. Le centurion M. Porcius Iasucthan à Bu Njem (Notes et documents XI). *Libya Antiqua* n.s. 1: 79–131.

Rebuffat, R. 1997. Les marques d'amphores de Bu Njem (notes et documents XII). *Libya Antiqua* n.s. 3: 163–75.

Rebuffat, R. 1998. L'armée de la Maurétanie Tingitane. *Mélanges de l'Ecole Française de Rome. Antiquité* 110(1): 193–242

Rebuffat, R. 1999. La frontière de la Tingitane. In Lepelley and Dupuis 1999, 265–93.

Rebuffat, R. 2000. L'armée romaine à Gholaia. In G. Alföldy, B. Dobson and W. Eck (eds), *Kaiser, Heer und Gesellschaft in der Römischen Kaiserzeit*, 227–59. Stuttgart: Franz Steiner Verlag.

Rebuffat, R. 2001. Les *gentes* en Maurétanie Tingitane. *Antiquités africaines* 37: 23–44.

Rebuffat, R. 2003. Les romains et les routes caravanières africaines. In M.H. Fantar (ed), *Le Sahara: Lien entre les peuples et les cultures*. Actes du colloque organisé à Douz, 29–22 décembre 2002, 221–60. Tunis: Université de Tunis El Manar.

Rebuffat, R. 2005. Le veteran gétule de Thullium. In Briand-Ponsart 2005a, 193–233.

Rebuffat, R. 2007. Pour un corpus des bilingues punico-libyques et latino-libyques. In M.H. Fantar (ed), *Osmose ethno-culturelle en Mediterranée*, 183–242. Tunis: Université de Tunis El Manar.

Rebuffat, R. 2011a. Les peuples du nord du Maroc. In Briand-Ponsart and Modéran 2011, 63–86.

Rebuffat, R. 2011b. La carte archéologique du Maroc. *Les Nouvelles de l'archéologie* 124: 16–20.

Rebuffat, R. 2012a. Qui va payer l'enceinte urbaine? In Déroche and Leclant 2012, 25–74.

Rebuffat, R. 2012b. *Carte archéologique du Maroc antique: Le Bassin de Sebou, vol. 2: À l'embouchure du Sebou. Cartes Kénitra – Sidi Yahia du Gharb*. Rabat: INSAP.

Rebuffat, R. 2013. Recueil des inscriptions libyques 1940–2012: Supplément à J.-B. Chabot, Recueil des inscriptions libyques, Paris 1940. Archéologie et Philologie d'Orient et d'Occident, CNRS/PSL. Accessed on 26 March 2020. https://halshs.archives-ouvertes.fr/halshs-00841800.

Rebuffat, R. 2014. La gestion du royaume en Afrique. In Briand-Ponsart 2014, 43–64.

Rebuffat, R. and Gabard, I. 1988. La vigne et la vin au Maroc. *Caesarodunum*. 24: 219–36.

Rebuffat, R. and Limane, H. 2011. *Carte archéologique du Maroc antique: Le bassin du Sebou, vol. 1: Au sud du Loukkos, Cartes Arbaoua, Lalla Mimouna, Moulay Bou Selham*. Rabat: INSAP.

Rebuffat, R. and Marichal, R. 1973. Les ostraca de Bu Njem. *Revue des Études latines* 51: 281–86.

Rebuffat, R., Gabard, I, and Le Bohec, Y. 1980. *Bibliographie de l'Afrique du Nord antique. Périodique et séries*. Paris: Presses de l'Ecole normale supérieure.

Rebuffat, R. Lenoir, M. and Akerraz, A. 1986. Plaine et montagne en Tingitane méridionale. In CTHS Montpellier 1986, 219–55.

Reddé, M. 1985. Occupation humaine et mise en valeur économique dans les vallées du nord de la Libye: L'exemple de la wadi Tlal. *Bulletin archéologique du comité des travaux historiques et scientifiques: Afrique du Nord* n.s. 19B: 173–82.

Reddé, M. 1988. *Prospections des vallées du nord de la Libye (1979–1980). La région de Syrte à l'époque romaine*. Cahiers du Groupe de Recherche sur l'armée romaine et les provinces, vol. 4. Paris: Presses de l'Ecole Normale Supérieure.

Reddé, M. 2012. Entre Afrique et Égypte. Les installations hydrauliques dans le désert et le prédésert à l'époque romaine. In Guédon 2012, 145–56.

Reddé, M. 2014. *Les frontières de l'Empire romain (1er siècle avant J.-C. – 5e siècle après J.-C.)*. Lacapelle-Marival: Éditions Archéologie Nouvelle.

Reddé, M. 2018. Il y a frontières et frontières … Les franges sahariennes de Rome, de la mer Rouge à la Tripolitaine. In Guédon 2018b, 139–59.

Rekowska, M. 2016. *In Pursuit of Ancient Cyrenaica … Two Hundred Years of Exploration Set against the History of Archaeology in Europe (1706–1911)*. Translated by M. Rekowska. Oxford: Archaeopress.

Revell, L. 2009. *Roman Imperialism and Local Identities*. Cambridge: Cambridge University Press.

Revell, L. 2013. Code-switching and identity in the western provinces. *HEROM: Journal on Hellenistic and Roman Material Culture* 2: 123–41.

Revell, L. 2016. *Ways of Being Roman: Discourses of Identity in the Roman West*. Oxford: Oxbow Books.

Reygasse, M. 1950. *Monuments funéraires préislamiques de l'Afrique du Nord*. Paris: Arts et métiers graphiques.

Ribichini, S. 1987. *Il tofet e il sacrificio dei fanciulli*. Sassari: Chiarella.

Ricci, C. 2011. *In custodiam urbis*: Notes on the *cohortes urbanae* (1968–2010). *Historia* 60(4): 484–508.

Ricci, F. Tafuri, M.A., Castorina, F., Di Vincenzo, F. Mori, L. and Manzi, G. 2019. The Garamantes from Fewet (Ghat, Fazzan, Libya): A skeletal perspective. In Gatto et al. 2019a, 162–92.

Ricciardi, M. 2018. *L'anfiteatro di Leptis Magna*. Rome: L'Erma di Bretschneider.

Richard, F.G. and MacDonald, K.C. (eds). 2015. *Ethnic Ambiguity and the African Past: Materiality, History, and the Shaping of Cultural Identities*. Walnut Creek: Left Coast Press.

Rickman, G. 1980. *The Corn Supply of Ancient Rome*. Oxford: Clarendon Press.

Ridgway, D. (1992) *The First Western Greeks*. Cambridge: Cambridge University Press.

Rieger, A.-K. 2017. Text and landscape: The complementarity of the Papiro Vaticano Greco 11 R (*PMarm*) to landscape-archaeological results from the arid Marmarica (NW-Egypt/NE-Libya). *Topoi. Orient-Occident* 21(1): 105–46.

Rieger, A.-K. and Möller, H. 2011. Kilns, commodities and consumers: Greco-Roman pottery production in eastern Marmarica (northwestern Egypt). *Archäologischer Anzeiger* 2011(1): 141–70

Rieger, A.-K., Vetter, T. and Möller, H. 2012. The desert dwellers of Marmarica, Western Desert: Second millennium BCE to first millennium CE. In H. Barnard and K. Duistermaat (eds), *The History of the Peoples of the Eastern Desert*, 156–73. Los Angeles: Cotsen Institute of Archaeology Press at UCLA.

Rife, J. 2001. The human remains from Site 250. In Stirling et al. 2001, 325–41.

RIL = Chabot 1940.

RIL 2 = Rebuffat 2013

Rind, M. 2009. *Römische Villen in Nordafrika: Untersuchungen zu Architektur und Wirtschaftsweise*. British Archaeological Reports, International Series 2012. Oxford: Archaeopress.

Ritter, S. and Ben Tahar, S. 2020. New insights into the urban history of *Meninx* (Jerba): Preliminary report on the Tunisian–German investigations in 2017 and 2018. *Antiquités africaines* 56: 101–28.

Ritter, S. and Von Rummel, P. (eds). 2015, *Thugga 3: Archäologische Untersuchungen zur Siedlungsgeschichte von Thugga. Die Ausgrabungen südlich der Maison du Trifolium 2001–2003*. Wiesbaden: Ludwig Reichert Verlag.

Ritter, S., Ben Tahar, S., Fassbinder, J.W.E. and Lambers, L. 2018. Landscape archaeology and urbanism at Meninx: Results of geophysical prospection on Jerba (2015). *Journal of Roman Archaeology* 31: 357–72.

Rives, J.B. 1995. *Religion and Authority in Roman Carthage from Augustus to Constantine*. Oxford: Clarendon Press.

Rives, J.B. 2007. *Religion in the Roman Empire*. Oxford: Blackwell.

Rivet, A.L.F. 1980. Celtic names and Roman places. *Britannia* 11: 1–19.

RMD 1–4 = Roxan, M.M. 1978/1985/1994/2003. *Roman Military Diplomas, vols. 1–4* London: Institute of Archaeology

Roddaz, J.-M. 2004. Auguste et les confins. *L'Africa romana* 15: 261–76.

Roller, D.W. 2003. *The World of Juba II and Kleopatra Selene: Royal Scholarship on Rome's African Frontier*. London: Routledge.

Romanelli, P. 1925. *Leptis Magna*. Rome: Ministero delle colonie.

Romanelli, P. 1959. *Storia delle province romane dell' Africa*. Rome: L'Erma di Bretschneider.

Romanelli, P. 1970. *Tipografia e archeologia dell'Africa Romana*. In Enciclopedia classica, 3: Archeologia e storia dell'arte classica, 10.7. Torino: Società Editrice Internazionale.

Romanelli, P. 1974. Le condizioni giuridiche del suolo in Africa. *Atti del convegno internazionale sul tema: I diritti locali nelle provincie romane con particolare riguardo alle condizioni giuridiche del suolo (Roma 26–28 ottobre 1971)*, 171–215. Rome: Accademia nazionale dei Lincei.

Romanelli, P. 1981. *In Africa e a Roma. Scripta minora selecta*. Rome: L'Erma di Bretschneider.

Rosignol, B. and Dana, D. 2020. Introduction: Mobilité, garnisons et nouveautés en épigraphie militaire: Les unités auxiliaires et l'Afrique romaine. *Antiquités africaines* 56: 275–84.

Ross, D. 2005. *Kbor Klib and the Battle of Zama: An Analysis of the Monument in Tunisia and Its Possible Connection with the Battle Waged between Hannibal and Scipio in 202BC*. British Archaeological Reports International Series S1399. Oxford: Archaeopress.

Rossignoli, C. 1994. Templi periurbani di Africa Proconsulare e Numidia: Alcuni esempli. *L'Africa romana* 10(2): 559–95.

Rothenhöfer, P. and Blänsdorf, J. 2016. Sana mente sanaque memoria testamentum feci: Eine testamentarische Verfügung vom 12. April 340 n. Chr. *Gephyra* 13: 153–63

Rothe, U. 2009. *Dress and Cultural Identity in the Rhine-Moselle Region of the Roman Empire.* British Archaeological Reports International Series S2038. Oxford: Archaeopress.

Rouighi, R. 2019. *Inventing the Berbers: History and Ideology in the Maghrib.* Pennsylvania: University of Pennsylvania Press.

Rousselle, A. (ed). 1995. *Frontières terrestres, frontières célestes dans l'Antiquité.* Perpignan: Presses Universitaires de Perpignan.

Rouvillois-Brigol, M. 1986. Quelques remarques sur la variation de l'occupation du sol dans le sud-est algérien. In CTHS Montpellier 1986, 35–53.

Roxan, M. 1973. The *auxilia* of Mauretania Tingitana. *Latomus* 32(4): 838–55.

Roymans, N. 2004. *Ethnic Identity and Imperial Power: The Batavians in the Early Roman Empire.* Amsterdam: Amsterdam University Press.

Rushworth, A., 2000. From periphery to core in late antique Mauretania. In G. Fincham, G. Harrison, R. Holland and L. Revell (eds), *TRAC 99: Proceedings of the Ninth Annual Theoretical Roman Archaeology Conference*, 90–103. Oxford: Oxbow Books.

Rushworth, A. 2004. From Arzuges to Rustamids: State formation and regional identity in the Pre-Saharan Zone. In Merrills 2004, 77–98.

Rushworth, A. 2015. Castra or centenaria? Interpreting the later forts of the North African frontier. In R. Collins, M. Symonds and M. Weber (eds), *Roman Military Architecture on the Frontiers: Armies and Their Architecture in Late Antiquity*, 123–39. Oxford: Oxbow Books.

Russell, B. 2013. *The Economics of the Roman Stone Trade.* Oxford Studies on the Roman Economy. Oxford: Oxford University Press.

Said, E.W. 1978. *Orientalism.* Harmondsworth: Penguin.

Said, E.W. 1992. *Culture and Imperialism.* London: Vintage.

Saidi, O. 1980. *Les grandes plaines de la haute vallée de la Medjerda et de la Kroumirie: Contribution à une monographie régionale du nord-ouest de la Tunisie.* Tunis: Imprimerie officielle de la République Tunisienne.

Saint-Amans, S. 2004. *Topographie religieuse de* Thugga *(Dougga): Ville romaine d'Afrique proconsulaire (Tunisie).* Bordeaux: Ausonius.

Salama, P. 1951. *Les Voies romaines de l'Afrique du Nord.* Algiers: Gouvernement général de l'Algérie.

Salama, P. 1966. Occupation de la Maurétanie Césarienne occidentale sous le Bas-Empire romain. In R. Chevalier (ed), *Mélanges d'archéologie et d'histoire offerts à A. Piganiol*, 1291–311. Paris: Centre de recherches historiques.

Salama, P. 1977. Les déplacements succesifs en Maurétanie Césarienne. Essai de synthèse. In Fitz 1977, 577–95.

Salama, P. 1981. The Sahara in classical antiquity. In Mokhtar 1981, 513–32.

Salama, P. 1987. *Bornes milliaires d'Afrique proconsulaire: Un panorama historique du Bas-Empire romain.* CEFR 101. Rome: École française de Rome.

Salama, P. 1999a. Cinquantenaire de la Carte du réseau routier de l'Afrique romaine 1947–1997. Problème de frontières administratives et militaires: Additions et corrections. In Lepelley and Dupuis 1999, 23–26.

Salama, P. 1999b. Tableaux de maîtres. In Lepelley and Dupuis 1999, 295–310.

Salcedo, F. 1996. *Africa: Iconografía de una provincia romana.* Rome/Madrid: Consejo superior de investigaciones científicas.

Salza Prina Ricotti, E. 1971. Le ville marittime di Silin (Leptis Magna). *Atti della Pontificia Accademia Romana di Archeologia. Rendiconti* 43: 135–63.

Sanghera, S. 2021. *Empireland: How Imperialism has Shaped Modern Britain*. London: Penguin.

Sanmartí, J. 2022. Libyan culture and society. In Hitchner 2022a, 41–63.

Sanmartí, J., Kallala, N., Belarte, M.C., Ramon, J. Telmini, B.M., Jornet, R. and Miniaoui, S. 2012. Filling gaps in the protohistory of the eastern Maghreb: The *Althiburos* Archaeological Project (El Kef, Tunisia). *Journal of African Archaeology* 10(1): 21–44.

Sanmartí, J., Kallala, N., Jornet, R., Belarte, M.C., Canela, J., Chérif, S., Campillo, J., Montanero, D., Bermúdez, X., Fadrique, T., Revilla, V., Ramon, J. and Ben Moussa, M. 2015. Roman Dolmens? The Megalithic necropolises of Eastern Maghreb revisited. In M. Díaz-Guardamino, L. García Sanjuán and D. Wheatley (eds), *The Lives of Prehistoric Monuments in Iron Age, Roman, and Medieval Europe*, 287–304. Oxford: Oxford University Press.

Sanmartí, J., Cruz Folch, I., Campillo, J. and Montanero, D. 2019. Numidian burial practices. In Gatto et al. 2019a, 249–90.

Sanmartí, J., Kallala, N., Belarte, M.C., Ramon, J., Cantero, F.J., López, D., Portillo, M. and Valenzuela, S. 2020. Numidian state formation in the Tunisian High Tell. In Sterry and Mattingly 2020a, 438–75.

Santangelo, F. 2008. Le quotidien d'une cité exceptionnelle: Élites et évergétisme dans la Carthage romaine. In C. Berrendonner, M. Cébeillac-Gervasoni and L. Lamoine (eds), *Le quotidien municipal dans l'Occident romain*, 459–71. Clermont-Ferrand: Presses universitaires Blaise-Pascal.

Saumagne, C. 1929. Les vestiges d'une centuriation romaine à l'est d'El-Djem. *Comptes rendus des séances de l'Académie des Inscriptions et Belles-Lettres* 73–4: 307–13.

Scarin, E. 1934. *Le oasi del Fezzàn: Ricerche ed osservazioni di geografia umana*. Bologna: Nicola Zanichelli.

Scheding, P. 2019. *Urbaner Ballungsraum im Römischen Nordafrika: Zum Einfluss von mikroregionalen Wirtschafts- und Sozialstrukturen auf den Städtebau in der Africa Proconsularis*. Studien zur Antiken Stadt 16. Weisbaden: Reichert Verlag.

Scheding, P. 2020. Micro-regional urbanism: An ancient urban landscape in Roman North Africa. In de Ligt and Bintliff 2020, 350–74.

Scheele, J. 2010. Traders, saints, and irrigation: Reflections on Saharan connectivity. *The Journal of African History* 51(3): 281–300.

Scheele, J. 2017. The need for nomads: Camel-herding, raiding, and Saharan trade. In Mattingly et al. 2017a, 55–79.

Scheele, J. 2020. Urbanisation, inequality and political authority in the Sahara. In Sterry and Mattingly 2020a, 667–91.

Scheidel, W. 2009. In search of Roman economic growth. *Journal of Roman Archaeology* 22.1: 46–70.

Scheidel, W., Morris, I. and Saller, R.P. (eds). 2007. *The Cambridge Economic History of the Greco-Roman World*. Cambridge: Cambridge University Press.

Schimmer, F. 2012. New evidence for a Roman fort and *vicus* at Mizda (Tripolitania). *Libyan Studies* 43: 33–39.

Schmid, S., Mackensen, M. and Stephani, M. 2019. The Roman watchtower near Gheriat el-Garbia, Tripolitania. *Libya Antiqua* n.s. 12: 69–83.

Schmidt, P.R. 2017. Decolonizing archaeological practice: Gazing into the past to transform the future. *Archaeologies: Journal of the World Archaeological Congress* 13(3): 392–411.

Schrüfer-Kolb, I.E. 2007a. Metallurgical and non-metallurgical industrial activities. In Mattingly 2007a, 448–62.

Schrüfer-Kolb, I.E. 2011. Iron production debris. In Stone et al. 2011a, 434–53.

Schwartz, J.H., Houghton, F.D., Macchiarelli, R. and Bondioli, L. 2010. Skeletal remains from Punic Carthage do not support systematic sacrifice of infants. *PloS ONE* 5(2): e9177.

Schwartz, J.H., Houghton, F.D., Bondioli, L. and Macchiarelli, R. 2012. Bones, teeth, and estimating age of perinates: Carthaginian infant sacrifice revisited. *Antiquity* 86(333): 738–45.

Schwarz, H. and Ray, S. (eds). 2000. *A Companion to Postcolonial Studies*. Oxford: Blackwell.

Scobie, A. 1986. Slums, sanitation, and mortality in the Roman world. *Klio* 68: 399–433.

Scott, J.-C. 1990. *Domination and the Arts of Resistance: Hidden Transcripts*. New Haven: Yale University Press.

Scott, S. and Webster, J. (eds). 2003. *Roman Imperialism and Provincial Art*. Cambridge: Cambridge University Press.

Sear, F. 2006. *Roman Theatres: An Archaeological Study*. Oxford: Oxford University Press.

Sears, G. 2007. *Late Roman African Urbanism: Continuity and Transformation in the City*. British Archaeological Reports International Series S1693. Oxford: BAR Archaeopress.

Sears, G. 2011. *The Cities of Roman Africa*. Stroud: History Press.

Sebaï, M. 2005. La romanisation en Afrique, retour sur un débat. La résistance africaine: Une approche libératrice? *Afrique & Histoire* 1(3): 39–56.

Sehili, S. 2002. Femme propriétaires de domaines en Afrique romaine. *Cahiers de Tunisie* 181: 49–64.

Sehili, S. 2008a. L'huile de la Byzacène. *L'Africa romana* 17: 777–92.

Sehili, S. 2008b. Henchir el Begar, centre du Saltus Beguenses: Étude archéologique et historique. In Bejaoui 2008, 85–106.

Sehili, S. 2009. *Huileries antiques de Jebel Semmama: Région de Kasserine*. Tunis: Centre de Publication Universitaire, Manouba.

Sehili, S. 2010. L'occupation humaine antique dans la Dorsale occidentale de la Tunisie. In Bejaoui 2010, 83–105.

Sehili, S. 2018. Bilan de la recherche archéologique sur l'oléiculture antique en Tunisie. In Sehili et al. 2018, 191–230

Sehili, S. and Ben Baaziz, S. (eds). 2011. *L'olivier en Méditerranée entre histoire et patrimoine*. Tunis: Université de la Manouba.

Sehili, S., Naddari, L., Grira, M. and Abid, H. 2018. *Mélanges d'histoire et d'archéologie de l'Afrique antique offerts à Sadok Ben Baaziz*. Tunis: Université de la Manouba.

Selkirk, A. 2006. Review of "An Imperial Possession: Britain in the Roman Empire" [Mattingly 2006a]. *Current Archaeology* 205: 30–31.

SEMPAM Tabarka 2003. *Protohistoire, cités de l'Afrique du Nord, fouilles et prospections récentes*, Actes du VIIIe Colloque international sur l'Histoire et l'Archéologie de l'Afrique du Nord antique et médiévale, Ier Colloque international sur l'histoire et l'archéologie du Maghreb (Tabarka, 8–13 mars 2000). Tunis: INP = Khanoussi 2003.

SEMPAM Tripoli 2008. *Lieux de cultes: Aires votives, temples, églises, mosquées*, Actes du IXe Colloque international sur l'histoire et l'archéologie de l'Afrique du Nord antique et médiévale (Tripoli, 19–25 février 2005). Paris: Éditions du CNRS = Blanc-Bijon 2008.

SEMPAM Caen 2014. *Centres de pouvoir et organisation de l'espace*. Actes du Xe colloque international sur l'histoire et l'archéologie de l'Afrique du Nord préhistorique, antique et médiévale (Caen, 25–28 mai 2009). Caen: Presses universitares de Caen = Briand-Ponsart 2014.

Sen, A. 2006. *Identity and Violence: The Illusion of Destiny*. New York: Norton.

Sennequier, G. and Colonna, C. 2003. *L'Algérie au temps des royaumes numides: Ve siècle avant J.-C. – Ier siècle après J.-C.* Paris: Somogy.

Seston, W. and Euzennat, M. 1971. Un dossier de la chancellerie romaine: La *Tabula Banasitana*. Étude de diplomatique. *Comptes rendus des séances de l'Académie des inscriptions et belles-lettres* 1971, 115(3): 468–90.

Sghaïer, Y. and Dammak-Latrach, O. 2020. La céramique préromaine de la nécropole du Nord-Ouest à Dougga: Un premier aperçu. *Antiquités africaines* 56: 207–19.

Shaw, B.D. 1979a. The camel in ancient North Africa and the Sahara: History, biology and human economy. *Bulletin de l'IFAN Serie B* 41(4): 663–721 = Shaw 1995a, chap.4.

Shaw, B.D. 1979b. Rural periodic markets in Roman North Africa as mechanisms of social integration and control. *Research in Economic Anthropology* 2: 91–117.

Shaw, B.D. 1980. Archaeology and knowledge: The history of the African provinces of the Roman empire. *Florilegium* 2: 28–60 = Shaw 1995a, chap.1.

Shaw, B.D. 1981a. Rural markets in North Africa and the political economy of the Roman Empire. *Antiquités africaines* 17: 37–83 = Shaw 1995b, chap.1.

Shaw, B.D. 1981b. Climate, environment and history: The case of Roman North Africa. In T.M.L. Wigley et al. (eds), *Climate and History*, 379–403. Cambridge: Cambridge University Press = Shaw 1995a, chap.3.

Shaw, B.D. 1981c. Fear and loathing: The nomad menace in Roman Africa. In Wells 1981, 29–50 = Shaw 1995b, chap.7.

Shaw, B.D. 1981d. The Elder Pliny's African geography. *Historia* 30(4): 424–71 = Shaw 1995b, chap.4.

Shaw, B.D. 1982. Lamasba: An ancient irrigation community. *Antiquités africaines* 18: 61–103 = Shaw 1995a, chap.4.

Shaw, B.D. 1983a. "Eaters of flesh, drinkers of milk": The ancient Mediterranean ideology of the pastoral nomad. *Ancient Society* 13/14: 5–31 = Shaw 1995b, chap.6.

Shaw, B.D. 1983b. Soldiers and society: The army in Numidia. *Opus: Rivista internazionale per la storia economica e sociale dell'antichità* 2: 133–60 = Shaw 1995b, chap. 9.

Shaw, B.D. 1984. Water and society in the ancient Maghrib: Technology, property and development. *Antiquités africaines* 20: 121–73 = Shaw 1995a, chap.5.

Shaw, B.D. 1987. Autonomy and tribute: Mountain and plain in Mauretania Tingitana. *Revue des mondes musulmans et de la Méditerranée* 41–42: 66–89 = Shaw 1995b, chap. 8.

Shaw, B.D. 1991a. The noblest monuments and the smallest things: Wells, walls and aqueducts in the making of Roman Africa. In Hodge 1991, 63–91 = Shaw 1995a, chap. 7.

Shaw, B.D. 1991b. The structures of local society in the early Maghrib: The elders. *The Maghreb Review* 16: 18–54 = Shaw 1995b, chap.2.

Shaw, B.D. 1995a. *Environment and Society in Roman North Africa*. London: Variorum.

Shaw, B.D. 1995b. *Rulers, Nomads, and Christians in Roman North Africa*. London: Variorum.

Shaw, B.D. 2000. Rebels and outsiders. In Bowman et al. 2000, 361–403.

Shaw, B.D. 2001. Challenging Braudel: A new vision of the Mediterranean. *Journal of Roman Archaeology* 14: 419–53.

Shaw, B.D. 2003. A peculiar island: Maghrib and Mediterranean. *Mediterranean Historical Review* 18(2): 93–125; reprinted in I. Malkin (ed), 2005, *Mediterranean Paradigms and Classical Antiquity*, 93–125. London/New York: Routledge.

Shaw, B.D. 2006. *At the Edge of the Corrupting Sea*. [The 23rd J.L. Myers Memorial Lecture.] Oxford: University of Oxford.

Shaw, B.D. 2011. *Sacred Violence: African Christians and Sectarian Hatred in the Age of Augustine*. Cambridge: Cambridge University Press.

Shaw, B.D. 2013a. *Bringing in the Sheaves: Economy and Metaphor in the Roman World*. Toronto: University of Toronto Press.

Shaw, B.D. 2013b. Cult and belief in Punic and Roman Africa. In W. Adler (ed), *The Cambridge History of Religions in the Ancient World, vol. 2: From the Hellenistic Age to Late Antiquity*, 235–63. Cambridge: Cambridge University Press.

Shaw, B.D. 2014. Who are you? Africa and Africans. In J. McInerney (ed), *A Companion to Ethnicity in the Ancient Mediterranean*, 527–40. Oxford: Wiley-Blackwell.

Shaw, B.D. 2021. Keti, Son of Maswalat. Ethnicity and empire. In J.J. Price, M. Finkelberg and Y. Shahar (eds), *Rome: An Empire of Many Nations: New Perspectives on Ethnic Diversity and Cultural Identity*, 58–83. Cambridge: Cambridge University Press.

Sheldon, R. 1982. Romanizzazione, acculturazione e resistenza: Problemi concettuali nella storia del Nordafrica. *Dialoghi di Archeologia* n.s. 4.1: 102–06.

Sheldrick, N. 2016. *Building the Countryside: A Regional Perspective on the Architecture and Settlement of Rural Tripolitania from the 1st c. BC to the 7th c. AD*. Unpublished DPhil thesis, University of Oxford.

Sheldrick, N. 2021. *Building the Countryside: Rural Architecture and Settlement in Tripolitania during the Roman and Late Antique Periods*. London: Society for Libyan Studies.

Shennan, S.J. (ed). 1994. *Archaeological Approaches to Cultural Identity*. 2nd edition. London: Routledge.

Sherwin-White, A.N. 1944. Geographical factors in Roman Algeria. *Journal of Roman Studies* 34(1–2): 1–10.

Sherwin-White, A.N. 1973. The *Tabula* of Banasa and the *Constitutio Antoniniana*. *Journal of Roman Studies* 63: 86–98.

Shipley, G. 2011. *Pseudo-Skylax's Periplous: The Circumnavigation of the Inhabited World: Text, Translation and Commentary*. Exeter: Bristol Phoenix Press.

Sigman, M.C. 1977. The Romans and the indigenous tribes of Mauretania Tingitana. *Historia* 26(4): 415–39.

Sintes, C. 2010. *Libye Antique: Un rêve de marbre*. Paris: Imprimerie nationale Éditions.

Sintes, C. and Rebahi, Y. 2003. *Algérie antique: Catalogue de l'exposition 26 avril au 17 août 2003, Musée de l'Arles et de la Provence antiques*. Arles: Éditions du Musée d'Arles antique.

Sirago, V.A. 1987. Contadini liberi nelle province africane. *L'Africa romana* 4: 253–65.

Sirago, V.A. 1990. Aspetti del colonialismo romano in Africa. *L'Africa romana* 7: 973–92.

Sirks, A.J.B. 1991. *Food for Rome: The Legal Structure of the Transportation and Processing of Supplies for the Imperial Distributions in Rome and Constantinople*. Amsterdam: Gieben.

Skounti, A. 2012. Les Berbères du Maroc. Qui sont ils, que sont ils? *Les Cahiers du Musée Berbère* 1: 79–96.

Slim, H. 1984. Recherches préliminaires sur les amphithéâtres romains de Tunisie. *L'Africa romana* 1: 129–65.

Slim, H. 1986. Les amphithéâtres d'El-Jem. *Comptes rendus des séances de l'Académie des inscriptions et belles-lettres* 1986, 130(3): 440–69.

Slim, H. 1988. La Sauvegarde et la mise en valeur du grand amphithéâtre d'El-Jem. *Africa* 10: 325–58.

Slim, H. 1992. Maîtrise de l'eau en Tunisie dans l'Afrique romain. In Argoud et al. 1992, 513–32.

Slim, H. 2004. *La Tunisie antique: De Hannibal à St Augustin*. Paris: Menges.

Slim, H., Bonifay, M. and Trousset, P. 1999. L'usine de salaison de Neapolis (Nabeul): Premiers résultats des fouilles 1995–1998. *Africa* 17: 153–97.

Slim, H., Trousset, P., Paskoff, R. and Oueslati, A. 2004. *Le littoral de la Tunisie: Étude géoarchéologique et historique*. Paris: CNRS Éditions.

Slim, L. 1984. A propos d'un cimetière d'enfants à *Thysdrus*. *L'Africa romana* 1, 167–77.

Slimani, S. 2015. Des sites inédites dans la region du Hodna: Quelques exemples aux alentours de Zabi. In Mrabet 2015, 41–60 (in Arabic).

Slimani, S. and Kherbouche, H. 2018. Les formes d'occupation antique dans le Hodna: État des lieux. In Guédon 2018b, 193–206.

Smajda, E. 1983. Modes de contact, sociétés indigènes et formation de l'état numide au second siècle avant notre ère. In *Modes de contacts et processus de transformation dans les sociétés antiques*, 685–702. CEFR 67. Rome: École française de Rome.

Smith, A.T., Allen, M.G., Brindle, T. and Fulford, M. 2016. *New Visions of the Countryside of Roman Britain, vol. 1: The Rural Settlement of Roman Britain*. Britannia Monograph 29. London: Society for the Promotion of Roman Studies.

Smith, A.T., Allen, M.G., Brindle, T., Fulford, M., Lodwick, L. and Rohnbogner, A. 2018. *New Visions of the Countryside of Roman Britain, vol. 3: Life and Death in the Countryside of Roman Britain*. Britannia Monograph 31. London: Society for the Promotion of Roman Studies.

Smith, D.J. 1971. The centenaria of Tripolitania and their antecedents. In Gadallah 1971, 299–321.

Smith, P., Avishai, G., Greene, J.A. and Stager, L.E. 2011. Aging cremated infants: The problem of sacrifice at the Tophet of Carthage. *Antiquity* 85(329): 859–74.

Snowden, F.M. 1970. *Blacks in Antiquity: Ethiopians in the Greco-Roman Experience*. Cambridge, MA: Harvard University Press.

Sommer, M. 2010. Shaping Mediterranean economy and trade: Phoenician cultural identities in the Iron Age. In Hales and Hodos 2010, 114–37.

Souville, G. 1973. *Atlas préhistorique du Maroc, 1. Le Maroc atlantique*. Paris: CNRS Éditions.

Soyer, J. 1973. Les cadastres anciens de région de Saint-Donat (Algérie). *Antiquités africaines* 7: 275–96.

Soyer, J. 1976. Les centuriations romaines en Algérie orientale. *Antiquités africaines* 10: 107–80.

Speidel, M.P. 1975. Africa and Rome: Continuous resistance? (A vexillation of the Norican Ala Augusta in Mauretania). *Proceedings of the African Classical Associations* 13: 36–38.

Speidel, M.P. 1982. Legionary cohorts in Mauretania: The role of legionary cohorts in the structure of expeditionary armies. In H. Temporini (ed), *Aufstieg und Niedergang der römischen Welt: Principat, vol. 10/2: Teilband Politische Geschichte (Provinzen und Randvölker: Afrika mit Ägypten [Forts.])*, 850–60. Berlin: De Gruyter.

Speidel, M.P. 1988. Outpost duty in the desert. Building the fort at Gholaia (Bu Njem, Libya). *Antiquités africaines* 24: 99–102.

Speidel, M.P. 1993. Mauri equites: The tactics of light cavalry in Mauretania. *Antiquités africaines* 29: 121–26.

Speidel, M.P. 2006. *Emperor Hadrian's Speeches to the African Army: A New Text*. Mainz: Verlag des Römisch-Germanischen Zentralmuseums.

Squarciapino, M.F. 1974. *Sculture del foro Severiano di Leptis Magna*. Rome: L'Erma di Bretschneider.

Stager, L. 1980. The rise of child sacrifice at Carthage. In Pedley 1980, 1–11.

Stager, L.E. 1992. Le tophet et le port commercial. In Ennabli 1992, 73–78

Stark, B.L. and Chance, J.K. 2012. The strategies of provincials in empires. In M.E. Smith (ed), *The Comparative Archaeology of Complex Societies*, 192–237. Cambridge: Cambridge University Press.

Stein, G.J. (ed). 2005. *The Archaeology of Colonial Encounters: Comparative Perspectives*. Santa Fe: School of American Research Press.

Stern, K.B. 2007. *Inscribing Devotion and Death: Archaeological Evidence for Jewish Populations of North Africa*. Religions of the Greco-Roman World 161. Leiden: Brill.

Sterret-Krause, A.E. 2012. *The Impacts of Private Donations on the Civic Landscapes of Roman Africa Proconsularis*. Unpublished PhD thesis, University of Cincinnati.

Sterry, M. and Mattingly, D.J. 2011. DMP XIII: Reconnaissance survey of archaeological sites in the Murzuq area. *Libyan Studies* 42: 103–16.

Sterry, M. and Mattingly, D.J. 2013. Desert Migrations Project XVII: Further AMS dates for historic settlements from Fazzan, south-west Libya. *Libyan Studies* 44: 127–40.

Sterry, M. and Mattingly, D.J. (eds). 2020a. *Urbanisation and State Formation in the Ancient Sahara and Beyond*. Cambridge: Cambridge University Press and The Society for Libyan Studies.

Sterry, M. and Mattingly, D.J. 2020b. Pre-Islamic oasis settlements in the southern Sahara. In Sterry and Mattingly 2020a, 277–329.

Sterry, M. and Mattingly, D.J. 2020c. Discussion: Sedentarisation and urbanisation in the Sahara. In Sterry and Mattingly 2020a, 330–55.

Sterry, M., Mattingly, D.J., Gatto, M.C. and Ray, N. 2019. Concluding discussion. In Gatto et al. 2019a, 525–48.

Sterry, M., Mattingly, D.J. and Bokbot, Y. 2020. Pre-Islamic oasis settlements in the north-western Sahara. In Sterry and Mattingly 2020a, 239–76.

Sterry, M., Mattingly, D.J. and Wilson, A.I. 2022. Foggaras and the Garamantes: Hydraulic landscapes in the Central Sahara. In S. Rost (ed), *Irrigation in Early States: New Directions*, 41–61. Oriental Institute Seminars 13. Chicago: Oriental Institute of the University of Chicago.

Stevens, S.T. 1995. A late-Roman urban population in a cemetery of Vandalic date at Carthage. *Journal of Roman Archaeology* 8: 263–70.

Stoll-Simon, C. 2006. Parcours nomades dans l'imaginaire occidental des 19e et 20e siècle. Sahara: Le refuge du "tout Autre". In M.H. Fantar 2006, 147–56.

Stirling, L.M. 2007. The koine of the cupula in Roman North Africa and the transition from cremation to inhumation. In Stone and Stirling 2007a, 110–37.

Stirling, L.M., Mattingly, D.J. and Ben Lazreg, N. (eds). 2001. *Leptiminus (Lamta): A Roman Port City in Tunisia. Report no. 2. The East Baths, Cemeteries, Kilns, Venus Mosaic, Site Museum, and Other Studies*. JRA supplement 41. Portsmouth, RI: Journal of Roman Archaeology.

Stirling, L.M., Stone, D.L. and Ben Lazreg, N. 2000. Roman kilns and rural settlement: Interim report of the 1999 season of the Leptiminus Archaeological Project. *Echos du Monde Classique / Classical Views* 44, n.s. 19(2): 179–224.

Stone, D.L. 1997. *The Development of an Imperial Territory: Romans, Africans, and the Transformation of the Rural Landscape of Tunisia.* Unpublished PhD thesis, University of Michigan.

Stone, D.L. 1998. Culture and investment in the rural landscape: The North African *bonus agricola*. *Antiquités africaines* 34: 103–13.

Stone, D.L. 2004. Problems and possibilities in comparative survey: A North African perspective. In Alcock and Cherry 2004, 132–43.

Stone, D.L. 2007a. Monuments on the margins: Interpreting the first millennium BCE rock-cut tombs (Haouanet) of North Africa. In Stone and Stirling 2007a, 43–74.

Stone, D.L. 2007b. Burial, identity and local culture in North Africa. In P. van Dommelen and N. Terrenato (eds), *Articulating Local Cultures: Power and Identity Under the Expanding Roman Republic*, 126–44. JRA supplement 63. Portsmouth, RI: Journal of Roman Archaeology.

Stone, D.L. 2008. Coloni and the imperial cult in the countryside of Sitifis. *L'Africa romana* 17: 2157–70.

Stone, D.L. 2010. Supplying Rome and the empire: The distribution of stamped amphoras from *Byzacena*. In J.H. Humphrey (ed), *Studies on Roman Pottery of the Provinces of* Africa Proconsularis *and* Byzacena *(Tunisia)*, 127–49. JRA supplement 76. Portsmouth, RI: Journal of Roman Archaeology.

Stone, D.L. 2013a. The economy of early cities. In P. Clark (ed), *The Oxford Handbook of Cities In World History*. Oxford: Oxford University Press, 127–46.

Stone, D.L. 2013b. The archaeology of Africa in the Roman Republic. In J. DeRose Evans (ed), *A Companion to Roman Republican Archaeology*, 505–21. Chichester: Wiley-Blackwell.

Stone, D.L. 2014a. Identity and identification in Apuleius' *Apology*, *Florida*, and *Metamorphoses*. In Lee et al. 2014, 154–73.

Stone, D.L. 2014b. Africa in the Roman Empire: Connectivity, the economy, and artificial port structures. *American Journal of Archaeology* 118(4): 565–600.

Stone, D.L. 2016a. The jetty with platform: A distinctive port structure from North Africa. *Antiquités africaines* 52: 125–39

Stone, D.L. 2016b. Burial mounds and state formation in North Africa: A volumetric and energetic approach. In Mugnai et al. 2016, 39–53.

Stone, D.L. 2020. A diachronic and regional approach to North African urbanism. In de Ligt and Bintliff 2020, 324–49.

Stone, D.L. 2022. Archaeology. In Hitchner 2022a, 9–23.

Stone, D.L. Forthcoming. Isolation and connectivity: The Maghrib and the Mediterranean in the first Millennium BC. In L. Gosner and J. Hayne, (eds), *Local Experiences of Connectivity and Mobility in the Ancient West-Central Mediterranean*. Monographs in Mediterranean Archaeology. Sheffield: Equinox Publishing.

Stone, D.L. and Carr, K.E. 2011. Gazetteer of sites and catalogue of pottery from the rural survey. In Stone et al. 2011a, 629–60.

Stone, D.L. and Mattingly, D.J. 2011. Moderate economic growth in a port city: Investment and workshops at Leptiminus. *FACTA: A Journal of Roman Material Culture Studies* 5: 31–63.

Stone, D.L. and Stirling, L.M. (eds). 2007a. *Mortuary Landscapes of North Africa*. Toronto: University of Toronto Press.

Stone, D.L. and Stirling, L.M. 2007b. Funerary monuments and mortuary practices in the landscapes of North Africa. In Stone and Stirling 2007a, 3–31.

Stone, D.L., Mattingly, D.J. and Ben Lazreg, N. 2011a. *Leptiminus (Lamta). Report No. 3: The Field Survey*. JRA supplement 87. Portsmouth, RI: Journal of Roman Archaeology.

Stone, D.L., Mattingly, D.J. and Dore, J. 2011b. Methodology and fieldwalking data. In Stone et al. 2011a, 49–89.

Stone, D.L., Mattingly, D.J., Wilson, A.I., Stirling, L., and Ben Lazreg, N. 2011c. Urban morphology, infrastructure and amenities. In Stone et al. 2011a, 120–204.

Stucchi, S. 1975. *Architettura cirenaica*. Rome: L'Erma di Bretschneider.

Stucchi, S. (ed). 1976. *Cirene e la Grecia = Quaderni di Archeologia della Libya* 8.

Stucchi, S. and Luni, M. (eds). 1987. *Cirene e I Libyi = Quaderni di Archeologia della Libya* 12.

Syme, R. 1951. Tacfarinas, the Musulamii and Thubursicu. In P.R. Coleman-Norton (ed), *Studies in Roman Economic History in Honor of Allen Chester Johnson*, 113–31. Princeton: Princeton University Press.

Stutz, R. 2007. *Thugga 2: Drei Hanghaüser in Thugga: Maison des trois Masques, Maison du Labyrinthe, Maison de Dionysos et d'Ulysse*. Mainz: Philipp von Zabern.

Suder, W. 1984. Le città dell'Africa romana: Mortalità. *Bulletin archéologique du comité des travaux historiques et scientifiques: Afrique du Nord* n.s. 17B: 225–35.

Suder, W. 1985. La demografia dell'Africa romana: Rassegna delle richerche e della bibliografia. *Bulletin archéologique du comité des travaux historiques et scientifiques: Afrique du Nord* n.s. 19B: 505–10.

Sycamore, R.A. and Buchanan, B.G. 2016. Rediscovering the rural landscape of Carthage's hinterland: A reassessment of the Carthaginian Countryside survey. *Libyan Studies* 47: 117–27.

Sznycer, M. 1976. L'expansion phénico-punique dans la méditerranée occidentale (problemes et methodes). In M. Galley (ed), *Actes du 2e congrès international. D'étude des cultures de la Méditerranée occidentale, vol. 1*, 35–48. Alger: Société Nationale d'Edition et de Diffusion.

Sznycer M. 2003. Nouvelles observations et nouvelles réflexions sur le bilinguisme punicolatin: Langue de culture et langue d'usage. *Antiquités africaines* 38–39: 275–80.

Tahar, M.A. 2005. L'hellénisme dans le royaume numide au IIe siècle av J.-C. *Antiquités africaines* 40–41: 29–41.

Talbert, R.J.A. (ed). 2000. *Barrington Atlas of the Greek and Roman World*. Princeton: Princeton University Press.

Tanda, G., Ghaki, M. and Cicilloni, R. (eds). 2009. *Storia dei paesaggi preistorici e protostorici nell'Alto Tell tunisino: Missione 2002–2003*. Cagliari: Edizioni AV.

Tengström, E. 1974. *Bread for the People: Studies of the Corn-Supply of Rome during the Late Empire*. Acta Instituti Romani Regni Sueciae 12. Stockholm: Astrom Editions AB.

Terrenato, N. 2005. The deceptive archetype: Roman colonialism in Italy and postcolonial thought. In Hurst and Owen 2005, 59–72.

Terrenato, N. 2008. The cultural implications of the Roman conquest. In E. Bispham (ed), *Roman Europe*, Short Oxford History of Europe, 234–64. Oxford: Oxford University Press.

Terrenato, N. 2019. *The Early Roman Expansion into Italy: Elite Negotiation and Family Agendas*. Cambridge: Cambridge University Press.

Thébert, Y. 1978. Romanisation et déromanisation en Afrique: Histoire décolonisée ou histoire inversée? *Annales. Economies, sociétés, civilisations* 33(1): 64–82.

Thébert, Y. 1987. Private life and domestic architecture in Roman Africa. In P. Veyne (ed), *A History of Private Life, vol. 1: From Pagan Rome to Byzantium*, 313–409. Cambridge, MA: Harvard University Press.

Thébert, Y. 2003. *Thermes romains d'Afrique du Nord et leur contexte méditerranéen.* Rome: École française de Rome.

Thompson, L.A. 1971. Roman and native in the Tripolitanian cities in the early Empire. In Gadallah 1971, 235–50.

Thompson, L.A. 1982. On "development" and "underdevelopment" in the early Roman Empire. *Klio* 64(1–2): 383–401.

Thorn, J.-C. 2005. *The Necropolis of Cyrene: Two Hundred Years of Exploration.* Rome: L'Erma di Bretschneider.

Thouvenot, R 1941. *Une colonie romaine de Maurétanie Tingitane: Valentia Banasa.* Paris: Presses universitaires de France.

Thouvenot, R. 1958. *Maisons de Volubilis: Le palais dit de Gordien et la maison à la mosaïque de Vénus.* Rabat: Service des antiquités de Maroc.

Tomasello, F. 2005. *Fontane e ninfei minori di Leptis Magna.* Rome: L'Erma di Bretschneider.

Tomasello, F. 2011. *Il tempio sul decumano maggiore di Leptis Magna.* Rome: L'Erma di Bretschneider.

Toubal, A. 1995. Les mines et carrières en Numidie. Exploitations antiques. In Trousset 1995c, 57–63.

Toutain, J. 1895. *Les cités romaines de la Tunisie: Essai sur l'histoire de la colonisation romaine dans l'Afrique du Nord.* Paris: Fontemoing.

Toutain, J. 1912. Les progrès de la vie urbaine dans l'Afrique du Nord sous la domination romaine. In *Mélanges Cagnat: Recueil de mémoires concernant l'épigraphie et les antiquités romaines*, 319–47. Paris: E. Leroux.

Trakadas, A. 2015. *Fish-Salting in the Northwest Maghreb in Antiquity: A Gazetteer of Sites and Resources.* Oxford: Archaeopress.

Trakadas, A. 2018. *In Mauretaniae Maritimis: Marine Resource Exploitation in a Roman North African Province.* Geographica Historica 40. Stuttgart: Franz Steiner Verlag.

Tran, N. 2005. Les grandes productions africaines dans les échanges méditerranéens de la fin du Ier s. au début du Ve s. ap. J.-C. In Cabouret 2005, 168–89.

Traversari, G. 1960. *Statue iconiche femminili cirenaiche.* Rome: L'Erma di Bretschneider.

Tréziny, H. (ed). 2010. *Grecs et indigènes de la Catalogne à la mer Noire.* Aix-en-Provence: Publications du Centre Camille Jullian, Éditions Errance.

Trimble, J. 2016. The Zoninus collar and the archaeology of Roman slavery. *American Journal of Archaeology* 120(3): 447–72.

Trousset, P. 1974. *Recherches sur le "limes tripolitanus" du Chott El-Djerid à la frontière tuniso-libyenne.* Paris: CNRS Éditions.

Trousset, P. 1976. Reconnaissance archéologiques sur la frontière saharienne de l'empire romain dans le sud-ouest de la Tunisie. In *Archéologie militaire: Les pays du nord.* Actes du 101e Congrès national des Societés savantes, Lille, 1976, 21–33. Paris: Bibliothèque nationale.

Trousset, P. 1977a. Le camp de Gemellae sur le *limes* de Numidie d'après les fouilles de Colonel Baradez (1947–50). In Fitz 1977, 559–76.

Trousset, P. 1977b. Nouvelles observations sur la centuriation romaine à l'est d'El Jem. *Antiquités africaines* 11: 175–207.

Trousset, P. 1978. Les bornes du Bled Segui. Nouveaux aperçus sur la centuriation romaine du Sud tunisien. *Antiquités africaines* 12: 125–77.

Trousset, P. 1980a. Signification d'une frontière: Nomades et sédentaires dans la zone du 'limes' d'Afrique. In W.S. Hanson and L.J.F. Keppie (eds), *Roman Frontier Studies 1979. Papers presented to the 12th International Congress of Roman Frontier Studies*, 931–43. British Archaeological Reports International Series S71. Oxford: BAR Publications.

Trousset, P. 1980b. Les milliaires de Chebika (Sud tunisien). *Antiquités africaines* 15: 135–54.

Trousset, P. 1980c. Villes, campagnes et nomadisme dans l'Afrique du Nord antique: Répresentations et réalités. *Villes et campagnes dans l'empire romain.* Actes du colloque organisé à Aix-en-Provence par l'UER d'histoire, 16–17 mai 1980, 195–205. Aix-en-Provence: Université de Provence.

Trousset, P. 1982a. Le franchissement des chotts du sud Tunisien dans l'antiquité. *Antiquités africaines* 18: 45–59.

Trousset, P. 1982b. L'image du nomade saharien dans l'historiographie antique. *Production pastorale et société*: Bulletin de l'équipe écologie et anthropologie des sociétés pastorales 10: 97–105.

Trousset, P. 1984a. L'idée de frontière au Sahara d'après les données archéologiques. In P.-R. Baduel (ed), *Enjeux Sahariens*, 47–78. Paris: Éditions CNRS.

Trousset, P. 1984b. Note sur un type d'ouvrage linéaire du *limes* d'Afrique. *Bulletin archéologique du comité des travaux historiques et scientifiques: Afrique du Nord* n.s. 17B: 383–98.

Trousset, P. 1985. Les "fines antiquae" et la reconquête byzantine en Afrique. *Bulletin archéologique du comité des travaux historiques et scientifiques: Afrique du Nord* n.s. 19B: 361–76.

Trousset, P. 1986a. Les oasis présahariennes dans l'Antiquité: Partage de l'eau et division du temps. *Antiquités africaines* 22: 163–93.

Trousset, P. 1986b. Limes et "frontière climatique." In CTHS Montpellier, 55–84.

Trousset, P. 1987a. De la montagne au désert: *Limes* et maitrise de l'eau. *Revue des mondes musulman et de la Méditerranée* 41–42: 90–115.

Trousset, P. 1987b. L'organisation de l'oasis dans l'antiquité (exemples de Gabes et du Jerid). In A. de Reparaz (ed), *L'eau et les hommes en Méditerranée*, 25–41, Paris: CNRS Éditions.

Trousset, P. 1990. Tours de guet (watch-towers) et système de liason optique sur le limes Tripolitanus. In *Der römischen limes in Österreich.* Akten des 14. Internationalen Limeskongresses 1986 in Carnuntum, 249–77. Vienna: Verlag der österreichischen Akademie der Wissenschaften.

Trousset, P. 1992. La vie littorale et les ports dans la petite Syrte à l'époque romaine. In CTHS Avignon 1992, 317–32.

Trousset, P. (ed). 1995a. *Monuments funéraires, institutions autochtones en Afrique du Nord antique et médiévale. Actes du VIe Colloque international de CTHS, vol. 1.* 118e Congrès national des sociétés historiques et scientifiques (Pau, 1993). Paris: Éditions du CTHS.

Trousset, P. 1995b. Djerid. *Encyclopédie Berbère* 16: 2461–65.

Trousset, P. (ed). 1995c. *Productions et exportations africaines, actualités archéologiques en Afrique du Nord antique et médiévale*. Paris: Éditions du CTHS.

Trousset, P. 1997a. Les centuriations de Tunisie et l'orientation solaire. *Antiquités africaines* 33: 95–109.

Trousset, P. 1997b. Nouvelles barrières romaines de contrôle dans l'extrême sud tunisien. *Bulletin archéologique du comité des travaux historiques et scientifiques: Afrique du Nord* n.s. 24B: 155–63.

Trousset, P. 1997c. Un nouveau document sur la *limitatio* de C. Vibius Marsus (Sud tunisien). In W. Groenman-van Waateringe (ed), *Roman Frontier Studies 1995*, Proceedings of the 16th International Congress of Roman Frontier Studies, 3–11. Oxford: Oxbow Books.

Trousset, P. 1998a. Fossatum. *Encyclopédie Berbère* 19: 2911–18.

Trousset, P. 1998b. La pêche et ses techniques sur les côtes de l'Africa. In É. Rieth (ed), *Méditerranée antique: Pêche, navigation, commerce*, 13–32. Paris: Éditions du CTHS.

Trousset, P. 2001. Territoires de tribus et frontière au sud de *l'Africa Proconsularis*. In Bejaoui 2001, 59–68.

Trousset, P. 2003. Le tarif de Zaraï: Essai sur les circuits commerciaux dans la zone présaharienne. *Antiquités africaines* 38–39: 355–73.

Trousset, P. 2004. Pénétration romaine et organisation de la zone frontière dans le prédésert tunisien. *L'Africa romana* 15: 59–88.

Trousset, P. 2011. Une entité frontalière tardive et sa genèse: Des Nybgenii aux Arzuges. In Briand-Ponsart and Modéran 2011, 201–19.

Trousset, P. 2012a. Nefzaoua: Antiquité. *Encyclopédie Berbère* 33: 5382–89.

Trousset, P. 2012b. Nomadisme (Saharien en Afrique du Nord dans l'antiquité). *Encyclopédie Berbère* 34: 5578–89.

Tsetskhladze, G.R. (ed). 2006a. *Greek Colonisation: An Account of Greek Colonies and Other Settlements Overseas*. Vol 1. Leiden: Brill.

Tsetskhladze, G.R. (ed). 2006b. *Greek Colonisation: An Account of Greek Colonies and Other Settlements Overseas*. Vol 2. Leiden: Brill.

Tuck, E. and Yang, K.W. 2012. Decolonization is not a metaphor. *Decolonization: Indigeneity, Education and Society* 1(1): 1–40.

Van Beek, C.I.M.I. 1936. *Passio Sanctarum Perpetuae et Felicitatis, vol. 1: Textum Graecum et Latinum ad fidem codicum MSS*. Nijmegen: Dekker en van de Vegt.

Van der Veen, M. 1995. Ancient agriculture in Libya: A review of the evidence. *Acta Palaeobotanica* 35(1): 85–98.

Van der Veen, M. 2010. Agricultural innovation: Invention and adoption or change and adaptation. *World Archaeology* 42(1): 1–12.

Van der Veen, M. and Westley, B. 2010. Palaeoeconomic studies. In Mattingly 2010a, 488–522.

Van Dommelen, P.A.R. 1998. *On Colonial Grounds: A Comparative Study of Colonialism and Rural Settlement in the 1st Millennium BC in West Central Sardinia*. Leiden: University of Leiden.

Van Dommelen, P.A.R. 2002. Ambiguous matters: Colonialism and local identities in Punic Sardinia. In Lyons and Papadopoulos 2002, 121–47.

Van Dommelen, P.A.R. 2014. Punic identities and modern perceptions in the western Mediterranean. In Quinn and Vella 2014, 42–57.

Van Dommelen, P.A.R. and Gómez Bellard, C. 2008. Defining the Punic world and its rural contexts. In P.A.R. van Dommelen and C. Gómez Bellard (eds), *Rural Landscapes of the Punic World*, 1–21. London: Equinox.

Van Dommelen, P.A.R. and Knapp, A.B. (eds). 2010. *Material Connections in the Ancient Mediterranean: Mobility, Materiality and Identity*. London: Routledge.

Van Dommelen, P.A.R. and Terrenato, N. 2007. *Articulating Local Cultures: Power and Identity under the Expanding Roman Republic*. JRA supplement 63. Portsmouth, RI: Journal of Roman Archaeology.

Van Oyen, A. 2015. Deconstructing and reassembling the Romanization debate through the lens of postcolonial theory: From global to local and back? *Terra Incognita* 6: 205–26.

Van Oyen, A. and Pitts, M. (eds). 2017. *Materialising Roman Histories*. Oxford: Oxbow Books.

Van Wyk Smith, M. 2009. *The First Ethiopians. The Image of Africa and Africans in the Early Mediterranean World*. Johannesburg: Wits University Press

Vanacker W. 2013. Ties of resistance and cooperation: Aedemon, Lusius Quietus and the Baquates. *Mnemosyne* 66(4–5): 708–33.

Vanacker W. 2014. Many paths to walk. The political and economic integration of nomadic communities in Roman North Africa (I–III cent. A.D.). *Afrika Focus* 27(2): 98–104.

Vanacker, W. 2015. *Adhuc Tacfarinas*. Causes of the Tiberian war in North Africa (A.D. ca.15–24) and the impact of the conflict on Roman imperial policy. *Historia*. 64(3): 336–356.

Várhelyi, Z. and Bagnall, R.S. 2009. Ostraka. In Fentress et al. 2009, 334–44.

Vasunia, P. 2013. *The Classics and Colonial India*. Oxford: Oxford University Press.

Vatin, J.-C. (ed). 1984. *Connaissances du Maghreb: Science sociales et colonisation*. Paris: CNRS Éditions.

Vattioni, F. 1979. Per una ricerca sull'antroponima fenicio-punica. *Studi Magrebini* 11: 43–123.

Vattioni, F. 1980. Per una ricerca sull'antroponima fenicio-punica. *Studi Magrebini* 12: 1–82.

Vattioni, F. 1981. La bilingue latine e neopunica di El-Amrouni. *Helikon* 20/21: 293–99.

Vella, N.C. 2014. The invention of the Phoenicians: On object definition, decontextualization and display. In Quinn and Vella 2014, 24–41.

Vera, D. 1988. Terra e lavoro nell'Africa romana. *Studi Storici* 29(4): 967–92.

Vera, D. 1987. Enfiteusi, colonato e trasformazioni agrarie nell'Africa proconsolare del tardo impero. *L'Africa romana* 4: 267–93.

Vernel, R. 1995. *Climats anciens du nord de l'Afrique*. Paris: Éditions L'Harmattan.

Versluys, M.J. 2014. Understanding objects in motion: An *archaeological* dialogue on Romanization. *Archaeological Dialogues* 21(1): 1–64 [includes responses by Hingley, Hodos, Stek, van Dommelen, Woolf].

Villaverde Vega, N. 2001. *Tingitana en la Antigüedad tardía (siglos III–VII)*. Madrid: Real Academia de la Historia.

Vismara, C. 1998. L'organizzazione dello spazio rurale nelle province del Nord Africa. *L'Africa romana* 12: 51–84.

Vismara, C. 2007. *Uchi Maius 3: I frantoi, miscellanea*. Sassari: Editrice Democratica Sarda.

Vismara, C. 2014. Le Rif oriental côtier dans les pages de voyageurs, explorateurs, historiens, archéologues, géographes: De Jean-Léon l'Africain à nos jours. *Antiquités africaines* 50: 141–99.

Vismara, C. 2021. Des bêtes pour l'arène. In Blanc-Bijon et al. 2021, 289–96.

Von Rummel, P. 2014. Chimtou, Tunesien: Die Arbeiten der Jahre 2012 und 2013. *E-Forschungsberichte* 2014.1: 125–30.

Von Rummel, P., Broisch, M. and Schöne, C.A. 2013. Geophysikalische Prospektionen in Simitthus (Chimtou, Tunisien). Vorbericht zu den Kampagnen 2010–2013. *Kölner und Bonner Archaeologica* 3: 203–16.

Von Rummel, P., Wulf-Rheidt, U., Ardeleanu, S., Beck, D., Chaouali, M., Goischke, J., Möller, M. and Scheding, P. 2016. Chimtou, Tunesien: Die Arbeiten der Jahre 2014 und 2015. *E-Forschungsberichte* 2016.2: 99–109.

Vuillemot, G. 1965. *Reconnaissances aux échelles puniques d'Oranie.* Autun: Musée Rolin.

Wagner, G. 2000. Oasis Magna. In Talbert 2000, Map 79 and map-by-map directory, 1164–69.

Waldherr, G.H. 2003. Frauen auf Kaiserzeitlichen Bauinschirften im Römischen Nordafrika. In Khanoussi 2003, 335–50.

Wallace-Hadrill, A. 2008. *Rome's Cultural Revolution.* Cambridge: Cambridge University Press.

Wallace-Hadrill, A. 2012. Romanizzazione. In Giardina and Pesando 2012a, 111–16.

Walth, C.K. 2001. The human remains from Site 10 (1991). In Stirling et al. 2001, 169–73.

Walth, C.K. 2005. Human bone. In S.T. Stevens, A.V. Kalinowski and H. vanderLeest (eds), *Bir Ftouha: A Pilgrimage Church Complex at Carthage*, 474–86. JRA supplement 59. Portsmouth, R.I.: Journal of Roman Archaeology.

Walth, C.K., and Mattingly, D.J. 2001. Catalogue of burials, Site 10, 1991. In Stirling et al. 2001, 175–201.

Walth, C.K., and Miller. L.J. 1993. Burials and disarticulated human bone (1990). In S.T. Stevens (ed), *Bir el Knissia at Carthage: A Rediscovered Cemetery Extramural Church. Report 1*, 191–200. JRA supplement 7. Portsmouth, RI: Journal of Roman Archaeology.

Ward, P. 1968. *Apuleius on Trial at Sabratha.* Cambridge: Oleander Press.

Ward-Perkins, J.B. 1971. Pre-Roman elements in the architecture of Roman Tripolitania. In Gadallah 1971:101–16.

Ward-Perkins, J.B. 1981. *Roman Imperial Architecture.* Harmondsworth: Penguin.

Ward-Perkins, J.B. 1982. Town planning in North Africa during the first two centuries of the Empire. *150-Jahr-Feier Deutches Archäologisches Institut Rom, Mitteilungen des Deutschen Archäologischen Instituts, Römische Abteilung* 25: 29–49.

Ward-Perkins, J.B. 1993. *The Severan Buildings of Lepcis Magna: An Architecturaal Survey.* London: Society for Libyan Studies.

Ward-Perkins, J.B. and Goodchild, R.G. 1949. The *limes Tripolitanus* in the light of recent discoveries. *Journal of Roman Studies* 39(1–2): 81–95 = Goodchild 1976, 17–34.

Ward-Perkins, J.B. and Goodchild, R.G. 2003. *Christian Monuments of Cyrenaica.* (Edited by J.M. Reynolds). London: Society for Libyan Studies.

Ward-Perkins, J.B., Little, J.H., Mattingly, D.J. and Gibson, S.C. 1986. Town houses at Ptolemais, Cyrenaica: A summary report of survey and excavation work in 1971, 1978–1979. *Libyan Studies* 17: 109–53.

Warmington, B.H. 1954. *The North African Provinces from Diocletian to the Vandal Conquest.* Cambridge: Cambridge University Press.

Warmington, B.H. 1956. The career of Romanus, *comes Africae*. *Byzantine Zeitschrift* 49(1): 55–64.

Warmington, B.H. 1969. *Carthage.* 2nd edition. London: Robert Hale.

Weber, M. and Schmid, S. 2012. Supplying a desert garrison. Pottery from the Roman fort at Gheriat el-Garbia (Libya). *Rei Cretariae Romanae Fautorum Acta* 42: 327–35.

Webster, J. 1995. *Interpretatio*: Roman word power and the Celtic gods. *Britannia* 26: 153–61.

Webster, J. 1997a. Necessary comparisons: A post-colonial approach to religious syncretism in the Roman provinces. *World Archaeology* 28(3): 324–38.

Webster, J. 1997b. A negotiated syncretism: Readings on the development of Romano-Celtic religion. In Mattingly 1997a, 165–84.

Webster, J. 1999. At the end of the World: Druidic and other revitalization movements in post-conquest Gaul and Britain. *Britannia* 30: 1–20.

Webster, J. 2001. Creolizing the Roman provinces. *American Journal of Archaeology* 105(2): 209–25.

Webster, J. 2005. Archaeologies of slavery and servitude: Bringing "New World" perspectives to Roman Britain. *Journal of Roman Archaeology* 18: 161–79.

Webster, J. 2007. Linking with a wider world. Rome and "barbarians". In S.E. Alcock and R. Osborne (eds), *Classical Archaeology*, 415–38. Malden: Blackwell.

Webster, J. 2008. Less beloved: Roman archaeology, slavery and the failure to compare. *Archaeological Dialogues* 15(2): 103–49 [with discussants' comments and response].

Webster, J. and Cooper, N. (eds). 1996. *Roman Imperialism: Post-Colonial Perspectives*. Leicester: School of Archaeological Studies.

Wells, C.M. (ed). 1982. *Roman Africa/L'Afrique Romaine: The Vanier Lectures 1980*. Ottawa: University of Ottawa.

Wells, P.S. 1999. *The Barbarians Speak: How the Conquered Peoples Shaped Roman Europe*. Princeton: Princeton University Press.

Welsby, D. 1983. The Roman fort at Gheriat el-Garbia. *Libyan Studies* 14: 57–64.

Welsby, D. 1988. The defences of the Roman forts at Bu Ngem and Gheriat el-Garbia. In P. Bidwell, R. Miket and B. Ford (eds), *Portae cum turribus. Studies of Roman fort gates*, 63–82. British Archaeological Reports British Series B206. Oxford: BAR Publishing.

Welsby, D. 1990. Observations on the defences of Roman forts in North Africa. *Antiquités africaines* 26: 113–29.

Welsby, D. 1992. ULVS XXV: The *gsur* and associated settlements in the Wadi Umm el Kharab: An architectural survey. *Libyan Studies* 23: 73–99.

Wheeler, M. 1954. *Rome Beyond the Imperial Frontiers*. London: G Bell and Sons.

Whelan, R. 2018. *Being Christian in Vandal Africa: The Politics of Orthodoxy in the Post-Imperial West*. Berkeley: University of California Press.

White, D. 1984–2012. *The Extramural Sanctuary of Demeter and Persephone at Cyrene, Libya. Final Reports 1–8*. Philadelphia: Penn Press.

Whitehead, N. 1992. Tribes make states and states make tribes: Warfare and the creation of colonial tribes and states in northeastern South America. In Ferguson and Whitehead 1992, 127–50.

Whitmarsh, T. (ed). 2010. *Local Knowledge and Microidentities in the Imperial Greek World*. Cambridge: Cambridge University Press.

Whittaker, C.R. 1974. The western Phoenicians: Colonisation and assimilation. *Proceedings of the Cambridge Philological Society* (second series) 20: 58–79.

Whittaker, C.R. 1978a. Land and labour in North Africa. *Klio* 60(60): 331–62.

Whittaker, C.R. 1978b. Marcel Bénabou, *La resistance africaine à la romanisation*. *Journal of Roman Studies* 68: 190–92.

Whittaker, C.R. 1978c. Carthaginian imperialism in the fifth and fourth centuries. In P.D.A. Garnsey and C.R. Whittaker (eds), *Imperialism in the Ancient World*, 59–90. Cambridge: Cambridge University Press.

Whittaker, C.R. 1994. *Frontiers of the Roman Empire: A Social and Economic Study*. Baltimore: Johns Hopkins.

Whittaker, C.R. 1995. Do theories of the ancient city matter? In T.J. Cornell and K. Lomas (eds), *Urban Society in Roman Italy*, 9–26. London: Routledge.

Whittaker, C.R. 1996. Roman Africa: Augustus to Vespasian. In Bowman et al. 1996, 586–618.

Whittaker, C.R. 1997. Imperialism and culture: The Roman initiative. In Mattingly 1997a: 143–63.

Whittaker, C.R. 2000. Africa. In Bowman et al. 2000, 514–46.

Whittaker, C.R. 2004. *Rome and its Frontiers: The Dynamics of Empire*. London: Routledge.

Whittaker, C.R. 2009. Ethnic discourses on the frontiers of Roman Africa. In Derks and Roymans 2009, 189–206.

Wickham, C. 2005. *Framing the Early Middle Ages: Europe and the Mediterranean, 400–800*. Oxford: Oxford University Press.

Wild, J.P., Wild. F.C. and Clapham, A.J. 2007. Irrigation and the spread of cotton growing in Roman times. *Archaeological Textiles Newsletter* 44: 16–18.

Wild, J.P., Wild, F.C. and Clapham, A.J. 2011. Roman Cotton Revisited. In C. Alfaro and L. Karali (eds), *Purpureae Vestes 2: Textiles y tintes del Mediterráneo en el mundo antiguo*, 143–47. Valencia: Universitat de Valencia.

Willet, R. 2012. *Red Slipped Complexity: The Socio-Cultural Context of the Concept and Use of Tableware in the Roman East (Second Century BC – Seventh Century AD)*. Unpublished PhD thesis, Leuven University.

Wilson, A. I. 1997. *Water Management and Usage in Roman North Africa: A Social and Technological Study*. Unpublished DPhil thesis, University of Oxford.

Wilson, A.I. 1998. Water supply in ancient Carthage. In *Carthage Papers: The Early Colony's Economy, Water Supply, A Private Bath, and the Mobilization of State Olive Oil*, 65–102. JRA supplement 28. Portsmouth, RI: Journal of Roman Archaeology.

Wilson, A.I. 2001a. Timgad and textile production. In D.J. Mattingly and J. Salmon (eds), *Economies Beyond Agriculture in the Classical World*, 271–96. London: Routledge.

Wilson, A.I. 2001b. Urban water storage, distribution, and usage in Roman North Africa. In A.O. Koloski-Ostrow (ed), *Water Use and Hydraulics in the Roman City*, 83–96. Boston, MA: Archaeological Institute of America.

Wilson, A.I. 2002a. Marine resource exploitation in the cities of coastal Tripolitania. *L'Africa romana* 14: 429–36.

Wilson, A.I. 2002b. Urban production in the Roman world: The view from North Africa. *Papers of the British School at Rome* 70: 231–73.

Wilson, A.I. 2005. Une cité grecque de Libye: Fouilles d'Euhésperidès (Benghazi). *Comptes rendus des séances de l'Académie des inscriptions et belles-lettres* 2003, 147(4): 1647–75.

Wilson, A.I. 2006a. The spread of foggara-based irrigation in the ancient Sahara. In Mattingly et al. 2006, 205–16.

Wilson, A.I. 2006b. New light on a Greek city: Archaeology and history at Euesperides. In Fabbricotti and Menozzi 2006, 141–52.

Wilson, A.I. 2009a. Foggaras in ancient North Africa: Or how to marry a Berber princess. In V. Bridoux (ed), *Contrôle et distribution de l'eau dans le Maghreb antique et médiéval*, 19–39. CEFR 426. Rome: École française de Rome.

Wilson, A.I. 2009b. Approaches to quantifying Roman trade. In Bowman and Wilson 2009, 213–49.

Wilson, A.I. 2009c. Indicators of Roman economic growth: A response to Walter Scheidel. *Journal of Roman Archaeology* 22: 71–82.

Wilson, A.I. 2011. City sizes and urbanization in the Roman Empire. In Bowman and Wilson 2011, 161–95.

Wilson, A.I. 2012a. Saharan trade in the Roman period: Short-, medium-, and long-distance trade networks. *Azania: Archaeological Research in Africa* 47(4): 409–49.

Wilson, A.I. 2012b. Neo-Punic and Latin inscriptions in Roman North Africa: function and display. In Mullen and James 2012, 265–316.

Wilson, A.I. 2013. Trading across the Syrtes: Euesperides and the Punic world. In Prag and Quinn 2013, 120–56.

Wilson, A.I. 2017. Saharan exports to the Roman world. In Mattingly et al. 2017a, 189–208.

Wilson, A.I. 2020. Mediterranean urbanisation in North Africa: Greek, Punic and Roman models. In Sterry and Mattingly 2020a, 396–437.

Wilson, A.I. Forthcoming. Aquaria and the landscape of the Albertini Tablets. (Draft text of article).

Wilson, A. I. and Flohr, M. (eds). 2016. *Urban Craftsmen and Traders in the Roman World*. Oxford Studies on the Roman Economy. Oxford: Oxford University Press.

Wilson, A.I. and Mattingly, D.J. 2003. Irrigation technologies: Foggaras, wells and field systems. In Mattingly 2003a, 234–78.

Wilson, A.I., Mattingly, D.J. and Sterry, M. 2020. The diffusion of irrigation technologies in the Sahara in antiquity: Settlement, trade and migration. In Duckworth et al. 2020a, 69–114.

Wilson, P.R. 2002. *Cataractonium: Roman Catterick and its Hinterland. Excavations and Research, 1958–1997*. 2 vols. CBA Research Reports 128–129. York: Council for British Archaeology.

Wilson, R.J.A. 2018. Roman villas in North Africa. In A. Marzano and G.P.R. Métraux (eds), *The Roman Villa in the Mediterranean Basin: Late Republic to Late Antiquity*, 266–307. Cambridge: Cambridge University Press.

Winther-Jacobsen, K. 2013. Artefact variability, assemblage differentiation and identity negotiation: Debating code-switching in material culture: Introduction. *HEROM: Journal on Hellenistic and Roman Material Culture* 2: 11–20.

Witcher, R. 2000. Globalisation and Roman imperialism. Perspectives on identities in Roman Italy. In E. Herring and K. Lomas (eds), *The Emergence of State Identities in Italy in the First Millennium BC*, 213–25. Specialist Studies on Italy 8. London: Accordia.

Wolff, C. 2014. La guerre de Tacfarinas (17–24). In Coltelloni-Trannoy and Le Bohec 2014, 53–67.

Woolf, G. 1992a. Imperialism, empire and the integration of the Roman economy. *World Archaeology* 23(3): 283–93.

Woolf, G. 1992b. The unity and diversity of Romanisation. *Journal of Roman Archaeology* 5: 349–52.

Woolf, G. 1994. Becoming Roman, staying Greek: Culture, identity and the civilizing process in the Roman East. *Proceedings of the Cambridge Philological Society* 40: 116–143.

Woolf, G. 1995. Romans as civilizers: The ideological pre-conditions of Romanization. In Metzler et al. 1995, 9–18.

Woolf, G. 1997. Beyond Romans and natives. *World Archaeology* 28(3): 339–50.

Woolf, G. 1998. *Becoming Roman: The Origins of Provincial Civilization in Gaul*. Cambridge: Cambridge University Press.

Woolf, G. 2012. *Rome: An Empire's Story*. Oxford: Oxford University Press.

Woolf, G. 2014. *Tales of the Barbarians: Ethnography and Empire in the Roman West*. Oxford: Wiley Blackwell.

Woolf, G. 2020. *The Life and Death of Ancient Cities: A Natural History*. Oxford: Oxford University Press.

Xella, P. 1991. *Baal Hammon. Recherches sur l'identité et l'histoire d'un dieu phénico-punique.* Rome: CNR.

Xella, P. 2009. Sacrifici di bambini nel mondo fenicio e punico nelle testimonianze in lingua greca e latina—I. *Studi epigrafici e linguistici sul Vicino Oriente antico* 26: 59–100.

Xella, P. (ed). 2013. *The Tophet in the Phoenician Mediterranean.* Verona: Essedue Edizioni.

Xella, P., Quinn, J.-C., Melchiorri, V. and Van Dommelen, P. 2013. Cemetery or sacrifice? Infant burials at the Carthage Tophet: Phoenician bones of contention. *Antiquity* 87(338): 1199–207.

Yacoub, M. 1996. *Le musée du Bardo.* Tunis: Agence Nationale de la Patrimoine.

Yasin, A.M. 2009. *Saints and Church Spaces in the Late Antique Mediterranean: Architecture, Cult, and Community.* Cambridge: Cambridge University Press.

Yegül, F.K. 1992. *Baths and Bathing in Classical Antiquity.* New York: MIT Press.

Yegül, F.K. and Favro, D.G. 2018. *Roman Architecture and Urbanism: From the Origins to Late Antiquity.* New York: Cambridge University Press.

Yelles, A. 2020. *Aux origines de la photographie archéologique. De Rome en Afrique.* Paris: Éditions Mergoil.

Yoffee, N. 2005. *Myths of the Archaic State: Evolution of the Earliest Cities, States, and Civilisations.* Cambridge: Cambridge University Press.

Younes, A. 1999. *Recherches sur la ville portuaire de Thapsus et son territoire en Byzacène dans l'Antiquité.* 2 volumes. Tunis: Centre d'Etudes et de Recherches Economiques et Sociales.

Younes, A. 2012. *Recherches sur l'urbanisation et l'architecture dans le Sahel méridional tunisien de l'Antiquité au Haut Moyen âge.* Tunis: Faculté des Science Humaines et Sociales de Tunis.

Zanker, P. 1988. *The Power of Images in the Age of Augustus.* Translated by A. Shapiro. Ann Arbor: University of Michigan Press.

Zanker, P. 2008. Selbstdarstellung am Rand der libyschen Wüste: Die Reliefs an den Häuptlings-Mausoleen in der Nordnekropole von Ghirza. In F. Pirson and U. Wulf-Rheidt (eds), *Austausch und Inspiration: Kulturkontakt als Impuls architektonischer Innovation*, 214–26. Mainz: Phillip von Zabern.

Zapata, L., López-Sáez, J.A., Ruiz-Alonso, M., Linstädter, J., Pérez-Jordà, G., Morales, J., Kehl, M. and Peña-Chocarro, L. 2013. Holocene environmental change and human impact in NE Morocco: Palaeobotanical evidence from Ifri Oudadane. *The Holocene* 23(9): 1286–96.

Zelazowski, J. (ed). 2012. *Ptolemais in Cyrenaica: Studies in Memory of Tomasz Mikocki.* Warsaw: Institute of Archaeology.

Zevi, F. and Tchernia, A. 1969. Amphores de Byzacène au Bas-Empire. *Antiquités africaines* 3: 173–214.

Ziegler, S. and Mackensen, M. 2014. Spätantike Ostraka aus Gheriat el-Garbia (al-Qaryāt al-Garbīyah) in der Provinz Tripolitana (Libyen). Belege für eine regionale Variante des Punischen. *Mitteilungen des Deutschen Archaeologischen Instituts: Römische Abteilung* 120: 313–40.

Zocchi, A. 2018a. *The Periphery of Lepcis Magna. Suburban Topography and Land Use of a Roman City.* Unpublished PhD Thesis, University of Leicester.

Zocchi, A. 2018b. The periphery of Lepcis Magna: New data related to the ancient road network and land partition. *Libyan Studies* 49: 51–79.

INDEX

Page numbers in italics are figures; with 'n' are notes; with 't' are tables. Ancient place names are in italics.